MAYSON, FRENCH & RYAN ON COMPANY LAW

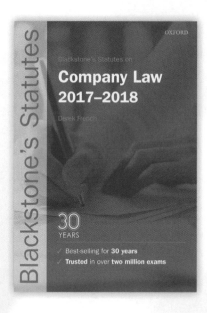

MAYSON, FRENCH & RYAN ON
COMPANY LAW

2017–2018 Edition

DEREK FRENCH BSC

OXFORD
UNIVERSITY PRESS

OXFORD
UNIVERSITY PRESS

Great Clarendon Street, Oxford, OX2 6DP,
United Kingdom

Oxford University Press is a department of the University of Oxford.
It furthers the University's objective of excellence in research, scholarship,
and education by publishing worldwide. Oxford is a registered trade mark of
Oxford University Press in the UK and in certain other countries

Thirty-first edition 2014
Thirty-second edition 2015
Thirty-third edition 2016

Impression: 1

Published in the United States of America by Oxford University Press
198 Madison Avenue, New York, NY 10016, United States of America

British Library Cataloguing in Publication Data
Data available

ISBN 978–0–19–879723–4

Printed in Great Britain by
Bell & Bain Ltd., Glasgow

CONTENTS

PART 2 ESTABLISHMENT

PART 4 GOVERNANCE

PART 5 INSOLVENCY AND LIQUIDATION

PREFACE

This book is intended to be a clear, straightforward, up-to-date introduction to English company law.

Readers of the book are assumed to have had an introduction to English law, but no special knowledge of any other branch of the law is assumed.

Although it is inevitable that a book of this character will be used mainly by students, it is hoped that it can also serve as a useful, compact and up-to-date statement of the law for lawyers, accountants, bankers, insolvency practitioners and other professionals.

Our primary aim in this book is to state what the law currently is with as much technical accuracy as can be achieved in the process of writing a textbook, but we also try to present something of the context in which the law has developed, looking at its purpose and history, and introducing some of the debate about both the controversial details and the fundamental nature of company law.

The greatest challenge in the study of company law is that it is a very large subject. An introductory book like this must concentrate on providing a framework of basic principles with some detail of how these principles are worked out in practice. The practice of company law involves the use of a very large legislative code, and requires familiarity with the way the courts interpret the legislation and how they fill in missing details. It is also necessary to know how the principles of equity are applied by judges and lawyers in the areas of company law which are not exclusively governed by statute. This book deals with the main topics of company law, stating what the legislative provisions are and giving examples of how problems have been dealt with by the courts. The number of references to primary sources (legislation, cases, articles) is very large. For most chapters the 'What is in this chapter' section gives a list of the key legislation for the chapter and a very select list of the most significant cases which are recommended further reading. Quotations of significant passages from legislation and judgments are given in this book where appropriate. To aid navigation, the titles of quoted cases, articles and books are in bold type. The text of relevant enactments, incorporating all amendments and repeals enacted up to 1 April 2017, will be found in D French, *Blackstone's Statutes on Company Law 2017–2018* (Oxford: Oxford University Press, 2017). It is hoped that the present book will provide its readers with the techniques required to use the original sources successfully.

This edition was completed on 4 April 2017. For news on subsequent developments in company law, please consult the Online Resource Centre for this book at **http://global.oup.com/uk/orc/law/company/mayson17_18/**.

Derek French

NEW TO THIS EDITION

- Effect of Brexit
- New EU Market Abuse Regulation
- New EU Audit Regulation
- Insolvency (England and Wales) Rules 2016

New cases including:

- *BAT Industries plc v Sequana SA*
- *Re Dee Valley Group plc*
- *Granada Group Ltd v Law Debenture Pension Trust Corp plc*
- *Gunewardena v Conran Holdings Ltd*
- *Re Sherlock Holmes International Society Ltd*
- *Re Zavarco plc (No 2)*

TABLE OF CASES

TABLE OF STATUTES

TABLE OF STATUTORY INSTRUMENTS

TABLE OF TREATIES AND CONVENTIONS

TABLE OF EUROPEAN SECONDARY LEGISLATION

REGULATIONS

TABLE OF REFERENCES TO THE FCA HANDBOOK

TABLE OF REFERENCES TO THE UK CORPORATE GOVERNANCE CODE

ABBREVIATIONS

AD	Appellate Division
BIS	Department for Business, Innovation and Skills
CA	Companies Act, Court of Appeal
C(AI&CE)A 2004	Companies (Audit, Investigations and Community Enterprise) Act 2004
CDDA	Company Directors Disqualification Act
ChD	Chancery Division
ChDC	Divisional Court of the Chancery Division
CIC	community interest company
CJEU	Court of Justice of the European Union
CP	Common Pleas
CPD	Common Pleas Division
CPDC	Divisional Court of the Common Pleas Division
CSD	central securities depository
CSess 1st Div	Court of Session First Division
CSess 2nd Div	Court of Session Second Division
CSess Extra Div	Court of Session Extra Division
CSess IH	Court of Session Inner House
CSess OH	Court of Session Outer House
CSR	corporate social responsibility
DC	Divisional Court
DTI	Department of Trade and Industry
DVP	delivery versus payment
EAT	Employment Appeal Tribunal
EEA	European Economic Area
ESV	enlightened shareholder value
ExDC	Divisional Court of the Exchequer Division
FC	Full Court
FCA	Financial Conduct Authority
FedC	Federal Court
FRC	Financial Reporting Council
FRS	Financial Reporting Standard
FSA	Financial Services Authority
FSMA 2000	Financial Services and Markets Act 2000

HC	High Court
HL	House of Lords
LSE	London Stock Exchange
PSM	Professional Securities Market

PART 1

INTRODUCTION

1
INTRODUCTION

SUMMARY OF POINTS COVERED

- What this book is about
- What is in the rest of this chapter
- Incorporation
- Other legal forms for businesses

- Sources of company law
- Purpose of company law
- Morality, economics, democracy and company law

1.1 WHAT THIS BOOK IS ABOUT

1.1.1 THE LEGAL CONCEPT OF A COMPANY

In a modern capitalist market economy, companies are a familiar part of everyday life. Companies own the supermarkets from which people buy their food; companies supply the water, gas, electricity and petroleum products we depend on; companies publish the newspapers we read and provide our Internet services. We deal with companies so often as purchasers and users of their products and services that the image which the word 'company' brings to mind is usually of an organisation concerned with marketing and collecting payment for products which the company has made (or bought in) or services it has provided. It is necessary to go behind this image to get to the company which is the subject of company law.

1.1.2 THE BIG IDEA

The company with which lawyers are concerned is the legal entity which owns the business which the organisation has been created to carry on. The remarkable thing about this entity is that it is created by process of law and exists only by virtue of the law.

The big idea of company law is the separate personality of the company as an artificial person. The separate artificial person is capable of owning property, being a party to contracts and being a claimant or defendant in legal proceedings. This big idea is not easy to get used to. There is a further introduction to it in **1.3**. It is the main theme of **Chapters 2, 5 and 19**, and is referred to throughout the book. **Chapter 5** also examines some of the arguments against the big idea of separate personality and when it can be ignored.

1.1.3 OTHER MAIN THEMES

1.1.3.1 Introduction

This book is organised to follow the life of a company roughly chronologically from formation to dissolution, but there are some main themes which keep recurring. One of them, the big idea of separate personality, has already been identified (see **1.1.2**). Other recurring main themes are: ownership and control of a company and corporate governance (**1.1.3.2**), corporate finance (**1.1.3.3**), transparency and disclosure (**1.1.3.4**), the differences between public and private companies (**1.1.3.5**) and picking up the pieces after things go wrong (**1.1.3.6**).

1.1.3.2 Ownership and control

A company is an artificial person, which is capable of owning property. Who owns the company and benefits from the wealth which the company has? Who controls what the company does with its assets? The basic company model is that a company has *members* (also known as shareholders) who, in effect, own it and it has *directors* who control what the company does. Rules about ownership and control of companies and about how they are controlled, what is generally known as corporate governance, are the main themes of **Chapters 3** and **14 to 17**. In practice, it is common for a company to be owner-managed, with all its members serving as directors (see **2.7**).

1.1.3.3 Corporate finance

A company as a separate person is capable of owning property, conducting a business and employing people. How does it acquire money to buy property, run a business and pay employees? Corporate finance is the main theme of **Chapters 6 to 13**. Two principal sources of corporate finance are (a) capital contributed for shares and (b) borrowings. The concept of share capital is introduced in **Chapter 2** (**2.3.2**). Issuing and dealing in shares are the subjects of **Chapters 6, 7** and **8**. Borrowing is the subject of **Chapters 11** and **12**.

1.1.3.4 Transparency

A company as a separate person has members, who are effectively its owners, and it has directors, who control what it does and manage its business. But only the company as a separate person is responsible for the debts incurred in carrying on its business. Members have what is called 'limited liability', which in practice they discharge when they contribute capital for their shares (see **2.3.2** and **6.5 to 6.7**). Directors of a company normally have no liability for its debts. This is a radical departure from the traditional view that the owner of a business must have unlimited liability for its debts. The price paid for limited liability for a company's debts is the obligation to make available to the public a great deal of information about the company (see **Chapter 4**), including its accounts (see **Chapter 9**). Rules on disclosure of information are referred to throughout this book.

1.1.3.5 Public and private companies

Public companies (plcs) are permitted to invite the general public to subscribe for their shares, whereas private companies are not. The shares of a public company may be officially listed for trading on a recognised investment exchange such as the London Stock Exchange. The shares of a private company may not. Offering shares to the public is the subject of **Chapter 7**. Some of the rules of company law, particularly on disclosure, are more stringent or onerous for public companies than for private companies. These are noted at appropriate points in **Chapters 2, 6, 9** and **10**. Public companies which are officially listed are subject to extra disclosure rules promulgated by the Financial Conduct Authority (FCA) for the protection of investors.

1.1.3.6 Picking up the pieces

Much of the function of company law is to prescribe rules which should be followed to avoid disputes and conflict in running companies. **Chapter 18** is about dispute resolution. The most common disputes resolved in company law are between a minority of members in a company and the majority, and the subject matter of **Chapter 18** is often called 'minority rights'. **Chapter 20** is concerned with the legal processes for dealing with companies whose businesses fail or otherwise cease. This is often a time for examining people's responsibility for a company's failure.

1.2 WHAT IS IN THE REST OF THIS CHAPTER

This introduction to the book begins with a short discussion of the nature of corporations in general, and companies as a particular type of corporation (**1.3**), and contrasts incorporated companies with two other legal forms used by businesses, the partnership and the sole proprietorship (**1.4**). The rest of this introduction looks at the sources of company law in statutes, case law, European law and so on (**1.5**), and asks what purposes company law should serve (**1.6**). This leads to an important political question which must be faced in company law, which is introduced in **1.6** and returned to in **1.7**. This question is whether company law should serve the interests only of those who contribute capital to companies or whether the activities of companies need to be controlled in the public interest.

1.3 INCORPORATION

1.3.1 THE NATURE OF INCORPORATION AND LEGAL PERSONALITY

The companies with which this book is concerned are called 'registered companies' because they are brought into existence by registration of documents with a public official (a registrar of companies) under the provisions of the Companies Act 2006 (CA 2006).

The most important legal characteristic of a registered company is that it is 'incorporated' and so has what is known as 'legal personality'. This is provided for in CA 2006, s 15(1), which provides that, on the registration of a company, the registrar must give a 'certificate that the company is incorporated'.

Describing a registered company as 'incorporated' means that it is a corporation or 'body corporate' (a company is described as a 'body corporate' in s 16(2) and (3)). The extraordinarily useful feature of a corporation is that it is an artificial entity which is treated in law as having the capacity to enter into legal relationships, such as being the owner of property, being a party to a contract or being a claimant or defendant in legal proceedings.

The law is concerned with relationships, such as contracts, ownership of property and duties of care, which are entered into by 'persons', who have the duties and rights attached to the relationships they enter into. The types of relationship studied in law are based on the transactions and activities of human beings, who are described as 'natural' or 'real' persons. But legal principles are concerned with the nature of a legal relationship, such as contract or the ownership of property, and can be applied not only when a human being enters into the relationship but also when another entity does. English law, like other legal systems, recognises that some entities, such as corporations, which are not human beings can enter into at least some legal relationships. For the purposes of the relationships in which their participation is recognised, entities other than human beings are said to have 'legal' personality (sometimes called 'juristic' or 'juridical' personality).

The capacity of a corporation, such as a registered company, to enter into legal relationships is limited only by two factors:

(a) The fact that the entity is not human. For example, a corporation cannot have hurt feelings (*Collins Stewart Ltd v Financial Times Ltd* [2005] EWHC 262 (QB), [2006] EMLR 5), cannot drive a lorry (*Richmond London Borough Council v Pinn and Wheeler Ltd* [1989] RTR 354), and cannot be committed to prison (*Masri v Consolidated Contractors International Co SAL* [2011] EWCA Civ 898, [2012] 1 WLR 223).

(b) Any limitation imposed by the process of incorporation. Following recent reforms, only charitable companies suffer any limitations on capacity by being incorporated as registered companies (see **19.4**).

Section 16(3) says that a registered company 'is capable of exercising all the functions of an incorporated company'.

As well as having its own personality, a registered company is also seen as being an association of persons (natural or legal) who are called the 'members' of the company. This is why persons who wish to register a new company must subscribe their names to a 'memorandum of association' (s 8) stating that they wish to form a company under CA 2006, and s 16(2) states that, on registration:

> The subscribers to the memorandum, together with such other persons as may from time to time become members of the company, are a body corporate by the name stated in the certificate of incorporation.

In nearly every company, membership is based on holding shares in the company and so the terms 'member' and 'shareholder' are virtually synonymous.

Probably the most important legal feature of a body corporate is its dual nature as both an association of its members and a person separate from its members. The association of members may have only one member, as when a company is registered with a memorandum of association subscribed by only one person, as permitted by s 7(1). CA 2006 does not prohibit other members joining a company which was registered with only one member.

A corporation which is regarded as an association of members is called a 'corporation aggregate'. Its members are sometimes called 'corporators'.

Artificial entities with full legal personality are very useful (as is shown by the fact that at the end of March 2017 there were 3,896,755 registered companies in the United Kingdom):

(a) Where legal relationships have to be entered into for a particular purpose those relationships can be ascribed to a separate legal person so as not to be confused with other affairs. For example, where business is conducted in the name of a registered company, the affairs of the business are kept separate from the personal affairs of the human beings who conduct it, and separate from the affairs of any other business they may conduct in the name of another registered company.

(b) An artificial entity may continue in existence indefinitely.

(c) Not only does an entity with full legal personality have all the legal rights, obligations, duties and liabilities arising from the legal relationships it is put into, but no other person shares any of those rights, obligations, duties or liabilities unless the entity is found to be acting as agent for some other person (*J H Rayner (Mincing Lane) Ltd v Department of Trade and Industry* [1990] 2 AC 418 per Lord Templeman at pp 479–80, Lord Oliver of Aylmerton at p 511). Furthermore, the facts that the members of a corporation exercise control over it, or that the sole objective of the corporation's legal relationships is to benefit the members, are not in themselves sufficient to constitute the corporation an agent of its members (*Salomon v A Salomon and Co Ltd* [1897] AC 22; *J H Rayner (Mincing Lane) Ltd v Department of Trade and Industry* [1989] Ch 72, CA at pp 188–9, [1990] 2 AC 418, HL at p 515). This is the principle of 'separate personality'. As Alderson B said in **Bligh v Brent** (1837) 2 Y & C Ex 268: 'The individual members of a corporation are quite as distinct from the metaphysical body called "the corporation", as any others of his Majesty's subjects are'. This principle confers on the members of a corporation the benefit of not being responsible for the corporation's debts except to the extent that they are made responsible by statute or by the corporation's constitution. Lord Parker of Waddington summarised the law as follows in **Daimler Co Ltd v Continental Tyre and Rubber Co (Great Britain) Ltd** [1916] 2 AC 307 at p 338:

> No one can question that a corporation is a legal person distinct from its corporators; that the relation of a shareholder to a company . . . is not in itself the relation of principal and agent or the reverse; that the assets of the company belong to it and the acts of its servants and agents are its acts, while its shareholders, as such, have no property in the assets and no personal liability for those acts.

It follows that the members of a corporation cannot owe any duty of care in respect of the corporation's acts, that is, they cannot be liable in tort for the corporation's acts (*Kuwait Asia Bank EC v National Mutual Life Nominees Ltd* [1991] 1 AC 187).

1.3.2 TYPES OF CORPORATION

1.3.2.1 Methods of incorporation

In the law of England and Wales, a corporation may be:

(a)   incorporated by the Crown by the grant of a royal charter;

(b)   incorporated by Parliament by passing an Act;

(c)   incorporated by registration with a public official who has authority to incorporate delegated by Parliament;

(d)   incorporated by act of a person exercising authority delegated by Parliament;

(e)   found to be incorporated by prescription.

1.3.2.2 Royal charter

The English theory of corporations was developed in relation to the powers of self-government which were possessed by certain communities (known as municipal corporations) and which were stated in royal charters.

From the sixteenth century onwards, royal charters were granted to trading companies, especially for the purposes of overseas trading, exploration and colonisation. In the seventeenth and eighteenth centuries, and in the early nineteenth century, many domestic trading companies were incorporated by royal charter. Such companies are known as 'chartered companies'. The characteristic structure of the later chartered companies was that the members contributed capital to form the company's 'joint stock' which was then managed by 'governors' or 'directors' appointed by the members.

Since the mid-nineteenth century, with a few exceptions, corporations have been created by the Crown only for non-profit-making, charitable and educational purposes, for example, the Law Society, the Institute of Chartered Accountants in England and Wales and the Chartered Institute of Management Accountants.

1.3.2.3 Act of Parliament

Parliament may create a body corporate by an enactment referring specifically to that body. Corporations established for public purposes (for example, the Historic Buildings and Monuments Commission for England incorporated by the National Heritage Act 1983, s 32 and sch 3, para 1) are incorporated by public general Act. Parliament may be petitioned to pass a private Act to establish a corporation for the petitioners' commercial purposes, especially where powers are required to compulsorily purchase land for public utilities: corporations formed in this way are called 'statutory companies'.

1.3.2.4 Registration with a public official

The main problem with incorporation by royal charter or by private Act of Parliament is that the Crown and Parliament have been suspicious of lending their dignity and the benefits of separate personality to commercial organisations and have therefore imposed procedural and cost deterrents. In the early nineteenth century, legal advisers of business people were well aware that incorporation is a convenient method of conducting the affairs of a business but were usually unable to obtain a charter or an Act of Parliament. Most joint-stock companies therefore had to be organised as unincorporated associations, which was often very inconvenient. Without separate personality a joint-stock company could not own property, make contracts or be a party to legal proceedings: everything had to be done in the joint names of the shareholders of whom there might be several thousand. Legal proceedings, in particular, could collapse under the weight of paper, as in *Van Sandau v Moore* (1826) 1 Russ 441, in which there were 250 defendants. Parliament did become willing to allow selected unincorporated joint-stock companies to overcome the difficulties of taking part in legal proceedings. In the early part of the nineteenth century it became quite common for the members of an unincorporated joint-stock company to obtain a private Act of Parliament entitling the secretary or a director of their company to take part in legal proceedings on behalf of the company, as the company's 'public officer'. However, Parliament would pass such an Act only for an established company, and it required, as a condition, that the company had to file a list of its members in the Court of Chancery and keep the list up to date. A company which made public disclosure of its list of members in this way was known in the early nineteenth century as a 'public company' (see *Macintyre v Connell* (1851) 1 Sim NS 225). For the use of the term 'public company' in this old sense, see **4.2.5**. In company law, the term is nowadays used in the sense discussed in **2.3.3**.

Eventually Parliament conceded that it had been unnecessarily difficult and inconvenient for business people to obtain the benefits of incorporation. It passed the Joint Stock Companies Act 1844, which established the office of the Registrar of Joint Stock Companies and empowered the registrar to incorporate any company whose documents were duly registered with him. Under the 1844 Act, registration was a two-stage process: provisional registration (costing £5), which did not confer corporate status (*Womersley v Merritt* (1867) LR 4 Eq 695), followed by complete registration (a further £5) which did. The whole system was revised by the Joint Stock Companies Act 1856, which introduced the present system of single-stage registration (which still costs £10 if the application is delivered electronically by a company formation agent: SI 2012/1907, sch 1, para 8(a)(iii)). The latest statute governing registration of companies is CA 2006.

Incorporation by registration is in fact an old idea: a statute of 1597, 39 Eliz 1, c 5 (Hospitals for the Poor), enabled individuals to incorporate hospitals by registration of a deed in the Court of Chancery. At present there are, essentially, nine provisions under which incorporation may be achieved by registering documents with a public official or body. They are (in alphabetical order) the Building Societies Act 1986, the Charities Act 2011, CA 2006, the Co-operative and Community Benefit Societies Act 2014, the European Economic Interest Grouping Regulations 1989 (SI 1989/638), the European Public Limited-Liability Company Regulations 2004 (SI 2004/2326), the Friendly Societies Act 1992, the Industrial and Provident Societies Act 1965 and the Limited Liability Partnerships Act 2000. Of these, CA 2006 is by far the most important. The other provisions apply only to limited classes of association, but a company may be formed under CA 2006 for any purpose that is not unlawful (s 7). The Limited Liability Partnerships Act 2000 (see **1.4.1.3**) is another general incorporation statute. It enables the incorporation by registration of a limited liability partnership (LLP) 'for carrying on a lawful business with a view to profit' (s 2(1)(a)). This is slightly less general than CA 2006 in that an LLP can be incorporated only for a business purpose whereas a company can be registered under CA 2006 for a business or non-business purpose.

1.3.2.5 Incorporation by delegated authority

The Housing Act 1988, s 62, is an example of a statutory provision enabling incorporation by ministerial act. It empowers the Secretary of State to create bodies corporate called housing action trusts by order made by statutory instrument. However, a draft of the order must be approved by a resolution of each House of Parliament.

An open-ended investment company can be incorporated by an order (called an authorisation order) made by the FCA under the Open-Ended Investment Companies Regulations 2001 (SI 2001/1228).

Ministers and other authorities have powers to create corporations only insofar as they have been given such powers by Parliament.

1.3.2.6 Prescription

The essence of the doctrine of incorporation by prescription is that a body may be found by a court to be incorporated by a royal charter that has been lost if, for a sufficiently long time, it has been treated as though it were incorporated. See *Re Company or Fraternity of Free Fishermen of Faversham* (1887) 36 ChD 329.

1.3.2.7 Corporations sole

English common law adopted a theory that certain public and ecclesiastical offices (such as the Crown, a bishop or a parson of the Church of England) had a separate legal personality, originally to provide a legal framework for ownership of church land. As only one individual could hold such an office at any one time, the incorporated offices are known as corporations 'sole'. Occasionally, Parliament creates a corporation sole, for example, the public trustee (Public Trustee Act 1906, s 1(2)) and the Corporate Officer of each House of Parliament (Parliamentary Corporate Bodies Act 1992, ss 1(1) and 2(1)). There is no concept of corporation sole in Scots law.

1.3.3 CORPORATION TAX

Any body corporate which is resident in the United Kingdom (see **19.8.7.2**) is subject to corporation tax on its profits, and is not subject to income tax or capital gains tax (Corporation Tax Act 2009, ss 2, 3 and 4, and Corporation Tax Act 2010, s 1121(1)). The same applies to unincorporated associations (see **1.4.2**), but not to partnerships (**1.4.1**). Rather confusingly, in tax legislation, the term 'company' is used for any entity which is subject to corporation tax (Corporation Tax Act 2010, s 1121(1)).

1.4 OTHER LEGAL FORMS FOR BUSINESSES

1.4.1 PARTNERSHIP

1.4.1.1 General partnerships

Persons (natural or legal) carrying on a business or profession in common with a view of profit, without being incorporated, are said to be in 'partnership' (Partnership Act 1890, s 1) and their association is known as a partnership 'firm' (s 4(1)). The law of partnership in the United Kingdom has been codified in the Partnership Act 1890. The members of a corporation aggregate, such as a company registered under CA 2006, are not in partnership (Partnership Act 1890, s 1(2)).

Partnership is created by agreement between the partners without any action by the State. But it is not the agreement alone which creates a partnership. It is carrying on business in a particular way which creates a partnership, and a partnership comes into existence only when the partners begin to carry on business in accordance with their agreement (see *Khan v Miah* [2000] 1 WLR 2123 on what constitutes carrying on business for this purpose). This may be contrasted with a registered company, which comes into existence as soon as it is registered, regardless of whether it transacts any business.

The fundamental difference between carrying on business in partnership and being a member of an incorporated company is that being a member of a partnership imposes liability for all debts and obligations of the firm incurred during membership (Partnership Act 1890, s 9) regardless of any agreement to the contrary between the partners, whereas a member of a body corporate is not liable for the debts of the corporation unless liability is imposed on members by the constitution of the corporation or by statute. As Cave J said in **Re Sheffield and South Yorkshire Permanent Building Society** (1889) 22 QBD 470, at p 476:

> [Counsel] argued that persons who unite together for trading or making profits in any way are, at common law, liable for all debts which are incurred during the time they are members of the association, and that, if the association has ultimately to be wound up, past members must pay their shares of the debts. As a general rule—apart from legislation—that is perfectly true with respect to partners, and with respect to associations in the nature of partnership where there is no incorporation, but with respect to corporations the case is entirely different where the legislature has not thought fit to intervene, or where the charter under which the body is incorporated does not provide otherwise. A corporation is a legal persona just as much as an individual; and, if a man trusts a corporation, he trusts that legal persona, and must look to its assets for payment: he can only call upon the individual members to contribute in case the Act or charter has so provided.

Linked to this is the further important difference that every partner in a firm may act for the purposes of the firm's business, and the acts of any one member of a partnership bind all the partners (Partnership Act 1890, s 5); whereas in an incorporated company a board of directors must be appointed to act for the company in matters of business and no member of the company has, as a member, any authority to bind the company (see **15.1**).

Sometimes, partnership firms are described as 'companies'. Often the name of a firm consists of the name of one or more principal or founding partners followed by the words 'and Company' to represent the other partners.

The Law Commissions published a joint report on partnership law, proposing that English partnerships should have separate legal personality (Law Commission, *Partnership Law* (Law Com No 283, Cm 6015) (London: Stationery Office, 2003)). The government decided not to act on this report.

1.4.1.2 Limited partnerships

The general rule of partnership is that there is no limit on a partner's liability for the firm's debts and obligations. It is possible, however, under the Limited Partnerships Act 1907 to form a limited partnership consisting of (a) one or more persons called 'general partners', who are liable for all debts and obligations of the firm, and (b) one or more persons called 'limited partners', who contribute capital to the firm on entering into the partnership but are not liable to pay anything more to meet its debts and obligations (s 4(2)). A limited partner does not have power to bind the firm (s 6(1)). A limited partnership must be registered with the registrar of companies, otherwise the limited partner will be deemed to be a general partner with unlimited liability (ss 5 and 15). The limited partnership form has not been very popular for business and professional purposes, but is used as a vehicle for making investments, because of tax advantages. At the end of March 2016 only 39,601 limited partnerships were registered in the United Kingdom. As limited partners do not take part in the management of the firm and, at one time, could not have their names included in the firm name (so as to avoid suggesting they would be liable for the firm's debts), they are sometimes called 'anonymous' partners. The idea survives in some European languages in which a public company whose members have limited liability is called an 'anonymous company' (for example, *société anonyme* in French, *sociedad anónima* in Spanish).

The Partnership Act 1890 and the general law of partnership apply to limited partnerships, subject to the modifications made by the Limited Partnerships Act 1907. It seems that the tax advantages of limited partnerships might be lost in overseas jurisdictions, if they were given separate legal personality, as the Law Commissions recommended for general partnerships (see **1.4.1.1**). So they recommended that separate personality should be optional for English limited partnerships (*Partnership Law* (Law Com No 283, Cm 6015) (London: Stationery Office, 2003)).

1.4.1.3 Limited liability partnerships

The Limited Liability Partnerships Act 2000 introduced a new form of business association called the limited liability partnership (LLP). The relationship between the members of an LLP can be like that of members of a general partnership (see **1.4.1.1**). In particular, every member of an LLP is deemed to be an agent of the LLP (s 6). But, when it is registered with the registrar of companies, an LLP is incorporated and so has separate personality (s 1(2)). It follows that the members of an LLP are not directly responsible for its debts, and the law relating to partnerships does not apply to LLPs (s 1(4) and (5)). At the end of April 2017 there were 60,772 LLPs in the United Kingdom.

1.4.2 UNINCORPORATED ASSOCIATIONS

The term 'unincorporated association' is usually used to refer to any association of persons (natural or legal) which has not been incorporated but which is not a partnership firm (because the members of the association are not carrying on a business or profession in common with a view of profit).

1.4.3 SOLE PROPRIETORSHIP

An individual who carries on a business or profession personally without partners is said to bethe 'sole proprietor' of the business or profession. A professional person is usually described as a 'sole practitioner' whereas a sole proprietor of a business is usually described as a 'sole trader'.

In sole proprietorship there is no legal separation between the business and personal affairs of the proprietor, and he or she is directly responsible for all the debts incurred in carrying on the business or profession.

1.5 SOURCES OF COMPANY LAW

1.5.1 LEGISLATION

1.5.1.1 Importance of legislation

A registered company, as an artificial person separate from its members, exists only by virtue of the Companies Act under which it was incorporated. In *Welton v Saffery* [1897] AC 299 Lord Macnaghten said, at p 324, 'These companies are the creature of statute', and in *Ooregum Gold Mining Co of India Ltd v Roper* [1892] AC 125 Lord Halsbury LC said, at p 133: 'the whole structure of a limited company owes its existence to the Act of Parliament, and it is to the Act of Parliament one must refer to see what are its powers, and within what limits it is free to act'. The legislation on companies is therefore the primary source of company law.

1.5.1.2 History and current legislation

Incorporation of companies by registration was first legislated for in the Joint Stock Companies Act 1844. The Joint Stock Companies Act 1856 created a wholly revised system which has been developed by successive Companies Acts ever since. The latest Act is the Companies Act 2006 (CA 2006), which has been fully in force since 1 October 2009.

The principal piece of legislation in force immediately before CA 2006 was CA 1985. The only provisions of CA 1985 which remain in force are parts 14, 15 and 18, s 726(2) and the short title.

Parts 14 and 15 are concerned with company investigations and are considered in **18.8**. Part 18 will be repealed when the Bankruptcy and Diligence etc (Scotland) Act 2007 (asp 3), s 46(1), is brought into force. Section 726(2) concerns court proceedings in Scotland.

CA 2006, s 2, defines 'the Companies Acts' as:

(a) parts 1 to 39 of CA 2006;

(b) parts 45 to 47 of CA 2006 so far as they apply for the purposes of parts 1 to 39;

(c) part 2 of the Companies (Audit, Investigations and Community Enterprise) Act 2004 (CICs; see **2.3.1**); and

(d) the provisions of CA 1985 and of the Companies Consolidation (Consequential Provisions) Act 1985 which remain in force (see earlier). The whole of the Consequential Provisions Act has been repealed.

Legislation on company insolvency and liquidation is in the Insolvency Act 1986 (IA 1986) and the Company Directors Disqualification Act 1986 (CDDA 1986). (The Insolvency Act 1986 also deals with the insolvency of individuals, known as bankruptcy.)

The legislation on the control of public markets in company shares is contained in the Financial Services and Markets Act 2000 (FSMA 2000).

The primary legislation in CA 2006 authorises the Secretary of State to fill in details by making delegated legislation in statutory instruments. Sometimes, persons other than government ministers are empowered to make delegated legislation. For public companies the most significant pieces of delegated legislation of this type are the rules which are made by the FCA in the FCA Handbook.

In this book, a reference to a provision of legislation is a reference to that provision as amended, unless the words 'as originally enacted' are used. The text of legislation as amended may be found in D French, *Blackstone's Statutes on Company Law 2017–2018* (Oxford: Oxford University Press, 2017).

1.5.1.3 The Company Law Review and the Companies Act 2006

CA 2006 is the most extensive revision of company law ever undertaken. It is the result of the Company Law Review, which was set up by the Department of Trade and Industry (DTI) in March 1998, and which made its final report in June 2001. The terms of reference for the Review were:

(i) To consider how core company law can be modernised in order to provide a simple, efficient and cost-effective framework for carrying out business activity which:

    (a) permits the maximum amount of freedom and flexibility to those organising and directing the enterprise;

    (b) at the same time protects, through regulation where necessary, the interests of those involved with the enterprise, including shareholders, creditors and employees; and

    (c) is drafted in clear, concise and unambiguous language which can be readily understood by those involved in business enterprise.

(ii) To consider whether company law, partnership law and other legislation which establishes a legal form of business activity together provide an adequate choice of legal vehicle for business at all levels.

(iii) To consider the proper relationship between company law and non-statutory standards of corporate behaviour.

(iv) To review the extent to which foreign companies operating in Great Britain should be regulated under British company law.

(v) To make recommendations accordingly.

The first product of this review was a consultation document from the **Company Law Review Steering Group,** *Modern Company Law for a Competitive Economy: The Strategic Framework* (URN 99/654) (London: DTI, 1999), which summarised the Review's overall approach (para 2):

> The objective is modern law supporting a competitive economy, in a coherent and accessible form, providing maximum freedom for participants to perform their proper functions, but recognising the case for high standards and for ensuring appropriate protection for all interested parties. Account needs to be taken of current change, particularly globalisation, the impact of the EU's company law harmonisation programme, modern patterns of regulation and ownership, changing asset structures and the importance of small and closely held businesses. In principle there should be presumptions:
>
> • against interventionist legislation and in favour of facilitating markets, including provision for transparency of information, wherever possible;
>
> • in favour of minimising complexity and maximising accessibility of the rules—complexity should only arise where the substance demands it and the law should be structured on 'think small first' principles;
>
> • against creating criminal offences unless the subject matter demands it; and
>
> • in favour of allocating jurisdiction to the most suitable regulatory bodies, avoiding duplication and effort.

All the Review's reports may be downloaded at **http://webarchive.nationalarchives.gov. uk/20070603164510/http://www.dti.gov.uk/bbf/co-act-2006/clr-review/page22794. html**

The Review was 'wholly committed to proceeding by open consultation' (*Completing the Structure*, para 1.5): and

> the Review has sought to build consensus around its emerging conclusions, and to work towards an outcome which commands wide support; but it would be quite wrong to regard the consultative process as looking simply for some common denominator. The primary focus is on forming a view as to the best way forward in relation to the framework of company law as a whole. (*Completing the Structure*, para 1.6)

Consultation helped the Steering Group to refine their proposals and, in some cases, to change their position (for example, on no par value shares, see **6.2.7**).

The Review's final report was published in two volumes in July 2001 (*Modern Company Law for a Competitive Economy: Final Report* (URN 01/942 and 01/943) (London: DTI, 2001)).

On 15 July 2002 the government published a White Paper, *Modernising Company Law* (Cm 5553), in response to the Review's final report. *Modernising Company Law* is in two volumes, the second volume (Cm 5553-II) containing an incomplete draft Bill.

The Company Law Review proceeded on the basis that it would result in a completely new Companies Act and supporting regulations. *Modernising Company Law* noted that drafting a new Companies Act is 'a huge undertaking' (Cm 5553-I, part I, para 11). Rather than wait for the whole job to be completed, some reforms were made by statutory instruments and by the Companies (Audit, Investigations and Community Enterprise) Act 2004.

After nearly three years of further work, a second White Paper, *Company Law Reform* (Cm 6456, 2005), was published in March 2005, containing new draft clauses. The idea of completely replacing CA 1985 was abandoned and there were significant differences between the drafts in the two White Papers, so the earlier one should be regarded as of historical interest only.

The government introduced a complete Bill in the House of Lords on 1 November 2005 with the title Company Law Reform Bill. Following the plan in the second White Paper, much of it was drafted as amendments to CA 1985. Almost all non-government speakers in the second reading debate protested that this would make companies legislation needlessly complex and asked for a complete restatement of the law. Bearing in mind that the previous consolidation, CA 1985, had taken five years to prepare, it is remarkable that the government accepted this request and also accepted that the title of the Bill should be changed to Companies Bill, which received royal assent on 8 November 2006 and is now the Companies Act 2006.

1.5.1.4 Legislative process

The Companies Bills considered in the 1980s revealed problems with the legislative process. In the debate on the third reading of the Bill that became the Companies Act 1981 Mr Stanley Clinton Davis (a practising solicitor) said (Parliamentary Debates (Hansard), Commons, 6th ser, vol 10 (1980–81), col 68):

> Few honourable members who have served in committee on Companies Bills regard them as great examples of the efficiency of Parliamentary procedures. We are bogged down with an enormous welter of technical detail. Few of us, including myself, understand much of that detail when it is before the committee.
>
> . . .
>
> The bodies with a professional interest in such matters have a great deal to contribute—more, I fear, than honourable members when dealing with highly technical, non-contentious matters.

Companies Bills are invariably government Bills. The legislators in Parliament are required to consider Bills prepared by the civil service dealing with topics chosen by the civil service. There is a great deal of public consultation before drafting legislation. BIS 'is committed to undertaking public consultation on the development of company law' (Department of Trade and Industry, *Companies in 1992–93* (London: HMSO, 1993), p 2). Extensive consultation was a particular feature of the Company Law Review. But consultation consists merely of receiving views, not arguing over them as in Parliamentary debate. Obviously it is to be welcomed that proposals for changing the law are the product of careful consideration but it often seems that the system prevents Parliament fulfilling properly its representative function in arguing the causes of different groups and its role in protecting the public interest.

In what seems like an admission of defeat, Parliament has granted the Secretary of State extensive powers to amend CA 2006 by regulations made by statutory instrument. See ss 151, 385(4) and (5), 468, 484, 657, 737, 828, 948(4) and (5), 1101 and 1160. Of these, the power to amend the provisions on accounts (now in s 468) has been the one which was most extensively used to amend CA 1985. Parliament retains some control over the delegated amendment process, in that regulations must be laid before it, and cannot come into force until approved by a resolution of each House. This is the 'affirmative resolution procedure' (s 1290). It does not apply to regulations made under ss 948 and 1160 or to some regulations under ss 468 (accounts) and 484 (audit). Those are subject only to the 'negative resolution procedure', meaning that they come into force unless either House annuls them (s 1289). Regulations under ss 468 and 484 are subject only to the negative resolution procedure unless they restrict exemptions or require additional disclosure (accounts), impose new requirements (audit) or render existing requirements more onerous (ss 473 and 484(3) and (4)). There is no parliamentary procedure for amending a statutory instrument, which can only be approved or rejected as a whole. In 2015, one of these powers to amend company law, CA 2006, s 657, was used purely to bring an end to a method of tax avoidance (SI 2015/472, which inserted new subsections (2A), (2B) and (2C) in CA 2006, s 641; see **10.7.1**).

The Company Law Review Steering Group recommended that there should be a permanent Company Law and Reporting Commission (*Modern Company Law for a Competitive Economy: Final Report* (URN 01/942 and 01/943) (London: DTI, 2001), vol 1, paras 5.21 to 5.37). It was proposed that this Commission would keep company law and governance under review and submit an annual report to the Secretary of State. In turn, the Secretary of State would be under a duty to consult the Commission on proposed secondary legislation. In its White Paper, *Modernising Company Law* (Cm 5553, 2002), the government rejected this idea (Cm 5553-I, part II, paras 5.25 to 5.27).

The White Paper said (part II, para 5.26):

The government has already shown its willingness to consult intensively and inclusively through the Company Law Review. We remain committed to continuing consultation on company law, although we trust the need to consult will be less in the period following major reform; but we prefer to do so flexibly, as the need arises, rather than through a single, statutory body. The government believes it is right to be cautious about entrenching in statute arrangements which may themselves become outdated and inflexible.

The White Paper, *Company Law Reform* (Cm 6456, 2005), para 6.1, proposed that future reform and restatement of company law should be made by a special form of secondary legislation, using a procedure like that for regulatory reform orders under the Regulatory Reform Act 2001. This would involve examination of proposals by committees of both Houses of Parliament and final approval by resolution of each House. The Secretary of State would be required to consult on all proposals. This proposal was included in the Company Law Reform Bill when it was first presented to the House of Lords, but was withdrawn when it was decided to make more general provision for revision of all kinds of legislation in the Legislative and Regulatory Reform Act 2006.

The House of Lords responded to these difficulties in the best possible way with a high standard of legislative scrutiny in debates on the Company Law Reform Bill, in which Lord Clinton-Davis, as he now is, participated. The Liberal Democrat spokesperson, Lord Razzall (another solicitor) called it 'an absolute paradigm of how Bills should be conducted' (Hansard HL, 23 May 2006, col 794).

1.5.1.5 Complexity

The legislation on companies forms a very large and detailed code of rules. A company as an artificial separate person exists only in writing, and there is a need for precise instructions on how this artificial entity is to be used, especially to ensure uniformity of treatment of the very large number of companies now registered in the United Kingdom. As Lord Hoffmann said in *Meridian Global Funds Management Asia Ltd v Securities Commission* [1995] 2 AC 500 at p 506, 'Any proposition about a company necessarily involves a reference to a set of rules.' Another factor contributing to the size of the code is the detailed style of drafting customarily used in UK legislation.

There is no doubt that the legislation on companies became very much more complex in the 1980s and 1990s because of amending Acts and statutory instruments. CA 1948 consisted of 462 sections and 18 schedules. CA 1985 had 747 sections and 25 schedules. CA 2006 has 1,300 sections and 16 schedules. But CA 1948 and CA 1985 included the legislation which is now in the Insolvency Act 1986 and the Company Directors Disqualification Act 1986, and most of the schedules in the earlier Acts are not in CA 2006 at all, but are covered by regulations in statutory instruments.

With a code of this length and complexity there is a great danger that people will act in ignorance of some vital legislative provision. For example, in *Re Bradford Investments plc (No 2)* [1991] BCLC 688, four people transferred their business to a public company in return for shares in the company not knowing that what is now CA 2006, s 593 requires the preparation of an independent report on the value of the business (see **6.6.4.2**). Because the statute was not complied with, they became liable to pay more than £1 million plus interest. They had relied on advice from solicitors, accountants in public practice and the company's accountant. In *British Racing Drivers' Club Ltd v Hextall Erskine and Co* [1996] 3 All ER 667, a solicitor, described as 'a senior commercial partner with extensive experience of the Companies Acts', wrongly advised that it was not necessary for a company to obtain the approval of its members for a substantial property transaction with one of its directors as required by what is now CA 2006, s 190 (see **16.12**). Damages of more than £2.8 million were awarded for this negligent advice. Other examples are *Re Chez Nico (Restaurants) Ltd* [1992] BCLC 192 discussed by C Mercer, 'Compulsory acquisition of minorities' (1992) 13 Co Law 139 and *Brady v Brady* [1989] AC 755 (see **10.8.1.7**), in which the lawyers did not discover which statutory provision was relevant to the case until it reached the House of Lords.

All the cases just mentioned were concerned with changes introduced into the law during the 1980s. Similar problems do, however, arise in relation to rules that have been in existence for much longer. In *EIC Services Ltd v Phipps* [2004] EWCA Civ 1069, [2005] 1 WLR 1377, advisers of a company preparing for a Stock Exchange flotation failed to notice that its directors should have obtained authorisation from its existing shareholders before issuing them with bonus shares (see **10.4**). The resulting claim took up ten days of court time and produced a judgment of 226 paragraphs, which was reversed by the Court of Appeal, after hearing argument only from a shareholder who did not have professional legal representation.

1.5.1.6 New styles of legislation

Finding some way to reduce the complexity of companies legislation was one of the tasks of the Company Law Review. An early consultation document introducing the Review, *Modern Company Law for a Competitive Economy* (London: DTI, 1998), said that one of the first subjects for review would be 'the structure and style of new legislation and how it might be made more accessible to non-specialists' (p 19). In particular it noted two suggestions, which have often been made: (a) that the law on private and public companies should be in separate Acts (pp 7 and 15) and (b) that provisions should be transferred to secondary legislation, which can be revised more easily (pp 11 and 16), leaving a shorter principal statute which would be more readable. In *Modern Company Law for a Competitive Economy: The Strategic Framework* (URN 99/654) (London: DTI, 1999), Chapter 8, the Company Law Review Steering Group examined the difficulty of the legislative process and discussed ways of legislating without full parliamentary debate. However, this only raises the question whether company law is so non-political and irrelevant to the public interest that it can be altered in this way. In *Modern Company Law for a Competitive Economy: Completing the Structure* (URN 00/1335) (London: DTI, 2000), the Steering Group said, 'We fully recognise the need for proper parliamentary oversight of legislation and rules made under it' (para 12.39). Chapter 12 of *Completing the Structure* examined how best to divide company law into primary legislation, delegated legislation and codes of practice. There was further discussion of this in the *Final Report*, vol 1, paras 5.4 to 5.12.

Several years' experience of drafting the new Companies Act showed that:

> Company law does not always divide readily into 'principles' elements, which might remain in primary legislation, and more minor detail which might be appropriate for secondary. (*Flexibility and Accessibility: A Consultative Document* (URN 04/994) (London: DTI, 2004), p 7.)

Dividing a topic between two or more legislative documents does not necessarily make it easier to find. What it has been possible to do is to recognise that nowadays more than 99 per cent of companies are private companies and so statutes on company law should be arranged to deal with them first. Historically, company law was conceived as the law of public companies. As special simpler provisions for private companies were introduced, they were drafted as exceptions to the rules on public companies. In most areas, such as accounts and meetings, CA 2006 has been drafted so as to state the law applying to private companies first, with the additional requirements for public companies given in separate sections.

One disappointment is that the government too often accepted the view that if Parliament changes the wording of a provision when re-enacting it, then it is presumed that it was intended to change its meaning. Fears were expressed that any rewording of existing provisions would create uncertainty. The result is that some very badly worded provisions have been kept unaltered, instead of replacing them with better wording which would be clearer and make the legislation more accessible. For example, see the discussion of s 126 in **8.6.1**.

1.5.1.7 Studying legislation

It is not the purpose of this book to set out for our readers every legislative provision relating to companies. We have selected for discussion what we believe to be the most important provisions relating to the creation, financing and management of companies, and their insolvency and winding up. We want to show the legislative framework of company law. We believe that having this framework in mind is the best preparation for reading the legislation itself and the large commentaries on it written for practitioners (see **1.5.5**), which will provide the fine detail. For most chapters the 'What is in this chapter' section gives a list of the key legislation for the chapter. See further **2.6.1**.

1.5.2 CASE LAW

1.5.2.1 Types of case law studied in company law

Legal principles taken from judgments in court cases—known as case law, common law or, simply, law, as opposed to legislation—are of great significance in company law. Four types of case law may be distinguished:

(a) The courts are given a remarkably extensive supervisory role by the legislation relating to companies (see **1.5.2.2**) and a company's affairs must be conducted in the knowledge that they may be reviewed in court proceedings.

(b) Compliance with most of the legislation is enforced by criminal sanctions (see **1.5.2.3**).

(c) As in any area of statute law the courts have an important role in determining the meaning and application of the legislation and filling gaps in the legislative code (see **1.5.2.4**).

(d) There are certain types of dispute which regularly arise in relation to companies which it is appropriate to consider in a book on company law even though the principles of law involved come from other areas of law such as contract (for example, rescission of contracts of allotment of shares, see **6.8**) or tort (for example, the liability of auditors for negligence, see **17.5**).

1.5.2.2 Judicial supervision of companies

Parliament has relied heavily on court proceedings to control and supervise the operation of companies. But courts do not themselves seek out wrongdoing for investigation and punishment: their powers have to be invoked in proceedings brought by persons with the requisite standing.

The ultimate judicial sanction that may be invoked is the power to order a company to be wound up (Insolvency Act 1986, s 122). The legislation relating to companies gives many other supervisory functions to 'the court', which means, in England and Wales, the High Court or the County Court (CA 2006, s 1156). Examples of the court's supervisory functions are:

(a) The court has an important general power to make 'such order as it thinks fit' to give relief in respect of conduct of a company's affairs which is unfairly prejudicial to the interests of some or all of its members (ss 994 to 999; see **18.6**).

(b) The court has a significant power to disqualify a former director of a company from being a director of, or taking part in the management of, companies for a fixed period of up to 15 years (Company Directors Disqualification Act 1986; see **20.13**).

(c) If a company is, or is likely to become, unable to pay its debts, the court may make an administration order appointing an administrator to manage the company's affairs, business and property (Insolvency Act 1986, sch B1, paras 1(1) and 2(a); see **20.3**).

(d) A public company's issued share capital cannot be reduced unless the reduction is confirmed by the court (CA 2006, s 641; see **10.7**).

(e) The court may declare that a company's annual accounts do not comply with statutory requirements and order its directors to prepare revised accounts (s 456; see **9.10**).

(f) On three matters a dissentient minority of members of a company may apply to the court to have a resolution adopted by the majority set aside (see **14.4.3**).

The success of this wide supervisory jurisdiction depends on judges and barristers who specialise in company law. All matters involving the exercise of the High Court's jurisdiction under the enactments relating to companies are assigned to the Chancery Division by the Senior Courts Act 1981, sch 1, para 1. The Chancery Division in London has a separate registry for company cases, which are heard by specially designated judges, with routine applications being heard by the registrar. This is an administrative arrangement which has come to be known as the Companies Court.

The main reasons why it was appropriate for Chancery lawyers to add company law to their practice when the topic developed in the nineteenth century were that: (a) they had always handled partnership and insolvency matters, and (b) the Chancery court was able to deal with matters which involved continuing management, such as winding up the affairs of deceased and insolvent persons, and had available remedies such as injunction and taking accounts, which are particularly suited to dealing with long-term disputes concerning business relationships.

Because of the role of Chancery lawyers, equity has always been an important component of company law and with its emphasis on conscience and fairness has provided an extra-statutory source for judicial supervision of company affairs. This is particularly noticeable in the application to company directors of the equitable concept of fiduciary duty (see **Chapter 16**).

There are doubts about whether the amount of court time that has to be devoted to company matters is an effective use of resources. There has been repeated criticism of the length and cost of proceedings under CA 2006, ss 994 to 999, for relief of unfairly prejudicial conduct, and the Law Commission has made recommendations for improving the situation (*Shareholder Remedies* (Law Com No 246, Cm 3769) (London: Stationery Office, 1997)). As from 2 April 2001 the Secretary of State has been able to accept undertakings from former directors not to take part in the management of companies in place of going to court to obtain a disqualification order (see **20.13.3**).

For detailed consideration of procedure in the High Court and County Court on applications under CA 2006, IA 1986, CDDA 1986, and other legislation relating to companies see S Sime and D French (eds) *Blackstone's Civil Practice 2017* (Oxford: Oxford University Press), Chapters 82, 84, 85 and 86.

1.5.2.3 Criminal sanctions

Another aspect of Parliament's reliance on the courts in company law is the vast number of criminal offences (over 200) created by the companies, insolvency and financial services legislation. Most of these, in particular those under CA 2006, consist in failing to supply information to Companies House and such offences are normally triable only summarily (that is, by a magistrates' court) and the only penalty that may be imposed is a fine with a limit specified in the legislation creating the offence (though, of course, it is possible to be imprisoned for failing to pay a fine).

Other offences created by the legislation may be trivial or serious depending on the surrounding circumstances and are triable either way, that is, in a magistrates' court or in the Crown Court, depending on, among other things, the gravity of the particular allegation involved. Generally the Acts provide that a prison sentence may be imposed (if the court thinks it appropriate), instead of or in addition to a fine, for an offence triable either way, and the maximum term of imprisonment is usually set at two years. For a few serious offences (such as being a party to fraudulent trading) the maximum sentence may be seven years. There is no limit to the size of a fine that the Crown Court may impose (Criminal Law Act 1977, s 32(1)).

As well as the possibility of a fine or imprisonment for contravening provisions of the companies and insolvency legislation, a person may be disqualified from acting as a director of a company (see **20.13**).

In the consultation document introducing its review of company law (see **1.5.1.3**) the DTI said: 'One issue for the review will be the balance between civil and criminal sanctions: it is commonly suggested that the existing Companies Act too readily invokes criminal penalties, when civil remedies would be more appropriate' (*Modern Company Law for a Competitive Economy* (London: DTI, 1998), p 17). Despite this invitation to decriminalise, the Company Law Review Steering

Group found that the existing system of criminal penalties for minor regulatory offences works well. The threat of prosecution is very effective in securing compliance:

> It may be thought to bring the law into disrepute to provide so many criminal sanctions for technical offences for which prosecution is extremely rare. However, we believe that criminalising procedural requirements can underline the importance of compliance for directors and advisers. This strengthens the hand of advisers and employees responsible for ensuring compliance. Provided that such offences continue to be enforced in a sensible way, that seeks to promote maximum compliance rather than punishment, such a framework appears the most cost-effective available. It is very unlikely that an enforcement regime based on active monitoring and extensive use of reminders could operate effectively without underpinning criminal offences. (*Modern Company Law for a Competitive Economy: Completing the Structure* (URN 00/1335) (London: DTI, 2000), para 13.48)

The Steering Group maintained this view in their final report. Indeed, instead of considering decriminalisation the Steering Group suggested creating new offences and increasing penalties. See *Modern Company Law for a Competitive Economy: Final Report*, vol 1 (URN 01/942) (London: DTI, 2001), Chapter 15. In 2013, however, one criminal sanction was dropped because it was thought that there is a sufficient economic incentive to ensure compliance (see **11.7.3**).

1.5.2.4 Interpretation and gap-filling

The legislative code governing companies is very extensive and detailed and the justification for this is that it sets out in advance the rights and duties of persons who have dealings with companies and the formalities that must be observed so that all parties know what the position is and can act accordingly. However, (a) the natural limitations of language mean that questions may arise on the interpretation and application of the provisions of a legislative code; and (b) real life is complex and unpredictable and a legislative code cannot be complete, in the sense of deciding all possible questions within its scope.

The courts are often required to expound the meaning of a statutory provision by, for example, deciding whether or not it applies to a particular set of facts. For example, in *Neptune (Vehicle Washing Equipment) Ltd v Fitzgerald* [1996] Ch 274 it was held that CA 1985, s 317(1), which required a director of a company who was interested in a contract with the company to declare the nature of the interest at a meeting of the company's directors, applied when the director in question was the only director of the company. In the corresponding provisions of CA 2006, ss 177, 182 and 186, the wording has been changed so that the provisions will not apply to a sole director unless the company should have more than one director (see **16.11.1.2**).

In the late nineteenth century the courts were called upon to fill some rather substantial gaps in the legislation as it then existed (in CA 1862). The House of Lords established important principles of company law, which were not at that time stated in the legislation, in cases such as *Ashbury Railway Carriage and Iron Co Ltd v Riche* (1875) LR 7 HL 653, *Trevor v Whitworth* (1887) 12 App Cas 409, and *Ooregum Gold Mining Co of India Ltd v Roper* [1892] AC 125. The law established in all those three cases has now been replaced by fresh legislation. The legislation has reversed the effect of the *Ashbury Railway Carriage* case (see **19.4.1**), but the other two have been confirmed, though important exceptions have been created (see **Chapter 10**). In some areas, case law still attempts to fill notable gaps in the legislation, often very cautiously. A notable example is the liability of companies for crimes (see **19.8.4** to **19.8.6**).

For a review of judicial interpretation of companies legislation see D Milman, 'The courts and the Companies Acts: the judicial contribution to company law' [1990] LMCLQ 401.

1.5.2.5 Reports of cases

Since 1983, company law cases have been reported in two specialist series, *Butterworths Company Law Cases* (BCLC) and *British Company Cases* (BCC), the first five volumes of which were called

British Company Law Cases. The most significant decisions at first instance and in the Court of Appeal are also reported in the Chancery section of the *Law Reports*, that is, Ch in the current series, ChD in the second series (1875 to 1890), and LR Eq and LR Ch App in the first series (1865 to 1874). Supreme Court, Privy Council and House of Lords decisions are usually in the Appeal Cases section of the *Law Reports*.

1.5.2.6 Criticism of judicial approaches

A legal system is a set of principles on which courts base reasoned judgments. Company law appears to be a particularly intricate system of legislative and common law rules and equitable principles. This leads to two criticisms:

(a) Decisions of great practical importance to business people are made to depend on insignificant legal details. Business people may, for example, wonder why the agreement of all the members of a public company to a decision to reduce its capital is not considered a good enough agreement for the court to approve under CA 2006, s 645, if the members did not hold a meeting to come to the decision, whereas a decision come to at a meeting by a three-quarters majority is good enough even if only a quorum of members (typically two) attended the meeting. This rule was arrived at in *Re Barry Artist Ltd* [1985] 1 WLR 1305 purely by construction of the legislation. Many business people would think it ridiculous that learned judges interpreting the Insolvency Act 1986, s 123(1)(a), disagree over whether a statutory demand for a debt (which can be the first stage in a creditor's proceeding to have a company compulsorily wound up by the court) may or may not be sent by post (see **20.6.4**).

(b) When application of a legal rule produces an unwelcome result one reaction is to assert that judges should be free to disapply the rule whenever they like (usually expressed as 'whenever justice and equity require') and insistence on applying rules whatever the consequences is described as 'formalism' or 'purism', which is thought to be inherently wrong. The prime example of this in company law is the long-running controversy over the circumstances in which the separate personality of a company may be ignored (see **5.3**). But settled legal rules with predictable outcomes are also valued, especially when business arrangements are made relying on those rules. In the consultation document introducing its review of company law (see **1.5.1.3**) the DTI said, 'The new arrangements should be based on principles of consistency, predictability and transparency' (*Modern Company Law for a Competitive Economy* (London: DTI, 1998), p 6). The way in which a legal system should deal with a case in which the application of a rule would be unwelcome is to analyse what distinguishes the case from those in which the rule can be applied successfully and use that analysis to formulate an additional principle providing an exception to the rule. That new principle can then be followed in future cases and can be taken into account by people when planning their business transactions. See Lord Steyn, 'Does legal formalism hold sway in England?' *Current Legal Problems 1996*, part 2, pp 43–58.

1.5.2.7 Studying case law

The number of reported cases on company law is huge. The cases up to 1999 occupy two volumes (bound in five parts) of *The Digest*, taking up 2,707 pages. As with its treatment of legislation (see **1.5.1.7**), this book presents only a selection of the relevant reported cases. As with our treatment of the legislation, our aim is to provide a framework, which you can, if and when necessary, fill in with more detailed research of your own.

This book adopts the approach of setting out our statement of what the principles of law are, giving references to the cases from which we have derived those principles. This enables us to cite, and derive principles from, vastly more cases than could possibly be read during, for example, an undergraduate course on company law. For most chapters the 'What is in this chapter' section gives a very select list of the most significant cases which are recommended further reading. Your particular course of study may require you to read other cases.

1.5.3 EUROPEAN LAW

1.5.3.1 Brexit

This edition sets out the effect of European Union (EU) legislation on UK company law as at 1 April 2017. This book refers to EU legislation of three types:

(a) Directives. A Directive sets out principles which all member States must follow when legislating on a particular topic but leaves it to each member State to decide how to word their own legislation implementing the Directive. Directives have been very important in shaping UK company law and are discussed further in **1.5.3.2**.

(b) Regulations. A Regulation is directly effective EU legislation which is to be applied uniformly in every EU jurisdiction. Examples are Regulation No 2157/2001/EC (the Statute for a European Company) discussed at **2.9** and Regulation (EU) No 596/2014 (the Market Abuse Regulation) discussed in **Chapter 13**.

(c) Delegated Regulations. These are usually titled 'Commission Regulation' or 'Commission Implementing Regulation'. They are the equivalent of UK statutory instruments and provide technical details to supplement Regulations.

On 29 March 2017 the United Kingdom began the process of leaving the EU (Brexit). The EU legislation discussed in this book remains in force until the United Kingdom actually leaves the EU, which may be in mid-2019 after a two-year negotiation period. The government has established a Department for Exiting the European Union. Its website is **www.gov.uk/government/organisations/department-for-exiting-the-european-union**. On 30 March 2017 the Department issued a White Paper, *Legislating for the United Kingdom's Withdrawal from the European Union* (Cm 9446). This makes clear that, as far as possible, EU law, as it applies in the United Kingdom immediately before Brexit, will continue as UK law after Brexit. It will be necessary to make textual changes, for example, to remove references to EU legislation. The White Paper, para 3.24, says that these changes are to be ready before Brexit day so that they can come into effect as soon as the United Kingdom leaves.

Up until the United Kingdom actually leaves, EU company law as it affects the United Kingdom can be amended or added to by the usual EU legislative processes. Information about developments in EU company law is available at the website of the Directorate-General for Financial Stability, Financial Services and Capital Markets Union (DG FISMA): **https://ec.europa.eu/dgs/finance/index_en.htm**. After the United Kingdom leaves, EU law as it applies in the United Kingdom will be converted into UK law and can be amended by the UK legislature.

One problem that may need to be addressed in the Brexit negotiations is the future of 'passporting'. This is where regulatory approval or legal status conferred in one EU State has to be recognised in all other EU States. If such reciprocal arrangements are not secured as a part of the UK's new relationship with the EU, it may not be in the national interest, or workable, to continue to operate those arrangements alone (White Paper, para. 3.3). For an example in company law, see **7.4.1.1**.

All of the Directives and some of the Regulations discussed in this book have been extended under the EEA Agreement to apply to the non-EU members of the European Economic Area (EEA), Iceland, Liechtenstein and Norway. The UK government has indicated that the United Kingdom will be withdrawing from the EEA as well as from the EU.

1.5.3.2 Harmonisation Directives

In order to establish a common market for goods and services throughout the EU it was necessary to ensure that member States do not have significantly different laws governing the establishment of businesses. The initial concern was that all States should have at least minimum safeguards 'for the protection of the interests of members [of companies] and others'. What is now the Treaty on the Functioning of the European Union (TFEU) therefore authorises the European Council and the European Commission to coordinate 'to the necessary extent' such safeguards with a view to making them equivalent throughout the EU (art 50(2)(g)). The process of coordination required by art 50(2)(g) is usually referred to as 'harmonisation' of company law.

The common market would be distorted if a member State could adopt laws restricting business within its territory conducted by companies incorporated in other EU States. So art 49 of the TFEU prohibits restrictions on the freedom of establishment of nationals of one member State in the territory of another member State. Furthermore, art 54 requires companies or firms formed in accordance with the law of a member State, and having their registered office, central administration or principal place of business within the EU, to be accorded the same rights of freedom of establishment as natural persons who are nationals of member States. See I G F Cath, 'Freedom of establishment of companies: a new step towards completion of the internal market' 6 YEL 1986 247. The programme of company law harmonisation is undertaken to promote freedom of establishment (see the opening words of art 50 and F G Jacobs, 'The basic freedoms of the EEC Treaty and company law' (1992) 13 Co Law 4).

Harmonisation of company law is carried out by Directives, issued by the European Parliament and the Council, which set out requirements which member States must enact in their domestic legislation. A Directive is initiated by a proposal from the Commission, which must be jointly approved, with amendments if necessary, by the Council and the Parliament, following the ordinary legislative procedure of art 294 of the TFEU. In the past the harmonisation Directives have been referred to as the 'First', 'Second', etc Directives in the order in which they were proposed by the Commission. However, the Commission is reissuing the earlier Directives in codified versions incorporating all subsequent amendments and has omitted the ordinal numbers from the titles of these new versions. In this book, therefore, we refer to the Directives by their EU document numbers (for example, Directive 2009/101/EC).

All the company law Directives have been extended to apply throughout the EEA.

Implementation of Directives on company law in the United Kingdom has usually been by Act of Parliament, but some detailed amendments have recently been made by Regulations (SI 2007/3494) made by the Secretary of State under the European Communities Act 1972, s 2(2). The White Paper, *Legislating for the United Kingdom's Withdrawal from the European Union* (Cm 9446) says that such regulations will remain in force after Brexit despite the repeal of the 1972 Act (para 2.5).

1.5.3.3 Jurisdictional competition or cooperation?

Companies legislation is long and complex and involves both enabling provisions, which provide corporate forms for businesses to use, and mandatory provisions, which restrict how those forms may be used. Different jurisdictions which have the ability to create different forms of company law may produce laws with more or fewer mandatory provisions or with different enabling provisions. This may make some jurisdictions more attractive than others to business people wishing to form companies. There is little doubt that most business people incorporate their businesses in the jurisdictions in which they are based. This saves having to hire foreign lawyers to deal with compliance with the law of the jurisdiction of incorporation, and saves having to file documents both in the place of incorporation and the place of business. Nevertheless, where a choice is available some people will seek to evaluate the alternatives and choose the one that seems best.

The problems of having different companies legislation in different neighbouring jurisdictions which are closely linked economically and politically, so that it is easy to choose where to incorporate a business, have been faced in several areas of the world. In the United Kingdom (see **1.5.3.4**) and Australia (see **1.5.3.5**) the answer has been to adopt a uniform code. In the USA (see **1.5.3.6**) the opposite solution has been adopted and States have been allowed complete freedom to enact whatever corporations laws they want. The European Union (see 1.5.3.7 and 1.5.3.8) has compromised on a programme of harmonisation but not uniformity. Perhaps naturally, Americans have sought to show that their system would be better for the EU than the one it has chosen.

1.5.3.4 United Kingdom: uniformity of companies legislation

CA 2006 is a single legislative code for the whole United Kingdom, though some of its provisions have alternative formulations adapted to the different legal systems of the three jurisdictions (England and Wales, Scotland and Northern Ireland).

The creation, operation, regulation and dissolution of types of business association are reserved matters on which the Scottish Parliament is not competent to legislate (Scotland Act 1998, ss 29 and 30 and sch 5, part II, s C1).

The Northern Ireland Assembly is competent to enact separate companies legislation for Northern Ireland. Its predecessor, the Northern Ireland Parliament, did enact companies legislation, but it simply repeated the provisions of the contemporary English legislation with adjustments to suit its legal system. Under CA 2006 there is no longer separate companies legislation for Northern Ireland, but there is still separate insolvency and director disqualification legislation.

Companies can be registered under separate codes in Guernsey, Jersey and the Isle of Man. The fact that the separate jurisdiction of Sark has no company law at all, and so no controls on the activities of company directors, has sometimes been seen as a way of avoiding the provisions of UK company law (see *Official Receiver v Vass* [1999] BCC 516).

1.5.3.5 Australia: uniformity of companies legislation

In Australia, the Federal Parliament does not have power to legislate for the incorporation of companies (*New South Wales v The Commonwealth, The Incorporation Case* (1990) 169 CLR 482), but, since 1961, the States have agreed to adopt a uniform companies code (now called the Corporations Act 2001). Among the reasons for preferring uniformity appear to be the convenience of professional advisers who have to learn only one code for application throughout the country (an obvious advantage given the length and complexity of modern companies legislation), and frustration under the old system of different laws in different States that when one State improved its legislation, other States could not benefit from those improvements until their own legislatures could find time to enact them (see R McQueen, 'Why High Court judges make poor historians: the Corporations Act case and early attempts to establish a national system of company regulation in Australia' (1990) 19 Fed Law Rev 245).

1.5.3.6 USA: competition for incorporation fees

In the USA, corporations are incorporated (or 'chartered', as it is said there) under State laws and there is no system of Federal chartering. In the nineteenth century there was great popular suspicion of monopolistic big business, and all States imposed upper limits on the amount of capital a corporation could have. At the end of the nineteenth century, States one by one abandoned those limits and other restrictions as they competed with each other for the fees they could obtain from new incorporations. The history was described in *Louis K Liggett Co v Lee* (1933) 288 US 517 by Brandeis J, who talked of 'the traffic in charters' (at p 557) and of a 'race' between States which 'was one not of diligence but of laxity' (at p 559). The process has since become known as the 'race to the bottom'. It has been claimed that States have continued the race to the bottom by favouring the interests of the people who decide where to incorporate, typically those who are to be, or will control the appointment of, the directors. Delaware—the second smallest of the States—is the acknowledged winner of the race: in some years corporate fees have made up one-quarter of Delaware's State revenues. Over 40 per cent of corporations listed on the New York Stock Exchange in 1987 were incorporated in Delaware. This leadership means that Delaware lawyers benefit from the fees generated by corporate litigation. W L Cary, 'Federalism and corporate law: reflections upon Delaware' (1974) 83 Yale LJ 663 is a notable attack on the system. Others, however, defend Delaware: see C Alva, 'Delaware and the market for corporate charters: history and agency' (1990) 15 Del J Corp L 885, which reveals that Delaware's statutes on corporate law are drafted by the Delaware Bar Association and automatically adopted by the legislature, which has no members with any expertise in the subject. For further criticism and a detailed description of Delaware's legislation procedures see 'Law for sale: a study of the Delaware Corporation Law of 1967' (1969) 117 U Pa L Rev 861.

The American system is commonly defended on the ground that competition is a good thing and in a market for incorporation where State laws are a 'product', competition must result in a better product. Fears that the most successful laws are those that favour a particular interest group are countered by saying that if other interest groups really felt disadvantaged they would stop dealing with companies incorporated under the disadvantageous laws, and those laws would cease to be the most successful. In particular, it is argued that if different State laws had different effects on shareholders then this would be reflected in share prices but in fact there seems to be no evidence that moving to Delaware, for example, affects a company's share price. It may be that shareholders and directors in the USA pay less attention to state corporation laws than lawyers do. The real reason for Delaware's success at attracting corporations may just be that it has become a centre of expertise in corporate law and that the lawyers advising business people tell them to incorporate in Delaware because the lawyers' future work will be made easier if they are in a legal environment with which they are familiar and can trust (see W Bratton, 'Corporate law's race to nowhere in particular' (1994) 44 UTLJ 401, which is a valuable review of the debate in this area; D G Kaouris, 'Is Delaware still a haven for incorporation?' (1995) 20 Del J Corp L 965; M B Hemraj, 'The US corporations' preference to incorporate in Delaware: the search for justification' (2016) 37 Co Law 256).

1.5.3.7 Should the EU learn from the USA?

The idea of legislation as a product which is periodically redesigned to make it more attractive to consumers who may choose whether or not to adopt it is a challenge to the traditional concept of legislation as expressing inescapable basic standards for public life enacted in the public interest by the people's representatives in the legislature. It raises the question whether the public interest does require any minimum standards in company law. In Europe there is some minimum standard setting by Directives which harmonise, in the words of art 50(2)(g) of the TFEU, 'the safeguards which, for the protection of the interests of members *and others*, are required by member States of companies' (emphasis added). If there is no element of public interest in company law then it can be made by legally expert product designers and, as in Delaware, the legislators can adopt it without worrying about its effect on the people they represent. As companies are of such pervasive influence in everyday life it is unlikely that there can be no public interest in their activities or that voters would want to give up political control over them. What is in the public interest is a political question which must be determined by political institutions in which, often, conflicting interests must be reconciled. Comparing EU and US company law, W J Carney, 'The political economy of competition for corporate charters' (1997) 26 J Legal Stud 303 says that EU company law Directives (and hence UK company law) have far more mandatory provisions than equivalent US law. He attributes this to the lack of competition among European jurisdictions allowing interest groups to obtain legislation in their favour which he claims would be removed by market forces in the competitive USA. But another way of looking at it is that European company law is produced by democratic political institutions representing a wide range of interests, whereas Delaware corporate law is not.

1.5.3.8 Current state of EU company law

At present there are no plans for a uniform company law in Europe as there is in the United Kingdom and Australia. Article 50(2)(g) of the TFEU requires laws to be made 'equivalent', not 'uniform'. So far the policy has been to create a system of minimum standards for company law. According to

I G F Cath, 'Freedom of establishment of companies: a new step towards completion of the internal market' 6 YEL 1986 247 at p 255:

> Though often limited in scope and having a 'compromising' character, reflecting the different schools of thought which had to be reconciled, these Directives have brought some alignment of company law and have generally raised the existing standards to a common Community level.

Directives have made some startling administrative changes to UK company law—for example, introducing uniform formats for the publicly available accounts of companies, introducing a new system for recognition of the qualifications of auditors and introducing single-member companies. Substantive changes, altering the balance between various interest groups, are far fewer. The most significant example is the rules on security of transactions, which improve the position of persons dealing with companies and which are discussed in **Chapter 19**, especially **19.5** and **19.6**. These rules were originally made in Directive 68/151/EEC, which was adopted before the United Kingdom joined what was then the EEC, and it has been very difficult to amend UK company law to comply with the rules. (Directive 68/151/EEC has now been codified as Directive 2009/101/EC.)

There is little evidence that any EEA country is bidding to become the Delaware of Europe by diluting company law—low taxation seems to be a much more effective incentive. However, there are significant differences between national laws. For example, Germany insists on employee participation in any company with more than 500 employees; in the United Kingdom there is no minimum capital requirement for a private company whereas there is in Germany. American commentators, reflecting experience in their own country, suggest that these differences will increasingly influence the choice of jurisdiction of incorporation (see A F Conard, 'The European alternative to uniformity in corporation laws' (1991) 89 Mich L Rev 2150; C D Stith, 'Federalism and company law: a "race to the bottom" in the European Community' (1991) 79 Geo LJ 1581). But the European Commission has said that the prospect of companies moving within the EEA to countries with less stringent company laws 'would be unacceptable to member States' (*Commission Consultation Paper on Company Law* (1997), p 3).

In *Centros Ltd v Erhvervs- og Selskabsstyrelsen* (case C-212/97) [2000] Ch 446 two Danish citizens, Mr and Mrs Bryde, registered a company, Centros Ltd, in England and Wales, intending that it would not trade in the United Kingdom but through a branch in Denmark. Danish companies legislation required companies registered there to have a minimum paid-up capital of DKr 200,000 (about £20,000), whereas UK companies legislation does not have any minimum capital requirement for a private company such as Centros Ltd. The Danish authorities refused to register Centros Ltd's Danish branch, saying that this would enable Mr and Mrs Bryde to evade Danish law on the minimum capital of a private company, which was a law designed to protect persons dealing with companies. The European Court of Justice held that the refusal to register the branch contravened what is now art 49 of the TFEU, which (when read with what is now art 54) prohibits restrictions on freedom of establishment. The court said:

> 26 . . . The provisions of the Treaty on freedom of establishment are intended specifically to enable companies formed in accordance with the law of a member State and having their registered office, central administration or principal place of business within the Community to pursue activities in other member States through an agency, branch or subsidiary.
>
> 27 That being so, the fact that a national of a member State who wishes to set up a company chooses to form it in the member State whose rules of company law seem to him the least restrictive and to set up branches in other member States cannot, in itself, constitute an abuse of the right of establishment. The right to form a company in accordance with the law of a member State and to set up branches in other member States is inherent in the exercise, in a single market, of the freedom of establishment guaranteed by the Treaty.
>
> 28 In this connection, the fact that company law is not completely harmonised in the Community is of little consequence. Moreover, it is always open to the Council, on the basis of the powers conferred upon it by [art 50(2)(g) of the TFEU], to achieve complete harmonisation.

The **Company Law Review Steering Group,** *Modern Company Law for a Competitive Economy: The Strategic Framework* (London: DTI, 1999), noted that investment in Britain by foreign firms is of great importance to our economy and that this must be taken into account by UK company law. They said (para 2.11): 'We have to recognise that it is increasingly possible that, if we make our law unduly prescriptive, inflexible, inaccessible or onerous, businesses will choose to incorporate elsewhere.' However, they do not discuss whether choosing to incorporate in the United Kingdom has anything to do with choosing to invest in the United Kingdom. The Department for International Trade's document, 'Why overseas companies should set up in the UK' (updated 19 February 2017) does not mention company registration until topic 20 and the only point made about it is that it costs only £20. By contrast, the much lengthier topic 4 is all about how favourable the UK's tax system is.

See generally, R Drury, 'A review of the European Community's company law harmonisation programme' (1992) 24 Bracton Law J 45; M Andenas, 'The future of EC law harmonisation' (1994) 15 Co Law 121. For an attempt to analyse why some company law rules should be set centrally in the EU and others left to local jurisdictions see D Charny, 'Competition among jurisdictions in formulating corporate law rules: an American perspective on the "race to the bottom" in the European Communities' (1991) 32 Harv Int'l LJ 423 (reprinted in S Wheeler, *A Reader on the Law of Business Enterprise* (Oxford: Oxford University Press, 1994)).

1.5.4 OTHER RULES

In addition to legislation and judge-made law there are carefully composed codes of rules which are of great importance in some areas of company activity, particularly for larger companies. Examples are Financial Reporting Standards and International Financial Reporting Standards (see **9.5.7**), the City Code on Takeovers and Mergers (see **8.7.1**) and the UK Corporate Governance Code (see **15.2.2**). All these were originally private initiatives by non-governmental bodies to issue statements of best practice, but all have been recognised in legislation which either requires at least larger companies to comply with the codes (International Financial Reporting Standards; the City Code) or requires them to explain why they have not complied (Financial Reporting Standards, UK Corporate Governance Code). The Company Law Review Steering Group, *Modern Company Law for a Competitive Economy: The Strategic Framework* (London: DTI, 1999), Chapter 5.5, discussed the range of regulations affecting companies, and they are summarised in a table in annex F to the consultation document.

1.5.5 PRACTITIONERS' BOOKS AND OTHER LITERATURE

There are three practitioners' works which deal with company law at length and in detail. *Buckley on the Companies Acts* (Butterworths) first appeared in 1873 when its author, Henry Burton Buckley, was a barrister of only four years' standing. He became Buckley J in 1900 and Buckley LJ in 1906 until he retired and became the First Baron Wrenbury: many of his judgments are quoted in this book as are those of his son, Sir Denys Buckley. *Palmer's Company Law* (Sweet and Maxwell) first appeared in 1898. Its author, Francis Beaufort Palmer (1845–1917), was a barrister and legal author. The work now known as *Gore-Browne on Companies* (Jordans) was originally written by Richard Jordan and first published in 1867 by Jordan and Sons Ltd, company registration agents. It was later edited by a barrister, Francis Gore-Browne (1860–1922).

Many academic lawyers specialise in company law. Scholarly articles and case notes will be found in the general legal journals, especially the *Cambridge Law Journal* (CLJ), the *Law Quarterly Review* (LQR) and the *Modern Law Review* (MLR). There is always much that is relevant to company law in the *Journal of Business Law* (JBL). However, probably the most important forum for academic discussion of company law is the *Company Lawyer* (Co Law), which was established in 1980. There is a similar journal published in Australia, *Company and Securities Law Journal* (C & SLJ).

Articles of a more practical nature will be found in the *Solicitors' Journal* (SJ) and the *Gazette*, and in the specialist publication *PLC: Practical Law for Companies*.

1.6 PURPOSE OF COMPANY LAW

1.6.1 SERVICE TO BUSINESS

Incorporation of companies has been made readily available by Parliament as a service to those who wish to take advantage of artificial entities with separate legal personality which they can control and put into legal relationships without being directly responsible for them.

Legislation providing for the incorporation of companies by registration is often described as 'enabling' or 'facilitative' legislation: it enables people to use the corporate form.

Most companies are incorporated for business purposes, which Parliament has wished to encourage. Business is risky. A venture may succeed and return profits to the providers of capital, and this is an incentive for investment. There is, however, always a risk that a venture may fail.

The common law principle is that those who provide the capital for a business on the basis of taking or sharing in its profits, as sole proprietors or partners, are liable for all the debts incurred in the course of the business. Parliament has considered that people are more likely to venture their capital in business if they know that their potential loss from failure of the business is limited to loss of the amount of capital they have ventured without any further liability to pay the business's outstanding debts. CA 2006 permits the incorporation of companies with limited liability. As will be explained in more detail in **2.3.2**, persons who contribute capital to a limited company, as members of the company, in return for a share in the profits made in the company's business are not liable, if the business should fail, to lose anything more than the amount of capital they have undertaken to contribute. In its White Paper, ***Modernising Company Law*** (Cm 5553, 2002), the government said:

> Company law has a direct impact on enterprise. It can actively promote and encourage enterprise—or hold it back. The government is strongly committed to promoting enterprise and believes that company law reform has an important part to play in making it as easy as possible to start and run companies while maintaining adequate safeguards against abuse. (Cm 5553-I, part I, para 3)

If business people are to be encouraged to create new businesses for which they require new companies, the creation of companies ought to be made as cheap and straightforward as possible. So one important aspect of company law which must be examined is how new companies are created (see **Chapters 2** and **3**). Once created, the continuing operation of a company is governed by the law, and the other important aspect of company law is the operation of existing companies, which takes up most of this book. The law on existing companies is also significant for the creation of new businesses because people might be discouraged from creating new companies if they felt that the law on operating them was unsatisfactory.

1.6.2 IS COMPANY LAW SUITED TO ALL USERS?

One reason for the popularity of registered companies is that CA 2006 permits a wide measure of choice in the constitution of a company, and the company format can be adapted to many different uses. Registered companies range in size and nature from huge industrial and commercial concerns like British Telecommunications plc to associations of people following a common hobby. Many companies exist only to hold one asset such as a building or a ship. Many individuals and companies divide up their business interests into scores or even hundreds of separate companies. The separate personality which incorporation of a company provides is widely exploited in tax-saving schemes. Many companies are bound by their constitutions to follow only charitable objectives.

Nevertheless, there have been complaints that the registered company is unsuitable in some circumstances. In particular it has for some time been argued that the company is not a suitable form for charities and they require a special legal form (J Warburton, 'Charity corporations: the framework for the future?' [1990] Conv 95). A report from the Cabinet Office Strategy Unit, *Private Action, Public Benefit* (2002), suggested two new legal forms, the charitable incorporated organisation (CIO) for charities generally, and the community interest company (CIC) for social enterprises. Legislation for CIOs is in the Charities Act 2011, part 11, and the implementing regulations came into force on 2 January 2013. (Equivalent legislation in Scotland came into force on 1 April 2011.) Legislation for CICs is in the Companies (Audit, Investigations and Community Enterprise) Act 2004, part 2 (see **2.3.1**).

The most persistent complaint has been that the company is an unsuitable form for small businesses. It has been argued that what is believed to be a 'simpler' legal form than a company could be used by presently unincorporated businesses and by small businesses which are presently companies but for which the company form is unsuitable. A proposal in *A New Form of Incorporation for Small Firms: a Consultative Document* (Cmnd 8171) (London: HMSO, 1981) received little support. Discussion continued. J Freedman, 'Small businesses and the corporate form: burden or privilege?' (1994) 57 MLR 555 reports empirical research on what business people actually want. As might be expected they are in practice indifferent about legal forms, which they leave to their professional advisers (apart from some who are aware of positive or negative effects of incorporation on the image of their business). What business people are concerned about are financial matters such as the cost of complying with the accounting requirements of CA 2006 (since the survey, companies with small turnovers have been exempted from compulsory auditing of their accounts) and the tax effects of incorporation. Freedman also points out that small businesses have widely differing ownership structures, from single individuals through small or extended families to business associates with or without investors who do not participate in management. It would not be easy to decide which particular group to design a new legal form for and it is not obvious what features would make a new design attractive.

In April 1994 the Department of Trade and Industry asked the Law Commission to undertake a preliminary investigation of the problem. The Commission's report was printed in Department of Trade and Industry, *Company Law Review: The Law Applicable to Private Companies* (URN 94/529) (London: DTI, 1994). The Commission noted the difficulty of defining what a small business is and that business people do not put company law high on their list of problems. It was sympathetic to the view that creating a new legal form for small businesses would merely complicate the law and, by confining businesses to a small form, would discourage growth. It concluded that there was no need for a new legal form for small businesses.

In its White Paper, *Modernising Company Law* (Cm 5553, 2002), the government rejected the idea of a separate corporate form for small businesses, principally because it might create a barrier to small companies growing. It preferred the approach of drafting companies legislation so that it is primarily suitable for small companies, with provisions for larger companies added on as necessary (Cm 5553-I, part II, paras 1.5 and 1.6). This has been done in CA 2006 to a great extent.

Further empirical research reported by A Hicks, R Drury and J Smallcombe, *Alternative Company Structures for the Small Business* (London: Certified Accountants Educational Trust, 1995) confirms the general picture found by Freedman but makes the interesting point that most small businesses are incorporated on the advice of accountants rather than lawyers. Accountants may well emphasise the taxation effects of incorporating. Hicks et al do support a special simple form of legal organisation for small businesses. They believe that limited liability is the cause of much of the complexity and compliance costs of the company form and their proposed 'business corporation' would have separate personality but unlimited liability and would be based on partnership concepts.

1.6.3 MANDATORY AND DEFAULT RULES

Those who register a company under CA 2006 gain the advantages of incorporating a company with artificial separate personality. In return, Parliament requires the observance of mandatory rules on the operation of the company. These include both the legislated rules (see **1.5.1**) and the judge-made rules of case law described in **1.5.2**.

Requiring the observance of rules in return for granting the privilege of incorporation has sometimes led to incorporation being described as a contract between Parliament and corporators. For an early example of the characterisation of incorporation as a contract see the US Supreme Court case of *Trustees of Dartmouth College v Woodward* (1819) 17 US (4 Wheat) 518, in which it was held that the state legislature of New Hampshire could not enact laws altering Dartmouth College's charter of incorporation (which was granted by the British Crown before the independence of the USA) without the College's agreement, because the charter was a contract between the Crown and the corporators protected by the US Constitution, art 1, s 10, cl 1 (the contracts clause), which prohibits States passing laws 'impairing the obligation of contracts'.

Because the separate personality of a company is artificial, it can be put into legal relationships only by the actions of human beings who will not, however, be directly responsible for those relationships. The persons who can put a company into legal relationships are its directors and persons they have authorised. Mandatory rules of company law regulate this situation for the protection of (a) the members of companies, (b) persons who deal with companies, especially those who become creditors of companies and (c) the public interest. A related area of law is concerned with public trading in company shares on the stock market.

Some people believe that the law should never interfere with the freedom of business people to make any contracts they choose. People with these beliefs disapprove of mandatory rules of company law. Often they deny the concession theory of incorporation and say that incorporation should be recognised as arising from private contract only. However, they usually allow that it is useful to have a model set of rules which will apply in default of other rules being chosen and will save people the costs of drafting their own rules. This has been the traditional British attitude to the regulations, known as the articles of association, governing a company's internal affairs and management (sometimes called the 'governance' of the company). Legislation provides model articles, which apply in default of other rules being chosen for a particular company, but any company is almost entirely free to choose any alternative articles (see **Chapter 3**). However, in other areas UK company law has a large mandatory content, particularly with regard to disclosure of information (see **Chapter 4**), preparation and disclosure of accounts (see **Chapter 9**), capital maintenance (see **Chapter 10**) and the duties of directors (see **Chapter 16**).

People who object to mandatory rules in company law usually believe that the rules which companies will have to adopt in order not to fail in a competitive market will be rules which will be of greatest benefit to the economy in which they operate. Market economists sometimes use their economic theories to work out what these theoretically wealth-maximising rules would be and propose them for adoption either as default rules or as mandatory rules. These issues were debated (in the context of US law) in a symposium issue of the *Columbia Law Review* (vol 89, No 7, November 1989). For the argument that there must be mandatory rules in certain areas of company law, see M A Eisenberg, 'The structure of corporation law' (1989) 89 Colum L Rev 1461 (reprinted in S Wheeler, *A Reader on the Law of Business Enterprise* (Oxford: Oxford University Press, 1994)). For the contrary view, see F S McChesney, 'Economics, law, and science in the corporate field: a critique of Eisenberg' (1989) 89 Colum L Rev 1530. The professors continued their debate in M A

Eisenberg, 'Contractarianism without contracts: a response to Professor McChesney' (1990) 90 Colum L Rev 1321 and F S McChesney, 'Contractarianism without contracts? Yet another critique of Eisenberg' (1990) 90 Colum L Rev 1332. For a parting shot, see M A Eisenberg, 'Bad arguments in corporate law' (1990) 78 Geo LJ 1551.

1.6.4 THE COMPANY'S POSITION IN SOCIETY

1.6.4.1 Corporate social responsibility

Corporate social responsibility (CSR) is the responsibility of each company for its effect on the society in which it operates.

There are sharply opposed views on the nature of a company's social responsibility and how that responsibility should be reflected in company law. UK company law has traditionally paid little attention to how anyone other than the members and creditors of a company may be affected by it. Persons other than members and creditors (often referred to as 'other constituencies') are affected by the activities of companies but not, it is said, specially affected by the particular legal form of the registered company, so that their concerns are not a matter for company law: the dealings between employer and employee, for example, are the same whether the employer is a company, an individual or a partnership, and should be dealt with in employment law. Furthermore, company law is by no means just the law of companies that own large business organisations. Incorporation of companies under CA 2006 is allowed for any lawful purpose. Companies are not required to own large business organisations and to have publicly traded shares—they are not required to have any business purpose at all. UK company law has to be adaptable to a wide variety of uses. Companies will always be a focus for any debate on the control of business activities because most business activity is conducted by companies. If, however, companies are singled out for regulation then incorporated businesses will be at a disadvantage compared with partnerships and sole proprietors.

1.6.4.2 Shareholder primacy

What is special about a company is that decisions about its activities are taken by its directors. Sole proprietors and partners can, if they wish, operate their businesses in the interests of any objectives they choose, and so can be persuaded to act as good citizens and operate their businesses for the public good, but directors of a company can act only in the way they consider, in good faith, would be most likely to promote the success of the company for the benefit of its members as a whole (CA 2006, s 172(1); see **16.6**), and for a business company this probably means only their financial benefit (see **16.6.5**). Directors are required to have regard to the interests of the company's employees (s 172(1)(b)) and, when the company is insolvent or near to insolvency, the interests of its creditors (see **16.6.9**). But neither employees nor creditors can take legal proceedings to force directors to have regard to their interests, whereas members with a simple majority of votes have a statutory right to dismiss directors (s 168; see **15.6.3**) and even a minority of members may petition the court for relief if the conduct of the company's affairs is unfairly prejudicial to their interests (s 994; see **18.6**). Company law is often described as 'shareholder-centred' or based on a principle of shareholder primacy.

Shareholder primacy is the subject of considerable political debate. On one side it is claimed that incorporation is made available to encourage business for the good of society generally and not simply for the private profit of shareholders:

> business is permitted and encouraged by the law primarily because it is of service to the community rather than because it is a source of profit to its owners. (E M Dodd Jr, 'For whom are corporate managers trustees?' (1932) 45 Harv L Rev 1145 at p 1149)
>
> One must remember that the corporation is a legal fiction—a creature of the law—and the benefits of participation in enterprise with limited liability are provided for the benefit of society, not of the

shareholders themselves. (T S Norwitz, '"The metaphysics of *Time*": a radical corporate vision' (1991) 46 Bus Law 377 at p 387)

It is pointed out that requiring people working for companies to restrict the purpose of their working lives to maximising shareholder wealth is unhealthy, demeaning and morally corrupting (L E Mitchell, 'Groundwork of the metaphysics of corporate law' (1993) 50 Wash and Lee L Rev 1477; A Wolfe, 'The modern corporation: private agent or public actor?' (1993) 50 Wash and Lee L Rev 1673; L E Mitchell, 'Cooperation and constraint in the modern corporation: an inquiry into the causes of corporate immorality' (1995) 73 Tex L Rev 477).

On the other side, it is claimed that restricting company management to the single objective of maximising shareholder wealth is the most efficient means of using companies to increase the wealth of society as a whole:

maximising profits for equity investors assists the other 'constituencies' automatically. The participants in the venture play complementary rather than antagonistic roles. In a market economy each party to a transaction is better off. A successful firm provides jobs for workers and goods and services for consumers. The more appealing the goods to consumers, the more profits (and jobs).

Prosperity for stockholders, workers and communities goes hand in glove with better products for consumers.

Frequently the harmony of interest between profit maximisation and other objectives escapes attention. (F H Easterbrook and D R Fischel, *The Economic Structure of Corporate Law* (Cambridge, MA: Harvard University Press, 1991), p 38)

For another expression of this view see M E DeBow and D R Lee, 'Shareholders, nonshareholders and corporate law: communitarianism and resource allocation' (1993) 18 Del J Corp L 393. Easterbrook and Fischel believe that if difficult moral and social questions were priced and expressed as costs to the company, they could be taken into account in corporate decision-making:

Far better to alter incentives by establishing rules that attach prices to acts (such as pollution and layoffs) while leaving managers free to maximise the wealth of the residual claimants [ie, the shareholders—see **15.2.6**] subject to the social constraints. (Easterbrook and Fischel, *The Economic Structure of Corporate Law*)

Treating corporate managers as capable only of profit-making but incapable of taking moral and social decisions is regarded by Mitchell as unnatural and objectionable. Requiring managers to take moral and social factors into account is characterised by followers of Easterbrook and Fischel as unnatural and objectionable 'social engineering' (DeBow and Lee, 'Shareholders, nonshareholders and corporate law' at p 404).

These issues are explored at length and in detail in J E Parkinson, *Corporate Power and Responsibility* (Oxford: Clarendon Press, 1993), which argues in favour of the thesis that 'every large corporation should be thought of as a social enterprise; that is, as an entity whose existence and decisions can be justified only in so far as they serve public or social purposes' (p 23, quoting R A Dahl, 'A prelude to corporate reform' in R L Heilbroner and P London (eds), *Corporate Social Policy* (Reading Mass: Addison-Wesley, 1975), pp 18–24 at p 18). For the opposing point of view see A Alcock, 'Corporate governance: a defence of the status quo' (1995) 58 MLR 898. The description of large American corporations as more nearly social institutions than private enterprise was made by A A Berle Jr and G C Means in *The Modern Corporation and Private Property* (New York: Commerce Clearing House, 1932), p 46.

The political debate in Britain was encapsulated by John Kay in his column in *The Daily Telegraph*, 11 September 1995 (reprinted in his book *The Business of Economics* (Oxford: Oxford University Press, 1996), p 86):

Is the purpose of a large public company to maximize its profits? Or to develop its business, in the interests of customers, employees, suppliers, investors, and the wider community? Like most people, I think the right answer is the second, but when I said so a few weeks ago institutions like the Institute of Directors denounced the prescription as wet, woolly, and vacuous.

Recognition by a company of the other interests listed by Kay is often seen as an element of the political idea of the stakeholding society (see J Plender, *A Stake in the Future: The Stakeholding Solution* (London: Nicholas Brealey, 1997); P Goldenberg, 'IALS Company Law Lecture—shareholders *v* stakeholders: the bogus argument' (1998) 19 Co Law 34). For a discussion of arguments for and against the stakeholder analysis of companies, see D Arnold, T Beauchamp and N Bowie (eds), *Ethical Theory and Business* (Harlow: Pearson, 2014), Chapter 2.

1.6.4.3 Enlightened shareholder value

In their first consultation document the Company Law Review Steering Group (see **1.5.1.3**), whose 12 members included both Kay and Parkinson, declared their preference for shareholder primacy, adopting the Easterbrook and Fischel line that 'the ultimate objective of companies as currently enshrined in law—ie to generate maximum value for shareholders—is in principle the best means of securing overall prosperity and welfare' (***Modern Company Law for a Competitive Economy: the Strategic Framework*** (London: DTI, 1999), para 5.1.12). Responses to that 1999 consultation document prompted a slight modification of this line. In ***Modern Company Law for a Competitive Economy: Developing the Framework*** (URN 00/656) (London: DTI, 2000) the group said, at para 2.11:

> A very substantial majority of responses (in number and in weight) favoured retaining the basic rule that directors should operate companies for the benefit of members (ie, normally shareholders). However, there was also very strong support for the view that this needed to be framed in an 'inclusive' way. There was concern that in many companies there was not sufficient appreciation (either by directors or by shareholders) of the importance of running businesses with a strategic balanced view of the implications of decisions over time, with proper emphasis on the long term. Due recognition was also needed of the importance in modern business of fostering effective relationships over time, with employees, customers and suppliers, and in the community more widely. If companies failed to address these interests effectively, then neither their own success, nor the overall competitiveness of the economy, which is the object of the Review, could be secured. Many favoured reform to reflect these imperatives, both in framing duties of directors and in the form in which companies account publicly for their achievement, prospects and intentions.

This is known as the 'enlightened shareholder value' (ESV) approach to directors' responsibilities. The then Secretary of State for Trade and Industry, Patricia Hewitt, said in her foreword to ***Draft Regulations on the Operating and Financial Review and Directors' Report: A Consultative Document*** (URN 04/1003) (London: DTI, 2004):

> What are companies for? The primary goal is to make a profit for their shareholders, certainly. But the days when that was the whole answer are long gone. We all have higher expectations of companies in the modern economy.
>
> We expect companies not simply to perform well in the short term, but to have an effective strategy for delivering long-term profitability. This is essential to the millions of us who invest our savings in companies through pension funds, life assurance, unit trusts and other forms of investment. We save for the years ahead, not the months ahead, and we need the companies in which we invest to share our own horizons.
>
> We expect companies to generate the wealth that provides good public services and a decent standard of living for everyone. We need continuing recognition that wealth-creation demands honest and fair dealings with employees, customers, suppliers and creditors. Good working conditions, good products and services and successful relationships with a wide range of other stakeholders are important assets, crucial to stable, long-term performance and shareholder value.

> We expect companies to create wealth while respecting the environment and exercising responsibility towards the society and the local communities in which they operate. The reputation and performance of companies which fail to do these things will suffer.
>
> The people who invest in companies are the same people who are employed by them, buy their products, live in the communities around them, and are concerned about their effect on the environment. So, we have multiple reasons for wanting to see good companies.

The enlightened shareholder value approach is adopted in CA 2006, s 172, which provides:

(1) A director of a company must act in the way he considers, in good faith, would be most likely to promote the success of the company for the benefit of its members as a whole, and in doing so have regard (amongst other matters) to—

    (a) the likely consequences of any decision in the long term,

    (b) the interests of the company's employees,

    (c) the need to foster the company's business relationships with suppliers, customers and others,

    (d) the impact of the company's operations on the community and the environment,

    (e) the desirability of the company maintaining a reputation for high standards of business conduct, and

    (f) the need to act fairly as between members of the company.

This preserves shareholder primacy while recognising that a company is both an association of its members and a person separate from them. Directors of a company must act to promote its success as a separate person, but for the benefit of its members, having regard to the matters listed in paras (a) to (f) among others. It is the members who have the benefit while other constituencies have only regard. Section 172 is considered in more detail at **16.6**.

1.6.4.4 Entity maximisation and sustainability

Andrew Keay has criticised both shareholder primacy (and its modified form, enlightened shareholder value) and the stakeholder analysis ('**Ascertaining the corporate objective: an entity maximisation and sustainability model**' (2008) 71 MLR 663). Professor Keay proposes an entity maximisation and sustainability theory, which he summarises, at p 698, as follows:

> This focuses on the company as a separate legal entity and maintains that the objective of the company is to maximise the wealth of the entity as an entity and, at the same time, to ensure that the company is sustained financially. The theory involves directors endeavouring to increase the overall long-run market value of the company as a whole, taking into account the investment made by various people and groups. But it maintains that maximisation must be combined with aiming to ensure entity survival and feasible development.

This theory does not specify any other persons as the intended beneficiaries of the company's wealth. Instead, it requires the company's directors to treat shareholders, employees, suppliers, lenders and so on as well as is necessary to ensure the company's prosperity and longevity. As beneficiaries are not specified, the theory avoids having to resolve conflicts of interest between the company and its members or other constituents, or between different groups of persons interested in the company's prosperity (see **16.6.4** to **16.6.12**).

1.6.4.5 Legitimacy of corporate power

Because most economic activity is conducted by companies, company law has a large potential impact on people's lives. People are naturally concerned by the power that companies have to affect their lives and wish to be assured that corporate power is legitimate and is properly controlled, just as they wish to see proper controls on the power of other institutions, such as national and local government, trade unions and educational institutions. People naturally look to the law to provide the framework for legitimation and control of power. For some people, the power of a company will be legitimate only if it is exercised in the interest of all those whom it affects. They want the law to require companies to give due consideration to all relevant interests. Other people believe that corporate power is legitimated by the contribution that companies make to the economy and that the market provides adequate control of economic activity so that legal controls are either superfluous or produce damaging distortions of the market.

1.6.4.6 Social, environmental and ethical considerations

CA 2006, s 414C(4), requires companies whose shares are traded on the London Stock Exchange and some other exchanges (quoted companies, see **7.3.4.6**) to give information in a strategic report about the following matters to the extent necessary for an understanding of the development, performance or position of the company's business:

(a) environmental matters, including the impact of the company's business on the environment;

(b) the company's employees; and

(c) social and community issues.

The information must include information about any policies of the company in relation to those matters and the effectiveness of those policies. See **9.9.2**. The directors' report of a quoted company must report its greenhouse gas emissions (SI 2008/410, sch 7, para 15; see **9.9.4.11**).

The largest traded companies (500 or more employees) must also provide a non-financial information statement on these matters and on respect for human rights and anti-bribery and anti-corruption policies (ss 414CA and 414CB; see **9.9.2**).

Pension funds are very significant as shareholders of companies whose shares are traded on the London Stock Exchange. The trustees of occupational pension schemes are required by the Pensions Act 1995, s 35, to produce a statement of their investment principles. This must state the extent to which (if at all) social, environmental or ethical considerations are taken into account in the selection, retention and realisation of investments (SI 1996/3127, reg 11A(a)). This may, at least, require companies to explain to those of their shareholders who are trustees of pension funds what effect they think that social, environmental and ethical (SEE) considerations may have on them, and may require them to reflect on the long-term effect of ignoring SEE considerations (see **16.6.5**).

1.6.4.7 Other styles of capitalism

The shareholder-centred vision of the company is not universally held among advanced economies. In Germany companies are seen as serving both shareholders and employees, and in German company law this is reflected in the 'co-determination' principle that both shareholders and workers should take part in the governance of large companies. The conflict between the German and British views of the company has caused significant difficulties in the harmonisation of EU company law. In Japan a company is seen as a long-term coalition of investors, employees and trading partners, who are all concerned with the company's continuing prosperity. Japan's company law is modelled on Germany's, and the concern in both countries with the position of the company in society has been heavily influenced by the thinking of the German industrialist and statesman, Walther Rathenau (1867–1922), whose writings are cited by and clearly influenced Berle and Means. See M Yoshimori, 'Whose company is it? The concept of the corporation in Japan and the West' (1995) 28(4) Long Range Planning 33; J Groenewegen, 'Institutions of capitalisms: American, European, and Japanese systems compared' (1997) 31 J Economic Issues 333; M Yavasi, 'Shareholding and board structures of German and UK companies' (2001) 22 Co Law 47. The German and Japanese experience has influenced the development of the idea of the stakeholding society.

For discussions of differing forms of capitalism in different national cultures see J Groenewegen, 'Institutions of capitalisms' in C Crouch and W Streeck (eds), *Political Economy of Modern Capitalism* (London: Sage, 1997).

1.6.4.8 International standards of corporate behaviour

In many parts of the world, businesses are seen to benefit from repressive governments which create a compliant and cheap workforce, while government personnel benefit from bribes paid by businesses.

Attempts have been made to require multinational (or transnational) companies to adopt higher standards than those of the governments of the countries in which they operate.

The United Kingdom, together with the other members of the Organisation for Economic Cooperation and Development (OECD), has recommended the **OECD Guidelines for Multi-national Enterprises** to multinational enterprises operating in or from its territory. The first general policy set out in these Guidelines is that enterprises should contribute to economic, social and environmental progress with a view to achieving sustainable development. As Chapter 1, para 4, of the Guidelines points out:

> The Guidelines are not aimed at introducing differences of treatment between multinational and domestic enterprises; they reflect good practice for all. Accordingly, multinational and domestic enterprises are subject to the same expectations in respect of their conduct wherever the Guidelines are relevant to both.

The Guidelines do not have the force of law, but are a statement of internationally recognised good practice. The UK National Contact Point for OECD Guidelines for Multinational Enterprises is at **www.gov.uk/guidance/uk-national-contact-point-for-the-organisation-for-economic-co-operation-and-development-oecd-guidelines-for-multinational-enterprises**.

A United Nations (UN) initiative launched in 2000, the Global Compact, is a voluntary network which seeks to promote responsible corporate citizenship. The Global Compact has ten principles in the areas of human rights, labour, the environment and anti-corruption, which it invites companies to adopt. See **www.unglobalcompact.org**.

Attempts to create a United Nations statement of companies' obligations to observe human rights have foundered, because it would have gone far beyond the current principle that legal responsibility for observance of human rights rests on governments alone. The statement was to be of 'norms on the responsibilities of transnational corporations and other business enterprises with regard to human rights'. A final draft (E/CN.4/Sub2/2003/12/Rev.2) was adopted by a sub-commission of the United Nations Commission on Human Rights in August 2003. It became clear that governments would not adopt the norms, which were expressed as positive obligations of enterprises. Instead, the Secretary-General appointed a special representative mandated, among other things, to identify and clarify standards of corporate responsibility and accountability and compile a compendium of best practices. See the website of the Business and Human Rights Resource Centre, **business-humanrights.org**, which includes the special representative's portal.

1.7 MORALITY, ECONOMICS, DEMOCRACY AND COMPANY LAW

The principal object of this book is to provide an introductory description of the current rules of English company law. Those rules are intended to support and serve the country's economic system, and different views are possible on how law should do this. Some of these differences of opinion reflect differences about the function of law generally.

Law influences human behaviour (a) by prescribing the limits of acceptable behaviour (for example, insider dealing is a criminal offence—see **13.6**; a director of a company who takes one of the company's business opportunities for him or herself is in breach of duty to the company—see **16.9.4**), and (b) by providing for sanctions to punish or deter unacceptable behaviour (a court may fine or imprison an insider dealer; may require a profit made in breach of fiduciary duty to be handed over to the company). Human behaviour is also influenced by moral judgement (which may, for example, limit actions by a human that harm other humans, the actor or other animals). It is natural to regard moral judgement as a precursor of law. So a Law Lord can say that: 'The law and morality are inextricably interwoven. To a large extent the law is simply formulated and declared morality' (Lord Steyn in *Smith New Court Securities Ltd v Citibank NA* [1997] AC 254 at p 280). Certainly laws command greatest respect when they reflect moral judgements held almost universally and without substantial objection (for example, laws punishing murder). But laws are often controversial in areas where a variety of moral views exist, and where the variety continues despite extensive public discussion, for example, on the subjects of abortion, drug use, euthanasia, sexual activity and the uses humans make of other animals. The relationship of morality to law has been particularly illuminated by the work of the legal philosopher H L A Hart, who argued for the autonomy of law and that there are some moral judgements which it is not appropriate to translate into laws. In the United Kingdom the theory of parliamentary sovereignty over law means that we look to the political forum to decide what laws to make in the knowledge of conflicting moral views.

Some legal philosophers have hoped to find a natural law, which would be a law that is a universal requirement of human societal life and which might be found by examining that life and, for some, by revelation from a deity.

Other jurists claim to have found a different underlying principle for law in the neoclassical economics of the Chicago school (so-called because its leading exponents, including Milton Friedman, George Stigler and Ronald Coase, taught at the University of Chicago). Jurists taking that view are usually known as the Chicago law and economics movement. A detailed and sympathetic account of the history of this movement, which nevertheless gives room to the criticism that has been made of it, is in N Duxbury, *Patterns of American Jurisprudence* (Oxford: Clarendon Press, 1995), Chapter 5. The best-known presentation of the movement's views is R A Posner, *Economic Analysis of Law*, 7th edn (New York: Aspen Publishers, 2007).

Chicago neoclassical economics is founded on the assumption that those who undertake economic activity do so for the sole purpose of maximising their wealth and they have both complete knowledge of what has to be done to achieve that and unfettered ability to do it—they are described as rational economic actors. If they undertake their economic activity by freely contracting in a market whose other participants also have the same knowledge and ability (known as a perfect market), it is predicted that productive resources will be acquired by those who use them to produce the greatest wealth, and so the overall wealth of the economy is maximised. It is assumed that freely contracting in markets is the best way of conducting economic activity. To the extent that law and other forms of State regulation are found to distort free contracting in a perfect market (which it is assumed they will do), they are wrong. As Milton Friedman put it in 1974 (quoted in Duxbury, *Patterns of American Jurisprudence*, p 366):

> In discussions of economic policy, 'Chicago' stands for belief in the efficacy of the free market as a means of organising resources, for scepticism about government intervention into economic affairs, and for emphasis on the quantity of money as a key factor in producing inflation.

The fact that real people do not have the knowledge and ability assumed in the theory (they have what is called bounded rationality) is not thought to affect the value of the theory. It is assumed that real people will want to become more and more like rational economic actors in perfect markets so that they can maximise their wealth. Many who disagree with the law and economics movement are content not to be rational economic actors in perfect markets, which is a profound difference in world views that may explain why supporters and opponents of the theory often do not take each other seriously (D Millon, 'Communitarians, contractarians and the crisis in corporate law' (1993) 50 Wash and Lee L Rev 1373 at p 1382). As Posner points out (*Economic Analysis of Law*, 3rd edn at p 22), 'The most frequent criticism is that the normative underpinnings of the economic approach are so repulsive that it is inconceivable that the legal system would (let alone should) embrace them.'

Promotion of collective wealth maximisation is proposed in Chicago law and economics apparently despite individual casualties. This is counter to the view of the law as the upholder of each subject's individual rights (see G J Stigler, 'Law or economics?' (1992) 35 J Law & Econ 455). For example, neoclassical economists assert that laws to prevent wage discrimination between workers of different gender or ethnicity prevent wealth maximisation (H Demsetz, 'Minorities in the market place'(1965) 43 NC L Rev 271, reprinted in *Ownership, Control and the Firm*, vol 1 (Oxford: Blackwell, 1988), pp 82–103; R A Posner, 'An economic analysis of sex discrimination laws' (1989) 56 U Chi L Rev 1311) and that the economy's wealth would be increased if women could sell their babies (E M Landes and R A Posner, 'The economics of the baby shortage' (1978) 7 J Legal Stud 323). A theory that leads to these results may look like the antithesis of law rather than a basis for it. Discrimination and baby-selling are illegal because they are disapproved of morally, not because of the effects they are predicted to have by a theory of economics. Proposing that they should be made legal because of a theory of economics supposes that the theory is superior to national moral judgement. Choosing whether to base a nation's laws on moral judgement or economic theory is a political choice.

Part of the problem is that, like much of economics, neoclassical theory is about static equilibrium states, not dynamic changing states: it predicts the ideal final state, but is not much concerned with getting there, or who might get hurt on the way (a point made by, among others, Guido Calabresi in, for example, 'The pointlessness of Pareto: carrying Coase further' (1991) 100 Yale LJ 1211). The most common criticism of the theory is that it maximises the wealth of an economy only for a given distribution of wealth within that economy, which it is not concerned to change. But in reality the present distribution of wealth gives some persons—particularly large companies—overwhelming power over others, so that there is no possibility of free contracting between them, and it is the underprivileged in this situation who require the protection of the law. For discussion of wealth maximisation as a guiding principle of public life see R M Dworkin, 'Is wealth a value?' (1980) 9 J Legal Stud 191; J L Coleman, 'Efficiency, utility and wealth maximisation' (1980) 8 Hofstra L Rev 509' and R A Posner, 'The value of wealth: a comment on Dworkin and Kronman' (1980) 9 J Legal Stud 243.

Supporters of the law and economics movement meet the controversy over its conclusions by claiming that they are arrived at scientifically. They say that their arguments are derived from scientific economics and they claim to have demonstrated the truth of their theory because it correctly predicts rules of common law arrived at before the theory was invented. The congruence of law and economics with common law is a central thesis of Posner. It has been elaborated in the company law context by B S Black, 'Is corporate law trivial? A political and economic analysis' (1990) 84 Nw U L Rev 542 and in relation to equity, which is of great significance to company law, by A J Duggan, 'Is equity efficient?' (1997) 113 LQR 601. However, in reality there seems to be only a coincidental overlap of common law and Chicago law and economics. There are common law doctrines of which Chicago law and economics disapproves and much of the law desired by Chicago law and economics does not exist. That the overlap is fortuitous is hardly surprising: both the common law and Chicago law and economics arrive at their results by systematic reasoning, but from different premises. Whether the common law should adopt the same premises as Chicago law and economics, and so produce exactly the same results, is an essentially political question. For more on the scientific status of law and economics see G S Crespi, 'The mid-life crisis of the law and economics movement: confronting the problems of nonfalsifiability and normative bias' (1991) 67 Notre Dame L Rev 231 (which, incidentally, suggests that law and economics is best characterised as a literary genre); R C Downs, 'Law and economics: nexus of science and belief' (1995) 27 Pac LJ 1 (which, incidentally, notes the quasi-religious tone of much of law and economics: a tone that is particularly apparent in the more fundamentalist writings on American corporate law and which is discussed in M A Eisenberg, 'New modes of discourse in the corporate law literature' (1984) 52 Geo Wash L Rev 582); G De Geest, 'The debate on the scientific status of law and economics' (1996) 40 European Economic Review 999 (which responds that law and economics is scientific if it is judged by weaker criteria than other sciences).

The fact that some predictions of Chicago law and economics are so obviously controversial shows that the theory cannot be relied on to produce laws to which there will be almost universal agreement and no substantial opposition. There are undoubtedly people who believe in it as a source of law, but equally there are many who do not. In a democratic society the law that will be made in the light of these conflicts of opinion will be the result of a political solution of the conflicts.

Many in the American law and economics movement extend their scepticism of government to scepticism about the political process of legislation, which they see as merely favouring interest groups whose aims they disapprove of, rather than achieving political solutions to the conflict between their aims and those of others. For example, Delaware's success in attracting incorporations is attributed by one author to the fact that its tiny legislature accepts the proposals of the Delaware Bar Association: 'Many of the legislative pressures, which could disrupt the development of corporate law, from environmental groups, unions, and local communities, are not present in Delaware' (**D G Kaouris, 'Is Delaware still a haven for incorporation?'** (1995) 20 Del J Corp L 965 at p 1005).

As companies are so important in economic life the Chicago law and economics movement has paid much attention to company law. The leading text in America is **F H Easterbrook and D R Fischel**, *The Economic Structure of Corporate Law* (Cambridge, MA: Harvard University Press, 1991). This is by two convinced believers in the neoclassical economics of Chicago (where Fischel teaches). As they say in their Preface: 'we take a few economic principles and preach to legislatures and judges about what the law ought to be if it is to promote social welfare' (p viii). The theory is applied in the context of English company law in B R Cheffins, *Company Law: Theory, Structure and Operation* (Oxford: Clarendon Press, 1997). Critics who argue that corporate law should not be captured by Easterbrook and Fischel include L Johnson, 'Individual and collective sovereignty in the corporate enterprise' (1992) 92 Colum L Rev 2215 at p 2217 and L E Mitchell, 'The cult of efficiency' (1992) 71 Tex L Rev 217 at p 219.

In the USA many of the legal scholars who apply Chicago law and economics to company law have adopted from economists the description of a company as a 'nexus of contracts' (see **5.5.4**), and such scholars are often called 'contractarians'. The following quotation from **H N Butler, 'The contractual theory of the corporation'** (1989) 11 Geo Mason U L Rev 99 at p 100, explains the contractarian position that corporations should be regarded as created by private contract with which the State must not interfere:

> The contractual theory of the corporation is in stark contrast to the legal concept of the corporation as an entity created by the State. The entity theory of the corporation supports State intervention—in the form of either direct regulation or the facilitation of shareholder litigation—in the corporation on the ground that the State created the corporation by granting it a charter. The contractual theory views the corporation as founded in private contract, where the role of the State is limited to enforcing contracts. In this regard, a State charter merely recognises the existence of a 'nexus of contracts' called a corporation. Each contract in the 'nexus of contracts' warrants the same legal and constitutional protections as other legally enforceable contracts. Moreover freedom of contract requires that parties to the 'nexus of contracts' must be allowed to structure their relations as they please.

As explained in **1.3** our view is that the most significant legal feature of incorporation is the creation of an artificial separate personality, and, in English law, this can only be done by grant from the State.

People who have disagreed with the conclusions of the Chicago law and economics analysis of company law have, in the USA, been called 'communitarians' (M E DeBow and D R Lee, 'Shareholders, nonshareholders and corporate law: communitarianism and resource allocation' (1993) 18 Del J Corp L 393). This has been accepted by a leading critic of that analysis (D Millon, 'Communitarians, contractarians and the crisis in corporate law' (1993) 50 Wash and Lee L Rev 1373 at p 1378), but it implies (and was perhaps intended to imply) that the only people who disagree with the analysis are those who adopt the political philosophy of communitarianism, which is not the case. Two articles which place arguments over the economic approach to company law into the context of a very long history of opposed political values are F R Kaen, A Kaufman and L Zacharias, 'American political values and agency theory: a perspective' (1988) 7 J Bus Ethics 805; and P N Cox, 'The public, the private and the corporation' (1997) 80 Marq L Rev 391.

PART 2

ESTABLISHMENT

2

REGISTRATION

SUMMARY OF POINTS COVERED

- What is in this chapter
- Registration procedure
- Classification of companies
- Company names
- Registered office

- Re-registration to change the classification of a company
- Quasi-partnership companies
- Numbers of companies
- European public limited-liability companies and single-member companies

2.1 WHAT IS IN THIS CHAPTER

The Companies Act 2006 (CA 2006) provides for the incorporation of companies by a simple process of registration which is described in this chapter. The companies thus incorporated are known as 'registered companies'. Registration under CA 2006 makes readily available the benefits of separate corporate personality which were described in **1.3.1**. Incorporation of a registered company does not confer on its members the benefit of not being liable for the company's debts, but:

- the liability is only to the company, not to the creditors; and
- persons who form a company have the option (which is taken for nearly all companies) of limiting its members' liability (see **2.3.2**).

CA 2006 offers a wide variety of basic structures for companies (see **2.3.1**), but nearly all companies are private companies limited by shares. The numerically much smaller class of public limited companies are of enormous economic significance, and the distinction between private and public companies (see **2.3.3**) is fundamental to company law.

The registration procedure (see **2.2**) creates a company with:

- separate corporate personality (see **2.2.2** and **Chapter 5**);
- members (see **2.2.1.7** and **Chapter 14**);
- a shareholding (see **2.2.1.7** and **Chapter 6**);
- directors (see **2.2.1.8** and **Chapter 15**);
- a secretary (see **2.2.1.8** and **17.3**; appointment of a secretary is optional for private companies);
- a name (see **2.4**);
- a constitution (see **2.2.1.6** and **Chapter 3**); and
- a registered office and domicile (see **2.5**).

Re-registration (**2.6**) can be used to change from one company type to another.

There is a legally very interesting class of private companies called quasi-partnership companies which are introduced in **2.7** and will be considered throughout this book.

There are statistics of the numbers of companies in **2.8**. There is a short note on European public limited-liability companies (SEs) and the new proposal for easily registered single-member companies throughout the EEA (SUPs) in **2.9**.

Key legislation which you should be able to consult when reading this chapter:

- CA 2006, ss 3–20, 53–81, 86–111, 1060, 1064–1066, 1079B, 1095, 1099, 1100, 1139; and

- Insolvency Act 1986 (IA 1986), s 74.

All that legislation is in *Blackstone's Statutes on Company Law*.

The following case, which is considered in this chapter, is particularly significant and is recommended further reading:

- *Ebrahimi v Westbourne Galleries Ltd* [1973] AC 360 (for **2.7**).

Your particular course of study may require you to read other source materials.

2.2 REGISTRATION PROCEDURE

2.2.1 FORMATION AND REGISTRATION OF A COMPANY

2.2.1.1 Companies House

In the United Kingdom, a company is created by registering it with a government agency called Companies House. In April 2015, 98.8 per cent of registrations were carried out electronically. Companies House runs two electronic services for registering companies: the software incorporation service, which can be used only by accredited company formation agents, and the web incorporation service, which anyone may use. There are limits on the types of company that may be registered by the web incorporation service (see **2.2.1.5** and **2.2.1.6**). Registration using paper forms is also still possible.

Companies House is an executive agency of the Department for Business, Energy and Industrial Strategy. Its main office is at Crown Way, Cardiff CF14 3UZ. An executive agency is a distinct part of a government department with its own budget. Companies House is funded entirely by the fees it charges, which include fees for registering new companies (see **2.2.1.12**), changes of companies' names (see **2.4.12**) and charges on companies' property (see **11.7.2**) together with fees for allowing inspection of all this information and providing copies (see **4.2.2.1**). Information about Companies House, including details of the procedure for registering new companies, is available at its website, **www.companieshouse.gov.uk**.

The chief executive of Companies House is the registrar of companies for England and Wales. CA 2006, s 1060, requires the Secretary of State to appoint registrars of companies for England and Wales, Scotland and Northern Ireland. The Act speaks of duties such as registration of companies being performed by 'the registrar'. In practice, of course, those duties are performed by members of the staff of Companies House. In this book we generally refer to these duties being performed by 'Companies House'.

2.2.1.2 Contents of an application

The following items must be filed in order to register a new company:

(a) a memorandum of association, which forms the company (see **2.2.1.3**);

(b) an application for registration (see **2.2.1.5**);

(c) the company's constitution, contained in articles of association, unless model articles are to be used (see **2.2.1.6**);

(d) a statement of capital and initial shareholdings (this is not required for a small minority of companies; see **2.2.1.7**);

(e) a statement of the company's proposed officers (see **2.2.1.8**);

(f) a statement of initial significant control (see **2.2.1.9**);

(g) notice or notices of election to keep registers at Companies House (such notices are optional) (see **2.2.1.10**); and

(h) a statement of compliance (see **2.2.1.11**).

2.2.1.3 Memorandum of association and subscribers

Persons who wish to form a company under CA 2006 must subscribe their names to a memorandum of association (s 7(1)(a)). This states that the subscribers wish to form a company under CA 2006 and agree to become members of it (s 8(1)). If the company is to have a share capital (as is usual), the memorandum must state that the subscribers agree to take at least one share each (s 8(1)(b)). A memorandum must be in prescribed form and must be authenticated by each subscriber (s 8(2)). The prescribed forms are in SI 2008/3014. One subscriber is sufficient (CA 2006, s 7(1)) but there is no upper limit to the number of subscribers.

The subscribers of a company's memorandum will be the company's first members when it is registered (s 16(2)). They are the persons who wish to be associated together as members of the company, which is why the document they sign is called a memorandum of association, though it is possible for the association to have only one member.

The memorandum of association of a company registered before 1 October 2009 was a radically different document (an 'old-style memorandum') which formed part of the company's constitution. The provisions of the old-style memorandum of a company registered before 1 October 2009 are now treated as provisions of its articles (s 28).

2.2.1.4 Who may be a subscriber

The subscribers of a memorandum of association may be foreigners: there is no requirement that the subscribers be domiciled in the part of the United Kingdom in which the company is to be registered (*Princess of Reuss v Bos* (1871) LR 5 HL 176), but an association which is already completely constituted as a partnership or a corporation under another legal system cannot be registered as a company under CA 2006 (*Bulkeley v Schutz* (1871) LR 3 PC 764). In particular, a company already registered in one part of the United Kingdom cannot register in another (see *Bateman v Service* (1881) 6 App Cas 386 on the inability of a company registered in one state of Australia to register in another).

Subscription of a memorandum by an individual under 18 is valid unless the individual has repudiated the subscription before registration (*Re Nassau Phosphate Co* (1876) 2 ChD 610; *Re Laxon and Co (No 2)* [1892] 3 Ch 555).

2.2.1.5 Application for registration

Persons wishing to form a company under CA 2006 must deliver their memorandum of association to Companies House with an application for registration (s 9(1) and (2)). The application for registration must state (s 9(2)):

(a) the company's proposed name (see **2.4**; it may be necessary to check before registering that there will be no objection to the name: see **2.4.6**);

(b) whether the company's registered office is to be situated in England and Wales (or in Wales), in Scotland or in Northern Ireland (see **2.5**);

(c) whether the liability of the members of the company is to be limited, and if so whether it is to be limited by shares or by guarantee (see **2.3.2**); and

(d) whether the company is to be a private or a public company (see **2.3.3**).

When the company is registered, these details will appear on its certificate of incorporation (s 15(2)).

The application must also state the intended address of the registered office (s 9(5)(a)), the type of company it is to be and its intended principal business activities (s 9(5)(c)).

The publicly available web incorporation service can only be used to register a private company limited by shares (in practice this is by far the most common type of UK company). The company formation agents who use the software incorporation service are able to register any of the five possible types of company (see **2.3.1**).

2.2.1.6 Articles of association

Articles of association set out the internal regulations of a company (see **Chapter 3**). A company's articles are its constitution (CA 2006, s 17) and one of its constitutional documents (s 32(1)(a); see **3.2.1**).

An application for registration of a company must contain a copy of its proposed articles (s 9(5)(b)). But when registering a private limited company or a public company, articles of association need not be registered if the company is to use the model articles promulgated by the Secretary of State—see **3.3.1**. A company registered by the publicly available web incorporation service must be registered with model articles. The company formation agents who use the software incorporation service are able to register articles of association specifically drafted for each company.

The articles of association of any company (whether or not they are model articles) can be altered after registration (see **3.5**), unless they contain a provision for entrenchment (see **3.6.2.1**). A company whose articles of association, on formation, contain a provision for entrenchment must give notice of that fact to Companies House (s 23(1)). When this notice has to be given is not specified, but it cannot be given on application for registration, because it has to be given by 'the company', and the company does not exist until it has been registered.

2.2.1.7 Statement of capital and initial shareholdings

If a company is to have a share capital (see **2.3.2**), the application to register it must contain a statement of capital and initial shareholdings (CA 2006, s 9(4)(a)). This statement is not required if a company is not to have a share capital. A company without a share capital is either a guarantee company, which must instead file a statement of guarantee (s 9(4)(b); see **2.3.2.3**), or an unlimited company without a share capital.

The statement of capital and initial shareholdings records what shares the company will issue when it is registered and who will own them.

The statement of capital section must be updated every time the company issues shares (s 555; see **6.3.6**) or otherwise alters its share capital. The terms and concepts used in the statement of capital are discussed in detail in **2.3.2** and in **Chapter 6**. The statement of capital must give the following details of the share capital to be taken on formation by the subscribers to the memorandum (s 10(2)):

(a) the total number of shares of the company to be taken on formation by the subscribers;

(b) the aggregate nominal value of those shares;

(c) the aggregate amount (if any) to be unpaid on those shares (whether on account of their nominal value or by way of premium); and

(d) for each class of shares:

(i) prescribed particulars of the rights attached to the shares (see **6.2.3**);

(ii) the total number of shares of that class; and

(iii) the aggregate nominal value of shares of that class.

A current statement of capital is one of a company's constitutional documents (s 32(1)(g); see **3.2.1**).

The statement of initial shareholdings section of the statement of capital and initial shareholdings must state:

(a) the name and address of each subscriber to the memorandum (s 10(3); SI 2008/3014, reg 3);

(b) the number, nominal value and class of the shares each subscriber will take on formation of the company (CA 2006, s 10(4)(a))—each subscriber must take at least one share (s 8(1)(b)); and

(c) the amount to be paid up and the amount, if any, to be unpaid on each share (whether on account of nominal value or by way of premium) (s 10(4)(b)).

2.2.1.8 Statement of the company's proposed officers

An application for registration of a company must contain a statement of the company's proposed officers (CA 2006, s 9(4)(c)). This must contain (s 12):

(a) the particulars of each proposed director of the company which must be stated in the company's register of directors and register of directors' residential addresses (these particulars are specified in ss 162 to 166—see **15.7**);

(b) the particulars of the secretary which must be stated in the company's register of secretaries (these particulars are specified in ss 277 to 279—see **17.3.2**); and

(c) a statement by the subscribers that each of the persons named as an officer has consented to act in the relevant capacity.

On registration of the company, the persons named in this statement will take up office as from the date of incorporation (s 16(1) and (6)). Appointment of a secretary is optional for a private company, and particulars of a secretary are not required for a private company if it is not proposed to have a secretary on registration.

Companies House must notify everyone who is named as a proposed director in a statement of a company's proposed officers (s 1079B). Anyone so notified may advise Companies House that they did not consent to act as a director and ask for their name to be removed from the register (s 1095(4A) to (4D)).

2.2.1.9 Statement of initial significant control

An application for registration of a company must contain a statement of initial significant control (CA 2006, ss 9(4)(d) and 12A; see **8.10.5**).

2.2.1.10 Notice of election to keep registers at Companies House

If subscribers are opting to have any registers held at Companies House, they must give notice of election when they deliver the registration documents (CA 2006, ss 128B(1), 167A(2), 279A(1) and 790X(1)).

2.2.1.11 Statement of compliance

An application for registration of a company must be accompanied by a statement of compliance (CA 2006, s 9(1)) which states that the requirements of CA 2006 as to registration have been complied with (s 13(1)).

2.2.1.12 Fee

Registration by the publicly available web incorporation service (which can only be used for a private company limited by shares with model articles) costs £12 (SI 2012/1907, sch 1, para 8(a)(i)). Company formation agents registered with Companies House are able to use the electronic software incorporation service which costs only £10, or £30 for same-day registration (paras 8(a)(ii) and (iii)). Non-electronic registration is more expensive: £40 (para 8(a)(v)) or £20 for an unlimited company or a CIC (para 8(a)(vii) and (viii)). Same-day non-electronic registration is £100 (para 8(a)(iv)).

2.2.1.13 Streamlined company registration

The Small Business, Enterprise and Employment Act 2015, s 15 (which came into force on 26 May 2015), requires Companies House and Her Majesty's Revenue and Customs to establish a single process to incorporate a new company and register it for VAT, corporation tax and PAYE. This was to be in place by 31 May 2017.

2.2.2 REGISTRATION AND CERTIFICATE OF INCORPORATION

Companies House must register an application for registration of a company, if satisfied that the requirements of CA 2006 as to registration are complied with (s 14). Companies House is entitled to accept the statement of compliance delivered with the application (see **2.2.1.11**) as sufficient evidence of compliance (s 13(2)).

On registering a company, Companies House must allocate to the company a number, called its 'registered number' (s 1066), and must give a certificate that the company is incorporated (s 15(1)). A certificate of incorporation is conclusive evidence that the requirements of CA 2006 as to registration have been complied with, and that the company is duly registered under the Act (s 15(4)). The certificate of incorporation must state (s 15(2)):

(a) the name and registered number of the company;

(b) the date of its incorporation;

(c) whether it is a limited or unlimited company, and if it is limited whether it is limited by shares or limited by guarantee;

(d) whether it is a private or a public company; and

(e) whether the company's registered office is situated in England and Wales (or in Wales), in Scotland or in Northern Ireland.

Companies House must give public notice (see **4.3**) of issuing a certificate of incorporation (s 1064). Any person may obtain from Companies House a copy of any company's certificate of incorporation (s 1065).

From the date of incorporation stated on the certificate, the company is a body corporate (s 16(1) to (3)) with its registered office at the address stated in the application for registration (s 16(4)), and the persons listed in the statement of proposed officers take office (s 16(6)). All this takes effect from the first moment of that day (*Jubilee Cotton Mills Ltd v Lewis* [1924] AC 958). A registered company exists as from the date of its incorporation as recorded on its certificate of incorporation without any further formalities and regardless of whether it undertakes any business. There is no need for a meeting of members or directors to ratify its incorporation.

A company's certificate of incorporation is one of its constitutional documents (s 32(1)(f); see **3.2.1**).

2.2.3 LAWFUL PURPOSE OF FORMATION

A company may not be formed under CA 2006 for an unlawful purpose (s 7(2)). In addition, a trade union must not be registered as a company (Trade Union and Labour Relations (Consolidation) Act 1992, s 10(3), repeating provisions made in earlier trade union legislation). The latter provision has caused problems: see M A Hickling, 'Trade unions in disguise' (1964) 27 MLR 625; R R Drury, 'Nullity of companies in English law' (1985) 48 MLR 644.

Companies House is entitled to refuse to register a company formed for an unlawful purpose. Before CA 2006 Companies House had an opportunity to discern the purpose for which a company was being registered because every company was required to state its objects in its old-style memorandum. Under CA 2006, however, a statement of objects (in the articles) is optional (s 31).

A refusal by Companies House to register a company is subject to judicial review. For example, in *R v Registrar of Joint Stock Companies, ex parte More* [1931] 2 KB 197 the registrar refused to register a company because its main object was stated to be to sell in Great Britain tickets in a lottery (popularly known as the Irish Sweep) run in what was then the Irish Free State. The promoters of the company sought judicial review of this decision. The Court of Appeal held that selling such tickets in England would have been an offence under statutes then in force (it would now be an offence under the Lotteries and Amusements Act 1976, s 2) so that the registrar was right to refuse to register the company, which was not formed 'for a lawful purpose'. (The Irish Sweep has been discontinued.)

In *R v Registrar of Companies, ex parte Bowen* [1914] 3 KB 1161 the court held that the registrar's refusal to register a company had been wrong. The registrar had doubted that the company's name, 'The United Dental Service Ltd', was legal because of statutory restrictions on advertising oneself as a qualified dental practitioner. However, the court held that the name was legal. There is now a procedure for vetting some company names before registration and if Mr Bowen were registering The United Dental Service Ltd today he would have to go through that procedure—see **2.4.6**.

Requiring something to be 'lawful' gives the courts the opportunity to exclude things not only because they constitute criminal offences or civil wrongs, but also because they offend against a wider moral code, especially in sexual matters. So, although trading as a prostitute is not a criminal offence, and the profits of the trade are subject to income tax (*Commissioners of Inland Revenue v Aken* [1990] 1 WLR 1374), to carry on the business of prostitution is not a lawful purpose for which a company may be registered (*R v Registrar of Companies, ex parte Attorney-General* [1991] BCLC 476).

A positive decision by Companies House to register a company is less amenable to judicial review than a refusal to register, because the applicant in the review proceedings would have to present evidence to the court that the requirements of CA 2006 in respect of registration had not been complied with, whereas the certificate of incorporation is conclusive evidence that they have been complied with (CA 2006, s 15(4)). Accordingly, the court cannot hear any application for review of a decision to register a company unless the applicant is the Attorney-General, whose evidence the court must hear because s 15(4) does not bind the Crown (per Lord Parker of Waddington in *Bowman v Secular Society Ltd* [1917] AC 406 at pp 438–40 and in *Cotman v Brougham* [1918] AC 514 at p 519; *R v Registrar of Companies, ex parte Central Bank of India* [1986] QB 1114). It is important for persons who deal with a company to be confident that the company's existence cannot easily be challenged. This applies even if registration was procured by fraud (*Bank of Beirut SAL v HRH Prince Adel El-Hashemite* [2015] EWHC 1451 (Ch), [2016] Ch 1, discussed at **4.2.3**).

Provided the fact of its incorporation is not questioned, the legality of the objects of a company with restricted objects may be questioned in legal proceedings and its certificate of incorporation is not conclusive that they are legal (*Bowman v Secular Society Ltd*).

2.2.4 COMPANY FORMATION AGENTS

The preparation of documents for the registration of a new company requires careful consideration and specialist knowledge of company law and procedures. Enterprises exist which specialise in company formation. It has been estimated that they are responsible for approximately 60 per cent of company registrations (Company Law Review Steering Group, *Modern Company Law for a Competitive Economy: Developing the Framework* (URN 00/656) (London: DTI, 2000), para 11.32). Company formation agents with systems approved by Companies House are able to register any kind of company electronically so they can meet customers' specific requirements very quickly. They have therefore moved away from their traditional method of business, which was to register a large number of companies and hold them ready for sale to anyone who wants a new company. This kind of company was called an 'off-the-shelf' or 'shelf' or 'ready-made' company.

2.2.5 COMPANIES FORMED AND REGISTERED UNDER THE FORMER COMPANIES ACTS

In Great Britain, before 1 October 2009, companies could be registered under the Companies Act 1985, which came into force on 1 July 1985.

From 1 July 1948 to 30 June 1985, companies could be registered under the Companies Act 1948. From 1 November 1929 to 30 June 1948, companies could be registered under the Companies Act 1929.

From 1 April 1909 to 31 October 1929, companies could be registered under the Companies (Consolidation) Act 1908.

From 2 November 1862 to 31 March 1909, companies could be registered under the Companies Act 1862.

From 14 July 1856 to 1 November 1862, companies could be registered under the Joint Stock Companies Act 1856, though, by virtue of s 2 of the 1856 Act, banking companies could not register until the Joint Stock Banking Companies Act 1857 came into force, and insurance companies never could register under the 1856 Act (they were allowed to register under the Companies Act 1862 and subsequent Acts). Insurance companies were excluded from the 1856 Act so as to prevent them being registered with limited liability (see **2.3.2.8**).

In the Companies Acts (see **1.5.1.2**) the word 'company' means a company registered under any of the Acts from 1856 to 2006 and corresponding Northern Ireland legislation (CA 2006, s 1(1)). For convenience of drafting these are referred to in the Act as companies formed and registered under CA 2006 (even if they were formed and registered under earlier Acts) (s 1(1)). It is also possible for existing companies formed under other legislation to convert themselves into registered companies and such companies are described as registered, but not formed, under CA 2006. Companies formed and registered under CA 2006 together with companies registered, but not formed, under the Act are referred to as UK-registered companies (s 1158).

The first Act enabling incorporation of companies by registration was the Joint Stock Companies Act 1844, which permitted registration as from 1 November 1844 (though it did not apply in Scotland). The system under the 1844 Act was very different from that under the 1856 Act and its successors. Accordingly, all companies registered under the 1844 Act were required to re-register under the 1856 Act on or before 3 November 1856 (Joint Stock Companies Act 1856, s 110), though this was later extended to 2 November 1857 by the Joint Stock Companies Act 1857, ss 25 to 27. Insurance companies registered under the 1844 Act were excluded from re-registering under the 1856 Act but were required to re-register under the 1862 Act. Banking companies were not allowed to register under the 1844 Act, and the Joint Stock Banks Act 1844 prevented any association of more than six persons setting up a banking business without obtaining a royal charter of incorporation under the Act.

2.3 CLASSIFICATION OF COMPANIES

2.3.1 FIVE TYPES OF COMPANY

CA 2006 provides for the registration of five different types of company. The contents of an application to register a new company depend on which type of company it is to be, so this must be decided before registering it. There are provisions for re-registration so that a company can be changed from one type to another, though there are certain changes that are not possible by re-registration—see **2.6**.

Three characteristics of a company determine which type it is:

(a) Whether the members have limited or unlimited liability (see **2.3.2**).

(b) Whether the company is public or private (see **2.3.3**). Companies whose members have unlimited liability must be private companies.

(c) Whether the company does or does not have a share capital (see **2.3.2**). A company without a share capital must be a private company.

This means that the following kinds of new company may now be registered:

(a) Public limited company (plc) with share capital.

(b) Private limited company with share capital (by far the most numerous type and often called a private company limited by shares).

(c) Private limited company without share capital (called a 'company limited by guarantee' or 'guarantee company').

(d) Private unlimited company with share capital.

(e) Private unlimited company without share capital.

The possible types of company are summarised in **Table 2.1**.

The features which have proved most popular have been limited liability and the capacity to have a share capital—see **2.3.2**. Both features are particularly attractive to business enterprises. The share capital of a company is capital contributed by members (shareholders) for use in the company's operations. The distinction between public and private companies is that a public company may invite the public generally to contribute to its share capital whereas a private company cannot (see **2.3.3.1**).

Guarantee and unlimited companies have been found appropriate for some specialised uses but the limited company with share capital is by far the most common form of company and this book will hardly mention other kinds of company.

Under part 2 (ss 26 to 63) of the Companies (Audit, Investigations and Community Enterprise) Act 2004, it is possible to register any type of limited company as a community interest company

Table 2.1 Possible types of company

	Limited or unlimited	Public or private	Share capital
(a) public limited company (plc)	limited	public	yes
(b) private company limited by shares (Ltd)	limited	private	yes
(c) guarantee company	limited	private	no
(d) unlimited company with share capital	unlimited	private	yes
(e) unlimited company without share capital	unlimited	private	no

(CIC). The registration of a CIC cannot go ahead until approved by the Regulator of Community Interest Companies (s 36), who must be satisfied that the company will satisfy the 'community interest test' and is not an excluded company (s 36(5)(b)). A company satisfies the community interest test if a reasonable person might consider that its activities are being carried on for the benefit of the community (s 35(2)). Excluded companies, which cannot be registered as CICs, are companies which are, or would be when formed, a political party or political campaigning organisation, or a subsidiary of such a party or organisation (SI 2005/1788, reg 6). CICs are subject to limitations on the dividends which they may pay their members. See **www.gov.uk/government/organisations/ office-of-the-regulator-of-community-interest-companies**.

2.3.2 LIMITED OR UNLIMITED COMPANIES AND SHARE CAPITAL

2.3.2.1 Liability of company members

An application for registration of a company must state whether the liability of the members of the company is to be limited (CA 2006, s 9(2)(c)). Almost all registered companies are incorporated with limited liability. A registered company with limited liability is called a 'limited company' and a registered company without limited liability is called an 'unlimited company'.

The principle of separate personality of a body corporate such as a registered company means that the company as a separate person incurs the company's debts. The members do not incur them. The result is, as Lord Cranworth said in *Oakes v Turquand and Harding* (1867) LR 2 HL 325 at p 357:

> There is no doubt that the direct remedy of a creditor is solely against the incorporated company. He has no dealing with any individual shareholder, and if he is driven to bring any action to enforce any right he may have acquired, he must sue the company, and not any of the members of whom it is composed.

Instead of being made directly liable to creditors of the company, the members are made liable by statute if, but only if, the company is wound up, and their liability then is *to the company as a separate person*, and is a liability to contribute money for the payment of the company's debts and liabilities, and settling its affairs (Insolvency Act 1986, s 74(1)).

In an unlimited company, the liability of members at this point is unlimited. Only a very small proportion of registered companies are unlimited companies and they will be almost completely ignored in this book.

The vast majority of companies are limited companies. In a limited company the members' liability when the company is wound up is limited to a fixed amount agreed with the company when they became members. The fixed amount is either an amount payable on shares or an amount payable by guarantee (Insolvency Act 1986, s 74(2)(d) and (3)). When applying for registration of a limited company, a choice must be made (CA 2006, s 9(2)(c)) between liability limited by shares (Insolvency Act 1986, s 74(2)(d)) and liability limited by guarantee (s 74(3)). Almost all limited companies are limited by shares.

The certificate of incorporation of a company states whether it is a limited or unlimited company, and, if it is limited, whether it is limited by shares or by guarantee (s 15(2)(c)).

One practical difference between limitation by guarantee and limitation by shares is that in a guarantee company, the limited amount that the members are liable to pay is payable only on the winding up of the company (s 11(3)) whereas in a company limited by shares it is expected that part at least of the payment will be made while the company is a going concern and will form the contributed capital of the company (known as its 'share capital'). In practice, nowadays, in a company limited by shares, the whole amount that the members are liable to pay is paid as contributed capital while the company is a going concern so that the members have no further liability on winding up. The creditors of a company limited by shares have to bear the risk that its capital contributed while it is a going concern may be lost in trading before it is wound up.

The position is, then, that in the statute permitting incorporation of companies by registration, Parliament has insisted that members of a registered company must be liable to contribute to its assets, but it permits that liability to be limited.

In relation to a company the terms 'limited' and 'unlimited' refer to the liability of the company's members, not the liability of the company as a separate person. Saying that a person has liability for an obligation does not mean that the person will actually meet the obligation when required to do so. A person who has run out of money cannot meet any liabilities. A limited company as a separate person has unlimited liability to pay all its debts and can be forced to pay them until it runs out of money. But if it is wound up, its members have only limited liability to contribute further money for the payment of those debts. They cannot be required to pay more than the limit on their liability.

2.3.2.2 Companies limited by shares

The liability of members of a company limited by shares is based on the company having a 'share capital' and the members taking 'shares' issued to them by the company. Each share is assigned a 'nominal value' or 'par value' (CA 2006, s 542). The nominal value of a share in a company is a sum of money that must be paid on it to the company (though, when a share is issued, the company and the person to whom it is issued may agree that an additional amount, called a 'share premium', is to be paid).

The Insolvency Act 1986, s 74(2)(d), provides that 'in the case of a company limited by shares, no contribution is required [when the company is wound up] from any member exceeding the amount (if any) unpaid on the shares in respect of which he is liable'. This means the amount of the *nominal value* of the shares that has not been paid (*Ooregum Gold Mining Co of India Ltd v Roper* [1892] AC 125 per Lord Watson at p 136), and a limited company cannot agree with its members that they may pay less than the nominal value of their shares (*Ooregum Gold Mining Co of India Ltd v Roper*; CA 2006, s 580). The liability of a member under the Insolvency Act 1986, s 74(2)(d), to pay whatever is unpaid of the nominal value of shares is a statutory liability (*Hansraj Gupta v Asthana* (1932) LR 60 Ind App 1) but it does not extend to share premium, which is a matter for contract between the member and the company (*Niemann v Smedley* [1973] VR 769; *Re Vedelago* (1992) 8 ACSR 135).

So, if Textbook Examples Co plc issues shares with a nominal value of 50p each, every member of the company must contribute to the company's capital at least 50p for each share. There could be a separate agreement between the company and a member that the member would pay, say, an extra £1 for each share, which would be a share premium and would reflect the investment value of the shares at the time of taking them. If when Textbook Examples Co plc is wound up a member has contributed, say, only 30p for each 50p share held, the member can be required to pay the remaining 20p per share in order to pay the company's debts and liabilities.

It is usual nowadays for an undertaking to contribute capital for shares to be fulfilled at the time when the shares are issued. When all the capital represented by a share has been contributed the share is said to be fully paid. In the nineteenth century it was common for only part of the nominal value of a share to be contributed on issue, leaving the company with the right to make a call for the remainder when it required more capital. Shares for which some of the capital has not been contributed are said to be partly paid.

For the first 20 years or so after registration of companies was introduced in 1844, it was thought to be essential to a company's creditworthiness that its shares should be partly paid. Shareholders were usually wealthy individuals who were known in the commercial world. The list of members of a company was available for public inspection and the presence on the list of well-known individuals of substantial means who still had a large liability to contribute to the assets of the company was thought to be a good way of encouraging traders to grant it credit. Accordingly, companies typically had shares with nominal values of £10 to £100 on which only a small amount was paid up, leaving a potentially huge liability for some shareholders. More than 30 companies in this period had shares of £1,000 or more.

The disadvantage for companies of partly paid shares was that there were very few investors wealthy enough to be able to meet the liabilities on their shares and they would only invest in companies if they knew the directors personally and could keep a close watch on the companies they were liable for.

Investors became alarmed at the large amounts they had to pay up during the financial crisis of 1866–67 and the depression years of 1873–86. They realised that, in effect, they were not benefiting from limited liability. Equally, companies realised that there were many middle-class, small-scale investors who would be willing to invest in company shares if they could have effective limited liability. Accordingly, during the 1880s it became normal for company shares to be fully paid £1 shares. For a more detailed history see J B Jefferys, 'The denomination and character of shares, 1855–1885' in *Essays in Economic History*, E M Carus-Wilson (ed) (London: Edward Arnold, 1954), pp 344–57.

CA 2006, s 3(2), describes a company limited by shares as a company whose members' liability is limited by its constitution to the amount, if any, unpaid on the shares held by them. There is such a statement in art 2 of the model articles both for private and for public companies in SI 2008/3229. The fact that a company is limited by shares is stated in its certificate of incorporation (CA 2006, s 15(2)(c)), which is one of the company's constitutional documents (s 32(1)(f)).

Each subscriber of the memorandum of association of a company limited by shares must agree to take at least one share (s 8(1)(b)) and there must be at least one subscriber (s 7(1)). The total number of shares to be taken by the subscribers must be stated in the statement of capital and initial shareholdings (s 10(2)(a)), and the subscribers become the holders of those shares as from the date of incorporation of the company (s 16(1) and (5)). These rules ensure that in any company limited by shares there is at least one share on which a payment must be made to the company by a member.

A person holding shares in a company limited by shares knows that liability to contribute to the assets of the company in respect of the shares is limited to a certain amount which the member has agreed with the company. Parliament has not put any restrictions on what that amount must be, apart from a rule that in a *public limited company* the *total liability of all the members* must be at least the 'authorised minimum' (ss 91(1)(a) and 761(2)), which is £50,000 or €57,100 (s 763; SI 2009/2425, reg 2). In private limited companies, it is common for the total liability of members to be a trivial amount, typically £1.

Nominal values of shares must be stated in monetary terms but not necessarily in sterling (*Re Scandinavian Bank Group plc* [1988] Ch 87; *Re Anglo-American Insurance Co Ltd* [1991] BCLC 564). The nominal value of a share may be an amount such as ½p which cannot be paid in legal tender (*Re Scandinavian Bank Group plc* at pp 99–100; *Re Australian Pacific Technology Ltd* [1995] 1 VR 457, in which the court approved the issue of shares with a nominal value of 0.01 cent each).

Almost all registered companies are companies limited by shares and in the rest of this book the term 'company' without further qualification will be used to mean a registered company limited by shares.

2.3.2.3 Companies limited by guarantee

A company limited by guarantee is defined as a company whose members' liability is limited by its constitution to such amount as they undertake to contribute to the assets of the company in the event of its being wound up (CA 2006, s 3(1) and (3)). When registering a company limited by guarantee, a statement of guarantee must be delivered with the application for registration (s 9(4) (b)) and is one of the company's constitutional documents (s 32(1)(g)). The statement of guarantee must, by s 11, state that each member undertakes that, if the company is wound up while he is a member, or within one year after he ceases to be a member, he will contribute, to the assets of the company, an amount not exceeding a sum specified in the statement of guarantee. The contribution is to be made for the payment of the debts and liabilities of the company, and of the costs, charges and expenses of winding up and for the adjustment of the rights of the contributories among themselves. The Insolvency Act 1986, s 74(3), confirms that in the case of a guarantee company, 'no contribution is required [when the company is wound up] from any member exceeding the amount undertaken to be contributed by him to the company's assets in the event of its being wound up'.

The limit on the liability of a member of a company limited by guarantee is the amount specified in the statement of guarantee.

The total amount that members of a guarantee company are liable to contribute under its statement of guarantee is sometimes called the company's 'guarantee fund'. A guarantee company does not have any contributed capital while it is a going concern—the guarantee fund comes into existence only when the company is wound up—and this is usually considered inappropriate for a business enterprise. Accordingly, guarantee companies are usually formed only to undertake charitable objects or to carry on some non-commercial undertaking. Only a very small proportion of registered companies are guarantee companies and so, like unlimited companies, they will hardly ever be mentioned again in this book.

A member of a company limited by guarantee knows that liability to contribute to the assets of the company under the guarantee is limited to a certain amount which the member has agreed with the company. Parliament has not put any restrictions on what that amount must be, and in practice it is usually nominal—typically it is £1.

2.3.2.4 Collateral liability

Parliament has insisted that every limited company must require each of its members to pay up to a fixed amount to the company on shares or under guarantee, but there must be a certain maximum amount—a company may be able to obtain a share premium when a member joins (see **2.3.2.2**) but it cannot make the amount payable on its shares or under guarantee variable at its option: this is the essence of limited liability. This is emphasised by CA 2006, s 25, which provides that a member of a company is not bound by any change in the company's articles which requires the member to take or subscribe for more shares or in any way increases the member's liability to contribute to the company's share capital or otherwise pay money to the company, unless (by s 25(2)) the member gives express written agreement to be bound.

In some English cases the court has accepted that it is possible for the constitution of a limited company to impose on its members a collateral liability to pay money to the company otherwise than on shares held or under guarantee. Examples are:

(a) *Peninsular Co Ltd v Fleming* (1872) 27 LT 93, in which the collateral liability was to lend money to the company; and

(b) *Lion Mutual Marine Insurance Association Ltd v Tucker* (1883) 12 QBD 176 and *Re Bangor and North Wales Mutual Marine Protection Association, Baird's Case* [1899] 2 Ch 593, in both of which the collateral liability was to contribute to a fund for insuring the marine losses of members of the company.

In *Galloway v Hallé Concerts Society* [1915] 2 Ch 233, each member had a collateral liability to contribute to the society (which was a guarantee company) such sum as the committee (equivalent to a board of directors) might determine, not exceeding in the aggregate £100: it was held that the directors could not call for different contributions from different members because of a general rule of law that members of a company must be treated equally.

In some cases in the Commonwealth it has been asserted that even a collateral liability offends against the principle of limited liability and so cannot be imposed (for example, Salmond J in *Shalfoon v Cheddar Valley Cooperative Dairy Co Ltd* [1924] NZLR 561 at p 577; *Edmonton Country Club Ltd v Case* (1974) 44 DLR (3d) 554). In England, the question has been debated in the context of what are now called registered societies (previously industrial and provident societies). Members of such societies have limited liability (limited by shares) in the same form as members of limited registered companies. In *Dibble v Wilts and Somerset Farmers Ltd* [1923] 1 Ch 342, P O Lawrence J held that such a society could not impose a collateral liability (and Salmond J in *Shalfoon v Cheddar Valley Cooperative Dairy Co Ltd* cited that case in support of his view). However, in *Agricultural Wholesale Society Ltd v Biddulph and District Agricultural Society Ltd* [1925] Ch 769, the Court of Appeal held that P O Lawrence J had been wrong, and the Court of Appeal's view was confirmed by the House of Lords in *Hole v Garnsey* [1930] AC 472; see especially the speech of Viscount Dunedin.

2.3.2.5 Hybrid companies

It was possible before 22 December 1980 in Great Britain (1 July 1983 in Northern Ireland) to register a company limited by guarantee with a share capital (known as a 'hybrid' company). Hybrid companies in existence on that date continue in existence as hybrids but no new hybrid company may be registered (CA 2006, s 5).

2.3.2.6 Share capital of unlimited companies

An unlimited company may have a share capital, which will be capital contributed for the company's day-to-day operations.

2.3.2.7 No liability companies

In the United Kingdom, the constitution of a registered company must impose liability on at least some of its members to contribute capital, either unlimited liability or liability limited by shares or by guarantee. In Australia, it is possible to register a no liability (NL) company, in which there is no obligation to pay calls on shares. However, a company can be registered with no liability only if its objects are confined to mining. In a no liability mining company, shareholders pay an initial small part of the nominal value of their shares to pay for investigation of a new mine, and further instalments to fund development and eventually operation of the mine if it appears to be worth going further. At any stage, shareholders can refuse to pay anything more on their shares, which will then be forfeited.

2.3.2.8 History of limited liability

When incorporation of companies by registration was first introduced by the Joint Stock Companies Act 1844, the most significant political dispute was about limited liability, which many saw as contrary to the established business ethic that a trader should be personally responsible, to the full extent of his or her fortune, for debts incurred in trading: unlimited liability was thought to be the best way of ensuring the standards of behaviour in business sought by the community.

Accordingly, the Joint Stock Companies Act 1844 imposed on the members of a company a form of direct and unlimited liability for its debts: a judgment creditor of a company registered under the Act was permitted to levy execution on individual members of the company if the judgment debt was not paid by the company itself (see *Re Sea Fire and Life Assurance Co, Greenwood's Case* (1854) 3 De G M & G 459).

The argument in favour of limited liability in joint-stock companies was that normally members were only investors who did not take part in the management of the company and so should not be held responsible for it. It was for the good of the community that capital in the hands of private investors should be made available to set up new businesses; such investment would be encouraged by removing the possibility of complete disaster if the business invested in should fail.

This argument was eventually won when the Limited Liability Act 1855 allowed any registered company (other than an insurance company) with at least 25 members to limit the liability of its members to the amounts unpaid on their shares, provided it put 'limited' as the last word of its name. Shortly afterwards, the Joint Stock Companies Act 1856 reduced the minimum number of members to seven (it is now one).

Insurance companies were not permitted to register with limited liability until CA 1862 came into force. In practice, though, a company incorporated under the Joint Stock Companies Act 1844 carrying on insurance business would include in every policy a provision precluding the levying of execution against the members of the company personally for any money payable under the policy. An insurance company's deed of settlement (equivalent to present-day articles, see 3.2.2) would usually forbid its directors from issuing policies without such a provision, and this was the basis on which members took shares in the company. The effectiveness of such a policy provision as a method of contracting out of the personal liability imposed by the 1844 Act was confirmed in *Halket v Merchant Traders' Ship Loan and Insurance Association* (1849) 13 QB 960 and *Hassell v Merchant Traders' Ship Loan and Insurance Association* (1849) 4 Ex 525. The device was also effective when used by unincorporated insurance companies (*Hallett v Dowdall* (1852) 18 QB 2).

Under the 1855 Act, the liability of members was still direct to creditors but the 1856 Act introduced the principle that the liability of members of a registered company should be to the company only and should be enforced for the benefit of creditors on the winding up of the company. Guarantee companies were first allowed for in CA 1862. For more detail of the history up to 1862 see H A Shannon, 'The coming of general limited liability' in E M Carus-Wilson (ed), *Essays in Economic History*, vol 1 (London: Edward Arnold, 1954), pp 358–79 (reprinted from *Economic History*, vol 2 (1931), pp 267–91); J Saville, 'Sleeping partnership and limited liability, 1850–1856', *Economic History Review*, 2nd ser, vol 8 (1956), pp 418–33; C E Amsler, R L Bartlett and C J Bolton, 'Thoughts of some British economists on early limited liability and corporate legislation', *History of Political Economy*, vol 13 (1981), pp 774–93. Saville's article reveals the wide variety of arguments for and against wider availability of limited liability that were advanced by various interest groups.

During the second half of the nineteenth century, believers in the moral superiority of unlimited liability, who nevertheless recognised that it was not appropriate to make mere investors in an enterprise liable for its debts to an unlimited extent, promoted the compromise of limited liability for investors but unlimited liability for the directors or managers who actually conducted the enterprise's business. Their model was the French partnership *en commandite*. A business may be conducted on these lines as a limited partnership (introduced in 1907; see 1.4.1.2). See M Lobban, 'Corporate identity and limited liability in France and England 1825–67' (1996) 25 Anglo-Am L Rev 397.

As will be explained in 2.3.3.2, in the late nineteenth century it was realised that, although limited liability encouraged capitalists to invest money in companies which they did not manage, nothing in the law required a limited liability company to have members who did not take part in management. It became increasingly popular for small businesses to be carried on by companies whose only members were the people who operated the business. Thus business people could obtain limited liability for their own trading.

Limited liability became the dominant business ethic in the European Community in 1989 when the Council adopted its Twelfth Company Law Directive (89/667/EEC, now consolidated as Directive 2009/102/EC). This required member States to provide a legal form for *individuals* to trade with limited liability, finally abandoning the view that limited liability is only appropriate for people who merely invest in a business without taking part in its management. The Directive has been implemented in the United Kingdom by permitting the registration of single-member private limited companies since 15 July 1992 in Great Britain (SI 1992/1699) and 19 October 1992 in Northern Ireland (SR 1992/405), and, from 1 October 2009, permitting any kind of registered company to have only one member. For background to the Directive see V Edwards, 'The EU Twelfth Company Law Directive' (1998) 19 Co Law 211.

The justification for making limited liability freely available is that it encourages people to set up in business by making it less risky. However, making it easier to carry on businesses that become insolvent makes economic activity more risky for the community generally if it becomes more likely that money will be lost dealing with insolvent limited liability companies. Any creditor of a small company in a strong enough negotiating position (such as a bank or a landlord) usually requires personal guarantees from the individuals controlling the company and this makes limited liability meaningless for them. In times of economic recession, ordinary trade creditors and customers who cannot negotiate special protection for themselves become discontented with limited liability. This has led to suggestions that it is necessary to return to the concept that limited liability should be available only for non-managing investors. See, for example, A Hicks, R Drury and J Smallcombe, *Alternative Company Structures for the Small Business* (London: Certified Accountants Educational Trust, 1995). A policy of restricting the availability of limited liability was rejected by the Company Law Review (*Modern Company Law for a Competitive Economy: Developing the Framework* (URN 00/656) (London: DTI, 2000), paras 9.61 to 9.71).

Merely imposing unlimited liability on a company's shareholders does not make dealing with the company free of risk for creditors. They still have the risk that their debts will exceed the shareholders' assets.

So far the main legislative response to discontent with freely available limited liability has been that business people need to be made responsible for their dishonest business practices not their economic misfortunes. Accordingly, in contrast to the limited liability of members of companies, statute has increasingly exposed directors to liability if they fail to meet publicly required standards of behaviour in business—see the Insolvency Act 1986, s 214 (wrongful trading) discussed in **20.12**, and s 217 discussed in **20.14** and the provisions on disqualification of directors discussed in **20.13**.

For a discussion of many issues related to limited liability, see T Orhnial (ed), *Limited Liability and the Corporation* (London: Croom Helm, 1982). There have been some discussions in terms of economic theory of the possible advantages of limited liability. See, for example, R E Meiners, J S Mofsky and R D Tollison, 'Piercing the veil of limited liability' (1979) 4 Delaware J Corp L 351; P Halpern, M Trebilcock and S Turnbull, 'An economic analysis of limited liability in corporation law' (1980) 30 UTLJ 117; and F H Easterbrook and D R Fischel, 'Limited liability and the corporation' (1985) 52 U Chi L Rev 89.

Halpern et al suggest that, as far as public companies are concerned, if they could not offer members limited liability then the market for their shares would be hampered. Shareholding would be concentrated in a few wealthy investors who were able to monitor closely the companies they invested in. Small investors would refuse to buy shares that could lead to catastrophic liability unless they could buy insurance against losses. (Insurers would depend on the effectiveness of the close monitoring by the large shareholders.) The poor experience of the English stock market with partly paid shares of high nominal value (which impose a liability that is practically unlimited), described in **2.3.2.2**, shows that this analysis is probably correct, at least in times of economic uncertainty. If, however, investors are confident that a company is sound and the risk of catastrophe is negligible then they will buy and trade in unlimited liability shares as though they had limited liability, as they did with the American Express Company in the 1950s (P Z Grossman, 'The market for shares of companies with unlimited liability: the case of American Express' (1995) 24 J Legal Stud 63).

In relation to private companies, Halpern et al support the criticism that if limited liability is too readily available then it encourages the setting up of too many businesses that will fail.

If a company's members have unlimited liability, or a high liability on partly paid shares, the company's creditors will want to check the wealth of its members, which is why it has always been considered important that a list of a company's members should be available for public inspection. If a company's members have limited liability, its creditors must turn to monitoring the company's own financial health, which is why accounting and auditing requirements are such an important feature of company law, and why limited, but not unlimited, companies must file their annual accounts with Companies House.

In the USA it has been suggested that although limited liability for contract debts may be an acceptable price for the business community, as creditors, to pay for giving enterprises the ability to raise capital easily, it is not acceptable that shareholders should have limited liability for tort when the activities of companies can do massive harm to the environment (for example, oil spills, explosions at chemical plants) and can cause serious personal injury to large numbers of consumers (for example, product negligence in vehicle and pharmaceutical manufacture, use of harmful materials such as asbestos). Clearly there is a qualitative difference between hardship caused because trading debts are not paid and hardship caused by personal injury or environmental damage. See H Hansmann and R Kraakman, 'Toward unlimited shareholder liability for corporate torts' (1991) 100 Yale LJ 1879. J A Grundfest, 'The limited future of unlimited liability: a capital markets perspective' (1992) 102 Yale LJ 387 suggests that the financial markets could invent ways of avoiding the imposition of unlimited liability but see the response by Hansmann and Kraakman (1992) 102 Yale LJ 427 and the article by Grossman cited earlier.

2.3.3 PRIVATE OR PUBLIC COMPANIES

2.3.3.1 Definitions

A limited company with a share capital is a public company if its certificate of incorporation states that it is, and it was registered or re-registered as, a public company on or after 22 December 1980 in Great Britain (1 July 1983 in Northern Ireland) (CA 2006, s 4(2) and (3)). (Re-registration is dealt with in **2.6.**) In addition, the name of a public company must end with the words 'public limited company' or the abbreviation 'plc' (s 58(1)) or, if it is a Welsh company, the equivalent in Welsh (s 58(2)).

The class of public companies includes hybrid companies (see **2.3.2.5**) which were in existence on 22 December 1980 in Great Britain (1 July 1983 in Northern Ireland) and which have re-registered as public companies.

A company that is not a public company is called a 'private' company (s 4(1)).

A private limited company's shares must not be offered to the public (s 755; see **7.4.7**) and the shares of a private company (whether limited or unlimited) cannot be listed (FSMA 2000, s 75(3); SI 2001/2956, reg 3) and so cannot be admitted to trading on the London Stock Exchange's Main Market (see **7.3.3.2**). A public company's shares can be offered to the public and listed, and the principal practical difference between public and private companies is that a public company can, if it is large enough and satisfies the conditions for listing, obtain large amounts of low-cost capital through public issues of shares on the London Stock Exchange. Although a company must have the legal form of a plc if it is to have its shares listed, the listing process is entirely independent of the company registration process, and it is not unusual for a plc to have no publicly traded shares.

A further difference between a public company and a private company is that, whereas a private company may have only a trivial amount of contributed capital (such as £1), the legislation sets a comparatively substantial minimum requirement for the members' liability to contribute capital to a public company, as measured by the nominal value of the shares they hold. This is required by Directive 2012/30/EU, art 6, which sets the minimum at €25,000. In the United Kingdom the minimum is expressed in terms of the 'authorised minimum', which is £50,000 or €57,100 (CA 2006, s 763; SI 2009/2425, reg 2). However, a public company is not actually required to have contributed capital of £50,000. The requirement is that a public company must allot to its members shares with a nominal value of at least £50,000 but it is permissible for the members to pay up only one-quarter of the nominal value of each share allotted. Thus the amount of contributed capital of a public company may be as little as £12,500 with a right to call on members for a further £37,500.

If a company is registered as a public company when it is first incorporated, CA 2006 ensures that it satisfies the minimum capital requirements by forbidding the company from doing any business or borrowing any money until it has been issued with a trading certificate under s 761. Failure of the company to obtain a certificate within a year of registration is a ground for petitioning the court to wind it up (Insolvency Act 1986, s 122(1)(b)). The main condition for the issue of a certificate is the allotment by the company of shares with a nominal value of at least £50,000 (CA 2006, s 761(2)), for each of which the company must have received at least one-quarter of the nominal value (ss 586(1) and (2) and 761(3)). For further details, see **6.7.1**. There is an alternative procedure for ensuring that a private company which re-registers as a public company has the minimum capital (see **6.7.2**).

The High Level Group of Company Law Experts appointed by the European Commission has noted that €25,000 'is not enough to ensure that companies have sufficient financial means to carry out substantial economic activities' (*A Modern Regulatory Framework for Company Law in Europe*, para 3.3.7). The only function of the minimum requirement seems to be to deter people from setting up a public company light-heartedly.

Under Regulation (EC) No 2157/2001, art 4, the capital of a European public limited-liability company (an SE) must be at least €120,000.

2.3.3.2　History of the distinction between private and public companies

When incorporation of companies by registration was first introduced in 1844, it was assumed that the typical registered company would have a large membership of investors who would entrust the management of the company's affairs to its directors. It was also presumed that there would be public dealings in the shares of registered companies.

The Joint Stock Companies Act 1856 set the minimum number of members of a registered company at seven. Within 20 years or so it was realised that it was unnecessary for a company to have a large membership. The practice grew of incorporating what were informally known as 'private' companies, as described in Francis Palmer's book, *Private Companies; or, How to Convert Your Business into a Private Company, and the Benefit of So Doing*, first published in 1877. An individual in business on his or her own (a 'sole trader') would find six nominees to make up the required minimum of seven subscribers and incorporate a company to take over the business, thus achieving a separation of business and private affairs and, most importantly, limited liability. In *Salomon v A Salomon and Co Ltd* [1897] AC 22 the House of Lords confirmed that this was permitted by CA 1862 and that the members of such a company had limited liability. The popularity of the 'private' company was recognised by Parliament, which in CA 1907 created a statutory category of 'private companies' for which the minimum membership was two. From 1908, it was possible to register a company as a private company but such a company was forbidden to offer its shares to the public and was required to restrict the right to transfer its shares and to limit its membership to 50 persons (excluding employees). This definition of 'private company' was last re-enacted in CA 1948, s 28. (In some Commonwealth countries in which similar legislation was introduced, private companies were called 'proprietary' companies, and their names included the abbreviation 'Pty'.) By 1979, nearly 98 per cent of British registered companies were private companies. See further P W Ireland, 'The rise of the limited liability company' (1984) 12 Int J Sociol Law 239.

The system was changed by CA 1980 so that now every registered company is defined to be a private company *unless* it is registered or re-registered as a public company (CA 2006, s 4). CA 1980 removed the requirement that a private company must limit the number of its members and reduced the minimum number of members of a public company from seven to two (for private companies the minimum number of members had been reduced to two in 1908). In 1992 the minimum number of members of a private company was reduced from two to one in accordance with Directive 89/667/EEC (now Directive 2009/102/EC). As from 1 October 2009, the minimum number for public companies has also been reduced to one by CA 2006. At the end of March 2017, 99.8 per cent of UK companies were private companies. Research carried out for the Company Law Review shows that about 90 per cent of companies have four or fewer members (*Modern Company Law for a Competitive Economy: Developing the Framework* (URN 00/656) (London: DTI, 2000), para 11.6).

British company law traditionally regards private and public companies as two variants of the same basic form of legal organisation, unlike legal systems in Continental Europe which tend to treat them as different forms of organisation. Since joining what was then the European Community, British law has made more differences between public and private companies. Before 1980 people dealing with companies did not usually know, or care, whether they were public or private. Now, the use of the two different terminations to names—plc for a public company, Ltd for a private company—makes it obvious. This is in accord with Continental practice, for example, in France the name of a public limited company (*société anonyme*) ends SA while that of a private limited company (*société à responsabilité limitée*) ends Sàrl.

Law and economics analysts, who are much concerned with companies as the subject of stock-market trading, draw a sharp distinction between companies whose shares are publicly traded and those which are not—see, for example, H G Manne, 'Our two corporation systems: law and economics' (1967) 53 Va L Rev 259.

2.4 COMPANY NAMES

2.4.1 INTRODUCTION

Since a company is an artificial person, it can be identified only by its name, which is thus of considerable importance. A limited company is required to indicate its status in its name and whether it is a public or a private company (**2.4.2**), with some exceptions (**2.4.3**). The Secretary of State has power to prescribe what characters can be used in company names (**2.4.4**). There are various statutes which prohibit the use of certain words in company names (**2.4.5**). There is a long list of words which cannot be used without permission (**2.4.6**). There are provisions to prevent companies being registered with confusingly similar names (**2.4.7**). The goodwill and reputation attached to an existing business's name may be damaged by a new company using the same or a similar name. The existing business can use the law of passing off (**2.4.8**) to prevent the use of the name and recover damages, and there is a system of company names adjudication to deal with these problems (**2.4.9**). It is common for a company to use a trading name or business name which is not the name under which it is registered. There are rules to ensure that the registered name is disclosed (**2.4.10**). There are further rules which require a company's registered name to be stated on business documents (**4.5.1**).

2.4.2 INDICATION OF LIMITED LIABILITY AND COMPANY TYPE

If a company limited by shares is to be a private company, the last word of its name must be 'limited' or 'Ltd' (CA 2006, s 59(1)), and if it is to be a public company, the name must end with the words 'public limited company' or 'plc' (s 58(1)). A Welsh company (which is registered as requiring its registered office to be in Wales: s 88) may use the Welsh equivalents of these words and abbreviations (ss 58(2) and 59(2)).

SI 2015/17 prohibits carrying on business in the United Kingdom under any name which concludes with one of the statutory indicators of corporate status unless the person carrying on the business has that status (regs 16 and 17). SI 2015/17 also prevents an unlimited company being registered with a name ending 'Ltd' or 'plc' (reg 6).

The name of an SE must begin or end with the abbreviation 'SE', and no other company or firm formed on or after 8 October 2004 may use that abbreviation in its name (Regulation (EC) No 2157/2001, art 11).

2.4.3 OMISSION OF 'LIMITED' FROM THE NAME OF A LIMITED COMPANY

CA 2006, s 60, permits registration of a company limited by guarantee with a name that does not include the word 'limited' or its Welsh equivalent, provided the company is a charity and complies with regulations made under s 60. Those regulations restrict the exemption to not-for-profit companies that limit their objects to the promotion or regulation of commerce, art, science, education, religion, charity or any profession (SI 2015/17, reg 3). Companies House must be provided with a statement that the company meets the conditions for exemption (CA 2006, s 60(2)), which Companies House may accept as sufficient evidence of the matters stated in it (s 60(3)). Guarantee companies exempted under more wide-ranging provisions of previous legislation continue to be exempted if they satisfy relevant conditions (ss 61 and 62).

2.4.4 PERMITTED CHARACTERS

CA 2006, s 57, gives the Secretary of State power to make regulations to specify what letters, characters, signs, symbols, accents and punctuation can be used in a company name. SI 2015/17, reg 2, lists as permitted characters the Latin alphabet (including extra characters and accents used in other EEA countries), Arabic numerals, punctuation marks, and some signs and symbols. The length of names is limited to 160 characters including spaces (reg 2(4)). Characters not allowed in company names can still be used in business names.

2.4.5 ILLEGAL OR OFFENSIVE NAMES

By CA 2006, s 53(a), a company must not be registered by a name if, in the opinion of the Secretary of State, the use of the name by the company would be a criminal offence.

Statute has prohibited the use of certain words that have an association with recognised charitable organisations. For example, a company's name may not include the words 'Red Cross' or 'Geneva Cross' without the authority of the Army Council (Geneva Convention Act 1957, s 6), nor the word 'Anzac' without the authority of the Secretary of State for Foreign and Commonwealth Affairs ('Anzac' (Restriction on Trade Use of Word) Act 1916, s 1).

Under the Chartered Associations (Protection of Names and Uniforms) Act 1926, s 1, it is unlawful to use or imitate the names of the Boy Scouts and Girl Guides Associations, the Order of St John of Jerusalem, the Royal Life Saving Society and the National Society for the Prevention of Cruelty to Children.

It is an offence to use a name including the words 'credit union' or any cognate term or derivative of those words without being registered, under the Co-operative and Community Benefit Societies Act 2014, as a credit union (Credit Unions Act 1979, s 3).

It is an offence to represent oneself as being a building society without being registered as one (Building Societies Act 1986, s 107).

In *R v Registrar of Companies, ex parte Bowen* [1914] 3 KB 1161, it was held that the registrar has no authority to refuse to register a company with a name which the registrar considers to be misleading, but Lord Reading CJ said, at p 1167, that the registrar could refuse registration if a company's name contained scandalous or obscene words. Now CA 2006, s 53(b), prohibits registration of a company with a name which, in the opinion of the Secretary of State, is offensive. This would appear to mean offensive to people generally rather than offensive to a particular section of the public. In Australia, a name cannot be used if it is likely to be offensive to members of any section of the public, and in *Little v Australian Securities Commission* (1996) 22 ACSR 226 it was held that the name 'Virgin Mary's Pty Ltd' could not be used because it was likely to offend a section of the public. (The company operated a nightclub: the objectors were represented at the hearing by J Santamaria QC.)

2.4.6 WORDS REQUIRING PERMISSION

By CA 2006, s 54, the Secretary of State's approval is required in order to register a company with a name likely to give the impression that the company is connected in any way with the government, with any local authority or with any public authority specified in SI 2015/17, sch 4 (see reg 9). By CA 2006, s 55, the Secretary of State's approval is required to register a company with a name that includes any word or phrase specified in SI 2014/3140. An applicant for approval must seek the views of a government department or other body specified in the relevant SI. For example, anyone wishing to register a company with a name that includes the word 'bank' requires the Secretary of State's approval and must seek the views of the Financial Conduct Authority (FCA).

2.4.7 EXISTING CORPORATIONS AND LIMITED PARTNERSHIPS

Companies House is required by CA 2006, s 1099, to keep an index of the names of:

(a) All corporations incorporated by registration as companies under the laws of England and Wales, Northern Ireland and Scotland.

(b) All corporations incorporated by registration as industrial and provident societies under the laws of England and Wales, Northern Ireland and Scotland.

(c) Certain chartered and statutory companies specified in regulations made under s 1043.

(d) Limited partnerships registered in the United Kingdom. Limited partnerships are not incorporated.

(e) Limited liability partnerships incorporated in the United Kingdom.

(f) Corporations incorporated outside the United Kingdom ('overseas companies') that have registered with Companies House under s 1046.

(g) European economic interest groupings registered in the United Kingdom.

(h) Open-ended investment companies authorised in the United Kingdom.

The index may be searched (as required by s 1100) online, free of charge, at **www.companieshouse.gov.uk**, click on Find Company Information.

By s 66, a company must not be registered with a name that is the same as one appearing in this index, or where there are only trivial differences, specified in SI 2015/17, reg 7 and sch 3. Under reg 8, though, it is possible to register a company with a name that is the same as an existing company, except for the presence of any word listed in sch 3, para 5, provided the existing company gives its consent and the new company will be in the same group as the existing company. The words listed in sch 3, para 5, include local top-level domain names such as 'co.uk' and words such as 'holdings', 'group' and 'Great Britain'.

CA 2006, ss 67 and 68, deal with erroneous registration of a company with a name too like that of an existing company, either because of Companies House's failure to appreciate the similarity or because the existing company was omitted from the index. In those circumstances the Secretary of State can, within 12 months of the erroneous registration, direct the company to change its name (see **2.4.12**).

2.4.8 PASSING OFF

Using a name for one's business which is deceptively similar to the name of another business so that actual damage has been, or is likely to be, caused to the goodwill and reputation of that other business is a form of the tort of passing off, which may be restrained by injunction. Thus, in *Hendriks v Montagu* (1881) 17 ChD 638 the Universal Life Assurance Society (which was not incorporated) obtained an injunction to prevent Montagu and his associates registering a company with the name Universe Life Assurance Association Ltd. It is not necessary to prove that the deception was intended (*British Diabetic Association v Diabetic Society Ltd* [1995] 4 All ER 812).

To counter passing off by a company that has already been registered, an injunction may be obtained requiring the company's controllers not to allow the company to continue to be registered with a deceptive name (specifying words which must not be used), so that they must either change the company's name (see **2.4.12**) or dissolve it (*La Société Anonyme des Anciens Établissements Pan-hard et Levassor v Panhard Levassor Motor Co Ltd* [1901] 2 Ch 513; *Exxon Corporation v Exxon Insurance Consultants International Ltd* [1982] Ch 119). The court cannot order the registrar to change a company's name, because a company's name can be changed only by one of the methods permitted by statute (see **2.4.12**) (*Halifax plc v Halifax Repossessions Ltd* [2004] EWCA Civ 331, [2004] BCC 281).

The court will not restrain an individual from trading under his or her own surname, provided the individual is acting honestly. However, a company is not entitled to the same immunity in respect of using the name of one of its members. A company does not have a right to trade under the name of one of its shareholders if to do so would damage another business (*M P Guimaraens and Son v Fonseca and Vasconcellos Ltd* (1921) 38 RPC 388, in which the defendant company was prohibited from trading in port wine under its name, which included the surname of one of its shareholders and directors, R A da Fonseca, because to do so would cause confusion with the claimant firm's old-established trade in 'Fonseca's port'). This emphasises that the business of a company is owned by the company as a separate person, not by its members. See also *Tussaud v Tussaud* (1890) 44 ChD 678, in which the company that owned Madame Tussaud's waxworks was granted an injunction to prevent a member of the Tussaud family from registering a company called Louis Tussaud Ltd to put on a similar waxworks show.

It is only *business* reputation and trading goodwill that can be protected by a claim for pass-ing off, not, for example, the reputation of a political party (*Kean v McGivan* [1982] FSR 119). However, 'trade' is interpreted widely, so as to include professional and artistic work and the activities of a pressure group such as the Countryside Alliance (*Burge v Haycock* [2001] EWCA Civ 900, [2002] RPC 28). A claimant can obtain an injunction to prevent passing off in England and Wales in relation to a product only if the claimant has customers among the general public in England and Wales for that product, merely having a reputation here is not enough. There has been controversy over whether this rule is appropriate for business in the Internet age, but it has now been confirmed by the Supreme Court (*Starbucks (HK) Ltd v British Sky Broadcasting Group (No 2)* [2015] UKSC 31, [2015] 1 WLR 2628).

Use of the name of a person, whether an individual or a company, to mark goods so that people may believe they are the goods of another trader is another form of passing off, and is regarded particularly seriously by the courts—it is no defence that all that has been done is honestly to put on the goods the name of their maker (*Baume and Co Ltd v A H Moore Ltd* [1958] RPC 226, in which the defendant company was prohibited from continuing to import watches made by a Swiss company, Baume & Mercier SA, marked 'Baume and Mercier', which the public might confuse with the 'Baume' watches which the plaintiff company had sold for about 80 years; *Parker-Knoll Ltd v Knoll International Ltd* [1962] RPC 243).

A recent development is the use of the law of passing off to counter people who register companies with names which existing traders or famous people might want to use as trading names in the future and who are then asked to pay large sums to buy the companies. This has been described as an abuse of the registration process, and a mandatory injunction will be issued in such a case to require the company to change its name (*Glaxo plc v Glaxowellcome Ltd* [1996] FSR 388; *Direct Line Group Ltd v Direct Line Estate Agency Ltd* [1997] FSR 374). In *British Telecommunications plc v One In A Million Ltd* [1999] 1 WLR 903, which concerned the registration of Internet domain names, Aldous LJ said, at p 925, that what the defendants in these cases had done wrong was to register names which were capable of being used for passing off and so could be described as 'instruments of fraud', which the courts had jurisdiction to restrain. See **2.4.9**.

2.4.9 COMPANY NAMES ADJUDICATORS

The Company Names Tribunal deals with complaints that a company name has been registered for the primary purpose of preventing someone with a legitimate interest from registering it, or demanding payment from them to release it (CA 2006, ss 69 to 74). The adjudicators are appointed, and may be dismissed, by the Secretary of State (s 70). A person may apply to the tribunal for an order that a company's name must be changed, because it wrongfully exploits goodwill in a name associated with the applicant (s 69). The two possible grounds for an application, specified in s 69(1), are:

(a) that the company's name is the same as a name associated with the applicant and in which the applicant has goodwill; or

(b) that the company's name is sufficiently similar to such a name that its use in the United Kingdom would be likely to mislead by suggesting a connection between the company and the applicant.

By s 69(4), if either of these grounds is established, an objection to a company's name will be upheld unless it is shown by the company (and any of its members or directors who are joined as respondents) that:

(a) the company was registered before commencement of the activities creating the applicant's goodwill; or

(b) the company is operating under the name, or is proposing to do so and has incurred substantial start-up costs, or has done so but is now dormant—in any of these circumstances a claim for passing off (see **2.4.8**) is more appropriate; or

(c) the company was registered in the ordinary course of a company formation business and is for sale to the applicant on the standard terms of that business; or

(d) the name was adopted in good faith (it is unclear why this should be a defence, as it would not be a defence to a passing-off claim); or

(e) the applicant's interests are not adversely affected to any significant extent.

Even if one of defences (a), (b) or (c) is established, the objection will be upheld if the applicant shows that the main purpose of registering the company was to obtain money (or other consideration) from the applicant or prevent the applicant from registering a company with that name (s 69(5)).

If an application is upheld, the tribunal will order the company to change its name by a specified date and, if that order is not complied with, may determine a new name for the company (s 73).

There is a right of appeal to the court from a decision of the tribunal (s 74).

2.4.10 USE OF A BUSINESS NAME OTHER THAN THE CORPORATE NAME

A company may conduct its business under a name which is not its corporate name (the name under which it is registered at Companies House and which appears on its certificate of incorporation). Under CA 2006, part 41, Chapter 1 (ss 1192 to 1199), a business name used by a company is subject to the same requirements for permission as a company's corporate name (see **2.4.6**).

2.4.11 USE OF AN INSOLVENT COMPANY'S NAME

When choosing a name for a company, it is necessary to consider the persons who are to be its directors or take part in its management. Any such person who was a director or shadow director of a company that went into insolvent liquidation less than five years previously is in danger of committing an offence under IA 1986, s 216, if the new company uses a name suggesting an association with the insolvent company. See **20.14**.

2.4.12 CHANGE OF NAME

2.4.12.1 Procedure for changing a company's name

A company may change its name by special resolution (75 per cent majority; see **14.4.3**) or by any other means provided by its articles (CA 2006, s 77(1)). The same restrictions apply to the choice of a new name as to the choice of the original name (see **2.4.2** to **2.4.11**). Notice of a change of name must be given to Companies House (ss 78(1) and 79), which must give public notice (see **4.3**) of receipt (ss 1077 and 1078(2)). Provided it is satisfied that the new name is legal and the correct procedure for changing the name has been followed, Companies House will enter the new name on the register in place of the old name (s 80(2)), and issue an altered certificate of incorporation (s 80(3)). Public notice is given of issuing the altered certificate (s 1064). The change of name takes effect on the date of issue of the altered certificate (s 81(1)). If a company's notice of change of name is delivered to Companies House electronically, a fee of £8 is charged for issuing the altered certificate of incorporation, or £30 for processing on the same day (SI 2012/1907, sch 1, para 8(g)(iii) and (iv)). The equivalent fees for non-electronic registration are £10 and £50 (para 8(g)(i) and (ii)).

If a premium listed company changes its name, it must inform the FCA and a regulatory information service, and send a copy of the new certificate of incorporation to the FCA (FCA Handbook, LR 9.6.19R).

A company's name may also be changed by a company names adjudicator, or by the court on appeal from an adjudicator (see **2.4.9**). The registrar of companies does not have an independent power to rename a company and cannot be ordered by the court to do so (*Halifax plc v Halifax Repossessions Ltd* [2004] EWCA Civ 331, [2004] BCC 281).

A change of name by a company does not affect the company's rights or obligations or render defective any legal proceedings by or against the company (which may be continued or commenced against it by its new name) (s 81(2) and (3)). The company with the altered name and altered certificate of incorporation is still the company it was under its previous name; the company is not 'formed' with the new name at the time of issuing the new certificate; it was formed when it was first registered (*Oshkosh B'Gosh Inc v Dan Marbel Inc Ltd* [1989] BCLC 507). Similarly, although the document issued by Companies House on registering a company's change of name is called a 'certificate of incorporation', it only records the change of name: the company is not incorporated anew—it was incorporated when it was first registered (*Cross v Aurora Group Ltd* (1988) 4 NZCLC 64,909).

2.4.12.2 Secretary of State's direction to change name

The Secretary of State has a power to direct a company to change its name in the following circumstances:

(a) If the company is exempt from the requirement to include the word 'limited' in its name but it appears to the Secretary of State that the company has ceased to be entitled to the exemption (s 64). The only change which can be directed under s 64 is to add the word 'limited' at the end of the name and, exceptionally, this may be resolved by the directors rather than the members (s 64(3)).

(b) If the company's name is the same as, or too like, a name which was, or should have been, on the Companies House index of names when the company was registered (ss 67 and 68).

(c) If the company, for the purpose of being registered with a particular name, provided misleading information, or gave undertakings or assurances which have not been fulfilled (s 75).

(d) If the company's name gives so misleading an indication of the nature of its activities as to be likely to cause harm to the public (s 76).

There are criminal sanctions for failure to comply with a direction (ss 64(5) and (6), 68(5) and (6), 75(5) and (6), and 76(6) and (7)).

In *Association of Certified Public Accountants of Britain v Secretary of State for Trade and Industry* [1998] 1 WLR 164 the court confirmed a direction to the Association to change its name because of a misleading indication of activities. The form of harm to the public which was identified in the case was that people would be likely to pay more for the services of members of the Association because of the word 'Certified' in its name, which was said to give a misleading impression of the level of qualification required of members.

2.5 REGISTERED OFFICE

2.5.1 PARTS OF THE UNITED KINGDOM

An application for the registration of a company must state whether the company's registered office is to be situated in England and Wales (or in Wales), in Scotland or in Northern Ireland (CA 2006, s 9(2)(b)). This statement determines whether the company is to be registered in England and Wales, in Scotland or in Northern Ireland (s 9(6)). These parts of the United Kingdom have separate legal systems and separate court systems. Registration of a company in a particular part of the United Kingdom means that the courts of that part will have jurisdiction over the internal affairs of the company—that is, the rights and duties, in relation to the company's affairs, of its members and directors. CA 2006 applies throughout the United Kingdom, with some special provisions for each of the three legal systems. Company law has to be seen in the context of the particular legal system in which a company is registered, and this book looks at company law from the perspective of the legal system of England and Wales.

The purpose of stating that a company's registered office is to be in Wales, rather than England and Wales, is that the company will be a Welsh company for the purposes of CA 2006 (s 88) and will be entitled to use the Welsh language in its name (see **2.4.2**) and in communications with Companies House (see **4.2.1.3**). A company whose registered office is in fact situated in Wales, but which is registered as having a registered office in England and Wales, may pass a special resolution (which requires a 75 per cent majority; see **14.4.3**) to alter the registration so as to provide that the registered office is to be situated in Wales (s 88(2)). The company will then be a Welsh company (s 88(1)). A Welsh company can relinquish that status by special resolution (s 88(3)). On becoming or ceasing to be a Welsh company, a new certificate of incorporation is issued (s 88(4)) and public notice is given (s 1064; see **4.3**).

As there is a single legal system for England and Wales, a Welsh company is correctly described as 'registered in England and Wales' and should not be referred to as 'incorporated in Wales' (Joint Committee on Statutory Instruments, *Twenty-second Report of Session 2013–14*, para 35). For the argument that Wales should have its own legal system see *Justice for Wales. In Support of a Welsh Jurisdiction* (September 2015).

2.5.2 REGISTERED OFFICE ADDRESS

The situation of a company's registered office is of great importance to persons dealing with the company because, by CA 2006, s 1139(1): 'A document may be served on a company registered under this Act by leaving it at, or sending it by post to, the company's registered office'. Section 1139(1) provides one method by which a document may be served on a company, but it does not state that this is the only valid method of service (*Spring Salmon and Seafood Ltd* 2004 SLT 501). In many circumstances in which service of a document is legally significant, legislation prescribes methods of service which may be used as alternatives to service under s 1139(1). For example, part 6 of the Civil Procedure Rules 1998 (SI 1998/3132) provides (as stated in r 6.3(2)) alternative methods for service on companies of documents in civil court proceedings.

An application for registration of a company must contain a statement of the intended address of the company's registered office (CA 2006, s 9(5)(a)). As from the date of the company's incorporation, its registered office will be at that address (s 16(1) and (4)). In order for a company to change the situation of its registered office, the company must give notice to Companies House (s 87(1)), which must give public notice (see **4.3**) of receipt (ss 1077 and 1078(2)). The change takes effect when the notice is registered at Companies House, but until the end of the period of 14 days beginning with the date on which it is registered, a person may validly serve any document on the company at its previous registered office (s 87(2)).

If a company is using an address for its registered office without authorisation, an application may be made for Companies House to be the company's registered office instead (s 1097A and SI 2016/423).

2.5.3 DOMICILE AND REDOMICILE

The legal system under which a company is incorporated is its domicile in private international law (*Gasque v Commissioners of Inland Revenue* [1940] 2 KB 80). A company incorporated by registration in one part of the United Kingdom has no power under the Companies Acts or the general law to have itself incorporated in any other jurisdiction (*Tayside Floorcloth Co Ltd* 1923 SC 590; see *Bateman v Service* (1881) 6 App Cas 386 on the inability of a company registered in one Australian colony to register in another). To put it another way, a company cannot, of its own volition, abandon one domicile and adopt another, as a natural person can (*Carl Zeiss Stiftung v Rayner and Keeler Ltd (No 3)* [1970] Ch 506 per Buckley J at p 544). A company exists as a person separate from its members only by virtue of the law under which it was incorporated, and the company itself cannot alter that law.

If the members of a company wish to move it from one jurisdiction to another, they must promote a private Act of Parliament for the purpose. The British Olivetti Limited Act 1980, for example, transferred a company from Scotland to England. The Henry Johnson, Sons & Co, Limited Act 1996 moved a company from England to France.

See further, P StJ Smart, 'Corporate domicile and multiple incorporation in English private international law' [1990] JBL 126; D Lewis, 'Corporate redomicile' (1995) 16 Co Law 295.

An SE (see **2.9**) can move freely within the EEA, and the European Commission considered making a proposal for a Fourteenth Company Law Directive, which would enable all EEA companies to move within the EEA. The UK government has delayed introducing provisions to enable a company to move from one part of the United Kingdom to another until the Fourteenth Directive is enacted, but the Commission has not reported any progress on the Fourteenth Directive since a public consultation in 2004.

In *Re Baby Moon (UK) Ltd* (1984) 1 BCC 99,298 the registrar of companies for England and Wales had registered in 1981 a company whose old-style memorandum stated its registered office was to be in England but the statement of intended address of the registered office said that it would be in Livingston, which is in Scotland. When a petition for the compulsory winding up of the company was presented to the High Court in London that court held that, by virtue of what is now CA 2006, s 15(4), the company's certificate of incorporation was conclusive evidence that the company was registered in England and Wales so that the High Court had jurisdiction to wind it up under what is now the Insolvency Act 1986, s 117(1).

2.6 RE-REGISTRATION TO CHANGE THE CLASSIFICATION OF A COMPANY

2.6.1 INTRODUCTION

CA 2006, part 7 (ss 89 to 111), provides procedures for a company to change its classification by re-registering. When a company changes classification from public to private or vice versa, or from limited to unlimited, or vice versa, a new certificate of registration must be issued because the certificate is required to state if a company is limited (s 15(2)(c)) and if it is a public company (s 15(2)(d)). Curiously, although a new certificate of registration must be issued when a company changes its name (see **2.4.12.1**), the procedure for changing a company's name is not referred to as 're-registration'.

The re-registration provisions are a very good example of the way in which the UK companies legislation attempts to prescribe every detail of a procedure, even if the procedure (like that for re-registering an unlimited company as a limited one) is hardly ever used. We will spend about three pages outlining the re-registration procedures in what we believe is enough detail for an introductory textbook like this. The legislation itself, with all its detailed provisions, occupies 13 pages of the Act.

The specific procedures set out in CA 2006, part 7, do not cover all the possible changes of status though some changes for which there is no direct procedure can be achieved by two successive re-registrations. For example, a public company can be re-registered as an unlimited company by two re-registrations (see **2.6.2**) but there is no procedure at all by which a guarantee company can be re-registered as a company limited by shares (see **2.6.4**). In Australia there has been controversy over whether a court-sanctioned arrangement with members (the UK provisions for which are in CA 2006, ss 895 to 901) can be used to effect a change of status for which there is no specific statutory procedure. In *Windsor v National Mutual Life Association of Australasia* (1992) 106 ALR 282 a full court of the Federal Court said that the specific procedures are the only ways of changing status; in *Australian Securities Commission v Marlborough Gold Mines Ltd* (1993) 177 CLR 485 the High Court of Australia would not go that far but held that there was a legislative intention that the particular change of status desired by the company—from limited to no liability—should not be carried out at all. The Company Law Review Steering Group recommended creating procedures for three further changes of status—public to unlimited, private company limited by shares to guarantee, and limited by guarantee to limited by shares (*Modern Company Law for a Competitive Economy: Final Report*, vol 1 (URN 01/942) (London: DTI, 2001), paras 11.11 to 11.15). CA 2006 has provided a procedure for the first of these (ss 109 to 111), but the government decided there was insufficient need for the other two.

2.6.2 CHANGE FROM BEING A PUBLIC COMPANY

A public company may re-register as a private limited company under CA 2006, ss 97 to 101. This is a common form of re-registration. It is used, for example, when a public company is taken over by, and becomes a subsidiary of, another company. In order for a public company to be re-registered as a private limited company, the members must adopt a special resolution (which requires a 75 per cent majority; see **14.4.3**) that it should be so re-registered (s 97(1)(a)).

A change from public to private status may be very unwelcome to a minority who object to the change if their shares lose their marketability. Provision is therefore made for accommodating a dissentient minority who object to re-registration as a private company.

The holders of 5 per cent or more of the nominal value of a public company's issued share capital or of any class thereof (not counting shares held by the company as treasury shares—see **10.6.6**), or 50 or more of its members, may apply to the court for the cancellation of a special resolution to request re-registration as a private company, provided that the applicants did not consent to or vote in favour of the resolution (s 98(1)). The application must be made within 28 days of the passing of the resolution (s 98(2)). On the hearing of a s 98 application the court may either cancel or confirm the resolution, and in any event may make its order on such terms and conditions as it thinks fit, adjourn the proceedings to enable an arrangement to be made which it finds satisfactory for the purchase of the applicants' interests in the company and give any directions or orders which are expedient for facilitating or carrying the arrangement into effect (s 98(4)). The court's order may provide for the purchase by the company of the shares of any members (s 98(5)).

Where shares are held by a nominee or trustee on behalf of others, only the registered shareholder can apply under s 98, unless the company's articles provide for indirect investor enfranchisement so that s 145(2) applies (see **14.7.3**; *Re DNick Holding plc* [2013] EWHC 68 (Ch), [2014] Ch 196). Usually, a nominee will hold shares for many different investors and may well have been instructed to vote some of those shares in favour of the privatisation resolution. If so, the nominee will be disqualified by s 98(1) from applying on behalf of other investors who oppose the resolution (*Re DNick Holding plc* at [32]).

A public company may re-register as an unlimited private company with a share capital under CA 2006, ss 109 to 111. All members of the company must have consented to this form of re-registration (s 109(1)(a)). This form of re-registration is not available to a company which has already had a re-registration to change from unlimited to limited or limited to unlimited (s 109(2)).

A public company limited by guarantee with a share capital (a public hybrid company) may re-register under s 97 as a private limited company or under s 109 as a private unlimited company, but must give up its hybrid status and choose between having a share capital or being a guarantee company.

There is no express provision for a public hybrid company to become a public company limited by shares. In principle this could be achieved by first re-registering as a private company limited by shares and then re-registering again as a public company under s 90 (see **2.6.3**), but this is unlikely to be a practical possibility because shareholders would lose the marketability of their shares in the interval between re-registrations without being certain that a special resolution for the second re-registration would be adopted.

2.6.3 CHANGE FROM BEING A PRIVATE COMPANY LIMITED BY SHARES

A private company limited by shares may be re-registered as a public company under CA 2006, ss 90 to 96. This is a common form of re-registration. It may be used, for example, when a private company decides to 'go public' in order to obtain more capital for growth by inviting the public to subscribe for its shares.

In order for a private company to be re-registered as a public company, the members must adopt a special resolution (which requires a 75 per cent majority; see **14.4.3**) that it should be so re-registered (s 90(1)(a)).

There are detailed provisions which ensure that a private company re-registering as public has the authorised minimum issued capital (see **6.7.2**).

A private limited company may, with the consent of all its members, re-register as an unlimited company (either with or without a share capital) under ss 102 to 104. Having changed from limited to unlimited, a company cannot change back again, to become either a public limited company (s 90(1)(b) and (2)(e)) or a private limited company (s 105(1)(b) and (2)).

Although a public company limited by shares may be re-registered as a company limited by guarantee (though it must be as a guarantee company without a share capital: s 97(3)), there is no express provision under which a private company limited by shares can become a company limited by guarantee. However, it seems that this change can be achieved by first re-registering the private company as a public company under ss 90 to 96 and then re-registering again as a private company limited by guarantee (see **2.6.2**).

2.6.4 CHANGE FROM BEING A PRIVATE COMPANY LIMITED BY GUARANTEE

A private guarantee company may be re-registered as an unlimited company under CA 2006, ss 102 to 104 (see **2.6.3**).

There is no provision for a guarantee company without a share capital to become a company limited by shares. It cannot become a hybrid company (s 5(1)) and it is forbidden from re-registering as a public company (s 90(1)(b) and (2)(a)). It could re-register as an unlimited company but could not then re-register again as a limited company (ss 90(1)(b) and (2)(e) and 105(1)(b) and (2)).

2.6.5 CHANGE FROM BEING A HYBRID PRIVATE COMPANY

A private hybrid company can be re-registered as a public company or as an unlimited company (see **2.6.3**) but there is no express provision for a private hybrid company to become a private company limited by shares (though this could be achieved by first re-registering as public and then re-registering again as a private company limited by shares). A private hybrid company could become a pure guarantee company by reducing its share capital to zero under the procedure described in **10.7**.

2.6.6 CHANGE FROM BEING AN UNLIMITED COMPANY

An unlimited company with a share capital may, if its members adopt a special resolution (which requires a 75 per cent majority; see **14.4.3**), re-register as a public limited company under CA 2006, ss 90 to 96 (this must be a company limited by shares: s 90(4)). An unlimited company, with or without a share capital, may, following a special resolution, re-register as a private limited company (either limited by shares or by guarantee) under ss 105 to 108. Having changed from unlimited to limited, a company cannot change back again (s 102(1)(b) and (2)). An unlimited company cannot be re-registered as a hybrid company (s 5(1)).

2.6.7 COMMON PROCEDURAL PROVISIONS

A company wishing to re-register must change its name and articles so that they are appropriate to its new status (CA 2006, s 90(3) (private to public); s 97(3) (public to private limited); s 102(3) (private limited to unlimited); s 105(4) (unlimited to private limited); s 109(3) (public to unlimited)). The company must submit an application to Companies House together with documents prescribed for the particular form of re-registration (s 94 (private to public); s 100 (public to private limited); s 103 (private limited to unlimited); s 106 (unlimited to private limited); s 110 (public to unlimited)). For all forms of re-registration the required documents include the company's articles as proposed to be amended (ss 94(2)(b), 100(2)(b), 103(2)(b), 106(2)(c) and 110(2)(b)), and a statement of compliance with the relevant requirements of part 7 (ss 90(1)(c)(ii) and 94(3) and (4), 97(1)(c)(ii) and 103(3) to (5), 105(1)(c)(ii) and 106(4) and (5), 109(1)(c)(ii) and 110(3) to (5)). For the re-registrations which require the assent of all members, a prescribed form of assent, authenticated by or on behalf of all members, must be delivered (s 103(2)(a) (private limited to unlimited); s 110(2)(a) (public to unlimited)). For the other re-registrations a copy of the special resolution must be delivered unless it has already been delivered under ss 29 and 30.

   If satisfied that the company is entitled to be re-registered, Companies House must issue a new certificate of incorporation, which must state that it is issued on re-registration and the date on which it is issued (s 96(1) to (3) (private to public); s 101(1) to (3) (public to private limited); s 104(1) to (3) (private limited to unlimited); s 107(1) to (3) (unlimited to private limited); and s 111(1) to (3) (public to unlimited)).

   On the issue of the certificate the company has its new status, new name and new articles (ss 96(4), 101(4), 104(4), 107(4) and 111(4)). The certificate is conclusive evidence that the requirements of CA 2006 as to re-registration have been complied with (ss 96(5), 101(5), 104(5), 107(5) and 111(5)). Companies House must give public notice (see **4.3**) of issuing a certificate of incorporation on re-registration (s 1064).

2.7 QUASI-PARTNERSHIP COMPANIES

The Companies Act classifications of companies do not necessarily reflect the varieties of relationships between members and especially between members and directors. The roles assigned by the law to members and directors are that members are investors who do not wish to be involved in day-to-day management, which is the province of the directors. Members are expected to see each other only at annual general meetings. In the case of a plc members are expected to have taken their shares as a result of a public advertisement. (Before 1908 this was expected of the members of any company.) Nevertheless, it is common for members to be directors, and soon after incorporation of companies by registration was first allowed it was found that, contrary to expectation, many companies were formed with very small numbers of members. This trend increased when the statutory minimum number of members for private companies was reduced from seven to two in 1908.

The courts have paid particular attention to companies formed on the basis of a personal relationship between members involving mutual confidence and the understanding that certain members will be directors. Such companies are known as 'quasi-partnership' companies and the courts are willing to take into consideration the mutual understandings between members of quasi-partnership companies even if they have not been stated in the company's articles or in separate contracts between the members.

The leading case on this topic is *Ebrahimi v Westbourne Galleries Ltd* [1973] AC 360, in which a member of a quasi-partnership company successfully invoked a provision which is now the Insolvency Act 1986, s 122(1)(g), under which the court can order a company to be wound up if it is 'just and equitable' to do so. Commenting on the phrase 'just and equitable', Lord Wilberforce said, at p 379:

> The words are a recognition of the fact that a limited company is more than a mere legal entity, with a personality in law of its own: that there is room in company law for recognition of the fact that behind it, or among it, there are individuals, with rights, expectations and obligations *inter se* which are not necessarily submerged in the company structure. That structure is defined by the Companies Act and by the articles of association by which shareholders agree to be bound. In most companies and in most contexts, this definition is sufficient and exhaustive, equally so whether the company is large or small. The 'just and equitable' provision does not . . . entitle one party to disregard the obligation he assumes by entering a company, nor the court to dispense him from it. It does, as equity always does, enable the court to subject the exercise of legal rights to equitable considerations; considerations, that is, of a personal character arising between one individual and another, which may make it unjust, or inequitable, to insist on legal rights, or to exercise them in a particular way.

In *Ebrahimi v Westbourne Galleries Ltd* the majority shareholders in a company (who were also directors of it) had the legal right, under what is now CA 2006, s 168 (see **15.6.3**), to dismiss Mr Ebrahimi, the minority shareholder, from his position as a full-time working director of the company. This dismissal in effect deprived him of his livelihood, because the company's profits were always distributed as directors' fees, not as share dividends. But the company had been formed on the basis that Mr Ebrahimi would be a full-time working director. The House of Lords found that the exercise of the legal right to dismiss Mr Ebrahimi breached this mutual understanding and was unjust and inequitable. So the House affirmed that the company should be wound up by the court, meaning that its business and assets would be sold and the surplus after paying its debts would be shared by all the members, including Mr Ebrahimi. (The law has subsequently been developed so that the normal remedy provided by the court in cases like this is that the majority shareholders must buy out the minority member at an independently fixed fair valuation of the minority member's share of the value of the company—see **18.6**.)

By asking the court to find that it is 'just and equitable' for a company to be wound up, IA 1986, s 122(1)(g), is expressly inviting the court to 'subject the exercise of legal rights to equitable considerations' (in the words of Lord Wilberforce quoted earlier). Similarly, when CA 2006, s 994(1), asks the court to provide relief when a company's affairs have been conducted in a manner that is 'unfairly prejudicial' to a member's interests (see **18.6**) the court may give relief on finding that legal rights have been exercised by some members contrary to the legitimate expectations of others (*Re a Company (No 00477 of 1986)* [1986] BCLC 376) because 'what is unjust and inequitable is obviously also unfairly prejudicial' (per Fulton J in *Diligenti v RWMD Operations Kelowna Ltd* (1976) 1 BCLR 36 at p 46). See also *Caratti Holding Co Pty Ltd v Zampatti* (1978) 52 ALJR 732, discussed in **3.4.3**.

In cases like *Ebrahimi v Westbourne Galleries Ltd*, what has been enforced by the courts is a mutual understanding by all the members of a company, not expressed in its constitution, that its affairs will be conducted in a particular way. This kind of mutual understanding will not exist in many companies. For example, it would be practically impossible for it to exist in a listed public company. The conventional way of approaching the cases is to say that it must be shown that a company satisfies certain conditions before a court will enforce mutual understandings not expressed in its constitution. Companies that satisfy these conditions are called quasi-partnership companies. Defining a quasi-partnership company depends on identifying what conditions must be satisfied before mutual understandings about it will be enforced.

The term 'quasi-partnership' is used because the recognition that it is unjust and inequitable to breach mutual understandings not expressed in the constitution developed from cases in which it was considered just and equitable to wind up a company in circumstances which would justify the dissolution of a partnership. It was considered appropriate to apply this partnership analogy to a company if, in the words of Lord Cozens-Hardy MR in *Re Yenidje Tobacco Co Ltd* [1916] 2 Ch 426 at p 432, 'in substance it is a partnership in the form or the guise of a private company'. This will clearly be so if the company was incorporated to carry on the business of a pre-existing partnership (as happened in *Ebrahimi v Westbourne Galleries Ltd*) and the members of the company are the members of the former partnership.

In *Ebrahimi v Westbourne Galleries Ltd* Lord Wilberforce widened the scope of the law by saying that the test of whether a company is a quasi-partnership company is whether it is appropriate to subject the legal rights of the members of the company to equitable considerations. In many companies it is not appropriate to look beyond the legal rights of members. Lord Wilberforce said ([1973] AC 360 at p 379) that it was impossible, and wholly undesirable, to define the circumstances in which it is appropriate. His Lordship went on to say:

> Certainly the fact that a company is a small one, or a private company, is not enough. There are very many of these where the association is a purely commercial one, of which it can safely be said that the basis of association is adequately and exhaustively laid down in the articles. The superimposition of equitable considerations requires something more, which typically may include one, or probably more, of the following elements: (i) an association formed or continued on the basis of a personal relationship, involving mutual confidence—this element will often be found where a pre-existing partnership has been converted into a limited company; (ii) an agreement, or understanding, that all, or some (for there may be 'sleeping' members), of the shareholders shall participate in the conduct of the business; (iii) restriction upon the transfer of the members' interest in the company—so that if confidence is lost, or one member is removed from management, he cannot take out his stake and go elsewhere.

It may well be that the essential question in the cases is whether it can be shown that the particular mutual understandings alleged to have been breached actually existed. It may be that the only purpose of showing that a company fits into a defined category of quasi-partnership companies is that the court can readily infer that in any company of that type such mutual understandings must have existed.

Just as many people would think that a company is not truly a 'public company' unless its shares are traded on the London Stock Exchange, but not all companies registered as plcs are traded, so the concept of the quasi-partnership company, with its emphasis on personal rather than financial association, may be thought to contain the essence of the truly 'private' company. See C M

Schmitthoff, 'How the English discovered the private company', in *Quo vadis ius societatum*, P Zonderland (ed) (Deventer: Kluwer, 1972), pp 183–93.

That company law may not exhaustively define the relationship between members of a company has been recognised in other contexts. For example, in *Lion Mutual Marine Insurance Association Ltd v Tucker* (1883) 12 QBD 176, the relationship between the members of a guarantee company was that of a mutual marine insurance association and the Court of Appeal held that the company law limitation on liability of members under CA 2006, s 11(3), did not apply to their liability among themselves to insure each other's marine losses. For other examples, see *Trebanog Working Men's Club and Institute Ltd v Macdonald* [1940] 1 KB 576, discussed in **5.4.2**, and *Elliott v Wheeldon* [1993] BCLC 53 discussed in **16.3.3**.

2.8 NUMBERS OF COMPANIES

At the end of March 2017 there were 3,896,755 companies registered in the United Kingdom, of which 3,639,818 were registered in England and Wales, 201,737 in Scotland and 55,200 in Northern Ireland. The figures include 248,277 companies in the course of liquidation or removal. Of the total number of companies in the United Kingdom, 0.2 per cent are public companies.

These figures give a slightly misleading impression because some companies are members of groups controlled by holding companies. Research carried out for the Company Law Review shows that about 13 per cent of companies are in groups (*Modern Company Law for a Competitive Economy: Developing the Framework* (URN 00/656) (London: DTI, 2000), para 11.6).

2.9 EUROPEAN PUBLIC LIMITED-LIABILITY COMPANIES AND SINGLE-MEMBER COMPANIES

A European public limited-liability company (SE, taken from the linguistically neutral Latin, *societas europaea*) may be registered in any EEA State under Regulation (EC) No 2157/2001. It must be registered in the member State in which it has its registered office (art 12(1)). An SE must be treated in every member State as if it were a public limited-liability company formed in accordance with the law of the member State in which it has its registered office (art 10).

The formation of an SE is governed by the law applicable to public limited-liability companies in the State in which it establishes its registered office, subject to the provisions of Regulation (EC) No 2157/2001 (art 15(1)). Registration of an SE in the United Kingdom is performed by the registrar of companies under SI 2004/2326. The provisions of Regulation (EC) No 2157/2001 mean that an SE, unlike a domestic public company, cannot be formed by the agreement of the subscribers to its memorandum (called the instrument of incorporation in the Regulation). Instead, an SE can be formed only by an existing SE (which may form an SE as a subsidiary) or by existing companies, at least two of which must be governed by the law of different member States. This considerably limits the circumstances in which SEs may be formed, when compared with companies formed under national law. The SE is conceived as a form into which companies can grow, rather than a form to be used when establishing a new business.

More than 2,500 SEs have been registered across Europe, but they have been more popular in some States than others. At the end of March 2016, only 53 SEs were registered in the United Kingdom.

Under the present plans for the United Kingdom's departure from the EU and EEA, no UK-registered SEs can be formed after Brexit and existing UK-registered SEs will not be able to move to another EEA State as they can now.

The European Commission has proposed (COM (2014) 212) a Directive requiring every EEA nation to provide for the electronic registration of a single-member company which could have its registered office in any EEA State. This form of single-member company would be known as an SUP (*societas unius personae*). The default articles of association of an SUP would be the same in all EEA States. This would make it easy for small and medium-sized enterprises to establish subsidiaries in each State in which they wished to do business. An SUP would be governed by the company law of the State in which it was registered.

3

ARTICLES OF ASSOCIATION

SUMMARY OF POINTS COVERED

- What is in this chapter
- Constitution
- Content of articles of association
- Effect of articles
- Amendment of articles
- Restrictions on amendment of articles
- Amendment of articles which are terms of another contract
- Restricted objects

3.1 WHAT IS IN THIS CHAPTER

A company's articles of association are the principal element of its constitution (CA 2006, s 17; see **3.2**). Every company must have articles of association, which form the company's rule book (s 18(1)). The Secretary of State has prescribed model articles of association which limited companies can adopt, in whole or in part, on registration (see **3.3.1** and **3.3.2**).

A company's articles operate as a contract between the company and its members and between the members themselves (see **3.4**). Provisions of articles may be incorporated in other contracts (see **3.4.2.3** to **3.4.2.8** and **3.7**).

The members of a company can, by special resolution, amend its articles (see **3.5**), except for entrenched provisions (see **3.6.2**). The courts have created a rule that an amendment must be bona fide for the benefit of the company as a whole, but they have run into difficulties in applying that rule (see **3.6.5**).

A company has the option of including in its articles a provision restricting its objects. Such a provision was compulsory before 1 October 2009 and generated a vast amount of case law which is discussed in **3.8**.

Key legislation which you should be able to consult when reading this chapter:

- CA 2006, ss 17–38; and
- the model articles for private companies limited by shares and for public companies in SI 2008/3229.

All that legislation is in *Blackstone's Statutes on Company Law*.

The following cases, which are considered in this chapter, are particularly significant and are recommended further reading:

- *Allen v Gold Reefs of West Africa Ltd* [1900] 1 Ch 656 (also a key case for **Chapter 14**);
- *Attorney-General of Belize v Belize Telecom Ltd* [2009] UKPC 10, [2009] 1 WLR 1988;
- *Beattie v E and F Beattie Ltd* [1938] Ch 708;
- *Bushell v Faith* [1969] 2 Ch 438 and [1970] AC 1099 (also a key case for **Chapter 15**);

- *Citco Banking Corporation NV v Pusser's Ltd* [2007] UKPC 13, [2007] Bus LR 960;
- *Hickman v Kent or Romney Marsh Sheep-Breeders' Association* [1915] 1 Ch 881; and
- *Salmon v Quin and Axtens Ltd* [1909] 1 Ch 311 and *Quin and Axtens Ltd v Salmon* [1909] AC 442.

Your particular course of study may require you to read other source materials.

3.2 CONSTITUTION

3.2.1 CONSTITUTION AND CONSTITUTIONAL DOCUMENTS UNDER CA 2006

CA 2006, s 17, provides that, in the Act, references to a company's constitution include:

(a) the company's articles; and

(b) the resolutions and agreements affecting a company's constitution which must be forwarded to Companies House under ss 29 and 30 (see **14.12.3**). These include all resolutions and agreements amending the articles.

Section 32 gives a slightly longer list of 'constitutional documents' which a company must send to a member on request. This adds:

(a) a copy of the company's certificate of incorporation, and of any past certificates;

(b) a current statement of capital (or statement of guarantee for a guarantee company); and

(c) copies of any court orders or enactments altering the company's constitution or sanctioning a compromise, arrangement, reconstruction or amalgamation.

A current statement of capital is (s 32(2)) a statement of:

(a) the total number of shares of the company;

(b) the aggregate nominal value of those shares;

(c) the aggregate amount (if any) unpaid on those shares (whether on account of their nominal value or by way of premium); and

(d) for each class of shares:

    (i) prescribed particulars of the rights attached to the shares (see **6.2.3**);

    (ii) the total number of shares of that class; and

    (iii) the aggregate nominal value of shares of that class.

The terms and concepts used in the statement of capital are discussed in detail in **2.3.2** and in **Chapter 6**.
     There are criminal sanctions for not complying with a request to be sent constitutional documents (s 32(3) and (4)).

3.2.2 BEFORE CA 2006

Before incorporation of companies by registration was introduced in 1844, the partnership agreement of an unincorporated joint-stock company was usually called its 'deed of settlement' and this term was used in the Joint Stock Companies Act 1844 for the constitutional document which every company registered under that Act was required to have. The Joint Stock Companies Act 1856 divided the constitution of a company into two documents, called the memorandum of association and the articles of association. In this arrangement, which continued until 30 September 2009, the memorandum (an 'old-style memorandum') was a continuing constitutional document which stated the company's name, domicile, objects, that it was a limited company (if that was the case), that it was a public company (if that was the case), and its authorised capital (unless it was an unlimited or guarantee company). As from 1 October 2009, the provisions of the old-style memorandum of an existing company are to be treated as provisions of its articles (CA 2006, s 28).

At first, the significant difference between the old-style memorandum and the articles was in the company's power to amend the documents. A company has a general power to amend any provision in its articles, except entrenched provisions, by special resolution (see **3.5** and **3.6**). However, the 1856 Act made no provision for amending the memorandum. This was relaxed by CA 1862, which allowed amendment of the name and capital clauses, but prohibited any other amendment. Subsequent legislation increased the range of amendments that could be made to an old-style memorandum of a company, but never gave a general power of amendment like the power to amend the articles, and imposed special procedural requirements on each power to amend an old-style memorandum.

3.2.3 UNANIMOUS SHAREHOLDERS' AGREEMENT

It is common for the members for the time being of a private company to make among themselves a separate contract, called a unanimous shareholders' agreement (USA), which supplements the articles and binds the members to operate the articles in a particular way. This is a private contract between the members for the time being of the company and does not form part of the company's constitution.

3.3 CONTENT OF ARTICLES OF ASSOCIATION

3.3.1 MODEL ARTICLES

Articles of association prescribe regulations for a company and every company must have articles (CA 2006, s 18(1)). They form the rule book of the association of members and therefore ought to deal with many situations which commonly arise. Although in principle the incorporators of a new company are free to make any rules they please (subject to some overriding statutory provisions, see **3.3.3**), they are usually content to adopt rules which have been found to work for similar companies and which have been professionally drafted. So CA 2006, s 19, empowers the Secretary of State to prescribe model articles of association for companies. This repeats a provision which has been made in every Companies Act since the Joint Stock Companies Act 1856. Until CA 1985, the model articles were in a schedule to each Companies Act. Under CA 1985 and CA 2006 the model articles are issued in statutory instruments. From CA 1862 to CA 1985 the model articles for a company limited by shares were called 'Table A'.

SI 2008/3229 contains model articles prescribed under CA 2006, s 19, for three types of company: private companies limited by shares, private companies limited by guarantee and public companies. This edition comments on the model articles for private companies limited by shares (referred to in this book as the model articles for private companies) and the model articles for public companies. The texts of those models are in D French, *Blackstone's Statutes on Company Law 2017–2018* (Oxford: Oxford University Press, 2017). The complete texts of all model articles prescribed since 1856 in the United Kingdom and the Republic of Ireland are in D French, *Model Articles of Association for Companies* (Oxford: Oxford University Press, 2009).

If the incorporators of a company do not wish to have model articles in their entirety as their articles of association they may, when they register their company, also register their own articles of association (s 18(2)). These must be contained in a single document and divided into paragraphs numbered consecutively (s 18(3)). If articles are not registered under s 18(2), then s 20 provides that the model articles will be the company's articles.

Section 19(3) permits a company to 'adopt all or any of the provisions of model articles'. This is taken to authorise the registration as articles for a company, under s 18(2), of a document which states that the articles of the company are to consist of all or part of relevant model articles (without reproducing them) together with the additional articles set out in the document. This has the great advantage that it makes immediately clear in what respect the company's articles differ from the model. The model articles also, in effect, prescribe what topics must be dealt with in any alternative set of articles registered under s 18(2). This is because, insofar as any articles do not exclude or modify the relevant model articles, those articles, so far as applicable, will constitute the company's articles 'in the same manner and to the same extent as if articles in the form of those articles had been duly registered' (s 20(1)). A statement in articles that only part of the relevant model articles is being adopted would, it seems, mean that the articles have excluded the part not adopted. The model articles that a company has for its articles, either in whole because no alternative articles were registered or in part insofar as alternative articles did not exclude or modify the model, are the articles that were prescribed for use at the date of the company's registration, notwithstanding any subsequent changes made by the Secretary of State in the prescribed form (s 19(4)).

There is no need to register a unanimous shareholders' agreement, unless it modifies the articles, so the members of a company could use a USA to set out matters which the members would prefer not to be in the publicly inspectable articles (see A Marsden, 'Does a shareholders' agreement require filing with the Registrar of Companies?' (1994) 15 Co Law 19).

3.3.2 CONTENT OF MODEL ARTICLES

Table 3.1 sets out the main topics dealt with in the model articles for private companies and the model for public companies in SI 2008/3229.

Table 3.1 Topics dealt with in model articles in SI 2008/3229

	Private companies	Public companies
Defined terms	art 1	art 1
Limitation of members' liability	art 2	art 2
Directors		
Directors' powers and responsibilities	arts 3–6	arts 3–6
Decision-making by directors	arts 7–16	arts 7–19
Appointment of directors	arts 17–20	arts 20–4
Alternate directors	—	arts 25–7
Shares and distributions		
Shares	arts 21–5	arts 43–51
Transfer and transmission	arts 26–9	arts 63–8
Consolidation	—	art 69
Partly paid shares	—	arts 52–62
Dividends and other distributions	arts 30–5	arts 70–7
Capitalisation of profits	art 36	art 78
Decision-making by shareholders		
Organisation of general meetings	arts 37–41	arts 28–33
Voting at general meetings	arts 42–7	arts 34–41
Class meetings	—	art 42

Administrative arrangements		
Communications	art 48	arts 79–80
Company seals	art 49	art 81
Destruction of documents	—	art 82
No right to inspect accounts and other records	art 50	art 83
Provision for employees on cessation of business	art 51	art 84
Directors' indemnity and insurance	arts 52–3	arts 85–6

3.3.3 CONTENT OF ALTERNATIVE ARTICLES

Apart from the possibility that provisions of the relevant model articles will be deemed by CA 2006, s 20, to be incorporated in alternative articles (see **3.3.1**), the model articles may be regarded as a model of form not content: alternative articles for a company may include any provisions thought to be appropriate to the company (*Gaiman v National Association for Mental Health* [1971] Ch 317 per Megarry J at p 328), subject to the following:

(a) Any provision in a company's articles which is inconsistent with the general law is void (*Welton v Saffery* [1897] AC 299 per Lord Davey at p 329).

(b) Any provision in a company's articles which is inconsistent with the legislation governing companies is void (*Re Peveril Gold Mines Ltd* [1898] 1 Ch 122, in which the articles purported to limit the circumstances in which the company could be wound up by the court; *Re Greene* [1949] Ch 333, in which the articles purported to make a transfer of shares without a proper instrument of transfer as required by what is now CA 2006, s 770(1)).

(c) It may be a waste of time including provisions not relating to membership because the members will not be contractually bound to observe such provisions (see **3.4.2.2**).

(d) Under the Stock Transfer Act 1963 (see **8.3.1**), members can ignore provisions in articles requiring them to use forms other than those specified in the Act to transfer their fully paid shares.

(e) Any limitation in the articles on the power of the board of directors to bind the company, or to authorise others to do so, cannot affect the rights, under any transaction or other act to which the company is a party, of a person dealing with the company in good faith (CA 2006, s 40(1) and (2)(a); see **19.5.5**). The fact that the person knows that an act is beyond the directors' powers under the articles does not mean that the person is acting in bad faith (s 40(2)(b)(iii)).

Articles of association can be in any language other than English, provided a certified translation into English is filed at Companies House (SI 2009/1803, reg 7).

3.3.4 CONSTRUCTION

Because they are prescribed in a piece of subordinate legislation (SI 2008/3229), the model articles must be interpreted in accordance with the Interpretation Act 1978 (by s 23(1) of that Act). If alternative articles adopt all or part of the model articles, the provisions that are added to or substituted for provisions of the model articles must also be interpreted in accordance with the Interpretation Act 1978, unless there is a statement to the contrary (*Fell v Derby Leather Co Ltd* [1931] 2 Ch 252).

When construing alternative articles, the court will apply the general principles of construction which apply to all texts that are intended to have legal effect, referred to by Lord Hodge in *Trump*

International Golf Club Scotland Ltd v Scottish Ministers [2015] UKSC 74, [2016] 1 WLR 85, at [33]. In ***Attorney-General of Belize v Belize Telecom Ltd*** [2009] UKPC 10, [2009] 1 WLR 1988, the Privy Council, per Lord Hoffmann, said, at [16]:

> The court has no power to improve upon the instrument which it is called upon to construe, whether it be a contract, a statute, or articles of association. It cannot introduce terms to make it fairer or more reasonable. It is concerned only to discover what the instrument means. However, that meaning is not necessarily or always what the authors or parties to the document would have intended. It is the meaning which the instrument would convey to a reasonable person having all the background knowledge which would reasonably be available to the audience to whom the instrument is addressed.

There is one respect in which general principles of construction have to be adapted to different classes of documents. This is that the extent to which the court may look at the factual background depends on the document's intended audience (Lord Hodge in *Trump International Golf Club Scotland Ltd v Scottish Ministers* at [33]). The articles of association of a company are a public document which is registered at Companies House for anyone to inspect. Whereas the construction of a private commercial contract may take into account circumstances of which the parties alone were aware, articles of association are a public document and the only background information which may be taken into account is that which is public knowledge (*Attorney-General of Belize v Belize Telecom Ltd* [2009] UKPC 10, [2009] 1 WLR 1988). The statement in *Cosmetic Warriors Ltd v Gerrie* [2015] EWHC 3718 (Ch), LTL 5/1/2016, at [7] that articles of association 'must be construed in accordance with the ordinary principles that apply to the interpretation of any contract' is, as is made clear in the rest of the judgment, an oversimplification. In *Cosmetic Warriors Ltd v Gerrie* the learned deputy judge accepted (at [26]–[27]) that information about the company which was filed at Companies House and was available for public inspection could be used to interpret its articles (but his Lordship ruled that none of it was relevant anyway).

When construing the meaning of alternative articles, the court will not consider matters known only to those who formed the company. The court will not, for example, in relation to articles of association, exercise its power to rectify a document to give effect to the true intent of those who made it (*Evans v Chapman* (1902) 86 LT 381; *Scott v Frank F Scott (London) Ltd* [1940] Ch 794). The court will not imply terms into articles so as to give business efficacy to a scheme which those who registered the articles had in mind, but which is not apparent from the wording of the articles themselves (*Bratton Seymour Service Co Ltd v Oxborough* [1992] BCLC 693). When determining the meaning of an amendment made to articles, the court will not consider the effect which the amendment was intended to have or the circumstances in which it was made (*Folkes Group plc v Alexander* [2002] EWHC 51 (Ch), [2002] 2 BCLC 254; *Rose v Lynx Express Ltd* [2004] EWCA Civ 447, [2004] 1 BCLC, 455, at [21]), though it will consider the wording of the articles before amendment (*Folkes Group plc v Alexander*). What the court will do is add words to avoid absurdity (*Folkes Group plc v Alexander*) or imply a term which is strictly necessary, proceeding from the express words of the articles, viewed objectively in their commercial setting (*Equitable Life Assurance Society v Hyman* [2002] 1 AC 408).

When construing the words actually used in alternative articles of association of a company, the articles should be regarded as a commercial or business document to which the maxim 'validate if possible' applies (*Rayfield v Hands* [1960] Ch 1 per Vaisey J). Another way of putting this is to say that the articles should be construed so as to give them reasonable business efficacy (*Holmes v Keyes* [1959] Ch 199 per Jenkins LJ at p 215). The court must reject even the plain and obvious meaning of the words if that meaning would be commercially absurd (*Thompson v Goblin Hill Hotels Ltd* [2011] UKPC 8, [2011] 1 BCLC 587).

When considering whether a provision ought to be implied in alternative articles, the question for the court is whether the provision would spell out in express words what the articles, read against the relevant background, would reasonably be understood to mean (*Attorney-General of*

Belize v Belize Telecom Ltd at [21]). In *Attorney-General of Belize v Belize Telecom Ltd* that background included the fact that the company had been formed to privatise a State-owned business, a fact which the Privy Council thought was known to everyone in Belize. In *Marks and Spencer plc v BNP Paribas Securities Trust Co (Jersey) Ltd* [2015] UKSC 72, [2016] AC 742, the Supreme Court stated that *Attorney-General of Belize v Belize Telecom Ltd* should not be regarded as relaxing the test to be applied before implying a term into a text such as a contract or articles of association. The judgment of the majority of the Supreme Court, given by Lord Neuberger PSC, looked at the test stated in *Belize Telecom* at [21], that the question is whether the implied term would spell out in express terms what the document, read against the relevant background, would reasonably be understood to mean. Lord Neuberger said ([2015] UKSC 72 at [23]):

> the notion that a term will be implied if a reasonable reader of the contract, knowing all its provisions and the surrounding circumstances, would understand it to be implied is quite acceptable, provided that (i) the reasonable reader is treated as reading the contract at the time it was made and (ii) he would consider the term to be so obvious as to go without saying or to be necessary for business efficacy. (The difference between what the reasonable reader would understand and what the parties, acting reasonably, would agree, appears to me to be a notional distinction without a practical difference.) The first proviso emphasises that the question whether a term is implied is to be judged at the date the contract is made. The second proviso is important because otherwise Lord Hoffmann's formulation may be interpreted as suggesting that reasonableness is a sufficient ground for implying a term. (For the same reason, it would be wrong to treat Lord Steyn's statement in *Equitable Life Assurance Society v Hyman* [2002] 1 AC 408, 459 that a term will be implied if it is 'essential to give effect to the reasonable expectations of the parties' as diluting the test of necessity. That is clear from what Lord Steyn said earlier on the same page, namely that '[t]he legal test for the implication of . . . a term is . . . strict necessity', which he described as a 'stringent test'.)

Lord Neuberger went on to say (at [26]) that construing the words actually used in a document and implying additional words are different processes governed by different rules, a point which is discussed further in *Trump International Golf Club Scotland Ltd v Scottish Ministers* at [31]–[37] and [41]–[44].

Common intentions which are not reflected in the wording of the articles may be taken into account when providing relief for unfairly prejudicial conduct of the affairs of a quasi-partnership company (see **18.6.7**; *Caratti Holding Co Pty Ltd v Zampatti* (1978) 52 ALJR 732 discussed in **3.4.3**).

3.4 EFFECT OF ARTICLES

3.4.1 CONTRACTUAL ANALYSIS OF COMPANIES

3.4.1.1 Companies Act 2006, section 33

The normal legal analysis of the nature of an association of persons is in terms of a contract between the members of the association. As Lawton LJ said in **Conservative and Unionist Central Office v Burrell** [1982] 1 WLR 522 at p 525: 'The bond of union between the members of an unincorporated association has to be contractual'. There are numerous dicta treating the articles of association of a company incorporated by registration as a contract between the members of the company. In **Re Tavarone Mining Co, Pritchard's Case** (1873) LR 8 Ch App 956, Mellish LJ said, at p 960:

> the articles of association are simply a contract as between the shareholders *inter se* [between themselves] in respect of their rights as shareholders. They are the deed of partnership by which the shareholders agree *inter se*.

A registered company, because it is a body corporate, has a dual aspect as both an association of its members and a person separate from its members. It is appropriate to introduce the company as a separate person into the contractual analysis by saying that the members also have a contract with the company as a separate person. For the first time in UK company law this has been done by CA 2006, s 33(1), which provides:

> The provisions of a company's constitution bind the company and its members to the same extent as if there were covenants on the part of the company and of each member to observe those provisions.

Previous versions of this subsection had referred only to covenants by the members, not by the company. The addition of the company as a covenantor, which was made on the initiative of Lord Wedderburn of Charlton, then the doyen of academic company lawyers, ended more than a century of controversy and has considerably shortened the following discussion.

3.4.1.2 Unusual features of the contract formed by the articles

The contract formed by the articles of association is not like, for example, a contract of sale of goods or a contract for the construction of a building. It does not provide for each party to perform a specified list of obligations after which the contract ends. The articles of association of a company are part of the company's constitution, which provides the rules governing decision-making in the company. It is the framework within which the company operates. The constitution provides a mechanism for deciding on questions that will arise in the future concerning the company. Questions about the day-to-day management of the company's business are to be determined by the directors while more fundamental matters are to be decided by the members (see **15.10**), in either case in accordance with the procedures, voting rights, etc set out in the articles.

The contract formed by articles of association is of a type sometimes called a 'relational contract', which is characterised by longevity and incompleteness, that is, the contract does not specify what is to happen in every possible circumstance. The articles of a company are not intended to be a complete statement of what is to happen in the relationship between the company and its members and between the members themselves. Instead the articles provide the procedure for deciding on each question that arises in those relationships as and when it arises.

The long-term, dynamic nature of the relationship between a company and its members, and between the members themselves, means that eventually the articles of association of the company may need amendment. CA 2006, s 21(1), provides that, subject to any provision for entrenchment, articles can be amended by the members by a 75 per cent majority (see **3.5.1**). Thus the contract formed by the articles is very unusual in that its provisions may be amended by a majority of the contracting parties against the wishes of the minority, subject to any provision for entrenchment.

In relation to articles of association, unlike a normal contract, the court will not exercise its power to rectify a document, and, when construing articles, will not take into account surrounding circumstances known to those who registered or amended them (see **3.3.4**).

3.4.2 ARTICLES AS A CONTRACT BETWEEN THE COMPANY AND ITS MEMBERS

3.4.2.1 Articles cannot remove members' statutory rights

A provision in the articles of a company cannot limit a right given to the members by statute, that is, the members of a company cannot agree with the company to contract out of the statute (*Re Peveril Gold Mines Ltd* [1898] 1 Ch 122, in which the articles purported to limit members' rights to petition under what is now the Insolvency Act 1986, s 124(1), for the company to be wound up; *Baring-Gould v Sharpington Combined Pick and Shovel Syndicate* [1899] 2 Ch 80, in which the articles purported to limit members' rights under what is now the Insolvency Act 1986, s 111(2), to have the value of their shares determined by arbitration in the event of a reconstruction of the company by liquidation agreement).

3.4.2.2 Only provisions relating to membership are contractual by virtue of section 33

In *Bisgood v Henderson's Transvaal Estates Ltd* [1908] 1 Ch 743, Buckley LJ said, at p 759:

> The purpose of the ... articles is to define the position of the shareholder as shareholder, not to bind him in his capacity as an individual.

The effect of CA 2006, s 33, in making the articles of association of a company contractual is limited to provisions of the articles concerned with the membership and constitution of the company. As Greene MR put it in *Beattie v E and F Beattie Ltd* [1938] Ch 708 at p 721:

> the contractual force given to the articles of association by the section is limited to such provisions of the articles as apply to the relationship of the members in their capacity as members.

Non-membership rights are often called outsider rights (and membership rights are insider rights). This terminology reflects the fact that membership rights are conferred on members whereas non-membership rights may be given to members or non-members. But it is the content of rights which determines whether or not they are membership rights. A non-membership right is not made contractual by s 33, whether it is asserted by a member or a non-member.

In *Beattie v E and F Beattie Ltd* a company brought legal proceedings against one of its directors, who was also a member of the company, concerning his conduct as a director. He asked the court to stay the proceedings in favour of arbitration. To do this, he had to prove that the proceedings were covered by an agreement in writing to submit present or future disputes to arbitration (see now the Arbitration Act 1996, ss 5, 6 and 9). He claimed that the proceedings were covered by a provision in the company's articles that any dispute between the company and a member was to be referred to arbitration. The Court of Appeal held that the arbitration article did not apply to a member's activities as a director, because the articles were an enforceable contract only in relation to membership matters.

In subsequent cases it was said that in a quasi-partnership company, which is formed on the basis that certain members shall be directors, provisions in the articles referring to 'directors' can be interpreted as referring to the class of members who are directors and therefore can be regarded as being concerned with membership rights: see *Rayfield v Hands* [1960] Ch 1 and *Caratti Holding Co Pty Ltd v Zampatti* (1978) 52 ALJR 732, discussed in 3.4.3. Otherwise, a non-membership right which is given to some members but not others does not create a class right (*Cumbrian Newspapers Group Ltd v Cumberland and Westmorland Herald Newspaper and Printing Co Ltd* [1987] Ch 1).

3.4.2.3 Has a non-membership provision been incorporated in a separate contract?

A provision of articles which is not a membership provision, and so is not contractual by virtue of CA 2006, s 33, is usually treated as specifying the terms on which a separate contract may be made by the company. It is a question of fact whether that separate contract is ever made. Although each case depends on its particular facts, there are three types of case which have often been reported:

(a) In some cases (see **3.4.2.4**) the non-membership provision concerns a contract with a specific person, and reflects a pre-incorporation contract made by promoters. Very clear evidence of a new separate contract made between the company and that person is required in these cases.

(b) In some cases (see **3.4.2.5**) the non-membership provision states terms on which officers or auditors will be appointed. Unless this reflects a pre-incorporation contract with a specific person (see para (a)), the court will usually infer that such a provision is incorporated in the contract of employment or services of anyone appointed to the specified position.

(c) In some cases (see **3.4.2.6**) the non-membership provision applies to substantially all members, and is concerned with trading between the company and its members. Usually the mere fact of becoming a member completes the formation of a separate contract on the terms of such a provision.

A person who is not a member of a company cannot rely on the Contracts (Rights of Third Parties) Act 1999 to enforce a term of the company's articles, because the contract formed by CA 2006, s 33, is exempt from the 1999 Act (by s 6(2) of the 1999 Act).

3.4.2.4 Provision reflecting pre-incorporation contract with specific person

If a non-membership provision in a company's articles states the terms of an agreement which was made, before the company was incorporated, between a specific person and those forming the company, in the expectation that the company would adopt the agreement, the courts usually require very clear evidence that the company, after incorporation, has made a new contract (novation) to make itself liable (see **19.6.2**). The mere fact that the alleged contractor has become a member of the company does not prove that a new contract has been made.

In *Browne v La Trinidad* (1887) 37 ChD 1, Mr Browne had agreed with the promoters of a company called La Trinidad Ltd that when the company was incorporated, he would sell a mine in Mexico to it in return for fully paid shares and that he should become a director of the company for a period of four years at least. The company was registered with articles which provided that this agreement was 'incorporated with and shall be construed as part of' the articles. Mr Browne was allotted his shares and was appointed a director of the company, but, before the end of the four-year period mentioned in his agreement with the promoters, the company's members adopted an extraordinary resolution (see **14.4.3**) dismissing Mr Browne from his directorship. (The company's articles provided that any director could be removed by extraordinary resolution: the statutory provision that members can remove directors by ordinary resolution—now CA 2006, s 168; see **15.6.3**—had not been enacted at that time.) Mr Browne claimed that the company could not dismiss him from his directorship until the agreed four-year period had ended. The Court of Appeal refused the injunction. Lindley LJ said, at pp 14–15:

> Having regard to the terms of [CA 2006, s 33], there would be some force, or at all events some plausibility, in the argument that, being a member, the contract which is referred to in the articles has become binding between the company and him. Of course that argument is open to this difficulty that there could be no contract between him and the company until the shares were allotted to him, and it would be remarkable that, upon the shares being allotted to him, a contract between him and the company, as to a matter not connected with the holding of shares, should arise.

Browne v La Trinidad may be contrasted with *Imperial Hydropathic Hotel Co, Blackpool v Hampson* (1882) 23 ChD 1, in which the company claimed to have dismissed Mr Hampson from his directorship. It was held that the company had not dismissed him, because there was no power in its articles to dismiss any of its directors. This was not because there was any special restriction in the articles agreed between the directors and the company or its promoters (as there was claimed to be in *Browne v La Trinidad*); it was merely that the members had failed to include the necessary power in their articles. Had they gone through the correct procedure of passing a special resolution to amend the articles, they could have inserted the necessary power and then dismissed Mr Hampson properly.

In *Eley v Positive Government Security Life Assurance Co Ltd* (1876) 1 ExD 88, the company's articles provided that Mr Eley should be the company's solicitor and should not be removed from office except for misconduct. Mr Eley had drafted the articles but he was not a subscriber of the memorandum. Mr Eley became a member of the company about a year after its incorporation.

The directors of the company stopped employing Mr Eley as solicitor and used other solicitors instead. Mr Eley sued the company for damages for breach of the contract, which he alleged existed between himself and the company, that only he should be employed as the company's solicitor. His claim failed as the articles could not prove that such a contract had ever been made and he did not produce any other evidence that the contract existed.

Similarly, if a company's articles provide that a specific person shall be a director at a specified remuneration, but that person is never appointed, that person cannot sue for breach of contract, even if a member of the company (per Jenkins LJ in *Read v Astoria Garage (Streatham) Ltd* [1952] Ch 637 at p 641).

In *Hickman v Kent or Romney Marsh Sheep-Breeders' Association* [1915] 1 Ch 881, Astbury J summarised the law as follows, at p 897:

> An outsider to whom rights purport to be given by the articles in his capacity as such outsider, whether he is or subsequently becomes a member, cannot sue on those articles treating them as contracts between himself and the company to enforce those rights. Those rights are not part of the general regulations of the company applicable alike to all shareholders and can only exist by virtue of some contract between such person and the company, and the subsequent allotment of shares to an outsider in whose favour such an article is inserted does not enable him to sue the company on such an article.

3.4.2.5 Appointment of auditor or officer upon the terms of the articles

Where a non-membership provision in a company's articles states terms on which officers or auditors will be appointed, the court will usually infer that the provision is incorporated in the contract of anyone appointed to the specified position. In *Guinness plc v Saunders* [1990] 2 AC 663 Lord Templeman said, at p 692:

> A director accepts office subject to and with the benefit of the provisions of the articles relating to directors.

In *Re Anglo-Austrian Printing and Publishing Union, Isaacs's Case* [1892] 2 Ch 158, Sir Henry Isaacs had been one of the first directors of the company. The articles of the company provided that a first director had to acquire 100 of the company's £10 shares within one month of being appointed, and if he did not do so, he would 'be deemed to have agreed to take the said shares from the company, and the same shall be forthwith allotted to him accordingly'. The company was ordered to be wound up 18 months after it was incorporated. No shares had ever been allotted to Sir Henry but the liquidator sought to hold him liable as if he were the holder of 100 shares. The Court of Appeal confirmed that he was liable. Bowen LJ said, at pp 167–8:

> [These articles] amount to an offer put forward by the company to persons intending to become directors of the terms on which the directors are to act. It is perfectly true that the offer is contained in articles, which are not drawn up between the company and the directors, but nevertheless the company puts forward the terms of the articles as the terms by which it will be bound; and the director by becoming and acting as director of the company accepts that position.

Earlier, Lord Esher MR had said in *Swabey v Port Darwin Gold Mining Co* (1889) 1 Meg 385, at p 387:

> The articles do not themselves form a contract, but from them you get the terms upon which the directors are serving.

See also *Salton v New Beeston Cycle Co* [1899] 1 Ch 775.

The courts will be more reluctant to find that there is a separate contract where the provision in the articles reflects a pre-incorporation contract concerning the appointment of a specific director: see *Browne v La Trinidad* (1887) 37 ChD 1 discussed in **3.4.2.4**.

An individually negotiated contract of appointment of an officer or auditor may displace general terms in the articles (per Warrington LJ in *Re City Equitable Fire Insurance Co Ltd* [1925] Ch 407 at pp 520–1; *John v Price Waterhouse* [2002] 1 WLR 953).

Incorporation into a contract with a director of terms from the articles of association can be particularly significant in relation to remuneration; see **3.4.2.7**.

3.4.2.6 Provisions in articles concerning trading between the company and its members

The question of whether a provision in the articles of a company relates to membership or not has been particularly difficult to answer in relation to companies formed on the basis that members will trade with the company as a separate person, as in agricultural producers' cooperatives. If provisions of the articles of such a company prescribe the terms on which members are to trade with the company, are those provisions contractually enforceable by virtue of CA 2006, s 33, because they concern membership (see **3.4.2.2**) or are they the terms of a separate 'special contract' made by express agreement between the company and each member when the member joins? If they are membership provisions, they can be amended by special resolution and the amendment will be binding on any member whether that member voted for it or not. If the provisions are the terms of a separate contract then it is a question of construction of that contract whether it is amended when the articles are amended.

In *Gore Bros v Newbury Dairy Co Ltd* [1919] NZLR 205, Chapman J thought that a provision in the articles of a producers' cooperative company concerning trading with the company was 'intimately connected with the very purpose of the incorporation of the company' and therefore was a membership provision. But in *Heron v Port Huon Fruitgrowers' Co-operative Association Ltd* (1922) 30 CLR 315, Isaacs J in the High Court of Australia doubted whether such a provision could be regarded as relating to membership: it was thought to be unnecessary to decide the question finally because the court held that the provision in question was in any event void as an unreasonable restraint of trade. The similar House of Lords case of *McEllistrim v Ballymacelligott Co-operative Agricultural and Dairy Society Ltd* [1919] AC 548 concerned a producers' cooperative incorporated by registration under the industrial and provident societies legislation. The provisions of the society's rules concerning trading with members were held to be void as an unreasonable restraint on trade, but their Lordships assumed that those provisions were otherwise part of the contract formed by the rules, which Lord Atkinson pointed out, at p 575, are analogous to the articles of a registered company.

Isaacs J in *Heron v Port Huon Fruitgrowers' Co-operative Association Ltd* and Salmond J in *Shalfoon v Cheddar Valley Co-operative Dairy Co Ltd* [1924] NZLR 561, at p 581, doubted whether the Law Lords in *McEllistrim v Ballymacelligott Co-operative Agricultural and Dairy Society Ltd* considered whether the provisions concerning trading with members were part of the contract formed by the rules, but in *Agricultural Wholesale Society Ltd v Biddulph and District Agricultural Society Ltd* [1925] Ch 769 Warrington LJ said, at pp 785–6, that he was quite sure that it was deliberately assumed that the provisions were contractually enforceable.

In *Eltham Co-operative Dairy Factory Co Ltd v Johnson* [1931] NZLR 216, the articles purported to prescribe the terms on which 'suppliers' could contract with the company, but the point was taken that a supplier did not have to be a member and a member did not have to be a supplier, even though in practice there must have been a substantial identity between the two categories. Accordingly the provisions relating to 'suppliers' were held to be not part of the contract formed by the articles.

It seems that provisions of articles which impose a collateral liability (see **2.3.2.4**), for example, to pay an annual subscription or service charge, can only operate by way of special contracts requiring individual acceptance by members and are not made contractual by s 33 (*Hole v Garnsey* [1930] AC 472; *Ding v Sylvania Waterways Ltd* (1999) 30 ACSR 301).

See also *Bailey v New South Wales Medical Defence Union Ltd* (1995) 184 CLR 399 discussed in **3.7**.

These cases show that it is dangerous to try to make the articles of association of a company do work which should be done by express contracts entered into between the company and its members.

3.4.2.7 Directors' remuneration

The analysis that provisions of a company's articles relating to directors are not membership provisions and are incorporated in a separate contract with a director on appointment has been adopted in cases in which a company has gone into insolvent liquidation owing fees to directors who were also members of the company and the amount payable was fixed by the company's articles. It is crucial in such a case to determine whether the fees are owed to the directors in their character as members, for if so they cannot be paid until all other creditors have been paid (Insolvency Act 1986, s 74(2)(f)). If the fees are not owed to them in their character as members, they will be paid along with other unsecured creditors. It has been held that if a member of a company is appointed one of its directors and the articles specify directors' remuneration then that remuneration is *not* payable to the director qua member even if the articles require a director to be a member (*Re Dale and Plant Ltd* (1889) 43 ChD 255; *Re New British Iron Co, ex parte Beckwith* [1898] 1 Ch 324; *Re A1 Biscuit Co* [1899] WN 115). This confirms that the remuneration is payable by virtue of the terms of the director's appointment which come into operation on acceptance of that appointment, the terms being the relevant provisions from the articles (*Re New British Iron Co, ex parte Beckwith*).

The earlier analysis in *Orton v Cleveland Fire Brick and Pottery Co Ltd* (1865) 3 Hurl & C 868 that such a payment was made under a contractually enforceable term of the articles to the director qua member (see also *Re Leicester Club and County Racecourse Co* (1885) 30 ChD 629 and *Re Iceland Sulphur and Copper Co Ltd* (1886) 2 TLR 509) was described as 'no longer law' by Wright J during argument in **Re Peruvian Guano Co, ex parte Kemp** [1894] 3 Ch 690 at p 701.

In **Re New British Iron Co, ex parte Beckwith** the company's articles fixed the remuneration of the directors at a total figure of £1,000, which was to be divided between the directors as they thought fit. Certain shareholders acted as directors and without any express agreement between the company and the directors as to remuneration. Wright J in upholding the directors' claim to £1,000 said, at pp 326–7:

> In this case there is a provision in the articles of association which . . . fixes the remuneration of the directors at the annual sum of £1,000. That article is not in itself a contract between the company and the directors; it is only part of the contract constituted by the articles of association between the members of the company *inter se*. But where on the footing of that article the directors are employed by the company and accept office the terms of [the article] are embodied in and form part of the contract between the company and the directors. Under the article as thus embodied the directors obtain a contractual right to an annual sum of £1,000 as remuneration . . . the remuneration is not due to the directors in their character as members. It is not due to them by their being members of the company, but under a distinct contract with the company.

In *Guinness plc v Saunders* [1990] 2 AC 663, Mr Ward was a director of Guinness plc. The articles of the company provided that special remuneration to directors for services outside the scope of the ordinary duties of a director had to be fixed by the board as a whole. Mr Ward had been given special remuneration by a committee of the board, an act which the committee had no authority to perform. Accordingly Mr Ward had to return that remuneration. If one person provides a service to another and the two have not agreed on the payment for that service, the court may order payment of an amount known as a *quantum meruit* (as much as he deserved). Mr Ward claimed a *quantum meruit* for the special services he had provided. However, a court will not award a *quantum meruit* if the parties have themselves agreed how remuneration is to be determined, even if they have not implemented that agreement. Mr Ward's appointment as a director of Guinness plc was upon the terms of the articles that remuneration was to be determined by the board. Accordingly the court would not grant a *quantum meruit*. If Mr Ward wanted special remuneration he had to ask the board for it. *Guinness plc v Saunders* is analysed in great detail in G McCormack, 'The Guinness saga: in Tom we trust' (1991) 12 Co Law 90.

It is notable that the Law Lords in *Guinness plc v Saunders* paid no attention at all to whether or not Mr Ward was a *member* of Guinness plc. This shows that it was not the contract between the members of Guinness plc and the company as a separate person formed by the company's articles which prevented Mr Ward being awarded a *quantum meruit*. It was the appointment, upon the terms of the articles, of Mr Ward as a director of the company which precluded a *quantum meruit* award.

In *Re Richmond Gate Property Co Ltd* [1965] 1 WLR 335, Mr Walker, one of the subscribers of the memorandum of the company, was appointed by art 9 of its articles joint managing director for life. However, after seven months, the company was wound up and he applied for payment for his services as joint managing director. The articles provided that 'A managing director shall receive such remuneration . . . as the directors may determine'. The directors had never determined Mr Walker's remuneration. Plowman J refused to award Mr Walker a *quantum meruit* because the way in which Mr Walker's remuneration was to be determined had already been fixed by contract. Plowman J's judgment in the case can be interpreted as holding that the contract which precluded the award of a *quantum meruit* was the contract formed between the members of the company and the company as a separate person by the company's articles (see the casenote by K W Wedderburn, 'Contractual rights under articles of association—an overlooked principle illustrated' (1965) 28 MLR 347). As has been said in previous editions of this work, this would be an unnecessary departure from the analysis of the relationship between director and company as an appointment upon the terms of the articles which was established by the Court of Appeal in *Swabey v Port Darwin Gold Mining Co* (1889) 1 Meg 385 and *Re Anglo-Austrian Printing and Publishing Union, Isaacs's Case* [1892] 2 Ch 158. It is submitted that it would be more consistent with the other cases to say that it was Mr Walker's appointment as managing director, upon the terms of the articles, which prevented Mr Walker, as managing director, being awarded a *quantum meruit*. This would be consistent with the analysis adopted by the Law Lords in *Guinness plc v Saunders*. The one problem with this analysis is that it assumes that a promise to pay an amount to be determined by the payer is sufficient to constitute contractual consideration.

3.4.2.8 A separate contract is different from the articles

When it is inferred (see **3.4.2.3**) that a contract (such as a director's contract of service) exists which incorporates one or more provisions of a company's articles, that contract is, as the terminology used in this discussion implies, not the articles themselves, but a separate contract. If that separate contract is not in writing, but is required to be, the requirement will not be satisfied by producing the written articles.

In *Beattie v E and F Beattie Ltd* [1938] Ch 708 (see **3.4.2.2**), the director could have asserted that the arbitration provision in the articles, insofar as it related to disputes concerning what a member did as a director, was incorporated in the separate contract under which he served as a director, but that separate contract, which was never put in writing, would not be an 'agreement in writing' as required by the statute to invoke the power to stay legal proceedings in favour of arbitration (per Greene MR at p 720).

This used to be very important when CA 1867, s 25, was in force (it was repealed by CA 1900). This section provided that if a company allotted shares to a member wholly or partly for a non-cash consideration, the non-cash part of the consideration would be deemed not to have been paid (leaving the member still liable to pay up to the full nominal value of the shares in cash) unless a written contract of allotment was filed with the registrar on or before allotment. The contract could be a pre-incorporation contract with a promoter (*Re Poole Firebrick and Blue Clay Co* (1875) as reported in 44 LJ Ch 240; *Smith v Brown* [1896] AC 614). However, a statement in the articles of a company (which are filed on registration of the company) that the company shall make a contract to allot shares to a person for a non-cash consideration was held to be not in itself a contract made with that person, and merely filing such articles was not sufficient to comply with s 25 (*Re Tavarone Mining Co, Pritchard's Case* (1873) LR 8 Ch App 956; *Re Malaga Lead Co, Firmstone's Case* (1875) LR 20 Eq 524; *Re Carribean [sic] Co Ltd, Crickmer's Case* (1875) 46 LJ Ch 870). The statement in the articles was merely an authorisation for the making of a contract with an outsider.

In *Re Appletreewick Lead Mining Co* (1874) LR 18 Eq 95, the articles provided that all the company's shares were to be allotted to the subscribers of the memorandum. Malins V-C held that filing those articles was sufficient to comply with CA 1867, s 25, but in *Crickmer's Case* at first instance (1875) 44 LJ Ch 595, he said that *Re Appletreewick Lead Mining Co* was a 'peculiar' case and that his decision depended on its unusual facts.

The law under which the cases on contracts of allotment were decided was repealed long ago and it is difficult now to appreciate the context in which they were decided. Nevertheless they are still relied on by judges and academic commentators as sources of the law on the contractual effect of the articles, which is why they have been discussed here.

3.4.2.9 Other effects of a non-membership provision in a company's articles

It is possible for a member of a company to obtain an injunction to prevent it acting in a way that is inconsistent with a non-membership provision of the articles.

In ***Salmon v Quin and Axtens Ltd*** [1909] 1 Ch 311 (affirmed by the House of Lords sub nom *Quin and Axtens Ltd v Salmon* [1909] AC 442) the bulk of the shares in Quin and Axtens Ltd were held by William Raymond Axtens and Joseph Salmon. The articles appointed them and one other person directors of the company and also appointed Axtens and Salmon 'managing directors'. There was a provision in the articles that either of 'the managing directors, the said William Raymond Axtens and Joseph Salmon' could veto any board decision on a wide range of matters. Salmon did issue such a veto but the other directors went ahead with their decision and got the members of the company to approve it by ordinary resolution (see further **15.10.2.3**). Salmon claimed, as a member of the company, an injunction restraining it and the other directors from acting on the decision and the Court of Appeal granted the injunction: the company was trying to bypass rules on decision-making contained in its constitution without following the procedure for amending the constitution—'in truth this is an attempt to alter the terms of the contract between the parties by a simple resolution instead of by a special resolution' (per Farwell LJ at p 319). The court would prevent the company acting on a decision taken unconstitutionally. Indirectly, Salmon enforced his outsider right as a managing director to veto certain board decisions by suing as a member for the enforcement of the relevant articles.

In *Beattie v E and F Beattie Ltd* [1938] Ch 708 (see **3.4.2.2**), Greene MR said, at p 722, that every member of the company (including Mr Beattie) might have had a membership right to require the company to submit the dispute with Mr Beattie to arbitration but this would have to be asserted in proceedings for an injunction, not in the application for a stay under the Arbitration Act which was before the court. In ***Eley v Positive Government Security Life Assurance Co Ltd*** (1876) 1 ExD 88 (see **3.4.2.4**), Lord Cairns LC said, at p 90, that the article requiring the company to employ Mr Eley as its solicitor was 'a matter between the directors and shareholders, and not between them and the plaintiff' which might suggest that every member of the company (including Mr Eley) had a membership right to prevent the directors appointing anyone else as solicitor (though his Lordship, at p 89, suggested that such a requirement was in any case against public policy; cf *Re Rhodesian Properties Ltd* [1901] WN 130). Mr Beattie and Mr Eley failed because they confined themselves to relying on contracts that turned out not to exist.

On the other hand, in *Salmon v Quin and Axtens Ltd*, Mr Salmon succeeded because he sued, as a member of the company, to prevent the company acting on a decision which had been taken unconstitutionally. Similarly, in *Ram Kissendas Dhanuka v Satya Charan Law* (1949) LR 77 Ind App 128 the articles of Lothian Jute Mills Ltd provided for the general management of the affairs of the company to be entrusted to managing agents, and provided that Andrew Yule and Co Ltd were to be the managing agents until removed by extraordinary resolution (three-quarters majority). The members of

Lothian Jute Mills Ltd passed an ordinary resolution (simple majority) removing Andrew Yule and Co Ltd from the position of managing agents and the Privy Council granted a dissentient member, Dr Law, a declaration that this resolution was invalid. Again, a member of a company succeeded in preventing it acting on a decision which had been taken unconstitutionally. (This Privy Council case escaped the notice of academic commentators until it was rediscovered by P StJ Smart, 'The enforcement of outsider rights: Lord Greene and the Privy Council' [1989] JBL 143.)

If a non-membership right is a right to do something, exercise of that right is effective, according to the New Zealand case of *Woodlands Ltd v Logan* [1948] NZLR 230. In that case, the company's articles provided that, in certain circumstances, the personal representatives of the company's founder could appoint its managing director, and another provision defined the powers of a managing director. It was held that when the personal representatives, who were not members of the company, exercised the right to appoint a managing director he was validly appointed and had all the powers of a managing director conferred by the articles. But the opposite view was taken in Singapore in *Malayan Banking Ltd v Raffles Hotel Ltd* [1966] 1 MLJ 206, in which the landlord of a company was given by the company's articles a right to appoint a director: when the landlord exercised that right it was held that the appointment was invalid and of no legal effect. It seems that *Woodlands Ltd v Logan* was not cited to the Singapore court.

3.4.2.10 Explanations by academics

Legal action by a member of a company to enforce the provisions of the company's articles is taken in the shadow of the 'internal management principle' that the company is the proper claimant in a matter concerning its internal management (see **18.4.4**). It is difficult to explain why, despite the internal management principle, a member of a company can succeed in a case like *Salmon v Quin and Axtens Ltd* [1909] 1 Ch 311 or *Ram Kissendas Dhanuka v Satya Charan Law* (1949) LR 77 Ind App 128 (discussed in **3.4.2.9**), both of which seemed to be about the internal affairs of companies so that the principle would require the companies to be the claimants. In **18.4.8** we will suggest that the common feature of the cases in which members are allowed to bring legal proceedings in respect of their companies' internal affairs, as an exception to the internal management principle, is that they are proceedings about decisions taken unlawfully.

A second difficulty is to explain how a non-membership provision of articles, which is not contractual by virtue of CA 2006, s 33, is nevertheless enforceable by the members, as happened in *Salmon v Quin and Axtens Ltd* and *Ram Kissendas Dhanuka v Satya Charan Law*.

The thesis advanced by K W Wedderburn, 'Shareholders' rights and the rule in *Foss v Harbottle*' [1957] CLJ 194 is that in *Salmon v Quin and Axtens Ltd*, Mr Salmon enforced a *contractual* right which Jordan CJ in *Australian Coal and Shale Employees' Federation v Smith* (1937) 38 SR (NSW) 48 at p 55 identified as 'the shareholder's right to have the articles observed by the company'. Wedderburn concluded ([1957] CLJ at pp 212–13) that:

> a member can compel the company not to depart from the contract with him under the articles, even if that means indirectly the enforcement of 'outsider' rights vested either in third parties or himself, so long as, but only so long as, he sues qua member and not qua 'outsider'.

A member sues 'qua member' if 'seeking to enforce a right which is common to himself and all other members' (in the words of Greene MR in *Beattie v E and F Beattie Ltd* [1938] Ch 708 at p 722).

Wedderburn also states ([1957] CLJ 194 at pp 214–15) that a member can enforce '*every* [his emphasis] provision of the contract found in the articles . . . subject only to those matters of "internal management" on which the courts have seen fit to displace his contractual rights in favour of majority rule' (this is a reference to the internal management principle discussed in **18.4.4**). This aspect of Wedderburn's thesis has been controversial. It is supported by

R Gregory, 'The section 20 contract' (1981) 44 MLR 526, in a radical reappraisal of the cases. Gregory's analysis asserts that all provisions of the articles are contractual, not just those relating to membership.

G N Prentice, 'The enforcement of "outsider rights"' (1980) 1 Co Law 179, asserts that not every provision of the articles is contractual but only the provisions 'definitive of the power of the company to function'. G D Goldberg, 'The enforcement of outsider rights under section 20(1) of the Companies Act 1948' (1972) 35 MLR 362 and 'The controversy on the section 20 contract revisited' (1985) 48 MLR 158, asserts that the crucial point is the remedy sought by the member, saying that:

> A member of a company has . . . a contractual right to have any of the affairs of the company conducted by the particular organ of the company specified in the Act or the company's memorandum or articles.

For a review of the controversy, see R R Drury, 'The relative nature of a shareholder's right to enforce the company contract' [1986] CLJ 219.

The fact that Gregory, Prentice and Goldberg can produce three different descriptions of the contractual effect of the articles shows that contract concepts are not easily applied to the articles of association. The articles of a company are part of its constitution, and what members require is that the company's affairs should be conducted constitutionally. Unfortunately, English law does not have a developed concept of enforcement of a constitution for an organisation, perhaps because the British constitution is largely unwritten. The only available legal concept is contract law, but it may be that it is not very appropriate. It is notable that in *Ram Kissendas Dhanuka v Satya Charan Law* the Privy Council did not refer to contractual concepts at all.

3.4.2.11 Debts under the contract formed by the articles

CA 2006, s 33(2), provides that money payable by a member of a company to the company under its constitution is a debt due from the member to the company, and is of the nature of an ordinary contract debt, for which the limitation period is six years (Limitation Act 1980, s 5). This is a change from the previous law, under which the limitation period was 12 years. CA 2006, s 33(2), applies to collateral liabilities (see **2.3.2.4**) (*Peninsular Co Ltd v Fleming* (1872) 27 LT 93).

3.4.3 ARTICLES AS A CONTRACT BETWEEN THE COMPANY'S MEMBERS

In *Eley v Positive Government Security Life Assurance Co Ltd* (1876) 2 ExD 88, Lord Cairns LC said, at pp 89–90:

> Articles of association . . . state the arrangement between the members. They are an agreement *inter socios* [that is, between business partners].

In *Welton v Saffery* [1897] AC 299, Lord Macnaghten (at p 321) and Lord Davey (at p 329) used the phrase 'social contract' as a literal translation of 'contract *inter socios*' but they were obviously not implying that any of the theory of the social contract of government, found in the writings of Locke, Hobbes and Rousseau, should be imported into company law, intriguing though that possibility is. It seems that Isaacs J was also using 'social contract' and 'social compact' merely as equivalents of 'partnership agreement' in *Dutton v Gorton* (1917) 23 CLR 362, especially at p 395, and *Wood v W and G Dean Pty Ltd* (1929) 43 CLR 77. The much-quoted remark by Fullagar J in *Re Chas Jeffries and Sons Pty Ltd* [1949] VLR 190 at p 194 that he took 'social contract' as used by Isaacs J in *Wood v W and G Dean Pty Ltd*: 'to be a Rousseau-esque synonym for the articles of association' is probably no more than a jest (his Honour was counsel in *Wood v W and G Dean Pty Ltd*).

See also the statement of Mellish LJ in *Re Tavarone Mining Co, Pritchard's Case* (1873) LR 8 Ch App 956 at p 960 quoted at **3.4.1.1**.

In *Wood v Odessa Waterworks Co* (1889) 42 ChD 636, Stirling J said:

> The articles of association constitute a contract not merely between the shareholders and the company, but between each individual shareholder and every other.

In *Automatic Self-Cleansing Filter Syndicate Co Ltd v Cuninghame* [1906] 2 Ch 34, Cozens-Hardy LJ said, at p 44:

> It has been decided that the articles of association are a contract between the members of the company *inter se* [between themselves]. That was settled finally by the case of *Browne v La Trinidad*, if it was not settled before.

(In fact, it is very difficult to see that the question was settled by *Browne v La Trinidad* because it was not in issue in that case.)

Section 33 has been interpreted as making the articles of a company a contract between the company and its members only in relation to membership matters (see **3.4.2.2**), and the same restriction has been put on the contractual effect of the articles between the members. In ***London Sack and Bag Co Ltd v Dixon and Lugton Ltd*** [1943] 2 All ER 763, Scott LJ said, at p 765:

> It may well be . . . as between . . . members of a company . . . that [s 33] adjusts their legal relations *inter se* in the same way as a contract in a single document would if signed by all; and yet the statutory result may not be to constitute a contract between them about rights of action created entirely outside the company relationship, such as trading transactions between members.

However, the courts have been reluctant to provide members of companies with contractual remedies in disputes between members. In *Welton v Saffery* [1897] AC 299, Lord Herschell said, at p 315:

> It is quite true that the articles constitute a contract between each member and the company, and that there is no contract in terms between the individual members of the company; but the articles do not any the less, in my opinion, regulate their rights *inter se*. Such rights can only be enforced by or against a member through the company, or through the liquidator representing the company; but I think that no member has, as between himself and another member, any right beyond that which the contract with the company gives.

The idea that rights can be enforced only 'through the company' derives from the proper claimant aspect of the internal management principle enunciated in *MacDougall v Gardiner* (1875) 1 ChD 13 and discussed in **18.4.4**.

In *Salmon v Quin and Axtens Ltd* [1909] 1 Ch 311, Farwell LJ, at p 318, after citing with approval the dictum of Stirling J quoted earlier, said: 'it may well be that the court would not enforce the covenant as between individual shareholders in most cases'.

The only directly relevant case is ***Rayfield v Hands*** [1960] Ch 1, which will be more intelligible if read in conjunction with the two casenotes by L C B Gower, 'The contractual effect of articles of association' (1958) 21 MLR 401 and '*Rayfield v Hands*—a postscript and a drop of Scotch' (1958) 21 MLR 657. Mr Rayfield was a member of a company whose articles of association provided that a member who intended to transfer his shares had to inform the directors of the company who would take the shares equally between them at a fair value. Mr Rayfield wanted to transfer his 725 shares but Mr Hands and his fellow directors refused to take them. Vaisey J interpreted the reference to the directors in the article as a reference to the class of members who were directors and so held that the article concerned membership and had contractual force. He granted Mr Rayfield an order requiring the directors to take the shares but said, at p 9:

> The conclusion to which I have come may not be of so general application as to extend to the articles of association of every company, for it is, I think, material to remember that this private company is one of that class of companies which bears a close analogy to a partnership.

In *Caratti Holding Co Pty Ltd v Zampatti* (1978) 52 ALJR 732, Mr Caratti and Mr Zampatti had carried on business in partnership, with each partner entitled to a stated proportion of assets and profits. Zampatti's share was 10 per cent. The assets of the partnership were sold to a new company, the holding company, and leased back to the partnership. Caratti and Zampatti held shares in the company in the same proportions as their interests in the partnership. However, the articles of association of the company included art 32, which entitled Caratti 'whilst he is the registered holder of the life governor's share' to compulsorily purchase any other member's share on payment of the amount paid up on it. Caratti attempted to invoke this article so as to purchase Zampatti's shares, then worth at least A$400,000, for A$3,000. At first instance ((1975) 1 ACLR 87) it was held that this provision had contractual force ('life governor' defining a class of shareholder) and there was no appeal on this point. (Clearly it was a quasi-partnership company but the judge did not say that this was crucial to his finding that the article was contractually enforceable.) It was held that Caratti's attempted exercise of the powers given him by the articles was conduct of the company's affairs in a manner oppressive to Zampatti (see **18.6**), and Caratti was ordered to buy the shares at a price to be determined by the court. The Privy Council upheld the order. Lord Scarman said:

> The interest offered to and accepted by Mr Zampatti was a 10% share of 'the business'. Questions as to the legal structure of the business or as to the legal entities created to hold its assets were, so far as Mr Caratti and Mr Zampatti gave any thought to them, matters for the accountant: they did not touch upon the basic agreement of the business, however matters were arranged, Mr Zampatti's interest was 10% of the profits earned and capital employed in the business. It would be contrary to the whole basis of such agreement for Mr Caratti to invoke art 32, since to do so would be to seek to deprive Mr Zampatti of that which it had been agreed he should have, a 10% share in the profits and capital of the business.
>
> Though at first sight strange, there is nothing incredible or unique in two self-made businessmen getting on with the job of running the business on an agreed basis as to their respective shares in its profits and capital, while leaving its legal structure or pattern to a trusted accountant.
>
> Article 32 was neither understood nor accepted by Mr Caratti and Mr Zampatti as having any reference to the business agreement between them: and the use of its provisions against Mr Zampatti is inconsistent with that agreement.

3.4.4 DEEMED NOTICE

A person who deals with a company has constructive notice of the contents of the company's articles of association because they are publicly registered and available for inspection (per Lord Wensleydale in *Ernest v Nicholls* (1857) 6 HL Cas 401 at p 419; per Lord Hatherley in *Mahony v East Holyford Mining Co Ltd* (1875) LR 7 HL 869 at p 893). A statutory exception to this general rule is provided by CA 2006, s 40(2)(b)(i), which provides that a person dealing with a company is not bound to inquire whether there is any limitation on the power of the board of directors to bind the company, or authorise others to do so.

3.5 AMENDMENT OF ARTICLES

3.5.1 POWER TO AMEND

The articles of association are concerned with the internal administration of a company. Such matters cannot remain static for all time and so amendments must be possible. The general power of amendment is contained in CA 2006, s 21(1):

> A company may amend its articles by special resolution.

A special resolution requires a 75 per cent majority; see **14.4.3**. This provision allows *some* of the shareholders to amend the articles. Agreement by *all* the shareholders to an amendment (whether or not they attend a meeting or pass a resolution) will also be effective (*Ho Tung v Man On Insurance Co Ltd* [1902] AC 232; *Cane v Jones* [1980] 1 WLR 1451). Agreement may be inferred from the way the members have acted. In *Re Sherlock Holmes International Society Ltd* [2016] EWHC 1076, LTL 1/6/2016, the company's articles provided that only a member could be a director. The members repeatedly appointed directors who were not members. The court inferred that they had amended the articles to permit this and so the appointments were valid.

Authority to allot a company's shares which is given to its directors by its articles may be revoked, varied or renewed by ordinary resolution, even though the resolution amends the articles (s 551(4) (b) and (8); see **6.3.4.2**). A resolution authorising a company's directors to determine the terms, conditions and manner of redemption of shares may be an ordinary resolution even if it amends the company's articles (s 685(2); see **6.2.4.5**). A company can amend its articles to remove a provision for issuing share warrants (which are now prohibited) without passing a special resolution (Small Business, Enterprise and Employment Act 2015, s 85).

The directors of a public company are empowered to amend its articles so as to convert the company into a private company if they have to do so because the cancellation of shares in certain circumstances has reduced the nominal value of the company's allotted shares to less than £50,000 (s 664; see **6.5.2.7**).

The court has power to amend a company's articles:

(a) on the application of members objecting to a public company re-registering as private (s 98(5)(b); see **2.6.2**);

(b) to convert a public company to a private company after confirming a reduction of its capital to below £50,000 (s 651; see **10.7.6**); and

(c) on the application of a creditor or member of a private company objecting to payment out of capital for purchase or redemption of its shares (s 721(6)(b); see **10.5.3**).

If a thing cannot be done by a company without an authorisation contained in its articles, and there is no such authorisation, a special resolution to do that thing will not be interpreted as impliedly amending the articles to provide the necessary power (*Hutton v Scarborough Cliff Hotel Co Ltd* (1865) 4 De G J & S 672). For example, before CA 2006, a company could not reduce its capital unless it was authorised to do so by its articles. In several cases, companies adopted special resolutions to reduce capital at a time when there was no authority in their articles, and the court refused to confirm the reductions (*Re West India and Pacific Steamship Co* (1868) LR 9 Ch App 11 n; *Re Patent Invert Sugar Co* (1885) 31 ChD 166; *Re Dexine Patent Packing and Rubber Co* (1903) 88 LT 791; *Oregon Mortgage Co Ltd* 1910 SC 964—the second and fourth of these cases were concerned with the old requirement that a special resolution had to be confirmed at a subsequent meeting: see **14.4.3**). See also *Imperial Hydropathic Hotel Co, Blackpool v Hampson* (1882) 23 ChD 1 discussed in **3.4.2.4** and *Boschoek Proprietary Co Ltd v Fuke* [1906] 1 Ch 148 (another case involving confirmation of a special resolution).

On the other hand, if the articles prevent a thing being done, a special resolution to do that thing 'notwithstanding anything contained in the articles' will be effective (*Taylor v Pilsen Joel and General Electric Light Co* (1884) 27 ChD 268).

The general power of a company to amend its articles may be affected by the restrictions discussed in **3.6**.

3.5.2 NOTIFICATION OF AMENDMENT

3.5.2.1 Notification to Companies House

Whenever the articles of a company are amended by special resolution under CA 2006, s 21, or by ordinary resolution under s 551, or by unanimous agreement, a copy of the resolution or agreement must be forwarded to Companies House within 15 days of being adopted or made (ss 29, 30 and 551(9)). The same applies to a court order made under the powers mentioned in **3.5.1** (ss 99(3), 651(3)(a) and 722(3)) or on a petition for relief of unfairly prejudicial conduct of the company's affairs (s 998(1) and (2), where the time limit is 14 days). The court may extend the time limit for filing an order that it has made under any of these powers. Any other court order altering a company's constitution must also be notified to Companies House, with a copy of the order, not later than 15 days after it takes effect (s 35(1), (2) and (5)), as must any enactment which alters the constitution, other than one which amends the general law (s 34(1) to (4)).

Whenever a company amends its articles, it must send to Companies House a copy of the articles as amended, and must do so not later than 15 days after the amendment takes effect (s 26). Amended articles must also be sent to Companies House when a court order amends articles to convert a public company to a private company (s 651(3)(b)) or as a remedy for unfairly prejudicial conduct of the company's affairs (s 999(1) and (2)) or in any other way alters a company's constitution (s 35(1), (2) and (5)).

There are criminal sanctions for failure to comply with these requirements (ss 26(3) and (4), 30(2) and (3), 34(5) and (6), 35(3) and (4), 99(4) and (5), 722(4) and (5), 998(3) and (4), and 999(4) and (5)). Companies House may send a notice requiring compliance with an obligation to send it amendments to articles, or amended articles, within 28 days, and may impose a civil penalty of £200 for failure to comply (s 27). But failure to register an amendment does not mean that it is ineffective. Members are bound by an amendment as from the time of adopting it, regardless of whether it is registered (*Gunewardena v Conran Holdings Ltd* [2016] EWHC 2983 (Ch), [2017] Bus LR 301).

If a company makes an application for re-registration, it must, as part of the application, supply Companies House with a copy of its articles as proposed to be amended to provide for its new status (ss 94(2)(b) (private to public), 100(2)(b) (public to private limited), 103(2)(b) (limited to unlimited), 106(2)(c) (unlimited to limited), 110(2)(b) (public to private unlimited), and 651(3)(b) (court order to convert public company to private company)).

3.5.2.2 Public notice

Companies House must give public notice (see **4.3**) of receipt of any amendment of a company's articles and the text of the articles as amended (CA 2006, ss 1077 and 1078(2)).

A company may not rely on any amendment in its articles against any other person until official notification of receipt of both the amendment and the text of the articles as amended, unless the company can show that the amendment was known to the person concerned (s 1079(1), (2)(a) and (4)(a)). Additionally, the company may not rely on an amendment within 15 days *after* official notification if it is shown that the person concerned was unavoidably prevented from knowing of the amendment within that period (s 1079(3)).

3.5.2.3 Issued copies of articles must include amendments

Every copy of a company's articles which the company issues after amending its articles must either incorporate all amendments or must be accompanied by a copy of the resolution, agreement, court order or enactment making the amendment (CA 2006, s 36).

3.6 RESTRICTIONS ON AMENDMENT OF ARTICLES

3.6.1 STATUTORY RESTRICTIONS

A company's power to amend its articles is limited by the provisions of CA 2006 (per Lindley MR in *Allen v Gold Reefs of West Africa Ltd* [1900] 1 Ch 656 at p 671).

Section 25 of the Act provides that a member of a company is not bound by any change in the company's articles which requires the member to take or subscribe for more shares or in any way increases the member's liability to contribute to the company's share capital or otherwise pay money to the company, unless (by s 25(2)) the member gives express written agreement to be bound.

A company which was registered before 1 October 2009 and permitted to omit the word 'limited' from its name on condition that its constitution made certain provisions (see **2.4.3**) may not amend its articles so as to remove those provisions (s 63).

3.6.2 RESTRICTIONS IMPOSED BY THE COMPANY ITSELF OR ITS MEMBERS

3.6.2.1 Entrenchment

The articles of association of a company may contain a provision which requires that specified provisions of the articles can be amended or deleted only if conditions are met, or procedures complied with, that are more restrictive than the conditions for passing a special resolution: such a provision is called a provision for entrenchment (CA 2006, s 22(1)). Notice must be given to Companies House if a company's articles contain a provision for entrenchment on registration or if one is inserted (s 23(1)). Whenever a company which has a provision for entrenchment in its articles makes any kind of amendment to the articles, the notification to Companies House of the amendment (see **3.5.2.1**) must include a statement of compliance, that is a statement that the amendment has been made in accordance with the articles (s 24). Notice must also be given to Companies House of deletion of a provision for entrenchment, accompanied by a statement of compliance (ss 23(2) and 24).

3.6.2.2 Old companies: provision for entrenchment

Any provision for entrenchment in an old-style memorandum of a company registered before 1 October 2009 is now treated as being in its articles (CA 2006, s 28).

3.6.2.3 Weighted voting

Any member who controls sufficient votes to prevent a special resolution (75 per cent majority) being adopted can always prevent any amendment of the articles. The articles may provide for votes to be specially weighted so as to provide members with a power to block special resolutions out of proportion to their shareholding. In *Bushell v Faith* [1970] AC 1099, the company's articles weighted a shareholder's voting rights on a certain issue (for which see **15.6.3**) and had the effect of preventing a resolution on that issue being passed. The Court of Appeal ([1969] 2 Ch 438) and the House of Lords upheld the weighted voting rights given by the articles. In the Court of Appeal, Russell LJ considered the problem of such weighted rights preventing the company from amending its articles. He said, at pp 447–8:

> [Counsel for the plaintiff] argued by reference to [CA 2006, s 21(1)], and the well-known proposition that a company cannot by its articles or otherwise deprive itself of the power by special resolution to alter its articles or any of them. But the point is the same one. An article purporting to do this is ineffective. But a provision as to voting rights which has the effect of making a special resolution incapable of being passed, if a particular shareholder or group of shareholders exercises his or their voting rights against a proposed alteration, is not such a provision. An article in terms providing that no alteration shall be made without the consent of X is contrary to [CA 2006, s 21(1)] and ineffective. But the provision as to voting rights that I have mentioned is wholly different, and it does not serve to say that it can have the same result.

Following this, in *Amalgamated Pest Control Pty Ltd v McCarron* [1995] 1 QdR 583, the court found nothing invalid about a provision in a company's articles giving a particular member 26 per cent of the votes on any special resolution.

3.6.3 RESTRICTIONS IMPOSED BY THE COURT UNDER STATUTORY POWERS

The court has power to order a company not to make any, or any specified, amendments to its articles without the court's leave:

(a) on the application of members objecting to a public company re-registering as private (CA 2006, s 98(6); see **2.6.2**);

(b) on the application of a creditor or member of a private company objecting to payment out of capital for purchase or redemption of its shares (s 721(7); see **10.5.3**);

(c) on a member's petition for relief of unfairly prejudicial conduct of the company's affairs (s 996(2)(d); see **18.6.11.1**).

Such an order has the same effect as a provision for entrenchment (see **3.6.2.1**) and is subject to the same requirements to notify Companies House (ss 23 and 24).

3.6.4 RESTRICTIONS IMPOSED BY CONTRACT

A contract made by a company that it will not exercise its statutory power to amend its articles is unenforceable (*Russell v Northern Bank Development Corporation Ltd* [1992] 1 WLR 588). Amendment of a company's articles may put it in breach of contract or make it impossible for the company to carry out its obligations under a contract. In two early cases, injunctions were granted to prevent companies amending their articles in a way that would breach contracts (*Baily v British Equitable Assurance Co* [1904] 1 Ch 374, CA (though the House of Lords [1906] AC 35 subsequently held that the proposed amendment would not be in breach of contract); *British Murac Syndicate Ltd v Alperton Rubber Co Ltd* [1915] 2 Ch 186). However, it is now accepted that the statutory right of a company to amend its articles cannot be taken away by injunction (this was originally held in *Punt v Symons and Co Ltd* [1903] 2 Ch 506; see per Lord Porter in *Southern Foundries (1926) Ltd v Shirlaw* [1940] AC 701 at pp 740–1; per Scott J in *Cumbrian Newspapers Group Ltd v Cumberland and Westmorland Herald Newspaper and Printing Co Ltd* [1987] Ch 1 at p 24).

3.6.5 LIMITS OF MAJORITY RULE

3.6.5.1 Bona fide for the benefit of the company as a whole

The members of a company must not exercise the company's power to amend its articles otherwise than bona fide for the benefit of the company as a whole. The classic statement of this restriction placed on the ability of majority shareholders to vote as they please, is to be found in the judgment of Lindley MR in **Allen v Gold Reefs of West Africa Ltd** [1900] 1 Ch 656 at pp 671–2:

> The power thus conferred on companies to alter the regulations contained in their articles is limited only by the provisions contained in the statute and the conditions contained in the company's memorandum of association. Wide, however, as the language of [CA 2006, s 21(1)] is, the power conferred by it must, like all other powers, be exercised subject to those general principles of law and equity which are applicable to all powers conferred on majorities and enabling them to bind minorities. It must be exercised, not only in the manner required by law, but also bona fide for the benefit of the company as a whole, and it must not be exceeded. These conditions are always implied, and are seldom, if ever, expressed. But if they are complied with I can discover no ground for judicially putting any other restrictions on the power conferred by the section than those contained in it.

The phrase 'bona fide for the benefit of the company as a whole' is a single criterion only. If the court accepts that the majority members' subjective bona fide view was that the amendment was for the benefit of the company, it cannot overrule the decision on the ground that in the court's view it was not for the benefit of the company—it is not the court's task to take business decisions (*Shuttleworth v Cox Brothers and Co (Maidenhead) Ltd* [1927] 2 KB 9; *Citco Banking Corporation NV v Pusser's Ltd* [2007] UKPC 13, [2007] Bus LR 960). Nevertheless, there is an objective minimum standard below which the members' subjective view will not be accepted. In ***Shuttleworth's* case,** Bankes LJ said, at pp 18–19:

> The alteration may be so oppressive as to cast suspicion on the honesty of the persons responsible for it, or so extravagant that no reasonable men could really consider it for the benefit of the company. In such cases the court is, I think, entitled to treat the conduct of shareholders as it does the verdict of a jury, and to say that the alteration of a company's articles shall not stand if it is such that no reasonable men could consider it for the benefit of the company. Or, if the facts should raise the question, the court may be able to apply another test—namely, whether or not the action of the shareholders is capable of being considered for the benefit of the company.

In the same case, Scrutton LJ said, at p 23:

> Now when persons, honestly endeavouring to decide what will be for the benefit of the company and to act accordingly, decide upon a particular course, then, provided there are grounds on which reasonable men could come to the same decision, it does not matter whether the court would or would not come to the same decision or a different decision. It is not the business of the court to manage the affairs of the company. That is for the shareholders and directors. The absence of any reasonable ground for deciding that a certain course of action is conducive to the benefit of the company may be a ground for finding lack of good faith or for finding that the shareholders, with the best motives, have not considered the matters which they ought to have considered. On either of these findings their decision might be set aside.

Where an amendment of articles will benefit a particular shareholder, that shareholder is under no obligation to abstain from voting, and the validity of the amendment does not depend on it being passed by a majority of disinterested members (*Citco Banking Corporation NV v Pusser's Ltd* [2007] UKPC 13, [2007] Bus LR 960).

The benefit of the company test is not appropriate if the company as a separate person has no interest in the amendment (see **3.6.5.2**); and the application of the test to one particular kind of amendment, namely provisions for the expulsion of members, has been inconsistent (see **3.6.5.3**). So, courts have sought other ways of judging whether they should overrule a majority in a company (see **3.6.5.4** and **3.6.5.5**). It may well be that the best concept to use is that of unfair prejudice (see **3.6.5.6** and **18.6**).

3.6.5.2 What is the company?

A company has a dual aspect as an association of its members and as a person separate from its members. The phrase 'the benefit of the company as a whole' might refer to either (or both) of these aspects. A feature of a number of leading English cases in which the court upheld the validity of an amendment of articles is that the amendment was made primarily for the benefit of the company as a corporate entity separate from its members.

In *Allen v Gold Reefs of West Africa Ltd* [1900] 1 Ch 656 the object of the change was to obtain payment to the company of calls due from the estate of a deceased member.

In *Sidebottom v Kershaw, Leese and Co Ltd* [1920] 1 Ch 154 the object of the alteration was to give the directors power to expel any member who carried on a business in direct competition with the company's business.

In *Shuttleworth v Cox Brothers and Co (Maidenhead) Ltd* [1927] 2 KB 9 the object of the alteration was to provide that a director should resign if requested in writing to do so by all his co-directors.

In all these cases, in assessing whether the majority have acted 'bona fide for the benefit of the company as a whole', it is the company as a separate person whose benefit is to be considered. But amendments of articles can concern matters, such as the distribution of dividends or capital or the power to dispose of shares, in which the company as a separate person has no interest, and the benefit of the company test is not relevant to such amendments (*Citco Banking Corporation NV v Pusser's Ltd* [2007] UKPC 13, [2007] Bus LR 960). As Latham CJ said, in **Peters' American Delicacy Co Ltd v Heath** (1939) 61 CLR 457, at p 481:

> The benefit of the company as a corporation cannot be adopted as a criterion which is capable of solving all the problems in this branch of the law . . . In cases where the question which arises is simply a question as to the relative rights of different classes of shareholders the problem cannot be solved by regarding merely the benefit of the corporation.

3.6.5.3 Expulsion cases

Several of the cases in which an amendment of articles has been challenged concerned the addition of a power to expel a member from a company (by compulsory purchase of shares) or remove a director from office. In *Sidebottom v Kershaw, Leese and Co Ltd* [1920] 1 Ch 154 and *Shuttleworth v Cox Brothers and Co (Maidenhead) Ltd* [1927] 2 KB 9, the challenge did not succeed and the expulsion or removal was valid, but in *Brown v British Abrasive Wheel Co Ltd* [1919] 1 Ch 290 and *Dafen Tinplate Co Ltd v Llanelly Steel Co (1907) Ltd* [1920] 2 Ch 124 expulsion was held to be invalid. All those cases were decided using the benefit of the company test, though in *Shuttleworth v Cox Brothers and Co (Maidenhead) Ltd* the Court of Appeal criticised the *Dafen Tinplate* case as a wrong application of that test. In an interim application in **Constable v Executive Connections Ltd** [2005] EWHC 3 (Ch), [2005] 2 BCLC 638, the learned deputy judge said, at [29]:

> I do not regard the law in this area as clear or easy to apply. There are no recent English cases and the older ones are to my mind quite difficult. Indeed the more one looks at the decided cases, the harder it is to know precisely where the line is to be drawn between those cases where the introduction of a compulsory transfer provision will be upheld and those where it will not.

3.6.5.4 Discrimination and hypothetical member tests

In **Greenhalgh v Arderne Cinemas Ltd** [1951] Ch 286 a provision in the articles of Arderne Cinemas Ltd which gave existing members a pre-emption right to buy any shares that a member wanted to sell was amended by adding a provision that, notwithstanding the pre-emption rights, any member could transfer shares if the transfer was approved by an ordinary resolution of the members. The managing director, Mr Mallard, controlled a majority of votes and intended to sell his controlling interest to an outsider, apparently to spite Mr Greenhalgh, a minority shareholder. Mr Mallard and his supporters had already successfully defended at least four legal actions brought by Mr Greenhalgh which had been taken to the Court of Appeal. In voting for the change in articles, Mr Mallard and his supporters did not claim to have acted in the company's interest because they did not allege that the company as a separate person had any interest in who its shareholders were. They apparently acted in Mr Mallard's interest, though it seems that he was interested in emotional rather than financial gratification. How then could the court decide whether the majority had abused their power? Evershed MR said, at p 291:

> the phrase, 'the company as a whole', does not (at any rate in such a case as the present) mean the company as a commercial entity, distinct from the corporators: it means the corporators as a general body. That is to say, the case may be taken of an individual hypothetical member and it may be asked whether what is proposed is, in the honest opinion of those who voted in its favour, for that person's benefit.
>
> I think that the matter can, in practice, be more accurately and precisely stated by looking at the converse and by saying that a special resolution of this kind would be liable to be impeached if the effect of it were to discriminate between the majority shareholders and the minority shareholders, so as to give the former an advantage of which the latter were deprived.

The court unanimously affirmed Roxburgh J's decision that the amendment of the articles of Arderne Cinemas Ltd was valid. The amendment took away from the minority the right to acquire other members' shares if those other members could secure an ordinary resolution approving a transfer to an outsider. But in Evershed MR's view (at p 292): 'I do not think that it can be said that that is such a discrimination as falls within the scope of the principle which I have stated'. It is difficult to follow the court's application of the discrimination principle in this case, though it may be that Mr Mallard's malevolent self-interest was an unusual factor. (For an earlier case in the Arderne Cinemas affair—*Greenhalgh v Arderne Cinemas Ltd* [1946] 1 All ER 512—see **14.10.5**.)

Evershed MR claimed that the discrimination test would explain two English cases in which amendments of articles were held to be invalid: *Brown v British Abrasive Wheel Co Ltd* [1919] 1 Ch 290 and *Dafen Tinplate Co Ltd v Llanelly Steel Co (1907) Ltd* [1920] 2 Ch 124 (the latter case was criticised in *Shuttleworth v Cox Brothers and Co (Maidenhead) Ltd* [1927] 2 KB 9 as a wrong application of the interest of the company test, see **3.6.5.3**). The discrimination test would also apparently explain the Scottish case of *Crookston v Lindsay, Crookston and Co Ltd* 1922 SLT 62.

In *Rights and Issues Investment Trust Ltd v Stylo Shoes Ltd* [1965] Ch 250 the company had two classes of shares, ordinary shares and management shares. It was proposed to issue new ordinary shares but also to double the number of votes attached to each management share so that the holders of the management shares would retain control of the company. The proposal was adopted by a very large majority at a general meeting—the holders of the management shares did not vote. Pennycuick J said (at p 255) that he was 'not persuaded that there has been here any discrimination against or oppression of the holders of the ordinary shares'.

In *Australian Fixed Trusts Pty Ltd v Clyde Industries Ltd* [1959] SR (NSW) 33, the directors of Clyde Industries Ltd proposed to amend its articles so as to make it virtually impossible for votes to be cast in relation to shares held on behalf of unit trusts (as 14.6 per cent of its shares were). The court was unable to discern any 'company purpose' for the amendment and so relied on the discrimination test. It was held that the proposed amendment would be invalid because it discriminated by reducing the voting power of specific shareholders and thereby increasing the voting power of the other shareholders.

Commentators often ignore the second paragraph (the discrimination test) in the passage from Evershed MR's judgment quoted earlier and suggest that the test to be applied is the hypothetical member test stated in the first paragraph quoted. But it is very difficult to understand how this test could be applied in practice. Is a hypothetical member different from a real member, and, if so, in what way? What is the hypothesis? As Evershed MR said, the discrimination test 'more accurately and precisely' tests whether an amendment of articles is valid, and that is the test which has in practice been used by subsequent courts. Commentators also ignore the words 'at any rate in such a case as the present' and assume that Evershed MR intended his test to be applied in all future cases. The true position is that the discrimination test is only necessary in cases where it is inappropriate to apply the test of benefit to the company as a whole.

3.6.5.5 Proper purpose test

In *Gambotto v WCP Ltd* (1995) 182 CLR 432, the High Court of Australia suggested that it was time to replace the 'benefit of the company as a whole' test entirely. The majority of the court said, at p 444, that the test of whether an amendment of a company's articles is valid should be whether the amendment is 'beyond any purpose contemplated by the articles or oppressive as that expression is understood in the law relating to corporations'. The court refused to allow a company to amend its articles so as to give the holder of 99.7 per cent of its shares a right to purchase the remainder compulsorily so as to make the company a wholly owned subsidiary and so obtain tax advantages and administrative savings. The majority of the court said that amendment of the articles of a company so as to give the majority in the company power to expropriate the minority is a special case in which the test should be that the amendment is valid only if (a) the power could be exercised 'for a proper purpose' and (b) exercising the power would not be oppressive to the minority. The majority of the court also held that the onus was on those proposing the amendment to show that it satisfies the test. In *Gambotto v WCP Ltd*, achieving tax and administrative savings was not a proper purpose and so the amendment was invalid. Although *Gambotto v WCP Ltd* now governs the law on this subject in Australia, it is not a precedent in England. It seems, with respect, to have introduced yet another vague test which does not clarify the law in this difficult area where the courts are trying to protect minorities without giving them disproportionate power.

3.6.5.6 Present significance of the various tests

In *Citco Banking Corporation NV v Pusser's Ltd* [2007] UKPC 13, [2007] Bus LR 960, the Privy Council (per Lord Hoffmann) affirmed that the primary test of validity of an amendment of a company's articles is the benefit of the company test (see **3.6.5.1**). Lord Hoffmann acknowledged that the test cannot be used where an amendment is only for the purpose of regulating the rights of shareholders in matters in which the company as a corporate entity has no interest, such as the distribution of dividends or capital or the power to dispose of shares (see **3.6.5.2**). His Lordship noted that the hypothetical member test proposed for use in these circumstances has not been found to be entirely illuminating by some commentators (see **3.6.5.4**). As the case before the Privy Council could be dealt with using the benefit of the company test, it was unnecessary to consider this problem any further. Lord Hoffmann also noted that the proper purpose test proposed by the High Court of Australia (see **3.6.5.5**) has no support in English authority.

This topic has been reviewed in detail by F G Rixon, 'Competing interests and conflicting principles: an examination of the power of alteration of articles of association' (1986) 49 MLR 446, who concludes by observing that, in future, minority shareholders who dispute a change in articles will petition for relief of unfairly prejudicial conduct (see **18.6**) rather than attempting to prove that the amendment was invalid under either the interest of the company test or the discrimination test. But using a different procedure does not avoid the problem of finding a rational test of whether an amendment of articles should be overruled by the court. The topic is also examined by P G Xuereb, 'The limitation on the exercise of majority power' (1985) 6 Co Law 199; H H Mason, 'Fraud on the minority. The problem of a single formulation of the principle' (1972) 46 ALJ 67; and S Satish, 'The alteration of the articles of association: tracing the trajectory from *Allen* to *Citco*' (2014) 35 Co Law 275. In *Re Charterhouse Capital Ltd* [2015] EWCA Civ 536, [2015] 2 BCLC 627, at [90], Sir Terence Etherton C gave a list of nine principles he derived from the cases. See also the general discussion in **14.10.3** to **14.10.6** of reasons for invalidating decisions of members.

3.7 AMENDMENT OF ARTICLES WHICH ARE TERMS OF ANOTHER CONTRACT

The contract between a company and its members which is formed by the membership provisions of the articles may be amended by special resolution and all members will be bound by the amendment, whether they voted for it or not. But if provisions of a company's articles are also terms of a separate contract which the company has made with a person (whether a member or not), then it is a question of construction of that separate contract whether or not it is amended by an amendment of the articles (*Allen v Gold Reefs of West Africa Ltd* [1900] 1 Ch 656 per Lindley MR at pp 673–4).

In *Shuttleworth v Cox Brothers and Co (Maidenhead) Ltd* [1927] 2 KB 9 the company's articles provided for five people to be its directors for life unless disqualified in any of six specified ways. The articles were subsequently amended by adding a seventh disqualifying circumstance and one of the directors was asked to resign when this seventh circumstance occurred. The director concerned claimed a declaration that he was still a director of the company but the Court of Appeal held that the company did have a power to dismiss him. Atkin LJ, at pp 25–6, said:

the proper inference appears to be that there was a contract that the plaintiff should be a permanent director, but a contract contained in articles which could be altered by a special resolution of the company in accordance with the provisions of the Companies Act; and inasmuch as the contract contemplated the permanent office being vacated in one of six contingencies, it is not inconsistent with the contract that the article should be altered so as to add a seventh contingency. In other words, it is a contract made upon the terms of an alterable article, and therefore neither of the contracting parties can complain if the article is altered.

In *Southern Foundries (1926) Ltd v Shirlaw* [1940] AC 701, Mr Shirlaw was a director of Southern Foundries and had been appointed its managing director for a fixed term of ten years. The articles of Southern Foundries were amended so as to provide that any of its directors could be removed from office by written notice signed by officers of its new parent company. When Mr Shirlaw was dismissed from his directorship of Southern Foundries using this provision it meant that he could not continue to be managing director, because both the old and the new articles specified that the office of managing director could be held only by a director of the company and that a managing director would cease to hold office on ceasing to be a director. Mr Shirlaw's ten-year contract was only in its fourth year when he was dismissed. A majority of the House of Lords (including Lord Atkin, as Atkin LJ had then become), held that, by making it impossible for Mr Shirlaw to continue as managing director, the company had breached its ten-year contract with him and had to pay damages. Even though the dismissal was actually effected by the parent company, in the view of the majority of the House, Southern Foundries was responsible for the breach of contract because it had granted the parent company the right to dismiss. (The minority held that Southern Foundries was not responsible for the dismissal.) In Mr Shirlaw's case, as in Mr Shuttleworth's case, using amended articles to dismiss a director was not in itself wrong but in Mr Shirlaw's case it caused a separate contract (the one relating to his office as managing director) to be breached, for which damages had to be paid.

In *Bailey v New South Wales Medical Defence Union Ltd* (1995) 184 CLR 399, the union provided professional negligence insurance to its medical-practitioner members on terms set out in its articles of association. The High Court of Australia held that the provisions of the articles relating to insurance were not membership provisions: it was possible for people to be members but not insured, and members had to pay annual subscriptions which were fixed by the union's council and depended on the extent of insurance cover required. The union amended its articles to give it the right to discontinue assistance to any member at the sole and absolute discretion of its council. A member, who had joined before the articles were amended, had been sued for damages for his professional negligence, which was alleged to have occurred before the articles were amended. The union claimed to relieve itself of liability by acting under the amended article. It was held that it was not a term of the insurance contract that the union could amend it retrospectively by amending its articles, so the member was still insured by the union.

3.8 RESTRICTED OBJECTS

3.8.1 OPTION TO RESTRICT OBJECTS OF COMPANY

A company may restrict its objects, that is, the purposes for which its powers may be exercised, by a provision in its articles. Unless its articles specifically restrict its objects, they are unrestricted (CA 2006, s 31(1)). CA 2006 does not implement the requirement in Directive 2012/30/EU, art 2, that a public company must state its objects in its constitution. Until 30 September 2009 it was compulsory for every company to state its objects in its old-style memorandum and every company was restricted to pursuing its stated objects. On 1 October 2009 the objects clause of any existing company became a provision of its articles (CA 2006, s 28), from which it may be deleted by special resolution (s 21) unless it is subject to a provision for entrenchment.

3.8.2 *ULTRA VIRES* TRANSACTIONS BEYOND A COMPANY'S RESTRICTED OBJECTS

3.8.2.1 Effect on directors' authority

If a company's objects are restricted by its articles, its powers cannot be exercised for a purpose which is beyond the restriction. Acting for such a purpose is said to be *ultra vires* (beyond the powers of) the company. (Conversely, a transaction for a purpose that is an object of the company is described as *intra vires*—within the powers.) The directors of a company have a duty to act within powers (CA 2006, s 171). It is not possible for a company with restricted objects to give its directors or other agents authority to cause it to enter into any transaction which is not for the purpose of, or reasonably incidental to, attaining or pursuing those objects (*Rolled Steel Products (Holdings) Ltd v British Steel Corporation* [1986] Ch 246 per Slade LJ at p 295).

Any director of a company who is responsible for it entering into a transaction outside its restricted objects is liable to replace the money the company expended on the transaction (*Re Lands Allotment Co* [1894] 1 Ch 616) unless the members of the company ratify the transaction (see **16.16.2** and **19.5.7**). In *Re Samuel Sherman plc* [1991] 1 WLR 1070 a director of a company who invested its money in loss-making activities outside its restricted objects was disqualified from being a director for five years.

3.8.2.2 Injunction

On the application of any member of a company, the court may order the company not to enter into a proposed transaction beyond the company's restricted objects (*Simpson v Westminster Palace Hotel Co* (1860) 8 HL Cas 712). If a proposed transaction is found to be beyond the company's restricted objects, but the members approve of the transaction, they can alter the objects to accommodate it.

The rule that a member of a *registered* company can prevent it entering into a transaction beyond its objects follows the rule that a member of a *statutory* company is entitled to prevent it entering into a transaction for a purpose that is not one of the objects of the company set out in its incorporating Act of Parliament. For example, in *Colman v Eastern Counties Railway Co* (1846) 10 Beav 1, the claimant succeeded in stopping the company (which operated the railway from London to Harwich) from giving financial support to a company it was promoting to operate a shipping service from Harwich to Rotterdam and other northern European ports—the plaintiff was probably acting for rival shipping interests.

In *Simpson v Westminster Palace Hotel Co*, the company had been incorporated to build and operate what for that time was an unusually large hotel. The directors decided that for the first three years they would lease part of the hotel to the Civil Service so as to provide a guaranteed income. A member of the company sought an injunction to prevent this but the House of Lords refused the injunction, finding that the proposed lease did not take the company outside the business of running a hotel. In *Stephens v Mysore Reefs (Kangundy) Mining Co Ltd* [1902] 1 Ch 745, a company formed to acquire a gold mine in India was restrained from acquiring an interest in a gold mining property in West Africa.

3.8.2.3 Repudiation of transactions

It is possible, in some circumstances, for a company with restricted objects to repudiate a transaction entered into on its behalf outside those objects. It can do this on the ground that the person who acted on its behalf could not have actual authority to act on its behalf outside its objects. However, the circumstances in which this can be done have been increasingly limited by statute in recent years so as to protect people who deal with companies from having their transactions repudiated—see **19.5.5**.

In the nineteenth century the courts established a rule (known as the '*ultra vires* rule') that a company did not have capacity to enter into a transaction which was not capable of being within its objects, so that such a transaction was void and did not bind the company (*Ashbury Railway*

Carriage and Iron Co Ltd v Riche (1875) LR 7 HL 653), but this rule was nullified as from 4 February 1991 by what is now CA 2006, s 39(1) (see **19.4.1**).

3.8.3 SUBSTRATUM

Where a company has restricted objects, its members take shares in the company and contribute capital to it on the basis that it will use its money to pursue those objects. Accordingly, it is just and equitable for the court to order the winding up of a company (under the Insolvency Act 1986, s 122(1)(g)) if 'that which the company was formed to do can no longer be done' (per Kekewich J in **Re Bristol Joint Stock Bank** (1890) 44 ChD 703 at p 712) so that anything it might do would be outside its objects. It is usually said in such a case that the company's 'substratum' has gone, using terminology apparently coined by Lord Cairns LJ in *Re Suburban Hotel Co* (1867) LR 2 Ch App 737 at p 750. For example, in *Re Baku Consolidated Oilfields Ltd* [1944] 1 All ER 24, the company was formed to purchase the undertakings of four companies whose undertakings were expropriated without compensation in 1920 shortly after the company was formed. Compulsory winding up was ordered. In 1990, compensation was finally agreed (see *Re Baku Consolidated Oilfields Ltd* [1994] 1 BCLC 173). See also **3.8.6**.

3.8.4 AN ACTION MAY BE *ULTRA VIRES* FOR SOME PURPOSES BUT NOT FOR OTHERS

According to Lord Parker of Waddington in *Cotman v Brougham* [1918] AC 514 at p 520, a court may take a different view of what is within or outside a company's restricted objects depending on whether the question before it is:

(a) one of equity between the company and its members (for example, when deciding, at the instance of a member of a company, whether to restrain a proposed action of the company—see **3.8.2.2** and **3.8.5**—or whether to wind up the company for loss of substratum—see **3.8.3**); or

(b) one of law between the company and another person (for example, whether the company is bound by a particular contract—see **3.8.2.3**).

When deciding whether a transaction between a company and an outsider can be repudiated, a court is likely to take a wide view of what is within the company's objects, and consequently a narrow view of what is *ultra vires*.

When deciding what is equitable between a company and its members, a court is likely to take a narrower view of what is within the company's objects, and consequently a wider view of what is *ultra vires*. In particular, when deciding a question of equity between a company and its members, a court may consider an action to be within the company's objects only if it is within what the court considers to be the company's 'main object' (see **3.8.6**).

3.8.5 IMPLIED POWERS FOR INCIDENTAL PURPOSES

3.8.5.1 Implied powers for incidental purposes

In **Attorney-General v Great Eastern Railway Co** (1880) 5 App Cas 473, Lord Selborne LC made the important statement, at p 478, that the *ultra vires* rule (see **3.8.2.3**):

> ought to be reasonably, and not unreasonably, understood and applied [to statutory companies], and that whatever may fairly be regarded as incidental to, or consequential upon, those things which the legislature has authorised, ought not (unless expressly prohibited) to be held, by judicial construction, to be *ultra vires*.

Accordingly, in *Deuchar v Gas Light and Coke Co* [1925] AC 691 it was held that the Gas Light and Coke Co (a statutory company formed to make gas from coal) could itself manufacture caustic soda (sodium hydroxide) for use in converting one of the by-products of its gas-making process into a substance that could be sold to dyestuff manufacturers. Mr Deuchar had acquired shares in the company to challenge the *vires* of this activity: he was the secretary of a company that made caustic soda.

The same rule is applied to registered companies with restricted objects. 'Any such company is treated as having implied powers to do any act which is reasonably incidental to the attainment or pursuit of any of its express objects, unless such act is expressly prohibited by the [articles]' (per Slade LJ in **Rolled Steel Products (Holdings) Ltd v British Steel Corporation** [1986] Ch 246 at p 287, re-expressing a statement of Buckley LJ in *Re Horsley and Weight Ltd* [1982] Ch 442 at p 448).

In *Johns v Balfour* (1889) 5 TLR 389, a company's object was to conduct mining operations in Russia and it did so on the estate of a landowner as tenant of the landowner. When the landowner died, it was proposed to buy the whole estate of 17,000 hectares so as to secure the company's right to mine the land. A shareholder objected that a purchase on such a scale would make the company a landowning company, which would be outside its objects, but the court held that the land purchase was merely in furtherance of the company's stated objects and so was *intra vires*.

Courts have made the following decisions about the implied powers of companies with restricted objects. A trading company must have an implied power to borrow money (*General Auction Estate and Monetary Co v Smith* [1891] 3 Ch 432), and a company that has power to borrow money must have an implied power to give security for its repayment (*Re Patent File Co* (1870) LR 6 Ch App 83). A company has an implied power to invest its surplus funds (*Burland v Earle* [1902] AC 83). There is an implied power to pay gratuities to employees while a company is a going concern (*Hampson v Price's Patent Candle Co* (1876) 45 LJ Ch 437 (which concerned a statutory company); *Cameron v Glenmorangie Distillery Co Ltd* (1896) 23 R 1092; *Cyclists' Touring Club v Hopkinson* [1910] 1 Ch 179). Any company with restricted objects has an implied power to compromise claims against itself (*Re Norwich Provident Insurance Society, Bath's Case* (1878) 8 ChD 334). If a claim is brought alleging that an individual committed a tort in the course of employment by a company with restricted objects, the company has an implied power to pay for the individual's defence (*Breay v Royal British Nurses' Association* [1897] 2 Ch 272 (which concerned a chartered corporation)).

On the other hand, a company with restricted objects does not necessarily have a power to issue negotiable instruments (for example, to accept bills of exchange) (*Peruvian Railways Co v Thames and Mersey Marine Insurance Co* (1867) LR 2 Ch App 617). No company with restricted objects has an implied power to sell or dispose of its whole undertaking: such a sale or disposal could not be incidental to the attainment or pursuit of the object of carrying on the undertaking (*Re Oceanic Steam Navigation Co Ltd* [1939] Ch 41). No company with restricted objects has an implied power to pay the costs of legal proceedings arising out of a dispute between its members (*Pickering v Stephenson* (1872) LR 14 Eq 322; see **18.6.4**).

3.8.5.2 Express powers in objects clauses

In the nineteenth century there was considerable uncertainty over whether the courts would accept that a company had an incidental power to engage in even the simplest commercial transaction such as issuing a bill of exchange, and it became the practice to include in the objects clause of every company's old-style memorandum of association a statement that the company's objects included engaging in a long list of classes of transaction. In **Cotman v Brougham** [1918] AC 514 at pp 522–3, Lord Wrenbury protested against this:

> The objects of the company and the powers of the company to be exercised in effecting the objects are different things. Powers are not required to be, and ought not to be, specified in the memorandum. The Act [ie, CA 1862] intended that the company, if it be a trading company, should by its memorandum define the

trade, not that it should specify the various acts which it should be within the power of the company to do in carrying on the trade.

There has grown up a pernicious practice of registering memoranda of association which, under the clause relating to objects, contain paragraph after paragraph not specifying or delimiting the proposed trade or purpose, but confusing power with purpose and indicating every class of act which the corporation is to have power to do. The practice is not one of recent growth. It was in active operation when I was a junior at the Bar. After a vain struggle I had to yield to it, contrary to my own convictions.

Lord Wrenbury's protest went unheeded, and long objects clauses with express powers for incidental purposes have since become normal in practice.

3.8.5.3 'Incidental and conducive' charitable and political donations

Although there is a legal rule that a company has implied powers to do any act reasonably incidental to the attainment or pursuit of its express objects (see 3.8.5.1), it is usual to conclude an objects clause with the words 'and the doing of all such other things as are incidental or conducive to the attainment of those objects'. In *Evans v Brunner, Mond and Co Ltd* [1921] 1 Ch 359, Eve J accepted the evidence of the company's directors that donating £100,000 to universities or scientific institutions for the furtherance of scientific education and research would be 'conducive to, and indeed necessary for, [the company's] continued progress as chemical manufacturers', and refused to restrain such donations at the instance of a shareholder, finding that they would be within the 'incidental or conducive' provision of the objects clause in the company's old-style memorandum. But in *Simmonds v Heffer* [1983] BCLC 298, Mervyn Davies J emphasised that doing something outside the main objects of a company cannot be incidental or conducive to those main objects: accordingly, contributing to a fund for the election of a Labour government was not within the objects of the League against Cruel Sports, despite a Labour Party commitment to promote legislation which would achieve many of the League's aims. It is probably impossible to explain the different results in *Evans v Brunner, Mond and Co Ltd* and *Simmonds v Heffer* except on the basis of the judges' personal choices.

In *Tomkinson v South-Eastern Railway Co* (1887) 35 ChD 675 (which concerned a statutory company), it was held that donating money to exhibitions, sporting events, and so on was not within the objects of the railway company, and would be restrained. The company had argued that encouraging such events was incidental to its railway business because people would want to travel to them by railway so that encouraging the events would increase the railway's traffic. However, Kay J said, at p 680: 'To say . . . that any expenditure which may indirectly conduce to the benefit of the company is *intra vires*, seems to me extravagant'.

Potential benefit to the company, then, is not enough: a proposed act of a company may be restrained, at the instance of a dissentient member, as being outside the company's restricted objects even if it is thought by the majority of members to be beneficial to the company. In *Evans v Brunner, Mond and Co Ltd* [1921] 1 Ch 359, Eve J said, at pp 368–9:

> When an act of the company is challenged on the ground that it is beyond the powers of the company the challenge is not disposed of by proving that the act is beneficial to the company, it must be established that it is an act the doing of which is authorised by the company's constitution.

Similarly, the fact that something is done in good faith does not bring it within the restricted objects of a company (per North J in *Henderson v Bank of Australasia* (1888) 40 ChD 170 at p 173). As Bowen LJ said in *Hutton v West Cork Railway Co* (1883) 23 ChD 654 (which concerned a statutory company) at p 671:

> Bona fides cannot be the sole test, otherwise you might have a lunatic conducting the affairs of the company, and paying away its money with both hands in a manner perfectly bona fide yet perfectly irrational. The test must be what is reasonably incidental to, and within the reasonable scope of carrying on, the business of the company.

Cases such as *Tomkinson v South-Eastern Railway Co* and *Evans v Brunner, Mond and Co Ltd* show that, unless the articles of a company with restricted objects expressly provide a power to make charitable and political donations, it is always questionable whether they are within the company's objects. It has been suggested that, as charitable giving is a good thing which deserves encouragement, companies should be given a statutory power to make charitable donations (P Graham, 'Removing the Scrooge principle from company law' (1998) 19 Co Law 54).

Under CA 2006, part 14 (which succeeds provisions which first came into force on 16 February 2001), a company may not make political contributions exceeding £5,000 a year without an authorising resolution (see **14.16**).

3.8.5.4 Acts that are not for the company's benefit

In considering a company's restricted objects, a court will not *imply* a power to do something that is not for the benefit of the company (*Hutton v West Cork Railway Co* (1883) 23 ChD 654; *Stroud v Royal Aquarium and Summer and Winter Garden Society Ltd* (1903) 89 LT 243; *Parke v Daily News Ltd* [1962] Ch 927). On the other hand, if the provision of the articles of a company which restricts its objects confers an express power to do something, any exercise by the directors of that express power is valid, whether it benefits the company or not, subject only to the directors' general duty to promote the success of the company (*Re Horsley and Weight Ltd* [1982] Ch 442).

In each of *Hutton v West Cork Railway Co*, *Stroud v Royal Aquarium and Summer and Winter Garden Society Ltd*, and *Parke v Daily News Ltd*, a company had ceased to carry on all, or a major part, of its business and it was proposed to make severance payments to former directors or employees which the company was not contractually obliged to make and which could not be regarded as payment for past services. The courts decided that these payments could not possibly benefit the companies, unlike gratuities paid to employees by a company continuing in business which would benefit from improved relations with the employees or an enhanced reputation as an employer which would attract higher-quality employees in future. CA 2006, s 247(1) (which was first enacted as CA 1980, s 74(1)), now gives directors an express power (if they would not otherwise have it, because of a provision in the company's articles restricting its objects) to provide for employees or former employees on cessation or transfer of the whole or part of the company's undertaking. Section 247(2) expressly provides that the general duty of directors to promote the success of the company does not apply to the exercise of this power.

It is possible for a provision of a company's articles, restricting its objects, to be worded in such a way that making gifts of the company's property is within its objects. As Buckley LJ said in **Re Horsley and Weight Ltd** at p 450:

> The objects of a company do not need to be commercial: they can be charitable or philanthropic . . . Nor is there any reason why a company should not part with its funds gratuitously or for noncommercial reasons if to do so is within its declared objects.

3.8.6 MAIN OBJECTS

When deciding a question of equity between a company with restricted objects and its members, a court may consider an action to be within the company's objects only if it is within what it considers to be the company's 'main object'. This is particularly apparent in cases in which members have petitioned the court for their company to be wound up compulsorily because its substratum has gone (see **3.8.3**). The court may accept in such a case that, because the 'main object' of the company has failed, whatever else the company might do is sufficiently outside its objects to justify compulsory winding up.

For example, in **Re German Date Coffee Co** (1882) 20 ChD 169 the first paragraph of the company's objects clause stated that the company was formed to 'acquire and purchase, and to use, exercise, and vend certain inventions for manufacturing from dates a substitute for coffee, for which a patent has or will be granted by the Empire of Germany to Thomas Frederick Henley'. The second paragraph stated that the company was to 'make and use the said inventions'. In fact, the Empire of Germany refused to grant a patent to Mr Henley for his method of manufacturing date coffee, but the company nevertheless acquired a factory in Hamburg and made date coffee there without patent protection. Two shareholders petitioned for the compulsory winding up of the company on the ground that its substratum had failed. The company opposed the petition, saying that using Mr Henley's *invention* was within its objects even if the invention was not protected by a patent. A winding-up order was made, and was affirmed by the Court of Appeal, where Jessel MR explained that the company's business was not 'to make a substitute for coffee from dates, but to work a particular patent, and as that particular patent does not exist, and cannot now exist, [the petitioners] are entitled to say the company ought to be wound up'. There was some discussion of whether the company's activities were within para 8 of its objects clause, which referred to it being formed 'to import all descriptions of produce for the purposes of food, and the exporting of the same, and the selling and disposing thereof respectively'. Lindley LJ said, at p 188:

> General words construed literally may mean anything; but they must be taken in connection with what are shown by the context to be the dominant or main objects. It will not do under general words to turn a company for manufacturing one thing into a company for importing something else, however general the words are.

Similarly, in deciding whether to restrain a proposed action of a company it may be sufficient that the action is outside what the court finds to be the company's main object (*Stephens v Mysore Reefs (Kangundy) Mining Co Ltd* [1902] 1 Ch 745, in which an injunction was granted; *Pedlar v Road Block Gold Mines of India Ltd* [1905] 2 Ch 427, in which an injunction was refused).

For further discussion of the identification of a company's main objects, see *Re Coolgardie Consolidated Gold Mines Ltd* (1897) 76 LT 269 and *Re Amalgamated Syndicate* [1897] 2 Ch 600.

There is sometimes said to be a 'main objects rule', which was described by Salmon J in **Anglo-Overseas Agencies Ltd v Green** [1961] 1 QB 1 at p 8 as follows:

> where [articles of association express] the objects of the company in a series of paragraphs, and one paragraph, or the first two or three paragraphs, appear to embody the 'main object' of the company, all the other paragraphs are treated as merely ancillary to this 'main object', and as limited or controlled thereby.

In the case of a quasi-partnership company the court may go beyond the articles to determine the members' general intention and common understanding (*Virdi v Abbey Leisure Ltd* [1990] BCLC 342; *Bernhardt v Beau Rivage Pty Ltd* (1989) 15 ACLR 160). Thus, if it was originally the common understanding of the members of a quasi-partnership company that the company should undertake one project only but, on completion of that project, a member who wants the company to be wound up cannot get a special resolution for voluntary winding up adopted because some members wish to go on to another project, then it may be just and equitable to order the compulsory liquidation of the company on the petition of the member who does not want to go on, even if continuing with other projects would be within the objects set out in the company's articles.

3.8.7 SEPARATE-OBJECTS PROVISIONS AND EXPRESS POWERS

To counter the main objects rule (see **3.8.6**), it was usual to list a wide variety of objects in different paragraphs of the objects clause of an old-style memorandum and conclude with a statement to the effect that 'each and every one of the above paragraphs states a separate and independent object of the company'. Such provisions were discussed in *Cotman v Brougham* [1918] AC 514 (which concerned a question between a company and a third party) and have become known as '*Cotman v Brougham*', or 'separate-objects', provisions.

The cautious drafter of an old-style memorandum would usually include dozens of 'separate objects'. However, the courts have decided that some of these are not independent objects but are instead express powers for purposes incidental to the company's true objects. In *Re Horsley and Weight Ltd* [1982] Ch 442 Buckley LJ said, at p 448:

> It has now long been a common practice to set out in memoranda of association a great number and variety of 'objects', so called, some of which (for example, to borrow money, to promote the company's interests by advertising its products or services, or to do acts or things conducive or incidental to the company's objects) are by their very nature incapable of standing as independent objects which can be pursued in isolation as the sole activity of the company. Such 'objects' must, by reason of their very nature, be interpreted merely as powers incidental to the true objects of the company and must be so treated notwithstanding the presence of a separate-objects clause.

In *Rolled Steel Products (Holdings) Ltd v British Steel Corporation* [1986] Ch 246 the Court of Appeal considered how a provision for restricted objects should be interpreted for the purpose of deciding whether or not a transaction is within the company's objects in order to determine whether the company is bound by the transaction. Slade LJ said, at pp 288–9, that full force must be given, so far as possible, to a separate-objects provision. Each paragraph of an objects clause with a separate-objects provision must be treated as containing a substantive object, unless either:

(a) the subject matter of the paragraph is by its nature incapable of constituting a separate object, or

(b) the wording of the objects clause shows expressly or by implication that the paragraph was intended merely to constitute an ancillary power.

In *Re Introductions Ltd* [1970] Ch 199 the first exception was applied to the company's express power to borrow money. Despite a separate-objects provision it was held that borrowing money could not be a substantive object but that money could be borrowed only for the purposes of the company's true objects. At the time of the borrowing in question, the company's only business was one that was not within its restricted objects and so the borrowing was not for the purpose of, or reasonably incidental to, attaining or pursuing the company's objects. It was therefore outside the scope of the directors' actual authority. The construction of the objects clause in *Re Introductions Ltd* seems to be somewhat arbitrary: it may be contrasted with the decision in *Re Horsley and Weight Ltd*, that granting pensions to past and present employees and directors and their dependants and promoting charitable purposes was a substantive object of the company in the case. See further K W Wedderburn, 'Unreformed company law' (1969) 32 MLR 563 at pp 565–6 and '*Ultra vires* in modern company law' (1983) 46 MLR 204 at pp 207–8.

In *Rolled Steel Products (Holdings) Ltd v British Steel Corporation*, the second exception applied. The provision of the objects clause of Rolled Steel Products (Holdings) Ltd (RSP) that it could give guarantees or become security for 'such persons, firms or companies . . . as may seem expedient' was merely a power ancillary to its true objects, despite the presence of a separate-objects provision. The words 'as may seem expedient' could only mean 'as may seem expedient for the furtherance of the objects of the company'. RSP had given a guarantee of a debt (which had already been incurred) owed by another company to the British Steel Corporation. The other company was owned by RSP's managing director and majority shareholder, who had himself already guaranteed the debt but was unable to honour his guarantee (he was subsequently adjudicated bankrupt). RSP's guarantee was secured by a floating charge on its entire property. It was held that the guarantee and charge were not for the purpose of, or reasonably incidental to, attaining or pursuing RSP's objects, so that giving them was beyond the actual authority of its directors.

4

TRANSPARENCY

SUMMARY OF POINTS COVERED

- What is in this chapter
- Information at Companies House
- Public notice of receipt of documents

- Company registers and documents
- Trading disclosures

4.1 WHAT IS IN THIS CHAPTER

The requirements for provision of information about a company are a significant price that must be paid for the benefits of corporate separate personality and, especially, limited liability. Information about a company's constitution, membership, officers and finances must be provided to Companies House (see **4.2** and **4.3**), where it is available for inspection by anyone on payment of prescribed fees. The requirements for filing accounts are considered in detail in **Chapter 9**. Much of this information must also be made available for inspection at the company's registered office or an alternative inspection place (**4.4**). Some other information, including directors' service contracts, must be kept available for inspection by the company's members at its registered office or inspection place (**4.4.3** and **4.4.4**). Any company must identify itself by its registered name at its registered office, inspection place, and places of business. Further identifying information, including its registered number, must be given on business letters, order forms and websites (see **4.5**).

This chapter gives general information about the transparency requirements. Details of what must be disclosed about particular events and transactions are given where those matters are discussed in this book. See, in particular, **2.2** on the information to be provided on registration, **3.5.2** on disclosure of amendments to articles, **6.2.3** and **6.3.6** on disclosures about shares, **Chapter 9** on accounts, **11.7** on registration of charges, **14.3** on the register of members, **15.7** on the register of directors and **17.3.2** on the register of secretaries.

Key legislation which you should be able to consult when reading this chapter:

- CA 2006, ss 82–85, 113–120, 128A–128J, 279A–279E, 790M–790S, 790W–790ZD, 853A–853L, 859P, 859Q, 1064, 1071–1087, 1093–1098, 1103–1105, 1112, 1113. All this legislation is in *Blackstone's Statutes on Company Law*.

- SI 2015/17, which is at the Online Resource Centre for *Blackstone's Statutes on Company Law*: **www.oxfordtextbooks.co.uk/orc/statutes**.

Your particular course of study may require you to read other source materials.

4.2 INFORMATION AT COMPANIES HOUSE

4.2.1 PROVISION OF INFORMATION TO THE REGISTRAR

4.2.1.1 Requirements

The Companies Act 2006 (CA 2006), the Insolvency Act 1986 (IA 1986), the Insolvency (England and Wales) Rules 2016 (SI 2016/1024) and associated statutory instruments require a vast quantity of information to be provided by companies to the registrar of companies at Companies House. CA 2006 usually refers to information being 'delivered' to the registrar, sometimes to notice being 'given' or documents 'sent'. A document is not delivered until it is received and the registrar may prescribe what amounts to receipt (s 1071). The Act often requires the registrar to 'register' a document which has been delivered. The records of information contained in documents delivered to Companies House are referred to collectively in CA 2006 as 'the register' (s 1080).

Some of the requirements in CA 2006 to deliver information are derived from what is now Directive 2009/101/EC, arts 2 and 3(3). Article 2 contains a minimum list of documents which must be filed in companies registries throughout the EEA. In CA 2006 these are referred to as documents subject to the Directive disclosure requirements and they are listed in s 1078.

Requirements to provide information to Companies House are noted in this book when the events giving rise to the requirements are discussed. Two of the most important documents that have to be delivered to Companies House are the annual confirmation statement (see **4.2.5**) and the annual accounts (see **9.5**).

Delivery and registration of a document are two separate events. Registration of a document that has been delivered does not occur until Companies House has checked that the document is acceptable and has completed the administrative process of registering it. On average, this takes three working days. The day on which the process is completed is recorded by Companies House as the date of registration and it is the first day on which the document will be seen by a person who searches the register. Where legislation provides that legal consequences take effect from the date of registration, they do so from the actual date on which Companies House registers the document, not the date on which it is delivered (*Re Globespan Airways Ltd* [2012] EWCA Civ 1159, [2013] 1 WLR 1122). This means that the person who delivers such a document cannot control when it becomes effective.

4.2.1.2 Form

The information that has to be provided to the registrar is recorded and kept at Companies House for inspection by the public. CA 2006, s 1068, therefore entitles the registrar to insist that information is delivered in a form that is convenient for processing. The registrar's current requirement is that documents must be capable of being scanned to produce a digital electronic record (Directive 2009/101/EC, art 3(3)). The registrar must allow electronic submission of documents which are subject to the Directive disclosure requirements (Directive 2009/101/EC, art 3(3); CA 2006, s 1068(5)), but the registrar cannot insist that documents be sent electronically (s 1068(6)). The Secretary of State is empowered to impose that requirement (s 1069), but it is not intended to use the power until electronic communication has become so commonplace that the requirement would be no real burden on companies (Lord McKenzie of Luton, Hansard HL, 28 March 2006, cols GC 348–9). It is not possible to submit documents by fax.

Requirements for proper delivery of documents are listed in s 1072(1). A document which is received by the registrar but does not meet these requirements is to be treated as not delivered (s 1072(2)), unless the registrar decides to accept and register it (s 1073). If Companies House receives a document which appears to be inconsistent with information already registered, it may give notice to the company (s 1093). The notice will require the delivery of such replacement or additional documents as may be required to resolve the inconsistency, and failure to supply those documents is an offence.

4.2.1.3 Language

Documents which are required to be delivered to the registrar must be drawn up and delivered in English (CA 2006, s 1103). An exception is made by s 1105 and SI 2009/1803, reg 7, where documents such as articles of association, contracts or foreign companies' accounts must be delivered. These can be in the original language provided they are accompanied by a certified translation. A Welsh company (see **2.5.1**) may draw up and file documents in Welsh, and may file a certified translation into Welsh of any document that it files in English (s 1104). A document delivered in Welsh must generally be accompanied by a certified translation into English (s 1104(2)), but this translation will be supplied by Companies House for the documents listed in SI 2009/1803, reg 6 (CA 2006, s 1104(3)). Any company may deliver a certified translation into any EU official language of any document that is subject to the Directive disclosure requirements (s 1106; SI 2006/3429, reg 5; Directive 2009/101/EC, art 4(2)).

4.2.1.4 Sanctions

A legislative provision imposing an obligation to deliver information to Companies House is usually backed up by a criminal sanction for failure to deliver.

If a company is in default of any of the provisions requiring information to be delivered to Companies House and fails to comply with a notice requiring the failure to be made good within 14 days, the registrar or any member or creditor of the company may apply to the court for an order requiring the company and any of its officers to make good the default (CA 2006, s 1113). This remedy is in addition to any criminal sanction (s 1113(5)). A similar power is contained in s 452, relating to the presentation of accounts. In addition, a failure to provide information to Companies House may give the registrar reasonable cause to believe that a company is not carrying on business or is not in operation, which may lead to the company being struck off the register under s 1000 (see **20.16.2.4**). A director disqualification order may be made against a person who is persistently in default in delivering information to Companies House (Company Directors Disqualification Act 1986 (CDDA 1986), ss 3 and 5; see **20.13.2.2** and **20.13.2.4**). See also CA 2006, s 27 (notice to comply with obligation to file an amendment to articles), discussed in **3.5.2.1**.

Every director of a company has a duty to ensure that it complies with its obligations to provide information to Companies House and cannot opt out of that responsibility by delegating it or refusing to deal with the matter (*Secretary of State for Trade and Industry v Hall* [2006] EWHC 1995 (Ch), [2009] BCC 190, at [17]).

It is an offence for a person, knowingly or recklessly, to deliver or cause to be delivered, to Companies House a document that is misleading, false or deceptive in a material particular (s 1112).

4.2.2 INSPECTION OF INFORMATION AT COMPANIES HOUSE

4.2.2.1 Rights to inspect and copy

The information that is provided about companies, in accordance with the legislation, to Companies House is recorded and kept for inspection by the public. Any person may inspect the register (CA 2006, s 1085(1)) and require a copy of any material on the register (s 1086(1)). Any person may obtain from Companies House a copy of any company's certificate of incorporation (s 1065). There is no right to inspect an original document unless the record that the registrar has of the contents of the document is illegible or unavailable (s 1085(2)) and Companies House is not required to keep original documents for more than three years (s 1083(2)). Records relating to dissolved companies may be sent to the Public Record Office (part of the National Archives) two years after the dissolution (s 1084(3)). Fees are payable to Companies House for inspection and copies (s 1063; SI 2012/1907).

4.2.2.2 Material not available for inspection

CA 2006, s 1087(1), lists classes of information which Companies House must not make available for public inspection. The most significant class is protected information about residential addresses of directors (see **15.7.3.2**). In addition to the classes listed in s 1087(1), if a company is in administration or administrative receivership, it is possible to obtain a court order of limited disclosure of the company's statement of affairs (see **20.9.2**).

4.2.3 LIABILITY FOR ERRORS IN THE REGISTER

Companies House is required to register the information that is provided to it by companies, but is not required to check that it is accurate, except when registering a new director, and then only the director's consent to act is verified, not his or her identity. The person providing the information is responsible for its accuracy and it is an offence for a person, knowingly or recklessly, to deliver or cause to be delivered, to Companies House a document that is misleading, false or deceptive in a material particular (CA 2006, s 1112). The registrar cannot have any liability to persons inspecting the register for errors and inaccuracies in the information that has been supplied for registration.

Different considerations arise when an inaccuracy is caused by an error in the registration process. In the disturbing case of *Sebry v Companies House* [2015] EWHC 115 (QB), [2015] 1 BCLC 670, a court order for the compulsory winding up of a company called Taylor and Son Ltd was carelessly registered against a long-established company called Taylor and Sons Ltd. The information that Taylor and Sons Ltd was being wound up was picked up immediately by credit reference agencies and suppliers of company information. As a result, Taylor and Sons Ltd's bank ended its overdraft facilities and the company's suppliers refused to deal with it on usual credit terms, insisting on immediate payment of all outstanding debts. The company was forced into administration. At first instance it was held (at [118]) that:

> the Registrar owes a duty of care when entering a winding up order on the Register to take reasonable care to ensure that the order is not registered against the wrong company. That duty is owed to any Company which is not in liquidation but which is wrongly recorded on the Register as having been wound up by order of the court. The duty extends to taking reasonable care to enter the order on the record of the Company named in the order, and not any other company.

It was emphasised that liability is owed only to the company, not to persons who have found inaccurate information by inspecting the register (at [92], [96] and [106]). It was also emphasised that there is no duty to check information supplied by other persons for registration by Companies House (at [118]).

The simple fact that Companies House registers, but does not check the veracity of, filed information is illustrated by *Bank of Beirut SAL v HRH Prince Adel El-Hashemite* [2015] EWHC 1451 (Ch), [2016] Ch 1. A man resident in Germany, HRH Prince Adel El-Hashemite, used forged powers of attorney purportedly given by Lebanese banks, to register limited partnerships at Companies House. In each partnership, a bank was registered as the general partner (with unlimited liability for the firm's debts) and he was the limited partner (with no liability). It was alleged that he used the registration of these limited partnerships to back up his claims to represent the banks and did so for fraudulent purposes. The Limited Partnerships Act 1908, s 8C, provides that a certificate of registration of a limited partnership is conclusive evidence that it came into existence on the date of registration. Nugee J held this means that the court cannot order a certified registration to be cancelled, even if procured by fraud (though this can be done on an application by the Attorney General, see **2.2.3**). Unlike the position with companies, there is currently no provision at all for removing a limited partnership from the register. Nugee J made a declaration that the limited partnerships in this case were registered fraudulently and this is now recorded on the register. The Treasury have proposed amending the law so that dormant limited partnerships can be removed from the register (HM Treasury, *Proposal on using Legislative Reform Order to change partnership legislation for private equity investments. Consultation on draft legislation* (July 2015)).

4.2.4 REMOVAL OF INACCURATE OR SUPERFLUOUS INFORMATION

Companies House may object to the inclusion of unnecessary material in a document when the document is submitted for filing (CA 2006, s 1074). 'Unnecessary material' means material that is not needed to comply with any statutory obligation and for which there is no specific authorisation for its delivery to Companies House (s 1074(2)). Companies House can either reject the document or, if it can be done readily, separate the unnecessary material and register the document without it (s 1074(5)).

Companies House may remove from the register anything that there was power, but no duty, to include (s 1094). Unless removal is requested by the company, notice must be given to a company of intention to remove anything relating to it, and notice will also have to be given to the person who filed the material (s 1094(4) and (5)).

It seems that some users do think it important to include extra information on the register and the Secretary of State has now been given power to make regulations for the recording of 'optional information', meaning information that a company is neither obliged nor authorised under any enactment to deliver to Companies House (s 1084A).

Under s 1095 a procedure has been prescribed in SI 2009/1803, regs 4 and 5, for applying to Companies House to remove from the register material:

(a) that derives from anything invalid or ineffective or that was done without the authority of the company to which it relates; or

(b) that is factually inaccurate, or is derived from something that is factually inaccurate or forged.

If there is a dispute about whether material qualifies for removal under these regulations, the court has a power (CA 2006, s 1096) to direct removal from the register of any material:

(a) that derives from anything which the court has declared to be invalid or ineffective, or to have been done without the authority of the company to which it relates; or

(b) that the court declares to be factually inaccurate, or to be derived from something that is factually inaccurate, or forged.

The court has statutory powers to correct errors in the registration of company charges (ss 859M and 859N; see **11.7.9**).

Anything that appears on the register as the result of a mistake made by Companies House staff will be removed (Adjudicator for Companies House, Annual Report 2007, para 8(b), *Register*, No 68).

4.2.5 CONFIRMATION STATEMENTS

Every company must deliver an annual confirmation statement to Companies House (CA 2006, s 853A(1)). This replaces the previous requirement to deliver much the same information in an annual return.

A confirmation statement confirms that all information required to be delivered by the company to Companies House in relation to the confirmation period concerned either has been delivered or is being delivered at the same time as the confirmation statement (s 853A(1)(b)).

Each confirmation statement must specify a confirmation date. The confirmation period is the period from the day after the previous statement's confirmation date to the present statement's confirmation date (or from the day of the company's incorporation if this is the first confirmation statement) (s 853A(3)). A confirmation date must be no later than the last day of the review period concerned (s 853A(4)). A company's review periods are the successive periods of 12 months from its date of incorporation unless, in a confirmation statement, it gives a confirmation date earlier than the end of a review period. If that happens, the next review period is 12 months starting with the day after that confirmation date (s 853A(5) and (6)).

Information required to be delivered is listed in ss 853B to 853I. Section 853B lists provisions of CA 2006 that require notification of particular events when they occur, for example, the requirement in s 87 to give notice of a change in the address of the company's registered office. The confirmation statement will confirm that any of those events that did occur during the confirmation period were properly notified at the time. Sections 853C to 853I list requirements to notify or state certain features of the company as they are at the date of the confirmation statement. The company must state:

(a) its principal business activities, unless there has been no change in the confirmation period (s 853C);

(b) its capital as set out in a statement of capital, unless there has been no change since the last statement of capital was delivered to Companies House (s 853D);

(c) whether any of the company's shares are publicly traded anywhere and, if so, whether they were admitted to trading on a 'relevant market' and the company was a DTR5 issuer (s 835E);

(d) depending on which category the company is in, information about the company's members (ss 853F and 853G);

(e) if the company is not a DTR5 issuer, but is exempt from keeping a PSC register (of persons with significant control; see **4.4.2.2** and **8.10**), there must be a statement of that fact, unless a previous statement is equally applicable (s 853H); and

(f) the information stated in its PSC register, unless that register is held at Companies House or the company is exempt from keeping one (s 853I).

Section 853E(6) defines a 'relevant market' as any of the markets mentioned in SI 2001/996, art 4(1), that is, any regulated market (see **7.3.4.3**) anywhere in the EEA and all other markets operated by UK recognised investment exchanges (see **7.3.4.2**) including AIM and the ISDX Growth Market. A 'DTR5 issuer' is a company subject to the disclosure requirements of DTR 5 in the FCA Handbook (see **8.9**) (CA 2006, s 853E(6): the Handbook puts a space in DTR 5 but CA 2006 does not). The information required about a company's members depends on which of the following categories the company is in:

(a) If none of the company's shares were, at any time during the confirmation period, shares admitted to trading on a relevant market or on any other market which is outside the United Kingdom, full details must be given (s 853F), see later. Companies in this category are called 'non-traded companies'.

(b) If any of the company's shares were, at any time during the confirmation period, shares admitted to trading on a relevant market or on any other market which is outside the United Kingdom, and the company is not in category (c), information (which is less detailed than is required for non-traded companies) is required only for members who held 5 per cent or more of the issued shares of any class (whether that class is admitted to trading or not) at any time during the confirmation period (s 853G).

(c) If throughout the confirmation period there were shares of the company which were shares admitted to trading on a relevant market, and the company was a DTR5 issuer, no information about members is required. Such companies already make information about major shareholders public as required by DTR 5 in the FCA Handbook (see **8.9**).

A company in category (a) must deliver with its confirmation statement a list of the names of all persons who were members of the company at any time during the confirmation period, stating the number of shares of each class that they held at the end of the confirmation date (s 853F(5)(a) and (b)). For each person who was a member at any time during the confirmation period, the numbers of each class of shares transferred by or to the member during the confirmation period must be stated and the dates of registration of the transfers (s 853F(5)(c) and (d)).

A company in category (b) is required to state only the name and address of each member who held at least 5 per cent of the issued shares of any class of the company at the end of the confirmation date and the number of shares of each class held by the person at that time (s 853G(6)).

Information about members is not required if and to the extent that it is the same as the information most recently delivered with a confirmation statement (ss 853F(4) and 853G(5)).

There are criminal sanctions for failure to deliver a confirmation statement within 14 days after the end of a review period (s 853L).

Companies House must give public notice of receipt of a company's confirmation statement (ss 1077 and 1078(2); see **4.3**).

As explained in **1.3.2.4**, in the early nineteenth century, any company which was under a statutory duty to supply a list of its members to a public office was regarded as being a 'public company'. Accordingly, any registered company with a share capital is a 'public company' for the purposes of legislation in which that term is used without further definition, for example the Apportionment Act 1870, s 5 (*Re Lysaght* [1898] 1 Ch 115). This is so even if the company is a 'private company' for the purposes of the companies legislation (*Re White* [1913] 1 Ch 231).

The original reason for requiring companies to reveal the names of their members was that a company's members usually had only partly paid shares and their ability to pay any calls which might be made was an important element of the company's creditworthiness. Now that partly paid shares are no longer in use this reason has disappeared.

It is not correct to try to resolve a dispute with a company about the accuracy of information in a confirmation statement by bringing a claim requiring Companies House to correct the information: the claim should be brought against the company and those asserting that the information is correct (*Archer v Registrar General* [2004] UKPC 31, 64 WIR 308).

4.3 PUBLIC NOTICE OF RECEIPT OF DOCUMENTS

Directive 2009/101/EC, art 3(5), requires disclosure of the documents listed in art 2 by publication in the national gazette, or by equally effective electronic means, of either the text of the document or a reference to its entry in the register. The UK forms of the documents required to be disclosed in this way are the documents subject to Directive disclosure requirements listed in CA 2006, s 1078. Companies House must cause to be published notice of receipt of any document which is subject to the Directive disclosure requirements (s 1077(1)). The notice must state the name and registered number of the company, the description of the document, and the date of receipt (s 1077(2)).

At present, for companies registered in England and Wales, these notices are published in weekly supplements to the *London Gazette*. Section 1116 gives the Secretary of State power to provide for publication by electronic means.

Companies House notifies in the same way the issue of a certificate of incorporation when a company is registered or re-registered, or changes its name, or becomes or ceases to be a Welsh company (s 1064). This notification is not required by the Directive.

Certain events affecting companies have profound effects on how other persons deal with them. Persons who deal with companies are given some protection by s 1079. This provides that a company cannot rely, against another person, on the happening of any event listed in s 1079(2) if, at the material time, the event had not been officially notified, unless the company can prove that the other person knew of the event. The events are:

(a) an amendment of the company's articles;

(b) a change among the company's directors;

(c) (as regards service of any document on the company) a change of the company's registered office;

(d) the making of a winding-up order in respect of the company; and

(e) the appointment of a liquidator in a voluntary winding up of the company.

In relation to events (a) to (d), 'official notification' means publication of notice of the receipt of the relevant document by Companies House as required by s 1077 (s 1079(4)(a) and (b)). In the case of an amendment of the company's articles, receipt of both the amendment and the amended articles must have been notified (s 1079(4)(a)). For event (e), 'official notification' means publication of a notice in the *London Gazette*, as required by the Insolvency Act 1986, s 109.

In addition, if the material time was on or before the fifteenth day after official notification (or the next business day if the fifteenth day is not a business day), the company will not be able to rely on an event if it is shown that the other person was unavoidably prevented from knowing of it at that time (CA 2006, s 1079(3)).

Section 1079 is primarily intended to protect persons dealing with companies rather than to protect companies themselves, and so a company cannot rely on official notification of any event specified in s 1079(2) as being constructive notice to other persons that the event has occurred (*Official Custodian for Charities v Parway Estates Developments Ltd* [1985] Ch 151).

In addition, people are not deemed to have constructive notice of any information published in the *Gazette* but not covered by s 1079 (*Ewart v Fryer* [1901] 1 Ch 499—reported on this point only in 82 LT 415 at pp 416–17; see also the same case in the House of Lords [1902] AC 187 per Lord Macnaghten at p 193 and Lord Lindley at p 194). In *Re Mawcon Ltd* [1969] 1 WLR 78, Pennycuick J said that the notice in the *Gazette* that a provisional liquidator had been appointed (required at that time by SI 1949/330, regs 42(1)(a) and (c)) was notice to all of the appointment; but *Ewart v Fryer* was not cited to his lordship and it is submitted that his decision on this point is wrong.

4.4 COMPANY REGISTERS AND DOCUMENTS

4.4.1 GENERAL REQUIREMENTS

A company is required to maintain registers and certain documents relating to its affairs for inspection by various people. Some of this information may duplicate information recorded and available for inspection at Companies House (see **4.2**). Apart from the statutory provisions discussed here, the members of a company have no legal right to inspect or take copies of its documents (*Lonrho Ltd v Shell Petroleum Co Ltd* [1980] 1 WLR 627 per Lord Diplock at p 634).

The legislation makes provision for:

(a) Who may inspect. Some registers and documents may be inspected by any person (**4.4.2**), some by members and creditors only (**4.4.3**), some by members only (**4.4.4**) and some only by company officers (**4.4.5**).

(b) Where inspection may be made. Each provision requiring a company to keep something available for inspection provides that it may be kept at the company's registered office or at some other inspection place permitted by regulations made under CA 2006, s 1136. Those regulations are in SI 2008/3006 and they provide that, apart from its registered office, a company can have only one other inspection place (reg 3). This is called the single alternative inspection location (SAIL). It must be in the part of the United Kingdom in which the company is registered and it must be notified to Companies House. Any person with whom a company deals in the course of business may require it to disclose, within five working days, the addresses of its registered office and inspection place and identify the records it keeps for inspection at each place (SI 2015/17, reg 27). Private companies may opt to keep some registers for inspection only at Companies House (see **4.4.2.9**).

(c) Whether a fee may be charged for inspection. The fees that may be charged are specified in SI 2007/2612, SI 2007/3535 and SI 2008/3007.

(d) Whether a person making an inspection may, on payment of a fee, require the company to supply a copy of the register or document. The fees that may be charged are specified in SI 2007/2612, SI 2007/3535 and SI 2008/3007. Whether or not there is a right to ask the company to supply a copy, a person with a right to inspect a register or document has a right to make a copy personally (*Mutter v Eastern and Midlands Railway Co* (1888) 38 ChD 92; *Nelson v Anglo-American Land Mortgage Agency Co* [1897] 1 Ch 130).

(e) The court to order immediate inspection or direct that a copy be supplied, if inspection is refused or a copy is not provided.

(f) A criminal sanction for not keeping the register or document available.

(g) A criminal sanction for not informing Companies House where the register is kept.

(h) A criminal sanction for refusing inspection by someone entitled to inspect or refusing to supply copies to a person entitled to ask for them.

4.4.2 REGISTERS AND DOCUMENTS THAT MAY BE INSPECTED BY ANY PERSON

4.4.2.1 Register of members

Every company must keep a register of its members (CA 2006, s 113), which must be kept available for inspection (s 114) by any person (s 116(1)). If there are more than 50 members, there must be an index of their names, unless the register of members is itself arranged in name order (s 115) and the index must be kept available for inspection with the register (s 115(4)). Private companies will be able to keep this register at Companies House (see **4.4.2.9**).

If the register of members of a British company was created before 1 July 1948 (when CA 1948 came into force), exemption from the obligation to give Companies House notice of the place where the register is available for inspection is available if it has been kept at the company's registered office since 1 July 1948 (for Northern Ireland companies the date is 1 April 1961) (s 114(3) and (4)).

Any member of a company may inspect its register of members free of charge; any other person may be charged a fee (s 116(1)). Any person may require a copy of the register on payment of a fee (s 116(2)).

Anyone seeking to inspect or copy a register of members must make a request to the company (s 116(3)) giving his or her name and address (an individual must be named when an application is made by an organisation), specifying the purpose for which the information is to be used, and stating whether the information will be disclosed to any other person (s 116(4)). If the information is to be disclosed to another person, that person's name and address must be given and the purpose for which that other person will use the information must be stated (s 116(4)(d)). It is an offence, triable either way, to make knowingly or recklessly a statement in such a request that is misleading, false or deceptive in a material particular (s 119). By s 117, the company has five working days either to comply with the request or apply to the court for a direction under s 117(3) that it need not comply because the inspection or copy is not sought for a proper purpose. Identifying persons as targets for violence, harassment or intimidation would obviously not be a proper purpose. The court has a power, on finding that a company need not comply with an inspection request, to direct the company not to comply with similar requests, whether from the same person or other persons (s 117(4)).

There is no guidance in the Act on what would or would not be a proper purpose, though the Institute of Chartered Secretaries and Administrators (ICSA) has published suggestions in *ICSA Guidance on Access to the Register of Members: Proper Purpose Test*. The onus is on the company to satisfy the court on a balance of probabilities that the purpose for which access is sought is not a proper one (*Re Burry and Knight Ltd* [2014] EWCA Civ 604, [2014] 1 WLR 4046, at [22]). The court may conclude that the true purpose is not that stated in the request for access (*Re Burry and Knight Ltd* at [21]). Communicating to members something that has no value or utility to them as members is not a proper purpose (*Re Burry and Knight Ltd* in which the request was from a member who had become obsessed with unsubstantiated allegations of wrongdoing long ago and wanted to communicate them to other members). Exploitation of a list of members for commercial gain is not a proper purpose unless it advances their interests in some way (*Burberry Group plc v Fox-Davies* [2015] EWHC 222 (Ch), [2015] 2 BCLC 66).

When a company allows inspection, or supplies a copy, of its register of members, it must state the date to which the register has been made up (s 120).

If a company has uncertificated shares, the rules on inspection of the register of members apply instead to the company's issuer register of members and its record of uncertificated shares (SI 2001/3755, sch 4, para 9) (see **14.3.2**). The Operator register of members is not open to public inspection.

4.4.2.2 PSC register

CA 2006, s 790M, requires every company which is not a DTR 5 issuer to keep a register of people with significant control over the company, known as a PSC register (see **8.10**). This must be kept available for inspection (s 790N) by any person without charge (s 790O(1)). Sections 790O to 790R make the same provision for inspections to be for a proper purpose as is made in relation to the register of members (see **4.4.2.1**). Private companies may keep this register at Companies House (see **4.4.2.9**). When a company allows inspection, or supplies a copy, of its PSC register, it must state the most recent date (if any) on which alterations were made to the register and whether there are further alterations to be made (s 790S).

4.4.2.3 Register of directors

Every company must keep a register of its directors (see **15.7.1**) available for inspection (CA 2006, s 162). Any member of a company may inspect its register of directors free of charge; any other person may be charged a fee (s 162(5)). A company's register of directors does not include their residential addresses. Those are in a separate register (s 165), which is not open to inspection (see **15.7.3**). Private companies will be able to keep these registers at Companies House (see **4.4.2.9**).

4.4.2.4 Register of secretaries

Every public company, and every private company which has a secretary, must keep a register of secretaries available for inspection (CA 2006, s 275). Any member of a company may inspect its register of secretaries free of charge; any other person may be charged a fee (s 275(5)). Private companies will be able to keep this register at Companies House (see **4.4.2.9**).

4.4.2.5 Public company's contract to purchase its own shares

Any person may inspect a copy of every contract (or memorandum of the terms of an unwritten contract) made by a public company to purchase its own shares (CA 2006, s 702(6)). A copy or memorandum of a contract must be kept available for inspection from the time it is concluded until ten years after the date on which the purchase under the contract was completed or the contract otherwise determined (s 702). No fee may be charged for inspection (s 702(6)).

4.4.2.6 Register of debentures

It is not compulsory to keep a register of debentures (see **12.4**), but if one is kept, it must be open to inspection by any person (CA 2006, s 744). As with registers of members (see **4.4.2.1**), there are provisions to ensure that inspection and copying are for a proper purpose (ss 744 to 747).

4.4.2.7 Investigation into interests in public company's shares

A public company must keep a register of interests disclosed in response to notices under CA 2006, s 793, requiring information about interests in its shares (s 808). The register must be kept available for inspection (s 809) by any person without charge (s 811(1)). Any person may require a copy of the register on payment of a fee (s 811(2)). As with the register of members (see **4.4.2.1**), there are provisions to ensure that inspection and copying are for a proper purpose (ss 811, 812 and 814).

If the members of a public company requisition an investigation into interests in shares, the company's report of the information received must be kept available for at least six years for inspection (s 805) by any person without charge (s 807(1)). Any person may require a copy of the report on payment of a fee (s 807(2)).

4.4.2.8 Charges

By CA 2006, s 859P, every company must keep available for inspection a copy of every instrument creating a charge capable of registration under part 25, ch A1 (ss 859A to 859Q; see **11.7.15**), but there is no criminal sanction for not doing so. Any creditor or member of a company may inspect the copy instruments free of charge; any other person may be charged a fee (s 859Q(4)).

4.4.2.9 Central registration

Private companies may opt to keep any (or all) of the following registers at Companies House, on what is called the 'central register': register of members (CA 2006, ss 128A to 128J), of directors and/or directors' residential addresses (ss 167A to 167E), of secretaries (ss 279A to 279E), and a PSC register (of people with significant control) (ss 790W to 790ZD). A company's registers of directors, directors' residential addresses and secretaries simply duplicate records that are held at Companies House anyway. The Secretary of State has power to permit public companies or a particular class of public companies, to keep PSC registers at Companies House (s 790ZE).

An election to keep a register centrally is made by giving notice to Companies House (ss 128B(3), 167A(3), 279A(2) and 790X(4)). The election may be made by the subscribers when they form a private company or by the company itself after it has been registered (ss 128B(1), 167A(2), 279A(1) and 790X(1)). An election to keep the register of members centrally can be made after a company is registered only if all members of the company assent (s 128B(2)). An election at any time to keep the PSC register centrally can only be made if persons who are to be, or are, on the register have not objected (s 790X(2) and (3)). An election may be withdrawn by giving notice to Companies House (ss 128J, 167E, 279E and 790ZD).

While an election for central registration is in force, the company has a duty to notify Companies House of any changes that it would otherwise have to record in its own register (ss 128E, 167D, 279D and 790ZA). Anyone inspecting a register of members on the central register is entitled to ask the company to confirm that it has complied with this requirement and failure to respond to such a request is an offence (s 128F).

An election in respect of a register of members made by a company after it has been registered only transfers to Companies House entries in the register in respect of matters that are current when the election takes effect (s 128B(5) and (6)). The company must still keep a 'historic' register containing all the information that was required to be stated in the register of members immediately before the election took effect. However, the company does not have to update that register to reflect any changes that occur after that time (s 128D(3)). The same applies to a PSC register (ss 790X(6)(b) and (7) and 790Z(3)).

4.4.3 DOCUMENTS THAT MAY BE INSPECTED BY MEMBERS AND CREDITORS ONLY

Any member or creditor of a company may inspect the directors' statement and auditor's report required in connection with a payment out of capital by a company for the redemption or purchase of its own shares (CA 2006, s 720). These documents must be kept available for inspection for a period of five weeks after adopting the resolution to make the payment (s 720(1)), but there is no criminal sanction for not doing so. No fee may be charged for inspection (s 720(4)).

Any member and any debenture holder of a company is entitled, on request, to be sent a copy of its last annual accounts and reports (ss 431 and 432; see **9.6.1.2**).

4.4.4 DOCUMENTS AND RECORDS THAT MAY BE INSPECTED BY MEMBERS ONLY

4.4.4.1 Directors' service contracts

Every company must keep a copy of every director's service contract with the company or any of its subsidiaries (CA 2006, s 228) available for inspection by its members free of charge (s 229(1)). If a service contract is not in writing, a written memorandum setting out its terms must be available for inspection (s 228(1)(b)). Availability for inspection must continue for at least one year from the date of termination or expiry of the contract (s 228(3)). This provision applies to shadow directors (s 230). Any member may require a copy of a contract or memorandum on payment of a fee (s 229(2)).

4.4.4.2 Qualifying indemnity provision

Every company must keep a copy of any qualifying indemnity provision made for any of its directors or a director of an associated company (CA 2006, s 237) available for inspection by its members free of charge (s 229(1)). If the provision is not in writing, a written memorandum setting out its terms must be available for inspection (s 237(2)(b)). Availability for inspection must continue for at least one year from the date of termination or expiry of the provision (s 237(4)). Any member may require a copy of a provision or memorandum on payment of a fee (s 238(2)).

4.4.4.3 Records of resolutions and meetings

The records of resolutions and meetings which a company must keep for ten years (CA 2006, s 355) must be kept available for inspection by any member of the company (s 358(1)). Any member may require a copy of the records on payment of a fee (s 116(2)).

4.4.4.4 Private company's contract to purchase its own shares

The provisions concerning inspection of contracts made by a company to purchase its own shares (CA 2006, ss 702 and 703; see **4.4.2.5**) also apply to private companies, except that only a member of a private company has a right of inspection (s 702(6)).

4.4.4.5 Documents in connection with resolutions

There are provisions of CA 2006 under which resolutions on certain matters will be ineffective unless documents relating to those matters are available for inspection by members when they consider the resolution. See s 188(5) (approval of director's service contract, discussed in **15.9.4**), s 696 (resolutions relating to off-market purchases of the company's own shares, discussed in **10.6.4**), and s 718 (approval of payment out of capital for redemption or purchase of company's own shares, discussed in **10.5.3**).

4.4.4.6 Right to copies of constitutional documents

A member of a company is entitled, on request, to be sent a copy of the company's constitutional documents (CA 2006, s 32; see **3.2.1**).

4.4.5 RECORDS THAT MAY BE INSPECTED BY OFFICERS ONLY

A company must keep accounting records at its registered office or at such other place as the directors may determine, and these records must be open to inspection at all times by the officers of the company (CA 2006, s 388(1); see further **9.3.3**).

4.5 TRADING DISCLOSURES

4.5.1 IDENTIFICATION OF A COMPANY

Every company must disclose the following information about itself on its business letters, its order forms and its websites:

(a) its registered name;

(b) the part of the United Kingdom in which it is registered;

(c) its registered number; and

(d) the address of its registered office.

These requirements are imposed by SI 2015/17 regs 24 and 25. Those regulations have been made under CA 2006, s 82, implementing Directive 2009/101/EC, art 5.

If a company with a share capital mentions its capital in any of these places, the reference must be to the paid-up capital (see **6.5.5**) (Directive 2009/101/EC, art 5; SI 2015/17, reg 25(3)).

A company's registered name must be displayed at its registered office, at any inspection place (see **4.4.1**) (SI 2015/17, reg 21(1)), and at any other location where it carries on business, except one primarily used for living accommodation (reg 22). Regulation 21(1) does not apply to dormant companies (reg 21(2)). For other exemptions see **4.5.4** and **15.7.3.2**.

SI 2015/17, reg 24(1), requires a company's registered name to be disclosed on all its business correspondence and documentation (reg 24(1)(g)) and provides a long list of particular types of document on which the name must be disclosed. These include cheques purporting to be signed by or on behalf of the company (reg 24(1)(c)), invoices and other demands for payment (reg 24(1)(e)), and applications for licences to carry on a trade or activity (reg 24(1)(f)).

Display or disclosure required by SI 2015/17 must be in characters that can be read with the naked eye (reg 20). A display at an office or other location must be positioned so that it may easily be seen by any visitor (reg 23). There can be a rolling or scrolling display if the office or location is shared by six or more companies (reg 23(3)).

CA 2006, s 45(2), requires a company to have its name engraved in legible characters on its common seal (see **19.2.2**).

Failure to comply with any of these requirements is a summary offence (SI 2015/17, reg 28; CA 2006, s 45(3) to (5)).

Contravention of these rules has been specified in SI 2003/1593, sch, part 1, as a domestic infringement for the purposes of the Enterprise Act 2002, part 8 (ss 210 to 236). This means that the Competition and Markets Authority, or any local weights and measures authority (trading standards), can take action under part 8 if an infringement harms the collective interests of consumers in the United Kingdom. The court may make an enforcement order requiring the infringer not to continue or repeat the infringing conduct (s 217) or the enforcing authority may accept an undertaking not to do so (s 219).

4.5.2 USING AN INCORRECT NAME: EFFECT ON VALIDITY OF TRANSACTION

In general, a failure by those acting on behalf of a company to state its name correctly when causing the company to enter into a transaction will not invalidate the transaction. For example, in *OTV Birwelco Ltd v Technical and General Guarantee Co Ltd* [2002] EWHC 2240 (TCC), [2002] 4 All ER 668, a company called Woodbank UK (Mechanical and Electrical) Ltd continued to use the name and company seal of a company called Woodbank UK Ltd, whose business it had bought. It was held that when the old seal was used to execute a deed, it was used as the new company's seal, and the fact that it had what was in effect the new company's trading name rather than its corporate name, as required by CA 2006, s 45(2) (see **19.2.2**), did not invalidate the deed. The fact that all documentation relating to a contract with a company is in the company's trading name without mentioning its registered name does not in itself make the contract illegal and unenforceable (*Moreland Metal Co Ltd v Cowlishaw* (1919) 19 SR (NSW) 231). The fact that a company has illegally used a business name without mentioning its corporate name does not mean that the company is precluded from bringing a claim for passing off against a rival who has used a similar business name (*Pearks, Gunston and Tee Ltd v Thompson, Talmey and Co* (1901) 18 RPC 185; *H E Randall Ltd v British and American Shoe Co* [1902] 2 Ch 354). However, it is possible that refusing to disclose the true name of a company in connection with a transaction will lead to dismissal of proceedings to enforce the transaction (CA 2006, s 1206).

The fact that a company is misnamed in a document does not make the document ineffective, provided it is clear that it was intended to name that company (*Bird and Co (London) Ltd v Thomas Cook and Son (Bankers) Ltd* [1937] 2 All ER 227; *F Goldsmith (Sicklesmere) Ltd v Baxter* [1970] Ch 85; *Badgerhill Properties Ltd v Cottrell* [1991] BCLC 805). If, however, it is not clear that it was intended to name the company, the document will not be effective (*Davies v Elsby Brothers Ltd* [1961] 1 WLR 170).

4.5.3 DIRECTORS

Under a law introduced in the middle of the First World War, and intended to force businesses to reveal whether they were controlled by foreigners, every company registered on or after

23 November 1916 was required to list the names and nationalities of all its directors on all its business letters. This was usually done by listing them on pre-printed stationery, but in practice companies found it difficult to comply with the law and ensure that stationery was changed every time board membership changed. So CA 1981 made a statement of directors' names on stationery optional. It introduced a rule that if directors are named on stationery (other than in the body of the letter or as signatory), all directors, including shadow directors (see **15.3.3**), must be named. The rule continued to apply only to companies registered on or after 23 November 1916, but the requirement to state directors' nationalities was dropped. The rule introduced by CA 1981 is continued by SI 2015/17, reg 26, but no longer requires shadow directors to be named.

4.5.4 INSOLVENCY

If a company is the subject of various insolvency and liquidation procedures, that fact must be stated on all invoices, orders for goods and services and business letters, if they are issued by or on behalf of the company or its receiver, manager, liquidator or administrator, and on all its websites. The facts which, if they exist, must be mentioned are:

(a) that a receiver or manager of the company's property (including an administrative receiver) has been appointed (IA 1986, s 39);

(b) that the company is being wound up (s 188);

(c) that a moratorium to enable preparation of a voluntary arrangement is in force, in which case the nominee's name must be given (sch A1, para 16); and

(d) that the company is in administration, in which case the administrator's name must be given (sch B1, para 45).

Failure to state the appropriate facts is a summary offence (IA 1986, sch 10).

If a company's registered office, inspection place or place at which it carries on business is at a place of business of its liquidator, administrator or administrative receiver, its registered name need not be displayed there (SI 2015/17, regs 21(3) and 22(4)).

4.5.5 CHARITABLE COMPANIES

By the Charities Act 2011, ss 193 and 194(1), if a company is a charity and its name does not include the word 'charity' or the word 'charitable', the fact that the company is a charity must be stated in legible characters:

(a) in every location, and in every document or communication, where it is required by SI 2015/17 to state its name (see **4.5.1**); and

(b) in all conveyances purporting to be executed by the company.

In this provision, 'conveyance' means any instrument creating, transferring, varying or extinguishing an interest in land (s 194(4)). The statement must be in English, or in Welsh in a document that is wholly in Welsh (s 194(2) and (3)).

It is important for persons dealing with a charitable company to appreciate that it is a charitable company because, unlike other companies, a charitable company's contractual capacity is limited (see **19.4.2**).

5

CORPORATE PERSONALITY

SUMMARY OF POINTS COVERED

- What is in this chapter
- Effects of separate corporate personality
- Piercing the corporate veil

- Connections between a company and other persons
- Corporate law theory
- Company linguistics
- Companies' human rights

5.1 WHAT IS IN THIS CHAPTER

Legally, the most important feature of a company is that it is both an association of its members and a person separate from its members (see **1.3.1**). This is reflected by grammatically treating a company sometimes as plural, sometimes as singular (see **5.6**). As a person separate from its members, a company can own property, enter into contracts and be a party to legal proceedings. As persons separate from the company, the members do not own the company's property, do not carry on its business and do not owe its debts. In *Salomon v A Salomon and Co Ltd* [1897] AC 22 (see **5.2.1**) every effort was made, on behalf of creditors of a failed company, to impose liability for the company's debts on its controlling shareholder. All the efforts failed, because the House of Lords affirmed the separate corporate personality of a company. Further consequences of separate corporate personality are discussed in **5.2.2** to **5.2.7**.

Although *Salomon v A Salomon and Co Ltd* affirmed separate corporate personality, it was often asserted that courts are able to ignore it, a process known as 'piercing the corporate veil' (see **5.3**). The Supreme Court, in *Prest v Petrodel Resources Ltd* [2013] UKSC 34, [2013] 2 AC 415, has shown that this is almost entirely mythical. There is probably only one circumstance in which veil piercing is possible. That is where veil piercing is necessary in order to apply the evasion principle (see **5.3.6.2**). In practice, veil piercing is never necessary. Inquiring into connections between a company and its members, directors or others does not ignore separate corporate personality and does not amount to piercing the corporate veil (see **5.3.6.1** and **5.4**).

Section **5.5** moves to the deeper question of how an artificial entity can have legal personality. The section examines some of the theories advanced in the philosophy of law to deal with this question.

One consequence of the separate personality of a company is that it can sometimes claim human rights, which, for this purpose, might be better described as personal rights (see **5.7**).

The following cases, which are considered in this chapter, are particularly significant and are recommended further reading:

- *Lee v Lee's Air Farming Ltd* [1961] AC 12 (also a key case for **Chapter 15**);
- *Macaura v Northern Assurance Co Ltd* [1925] AC 619;

- *Prest v Petrodel Resources Ltd* [2013] UKSC 34, [2013] 2 AC 415;

- *Salomon v A Salomon and Co Ltd* [1897] AC 22; and

- *VTB Capital plc v Nutritek International Corporation* [2013] UKSC 5, [2013] 2 AC 337.

Your particular course of study may require you to read other source materials.

5.2 EFFECTS OF SEPARATE CORPORATE PERSONALITY

5.2.1 *SALOMON'S* CASE

A company has a dual nature as both an association of its members and a person separate from its members. A company's property is owned by the company as a separate person, not by the members; the company's business is conducted by the company as a separate person, not by the members; it is the company as a separate person that enters into contracts in relation to the company's business and property.

The leading case on the fundamental importance of the separate personality of a company is **Salomon v A Salomon and Co Ltd** [1897] AC 22. In a poll of subscribers to the Law Reports, this was chosen as one of the 15 most significant cases reported in the period 1865–2015.

As explained in **2.3.3.2**, it was common in the late nineteenth century for businesses previously conducted by sole proprietors or partnerships to be 'incorporated'. The business would be sold to a company whose only members were its previous owner or owners and sufficient nominees to make up the then minimum number of seven members (the minimum number of members of a company is now one). Mr Salomon had conducted his bootmaking business as a sole trader. He sold it to a company incorporated for the purpose called A Salomon and Co Ltd whose only members were himself, his wife, a daughter and four sons. These seven individuals were the subscribers of the company's memorandum and took one £1 share each. The business was sold to the company for over £39,000. Part of the purchase price was used by Mr Salomon to subscribe for 20,000 further £1 shares in the company, but £10,000 of the purchase price was not paid by the company. Instead, the company issued Mr Salomon with a series of debentures (written acknowledgements of indebtedness) for £10,000 and gave him a floating charge on its assets as security for the debt (floating charges are explained in **11.6**). Unfortunately the company's business failed and the company went into liquidation. As will be explained in **11.6**, the holder of a floating charge on a company's assets is entitled, on the liquidation of the company, to have the assets covered by the charge applied to the payment of the debt secured by the charge. If Mr Salomon had been able to enforce his floating charge, the company's other creditors would have got nothing. The company's liquidator took a stand on behalf of the other creditors. He resisted Mr Salomon's claim and suggested that, rather than take money from his company, Mr Salomon should be made responsible for paying all its debts, just as he would have if he had continued to conduct the business as a sole trader. The liquidator wanted somehow to ignore the fact that Mr Salomon had sold his business to a separate person, A Salomon and Co Ltd, and that Mr Salomon now had only limited liability to that company instead of the unlimited liability he had when he conducted the business as a sole trader.

At first instance (sub nom *Broderip v Salomon* [1895] 2 Ch 323), it was held that the company had conducted the business as agent for Mr Salomon, so that he was responsible for all debts incurred in the course of the agency for him. The House of Lords rejected this approach. Lord Herschell said ([1897] AC 22 at p 43):

> In a popular sense, a company may in every case be said to carry on business for and on behalf of its shareholders; but this certainly does not in point of law constitute the relation of principal and agent between them or render the shareholders liable to indemnify the company against the debts which it incurs.

In the Court of Appeal (sub nom *Broderip v Salomon* [1895] 2 Ch 323 at p 333), it was held that Mr Salomon had incorporated the company contrary to the true intent and meaning of CA 1862, and that, because of Mr Salomon's fraud, the company should be declared to have operated the business as trustee for Mr Salomon, who should therefore indemnify the company for all debts incurred in carrying out the trust. The House of Lords also rejected this argument. There was nothing at all in the Act to show that what Mr Salomon had done was prohibited. Indeed, Lord Macnaghten pointed out ([1897] AC 22 at p 52) that in an earlier case (*Re Baglan Hall Colliery Co* (1870) LR 5 Ch App 346), Giffard LJ had said (at p 356) that it was 'the policy of the Companies Act' to enable business people to incorporate their businesses and so avoid incurring further personal liability. Lord Macnaghten said ([1897] AC 22 at p 51):

> When the memorandum is duly signed and registered . . . the subscribers are a body corporate 'capable forthwith', to use the words of the enactment, 'of exercising all the functions of an incorporated company'. Those are strong words. The company attains maturity on its birth. There is no period of minority—no interval of incapacity. I cannot understand how a body corporate thus made 'capable' by statute can lose its individuality by issuing the bulk of its capital to one person, whether he be a subscriber to the memorandum or not. The company is at law a different person altogether from the subscribers to the memorandum; and, though it may be that after incorporation the business is precisely the same as it was before, and the same persons are managers, and the same hands receive the profits, the company is not in law the agent of the subscribers or trustee for them. Nor are the subscribers as members liable, in any shape or form, except to the extent and in the manner provided by the Act. That is, I think, the declared intention of the enactment.

Lord Halsbury LC said, at pp 30–1:

> it seems to me impossible to dispute that once the company is legally incorporated it must be treated like any other independent person with its rights and liabilities appropriate to itself, and that the motives of those who took part in the promotion of the company are absolutely irrelevant in discussing what those rights and liabilities are.

For the background to *Salomon v A Salomon and Co Ltd*, which is probably the most famous case in company law, see G R Rubin, 'Aron Salomon and his circle', in *Essays for Clive Schmitthoff*, John Adams (ed) (Abingdon: Professional Books, 1983), pp 99–120. Following the case, Parliament enacted provisions in the Companies Act 1900 requiring the public registration of charges on company property (see **11.7**) and in the Companies Act 1907 enabling liquidators to avoid floating charges given to secure pre-existing debts (see **11.6.7.1**). L S Sealy, 'Modern insolvency laws and Mr Salomon' (1998) 16 C & SLJ 176, discusses various statutory provisions which might have applied if *Salomon*'s case had occurred a century later than it did, but concludes that it is unlikely Mr Salomon could be made liable under them.

5.2.2 A COMPANY'S BUSINESS IS ITS BUSINESS

The House of Lords in *Salomon v A Salomon and Co Ltd* [1897] AC 22 recognised that a company's business is conducted by the company as a separate person (see also per Lord Sumner in *Gas Lighting Improvement Co Ltd v Commissioners of Inland Revenue* [1923] AC 723 quoted in **5.5.2**). It is the company as a separate person that owns the company's property and enters into contracts and incurs debts. This has been affirmed in many different contexts.

It is the company as a separate person that conducts the company's business and so any defamatory statement made about that business defames the company as a separate person, which may sue for libel or slander (*Metropolitan Saloon Omnibus Co Ltd v Hawkins* (1859) 4 Hurl & N 87; *South Hetton Coal Co Ltd v North-Eastern News Association Ltd* [1894] 1 QB 133; *Jameel v Wall Street Journal Europe SPRL* [2006] UKHL 44, [2007] 1 AC 359). A company, as a person separate from its members, may even sue one of its own members for libel (*Metropolitan Saloon Omnibus Co Ltd v*

Hawkins). However, a company cannot be awarded aggravated damages, because aggravated damages compensate for injury to feelings caused by the manner in which a wrong was committed, and a company has no feelings to be injured (*Collins Stewart Ltd v Financial Times Ltd* [2005] EWHC 262 (QB), [2006] EMLR 5).

In *Cristina v Seear* [1985] 2 EGLR 128, Mr and Mrs Cristina claimed the protection of part II of the Landlord and Tenant Act 1954, which gives security of tenure when leased land is occupied for the purposes of a business carried on by the tenant. The Cristinas were the tenants of premises on which a business was conducted but the business was carried on by a company whose shares were all owned by the Cristinas, so the business was not carried on by the tenants of the premises and the tenancy was not covered by the Act.

A company may operate its business in separate branches at geographically separate locations. It is possible for a company to incorporate separate companies, as subsidiaries, to operate each branch and each of those subsidiaries will be a separate legal person. If that is not done, company law does not treat each branch as a separate person, even if it is in another country: instead there is just one legal person operating the whole business (*Appeal Commissioners v Bank of Nova Scotia* [2013] UKPC 19, [2013] STI 2863).

There is a danger that the principle that a company's business is conducted by the company rather than its members or directors could be misused in criminal law. It might be argued that people who are responsible for making a company commit criminal offences should be excused on the ground that the company committed the crime, not them. As will be explained in **19.8.4.11**, statutes creating criminal offences for the regulation of economic activity usually deal with this argument by providing that a director or other officer of a company who consented to or connived at the company's commission of an offence may be prosecuted along with the company.

Normally, when one person, A, buys all the shares in a company, B, there is no transfer of the undertaking or business of B to A for the purposes of the Transfer of Undertakings (Protection of Employment) Regulations 2006 (SI 2006/246) (*Brookes v Borough Care Services Ltd* [1998] ICR 1198). In *Print Factory (London) 1991 Ltd v Millam* [2007] EWCA Civ 322, [2007] ICR 1331, though, the Court of Appeal upheld the employment tribunal's finding that there had been a transfer on the purchase of a company's shares because of the extent to which that business had been integrated into the purchaser's business.

5.2.3 MEMBERS OF A COMPANY HAVE NO INTEREST IN ITS PROPERTY

A company's property is the property of the company as a separate person, not the members. This is illustrated by **Macaura v Northern Assurance Co Ltd** [1925] AC 619. The owner of a timber estate sold all the timber to a company in which he owned almost all the shares. He was also the company's largest creditor. He insured the timber against fire by policies taken out in his own name. The timber was destroyed by fire and he sued the insurance company. The House of Lords held that in order to have an insurable interest in property a person must have a legal or equitable interest in the property and not merely a moral certainty of profiting or losing from the property (the latter is sometimes called the 'factual expectancy test' of insurable interest). Accordingly, Macaura's claim failed because, as Lord Wrenbury said, at p 633:

> My Lords, this appeal may be disposed of by saying that the corporator even if he holds all the shares is not the corporation, and that neither he nor any creditor of the company has any property legal or equitable in the assets of the corporation.

See also *Acatos and Hutcheson plc v Watson* [1995] 1 BCLC 218 discussed in **10.6.9**.

A freezing injunction, which prohibits an individual from disposing of, dealing with or diminishing the value of any of his assets, does not apply to the assets of a company of which the individual is director and sole shareholder (*Group Seven Ltd v Allied Investment Corporation Ltd* [2013] EWHC 1509 (Ch), [2014] 1 WLR 735).

A company is normally both the legal and the beneficial owner of its property: there is no rule of company law which constitutes a company trustee of its property, with the members (or any other person) as beneficiaries of the trust (*J J Harrison (Properties) Ltd v Harrison* [2001] EWCA Civ 1467, [2002] 1 BCLC 162, at [25]). It follows that the members of a company cannot normally be described as the 'beneficial owners' of its property (*The Maritime Trader* [1981] 2 Lloyd's Rep 153). The fact that the members of a company hold their shares in the company in trust for others does not make the beneficiaries of that trust beneficial owners of the company's property (*Ayton Ltd v Popely* [2005] EWHC 810 (Ch), LTL 19/9/2005). However, a company, like any other person, can become a trustee of property under the usual rules on the creation of trusts and appointment of trustees.

In *Farrar v Farrars Ltd* (1888) 40 ChD 395 three individuals were joint mortgagees of a stone quarry. When the interest on the mortgage debt was not paid they decided to exercise their power of sale. They sold the quarry to Farrars Ltd, a company in which two of them held shares. The mortgagors asked for the sale to be rescinded but the court refused. Lindley LJ explained, at pp 409–10:

> It is perfectly well settled that a mortgagee with a power of sale cannot sell to himself either alone or with others, nor to a trustee for himself . . . A sale by a person to himself is no sale at all.
>
> A sale by a person to a corporation of which he is a member is not, either in form or in substance, a sale by a person to himself. To hold that it is, would be to ignore the principle which lies at the root of the legal idea of a corporate body, and that idea is that the corporate body is distinct from the persons composing it.

(A mortgagee exercising a power of sale does have a duty to take reasonable precautions to obtain the best price reasonably obtainable at the time of sale: the mortgagees in *Farrar v Farrars Ltd* had complied with this duty, but in the similar case of *Tse Kwong Lam v Wong Chit Sen* [1983] 1 WLR 1349 the mortgagee failed to prove he had discharged the duty, and damages were awarded to the mortgagor.)

In *Re Lewis's Will Trusts* [1985] 1 WLR 102, Mr Tudor Rhys Lewis had made a will dated 11 August 1964 by which he gave 'my freehold farm and premises, known as Talygarn, Pontyclun . . . to my son'. However, since January 1961 the farm had actually been owned by G R Lewis (Talygarn) Ltd in which Mr Lewis had a majority shareholding. On his death in 1978, Mr Lewis owned 750 of the 1,000 shares in the company; the remainder were owned by the son, to whom the will gave the farm, and the son's wife. As Mr Lewis did not own the farm at his death, it was not given by his will and it was held that the statement in the will could not be taken as referring to Mr Lewis's shares in the company. Those shares were therefore to be divided between Mr Lewis's son and daughter under the rules on intestate succession.

A member of a limited company, who has no liability for its debts, is not, merely by being a member, 'directly affected' by a judgment ordering the company to pay money, and so cannot apply under the Civil Procedure Rules 1998, r 40.9, to have the judgment set aside (*Abdelmamoud v The Egyptian Association in Great Britain Ltd* [2015] EWHC 1013 (Ch), [2015] Bus LR 928).

5.2.4 MEMBERS OF A COMPANY CANNOT SUE ON ITS BEHALF

The legal rights of a company belong to the company as a separate person and not to its members. So the members of a company do not have standing to claim remedies for wrongs done to the company (see **18.4.1**).

5.2.5 A COMPANY MAY CONTRACT WITH ITS MEMBERS

Because a company is a person separate from its members, a company can enter into transactions with its members (see *Farrar v Farrars Ltd* (1888) 40 ChD 395 discussed in **5.2.3**). In particular, money which the members of a company pay to the company for their shares belongs to the company as a separate person (see **Chapter 10** on restrictions on the return of capital to members), and when a company has paid a dividend to its members the money paid no longer belongs to the company as a separate person (see per Cotton LJ in *Re Exchange Banking Co, Flitcroft's Case* (1882) 21 ChD 519 at p 536 where his Lordship summarised the position by saying that: 'The corporation is not a mere aggregate of shareholders').

In *Wurzel v Houghton Main Home Delivery Service Ltd* [1937] 1 KB 380 a vehicle owned by the defendant company was used to deliver coal to its members. The members paid delivery charges to the company. It was held that the vehicle was used for the carriage of goods for hire or reward, which went beyond the use allowed for the vehicle under the statutory scheme then in force for licensing road haulage.

Similarly, a company can employ one of its members under a contract of service. In *Lee v Lee's Air Farming Ltd* [1961] AC 12 the company employed Mr Lee who owned 2,999 of the company's 3,000 shares, was its only director and had been appointed 'governing director' for life. Mr Lee was killed in the course of his work for the company. The company's insurers alleged that there was no contract of service so that no claim could be made under legislation which made employers liable to pay compensation for accidental personal injury suffered by their employees at work. The insurers said that it was impossible for Mr Lee, as the director of the company, to make, on its behalf, a contract with himself. But Lord Morris of Borth-y-Gest said, at p 26:

> In their lordships' view it is a logical consequence of the decision in *Salomon v A Salomon and Co Ltd* [1897] AC 22 that one person may function in dual capacities. There is no reason, therefore, to deny the possibility of a contractual relationship being created as between the deceased and the company.

The Privy Council also rejected the insurers' argument that Mr Lee as governing director could not give orders to himself as employee. Lord Morris said, at p 30:

> There appears to be no greater difficulty in holding that a man acting in one capacity can give orders to himself in another capacity than there is in holding that a man acting in one capacity can make a contract with himself in another capacity.

The law stated by the Privy Council in *Lee v Lee's Air Farming Ltd* is also the law of England and Wales (*Secretary of State for Business, Enterprise and Regulatory Reform v Neufeld* [2009] EWCA Civ 280, [2009] ICR 1183, at [29]). See also **15.9.1.5**.

5.2.6 A COMPANY SURVIVES THE DEATH OF ITS MEMBERS

The Australian case of *Re Noel Tedman Holdings Pty Ltd* [1967] QdR 561 is a striking illustration of the consequences of separate personality. Noel Tedman and his wife were the sole shareholders and directors of two companies. They both died as a result of a road traffic accident. However, their deaths did not bring to an end the legal existence of their companies. The companies continued as owners of property and parties to uncompleted contracts. Because of the particular wording of the companies' articles, the deceased shareholders' personal representatives had to seek the court's assistance to enable them to appoint new directors of the companies so as to realise their property for the benefit of the deceaseds' estates. (The problem in the case and the solution found by the court depended on the special wording of the companies' articles and will not be of general application.)

The fact that membership can be inherited distinguishes registered companies from the municipal corporations considered in old cases which were dissolved because it was impossible to replace deceased members (*R v Pasmore* (1789) 3 TR 199; *R v Hughes* (1828) 7 B & C 708 per Lord Tenterden CJ at p 717). There are also now procedures for winding up insolvent companies (see **20.6.1**) and dissolving defunct ones (see **20.16.2.4**) which can be used to deal with companies lacking active management.

5.2.7 DETRIMENT OF MEMBERS

Persons are entitled to incorporate companies for the purpose of separating their business affairs from their personal affairs or for the purpose of separating the affairs of one part of a business from another part. In doing so they are relying on the separate personalities of the companies they incorporate and this separate personality is respected by the courts, even if it is to the detriment of the incorporators. For example, in *Sociedade Nacional de Combustiveis de Angola UEE v Lundqvist* [1991] 2 QB 310, the claimants in a claim against Mr Lundqvist had obtained a court order requiring a Liberian company, which was controlled by and was the employer of Mr Lundqvist, to give details of Mr Lundqvist's assets so that the claimants could check that he complied with a freezing injunction they had obtained against him. The order requiring this information nominated Mr Lundqvist to give it on behalf of his company, but Mr Lundqvist claimed that the information would incriminate him, and that he should be excused from giving it. The Court of Appeal, however, observed that the order could be amended by nominating someone else to give the information on behalf of the company. In the similar case of *Tate Access Floors Inc v Boswell* [1991] Ch 512, Browne-Wilkinson V-C said, at p 531:

> If people choose to conduct their affairs through the medium of corporations, they are taking advantage of the fact that in law those corporations are separate legal entities, whose property and actions are in law not the property or actions of their incorporators or controlling shareholders. In my judgment controlling shareholders cannot, for all purposes beneficial to them, insist on the separate identity of such corporations but then be heard to say the contrary when [disclosure of documents] is sought against such corporations.

5.3 PIERCING THE CORPORATE VEIL

5.3.1 WAYS OF AVOIDING EFFECTS OF SEPARATE CORPORATE PERSONALITY

The big idea of company law is that a company is a separate legal person, which can own property, be a party to contracts and legal proceedings, and have its own legal rights and obligations. The cases discussed in **5.2** confirm it is a basic principle of company law that the members of a company cannot claim its property or its legal rights. It is also a basic principle that the members of a company are not responsible for its liabilities (see **1.3.1**). These basic principles of company law follow from the rule stated by Lord Halsbury LC in *Salomon v A Salomon and Co Ltd* [1897] AC 22 at p 30 that

> once the company is legally incorporated it must be treated like any other independent person with its rights and liabilities appropriate to itself.

For many years, there has been extensive discussion of whether a court can ignore this separate legal personality and can treat a company's property, rights and obligations as belonging to a person who owns and controls the company. This has been called 'piercing the corporate veil'.

A number of specific legal principles can be used to attribute one person's property, rights or liabilities to another person, whether the persons are natural or legal persons. They include:

(a) statutory provisions (see **5.3.2**);

(b) contractual provisions (see **5.3.3**);

(c) liability of a person for the acts of an agent (see **5.3.4**); and

(d) beneficial ownership of trust property (see **5.3.5**).

In *Prest v Petrodel Resources Ltd* [2013] UKSC 34, [2013] 2 AC 415, at [16], Lord Sumption identi-fied other specific principles:

> There is a range of situations in which the law attributes the acts or property of a company to those who control it, without disregarding its separate legal personality. The controller may be personally liable, gener-ally in addition to the company, for something that he has done as its agent or as a joint actor [see **19.7.1**]. Property legally vested in a company may belong beneficially to the controller, if the arrangements in rela-tion to the property are such as to make the company its controller's nominee or trustee for that purpose [as was held in *Prest v Petrodel Resources Ltd* itself, see **5.3.5**]. For specific statutory purposes, a company's legal responsibility may be engaged by the acts or business of an associated company. Examples are the provisions of the Companies Acts governing group accounts [see **9.8**] or the rules governing infringements of competition law by 'firms', which may include groups of companies conducting the relevant business as an economic unit [see **5.4.7.2**]. Equitable remedies, such as an injunction or specific performance may be available to compel the controller whose personal legal responsibility is engaged to exercise his control in a particular way [see **5.3.6.2**]. But when we speak of piercing the corporate veil, we are not (or should not be) speaking of any of these situations, but only of those cases which are true exceptions to the rule in *Salomon v A Salomon and Co Ltd* [1897] AC 22, ie where a person who owns and controls a company is said in certain circumstances to be identified with it in law by virtue of that ownership and control.

It is clear that, in the last sentence of that extract, as in the first sentence of it, Lord Sumption intended to refer only to identification for the purpose of transferring a company's property, liabilities or obligations to its controller. The rest of his Lordship's judgment is only concerned with that situation. But Lady Hale and Lord Wilson pointed out (at [95]) that identification is also used to attribute to a company the knowledge and/or intention of an individual so as to provide the company with mental capacity where that is required for legal purposes (see **19.8**). That is often seen as disregarding the company's separate personality, but really it is just making up for a defect in that personality. That is a very different issue which the following discussion does not address.

In *Prest v Petrodel Resources Ltd* the Supreme Court considered whether the court has a general power to pierce the corporate veil in circumstances where these specific legal principles do not apply. It was held that there is such a power but it can only be used when applying the evasion prin-ciple, which is discussed at **5.3.6.2**, and can only be used if there is no alternative (see also **5.3.7**).

The terms 'piercing', 'setting aside', 'lifting' or 'going behind' the corporate veil have been used in the past to describe many court decisions which involve acknowledging connections between a company and its members, directors or other persons, but do not involve any contravention of principles of company law (see **5.4**). Following Lord Sumption in *Prest v Petrodel Resources Ltd* at [16], the term 'piercing the corporate veil' will be used in this chapter only for true exceptions to the rule that a company has separate legal personality.

Companies, like individuals, are persons in law. Saying that a company and its members are separate persons is the same as saying that you and I are separate persons. Whenever it is claimed that a court decision ignores a company's separate personality, the question that should be asked is: Would the decision have been the same if the company had been a human being? If the answer is yes, the company is being treated as a person and no principle of company law has been over-ridden. If the answer is no, the company is being treated in some way differently from other persons.

This central problem was summarised by Lord Neuberger in *VTB Capital plc v Nutritek Inter-national Corporation* [2013] UKSC 5, [2013] 2 AC 337, at [138]:

> A company should be treated as being a person by the law in the same way as a human being. The fact that a company can only act or think through humans does not call that point into question: it just means that the law of agency will always potentially be in play, but, it will, at least normally, be the company which is the principal, not an agent.

5.3.2 STATUTORY PROVISIONS

The separate corporate personality of a company is created by a statute, CA 2006, and can be modified by other statutes. In **Dimbleby and Sons Ltd v National Union of Journalists** [1984] 1 WLR 427 Lord Diplock said, at p 435:

> The 'corporate veil' in the case of companies incorporated under the Companies Act is drawn by statute and it can be pierced by some other statute if such other statute so provides; but, in view of its *raison d'être* and its consistent recognition by the courts since *Salomon v A Salomon and Co Ltd* [1897] AC 22, one would expect that any parliamentary intention to pierce the corporate veil would be expressed in clear and unequivocal language. I do not wholly exclude the possibility that even in the absence of express words stating that in specified circumstances one company, although separately incorporated, is to be treated as sharing the same legal personality of another, a purposive construction of the statute may nevertheless lead inexorably to the conclusion that such must have been the intention of Parliament.

Examples can be found in statutes conferring benefits on occupiers of land. One example is the Landlord and Tenant Act 1954, s 30, which sets out the circumstances in which a landlord of a business tenant can oppose renewal of the tenant's lease. One of these circumstances is where it is intended that the premises will be occupied for the purposes of a business to be carried on by the landlord. In *Tunstall v Steigmann* [1962] 2 QB 539 it was held that, under the section as originally enacted, an intention that a company which the landlord controlled should occupy the premises for the purposes of its business was not sufficient to provide a ground for opposition. The Act has since been amended and now covers that circumstance (s 30(1A)). It also now covers the situation where the landlord is a company and the intention is that a person with a controlling interest in the company is to occupy the premises for the purposes of that person's business (s 30(1B)), but only if the controlling interest has been held for at least five years (s 30(2A)). A second example is the statutory provision that, for the purposes of relief from inheritance tax for agricultural property, occupation of such property by a company controlled by an individual can count as occupation by the individual (Inheritance Tax Act 1984, ss 116, 117, 122 and 123).

Since the separate legal personality of a company arises only when the formal requirements of the Companies Act are complied with, it is not perhaps surprising that the legislature should wish to impose sanctions, including personal liability, on persons in breach of certain fundamental requirements. For example, the Insolvency Act 1986 (IA 1986), s 213, imposes personal liability on any person (not just a member) who knowingly carries on a company's business with intent to defraud creditors or for any other fraudulent purpose (see **20.11**). But it is significant that the liability is to make a payment *to the company*, which is hardly a denial of the company's separate personality. The same applies to IA 1986, s 214 (liability of directors for wrongful trading).

A public company may not do business or exercise any borrowing powers unless it has complied with the requirements as to minimum share capital (see CA 2006, s 761, discussed in **6.7.1**). Since the power to trade or borrow in this situation is denied and is regarded by Parliament as a fundamental requirement of company law, it is not surprising that personal liability should be imposed on the directors for any loss or damage suffered by a third party who has entered into a transaction with a company which is in contravention of the provision (s 767(3)). This liability is only imposed, however, if the company itself fails to comply with its obligations under the transaction.

In enacting these statutory provisions, Parliament has decided to override some effects of separate corporate personality which it has determined are unwanted. However, it is submitted that these provisions do not represent a desire on the part of the legislature to disregard the company's separate personality, but merely impose *additional* liability on those responsible for *the expression of* the corporate personality in these circumstances.

5.3.3 CONTRACT

It is very common for the members of an owner-managed company to make contracts agreeing to guarantee its obligations. Banks and landlords, for example, are usually able to insist on guarantees which effectively nullify the limited liability that the members have in company law. Nothing in company law prevents a person contracting out of any benefit the person could derive from the principle of separate corporate personality.

5.3.4 AGENCY

5.3.4.1 Company as agent of its members

If the legal relationship of agency exists between two persons, called the principal and the agent, then the principal is responsible for whatever the agent does within the scope of the agency. Also the agent has authority to create legal relations, such as contracts, between the principal and third parties. Whether one person is an agent of another is a question of fact, and agency can be inferred from the surrounding circumstances, though it can only be established by the consent of the principal and the agent (*Garnac Grain Co Inc v H M F Faure and Fairclough Ltd* [1968] AC 1130). Nothing in company law prevents a person agreeing that a company is to be his, her or its agent, making that person liable for what the company does within the agency. The liability arises under agency law, not company law, and agency law is the same whether the agent (or the principal) is a natural person or a corporation.

In the absence of agreement to an agency relationship, *Salomon v A Salomon and Co Ltd* [1897] AC 22 established that the circumstance that a person is a member of a company does not in itself make the company an agent of that person (and see per Viscount Cave LC in *Gas Lighting Improvement Co Ltd v Commissioners of Inland Revenue* [1923] AC 723 at p 732). Agency cannot be inferred from the control exercisable by the members over the company—either by virtue of their votes in general meeting or because they are also directors—or from the fact that the sole objective of the company is to benefit the members (per Tomlin J in *British Thomson-Houston Co Ltd v Sterling Accessories Ltd* [1924] 2 Ch 33 at p 38; Kerr LJ in *J H Rayner (Mincing Lane) Ltd v Department of Trade and Industry* [1989] Ch 72, CA, at pp 188–9; [1990] 2 AC 418, HL, per Lord Oliver of Aylmerton at p 515). Usually the fact that the members of a company do not intend that it is to be their agent is sufficient to show that no agency relationship exists, because there has been no consent to one being created (*Yukong Line Ltd v Rendsburg Investments Corporation (No 2)* [1998] 1 WLR 294 at p 304).

The fact that one company is a subsidiary of another company (see **14.15**) does not in itself make the subsidiary an agent of its parent company. In *Ebbw Vale Urban District Council v South Wales Traffic Area Licensing Authority* [1951] 2 KB 366 Cohen LJ said, at p 370:

> Under the ordinary rules of law, a parent company and a subsidiary company, even a 100 per cent subsidiary company, are distinct legal entities, and in the absence of an agency contract between the two companies one cannot be said to be the agent of the other. That seems to me to be clearly established by *Salomon v A Salomon and Co Ltd* and by the observations of Tomlin J in *British Thomson-Houston Co Ltd v Sterling Accessories Ltd*.

In practice, it is very unlikely that a company will be found to be the agent of its members, see *Yukong Line Ltd v Rendsburg Investments Corporation (No 2)* and *Bank of Montreal v Canadian Westgrowth Ltd* (1990) 72 Alta LR (2d) 319, which is discussed in **5.4.7.4**. See, however, the discussion in **5.3.4.2**.

5.3.4.2 Company carrying on business as agent of its members

The characteristic feature of agency is that the agent has authority or capacity to create legal relations between the principal and third parties. In order to find that a company is the agent of one or more of its members, this authority or capacity must be present. In practice, though, the whole object of creating a company to carry on a business is that the business will be the company's business and not the members' business. It will be very rare to find that members have set up a company to run a business which they have retained ownership of, but this was what happened in *Smith, Stone and Knight Ltd v Birmingham Corporation* [1939] 4 All ER 116. Smith, Stone and Knight Ltd carried on a business manufacturing paper. It acquired from a partnership a business of dealing in waste paper. It incorporated a wholly owned subsidiary company called Birmingham Waste Co Ltd, which nominally operated the waste-paper business, but it never actually transferred ownership of the waste-paper business to that subsidiary, and it retained ownership of the land on which the waste-paper business was operated. Atkinson J found that the waste-paper business was still the business of the parent company and that it was operated by the subsidiary as agent of the parent company. Accordingly, on the compulsory purchase of the land on which the waste-paper business was operated, the parent company was entitled to compensation both for the value of the land and for disturbance of the business because it owned both the land and the business. Smith, Stone and Knight Ltd owned 497 of the 502 issued shares of Birmingham Waste Co Ltd. The other five were held by nominees of Smith, Stone and Knight Ltd. In this case, unlike the position in *Salomon v A Salomon and Co Ltd* [1897] AC 22, Birmingham Waste Co Ltd was found to be carrying on business as agent of its principal member. The crucial difference is that the business of A Salomon and Co Ltd was formally transferred to it by its principal member, Mr Salomon, and so had become the business of the company, whereas the business which Birmingham Waste Co Ltd operated was never transferred to it and remained the property of its principal member.

5.3.4.3 Agent of a person who is not a member

Because of the surrounding circumstances, a company may be found to be an agent of some person who is not a member of the company. For example, in *William Cory and Son Ltd v Dorman Long and Co Ltd* [1936] 2 All ER 386, a holding company was found to be carrying on a business as agent of its wholly owned subsidiary. The situation was the reverse of that in *Smith, Stone and Knight Ltd v Birmingham Corporation* [1939] 4 All ER 116 (see **5.3.4.2**) in that instead of the company being the agent of its principal member, the principal member was agent of the company.

5.3.4.4 Company as agent for tax purposes

Deciding who owns a business can be important for tax purposes. Normally, for tax purposes, the business of a company is not the business of its members (*Gramophone and Typewriter Ltd v Stanley* [1908] 2 KB 89) or of any person other than the company itself. Therefore, it is the company, not its members or any other person, which is liable to pay tax on the profits of its business.

In *Firestone Tyre and Rubber Co Ltd v Lewellin* [1957] 1 WLR 464, the appellant company was the wholly owned subsidiary of a US company. The appellant company manufactured tyres for sale to distributors in Europe. Its parent company had arranged special contracts with these distributors, and with the appellant company, which were claimed to have the effect that the business of selling tyres to European distributors was not carried on in the United Kingdom and so not subject to UK tax. It was held, however, that the true effect of the arrangements was that the business was the business of the parent company carried on in the United Kingdom through the appellant company acting as its parent company's agent. Tax on the profits or gains arising through or from the agency was therefore properly assessable and chargeable in the name of the agent (the appellant company) under what is now the Income Tax Act 2007, s 835E. The agency in this case resulted from the trading arrangements set up by the parent company. Those arrangements would have successfully avoided UK tax had it not been found, as a fact, that the business was carried on in the United Kingdom.

In *Smith, Stone and Knight Ltd v Birmingham Corporation* [1939] 4 All ER 116, Atkinson J, at p 121, analysed cases in which the question was whether business carried on by a subsidiary company was the business of its parent company on which the parent was liable to pay tax. His Lordship found six points which had to be taken into consideration in answering that question. In *Yukong Line Ltd v Rendsburg Investments Corporation (No 2)* [1998] 1 WLR 294, Toulson J rejected the submission that these points should determine whether a company is carrying on business as another person's agent. In *Alberta Gas Ethylene Co Ltd v Minister of National Revenue* (1988) 24 FTR 309, Reed J rejected the submission that whenever the six criteria are met the company's separate personality can be ignored. The six points were, however, used to establish agency in *Spreag v Paeson Pty Ltd* (1990) 94 ALR 679 in the Federal Court of Australia.

5.3.4.5 Agency does not deny separate corporate personality

It is submitted that treating a company as the agent of its controllers is a complete affirmation of the corporate entity principle since the agency relationship demands two legally recognisable parties.

5.3.4.6 'Agent' in a general sense: validating agreement in restraint of trade

In *Stenhouse Australia Ltd v Phillips* [1974] AC 391 a company and one of its employees made a contract providing that, after termination of the employment, the employee would not do business with any clients of the company or its subsidiaries for five years. The employee argued that this was an illegal restraint of trade, because it protected the interests of subsidiary companies, which were separate persons and did not employ him. The Privy Council (per Lord Wilberforce) rejected this, saying, at p 404:

> The evidence is clear that the business of the Stenhouse Group was controlled and coordinated by the appellant company, and all funds generated by each of the companies were received by the appellant. The subsidiaries were merely agencies or instrumentalities through which the appellant company directed its integrated business.

Lord Wilberforce used 'agencies and instrumentalities' here to characterise a situation in which a restraint of trade is permissible, not to identify a subsidiary as an agent, in law, of its holding company, with authority to put the holding company into contractual relations with other persons. That would be inconsistent with the cases discussed in **5.3.4.1**.

In *Beckett Investment Management Group Ltd v Hall* [2007] EWCA Civ 613, [2007] ICR 1539, it was held that a restraint-of-trade contract which referred only to clients of a holding company was to be construed as also restraining trade with clients of that company's subsidiaries. The court found that the parties intended the contract to have that construction. Lord Wilberforce's statement was invoked in order to reject an argument that the construction should not be adopted because of the separate personalities of the holding company and its subsidiaries.

It is submitted that these are cases in which the court has acknowledged connections between companies rather than ignored their separate personalities. These cases may be contrasted with *Newton-Sealy v Armorgroup Services Ltd* [2008] EWHC 233 (QB), LTL 21/2/2008, in which it was held that a contract of employment with one company in a group cannot be treated as a contract with other companies in the group.

5.3.5 PROPERTY HELD IN TRUST

Prest v Petrodel Resources Ltd [2013] UKSC 34, [2013] 2 AC 415, concerned proceedings for ancillary financial relief following the divorce of Yasmin and Michael Prest. Michael Prest owned and controlled a number of companies which owned residential properties. The question was whether Mr Prest was 'entitled' to those properties, for the purposes of the Matrimonial Causes Act 1973, s 24(1)(a), so that the court could exercise its power under that provision to order the transfer of the properties to Yasmin. The Supreme Court held, unanimously, that piercing the corporate veil could not be used to treat the companies' assets as belonging to Mr Prest. However, the evidence showed that the companies held the properties as a trustee for Michael Prest, not simply because he was the owner and controller of the companies, but because of the circumstances in which the properties were acquired by the companies. One of them was the Prests' matrimonial home, for which they paid no rent. Three others had been bought by the company for £1 each. Others seem to have been bought by the company using money provided by Mr Prest. So under ordinary principles of trust law, Mr Prest was entitled to the properties and an order could be made under s 24(1)(a). See also **5.3.6.1**.

5.3.6 CONCEALING OR EVADING LIABILITY

5.3.6.1 Concealment principle

In *Prest v Petrodel Resources Ltd* [2013] UKSC 34, [2013] 2 AC 415, at [28] Lord Sumption identified what he called the 'concealment principle' which exists to deal with a company that is being used as a device or facade to conceal the true facts and avoid or conceal the liability of the individual controlling the company. The concealment principle:

> is that the interposition of a company or perhaps several companies so as to conceal the identity of the real actors will not deter the courts from identifying them, assuming that their identity is legally relevant. In these cases the court is not disregarding the 'facade', but only looking behind it to discover the facts which the corporate structure is concealing.

Applying this principle may reveal, for example, that the company is holding property as agent or trustee for a controller. So where a wrongdoer banks ill-gotten gains in his company's bank account rather than his own, the company will have received the money as agent or nominee of the wrongdoer. So the court may order repayment to the defrauded person, just as it would if the money had been passed to another individual. See the discussion by Lord Sumption in *Prest v Petrodel Resources Ltd* at [31]–[33] of *Gencor ACP Ltd v Dalby* [2000] 2 BCLC 734 and *Trustor AB v Smallbone (No 2)* [2001] 1 WLR 1177. In that discussion Lord Sumption emphasised that application of the concealment principle does not involve piercing the corporate veil (Lord Neuberger agreed at [61]). The judges who decided *Gencor ACP Ltd v Dalby* and *Trustor AB v Smallbone (No 2)* were wrong to say that they were piercing the corporate veil. For a case decided after *Prest v Petrodel Resources Ltd* in which these principles were applied, see *Pennyfeathers Ltd v Pennyfeathers Property Co Ltd* [2013] EWHC 3530 (Ch), LTL 26/11/2013.

5.3.6.2 Evasion principle

More difficult legal considerations occur when an individual interposes a company so as to evade, or frustrate the enforcement of, an existing legal obligation, liability or restriction. In that circumstance the court may apply what Lord Sumption described (**Prest v Petrodel Resources Ltd** [2013] UKSC 34, [2013] 2 AC 415, at [28]) as the 'evasion principle' and may:

> pierce the corporate veil for the purpose, and only for the purpose, of depriving the company or its controller of the advantage that they would otherwise have obtained by the company's separate legal personality (Lord Sumption at [35], Lord Neuberger at [81]).

The leading example is **Gilford Motor Co Ltd v Horne** [1933] Ch 935, in which the defendant, Mr E B Horne, attempted to evade a covenant not to compete in business with the claimant. Mr Horne arranged for his wife, J M Horne, to form a company, J M Horne and Co Ltd, which carried on business in competition with the claimant. Lord Hanworth MR said, at p 956:

> I am quite satisfied that this company was formed as a device, a stratagem, in order to mask the effective carrying on of a business of Mr E B Horne. The purpose of it was to try to enable him, under what is a cloak or a sham, to engage in business which, on consideration of the agreement which had been sent to him just about seven days before the company was incorporated, was a business in respect of which he had a fear that the [claimant] might intervene and object.

The court restrained both Mr Horne and the company from enticing away the claimant's customers.

In *Jones v Lipman* [1962] 1 WLR 832, Mr Lipman contracted to sell land to Mr Jones. Before completion of the contract for sale, Mr Lipman decided not to go through with it. Instead, he transferred the land to a company of which he and a nominee were the sole shareholders and directors. Russell J ordered specific performance of the contract for sale against Mr Lipman and the company. It was accepted that an order for specific performance could be made against Mr Lipman because he was in effective control of the property (see **5.4.6**) but Russell J went on to say, perhaps with unnecessary mysticism, that:

> The defendant company is the creature of the first defendant, a device and a sham, a mask which he holds before his face in an attempt to avoid recognition by the eye of equity.

For other examples see *Albert Locke (1940) Ltd v Winsford Urban District Council* (1973) 71 LGR 308 and *Anglo German Breweries Ltd v Chelsea Corporation Inc* [2012] EWHC 1481 (Ch), [2012] 2 BCLC 632.

The evasion principle was applied in these cases to pierce the corporate veil (see the discussion of *Gilford Motor Co Ltd v Horne* and *Jones v Lipman* in *Prest v Petrodel Resources Ltd* by Lord Sumption at [29]–[30] and Lord Neuberger at [69]–[73]). However, it has been pointed out that piercing the corporate veil was not necessary in *Gilford Motor Co Ltd v Horne* or *Jones v Lipman*. See *Antonio Gramsci Shipping Corporation v Stepanovs* [2011] EWHC 333 (Comm), [2012] 1 All ER (Comm) 293, at [18], and *Prest v Petrodel Resources Ltd* at [69]–[73]. Liability for causing a company's wrongdoing may be imposed on a company's controller in other ways, for example as a joint tortfeasor (see **19.7.1**) or under IA 1986, s 213 (fraudulent trading; see **20.11.1**). In *Prest v Petrodel Resources Ltd* it was said that the court can pierce the corporate veil only if it is necessary to do so (Lord Sumption at [35], Lord Neuberger at [62] and Lord Clarke at [103]), that is, only 'when all other, more conventional remedies have proved to be of no assistance' (Lord Neuberger at [63]).

It is clearly irrelevant that the entities used to evade the obligations in these cases were companies. In *Gilford Motor Co Ltd v Horne*, for example, the court would have come to exactly the same conclusion if the competing business had been in the name of Mrs Horne personally rather than in the name of J M Horne and Co Ltd (*Yukong Line Ltd v Rendsburg Investments Corporation (No 2)* [1998] 1 WLR 294 at p 308). In both *Gilford Motor Co Ltd v Horne* and *Jones v Lipman* the court made orders against both the individual defendant and the company, thus recognising rather than ignoring the company's separate personality.

Equitable remedies were granted against companies in *Gilford Motor Co Ltd v Horne* and *Jones v Lipman* to deal with wrongs perpetrated by persons controlling the companies. So the principle of these cases will be applied only where there is both control and impropriety (**Ben Hashem v Shayif** [2008] EWHC 2380 (Fam), [2009] 1 FLR 115, at [163]). That impropriety must be a wrongdoing by the controller that is 'entirely dehors [outside, apart from] the company' (*Ben Hashem v Shayif* at [199]). In other words it is the controller's wrongdoing, not the company's, which triggers the use of the principle. The principle cannot be used to make a controller of a company liable for the company's wrongdoing, even if the controller caused it (*Lindsay v O'Loughnane* [2010] EWHC 529 (QB), [2012] BCC 153).

In *Pennyfeathers Ltd v Pennyfeathers Property Co Ltd* [2013] EWHC 3530 (Ch), LTL 26/11/2013, the wrongdoing controllers did not own the shares in, and were not directors of, the company concerned, which was incorporated in Jersey for tax purposes. It was sufficient that the shares were owned by a trust of which they were the only beneficiaries. They gave instructions to the company's directors and the directors displayed their independence for tax purposes by considering the instructions before implementing them (see **19.8.7.2**). None of this could prevent the court making orders against the company.

The principle of *Gilford Motor Co Ltd v Horne* and *Jones v Lipman* is not applied where other persons, not complicit in the impropriety, are interested in the company. *Ben Hashem v Shayif* was an application for ancillary relief in divorce proceedings. The husband was alleged to control a company which owned two apartments and an order was sought transferring them to the wife. The order was refused because: (a) there was no allegation of any impropriety by the husband in using the company to invest in property; and (b) the husband held only 30 per cent of the shares. The court rejected an argument that the other shares were held in trust for him.

The court's ability to prevent persons evading their obligations by transferring their property to others is also illustrated by cases concerning freezing injunctions. A freezing injunction prohibits a defendant in legal proceedings from disposing of assets which could be used to meet any award of damages in the proceedings. To prevent a defendant avoiding the effect of a freezing injunction by putting assets into the ownership of companies, the court will extend the injunction to cover assets owned by companies controlled by the defendant, and will similarly extend the scope of supporting orders requiring the defendant to disclose information (*Re a Company* [1985] BCLC 333) or for the appointment of a receiver (*International Credit and Investment Co (Overseas) Ltd v Adham* [1998] BCC 134). *Re H (Restraint Order: Realisable Property)* [1996] 2 All ER 391 is a similar case involving seizure of the proceeds of alleged criminal activity.

The cases on freezing injunctions are not concerned with a special rule of company law. *Re a Company* [1985] BCLC 333, for example, was concerned with a defendant's assets transferred to both companies and trusts. See also per Laws LJ in *Re K* [2005] EWCA Crim 619, [2006] BCC 362, at [23].

The cases discussed so far have all involved the court granting equitable remedies. In *VTB Capital plc v Nutritek International Corporation* [2013] UKSC 5, [2013] 2 AC 337, the Supreme Court refused to extend veil piercing to contract law. It was held that there is no power to make a controller of a company liable on a contract to which the company is a party but the controller is not. Lord Neuberger said, at [139]:

> Subject to some other rule (such as that of undisclosed principal), where B and C are the contracting parties and A is not, there is simply no justification for holding A responsible for B's contractual liabilities to C simply because A controls B and has made misrepresentations about B to induce C to enter into the contract. This could not be said to result in unfairness to C: the law provides redress for C against A, in the form of a cause of action in negligent or fraudulent misrepresentation.

5.3.6.3 Evasion of a company's obligations by removing its property

In *The Tjaskemolen* [1997] 2 Lloyd's Rep 465 Clarke J was concerned with a company against which a claim was pending for breach of contract to charter (hire out) the one ship that it owned. In maritime law, a person making such a claim is entitled to ask the court to 'arrest' (hold as security) any ship beneficially owned by the defendant. The defendant company had transferred legal title to its ship to another company controlled by the same person. The question was whether the claimant was still entitled to arrest the ship. Clarke J held, at p 469, that:

> where an alleged transfer of a vessel is in the relevant sense a sham or facade, the court will hold that the original owners retain the beneficial ownership in the vessel.
>
> That approach is consistent with a number of authorities which have considered the circumstances in which it may be appropriate, as it is sometimes put, to pierce the corporate veil.

His lordship found that the transfer was not a genuine commercial transaction. Its purpose was to avoid arrest of the ship and it was never intended that the transferee company should pay the full purchase price. So the defendant company retained beneficial ownership of the ship and it could be arrested. Obviously, the fact that the transfer was between two companies was of no significance in this case. The decision would have been the same if the transfer had been from one individual to another (see *Yukong Line Ltd v Rendsburg Investments Corporation (No 2)* [1998] 1 WLR 294 at p 308).

Other attempted solutions to the problem of removing assets from a company to evade its obligations have not succeeded. For example, if a company is sued for damages for a wrong it has committed and the claimant alleges that the company's controller has deliberately ensured that the company has no money to pay any damages which may be awarded, the court will not make the controller liable directly to the claimant for the damages: the wrong was done by the company and only the company can be sued for it (*B G Preeco I (Pacific Coast) Ltd v Bon Street Holdings Ltd* (1989) 60 DLR (4th) 30; *Yukong Line Ltd v Rendsburg Investments Corporation (No 2)* [1998] 1 WLR 294; *Ord v Belhaven Pubs Ltd* [1998] 2 BCLC 447). It is possible that directors of a company who have removed its assets so as to defeat claims against it may be liable to the company, either for breaching their duty to act within powers (CA 2006, s 171) or under the wrongful trading provisions of the Insolvency Act 1986, s 214 (see **16.5** and **20.12**). However, this is a matter between the company (or its liquidator) and the directors, not between the directors and the person whose claim is against the company. In *Creasey v Breachwood Motors Ltd* [1993] BCLC 480 the directors of a company which was defending a claim by a former employee transferred all its assets to another company, of which they were also directors and shareholders, leaving the original company with nothing to pay the claim. The deputy High Court judge substituted the transferee company as the defendant to the claim, thus making one person liable to defend a claim brought to remedy a wrong done by another person. This was done so as to avoid the cost of separate proceedings between the original defendant company and its directors and the transferee company for the recovery of money to pay for any damages the claimant might be awarded. In *Ord v Belhaven Pubs Ltd* the Court of Appeal held that *Creasey v Breachwood Motors Ltd* was wrongly decided. Hobhouse LJ said, at p 458, that the case 'represents a wrong adoption of the principle of piercing the corporate veil'. It is, however, defended for its cost saving by D Bromilow, '*Creasey v Breachwood Motors*: mistaken identity leads to untimely death' (1998) 19 Co Law 198.

5.3.6.4 Can a company be a sham?

The colourful epithets 'sham', 'cloak' and 'mask' seem to be used in these cases:

(a) to indicate that a company is completely controlled by a person who can therefore use it for his or her own purposes and is able to make it comply with court orders; and

(b) to show that there was some impropriety in the use of the company which justifies the court in making an order to override a transaction which is otherwise legally effective (see L Linklater, '"Piercing the corporate veil"—the never-ending story' (2006) 27 Co Law 65). The impropriety is that the company has been used to evade its controller's legal obligations. This is sometimes described as 'abuse of the corporate form' (see C M Schmitthoff, '*Salomon* in the shadow' [1976] JBL 305).

In *Re G (Restraint Order)* [2001] EWHC 606 (Admin), [2002] STC 391, the judge referred, at [11], to a company which 'has no genuine separate existence from the defendant, and is used by him as a device for fraud'. Courts often say that they are treating a company itself as a sham (as in the remark by Russell J in *Jones v Lipman* [1962] 1 WLR 832 quoted in **5.3.6.2**), implying that the company's existence or separate personality is being ignored. However, a company's certificate of incorporation is conclusive evidence that its existence is genuine and not a sham (CA 2006, s 15(4)). As is made clear in *The Tjaskemolen* [1997] 2 Lloyd's Rep 465 discussed in **5.3.6.3**, what is really being objected to in these cases is a transaction to which the company is a party (such as the house sale in *Jones v Lipman*), or the business it is carrying on (as in *Gilford Motor Co Ltd v Horne* [1933] Ch 935). The most commonly cited definition of sham (given in a case that did not involve any question of corporate personality) is concerned with transactions, not parties to transactions.

In *Snook v London and West Riding Investments Ltd* [1967] 2 QB 786 Diplock J said, at p 802, that if 'the popular and pejorative word' sham:

> has any meaning in law, it means acts done or documents executed by parties to the 'sham' which are intended by them to give to third parties or to the court the appearance of creating between the parties legal rights and obligations different from the actual legal rights and obligations (if any) which the parties intend to create.

Forming a company to carry on a business or own property is entirely legal. It is the misuse of a company to evade enforcement of existing rights which the courts overcome by requiring the company to be used to comply with those rights. It seems that the true function of a characterisation of a company as a sham, cloak, mask, puppet, clone or alter ego of the person who is misusing the company is as evidence that a *transaction* with the company carried out by that person is a sham.

Nevertheless, the possibility of finding that a company itself is a sham is considered in *Secretary of State for Business, Enterprise and Regulatory Reform v Neufeld* [2009] EWCA Civ 280, [2009] ICR 1183. In this case, the Court of Appeal dealt with the problem of deciding whether a controlling shareholder and director of a company has a contract of employment with the company. It gave guidance, at [82]–[83], on deciding whether an alleged contract of employment with a company is a sham. It also discussed what it identified as the separate problem of whether the company itself could be a sham, saying, at [34], that describing a company as 'a sham or a mere simulacrum' (*Lee v Lee's Air Farming Ltd* [1961] AC 12 at p 25) means that it is:

> right for policy reasons to 'pierce the veil' of incorporation and treat the company as the alter ego of the controlling shareholder, that is to treat them as one.

Treating a company and its controlling shareholder as one would mean that they are not two separate persons who could make a contract with each other. In particular, the shareholder could not be an employee of the company under a contract of employment. This would completely ignore the separate personality of the company and would now only be permissible when applying the evasion principle.

5.3.7 FUTURE OF VEIL PIERCING

In *Prest v Petrodel Resources Ltd* [2013] UKSC 34, [2013] 2 AC 415, Lords Sumption (at [35]) and Neuberger (at [81]) held that piercing the corporate veil can only be used when applying the evasion principle (see **5.3.6.2**) and Lords Sumption (at [35]), Neuberger (at [62]) and Clarke (at [103]) held that the court can pierce the corporate veil only if it is necessary to do so. Lord Neuberger analysed examples of veil piercing in the past and said that whenever it had been done, it had been unnecessary. His Lordship concluded (at [64]) that:

> there is not a single instance in this jurisdiction where the doctrine [that it is open to a court to pierce the veil of incorporation] has been invoked properly and successfully.

Given this history, it seems unlikely that the doctrine could ever be invoked properly and successfully in the future.

Lord Mance (at [100]) and Lord Clarke (at [103]) said that they would not want to prevent the courts extending veil-piercing to situations other than those covered by the evasion principle. However, Lord Mance went on to say that:

> the strength of the principle in *Salomon v A Salomon and Co Ltd* [1897] AC 22 and the number of other tools which the law has available mean that, if there are other situations in which piercing the veil may be relevant as a final fall-back, they are likely to be novel and very rare.

In *Antonio Gramsci Shipping Corporation v Recoletos Ltd* [2013] EWCA Civ 730, [2014] Bus LR 239, at [66], Beatson LJ doubted whether it would be possible to develop the law in this way, because of the difficulty of finding any underlying principles for the doctrine of piercing the corporate veil. He pointed out that Lord Walker in *Prest v Petrodel Resources Ltd* at [106] said that it was not a doctrine in the sense of a coherent principle or rule of law. Beatson LJ predicted that piercing the corporate veil would come to be seen as an anomaly incapable of further development.

In Crown Court proceedings concerning confiscation of proceeds of crime there has been considerable difficulty in dealing with money earned by a company as a result of a crime committed by a controlling director. The problem arises because of a policy of not prosecuting the company so the proceeds cannot be confiscated directly from it, but have to be treated as the proceeds of the controller's crime. In *R v Boyle Transport (Northern Ireland) Ltd* [2016] EWCA Crim 19, [2016] 4 WLR 63, the Court of Appeal examined this problem at length. It emphasised that the Crown Court must apply *Prest v Petrodel Resources Ltd* and cannot evade it by reference to 'the reality of the situation'.

5.4 CONNECTIONS BETWEEN A COMPANY AND OTHER PERSONS

5.4.1 INTRODUCTION

There are many situations in which the court considers connections between a company and its members, directors or other persons, including companies in the same group. In itself, this does not involve transferring the property, rights or obligations of the company to other persons and so, as with the concealment principle (see **5.3.6.1**), there is no piercing of the corporate veil and there is no conflict with any principle of company law.

5.4.2 DETERMINING LEGAL STATUS

In a large number of cases, a court determines the character of a company's status or legal relationships by reference to persons connected with the company.

While the courts in this situation are undeniably looking at the actions and intentions of persons other than the company, it is submitted that this is not a denial of corporate personality, but a recognition of it. The courts are trying to discover the true expression of that personality and, being conscious of the necessary limitations attaching to an artificial entity, are looking to the company's controllers to determine how the company expresses its independent personality.

By far the most important example of using information about persons connected with a company to determine the character of the company's acts is when a human being is identified with the company and the human's knowledge, actions, criminal intent or other physical or mental attributes are taken to be those of the company. (See **19.8.**)

The following three cases are examples of information about persons connected with a company being used to characterise the company's status or legal relationships.

In *Newell v Hemingway* (1888) 53 JP 324 and *Trebanog Working Men's Club and Institute Ltd v Macdonald* [1940] 1 KB 567 the fact that the members of a company, by their membership, constituted themselves a members' club determined that when members paid for their drinks in the club it was not a sale by retail by the company such as to be subject to the law then in force which required retailers of intoxicating liquor to purchase excise duty licences.

In *The Abbey Malvern Wells Ltd v Ministry of Local Government and Planning* [1951] Ch 728 the fact that, by virtue of provisions of its articles, the only persons who could be directors of the company were the trustees of a deed which required them to operate the company for charitable purposes, determined that land held by the company was held for charitable purposes and so exempt from a now-abolished land tax.

Information about a subsidiary company's holding company and the way it finances its subsidiary may be taken into account in determining whether the subsidiary is a 'responsible' person to take an assignment of a lease (*Re Greater London Properties Ltd's lease* [1959] 1 WLR 503). In *R (Healy) v Vehicle Inspectorate* [2001] RTR 253 a company acquired a vehicle testing business previously operated by a partnership. The Vehicle Inspectorate withdrew the company's authorisation to perform MoT tests, taking into account incidents occurring before and after the transfer of the business, which had been conducted by the same individual throughout. It was held that there was nothing objectionable in the Inspectorate's decision-making. But in *R v Crown Court at Warrington, ex parte RBNB* [2002] UKHL 24, [2002] 1 WLR 1954, it was held to be wrong for the Crown Court to conclude that an individual was not a fit and proper person to hold a licence to sell intoxicating liquor merely because no information was available about who were the beneficial owners of the shares in the company which employed the individual.

There are other examples of when, as in *R v Crown Court at Warrington, ex parte RBNB*, it is not appropriate to consider a company's members when determining its legal status. In Canada the amount of local tax payable on the occupation of land depends on whether the occupier is using it for the purposes of a business. The key characteristic of a business, for the purposes of this tax, is that its preponderant purpose is the making of a profit. There has been difficulty in determining the correct rate of tax when land is occupied by a non-profit-making company providing its members with facilities for the purposes of their own businesses, for example, where market premises are owned by a non-profit company whose members are the firms which trade on the premises. It has now been held by the Ontario Court of Appeal, disagreeing with an earlier view by a lower Ontario court, that if the predominant purpose of a company which occupies land is not to make profits for itself but to enable its members to make profits then the company is not itself carrying on a business on the land and should not be assessed at the business rate (*Toronto Stock Exchange v Regional Assessment Commissioner, Region No 9* (1996) 136 DLR (4th) 362).

5.4.3 EXERCISE OF JUDICIAL DISCRETION

If a court has a discretion whether to make an order in relation to a company then it has a duty to consider all relevant matters. One of the matters which the court may take into consideration is information about persons connected with the company.

In **Merchandise Transport Ltd v British Transport Commission** [1962] 2 QB 173, Merchandise Transport Ltd had applied, under the statutory system then in force for licensing road haulage, for a licence to operate over 100 vehicles as a public carrier. The statute gave the 'licensing authority' (in fact, one man) discretion whether to grant a licence or not. In deciding to refuse the licence, the licensing authority took into account the fact that Merchandise Transport Ltd was the wholly owned subsidiary of a large company manufacturing furniture, Harris Lebus Ltd, and the vehicles were at the time owned by the manufacturing company and used to deliver its products. The holding company could not obtain a licence to use these vehicles for public carrier business on return journeys after delivering its goods because it could afford to charge lower rates for such journeys than full-time public carriers whom the licensing system was intended to protect. It was clear that after being transferred to the subsidiary the vehicles would continue to be used to deliver the holding company's products and would only be available for public carrier business on return journeys for which low charges would be made. Devlin LJ said, at pp 201–2:

> The reasoning of the licensing authority is said to conflict with [the proposition that a company is a legal entity distinct from its shareholders]. I cannot see that it does. If he had refused a licence to Merchandise

Transport on the ground that it had no legal existence apart from Harris Lebus Ltd and that the latter ought to have applied themselves, that would be wrong.

But the fact that two persons are separate in law does not mean that one may not be under the control of the other to such an extent that they constitute one commercial unit . . . Whenever a licensing authority is satisfied that that sort of relationship exists, and that the dominant party is using it to obtain contrary to the intent of the Act an advantage which he would not otherwise get, he is entitled, if not bound, to exercise his discretion so as to ensure that the scheme of the Act is complied with in the spirit as well as in the letter.

For other examples of the exercise of judicial discretion, see *Re Bugle Press Ltd* [1961] Ch 270 and *Esso Standard (Inter-America) Inc v JW Enterprises Inc* (1963) 37 DLR (2d) 598, discussed in **8.7.2.4**. Another example is *Burnet v Francis Industries plc* [1987] 1 WLR 802, in which the court exercised its discretion to stay execution of a judgment obtained against a company pending determination of a separate claim against the judgment creditor made by the company's parent company. (See also *Canada Enterprises Corporation Ltd v MacNab Distilleries Ltd* [1987] 1 WLR 813.) In *Atlas Maritime Co SA v Avalon Maritime Ltd (No 1)* [1991] 4 All ER 769 one company had used a wholly owned subsidiary to conduct a particular business operation which became the subject of legal proceedings against the subsidiary. In those proceedings the subsidiary's assets were made subject to a freezing injunction, and the court refused to allow the subsidiary to repay to the parent company the money which it had provided as working capital for the venture. Neill and Staughton LJJ both said that this was not 'piercing' the corporate veil (though Stocker LJ did use that phrase). Staughton LJ said (at p 780) that the relationship of holding and subsidiary company was a factor to be taken into account in exercising the court's discretion and preferred to describe this as 'lifting' the corporate veil. It was held that the subsidiary was not an agent of the parent company.

If a company claims that an order for it to give security for the costs of an appeal in civil proceedings would mean that it could not afford to continue with the appeal, the court may require it to show that it could not obtain finance from another party such as its directors, shareholders or other backers (*Hammond Suddards Solicitors v Agrichem International Holdings Ltd* [2001] EWCA Civ 2065, [2002] CP Rep 21, at [27]–[28]). The same applies to an order requiring a judgment debt under appeal to be paid into court (*Hammond Suddards Solicitors v Agrichem International Holdings Ltd*).

It is not always proper to take into account the membership of a company when exercising a discretion in relation to that company. **Pioneer Laundry and Dry Cleaners Ltd v Minister of National Revenue** [1940] AC 127 concerned a Canadian tax statute which gave the Minister discretion to decide how much a taxpayer could deduct from income for depreciation of fixed assets when computing taxable profit. The Minister decided that Pioneer Laundry and Dry Cleaners Ltd could not deduct any depreciation for some of its assets because they had previously been owned by another company with the same shareholders and that company had already been allowed 100 per cent depreciation on them. The Privy Council held that this was wrong, saying (per Lord Thankerton), 'The taxpayer is the company, and not its shareholders'. Lord Thankerton said that the Minister was wrong 'to disregard the separate legal existence of the appellant company and to inquire as to who its shareholders were and its relation to its predecessors'. It is submitted that taking into account the company's membership in exercising the discretion did not disregard the company's separate personality. But the Minister's erroneous reason for taking the membership into account, that the members were the taxpayers rather than the company, did ignore the company's separate personality.

5.4.4 JUDICIAL BIAS

It is a fundamental principle of the proper administration of justice that an individual who is a party to legal proceedings should not be a member of a tribunal which deals with those proceedings. This is naturally extended to prevent the trial of legal proceedings by an individual who, though not a party, has an interest in the proceedings. In order to disqualify a person because of an interest there is no need to prove actual bias, because disqualification is required to remove the appearance of bias, and the harm which that would do to public confidence in the legal system. According to the Court of Appeal in *Taylor v Lawrence* [2002] EWCA Civ 90, [2003] QB 528, at [60], the test of bias is as follows:

> The court must first ascertain all the circumstances which have a bearing on the suggestion that the judge was biased. It must then ask whether those circumstances would lead a fair-minded and informed observer to conclude that there was a real possibility that the tribunal was biased.

As the principal reason for holding shares in a company is to benefit financially from the company's activities, this rule means that a shareholder in a company cannot judge a case in which the company is a party. Thus it was wrong for Lord Cottenham LC to hear an appeal in a case brought by the Grand Junction Canal Co (a statutory company) at a time when he held shares in that company (*Dimes v Grand Junction Canal Co* (1852) 3 HL Cas 759). An exception may be made where the judge's shareholding is so small that it is incapable of affecting his or her decision one way or the other (*Locabail (UK) Ltd v Bayfield Properties Ltd* [2000] QB 451 at p 473). So in *Weatherill v Lloyds TSB Bank plc* (2000) LTL 4/10/2000 it was unnecessary for the judge to abandon hearing a case when he discovered that, of the defendant company's 5.5 billion shares, he owned 570 (which he immediately sold). Normally the type of apparent interest which leads to disqualification is a financial interest, but in *R v Bow Street Metropolitan Stipendiary Magistrate, ex parte Pinochet Ugarte (No 2)* [2000] 1 AC 119 the House of Lords held that the rule also disqualifies someone whose connection with a pressure group which is a party to proceedings (in this case the connection was as director and chairperson of a company which ran the group's charitable activities) gave a sufficient appearance of bias to warrant disqualification.

5.4.5 STANDING TO CLAIM JUDICIAL REVIEW

A claim for judicial review may be made only if the claimant has a sufficient interest in the matter to which the claim relates (Senior Courts Act 1981, s 31(3)). It has been held that a company may make a claim if its members have a sufficient interest, at least where the company was formed to promote that interest (*R v Hammersmith and Fulham London Borough Council, ex parte People Before Profit Ltd* (1981) 80 LGR 322; *R v Secretary of State for the Environment, ex parte Rose Theatre Trust Co* [1990] 1 QB 504). In the first of these cases People Before Profit Ltd was held to be capable of making a claim, but the claim failed; in the second case Rose Theatre Trust Co was held not to be capable of making a claim because none of its members had a sufficient interest.

For the ability of a member of a company to claim judicial review on behalf of the company, see 18.4.3.5.

5.4.6 CONTROL OF A COMPANY'S PROPERTY

In some circumstances, a court may require a person to deal with property over which that person has control even though that person does not have legal title to it. The fact that the person controls a company which owns the property may be enough to put the property within the person's control.

For example, a person who is a party to legal proceedings and has 'control' of relevant documents may be ordered to disclose them and allow inspection of them (Civil Procedure Rules 1998, Part 31, particularly r 31.8). The court may recognise that the requisite degree of control exists where the document belongs to a company controlled by the person ordered to give disclosure, because the court may recognise that a company cannot prevent a person who controls it dealing with its documents (*Dallas v Dallas* (1960) 24 DLR (2d) 746; see further *Lonrho Ltd v Shell Petroleum Co Ltd* [1980] 1 WLR 627 and *Re Tecnion Investments Ltd* [1985] BCLC 434, in which it was found that the requisite degree of control was not present).

Another example is where a court orders specific performance of a contract of sale of property which is controlled by but not owned by the defendant. Again the requisite degree of control may be found where the property is owned by a company controlled by the defendant (*Elliott v Pierson* [1948] Ch 452; *Jones v Lipman* [1962] 1 WLR 832).

In *Littlewoods Mail Order Stores Ltd v Commissioners of Inland Revenue* [1969] 1 WLR 1241 Littlewoods had spent money acquiring a fixed asset (the freehold of its headquarters building) for a wholly owned subsidiary. It claimed that this was a revenue expenditure for the use of property owned by another (and so deductible from income when computing taxable profits) rather than capital to be employed in its trade (which was not deductible), but the Court of Appeal rejected the claim. Sachs LJ said, at p 1256:

> [The money] was clearly expended for the purpose of acquiring a capital asset which happened to have been put into the ownership of [the subsidiary]. It is thus in truth expenditure of a capital nature to secure the advantage of an enduring benefit.

Karminski LJ said, at p 1256:

> It is necessary . . . to ask . . . who really benefited from getting hold of the freehold. To that in my view there can be only one answer, that it is Littlewoods and not [the subsidiary].

Both judges clearly assumed that the parent company would use its control over the subsidiary to ensure that the freehold was held for its benefit. Lord Denning MR said, at p 1254, that he declined to treat the subsidiary as 'a separate and independent entity' and held that Littlewoods had acquired the freehold. The majority of the court, though, showed that it was unnecessary to take the drastic step of depriving the subsidiary of its property and giving that property to its parent: it was sufficient to accept that buying a capital asset for another to be held for one's own benefit amounted to non-deductible capital expenditure. Similarly in *R v MerBan Capital Corporation Ltd* [1985] 1 CTC 1 a company paid interest on a loan to its wholly owned subsidiary which was made so that the subsidiary could acquire assets and it was held that the interest could be deducted from the parent company's taxable income because it was paid for the holding company's business purposes. The fact that the revenue authorities ended up gaining tax in *Littlewoods Mail Order Stores Ltd v Commissioners of Inland Revenue* and losing it in *R v MerBan Capital Corporation Ltd* illustrates that the distinction between income and capital is of crucial importance for the purposes of income tax, which taxes one but not the other.

In *Revlon Inc v Cripps and Lee Ltd* [1980] FSR 85, Revlon Inc was the American parent of an international group of companies. Trade marks used by the companies had been assigned to Revlon Suisse SA, which was the wholly owned subsidiary of a wholly owned subsidiary of Revlon Inc. Under UK trade marks legislation Revlon Suisse was registered in the United Kingdom as the 'proprietor' of a trade mark and claimed that the defendant had infringed it by bringing into the United Kingdom goods to which that mark had been applied by Revlon Inc in the USA. Buckley LJ, at p 107, said that Revlon Suisse held the trade marks for the purposes of the trade carried on by companies in the group and so had impliedly consented to Revlon Inc's use of the mark on its goods, which was a use 'in relation to goods connected in the course of trade with the proprietor', which was deemed by the Trade Marks Act 1938, s 4(3), not to be an infringement. (The law on trade marks has since been changed and there is now no provision equivalent to s 4(3) of the 1938 Act.) His Lordship said, at p 105:

> Since, however, all the relevant companies are wholly owned subsidiaries of [Revlon Inc], it is undoubted that the mark is, albeit remotely, an asset of Revlon and its exploitation is for the ultimate benefit of no one but Revlon. It therefore seems to me to be realistic and wholly justifiable to regard [Revlon Suisse] as holding the mark at the disposal of Revlon and for Revlon's benefit . . . This view does not, in my opinion, constitute what is sometimes called 'piercing the corporate veil'; it recognises the legal and factual position resulting from the mutual relationship of the various companies.

5.4.7 GROUPS OF COMPANIES

5.4.7.1 Separate personalities of companies in a group

The Albazero [1977] AC 774 concerned a cargo of crude oil which Concord Petroleum Corporation, a wholly owned subsidiary of Occidental Petroleum Corporation, had consigned on a ship for shipment from Venezuela to Europe. During the voyage, the consigning company, Concord, transferred ownership of the cargo to another wholly owned subsidiary of Occidental Petroleum Corporation. After the transfer of ownership the ship and cargo were totally lost. Concord sued the shipowner for the loss. The shipowner argued that the true loser of the cargo was the company to which ownership had been transferred and only that company could sue for the loss. (Proceedings could not be restarted with that company as claimant because the limitation period had expired.) At first instance, Concord submitted that it and the company to which the cargo had been sold should be treated as one because they were both wholly owned subsidiaries of the same company. This argument was rejected. In the Court of Appeal, Roskill LJ said, at p 807, that it was a fundamental principle of English law:

> long established and now unchallengeable by judicial decision . . . that each company in a group of companies . . . is a separate legal entity possessed of separate legal rights and liabilities so that the rights of one company in a group cannot be exercised by another company in that group even though the ultimate benefit of the exercise of those rights would enure beneficially to the same person or corporate body irrespective of the person or body in whom those rights were vested in law.

The argument was not pursued in the House of Lords where Concord succeeded (as it had at first instance and in the Court of Appeal) on the alternative argument that it was an established rule of maritime law that the consignor of cargo could sue for its loss regardless of who owned the cargo.

It follows that a parent company is not responsible for the debts of its subsidiary (*Re Southard and Co Ltd* [1979] 1 WLR 1198 per Templeman LJ at p 1208) even if it has in the past expressed in a comfort letter a policy of supporting the subsidiary (*Kleinwort Benson Ltd v Malaysia Mining Corporation Bhd* [1989] 1 WLR 379; *Re Atlantic Computers plc, National Australia Bank Ltd v Soden* [1995] BCC 696). In *Reed v Nova Securities Ltd* [1985] 1 WLR 193, Lord Templeman said, at p 201: 'the theoretical independent existence of every corporation enables a group of companies to escape liability at common law for the losses of an individual member of the group'.

In *Bank of Tokyo Ltd v Karoon* [1987] AC 45, Bank of Tokyo Ltd carried on a banking business in London, and its wholly owned subsidiary, Bank of Tokyo Trust Co (BTTC), carried on a banking business in New York. Mr Karoon was a customer of both banks. He complained that details of his account with BTTC had been disclosed by BTTC to its parent company without his permission in breach of a bank's duty of confidence, and sued BTTC in the New York courts for damages. The disclosure was made for the purposes of legal proceedings in the High Court in London to which Mr Karoon and the parent company were parties. The parent company sought an order restraining the action against its subsidiary. Robert Goff LJ said, at p 64:

> [Counsel for the Bank of Tokyo Ltd] suggested beguilingly that it would be technical for us to distinguish between parent and subsidiary company in this context; economically, he said, they were one. But we are concerned not with economics but with law. The distinction between the two is, in law, fundamental and cannot here be bridged.

The same approach was taken by the Court of Appeal in *Adams v Cape Industries plc* [1990] Ch 433 at pp 532–9.

In *Newton-Sealy v Armorgroup Services Ltd* [2008] EWHC 233 (QB), LTL 21/2/2008, the claimant had been injured in the course of his employment with one company in a group. As that company was incorporated in Jersey, its contract of employment could exclude liability for personal injury. The court struck out a claim that the contract of employment was also with other companies in the group incorporated in England and Germany, where such liability cannot be excluded. Although the employee's contract was with the Jersey company only, the other companies dealt with him day to day. The court accepted it was arguable that these day-to-day dealings created a relationship of proximity or assumption of liability, so that the other companies had a duty of care in the law of negligence.

5.4.7.2 EU competition law

EU competition law can treat a parent company and its subsidiaries as an economic unit. The rules on competition in arts 101 to 106 of the Treaty on the Functioning of the European Union (TFEU) are 'rules applying to undertakings' and the Court of Justice of the European Union has held that the use of the word 'undertakings' means that the rules are 'aimed at economic units which consist of a unitary organisation of personal, tangible and intangible elements which pursues a specific economic aim on a long-term basis' (*Shell International Chemical Co Ltd v Commission* (case T-11/89) [1992] ECR II-757 at para 311). Where a group of companies forms an 'undertaking', the whole undertaking can be found to have broken the competition rules. Even so, because a group of companies does not have legal personality, the European Commission must select a specific company in the group to be the addressee of its Decision and to be responsible for payment of any penalty (see *Provimi Ltd v Roche Products Ltd* [2003] EWHC 961 (Comm), [2003] 2 All ER (Comm) 683, at [6]). Where the companies in a group form one undertaking, agreements between them, for example fixing prices, cannot be anti-competitive agreements contrary to art 101(1) of the TFEU, because they are not agreements 'between undertakings', only agreements within one undertaking (*Centrafarm BV v Sterling Drug Inc* (case 15/74) [1974] ECR 1147; *Viho Europe BV v Commission* (case C-73/95 P) [1996] ECR I-5457). In *Imperial Chemical Industries Ltd v Commission* (case 48/69) [1972] ECR 619 it was held that anti-competitive behaviour of a subsidiary company within what was then the European Economic Community, acting on the instructions of its parent company outside the Community, could be attributed to the parent company so as to bring the parent company within the jurisdiction of the Commission and allow the Commission to fine it. Taking extraterritorial jurisdiction in this way was seen by the European Court of Justice as necessary for the effective enforcement of competition law. This decision in EU competition law may be contrasted with *Adams v Cape Industries plc* [1990] Ch 433, in which the English Court of Appeal held that the fact that a subsidiary of an English company was present in the jurisdiction of a Texas court did not mean that the parent company was present in that jurisdiction, so that the parent company was not liable for a judgment which the Texas court had given against the subsidiary.

5.4.7.3 Parent company's duty of care to its subsidiary's employees

In some groups of companies, a parent company plays a considerable part in managing the operations of a subsidiary. In the common law of tort this may lead to a finding that the parent company has assumed a duty, owed to the subsidiary's employees, of care for their safety. (See **17.5.2** for discussion of the concept of assumption of responsibility in tort law.) In *Chandler v Cape plc* [2012] EWCA Civ 525, [2012] ICR 1293, at [69], Arden LJ 'emphatically' rejected any suggestion that this involved piercing the corporate veil. A duty is not attached to the parent company simply because it is a parent company but because what it did amounted to taking on a direct duty to the subsidiary's employees. Her Ladyship listed, at [80], four factors which justified finding that the parent assumed a duty of care:

(a) the businesses of the parent and subsidiary are in a relevant respect the same;

(b) the parent has, or ought to have, superior knowledge on some relevant aspect of health and safety in the particular industry;

(c) the subsidiary's system of work is unsafe as the parent company knew, or ought to have known; and

(d) the parent knew or ought to have foreseen that the subsidiary or its employees would rely on its using that superior knowledge for the employees' protection.

The mere fact that a parent company has appointed a director of a subsidiary with responsibility for health and safety is not enough to establish assumption of a duty of care for the health and safety of a subsidiary's employees (*Thompson v Renwick Group plc* [2014] EWCA Civ 635, [2014] 2 BCLC 97). *Thompson v Renwick Group plc* showed that in the very common situation of a parent company being only a holding company with no business activities of its own, there will be no evidence that the parent company has superior expertise in, for example, health and safety, on which it would be reasonable for a subsidiary's employees to rely.

5.4.7.4 Challenging arrangements of affairs

Usually, the whole point of using a company to conduct transactions is to separate those trans-actions from other affairs of the company's owners so that liabilities incurred in the course of those transactions are the liabilities of the company rather than of its owners, who have such lim-ited liability for the company's affairs as legislation permits. Parliament has made limited compan-ies available for this purpose because it believes that it will encourage economic activity. Many demands for the separate personality of companies to be ignored are simply attempts to challenge advantageous uses of companies to limit liability. Since *Salomon v A Salomon and Co Ltd* [1897] AC 22, the courts consistently reject such challenges. In **Adams v Cape Industries plc** [1990] Ch 433 the Court of Appeal said, at p 544:

> we do not accept as a matter of law that the court is entitled to lift the corporate veil as against a defend-ant company which is the member of a corporate group merely because the corporate structure has been used so as to ensure that the legal liability (if any) in respect of particular future activities of the group (and correspondingly the risk of enforcement of that liability) will fall on another member of the group rather than the defendant company. Whether or not this is desirable, the right to use a corporate structure in this manner is inherent in our corporate law.

It is a feature of company law that it permits a group of companies to be arranged so as to separate liabilities for the various activities of the group. The unlikelihood of a court ever overriding such an arrangement and transferring liability from a company which incurred it to a company more able to meet it is demonstrated by the Canadian case of **Bank of Montreal v Canadian Westgrowth Ltd** (1990) 72 Alta LR (2d) 319. The plaintiff sought to make a parent company liable on a contract entered into by its wholly owned subsidiary, because: (a) the officers and directors of the two companies were identical and meetings of their two boards were held concurrently; (b) the subsidiary was funded entirely by the parent and its assets were purchased with money loaned by the parent interest free and with no terms for repayment; (c) the audits for both companies were performed by the same auditor and they had identical financial years; (d) most of the dealings and correspondence concerning the contract were with the parent's personnel and correspondence was on the parent's headed paper; and (e) the parent provided management services to the subsidiary without cost. Brennan J said, at p 327:

> In the present case there was no express contract of agency between [parent and subsidiary], and I am not prepared to find an implied contract of agency from the facts before me.
>
> In my view the facts relied upon by the plaintiff to support its argument for a piercing of the corporate veil do not justify a finding that [parent and subsidiary] were one and the same and that [the parent] was the *de facto* contracting party, being the alter ego of [the subsidiary].
>
> With respect to both grounds argued by the plaintiff it is my view that the facts relied upon by the plaintiff in support thereof are nothing more than one would expect to find in the operation of two associated com-panies, and in particular where, as here, [the parent] provided management services for [the subsidiary].

On appeal ((1992) 2 Alta LR (3d) 221) Fraser CJA said, at p 223:

> In this case we have a written contract which clearly says it is with one party, [the subsidiary]. In order to find that (in some way by agency or otherwise) it is not really with [the subsidiary], it is really with [the parent], one would need pretty clear—possibly overwhelming—evidence of agency or something else. The evidence which has been pointed out to us is not of that nature.

It is common for a contract of sale to provide that the purchaser can nominate a company to take legal title to the property on completion of the sale. This in itself does not constitute the nominated company an agent, trustee or partner of the nominator or otherwise justify ignoring the nominated company's separate personality, even where the purchaser and the nominated company are in the same group of companies (*Attorney-General v Equiticorp Industries Group Ltd* [1996] 1 NZLR 528).

It is common for each vessel in a merchant shipping fleet to be in the registered ownership of a separate company—known as a 'one-ship company'—so as to limit the liability of the fleet owner in respect of each vessel. The court will not ignore the separate personality of a one-ship company so as to transfer its liabilities to the fleet owner just because this corporate structure has been used (*The Evpo Agnic* [1988] 1 WLR 1090; *The Skaw Prince* [1994] 3 SLR 379).

5.5 CORPORATE LAW THEORY

5.5.1 INTRODUCTION

Probably the most important legal feature of a body corporate is its dual nature as both an association of its members and a person separate from its members. Separate personality is a powerful but perplexing legal concept and has attracted a great deal of argument. This section offers a very brief introduction to the main themes of this argument.

5.5.2 CRITICISM OF ARTIFICIAL SEPARATE PERSONALITY

This book adopts what is often called the 'artificial-entity' theory of corporate personality, which is that incorporation creates an artificial separate person. That separate person, though artificial (that is, produced by human artifice rather than occurring naturally), is treated by the law as being, as far as possible, a person with the same capacity to engage in legal relationships as a human person. It is an important feature of the legal systems of the United Kingdom and many other jurisdictions that they treat artificial persons in this way.

The description of corporate personality as artificial has been adopted by some judges. In **Trustees of Dartmouth College v Woodward** (1819) 17 US (4 Wheat) 518 Marshall CJ said, at p 636:

> A corporation is an artificial being, invisible, intangible, and existing only in contemplation of law. Being the mere creature of law, it possesses only those properties which the charter of its creation confers upon it, either expressly or as incidental to its very existence ... Among the most important are immortality, and, if the expression be allowed, individuality; properties by which a perpetual succession of many persons are considered as the same, and may act as a single individual.

In *Welton v Saffery* [1897] AC 299 Lord Halsbury LC described a registered company as an 'artificial creature', which must be dealt with 'as an artificial creation' (at p 305).

There has been considerable criticism of what is called the 'fiction' that the process of incorporation creates a separate, artificial person.

One group of critics belongs to a long tradition of holding what may be called an 'individualistic' view, that only human beings can claim legal rights and obligations and have rights and duties arising from legal relationships. As Max Radin put it, in **'The endless problem of corporate personality'** (1932) 32 Colum L Rev 643 at p 665:

There is always a danger of indirection and confusion when, for any purpose and even for a moment, lawyers or publicists lose sight of the fact that their fundamental units are human beings, nearly all human beings but nothing but human beings. These are persons in the proper sense of the term. Law exists for them to express their relations and subserve their needs. One of these needs is to speak of collectivities as though they too were persons. But an equal need is not to forget that they are not.

Jurists adopting this view suggest that a corporation should be regarded merely as a collective name for its members. This is sometimes known as the 'symbolist' or 'bracket' theory of corporate personality because a corporation is seen as merely a symbol for, or brackets around, the names of its members. It is also known as the 'aggregate theory' of corporate personality because it regards a corporation as merely an aggregate of its members. Writers on jurisprudence who asserted this view include the German Rudolf von Jhering (1818–92) and the American Wesley N Hohfeld (1879–1918). For references to original German sources, see M Wolff, 'On the nature of legal persons' (1938) 54 LQR 494 at p 497, nn 9 and 10. (Wolff's article generally gives more detail on this and other criticisms of artificial separate personality.) Hohfeld's views are discussed in the article by Radin cited earlier.

In recent times, there has been important individualist criticism of economics, social sciences and political theory, associated especially with the economist Friedrich von Hayek (1899–1992). This criticism seeks to require society to be studied in terms of individual human beings and not as an entity in itself. This has been called 'methodological individualism'. See S Lukes, *Individualism* (Oxford: Basil Blackwell, 1973), especially Chapter 17.

The individualistic view cannot be regarded as an accurate description of the common law theory of the corporation. It ignores the fact that the corporation is a useful legal concept precisely because it is regarded by common law both as a separate person and an association of its members. As Lord Sumner said in *Gas Lighting Improvement Co Ltd v Commissioners of Inland Revenue* [1923] AC 723 at p 741:

> Between the investor, who participates as a shareholder, and the undertaking carried on, the law interposes another person, real though artificial, the company itself, and the business carried on is the business of that company, and the capital employed is its capital and not in either case the business or the capital of the shareholders . . . the idea that [the company] is mere machinery for effecting the purposes of the shareholders is a layman's fallacy. It is a figure of speech, which cannot alter the legal aspect.

The relationship between the members of a company and the company as a separate person is the subject of a great deal of law. The individualistic view does, however, serve as a reminder that the common law principle of legal personality is not without problems, which are manifested in the controversy over lifting or piercing the veil (that is, ignoring the separate personality of a company), discussed in 5.3. Other problems are the extent to which a company, as a separate person, can be said to have interests (see 3.6.5.2 and 16.6.4) or should have criminal liability (see 19.8), and the extent to which companies should be accorded human rights such as freedom of speech (see 5.7), freedom of religion (see 19.8.9), or the right not to give evidence incriminating oneself (see 19.9.3).

Another group of critics assert that an association of persons has a real personality which is merely recognised, and not created, by the process of incorporation. This assertion is called the 'realist' theory or 'natural-entity' theory and is particularly associated with the German legal historian Otto von Gierke (1841–1921). The realist theory of corporate personality is associated with opposition to the concession theory of incorporation. Supporters of the realist theory refer to the artificial-entity theory, rather scornfully, as the 'fiction theory', because they see it mainly as a denial of the reality of corporate personality.

The best-known exposition in English of Gierke's work is by the legal historian Frederick Maitland (1850–1906); see **F W Maitland, 'Introduction'**, in O Gierke, *Political Theories of the Middle Age*, transl. F W Maitland (Cambridge: Cambridge University Press, 1900), pp vii–xlv. Like many writers on corporate law theory, Gierke was interested in both legal theory and political theory. He was interested in the position of the corporation in the polity and also in the links between theories of corporations and theories of the State. For a detailed, if at times overheated, discussion of theories of the corporation and theories of the State, see F Hallis, *Corporate Personality* (Oxford: Oxford University Press, 1930). The development of these ideas in the Middle Ages is considered with a brilliant cascade of medievalistic scholarship in E H Kantorowicz, *The King's Two Bodies* (Princeton NJ: Princeton University Press, 1957).

The great difficulty for realists is to describe the personality which they ascribe to a corporation. Is corporate personality comparable to human personality? Sometimes a body corporate is described in terms of a human body (see **19.8.2.2**). Some commentators have seen the real personality of a group of persons in terms of a group psyche—a mind and will created by the group. Maitland ('**Introduction**', pp xxv–xxvi) said that Gierke's theory:

> seems to say . . . our German Fellowship is no fiction, no symbol, no piece of the State's machinery, no collective name for individuals, but a living organism and a real person, with body and members and a will of its own. Itself can will, itself can act; it wills and acts by the men who are its organs as a man wills and acts by brain, mouth and hand. It is not a fictitious person . . . it is a group-person, and its will is a group-will.

W M Geldart, 'Legal personality' (1911) 27 LQR 90 quoted the above passage, without the cautionary first three words, and said (at p 93) that it stated the 'essence' of the realist theory and talked (at p 94) of 'the reality of a group-personality' which was to be investigated by political science, ethics, psychology and metaphysics. J A Mack, 'Group personality—a footnote to Maitland' (1952) 2 Philos Q 249, suggested that Maitland did not believe the theory of the group-person and the group-will, and that what Gierke meant by it 'is not altogether clear' (p 250, n 6). Between Geldart's expression of support for Gierke and Mack's attempt to separate Maitland from Gierke, it had been said that Gierke's views were used in Fascist political theory to justify the dictatorial Fascist State as an organism superior to the individuals of whom it is composed (see E Barker, 'Introduction', in O Gierke, *Natural Law and the Theory of Society 1550 to 1800*, transl. E Barker (Cambridge: Cambridge University Press, 1934) at pp lxxxiv–lxxxvii; J D Lewis, *The Genossenschaft-Theory of Otto von Gierke* (University of Wisconsin Studies in the Social Sciences and History, No 25) (Madison, Wis: University of Wisconsin, 1935)).

As in the passage from Maitland quoted earlier, realists sometimes assert that a distinction should be drawn between a company acting by an agent and a company acting by an organ, and it is only with a realist conception of the corporation that it can be said to act by an organ (which is why the realist theory is sometimes called the 'organic' theory). English law does not, however, seem to make this distinction (see **14.4.5**, **19.5.6** and **19.8.2.4**).

The idea of a company as an entity with its own personality and will has recently emerged again through applying the political philosophy of communitarianism to companies (see D J Morrissey, 'Toward a new/old theory of corporate social responsibility' (1989) 40 Syracuse L Rev 1005, especially at pp 1033–6).

A more recent approach is to say that an entity's real personality derives from the mere fact of its being referred to as a unit. This is known as the 'autopoietic' ('self-creating') theory (see G Teubner, 'Enterprise corporatism: new industrial policy and the "essence" of the legal person' (1988) 36 Am J Comp Law 130 (reprinted in S Wheeler, *A Reader on the Law of Business Enterprise* (Oxford: Oxford University Press, 1994))). This approach can also be seen in the statement by F W Maitland, 'if n men unite themselves in an organised body, jurisprudence, unless it wishes to pulverise the group, must see $n + 1$ persons' ('**Moral personality and legal personality**', in *Collected Papers*, H A L Fisher (ed), vol 3 (Cambridge: Cambridge University Press, 1911), pp 304–20, at p 316). Maitland, giving the 1903 Sidgwick Lecture, was discussing a statement in the previous year's lecture by Professor A V Dicey (1835–1922), 'When a body of 20 or 2,000 or 200,000 men bind themselves together to act in a particular way for some common purpose, they create a body which, by no fiction of law but from the very nature of things, differs from the individuals of whom it is constituted' (**A V Dicey, 'The combination laws as illustrating the rela-tion between law and public opinion in England during the 19th century'** (1904) 16 Harv L Rev 511 at p 513). Dicey was discussing the personality of trade unions. In *Bonsor v Musicians' Union* [1954] Ch 479, Denning LJ quoted Dicey to support his view that a trade union did have legal personality (the Trade Union and Labour Relations (Consolidation) Act 1992, s 10, now provides that it does not), and in *Willis v Association of Universities of the British Commonwealth* [1965] 1 QB 140, his Lordship held (again quoting Dicey) that a department of a company was 'a separate entity' (but then proceeded to find that this did not affect the case before him), claiming that his view in *Bonsor v Musicians' Union* had been upheld by the House of Lords on appeal [1956] AC 104. In fact, as Mocatta J pointed out in *Knight and Searle v Dove* [1964] 2 QB 631 at p 635, the Law Lords in *Bonsor v Musicians' Union* were divided on the question. For a full discussion of these cases, see K W Wedderburn, 'Corporate personality and social policy: the problem of the quasi-corporation' (1965) 28 MLR 62.

Realist critics would generally admit that the common law does not give full legal personality to entities that they think should have full legal personality, for example, partnerships and most unincorporated associations (though Scots law does confer full legal personality on partnerships: Partnership Act 1890, s 4(2)). It is also difficult to accept that such entities as wholly owned subsid-iaries, shelf companies waiting to be bought, dormant companies and single-member companies have 'real' personality. Realist critics would say that this is the fault of the legal system, which ought to change its rules for conferring legal personality. They say that it is wrong for the legal system to confer personality on entities that do not have a 'real' personality while denying legal personality to entities that do have a real personality (see, for example, H J Laski, 'The personality of associations' (1916) 29 Harv L Rev 404). The counter-argument of the artificial-entity theory is that it is better not to seek some characteristic of entities (such as being a group-person with a group-will) which justifies them being granted legal personality, rather it should be left to the legal system to decide which entities are to have legal personality (see J Dewey, 'The historic background of legal per-sonality' (1926) 35 Yale LJ 655; M Wolff, 'On the nature of legal persons' (1938) 54 LQR 494). H L A Hart, 'Definition and theory in jurisprudence' (1954) 70 LQR 37 took this counterargument further and suggested that it is misguided to search for the meaning of the legal concept of 'corpor-ation' in terms of what it is that the word by itself refers to, because, like many legal concepts, it is a product of human thought rather than a description of some pre-existing entity. One should instead seek the meaning of the concept in the way in which it is used (this idea is also mentioned by Dewey, 'The historic background of legal personality' at pp 660–1). It seems that Hart was mak-ing an essentially philosophical point about the nature of definition. For a more abstract analysis on the same lines, see J Wrónblewski, 'Legal person: legal language and reality' (1982–83) 11/12 Quaderni Fiorentini per la Storia del Pensiero Giuridico Moderno 1035.

The natural-entity (realist) and artificial-entity (fiction) theories produce two different policies. In a realist legal system, all entities with 'real personality' would have legal personality, and entities without 'real personality' would not have legal personality. A fictionist legal system grants legal personality simply on the basis of whether it is beneficial to do so. It is clear that the English legal system is not realist. It does not grant legal personality to trade unions (Trade Union and Labour Relations (Consolidation) Act 1992, s 10) because trade unionists do not want it, though realists argued that trade unions do have real personality. It grants separate legal personality to wholly owned subsidiaries because of the commercial benefits of allowing them separate legal personality, though realists would argue that they do not have real personality. It grants separate legal personal-ity to single-member companies so as to enable individuals to trade with limited liability though realists would argue that a single-member company does not have a real personality separate from that of its member.

The realist–fictionist argument may be seen (especially in Maitland's presentation) as a manifestation of the clash of world-views which pervaded much of nineteenth century thought:

the traditional view of cultured Europeans based on an admiring vision of Classical Greece and Rome against the newer, more nationalistic view based on a vision of a glorious medieval past. The realist critics asserted that the fiction theory was a theory of Roman law but the realist theory represented medieval German and English jurisprudence. The discussion of realism and fictionism in the late nineteenth and early twentieth centuries was accompanied by vast amounts of history, but subsequent commentators have pointed out that there has been a search for a coherent theory of corporate personality only in modern times, and that there is no evidence of what theory ancient or medieval lawyers held because they never considered the issue (see P W Duff, *Personality in Roman Private Law* (Cambridge: Cambridge University Press, 1938), Chapter 9; H Lubasz, 'The corporate borough in the late Year-Book period' (1964) 80 LQR 228).

Some critics see the concept of the separate personality of a company as alienating people from their real conditions of existence by reifying social relationships. The view of A A Berle Jr and G C Means in *The Modern Corporation and Private Property* (New York: The Macmillan Company, 1932), at pp 66–7, was that:

> The spiritual values that formerly went with ownership have been separated from it. Physical property capable of being shaped by its owner could bring to him direct satisfaction apart from the income it yielded in more concrete form. It represented an extension of his own personality. With the corporate revolution, this quality has been lost to the property owner much as it has been lost to the worker through the Industrial revolution.

Later, at p 352, they quoted **W Rathenau, *In Days to Come*, transl E and C Paul (London: Allen & Unwin, 1921), pp 120–1, writing of public companies:

> No one is a permanent owner. The composition of the thousandfold complex which functions as lord of the undertaking is in a state of flux . . . This condition of things signifies that ownership has been depersonalised . . . The depersonalisation of ownership simultaneously implies the objectification of the thing owned. The claims to ownership are subdivided in such a fashion, and are so mobile, that the enterprise assumes an independent life, as if it belonged to no one.

Critical studies of company law, enlarging on the points just made, may be found in K A Lahey and S W Salter, 'Corporate law in legal theory and legal scholarship: from classicism to feminism' (1985) 23 Osgoode Hall LJ 543; P Ireland, I Grigg-Spall and D Kelly, 'The conceptual foundations of modern company law' (1987) 14 J Law and Soc 149; and C Stanley, 'Corporate personality and capitalist relations: a critical analysis of the artifice of company law' (1988) 19 Cambrian Law Review 98.

5.5.3 THE CONCESSION THEORY

The theory of English law, as set out in **1.3.2**, is that (ignoring corporations sole) an entity can be given separate personality only by or on the authority of the Crown or Parliament. A group of people who form an association cannot effectively declare it to have separate personality. The principle that corporations with separate personality can be created only by act of State is known as the 'concession theory'. It is true that, in contrast to the great reluctance of Crown or Parliament to grant the privileges of incorporation before 1844 (see **1.3.2.4**), the system of registration introduced by the Joint Stock Companies Act 1844 and now governed by CA 2006 offers virtually automatic incorporation. It has been said that UK companies 'are formed by contract . . . under memorandum and articles of association to which the Registrar of Joint-Stock Companies necessarily assents if the documents are regular in form' (per Sir Walter Phillimore in **Canada National Fire Insurance Co v Hutchings** [1918] AC 451 at p 456). Nevertheless, the issue of the registrar's certificate of incorporation is an essential step in the incorporation of a registered company, and the ease with which it can be obtained does not negate the concession theory. The registrar may refuse to register a company formed for an unlawful purpose, see **2.2.3**. As Lord Templeman said in *Arab Monetary Fund v Hashim (No 3)* [1991] 2 AC 114 at p 160:

> When the promoters of a company enter into an agreement to incorporate a company and the agreement takes the form of a memorandum and articles of association of the company, that agreement does not create a corporation. When the memorandum and articles are registered under the Companies Act 1985, that registration does not recognise a corporation but creates a corporation.

Different legal systems may confer full legal personality on different entities. For example, in Scots law, unlike the law of England and Wales, a partnership firm has legal personality (Partnership Act 1890, s 4(2)), that is its personality arises by virtue of the private contract between the partners and not by any act of State (though every partner in a partnership is directly responsible for the firm's debts in both English and Scots law). In Hindu law, a family idol has legal personality (*Pramatha Nath Mullick v Pradyumna Kumar Mullick* (1925) LR 52 Ind App 245; see P W Duff, 'The personality of an idol' (1927) 3 CLJ 42). In *Bumper Development Corporation v Commissioner of Police of the Metropolis* [1991] 1 WLR 1362, expert evidence was accepted that a Hindu temple has legal personality in Tamil Nadu. For a proposal that natural environmental features should be given legal personality so that they can bring proceedings to prevent, or obtain compensation for, damage, see C D Stone, 'Should trees have standing?—Toward legal rights for natural objects' (1972) 45 S Cal L Rev 450 and '"Should trees have standing?" revisited: how far will law and morals reach? A pluralist perspective' (1985) 59 S Cal L Rev 1. In New Zealand, the Te Awa Tupua (Whanganui River Claims Settlement) Act 2017, ss 12 and 14, give legal personality to all the physical and metaphysical elements of the Whanganui River under the name Te Awa Tupua.

Within a legal system, entities may be regarded as having partial legal personality, in the sense that they may be regarded as having a capacity to enter into some but not all legal relationships. For example, English rules of court procedure permit an English partnership firm to be a party to legal proceedings, and CA 2006, s 1216(2), empowers a company to appoint an English partnership firm as its auditor.

There has been a great deal of political debate about the concession theory. In various countries at various times, there have been fears that it may be used by governments as a means of curbing freedom to associate for political purposes. In Britain, the deliberate withholding of corporate personality from trade unions so that it would be difficult if not impossible to sue them for damage caused by industrial action was a serious political and legal issue for most of the twentieth century. In the USA, controversy over the concession theory of incorporation is associated with controversy over State regulation of business activity.

5.5.4 ECONOMISTS AND CONTRACTARIANS

Whether or not it is accepted that the law deals adequately with the separate personality and the membership as two aspects of the company, it is said by some critics of the common law theory of corporate personality that it pays insufficient attention to the business or other activity that the company pursues. These critics suggest that the law should have regard to the business enterprise rather than the individual company as a legal entity. This theory of enterprise entity seems to involve abandoning the concession theory of incorporation in favour of requiring courts to analyse in each case the economic structures they are asked to deal with and deciding for each of them where to allocate personality. This would seem to be unworkable in practice.

Economists are usually interested in companies only in so far as they engage in economic activity. Economists are not usually interested in dormant companies or shelf companies waiting to be bought. Economists are interested in economic actors regardless of their legal form. However, they are interested in the organisation of economic actors, especially where they are organised with systems of long-term relationships between factors of production—where, for example, investors put in permanent contributed capital, or the contracts of employment of employees last for longer than the production of a single item of output. These long-term relationships surprise economists who believe that factors of production would be more efficiently allocated in a continuous marketplace. R H Coase, 'The nature of the firm' (1937) 4 Economica NS 386 observed that not going to the marketplace for each and every particle of input saves on transaction costs. A A Alchian and H Demsetz, 'Production, information costs, and economic organization' (1972) 62 Am Econ Rev 777 focus on the necessity for teams of inputs (a multitude of investors to provide large amounts of capital; a team of employees to collaborate in making products) and deduce that the characteristic feature of an organised firm is not so much long-term contracting but the management coordination of teams of contractors. (O Hart, 'An economist's perspective on the theory of the firm' (1989) 89 Colum L Rev 1757 reviews these and other contributions and suggests that economists' theories of the firm have not yet got very far.) Economists who have concentrated on analysing organised firms as alternatives to markets have described a firm as a 'nexus of contracts', a catchphrase which seems to have originated with **M C Jensen and W H Meckling, 'Theory of the firm: managerial behavior, agency costs and ownership structure'** (1976) 3 J Fin Econ 305, who talk, at pp 310–11, of 'a nexus of contracting relationships'. The phrase has been adopted by many in the law and economics movement. If, as many in that movement believe, the law should not interfere with freedom of contract, the law should have little to do with a company which is only a 'nexus of contracts'. As a public service, the State may promulgate a standard-form contract to save people the expense of working out their own contracts (for example, the model articles of association in SI 2008/3229) but mandatory rules of company law are likely to be either superfluous or distortions of the free market. For expositions of the nexus of contracts view see F H Easterbrook and D R Fischel, 'The corporate contract' (1989) 89 Colum L Rev 1416 and H N Butler, 'The contractual theory of the corporation' (1989) 11 Geo Mason U L Rev 99. Writers adopting the nexus of contracts view are often called 'contractarians'. They scarcely mention corporate personality, which is largely irrelevant to their policy programme. Easterbrook and Fischel, for example, in the article just cited, seem to regard a company as merely a symbol for the names of its members (see p 1426) as in the aggregate theory discussed at the beginning of 5.5.2. But in an earlier article, **'Limited liability and the corporation'** (1985) 52 U Chi L Rev 89, they regard a company as a 'set of contracts among managers, workers, and contributors of capital', a view also taken in the economics literature by E F Fama, 'Agency problems and the theory of the firm' (1980) 88 J Polit Econ 288 at p 289. Many adherents of the nexus of contracts view see no need for the State to be involved in creating corporate personality and disapprove of the concession theory.

The metaphor of the nexus of contracts neatly encapsulates the law and economics approach to company law, but it is the application of economic theory to law which is the distinctive feature of that approach not the application of contract law. As explained in **3.4**, lawyers have long recognised a contractual analysis of companies but the practical application of contract law to company law has always been fraught with difficulty, partly because of contract law's unfamiliarity with the process of renegotiation to adjust to changes of circumstances and partly because contract law is inappropriate for handling constitutional questions (again because they involve adjustments in long-term arrangements). One problem with the nexus of contracts metaphor is that a lawyer's concept of contract is much narrower than an economist's and it is sometimes difficult to know whether people using the metaphor are talking only of legally enforceable contracts or of economically significant dealings generally.

Economists are interested in the contracts made with suppliers to a firm of goods, labour, energy and services, and in the contracts made with customers of the firm. Contractarian analysts of company law, though, generally do not want anyone other than shareholders to be regarded as having a stake in a company and tend to ignore contracts with persons other than shareholders except as aspects of markets in which the company operates, though they do devote considerable time to analysing the relationship between shareholders and directors.

An important difficulty with applying the legal concept of a contract to the constitution of a company is, as pointed out in **3.4.1.2**, that a constitution is only a framework of procedures for making decisions as and when decisions are required whereas a contract is traditionally thought of as a schedule of things to be done by the parties. Members of a company do not make a contract detailing what they and their company are to do: they enter into a relationship in which they expect to benefit from whatever it is their company does do, as settled from time to time by themselves and the directors, and they agree on the form of that relationship as set out in the company's constitution. For a discussion of these problems see C A Riley, 'Contracting out of company law: section 459 of the Companies Act 1985 and the role of the courts' (1992) 55 MLR 782.

The idea that a company is a nexus of contracts has been useful to the law and economics movement and has been useful for promoting the application of the idea of freedom of contract to company law but it is an inadequate description of the company unless the concept of contract is expanded to take in the constitutional relationships between a company and its members and between the members themselves.

For a large-scale review, with copious references, see the pair of articles by W W Bratton Jr, 'The new economic theory of the firm: critical perspectives from history' (1989) 41 Stan L Rev 1471 (reprinted in S Wheeler, *A Reader on the Law of Business Enterprise* (Oxford: Oxford University Press, 1994)) and 'The "nexus of contracts" corporation: a critical appraisal' (1989) 74 Cornell L Rev 407. R Flannigan, 'The economic structure of the firm' (1995) 33 Osgoode Hall LJ 105 observes that the primary purpose of a firm is not to make contracts but to produce goods or services and that concentrating attention on the contracts a firm makes may not help in the analysis of its internal structure. Flannigan's article includes a valuable review of economic theories of the firm. There is another very helpful review of theories in S Douma and H Schreuder, *Economic Approaches to Organizations*, 4th edn (Harlow: Financial Times Prentice Hall, 2008).

5.5.5 WHAT INFLUENCE DOES THEORY HAVE?

We have never come across an instance of a judge or legislator saying that a case was being decided in a particular way, or an enactment was worded in a particular way, so as to be in accordance with one theory of corporate personality rather than another. None of the theories can be regarded by a court as a source of law, since none has been stated legislatively or pronounced in a court judgment. The theories themselves are in fact very malleable and can rarely decide a point one way or another. This is perhaps to be expected since the theories have come after company law itself and have all had to be capable of explaining existing company law in order to be taken seriously. However, as we have suggested in our comments, the theories are never complete explanations: none of them provides a base from which company law can be deduced. The philosopher John Dewey (whose philosophy was founded on suspicion about the practical value of abstract theories) suggested that apparently conflicting theories of corporate personality had been used to serve the same ends, while one theory alone could be used to serve opposing ends ('The historic background of corporate legal personality' (1926) 35 Yale LJ 655 at p 669). Nevertheless, the theories have always provoked great interest and are widely discussed. Some scholars have discerned the influence of one theory or another in cases or legislation but this is more a matter of identifying a sympathy for a theory than finding a logical consequence of it. In an article dedicated to Gierke, F Pollock, 'Has the common law received the fiction theory of corporations?' in *Essays in the Law* (London: Macmillan, 1922), pp 151–79, concluded that the fiction theory was not part of the common law. D H Bonham and D A Soberman, 'The nature of corporate personality' in *Studies in Canadian Company Law*, J S Ziegel (ed) (Toronto: Butterworths, 1967), pp 3–32, found some evidence that courts in England and Canada have sometimes adopted a line of reasoning which coincides with one or other of the realist or fictionist standpoints. D Millon, 'Theories of the corporation' [1990]

Duke LJ 201 examines the history of corporate law in the USA. There is a very detailed examination of the influence of realist theory in England and the USA at the end of the nineteenth and beginning of the twentieth centuries in M M Hager, 'Bodies politic: the progressive history of organizational "real entity" theory' (1989) 50 U Pitt L Rev 575; see also M J Horwitz, '*Santa Clara* revisited: the development of corporate theory' (1985) 88 W Va L Rev 173. Both Hager and Horwitz claim to demonstrate that realist theory had a consistent influence, but their articles seem better to support the view of John Dewey that different corporate theories could support similar arguments and the same theory could be used both for and against an argument. The articles by Hager and Horwitz do, however, show the inaccuracy of the crude association of corporate law theories with political views given by J C Coates IV, 'State takeover statutes and corporate theory: the revival of an old debate' (1989) 64 NYU L Rev 806 at p 809, n 18 (artificial-entity theory, liberal or leftist; natural-entity theory, traditional conservative; aggregate theory, neoconservative): the natural-entity theory was once the favourite of both the left and the right.

5.6 COMPANY LINGUISTICS

5.6.1 COMPANY SINGULAR OR PLURAL?

The idea of treating an incorporated company as a person separate from its members rather than as an aggregate of its members is a simple legal device that has very considerable consequences, as shown in this chapter. One consequence is linguistic: 'company' is always construed as a singular noun—at least by writers on company law nowadays. Anyone reading cases decided before the First World War will notice that judges in those days always construed 'company' as a plural noun: the company was 'they' rather than 'it'—linguistically, the judges seemed to have been thinking of a company as an aggregate of its members. The point is illustrated by *Prior v Sovereign Chicken Ltd* [1984] 1 WLR 921, in which a building would have been entitled to exclusion from rating if it had been occupied by 'persons'. It was occupied by a company so it was only occupied by one person, and in the circumstances the court held that in this instance the plural did not include the singular.

The linguistics of talking about companies, and the implications for jurisprudential theories of company law, are discussed in S A Schane, 'The corporation is a person: the language of a legal fiction' (1987) 61 Tul L Rev 563.

5.6.2 PERSONS AND INDIVIDUALS

The use in this book of the terms 'natural person' and 'legal person' for distinct categories corresponds to the way they are used in European Union documents (see *Gregg v Commissioners of Customs and Excise* (case C-216/97) [1999] ECR I-4947), and is the way in which 'legal person' was used when it was introduced into the language by the University of London's first professor of jurisprudence, John Austin (1790–1859). In French, what is here called a legal person is usually called a '*personne morale*', the adjective '*morale*' indicating that it is not a physical person but the product of human thought. In the past, this was sometimes rather inappropriately translated into English as 'moral person', but this usage seems to have died out and 'moral person' is nowadays used to refer to a person capable of moral responsibility and accountability—whether a corporation can be a moral person in this sense is an interesting philosophical and legal question: see the discussion of corporate criminal liability in **19.8**.

Some writers on jurisprudence adopt a more abstract analysis. They describe any entity that has legal rights and duties as a 'legal person' and say that the rules of a legal system determine whether any particular human being or non-human entity has a legal personality. This analysis has the advantage that it allows for an entity to have more than one legal personality.

Section 5 of and sch 1 to the Interpretation Act 1978 prescribe that in Acts of Parliament and subordinate legislation, unless the contrary intention appears, '"Person" includes a body of persons corporate or unincorporate.' This applies to Acts passed after 1889 (Interpretation Act 1978, sch 2, para 4(1)). In addition, 'person' is deemed to include a body corporate in any provision of an Act, whenever passed, relating to an offence, unless the contrary intention appears (sch 2, para 4(5)). In *R v Home Secretary, ex parte Atlantic Commercial Ltd* [1997] BCC 692 a contrary intention was found. It was held that in the Criminal Justice Act 1988, s 133 (which provides for the payment of compensation to 'a person' who has been wrongfully convicted of an offence), 'person' does not include a corporation. In all deeds, contracts, wills, orders and other instruments, unless the context otherwise requires, 'person' includes a corporation (Law of Property Act 1925, s 61; see *Deutsche Genossenschaftsbank v Burnhope* [1995] 1 WLR 1580 discussed in **19.8.4.4**).

In legislation, the word 'individual' is capable of including a company, if the context requires it, but the word does not usually bear that meaning (*Jasmine Trustees Ltd v Wells and Hind* [2007] EWHC 38 (Ch), [2008] Ch 194). In this book, 'individual' is used to mean an individual human being.

It is usual in drafting legislation to use the pronouns 'he' and 'him' for a 'person', and use of those pronouns does not show an intention to refer only to individuals (per Lord Simon of Glaisdale in *Applin v Race Relations Board* [1975] AC 259 at p 290).

In the United Kingdom and Ireland, the word 'company' is used for corporations which are incorporated by registration under a Companies Act. And 'company' is the term used in European Union documents in English for the equivalent entities throughout the EU. In some other English-speaking countries, including the USA, Canada and Australia, the equivalent entity is called a 'business corporation' or simply a 'corporation'.

5.7 COMPANIES' HUMAN RIGHTS

In many nations, laws define enforceable human rights so as to limit the power of government and State institutions to dispose of individuals and their property. One of the most important systems for the enforcement of human rights was established by the European Convention on Human Rights, which the United Kingdom was the first State to ratify. The Convention has been incorporated into the UK's domestic law by the Human Rights Act 1998.

Although human rights are always thought of as the rights of individual human beings, companies may be able to benefit from them and when they do, it might be better to refer to the rights as personal rights. For example, a company may invoke art 6 of the Convention to require a fair trial in the determination of its civil rights and obligations (as in *R (Alconbury Developments Ltd) v Secretary of State for the Environment, Transport and the Regions* [2001] UKHL 23, [2003] 2 AC 295) or of any criminal charge against it (as in *Marpa Zeeland BV v Netherlands* (application 46300/99) (2004) 40 EHRR 34). A company is entitled to the protection of art 10 (freedom of expression) (*Autronic AG v Switzerland* (application 12726/87) (1990) 12 EHRR 485 at para 47; *R (North Cyprus Tourism Centre Ltd) v Transport for London* [2005] EWHC 1698 (Admin), [2005] UKHRR 1231; *Meltex Ltd v Armenia* (application 32283/04) 49 EHRR 40). Article 1 (protection of property) of the First Protocol to the Convention is expressly stated to apply to every natural or legal person. However, in *R v Home Secretary, ex parte Atlantic Commercial Ltd* [1997] BCC 692 it was held that the Criminal Justice Act 1988, s 133, which provides for the payment of compensation to a person who has been wrongly convicted of an offence and which was intended to give effect to the United Nations International Covenant on Civil and Political Rights (1966), art 14(6), was not intended to apply to companies.

In *R v Broadcasting Standards Commission, ex parte British Broadcasting Corporation* [2001] QB 885 the Court of Appeal held that, under the Broadcasting Act 1996, a company could complain to the Broadcasting Standards Commission (now Ofcom) that there had been an unwarranted infringement of its privacy in connection with obtaining material included in broadcast programmes. Lord Woolf MR said, at p 897, that 'a company does have activities of a private nature which need protection from unwarranted intrusion'. However, all three members of the court said that the concept of privacy in the 1996 Act was different from the concept of 'respect for [someone's] private and family life, his home and his correspondence' in art 8 of the European Convention on Human Rights, and emphasised that they were not deciding that the Convention's concept could apply to a company. See E Weinert, '*Firma EDV v Germany*—do companies have feelings too?' (2015) 26 Entertainment Law Review 50.

If a company has been injured by a breach of the European Convention on Human Rights, a member of the company is not a victim of that breach and so has no standing to apply to the European Court of Human Rights or to bring proceedings under the Human Rights Act 1998, s 7 (*Agrotexim v Greece* (application 14807/89) (1995) 21 EHRR 250; *Weir v Secretary of State for Transport* [2005] EWHC 2192 (Ch), LTL 21/10/2005, at [294]–[298]). This is an application of the proper claimant principle discussed in **18.4.1**. The European Court of Human Rights has, however, allowed a form of derivative claim, in which a member of a company presents an application in its name, where it is clear that it is not possible for those responsible for the company's litigation to make the application (*Credit and Industrial Bank v Czech Republic* (application 29010/95) (2003) ECHR 2003-XI at paras 46–52).

PART 3

FINANCE

6

SHARES

SUMMARY OF POINTS COVERED

- What is in this chapter
- Shares and membership rights
- Allotment
- Principles of accounting
- Timing and size of the capital contribution
- Form of contribution
- Minimum capital of a public company
- Remedies of a wronged allottee
- Alteration of share capital

6.1 WHAT IS IN THIS CHAPTER

The legal form of the company limited by shares was designed primarily for use as a means of carrying on a business. Membership of a company limited by shares is based on contributing (or undertaking to contribute) capital for use in the business in return for the issue of shares. The shares that a member holds entitle the member to benefit from the company's business profits by receiving dividends and a share in any surplus when the company is wound up. Shares also entitle a member to participate in the governance of the company (see **Chapter 14**).

A member of a company who contributes more capital than another will want a proportionally greater share in distributions of the company's profits and also a greater influence on the company's affairs (ie, more votes at members' meetings). The extent of a member's undertaking to contribute capital, and of entitlement to share in distributions and vote at meetings, are all related to the number and class of shares of the company that the member holds (see **6.2**).

Normally, in a company limited by shares, every member is a shareholder, so that the terms 'member' and 'shareholder' are synonymous. Where a company limited by shares has uncertificated shares, there is legislative provision that only shareholders can be members (SI 2001/3755, reg 24(3); see **14.2**). In principle, a company limited by shares which had no uncertificated shares could have a class of members (perhaps called honorary members) who are not required to contribute any capital, and who each have one vote, and then no shares would be needed to measure the interests of any particular member of that class.

A person may become a shareholder of a company with a share capital:

(a) by taking shares from the company in exchange for a contribution of capital;

(b) through an employees' share scheme (see **10.9**);

(c) by taking a transfer of shares (on sale or gift or as a trustee) from an existing member (see **Chapter 8**);

(d) by operation of law under which the shares of an existing member devolve on, or are vested in, the person. (This happens, for example, when the shares of a deceased member devolve on personal representatives, or the shares of a bankrupt member are vested in a trustee in bankruptcy. Devolution or vesting of shares by operation of law is usually called *transmission* of shares.)

This chapter concentrates on the first method of becoming a shareholder. Shares are allotted (see **6.3**) in exchange for a capital contribution (see **6.4** to **6.6**). Public companies must have a minimum contributed capital (see **6.7**). The possible remedies where a person has been induced by a misrepresentation to take an allotment of shares are considered in **6.8**.

Ways of altering a company's share capital are considered in **6.9**.

Key legislation which you should be able to consult when reading this chapter:

- CA 2006, ss 540–551, 555–577, 580–597, 605–628. All this legislation is in *Blackstone's Statutes on Company Law*.

Your particular course of study may require you to read other source materials.

6.2 SHARES AND MEMBERSHIP RIGHTS

6.2.1 NOMINAL VALUE AND SHARE PREMIUM

A share is essentially a unit of account for measuring a member's interest in a company. Each share in a company limited by shares is required to have a sum of money assigned to it as its nominal value (CA 2006, s 542) and this is the size of the unit of account. The nominal value of a share is the minimum value that a company must demand to receive as contributed capital in exchange for the share.

So if Textbook Examples Co plc has only one class of members and the nominal value of each of its shares is 50p, and I undertake to contribute £5,000 worth of capital to the company, I cannot expect to be allotted more than 10,000 of its shares. Moreover, the company must not offer to allot me more than 10,000 of its 50p shares as an incentive to me to contribute only £5,000 worth of capital, because to do so would distort the way in which the shares allotted to me measure my interest in the company (s 580).

It is, however, permissible for a shareholder to undertake to contribute more for shares than their nominal value—the excess is called share premium. At any time, a member may agree to contribute more capital, either in return for further shares or as share premium (*Kellar v Williams* [2000] 2 BCLC 390). In a solvent winding up of a company, unless the articles provide otherwise, share premium is divisible among all members, even if it was contributed only by some of them.

Capital contributed in exchange for shares, apart from share premium, is called share capital.

Having undertaken to contribute capital to a limited company and thereby become a member, a person may transfer that membership to someone else either by gift or sale. In most private companies, however, the members give the directors power to control admission to membership and an attempted transfer by an existing member may fail because the directors refuse to accept the transferee as a new member.

An advantage of measuring a member's interest by the number of shares held is that it facilitates transfer of part of that interest. For example, a member who has been allotted two shares in a company can transfer half of that interest in the company to someone else: there will then be two members with one share each.

A company may have different classes of members with differing rights of membership if there is a provision to that effect in its articles of association (*Andrews v Gas Meter Co* [1897] 1 Ch 361). The model articles of association in SI 2008/3229 provide that shares may be issued with such rights or restrictions as may be determined by ordinary resolution (model articles for private companies, art 22(1); model articles for public companies, art 43(1)).

Shares in different classes may have different nominal values. Nominal values of different shares may be in different currencies (*Re Scandinavian Bank Group plc* [1988] Ch 87).

6.2.2 MEMBERSHIP RIGHTS

The nominal value of the shares held by a member of a company measures the member's liability to contribute capital to the company. In return for this liability membership confers benefits, of which the main ones are:

(a) The right to influence the way the company's affairs are conducted, by voting at meetings of members.

(b) The right to a return of contributed capital when the company is wound up (provided there is any property left after paying the company's creditors). Sometimes a company returns part of its contributed capital though continuing in business, but this is subject to rules which attempt to ensure that creditors are not jeopardised (see **Chapter 10**).

(c) The right to participate when the company makes a distribution of its profits to its members. If on winding up a company there is a surplus after paying all its creditors and repaying its contributed capital then the surplus is divided among the members. While a company is in existence it may anticipate an ultimate share-out of surplus by an annual (or more frequent) distribution of profits. A distribution of surplus or annual profits is called a dividend.

In a meeting, the general rule is that a vote must first be taken by show of hands, with each member entitled to exercise one vote. It is not possible to take into account different members having different voting strengths unless a written record is made stating how each member voted and how many votes were cast by each member: a vote taken in this way is called a 'poll'. CA 2006, s 284, provides that the default position (which may be changed by the articles) is that each member has one vote on a show of hands but one vote in respect of each share held on a poll. For the rules about demanding that a poll be taken, see **14.10.2**.

The default position at common law for entitlement to return of contributed capital or to dividends is that payments are proportional to the nominal values of shares held (*Oakbank Oil Co v Crum* (1882) 8 App Cas 65; *Birch v Cropper* (1889) 14 App Cas 525; *Re Anglo-Continental Corporation of Western Australia* [1898] 1 Ch 327). However, CA 2006, s 581(c), permits a company's articles to authorise dividends in proportion to amounts paid up on shares, and this is done by art 71 of the model articles for public companies in SI 2008/3229. Bonus shares are issued on the same basis (art 78(2)(b)). So, under these articles, dividends and bonus shares are proportional to capital contributed rather than capital which it has been undertaken to contribute, and nothing is distributed on totally unpaid shares.

6.2.3 PUBLIC NOTIFICATION OF MEMBERSHIP RIGHTS

The rights of a member that depend on the size and class of the member's shareholding may be specified in the contract for the allotment of the shares made between the company and the member. If a company is incorporated with only one class of members, it is likely that their rights will be specified in the articles. If such a company later creates a second class of membership, the rights of those members may be specified in the contracts for the allotment of their shares; alternatively, the rights of the new class may be added, by special resolution, as new provisions of the articles.

If a company is incorporated with two classes of members, the founders may state the rights of both classes in their articles or in a shareholders' agreement.

If membership rights are stated in the articles, a new member is automatically bound to them on taking up membership (CA 2006, s 33(1)), though the new member may join with the other members in altering the rights where that is possible (see **3.5** and **14.14**).

Before CA 1980, the rights of shareholders were not available for public inspection at Companies House unless they were contained in the old-style memorandum or articles, or were conferred by a resolution which had to be filed at Companies House under what is now CA 2006, s 30. However, CA 1980, s 33(5), required every company to file at Companies House, before 22 March 1981, details of all shareholders' rights not contained in documents already filed. Under CA 2006, an application to register a company limited by shares, and a return of allotment of a limited company's shares must be accompanied by a statement of capital (see **2.2.1.7** and **6.3.6**). A statement of capital on registration must state prescribed particulars of the rights attached to the shares that the company will issue to the subscribers (s 10(2)(c)(i)). A statement of capital on allotment must state the same particulars of the rights attached to the allotted shares (s 555(4)(c)(i)). The particulars are prescribed in SI 2009/388, art 2, as follows:

(a) particulars of any voting rights attached to the shares, including rights that arise only in certain circumstances;

(b) particulars of any rights attached to the shares, as respects dividends, to participate in a distribution;

(c) particulars of any rights attached to the shares, as respects capital, to participate in a distribution (including on winding up); and

(d) whether the shares are to be redeemed or are liable to be redeemed at the option of the company or the shareholder (see **10.5**).

For notification of variations of class rights see **14.14.2.6**.

6.2.4 PARTICULAR TYPES OF SHARES

6.2.4.1 Ordinary or equity shares

If there is no prior limit on the amount which the holder of a share may receive in a distribution, either as an annual dividend or as a distribution of surplus assets on winding up, the share is called an ordinary share (CA 2006, s 560(1)) or an equity share (s 548). The total nominal value of all the equity shares issued (see **6.3.1**) by a company is called its equity share capital (s 548). Equity shares and securities convertible into equity shares are together called equity securities in the Listing Rules (FCA Handbook, Glossary).

6.2.4.2 Preference shares

A preference share is a share which entitles the holder to an annual dividend, of a fixed amount per share (usually expressed as a percentage of the nominal value of the share), paid in priority to any dividend payments to other members.

Unless otherwise stated, the right to receive a preference dividend is 'cumulative', that is, if the dividend is not paid for one period, then double payment is due the next period, and so on (*Webb v Earle* (1875) LR 20 Eq 556). It is usual to make this clear by entitling the shares 'cumulative preference shares'. For an example of non-cumulative preference shares see *Staples v Eastman Photographic Materials Co* [1896] 2 Ch 303.

In the absence of any express provision in the agreement between a company and its members of a particular class concerning their class rights, all members must be treated equally (*Birch v Cropper* (1889) 14 App Cas 525). If, however, provision is made in the agreement concerning a particular matter then it is presumed to be exhaustive. For example, shares which carry a right to a fixed preference dividend cannot also receive the dividend paid on ordinary shares (*Will v United Lankat Plantations Co Ltd* [1914] AC 11). (Sometimes, preference shares are issued on the basis that they will carry the right to receive all or part of the ordinary shareholders' dividend and they are known as 'participating' preference shares.) Accordingly, if, as is usual, it is provided that when the company is wound up, any surplus after paying debts is to be devoted first to repaying the capital contributed for preference shares then the preference shareholders will not be entitled to any further share in the surplus (*Scottish Insurance Corporation Ltd v Wilsons and Clyde Coal Co Ltd* [1949] AC 462; *Re Isle of Thanet Electricity Supply Co Ltd* [1950] Ch 161). In practice it has been very difficult to define unambiguously the rights of preference shareholders and there is a large volume of litigation on the meaning of articles of association from the days when preference shares were more common than they are now—see M A Pickering, 'The problem of the preference share' (1963) 26 MLR 499.

Although preference shares are used to provide finance in some special situations their importance as a method of financing generally has declined in recent years, partly because of changes in taxation rules.

6.2.4.3 Deferred shares

A deferred share is a share bearing the restriction that no dividend can be paid to the shareholder for a financial year unless ordinary shareholders are paid a certain amount for that year. Companies that have issued deferred shares have often called them 'founders' shares' and issued them to the founders of a business that the company has been formed to purchase. Often the holders of founders' shares are entitled to a large proportion (for example, one-third or one-quarter) of all profits remaining after the ordinary shareholders have received their minimum dividend.

6.2.4.4 Non-voting ordinary shares

Some companies have a class of members whose rights to dividends and to share in surplus assets are like those of ordinary members but who have no right to vote at members' meetings. In such a company there is usually a small class of members who hold ordinary shares with a right to vote, and entry to this class is carefully controlled.

6.2.4.5 Redeemable shares

Redeemable shares in a company offer temporary membership of the company with repayment of the nominal value of the shares (and in some cases a redemption premium) at the end of the period of membership. The shares are redeemed and the membership comes to an end either after a fixed period or at the company's option, depending on the terms of redemption of the shares.

CA 2006, s 684(1), permits a limited company to issue redeemable shares, and they can be redeemed despite the general prohibition on a company acquiring its own shares (s 658(1)), but subject to rules concerning maintenance of capital, which are discussed at **10.5**. A public company can issue redeemable shares only if authorised to do so by its articles (s 684(3)). In the model articles for public companies in SI 2008/3229, authority is provided by art 43(2). A private company does not need authority in its articles to issue redeemable shares (though art 22(2) of the model articles for private companies does provide such authority), but its articles can exclude or restrict their issue (CA 2006, s 684(2)).

A company may, in its articles or by resolution, authorise its directors to determine the terms, conditions and manner of redemption of shares (CA 2006, s 685(1)). An authorising resolution may be an ordinary resolution even if it alters the company's articles (s 685(2)). Authority is given to directors by the model articles of association in SI 2008/3229 (model articles for private companies, art 22(2), and the model articles for public companies, art 43(2)).

Redeemable shares may not be issued by a company at a time when none of its members holds any non-redeemable shares (CA 2006, s 684(4)).

6.2.5 SHARES AS THINGS IN ACTION

The size of the shareholding of a company member is used to describe the relative importance of the member's interest in the company. It is also natural to think of shares as things in themselves, which are created, bought and sold. Instead of saying that a member of a company has transferred membership to someone else it is usual to say that the member has transferred shares in the company; instead of saying that the extent of a member's interest has changed it is usual to say that the member has acquired or disposed of some shares.

If a company owns real property, is a share in the company real or personal property? This was a difficult problem in the early history of company law—see C Stebbings, 'The legal nature of shares in landowning joint stock companies in the 19th century' (1987) 8 J Legal Hist 25. The solution depended on deciding that the members of a company are not the joint owners of its property, because the company is a separate person in law and property held in the name of the company belongs to the company and no one else (*Bligh v Brent* (1837) 2 Y & C Ex 268). So, whether a company share is real or personal property does not depend on the nature of the company's property. The matter is settled by CA 2006, s 541, which declares that the shares or other interest of any member in a company shall be personal property and are not in the nature of real estate.

Regarded as an item of property in itself, a company share comes into the class of personal property known as choses in action (or things in action) (*Colonial Bank v Whinney* (1886) 11 App Cas 426). This is because holding a company share confers an entitlement to certain benefits and privileges (which may be enforced by action in the courts if they are denied to a shareholder) but does not give possession of any tangible physical object. (A holder of certificated shares is entitled to a share certificate but that is merely a memorandum: membership is not lost by being without a share certificate.)

It is perhaps better not to regard shares as items of property in themselves but to regard membership of a company as an item of property of which the size is determined by the number of shares held. One can, perhaps, discern this view in the much quoted remark of Farwell J in *Borland's trustee v Steel Brothers and Co Ltd* [1901] 1 Ch 279:

> A share is the interest of a shareholder in the company measured by a sum of money, for the purpose of liability in the first place, and of interest in the second . . . A share is not a sum of money . . . but is an interest measured by a sum of money and made up of various rights.

It is also worth noting the (dissenting) judgment of Lord Russell of Killowen in *Commissioners of Inland Revenue v Crossman* [1937] AC 26 at p 66:

> A share in a limited company is a property the nature of which has been accurately expounded by Farwell J in *Borland's Trustee v Steel Brothers and Co Ltd*. It is the interest of a person in the company, that interest being composed of rights and obligations which are defined by the Companies Act and by the memorandum and articles of association of the company. A sale of a share is a sale of the interest so defined, and the subject-matter of the sale is effectively vested in the purchaser by the entry of his name in the register of members.

For a detailed historical discussion see Robert Pennington, 'Can shares in companies be defined?' (1989) 10 Co Law 140.

6.2.6 NATIONALITY OF SHAREHOLDERS

There is no general requirement that any shares in a UK company must be held by a person domiciled in the United Kingdom (or in the part of the United Kingdom in which the company is registered). A law that prevented shares being held by nationals of another EU State would contravene art 55 of the Treaty on the Functioning of the European Union (TFEU), which requires member States to 'accord nationals of the other member States the same treatment as their own nationals as regards participation in the capital of companies'. For example, the Merchant Shipping Act 1988, s 14, which prevented a boat being registered as a British fishing vessel if it was owned by a company in which less than 75 per cent of the shares were owned by British citizens, contravened art 55 (*R v Secretary of State for Transport, ex parte Factortame Ltd* (case C-221/89) [1991] ECR I-3905).

6.2.7 NO PAR VALUE SHARES

In practice, it is usual nowadays for a person who is issued shares in a limited company to contribute their entire nominal value at the time when they are issued, and the nominal value of shares is redundant as a measure of such a shareholder's liability. In the USA it is common for this to be recognised by issuing shares without any nominal value, known as shares of 'no par value'. Shares of no par value have never been permitted by British company law. In 1954 a committee reported in favour of introducing no par value shares in Britain but revealed strong opposition from trade unions, who regarded it as a device to disguise from workers the size of dividends being paid to shareholders (Board of Trade, *Report of the Committee on Shares of No Par Value* (Cmd 9112) (London: HMSO, 1954)). In Belgium the par value of a share need not be stated on the share certificate, but an 'accounting value' must be assigned to each share for the purposes of the company's accounts, and this is the only system of no par value shares permitted to public companies in the EEA under Directive 2012/30/EU. The 1954 committee said that the Belgian system could not be recommended for use in Britain. Perhaps the most revolutionary proposal of the Company Law Review Steering Group was that shares of no par value should be compulsory for private companies (*Modern Company Law for a Competitive Economy: Company Formation and Capital Maintenance* (URN 99/1145) (London: DTI, 1999), para 3.8). They proposed that all existing shares of private companies should be deemed to be of no par value. The majority of responses to the 1999 consultation document favoured making no par value shares optional rather than compulsory. Concern about requiring all existing private companies to change to no par value shares centred on: the constitutional change which would be required of the companies concerned; the redefinition of rights of third parties, including creditors and the holders of convertible securities, which are defined in terms of par value; and how a private company would convert back to par values on re-registration as a public company (*Modern Company Law for a Competitive Economy: Capital Maintenance: Other Issues* (URN 00/880) (London: DTI, 2001), para 9). In the light of these proposals the Steering Group decided not to go ahead with compulsory no par value shares. They also decided that introducing optional no par value shares 'would require a commitment of effort and resources out of proportion to the likely benefit' (*Modern Company Law for a Competitive Economy: Completing the Structure* (URN 00/1335) (London: DTI, 2000), para 7.3). Fixed nominal values are required only for shares of limited companies (CA 2006, s 542(1)), so unlimited companies can issue no par value shares.

6.3 ALLOTMENT

6.3.1 ISSUE AND ALLOTMENT

The process by which members take shares from a company is called *issuing* the shares. A previously unissued share is said to be *allotted* when a person acquires the unconditional right to be entered in the register of members in respect of that share (CA 2006, s 558). The person who has that right is called the *allottee* of the share. Until the statutory definition of 'allotment' was introduced by CA 1980, s 87(2), the term was usually used to refer to a decision by directors to issue shares to particular applicants. Such a decision would not necessarily give the applicants an unconditional right to be registered. For example, it might be conditional on the applicant paying a certain amount for the shares (*McEuen v West London Wharves and Warehouses Co* (1871) LR 6 Ch App 655). Under the statutory definition, shares are not regarded as allotted until such conditions are fulfilled.

The concept of allotment is irrelevant to the shares which are to be taken on formation of a company by the subscribers to its memorandum (CA 2006, s 559). The subscribers become the holders of those shares as from the date of incorporation (s 16(5)).

Otherwise, the time at which a person becomes an allottee of shares depends on the terms of the agreement under which the person has taken the shares, that is the contract for the allotment of the shares.

In *National Westminster Bank plc v Inland Revenue Commissioners* [1995] 1 AC 119, a tax advantage would have been obtained if certain shares of a company had been 'issued' before 16 March 1993. The shares had been allotted before that date but the shareholders had not been entered in the company's register of members until 2 April. A majority of the House of Lords held that the shares had not been issued before 16 March. On the other hand, shares will be regarded as issued if the holder's name has been entered in the register of members even if no share certificates have been issued (*Re Heaton's Steel and Iron Co, Blyth's Case* (1876) 4 ChD 140), so it seems that registration is the final stage in the 'issue' of shares. In relation to uncertificated shares, issuing a new share is defined in SI 2001/3755, reg 3(1), as conferring title to the new share on a person.

6.3.2 CONTRACTS OF ALLOTMENT

6.3.2.1 Essential terms

An exchange of capital contributed to a company for shares issued by the company is always the result of a contract, which is called a contract to subscribe for shares, or a contract for the allotment of shares. The important details of this contract which the two parties must agree are:

(a) The amount of capital to be contributed.

(b) The time at which the capital is to be contributed.

(c) The form in which the capital is to be contributed—money, goods, services, land or some other form.

(d) The time at which the potential shareholder is to have the unconditional right to the shares.

(e) The membership rights attached to each share.

6.3.2.2 Offer and acceptance

A contract for the allotment of shares, like any contract, is formed after acceptance by one party of an offer made by the other. There are two possibilities:

(a) The offer is made by the potential shareholder. In many issues of shares by public companies, prospective shareholders make offers on the basis of an invitation to treat (called a 'prospectus') issued by the company, which sets out standard terms and conditions on which the company will accept offers, and there is no negotiation of any of the terms. In other issues an individual investor and a company may conduct lengthy negotiations to establish the terms on which the investor will put money into the company.

(b) The offer is made by the company. This is usually done by means of a provisional allotment letter, which is a letter stating that the company has provisionally allotted certain shares to the addressee pending acceptance of the offer and specifying a date when the offer will lapse if not accepted. Usually offers of this kind are made only to existing members of a company.

If an offeror authorises acceptance of the offer by post (as is the case with most public issues of shares), the contract is formed when a properly addressed acceptance is put into the control of the Royal Mail (*Household Fire and Carriage Accident Insurance Co Ltd v Grant* (1879) 4 ExD 216; *Re London and Northern Bank, ex parte Jones* [1900] 1 Ch 220).

Unless a time limit is specified, an offer lapses if it is not accepted after a reasonable time. In *Ramsgate Victoria Hotel Co Ltd v Montefiore* (1866) LR 1 Ex 109, Mr Montefiore offered on 8 June

1864 to subscribe for shares in the company. On 23 November, the company decided to accept the offer but the court held that it had lapsed and so Mr Montefiore was not liable to pay for the shares, and the company had to return his deposit.

6.3.2.3 Renunciation of allotment

A contract between a company and a person for the allotment of shares to the person may provide that for a period after the contract is made (typically for six to eight weeks) the allottee's right to be entered on the register of members may be transferred by the allottee to another person. Such a transfer is called renunciation in favour of another person.

Renunciation is normally allowed for in public issues of shares.

6.3.3 OPTIONS AND CONVERTIBLES

A company may make a conditional contract for the allotment of shares to a person (called an option holder) under which the option holder is given an option to require the allotment of shares at a time specified in the contract. An option may be transferred from one holder to another. Sometimes public companies sell large numbers of options, embodied in documents called 'option warrants' or 'warrants to subscribe for shares' which are then traded on an investment exchange until they are converted or expire. Options have also been given by some companies to staff as part of remuneration.

Unsecured loan stock, or sometimes secured debenture stock, may carry a right to require an allotment of shares in exchange for the stock at some date in the future. Convertible securities like this are considered in **12.7**.

Preference shares may carry a right for the holder to convert them into ordinary shares. The terms of an option or convertible security must not result in the company receiving less than the nominal value of the shares issued (*Mosely v Koffyfontein Mines Ltd* [1904] 2 Ch 108; CA 2006, s 580).

When warrants to subscribe for shares are converted the company's share capital increases.

6.3.4 AUTHORISATION OF SHARE ISSUES

6.3.4.1 Principle

CA 2006, ss 549 to 551, provide the members of a company with the power to control how their directors allot new shares, or grant rights to subscribe for shares, or issue securities convertible into shares. If a company is a *private company* with only one class of shares, its articles *may* (but are not required to) restrict the directors' powers to allot etc (s 550). The directors of any other company cannot allot shares etc unless they are authorised to do so by the company's articles or by a resolution of the company (s 551(1)). It is a criminal offence, triable either way, to allot shares etc otherwise than in accordance with s 550 or s 551 (s 549(4) and (5)), but allotments etc to employees' shares schemes are exempt (s 549(2)). The fact that an allotment etc was not in accordance with s 550 or s 551 does not affect its validity (s 549(6)).

Directors can use their power of allotment of shares to determine the composition of the membership of the company: in particular they can ensure that the majority of members support them and will keep them in office. Some important cases concern directors' alleged misuse of their power of allotment and they are considered in the context of directors' duties generally in **16.5.3**.

6.3.4.2 Details

If a company is a private company with more than one class of shares, or is a public company, authority to allot shares which is given to its directors by its articles or a resolution:

(a) must specify the maximum number of shares that may be allotted (or in the case of an authority to grant subscription or conversion rights, the maximum number of shares that may be allotted as a result of the exercise of those rights) (CA 2006, s 551(3)(a) and (6));

(b) must expire after at most five years and must state the date on which it is to expire (s 551(3)(b)); and

(c) may in any case be revoked or varied by ordinary resolution of the members (even if the revocation or variation amends the articles, which would normally require a special resolution) (s 551(4)(b) and (8)).

Authority may be given either for a particular allotment (or grant of subscription or conversion rights) or generally (s 551(2)). Authority may be renewed or further renewed by ordinary resolution of the members but never for more than five years at a time (s 551(4)(a)). Each renewal resolution must state (or restate) the number of shares that may be allotted (or the number remaining to be allotted) and state the date on which the renewed authority will expire (s 551(5)).

If the authority allows the company to make an offer or agreement which will or may require shares to be allotted after the authority has expired, the directors may carry out such an offer or agreement after the authority has expired (s 551(7)).

6.3.4.3 Transparency

A copy of any resolution giving, varying, revoking or renewing authority to allot must be sent to Companies House within 15 days of being adopted (CA 2006, s 30 applied by s 551(9)).

6.3.4.4 Waiver of mandatory takeover bid

If a company which is subject to the City Code on Takeovers and Mergers (see **8.7.1**) intends to allot shares which would give the allottee 30 per cent or more of the voting rights in the company, it may apply to the Panel on Takeovers and Mergers to waive rule 9 of the Code, which would otherwise require the allottee to make a takeover bid for all of the voting shares. The Panel will usually waive rule 9 if the allotment is for cash or is itself made in connection with a takeover by share exchange (see **8.7.4**) and the members of the company approve it by ordinary resolution after full disclosure. The waiver is known as a 'whitewash'. The details of the procedure are printed at the end of rule 9 in the Code ('notes on dispensations from rule 9') and in app 1 to the Code.

6.3.4.5 Old companies' authorised share capital

Before CA 2006 the old-style memorandum of a company limited by shares had to state the maximum total nominal value of shares which the company could issue. This was known as the authorised share capital. It could be increased by ordinary resolution of the members if there was authority to do so in the company's articles. As from 1 October 2009, such a provision is treated as a provision of the company's articles setting the maximum amount of shares that may be allotted by the company (SI 2008/2860, sch 2, para 42). The provision may be amended or revoked by the company by ordinary resolution (para 42).

6.3.5 PRE-EMPTION RIGHTS

6.3.5.1 Principle

In order to ensure that existing shareholders' rights are not diluted by the issue of new shares, CA 2006, s 561, requires that before any equity securities (see **6.3.5.2**) are allotted for a wholly cash capital contribution they must first be offered to existing shareholders (excluding the company itself as holder of treasury shares—see **10.6.6**: s 561(4)). Each shareholder must be offered a number of shares which will (as far as practicable) maintain that shareholder's proportionate holding in the company. Such an offer is called a 'rights issue'. The shareholders are said to have 'pre-emption rights' (rights of first refusal). Pre-emption rights help to prevent control of a company being taken away from its existing members without their consent. The members of a company may disapply their pre-emption rights (see **6.3.5.3**).

An allotment in contravention of s 561 is not invalid, but the responsible directors are liable to compensate the shareholders to whom the new shares should have been offered (s 563).

The provisions on shareholders' pre-emption rights were introduced by CA 1980 to implement what is now Directive 2012/30/EU, art 33, which makes pre-emption rights mandatory for public companies. Before then, shareholders did not have pre-emption rights under the general law (*Ving v Robinson and Woodcock Ltd* (1912) 56 SJ 412) though a company's constitution might give such rights. The reasons for pre-emption rights (which are mandatory in the EU, but have been abandoned in the USA) are examined by Paul Myners (now Lord Myners) in *Pre-emption Rights: Final Report* (URN 05/679) (London: DTI, 2005).

6.3.5.2 Details

The scope of CA 2006, s 561, is defined in s 560. 'Equity securities' are ordinary shares (see **6.2.4.1**) or rights to subscribe for, or to convert securities into, ordinary shares (s 560(1)). 'Allotment of equity securities' includes the grant of a right to subscribe for, or to convert equity securities into, ordinary shares, and also includes a sale of ordinary shares held as treasury shares (s 560(3)). Section 561 does not apply to the allotment of bonus shares (s 564) or to allotments to an employees' share scheme (s 566). Section 561 also does not apply where shares are to be wholly or partly paid up otherwise than in cash (s 565).

Section 562 prescribes the manner in which a rights offer must be made. Its provisions may be excluded by the articles of a *private company* (s 567).

6.3.5.3 Disapplication

A *private company* may have a provision in its articles that any issue of shares (or any issue of a particular description) may be made without first offering them to existing members (CA 2006, s 567). If a private company has only one class of shares (so that directors are not required to be authorised to allot shares, see **6.3.4.1**), directors may be given, by the articles or by special resolution, power to allot equity securities either as if s 561 did not apply or as if it applied with such modifications as the directors may determine (s 569).

Section 568 allows any company to make its own provision in its articles for pre-emption rights in relation to shares of a particular class.

Sections 570 and 571 allow the members of any company, under certain conditions, to disapply their pre-emption rights, either generally (s 570) or in relation to a particular allotment (s 571).

A general disapplication (under s 570) may be made only if the directors of the company have a general authority to allot shares under s 551 (see **6.3.4**). Pre-emption rights may be generally disapplied by giving the directors a power to allot securities either as if s 561 did not apply or as if it applied with such modifications as the directors may determine. Such a power may be given either by the articles or by a special resolution of the members. It automatically ceases to have effect when the general authority to allot expires or is revoked (s 570(3)). (A general power to allot may be revoked by *ordinary* resolution: s 551(4)(b).) However, it may be renewed by special resolution if the general authority to allot is renewed (s 570(3)).

In relation to a particular allotment, provided the directors of the company are authorised under s 551 to make the allotment, the members may, by special resolution, resolve either that s 561 is not to apply to the allotment or that it is to apply with such modifications as are specified in the resolution (s 571). Such a special resolution automatically ceases to have effect when the directors' authority to make the allotment expires or is revoked but it may be renewed by special resolution if the authority to allot is renewed (s 571(3)). However, a special resolution under s 571 (or a special resolution to renew such a resolution) must not be proposed unless it is recommended by the directors (s 571(5)). The directors must make a written statement setting out:

(a) their reasons for making the recommendation;

(b) the amount to be paid to the company in respect of the securities to be allotted; and

(c) the directors' justification of that amount.

If the resolution is proposed as a written resolution, the statement must be sent or submitted to every eligible member at or before the time of submitting the resolution; if the resolution is to be proposed at a meeting, the statement must be circulated with notice of the meeting (s 571(7)). It is an offence triable either way knowingly or recklessly to authorise or permit the inclusion in such a statement of any matter which is misleading, false or deceptive in a material particular (s 572).

6.3.5.4 Transparency

As with any special resolution, a copy of a resolution under CA 2006, ss 570 or 571, disapplying pre-emption rights must be sent to Companies House within 15 days (s 30). If such a resolution relates to a *public company*, Companies House give public notice of receipt (ss 1077 and 1078(3); see **4.3**).

6.3.6 RETURN OF ALLOTMENT AND STATEMENT OF CAPITAL

Within one month of making an allotment of its shares, a limited company must make a return of allotment of shares to Companies House (CA 2006, s 555). This must be accompanied by a statement of capital. If the company is a public company, Companies House gives public notice of receipt (ss 1077 and 1078(3); see **4.3**). The return is required by SI 2009/388, art 3, to state:

(a) the number of shares allotted;

(b) the amount paid up and the amount (if any) unpaid on each allotted share (whether on account of the nominal value of the share or by way of premium); and

(c) where the shares are allotted as fully or partly paid up (as to their nominal value or any premium on them) otherwise than in cash, the consideration for the allotment.

The statement of capital states:

(a) the total number of shares of the company;

(b) the aggregate nominal value of those shares;

(c) the aggregate amount (if any) unpaid on those shares (whether on account of their nominal value or by way of premium); and

(d) for each class of shares

 (i) prescribed particulars of the rights attached to the shares (see **6.2.3**),

 (ii) the total number of shares of that class, and

 (iii) the aggregate nominal value of shares of that class.

An unlimited company is required to make a return of allotment only if the rights attached to the new shares are not the same as the rights attached to shares already allotted (CA 2006, s 556).

Failure to deliver a return of allotment when required is an offence (s 557), but an application may be made to the court for an extension of time for delivery (s 557(3)).

6.3.7 SHARE CERTIFICATES

Within two months after the allotment of a company's shares the company must, under penalty, complete, and have ready for delivery, share certificates for all the shares allotted, unless the conditions of issue of the shares provide otherwise (CA 2006, s 769). This does not apply if the shares are allotted in uncertificated form through CREST (SI 2001/3755, reg 38(2)).

An allottee who does not receive a share certificate as required by s 769 may serve a notice on the company requiring it to make good the default. If the company fails to do so within ten days, the allottee may obtain a court order directing the company or any officer to issue the certificate (s 782).

For more on share certificates, see **8.2**.

6.3.8 FAILURE TO CARRY OUT A CONTRACT OF ALLOTMENT

If a company fails to carry out a contract of allotment of shares, the person to whom the shares should have been allotted may obtain an order for specific performance of the contract if damages would not be an adequate remedy (for example, *Sri Lanka Omnibus Co Ltd v Perera* [1952] AC 76). However, damages are normally adequate if the company's shares are readily available in the market (*Re BTR plc* (1987) 4 BCC 45).

Insolvency or liquidation of a company does not frustrate a contract to subscribe for its shares (*Veremu Pty Ltd v Ezishop.Net Ltd* [2003] NSWCA 317, 47 ACSR 681). Persons who agree to take shares in a company do so knowing that there is a risk that the company will fail. The fact that it fails before their shares are allotted means 'only that the hope or expectation of the parties was disappointed at a time earlier than it might in any event have been disappointed' (at [21]).

6.4 PRINCIPLES OF ACCOUNTING

6.4.1 INTRODUCTION

In order to appreciate the remainder of this chapter it is necessary to know some of the terminology of financial accounting, and so a very brief statement of principles is given here.

6.4.2 BALANCE SHEETS

A balance sheet of a company is a statement of its financial position on a particular day, called the balance sheet date. As will be explained in **Chapter 9**, the directors of a company are required to draw up a balance sheet for their company once a year.

A balance sheet begins by summarising the value of the assets that the company had on the balance sheet date. Apart from called-up share capital not paid, the company would have acquired its assets by using its contributed capital, money that it has borrowed, and profits it has made from its operations. Some of the assets, such as stock in trade, are intended to be held for only a short time for the purposes of the company's business; others, such as debts owed to the company, arise as a result of the company's operations. The total value of assets shown in a balance sheet is called the balance sheet total (see CA 2006, s 382(5)).

A balance sheet then summarises the value of the company's liabilities at the balance sheet date. These include the company's obligations to repay loans and to pay for goods that have been supplied on credit. The value of goods supplied on credit, and the value of assets acquired with loaned money, are included in the assets section of the balance sheet.

It is also prudent to show *provisions* in the balance sheet. These are estimates of payments that the company is likely to be liable for though their size and/or timing is not yet certain.

Net assets is defined by CA 2006, s 831(2), as the total value of assets minus the total value of liabilities. In principle, this is the amount which would be left for the members of the company if it ceased trading on the balance sheet date, and its assets were then sold and its debts paid. The value of net assets is often called the *owners' equity*. Investment analysts often refer to net assets as the *net worth* of the company.

A final section of a balance sheet shows the value of its capital and reserves. An important item in this section is called profit and loss account: it records the amount of profit that the company has retained instead of distributing to members.

If the accounts have been prepared correctly, the sum of the liabilities section and the capital and reserves section will equal the total of the assets section. (This relationship is known as the 'accounting equation' or 'balance sheet equation'.)

6.4.3 DEPRECIATION AND REVALUATION

The net assets of a company may not be correctly represented by its balance sheet if the assets section does not correctly state the value of the company's assets. Two accounting devices used to adjust the values of fixed assets are revaluation and depreciation.

The fixed assets of a company are its assets that are intended for use on a continuing basis in its activities; all other assets of a company are current assets.

If any fixed asset of a company has a limited useful economic life then, for each year of that life, some of the company's income must be set aside as a provision (called a provision for depreciation) which may be regarded as providing for the future loss in value of the company's assets when the fixed asset is finally abandoned or disposed of. A provision for depreciation of a fixed asset may also be regarded as reflecting the consumption of the value of the asset by the company.

Systematic provision for depreciation must be made for every fixed asset with a limited useful economic life. The provision should be calculated so that over the estimated life of the asset the amount provided will add up to the difference between the purchase price or production cost of the asset (called the 'historical cost' of the asset) and its estimated residual (or scrap) value at the end of that life. A provision for depreciation is, it should be emphasised, a matter of accounting, not a physical setting aside of a sum of money. In the accounts, the provision is shown as an amount to be deducted from the historical cost of the asset.

In addition, it is sometimes necessary to recognise that a fixed asset has permanently lost value. If that occurs, a separate provision must be made for the amount of the loss in value and, in the assets section of the balance sheet, the value recorded for the asset must be altered to the lower amount that is now recognised as its value. A provision for diminution in value may have to be made for any fixed asset whether or not it has a limited useful economic life. However, if a provision for diminution in value is made for an asset with a limited useful economic life, the depreciation provision for that asset continues to be made on the basis of its historical cost.

The requirement, which was introduced by CA 1981, that fixed assets must be depreciated in accounts overturns the decision in *Lee v Neuchatel Asphalte Co* (1889) 41 ChD 1 that a company is not legally bound to allow in its accounts for depreciation.

As an example of a common method of depreciation, called the straight-line method, suppose a fixed asset is purchased for £12,500. It is expected that after five years it will be no longer useful to the company but will have a resale value of £2,500. The depreciation charge for each of those five years is then £2,000. At the end of the first year its value will be stated as £10,500; at the end of the second year as £8,500; and so on until the end of the fifth year when its value will be stated as £2,500 which is its expected sales value.

As an alternative to historical cost and depreciation, a balance sheet may state the market value of a company's fixed asset, as determined by valuation. An allowance for depreciation must be deducted from the valuation value (assuming the valuation was made before the balance sheet date).

When the value of a fixed asset to be shown in the accounts is altered by revaluation, the increase (or decrease) must be balanced by an equal change in the capital and reserves section of the balance sheet. This is achieved by crediting (or debiting) a separate item in that section called the revaluation reserve. In respect of a fixed asset that has been revalued the depreciation provision must be calculated on the basis of the new value and is called the 'adjusted amount'. However, the depreciation deducted from profit and loss account for a particular financial year may be calculated on the historical cost basis despite revaluation. The difference between the adjusted amount and the historical cost amount must be charged to revaluation reserve.

6.4.4 PROFIT AND LOSS ACCOUNT

A balance sheet of a company is normally supplemented by a profit and loss account which summarises the revenues and expenditures of the company during the period between the previous balance sheet date and the present one. The difference between revenues and expenditures for the period is a profit or loss of the period. It is added to (or subtracted from) the figure for profit and loss account in the balance sheet for the beginning of the period, to produce the figure for that item in the balance sheet for the end of the period.

6.5 TIMING AND SIZE OF THE CAPITAL CONTRIBUTION

6.5.1 DISCOUNTS, COMMISSION AND BROKERAGE

Parliament has insisted that members of a registered company must be liable to contribute to its assets, but a holder of shares in a company limited by shares has only a limited liability, which is to contribute the nominal value of the shares held. In the nineteenth century some companies tried to make membership more attractive by attempting to waive members' liability for the full nominal value of their shares. The courts slowly ruled each attempt to be unlawful. In one of the most important cases, *Ooregum Gold Mining Co of India Ltd v Roper* [1892] AC 125, Lord Halsbury LC said, at p 134:

> What is the nature of an agreement to take a share in a limited company? . . . it is an agreement to become liable to pay to the company the amount for which the share has been created. That agreement is one which the company itself has no authority to alter or qualify.

The Ooregum Gold Mining Co of India Ltd had run into temporary difficulties and the market value of its £1 shares was only 12½p. Its members adopted a special resolution that it should issue further £1 shares, which would be treated as having had 75p paid up on them, though the company had not in fact received that 75p. This is called 'issuing shares at a discount'. Although the Ooregum discounted shares were issued for 5p each, the company's register of members recorded that they had been issued at 80p each. Holders of the discounted Ooregum shares thought they were liable to contribute only a further 20p each for them. The company was successful but a holder of ordinary shares on which the full £1 had been paid took proceedings to have the company's register of members rectified to show that only 5p had been paid on the discounted shares instead of 80p. The House of Lords, affirming the decisions of the courts below, ordered the rectification asked for. Lord Halsbury LC said, at p 134, that 'the company were prohibited by law . . . from doing that which is compendiously described as issuing shares at a discount'. It follows that a company cannot give away its shares, treating shares as fully paid up though it has not received anything for them (*Re Eddystone Marine Insurance Co* [1893] 3 Ch 9).

The decisions of the courts have been superseded by statutory provisions. CA 2006, s 580(1), prohibits the allotment of shares at a discount. If a share is allotted at a discount, the allottee is liable to pay the company the amount of the discount plus interest at 5 per cent per year (ss 580(2) and 609).

However, a company may pay underwriting commission on the conditions laid down in s 552, and may pay brokerage. Underwriting and brokerage are discussed in 7.8.

6.5.2 PARTLY PAID SHARES

6.5.2.1 Definition

If a share is allotted to a member who does not contribute its whole nominal value, the share is said to be partly paid. Unlike fully paid shares, each partly paid share of a company must have a distinguishing number (CA 2006, s 543(2)) which is recorded against the holder's name in the register of members (s 113(3)(a)(i)).

If a *public company* issues shares partly paid, at least one-quarter of the nominal value must be paid on or before allotment (s 586(1)) unless the shares are being allotted in pursuance of an employees' share scheme (s 586(2)).

If a share is allotted in contravention of s 586(1), it must be treated as though the minimum amount had been paid up, and the allottee is liable to pay the deficiency plus interest at 5 per cent per annum (ss 586(3) and 592). Further, the company and any officer of the company in default will have committed an offence triable either way (s 590).

As explained in **2.3.2.2** it is now unusual to issue partly paid shares, but the law relating to them throws light on the nature of shareholding, and so a brief summary of it is given in **6.5.2.2** to **6.5.2.7**.

6.5.2.2 Calls

A company that has allotted a share partly paid has the right to make a call for any or all of the remainder of the agreed capital contribution at any time.

The articles of a company normally assign to its directors the power to make calls, but usually set out rules of procedure, as in the model articles for public companies, arts 54 to 62, in SI 2008/3229. In *Odessa Tramways Co v Mendel* (1878) 8 ChD 235 and in *Anglo-Universal Bank v Baragnon* (1881) 45 LT 362, the Court of Appeal said that it could not review the amount called up by directors of a company on partly paid shares because it would not question their judgement on what financial resources were required by the company. The decision to make a call could only be challenged for breach of what is now CA 2006, s 171 (see **16.5**) or s 172 (see **16.6**). Mr Mendel did not make such a challenge. Mr Baragnon did, but the court rejected it. (*Bailey v Birkenhead, Lancashire and Cheshire Junction Railway Co* (1850) 12 Beav 433 was a similar case concerning a statutory company.) These cases are examples of the court refusing to investigate questions of business judgment (see **18.3.3.1**).

It has been held that directors' power to make calls is limited by a rule of the general law that members must be treated equally: accordingly, directors cannot make different calls on different shares (*Preston v Grand Collier Dock Co* (1840) 11 Sim 327). However, CA 2006, s 581(a), permits contracts for the allotment of shares in a company to provide for different calls to be made on different shares, if there is an authorisation to that effect in the company's articles. Such an authorisation is given in the model articles for public companies, art 55(3).

6.5.2.3 Lien

In addition to the right to sue for payment of a call, articles commonly give a company a charge on partly paid shares as a security for the payment of calls. The charge is traditionally called a 'lien'. In the model articles for public companies in SI 2008/3229, arts 52 and 53 deal with lien and provide that the company may realise its security by selling the charged shares 14 days after giving a lien enforcement notice to the shareholder demanding payment of a call. In the case of a public company, a lien for an amount payable on partly paid shares is an exception to the general rule that any charge created in favour of a public company over its own shares is void (CA 2006, s 670(1) and (2)).

6.5.2.4 Forfeiture

Articles may give the company a right to forfeit shares if a demand for payment of a call is not met (CA 2006, s 659(2)(c)). In the model articles for public companies in SI 2008/3229, arts 58 to 61 deal with forfeiture. A company does not have an inherent right to forfeit shares: the power must be provided in the articles (*Re National Patent Steam Fuel Co, Barton's Case* (1859) 4 De G & J 46). A company is permitted to accept a surrender of shares in lieu of forfeiture if this is provided for in its articles (CA 2006, s 659(2)(c)). Article 62 of the model articles for public companies makes such a provision.

The courts have always interpreted any provision for the forfeiture of property strictly. The articles specify the procedure for forfeiture and that procedure must be followed or the forfeiture will be invalid (*Johnson v Little's Iron Agency* (1877) 5 ChD 687—wrong amount of interest demanded in demand for call so that forfeiture could not be grounded on failure to meet demand; *Goulton v London Architectural Brick and Tile Co* [1877] WN 141). In *Sweny v Smith* (1869) LR 7 Eq 324 a forfeiture was invalid because the company had wrongly refused a tender of the amount demanded.

Under the model articles for public companies, art 59, the directors have the power to forfeit shares, and the exercise of this power is subject to their statutory duty to exercise powers only for the purposes for which they are conferred (CA 2006, s 171) and to act in the way they consider, in good faith, would be most likely to promote the success of the company for the benefit of its members as a whole (s 172). Forfeitures have been held to be ineffective when carried out for the purpose of relieving members of liability (*Re National Provincial Marine Insurance Co, Gilbert's Case* (1870) LR 5 Ch App 559; *European Assurance Society Arbitration, Manisty's Case* (1873) 17 SJ 745; *Re Esparto Trading Co* (1879) 12 ChD 191).

In deciding whether to forfeit a member's shares for non-payment of a call, the directors must take into account all material considerations, and if they do not, the decision is voidable (*Hunter v Senate Support Services Ltd* [2004] EWHC 1085 (Ch), [2005] 1 BCLC 175, in which the directors had failed to consider other ways of convincing the obstreperous shareholder that it would be to his advantage to pay the calls).

6.5.2.5 Consequences of forfeiture

A member whose shares have been forfeited or surrendered loses whatever capital was contributed for those shares. However, in principle the member would also be relieved of liability to pay the amounts unpaid on the shares (*Re Blakely Ordnance Co, Stocken's Case* (1868) LR 3 Ch App 412 per Lord Cairns LJ at p 415). But this would amount to an acquisition by the company of its own shares for valuable consideration—namely, the forgiving of a debt due to the company (*Bellerby v Rowland and Marwood's Steamship Co* [1902] 2 Ch 14). By s 659(2)(c), forfeiture, or surrender in lieu of forfeiture, of shares is outside the general prohibition on acquisition of own shares for valuable consideration imposed by s 659(1) (see **10.6**). Article 60(3)(d) of the model articles for public companies avoids this problem by providing that a person whose shares have been forfeited 'remains liable to the company for all sums payable by that person under the articles at the date of forfeiture in respect of those shares'.

A person who has forfeited shares in a company ceases to be a member in respect of those shares (*Re China Steam Ship Co, Dawes's Case* (1868) LR 6 Eq 232) so that the money owed by such a person to the company under art 60 is owed as a debtor to the company and not as a member of it (*Ladies' Dress Association Ltd v Pulbrook* [1900] 2 QB 376). Similarly, damages due from the company to a person for wrongful forfeiture of shares are not owed to the person qua member (*Re New Chile Gold Mining Co* (1889) 45 ChD 598). Liability under art 60 arises at the time of forfeiture and the debt is owed by virtue of the articles of association (*Re Blakely Ordnance Co, Stocken's Case* per Lord Cairns LJ at p 416). However, the liability does not arise under the contract formed between the company and its members by the company's articles; it arises because the contract of allotment of the forfeited shares was upon the terms of the articles.

The company becomes the holder of shares that are forfeited or surrendered in lieu of forfeiture and must attempt to sell them to a new holder who will become liable for the whole amount unpaid on the shares including amounts left unpaid by the previous holder (*New Balkis Eersteling Ltd v Randt Gold Mining Co* [1904] AC 165). However, the new holder's liability is reduced by the amount of any money recovered from the previous holder under art 60 (*Re Randt Gold Mining Co* [1904] 2 Ch 468). Similarly, liability under art 60 is reduced by the amount the company receives from the new holder (*Re Bolton* [1930] 2 Ch 48).

6.5.2.6 Transparency

If a company holds any of its own shares on a balance sheet date, they must be shown as investments in the assets section of the balance sheet. And if the company is a public company, it must transfer an amount equal to the value of the shares from profit and loss account to an account called 'reserve for own shares' in the capital and reserves section of the balance sheet. A reserve for own shares may not be distributed to the company's members except in the liquidation of the company or in a duly authorised reduction of capital (CA 2006, s 669(1)).

6.5.2.7 Company's obligations with respect to forfeited shares

A public company must not exercise any voting rights in respect of shares it holds by forfeiture or surrender in lieu of forfeiture (CA 2006, s 662(1)(a) and (5)). If it fails to sell such shares within three years of forfeiture or surrender, it must cancel the shares and reduce its share capital account accordingly (s 662(2) and (3)(a)). If this reduces the nominal value of the company's allotted share capital to less than the authorised minimum, the company must re-register as a private company (s 662(2)(b)) and the directors are empowered to apply for re-registration and to make the necessary changes in the company's articles without consulting the members (s 664).

6.5.3 PAYMENT IN INSTALMENTS

A contract for the allotment of shares may provide for part payments to be made on definite dates. Sometimes one payment is made, as a deposit, on application for shares and the balance is payable on allotment, and allotment is agreed to be conditional on payment of the final instalment. Article 56 of the model articles for public companies in SI 2008/3229 provides that failure to make part payments due on definite dates (or on allotment) is to be treated in the same way as failure to comply with a call notice, so that all the company's remedies of lien and forfeiture can be employed against defaulters.

If a company does not have such a provision in its articles, it will be granted an order for specific performance of a contract to take shares (for example, *Odessa Tramways Co v Mendel* (1878) 8 ChD 235).

6.5.4 SHARE PREMIUM

A contract for the allotment of shares may provide that the value of assets to be contributed in exchange for the shares is to be greater than their nominal value: the difference is called share premium.

In a company's accounts, share premium is credited to a separate share premium account and is recorded under a separate subheading in a balance sheet. It may be paid before the whole of the nominal value is paid but if this is done, it cannot be treated by the company as payment of part of the nominal value. A premium may be payable on or before allotment, or at a time specified in the contract of allotment, or when called by the company. However, a premium payable to a *public company* must be paid on or before allotment (CA 2006, s 586(1)) unless the share is being allotted to an employees' share scheme (s 586(2)). If a share is allotted in contravention of this provision, it must be treated as though the premium had been paid up, and the allottee is liable to pay the deficiency plus interest at 5 per cent a year (ss 586(3) and 592). In addition, the company and any officer in default will have committed an offence triable either way (s 590).

Share premium received by a company may be used by it to pay the expenses of the issue or any commission paid on the issue (s 610(2)) or to pay up fully paid bonus shares (s 610(3); see **10.4**).

There are special provisions for the use of share premium received on the allotment of redeemable shares (see **10.5.2**).

6.5.5 WAYS OF MEASURING SHARE CAPITAL

The *issued share capital* of a company is the total nominal value of the shares which the company has issued (see **6.3.1**).

The *paid-up share capital* of a company is the amount of capital contributed for its issued shares, excluding share premium (see **6.2.1**).

The *called-up share capital* of a company is the amount actually contributed to its share capital plus amounts presently due to be contributed by members (CA 2006, s 547)—such amounts may arise either because the company has called for further contributions from holders of partly paid shares, or because members agreed to pay for their shares in instalments and the instalments are due on fixed dates.

The term 'equity share capital' is defined in **6.2.4.1**.

If a company states the amount of its capital in a letter or order form or on one of its websites, the amount stated must be the paid-up share capital (Directive 2009/101/EC, art 5; SI 2015/17, reg 25(3)).

6.6 FORM OF CONTRIBUTION

6.6.1 COMMON FORMS OF CAPITAL CONTRIBUTION

In *Re China Steamship and Labuan Coal Co, Drummond's Case* (1869) LR 4 Ch App 772, Giffard LJ said, at p 779:

> if a man contracts to take shares he must pay for them, to use a homely phrase, 'in meal or in malt'; he must either pay in money or in money's worth. If he pays in one or the other, that will be a satisfaction.

Brewer's Dictionary of Phrase and Fable explains Giffard LJ's homely phrase as meaning 'directly or indirectly; in one way or another'. The two commonest forms of capital contribution are:

(a) money; and

(b) an existing business (including shares in an existing company) or other fixed assets.

It is also possible to count services (for example, as managing director) or an agreement to forgive a debt as contributed capital.

6.6.2 VENDOR CONSIDERATION ISSUES

An issue of shares to purchase a business or other assets is called a vendor consideration issue. Such an issue is made when the owners of a business conducted by a sole trader or partnership incorporate a company which buys the business from them and then carries it on. An issue of shares may also be made to purchase the shares of an existing company in a takeover.

If the value of non-cash assets is higher than the nominal value of the shares issued for the assets, the excess value is share premium (*Henry Head and Co Ltd v Ropner Holdings Ltd* [1952] Ch 124; *Shearer v Bercain Ltd* [1980] 3 All ER 295). However, in a takeover, if the consideration for the issue of equity shares by a company is 90 per cent or more of another company's issued equity shares (excluding treasury shares; see **10.6.6**) then the difference between the nominal value of the shares issued and the value of the shares received for them is not to be regarded as share premium (CA 2006, s 612). Also, the difference in value may be ignored when recording the value of the shares received in the assets section of the company's balance sheet (s 615).

6.6.3 MEANING OF 'SUBSCRIPTION'

Arnison v Smith (1889) 41 ChD 348 and *Akerhielm v De Mare* [1959] AC 789 both concerned companies which, when negotiating new finance, said that their shares had been 'subscribed for'. In fact, they had both issued their shares in exchange for non-cash assets. In each case the new suppliers of finance lost their money and claimed that they had not been told the truth about earlier issues of shares. In *Arnison v Smith* the Court of Appeal agreed and held that saying a person 'subscribed for' shares meant that the person had undertaken to pay for them in cash. This was followed in *Governments Stock and Other Securities Investment Co Ltd v Christopher* [1956] 1 WLR 237.

In *Akerhielm v De Mare*, though, the Privy Council said that there was no effective difference between, on the one hand, issuing shares for cash and using that cash to purchase other assets, and on the other hand, buying assets directly by issuing shares for them. Therefore it was legitimate in either circumstance to say that the shares had been subscribed for.

However, a supplier of finance may take a very different view about a company that has previously persuaded people to part with cash for its shares and one that has been persuaded to issue its shares in exchange for a contribution of assets whose true value is unknown. In the first case, the shareholders have parted with their money to people who they believe can use it wisely, and any purchases of assets by the company can be assumed to have been made wisely. In the second case, nobody has put up any money and the whole transaction may be artificial.

A *public company* can allot its shares for non-cash assets only if those assets are independently valued, and this provision is discussed in **6.6.4.2**.

Acquiring shares by subscribing for them and being their original allottee is not 'purchasing' the shares for the purposes of CA 2006: a purchase of shares is an acquisition from an existing holder (*Re VGM Holdings Ltd* [1942] Ch 235).

6.6.4 VALUATION OF NON-CASH ASSETS

6.6.4.1 Private companies

If a company issues its shares in return for non-cash assets, crediting the shares as paid up to the extent of the value of the assets, it is possible that the assets have been overvalued, raising the possibility that further money should be paid on the shares. However, the court is generally very reluctant to decide the value of assets and will normally accept the valuation made at the time of allotment, unless it is shown to have been made dishonestly or colourably (that is, falsely for the sake of appearance), or the contract of allotment is itself set aside for fraud (*Re Wragg Ltd* [1897] 1 Ch 796).

Where, however, there is an express agreement to credit shares as paid up with more than the value of the contributed assets then the shares are issued at a discount. In *Hong Kong and China Gas Co Ltd v Glen* [1914] 1 Ch 527, the company had acquired from Mr Glen the right to supply gas in the city of Victoria, Hong Kong, in return for issuing 400 of its £10 shares paid up in full and had further promised that whenever it increased its capital it would allot to him 20 per cent of the newly created shares credited as fully paid up. It was held that although the allotment of 400 shares at the time of acquiring the concession was valid, the promise to treat shares allotted in the future as fully paid up was void and unenforceable.

These rules still apply to *private companies*.

6.6.4.2 Public companies

A *public company* must not allot shares for a consideration other than cash, unless the consideration has been independently valued as being worth at least as much as the amount to be credited as paid up by it on the shares to be allotted (CA 2006, ss 593(1)(a) and 596(3)(d)).

Section 593(1) does not apply to a takeover by a public company in which it issues its own shares to buy the shares of an existing company, provided that the offer to exchange shares is made to all shareholders (or all of a particular class) of the other company (s 594, which includes detailed provisions). This exception applies to a takeover bid for any kind of body corporate, whether UK or foreign (ss 594(6)(b) and 1173(1)).

The valuation required by s 593(1) must be by a person qualified to act as auditor of the company (see **17.4.2**) or by someone appointed by a person qualified to act as auditor. (In practice, of course, the company's own auditor would arrange for the valuation.) The report must have been made not earlier than six months before the date of the allotments (s 593(1)(b)) and must state that the value of the asset is at least the amount to be credited as paid up for it on the shares to be allotted (s 596(3)(d)). (The report does not have to state the value.) A copy of the report must be sent to the allottee (s 593(1)(c)).

A person who is allotted shares in a public company in return for non-cash assets without receiving any valuation report, or who knows (or ought to know) that some other provision of CA 2006, s 593 or 596, has been contravened, will be liable to pay the company in cash the amount treated as paid up by the alleged value of the assets plus interest at 5 per cent a year (ss 593(3) and 609). In addition, the company and any officer of the company in default will have committed an offence triable either way (s 607). But any promise by the allottee to the company is nevertheless enforceable by the company (s 608(1)). The knowledge that will make a person liable under these provisions is knowledge of the facts constituting the contravention: it is irrelevant that the person does not know the legal consequences of those facts (*System Controls plc v Munro Corporate plc* [1990] BCLC 659).

In this context, 'cash consideration' means cash received by the company, any cheque received by the company, in good faith, which the directors of the company have no reason for suspecting will not be paid, a release of a liability of the company for a liquidated sum, an undertaking to pay cash to the company at a future date, or payment by any other means giving rise to an entitlement to a payment in cash or to credit equivalent to payment in cash (s 583(3)), and may be in sterling or a foreign currency (s 583(6)). It does not include an assignment of a debt (*System Controls plc v Munro Corporate plc* [1990] BCLC 659).

6.6.5 PROMISES TO PERFORM SERVICES AND FUTURE UNDERTAKINGS

A *public company* may not accept, as part or all of the contribution in exchange for issuing shares, a promise to do work or perform services for the company or for any other person (CA 2006, s 585(1)). If a share is allotted in contravention of this provision, the allottee is liable to pay in cash the amount unlawfully credited as paid on the share, plus interest at 5 per cent per annum (ss 585(2) and 592); the company and any officer of the company in default will have committed an offence triable either way (s 590), but the allottee's promise is nevertheless enforceable by the company (s 591). Past services may be paid for in shares, provided the amount to be paid for the services is a liquidated debt of the company (and so counts as a cash contribution) or an independent valuation report can be made on the services (see 6.6.4.2).

A promise to pay cash in the future counts as cash (s 583(3)(d)) and so does not have to be valued for a public company (see 6.6.4.2).

A *public company* may not accept, as part or all of the contribution in exchange for issuing shares, an undertaking to provide a non-cash asset which is to be, or may be, performed more than five years after the allotment of the shares (s 587(1)). If a share is allotted in contravention of this provision, the allottee is liable to pay in cash the amount unlawfully credited as paid on the share, plus interest at 5 per cent per annum (ss 587(2) and 592); the company and any officer of the company will have committed an offence triable either way (s 590) but the allottee's promise is nevertheless enforceable by the company (s 591(1)).

The rules in ss 585(1) and 587, applying to public companies, are a statutory version of the judge-made rule, which still applies to private companies, that a company may not agree to accept as payment for shares a contractual obligation if breach of the contract would leave the company with only a claim for damages (*Re Richmond Hill Hotel Co, Pellatt's Case* (1867) LR 2 Ch App 527; *Gardner v Iredale* [1912] 1 Ch 700 at p 716).

6.6.6 EXEMPTION FROM LIABILITY TO COMPANY

A person who has a liability to a company by virtue of a contravention of any of the provisions discussed in 6.6.4.2 and 6.6.5 may apply to the court to be exempted from that liability under CA 2006, s 589. The court may grant exemption if it appears just and equitable to do so but must have regard to the overriding principle (s 589(5)(a)) that:

> a company that has allotted shares should receive money or money's worth at least equal in value to the aggregate of the nominal value of those shares and the whole of any premium or, if the case so requires, so much of that aggregate as is treated as paid up.

For the operation of this provision, see *Re Ossory Estates plc* [1988] BCLC 213, in which exemption was granted, and *Re Bradford Investments plc (No 2)* [1991] BCLC 688, in which it was not.

6.7 MINIMUM CAPITAL OF A PUBLIC COMPANY

6.7.1 COMPANY INITIALLY REGISTERED AS PUBLIC

A company registered as a public company on its original incorporation (as opposed to a private company which re-registers as public, see 6.7.2) may not do business or exercise any power to borrow money unless Companies House has issued it with a trading certificate under CA 2006, s 761. A trading certificate can only be issued after the company has allotted shares with a nominal value at least equal to the authorised minimum (£50,000 or €57,100) (ss 761(2) and 763(1); SI 2009/2425, reg 2). The assets contributed for those shares must satisfy the restrictions applicable to public companies (see 6.5.2.1, 6.5.4, 6.6.4.2 and 6.6.5). In addition, the nominal value of a share allotted to an employees' share scheme will not count towards the £50,000/€57,100 limit unless (s 761(3)) one-quarter of its nominal value and the whole of any share premium have been paid up (which is not normally compulsory: s 586(1) and (2)).

An application for a trading certificate must be accompanied by a certificate of compliance stating that the company meets the requirements for the issue of a trading certificate (s 762(1)(d) and

(2)). Companies House may accept that certificate of compliance as sufficient evidence (s 762(3)) and must give public notice of receiving it (ss 1077 and 1078(3); see **4.3**). A trading certificate is conclusive evidence that the company is entitled to do business and exercise borrowing powers (s 761(4)). There is no fee for the issue of a trading certificate.

If a company is registered as a public company on original incorporation but fails to obtain a trading certificate within one year, an application may be made for it to be wound up by the court (Insolvency Act 1986, s 122(1)(b)).

If a public company, registered as such on its original incorporation, transacts any business or makes any borrowing before the issue of its certificate to commence business, the company and any officer in default will have committed an offence triable either way (CA 2006, s 767). The transactions themselves are not invalid but, if the company fails to honour its obligations under them within 21 days of being called upon to do so, its directors become jointly and severally liable to indemnify the other parties to the transactions for their losses caused by the company's failure to honour its obligations (s 767(3)).

6.7.2 PRIVATE COMPANY RE-REGISTERED AS PUBLIC

In order for a private company to re-register as a public company, its members must adopt a special resolution (CA 2006, s 90(1)) and on the day that resolution is adopted the company must have allotted shares with a nominal value at least equal to the authorised minimum (£50,000 or €57,100) (ss 91(1)(a) and 763(1); SI 2009/2425, reg 2). The capital contributed for the company's allotted shares must, in effect, satisfy the restrictions applicable to forms of contribution that may be accepted by public companies. Thus at least a quarter of the nominal value of each share plus the whole of any share premium must be paid up (CA 2006, s 91(1)(b); see **6.5.2.1** and **6.5.4**). If the private company accepted, as part or all of the contribution in exchange for issuing shares, a promise to do work or perform services for the company or any other person, that promise must have been carried out (s 91(1)(c); see **6.6.5**). If the private company accepted any other form of future undertaking to contribute non-cash assets, the undertaking must either have been performed or there must be an enforceable obligation to perform it within five years from the date of adopting the special resolution to re-register (s 91(1)(d); see **6.6.5**).

In order to deal with the valuation of non-cash assets that may have been contributed for a private company's shares (see **6.6.4.2**), s 92(1)(a) requires that an application to re-register a private company as public must be accompanied by a balance sheet of the company, for a date no more than seven months before the date of the application, and an unqualified auditor's report on that balance sheet (s 92(1)(b)). The application must also be accompanied by a written statement that in the auditor's opinion the balance sheet shows that the company's net assets (see **6.4.2**) were, at the balance sheet date, not less than the sum of its called-up share capital and its undistributable reserves (see **10.3.6**) (s 92(1)(c)).

If, between that balance sheet date and the date of adopting the resolution to re-register, the company allotted shares for non-cash assets then it must have those assets valued in accordance with the procedure described in **6.6.4.2** (s 93).

A private company re-registered as public does not need a trading certificate.

6.8 REMEDIES OF A WRONGED ALLOTTEE

6.8.1 INTRODUCTION

This section describes the remedies available to a person who has been induced by a misrepresentation to subscribe for shares in a company. The law described here applies to misrepresentations made in any way. In **7.4** it will be explained that, when shares are offered to the public, a prospectus must be published and, when an application is made for listing on the Stock Exchange, either a prospectus or listing particulars must be published. There are special rules about liability for errors and omissions in those documents, which are described in 7.5. The law described in this section is most useful when an allotment has been made for which a prospectus or listing particulars was not required.

6.8.2 RESCISSION FOR MISREPRESENTATION

If one party to a contract was induced to make the contract by statements of fact made by the other party and any of those statements was untrue then there has been misrepresentation, and the misled party is entitled to rescind the contract.

The misled party may also ask a court for an order rescinding the contract—that is, declaring that the contract never created any rights or obligations so that each party must return to the other what was received under the contract. Though it finds rescission of a contract justifiable, the court may, at its discretion, reconstitute the contract or refuse to order rescission, and award damages in lieu of rescission (Misrepresentation Act 1967, s 2(2)).

Rescission of a contract of allotment of shares in a company means that the company must return whatever capital the shareholder has contributed for the shares; the shareholder will cease to have any liability to pay calls if the shares were partly paid; and the company must treat the shares as unissued. The claimant shareholder must be able to provide counter-restitution (what used to be called *restitutio in integrum*) to the defendant (*Erlanger v New Sombrero Phosphate Co* (1878) 3 App Cas 1218 per Lord Blackburn at p 1278) by returning the shares. This will not be possible after commencement of winding up of the company (*Oakes v Turquand* (1867) LR 2 HL 325; *Kent v Freehold Land and Brick-making Co* (1868) LR 3 Ch App 493) because the claimant will not be able to return what was received under the contract (a share in a going concern): the claimant will be able to return only a contributory's interest in a company in liquidation (*Re Hull and County Bank, Burgess's Case* (1880) 15 ChD 507). The fact that the company has gone into liquidation will not be a bar to rescission of an allotment if the allottee started proceedings for rescission before the commencement of the liquidation (*Reese River Silver Mining Co Ltd v Smith* (1869) LR 4 HL 64). An allottee will not be able to claim rescission of a contract of allotment of shares which were transferred to another person after allotment, unless they can be recovered. The mere fact that the market value of the shares has declined will not prevent rescission (*Armstrong v Jackson* [1917] 2 KB 822).

The right to rescission for misrepresentation does not depend on the motive or reason for making the misrepresentation. Rescission may be grounded on a wholly innocent mistake (per Lord Herschell in *Derry v Peek* (1889) 14 App Cas 337 at p 359) as in *Coles v White City (Manchester) Greyhound Association Ltd* (1929) 45 TLR 230.

A party who makes a misstatement is not permitted to say that the misled party could have checked it and discovered it was wrong (*Redgrave v Hurd* (1881) 20 ChD 1).

6.8.3 ATTRIBUTION OF MISREPRESENTATIONS TO A COMPANY

An allottee of shares who wants to rescind the contract for the allotment of the shares must show that a misrepresentation was made by the other party to that contract, namely the company. In practice, it is unlikely that a misrepresentation would be made in a notice given by the company, except in the listing particulars or prospectus for a public issue (see **Chapter 7**). In private negotiations between an investor and a company it is more likely that misrepresentations will be made by individuals negotiating on the company's side. How far should misstatements of fact by individuals be attributed to a company so as to make them misrepresentations made by the company? A comprehensive answer was given by Romer J in *Lynde v Anglo-Italian Hemp Spinning Co* [1896]

1 Ch 178, and slightly modified by Luxmoore J in *Collins v Associated Greyhound Racecourses Ltd* [1930] 1 Ch 1. The combined effect of the two judgments is that a company will be liable:

(a) where the misrepresentations are made by the directors or other general agents of the company entitled to act, and acting, on its behalf;

(b) where the misrepresentations are made by a special agent of the company while acting within the scope of his or her authority;

(c) where the company can be held affected, before the contract is made, with knowledge that the contract was induced by misrepresentations—for example, if the directors, when making an allotment, know that it was induced by misrepresentations, whether made with their authority or not;

(d) where, to the knowledge of the company or its agents, the contract is made on the basis of particular representations that later turn out to be untrue.

In *Re Metal Constituents Ltd, Lord Lurgan's Case* [1902] 1 Ch 707, Lord Lurgan had subscribed the company's old-style memorandum, in which he had undertaken to take 250 of the company's shares. He wished to be relieved of this obligation on the ground that he had been induced to give the undertaking by a misrepresentation made by one of the company's promoters. His claim failed because the company did not exist until its memorandum was registered, which was after Lord Lurgan had signed it and given his undertaking. Any misrepresentation inducing Lord Lurgan to sign could not be attributed to the company because at the time of the alleged misrepresentation, the company was not in existence.

6.8.4 LIMITATIONS ON THE STATEMENTS ON WHICH RESCISSION MAY BE GROUNDED

Only a misstatement of fact by the other party is a misrepresentation entitling a party to rescind.

A statement of an opinion that is wrong is not a misstatement of fact (*Bisset v Wilkinson* [1927] AC 177) though it may be difficult to distinguish between opinion and fact (*Smith v Land and House Property Corporation* (1884) 28 ChD 7).

A statement of an intention that is not carried out is not a misstatement of fact, but a statement of an intention that the maker of the statement actually does not have is a misstatement of fact. In *Edgington v Fitzmaurice* (1885) 29 ChD 459 directors of a company invited people to lend it money saying that the money would be used to finance the extension of the company's buildings and plant. In fact the company was in difficulties and most of the money lent was used to pay pressing liabilities. Soon afterwards the company failed. It was found that the directors had never intended to use the money in the way that they had stated, and Bowen LJ remarked: 'the state of a man's mind is as much a fact as the state of his digestion'.

A statement may be a misrepresentation because it is incomplete or ambiguous. Lord Halsbury LC said in *Aaron's Reefs Ltd v Twiss* [1896] AC 273, at p 281:

> It is said there is no specific allegation of fact which is proved to be false. Again I protest, as I have said, against that being the true test. I should say, taking the whole thing together, was there false representation? I do not care by what means it is conveyed—by what trick or device or ambiguous language: all those are expedients by which fraudulent people seem to think they can escape from the real substance of the transaction.

In *Greenwood v Leather Shod Wheel Co* [1900] 1 Ch 421 the company issued a prospectus inviting the public to subscribe for its shares. The company had been formed to exploit a new method of making wheels with leather tyres. One paragraph of the prospectus correctly listed important potential purchasers who had agreed to try sets of the new wheels. The following paragraph said that various other bodies 'have already given orders'. In fact the bodies mentioned in the second paragraph had also only agreed to try the new product. The court agreed with Greenwood's contention that the prospectus gave the impression that the company had numerous orders and so would be successful but this was a misstatement because it actually had no orders.

A misstatement does not justify rescission if it is not material. For example, in *Smith v Chadwick* (1882) 20 ChD 27, CA, affirmed by HL (1884) 9 App Cas 187, Chadwick and partners had promoted a company and in the prospectus had stated that Mr JJ Grieves MP would be a director. Smith took shares in the company. In fact, Grieves had withdrawn from the project the day before the prospectus was issued. On the other hand, Mr Smith admitted that he had never heard of Mr Grieves, and so it was held that the misstatement was not material to him.

The fact that a company has totally failed to mention a material fact does not justify rescission of a contract for the allotment of shares unless the omission makes what is said a misstatement (*McKeown v Boudard-Peveril Gear Co Ltd* (1896) 65 LJ Ch 735).

If a material statement of fact is made to induce the making of a contract but, before the contract is made circumstances change so that the statement is no longer true, then the maker of the statement has a duty to correct it, and failure to do so entitles the misled party to rescission (*With v O'Flanagan* [1936] Ch 575).

6.8.5 LOSS OF THE REMEDY OF RESCISSION

6.8.5.1 General rules

A court will not rescind a contract for misrepresentation if:

(a) The claimant cannot provide counter-restitution to the defendant (see **6.8.2**).

(b) After learning of the misrepresentation, the misled party acted as if the contract had nevertheless created rights and duties. With a contract of allotment the right to rescind will be lost if the allottee tries to sell the shares (*Re Hop and Malt Exchange and Warehouse Co* (1866) LR 1 Eq 483), or votes at a meeting of members (*Sharpley v Louth and East Coast Railway Co* (1876) 2 ChD 663) or pays calls on partly paid shares and accepts payment of dividends (*Scholey v Central Railway Co of Venezuela* (1868) LR 9 Eq 266 n).

(c) After learning of the misrepresentation, the misled party failed to act promptly to rescind (see **6.8.5.2**).

(d) Too long a time has elapsed since the misled party acted in reliance on the misrepresentation. This does not apply if it can be shown that the misrepresentation was fraudulent (*Armstrong v Jackson* [1917] 2 KB 822).

6.8.5.2 Promptness

The rule that a claim for rescission must be made promptly after learning of misrepresentation is enforced very strictly in relation to contracts for the allotment of shares. In *Re Estates Investment Co, Ashley's Case* (1870) LR 9 Eq 263, Lord Romilly MR said, at pp 268–9:

> whenever a misrepresentation is made of which any one of the shareholders has notice, and can take advantage to avoid his contract with the company, it is his duty to determine at once whether he will depart from the company, or whether he will remain a member.

Ashley had been present at a meeting of members at which allegations of misrepresentation were made. Some members formed a committee to take action against the company but Ashley did not join them, saying that he would await the outcome of their case. The case was finally decided in the shareholders' favour (though not until after the company commenced winding up) but it was held that Ashley had lost his right to rescind. On the other hand, all the allottees who did join the committee were entitled to rescind even though only one representative member actually took legal proceedings (*Re Estates Investment Co, Pawle's Case* (1869) LR 4 Ch App 497).

It has been suggested that a delay of two weeks between learning of a misrepresentation and rescission of the contract of allotment would be too long (*Re Scottish Petroleum Co* (1883) 23 ChD 413 per Baggallay LJ at p 434). In *Re Russian (Vyksounsky) Ironworks Co, Taite's Case* (1867) LR 3 Eq 795, a delay of one month in commencing proceedings after the company had refused to refund application money was held to be too long. In *Heymann v European Central Railway Co* (1868) LR 7 Eq 154, a delay of three months in commencing proceedings after discovering grounds for rescission was held to be too long. In *Re Snyder Dynamite Projectile Co Ltd, Skelton's Case* (1893) 68 LT 210, Stirling J said (at p 212) that in every case all the circumstances must be taken into account. In the past, when most shares were partly paid, it was thought that creditors of a company relied on its list of members as indicating that there were substantial persons able to contribute further capital if calls were to be made. The court's insistence that rescission of membership had to be done quickly if at all, minimised the risk of creditors being misled. Similarly, it minimises the risk of persons being misled into taking shares in a company on the strength of the list of others who have apparently thought the company a good investment. These considerations have less force in relation to a private company in which the shares are fully paid (*Haas Timber and Trading Co Pty Ltd v Wade* (1954) 94 CLR 593 at p 604).

6.8.6 DAMAGES

6.8.6.1 Bases for awarding damages for misrepresentation

A wronged allottee of shares may want damages instead of rescission if rescission is no longer possible (see **6.8.5**) or in addition to rescission if compensation is required for consequential loss. Under the common law, rescission of a contract induced by a misrepresentation is available whether the misrepresentation was fraudulent, negligent or wholly innocent. However, damages could be awarded in addition to or instead of rescission only where there was a fraudulent misrepresentation, in which case damages could be awarded for the tort of deceit (per Lord Bramwell in *Derry v Peek* (1889) 14 App Cas 337 at p 347). Subsequently, it has been recognised that damages can be awarded in tort for negligent misstatements (see **17.5.2**) but, as the reported cases on negligent misstatement have not so far involved subscriptions for new issues of shares, the discussion here will concentrate on the tort of deceit and the statutory liability for damages for misrepresentation introduced by the Misrepresentation Act 1967.

6.8.6.2 Deceit

A claim for damages for the tort of deceit is available to a claimant who has suffered harm in consequence of acting in reliance on a false statement which the defendant made with intent that persons should act in reliance on it. It is essential to prove that the statement was made fraudulently. For the purposes of the common law this means proving that the defendant knew the statement was untrue (or did not believe that it was true) or made the statement recklessly, without caring whether it was true or false. In *Derry v Peek* (1889) 14 App Cas 337 it was held that it is not fraudulent to make a statement, which is in fact false, in the honest belief that it is true, even if one did not have a reasonable ground for that belief. *Derry v Peek* concerned an untrue statement in a prospectus for a public offer of shares in a statutory company, but the directors were held not liable for the losses of people who took shares on the strength of the prospectus, because it was accepted that the directors honestly believed the statement was true.

Because of the policy of English law of imposing more extensive liability on intentional wrongdoers than on merely careless ones, the measure of damages for deceit is more generous than for negligence. Where a fraudulent misrepresentation has caused the claimant to enter into a transaction, damages must compensate the claimant for all the actual loss directly flowing from (that is, caused by) entering into the transaction, including consequential losses. There is no restriction to compensating only for foreseeable loss. These principles were established in *Smith New Court Securities Ltd v Citibank NA* [1997] AC 254.

The defence of contributory negligence is not available in a claim for deceit, so the fact that the claimant had other erroneous reasons for entering into a transaction does not affect the liability of the defendant whose fraudulent misrepresentation was a reason for entering into it (*Standard Chartered Bank v Pakistan National Shipping Corporation (Nos 2 and 4)* [2002] UKHL 43, [2003] 1 AC 959).

6.8.6.3 Statutory liability

The availability of damages for misrepresentation was extended by the Misrepresentation Act 1967, s 2(1), which has created a statutory liability for damages for misrepresentation unless the misrepresentor can prove that 'he had reasonable ground to believe and did believe up to the time the contract was made that the facts represented were true'. Section 2(1) applies only where the misrepresentor is a party to the contract. Accordingly, it applies to a contract for the allotment of shares in a company only if the misrepresentation which induced the shareholder to take the shares was made by, or can be attributed to, the company (see **6.8.3**). If the misrepresentation can be attributed to the company, it is unnecessary to resort to the torts of negligence or deceit because the statutory remedy will be more convenient.

The measure of damages to be awarded under s 2(1) has been held to be the same as for fraudulent misrepresentation (see **6.8.6.2**), even though it is unnecessary to prove fraud (*Royscot Trust Ltd v Rogerson* [1991] 2 QB 297). Trenchant academic criticism of this decision (Richard Hooley, 'Damages and the Misrepresentation Act 1967' (1991) 107 LQR 547) was noted by Lord Steyn in *Smith New Court Securities Ltd v Citibank NA* [1997] AC 254 at p 283.

6.8.6.4 No need for rescission

Formerly, there was a rule that damages for misrepresentation inducing a person to subscribe for shares could not be awarded unless the person rescinded the contract of allotment (*Houldsworth v City of Glasgow Bank* (1880) 5 App Cas 317). As rescission is not permitted if the allottee's claim is begun after the company has commenced winding up, an allottee who was not able to begin proceedings before commencement of winding up was deprived of any remedy. Now, CA 2006, s 655, provides that a person is not debarred from obtaining damages or other compensation from a company by reason only of holding shares in the company.

6.9 ALTERATION OF SHARE CAPITAL

6.9.1 PERMITTED WAYS OF ALTERING SHARE CAPITAL

A limited company with a share capital may not alter that share capital except in the ways permitted by CA 2006, s 617 (s 617(1)). Subsections (2), (3) and (4) of s 617 list seven permitted ways of altering share capital:

(a) increase by allotting new shares (see **6.3**);

(b) reduction (see **10.7**);

(c) subdivision (see **6.9.2**);

(d) consolidation (see **6.9.2**);

(e) reconversion of stock into shares (see **6.9.3**);

(f) redenomination (see **6.9.4**); and

(g) reduction in connection with redenomination (see **6.9.5**).

Section 617(5) lists other ways of altering share capital which are permitted by provisions of CA 2006. These are:

(a) purchase of own shares (see **10.6**);

(b) redemption of redeemable shares (see **10.5**);

(c) forfeiture of shares or surrender in lieu of forfeiture (see **6.5.2.5**);

(d) cancellation of shares under s 662; and

(e) alteration under a compromise or arrangement sanctioned by the court under part 26.

6.9.2 SUBDIVISION AND CONSOLIDATION

Subdivision and consolidation of a company's shares are permitted by CA 2006, ss 617(3)(a) and 618(1), but can only be done if authorised by a resolution of the company's members (s 618(3)). Subdivision of shares replaces each share with a number of shares of smaller nominal value. Consolidation is the reverse. Subdivision or consolidation of partly paid shares must not change the ratio of amount paid up to amount unpaid (s 618(2)). The usual reason for subdividing or consolidating is to improve marketability. A company's articles may exclude or restrict subdivision or consolidation (s 618(5)).

Within one month after a company subdivides or consolidates shares, it must give notice to Companies House accompanied by a statement of capital (s 619).

6.9.3 RECONVERSION OF STOCK INTO SHARES

Until CA 2006, a company could decide to treat its paid-up share capital as a 'stock' held by the members and having a value equal to the total nominal value of those paid-up shares. Each member of a company which has converted its shares into stock is regarded as being the holder of an amount of stock of a certain nominal value, rather than of a number of shares with that nominal value. In principle, any amount of stock may be transferred, though in practice it is usual to specify a 'stock unit' and require the nominal value of the amount transferred to be a multiple of the stock unit.

Rights of members who hold stock are reckoned by the nominal value of the stock held. For example, a member may be entitled to one vote for each £1 of stock held.

In the past, the advantage of stock over shares was that shares had to be numbered and this caused a great deal of extra work in public companies when registering transfers. Now, however, distinguishing numbers are not required if all the issued shares of a class are fully paid up and rank equally for all purposes (CA 2006, s 543).

CA 2006 does not permit conversion of shares into stock (s 540(2)) but it does allow a company which has done so to reconvert the stock into shares (ss 617(3)(b) and 620). Notice of reconversion must be given to Companies House within one month, with a statement of capital (s 621).

In CA 2006, the term 'share' is to be interpreted as including stock, except where a distinction between shares and stock is express or implied (s 540(4)).

6.9.4 REDENOMINATION

A limited company may, by resolution, convert the nominal value of its shares (or shares of a particular class) into a different currency (CA 2006, ss 617(4) and 622(1)), provided it uses the spot rate of exchange prevailing on a day specified in the resolution, or an average of the rates over a specified period (s 622(3)). This is called redenomination (s 622(1)). The day or period must be within the 28 days preceding the date of the resolution (s 622(3)). A company's articles may prohibit or restrict redenomination (s 622(7)). Notice of redenomination must be given to Companies House within one month, with a statement of capital (s 625). In the case of a public company, Companies House must give public notice of receipt of the statement of capital (ss 1077 and 1078(3); see **4.3**).

Redenomination of a company's shares does not affect any rights or obligations of its members under its constitution (s 624(1)). In particular, it does not affect entitlement to dividends, voting rights or liability in respect of amounts unpaid on shares (s 624(1)).

6.9.5 REDUCTION OF CAPITAL IN CONNECTION WITH REDENOMINATION

As redenomination must be carried out at a spot exchange rate, it is unlikely to produce a convenient round figure for the new nominal value. CA 2006, s 626, therefore permits a company, by special resolution, to reduce its capital, by not more than 10 per cent, in order to obtain a more suitable nominal value following redenomination. The resolution must be passed within three months of the resolution effecting redenomination (s 626(3)). The amount by which the share capital is reduced must be transferred to a redenomination reserve (s 628(1)), which must be treated as if it were paid-up share capital (s 628(3)), except that it can be used in paying up fully paid bonus shares (s 628(2)).

Notice of a resolution under s 626 must be given to Companies House within 15 days (s 627(1)), accompanied by a statement of capital (s 627(2) and (3)). In the case of a public company, Companies House must give public notice of receipt of the statement of capital (ss 1077 and 1078(3); see **4.3**).

The reduction of capital is not effective until the notice and statement of capital have been registered (s 627(5)).

Also within 15 days, Companies House must be sent a statement by the directors confirming that the reduction does not exceed the 10 per cent limit (s 627(6)).

7

OFFERING SHARES TO
THE PUBLIC

SUMMARY OF POINTS COVERED

- What is in this chapter
- Financial Services and Markets Act 2000
- Marketplaces for shares
- Prospectuses
- Misleading statements and omissions in prospectuses

- Official listing
- Investment advertisements
- Underwriting and commissions
- Inadequate response

7.1 WHAT IS IN THIS CHAPTER

In a company with a small number of members it is usually the case that all the members are closely concerned with the company and take part in its management. An important aspect of their control of the company is the ability to decide who to admit as new members. Sometimes, though, it is decided to open up membership of a company to anyone who wants to come in. The usual reason for opening membership of a company is that it needs contributed capital and is willing to accept money from anyone. Sometimes a founder, or the heir of a founder, of a successful company wishes to sell all or part of his or her stake in the company and offers it to the public: the company may first have to subdivide the shares or make a capitalisation issue (see **10.4**) in order to represent the stake by a sufficient number of shares to be able to sell it to a large number of buyers.

When a company's shares are widely held, individual shareholders tend to be personally uninterested in participating in management: they are simply investors who, depending on the purpose of their investment and their tax position, look for good dividend income or for a capital profit on selling shares.

Public investment in company shares is a very important source of finance for companies. But it is an inescapable fact of business life that some businesses are more successful than others, and some businesses fail entirely. Investors require information about companies in order to decide whether to invest in them, and much of this chapter is devoted to the legal requirements to provide that information (see **7.4** to **7.7**). Investors also need to know that they can easily sell their shares when they want to. So it is important that there is a marketplace which can be relied on to provide an opportunity to sell at the best possible price. That marketplace also requires information to set prices. A substantial financial services industry has grown up to facilitate the buying and selling of shares and is regulated by the Financial Services and Markets Act 2000 (see **7.2**). It is an important feature of the common market of the European Economic Area (EEA) that there should be no national barriers to the movement of capital for investment. Accordingly, the principles of regulation of financial services and capital markets are mostly formulated at EU level. It has been thought that this regulation has to be flexible so as to be affordable by companies of various sizes (see **7.3**). The Companies Act 2006 (CA 2006) provides two further national controls on share offers to the public: it restricts the payment of underwriting commission (see **7.8**) and it requires repayment of subscribers' money if a share offer is not completely successful (see **7.9**).

Key legislation which you should be able to consult when reading this chapter:

- Financial Services and Markets Act 2000 (FSMA 2000), ss 73A–103, sch 10;
- CA 2006, ss 552 and 553 (for **7.8**), s 578 (for **7.9**).

All that legislation is in *Blackstone's Statutes on Company Law*.

- SI 2005/1529 (for **7.7**), which is at the Online Resource Centre for *Blackstone's Statutes on Company Law*: **global.oup.com/uk/orc/law/company/company_statutes**.
- The Listing Rules (LR) and the Prospectus Rules (PR) in the FCA Handbook, which is at **handbook.fca.org.uk**.

7.2 FINANCIAL SERVICES AND MARKETS ACT 2000

7.2.1 FINANCIAL CONDUCT AUTHORITY

The industry that has grown up in the United Kingdom to persuade people to put their money into company shares and other investments and which provides facilities for doing so is subject to the Financial Services and Markets Act 2000 (FSMA 2000).

FSMA 2000 replaced the Financial Services Act 1986 and other legislation, under which different parts of the financial services industry were separately regulated by a mixture of public bodies, professional institutes and trade associations. Under FSMA 2000, one of those regulators, the Securities and Investments Board, was renamed the Financial Services Authority (FSA) and made the sole regulator of the whole industry. In particular it took over from the Bank of England the regulation of banks. The Bank of England had been criticised for its failings in the case of the Bank of Credit and Commerce International, which had collapsed as a result of widespread fraud. Subsequently, however, the FSA was seen as failing to anticipate the financial crisis of 2007–8, and the effect of that crisis on the Northern Rock and HBOS banks. As a result, FSMA 2000 was extensively amended by the Financial Services Act 2012. This divided the FSA into the Financial Conduct Authority (FCA) and the Prudential Regulation Authority (PRA). The PRA is responsible for the prudential regulation of banks, insurers and complex investment firms. Its objective is to prevent a failure of one firm damaging the entire financial system. Originally the PRA was a subsidiary of the Bank of England. As from 1 March 2017, the Bank of England is the PRA. The task of the FCA is to protect consumers and promote confidence in financial services and markets. The FCA deals with all the matters considered in **Chapter 7**.

The FCA is a company limited by guarantee. It is exempt from the requirement to have the word 'limited' at the end of its name (FSMA 2000, sch 1ZA, para 17), unless the Secretary of State removes the exemption because of action taken by the FCA which makes it no longer appropriate (para 18). The Bank of England's deputy governor for prudential regulation is automatically a member of the FCA's governing body. The other members are appointed by the Treasury and the Secretary of State (para 2). Information about the operation of the FCA can be obtained from its website, **www.fca.org.uk**. The FCA's regulations and guidance are in the FCA Handbook, which may be consulted at its website.

The FCA is financed by fees paid by the persons it regulates. It receives no money from the government.

7.2.2 REGULATED ACTIVITIES, AUTHORISED PERSONS, EXEMPT PERSONS

FSMA 2000 controls what it calls 'regulated activities'. These are defined in s 22 and sch 2 and in SI 2001/544 and 2001/1177 to include most forms of financial services provided by way of business. In particular, the definition of regulated activities includes dealing in securities as principal (SI 2001/544, art 14), dealing in securities as agent (art 21), arranging deals in securities (art 25), and advising on investments (art 53). Shares in a company are defined to be securities by arts 3(1) and 76.

Financial services is an area in which it has been seen to be particularly important to achieve harmonised regulation in the EEA. Requirements for authorisation of providers of investment services are governed by the recast Markets in Financial Instruments Directive (Directive 2014/65/EU, MiFID 2). The term 'financial instruments' is defined to include transferable securities (Directive 2014/65/EU, annex I, s C), and shares in companies are an example of transferable securities (art 4(1)(44)).

The 'general prohibition' made by FSMA 2000, s 19, is that regulated activities can be carried on in the United Kingdom only by authorised persons and exempt persons. The usual way of becoming an authorised person is by obtaining permission from the FCA under part 4A of the Act (a 'part 4A permission') to carry on one or more regulated activities (s 31). The FCA refers to authorised persons as 'firms' regardless of their legal form (FCA Handbook, Glossary). Authorised persons are able to employ agents, called 'appointed representatives', who are exempt persons under s 39 and SI 2001/1217. Some regulated activities are defined as 'PRA-regulated activities' by FSMA 2000, s 22A, and SI 2013/556. Part 4A permission to carry on PRA-regulated activities is given by the PRA instead of the FCA.

Solicitors, accountants, actuaries, licensed conveyancers and chartered surveyors ('professional firms') are exempt persons when they provide a limited range of financial services in a manner which is incidental to the provision of professional services (FSMA 2000, s 327; SI 2001/1227). Professional firms are exempt only when providing professional services subject to supervision and regulation by one of the designated professional bodies listed in SI 2001/1226 (FSMA 2000, ss 326 and 327(8)). Other exempt persons (mainly public bodies) are listed in SI 2001/1201.

The general prohibition does not generally apply to companies themselves in relation to their own shares. This is because the issue by a company of its own shares or share warrants is excluded by SI 2001/544, art 18, from the definition of regulated activity. Also the making of arrangements by a company for another person (whether as principal or agent) to buy, sell or subscribe for the company's own shares is excluded from the definition of regulated activity by art 34.

7.3 MARKETPLACES FOR SHARES

7.3.1 INTERMEDIARIES

In order to make a company's shares more attractive to investors it is necessary to assure them that they will be able to sell shares easily in order to realise capital profits, or liquidate the investment or switch to a different investment. Accordingly, enterprises have developed which specialise in acting as intermediaries to assist investors to sell (or, on the other hand, buy) company shares (or stocks) and associated investments such as subscription warrants and company marketable loans (see **Chapter 12**) which are collectively known as 'company securities'. (The 'security' provided by shares and similar investments used to be the certainty of title provided by share, stock or deben-ture certificates, but now evidence of ownership of most publicly traded shares is by computer record. The term 'security' is also used with a completely different meaning in connection with borrowing—see **Chapter 11**.)

The basic activity of securities intermediaries is 'broking'—that is acting as an agent for a client to sell or buy securities for the client, making a profit from a commission on each deal. A broker can assist the marketability of a particular security by being willing to attempt to buy or sell that security whenever asked to do so. This is known as acting as a 'matching broker'. A security will be even more marketable if there is a 'market maker' who is willing actually to buy or sell that security whenever asked to do so. If a security has market makers who are always willing to buy and sell, it will be particularly attractive to investors but, conversely, market mak-ers will only hold themselves out as willing to deal in the most actively traded securities since they must be assured of being able to sell, at a profit, what they are asked to buy and of being able to buy what they are asked to sell. The prices at which a market maker offers to buy and sell are called 'quotations' and if a security has a market maker it is described as 'quoted'. A company whose securities are quoted is generally described as a 'quoted company', but that term now has a statutory definition when it is used in CA 2006 (see **7.3.4.6**). A security will be even more attrac-tive to investors when there are two or more market makers competing with each other to offer the best quotations. Where there is a large volume of trading, which can be observed by brokers (either by using computer systems or by meeting for 'open outcry' trading), market makers are unnecessary. (Market makers used to be known as 'jobbers'. Sometimes, matching brokers are considered to be a type of market maker.)

In order to attract permanent clients, brokers offer extensive advice and investment manage-ment services. Even so, a broker may be willing to act for a client on an 'execution-only' basis, which means doing nothing but carrying out the client's instruction to buy or sell.

7.3.2 INVESTMENT EXCHANGES

Historically, it has been usual for securities intermediaries in a particular town to form an association to provide premises where they could transact business and establish rules for the conduct of business. Such associations have also been formed by intermediaries specialising in other forms of investment and they are generally known as 'investment exchanges'. An investment exchange whose members specialise in government stocks and company securities is often called a 'stock exchange'. An investor wishing to buy or sell securities can contact a member of a suitable exchange to carry out the transac-tion. The investor may deal directly with a member who is a market maker in the particular security. But where there are several competing market makers with rapidly changing quotations, the investor may prefer to employ a member of the exchange as a broker to find the best quotation.

Since the 1980s, running an investment exchange has been seen as a commercial activity in itself and enterprises have devised new forms of exchange and new markets to meet special needs and to compete with traditional exchanges by, for example, offering lower dealing costs. Some exchanges, such as the London Stock Exchange, operate several markets. The advent of sophisticated com-puter systems has transformed the operation of investment exchanges.

7.3.3 THE LONDON STOCK EXCHANGE

7.3.3.1 What is the LSE?

The London Stock Exchange (LSE) is a recognised investment exchange (see **7.3.4.2**) for buying and selling government stocks, securities of British and foreign companies, and options to buy and/or sell company securities.

Securities trading has been carried on in London since the seventeenth century, and the first traders' association was formed in 1762: it eventually became the London Stock Exchange, which, in March 1973, amalgamated with other exchanges in the United Kingdom and Ireland. At that time, trading on stock exchanges was conducted face to face in various premises known as 'trading floors'. In 1986 the London Stock Exchange abandoned the trading floor and switched to trading by telephone, relying on information about prices supplied by a computer system called SEAQ (Stock Exchange Automated Quotation System).

On 8 December 1995 the Irish Stock Exchange once again became a separate entity.

In 1997 the London Stock Exchange introduced fully automated trading for the most actively traded shares. Fully automated trading is carried out on a computer system called SETS (Stock Exchange Electronic Trading System) which executes a buy or sell order from a broker as soon as a matching sell or buy order is entered into the system. This is known as 'order book trading'. Market makers are unnecessary in order book trading.

Transactions on the London Stock Exchange are effected by its member firms and by approved SETS participants (who are member firms of other EU exchanges).

The London Stock Exchange is owned and operated by a registered company called London Stock Exchange plc, which itself has listed shares which are traded on its own Main Market.

7.3.3.2 The LSE's markets

The London Stock Exchange operates a number of markets, subject to various combinations of regulatory regimes (see **7.3.4**). The three most significant LSE markets on which UK companies' shares and debt securities are traded are the Main Market, AIM and the Professional Securities Market (PSM). The only securities that can be traded on each market are securities admitted to trading on that market in accordance with the LSE's rules for that market. The Main Market is the most important market for company shares and is the most heavily regulated market. It admits only listed securities to trading, and issuers and market participants must comply with EU requirements for regulated markets. AIM is not subject to either of these regulatory regimes. It provides a marketplace for shares of companies that are smaller or less mature than listed companies or have only a small proportion of their shares in public hands. PSM is a market for professional traders in debt securities: it is not an EU-regulated market but is a market for listed securities, although the listing regime is modified to suit it (see **12.9**).

7.3.3.3 FTSE

In terms of market capitalisation (share price multiplied by number of shares), 100 companies account for about 80 per cent of the value of shares on the LSE's Main Market. The FTSE 100 is an index of the share prices of the 100 largest companies by market capitalisation, the constituent companies being chosen quarterly. The FTSE 250 is an index of the next 250 companies, which account for about 14 per cent of market capitalisation. The FTSE 350 combines the FTSE 100 and FTSE 250. Only shares with a premium listing (see **7.6**) are eligible for inclusion in these indices. See **www.ftse.com**.

7.3.4 REGULATORY REGIMES FOR SECURITIES MARKETS

7.3.4.1 Choice of regulatory regime

Securities markets are regulated in the interests of investors so as to make them attractive to as many investors as possible and so maximise the amount of capital available to the issuers of the securities traded on the markets. But regulation imposes costs primarily on issuers who must provide information about themselves and must subject themselves to public scrutiny. The greater the regulation the higher the cost to issuers. The regulatory system allows for different levels of regulation designed to create costs appropriate to the size of the issue of securities being traded. So trading in the securities of smaller, less well-known, riskier companies is less regulated than trading in larger, better known, less risky ones.

The legislation on regulation of securities markets offers exchanges and issuers of securities a remarkable variety of regulatory regimes, allowing a choice of various combinations of regulation. The fact that regulators have been forced to offer a variety of regulatory regimes, from which markets and issuers can choose according to how much they are willing to pay, shows that the regulators do not have complete control over marketplaces for company securities. Nevertheless, the most expensive and extensive form of regulation, that of listed shares on the London Stock Exchange's Main Market, is a status that is much aspired to, partly because of the prestige it confers on a company and its directors, but mainly because of access to vast amounts of low-cost capital.

Four different aspects of securities markets may be regulated: (a) operators of markets (7.3.4.2); (b) markets (7.3.4.3); (c) securities (7.3.4.4); and (d) market participants (7.3.4.5).

7.3.4.2 Regulatory regimes for operators of markets

A person operating a securities market may be regulated, by the FCA, either as a recognised investment exchange (RIE) or as an operator of a multilateral trading facility. The status of RIE is conferred by a recognition order made under FSMA 2000, s 290 (or s 292 if the exchange is overseas), and it makes the exchange an exempt person. Permission to operate a multilateral trading facility is given under FSMA 2000, part 4A, and it makes the operator an authorised person. Requirements for recognition as an RIE are considerably more extensive than requirements for a part 4A permission. Requirements for recognition are set out in the schedule to SI 2001/995 and there are more details in the Recognised Investment Exchanges Sourcebook (REC) in the FCA Handbook.

The RIEs in the United Kingdom operating markets on which company securities are traded are the London Stock Exchange plc and ICAP Securities & Derivatives Exchange Ltd (ISDX).

The overseas RIEs recognised by the FCA include the NASDAQ Stock Market, which is based in the USA and is an electronic trading system for users worldwide.

The principal multilateral trading facility for UK company shares is BATS Chi-X Europe.

7.3.4.3 Regulatory regimes for markets

A securities exchange in the United Kingdom must operate its markets in accordance with the terms on which it has been granted recognition or part 4A permission (see 7.3.4.2). To that extent every market is supervised by the exchange which operates it, and is described as an 'exchange regulated market'. Exchanges may choose to operate markets in accordance with the further requirements of Title III of Directive 2014/65/EU. Those markets are usually described as 'EU regulated markets'. But in the Directive (art 4(1)(21)), in CA 2006 (s 1173(1)), and in this book they are called simply 'regulated markets'.

Title III of the Directive requires regulated markets to be authorised by member States (art 44) and requires each member State to draw up a list of the regulated markets for which it is the home member State and which comply with its regulations (art 56). In the United Kingdom, only RIEs are permitted to operate regulated markets. In the UK list of regulated markets, the markets on which shares of UK companies are traded are the London Stock Exchange Main Market and the ISDX Main Board. Only listed securities (see 7.6) are traded on these markets.

Unfortunately, the term 'regulated market' is also used with a different meaning in the Criminal Justice Act 1993, part V (see 13.6.3). There it refers to markets which are protected from insider trading by the 1993 Act. In this book the term will not be used in that sense, except in the discussion of the 1993 Act in **Chapter 13**.

7.3.4.4 Regulatory regimes for securities; listing

The only securities that can be traded on a market are those that have been admitted to trading in accordance with the rules governing the market. The securities admitted to trading on a market and their issuers may or may not be regulated by:

(a) requiring provision of information beyond the obligation of the issuer as a public company to produce annual accounts and reports, and to provide information to Companies House; and

(b) requiring compliance with additional standards of corporate governance.

There are three varieties of this form of regulation:

(a) at EU level for all securities admitted to trading on regulated markets (see **7.3.4.3**);

(b) at EU level for any security which is the subject of a public offer; and

(c) at national level (subject to EU minimum requirements) for a special range of securities called listed securities (see **7.6**).

All issuers of securities admitted to trading on regulated markets (or the subject of an application for admission) must comply with three principal EU requirements for extra information. The first is that a prospectus (see **7.4**) must be published, and must be approved by a national 'competent authority' (in the United Kingdom, the FCA), when an application is made for securities to be admitted to trading on a regulated market, with some exceptions (see **7.4.5**). The second is that an issuer of shares which are admitted to trading on a regulated market must issue half-yearly financial reports and interim management statements (see **9.7**). The third is that an issuer of shares which have been admitted to trading on a regulated market must ensure that inside information is publicly available (see **13.3**). In addition a company whose shares are admitted to trading on a regulated market must use international accounting standards for its group accounts (see **9.5.7.4**).

An approved prospectus is also required for a public offer of securities, with some exceptions (see **7.4.5**), whether or not the securities are to be traded on a regulated market. In the United Kingdom, this requirement affects public offers of securities which are admitted to trading on AIM (which is not a regulated market). There is an option of restricting a market (whether or not it is a regulated market) to trading in listed securities, whose issuers (called listed companies) are subject to EEA requirements or, if they have a UK premium listing, higher requirements set by the FCA. Premium listing requires information to be published after admission to trading and compliance with the governance standards set out in the UK Corporate Governance Code. Currently, both of the UK's regulated markets for UK company shares, the London Stock Exchange's Main Market and the ISDX Main Board, are restricted to listed shares.

A listed company will usually be a quoted company for the purposes of CA 2006 (see **7.3.4.6**) and so will be required to produce a directors' remuneration report (see **15.9.3.4**) for each financial year.

An RIE can admit a security to trading on one of its markets only if there is a proper market in the security (SI 2001/995, sch, para 4(2)(b)) and appropriate arrangements are made for information which is relevant in determining the current value of the security is made available to persons dealing on the market (para 4(2)(c) and (3)). The concepts of a proper market and proper information are amplified in FCA Handbook, REC 2.12.

The FCA has a power to require any market operator (or class of operators) to suspend or remove a company's shares, or any other financial instrument, from trading, for the purpose of protecting

the interests of investors or the orderly functioning of the financial markets (FSMA 2000, s 313A).
Either the operator or the issuer may appeal to the Upper Tribunal against an exercise of this power
(s 313A(2)).

7.3.4.5 Regulatory regimes for market participants

A market may or may not be protected by subjecting market participants to laws against insider
dealing and other forms of market abuse (see **Chapter 13**).

A regulated market (see **7.3.4.3**) has the additional protection of public notification when any
person discharging managerial responsibilities within an issuer of securities admitted to trading
on the market conducts transactions in its securities (see **13.3.3**).

7.3.4.6 Listed, quoted and traded companies

The term 'listed company', when used in the listing rules, is defined in the FCA Handbook Glossary
as a company that has any class of its securities officially listed in the United Kingdom (see **7.6**).

In CA 2006, the expression 'quoted company' means a company whose equity share capital (see
6.2.4.1) is officially listed in the United Kingdom or any other EEA State, or is admitted to dealing
on either the New York Stock Exchange (NYSE) or NASDAQ (ss 361 and 385(2)). Unfortunately,
the term 'quoted' has long been used to describe shares admitted to trading on any market, and this
use continues alongside the more restricted statutory definition. In this book the term will be used
only in that restricted statutory sense.

An 'unquoted company' is a company that is not a quoted company (s 385(3)).

In CA 2006, part 13 (resolutions and meetings), the term 'traded company' means a company
which has shares admitted to trading, by or with the consent of the company, on a regulated market
in any EEA State (see **7.3.4.3**), provided the shares admitted to trading carry rights to vote at general
meetings (s 360C). In particular, a UK company whose listed voting shares are admitted to trading
on the LSE Main Market or the ISDX Main Board is a traded company for the purposes of part 13.

Regulated markets in company shares in the United Kingdom admit only listed shares to trading.
So a company whose equity share capital is admitted to trading on the London Stock Exchange's
Main Market or the ISDX Main Board is simultaneously listed, quoted and traded. A company
whose shares are admitted to trading on AIM or the ISDX Growth Market is usually not listed, not
quoted and not traded.

It is possible for a company to be a listed company, but not a quoted company, if it has only debt
securities rather than equity share capital listed. It is also possible for a UK company to be quoted
but not listed if its shares are not listed but are admitted to dealing on NYSE or NASDAQ.

The term 'company whose transferable securities are admitted to trading on a regulated market'
refers to a company whose transferable securities (which includes shares, see **7.2.2**) are admitted
to trading on a regulated market anywhere in the EEA (see **7.3.4.3**). So it includes a UK company
whose listed shares are admitted to trading on the LSE Main Market or the ISDX Main Board.
Other UK companies will be included if they have transferable securities (whether listed or not)
other than shares admitted to trading on a regulated market, or if they have shares admitted to
trading on a regulated market outside the United Kingdom.

7.3.4.7 Prescribed markets

The FCA Handbook Glossary defines a prescribed market as one which had been prescribed by
the Treasury in SI 2001/996, art 4, as in force on 2 July 2016. In fact, art 4 was only concerned with
prescribed markets for the purposes of FSMA 2000, s 118 (now repealed), and it prescribed two
overlapping lists of markets for different provisions of that section. When the FCA Handbook uses
the term for other purposes (for example, in DTR, see **8.9**), it seems that the two lists must be combined. If that is correct, the term means all regulated markets (see **7.3.4.3**) throughout the EEA and
all other markets operated by UK RIEs (so, for example, AIM is a prescribed market).

7.3.5 CIRCUMSTANCES IN WHICH AN APPLICATION FOR ADMISSION TO TRADING MAY BE MADE

Usually, an application for admission to trading is made in respect of a new issue of securities, with allotment of those securities being conditional on them being admitted to trading. The forms of new issues most commonly made are:

(a) A public offer for subscription, in which there is a general invitation to the public to subscribe for the securities (ie, to contribute capital or make a loan directly to the company that is issuing the securities).

(b) A selective marketing (or 'placing'). This is where the bulk, or often all, of a new issue of securities is allotted to a small number of large investors who have been approached privately without any public offer being made.

(c) In a 'vendor consideration' placing, a company acquires a major asset (such as all the issued shares of another company it is taking over) from a vendor or vendors and treats the acquired asset as contributed capital for which it issues new shares to the vendor. These new shares are immediately placed and the cash proceeds go to the vendor.

(d) An intermediaries offer, in which shares are offered to a number of brokers and securities houses for them to place with their clients. An intermediaries offer is intended to create a wider spread of holdings than a placing.

(e) A rights issue. This is an offer by a company of new shares to its existing shareholders in proportion to their present holdings and is made by means of renounceable allotment letters (see **6.3.2.2, 6.3.2.3** and **6.3.5**). This is the normal method by which a company that is already listed raises extra capital.

(f) An open offer. This is an invitation to existing shareholders of a company to subscribe for a new issue in which they can take up as many or as few as they wish, rather than being restricted to a number in proportion to their existing holdings as in a rights issue.

An application for listing may also be made in relation to an 'offer for sale'. This is a general invitation to the public to buy, at a fixed price, a large block of shares already issued. The block of shares may be either those of a major shareholder who has decided to realise his investment or a new issue which has been made to an intermediary who takes the risk of the issue not succeeding with the public. A major shareholder wishing to sell may sell first to an intermediary for the same reason. Offers for sale through intermediaries are called 'secondary offers'.

If a new issue of equity shares is made by a company for a wholly cash consideration and it is not a rights issue, the members of the company must vote to disapply their pre-emption rights (see **6.3.5.3**). This applies to a public offer, a selective marketing (other than a vendor consideration placing, which, as far as the issuing company is concerned, is not for cash) and an open offer.

An application for admission to trading may also be made when a company increases the size of a class of securities already admitted to trading, for example by a capitalisation issue (see **10.4**), or when holders of convertible securities exercise their right to convert or when holders of subscription warrants exercise their right to subscribe for new shares.

7.3.6 GOING PUBLIC

There are several main reasons or advantages for seeking to have a company's shares traded publicly:

(a) It facilitates raising new finance for the company.

(b) Existing shareholders can readily realise all or part of their investment.

(c) It facilitates expansion of the company by way of takeovers in that its fully marketable securities may be used as consideration for such acquisition.

(d) It provides a higher public profile and thus may provide prestige and an enhanced trading status for the company.

There are also disadvantages, which include:

(a) The burden of meeting additional disclosure requirements which involves more expense for the company.

(b) The infliction on the company's management of increased scrutiny by investors, the press and the public.

(c) The price of the company's shares will be affected by market conditions over which the company has no control.

(d) The company's shares may suddenly become higher in value for taxation purposes and, in particular, inheritance tax which may be very disadvantageous—especially for family and individual shareholders whose tax affairs were not considered carefully prior to the decision to go public.

(e) The likelihood of a predator company making a takeover bid is enhanced, especially when a large portion of the company's equity is spread among the general public.

(f) The company's management is likely to be put under more pressure than before to take a short rather than a long-term view and to pay out a dividend or a higher dividend.

7.4 PROSPECTUSES

7.4.1 PRINCIPLE

7.4.1.1 Prospectus Directive

The principle of the Prospectus Directive (Directive 2003/71/EC) is that, with defined exceptions (art 4; see **7.4.5**), whenever there is, in the EEA, a public offer of transferable securities, or a request for admission of transferable securities to trading on a regulated market (see **7.3.4.3**), a prospectus must be published (art 3) which must have been approved by the competent authority in the issuer's home member State (art 13; see **7.4.2**). An issuer's home member State is usually the EEA State in which the issuer has its registered office (art 2(1)(m)). Once a prospectus is approved in the issuer's home member State it is valid throughout the EEA (art 17; see **7.4.3**). Once the United Kingdom leaves the EU, UK-approved prospectuses will no longer be valid elsewhere in the EEA and the United Kingdom will have no obligation to recognise prospectuses approved elsewhere, unless Brexit negotiations find some way of maintaining reciprocity.

The prospectus must contain all information required by investors to make an informed assessment of the securities (art 5; see **7.4.3**).

7.4.1.2 Application to UK registered companies

The rest of **7.4** will consider how the Prospectus Directive (Directive 2003/71/EC) applies to securities issued by UK registered companies.

The Prospectus Directive is implemented in the United Kingdom by provisions of FSMA 2000, part VI. The competent authority for the United Kingdom is the FCA. When the FCA acts as competent authority for the purposes of FSMA 2000, part VI, it sometimes uses the name United Kingdom Listing Authority (UKLA). There is more information about the UKLA on its website, **www.fca.org.uk/firms/markets/ukla**.

The FCA has extensive enforcement and disciplinary powers (see **7.4.6**).

7.4.1.3 Part 6 rules

The FCA is authorised by FSMA 2000, s 73A, to make rules, which are called 'Part 6 rules', for the purposes of FSMA 2000, part VI, and the Prospectus Directive. The rules concerning prospectuses are the Prospectus Rules (PR) in the FCA Handbook. Other Part 6 rules include corporate governance rules (FSMA 2000, s 89O(1)), listing rules (s 73A(2), see **7.6.1**) and transparency rules (s 89A).

7.4.2 DETAILS

7.4.2.1 When a prospectus is required

FSMA 2000, s 85, requires publication of an approved (see **7.4.2.2**) prospectus for transferable securities (see **7.2.2** and **7.4.2.3**) issued by a UK registered company when:

(a) the securities are offered to the public in the United Kingdom (see **7.4.2.4**) (Directive 2003/71/EC, art 3(1); FSMA 2000, s 85(1)); or

(b) a request is made for the securities to be admitted to trading on a regulated market (see **7.3.4.3**) situated or operating in the United Kingdom (Directive 2003/71/EC, art 3(3); FSMA 2000, s 85(2)).

A person who contravenes the requirement for a prospectus commits an offence (s 85(3)) and is liable to be sued for breach of statutory duty by anyone who suffers loss as a result of the contravention (s 85(4)).

There are exemptions from the requirement for a prospectus (see **7.4.5**).

7.4.2.2 Approval of a prospectus

A prospectus required by FSMA 2000, s 85, must be approved by the FCA as the competent authority of the issuer's home State (s 85(7)). The United Kingdom is the home State of a UK registered company, because the company will have its registered office in the UK (Directive 2003/71/EC, art 2(1)(m); FSMA 2000, s 102C). The competent authority for the United Kingdom is the FCA (s 87A(1)(a)).

The FCA must notify its decision on an application for approval of a prospectus within ten working days (s 87C(3)(a)), but this is extended to 20 days for a new applicant (s 87C(3)(b)). If the FCA requires further information, these time limits do not start until that information is received (s 87C(2)(b)). Failure to meet the time limit is not to be taken as approval (s 87C(10)).

7.4.2.3 Transferable securities

The Prospectus Directive uses the term 'securities' instead of 'transferable securities', because it does not cover some short-term money market instruments which are included in the usual definition of 'transferable securities' used in EU legislation (Directive 2003/71/EC, art 2(1)(a)). The UK legislation, however, uses the term 'transferable securities' (FSMA 2000, s 102A(3)). This is because FSMA 2000, part VI, already uses the term 'securities' to mean things which have been, or may be, admitted to the UK official list (s 102A(2)). In relation to securities issued by companies, for the Directive's term, 'non-equity securities' (debt securities, other than convertibles, see **12.7**), FSMA 2000, part VI, uses 'non-equity transferable securities' (s 102A(5)).

This chapter will deal with the legislation as it applies to shares. The special provisions for debt securities and convertibles are considered in **12.9**.

7.4.2.4 Offer to the public in the United Kingdom

There is an offer of transferable securities to the public in the United Kingdom if there is a communication, in any form or by any means, to any person in the United Kingdom which presents sufficient information on:

(a) the transferable securities to be offered; and

(b) terms on which they are offered,

to enable an investor to decide to buy or subscribe for the securities in question (Directive 2003/71/EC, art 2(1)(d); FSMA 2000, s 102B(1), (2) and (3)). This includes an intermediaries offer (s 102B(4)), but does not include a communication in connection with trading on a regulated market or a multilateral trading facility (see **7.3.4.2**) (s 102B(5) and (6)).

7.4.3 CONTENT OF A PROSPECTUS

The form and content of a prospectus are specified in Regulation (EC) No 809/2004, which has been transposed into prospectus rules. It is an important principle of Directive 2003/71/EC, art 17, that a prospectus approved in a company's home member State (the State where it has its registered office: art 2(1)(m)) is valid throughout the EEA. This is to facilitate development of a single European capital market in which an issue of shares can be offered to the public and traded throughout the EEA.

A prospectus must contain all information which is necessary to enable investors to make an informed assessment of the assets and liabilities, financial position, profits and losses, and prospects of the issuer of the securities and the rights attaching to them (Directive 2003/71/EC, art 5(1); FSMA 2000, s 87A(1)(b) and (2)). All this must be presented in a comprehensible and easily analysable form (s 87A(3)). The prospectus must include a brief summary in non-technical language (Directive 2003/71/EC, art 5(2); FSMA 2000, s 87A(5) and (6)).

A prospectus can be divided into three documents: the registration document, which contains information relating to the issuer, a securities note, which contains information relating to the particular securities being offered or admitted, and the summary (FCA Handbook, PR 2.2.2R). An issuer which already has an approved registration document needs to prepare only a securities note and summary (PR 2.2.4R). Alternatively the three elements can be combined in a single document (PR 2.2.1R). The requirements for the content of a prospectus relating to shares are set out in Commission Regulation (EC) No 809/2004, art 4 and annex I (registration document), and art 6 and annex III (securities note). These requirements are reproduced in PR 2.3.1EU and PR App 3EU.

In accordance with Directive 2003/71/EC, art 8(2), the FCA may authorise the omission from the prospectus for a company's securities of information otherwise required in any of the following circumstances (FSMA 2000, s 87B):

(a) If disclosure of the information would be contrary to the public interest. The FCA may rely on a certificate to that effect issued by the Secretary of State or the Treasury (s 87B(2) and (3)).

(b) If disclosure of the information would be seriously detrimental to the company, though authorisation can be given on this ground only if not disclosing the information would not be likely to mislead a person considering acquiring the securities about any facts, knowledge of which is essential for informed assessment of the securities.

(c) If the information is of minor importance only and is not such as will influence assessment of the assets and liabilities, financial position, profits and losses, and prospects of the company.

7.4.4 SUPPLEMENTARY PROSPECTUS

A supplementary prospectus must be submitted to the FCA and, with its approval, published if, between approval of a prospectus and the final closing of the offer of securities to the public or the beginning of trading on a regulated market, there arises or is noted a significant new factor, material mistake or inaccuracy relating to the information in the prospectus. The supplementary prospectus must contain details of the new factor, mistake or inaccuracy (Directive 2003/71/EC, art 16(1); FSMA 2000, s 87G). If there is both a public offer and admission to trading, a supplementary prospectus is required at any time up to the later of the two events specified in s 87G (s 87G(3A)). A person who agreed to buy or subscribe for the securities before the supplementary prospectus was published may withdraw before the second working day after the day of publication of the supplementary prospectus (Directive 2003/71/EC, art 16(2); FSMA 2000, s 87Q(4) to (6)). The supplementary prospectus may specify a later deadline (s 87Q(6)(b)). There is no right to withdraw if the significant new factor, material mistake or inaccuracy arose after the securities were delivered (s 87Q(5)(d)).

7.4.5 EXEMPTIONS FROM THE PROSPECTUS REQUIREMENT

7.4.5.1 Offers to qualified investors

An offer of securities addressed solely to qualified investors can be made without publishing an approved prospectus (Directive 2003/71/EC, art 3(2)(a); FSMA 2000, s 86(1)(a)). Qualified investors are professional investors identified by s 86(7) to (10), Directive 2003/71/EC, art 2(1)(e) and Directive 2014/65/EU, Annex II. Even though an offer of securities qualifies for this exemption, an application for admission of the securities to trading on a regulated market requires a prospectus, unless the application is exempted by the provisions discussed in 7.4.5.6 to 7.4.5.10.

7.4.5.2 Small number of offerees who are not qualified investors

The obligation to publish an approved prospectus does not apply to an offer to fewer than 150 persons (apart from qualified investors, see 7.4.5.1) per EEA State (Directive 2003/71/EC, art 3(2)(b); FSMA 2000, s 86(1)(b)).

Even though an offer of securities qualifies for this exemption, an application for admission of the securities to trading on a regulated market requires a prospectus, unless the application is exempted by the provisions discussed in 7.4.5.6 to 7.4.5.10.

7.4.5.3 Small issues

Publication of an approved prospectus for a public offer is optional if the total consideration for the offer in the EEA is less than €5 million (Directive 2003/71/EC, art 1(2)(h) and (3); FSMA 2000, ss 85(5)(a) and 87 and sch 11A, para 9). This limit can be used only once every 12 months (sch 11A, para 9(2)).

The obligation to publish an approved prospectus for a public offer does not apply if the total consideration in the EU cannot exceed €100,000, again only once every 12 months (Directive 2003/71/EC, art 3(2)(e); FSMA 2000, s 86(1)(e)).

Even though an offer of securities qualifies for either of these exemptions, an application for admission of the securities to trading on a regulated market requires a prospectus, unless the application is exempted by the provisions discussed in 7.4.5.6 to 7.4.5.10. It seems that this is the reason why the option to publish a prospectus for the offer as well is given in the first of the exemptions. It is unclear whether an issue for less than €100,000 can claim the option of publication of a prospectus, on the ground that it is an issue for less than €5 million, or whether it is excluded from that option by s 86(1)(e).

7.4.5.4 Large-denomination issues

The obligation to publish an approved prospectus does not apply to an offer if the minimum consideration payable by each investor is €100,000 (or the equivalent in another currency) or the nominal value of each security is at least €100,000 (or equivalent) (Directive 2003/71/EC, art 3(2)(c) and (d); FSMA 2000, s 86(1)(c) and (d)).

Even though an offer of securities qualifies for this exemption, an application for admission of the securities to trading on a regulated market requires a prospectus, unless the application is exempted by the provisions discussed in **7.4.5.6** to **7.4.5.10**.

In practice this exemption will apply to debt securities and convertibles, for which €100,000 is the boundary between securities intended for the retail market (the general public) and the wholesale market (professional investors) (see **12.9**).

7.4.5.5 Sale or placing through a financial intermediary

If shares have previously been the subject of one or more offers to the public, and one or more of those offers was exempt under any of the provisions discussed in **7.4.5.1** to **7.4.5.4**, a sale or placing of them through a financial intermediary may reuse any prospectus for them approved by the FCA within the preceding 12 months, provided it is accompanied by all required supplementary prospectuses and provided the issuer, or other person responsible for drawing up the prospectus, gives written permission (FSMA 2000, s 86(1)(f), (1A) and (1B)(a)).

7.4.5.6 Small increase in class admitted to trading; employee share schemes

Where a company has a class of shares admitted to trading on a regulated market it may apply for admission on the same market of additional shares of the same class without publishing a prospectus, provided the additional shares number less than 10 per cent of those already admitted: the 10 per cent limit can be used only once every 12 months (Directive 2003/71/EC, art 4(2)(a); FSMA 2000, s 85(6)(b); FCA Handbook, PR 1.2.3R(1)). However, a prospectus is required for an offer of those shares to the public. Shares of the same class offered or allotted to present or former employees or directors can be admitted to trading without a prospectus and the offer itself also does not require a prospectus, though a document must be made available stating the number and nature of the shares and the reasons for and details of the offer (Directive 2003/71/EC, art 4(1)(e); FSMA 2000, s 85(5)(b) and (6)(b); PR 1.2.2R(5); PR 1.2.3R(6)).

7.4.5.7 Substitute shares; exchange and conversion

The obligation to publish a prospectus does not apply to shares issued in substitution for shares of the same class already issued or admitted to trading, provided there is no increase in issued capital (Directive 2003/71/EC, art 4(1)(a) and (2)(b); FSMA 2000, s 85(5)(b) and (6)(b); PR 1.2.2R(1); PR 1.2.3R(2)). Where a company has a class of shares admitted to trading on a regulated market it may apply for admission on the same market of additional shares of the same class without publishing a prospectus, if the shares result from conversion or exchange of other transferable securities or from rights conferred by other transferable securities (Directive 2003/71/EC, art 4(2)(g); FSMA 2000, s 85(6)(b); PR 1.2.3R(7)).

7.4.5.8 Takeovers and mergers

The obligation to publish a prospectus does not apply to shares offered in connection with a takeover by share exchange or a merger, provided a document is available which the FCA considers contains information equivalent to a prospectus (Directive 2003/71/EC, art 4(1)(b) and (c) and (2)(c) and (d); FSMA 2000, s 85(5)(b) and (6)(b); PR 1.2.2R(2) and (3); PR 1.2.3R(3) and (4)).

7.4.5.9 Bonus shares and scrip dividends

The obligation to publish a prospectus does not apply to bonus shares or shares issued in lieu of dividend, provided a document is made available stating the number and nature of the shares and the reasons for and details of the offer (Directive 2003/71/EC, art 4(1)(d) and (2)(e); FSMA 2000, s 85(5)(b) and (6)(b); PR 1.2.2R(4); PR 1.2.3R(5)).

7.4.5.10 Shares admitted to trading on another regulated market

If shares have been admitted to trading on one EEA regulated market for more than 18 months, they can be admitted to trading on another regulated market without issuing a new prospectus (Directive 2003/71/EC, art 4(2)(h); FSMA 2000, s 85(6)(b); PR 1.2.3R(8)), subject to various conditions set out in PR 1.2.3R(8) and PR 1.2.4G.

7.4.6 FCA SANCTIONS

7.4.6.1 Suspension or prohibition

The FCA has various powers under FSMA 2000, ss 87K and 87L, to suspend or prevent a public offer of securities, or an application for admission to trading on a regulated market, if it reasonably suspects, or finds, that there has been a contravention of applicable provisions of FSMA 2000, part VI, or of prospectus rules, or of other provisions made in accordance with the Prospectus Directive.

7.4.6.2 Financial penalties or censure

Under FSMA 2000, s 91(1A), the FCA may impose a financial penalty, or issue a public statement of censure (s 91(3)), for contravention of:

(a) FSMA 2000, part VI;

(b) prospectus rules; and

(c) any provision otherwise made in accordance with the Prospectus Directive or a requirement imposed under such a provision.

Only the following persons are under the FCA's jurisdiction to penalise or censure under s 91(1A) or (3):

(a) an issuer of transferable securities;

(b) a person offering transferable securities to the public or requesting their admission to trading on a regulated market;

(c) an applicant for the approval of a prospectus in relation to transferable securities;

(d) a person on whom a requirement has been imposed under ss 87K or 87L;

(e) any other person to whom a provision of the Prospectus Directive applies; and

(f) a director, of any person in (a) to (e), who was knowingly concerned in the contravention (s 91(2)).

In relation to persons (a), (b) and (c) in this list, the FCA may alternatively issue a public statement of censure under s 87M for failure to comply with obligations under an applicable provision of FSMA 2000, part VI, or prospectus rules, or any other applicable provision made in accordance with the Prospectus Directive.

The FCA must pay to the Treasury all penalties it receives after deducting its enforcement costs (FSMA 2000, sch 1ZA, para 20). Details of the FCA's disciplinary and enforcement arrangements are in the Enforcement Guide (EG) in the FCA Handbook. See especially EG 7 (financial penalties and public censures).

7.4.6.3 Investigation

The FCA may, under FSMA 2000, s 97, appoint one or more investigators if it is apparent to it that there are circumstances suggesting that:

(a) there may have been a contravention of a provision of part VI or of Part 6 rules or a provision otherwise made in accordance with the Prospectus Directive;

(b) a person who was at the material time a director of a person mentioned in FSMA 2000, s 91(1A) (see **7.4.6.2**), has been knowingly concerned in a contravention by that person of one of the provisions listed in (a);

(c) there may have been a contravention of s 85 (requirement for a prospectus; see **7.4.2.1**) or s 87G (requirement for a supplementary prospectus; see **7.4.4**).

An investigator appointed under s 97 is treated under FSMA 2000 as if appointed under s 167(1) (s 97(3)). See **18.8.3.3** and FCA Handbook, EG 3 and EG 4.

7.4.7 RESTRICTION ON PUBLIC OFFERS BY PRIVATE COMPANIES

A private limited company must not offer its shares to the public (CA 2006, s 755), though an allotment made following an offer which has contravened the prohibition is not invalid (s 760). For this purpose, an offer of shares is not an offer to the public if it is not likely to result in the shares becoming available to persons other than those receiving the offer (s 756(3)(a)). An offer is not made to the public if it can properly be regarded as being a 'private concern of the person receiving it and the person making it' (s 756(3)(b)). An offer to a person already connected with the company is regarded as a private concern, unless the contrary is proved (s 756(4)). For this purpose, the persons connected with the company are: its existing members and employees; families of existing members and employees; widows, widowers and surviving civil partners of deceased members and employees; existing debenture holders; and trustees of trusts for such persons (s 756(5)). Otherwise, an offer to a section of the public, however selected, is an offer to the public (s 756(2)).

There is an exception from the prohibition (s 755(3) and (4)) where:

(a) a company acts in good faith in pursuance of arrangements under which it is to re-register as a public company before the shares are allotted; or

(b) as part of the terms of the offer, it undertakes to re-register as a public company within a specified period (not longer than six months from the day the offer is made), and it complies with that undertaking.

The court may make an order restraining a company from contravening the prohibition (s 757), order the company to re-register as a public company (see **2.6.3**), order it to be wound up (s 758) or make a remedial order for the purpose of putting a person affected by a contravention in the position he would have been in if there had been no contravention (s 759).

7.5 MISLEADING STATEMENTS AND OMISSIONS IN PROSPECTUSES

7.5.1 INTRODUCTION

In **6.8** it was explained that the common law and the Misrepresentation Act 1967 provide some remedies to a person who has been induced to subscribe for shares by a misrepresentation and these remedies are available in all circumstances in which shares are issued. This section will describe the remedies provided by legislation to persons who suffer loss as a result of any untrue or misleading statement in, or omission from, a prospectus or supplementary prospectus.

Because of its history, the relevant legislation in FSMA 2000, s 90 and sch 10, is drafted in terms of listing particulars and supplementary listing particulars (see **12.9.2**) and then applied to prospectuses and supplementary prospectuses by s 90(11).

The provisions are expressly stated not to affect liability under any other legislation or at common law (s 90(6)), so the remedies described in **6.8** may be available in addition to the remedies described here.

7.5.2 MISREPRESENTATION AND OMISSION

The first head of liability, in FSMA 2000, s 90(1), is for loss suffered as a result of:

(a) any untrue or misleading statement in a prospectus or supplement, or

(b) the omission from such a document of any matter required to be included by s 87A (prospectus) or s 87G (supplementary prospectus).

Where the listing rules require a statement of information about some matter or a statement that there is no such matter then omitting information is to be regarded as a statement that there is no such matter (FSMA 2000, s 90(3)).

By s 90(8) and (9), no one can be liable for an omission from a prospectus which has been authorised by the FCA under s 87B (omission because of public interest or serious detriment to the issuer).

7.5.3 RESPONSIBILITY FOR PROSPECTUSES

Compensation under the first head of liability (see **7.5.2**) is payable by any person 'responsible for' the prospectus or supplement which contained the untrue or misleading statement or from which required information was omitted (FSMA 2000, s 90(1)). The persons responsible for a prospectus are specified in the prospectus rules. Those rules identify the following persons as responsible for a prospectus for company shares published in relation to a public offer, or request for admission to trading, made by the company:

(a) the company (FCA Handbook, PR 5.5.3R(2)(a));

(b) every director of the company at the time when the prospectus is published (PR 5.5.3R(2)(b)(i)), unless it is published without the director's knowledge or consent and, on becoming aware of its publication, the director, as soon as practicable, gives reasonable public notice that it was published without his or her knowledge or consent (PR 5.5.6R);

(c) every person named in the prospectus as being, or having agreed to become, a director of the company, provided this was done with the person's authority (PR 5.5.3R(2)(b)(ii));

(d) if the company has appointed an external management company to perform functions that would ordinarily be performed by the company's officers and to make recommendations in relation to strategic matters, every senior executive of the external management company (PR 5.5.3R(2)(b)(iii), PR 5.5.3AR and PR 5.5.3BG);

(e) every person who accepts, and is stated in the prospectus as accepting, responsibility for the prospectus (PR 5.5.3R(2)(c))—such a person may limit responsibility to specified parts of the prospectus (PR 5.5.8R);

(f) any other person who has authorised the contents of the prospectus (PR 5.5.3R(2)(f))— such a person may limit responsibility to specified parts of the prospectus (PR 5.5.8R).

If another person is making the public offer or seeking admission to trading, that person is also responsible for the prospectus (PR 5.5.3R(2)(d)(i) and (e)(i)) and, if it is a body corporate, so are all its directors at the time when the prospectus is published (PR 5.5.3R(2)(d)(ii) and (e)(ii)). The company itself and its directors will not be responsible if it did not authorise the public offer or request for admission (PR 5.5.5R). However, in relation to a public offer, this will not apply if the offer is being made in association with the company and the prospectus was drawn up primarily by the company or by persons acting on its behalf (PR 5.5.7R).

Giving advice on the contents of a prospectus in a professional capacity does not make a person responsible for the prospectus (PR 5.5.9R).

7.5.4 DEFENCES IN RELATION TO MISREPRESENTATIONS AND OMISSIONS

7.5.4.1 Reasonable belief

It is a defence to liability for a misrepresentation or omission to prove that, after making reasonable inquiries, the defendant reasonably believed, at the time the document was submitted to the FCA, that the statement in question was true and not misleading or that the matter which was omitted was properly omitted (FSMA 2000, sch 10, para 1). One of the following four circumstances must also be proved:

(a) that the defendant continued in that belief until the shares were acquired; or

(b) that they were acquired before it was reasonably practicable to bring a correction to the attention of persons likely to acquire the shares in question; or

(c) that before the shares were acquired the defendant had taken all reasonable steps to secure that a correction was brought to the attention of persons likely to acquire the shares in question; or

(d) that the shares were acquired after such a lapse of time that the defendant ought in the circumstances reasonably to be excused, provided that the defendant continued to believe that the statement or omission was proper until after dealings in the shares commenced.

7.5.4.2 Expert's statement

It is a defence to liability for a loss caused by a statement purporting to be made, as an expert, by or on the authority of someone other than the defendant, which statement is, and is stated to be, included in the prospectus or particulars with that expert's consent, to prove that the defendant reasonably believed, on reasonable grounds, at the time the document was submitted to the FCA, that the expert was competent to make or authorise the statement and had consented to its inclusion in the form and context in which it was included (FSMA 2000, sch 10, para 2). One of the following four circumstances must also be proved:

(a) that the defendant continued in that belief until the shares were acquired; or

(b) that they were acquired before it was reasonably practicable to bring the fact that the expert was not competent or had not consented to the attention of persons likely to acquire the shares in question; or

(c) that before the shares were acquired the defendant had taken all reasonable steps to secure that that fact was brought to the attention of persons likely to acquire the shares in question; or

(d) that the shares were acquired after such a lapse of time that the defendant ought in the circumstances reasonably to be excused, provided that the defendant continued to believe in the expert until after dealings in the shares commenced.

The term 'expert' includes any engineer, valuer, accountant or other person whose statements are given authority by his or her profession, qualifications or experience (FSMA 2000, sch 10, para 8).

7.5.4.3 Reasonable steps taken to correct defect

Without prejudice to the defences in 7.5.4.1 and 7.5.4.2 it is a defence to prove that the defendant took reasonable steps to bring a correction, or the fact of an expert's lack of competence or consent, to the attention of potential investors before the claimant's shares were acquired (FSMA 2000, sch 10, paras 3 and 4).

7.5.4.4 Official statements and documents

It is a defence to prove that the statement which caused the loss accurately and fairly reproduces a statement made by an official person or contained in a public official document (FSMA 2000, sch 10, para 5).

7.5.4.5 Claimant's knowledge of the circumstances

It is a defence to prove that the person claiming compensation acquired the shares in question with knowledge, as the case may be, that the statement was false or misleading or of the omission (FSMA 2000, sch 10, para 6).

7.5.5 FAILURE TO ISSUE SUPPLEMENTS

The second head of liability, in FSMA 2000, s 90(4), is loss suffered in respect of a failure to comply with s 87G, which requires:

(a) publication of a supplementary prospectus in certain circumstances; and

(b) notification of any matter for which a supplementary document would be required.

The person who has the duty of publishing a supplement, and who would be liable under this head for not publishing when aware that one is required, is the person who applied for approval of the prospectus (s 87G(2)).

Any person who is responsible for a prospectus has the duty to inform the issuer and the person who applied for approval of the prospectus on becoming aware of any matter which requires a supplementary document (s 87G(5)).

It is a defence to liability under this head to show:

(a) that the person claiming compensation acquired the shares in question with knowledge of the change or new matter or (in the case of a prospectus for unlisted shares) inaccuracy for which a supplement should have been published (sch 10, para 6); and

(b) reasonable belief that the change, etc, was not such as to call for a supplement (sch 10, para 7).

7.5.6 PERSONS TO WHOM COMPENSATION IS PAYABLE

The provisions of FSMA 2000, s 90(1) and (4) (see 7.5.2 and 7.5.5), impose a liability to any person who has 'acquired' shares, which includes both original allottees and persons who have purchased shares in the market. This improves on the common law rule that only original allottees could sue for a misrepresentation made in a prospectus inviting subscriptions for new shares (*Peek v Gurney* (1873) LR 6 HL 377). This common law rule depended on the court finding that prospectuses were intended only for subscribers and not for subsequent purchasers. In *Possfund Custodian Trustee Ltd v Diamond* [1996] 1 WLR 1351, the claimants claimed that the court should now recognise that stock market practice has since changed and that prospectuses are now intended to encourage subsequent trading in shares so that those responsible for prospectuses should be liable at common law to subsequent purchasers for negligent or deceitful misrepresentations. In preliminary proceedings, Lightman J refused to strike out this claim. At p 1360, Lightman J seized on a difference in wording between the Financial Services Act 1986, s 150(1) (which imposed liability to pay compensation to any person 'who has acquired any of the securities in question'), and SI 1995/1537, reg 14(1) (which imposed liability to any person 'who has acquired the securities to which the prospectus relates'). His Lordship held, obiter, that this difference in wording meant that reg 14(1) applied only to original allottees and not to subsequent purchasers. With the greatest respect it is very difficult to see that the slightly different wording could have such a dramatic consequence. In any case, his Lordship ignored the fact that the Financial Services Act 1986, s 150(3), and SI 1995/1537, reg 14(3), both use the 'any of the securities in question' formula. If his Lordship's interpretation were correct, subsequent purchasers could claim under reg 14(3) for failure to publish a supplementary prospectus but not under reg 14(1) for a misrepresentation in or omission from the principal prospectus, which cannot have been the Treasury's intention when making the regulations. This difficulty with Lightman J's interpretation continues under FSMA 2000, in which s 90(1) refers to 'securities to which the particulars apply' and s 90(4) refers to 'securities of the kind in question'.

Making a contract to acquire shares or an interest in shares is deemed to be an 'acquisition' of the shares (FSMA 2000, s 90(7)).

These provisions of FSMA 2000 replace similar provisions first enacted in the Directors Liability Act 1890. In relation to the earlier provisions it was held in *Clark v Urquhart* [1930] AC 28 that the measure of the 'compensation' for which they provided was the same as the measure of damages in a claim for the tort of deceit (see **6.8.6.2**). The term 'compensation' is used in FSMA 2000, s 90(1) and (4), and there is no reason to doubt that the measure of this compensation is still the same as in a tort claim.

7.6 OFFICIAL LISTING

7.6.1 GENERAL DESCRIPTION

Official listing is an optional additional regulatory regime for a securities market. It imposes extra responsibilities on issuers of securities so as to provide a lower risk for investors, which leads to easier access to new capital for issuers. There are minimum standards for official listing in the EEA in Directive 2001/34/EC, but individual member States are free to add their own requirements, provided they are applied uniformly (art 8). The United Kingdom has always had particularly extensive additional, 'super-equivalent' requirements, which have been credited as being an important element in the success of the London Stock Exchange's Main Market, which is a market for listed securities. Since October 2009, compliance by issuers with the super-equivalent requirements has been optional. A company which chooses to comply is said to have a 'premium listing', while companies that opt for the minimum Directive requirements have a 'standard listing'.

Directive 2001/34/EC is a consolidated version of four earlier Directives and is sometimes known as the Consolidated Admissions and Reporting Directive (CARD). It is implemented in UK law by FSMA 2000, part VI.

Article 105 of Directive 2001/34/EC requires each member State to appoint one or more competent authorities for the purposes of the Directive, in particular with the power to decide on the admission of securities to official listing (art 11). The single competent authority nominated by the UK government is the FCA. It has made Part 6 rules (see **7.4.1.3**) concerning listing, which are the Listing Rules (LR) in the FCA Handbook.

The EEA-wide minimum requirements for listing are intended to ensure that admission to listing is restricted to securities of companies with a demonstrable track record (Directive 2001/34/EC, art 44) in issues which are large enough (art 43) and with a wide enough spread of public holding (art 48) to create a realistic market (see **7.6.2.1**).

In the listing rules, a company which has any class of its securities listed in the United Kingdom is called a listed company (FCA Handbook, Glossary).

7.6.2 APPLICATION FOR ADMISSION TO THE OFFICIAL LIST

7.6.2.1 Eligibility

The FCA admits both UK and foreign companies' securities to the UK Official List and various types of debt securities (marketable loans) and shares. The FCA may not entertain an application for official listing of securities to be issued by a private company (FSMA 2000, s 75(3); SI 2001/2956, reg 3).

The principal criteria for admission of a company's equity shares to standard listing are:

(a) *Legality.* The company must be duly incorporated and it must be operating within its constitution (Directive 2001/34/EC, art 42; LR 2.2.1R). The shares must conform with the law and be duly authorised under the company's constitution (Directive 2001/34/EC, art 45; LR 2.2.2R).

(b) *Admission to trading.* The shares must be admitted to trading on an RIE's regulated market for listed securities (LR 2.2.3R). This means that an application for official listing is often made in conjunction with a request for admission to trading. The request for admission to trading normally requires the issue of a prospectus which must be approved by the FCA (see 7.4; LR 2.2.10R). There is an exception to LR 2.2.3R for issues which are exempt from the requirement to issue a prospectus (LR 4; see 7.4.5).

(c) *Transferability.* The shares must be freely transferable and fully paid (LR 2.2.4R). A company whose shares are listed at its request is to be taken as representing that they are fully paid and will be estopped from claiming that they are not (*Re Zavarco plc (No 2)* [2016] EWHC 1143 (Ch), [2016] Bus LR 907). The FCA may allow partly paid shares to be listed if it is satisfied that their transferability is not restricted and investors have been provided with appropriate information to enable dealings in the securities to take place on an open and proper basis (LR 2.2.5G).

(d) *Minimum market value.* The expected aggregate market value of all the shares (excluding treasury shares) to be listed must be at least £700,000, unless shares of the same class are already listed (Directive 2001/34/EC, art 43; LR 2.2.7R). Shares of a lower value may be listed if the FCA is satisfied that there will be an adequate market for them (Directive 2001/34/EC, art 43(2); LR 2.2.8G).

(e) *Marketability.* The listing must be for all shares of the same class, both issued and proposed to be issued (Directive 2001/34/EC, art 49; LR 2.2.9R).

The following additional criteria apply to premium listing:

(a) *Marketability.* At least 25 per cent of the shares (excluding treasury shares) must be in public hands at the time of admission (Directive 2001/34/EC, art 48; LR 6.1.19R). It is unclear why this Directive requirement is not applied to standard listing in the United Kingdom.

(b) *Sufficient working capital.* The company must satisfy the FCA that it and its subsidiary undertakings have sufficient working capital available for the group's requirements for at least the next 12 months (LR 6.1.16R).

(c) *Sponsor.* The company must have an independent sponsor who is approved by the FCA (LR 8). The sponsor must assure the FCA, when required, that the company has met its responsibilities under the listing rules, explain and confirm to the FCA, when required, that the listing rules are being complied with, and must guide the company in understanding and meeting its responsibilities under the listing and disclosure rules (LR 8.3.1R).

(d) *Continuing obligations.* The company must meet the continuing obligations of listed companies set out in LR 9. The continuing obligations require extra information to be provided in a premium listed company's annual accounts and reports (see **9.9.1**). They also require a listed company to comply with the UK Corporate Governance Code (see **15.2.2**) or to explain why it has not complied.

(e) *Approval of significant transactions.* Shareholders must be informed of transactions that are outside the ordinary course of the listed company's business and may change a security holder's economic interest in the company's assets or liabilities (LR 10). Larger transactions must be conditional on shareholder approval (see **15.10.6**).

For a new applicant, that is one with no securities already listed, the following *track record* and *working capital* criteria apply to premium listing:

(a) *Three years' accounts.* The company must have published audited accounts covering at least three years with unqualified auditors' reports (Directive 2001/34/EC, art 44; LR 6.1.3R). It is unclear why this Directive requirement is not applied to standard listing in the United Kingdom.

(b) *Nature and duration of business activities.* The historical financial information must represent at least 75 per cent of the company's business for the whole of the three years and must put prospective investors in a position to make an informed assessment of the business (LR 6.1.3BR). The company must have controlled the majority of its assets for that period (LR 6.1.4R(2)). It must demonstrate that it will be carrying on an independent business as its main activity (LR 6.1.4R(3)).

(c) *Working capital.* The company must satisfy the FCA that it and its subsidiary undertakings have sufficient working capital for at least the 12 months following the date of the prospectus (LR 6.1.16R).

There are special dispensations from the track-record requirements for mineral companies (LR 6.1.8R, 6.1.9R, 6.1.10R), scientific research-based companies (LR 6.1.11R, 6.1.12R) and in any case if the FCA is satisfied that it is desirable in the interests of investors and that investors have the necessary information available to arrive at an informed judgement about the shares (Directive 2001/34/EC, art 44; LR 6.1.13G).

A company cannot change from premium listing to standard listing unless the change is approved by a 75 per cent majority in a general meeting (LR 5.4A.4R).

7.6.2.2 Application procedure

An application for the listing of securities cannot be made without the permission of the issuer of the securities (FSMA 2000, s 75(2)). Under s 75(5) and (6), the FCA may refuse an application to list a company's securities:

(a) if it considers that by reason of any matter relating to the company the admission of the securities would be detrimental to the interests of investors; or

(b) in the case of securities already officially listed in another EEA country, if the company has failed to comply with any obligations imposed by that listing.

Details of the application procedure are set out in LR 3.

The FCA must notify an applicant of its decision on the application within six months of receiving it (or within six months of receiving any further information it has requested) (FSMA 2000, s 76(1)) and a failure to inform within this time will be taken as a refusal of the application (s 76(2)).

Once a security has been listed, the listing cannot be called into question on the ground that any requirement or condition for admission to listing has not been complied with (s 76(7)).

7.6.3 LISTING PRINCIPLES

The following Listing Principles (LR 7.2.1R) apply to every premium listed company (LR 7.1.1R):

Principle 1   A listed company must take reasonable steps to enable its directors to understand their responsibilities and obligations as directors.

Principle 2   A listed company must take reasonable steps to establish and maintain adequate procedures, systems and controls to enable it to comply with its obligations.

Principle 3   A listed company must act with integrity towards holders and potential holders of its listed equity shares.

Principle 4   A listed company must communicate information to holders and potential holders of its listed equity shares in such a way as to avoid the creation or continuation of a false market in such listed equity shares.

Principle 5   A listed company must ensure that it treats all holders of the same class of its listed equity shares that are in the same position equally in respect of the rights attaching to such listed equity shares.

Principle 6   A listed company must deal with the FCA in an open and cooperative manner.

7.6.4 FCA SANCTIONS

7.6.4.1 Discontinuance or suspension of listing

The FCA may permanently discontinue or temporarily suspend a listing in accordance with the listing rules if it is satisfied that there are special circumstances which preclude normal regular dealings in the securities (Directive 2001/34/EC, art 18; FSMA 2000, s 77(1) and (2); LR 5). This can be done on the FCA's own initiative or at the request of the issuer (FSMA 2000, s 77(2A)). Listing would be discontinued only in exceptional circumstances which absolutely preclude normal, regular dealings in the securities in question. Listing of a security will be cancelled if it is no longer admitted to trading on an RIE's market for listed securities (LR 5.2.2G(1)). Suspension of listing, on the other hand, is not unusual and often occurs at the issuer's request, but it also can be used if the normal market in the shares is temporarily distorted or impaired, for example, where there are rumours of an imminent takeover bid.

The issuer has a right to appeal to the Upper Tribunal against a decision by the FCA on its own initiative to discontinue or suspend listing (FSMA 2000, s 77(5)). The FCA does not have to inform the shareholders of a company that it is considering suspending or discontinuing the company's listing, and does not have to give them an opportunity to make representations (*R v International Stock Exchange of the United Kingdom and the Republic of Ireland Ltd, ex parte Else (1982) Ltd* [1993] QB 534). Shareholders in a company do not have a right under Directive 2001/34/EC to appeal to a court against a decision by the FCA to suspend or discontinue the company's listing (*ex parte Else (1982) Ltd*).

If the listing of securities of a company is temporarily suspended, the company is nevertheless subject to the continuing obligations to disclose information and is still liable to pay fees for maintenance of listing (FSMA 2000, s 77(3)).

7.6.4.2 Financial penalties and censure

The FCA may, under FSMA 2000, s 91(1), impose a financial penalty on, or issue a statement of censure of (s 91(3)), any of the following persons who it considers has contravened a provision of listing rules:

(a)   the issuer of a listed security, or an applicant for listing (s 91(1)); or

(b)   a director of any person mentioned in (a) who was knowingly concerned in the contravention (s 91(2)).

Similar powers are available to discipline sponsors who contravene provisions of listing rules applying to them (s 88A). See **7.4.6.2**.

7.6.4.3 Investigation

The FCA may, under FSMA 2000, s 97, appoint one or more investigators if it is apparent to it that there are circumstances suggesting that:

(a) there may have been a contravention of a provision of part VI or of Part 6 rules; and

(b) a person who was at the material time a director of a person mentioned in s 91(1) (see **7.6.4.2**) has been knowingly concerned in a contravention by that person of one of the provisions listed in (a).

An investigator appointed under s 97 is treated under FSMA 2000 as if appointed under s 167(1) (s 97(3)). See **18.8.3** and FCA Handbook, EG, Chapters 3 and 4.

7.7 INVESTMENT ADVERTISEMENTS

Under FSMA 2000, s 21, 'an invitation or inducement to engage in investment activity', which is communicated in the course of business so as to be capable of having an effect in the United Kingdom, must be communicated by, or approved by, an authorised person; otherwise a criminal offence triable either way will be committed by the person making the communication (s 25). This is known as the 'financial promotion restriction' (SI 2005/1529, art 5). 'Engaging in investment activity' means entering or offering to enter into an agreement the making or performance of which by either party constitutes a controlled activity (FSMA 2000, s 21(8)(a)). Buying, selling and subscribing for company shares and debentures are controlled activities (SI 2005/1529, art 4 and sch 1, paras 3, 14, 15 and 28).

SI 2005/1529 specifies exemptions from the financial promotion restriction. This lengthy piece of delegated legislation specifies the exemptions in careful detail. The following paragraphs summarise the exemptions which are most significant for companies.

The restriction does not apply to any communication which is made only to recipients whom the communicator believes on reasonable grounds to be investment professionals (SI 2005/1529, art 19). Authorised persons are investment professionals, as is any person who ordinarily carries on the relevant controlled activity for the purpose of his, her or its business (art 19(5)). A communication can be regarded as directed only at professional investors if it states that it is and there are proper systems and procedures to prevent recipients who are not professionals from engaging in the investment activity to which it relates (art 19(1)(b), (2) and (4)).

The financial promotion restriction does not apply to what the regulations call 'non-real time communications' or to 'solicited real time communications' made by a company to certain persons. A non-real time communication is a communication other than one made in the course of a personal visit, telephone conversation or other interactive dialogue (art 7). A solicited real time communication is a communication made in the course of a personal visit, telephone call or other interactive dialogue which was initiated by, or takes place at the request of, the recipient of the communication (art 8). The restriction does not apply to such communications by a company to (a) its members or creditors concerning its own shares or debentures, or those of another undertaking in the same group (art 43), (b) its corporate customers for the purposes of, or in connection with, the sale of goods or supply of services (art 61), or (c) members of a common interest group concerning the company's own shares or debentures (art 52). A common interest group means an identified group of persons who, at the time the communication is made, might reasonably be regarded as having an existing and common interest with each other and with the company in (a) the affairs of the company, and (b) what is done with the proceeds arising from any investment to which the communication relates.

The financial promotion restriction does not apply to what the regulations call 'one-off communications' (arts 28 and 28A). A communication will be a one-off communication if it is not part of an organised marketing campaign, is made to one person (or to a group of persons who are expected to invest collectively) and concerns a product or service 'determined having regard to the particular circumstances of the recipient' (arts 28(2) and (3) and 28A(3)). A communication may also be a one-off communication without meeting all these criteria exactly (art 28(2)). To be exempt from the financial promotion restriction a one-off communication must be a non-real time communication or a solicited real time communication. An unsolicited real time communication is exempt under art 28A if it is a one-off communication made to a recipient who the communicator believes (a) understands the risks involved and (b) would expect to be contacted in relation to the investment referred to.

The financial promotion restriction does not apply to communications between companies in the same group (art 45), or communications for the purposes of an employee share scheme (art 60), or communications for the purposes of selling a controlling interest in a company (art 62) or in connection with a recommended takeover of a company which has been unlisted for the past ten years (arts 63 to 66 and sch 4).

The financial promotion restriction does not apply to communications to various rich persons who are supposed to be able to look after themselves, including certified high net worth individuals (art 48: they certify themselves), high net worth companies (art 49), certified sophisticated investors (art 50: the certification is by an authorised person) and associations of such persons (art 51), and self-certified sophisticated investors (art 50A). Promotions to certified high net worth individuals and self-certified sophisticated investors can relate to unlisted shares but not listed shares. Promotions to certified sophisticated investors can relate only to classes of investments for which they have been certified.

The financial promotion restriction does not apply to the publication of all or part of a company's annual accounts or an approved and signed strategic report or directors' report, provided it is not accompanied by an invitation to invest in the company's shares or debentures and otherwise complies with the restrictions in art 59. It is difficult to see how a communication which meets all the restrictions of art 59 could be an invitation or inducement to engage in investment activity subject to the financial promotion restriction. There is a similar exemption in arts 67 to 69 concerning communications required or permitted by stock exchanges.

The financial promotion restriction does not apply to the publication of listing particulars, a prospectus for new shares which are to be listed, a prospectus for unlisted shares, or any supplementary versions of these documents, communications relating to applications for listing, and formal advertisements of prospectuses for unlisted shares (arts 70 to 73).

The financial promotion restriction does not apply to a communication by a director or employee of a company speaking on a radio or television broadcast or webcast (art 20A).

7.8 UNDERWRITING AND COMMISSIONS

7.8.1 COMMISSIONS FOR FINDING SUBSCRIBERS OR UNDERWRITING NEW ISSUES

A company is permitted to pay commissions of various kinds to persons who find subscribers for new share issues, or underwrite or guarantee new issues, even though the effect of the commissions is to diminish the amount of capital contributed for the new shares. There are two main services for which commissions are paid: underwriting (see 7.8.2) and introducing subscribers (see 7.8.6). Payment of commission for these services is controlled by CA 2006, ss 552 and 553, and the prospectus rules.

7.8.2 DEFINITION OF UNDERWRITING

In relation to an offer of securities, an underwriting agreement is a contract by which a person, called an underwriter, agrees to take, and pay for, any securities that are not taken by the persons to whom the offer is made. The amount which the underwriter is paid for entering into this agreement is called an underwriting commission and is paid whether or not the underwriter has to take up any of the securities. An underwriting agreement for a securities issue is entered into before the offer is made.

One or more sub-underwriters may be brought in by the underwriter, who is then called the lead underwriter. A sub-underwriter agrees, in return for a fee, to take some or all of the securities which the lead underwriter has to take up.

When carried on by way of business, underwriting securities is a regulated activity. So underwriters carrying on business in the United Kingdom must be authorised by the FCA under FSMA 2000, part 4A. The definition of regulated activities in SI 2001/544 includes underwriting securities as principal (art 14) or as agent (art 21), and giving personal advice on the merits of underwriting a particular security (art 53). Making arrangements for another person to underwrite securities is also a regulated activity (art 25), except where the arrangements are made by the company issuing the securities (art 34).

7.8.3 PAYMENT OF UNDERWRITING COMMISSION

CA 2006, s 552(1), provides that a company may not 'apply any of its shares or capital money, either directly or indirectly' to pay a commission, discount or allowance for 'subscribing or agreeing to subscribe (whether absolutely or conditionally) for shares in the company'. Section 553 provides that such a commission may be paid, provided:

(a) the commission is authorised by the company's articles (authorisation is given by the model articles for public companies, art 44, in SI 2008/3229); and

(b) the commission does not exceed 10 per cent of the price at which the shares are issued, or the amount authorised by the articles, if that is less (no limit is specified in the model articles for public companies).

Unlike their predecessors, ss 552 and 553 never use the term 'underwriting'.

Disclosure of the overall amount of underwriting commission is required in any prospectus to be approved by the FCA (Commission Regulation (EC) No 809/2004, annex III, 5.4.3 and 5.4.4; reproduced in FCA Handbook, PR App 3EU).

7.8.4 METHODS OF PAYMENT

Underwriting commission may be paid by a company either from cash in hand (including cash received from subscribers for the issue) or by set-off from the money due for shares the underwriter has to take.

As a matter of accounting an underwriting commission may be written off share capital account, or profit and loss account, or (CA 2006, s 610(2)) any share premium received for the issue for which the commission was paid.

7.8.5 UNDERWRITING FIRM

An underwriting agreement may provide that the underwriter is to take a certain number of shares in any case. These shares are said to be underwritten firm, and, in effect, the underwriter obtains them at a discount. Where underwriting is shared the underwriting agreements should specify whether shares underwritten firm by one underwriter are to be regarded as taken by persons to whom the offer was made (thus reducing all underwriters' liabilities), or as credited against the individual underwriter's liability.

7.8.6 COMMISSIONS FOR INTRODUCING SUBSCRIBERS

The restrictions in CA 2006, ss 552 and 553 (see **7.8.3**), also apply to applications of a company's shares or capital money to payment of a commission, discount or allowance to a person for 'procuring or agreeing to procure subscriptions (whether absolute or conditional) for any shares in the company'. However, s 552(3) states that nothing in s 552 'affects the payment of such brokerage as has previously been lawful'. Brokerage is a fee paid for a broker's services. The lawfulness of paying brokerage was discussed in *Metropolitan Coal Consumers' Association v Scrimgeour* [1895] 2 QB 604, in which the Court of Appeal held that a payment by a company of a commission to stockbrokers for finding subscribers for the company's shares did not contravene the common law rule against issuing shares at a discount. However, the court pointed out that this would not apply where the commission is not bona fide or is not paid in the ordinary course of a stockbroker's business. In *Andreae v Zinc Mines of Great Britain Ltd* [1918] 2 KB 454 it was held that brokerage agreed to be paid for a one-off transaction to an individual who was not in business as a broker was illegal.

7.9 INADEQUATE RESPONSE

By CA 2006, s 578, whenever a public company offers shares for subscription it must not allot any of the shares if the issue is not subscribed for in full unless it has stated in the offer either that it will proceed to allotment in any event or that it will allot if certain conditions (such as a minimum proportion being subscribed for) are met and those conditions have been met.

If an offer is not fully subscribed as required by s 578, when 40 days have elapsed since the offer was first made, all money received from applicants for the shares must be repaid to them forthwith, but they are not entitled to interest (s 578(2)). If any money is not repaid by the forty-eighth day after the first issue of the prospectus, the directors of the company become jointly and severally liable to repay it, and interest starts to accrue (s 578(3)). A director can escape liability by proving that the default in repayment was not due to any misconduct or negligence on his or her part (s 578(3)). Any attempt to contract out of s 578 is void (s 578(6)).

If an allotment is made in contravention of s 578, the allottee may rescind it within one month of the date of allotment (s 579(1)), even if the company is in the course of being wound up (s 579(2)).

Under s 579(3), both the company and any allottee can recover any loss, damages or costs they sustain as a result of a contravention of s 578 from any director who knowingly committed, permitted or authorised the contravention.

8

SHARE TRANSFER AND COMPANY CONTROL

SUMMARY OF POINTS COVERED

- What is in this chapter
- Share certificates; uncertificated shares
- Transfer procedures
- Forged or fraudulent transfers
- Transmission of shares

- Third-party interests in shares
- Takeovers
- Public company's inquiry into share ownership
- Notification of major shareholdings
- People with significant control

8.1 WHAT IS IN THIS CHAPTER

This chapter describes some of the procedures involved when some or all of a company member's shares are transferred to another person. The procedure to be followed depends on three important factors: first whether or not the transfer is by a sale on the London Stock Exchange; secondly whether the whole of the member's holding is being transferred or only part of it; thirdly whether the shares are certificated or uncertificated (see **8.2** and **8.3**).

CA 2006, s 544(1), provides that shares in a company are transferable in accordance with the company's articles. This legislative provision states an essential feature of registered companies: that their shares are transferable. The shares of a registered company are transferable by virtue of the statutory provision and there is no need for any specific authority or permission to transfer to be stated in the company's constitution (*Re Smith, Knight and Co, Weston's Case* (1868) LR 4 Ch App 20). Buckley LJ said in ***Re Discoverers Finance Corporation Ltd, Lindlar's Case*** [1910] 1 Ch 312, at p 316:

> The regulations of the company may impose fetters upon the right of transfer. In the absence of restrictions in the articles the shareholder has by virtue of the statute the right to transfer his shares without the consent of anybody to any transferee.

However, the articles of nearly all (if not all) private companies restrict their members' right to transfer their shares (see **8.3.4**).

Specific performance of contracts for the sale of company shares will be ordered unless there is a ready market in the shares, so that a claimant could make a substitute contract and would be adequately compensated by damages for the additional cost of (or lower receipts from) the alternative contract (*Re Schwabacher* (1907) 98 LT 127).

The problem of who is to bear the loss when there is a forged or fraudulent transfer of shares is considered in **8.4**.

The other means by which share ownership can change is by transmission on death or bankruptcy (**8.5**).

There is a basic rule that a company is concerned only with the registered holder of a share, not with any third-party interest in it, though, in some circumstances, a third party can obtain a court order preventing transfer of a share (see **8.6**).

Transferring shares in a company may change who controls the company.

In a takeover of a company, usually, all its shares are acquired by a new owner. Takeovers of public companies have long been a notable feature of the UK capital market and are considered in **8.7**. There is statutory provision for compulsory acquisition of remaining shares when a takeover bid is 90 per cent successful (see **8.7.2**).

It is common for shares in public companies to be held by nominee owners. This may disguise the fact that one person is building up a significant holding. Statutory provisions enable a public company to obtain information about who has interests in its shares (see **8.8**). If a company's shares are admitted to trading on a regulated market, substantial interests in the shares must be notified to the company and to the FCA (see **8.9**).

It is in the public interest to reveal who is in control of every company. Companies are not to be a means of anonymising ownership. Since 6 April 2016 every company must keep what the legislation calls a PSC register, a register of people with significant control (see **8.10**), unless it has to provide the information under the provisions considered in **8.9**.

Key legislation which you should be able to consult when reading this chapter:

- CA 2006, ss 126, 543, 544, 768–828, 942–992, sch 1A, sch 2; and

- the model articles for private companies limited by shares and for public companies in SI 2008/3229.

All that legislation is in *Blackstone's Statutes on Company Law*.

- the Uncertificated Securities Regulations 2001 (SI 2001/3755), which are at the Online Resource Centre for *Blackstone's Statutes on Company Law*: **global.oup.com/uk/orc/law/company/company_statutes**; and

- DTR 5 in the FCA Handbook, which is at **handbook.fca.org.uk**.

Your particular course of study may require you to read other source materials.

8.2 SHARE CERTIFICATES; UNCERTIFICATED SHARES

8.2.1 DESCRIPTION

The primary record of ownership of a company's shares is in its register of members (see **14.3**). Companies also provide their shareholders with share certificates, which provide convenient evidence of ownership of shares. Until 1996 any shareholder who wanted to sell shares had to produce the share certificate relating to them in order to demonstrate the right to sell them. In 1996 share dealing on the London Stock Exchange was revolutionised by the introduction of a national central securities depository (CSD), called CREST, which is a computer-based system which records title to shares and enables title to be transferred. When the title to a share is recorded in CREST, no share certificate is issued in respect of it and it is said to be uncertificated or dematerialised. At present only listed companies need to have uncertificated shares.

A member's share certificate states the name, and in many cases the address, of the member and certifies that the member is the registered holder of a specified number of shares of a certain class. It either states that the shares are fully paid or, if they are partly paid, how much of their nominal value has been paid up. If all the shares of one class are fully paid, and rank equally for all purposes, they do not have to be individually numbered (CA 2006, s 543). Otherwise shares do have to be numbered and a share certificate should state the distinguishing numbers of the shares it represents (as is required by the model articles for private companies, art 24(2)(d), and the model articles for public companies, art 47(1)(d), in SI 2008/3229).

A share certificate must be issued by a company for its shares when allotting them (CA 2006, s 769; see **6.3.7**) or registering a transfer (s 776; see **8.3.4**). This obligation can be modified by the terms of issue of the shares and it does not apply to uncertificated shares, except where they were converted into certificated shares (rematerialised) on transfer (SI 2001/3755, reg 38(2)).

A share certificate may be sealed with the company's common seal, if it has one. By CA 2006, s 50, if a company has a common seal then it may have, for sealing share certificates, an official seal which is a facsimile of the company's common seal with the addition of the word 'Securities'. When duly affixed to a document, such an official seal has the same effect as the company's common seal. Whether or not a company has a common seal, signature of a share certificate can be equivalent to sealing it (s 44(4); see **19.2.4**).

8.2.2 ESTOPPEL

A share certificate under the common seal or securities seal of a company is prima facie evidence of the title of the named member to the shares specified in the certificate (CA 2006, ss 50 and 768). So the onus is on the person who disputes the member's title to prove that the title is defective.

Companies issue share certificates so as to provide their members with convenient evidence of ownership of shares to facilitate selling the shares. In issuing a share certificate a company must be taken to intend that people will act on the assumption that the statements in the certificate are true. If a company issues a share certificate which misstates facts and a person acts, in good faith, in reliance on the truth of the statement and suffers a detriment as a result then, in legal proceedings between the company and that person, the company must compensate that person for losses caused by relying on the company's erroneous statement (*Re Bahia and San Francisco Railway Co Ltd* (1868) LR 3 QB 584; *Balkis Consolidated Co Ltd v Tomkinson* [1893] AC 396, which is discussed in **8.4**). This is an application of the doctrine of estoppel by representation: the company is estopped (precluded) from denying its representation on which the other party relied.

The most common situation in which compensation is payable for an erroneous share certificate is where a person has, in good faith, paid, to the person erroneously named as holding shares, money to purchase those shares. When the transfer is presented for registration the company must refuse to register it, because the shares have not been transferred by their true owner, but the company must compensate the disappointed buyer who relied on the false share certificate (as in *Re Bahia and San Francisco Railway Co Ltd*). However, the company may be able to recover the damages from the person who caused it to issue the erroneous share certificate, see **8.4**.

If a share certificate states that shares are fully paid when in fact they are not and a holder of the shares has suffered a detriment by acting in reliance on the statement (for example, by parting with money to buy them or becoming a mortgagee of the shares as security for a loan), then that shareholder cannot be called upon to pay the unpaid part of the nominal value of the shares (*Burkinshaw v Nicolls* (1878) 3 App Cas 1004; *Bloomenthal v Ford* [1897] AC 156).

A statement creates an estoppel against a company only if it is made with the company's authority. In the following two cases it was held that the erroneous share certificates had been issued without authority and so did not create any estoppel.

In ***Ruben v Great Fingall Consolidated*** [1906] AC 439, the secretary of the defendant company issued what purported to be a share certificate of the company, having forged a transfer of shares belonging to one of the company's members. The purported share certificate bore the company's seal and the signatures of two directors, which the secretary had signed without their knowledge, and the secretary's signature. The certificate had been issued to a firm of stockbrokers to whom the secretary was pretending to mortgage the shares as security for money they had lent him. When the forgery was discovered the company refused to register the stockbrokers as holders of the shares and they sued for damages claiming that the company was estopped from denying the truth of the certificate. Lord Loreburn LC, however, said, at p 443:

> I cannot see upon what principle your Lordships can hold that the defendants are liable in this action. The forged certificate is a pure nullity.

In *South London Greyhound Racecourses Ltd v Wake* [1931] 1 Ch 496 a document purporting to be a share certificate of the company had been given to Mr Wake. It bore the company's seal and had been countersigned by the company's managing director and secretary. It related to shares which were owned by the English and Foreign Investment Trust Ltd, which in fact had never transferred the shares. The articles of association of South London Racecourses Ltd stated that the company's seal could be put on documents only when authorised by a resolution of the board of directors but the board had never authorised the issue of the certificate. Clauson J characterised the purported certificate as a forgery, which was of no effect.

It is disconcerting to find the concept of forgery being brought into a situation where one might have thought that officers of a company had an ostensible authority which the company could not deny (see **19.5.3** and **19.5.4**). However, the House of Lords in **Ruben v Great Fingall Consolidated** was convinced that a company secretary had no ostensible authority to represent that a share certificate he or she issued was genuine. Lord Macnaghten said, at p 444:

> The secretary of the company, who is a mere servant, may be the proper hand to deliver out certificates which the company issues in due course, but he can have no authority to guarantee the genuineness or validity of a document which is not the deed of the company.

Similarly, in *South London Greyhound Racecourses Ltd v Wake*, Clauson J pointed out that the managing director had no ostensible authority to seal documents for the company, and that the company had never represented that he had such authority.

Under the model articles for private companies, art 25, and the model articles for public companies, art 49, in SI 2008/3229, a member will be supplied with a replacement for a certificate that is damaged or defaced, or which is said to be lost, stolen or destroyed.

When issuing a replacement certificate for one supposed to have been lost, stolen or destroyed it is necessary to take precautions against fraudulent claims. It is usual to require:

(a) a statutory declaration from the shareholder setting out the circumstances of the loss or destruction of the original certificate;

(b) an indemnity under which the shareholder promises to make good to the company and its directors any loss they may suffer as a result of issuing a replacement certificate; and

(c) if the sum involved is large, a guarantee from a bank or insurance company.

When a replacement certificate is issued, it should be marked 'duplicate' and a note should be made on the register of members so that any future transfer of the shares concerned is made only on production of the duplicate certificate.

8.3 TRANSFER PROCEDURES

8.3.1 INSTRUMENT OF TRANSFER

A company may not register a transfer of its certificated shares unless a 'proper instrument of transfer' has been delivered to it (CA 2006, s 770(1)). This provision was enacted to ensure that a transfer of shares is made by a document on which stamp duty may be charged (stamp duty is levied on documents rather than transactions) (*Re Greene* [1949] Ch 333 per Harman J at p 339; *Re Paradise Motor Co Ltd* [1968] 1 WLR 1125). Accordingly, any instrument that will attract stamp duty is a 'proper' instrument for the purposes of s 770(1). However, a document is capable of being a proper instrument of transfer for the purpose of s 770(1) even though, contrary to the Stamp Act 1891, s 5, the amount of duty cannot be assessed from the document itself (because, for example, it gives insufficient information about the consideration for the transfer) (*Nisbet v Shepherd* [1994] 1 BCLC 300). A provision in a company's articles purporting to transfer shares of the company is not a proper instrument of transfer and so is void (*Re Greene*).

By the Stock Transfer Act 1963, s 1(1) and (4)(a), fully paid company shares may be transferred by executing a document in one of the forms set out in sch 1 to the Act (as amended by SI 1996/1571). By s 2(1) of the 1963 Act such a form may be used to transfer fully paid shares of a company notwithstanding a provision in the company's articles requiring the use of some other form (the model articles for private companies, art 26(1), and the model articles for public companies, art 63(1), in SI 2008/3229, refer to the use of 'any usual form or any other form approved by the directors') and may be executed under hand only notwithstanding a provision in the articles requiring execution as a deed.

The Stock Transfer Act 1963 does not apply to partly paid shares, and a company that has issued such shares may in its articles specify a transfer procedure for them.

CA 2006, s 770(1), does not apply to a transfer of uncertificated shares. This is because s 770(1) is expressed not to apply to a transfer which is in accordance with regulations made under part 21, Chapter 2 (ss 783 to 790), which are regulations concerning the transfer of uncertificated shares and other securities (see **8.3.3**). CA 2006, s 770(1), is also expressed not to apply to an exempt transfer within the Stock Transfer Act 1982, but that Act has never been applied to company shares.

8.3.2 TRANSFER OF CERTIFICATED SHARES

The procedure by which a holder of fully paid certificated shares in a company transfers them is as follows. The transferor makes out and signs a stock transfer form on which is stated:

(a) the name of the company whose shares are being transferred;

(b) the number, nominal value and class of the shares being transferred (shares of different classes should not be transferred on the same form—see Table A, art 24(b));

(c) the consideration being paid;

(d) the transferor's name and address; and

(e) the name and address of the transferee.

If the transferee is to hold the shares in uncertificated form, a special stock transfer form, known as a CREST transfer form, is used, which expressly requests transfer to a system-member and does not require the address of the transferee (SI 1996/1571, art 2). The transfer is then made under SI 2001/3755, reg 33 (see **8.3.3.5**).

If all the shares represented on a share certificate are being transferred to one transferee, the share certificate is sent with the transfer form to the transferee. The transferee pays the stamp duty and then sends the stock transfer form and the share certificate to the company for registration.

If only part of the holding represented by a share certificate is being transferred, or different parts of the holding are being transferred to different persons, the transferor will not want to send the certificate to one transferee, for fear of it being used fraudulently to obtain a transfer of the whole holding. Instead the transferor sends the certificate and all transfer forms to the company so that it can certify on the transfer forms that the transferor has produced a certificate covering the shares being transferred and forward the forms to the transferees. This procedure is known as 'certification' of the transfer forms. If some of the shares represented by the transferor's share certificate are not being transferred, the company will send the transferor a 'balance ticket', which is a temporary certificate for the shares not being transferred. A new certificate for those shares would not normally be issued until the transfers were registered.

If a transfer is falsely certificated and the false certification was made fraudulently, any person to whom detriment has been caused by acting in reliance on the false certification can claim damages for deceit from the person who made the false certification. Claims for deceit are discussed in more detail in **6.8.6.2**. By statute, a company which makes a false certification negligently is under the same liability as if it had been made fraudulently (CA 2006, s 775(3))—this is a statutory liability for economic loss caused by negligent misstatement introduced before the courts recognised such a liability in common law.

The common law took the view that, as in the cases on forged share certificates (see **8.2.2**), a company was not liable for a false certification of a transfer unless it had been made by someone with actual or ostensible authority to guarantee the authenticity of certifications, and that a company secretary does not have ostensible authority to do such a thing (*George Whitechurch Ltd v Cavanagh* [1902] AC 117; *Kleinwort Sons and Co v Associated Automatic Machine Corporation Ltd* (1934) 151 LT 1). However, this has been affected by statute. CA 2006, s 775(4)(b), deems a certification to have been made by a company if it was issued and signed by a person authorised to issue certifications.

If the transfer is a sale and purchase of shares on the London Stock Exchange, the stock transfer form and share certificate are sent to the member firm acting for the seller. The particulars of the consideration and of the transferee are not put on the stock transfer form by the seller: instead the member firm puts these particulars on one or more brokers transfer forms (Stock Transfer Act 1963, s 1(2) and sch 2).

8.3.3 TRANSFER OF UNCERTIFICATED SHARES

8.3.3.1 Uncertificated shares and CREST

Most shares traded on the London Stock Exchange are uncertificated shares (also known as dematerialised shares). When a share is uncertificated, there is no share certificate for it: instead, title to it is recorded in, and transferred by means of, a computer-based system, known as a central securities depository (CSD). A CSD is operated independently of the companies whose securities it records. Regulation (EU) No 909/2014 governs the operation of CSDs in the EEA. Provision for the operation of CSDs in the United Kingdom is made by the Uncertificated Securities Regulations 2001 (USR 2001, SI 2001/3755). In USR 2001 a CSD is referred to as a 'relevant system', which is defined in reg 2(1) as:

> a computer-based system, and procedures, which enable title to units of a security to be evidenced and transferred without a written instrument, and which facilitate supplementary and incidental matters.

In the terms of this definition, a class of shares is a security, and an individual share is a unit of that security.

The USR 2001 are concerned only with relevant systems operated by an Operator approved by the Bank of England. The only approved Operator is Euroclear UK & Ireland Ltd, which is also a recognised clearing house under the Financial Services and Markets Act 2000, s 285. The system which Euroclear UK & Ireland operates is called CREST. A great deal of information about Euroclear is given on its website: **www.euroclear.com**. Euroclear UK & Ireland is one of a group of companies providing a wide range of settlement services, including acting as CSD for Finland, France, the Netherlands and Sweden.

8.3.3.2 Participating securities and issuers

Title to shares in a particular class of shares can be transferred by means of CREST only if the issuer of the shares permits them to be held in uncertificated form and only if both the issuer and Euroclear permit title to them to be transferred by means of CREST (USR 2001, reg 14). Equity shares cannot have premium listing unless they are eligible for electronic settlement, such as by CREST (LR 6.1.23R and 6.1.24G), and that eligibility must be maintained at all times (LR 9.2.3R). Euroclear can permit title to a class of shares to be transferred using CREST only if:

(a) the issuer's articles of association are in all respects consistent with the use of CREST and with USR 2001 (regs 14(a) and 15); or

(b) the company's directors have resolved that title to shares of that class may be transferred using CREST (regs 14(a) and 16). The members of a company may, by ordinary resolution, prohibit or revoke a reg 16 directors' resolution (reg 16(6)). A reg 16 directors' resolution must be notified to every member of the company within 60 days of adoption (reg 16(4)).

If Euroclear has permitted title to shares in a class of shares to be transferred by means of CREST, the class is called a 'participating security' (reg 3(1)). The issuer of a participating security is called a 'participating issuer' (reg 3(1)).

A class of shares is described as 'wholly dematerialised' if its terms of issue, or the issuer's articles of association, provide that shares of the class can only be held in uncertificated form and that title to them can only be transferred by means of a relevant system (USR 2001, reg 3(1)). If a class of shares is not wholly dematerialised, holders of shares in that class can choose whether their shares are to be uncertificated or not.

8.3.3.3 System-members

The only persons who can be registered in CREST's Operator registers of members (see **14.3.2**) as holders of uncertificated shares are 'system-members'. A system-member must enter into an admission agreement with Euroclear and must nominate a bank to be its settlement bank. A member's settlement bank pays for the member's purchases and receives payment for sales. Any other person who wishes to invest in uncertificated shares must arrange for a system-member to hold them as trustee.

8.3.3.4 Transfers of uncertificated shares

When a UK company has uncertificated shares, its register of members is divided into two: the Operator register and the issuer register (see **14.3.2**). The Operator register is maintained in the CREST computer system and is used to register transfers of uncertificated shares. The issuer register records transfers of certificated shares.

Because it registers transfers of uncertificated shares, CREST provides delivery versus payment (DVP) to settle trades in shares: that is registration of the buyer as the new holder of purchased shares is made simultaneously with payment of the purchase price, and one aspect of the settlement cannot occur unless the other does. This is more secure than settlement of trades in certificated shares where payment normally has to be made before registration, which is done by the company or by a firm of registrars acting on its behalf, and the purchaser must bear the risk that the transfer might not be registered, because, for example, the seller did not own the shares.

The procedure for a sale and purchase of uncertificated shares is, in outline, as follows. When buyer and seller have both established the terms of the sale, instructions to make the transfer and pay for it are sent to CREST. These instructions are what the USR 2001 call 'dematerialised instructions', which are sent by computer over a specialised telecommunications network approved by Euroclear. Dematerialised instructions are in the format, and use security devices, specified by Euroclear.

Some system-members are 'system-participants', who are connected to the CREST computer through an approved network and can send dematerialised instructions to effect transfers of their own shareholdings. The other system-members (called 'sponsored members' by Euroclear) arrange for system participants to send instructions on their behalf. A system participant can send instructions on behalf of a sponsored member only if it has entered into a sponsors agreement with Euroclear.

The CREST computer matches the selling and buying instructions and settles the transaction on the nominated settlement day. Settlement is achieved by simultaneously (a) notifying the Bank of England's inter-bank payment system to transfer the purchase price from the buyer's to the seller's settlement bank and (b) transferring shares from the seller's account to the buyer's in the Operator register of members.

The rules governing a transfer of uncertificated shares which remain uncertificated after transfer are in USR 2001, reg 27. By reg 27(2), Euroclear must refuse to register a transfer if it has actual notice that the transfer is:

(a) prohibited by order of a UK court;

(b) prohibited or avoided by or under any enactment; or

(c) a transfer to a deceased person.

Under reg 27(4), Euroclear may refuse to register a transfer:

(a) to an entity which is not a natural or legal person;

(b) to a minor;

(c) to be held jointly in the names of more persons than permitted under the terms of issue of the shares; or

(d) where it has actual notice that the dematerialised instruction requesting the transfer is not authentic.

It is also possible for uncertificated shares to be transferred under reg 28 to a person who will hold them as certificated shares (this is known as a transfer with rematerialisation of the shares). A rematerialisation transfer is not completed until the transferee's name is in the issuer register of members, and the USR 2001 ensure that this registration is only performed in accordance with an instruction sent by CREST under reg 27(7), or a court order or statutory requirement (regs 28(2) and (6) and 32(1)). In the interval between deletion of the transferor's name from the Operator register of members and registration of the transferee's name in the issuer register, the transferor remains a member of the company and retains title to the shares, subject to the transferee's equitable interest in them as purchaser (regs 31(1) and (2) and 32(6)). Rematerialisation of shares is not possible if the shares are in a class which is wholly dematerialised (reg 45(b)). By reg 28(3), the issuer must refuse to register a rematerialisation transfer in the same circumstances as Euroclear must refuse under reg 27(2). By reg 28(4), the issuer may refuse to register in the same circumstances as Euroclear may refuse to register under reg 27(4).

By reg 29, registration in accordance with regs 27 or 28 is the only effective way of registering a transfer of title to an uncertificated share.

8.3.3.5 Transfer with dematerialisation

A share in a class of shares which is a participating security can be transferred by means of CREST only if title to it is already recorded on the Operator register of members for the issuing company, that is if it is already in uncertificated form (USR 2001, reg 14). A transfer of a share in certificated form to a transferee who wishes to hold it in uncertificated form is carried out under reg 33. The issuer, having received the stock transfer form and share certificate, must give a dematerialisation notice to CREST and record in the issuer register of members that the shares are no longer the transferor's. CREST must register the transferee as owner of the shares in the Operator register of members. In the interval between deletion of the transferor's name from the issuer register of members and registration of the transferee's name in the Operator register, the transferor remains a member of the company and retains title to the shares, subject to the transferee's equitable interest in them as purchaser (regs 33(8) and (9)). CREST must inform the issuing company within two months that it has made the required entry in the Operator register (reg 33(10)).

8.3.3.6 Central counterparty trading

In order book trading on the London Stock Exchange using SETS (see **7.3.3.1**), the seller of shares does not know who the buyer will be. To preserve this anonymity, trading is conducted through a central counterparty (CCP); that is, any trade is split into two: a sale from the seller to the CCP and a purchase from the CCP by the buyer. The CCP is LCH.Clearnet Ltd, which is a recognised clearing house under FSMA 2000, s 285. The undoubted creditworthiness of LCH.Clearnet Ltd removes the risk of not being paid which sellers might feel when dealing with unknown buyers.

8.3.3.7 Future developments

Experience of uncertificated shares has shown how cumbersome it is for brokers and registrars to handle sales of the remaining shares in listed companies which have not been dematerialised. In a report issued in December 2004 a working group from the securities industry recommended compulsory dematerialisation of the remaining certificated shares. CA 2006, s 786, gives the Secretary of State powers to make the necessary legislation. Regulation (EU) No 909/2014 sets a timetable for compulsory dematerialisation of shares admitted to trading, or traded, on regulated markets and multilateral trading facilities throughout the EEA. For these traded shares, compulsory dematerialisation will apply to new share issues from 1 January 2023 and for all other shares in issue from 1 January 2025 (arts 3(1) and 76(2)).

8.3.4 DIRECTORS' APPROVAL, RESTRICTIONS ON TRANSFER AND PRE-EMPTION RIGHTS

8.3.4.1 Registration of transfers

A transfer of certificated shares is not complete until the transferee is registered as the new owner in the company's register of members. After paying for shares and before registration, the transferee has an equitable interest only in the shares. Entries in the register of members are acts of the company which may only be taken with the approval of the directors (see, for example, *South London Greyhound Racecourses Ltd v Wake* [1931] 1 Ch 496) or of all the members (*Re Zinotty Properties Ltd* [1984] 1 WLR 1249). The company secretary, for example, does not have authority to decide what entries are to be made in the register (*Chida Mines Ltd v Anderson* (1905) 22 TLR 27; *Re Indo-China Steam Navigation Co* [1917] 2 Ch 100; *Re Zinotty Properties Ltd*).

Under the model articles for private companies, art 26(2), and the model articles for public companies, art 63(2), in SI 2008/3229, no fee is to be charged for registering a transfer.

8.3.4.2 Directors' power to refuse to register a transfer

Because it is an essential feature of registered companies that their shares are freely transferable, the directors of a company have no power to refuse to register a transfer unless they have been given such a power by the company's constitution (*Re Cawley and Co* (1889) 42 ChD 209; *Re Bede Steam Shipping Co Ltd* [1917] 1 Ch 123; *Re Copal Varnish Co Ltd* [1917] 2 Ch 349). As shares are prima facie transferable, a restriction on transfer must be clearly expressed and will not usually be implied by the courts (*Greenhalgh v Mallard* [1943] 2 All ER 234 per Lord Greene MR at p 237). The articles cannot be altered with retrospective effect so as to allow the directors to refuse to register a transfer that has already taken place (*W and A M'Arthur Ltd v Gulf Line Ltd* 1909 SC 732).

In the model articles for private companies in SI 2008/3229, art 26(5) gives the directors a general power to refuse to register a transfer. In the model articles for public companies, art 63(5) gives a general power of refusal only in relation to partly paid shares (this provision was originally introduced to enable directors to check on the creditworthiness of proposed transferees of partly paid shares). Article 63(5) also gives a power to refuse to register transfers that do not comply with administrative requirements.

A power to register a transfer of a company's shares must only be exercised for the purposes for which it is conferred (CA 2006, s 171). When deciding whether to register a transfer the directors can consider only factors which the company's constitution allows them to consider. Unless permitted to do so by the constitution, they cannot, for example, refuse to register a transfer because they believe the transferee will be acting as a trustee for the transferor (*Moffat v Farquhar* (1878) 7 ChD 591), or because they believe the transferee will be acting as a trustee for a person of whom they disapprove (*Re Bell Bros Ltd* (1891) 65 LT 245), or because the transferee is not a member of a particular family (*Re Bell Bros Ltd*) or because the transferee will hold only one share (*Re Bede Steam Shipping Co Ltd*).

A renunciation of allotment in favour of another person is not a transfer for the purposes of provisions in articles empowering directors to refuse to register a transfer (*Re Pool Shipping Co Ltd* [1920] 1 Ch 251; *System Controls plc v Munro Corporate plc* [1990] BCLC 659).

8.3.4.3 Time to decide to refuse to register a transfer

When a transfer has been lodged with a company, it must either register the transfer or give the transferee notice of refusal to register, together with its reasons for the refusal (CA 2006, s 771(1)). This must be done as soon as practicable and, in any event, within two months after the date of lodging the transfer (s 771(1)). Within those two months, unless the company has refused the transfer, it must complete and have ready for delivery new share certificates, unless the conditions of issue of the shares provide otherwise (s 776). Failure to comply with s 776 is a criminal offence (s 776(5) and (6)). The transferee may serve a notice on the company requiring it to supply a certificate and, if the company does not do so within ten days of service of the notice, the transferee may apply to the court to make an order requiring the company, and any officer, to make good the default (s 782).

If the transfer is refused, the company must provide the transferee with such further information about the reasons for the refusal as the transferee may reasonably request, apart from minutes of directors' meetings (s 771(2)).

Provided a decision to refuse registration has been taken within a reasonable time, the fact that notice of it was not sent within the statutory two-month period does not render the decision invalid (*Popely v Planarrive Ltd* [1997] 1 BCLC 8). If there is no board of directors to exercise a right of refusal, the transferee will be entitled to be registered after two months (*Re New Cedos Engineering Co Ltd* [1994] 1 BCLC 797, in which the acting directors had not been validly appointed).

The provisions of CA 2006 requiring a company to give reasons for refusing a transfer are new to company law. Before CA 2006, it was accepted that a company could refuse to give any reasons for transfer, and this made it difficult to challenge any refusal.

8.3.4.4 Pre-emption rights

It is common for the articles of a private company to provide that a member may not sell shares without first offering them to existing members for sale at a price to be determined by independent valuation, or according to a formula set out in the articles. (This is called a right of pre-emption.) It is the duty of directors to refuse to register a transfer to an outsider if the transferor has breached the company's articles by not offering the shares to other members first (*Tett v Phoenix Property and Investment Co Ltd* [1986] BCLC 149).

If a member of a company executes a transfer of a share despite the existence of other members' pre-emption rights in the articles of association, the other members have an equitable interest in the share, consisting of an option to purchase it. As this equitable interest was created by the articles, it takes priority over the transferee's equitable interest (*Tett v Phoenix Property and Investments Co Ltd* [1984] BCLC 599; *Cottrell v King* [2004] EWHC 397 (Ch), [2004] 2 BCLC 413).

8.3.4.5 Listed companies

It is an essential feature of listed shares that they are freely transferable (Directive 2001/34/EC, art 46(1); LR 2.2.4R(1)). In exceptional circumstances, restrictions on transfer may be accepted if they will not disturb the market in the shares (Directive 2001/34/EC, art 46(3); LR 2.2.6G).

As there are only limited circumstances in which Euroclear can refuse to register a transfer of uncertificated shares (SI 2001/3755, reg 27(2) and (4), see **8.3.3.4**), Euroclear does not permit shares to be transferred by means of CREST unless they are freely transferable.

8.4 FORGED OR FRAUDULENT TRANSFERS

If the signature of a shareholder is forged on an instrument of transfer of those shares, the instrument is void; the shares are not transferred; and the original holder still holds them.

A person who presents a forged or fraudulent transfer of shares for registration (whether knowing it is a forgery or not) and who receives a share certificate cannot use the doctrine of estoppel by representation (see **8.2.2**) to require the company to stand by its statement in the share certificate of who owns the shares because the representation merely repeated the information which that person provided (*Simm v Anglo-American Telegraph Co* (1879) 5 QBD 188).

In *Balkis Consolidated Co Ltd v Tomkinson* [1893] AC 396, the plaintiff had sent a transfer to the company for registration relying on the company's certification of the transfer. In fact the certification was false and the shares had already been sold to other buyers. Nevertheless the company issued the plaintiff with a share certificate, but when the plaintiff in turn tried to sell the shares the company had discovered the error and refused to register the purchasers, so the plaintiff had to buy equivalent shares to fulfil the contracts of sale. It was held that the plaintiff could rely on the representation of ownership in his share certificate because it repeated the representation made by the company in the certification of the transfer. This is now affected by statute. By CA 2006, s 775(2), a company's certification of a transfer of shares is not to be taken as a representation that the transferor has any title to the shares: it is only a representation that documents have been produced to the company showing prima facie that the transferor has title to the shares (s 775(1)). If a case like *Balkis Consolidated Co Ltd v Tomkinson* occurred today, the plaintiff could claim damages under s 775(3) for negligent false certification.

A person who presents a transfer for registration is required by common law to indemnify the company against any liability it incurs to other persons as a result of registering the transfer (*Sheffield Corporation v Barclay* [1905] AC 392; *Yeung v Hong Kong and Shanghai Banking Corporation* [1981] AC 787). So if A sends a forged or fraudulent transfer of a company's shares to the company for registration and receives a share certificate and subsequently B relies on the share certificate to buy the shares from A then B can sue the company for the value of the shares (*Re Bahia and San Francisco Railway Co Ltd* (1868) LR 3 QB 584, see **8.2.2**) but the company can recover the damages from A, even if A did not know of the fraud or forgery of the transfer (*Royal Bank of Scotland plc v Sandstone Properties Ltd* [1998] 2 BCLC 429). But where what is relied on is an erroneous statement by the company, on a share certificate, of who owns shares, the estoppel raised against the company by its share certificate overrides its right to an indemnity (*Cadbury Schweppes plc v Halifax Share Dealing Ltd* [2006] EWHC 1184 (Ch), [2007] 1 BCLC 497). In the *Cadbury Schweppes* case, shares in the claimant company had been fraudulently transferred to people who were not the true owners and the claimant issued new share certificates in their names. Stockbrokers who acted for subsequent buyers of the shares and presented transfers in reliance on the erroneous certificates were not liable to indemnify the company.

It is usual for a public company to insure itself against the consequences of acting on a forged instrument of transfer, or other document (such as a forged power of attorney) affecting share transfer.

If, as a result of a forged instruction within CREST, there is an error in a person's entry in a company's register of members which causes loss to that person, the court may make a compensation order against Euroclear (SI 2001/3755, reg 36). There are several limitations in reg 36 on compensation orders. Perhaps the most significant is the rule that if the perpetrator of the forgery is identified, no compensation order can be made against Euroclear even if the loss cannot be recovered from the perpetrator (reg 36(4)(a)).

8.5 TRANSMISSION OF SHARES

The term 'transmission' is used to describe the automatic transfer of ownership of an individual shareholder's shares which occurs by operation of law when the individual dies or is adjudged bankrupt. On death, an individual's shares are transmitted to his or her personal representatives or, if the individual was a co-owner of the shares, to the surviving co-owner or co-owners. In bankruptcy, shares go to the individual's trustee in bankruptcy (IA 1986, s 306).

Transmission of a share of a company to a personal representative or trustee in bankruptcy does not by itself make that person a member of the company: the status of membership is not achieved until the person has agreed to be registered as a member (*Re Bowling and Welby's Contract* [1895] 1 Ch 663 per Lindley LJ at p 670). Nevertheless, in the absence of a contrary provision, 'member' in articles of association must be read, as far as possible, as including the estate of a deceased member (*New Zealand Gold Extraction Co (Newbery-Vautin Process) Ltd v Peacock* [1894] 1 QB 622; *James v Buena Ventura Nitrate Grounds Syndicate Ltd* [1896] 1 Ch 456).

The personal representatives of a deceased shareholder, as representing his or her estate, are entitled to all the profits and advantages attaching to the deceased's shares, and are subject to all the incidental liabilities (*James v Buena Ventura Nitrate Grounds Syndicate Ltd*; *Llewellyn v Kasintoe Rubber Estates Ltd* [1914] 2 Ch 670).

The trustee in bankruptcy of a bankrupt shareholder in a company has a right to be registered as the holder of the bankrupt's shares in place of the bankrupt unless the company's articles restrict that right (*Wood v W and G Dean Pty Ltd* (1929) 43 CLR 77). The only reason for registering as the holder of the shares is that it enables the trustee to vote at general meetings but in practice it is rare for the trustee in bankruptcy of a shareholder in a company to wish to take part in the company's affairs. See further **14.10.1.3**.

The model articles for private companies, art 27, and the model articles for public companies, art 66, in SI 2008/3229, provide that a person to whom a shareholder's share is transmitted on death or bankruptcy (a transmittee) has the same rights as the holder, except that the transmittee cannot attend or vote at a general meeting until registered as the new holder of the share. Those articles provide that a transmittee of a share may choose either to become registered as the holder of the share or to have it transferred to another person.

8.6 THIRD-PARTY INTERESTS IN SHARES

8.6.1 NO NOTICE TO COMPANY OF THIRD-PARTY INTERESTS

Like any other item of property, it is possible for more than one person to have a property interest in a company share. For example, the owner of the legal title may be holding it in trust for one or more beneficiaries, or may be a mortgagee who is required to recognise the mortgagor's equity of redemption. It is very common for the shares of listed public companies to be held by nominees on behalf of the beneficial owners. An important reason for this is the need for uncertificated shares to be held by a system-member (see **8.3.3.3**). It is common for brokers to arrange for their clients' shares to be held by a nominee company which is a system-member. Some large listed companies arrange for their shareholders' uncertificated shares to be held by a nominee company which is a system-member.

It is an important principle of company law that if a person is named in a company's register of members as the owner of a share in the company then the company is entitled to regard that person as the only person interested in the share and to ignore the claims of anyone else, even if informed of those claims, unless the court intervenes. This is provided by CA 2006, s 126.

> No notice of any trust, expressed, implied or constructive, shall be entered on the register of members of a company registered in England and Wales or Northern Ireland, or be receivable by the registrar.

The mysterious phrase 'receivable by the registrar' in s 126 first appeared in CA 1862, s 30, and from its context in that Act it clearly means the registrar of companies. However, the provision enacted in the section first appeared in the Joint Stock Companies Act 1856, s 19, where the phrase used is 'receivable by the company'. It is pretty clear that the word 'registrar' was put in by mistake when the provision was re-enacted in 1862. In *Société Générale de Paris v Tramways Union Co Ltd* (1884) 14 QBD 424, Lindley LJ, commenting on CA 1862, s 30, said:

> The section in question appears to me . . . to relieve [registered companies] from the duty of attending to mere notices of equitable interests.

His Lordship rejected the argument that the wording of the provision in the 1862 Act meant only that a company must not record a notice of an equitable interest in the register of members but that it is affected by such notice and should record it somewhere else. See also the remarks of the Earl of Selborne in the same case in the House of Lords (1885) 11 App Cas 20. In effect, Lindley LJ's interpretation of the provision as enacted in 1862 (and re-enacted in CA 2006, s 126) gives it the meaning that its predecessor in the 1856 Act plainly had (see also *Re T H Saunders and Co Ltd* [1908] 1 Ch 415 per Warrington J at p 422).

In relation to uncertificated shares, which are recorded in the part of the register of members maintained by Euroclear (see **14.3.2**), a provision equivalent to s 126 is made by SI 2001/3755, reg 23(3).

8.6.2 STOP NOTICES

A person claiming to be interested in shares in a company may apply to the High Court to serve a 'stop notice' (Charging Orders Act 1979, s 5(2)(b); Civil Procedure Rules 1998, rr 73.16 to 73.21). A stop notice requires the company to refrain from registering a transfer of the shares in question and to refrain from paying any dividend without first sending a notice by first-class post to the person on whose behalf the stop notice was served and then waiting 14 days to see whether that person takes any action. If the company has heard nothing at the end of the 14 days it may safely go ahead with registering the transfer or paying the dividend.

A stop notice is also served by the High Court or County Court if the court has made a charging order on shares (Civil Procedure Rules 1998, r 73.8(3)). A charging order imposes a charge in order to secure payment of a judgment debt (Charging Orders Act 1979, s 1(1)) and while one is in force in relation to shares, the shares may not be transferred and no payment of dividend on them may be made without the court's authority.

8.6.3 STOP ORDERS

A person claiming to be interested in shares in a company may apply to the High Court to make a 'stop order' (Charging Orders Act 1979, s 5(2)(a); Civil Procedure Rules 1998, rr 73.11 to 73.15). A stop order on shares prohibits the registration of any transfer of the shares and/or payment of any dividend or other payment relating to the shares (r 73.14).

8.6.4 INTERIM CHARGING ORDERS

Pending determination of an application for a charging order on shares of a company, the court may make an interim charging order (Civil Procedure Rules 1998, r 73.4), which must be served on the company (r 73.5(1)(d)(iii)). Once the company has been served with the order, it must not permit any transfer of the shares or pay any dividend or redemption payment on them, unless the court gives permission (r 73.6(2)). The company may have to pay compensation if it acts contrary to an interim charging order (r 73.6(3)).

8.7 TAKEOVERS

8.7.1 TAKEOVERS AND THE CITY CODE

8.7.1.1 Definitions

If company A acquires sufficient shares in company B to control the board of directors and policies of B, there is a takeover of B by A. If B is a private company, it will probably have a provision in its articles authorising the directors to refuse to register a transfer of shares. So a takeover of a private company inevitably requires the approval of the directors. It is normally not possible to control a private company without holding more than 50 per cent of the voting shares. If B is a listed company with a large number of members then A will not normally be able to acquire sufficient shares to give it control merely by purchases on the Stock Exchange. So it is usually necessary to send a circular to B's shareholders offering to buy their shares. An offer of this kind is called a takeover bid; the company making the offer (A) is called the offeror company, and the company whose shares it is sought to acquire is called the offeree or target company. It is common for the offeror to offer to allot new shares in itself as the consideration for purchasing shares in the offeree company.

8.7.1.2 The Takeovers Directive

Directive 2004/25/EC (the Takeovers Directive) harmonises member States' laws on takeover bids for securities admitted to trading on a regulated market (see **7.3.4.3**). The Directive is implemented by CA 2006, ss 942 to 992 and sch 2.

8.7.1.3 The Takeover Panel and the City Code

Directive 2004/25/EC requires each member State to designate an authority competent to supervise bids (art 4(1)). In the United Kingdom the competent authority is the Panel on Takeovers and Mergers (**www.thetakeoverpanel.org.uk**), which was established in 1968 and took on its role as competent authority on 20 May 2006 (SI 2006/1183, reg 4(2)). The Panel itself appoints most of its members and chooses its chairman and two deputies. Eleven members of the Panel are appointed by bodies including the CBI, the ICAEW, the NAPF and the London Investment Banking Association.

The Panel is required to make rules to give effect to the provisions of the Directive listed in CA 2006, s 943(1), and may also make rules for other purposes mentioned in s 943. The Panel's rules are contained in the latest version of the City Code on Takeovers and Mergers, which can be seen at the Panel's website.

The Code reflects 'the collective opinion of those professionally involved in the field of takeovers as to appropriate business standards and as to how fairness to shareholders and an orderly framework for takeovers can be achieved' (Code, Introduction, s 2(a)).

A takeover bid is subject to the Panel's jurisdiction if the securities which are the subject of the offer are admitted to trading on a regulated market in the United Kingdom (Directive 2004/25/EC, art 4(2)(a) and (b)). If the securities have been admitted to trading on regulated markets in more than one State at different times, the competent authority is that of the State in which the securities were first admitted to trading (art 4(2)(b)). A company which has securities admitted to trading simultaneously in more than one State on or after 20 May 2006 can itself choose which State is to regulate any takeover offer for those securities: the choice must be made on the first day of trading (art 2(4)(c)). The competent authorities for companies whose securities were admitted to trading simultaneously in different States before 20 May 2006 were settled under art 4(2)(c) four weeks after 20 May 2006.

8.7.1.4 General principles

Directive 2004/25/EC, art 3(1), requires member States to comply with six general principles in implementing the Directive, and they are repeated as the General Principles of the City Code:

1. All holders of the securities of an offeree company of the same class must be afforded equivalent treatment; moreover, if a person acquires control of a company, the other holders of securities must be protected.

2. The holders of the securities of an offeree company must have sufficient time and information to enable them to reach a properly informed decision on the bid; where it advises the holders of securities, the board of the offeree company must give its views on the effects of implementation of the bid on employment, conditions of employment and the locations of the company's places of business.

3. The board of an offeree company must act in the interests of the company as a whole and must not deny the holders of securities the opportunity to decide on the merits of the bid.

4. False markets must not be created in the securities of the offeree company, of the offeror company or of any other company concerned by the bid in such a way that the rise or fall of the prices of the securities becomes artificial and the normal functioning of the markets is distorted.

5. An offeror must announce a bid only after ensuring that he/she can fulfil in full any cash consideration, if such is offered, and after taking all reasonable measures to secure the implementation of any other type of consideration.

6. An offeree company must not be hindered in the conduct of its affairs for longer than is reasonable by a bid for its securities.

8.7.1.5 Executive rulings

The day-to-day work of the Panel on Takeovers and Mergers is carried out by the Panel Executive headed by the Director General. Any person may consult the Panel Executive, before taking any action, for a ruling on whether a proposed course of conduct is in accordance with the General Principles or the rules in the Code. The Introduction to the Code, s 6, says:

> To take legal or other professional advice on the interpretation, application or effect of the Code is not an appropriate alternative to obtaining a ruling from the Executive.

A ruling can be challenged before the Hearings Committee, or the Executive may refer a matter for decision by the Hearings Committee without itself giving a ruling if it considers that the matter involves a particularly unusual, important or difficult point. A challenge to a ruling must be instigated as soon as possible. The Executive may stipulate what is a reasonable time within which a challenge must be made, which will not usually be longer than one month and may, depending on the circumstances, be just a few hours. The Hearings Committee is a committee of the Panel. Proceedings are informal and are usually in private.

A further appeal is possible to the Takeover Appeal Board, which is an independent body with a chairman and deputy chairman appointed by the Master of the Rolls.

Subject to any appeal, an unconditional ruling by the Panel Executive has binding effect (CA 2006, s 945).

8.7.1.6 Power to require documents and information

The Panel on Takeovers and Mergers has a power under CA 2006, s 947, to require a person to produce specified documents or information reasonably required in connection with the Panel's exercise of its functions. Documents or information subject to legal professional privilege need not be disclosed (s 947(10)). A statement made by a person in response to a requirement under s 947 cannot be used against that person in criminal proceedings other than for perjury (s 962). Disclosure of documents or information obtained by the Panel under s 947 is permitted by s 948 and sch 2 for the purpose of cooperation with other regulatory authorities in much the same way as information obtained in inspection or investigation of companies (see **18.8.5.2**).

8.7.1.7 Enforcement

The Panel on Takeovers and Mergers (but no one else) may apply to the court under CA 2006, s 955, for an order to secure compliance with a 'rule-based requirement', that is, a requirement imposed by or under the City Code (s 943(9)), or a requirement under s 947 to disclose documents or information (see **8.7.1.6**). The Panel may take part in legal proceedings in its own name despite being unincorporated (s 960). The court may make such order as it thinks fit if it is satisfied that there is a reasonable likelihood that a person will contravene a rule-based requirement or if satisfied that a rule-based requirement or a disclosure requirement has been contravened. Alternatively, the Panel itself may give directions (s 946). Contravention of a rule-based requirement does not in itself make any transaction void or unenforceable or affect the validity of any other thing (s 956(2)) and cannot be the subject of a claim for breach of statutory duty (s 956(1)).

The Panel Executive may institute disciplinary proceedings before the Hearings Committee (see **8.7.1.5**) when it considers that there has been a breach of the Code or of a ruling. The Hearings Committee may (Code, Introduction, s 11(b)):

(a) issue a private statement of censure; or

(b) issue a public statement of censure; or

(c) suspend, withdraw or impose conditions on any exemption, approval or other special status which the Panel has granted to a person; or

(d) report the offender's conduct to a regulatory authority or professional body; or

(e) publish a Panel statement indicating that the offender is someone who, in the Hearings Committee's opinion, is not likely to comply with the Code. Firms in the securities industry may be prohibited from dealing with or employing a person against whom such a finding has been stated (this is known as 'cold-shouldering').

If certain rules are breached, the Panel may require payment, to the holders, or former holders, of the offeree's securities, of an amount to ensure they receive what they would have been entitled to receive had the rule been complied with (Code, Introduction, s 10(c)).

There is a right of appeal from the Hearings Committee to the Takeover Appeal Board (see **8.7.1.5**).

8.7.1.8 Judicial review

Decisions of the Panel on Takeovers and Mergers are subject to judicial review, though the court is aware that it is important for the Panel to give firm decisions quickly and may exercise discretion to give declarations of the meaning of provisions of the Code for future guidance rather than reverse past decisions of the Panel (*R v Panel on Takeovers and Mergers, ex parte Datafin plc* [1987] QB 815; *R v Panel on Takeovers and Mergers, ex parte Guinness plc* [1990] 1 QB 146).

8.7.1.9 Mandatory offer

The City Code on Takeovers and Mergers recognises that a company may be controlled by the holders of less than 50 per cent of its voting rights because the fact that shares are dispersed among a large number of holders means that most members do not act in coordinated groups with agreed policies and voting strategies.

When a person holds 30 per cent of the voting rights in a public company other shareholders will find that they are effectively in a minority and may feel that their interest in the company has been devalued. The City Code therefore requires that a person who gains 30 per cent control must make a takeover bid for all of the voting shares. This is known as a mandatory offer (rule 9.1). The price that has to be offered in a mandatory offer is the highest price at which the offeror (or persons acting in concert with it) has dealt in the offeree company's shares in the 12 months preceding the announcement of the mandatory offer (rule 9.5). This rule is intended to prevent an offeror obtaining a controlling interest at a premium price from a few large shareholders and then later buying out all the small shareholders cheaply.

In any takeover bid, if the holders of 90 per cent of the shares which are the subject of the bid accept it then the offeror may compulsorily acquire the remainder under CA 2006, ss 974 to 991 (see **8.7.2**).

8.7.2 SQUEEZE-OUT AND SELL-OUT

8.7.2.1 Purpose and scope of the legislation

Sections 974 to 991 of CA 2006 provide a procedure by which a takeover bidder whose bid is almost completely successful (90 per cent) can acquire the remaining shares compulsorily (a squeeze-out), subject to a right given to the minority to apply to the court to set fairer terms than the bidder is offering. It also provides a procedure by which a minority left after a 90 per cent successful takeover bid can force the bidder to buy them out (a sell-out).

Speaking of an earlier version of these provisions, in **Re Greythorn Ltd** [2002] 1 BCLC 437, the learned deputy judge said, at pp 447–8:

> The purpose of the provisions . . . is to strike a fair balance between the interests of a bidder whose takeover offer has been sufficient to enable it to obtain acceptances from 90 per cent or more of the shares to which the offer relates and the interests of the minority who have refused the offer.
>
> The bidder's interest is to ensure that its takeover objectives are not undermined by a small minority or because some shareholders cannot be traced. On the other hand a dissenting shareholder is concerned to ensure that he is not compelled to accept terms that are objectively unfair. Similarly, shareholders who cannot be traced should be entitled to be treated fairly. Further, the dissenting shareholder may face an invidious choice between being isolated in a company controlled by a dominant shareholder whose objective has been partially thwarted and being compelled to sell at a price that may be less than fair.

In *Bramelid v Sweden* (applications 8588 and 8589/79) (1982) 5 EHRR 249, similar provisions of Swedish law were found not to offend the European Convention on Human Rights, protocol 1, art 1 (protection of property), which is incorporated in UK law in the Human Rights Act 1998, sch 1.

There is no general principle of EU law that a dominant shareholder must offer to buy a minority's shares on the same terms that applied when it acquired or strengthened its control (*Audiolux SA v Groupe Bruxelles Lambert SA* (case C-101/08) [2010] Bus LR 197).

8.7.2.2 Meaning of 'takeover offer'

The squeeze-out and sell-out provisions of CA 2006, ss 974 to 991, can be invoked only where there is a 'takeover offer' as defined in s 974. This is an offer to acquire all the shares, or all the shares of any class or classes, in a company, which have been allotted on the date of the offer and which are not already held by the offeror, with the same terms being offered for all shares (or all shares of the same class), apart from allowable variations which are described later.

The date of the offer is defined in s 991(1) as the date of publication, or where any notices are given before the date of publication, the date when notices of the offer (or the first such notices) are given. If the terms of the offer make provision for their revision, and for acceptances on the previous terms to be treated on the revised terms, then a revision of the offer is not a fresh offer and the date of the offer is not changed (s 974(7)).

The squeeze-out right cannot be exercised until the bid is 90 per cent successful. When calculating this percentage for squeeze-out (but not for sell-out), the following shares are not counted as being shares to which the offer relates:

(a) Shares already held by the offeror at the date of the offer, including shares the offeror has contracted to buy (whether conditionally or unconditionally), apart from shares subject to so-called 'irrevocable undertakings', that is a promise to sell to the offeror, for which no consideration is given and which is only enforceable by virtue of being under seal or for which the only consideration is a promise by the offeror to make the takeover offer (s 975(1) to (3)).

(b) Shares already held by 'associates' of the offeror (see **8.7.2.10**) at the date of the offer (including shares that associates have contracted to acquire, conditionally or unconditionally) (s 975(4)).

(c) 'Relevant treasury shares' (s 974(4)), which means (s 974(6)) shares held by the company as treasury shares on the date of the offer and shares which become held as treasury shares after the date of the offer but before a date specified in, or determined in accordance with, the terms of the offer.

So a person who has built up a holding of 30 per cent of a company's shares and then makes a takeover offer is only counted as offering for the remaining 70 per cent (assuming there are no treasury shares). The bid will be 90 per cent successful when it has been accepted by the owners of 63 per cent of the total number of shares (90 per cent of 70 per cent). At that point the offeror will have 93 per cent of the total and there will only be a 7 per cent minority to which the squeeze-out right will apply. This means that any person with a block of more than 7 per cent can prevent the threshold for squeeze-out ever being reached and can hold out for a higher price than has been offered to other shareholders (this is known as greenmail). Knowing about the existence of small but crucial blocks such as this can be very important in judging the potential success of a takeover bid.

The sell-out right arises when the offeror has acquired a total of 90 per cent of all the shares (or all of a particular class) (see **8.7.2.5**).

An offeror may, by s 974(5), choose to extend the offer to:

(a) all or any shares that are allotted after the date of the offer but before a specified date;

(b) all or any relevant treasury shares that cease to be held as treasury shares before a specified date; and

(c) all or any other relevant treasury shares.

The terms of the offer must be the same in relation to all the shares to which the offer relates (or the same for all shares of the same class where different classes are being bid for) (s 974(3)). This requires the primary contractual terms of the offer (such as the consideration) to be the same in relation to all the shares being bid for (or the same for all shares of the same class where different classes are being bid for), but provisions concerning the mechanics of the offer and how to accept it need not be uniform (*Re Joseph Holt plc* [2001] EWCA Civ 770, [2001] 2 BCLC 604). Provision is made in s 976(1) and (3) for an offer to include variations to ensure that it will not contravene the laws of jurisdictions outside the United Kingdom. For the way this provision operates in practice, see *Re Joseph Holt plc*. Further provision is made to allow a takeover offer to contain the following differences of treatment for different shareholders:

(a) Different consideration may be offered for shares of the same class only to reflect the fact that they have different entitlements to dividend, because of being allotted at different times (s 976(1) and (2)).

(b) The offer may not be sent to some shareholders, because they have no registered address in the United Kingdom and sending an offer would contravene the law of a jurisdiction outside the United Kingdom, but the offer must either be published in the *Gazette* or be available for inspection at a place in an EEA State or on a website whose address is notified in the *Gazette* (s 978(1)).

(c) It may be an offer which for some shareholders is more difficult or impossible to accept, because of the law of a jurisdiction outside the United Kingdom (s 978(2)).

A person who invites shareholders to offer their shares for purchase is not making a takeover offer as defined in s 974 (*Re Chez Nico (Restaurants) Ltd* [1992] BCLC 192).

8.7.2.3 Conditions for compulsory acquisition (squeeze-out)

The squeeze-out procedure in CA 2006, ss 974 to 991, is available to an offeror who has acquired, or unconditionally contracted to acquire, by virtue of acceptances of the offer, 90 per cent or more (in value) of the shares to which the offer relates and (unless they have no voting rights) 90 per cent or more of the voting rights carried by the shares to which the offer relates (s 979(1) and (2)). If an offer is for more than one class, the threshold can be achieved, and the squeeze-out rights can be exercised, for each class separately (s 979(3) and (4)). When the 90 per cent threshold is reached the offeror can acquire compulsorily the remaining shares (or the remaining shares of the particular class if the limit is reached only in relation to one class). The shares which may be compulsorily purchased include shares for which the offeror has a contract to acquire which is still conditional (s 979(2) and (4)), and those shares are not treated as shares of which there could be an acquisition by virtue of acceptance of the offer (s 979(6) and (7): the purpose of this latter provision is obscure, to say the least). There is no time limit for reaching the 90 per cent threshold, but the squeeze-out process must be started within three months after the last day on which the offer can be accepted (s 980(2); see **8.7.2.4**).

The 90 per cent acceptance limit is 90 per cent of the shares that are the subject of the offer, which excludes shares held or contracted for by the offeror or the offeror's associates at the time of the offer, as described in **8.7.2.2**. It also excludes any shares which the offeror, or any associate, acquires or contracts to acquire during the period within which the takeover offer can be accepted but otherwise than by virtue of acceptances of the offer and at a price exceeding the offer price (or the highest offer price if it is revised) (s 979(8), (9) and (10)). However, shares acquired (or contracted for) otherwise than by virtue of acceptances of the offer at a price less than or equal to the offer price (or the highest offer price if it is revised) can be counted as acquired or contracted for by virtue of the offer.

If the 90 per cent limit cannot be reached because the offeror has been unable, after reasonable inquiry, to trace one or more of the persons holding shares to which the offer relates, and the 90 per cent limit would be reached if such holders accepted it, then the court may authorise the offeror to carry out the squeeze-out procedure if it is satisfied that the consideration offered is fair and reasonable (s 986(9)). However, the court must not make an order under this provision unless it considers that it is just and equitable to do so having regard, in particular, to the number of share-holders who have been traced but who have not accepted the offer (s 986(10)).

In *Rock Nominees Ltd v RCO (Holdings) plc* [2004] EWCA Civ 118, [2004] 1 BCLC 439, two companies with which Lord Ashcroft was associated, Rock Nominees Ltd, which was the peti-tioner in this case, and Rapid Reef Ltd, which took no part in the litigation, held a small number of shares in RCO (Holdings) plc (RCO), sufficient to prevent an otherwise successful takeover offer of £2.80 per share for RCO passing the 90 per cent threshold. It seemed that Lord Ashcroft would hold out for a high price to be paid by the takeover bidder for these shares so as to reach the threshold (greenmail). The new board of RCO sold its operating companies to the takeover bidder at a price which reflected the price of £2.80 paid for its shares in the takeover bid, and RCO was then put into voluntary winding up (see **20.5**). In the winding up, Rock Nominees Ltd, like all other shareholders (including the takeover bidder), would receive its proportionate share of the proceeds of sale of the operating companies and other assets of RCO, which turned out to be about £3.18 per share. Rock Nominees Ltd claimed under s 994 (see **18.6**) that this was conduct of the company's affairs which was unfairly prejudicial to it. It was held that the sale of the operating companies was at a proper price and was not unfairly prejudicial.

8.7.2.4 Procedure for compulsory acquisition

A notice must be given in the prescribed manner by the offeror to each shareholder whose shares are to be compulsorily acquired and a copy must be given to the company together with a statutory declaration that the conditions for giving the notice are satisfied (CA 2006, s 980). The notice must be given before the end of the period of three months beginning with the day after the last day on which the offer can be accepted (s 980(2)).

The offeror is bound to acquire the shares on the terms of the offer (s 981(2)), subject to any court order made under s 986(1) (see later).

At the end of six weeks from the date of the notice the offeror must send a copy of it to the company, pay or transfer to the company the consideration for the shares and, if the shares are not uncertificated, provide an instrument of transfer of the shares executed by a person appointed by the offeror (or a statement that the shares are transferable by delivery) (s 981(6), (7) and (8); SI 2001/3755, reg 42). The company must then register the offeror as the holder of the shares (CA 2006, s 981(7) and (8)). If the shares are uncertificated, the procedure in SI 2001/3755, reg 42, must be followed.

Consideration received by the company is held by it on trust for the former holder of the shares acquired and monetary consideration must be paid into a separate interest-bearing bank account (ss 981(9) and 982(1) to (3)). The company should make reasonable inquiries at reasonable inter-vals to locate the person to whom the money is due (s 982(5)(a); the cost comes out of the money held in trust: s 982(9)) but if the person is not located after 12 years, the money must be paid into court (s 982(4)).

A shareholder who is given a squeeze-out notice may challenge it under s 986(1) by applying to the court, within six weeks after the notice was given (s 986(2)). On such an application the court may:

(a) order that the offeror shall not be entitled and bound to acquire the shares; or

(b) specify terms of acquisition different from those of the offer.

When specifying terms of acquisition, the court must not specify a consideration which is less than the offer price, and must not specify a higher consideration unless the holder of the shares shows that the offer price would be unfair (s 986(4)).

The offeror cannot carry out the transfer procedure until such an application is disposed of, and cannot withdraw the squeeze-out notice so as to end the application to the court (*Re Greythorn Ltd* [2002] 1 BCLC 437).

The onus is on the applicant to convince the court that it should interfere, and, in the absence of special circumstances, it must be shown that, despite acceptance by 90 per cent of the shareholders, the offer is unfair (*Re Hoare and Co Ltd* (1933) 150 LT 374; *Re Press Caps Ltd* [1949] Ch 434; *Nidditch v Calico Printers' Association Ltd* 1961 SLT 282). The test is of fairness to the body of shareholders, not the individual applicant (*Re Grierson, Oldham and Adams Ltd* [1968] Ch 17). It is not enough that the offer is open to criticism and could be improved; it must be 'obviously unfair, patently unfair, unfair to the meanest intelligence' (**Re Sussex Brick Co Ltd** [1961] Ch 289 per Vaisey J at p 292), though this has been described as a 'rather enthusiastic statement of what is required' (**Re Deans** [1986] 2 NZLR 271 per Hardie Boys J; His Honour went on to say that he was sure the applicant did not have to show the majority were morons).

One special circumstance in which acceptance by 90 per cent of shareholders will carry little weight is where insufficient information was given about the offer to enable shareholders to evaluate it properly (*Fiske Nominees Ltd v Dwyka Diamond Ltd* [2002] EWHC 770 (Ch), [2002] 2 BCLC 123). The minimum amount of information required depends on the circumstances of the case, but the requirements of the City Code on Takeovers and Mergers are a starting point (*Re Chez Nico (Restaurants) Ltd* [1992] BCLC 192; *Fiske Nominees Ltd v Dwyka Diamond Ltd*). The board of an offeree company should have taken independent advice on the offer and communicated it to shareholders (*Fiske Nominees Ltd v Dwyka Diamond Ltd*). The fact that acceptances were based on misleading or erroneous advice will reduce the weight to be given to the fact that 90 per cent have accepted (*Re Lifecare International plc* [1990] BCLC 222).

The fact that 90 per cent of the shareholders have accepted the offer will carry little weight as evidence that the court should not stop the compulsory purchase if in fact there is a substantial identity of interest between the offeror and the shareholders who have accepted (*Re Bugle Press Ltd* [1961] Ch 270; *Esso Standard (Inter-America) Inc v JW Enterprises Inc* (1963) 37 DLR (2d) 598; *Fiske Nominees Ltd v Dwyka Diamond Ltd*). In most cases of substantial identity of interest, the accepting shareholders will be associates of the offeror and so their shares will not count in the calculation of the 90 per cent acceptance limit. This would have been the case had *Esso Standard (Inter-America) Inc v JW Enterprises Inc* been decided under the present UK legislation. In that case, the offeror was a wholly owned subsidiary of a company which owned 96.75 per cent of the shares being bid for; it was not permitted to compulsorily purchase the remaining shares, even though some independent shareholders had accepted the offer. (Under CA 2006, s 988(1)(b), a holding company of the offeror is an associate of it.) In *Re Bugle Press Ltd* the offeror was a company whose only members and directors were two individuals who held 90 per cent of the shares being bid for (they would not be associates of the offeror under the current legislation): the offeror was not permitted to compulsorily purchase the remaining shares.

The court may not make an order for costs against an unsuccessful applicant unless the court considers that the application was unnecessary, improper or vexatious; or that there has been unreasonable delay in making the application, or unreasonable conduct on the applicant's part in conducting proceedings on the application (s 986(5)). The only applications that this provision is intended to discourage are applications which 'ought not properly to engage the attention of the court' (*Re Britoil plc* [1990] BCC 70 at p 74). An application is not vexatious unless it is 'so obviously unsustainable or so impossible of success as to amount to an abuse of the process of the court' (*Re Britoil plc* at p 75).

If the taken-over company holds treasury shares and receives a squeeze-out notice to acquire them, it must not sell or transfer the shares to any person other than the offeror (s 727(4)).

8.7.2.5 Requirement by shareholder to be bought out (sell-out)

If, in a takeover offer, the total holdings of the offeror and the offeror's associates (including shares held at the date of the offer) reach 90 per cent (both of value and of voting rights, if any) of the total number of shares in the company (or the total of a class being bid for if there is more than one class) before the end of the period within which the offer can be accepted, then the offeror can be required to acquire the shares of a shareholder who has not accepted the offer (CA 2006, s 983(1) to (4) and (8)).

In calculating the 90 per cent threshold, shares acquired or unconditionally contracted to be acquired otherwise than by virtue of acceptances of the offer can be counted as acquired by the offeror, provided that at least one share has been acquired or unconditionally contracted for by virtue of acceptance (s 983(1) to (4) and (8)). Shares which are only conditionally contracted for when the offer closes can be counted as acquired by the offeror if the 90 per cent threshold is reached by acquired and unconditionally contracted-for shares before the last day for exercising the sell-out right (s 983(6) and (7)). Also, shares held as treasury shares can be treated as having been acquired by the offeror (s 983(5)).

The requisition must be made in a written communication addressed to the offeror (s 984(1)) but there is no prescribed form. The offeror is bound to acquire the shares on the terms of the offer or on such other terms as may be agreed (s 985(2)) but either the holder or the offeror may apply to the court to fix the terms of acquisition (s 986(3)). The limits imposed by s 986(4) on what consideration the court may order, described in **8.7.2.4**, apply. The limit on awards of costs in s 986(5), discussed in **8.7.2.4**, applies.

Within one month of reaching the 90 per cent threshold for the exercise of the sell-out right, the offeror must either issue a squeeze-out notice to every shareholder who has not accepted the offer or give notice in the prescribed manner of the right to sell out (s 984(3) and (4)). Failure to do so is an offence triable either way (s 984(5), (6) and (7)). If the offeror's notice is issued before the time for acceptance of the takeover offer has expired, the notice must state that fact (s 984(3)). Sell-out rights cannot be exercised more than three months after the date of the offeror's notice given under s 984(3), if that is later than the end of the period within which the offer could have been accepted (s 984(2)).

8.7.2.6 Choice of consideration

If squeeze-out or sell-out rights are invoked after a takeover offer the terms of which provided for a choice of consideration, then:

(a) A squeeze-out notice to a shareholder by the offeror must give the shareholder six weeks in which to make a choice in respect of his own shares and must state which consideration will be given in default of a choice being made (CA 2006, s 981(3)).

(b) A shareholder's sell-out notice may indicate his choice (s 985(3)(a)).

(c) A notice to a shareholder of sell-out rights must give particulars of the choice and must state that a holder may indicate his choice in a sell-out notice, and may state which consideration will be given in default of a choice being made (s 985(3)(b)).

(d) If a time limit or other conditions set in the offer for making a choice has expired, the rules stated in (a), (b) and (c) apply nevertheless (ss 981(4) and 985(4)).

(e) If the consideration chosen by a holder, either in response to a squeeze-out notice or on requiring sell-out, is not cash and the offeror is no longer able to provide it, or was to have been provided by another person who is no longer bound or able to provide it, then the shareholder must be paid a cash equivalent (ss 981(5) and 985(5)).

8.7.2.7 Joint offers

The way in which the squeeze-out and sell-out rights operate when a takeover offer is made by two or more persons jointly is set out in CA 2006, s 987.

8.7.2.8 Convertible securities

Securities of a company convertible into the company's shares are to be treated as 'shares' for the purposes of the squeeze-out and sell-out provisions (CA 2006, s 989(1)). However, convertibles must be treated as a separate class from the shares into which they may be converted (s 989(2)).

8.7.2.9 Debentures carrying voting rights

Debentures carrying voting rights are treated as shares (CA 2006, s 990), but they are ignored when calculating the 90 per cent threshold for the exercise of the sell-out right (s 983(2)(b) and (3)(b)).

8.7.2.10 Associates of the offeror

Who is an associate of an offeror for the purposes of the squeeze-out and sell-out provisions is defined in detail in CA 2006, s 988. Briefly, any of the following is an associate of the offeror:

(a) A nominee of the offeror.

(b) A company in the same group as the offeror or a nominee of a company in the same group.

(c) A corporation in which the offeror has (or can control the exercise of) one-third or more of the voting rights.

(d) A corporation which is (or whose directors are) accustomed to act in accordance with the offeror's directions or instructions.

(e) Any party to an agreement with the offeror to acquire the shares that are the subject matter of the takeover offer (or any nominee of such a party) if the agreement imposes obligations or restrictions on any one or more of the parties with respect to their use, retention or disposal of shares acquired.

8.7.3 OVERRIDING TAKEOVER BARRIERS

8.7.3.1 Opting-in and opting-out resolutions

CA 2006, s 966, gives a company the option of adopting a special resolution to invalidate, during a takeover bid, various restrictions on share transfers and voting which might frustrate the bid and which are contained in agreements made between the company and its shareholders or between shareholders. The restrictions to be invalidated are listed in s 968 (see **8.7.3.2**), which is derived from Directive 2004/25/EC, art 11. Article 12 of the Directive allows member States to let companies choose whether to invalidate these restrictions. A resolution to invalidate such restrictions is called an 'opting-in resolution' (s 966(1)). It cannot be adopted if the restrictions are contained in the company's articles (s 966(3)) or if a minister in the UK, Scottish or Northern Ireland government holds shares conferring special rights in the company (a 'golden share') (s 966(4) and (7)). An opting-in resolution has the effect of invalidating restrictions agreed by other parties only if it is adopted by a company which has voting shares admitted to trading on a regulated market (see **7.3.4.3**) at the time when the resolution becomes effective (ss 966(2) and 967(3)). An opting-in resolution must specify a date from which it is to have effect (s 967(1)), which cannot be earlier than the day it is adopted (s 967(2)) but can be specified as a day in the future when shares are admitted to trading (s 967(3) and (4)).

A company for which an opting-in resolution is in force is called an opted-in company.

An opting-in resolution can be revoked by a special resolution called an opting-out resolution (s 966(5)), which cannot have an effective date earlier than the first anniversary of the date on which the opting-in resolution was forwarded to Companies House under s 30 (s 967(6)).

An opting-in or opting-out resolution must, under penalty, be notified to the Panel on Takeovers and Mergers (s 970).

8.7.3.2 Agreements invalidated

Agreements are, by CA 2006, s 968, invalidated when a takeover bid is made for an opted-in company insofar as they place any restriction:

(a) on transfer to the offeror, or at the offeror's direction to another person, of shares in the company during the offer period;

(b) on the transfer to any person of shares in the company at a time during the offer period when the offeror holds 75 per cent or more (in value) of all the voting shares in the company;

(c) on rights to vote at a general meeting of the company that decides whether to take any action which might result in the frustration of the bid;

(d) on rights to vote at a general meeting of the company that

(i) is the first such meeting to be held after the end of the offer period, and

(ii) is held at a time when the offeror holds shares amounting to 75 per cent or more (in value) of all the voting shares in the company.

This applies to any agreement entered into between the company and any of its shareholders and also to any agreement between shareholders entered into on or after 21 April 2004 (the day that Directive 2004/25/EC was made) (CA 2006, s 968(3)).

8.7.3.3 Compensation

The fact that an agreement is invalidated by an opt-in resolution does not affect liability for what would otherwise be a breach of the agreement (Directive 2004/25/EC, art 11(5); CA 2006, s 968(6)). A person who suffers loss by what would otherwise be a breach of an invalidated agreement is entitled to such compensation as the court considers just and equitable (s 968(6)).

8.7.3.4 Offeror's power to requisition meeting

An offeror in a takeover bid for an opted-in company who has acquired 75 per cent or more (in value) of all the voting shares has the right to requisition a general meeting of the target company under CA 2006, ss 303 to 305, as modified by s 969.

8.7.4 TAKEOVERS BY SHARE EXCHANGE

There are two methods of effecting a takeover by share exchange between companies A and B:

(a) The members of company B contribute to company A their shares in company B as assets in exchange for an allotment of A's shares. The result is that the members of B become members of A, and A not only owns its own business but also has B as a subsidiary. Neither A nor B is dissolved in this method. The members of A must approve an allotment of shares in their company (see **6.3.4**). However, the members of B do not have to meet to approve the merger because it necessarily involves the individual consent of each member to the exchange of his particular shares. If in fact the holders of 90 per cent of the shares in B accept the share exchange, the remainder may be compulsorily acquired by A under CA 2006, s 979 (see **8.7.2**). One possible problem is that the objects of B must be within the objects of A, otherwise A's long-term ownership of B will be *ultra vires* (*Joint Stock Discount Co v Brown* (1866) LR 3 Eq 139) unless holding shares is itself an object of A (*Re Barned's Banking Co, ex parte Contract Corporation* (1867) LR 3 Ch App 105).

(b) The members of B may agree to surrender their shares in B and for those shares to be cancelled. As compensation they will receive shares allotted by A. Meanwhile the reserve created by the cancellation of B's shares is used to pay up a capitalisation issue of shares which are all allotted to A. The result is the same as in method (b) but there may be a considerable saving in SDRT and/or stamp duty because there are no transfers of shares to A. The surrender and cancellation of shares in B is a reduction of capital which must be carried out under CA 2006, s 641 (see **10.7**). The whole scheme is an arrangement between B and its members which may be put through under the part 26 procedure. The advantage of the part 26 procedure is that it requires the approval of only the shareholders of B who attend (in person or by proxy) a meeting, and the majority at the meeting need hold only 75 per cent of the shares represented at the meeting (though shares already belonging to A cannot be counted—see *Re Hellenic and General Trust Ltd* [1976] 1 WLR 123). This contrasts with the 90 per cent approval needed before a compulsory purchase scheme may be put through under s 979. However, part 26 may only be used if the board of B approve the scheme (*Re Savoy Hotel Ltd* [1981] Ch 351) and the scheme may not be put into effect until it is approved by the court whereas a compulsory acquisition under s 979 goes ahead unless a successful application is made to the court to stop it under s 986(1). Therefore, in *Re National Bank Ltd* [1966] 1 WLR 819, Plowman J was prepared to sanction a part 26 takeover scheme which he was satisfied was fair despite the objection of the holders of just over 5 per cent of the shares of the company being taken over, whereas in *Re Hellenic and General Trust Ltd* Templeman J exercised his discretion the other way and refused to sanction a scheme objected to by the holders of 13.95 per cent of shares in the company being taken over.

8.7.5 TAKEOVER INDUCED BY MISREPRESENTATION

The law on liability for misrepresentation, which is discussed in **6.8** in relation to misrepresentation by a company to subscribers for its shares, also applies to misrepresentations by vendors of shares to their purchasers.

In *MAN Nutzfahrzeuge AG v Freightliner Ltd* [2007] EWCA Civ 910, [2007] 2 CLC 455, the claimant bought all the shares in ERF (Holdings) plc from its parent company, Western Star Trucks Holdings Ltd. When negotiating the sale, the directors of Western Star asked ERF's financial controller, Mr Ellis, to attend meetings with the purchasers to provide information about ERF's financial position. It was held that Mr Ellis acted as Western Star's agent in giving this information and that Western Star, as his principal, was vicariously liable for wrongs committed by him in the course of giving that information (see **19.7**). The directors of Western Star were unaware that Mr Ellis had been falsifying the accounts of ERF for several years, to disguise its losses and keep it in business. In not revealing this to the purchaser, he had fraudulently misrepresented the value of the shares and Western Star was held to be vicariously liable for the deceit.

ERF's auditor admitted negligence in not detecting Mr Ellis's false accounting, but it was held that the auditor had not assumed responsibility for Mr Ellis's misrepresentation that the accounts gave a true and fair view when he knew that he had falsified them, so the auditor was not liable to Western Star.

For claims by disappointed takeover bidders against the auditor of the company taken over see **17.5.2** to **17.5.4**.

8.8 PUBLIC COMPANY'S INQUIRY INTO SHARE OWNERSHIP

8.8.1 NEED TO IDENTIFY OWNERS OF SHARES

A company's register of members may not reveal the true identity of its shareholders. If a share is held by a nominee of the beneficial owner, the company is forbidden to state the name of the beneficial owner in the register (CA 2006, s 126; see **8.6.1**). One beneficial owner of shares can have them registered in the names of several nominees to disguise the fact that a substantial block of shares is controlled by one person. Substantial blocks are important. They can be used to prevent important resolutions (especially special resolutions) being adopted at general meetings. They can be a platform for a takeover bid, or can prevent another bid succeeding.

The directors of a private company are usually able to inquire into a new shareholder's identity when considering whether to register a transfer of shares. A public company which has any kind of public trading in its shares, whether or not on a regulated market, will have to accept all transfers of shares. It may need to know who nominee shareholders are acting for, especially where there is a suspicion that one person is building up a substantial holding.

CA 2006, part 22 (ss 791 to 828), which applies to public companies only (s 791), enables a company to inquire into the true ownership of its shares.

8.8.2 COMPANY'S NOTICE REQUIRING INFORMATION

If a public company has reasonable cause to believe that a person is interested in the company's shares, it may serve a notice on that person requiring the person to confirm that fact (CA 2006, s 793(1) and (2)). As well as present interests the company can inquire about interests held in the three years preceding the date on which the notice is issued. The notice can ask for particulars of the person's interest (s 793(3)). It can also ask for particulars of any other interest subsisting in the shares at the same time (s 793(4)), including the identity of persons interested (s 793(5)(a)).

The shares which a public company may inquire about are the company's issued shares of a class carrying rights to vote in all circumstances at general meetings, including shares held as treasury shares (s 792).

The term 'interest in shares' is given a very wide meaning by s 820, and the term is extended so that:

(a) A right to subscribe for shares counts as an interest in shares (s 821).

(b) An individual on whom a notice is served must report the interests of his or her spouse, civil partner, and infant children and stepchildren (s 822).

(c) A person is interested in shares if a company which the person controls is interested in them (s 823). There is control for this purpose if the person is a shadow director of the company or is entitled to exercise, or control the exercise, of one-third or more of the voting power at general meetings.

According to s 820(2)(a), 'a reference to an interest in shares includes an interest of any kind whatsoever in the shares'. It might be thought that nothing more need be said, but s 820 adds several more rules. Some of them are:

(a) Restraints or restrictions on the exercise of any right attached to an interest do not prevent it being an interest (s 820(2)(b)).

(b) If an interest in shares is held on trust, a beneficiary of the trust is interested in the shares (s 820(3)).

(c) A person who has made a contract to purchase shares has an interest in them (s 820(4)(a)), whether they are identified or not (s 820(8)).

(d) A person who has an option to purchase shares, or an interest in shares, has an interest in them (s 820(6)).

(e) A person who is not registered as the holder of shares but is entitled to exercise any right conferred by holding them or to control the exercise of any such right has an interest in them (s 820(4)(b)). Thus a person whose shares are held by another as nominee is interested in those shares.

(f) If an interest is held jointly, it must be counted as an interest of each of the joint holders (s 820(7)).

Special provision is made in ss 824 and 825 for agreements between two or more persons for the acquisition of shares in a particular company (the 'target company'). Persons who agree to cooperate to obtain or consolidate control of a company (or to frustrate another takeover bid) are known as 'persons acting in concert' or 'concert parties' in the City Code. If an agreement imposes obligations or restrictions on any one or more of the parties to it with respect to their use, retention or disposal of their interests in the shares of the target company acquired in pursuance of the agreement and an interest in the target company's shares is in fact acquired by any of the parties in pursuance of the agreement, then s 824 applies to the agreement. This means that each party to the agreement is interested in shares acquired by other parties under the agreement (s 824(1)) and is also treated as interested in all shares in the target company in which any other party is interested apart from the agreement (s 825(1)). A party to a share acquisition agreement who receives a s 793 notice from the target company must state the fact of being a party to the agreement, give the names and addresses of the other parties, and state how many shares he is deemed to have interests in by ss 824 and 825 (s 825(4)). A s 793 notice given to a person can ask whether other persons interested in shares in which that person is or has been interested are or were parties to a share acquisition agreement within s 824 (s 793(5)(b)(i)). It can also ask whether other interested persons are or were parties to an agreement or arrangement relating to the exercise of any rights conferred by holding the shares, for example, a voting agreement (s 793(5)(b)(ii)).

A company is empowered by s 793 to address notices to persons domiciled abroad who have no connection with the United Kingdom (*Re F H Lloyd Holdings plc* [1985] BCLC 293).

A s 793 notice must specify a 'reasonable time' within which a reply must be given. In the case of a person in the United Kingdom dealing in a listed company's shares on a large scale, it would be reasonable to require a reply within one working day, but foreigners must be given a further time to ask English solicitors to advise on what information must be provided: two clear working days is the longest period that need be allowed in all but very exceptional circumstances (*Re Lonrho plc (No 2)* [1989] BCLC 309, which includes an interesting description of the way in which a large company uses s 793).

A person may be exempted by the Secretary of State from having to reply to notices under s 793 but the Secretary of State must be satisfied that there are special reasons why the person should not be subject to the obligations imposed by s 793 and must consult with the Governor of the Bank of England (s 796).

A person who fails to comply with a s 793 notice, and who is not exempt from replying, is guilty of an offence triable either way (s 795) though it is a defence to prove that the requirement to give the information was frivolous or vexatious (s 795(2)).

8.8.3 REGISTER OF INTERESTS DISCLOSED

A company must, by CA 2006, s 808, keep a register of information received by it in response to any notice issued under s 793 (see **8.8.2**). The register must be available for inspection (s 809;

see **4.4**). Entries must be kept for at least six years (ss 815 and 816), even if the company ceases to be a public company (s 819). Information received must be entered in the register within three days of receipt (s 808(2)). Entry of information in the register does not constitute notice to the company of any person's rights in relation to shares (s 808(7)). The company is not entitled to add comments or information derived from sources other than a response to a s 793 notice (*Re TR Technology Investment Trust plc* [1988] BCLC 256). If the information includes the name and address of another person as being interested in shares, that other person may apply to have the entry removed (s 817(1) and (2)) and the company must remove it if satisfied that it was made in pursuance of incorrect information (s 817(3)). If the company refuses to remove the entry, the person may apply to the court for an order directing removal of the entry, and the court may make such an order if it thinks fit (s 817(4)).

8.8.4 MEMBERS' REQUISITION OF INVESTIGATION OF SHARE OWNERSHIP

The holders of shares representing 10 per cent or more of the amount paid up on shares (excluding treasury shares; see **10.6.6**) carrying a right to vote at general meetings of a public company may, under CA 2006, s 803, requisition it to exercise its powers under s 793 (see **8.8.2**). The requisition must specify the manner in which the powers are to be exercised and give reasonable grounds for requiring the company to exercise its powers in that manner (s 803(3)).

On deposit of a requisition complying with s 803 the company must exercise its powers under s 793 as required and if it does not then the company and every officer of the company in default is guilty of an offence triable either way (s 804).

On the conclusion of investigations made in response to a requisition, the company must prepare a report, which must be made available for inspection within a reasonable period (not more than 15 days) after the conclusion of that investigation (s 805(1)). Within three days of making a report available at the registered office, the company must inform the requisitionists of its availability (s 805(6)). A report must be kept for six years and be available for inspection (ss 805(4) and 807).

Alternatively, 200 or more members of a company, or members holding 10 per cent or more of the company's issued shares, may, under CA 1985, s 442(3), ask the Secretary of State to investigate ownership and control of the company—see **18.8.3.2**.

8.8.5 FREEZING ORDERS

If a company has served a notice on a person under CA 2006, s 793, and that person has failed to give the company any information required by the notice then the company may apply to the court for an order (a 'freezing order') imposing restrictions on the shares in question (s 794(1)). A person fails to give information if he does not, so far as lies within his knowledge, give a full and truthful answer to the question (*Re TR Technology Investment Trust plc* [1988] BCLC 256).

If restrictions are imposed on a share then the share may not be transferred, the votes attached to it may not be exercised, no dividend may be paid on it, there can be no return of capital unless the company is wound up and no pre-emptive subscription rights may be exercised (s 797).

If shares are subject to a freezing order, an application may be made to the court under s 800(1) to lift the restrictions. An application to disapply restrictions will be granted only if (s 800(3)):

(a) the relevant facts about the shares have been disclosed to the company and no unfair advantage has accrued to any person as a result of the earlier failure to make that disclosure; or

(b) the shares are to be transferred for valuable consideration and the court approves the transfer.

The wording of this provision does not mean that the shareholder can choose either to disclose facts or sell the shares; the court will normally not permit a sale if the company requires information and it has not been given (*Re Geers Gross plc* [1987] 1 WLR 1649) whether that information relates to the frozen shares or to other shares (*Re Lonrho plc* [1988] BCLC 53). On the other hand, a freezing order is imposed as a sanction to compel the provision of information to which the company is entitled and once the information is supplied there is no justification for continuing the sanction (*Re Ricardo Group plc* [1989] BCLC 566, in which Millett J reviewed in detail the procedure for making orders without notice).

It is not sufficient that information can be obtained from other sources because such information cannot be entered on the register of interests disclosed (*Re TR Technology Investment Trust plc*).

Restrictions may be imposed in respect of the interests of any person, even a person domiciled outside the United Kingdom having no connection with the United Kingdom (*Re F H Lloyd Holdings plc* [1985] BCLC 293). Restrictions may be imposed on shares that the holder has contracted to sell, and the buyer cannot then be registered as the new holder (*Re Geers Gross plc*).

It seems that many public companies provide in their articles of association that the directors can impose restrictions comparable to freezing orders without having to apply to the court. In *Eclairs Group Ltd v JKX Oil and Gas plc* [2015] UKSC 71, [2015] Bus LR 1395, it was found that directors had misused such a power for the purpose of influencing the outcome of resolutions at a general meeting. This was held to be an improper purpose, contrary to CA 2006, s 171(b) (see **16.5**).

For more details see D Milman and D Singh, 'The evolution of the freezing order in UK company law' (1992) 13 Co Law 51.

8.9 NOTIFICATION OF MAJOR SHAREHOLDINGS

If shares are traded on a regulated market (see **7.3.4.3**) or a prescribed market (see **7.3.4.7**), persons with interests in them are obliged to notify those interests, if they are substantial, to the company that issued the shares and, if the shares are traded on a regulated market, to the FCA. This requirement is imposed by rules in the FCA Handbook, DTR 5. The rules implement Directive 2004/109/EC (the Transparency Directive), arts 9 to 16.

The shares that are covered by DTR 5 are shares which carry rights to vote at general meetings in all circumstances (DTR 5.1.1R(3)). An interest is substantial and has to be notified if it is in 3 per cent or more of the issuer's voting rights (DTR 5.1.2R). Once a person has notified a substantial interest, every change in that interest must be notified when the percentage of voting rights reaches or crosses every 1 per cent threshold up to 100 per cent, going up or down (DTR 5.1.2R). This continues the requirements previously made by CA 1985 even though they are more stringent than the Directive, which has thresholds only at 5, 10, 15, 20, 25, 30, 50 and 75 per cent.

Notification of changes in a major shareholding in a company must be made, within two trading days (DTR 5.8.3R), to the company (DTR 5.1.2R) and, if the shares are admitted to trading on a regulated market, to the FCA (DTR 5.9.1R). Companies are not required to maintain a register of notifications.

8.10 PEOPLE WITH SIGNIFICANT CONTROL

8.10.1 INTRODUCTION

Companies must keep a register of people with significant control, known as a PSC register (CA 2006, ss 790A to 790ZG, sch 1A, and sch 1B; SI 2016/339), unless they are subject to similar disclosure requirements because their shares are traded. The government has said that:

This reform will increase transparency around who ultimately owns and controls UK companies. It will help deter, identify and sanction those who hide their interest in UK companies to facilitate illegal activities. Enhanced transparency will also promote good corporate behaviour. (Department for Business, Innovation and Skills, *Small Business, Enterprise and Employment Act: Companies: Transparency Fact Sheet*).

The companies that are exempt from keeping a PSC register, because they are already subject to similar disclosure requirements, are:

(a) any company which is subject to the DTR 5 requirements for notification of major share-holdings (CA 2006, s 790B(1)(a); see **8.9**);

(b) any company which has voting shares admitted to trading on a regulated market (see 7.3.4.3) in an EEA State other than the United Kingdom (s 790B(1)(b); SI 2016/339, reg 3(a)); and

(c) any company which has voting shares admitted to trading on a market listed in SI 2016/339, sch 1 (CA 2006, s 790B(1)(b); SI 2016/339, reg 3(b)).

8.10.2 SIGNIFICANT CONTROL

'Significant control' of a company means:

(a) holding, directly or indirectly, more than 25 per cent of the company's shares (CA 2006, sch 1A, para 2);

(b) holding, directly or indirectly, more than 25 per cent of the company's voting rights (sch 1A, para 3);

(c) holding the right, directly or indirectly, to appoint or remove a majority of the board of directors of the company (sch 1A, para 4);

(d) having the right to exercise, or actually exercising, significant influence or control over the company (sch 1A, para 5); and

(e) having the right to exercise, or actually exercising, significant influence or control over the activities of a trust whose trustees, or a firm whose members, meet any of conditions (a) to (d), or would do so if they were individuals (sch 1A, para 6).

An individual has significant control over a company if he or she meets at least one of conditions (a) to (e) (sch 1A, para 1). There are supplementary provisions in paras 10 to 25.

8.10.3 REGISTERING INDIRECT CONTROL

The purpose of a company's PSC register is to identify individuals who have significant control over the company. Very often such control is exercised indirectly, through one or more other companies. So as to avoid duplicating information in many registers, the scheme of the legislation is that if all the intermediary companies are themselves required to keep PSC registers or are subject to similar disclosure requirements then the individual is only registered (or reported under DTR 5) in the company in which he or she has a direct interest. Each other company registers only the company which is directly interested in it. Someone searching the register of the company at the bottom of the chain will have to follow up the references to each other company in the chain in order to find the individual who is the ultimate controller.

A company (or other entity with legal personality) is a 'relevant legal entity' (RLE) for a company preparing a PSC register if it would have come within the definition of a person with significant control over the company if it had been an individual, and it is subject to its own disclosure requirements (s 790C(5) to (7); SI 2016/339, reg 4). If an RLE does not hold any interest in the company preparing the PSC register except through one or more other legal entities over each of which it has significant control and each of which is also an RLE in relation to the company, it is non-registrable (s 790C(8)). Otherwise it is registrable (s 790C(8)) and its required particulars must be noted in the register once the company becomes aware of the entity's status as such (s 790M(5)).

Similarly, an individual who has significant control over a company is non-registrable (s 790C(4)) and must not be entered in the company's PSC register (s 790M(4)) if he or she does not hold any interest in the company except through one or more other legal entities over each of which he or she has significant control and each of which is an RLE in relation to the company. Otherwise the individual is registrable (s 790C(4)).

The concepts of holding an interest in a company and holding an interest through a legal entity are spelt out in sch 1A, paras 7 to 9, with supplementary provisions in paras 10 to 25.

8.10.4 PSC REGISTER

A PSC register must contain the particulars required by CA 2006, s 790K, and SI 2016/339, regs 7 and 9 to 17 and sch 2 (CA 2006, s 790M). The register must be kept available for inspection for a proper purpose (ss 790N to 790T; see 4.4). Residential addresses in this register have the same protection from disclosure as those in the registers of directors and of directors' residential addresses (s 790ZF; see 15.7.3.2). Private companies may keep this register at Companies House (see 4.4.2.8) and the Secretary of State has a power to extend this facility to public companies (s 790ZE). Provision for rectification of a PSC register by the court is made in s 790V in much the same terms as for rectification of a register of members in s 125 (see 14.3.3).

8.10.5 STATEMENT OF INITIAL SIGNIFICANT CONTROL

When registering a new company, Companies House must be supplied with a statement of initial significant control (CA 2006, ss 9(4)(d) and 12A). This must state whether, on incorporation, there will be anyone who will be a registrable person or registrable RLE in relation to the company and include required particulars of them (s 12A).

8.10.6 INVESTIGATION AND DISCLOSURE

A company must take reasonable steps to find out if there is anyone who is a registrable person or a registrable RLE in relation to the company, and if so, to identify them (CA 2006, s 790D(1)). It may serve notices requiring disclosure (s 790D). A person who is a registrable person or registrable RLE in relation to a company but is not on the company's PSC register must notify the company (s 790G). Where a person is on a PSC register and some change of circumstances occurs that should be registered, the company has a duty to keep the information up to date and may serve a notice requiring disclosure (s 790E), and the registrable person or RLE has a duty to inform the company (s 790H). If a company fails to do these things, there are criminal sanctions (s 790F). If a person fails to comply with a company's notice under s 790D or 790E, the company may issue a restrictions notice under sch 1B, restricting the exercise of shareholding or voting rights or the right to appoint or remove directors.

9

ACCOUNTS

SUMMARY OF POINTS COVERED

- What is in this chapter
- Financial Reporting Council
- Accounting records
- Reporting requirements for various classes of company
- Annual accounts and reports
- Distribution, filing and publication of annual accounts and reports

- Half-yearly reports
- Group accounts
- Contents of strategic report and directors' report
- Revision and external review of accounts and reports
- Reports on payment practices and performance

9.1 WHAT IS IN THIS CHAPTER

An important feature of the companies legislation is the requirement that the directors of a company must, once a year, prepare accounts and present them to the company's members and (unless the company is unlimited) file them at Companies House. In *Caparo Industries plc v Dickman* [1990] 2 AC 605, Lord Jauncey of Tullichettle said, at p 662:

> the purpose of annual accounts, so far as members are concerned, is to enable them to question the past management of the company, to exercise their voting rights, if so advised, and to influence future policy and management.

Financial results are required to be presented in a balance sheet and profit and loss account (or income statement), and there are elaborate technical rules on the preparation of these financial statements (see **9.4** and **9.5.7**). The Financial Reporting Council (FRC) is the regulator for accountancy, auditing and financial reporting (see **9.2**).

The elaborate requirements calling for directors to account to members seem highly unrealistic for the typical private company whose directors and members are the same persons. For such companies the more important purpose of insisting on annual accounts is so that outsiders can look at them to assess creditworthiness, assess tax liabilities or investigate financial dealings. Every limited company is required to file annual accounts at Companies House where they form part of the documentation available for inspection by anyone.

The fact that a limited company has to reveal its financial affairs by filing accounts at Companies House is often regarded as a price that must be paid for limited liability: people who trade with unlimited liability—whether as sole traders, in partnerships or in unlimited companies—do not have to make their financial affairs public. Accordingly, business people who use limited companies to conduct their businesses and act as directors but persistently fail to discharge their statutory obligations in respect of accounting, must expect to be disqualified from being directors or taking part in the management of companies so that they will have to trade with unlimited liability (per Nicholls V-C in *Secretary of State for Trade and Industry v Ettinger* [1993] BCLC 896 at p 900).

Examining arguments for and against mandatory public disclosure of accounts, the Department of Trade and Industry said in 1995 that in its view the accounts of all limited companies should continue to be available at a central registry and that this should apply in all European Union member States (*Accounting Simplifications: A Consultative Document* (URN 95/669) (London: DTI, 1995), para 4.18). Those dealing with limited companies should have access to this information, and normal business practice in the United Kingdom, especially in the provision of credit, depends on public availability of accounts in standardised form.

Accounting requirements of company law are harmonised in the EEA by Directive 2013/34/EU (the New Accounting Directive), which has replaced the Fourth and Seventh Company Law Directives.

In outline, the accounting requirements are as follows. Every company must keep reasonably accurate accounting records of all financial transactions (9.3). From these the directors must prepare annual accounts (9.5.1) for each of the company's financial years (9.5.2), giving a true and fair view (9.5.8) of the company's financial position. If the company is a parent company, the directors must also prepare group accounts consolidating the finances of the company and its subsidiary undertakings (9.8). A private company which is a parent company can opt out of preparing group accounts if its group qualifies as a small group (see 9.8.5). Directors must also prepare a strategic report and a directors' report (9.5.3 and 9.9). The directors of a quoted company (9.5.2) must prepare a directors' remuneration report (15.9.3.4). Most private companies are subject to the small companies regime (9.4.3), which exempts them from preparing a strategic report. Most companies subject to the small companies regime are micro-entities, which can prepare much less detailed micro-entity accounts (9.4.3) and are exempt from preparing a directors' report. The annual accounts must be audited (9.5.5), unless the company is a small private company which is not in a group containing a public company (9.4.6) or is dormant (9.4.7). The annual accounts and reports must be sent to the members and debenture holders (who may be given an option to receive only the strategic report and brief supplementary material) (9.6.1). The annual accounts and reports of a public company must be laid before a general meeting of its members (9.6.3). All companies must deliver their annual accounts and reports to Companies House (9.6.4 to 9.6.6), though most private companies can omit the profit and loss account and directors' report (9.6.6). A company whose transferable securities are admitted to trading on a regulated market (see 7.3.4.6) must make public a half-yearly financial report (9.7).

There are procedures for revising accounts that are found to be erroneous (9.10).

Key legislation which you should be able to consult when reading this chapter:

- CA 2006, ss 380–484, 1159–1162.

All that legislation is in *Blackstone's Statutes on Company Law*.

- Regulation (EC) No 1606/2002, which is at the EUR-Lex website: **eur-lex.europa.eu**.

- UK Corporate Governance Code, which is at **www.frc.org.uk/Our-Work/Corporate-Governance-Reporting/Corporate-governance.aspx**.

The following case, which is considered in this chapter, is particularly significant and is recommended further reading:

- *Caparo Industries plc v Dickman* [1990] 2 AC 605 (also a key case for **Chapter 17**). This case, like *Salomon v A Salomon and Co Ltd* [1897] AC 22 (see **5.2.1**), has been voted one of the 15 most significant cases in the period 1865–2015.

Your particular course of study may require you to read other source materials.

9.2 FINANCIAL REPORTING COUNCIL

The Financial Reporting Council (FRC) describes itself as the UK's independent regulator responsible for promoting high-quality corporate governance and reporting to foster investment. It sets UK standards for the form and content of company accounts (see **9.5.7.5**), for auditing and actuarial work. It issues the UK Corporate Governance and Stewardship Codes (see **15.2.2**) as well as UK standards for accounting, auditing and actuarial work. It monitors (see **9.10**) and takes action to promote the quality of corporate reporting and auditing. It operates independent disciplinary arrangements for accountants and actuaries. The chair and deputy chair of the FRC's board are appointed by the Secretary of State for Business, Energy and Industrial Strategy. Funding for the FRC's activities in relation to company accounts is provided by the six major professional bodies for accountants and by a preparers' levy, which public companies, large private companies and public sector bodies must contribute.

There is a great deal of information about the FRC's work on its website, **www.frc.org.uk**.

9.3 ACCOUNTING RECORDS

9.3.1 EVERY COMPANY MUST KEEP ACCOUNTING RECORDS

CA 2006, s 386, requires every company to keep accounting records which are sufficient to show and explain the company's transactions and also to disclose, with reasonable accuracy, the financial position of the company at any time. The accounting records must also be adequate to enable the directors to ensure that any accounts required to be prepared comply with the requirements of the Act and, where applicable, of Regulation (EC) No 1606/2002, art 4 (see **9.5.7.4**).

R v Bennett (1985) 2 NZCLC 99,279 concerned a similarly worded provision in the New Zealand companies legislation. The New Zealand Court of Appeal held that the obligation to cause accounting records to be 'kept' was not merely an obligation to retain and store records but also to create records conforming with the requirements of the section. It was also held that dealings between a company and its members, for example contributions of capital and payments of dividend, are transactions of the company that must be included in its accounting records.

There are criminal sanctions for failure to comply with CA 2006, s 386, subject to a defence of acting honestly where, in the circumstances in which the company's business was carried on, the default was excusable (s 387).

If a company's auditor is of opinion that adequate accounting records have not been kept by the company, that fact must be stated in the auditor's report (s 498(2)).

9.3.2 PRESERVATION OF RECORDS

The accounting records of a private company must be preserved for three years from the date on which they are made; those of a public company must be kept for six years (CA 2006, s 388(4)). An officer of a company who does not take all reasonable steps to ensure that the company complies with these requirements is guilty of an offence (s 389(3) and (4)).

9.3.3 ACCESS TO ACCOUNTING RECORDS

A company's accounting records must, at all times, be open to inspection by the company's officers (CA 2006, s 388(1); see **4.4.5**).

The court will order a company to allow one of its directors to inspect its accounting records (*Burn v London and South Wales Coal Co* (1890) 7 TLR 118; *Edman v Ross* (1922) 22 SR (NSW) 351; both decided before there was any statutory obligation to keep accounts open to inspection). An order can be made only for the purposes of enabling the director to carry out their duties as a director of the company (*Oxford Legal Group Ltd v Sibbasbridge Services plc* [2008] EWCA Civ 387, [2008] Bus LR 1244).

The sole statutory provision for enforcing s 388(1) is the criminal sanction imposed by s 389(1). The court grants orders for inspection under the common law as stated in *Burn v London and South Wales Coal Co* and, as with any injunctive relief, an order is granted at the court's discretion (*Conway v Petronius Clothing Co Ltd* [1978] 1 WLR 72). It has been argued that s 388 does create a statutory right to an order for inspection (*M'Cusker v M'Rae* 1966 SC 253, in which the petition was granted by consent; D D Prentice, 'A director's right of access to corporate books of account' (1978) 94 LQR 184; *Berlei Hestia (NZ) Ltd v Fernyhough* [1980] 2 NZLR 150—in which an injunction was granted—per Mahon J at p 163). In *Oxford Legal Group Ltd v Sibbasbridge Services plc* the Court of Appeal found it unnecessary to decide which of these views is correct.

Members of a company do not have a right of access to its accounting records (*R v Merchant Tailors' Co* (1831) 2 B & Ad 115; *Edman v Ross*; *Lonrho Ltd v Shell Petroleum Co Ltd* [1980] 1 WLR 627 per Lord Diplock at p 634; *Murray's Judicial Factor v Thomas Murray and Sons (Ice Merchants) Ltd* [1993] BCLC 1437). The model articles for private companies, art 50, and the model articles for public companies, art 83, in SI 2008/3229, repeat this common law rule, but also allow the directors, or the members by ordinary resolution, to authorise a member to inspect accounting or other records or documents.

A company's auditor has a right of access to its accounting records (CA 2006, s 499(1))—see **17.4.7**.

9.4 REPORTING REQUIREMENTS FOR VARIOUS CLASSES OF COMPANY

9.4.1 CLASSES

The requirements in CA 2006 for companies to report their financial position to their members and to the public vary according to whether the company is a micro-entity, or is small, medium-sized or large (see **9.4.2** to **9.4.5**). A company is subject to additional requirements if it is a quoted company (see **9.5.2**). Public companies cannot be micro-entities or small or medium-sized companies (see **9.4.4**). So all public companies must be large companies. All micro-entities, small and medium-sized companies must be private companies, but large companies can be public or private, quoted or unquoted.

Numerically the biggest class is micro-entities, of which there are estimated to be 1.56 million. They must be private companies and they have the least onerous reporting requirements. Quoted companies are subject to the most onerous requirements. In particular, they must publish accounts on a website (see **9.6.2.1**) and produce a detailed directors' remuneration report (see **9.5.4** and **15.9.3.4**) and a more detailed strategic report (see **9.9.2**).

Extra requirements are imposed on all companies whose shares are admitted to trading on a regulated market (see **7.3.4.3**). See **9.5.7.4** (group accounts must be IAS group accounts), **9.5.1** and **9.9.1** (statement of assurance in accounts and directors' report), **9.6.2.2** (public availability of accounts), **9.7** (half-yearly financial reports), **9.9.3** (corporate governance statement) and **9.9.4.6** (details of barriers to takeovers in directors' report). These requirements are imposed by EU legislation, mostly by Directives which are implemented by rules in the FCA Handbook, though the rule that group accounts must be IAS accounts is in the directly effective Regulation (EC) No 1606/2002.

Further requirements, in the listing rules in the FCA Handbook and in the UK Corporate Governance Code, affect the directors' report (see **9.9.1**) of a premium listed company (see **7.6**).

9.4.2 QUALIFYING CONDITIONS

The conditions for qualifying as a micro-entity, a small company or a medium-sized company are set out in CA 2006, ss 384A (micro-entity), 382 (small company) and 465 (medium-sized company). There are three size conditions relating to turnover, balance sheet total (that is, total assets) and weekly average number of employees for a financial year. They are set out in **Table 9.1**.

If a company is newly incorporated, it qualifies in its first financial year if it meets at least two of the requirements in that first year (ss 382(1) and 465(1)).

If a company does not qualify in one financial year, but then meets at least two of the requirements in two consecutive financial years, it qualifies in the second of those years (ss 382(2)(a) and 465(2)(a)).

Having qualified, a company remains qualified until it fails to satisfy at least two conditions in two consecutive financial years (ss 382(2) and 465(2)).

If a financial year is not 12 months, the turnover limit must be adjusted proportionately.

A company that qualifies as a micro-entity also qualifies as a small company.

A company that is neither a small company nor a medium-sized company is called a large company (though this term is not formally defined in the legislation).

Table 9.1 Size limits for micro-entities, small and medium-sized companies

	Turnover must not exceed	Balance sheet total must not exceed	Weekly average number of employees must not exceed
Micro-entity	£632,000	£316,000	10
Small company	£10.2 million	£5.1 million	50
Medium-sized company	£36 million	£18 million	250

9.4.3 BENEFITS

The 'small companies regime' for reporting requirements applies to a private company for a financial year if it qualifies as a small company in relation to that year (see **9.4.2**) and is not excluded from the regime (see **9.4.4**) (CA 2006, s 381). The small companies regime is considerably less onerous than the accounting and filing obligations imposed on large companies. In particular, preparation of group accounts (see **9.5.1**) is optional, a strategic report is not required, abridged formats can be used for the balance sheet and profit and loss account (see **9.5.7.7**) and the accounts filed at Companies House can omit the profit and loss account and directors' report (see **9.6.7**).

A company which qualifies as a micro-entity for a financial year is not only entitled to take advantage of the small companies regime but is also exempt from preparing a directors' report and can prepare its accounts as micro-entity accounts which are simpler and less detailed than the accounts required of larger companies.

9.4.4 EXCLUDED COMPANIES

Public companies are excluded both from the small companies regime (by CA 2006, s 384(1)(a)) and from being treated as medium-sized (by s 467(1)(a)). Some financial services companies are excluded from the small companies regime by s 384(1)(b) and all are excluded from being medium-sized (s 467(1)(b) and (ba)). In addition, a company is excluded from being either small or medium-sized if it is in an ineligible group (ss 384(1)(c) and (2) and 467(1)(c) and (2)). This means a group which includes a traded company (which means a company any of whose transferable securities are admitted to trading on a regulated market (see 7.3.4.3) anywhere in the EEA: s 474(1)), or a corporation (other than a company) whose shares are admitted to trading on a regulated market or a financial services company. 'Group' means a parent undertaking and its subsidiary undertakings (s 474(1)). If a company was, at any time during a financial year, excluded by s 384 from the small companies regime, it cannot prepare micro-entity accounts for that year (s 384B(1)(a)).

Charities cannot prepare micro-entity accounts, nor can many financial services companies (s 384B(1)(b) to (f)).

If a company is a parent company, it cannot qualify as a small company unless the group which it heads qualifies as a small group (s 383(1); see 9.4.5) and cannot qualify as a medium-sized company unless the group which it heads qualifies as a medium-sized group (s 466(1); see 9.4.5). Because micro-entity accounts cannot be integrated with group accounts, a company cannot prepare micro-entity accounts if it is in a group for which group accounts are prepared or if its parent company prepares group accounts despite being exempt from doing so (s 384B(2)).

9.4.5 SMALL AND MEDIUM-SIZED GROUPS

If a company is a parent company, it cannot qualify as a small company unless the group which it heads qualifies as a small group (CA 2006, s 383(1)). The conditions for qualifying as a small group are in s 383. A parent company cannot qualify as a medium-sized company unless the group which it heads qualifies as a medium-sized group (s 466(1)). The conditions for qualifying as a medium-sized group are in s 466.

The conditions for qualifying as a small or medium-sized group correspond to the conditions under which a company qualifies as a small or medium-sized company except that the relevant figures for turnover, assets and employees are aggregate figures for all the undertakings in the group. The aggregates of turnover and assets may be either the figures (described as 'net') that would appear in group accounts (that is, after set-offs and other adjustments to eliminate transactions within the group) or 'gross' (that is, without such adjustments) (ss 383(6) and 466(6)). Two or more of the requirements set out in **Table 9.2** must be met (ss 383(4) and 466(4)).

Table 9.2 Conditions for qualifying as a small or medium-sized group

	Small group
1. Aggregate turnover	Not more than £10.2 million net (or £12.2 million gross)
2. Aggregate balance sheet total	Not more than £5.1 million net (or £6.1 million gross)
3. Aggregate number of employees	Not more than 50
	Medium-sized group
1. Aggregate turnover	Not more than £36 million net (or £43.2 million gross)
2. Aggregate balance sheet total	Not more than £18 million net (or £21.6 million gross)
3. Aggregate number of employees	Not more than 250

9.4.6 SMALL COMPANIES AND SUBSIDIARY COMPANIES EXEMPTION FROM AUDIT

A company that qualifies as a small company in relation to a financial year (see **9.4.2**) is not required to have its annual accounts for that year audited (CA 2006, s 477).

If a small company is in a group as a parent company or a subsidiary undertaking (defined in **9.8.2**), it is exempt as a small company from the auditing requirements for a financial year only if it is a dormant subsidiary company (s 479(3); see **9.4.7**) or the group is a small group which was not an ineligible group (defined in **9.4.4**) at any time during that year (s 479(1)).

The financial services companies which are excluded from the small companies regime by s 384(1)(b) also cannot claim exemption from audit as small companies, nor can public companies (s 478).

A subsidiary company in a group of any size is exempt from having its individual accounts audited if it satisfies the conditions in ss 479A, 479B and 479C. The conditions for exemption are:

(a) The subsidiary's parent undertaking must be established under the law of an EEA State (s 479A(1)(b)).

(b) All members of the subsidiary must agree to the exemption in respect of the financial year in question (s 479A(2)(a)) and written notice of that agreement must be filed with the accounts (s 479A(2)(e)(i)).

(c) The parent undertaking must guarantee full payment of all the subsidiary's liabilities outstanding at the end of the financial year (ss 479A(2)(b) and 479C) and a written statement of the guarantee must be filed with the subsidiary's accounts (s 479A(2)(e)(ii)).

(d) The subsidiary must be included in consolidated accounts complying with EU or IAS accounting requirements (s 479A(2)(c)), those accounts must disclose the exemption (s 479A(2)(d)) and a copy of those accounts (with their auditor's report) and the parent undertaking's consolidated annual report must be filed with the subsidiary's accounts (s 479A(2)(e)(iii)–(v)).

Traded companies (see **9.4.4**) and financial services companies are excluded from this exemption (s 479B).

The exemption from audit given to small companies by s 477 and subsidiary companies by s 479A is expressed to be subject to s 476. Under s 476, if a company's accounts for a financial year will not be audited, any member or members holding 10 per cent or more in nominal value of the company's issued share capital, or any class of it, may require the company to obtain an audit of those accounts. A written notice requiring an audit must be deposited at the company's registered office during the financial year and not later than one month before the end of the year.

By s 475, a balance sheet of a company which is exempt from the audit requirements must include a statement by the directors that the conditions for exemption have been met and that they acknowledge their responsibility for keeping proper accounting records and preparing proper accounts.

9.4.7 DORMANT COMPANIES

A company is 'dormant' during a period in which 'no significant accounting transaction' occurs (CA 2006, s 1169(1)). Section 1169(2) defines significant accounting transactions as transactions that must be entered in the company's accounting records by virtue of s 386 (see **9.3.1**), apart from transactions relating to fulfilment of the undertaking of subscribers of the memorandum to take shares (s 1169(3)(a); see **2.2.1.3**) and the payment to Companies House of certain routine fees listed in s 1169(3)(b).

Section 480(1) exempts a dormant company from having its accounts for a financial year audited if:

(a) it has been dormant since its formation; or

(b) it has been dormant since the end of the previous financial year and, for the current financial year, it is entitled to prepare accounts in accordance with the small companies regime and is not required to prepare group accounts (see **9.8**) (s 480(2)).

The small companies regime does not apply to a public company (s 384(1)(a)) or a member of an ineligible group (s 384(1)(c)). Nevertheless, s 480(2)(a)(ii) allows a public company or a member of an ineligible group to be exempt from audit as a dormant company. Traded companies (see **9.4.4**) and the financial services companies which are excluded from the small companies regime by s 384(1)(b) cannot claim exemption from audit as dormant companies (s 481).

The exemption from audit given to dormant companies by s 480 is expressed to be subject to ss 475 and 476 (right of members to demand audit and directors' statement required on balance sheet). These provisions are described in **9.4.6**.

A subsidiary company which has been dormant for the whole of a financial year is exempt from having to prepare individual accounts for that year, subject to the same conditions as for exempting subsidiary companies from audit (see **9.4.6**). This exemption is made by CA 2006, ss 394A, 394B and 394C.

9.5 ANNUAL ACCOUNTS AND REPORTS

9.5.1 ANNUAL ACCOUNTS, INDIVIDUAL AND GROUP

For each financial year (see **9.5.2**) of a company, its directors must prepare its individual accounts (CA 2006, s 394). These consist of a balance sheet and profit and loss account and (except in micro-entity accounts) notes to the accounts.

If, at the end of the financial year, the company was a parent company, the directors may be required, or may choose, to prepare group accounts (see **9.8**).

According to s 471(1), the 'annual accounts' of a company are its individual accounts required by s 394 and any group accounts required by s 398 or 399. They are usually known as the annual financial statements.

The directors of a premium listed company must state in the annual financial statements that the business is a going concern, with supporting assumptions or qualifications as necessary (FCA Handbook, LR 9.8.6R(3)). This statement must be reviewed by the auditor (LR 9.8.10R(1)). The UK Corporate Governance Code says that the directors should state whether they consider it appropriate to adopt the going concern basis of accounting and identify any material uncertainties to the company's ability to continue to do so over a period of at least 12 months from the date of approval of the financial statements (para C.1.3).

A company's annual accounts must be approved by its board of directors, and signed on behalf of the board by a director of the company (s 414(1)). The signature must be on the company's balance sheet (s 414(2)). If the accounts are micro-entity accounts or were prepared under the small companies regime, that fact must be stated in a prominent position above the signature (s 414(3)). Every person who was a director of a company at the time that its annual accounts were signed on behalf of the board is responsible for those accounts and is taken to know what is stated in them (*Neville v Krikorian* [2006] EWCA Civ 943, [2007] 1 BCLC 1) and is responsible for compliance with relevant legislation (see s 414(4) and (5) at **9.5.7.4**). But a member of a company, who is not a director, does not have a duty to read its annual accounts (*Maidment v Attwood* [2012] EWCA Civ 998, [2013] Bus LR 753).

A company's accounts must give a true and fair view of its financial position (see **9.5.8**):

> the responsibility for the preparation of accounts giving a true and fair view of the company's financial state is placed fairly and squarely on the shoulders of the directors (per Lord Jauncey of Tullichettle in *Caparo Industries plc v Dickman* [1990] 2 AC 605 at p 660).

See **9.9.5** for the statement of assurance to be given by the directors of a company whose transferable securities are admitted to trading on a regulated market.

9.5.2 ACCOUNTING REFERENCE PERIODS, FINANCIAL YEARS AND QUOTED COMPANIES

The timetable for the production of the successive annual accounts of a company is based on the company's 'accounting reference periods'. Accounting reference periods are consecutive periods of, normally, 12 months each, ending on a date called the 'accounting reference date' (CA 2006, s 391(6)). Normally, this is the last day of the month in which the anniversary of the company's incorporation falls (s 391(4)).

The successive annual accounts of a company refer to consecutive periods known as 'financial years', each of which must end not more than seven days before or after the end of an accounting reference period (s 390).

A company may change its accounting reference date by following the procedure set out in s 392. Under s 390(5), it is the duty of directors of a parent company to ensure that the financial years of their company and its subsidiary undertakings coincide, unless in their opinion there are good reasons to the contrary.

A company is a quoted company in relation to a financial year if it is a quoted company (see **7.3.4.6**) immediately before the end of the accounting reference period by reference to which the financial year was determined (s 385(1)).

9.5.3 STRATEGIC REPORT AND DIRECTORS' REPORT

The directors of a company must prepare, for each financial year, a strategic report and a directors' report, with the contents described in **9.9** (CA 2006, ss 414A(1) and 415(1)). For a financial year in which the company is a parent company and the directors prepare group accounts (see **9.8**), these reports must be group reports relating to the undertakings included in the consolidation (ss 414A(3) and 415(2)).

The directors of a company do not have to prepare a strategic report for a financial year if the company is entitled to the small companies exemption for that year (s 414A(2)). They do have to prepare a directors' report but it does not have to be delivered to Companies House (s 444A) and need not state the recommended dividend (s 416(3)). Sections 414B and 415A provide that a company is entitled to small companies exemption in relation to the strategic report and the directors' report for a financial year if:

(a) it is entitled to prepare accounts for the year in accordance with the small companies regime (see **9.4.3**); or

(b) it would be so entitled but for being or having been a member of an ineligible group (see **9.4.4**).

Directors' reports are not required for micro-entities (s 415(1A)).

The strategic report and directors' report must be approved by the board of directors and signed on behalf of the board by a director or by the secretary (ss 414D(1) and 419(1)). If the directors' report was prepared under the small companies regime, that fact must be stated in a prominent position above the signature (s 419(2)).

Under s 463, a director of a company is liable to compensate it for any loss it suffers as a result of:

(a) any untrue or misleading statement in a strategic report, directors' report or directors' remuneration report; or

(b) the omission from any such report of anything required to be included in it.

A director is liable under s 463 only if he or she knew the statement was untrue or misleading, or was reckless as to whether it was untrue or misleading, or knew the omission was a dishonest concealment of a material fact (s 463(3)).

9.5.4 DIRECTORS' REMUNERATION REPORT

If a company is a quoted company in relation to a financial year (see **9.5.2**), its directors must prepare a directors' remuneration report (CA 2006, s 420; see **15.9.3.4**).

Section 463 (director's liability for untrue or misleading statements or omissions) applies to a directors' remuneration report. See **9.5.3**.

9.5.5 AUDITOR'S REPORT

It is usually assumed in company law that the members of a company are not directly active in managing the company. The annual accounts are prepared for the members by people who are directly concerned in management and there is an obvious danger that the accounts will deliberately or accidentally misrepresent the company's financial affairs. So members could benefit from an independent check on the adequacy of the accounts. Independent checks of financial accounts are normally provided by the process known as 'auditing' which has become a highly developed branch of accountancy. Under CA 1862, it was assumed that the members of a company would want to have its annual accounts audited and a provision to that effect was included in the model set of articles of association in Table A (CA 1862, sch 1) but, like any provision in the articles, this could be varied. CA 1900, ss 21 to 23, made the audit of companies' annual accounts a mandatory requirement of company law and this requirement is now contained in CA 2006, ss 475 to 484. Since 1900, users of accounts have demanded increasingly high standards of auditing, and the audit function has become more and more expensive. It has recently been recognised that in most small companies the members are directly concerned in management and regard a sophisticated audit of accounts as an unnecessarily costly protection. So ss 477 to 481 make exemptions from the mandatory audit requirement for small companies (see **9.4.6**) and dormant companies (see **9.4.7**).

If a company is not exempt from the mandatory auditing requirement, it must appoint an auditor in accordance with the rules set out in **17.4.1**.

The company's auditor is required by s 495(1) to report to the members on all annual accounts which are, during the auditor's tenure of office, to be sent to members under s 423 (see **9.6.1**) or, if the company is public, laid before the company in general meeting under s 437 (see **9.6.3**).

For the content of the auditor's report see **17.4.6**. The auditor's report must state the name of the auditor and be signed and dated (s 503; see **17.4.6**).

In *Caparo Industries plc v Dickman* [1990] 2 AC 605, Lord Oliver of Aylmerton said, at p 630:

> It is the auditors' function to ensure, so far as possible, that the financial information as to the company's affairs prepared by the directors accurately reflects the company's position in order, first, to protect the

company itself from the consequences of undetected errors or, possibly, wrongdoing (by, for instance, declaring dividends out of capital) and, secondly, to provide shareholders with reliable intelligence for the purpose of enabling them to scrutinise the conduct of the company's affairs and to exercise their collective powers to reward or control or remove those to whom that conduct has been confided.

9.5.6 ANNUAL ACCOUNTS AND REPORTS

By CA 2006, s 471(2) and (3), the annual accounts and reports of a company for a financial year consist of its annual accounts (see **9.5.1**), the directors' report (unless the company is a micro-entity), the strategic report (if any) and the auditor's report (unless the company is exempt from audit), plus, if the company is a quoted company (see **9.5.2**), the directors' remuneration report.

For a company whose transferable securities are admitted to trading on a regulated market (see **7.3.4.6**), the audited annual accounts (financial statements), directors' report and strategic report (management report) and responsibility statements constitute the annual financial report (Directive 2004/109/EC, art 4(2); FCA Handbook, DTR 4.1.5R to 4.1.12R). A listed public company's annual financial report will contain the following items:

(a) strategic report;

(b) corporate governance statement;

(c) directors' report;

(d) directors' remuneration report;

(e) directors' responsibility statement;

(f) auditor's report; and

(g) financial statements.

The corporate governance statement can be included in the directors' report.

9.5.7 FORM AND CONTENT OF ANNUAL ACCOUNTS

9.5.7.1 Legislation and professional codes

It is very important that annual accounts should be presented in a standard form so that users can locate the information they want and so that accounts of different companies can be compared.

Preparing accounts involves several processes such as valuation (giving a monetary value to non-money items) and classification (for example, into fixed assets and current assets) and users need to be assured that these processes have been carried out in an expected way. Rules for preparation and presentation of accounts are stated:

(a) in legislation, both at national level and at European level, in both harmonising Directives and directly applicable Regulations; and

(b) in accounting standards written by and for professional accountants, both at national and international level.

All of these sources provide different standards for different kinds of company, depending on size and on whether shares are publicly traded. There is an additional element of complexity in that a company may choose to prepare its accounts to a more exacting standard than the one prescribed for its class, subject to detailed conditions.

The rules that are prescribed for a particular company or group depend on:

(a) whether the company or group is small, medium-sized or large;

(b) whether the company is a micro-entity;

(c) whether the company's securities are admitted to trading on a regulated market;

(d) whether the accounts are prepared and/or audited by professional accountants; and

(e) whether the company is a charity.

9.5.7.2 UK and EU legislation

The UK legislation on form and content of annual accounts is in CA 2006, ss 380 to 474, and in two statutory instruments:

(a) SI 2008/409, parts 2 and 4, apply to small companies and groups. Part 2 deals with individual accounts and part 4 deals with group accounts. Part 2 also deals with micro-entity accounts.

(b) SI 2008/410, part 2, applies to large and medium-sized companies and groups.

This legislation implements Directive 2013/34/EU. Other parts of the statutory instruments deal with the directors' report and the directors' remuneration report.

In addition to the Directive implemented by the UK legislation, there is directly effective EU legislation in Regulation (EC) No 1606/2002 and Commission Regulation (EC) No 1725/2003. These regulations apply only to the group accounts of a company whose securities are admitted to trading on a regulated market (see **7.3.4.3**) on the balance sheet date. They are compulsory for such a company.

9.5.7.3 International accounting standards

International Financial Reporting Standards (IFRSs) are issued by the International Accounting Standards Board (IASB). See **www.ifrs.org**.

The IASB's international standards are primarily intended for use by large companies with publicly traded shares, but it has also issued an IFRS for small and medium-sized entities (SMEs).

9.5.7.4 Choice of financial reporting framework

Most companies may, by CA 2006, ss 395(1) and 403(2), choose whether their individual and group accounts are prepared:

(a) as 'Companies Act individual accounts' or 'Companies Act group accounts' in accordance with CA 2006, ss 380 to 474, and SI 2008/409, parts 2 and 4 (small companies and groups), or SI 2008/410, part 2 (large and medium-sized companies and groups); or

(b) as 'IAS individual accounts' or 'IAS group accounts' in accordance with international accounting standards. In this context, 'international accounting standards' means only those which have been adopted by the European Commission under Regulation (EC) No 1606/2002, art 3 (CA 2006, s 474(1)). The annex to Commission Regulation (EC) No 1725/2003, which has been amended several times, contains the complete texts of the standards which have been adopted. The European Financial Reporting Advisory Group maintains a report on the adoption status of all international standards at **www.efrag.org**.

These are called the two 'accounting frameworks'. The provisions of SI 2008/409, parts 2 and 4, and SI 2008/410, part 2, requiring information about related undertakings and directors' benefits, apply to both Companies Act accounts and IAS accounts.

A small company which chooses to prepare Companies Act accounts has the option of preparing them in accordance with the requirements in SI 2008/410 for large and medium-sized companies and groups, because such accounts are treated as satisfying the requirements for small companies and groups (SI 2008/409, regs 3(3) and 8(2)).

This general freedom of choice of financial reporting framework is subject to the following restrictions:

(a) The group accounts of a company whose securities are admitted to trading on a regulated market anywhere in the EEA (see **7.3.4.3**) on the balance sheet date must be IAS group accounts (Regulation (EC) No 1606/2002, art 4; CA 2006, s 403(1)).

(b) The accounts of a charitable company must be Companies Act accounts (ss 395(2) and 403(3)).

(c) The directors of a parent company who are required to prepare group accounts must normally ensure that the same framework is applied in preparing the individual accounts of the parent company and of its subsidiary undertakings whose accounts are required to be prepared under part 15 (s 407(1), (2) and (3)). Different frameworks for individual accounts within a group are allowed to the extent that:

  (i) in the opinion of the parent company's directors there are good reasons for applying different frameworks (s 407(1));

  (ii) a company is a charity which must prepare Companies Act accounts (s 407(4)); and

  (iii) the group and individual accounts of the parent company are both IAS accounts, but the individual accounts of subsidiary undertakings are Companies Act accounts (s 407(5)).

(d) Once a company has prepared IAS accounts (whether individual or group) for a financial year, it may change back to Companies Act accounts for a subsequent year, but this can be done only once every five years unless there is a 'relevant change of circumstances' (s 395(3) to (3B) (individual accounts); s 403(4) to (4B) (group accounts)). A relevant change of circumstances is (s 395(4) (individual); s 403(5) (group)):

  (i) in relation to individual accounts, the company becomes a subsidiary undertaking of another undertaking which does not prepare IAS individual accounts or the company ceases to be a subsidiary undertaking;

  (ii) in relation to group accounts, the company becomes a subsidiary undertaking of another undertaking which does not prepare IAS group accounts;

  (iii) the company ceases to be a company with securities admitted to trading on a regulated market; and

  (iv) a parent undertaking of the company ceases to be an undertaking with securities admitted to trading on a regulated market.

The notes to IAS accounts must state that they have been prepared in accordance with international accounting standards (s 397(2) (individual accounts); s 406(2) (group accounts)).

By s 414(4) and (5), if annual accounts of a company are approved by its directors but do not comply with the requirements of CA 2006 or of Regulation (EC) No 1606/2002, art 4, as appropriate, every director who is a party to their approval and who knows that they do not comply, or is reckless as to whether they comply, is guilty of an offence triable either way.

9.5.7.5 UK accounting standards

In the United Kingdom, Financial Reporting Standards (FRSs) are issued by the Financial Reporting Council (FRC). See **www.frc.org.uk/Our-Work/Codes-Standards/Accounting-and-Reporting-Policy.aspx**.

Notes to the Companies Act accounts of a large company must state whether the accounts have been prepared in accordance with applicable accounting standards, and particulars of any material departure from those standards, and the reasons for it, must be given (SI 2008/410, reg 4(2A) and sch 1, para 45). Applicable accounting standards are standards issued by the FRC or its predecessors which are relevant to the company's circumstances and to the accounts (CA 2006, s 464; SI 2012/1741, arts 23 and 24).

Although the Companies Act accounts of a small or medium-sized company are not required by legislation to follow FRC standards, a person preparing such accounts will wish to work to those standards, because they show what is 'generally accepted accounting practice' (GAAP). In the law of tort, a professional person's actions are not negligent if they are in accordance with a practice accepted as proper by a responsible body of fellow professionals (*Bolam v Friern Hospital Management Committee* [1957] 1 WLR 582).

The legislative provisions, standards and other commonly accepted professional practices applicable to Companies Act accounts are known as 'United Kingdom GAAP' while those applicable to IAS accounts are known as 'international GAAP'.

For small companies, the current version of the Financial Reporting Standard for Smaller Entities (FRSSE) was issued by the FRC to take effect from January 2015. This is a single comprehensive standard for the accounts of small companies. The Companies Act accounts of a small company will comply with UK GAAP if they are prepared in accordance with the FRSSE and no other FRC standards need to be applied.

Other companies which prepare Companies Act accounts must apply FRS 102 *The Financial Reporting Standard Applicable in the UK and Republic of Ireland*, which is based on the IFRS for SMEs (see **9.5.7.3**). Significant differences between the two standards are listed in FRS 102, appendix 2. A company which is a member of a group may prepare its individual accounts, as Companies Act accounts, in accordance with FRS 101 *Reduced Disclosure Framework*. The result is that since 2015 all UK companies not subject to the small companies regime apply IFRSs, either directly if they prepare IAS accounts or in the form of FRS 101 or 102 otherwise.

9.5.7.6 Off-balance sheet arrangements

A big problem for investors has been that companies have entered into risky transactions in ways which do not have to be reported in the annual accounts. CA 2006, s 410A, implementing Directive 2006/46/EC, deals with this. It requires a company to report, in a note to its annual accounts, the nature and business purpose of arrangements to which the company is or has been party but which are not reflected in its balance sheet, if the risks or benefits arising from the arrangements are material. Unless it is subject to the small companies regime, the company must also report the financial impact on it of the arrangements. The information need only be given to the extent necessary for enabling the financial position of the company to be assessed.

9.5.7.7 Abridged accounts of small companies

The directors of a company which is subject to the small companies regime may prepare its balance sheet and/or profit and loss account in an abridged form giving less analysis of the figures than would otherwise be required by SI 2008/409 (see sch 1, para 1A). This can only be done where it is appropriate to the circumstances of the company's business and only where all members of the company have consented to the accounts being drawn up in that way. This consent can only be given for the preparation of the accounts for the preceding financial year (sch 1, para 1A(3)).

9.5.8 'TRUE AND FAIR VIEW'

CA 2006, s 393(1), states a fundamental principle that the directors of a company must not approve its annual accounts unless satisfied that the accounts give a true and fair view of the assets, liabilities, financial position and profit or loss of the company, or, if they are group accounts, the undertakings included in the consolidation as a whole, so far as concerns members of the company. Auditors must have regard to this requirement when carrying out their functions (s 393(2)).

Items of information which are required by CA 2006, part 15, or SI 2008/409 to be contained in micro-entity accounts are presumed to give a true and fair view (CA 2006, ss 393(2A) and 474(1)).

The phrase 'true and fair view' was introduced into British company law in 1948 (CA 1948, s 149(1)). The phrase has since been adopted in EU law. Directive 2013/34/EU requires that 'The annual financial statements shall give a true and fair view of the undertaking's assets, liabilities, financial position and profit or loss' (art 4(3)). Regulation (EC) No 1606/2002, art 3(2), prevents the European Commission from adopting IASB standards which are contrary to the principle that accounts should show a true and fair view (IAS 1, para 13, uses the phrase 'fair presentation').

Earlier, the Companies (Consolidation) Act 1908, s 113(2), had required a company's auditors to certify whether in their opinion its balance sheet 'is properly drawn up so as to exhibit a true and correct view of the state of the company's affairs'. This repeated a phrase used in CA 1900, s 23. CA 1900 had reintroduced the requirement that every company must appoint an auditor. Under the Joint Stock Companies Act 1856 and CA 1862, auditing was a matter for the articles of association but the phrase 'true and correct view' was used in art 94 of the model set of articles, Table A in CA 1862, sch 1, though that article also referred to a 'full and fair balance sheet'. The phrase 'full and fair balance sheet' had appeared in the Joint Stock Companies Act 1844, s 35. R J Chambers and P W Wolnizer have found that in partnership agreements and deeds of settlement before 1844, phrases such as 'full, true and explicit' and 'fair, accurate and just' were used ('A true and fair view of financial position' (1990) 8 C & SLJ 353 at p 359). In *Re London and General Bank (No 2)* [1895] 2 Ch 673, Rigby LJ said, at p 692, that it was not easy to define what else was required of a 'full and fair' balance sheet for it to show a 'true and correct view'. His Lordship thought that:

> A full and fair balance sheet must be such a balance sheet as to convey a truthful statement as to the company's position. It must not conceal any known cause of weakness in the financial position, or suggest anything which cannot be supported as fairly correct in a business point of view.

Clearly, there has been some difficulty in finding the right words to express what is expected of accounts, and it may be that the present phrase, 'true and fair', cannot withstand too much analysis. H Evans, 'True and fair revisited' [1990] LMCLQ 255, for example, suggests that 'fair' could mean either 'tolerable, passable, of moderate quality, average', or 'impartial, just, unbiased, equitable' and, remarkably, prefers the first meaning: it seems unlikely that this is correct.

Whether or not accounts show a true and fair view must be determined by reference to applicable accounting standards. The law does not recognise any higher or more abstract principles (*Commissioners of HM Revenue and Customs v William Grant and Sons Distillers Ltd* [2007] UKHL 15, [2007] 1 WLR 1448).

See further K P E Lasok and E Grace, 'The true and fair view' (1989) 10 Co Law 13; A McGee, 'The "true and fair view" debate: a study in the legal regulation of accounting' (1991) 54 MLR 874; Martin Moore, 'The true and fair requirement revisited: opinion', **www.frc.org.uk/FRC-Documents/FRC/True-and-Fair-Opinion,-Moore,-21-April-2008.aspx**.

9.6 DISTRIBUTION, FILING AND PUBLICATION OF ANNUAL ACCOUNTS AND REPORTS

9.6.1 SENDING ANNUAL ACCOUNTS AND REPORTS TO MEMBERS

9.6.1.1 Obligation to circulate

Copies of a company's annual accounts and reports for a financial year must be sent to each of the company's members and debenture holders (CA 2006, s 423(1)(a) and (b)). Copies of the accounts and reports must also be sent to anyone else entitled to receive notice of general meetings (s 423(1) (c)), which includes the company's auditor (s 502(2)(a)). Copies need not be sent to a person for whom the company does not have a current address (s 423(2) and (3)). A company may give persons entitled to receive copies of its accounts and reports the option to receive instead a copy of the strategic report with supplementary material (s 426; see **9.6.1.3**).

For a *private company* the time limit for circulating the annual accounts and reports is the end of the period for filing them at Companies House (see **9.6.5**), or the actual date of filing, if that is earlier (s 424(2)). For a *public company* the limit is 21 days before the accounts meeting of the company at which the accounts and reports in question are to be laid (see **9.6.3**) (s 424(3) and (6)). Copies can be sent out later than the deadline for a public company if all the members entitled to attend and vote at the accounts meeting agree (s 424(4)).

9.6.1.2 Right to demand copies of annual accounts and reports

Any member of a company and any holder of its debentures is entitled to demand a copy of its most recent annual accounts and reports free of charge (CA 2006, ss 431 and 432). One person may demand only one copy of the annual accounts and reports for a year under s 431 or 432, but that is in addition to any right under s 423 (see **9.6.1.1**) to receive a copy (ss 431(2) and 432(2)).

9.6.1.3 Strategic report with supplementary material

Instead of sending the full annual accounts and reports, as required by CA 2006, s 423 (see **9.6.1.1**), a company may send its strategic report with supplementary material to persons who have indicated that they do not wish to receive full annual accounts and reports (s 426). A company is not compelled to give users of its accounts the option of being provided with the strategic report with supplementary material. Detailed provisions are made in SI 2013/1973.

The supplementary material to be supplied with the strategic report instead of the rest of the company's accounts and reports is quite brief. It must include a warning that the strategic report is only part of the company's annual accounts and reports (CA 2006, s 426A(2)(a)) and directions on how to obtain a full copy of the accounts and reports (s 426A(2)(b)). In the case of a quoted company (see **9.5.2**), the main table from the directors' remuneration report must be supplied (s 426A(2)(e)). The supplementary material must state whether the auditor's report on the annual accounts was qualified or unqualified (s 426A(2)(c)) and do the same for the auditor's statement whether the strategic report and directors' report are consistent with the accounts (s 426A(2)(d)). A qualified report must be set out in full together with any further material needed to understand the qualification.

Sections 426 and 426A make no reference to companies that do not produce a strategic report.

9.6.2 WIDER PUBLICATION OF PUBLICLY TRADED COMPANY'S ACCOUNTS

9.6.2.1 Publication on quoted company's website

A quoted company (see **9.5.2**) must make its annual accounts and reports available on a website (CA 2006, s 430(1)(a)). They must remain available until the accounts and reports for the next year are put on the website (s 430(1)(b)). There must be no restrictions on access to the website (other than to meet legal or regulatory requirements in this country or abroad) or requirement for payment (s 430(3)). The annual accounts and reports must be made available as soon as reasonably practicable (s 430(4)(a)) and must be available throughout the required period (s 430(4)(b)).

9.6.2.2 Public availability of accounts of company traded on regulated market

A company whose transferable securities are admitted to trading on a regulated market (see **7.3.4.6**) must make public its annual financial report within four months of the end of the financial year being reported on (Directive 2004/109/EC, art 4(1); FCA Handbook, DTR 4.1.3R) and the report must remain publicly available for at least five years (Directive 2004/109/EC, art 4(1); DTR 4.1.4R).

9.6.3 LAYING ANNUAL ACCOUNTS BEFORE GENERAL MEETING OF PUBLIC COMPANY

The directors of a *public company* must lay before a general meeting copies of the company's annual accounts and reports (CA 2006, s 437(1)). This must be done not later than the end of the period allowed for filing the accounts and reports (see **9.6.5**). A general meeting of a public company at which its annual accounts and reports are (or are to be) laid is called an 'accounts meeting' (s 437(3)). Normally it will be the company's annual general meeting (see **14.7.1**).

If the directors of a public company fail to lay copies of its annual accounts and reports before a general meeting before the end of the period allowed, every person who was a director of the company immediately before the period ended is guilty of an offence and may be fined (s 438). It is a defence to prove that one took all reasonable steps to get the accounts presented on time (s 438(2)) but not that the accounts were not in fact prepared in time (s 438(3)).

Exactly what has to be done to annual accounts and reports to constitute 'laying before' a general meeting partly depends on the practice of the company concerned. Annual accounts and reports must be sent to the members at least 21 days before the meeting (ss 423 and 424(3)), unless all members entitled to attend and vote at the meeting agree to them being sent later (s 424(4); see **9.6.1.1**). Usually, the notice convening the meeting will state that its business will include 'receiving' the accounts and it is conventional to propose a resolution that the meeting adopts or approves the accounts, so as to provide an opportunity for discussion. The UK Corporate Governance Code (see **15.2.2**), which applies to premium listed companies (see **7.6**), requires a resolution to be proposed relating to the report and accounts (para E.2.1). Rejection of a resolution to approve or adopt annual accounts and reports would have no legal effect: the documents are the accounts and reports of the directors and auditor, which are produced to inform the members, not to be adopted or rejected by them. However, refusal by the members to adopt the accounts and reports would signal a complete loss of confidence in the directors. The directors of a quoted company (see **9.5.2**) must ensure that a resolution approving the directors' remuneration report is put to the vote at the meeting before which the accounts are laid (CA 2006, ss 439 and 440), but this statutory requirement does not by itself mean that any director's remuneration depends on the outcome of the vote (s 439(5)).

9.6.4 DELIVERY OF ACCOUNTS AND REPORTS TO COMPANIES HOUSE

In respect of each financial year, the directors of a company must deliver a copy of the company's annual accounts and reports to Companies House (CA 2006, s 441). Companies House gives public notice of receipt of annual accounts and reports (ss 1077 and 1078(2); see **4.3**).

Delivery of accounts and reports to Companies House must be completed before the end of the period allowed for filing accounts and reports—see **9.6.5**.

Under s 453, fixed penalties, recoverable by the registrar in civil proceedings, are imposed for filing accounts late. The penalties are prescribed in SI 2008/497. A penalty is payable by virtue of the legislation when default occurs, and can be recovered by the registrar in County Court proceedings. The registrar may decide not to recover the penalty, but has announced that this will be done only in very exceptional cases. It has been held that the fixed penalty scheme legitimately promotes compliance with a vital regulatory requirement in the public interest and does so proportionately. Therefore, it is not contrary to the European Convention on Human Rights, Protocol 1, art 1 (protection of property), in the Human Rights Act 1998, sch 1 (*R (POW Trust) v Chief Executive and Registrar of Companies* [2002] EWHC 2783 (Admin), [2003] 2 BCLC 295). The penalty is paid into the Consolidated Fund rather than going to Companies House (s 453(3)).

The amount of the penalty depends on the length of the period 'between' the end of the period for filing the accounts and reports (see **9.6.5**) and the day on which they are filed (s 453(2)(a)). This period excludes both the day when the period for filing ended and the day on which the accounts were filed (*Registrar of Companies v Stonelee Developments Ltd* 2004 SLT (Sh Ct) 116).

In addition to the fixed civil penalties, CA 2006 provides that if the directors of a company fail to deliver copies of its accounts and reports to Companies House before the end of the period allowed, every person who was a director of the company immediately before the period ended is guilty of a criminal offence for which a fine may be imposed (s 451). It is a defence for a director to prove that he or she took all reasonable steps to get the accounts delivered on time (s 451(2)) but not that the accounts and reports were not in fact prepared in time (s 451(3)).

As well as imposing financial penalties for failure by a company's directors to deliver accounts and reports to Companies House, CA 2006 provides that a notice can be served on the directors requiring compliance (s 452(1)). If they have failed to make good the default within 14 days after service of the notice, the court may order them to do so (s 452(1)). Wilful refusal to comply with that order would be contempt of court. The notice may be served, and the order applied for, by any member or creditor of the company, or by the registrar (s 452(1)).

9.6.5 PERIOD ALLOWED FOR FILING ANNUAL ACCOUNTS AND REPORTS

The period allowed for filing annual accounts and reports is defined in CA 2006, ss 442 and 443. The period is defined by reference to the 'relevant accounting reference period', which is the accounting reference period by reference to which the financial year for the accounts in question was determined (see **9.5.2**). For a *private company*, the period allowed for filing is nine months after the end of the relevant accounting reference period (s 442(2)(a)). For a *public company* it is six months after the end of the relevant accounting reference period (s 442(2)(b)). Whether the private or the public company rule applies depends on the company's status immediately before the end of the relevant accounting reference period (s 442(6)).

Where a company's first accounting reference period is longer than 12 months, the period allowed for filing is calculated from the first anniversary of incorporation or is three months after the end of the accounting reference period, whichever expires later (s 442(3)).

Where a company has shortened the relevant accounting reference period by changing its accounting reference date, it is allowed up to three months from the date of the notice changing the reference date, if that is longer than the time which would otherwise apply (s 442(4)).

The Secretary of State may extend the period allowed for filing, for a special reason (s 442(5)). An application for extension must be made before the unextended period expires (s 442(5)). The maximum extension is to 12 months after the end of the relevant accounting reference period (s 442(5A)).

Because of the almost automatic imposition of civil penalties for late filing, arguments over exactly which day is the last day for filing are common. Section 443 specifies how to calculate the period allowed.

The calculation under s 443 is as follows. First, find the month in which the period ends by counting the number of months from the month in which the relevant accounting reference period ended (so nine months after an accounting reference period ending in May ends in the following

February). This is the 'appropriate month'. Secondly, the day in the appropriate month on which the period ends is the day with the same number as the day on which the accounting reference period ended (so nine months after 5 May ends on 5 February). This is the 'corresponding date'. Exceptionally, if the accounting reference period ended on the last day of a month, the period for delivering accounts ends on the last day of the appropriate month, whatever its number. So, if the accounting reference period of a public company ends on 30 September, the period for delivering accounts ends six months later on 31 March. (This modifies the common law corresponding date rule, under which it would end on 30 March.) If there is no day with the same number in the appropriate month, the end of the period is the last day of the appropriate month (so nine months after 30 May is 28 February, or 29 February in a leap year). A period 'after' an event ends at the last moment of the corresponding date, but a document is not delivered to Companies House until it is received and the registrar is now entitled to prescribe what amounts to receipt (s 1071) and may, for example, require delivery within office hours.

9.6.6 SMALL COMPANIES

If a company is subject to the small companies regime, it must deliver to Companies House copies of the company's annual accounts and reports (CA 2006, s 444(3)), but may omit the profit and loss account and/or directors' report (s 444(1); directors' reports are not required for micro-entities). If either of those documents is omitted, the filed balance sheet must contain in a prominent position a statement that the company's annual accounts and reports have been delivered in accordance with the provisions applicable to companies subject to the small companies regime (s 444(5)) and (unless they are micro-entity accounts) there must be a specific statement that a profit and loss account has not been filed, if that is the case (s 444(5A)(a) and (5C)). An auditor's report has to be filed only if a profit and loss account is filed and only if the company is not exempt from audit or the directors have not taken advantage of exemption (s 444(2)). However, if a profit and loss account is not filed and the company is not exempt from audit (or the directors have not taken advantage of exemption), notes to the filed balance sheet must disclose details of the audit report, including any qualifications or emphasised matters (s 444(5A) and (5B)).

If a filed balance sheet or profit and loss account is in abridged form (see **9.5.7.7**), it is also necessary to file a statement by the company that all the members of the company have consented to the abridgement (s 444(2A)).

As an exception to the rule that filed accounts must be copies of the accounts sent to members, filed small group accounts can omit disclosure of shares in the parent company held by subsidiaries (SI 2008/409, reg 11(b); preparation of group accounts is optional in the small companies regime).

If a company is entitled to the small companies exemption in relation to the directors' report for a financial year (see **9.5.3**), but is not subject to the small companies regime, it must deliver to Companies House its full accounts and reports, except that it need not deliver the directors' report (CA 2006, s 444A).

If the directors of a company have prepared accounts in accordance with the small companies regime and in the opinion of the company's auditor they were not entitled to do so, that fact must be stated in the auditor's report (s 498(5)). However, usually there will be no auditor's report, because if directors claim their company is small they will also claim it is exempt from audit (see **9.4.6**).

9.6.7 PUBLICATION OF ACCOUNTS

If a company wishes to publish financial statements relating to one of its financial years then, under CA 2006, ss 434 and 435, it has two options. It may publish either its 'statutory accounts' or 'non-statutory accounts'. In this context, a company 'publishes' a document if it publishes, issues or circulates it or otherwise makes it available for public inspection in a manner calculated (that is, likely) to invite members of the public generally, or any class of members of the public, to read it (s 436).

The statutory accounts for a financial year are the individual accounts or group accounts that are required to be delivered to Companies House (s 434(3)).

If a company publishes any of its statutory accounts, they must be accompanied by the relevant auditor's report (s 434(1)). If it is required to prepare group accounts, it must not publish its statutory individual accounts without also publishing with them its statutory group accounts (s 434(2)). (But it can publish its group accounts without its individual accounts.)

Copies of the balance sheet, strategic report, directors' report and directors' remuneration report must state the name of the person who signed the original on behalf of the board (s 433).

The term 'non-statutory accounts' means (s 435):

(a) any balance sheet or profit and loss account relating to, or purporting to deal with, a financial year of the company; or

(b) an account in any form purporting to be a balance sheet or profit and loss account for the group consisting of the company and its subsidiary undertakings relating to, or purporting to deal with, a financial year of the company.

If a company publishes non-statutory accounts, then, by s 435(1) and (2), it must not publish with them the auditor's report but it must publish with them a statement indicating:

(a) that they are not the company's statutory accounts;

(b) whether statutory accounts dealing with any financial year with which the non-statutory accounts purport to deal have been delivered to Companies House;

(c) whether the statutory accounts for any such financial year have been reported on by the company's auditor; and

(d) whether the auditor's report was qualified or unqualified, or drew attention to any matter by way of emphasis without qualifying the report, or contained a critical statement under s 498(2) or (3) (see **17.4.6**).

9.7 HALF-YEARLY REPORTS

A company whose transferable securities are admitted to trading on a regulated market (see **7.3.4.6**) must make public a half-yearly financial report covering the first six months of the financial year (Directive 2004/109/EC, art 5; FCA Handbook, DTR 4.2.1R, 4.2.2R(1) and 4.4.2R). It must be issued as soon as possible and no later than two months after the end of the period reported on (DTR 4.2.2R(2)). It must remain available to the public for at least five years (DTR 4.2.2R(3)).

A half-yearly financial report consists of (DTR 4.2.3R):

- a condensed set of financial statements (group accounts and the individual accounts of the parent company);
- an interim management report; and
- responsibility statements.

Details of the requirements are in DTR 4.2.4R to 4.2.11R.

9.8 GROUP ACCOUNTS

9.8.1 GROUP ACCOUNTS OF A PARENT COMPANY

When a company conducts parts of its business through separate undertakings that it owns or controls, its members will want an overall picture of the financial position of the whole business, not just the part that is carried out by the company of which they are members. Group accounts for a number of related undertakings treat them as one single entity and ignore transactions between undertakings within the group.

'Undertaking' in this context means (CA 2006, s 1161(1)):

(a) a body corporate or partnership firm, or

(b) an unincorporated association carrying on a trade or business, with or without a view to profit.

If, at the end of a financial year, a company is a parent company, and is not subject to the small companies regime, the directors must, as well as preparing individual accounts for the year, prepare group accounts (s 399(2) and (2A)(a)(i)), unless one of the exemptions provided by s 400 or 401 (see **9.8.4**) or s 402 (see **9.8.6**) applies. The exemption for companies in the small companies regime is extended to a company which would be a small company but for being a public company, provided it is not in the same group as a company of various economically significant types (s 399(2A)(b) and (2B)). A company that is exempt from preparing group accounts may nevertheless choose to do so (s 399(4)).

9.8.2 PARENT AND SUBSIDIARY UNDERTAKINGS; GROUP UNDERTAKINGS

The relationship of parent undertaking and subsidiary undertaking is defined in CA 2006, s 1162, in a way that is similar to the definition of the relationship of holding company and subsidiary in s 1159 (see **14.15**). A 'parent company' is a parent undertaking which is a company.

The relationship of parent undertaking and subsidiary undertaking may arise in the following ways:

(a) under s 1162(2)(a), where the parent undertaking holds a majority of the voting rights in the subsidiary undertaking;

(b) under s 1162(2)(b), where the parent undertaking is a member of the subsidiary undertaking and has the right to appoint or remove a majority of its board of directors;

(c) under s 1162(2)(c), where the parent undertaking has the right to exercise a dominant influence over the subsidiary undertaking

  (i) by virtue of provisions contained in the subsidiary undertaking's articles, or

  (ii) by virtue of a control contract;

(d) under s 1162(2)(d), where the parent undertaking is a member of the subsidiary undertaking and controls alone, pursuant to an agreement with other shareholders or members, a majority of the voting rights in the subsidiary undertaking;

(e) under s 1162(4), where

  (i) the parent undertaking has the power to exercise, or actually exercises, dominant influence or control over the subsidiary undertaking, or

  (ii) the parent company and the subsidiary undertaking are managed on a unified basis; or

(f) under s 1162(5), where the subsidiary undertaking is a subsidiary undertaking of an under-
     taking which is itself a subsidiary undertaking of the parent undertaking.

The definition of the relationship of parent undertaking and subsidiary undertaking corresponds
to the definition of holding company and subsidiary, except for s 1162(2)(c) and (4) (items (c) and
(e) in the above list), which have no equivalent in the definition of holding company and subsidiary.
     For the purposes of s 1162(2), an undertaking P is to be treated as a member of an undertaking S if:

(a) any subsidiary undertaking of P is a member of S (s 1162(3)(a)); or

(b) any shares in S are held by a person acting on behalf of P or any of its subsidiary undertakings
     (s 1162(3)(b)).

There is no equivalent of s 1162(3) in the definition of holding company and subsidiary.
     The definition in s 1162 is explained and supplemented by sch 7, which corresponds to sch 6 in
the definition of holding company and subsidiary.
     Schedule 7, para 4, explains s 1162(2)(c) (which has no equivalent in the definition of hold-
ing company and subsidiary). Under sch 7, para 4(1), an undertaking is not to be regarded as
having the right to exercise a dominant influence over another undertaking unless it has a right
to give directions with respect to the operating and financial policies of that other undertaking
which its directors are obliged to comply with whether or not they are for the benefit of that other
undertaking. 'Control contract' is defined by sch 7, para 4(2), to mean a written contract conferring
a right to exercise a dominant influence over another undertaking which:

(a) is of a kind authorised by the articles of the undertaking in relation to which the right is
     exercisable; and

(b) is permitted by the law under which that undertaking is established.

In relation to an undertaking which is not a company, expressions appropriate to companies are to
be construed as references to the corresponding persons, officers, documents or organs, as the case
may be, appropriate to undertakings of that description (s 1161(3)). By sch 7, para 4(3), the concept
of actual dominant influence of one undertaking over another in s 1162(4) is not to be interpreted
by reference to sch 7, para 4.
     In relation to an undertaking A, another undertaking B is a 'group undertaking' if (s 1161(5)):

(a) B is a parent undertaking or a subsidiary undertaking of A; or

(b) B is a subsidiary undertaking of any parent undertaking of A.

If a company is a member of a group, its annual accounts must disclose the name of the parent
company which draws up group accounts. If there is more than one such group, the parent companies of the largest and the smallest group must be identified. The accounts must also disclose the
name of the company which the directors regard as being the company's ultimate parent company
(if there is one). The country in which the ultimate parent company is incorporated must be given,
if it is known to the directors and is outside the United Kingdom. See SI 2008/409, sch 6, paras 35
and 36; SI 2008/410, sch 4, paras 8 and 9.

9.8.3 EFFECT ON INDIVIDUAL ACCOUNTS

A company that prepares group accounts does not have to include an individual profit and loss
account for itself in its published annual accounts, provided its individual balance sheet shows the
company's profit or loss for the financial year, and provided the accounts disclose that the exemption applies (CA 2006, s 408). However, by s 408(3), the full individual profit and loss account

(apart from some notes) must be considered and approved by the board, in accordance with s 414(1). In practice, a separate profit and loss account for a parent company rarely gives useful information and is normally omitted.

Full individual accounts must be prepared for each subsidiary included in a group consolidation.

9.8.4 EXEMPTION FOR SUBGROUPS

Provided it is not a traded company (see **9.4.4**), a parent company is exempt from the requirement to prepare group accounts for a financial year if it is itself a subsidiary undertaking and is included in consolidated accounts for a larger group. This exemption is given by CA 2006, s 400, if the group accounts which include the company are drawn up by a parent undertaking incorporated in an EEA State, or by s 401 otherwise. The two sections are in almost identical terms.

The group accounts which include the company must be drawn up to the same date, or to an earlier date in the same financial year (CA 2006, ss 400(2)(a) and 401(2)(a)). The group accounts must be prepared in accordance with Directive 2013/34/EU or, if they are prepared under the law of a non-EEA State, in an equivalent manner (CA 2006, ss 400(2)(b) and 401(2)(b)) and they must be audited (ss 400(2)(b) and 401(2)(c)).

A company which is exempt from preparing group accounts by virtue of s 400 or 401 must disclose in the notes to its individual accounts the fact that it is exempt (ss 400(2)(c) and 401(2) (d)). It must also disclose the name of the parent undertaking in whose accounts its affairs are consolidated and the address of its registered office or, if it is not incorporated, the address of its principal place of business (ss 400(2)(d) and 401(2)(e)). An exempt subgroup parent must deliver to Companies House, within the period allowed for delivering its individual accounts, copies of its parent undertaking's group accounts, annual report and auditor's report, with certified translations of any document not in English (ss 400(2)(e) and (f) and 401(2)(f) and (g)).

This exemption is qualified by ss 400(1) and 401(1) where the company is not a wholly owned subsidiary, that is, where there are minority interests. In that case, if the immediate parent undertaking holds more than 90 per cent of the shares in the company, all the remaining shareholders must have approved the exemption. If it holds between 50 and 90 per cent, shareholders holding in aggregate at least 5 per cent of the allotted shares in the company can block use of the exemption by serving notice at least six months before the end of the financial year to which it relates.

9.8.5 EXEMPTION FOR SMALL GROUPS

If a company is the parent company of a small group (see **9.4.5**), it will be subject to the small companies regime (CA 2006, s 383(1)), unless it is excluded by s 384 (see **9.4.4**). If it is subject to the small companies regime, preparation of group accounts is optional (s 399(2A)(a)(i) and (4)). If the only reason for being excluded by s 384 is that the company is a public company then, provided the group does not include a traded company (see **9.4.4**) or various other economically significant types of company, group accounts are not required (s 399(2A)(b) and (2B)).

9.8.6 SUBSIDIARIES THAT MAY BE EXCLUDED FROM GROUP ACCOUNTS

The general rule is that every subsidiary undertaking of a parent company must be included in the consolidation when Companies Act group accounts are prepared (CA 2006, s 405(1)). However, s 405 allows for some subsidiaries to be excluded. Under s 405(2) and (3), a subsidiary undertaking may be excluded from consolidation in the following circumstances:

(a) Under s 405(2), if including the subsidiary is not material for the purpose of giving a true and fair view; but two or more undertakings may be excluded on this ground only if they are not material taken together.

(b) Under s 405(3)(a), if severe long-term restrictions substantially hinder the exercise of all the rights of the reporting company over the assets or management of the subsidiary by virtue of which it is deemed to be the parent company.

(c) Under s 405(3)(b), if extremely rare circumstances mean that the information necessary for the preparation of group accounts cannot be obtained without disproportionate expense or undue delay.

(d) Under s 405(3)(c), if the interest of the parent company in the subsidiary undertaking by virtue of which it is deemed to be the parent company is held exclusively with a view to subsequent resale.

If all the subsidiary undertakings of a parent company fall within these exclusions, no group accounts (either IAS or Companies Act) are required (s 402).

9.8.7 INFORMATION ABOUT RELATED UNDERTAKINGS

Small group accounts and large or medium-sized individual and group accounts must give information about what the legislation refers to as 'related undertakings'. For small groups the information to be given is specified in SI 2008/409, reg 10 and sch 6, part 2. For large and medium-sized companies and groups the information to be given is specified in SI 2008/410, reg 7 and sch 4. Micro-entity accounts do not include this information (SI 2008/409, reg 5A).

Related undertakings include subsidiary undertakings and undertakings which are not subsidiaries but in which the company has a significant holding (20 per cent or more of the nominal value of any class of shares in the undertaking, or a holding whose value is more than 20 per cent of the reporting company's assets).

The rules require related undertakings to be named. The country of incorporation must be stated if it is not the United Kingdom. If the undertaking is not incorporated, the address of its principal place of business must be given. The company's shareholding in the related undertaking must be identified and certain financial information about the undertaking must be disclosed.

9.9 CONTENTS OF STRATEGIC REPORT AND DIRECTORS' REPORT

9.9.1 INTRODUCTION

The strategic report for a financial year of a company must comply with CA 2006, ss 414A to 414D. The directors' report must comply with ss 415 to 419, and with SI 2008/409, reg 7 and sch 5 (small companies) or SI 2008/410, reg 10 and sch 7 (medium-sized and large companies). These provisions implement the requirements of Directive 2013/34/EU, art 19, to include information in what the Directive calls a 'management report'. CA 2006 divides that information between the strategic report, which covers art 19(1) and the directors' report, which deals with the requirements of art 19(2) (see **9.9.4.7**). The United Kingdom legislation also contains UK requirements to provide information on matters of public interest including gender balance (see **9.9.2**), employment of disabled people (see **9.9.4.8**), involvement of employees (see **9.9.4.9**), political donations (see **9.9.4.10**) and greenhouse gas emissions (see **9.9.4.11**).

Premium listed companies (see **7.6**), as part of their continuing obligations, must include a large quantity of additional information in their annual financial reports (LR 9.8.4R to 9.8.12R). Apart from the corporate governance statement (see **9.9.3**), those requirements will not be considered here. Premium listed companies are also subject to the UK Corporate Governance Code (see **15.2.2**), which requires further information (see **9.9.3**, **9.9.4.2** and **9.9.4.3**).

If a company is a parent company and its directors prepare group accounts, their directors' report must be a group directors' report relating to all the companies included in the group accounts (CA 2006, s 415(2)). The same applies to the strategic report (s 414A(3)). Where appropriate, a group strategic report may give greater emphasis to the matters that are significant to the undertakings included in the consolidation, taken as a whole (s 414A(4)).

An auditor's report on a company's annual accounts must state whether, in the auditor's opinion, the information given in the strategic report (if any), the directors' report and any separate corporate governance statement is consistent with those accounts, whether the reports and statement have been prepared in accordance with applicable legal requirements, and whether the auditor has identified in them any material misstatements, giving an indication of the nature of each misstatement (ss 496 and 497A).

9.9.2 STRATEGIC REPORT

The statutory purpose of the strategic report is to inform members and help them assess how the directors have performed their duty under CA 2006, s 172, to promote the success of the company (s 414C(1)) or, in a group strategic report, the undertakings included in the consolidation. Specification of a statutory purpose may limit the persons who can claim that they are owed a duty not to be negligent in the preparation of the report (see **17.5.2** to **17.5.4**).

The strategic report of a quoted company (see **9.5.2**) must describe the company's business model and strategy (s 414C(8)(a) and (b)). This is not required by Directive 2013/34/EU, art 17(1), but it accords with the requirement in the UK Corporate Governance Code that the directors must state in the annual report the basis on which the company generates or preserves value over the longer term (its business model) and the strategy for delivering the company's objectives (UK Corporate Governance Code, para C.1.2).

Every strategic report must include a fair review of the company's or group's business and a description of the principal risks and uncertainties facing the company or group (s 414C(2) and (13)). The report must be a balanced and comprehensive analysis of the development and performance of the company's or group's business during the financial year, and its position at the end of the year, consistent with the size and complexity of the business (s 414C(3) and (13)). A strategic report is required by s 414C(4) to include analysis using financial key performance indicators (KPIs) and, where appropriate, other KPIs, including information relating to environmental matters and employee matters. 'Key performance indicator' is defined to mean a factor which effectively measures the development, performance or position of the company's or group's business (s 414C(5) and (9)). A medium-sized company need not deal with non-financial information in the analysis using KPIs (s 414C(6)). A strategic report must, where appropriate, include references to, and additional explanations of, amounts included in the annual accounts (s 414C(12)). It need not disclose information about impending developments or negotiations if disclosure would be seriously prejudicial to the company's interests (s 414C(14)).

The strategic report of a quoted company must also include (s 414C(7)):

(a) the main trends and factors likely to affect the future development, performance and position of the company's business;

(b) information about

    (i) environmental matters, including the impact of the company's business on the environment,

    (ii) the company's employees, and

    (iii) social and community issues, including information about any policies of the company in relation to those matters and the effectiveness of those policies; and

(c) information about persons with whom the company has contractual or other arrangements which are essential to the business of the company.

These points must be covered to the extent necessary for an understanding of the development, performance or position of the company's business (s 414C(7)). A strategic report which omits information about all or any of the environmental, employee and social issues must state which of them is omitted (s 414C(7)).

The strategic report of a quoted company is required by s 414C(8)(c) and (10)(a) to show its gender balance by giving a breakdown, as at the end of the year, of:

(a) the number of persons of each sex who were directors of the company (or, in a group report, directors of the parent company);

(b) the number of persons of each sex who were senior managers of the company (other than persons already counted as directors); and

(c) the number of persons of each sex who were employees of the company.

A 'senior manager' is defined (s 414C(9)) as an employee of the company, or of a group undertaking, who has responsibility for planning, directing or controlling the activities of the company or undertaking, or a strategically significant part of it. In a group strategic report, the breakdown of senior managers must include the number of persons of each sex who were the directors of the undertakings included in the consolidation (s 414C(10)(b)). The analysis of gender balance is not required by Directive 2013/34/EU, art 17(1), but is a matter of public interest in the United Kingdom.

The strategic report of a traded company (see **9.4.4**), bank or insurance company must include a non-financial information statement (s 414CA(1) and (2)). This applies only if the company or group has more than 500 employees (s 414CA(4)–(6)), is not subject to the small companies regime and does not qualify as medium-sized (s 414CA(3)).This statement must contain information (s 414CB(1) and (2) about the company's policies, and the outcome of those policies, in relation to, at least:

(a) environmental matters (including the impact of the company's business on the environment);

(b) the company's employees;

(c) social matters;

(d) respect for human rights; and

(e) anti-corruption and anti-bribery matters.

If the company does not have a policy in relation to any of these matters, it must provide a clear and reasoned explanation for not doing so (s 414CB(4)).

A strategic report may also include any matter required to be disclosed in the directors' report if the directors consider it is of strategic importance to the company (CA 2006, s 414C(11)). There must be a statement in the directors' report that the information will be found in the strategic report (SI 2008/410, sch 7, para 1A).

9.9.3 CORPORATE GOVERNANCE STATEMENT

If a company has transferable securities admitted to trading on a regulated market (see **7.3.4.6**), it must produce a corporate governance statement (Directive 2013/34/EU, art 20). The required content of the corporate governance statement is set out in the FCA Handbook DTR 7.2. A company's corporate governance statement must:

(a) Identify the corporate governance code to which the company is subject, and state whether it has departed from, or not applied, any aspects of the code and why (DTR 7.2.2R and 7.2.3R). Premium listed companies (see **7.6**) are subject to the UK Corporate Governance Code (see **15.2.2**) and are required to make the statement in relation to that code (LR 9.8.6R(5) and (6)).

(b) Describe the main features of the company's or group's internal control and risk management systems in relation to the financial reporting process (DTR 7.2.5R and 7.2.10R; see also UK Corporate Governance Code, C.2.1).

(c) Give details about capital structure which may be a barrier to takeovers (DTR 7.2.6R; see **9.9.4.6**).

(d) Describe the composition and operation of the company's administrative, management and supervisory bodies and their committees (DTR 7.2.7R). This requirement overlaps with the requirements of the UK Corporate Governance Code, A.1.1, A.1.2, B.2.4, C.3.3 and D.2.1.

A corporate governance statement must either be in the directors' report or in a separate statement which is either published together with the directors' report or is published on the company's website and referred to in the directors' report (DTR 7.2.9R).

A listed company should report its chairman's other significant commitments and explain the impact of any change in them (UK Corporate Governance Code, para B.3.1). There should be a statement of how performance evaluation of the board, its committees and its individual directors has been conducted (UK Corporate Governance Code, para B.6.1).

9.9.4 DIRECTORS' REPORT

9.9.4.1 Directors

A directors' report must state the names of all persons who, at any time during the financial year reported on, were directors of the company (CA 2006, s 416(1)(a)). Directors of subsidiary undertakings do not have to be named.

A directors' report for a company's financial year must disclose the qualifying indemnity provisions (see **16.16.5**) for the benefit of the company's directors and directors of associated companies that were in place both during the financial year reported on and (if different) at the time the report is approved by the board (s 236).

9.9.4.2 Auditor and audit committee

CA 2006, s 418, requires a directors' report to contain a statement by every person who is a director at the time when the report is approved by the board (s 418(2); see **9.5.3**) that:

(a) So far as the director is aware, there is no relevant audit information of which the company's auditor is unaware. 'Relevant audit information' means information needed by the auditor in connection with preparing the auditor's report (s 418(3)).

(b) The director has taken all the steps he or she ought to have taken, as a director, to make him or herself aware of any relevant audit information and to establish that the company's auditor is aware of that information. The director must have taken such steps for that purpose as were required by his or her duty to exercise due care, skill and diligence (s 418(4)) as assessed by the dual objective/subjective standard discussed in **16.8.1** (s 418(5)). In particular, the director must have made such inquiries of his or her fellow directors and of the company's auditor as are required by the dual objective/subjective standard (s 418(4) and (5)).

This statement is not required if the company is exempt from the auditing requirements, because it is a small company (see **9.4.6**), a subsidiary (see **9.4.6**) or a dormant company (see **9.4.7**) (s 418(1)).

There should be a statement in the directors' report of a listed company about the reporting responsibilities of its auditor (UK Corporate Governance Code, para C.1.1). If the auditor provides non-audit services, the directors' report should explain to shareholders how auditor objectivity and independence are safeguarded (para C.3.8). There should be a separate section of the report describing how the audit committee has discharged its responsibilities (para C.3.8). If the company has no internal audit function, there should be an explanation of its absence (para C.3.6).

9.9.4.3 Views of major shareholders of listed company

The directors' report of a listed company should state the steps the board has taken to ensure that directors, particularly non-executive directors, develop an understanding of the views of major shareholders, for example, through face-to-face contact, analysts' or brokers' briefings and surveys of shareholder opinion (UK Corporate Governance Code, para E.1.2).

9.9.4.4 Dividend recommendation

Unless the company is entitled to the small companies exemption (see **9.5.3**), a directors' report must state the amount (if any) that the directors recommend should be paid by way of dividend (CA 2006, s 416(3)).

9.9.4.5 Holdings of own shares

The directors' report of a public company must give details of acquisitions, by or on behalf of the company, of its own shares and the creation in its favour of charges or liens on its own shares (SI 2008/410, sch 7, paras 8 and 9).

9.9.4.6 Barriers to takeovers

If a company has securities which carry voting rights and are admitted to trading on a regulated market (see **7.3.4.3**), its directors' report must give details, as required by Directive 2004/25/EC, art 10, of capital structure which may be a barrier to takeovers (SI 2008/410, sch 7, paras 13 and 14). This information must also be given in the corporate governance statement (see **9.9.3**).

9.9.4.7 Information required by art 19(2)

Directive 2013/34/EU, art 19(2) requires the following information in the management report and United Kingdom legislation has allocated it to the directors' report. The directors' report of a medium-sized or large company must, by SI 2008/410, sch 7, para 7, contain:

    (a) particulars of any important events affecting the company or group which have occurred since the end of the financial year;

    (b) an indication of likely future developments in the business of the company or group;

    (c) an indication of the activities (if any) of the company or group in the field of research and development; and

    (d) (unless the company is an unlimited company) an indication of the existence of branches (as defined in CA 2006, s 1046(3)) of the company outside the United Kingdom.

The directors' report of a medium-sized or large company must contain an indication of the following matters in relation to its, or the group's, use of financial instruments:

    (a) the financial risk management objectives and policies of the company, including the policy for hedging each major type of forecasted transaction for which hedge accounting is used; and

(b) the exposure of the company to price risk, credit risk, liquidity risk and cash flow risk.

This information is required by SI 2008/410, sch 7, para 6, which reproduces the requirements of Directive 2013/34/EU, art 19(2)(e), which were formerly in Directive 78/660/EEC, art 46(2)(f) (individual accounts), and Directive 83/349/EEC, art 36(2)(e) (group accounts). SI 2008/410, sch 7, para 6(3), states that various terms used in para 6 'have the same meaning as they have' in those Directives, but the terms are not actually defined either in those Directives or in Directive 2013/34/EU.

This information is not required if it is not material for the assessment of the assets, liabilities, financial position and profit or loss of the company (SI 2008/410, sch 7, para 6(1)).

9.9.4.8 Employment of disabled persons

If the weekly average number of employees of a company in a financial year exceeded 250, its directors' report must describe its policy (if any) concerning the employment of disabled persons (SI 2008/409, sch 5, para 5; SI 2008/410, sch 7, para 10).

9.9.4.9 Employee involvement

If the weekly average number of employees of a medium-sized or large company in a financial year exceeded 250, its directors' report must describe the action taken to inform and consult employees, to involve them in the company's performance through an employees' share scheme or otherwise, and to achieve awareness of the financial and economic factors affecting the company's performance (SI 2008/410, sch 7, para 11).

9.9.4.10 Political donations and expenditure

Particulars of the political donations and expenditure of a company and its subsidiaries during a financial year must be given in its directors' report, unless the total amount did not exceed £2,000 (SI 2008/409, sch 5, para 2; SI 2008/410, sch 7, para 3). The parties or candidates who received donations must be named and the total amount given to each of them stated. The report must also state the amount given to any 'non-EU political party', meaning a political party which carries on, or proposes to carry on, its activities wholly outside the EU (SI 2008/409, sch 5, para 3; SI 2008/410, sch 7, para 4).

A company that is a wholly owned subsidiary of a company incorporated in the United Kingdom is not required to report political donations and expenditure.

9.9.4.11 Greenhouse gas emissions

SI 2008/410, sch 7, para 15(1), (2) and (3), require the directors' report of a quoted company (see 9.5.2) to state the annual quantity of emissions in tonnes of carbon dioxide equivalent:

(a) from activities for which that company is responsible, including the combustion of fuel and the operation of any facility; and

(b) resulting from the purchase of electricity, heat, steam or cooling by the company for its own use.

The terms 'emissions' and 'tonne of carbon dioxide equivalent' are defined in the Climate Change Act 2008, ss 92 and 93(2) (SI 2008/410, sch 7, para 20). The report must state the methodologies used to calculate these quantities (sch 7, para 16), which must be given both in absolute amounts and as a ratio to a quantifiable factor associated with the company's activities (sch 7, para 17). The figures reported for the preceding year must be given for comparison (sch 7, para 18).

This information is required only to the extent that it is practical for the company to obtain it (sch 7, para 15(4)). If it is not practical to obtain some or all of the information, the report must state what information is not included and why (sch 7, para 15(4)).

9.9.5 DIRECTORS' RESPONSIBILITY STATEMENT

The annual financial report of a company whose transferable securities are admitted to trading on a regulated market (see **7.3.4.6**) must include a statement of assurance (also called a responsibility statement) (Directive 2004/109/EC, art 4(2)(c); FCA Handbook, DTR 4.1.5R and 4.1.12R). This is a statement made by the persons responsible within the company, to the effect that, to the best of their knowledge:

(a) the accounts give a true and fair view of the assets, liabilities, financial position and profit or loss of the company and the undertakings included in group accounts; and

(b) the report includes a fair review of the development and performance of the business and the position of the company and the undertakings included in the group accounts taken as a whole, together with a description of the principal risks and uncertainties that they face.

For a premium listed company, the statement should explain the directors' responsibility for preparing the accounts and the directors' report, and that they consider that those documents, taken as a whole, are 'fair, balanced and understandable' and provide 'the information necessary for shareholders to assess the company's performance, business model and strategy' (UK Corporate Governance Code, C.1.1). The audit committee should provide the board with advice on this point if requested (C.3.4).

9.10 REVISION AND EXTERNAL REVIEW OF ACCOUNTS AND REPORTS

Under CA 2006, s 454, if the directors of a company discover that annual accounts which they have issued do not comply with the Act or, where applicable, with Regulation (EC) No 1606/2002, art 4, they may prepare a revised version (CA 2006, s 454(1)). The same applies to a non-compliant directors' report, directors' remuneration report or strategic report (s 454(1)) and to a revision of a directors' remuneration policy (s 422A(5)). The detailed procedure is set out in SI 2008/373.

Under CA 2006, s 456, an application may be made to the court for a declaration that the annual accounts, strategic report or directors' report of a company do not comply with the requirements of the Act or, where applicable, Regulation (EC) No 1606/2002, art 4 and for an order requiring the company's directors to revise them (CA 2006, s 456(1)). This modifies the decision in *Devlin v Slough Estates Ltd* [1983] BCLC 497 that, in the absence of bad faith or fraud, the court would not make declarations of how matters should be reported in a company's annual accounts. Section 456 is applied by s 422A(5) to a revision of a directors' remuneration policy. Notice of any application made under s 456, and a copy of any order made by the court on the application, must be filed by the applicant at Companies House (s 456(2) and (7)). The only persons who may apply under s 456 are the Secretary of State and the FRC's Conduct Committee, which is authorised for the purpose by SI 2012/1439, art 4. The Conduct Committee has powers under CA 2006, s 459, to require a company, its officers, employees and auditor, to produce documents or provide information or explanations so that the Committee can discover whether there are grounds for applying under s 456 or can determine whether or not to make an application. If the court orders revision of accounts, it may give directions with respect to the auditing of the accounts, the revision of any directors' report, directors' remuneration report, or strategic report and supplementary material and publicising the revision (s 456(3)). It may also make the directors liable for the costs of the application (s 456(5) and (6)). In practice, and as agreed with BIS, the Committee normally exercises this authority only in connection with the accounts of public companies and large private companies (*The Conduct Committee: Operating Procedures for Reviewing Corporate Reporting* (1 April 2016)).

Under s 455, the Secretary of State is empowered to notify directors of a company that he or she believes something is wrong with their annual accounts, strategic report or directors' report and give them one month to provide an explanation of the accounts or report or prepare revised accounts or a revised report (s 455(1) to (3)). This power can be exercised only after accounts have been sent out under s 423 or laid before a general meeting or delivered to Companies House (s 455(1)). An application to the court under s 456 may be made by the Secretary of State if there is no response to the notice within the time limit, or the response is unsatisfactory or any revision supplied is unsatisfactory (s 455(4)).

Sections 455 and 456 also apply to accounts which have already been voluntarily revised by directors (ss 455(5) and 456(8)).

The Conduct Committee keeps under review the annual accounts and half-yearly reports (see **9.7**) produced by issuers of shares and other transferable securities (see **7.4.2.3**) admitted to trading on a regulated market (defined in FSMA 2000, s 102A(3); see **7.3.4.3**) (Companies (Audit, Investigations and Community Enterprise) Act 2004, s 14; SI 2012/1439, art 2). The Committee may inform the FCA of any conclusions it reaches in relation to any such accounts or reports (Companies (Audit, Investigations and Community Enterprise) Act 2004, s 14(2)(b)). If the Committee considers that a company's accounts may not comply with Part 6 rules made by the FCA (see **7.4.1.3** and **7.6.1**), it may require the company, or any of its officers or employees, or its auditor, to produce documents or provide information or explanations (s 15B).

9.11 REPORTS ON PAYMENT PRACTICES AND PERFORMANCE

For the seven years from 2017 to 2024, large companies must publish a half-yearly report on their payment practices, policies and performance (Small Business, Enterprise and Employment Act 2015, s 3; SI 2017/395). Publication is on a web-based service provided by the Secretary of State.

10

DISTRIBUTIONS AND THE MAINTENANCE OF CAPITAL

SUMMARY OF POINTS COVERED

- What is in this chapter
- General principle
- Distributions
- Capitalisations and bonus shares
- Redeemable shares

- Purchase of own shares
- Reduction of capital
- Financial assistance for purchase of own shares
- Exemptions for employees' share schemes

10.1 WHAT IS IN THIS CHAPTER

The statutory liability of a member of a company limited by shares is a liability to contribute to its assets when it is wound up (Insolvency Act 1986, s 74). The nominal value of the shares held by a member is the limit on this liability. It is expected that all, or perhaps some, of the contribution will be made before winding up so as to form the company's capital while it is a going concern. If a member could contribute capital in respect of shares before winding up and have it returned before winding up, and then claim that, having made a contribution once, there is no requirement to make it again in winding up, this would evade the statutory liability. The amounts of issued and paid-up share capital that a company has are set out in the publicly available statement of capital (see **2.2.1.7** and **6.3.6**). Persons who deal with the company may rely on that statement as giving some indication of the company's financial strength. They could be deceived if the company could freely return the paid-up capital to its members. In *Guinness v Land Corporation of Ireland* (1882) 22 ChD 349, Cotton LJ said, at pp 375–6:

> That section [now the Insolvency Act 1986, s 74] provides that in the case of a company limited by shares being wound up, no contribution shall be required from any member exceeding the amount if any unpaid on the shares in respect of which he is liable as a present or past member; that the capital of the company as mentioned in the memorandum [now the statement of capital] is to be the fund which is to pay the creditors in the event of the company being wound up. From that it follows that whatever has been paid by a member cannot be returned to him. . . . [What is described in the statement of capital as the capital] is, of course, liable to be spent or lost in carrying on the business of the company, but no part of it can be returned to a member so as to take away from the fund to which the creditors have a right to look as that out of which they are to be paid. . . . no part of the capital mentioned in the [statement of capital] can be taken out of the fund to which the creditors have to look except for the purpose of employing it for the objects of the company.

This chapter considers the controls imposed on return of a company's capital to its members, beginning with the common law general principle that return of capital is illegal unless permitted by statute (**10.2**). Where members of a company have dealings with it, there is a problem of deciding whether there has been a genuine commercial transaction or an illegal return of capital.

The whole purpose of putting capital into a company is that the company will use the capital to make profits to be distributed among the members. The problem of distinguishing between a legal distribution of profits and an illegal return of capital is dealt with in statutory provisions (**10.3**). Statute also permits a transfer of profits to a capital redemption reserve and use of profits to pay up bonus shares (**10.4**).

It is often beneficial for a company to rearrange its share capital in changing circumstances and this may involve returning capital to some or all members. Statutory provisions permit a company to issue and redeem redeemable shares (**10.5**) or purchase its own shares (**10.6**). If purchased shares are publicly traded, they may be held as treasury shares (**10.6.6**). Redemption or purchase of shares by a public company must be done in a way that does not reduce its capital. A private company may make a payment out of capital to redeem or purchase shares. A company may reduce its issued share capital by special resolution, though a public company requires court approval (**10.7**). A return or reduction of a private company's capital must be approved by its members and must be supported by a solvency statement made by the directors and there are publicity requirements to ensure transparency. A public company's reduction of capital must be approved by its members and by the court. Approval by the court is also an alternative way of reducing a private company's capital.

Financial assistance cannot be given for the acquisition of shares if either the issuer of the shares or the assisting company is a public company, and the assisting company is either the issuing company or a subsidiary (see **10.8**).

Employees' share schemes are encouraged by exemptions from many of the controls on contributed capital (see **10.9**).

Where statutory provisions apply, they require the legality of transactions to be determined by objective analysis of accounts. When applying the common law rules, it may be necessary to consider the subjective intentions of the parties to the transaction (see **10.2**).

The collapse of the department store chain BHS in 2016 revealed that during 15 years of control by Sir Philip Green, astonishing amounts of the company's money had been transferred to benefit him, apparently completely legally. For a discussion of some of the resultant calls for reform of the law see Alastair Hudson, 'BHS and the reform of company law' (2016) 37 Co Law 364.

Key legislation which you should be able to consult when reading this chapter:

- Insolvency Act 1986, s 74;
- CA 2006, ss 641–737, 829–853, 1166;
- the model articles for private companies limited by shares and for public companies in SI 2008/3229.

All that legislation is in *Blackstone's Statutes on Company Law*.

The following cases, which are considered in this chapter, are particularly significant and are recommended further reading:

- *Bairstow v Queens Moat Houses plc* [2001] 2 BCLC 531;
- *Belmont Finance Corporation v Williams Furniture Ltd (No 2)* [1980] 1 All ER 393 (also a key case for **Chapter 16**); and
- *Progress Property Co Ltd v Moorgarth Group Ltd* [2010] UKSC 55, [2011] 1 WLR 1.

Your particular course of study may require you to read other source materials.

10.2 GENERAL PRINCIPLE

The judge-made rule of common law was summarised by Lord Russell of Killowen giving the opinion of the Privy Council in *Hill v Permanent Trustee Co of New South Wales Ltd* [1930] AC 720 at p 731:

> A limited company not in liquidation can make no payment by way of return of capital to its shareholders except as a step in an authorised reduction of capital [see **10.7**]. Any other payment made by it by means of which it parts with moneys to its shareholders must and can only be made by way of dividing profits [see **10.3**]. Whether the payment is called 'dividend' or 'bonus', or any other name, it still must remain a payment on division of profits.

At the time Lord Russell was speaking, the courts had arrived, after initial uncertainty, at an absolute prohibition on a company purchasing its own shares (*Trevor v Whitworth* (1887) 12 App Cas 409). This prohibition has been relaxed by statute, which now permits redemption (see **10.5**) and repurchase (see **10.6**) of shares as additional ways in which a company may legally return capital to its members.

In a small private company, the members may all be directors and/or employees of the company. They can remove the company's assets by paying themselves large salaries and directors' fees or buying the company's property for less than its true value. A holding company can require its subsidiary to pay large fees for 'group services'. The propriety of such practices cannot normally be determined objectively but depends on a subjective assessment of the intentions of those involved (*Progress Property Co Ltd v Moorgarth Group Ltd* [2010] UKSC 55, [2011] 1 WLR 1). The court must examine the substance rather than the form of the transaction or what description the parties have given to it (*Progress Property Co Ltd v Moorgarth Group Ltd* at [16]). For example, if the members of a company genuinely resolve to pay remuneration to a director for service as a director, the court will not inquire whether the remuneration is reasonable, though if it finds that the so-called remuneration is in fact a repayment of capital, it will order the money to be returned to the company (*Re Halt Garage (1964) Ltd* [1982] 3 All ER 1016; *MacPherson v European Strategic Bureau Ltd* [2000] 2 BCLC 683). There is no rule that directors' fees can be paid only out of profits (*Re Lundy Granite Co Ltd, Harvey Lewis's Case* (1872) 26 LT 673).

In *Progress Property Co Ltd v Moorgarth Group Ltd* the claimant company sold all the shares it held in a wholly owned subsidiary to the defendant company. Both claimant and defendant were controlled by the same man. However, because the transaction was part of a deal to refinance his companies, the claimant and defendant were represented by separate solicitors, there had been an independent professional valuation of the shares and the negotiations had gone on for several months. Unfortunately, everyone involved had misunderstood an important element of the valuation of the shares and it was alleged (though, in these proceedings, not proved) that they were worth about £4 million more than was paid for them. The Supreme Court held that as the judge at first instance and the Court of Appeal had found that there was a genuine commercial sale, it could not be characterised as an illegal return of capital. The transaction considered in this case took place before CA 2006, s 845 (see **10.3.5**), was enacted.

There is a more general rule that it is illegal for a company to make a gift to anyone of any of its assets otherwise than out of profits available for distribution (see **10.3.3**) or in furtherance of its objects. The rule is exemplified by *Re George Newman and Co* [1895] 1 Ch 674, in which a man who had been a director and chairman of the company had used £3,500 of its money for improvements to his own house. The Court of Appeal said, at p 686:

> The shareholders . . . can, if they think proper, remunerate directors for their trouble or make presents to them for their services out of assets properly divisible amongst the shareholders themselves. . . . But to make presents out of profits is one thing and to make them out of capital or out of money borrowed by the company is a very different matter. Such money cannot be lawfully divided amongst the shareholders themselves, nor can it be given away by them for nothing to their directors so as to bind the company in its corporate capacity.

10.3 DISTRIBUTIONS

10.3.1 DIVIDENDS

The law on distributions would be much simpler and easier to understand if every company was intended to run a business for a definite period of time and was not permitted to make payments to its members until the end of that period, when it would sell the business and be wound up. On winding up, a company's resources must be devoted first to paying its debts. Only the money left after paying debts (including long-term loans) is profit for distribution to the members. In practice the members of a company do not wish to wait until its liquidation before receiving a share of its profits: they wish to have a regular dividend income from the company. Although the payment of annual profit dividends to members is recognised as an essential feature of the financing of companies, the difficulty is to find a way of paying profit dividends before liquidation without jeopardising the payment of debts in liquidation. The answer adopted by CA 2006 depends on the concept of 'profits available for distribution' (see **10.3.3**).

Commercial companies are formed to earn profits for their shareholders and no express power is needed in the articles to make distributions of profits before winding up. However, there is no rule that all profits must be distributed each year (*Burland v Earle* [1902] AC 83).

Companies formed for charitable purposes usually have a provision in their articles that no distributions are to be made to members. The articles of an investment company must prohibit distribution of its capital profits (see **10.3.7**).

A payment of the profits of a company to its members is called a 'dividend'. To a Latinist, 'dividend' means an amount to be divided but in its ordinary use now it means each person's portion of the amount to be divided (*Henry v Great Northern Railway Co* (1857) 1 De G & J 606 per Lord Cranworth LC at pp 636–7, Knight Bruce LJ at pp 642–3).

Unless the articles provide otherwise, a dividend must be in cash (*Wood v Odessa Waterworks Co* (1889) 42 ChD 636). Power to make a distribution in kind is given in the model articles for private companies, art 34, and the model articles for public companies, art 76, in SI 2008/3229.

The directors of a company, unless it is entitled to the small companies exemption (see **9.5.3**), must include in their directors' report for each financial year the amount which they recommend should be paid as a dividend (CA 2006, s 416(3)).

In recommending the amount of a dividend, the directors must have regard to the general interest of all classes of shareholders and not favour one class at the expense of another (*Henry v Great Northern Railway Co* at p 637). However, in Canada, a majority of the Supreme Court has held that a company with more than one class of ordinary shares may have in its articles a so-called 'discretionary dividend provision' giving the directors a discretion to choose which class or classes of shareholders are to receive any dividend declared (*McClurg v Canada* (1990) 76 DLR (4th) 217). In *McClurg's* case, the directors of the company held all the shares in two of the company's classes of shares and their wives held all the shares in the other class. Dividends were allocated to classes purely on the basis of which class of shareholders would pay the least tax. Clearly, in practice, the directors allocated the dividends with due regard to the interests of all classes of shareholders.

As from the time when a dividend is payable to a member, it is a debt owed by the company to the member and is subject to the Limitation Act 1980 (*Re Severn and Wye and Severn Bridge Railway Co* [1896] 1 Ch 559). The limitation period is six years—see **3.4.2.11**. No dividend is payable on a company's shares, even on preference shares, unless and until the company has decided to pay one (*Bond v Barrow Haematite Steel Co* [1902] 1 Ch 353)—the decision is usually known as a 'declaration' of a dividend.

The model articles for private companies, art 30, and the model articles for public companies, art 70, require the members to 'declare' dividends by ordinary resolution. They must not do so unless the directors have made a recommendation, and the dividend they declare must not exceed the amount that the directors recommend. Although it is the members in general meeting who 'declare' a dividend, the actual payment can be made only on the authority of the directors, and they are responsible for seeing that the payment is properly made (*Re Exchange Banking Co, Flitcroft's Case* (1882) 21 ChD 519). Under the model articles for public companies, art 71, dividends are paid in proportion to the amounts paid up on shares, unless some other provision is made, for example, in the terms of issue of particular shares. This means that no dividends are paid to members whose shares are totally unpaid. (The model articles for private companies assume that all shares are fully paid.)

No dividend may be paid on treasury shares (see **10.6.6**) (CA 2006, s 726(3)).

10.3.2 RESTRICTIONS ON DIVIDENDS

The law has long sought to ensure that a dividend paid by a company to its members is not, in whole or in part, a return of the capital they have contributed, because this would enable the members to avoid their statutory liability to the company (see **10.1**). This is seen as a protection for creditors of the company.

The great difficulty in controlling payments of dividends is that contributed capital is not kept by the company as a fund of cash: it is used to buy a continually changing set of assets whose value may go up or down but rarely stays the same. The assets of the company may be augmented by profits it makes or diminished by losses. Ascertaining whether any particular dividend payment represents a return of capital is not, therefore, straightforward. The courts attempted to lay down rules on a case-by-case basis but the result was not satisfactory, and CA 1980 introduced statutory rules, which are now set out in CA 2006, part 23 (ss 829 to 853).

The statutory rules restricting distributions apply to 'every description of distribution of a company's assets to its members, whether in cash or otherwise' (s 829(1)) with the following exceptions (s 829(2)):

(a) issue of fully or partly paid bonus shares (see **10.4**);

(b) return of capital to members in a properly authorised reduction of capital (including the cancellation or reduction of liability on partly paid shares) (see **10.7**);

(c) purchase or redemption of the company's own shares (see **10.5** and **10.6**); and

(d) distribution of assets on winding up (see **20.15**).

The most common form of distribution is a dividend paid to members on their shares (whether ordinary or preference). In *Aveling Barford Ltd v Perion Ltd* [1989] BCLC 626, a sale at an undervalue of an asset of Aveling Barford Ltd to another company controlled by the sole beneficial shareholder of Aveling Barford was held to be a distribution to him (see **10.3.5**).

10.3.3 PROFITS AVAILABLE FOR DISTRIBUTION

The basic principle is that a company may make a distribution only out of profits available for the purpose (CA 2006, s 830(1)) and a company's profits available for distribution are (s 830(2)):

> its accumulated, realised profits, so far as not previously utilised by distribution or capitalisation, less its accumulated, realised losses, so far as not previously written off in a reduction or reorganisation of capital duly made.

Public companies are subject to a further requirement: see **10.3.6** and **10.3.7**.

10.3.4 REALISED AND UNREALISED PROFITS

It is provided by CA 2006, s 853(4), that whether or not a profit is a 'realised profit' is to be determined by the generally accepted accounting principles in use at the time the accounts showing the profit are prepared. Financial Reporting Standard 18 (FRS 18) Accounting Policies states:

> 28 It is generally accepted that profits shall be treated as realised, for these purposes, only when realised* in the form either of cash or of other assets the ultimate cash realisation of which can be assessed with reasonable certainty.
>
>   * In this context, 'realised' may also encompass profits relating to assets that are readily realisable.
>
> 29 The requirements in paragraph 28 relating to realised profits and the profit and loss account apply unless there are special reasons for departing from them. However, such reasons will not exist unless, as a minimum, it is possible to be reasonably certain that, although a gain is unrealised, it nevertheless exists, and to measure it with sufficient reliability.*
>
>   * In addition where there are special reasons for departing from the requirements described in paragraph 28, directors will also consider whether a departure would result in the use of valuation bases or other accounting treatments not permitted by companies legislation, which would be available only if use of the true and fair override was justified.

The Institute of Chartered Accountants in England and Wales (ICAEW) and the Institute of Chartered Accountants of Scotland (ICAS) have issued Technical Release Tech 02/10, Guidance on the Determination of Realised Profits and Losses in the Context of Distributions under the Companies Act 2006.

A related problem of accounting is when to recognise (that is, record in accounts) revenues and expenses (and hence profits or losses). The general rule is that expenses must be recognised when they are incurred (not when they are paid for). In respect of a cash sale, revenue is of course recognised at the time of the sale, which is the time when the cash is received. Most companies conduct their business on credit—that is, they allow their customers time to pay for goods and services supplied—but this does not affect the accounting recognition of the revenue from the sale: the revenue is recognised at the time of sale of goods or rendering of services, provided the amount to be charged is ascertained at that time, and provided it is not unreasonable to expect ultimate collection of the amount charged.

10.3.5 DISTRIBUTIONS IN KIND

A distribution of an asset in kind is to be taken to be a distribution of the asset's book value less any consideration received, provided the company has profits of that amount available for distribution (CA 2006, s 845). If the consideration received exceeds the book value, the amount of the distribution is zero. It may be necessary to obtain an independent professional valuation of an asset which is overvalued in a company's accounts in order to justify a distribution in kind. Section 845 is new to CA 2006 and the transactions considered in *Aveling Barford Ltd v Perion Ltd* [1989] BCLC 626 and *Progress Property Co Ltd v Moorgarth Group Ltd* [2010] UKSC 55, [2011] 1 WLR 1, would be dealt with under it if they had occurred after it came into force.

If the book value of a non-cash asset of a company includes an unrealised profit (because the asset has been revalued), the asset itself may be distributed as a dividend in kind to members and, for that purpose, the unrealised profit may be treated as a realised profit so as to make the distribution legal (CA 2006, s 846).

10.3.6 PUBLIC COMPANIES

A public company, like a private company, may not distribute more than its accumulated net real-ised profits but in addition, by CA 2006, s 831, a distribution by a public company may not exceed the following limit:

net assets *minus* sum of called-up share capital plus undistributable reserves.

The undistributable reserves of a company are various funds which are treated like contributed capital together with net unrealised profits. The full list is:

(a) the share premium account;

(b) the capital redemption reserve;

(c) accumulated unrealised profits (so far as they have not been capitalised as bonus shares) less accumulated unrealised losses (so far as not written off in a reduction of capital); and

(d) any other reserve which the company is forbidden to distribute, under its articles or legisla-tion, for example, a reserve for own shares (s 669).

Section 831 implements Directive 2012/30/EU, art 17(1).

10.3.7 INVESTMENT COMPANIES

By CA 2006, s 833(1), an investment company is a public company which has given notice to Companies House that it intends to operate as an investment company and has since complied with the requirement of s 833(2). This is that the business of the company consists of investing its funds in shares, land or other assets, with the aim of spreading risk and giving members of the company the benefit of the result of the management of its funds. An investment company is usually recognised as an investment trust by HM Revenue and Customs (see the Corporation Tax Act 2010, ss 1158 to 1165) in order to be exempt from capital gains tax (Taxation of Charge-able Gains Act 1992, s 100). So investment companies are usually known as 'investment trust companies' or ITCs.

As well as taxation advantages, ITCs benefit from a special definition, in CA 2006, s 832, of the limit for a distribution of an investment company, as:

assets *minus* 1½ times liabilities to creditors.

This special definition applies only if the company's shares are admitted to trading on a regulated market anywhere in the EEA (see **7.3.4.3**). ITCs have long functioned as collective investment schemes, enabling individuals to participate in a professionally managed portfolio of securities. Optional special provisions for ITCs are permitted by Directive 2012/30/EU, art 17(7).

10.3.8 ACCOUNTS JUSTIFYING A DISTRIBUTION

To establish whether a distribution by a company is lawful it is necessary to check that it is within the amount permitted by statute as determined from what the legislation calls 'relevant accounts' (CA 2006, s 836). Usually, these are the last individual accounts of the company to have been circulated to members (ss 836(2) and 837(1)). Accounts cannot be relied on unless they have been properly prepared in accordance with CA 2006 (s 837(2)). Unless the company is exempt from the audit requirements, the accounts must have been audited (s 837(3)) and, if the audit report is qualified, the auditor must have given a written statement of whether the matter in respect of which the report is qualified is material for determining whether the dis-tribution would contravene part 23 (s 837(4)). In the case of a private company, that statement must have been circulated in the same way as annual accounts; in the case of a public company, it must have been laid before the company in general meeting (s 837(4)). The members cannot waive these procedures, because they exist for the protection of creditors (*Precision Dippings Ltd v Precision Dippings Marketing Ltd* [1986] Ch 447; *Bairstow v Queens Moat Houses plc* [2001] 2 BCLC 531). If the auditor has made a qualified report on the last annual accounts, but was never asked to state that the qualification is immaterial, a distribution is invalid even if it is clear that the auditor would have stated that it was immaterial, if asked to do so (*BDG Roof-Bond Ltd v Douglas* [2000] 1 BCLC 401).

If a distribution would not be justified according to the most recent annual accounts, the company may justify it on the basis of (more recent) 'interim accounts' (s 836(2)(a)). In the case of a private company, the Act says nothing further about the way in which interim accounts used to justify a distribution should be prepared. In the case of a public company, interim accounts used to justify a distribution are required to be prepared as nearly as is practicable in the manner in which annual accounts are prepared under CA 2006, except that no auditor's report is required. Interim accounts used to justify a distribution of a public company must be filed at Companies House (s 838(6)).

If a company wishes to make a distribution soon after it is incorporated, so that no annual accounts have yet been required, it can justify the distribution on the basis of 'initial accounts' (s 836(2)(b)), to which the same conditions apply as for interim accounts (s 839) except that an auditor's report is required in the case of a public company (s 839(5)).

In *Mullins v Taylor* (2006) LTL 3/1/2007 it was argued that a distribution could be justified by the most recent audited accounts, even though another financial year had passed, for which the directors had failed to produce accounts which would have shown that the distribution was illegal. This argument was not accepted on an application to strike out the claim. The judge said that, if the argument were correct, it would allow 'the most extraordinary abuse' (at [27]) and he thought there was a realistic prospect that it would be held to be wrong at the trial of the claim.

10.3.9 CONSEQUENCES OF AN EXCESSIVE DISTRIBUTION

If a company has made an illegal distribution, the directors who authorised the payment are liable to repay the money to the company (*Re National Funds Assurance Co* (1878) 10 ChD 118; *Re Exchange Banking Co, Flitcroft's Case* (1882) 21 ChD 519). This applies whether the company is solvent or insolvent when it claims repayment (*Bairstow v Queens Moat Houses plc* [2001] 2 BCLC 531). The object of the remedy is restitution of what was wrongfully paid out by the company, not compensation for what the company has lost (*Commissioners of HM Revenue and Customs v Holland* [2010] UKSC 51, [2010] 1 WLR 2793, at [48]–[49]). Accordingly, where the dividend was unlawful because the accounts were erroneous, it is irrelevant that the dividends might have been lawful if the accounts had been drawn up correctly (*Allied Carpets Group plc v Nethercott* [2001] BCC 81; *Bairstow v Queens Moat Houses plc*; *Inn Spirit Ltd v Burns* [2002] EWHC 1731 (Ch), [2002] 2 BCLC 780). The fact that the illegal distribution was approved by the members does not cure its illegality, and the members' decision does not ratify the directors' act so as to absolve them from liability (*Re Exchange Banking Co, Flitcroft's Case*; *Aveling Barford Ltd v Perion Ltd* [1989] BCLC 626). Formerly, the position was that a director who took reasonable care to secure that accounts were properly prepared and who exercised commercial judgement in assessing whether dividends were properly payable on the basis of those accounts was not liable for an illegal distribution (*Dovey v Cory* [1901] AC 477). However, in *Commissioners of HM Revenue and Customs v Holland* [2010] UKSC 51, [2010] 1 WLR 2793, at [45]–[48], Lord Hope said, obiter, that the better view now is that directors are strictly liable for illegal distributions. The court may give relief from liability on an application under CA 2006, s 1157 (see **16.16.6**).

CA 2006, s 847(1) and (2), makes a member liable to repay a distribution received if the member knew, or had reasonable grounds for believing, that it was being paid in contravention of part 23. In order to establish liability under s 847(1) and (2) it is necessary to prove knowledge of, or reasonable grounds for believing, the fact which made the distribution contravene part 23, but it is not necessary to show any awareness of the legislation or how it applied to the distribution. In other words, ignorance of the law is no defence (*It's a Wrap (UK) Ltd v Gula* [2006] EWCA Civ 544, [2006] 2 BCLC 634).

If an illegal dividend has been paid by a company in reliance on erroneous accounts, the company's auditor may be liable to it for negligently failing to report the error (*Leeds Estate Building and Investment Co v Shepherd* (1887) 36 ChD 787; *Re London and General Bank (No 2)* [1895] 2 Ch 673; *Re Thomas Gerrard and Son Ltd* [1968] Ch 455; *Segenhoe Ltd v Akins* (1990) 29 NSWLR 569).

10.4 CAPITALISATIONS AND BONUS SHARES

Money that is reckoned in a company's accounts to be profit can be transferred to capital accounts and this is known as 'capitalisation'. Two ways of doing this are recognised in CA 2006, s 853(3):

(a) transferring the profits to capital redemption reserve on cancelling redeemable shares (see **10.5.1**); and

(b) transferring the profits to a share capital account and treating them as wholly or partly paying up new shares which are to be allotted to the company's members as 'bonus shares'.

An issue of bonus shares is known as a 'capitalisation issue' but bonus shares can also be paid up by a transfer from share premium account (s 610(3)), redenomination reserve (s 628(2)) or capital redemption reserve (s 733(5)).

If profit that could be distributed to members is capitalised, it can no longer be distributed, and it is considered that such a use of profit should be specially authorised by the articles, as in the model articles for private companies, art 36, and the model articles for public companies, art 78, in SI 2008/3229. These articles specify that the number of bonus shares to be allotted to a particular member is to be determined in the same way as entitlement to dividend. For public companies, by art 71, this is in proportion to the amount paid up on shares, so holders of totally unpaid shares are not entitled to any bonus shares. (The model articles for private companies assume that all shares are fully paid.)

Under the model articles for private companies, art 36, and the model articles for public companies, art 78, a decision to make a capitalisation issue is to be taken by the directors on the authority of an ordinary resolution of the members.

It is not necessary for a public company to obtain a valuation report (CA 2006, s 593(2)).

In *Re Cleveland Trust plc* [1991] BCLC 424 and *EIC Services Ltd v Phipps* [2004] EWCA Civ 1069, [2005] 1 WLR 1377, an issue of bonus shares was held to be void for mistake. In *Re Cleveland Trust plc* the bonus shares were paid up by capitalisation of the balance on profit and loss account, without realising that the accounts were wrong and the true profit was nowhere near enough to pay up the shares. In *EIC Services Ltd v Phipps*, directors issued bonus shares to members whose existing shares were totally unpaid and who had never adopted a resolution authorising the issue. The idea of a transaction being void for mistake is taken from contract law, on the basis that issuing bonus shares involves a relationship between shareholder and company analogous to a contractual relationship ([2004] EWCA Civ 1069 at [12]).

Members may be issued with bonus shares of the same class as the shares they already hold or bonus shares of a different class (*White v Bristol Aeroplane Co Ltd* [1953] Ch 65).

10.5 REDEEMABLE SHARES

10.5.1 DESCRIPTION

When redeemable shares (see **6.2.4.5**) are redeemed, they must be cancelled (CA 2006, s 688). On cancellation of its redeemed shares, a company must reduce its issued share capital by the nominal value of the cancelled shares (s 688) and transfer that amount, to the extent that it is not made up from the proceeds of a fresh issue, to a new capital account called capital redemption reserve (s 733). The increase in capital redemption reserve is balanced by the money paid out of profit and loss account to redeem the shares.

The amount recorded in a capital redemption reserve may be reduced by transfer to a share capital account to pay up fully paid bonus shares (s 733(5); see **10.4**) but otherwise capital redemption reserve is subject to the same rules on reduction as issued share capital (s 733(6); see **10.7.1**).

The money to redeem a *public company's* redeemable shares must come either from 'distributable profits', or from the proceeds of a new share issue (s 687(1) and (2)). In relation to the making of a payment by a company, 'distributable profits' means profits out of which the company could lawfully make a distribution equal in value to that payment (s 736). For the conditions under which a distribution may be made lawfully, see **10.3.3** to **10.3.8**. A new share issue could be used to convert redeemable shares into ordinary shares or to roll over the redemption period.

Section 709(1) permits a *private company* to make a payment in respect of the redemption of its own shares otherwise than out of its distributable profits or the proceeds of a fresh issue of shares. Such a payment is called a 'payment out of capital' (s 709(2); see **10.5.3**). A private company's articles may restrict or prohibit payments out of capital (s 709(1)).

Redeemable shares cannot be redeemed unless they are fully paid (s 686(1)). The money to be paid by the company for redemption must be paid in full on redemption (s 686(3); *Peña v Dale* [2004] EWHC 1065 (Ch), [2004] 2 BCLC 508, at [107] to [114]; *Kinlan v Crimmin* [2006] EWHC 779 (Ch), [2007] 2 BCLC 67, at [46] to [50]), unless the terms of redemption permit the company to agree with a shareholder to pay at a later date (s 686(2)).

Within one month of redeeming any of its shares a company must give notice to Companies House accompanied by a statement of capital (CA 2006, s 689).

10.5.2 REDEMPTION PREMIUM

Redemption premium payable by a *public company* must be paid out of its distributable profits (CA 2006, s 687(3)) unless the premium effectively represents a repayment of capital because it was a share premium contributed when the shares were issued. In that case the amount may be deducted from the share premium account (provided, of course, there is an adequate balance on the account—ie, it has not been used for other purposes, see **6.5.4**) (s 687(4)(b) and (5)). It is clear from the debates in committee, when what is now s 687(5) was introduced as an amendment to the Bill that became CA 1981, that it was assumed that the amount written off share premium account under the subsection would have to be replaced by new contributed capital or share premium from a new issue of shares. However, this could only have been achieved by also amending what is now s 733(3), and that was not done. Accordingly there are circumstances in which share premium account will be reduced on redemption of shares. See Jamieson, *Accountancy*, July 1983, p 103; the reply by Anderson and Keenan, *Accountancy*, October 1983, p 75 is unconvincing. The result is not much different from the position under CA 1948.

If a private company decides to pay for redemption otherwise than from the proceeds of a fresh issue of shares or from distributable profits then redemption premium may have to be written off any available capital account or the revaluation reserve (CA 2006, s 734(3)).

10.5.3 MAKING A PAYMENT OUT OF CAPITAL

When a redeemable share is redeemed it must be cancelled (CA 2006, s 688) and this means that its nominal value must be deducted from the balance on share capital account. (It must be the whole nominal value because only a fully paid share may be redeemed: s 686(1).) The general policy is that the amount thus written off share capital account must be made up by a counterbalancing increase either in share capital and premium from the issue of new shares or in capital redemption reserve by a transfer from profit and loss. However, the members of a *private company* may, under s 709(1), adopt a special resolution to enable the company's shares to be redeemed with less than the full counterbalancing increase in capital accounts. This is called a resolution to make a 'payment out of capital' (s 709(2)). It will mean that some or all of the cancelled capital written off will not be replaced and so the company will reduce its capital. The extent to which the counterbalancing is not done (ie, the extent of the capital reduction) is limited to the 'permissible capital payment' (s 710) and this is computed in such a way that the company is forced to use all its available profits and all proceeds of a new issue of shares in making counterbalancing transfers to capital accounts (ss 710, 711 and 712).

The articles of a private company may restrict or prohibit payments out of capital (s 709(1)).

The prescribed procedure for approving a redemption of shares with a payment out of capital is designed to ensure that the return of capital does not make the company unable to pay its debts, there is transparency, and there is approval by members. The same procedure is used for approving a repurchase of shares with a payment out of capital (see **10.6**).

Members' approval of a redemption of shares with a payment out of capital must be given by special resolution (75 per cent majority), ignoring votes attached to the shares that are to be redeemed. Where the resolution is proposed as a written resolution, a member who holds shares to which the resolution relates is not an eligible member (s 717(2)). At a meeting, the resolution must be passed without the votes attached to the shares to which it relates (s 717(3)), whether exercised on a show of hands or a poll (s 717(4)(a)), in person or by proxy (s 717(4)(c)). At a meeting, any member may, in person or by proxy, demand a poll on the resolution (s 717(4)(b) and (c)).

A special resolution to redeem shares with a payment out of capital must be adopted between five and seven weeks before the payment is to be made (s 723(1)).

Directors and members are forced to consider the effect of the return of capital on the company's ability to pay its debts by a requirement for a solvency statement. Not more than a week before passing the resolution (s 716(2)) the directors must make a statement which complies with SI 2009/388, art 5. This statement must specify the permissible capital payment (CA 2006, s 714(1) and (2)), and must include a solvency statement (s 714(3) and (4)). It must be accompanied by a confirmatory report by the company's auditor (s 714(6)). If the resolution is to be adopted as a written resolution, the directors' statement and auditor's report must be sent or submitted to every eligible member before or with the resolution; if the resolution is to be adopted at a meeting, the statement and report must be available for inspection by members at the meeting (s 718(2)). If the statement and report are not made available to the members, the resolution will be ineffective (s 718(3)).

By s 714(3) the directors' solvency statement is a statement that in their opinion:

(a) there will be no grounds on which the company could be found unable to pay its debts immediately after the payment out of capital is made; and

(b) the company will continue in business as a going concern for the whole of the following year and during that year will be able to pay its debts as they fall due.

In forming their opinion of the company's ability to pay its debts immediately after the payment is made, the directors must take into account all of the company's liabilities (including any contingent or prospective liabilities) (s 714(4)). Making a solvency statement without having reasonable grounds for the opinion expressed in it is an offence triable either way; if tried on indictment the penalty is imprisonment for up to two years and/or a fine for which there is no limit (s 715).

If a company goes into insolvent liquidation within a year of making a payment out of capital, the member from whom the shares were purchased and the directors who made the solvency statement are liable to repay the amount paid out of capital in so far as this is necessary to pay the company's debts—see IA 1986, s 76.

The transparency requirements are:

(a) If the resolution is adopted, the company must deliver a copy of the directors' statement and the auditor's report to Companies House (CA 2006, s 719(4)).

(b) Within one week of adopting the special resolution the company must advertise its adoption in the *Gazette* (s 719(1)) and must either insert a similar advertisement in a national newspaper or notify all of its creditors by letter (s 719(2) and (3)). The copy of the directors' statement and auditor's report must be received at Companies House on or before the day the first of these advertisements or notifications appears (s 719(4)).

(c) From that day until five weeks after the special resolution was adopted, the statement and report must be available for inspection, free of charge, by any member or creditor of the company (s 720).

Within the period of five weeks following the adoption of the special resolution any creditor of the company, or any of its members who did not vote in favour of the resolution, may apply to the court for cancellation of the resolution (s 721). On the hearing of a s 721 application the court may either cancel or confirm the resolution, and in any event may make its order on such terms and conditions as it thinks fit (s 721(4)), adjourn the proceedings to enable an arrangement to be made which it finds satisfactory for the purchase of the applicants' interests in the company or the protection of dissentient creditors, and give any directions or orders which are expedient for facilitating or carrying the arrangement into effect (s 721(3)). The court's order may provide for the purchase by the company of the shares of any members and, if necessary, amend its articles (s 721(6)). The court may order the company not to amend its articles without the court's permission (s 721(7)).

10.6 PURCHASE OF OWN SHARES

10.6.1 AUTHORITY TO REPURCHASE SHARES

The general rule stated in CA 2006, s 658(1), is that a company must not acquire its own shares. However, s 690(1) permits a company to purchase its own shares (including redeemable shares) in the circumstances set out in ss 690 to 708. A company's articles may restrict or prohibit purchase of its own shares (s 690(1)). A company may not purchase its own shares if doing so would result in there being no issued shares of the company other than redeemable shares (see **10.5**) and treasury shares (see **10.6.6**) (s 690(2)). In other words, after the purchase there must be at least one member who is not the company itself and who holds a share that is not a redeemable share. Only fully paid shares can be purchased (s 691(1)).

Members are required to approve the terms of purchases, and there are different approval requirements depending on whether the purchase is to be made on a UK recognised investment exchange (a 'market purchase', see **10.6.3**) or otherwise (an 'off-market purchase', see **10.6.4**) (s 693).

Shares may not be purchased unless they are fully paid (s 691(1)), which means that a company cannot subscribe for its own shares but can only repurchase them from existing members. This also follows from the use in s 690(1) of the word 'purchase', which does not include subscription (*Re VGM Holdings Ltd* [1942] Ch 235).

An important restriction on repurchasing shares is that the company must pay for them in full at the time of repurchase: payment in instalments or at a later date is not permitted (s 691(2); *Peña v Dale* [2004] EWHC 1065 (Ch), [2004] 2 BCLC 508, at [107] to [114]; *Kinlan v Crimmin* [2006] EWHC 779 (Ch), [2007] 2 BCLC 67, at [46] to [50]).

If a company's shares have been admitted to trading on a regulated market (or if a request for admission to trading has been made), a purchase of the shares by the company itself (buy-back or stabilisation) is not market abuse if it meets the conditions set out in Regulation 596/2014/EU, art 5, and Commission Delegated Regulation (EU) 2016/1052 (see **13.2.6**).

For other exceptions to the rule against acquiring own shares, see **10.6.8**.

Many of the controls on company share buy-backs are relaxed if a purchase is for the purposes of or pursuant to an employees' share scheme (see **10.9**).

10.6.2 FINANCING REPURCHASE

The money to buy back a public company's shares must come from distributable profits (see **10.5.1**) or, provided the repurchased shares are to be cancelled rather than held as treasury shares, from the proceeds of a new share issue (CA 2006, s 692(2)(a); treasury shares must be purchased out of distributable profits, see s 724(1)(b)(i)). A new share issue might be used to convert a class of shares with undesirable membership rights to more favourable shares. A *private company* may make a payment out of capital to repurchase its own shares under the same conditions as for redemption of shares out of capital (see **10.5.1** and **10.5.3**) (s 692(1)). A private company may purchase a small quantity of its shares with cash, without having to identify it as distributable profits, if authorised to do so by its articles (s 692(1ZA)). The annual limit for cash purchases is £15,000 or the nominal value of 5 per cent of its share capital, whichever is less.

10.6.3 AUTHORITY FOR MARKET PURCHASES

A company may purchase its own shares on a UK recognised investment exchange (a market purchase: CA 2006, s 693) only if the purchase has been authorised beforehand by a resolution of the company (s 701(1)). The resolution must specify the maximum number of shares authorised to be acquired and the maximum and minimum prices to be paid (s 701(3)). The maximum and minimum prices may be expressed as a formula, for example, linking them to the average market quotation over a period (s 701(6)(b)). The resolution must state a date on which the authority will expire, which must not be later than five years after the date on which the resolution is passed (s 701(5)). Authority may be varied, revoked or renewed by a resolution of the company (s 701(4)).

A copy of any resolution giving, varying, revoking or renewing authority for a market purchase must be forwarded to Companies House within 15 days of adoption (s 701(8), applying s 30).

10.6.4 AUTHORITY FOR OFF-MARKET PURCHASES

A company cannot make an off-market purchase of its own shares unless the terms of the purchase contract have been approved by the members prior to purchase (CA 2006, s 694(1)). Authority to make an off-market purchase must be conferred by a resolution under s 694(2). Section 694(2) provides two ways of approving a contract:

(a) the resolution is adopted before the company enters into the contract; or

(b) the contract provides that no purchase may take place until its terms have been approved by resolution.

Under option (a), there is no minimum time interval between adopting the resolution and entering into the contract, and it has been held that the two may be done simultaneously (*Dashfield v*

Davidson [2008] BCC 222). In the case of a public company this resolution must specify a date on which the authority is to expire, which must not be later than five years after the date of adopting the resolution (s 694(5)).

Where the resolution is proposed as a written resolution, a member who holds shares to which the resolution relates is not an eligible member (s 695(2)). At a meeting, any member may, in person or by proxy, demand a poll on the resolution (s 695(4)(b) and (c)), and the resolution must be passed without the votes attached to the shares to which it relates (s 695(3)), whether exercised on a show of hands or a poll (s 695(4)(a)), in person or by proxy (s 695(4)(c)).

If the resolution is to be adopted as a written resolution, a copy of the contract must be sent or submitted to every eligible member before or with the resolution; if the resolution is to be adopted at a meeting, the contract must be available for inspection by members at the company's registered office for 15 days before the meeting and at the meeting (s 696(2)). If the contract is not made available to the members, the resolution will be ineffective (s 696(5)). If the contract is not in writing, a memorandum of its terms must be made available. The names of the members holding shares to which the contract relates must be revealed if they are not stated in the contract (s 696(3) and (4)).

The procedure for varying a contract is set out in ss 697 to 699.

10.6.5 PUBLICITY FOR PURCHASES

Every purchase of its shares by a company must be reported to Companies House within 28 days of completion (CA 2006, s 707). The return must state the number and nominal value of shares purchased and the date of delivery (s 707(3)). A public company must also give details of the price paid (s 707(4)).

A copy of every contract (or memorandum of the terms of an unwritten contract) made by a company to purchase its own shares must be kept available for inspection by anyone if the company is public, or to members only if the company is private, until ten years from the date on which the transfer under the contract was completed or the contract otherwise determined (CA 2006, s 702).

A premium listed company must notify a regulatory information service when it purchases, redeems or cancels more than 10 per cent of a class of shares, and every 5 per cent thereafter (LR 12.5.2R).

10.6.6 TREASURY SHARES

Shares which a company has repurchased in accordance with CA 2006, ss 690 to 708, out of distributable profits (see **10.5.1**), and which it has held continuously since repurchase are called 'treasury shares' (s 724(1) and (5)). A company holding treasury shares must register itself as the member holding the shares (s 724(4)).

Although a company which holds treasury shares is listed in its register of members as being the member holding the shares (s 724(4)), it must not exercise any membership rights (s 726(2)). Any purported exercise of those rights is void (s 726(2)) and responsible officers are liable to a fine (s 732). In particular, the company cannot attend or vote at meetings (s 726(2)) and it cannot pay itself a dividend (s 726(3)). It can, however, receive an allotment of fully paid bonus shares (s 726(4)(a)), which will be treated as if, at the time they were allotted, they were purchased for the purposes of s 724(1) (s 726(5)) for a nil purchase price (s 731(4)(b)). A company which holds redeemable shares as treasury shares may redeem them from itself and pay itself the redemption price (s 726(4)(b)).

A company which holds treasury shares may sell them for a cash consideration, transfer them to an employees' share scheme (s 727(1)) or cancel them (s 729(1)). Any of these events must be reported to Companies House with a statement of capital (ss 728 and 730). For this purpose, 'cash consideration' is defined in s 727(2) in the same way as in s 583(3) (payment in cash for shares, see **6.6.4.2**) except that an undertaking to pay cash at a future date counts only if the date is not more than 90 days after the date on which the company agrees to sell the shares.

As the money used to repurchase treasury shares came from distributable profits, the proceeds of selling them again, up to the average price which the company paid for repurchasing them, are realised profits (s 731). Proceeds of sale in excess of the average repurchase price must be transferred to the company's share premium account (s 731(3)). A sale of treasury shares is subject to members' pre-emption rights (s 560(3); see **6.3.5**).

As far as a company is concerned, its purchase of its shares to be held as treasury shares, and its dealings in its treasury shares as permitted by s 727, are excluded from the definition of regulated activities for the purposes of FSMA 2000, so that the company does not require permission from the FCA (SI 2001/544, art 18A).

10.6.7 CANCELLATION OF REPURCHASED SHARES

A company which repurchases shares which do not qualify as treasury shares (see **10.6.6**) must cancel them (CA 2006, s 706). A company which holds treasury shares may cancel them (s 729(1)).

On cancellation of a company's repurchased shares (whether or not held as treasury shares), the company must reduce its issued share capital by the nominal value of the cancelled shares (ss 706 and 729(4)) and transfer that amount, to the extent that it is not made up from the proceeds of a fresh issue, to capital redemption reserve (s 733(1) to (4)). The increase in capital redemption reserve is balanced by the money paid out of profit and loss account to repurchase the shares. A cancellation of repurchased shares is done without going through the statutory procedure for reducing capital described in **10.7** (s 729(5)). This is because capital redemption reserve is itself treated as paid-up share capital and can only be reduced by going through that procedure (s 733(6)), except that it can be used for paying up fully paid bonus shares (s 733(5)).

10.6.8 EXCEPTIONS TO THE PROHIBITION ON ACQUIRING OWN SHARES

10.6.8.1 Repurchase under court order

The court has powers to order a company to repurchase its shares as a remedy when dissentient members apply for the cancellation of a resolution of a public company to re-register as a private company (CA 2006, s 98(5)), or a resolution of a private company to make a payment out of capital to redeem or repurchase shares (s 721(6)). It is also a possible remedy for unfairly prejudicial conduct of a company's affairs (s 996(2)(e)) or for contravening the prohibition of public offers of securities by private companies (s 759(3) and (5)). When ordering a company to repurchase its shares in these circumstances the court may provide for the reduction of the company's capital accordingly, and purchase of shares in pursuance of such a court order is an exception to the general rule that a limited company must not acquire its own shares (s 659(2)(b)).

10.6.8.2 Gift, forfeiture and surrender

A company may accept a gift of its own fully paid shares (CA 2006, s 659(1)). A company may forfeit shares, or accept a surrender in lieu of forfeiture, for non-payment of amounts payable in respect of the shares (s 659(2)(c)).

10.6.9 HOLDING SHARES IN A HOLDING COMPANY

If a body corporate is a subsidiary of a registered company (see **14.15**), it is not permitted to be a member of that company and it must not appoint a nominee to membership of that company (CA 2006, ss 136 and 144). Therefore, a subsidiary of a registered company with a share capital must not hold shares in its holding company.

This rule was introduced in England and Wales and Scotland by CA 1947, s 80, in order to prevent a registered company evading the rule against purchase of own shares (now CA 2006, s 658(1)) by having a subsidiary company buy its shares. The section was not retrospective, so a subsidiary which held shares (either directly or through a nominee) in its holding company before 1 July 1948 is permitted to continue holding them (s 137) but must not exercise any voting rights attached to the shares (s 137(4)). Similarly, where a company holds shares in another company legally but circumstances change to make the holding illegal, it may continue, under s 137, to hold the shares but may not vote them. So the fact that company B owns shares in company A is not a bar to company A buying all shares in B and turning it into a subsidiary (*Acatos and Hutcheson plc v Watson* [1995] 1 BCLC 218). The fact that A becomes a member of B does not mean that it 'acquires' B's assets so it has not acquired B's shares in A in contravention of s 658(1) (*Acatos and Hutcheson plc v Watson*; R Nolan, 'The veil intact' (1995) 16 Co Law 180).

The prohibition does not apply where the subsidiary holds shares in the ordinary course of a bona fide business of dealing in securities on a regulated market in the United Kingdom or any other EEA State (s 141).

There is an exception in favour (principally) of banks. It is quite common for a bank to take a mortgage of shares as security for a loan. In the usual form of mortgage in use in Scotland, the bank as mortgagee of shares in a company becomes a member of that company. As shares in the major UK banks are widely held by the public, sooner or later a bank will find itself as mortgagee of its own shares. To avoid being a holder of its own shares, shares mortgaged to a bank are always held by a subsidiary company as nominee. By s 138(2)(a), this is a permissible exception to the rule that a subsidiary must not hold shares in its holding company. There is a similar exception for shares held by a subsidiary (or its nominee) as personal representative of a deceased individual.

There is a further exception under s 138 for shares in a company held by a subsidiary of that company as a trustee unless the company has a beneficial interest in the trust (apart from the security interest mentioned in the preceding paragraph and various residuary interests that may exist when a subsidiary of a company holds its shares for the purposes of a pension scheme or employees' share scheme—see ss 139 and 140).

A large or medium-sized parent company must report, in notes to its annual accounts, holdings of the company's shares by or on behalf of its subsidiary undertakings, with the same exceptions as are made by ss 138 to 140 (SI 2008/410, sch 4, paras 3 and 24 to 27). A subsidiary undertaking may be a partnership firm or unincorporated association (see **9.8.1** and **9.8.2**), for which shares may be held without contravening CA 2006, ss 136 and 144, because those provisions apply only to incorporated subsidiaries.

10.7 REDUCTION OF CAPITAL

10.7.1 POWER TO REDUCE

A company cannot reduce its issued share capital (see **6.5.5**) unless authorised by statute (*Trevor v Whitworth* (1887) 12 App Cas 409). CA 2006, s 641, permits a company to carry out a reduction of capital by special resolution (which requires a 75 per cent majority, see **14.4.3**), provided the resolution is either supported by a solvency statement (see **10.7.2**) or is confirmed by the court (s 641(1)). The option of a solvency statement without court confirmation is not available to a public company (s 641(1)).

It is also possible, within statutory restrictions, to reduce issued share capital by cancelling shares on redemption (see **10.5.1**) or repurchase (see **10.6.7**), but a reduction by either of these procedures must be balanced by the issue of new shares or the creation of a capital redemption reserve, so that there is no overall reduction of capital. Exceptionally, a private company may, unless forbidden to do so by its articles, redeem or repurchase its own shares by a payment out of capital under the procedure in ss 709 to 723, which involves making a solvency statement (see **10.5.3** and **10.6.2**). In certain circumstances the court may order repurchase of shares and consequential reduction of capital (see **10.6.8.1**).

Reductions of share premium account (s 610(4)), reserve for own shares (s 669(1)) and capital redemption reserve (s 733(6)) are subject to the same rules as reductions of issued share capital, except that share premium account and capital redemption reserve can be used to pay up new shares to be issued as fully paid bonus shares (ss 610(3) and 733(5); see **10.4**).

The remainder of **10.7** is concerned with reductions of capital by special resolution under s 641.

A company may reduce its capital by special resolution in any way (s 641(3)), provided it does not result in no members holding shares that are not redeemable shares (s 641(2)).

There are only two restrictions on the purposes for which a reduction may be made. The first is that a reduction for the purpose of reducing the stamp duty payable by a person who is taking over a company by purchasing all its shares is prohibited (s 641(2A), (2B) and (2C)). The second is that the court will not approve a reduction that has no discernible purpose (per Harman J in *Re Ratners Group plc* [1988] BCLC 685 and in *Re Thorn EMI plc* [1989] BCLC 612 at p 616).

Section 641(4) gives some examples of circumstances in which a company may want to reduce its capital, including returning to members contributed capital which is 'in excess of the company's wants', reducing members' liability to pay uncalled capital and reflecting a diminution in the value of the company's assets. This list is not exhaustive and it is not necessary to prove that a reduction of capital is for one of the reasons listed. In particular, it is not necessary to show that capital which is to be returned to members is in excess of the company's wants (*Re Hunting plc* [2004] EWHC 2591 (Ch), [2005] 2 BCLC 211).

It is for the members to decide how to carry out a reduction of capital by special resolution (*Ex parte Westburn Sugar Refineries Ltd* [1951] AC 625 at p 629). Any method of reducing capital is legal if carried out in accordance with the statutory provisions, and the court has jurisdiction to confirm any kind of reduction. For example, in *British and American Trustee and Finance Corporation Ltd and Reduced v Couper* [1894] AC 399 it was held that a reduction could be carried out by purchasing the company's own shares, a procedure which was otherwise prohibited by company law (*Trevor v Whitworth* (1887) 12 App Cas 409). In relation to the statutory provision forbidding a company to purchase its own shares now made by CA 2006, s 658(1), there is now an express exemption for the acquisition of shares in a reduction of capital duly made (s 659(2)(a)).

It is possible to arrange for a 'deferred' reduction by converting shares into redeemable shares, which will be redeemed at some time in the future in a way that will reduce capital (*Forth Wines Ltd* [1991] BCC 638).

It is not necessary that all the issued shares of a class should be treated in exactly the same way. For example, a reduction may involve the company purchasing the shares of specific shareholders (*British and American Trustee and Finance Corporation Ltd and Reduced v Couper*).

If surplus capital is to be returned to members, it is not necessary that it be returned in cash, and the value of what is returned may exceed the amount by which the nominal values of the shares are reduced (*Ex parte Westburn Sugar Refineries Ltd*, in which members of Westburn Sugar Refineries Ltd whose shares in that company were being reduced from £1 to 90p each in nominal value received 10p shares in another company to which assets of Westburn Sugar Refineries Ltd had been transferred).

10.7.2 REDUCTION OF CAPITAL SUPPORTED BY SOLVENCY STATEMENT

CA 2006, s 642, provides *private companies* limited by shares with an optional procedure for reducing capital without having to apply to the court for confirmation. A company wishing to use this procedure must adopt a special resolution detailing the reduction that is to be made, but, no more than 15 days before the resolution is passed, the directors must make a solvency statement. By s 643(1) and SI 2008/1915, art 2, this is a written statement that each of the directors has formed the opinion that, at the date of the statement:

(a) there is no ground on which the company could be found to be unable to pay, or otherwise discharge, its debts; and

(b) the company will be able to pay, or otherwise discharge, its debts as they fall due during the following year. If it is intended to wind the company up within that year, the directors must be of the opinion that the company will pay or discharge its debts in full within 12 months of the commencement of winding up.

In forming their opinions the directors must take into account all the company's liabilities, including any contingent or prospective liabilities (CA 2006, s 643(2)). If a liability must be estimated, the directors are not restricted to using only the worst-case amount (*BAT Industries plc v Sequana SA* [2016] EWHC 1686 (Ch), [2017] Bus LR 82). If the reduction resolution is to be adopted as a written resolution, the solvency statement must be sent or submitted to every eligible member before or with the resolution (s 642(2)); if the resolution is to be adopted at a meeting, the statement must be available for inspection by members throughout the meeting (s 642(3)). Each of the directors must sign the statement and it must indicate that it is a solvency statement made for the purposes of s 642 (SI 2008/1915, art 2).

Within 15 days of adopting the resolution for reduction of capital, a copy of the solvency statement must be sent to Companies House, together with a statement of capital (s 644), and the resolution for reduction will not take effect until those documents are registered (s 644(4)). Companies House must also be sent a statement by the directors confirming that the solvency statement was made within 15 days of the reduction resolution being passed, and that it was provided to members as required by s 642(2) or (3) (s 644(5)).

It is an offence for directors to send a solvency statement to Companies House without having reasonable grounds for the opinions expressed in it (s 643(4) and (5)) or without submitting it to members (s 644(7) and (9)). Failure to submit the statement to members does not invalidate the reduction resolution (s 642(4)), nor does failure to deliver statements to Companies House (s 644(6)). Absence of reasonable grounds for the opinions expressed in the statement does not invalidate the reduction resolution, unless it shows that the directors did not 'form' their opinions (*BAT Industries plc v Sequana SA*).

10.7.3 REDUCTION OF CAPITAL CONFIRMED BY THE COURT

A resolution for reduction of capital of a public company must be confirmed by the court (CA 2006, s 641(1)). For a private company, confirmation by the court is an optional alternative to issuing a solvency statement (see **10.7.2**).

In deciding whether or not to confirm a resolution for the reduction of capital the primary concern of the court is to be assured that the interests of existing creditors are protected (see **10.7.4**) and that the procedure by which the reduction is carried out is formally correct (per Lord Simonds in *Scottish Insurance Corporation Ltd v Wilsons and Clyde Coal Co Ltd* [1949] AC 462 at p 486).

The court must be satisfied that, in obtaining the special resolution of members for reducing capital, the cause of the reduction was properly put to the members so that they could exercise an informed choice, and that the cause is proved by the evidence before the court (per Harman J in *Re Jupiter House Investments (Cambridge) Ltd* [1985] 1 WLR 975 at p 978). Information should be given to the members in a circular accompanying the notice of the meeting at which the special resolution is to be proposed (per Harman J in *Re Thorn EMI plc* [1989] BCLC 612 at p 616).

In *Re European Home Products plc* [1988] BCLC 690, the court confirmed a reduction despite a significant error in the circular sent to members (a sum of US$38 million had been mistakenly treated as £38 million) because members had been informed of the error and invited to appear at the hearing to object but had not done so. Giving inadequate information may lead to time and costs being wasted on making unnecessary objections to the court. However, the court may sanction a reduction despite the fact that inadequate information has been given to members if the reduction is otherwise fair and equitable and it is clear that the resolution in favour of it would not have been lost if fuller information had been circulated (*Re Ransomes plc* [1999] 1 BCLC 775).

The court will also consider the public interest (per Lord Reid in *Ex parte Westburn Sugar Refineries Ltd* [1951] AC 625 at p 632), which will include the interests of members of the public who may be induced to take shares in the company (per Lord Macnaghten in *Poole v National Bank of China Ltd* [1907] AC 229 at p 239; per Lord Normand in *Ex parte Westburn Sugar Refineries Ltd* at p 629 and Lord Reid at p 632) and future creditors of the company (per Lord Reid in *Ex parte Westburn Sugar Refineries Ltd* at p 632). Normally, future investors and creditors are adequately protected by the statutory requirements for publicising the reduction and the requirement that accounts must show a true and fair view of the company's position (*Re Grosvenor Press plc* [1985] 1 WLR 980).

As far as the existing members of a company proposing a reduction of capital are concerned, the court will refuse its sanction if the scheme is unfair (*Poole v National Bank of China Ltd* per Lord Loreburn LC at p 236). The court must consider whether the scheme is 'fair and equitable', either as between different classes of shareholders (*Poole v National Bank of China Ltd*, per Lord Macnaghten at p 239; *Scottish Insurance Corporation Ltd v Wilsons and Clyde Coal Co Ltd* per Lord Simonds at p 486) or as between different shareholders of the same class (*British and American Trustee and Finance Corporation Ltd and reduced v Couper* [1894] AC 399 per Lord Herschell LC at p 406). In *Re Jupiter House Investments (Cambridge) Ltd* [1985] 1 WLR 975, Harman J said, at p 978, that the court had to be satisfied that a proposed reduction affects all shareholders of equal standing in a similar manner, or that those treated in a different manner from their equals have consented to that different treatment. The onus is on those opposing the reduction to show that it is unfair: the company is not bound to satisfy the court that its proposals are not unfair (per Lord Normand in *Scottish Insurance Corporation Ltd v Wilsons and Clyde Coal Co Ltd* at p 498; per Evershed MR in *Re Old Silkstone Collieries Ltd* [1954] Ch 169).

10.7.4 INTERESTS OF CREDITORS

On an application for confirmation of a reduction of capital a procedure is provided in CA 2006, ss 645(2) and (4) and 646, for settling a list of creditors and checking that each one of them has consented to the reduction or has been adequately provided for. The court has discretion to dispense with the creditors' procedure (s 645(3)). A consultation paper, *Access to Justice: Proposed New Procedures for the Specialist Jurisdictions of the High Court*, issued by the Lord Chancellor's Department in December 1997, noted that the procedure had not been used since 1949. This is because companies seeking confirmation of a reduction of capital have been able to provide evidence of consent and adequate provision sufficient to persuade the court that an expensive and time-consuming formal investigation is unnecessary. From 6 April 2008, there has been an additional condition that the list of creditors will include only those who can show that there is a real likelihood that the proposed reduction in capital would result in the company being unable to discharge their debts or claims as they fall due.

Generally the information about creditors of a company seeking confirmation of a reduction of capital will come from the company itself and so s 647 makes it an offence triable either way for an officer of the company wilfully to conceal the names of creditors entitled to object to the reduction or to misrepresent the nature of their claims.

10.7.5 TREATMENT OF DIFFERENT CLASSES

When a company issues preference shares it is usual to provide that if the company is wound up, any surplus after paying debts is to be devoted first to repaying the capital contributed for the preference shares. Where this is so then, on a reduction of capital to reflect a loss of capital, the preference shares should be the last to be reduced (*Re Floating Dock Co of St Thomas Ltd* [1895] 1 Ch 691). But on a return of surplus capital, the capital contributed for the preference shares should be returned first (*Scottish Insurance Corporation Ltd v Wilsons and Clyde Coal Co Ltd* [1949] AC 462; *Prudential Assurance Co Ltd v Chatterley-Whitfield Collieries Ltd* [1949] AC 512). For alteration of class rights, see **14.14**.

If, as is usual, the preference shareholders in a company are not entitled, when the company is wound up, to any share in a surplus beyond the return of their capital for which they have priority, then a reduction of capital which involves returning capital to, and cancelling the shares of, the preference shareholders will be in accordance with their rights and not in abrogation of them, so it is unnecessary to follow the procedures for the variation of rights described at **14.14** (*Re Saltdean Estate Co Ltd* [1968] 1 WLR 1844; *House of Fraser plc v ACGE Investments Ltd* [1987] AC 387). This means that, provided it has the resources, a company can buy out its preference shareholders when it finds that it can obtain fresh capital more cheaply elsewhere, which means that the preference shareholders will have their investment terminated just when it starts to show better returns than would be available on new investments. In *Re Northern Engineering Industries plc* [1994] 2 BCLC 709, the preference shareholders in a company had sought to protect themselves by having a provision inserted in the company's articles that a reduction of capital paid up on their shares was deemed to be a variation of their rights which had to be approved by them in a separate class meeting. It was held that this was effective to prevent them being bought out without their permission because 'reduction' was held to include 'extinction'.

10.7.6 PROCEDURE

A company may reduce its issued capital by special resolution of the members (CA 2006, s 641(1)). If the company is a public company, so that the resolution must be confirmed by the court (s 641(1)), a resolution adopted unanimously without meeting is not acceptable, because it is not within the statutory definition of a special resolution in s 283 (*Re Barry Artist Ltd* [1985] 1 WLR 1305; see **14.13.4**).

After the special resolution for a reduction has been passed, the company applies to the court to confirm the reduction. If the court confirms the reduction, it may do so on such terms and conditions as it thinks fit (s 648(1)). It may, for example, insist on the company adding 'and reduced' to its name (s 648(4)) or publishing an explanation of the reduction (s 648(3)), but it is not now usual for this to be done. The court's order can correct an error in the resolution if the error is insignificant, if no one will be prejudiced by the correction, and if it is clear how the error should be corrected (*Re Willaire Systems plc* [1987] BCLC 67).

It is common for companies to carry out complicated rearrangements of capital in which a reduction of one or more capital accounts is only one step. It is convenient to adopt all the necessary resolutions together. However, if a scheme involving an increase of a capital account followed by its reduction is to be confirmed, the increase must have taken place by the time the court is asked to confirm the reduction (*Re Transfesa Terminals Ltd* (1987) 3 BCC 647; *Re TIP-Europe Ltd* (1987) 3 BCC 647).

When the court's confirmation of the reduction has been given, a copy of the court's order and a statement of capital approved by the court must be delivered for registration at Companies House under s 649. Companies House will issue a certificate, which is conclusive evidence that all the requirements of the Act have been complied with, and that the company's share capital is as stated in the statement of capital (s 649(5) and (6)). The reduction of capital does not take effect until the order and statement are registered (s 649(3); *Re Castiglione, Erskine and Co Ltd* [1958] 1 WLR 688).

If a reduction of a public company's capital brings the nominal value of the company's allotted share capital below £50,000, the company must be re-registered as a private company and Companies House must not register the reduction of capital unless the change of status takes place (s 650) though the court is given a discretion to direct otherwise, for example where the reduction is to be followed immediately by an increase of capital to the authorised minimum or more (as part of a scheme for changing the company's shares from one type to another) (s 650(2)(a); *Re MB Group plc* [1989] BCLC 672; *Re Anglo-American Insurance Co Ltd* [1991] BCLC 564). The change of status may be resolved by the company following the procedure of s 97 (see **2.6.2**) or it can be incorporated in the order of the court confirming the resolution for reducing share capital (s 651).

10.7.7 ALERTING MEMBERS TO A SERIOUS LOSS OF CAPITAL

CA 2006, s 656, provides that, if the net assets of a *public company* fall to half or less of its called-up share capital, the directors must, within 28 days of a director first becoming aware of this fact, convene a general meeting. The meeting must take place not later than 56 days from the day on which a director became aware of the serious loss. The purpose of the meeting is to consider what measures should be taken to deal with that situation. Any director who knowingly and wilfully fails to comply with these requirements commits an offence triable either way (s 656(4) and (5)).

10.8 FINANCIAL ASSISTANCE FOR PURCHASE OF OWN SHARES

10.8.1 PROHIBITION ON ASSISTANCE BY PUBLIC COMPANY FOR PURCHASE OF OWN SHARES

10.8.1.1 Principle

Financial assistance (see **10.8.1.2**) must not be given by a public company, or by any of its subsidiaries, for the acquisition of its shares (CA 2006, s 678). Financial assistance must not be given for the acquisition of a private company's shares by any subsidiary of the private company which is a public company (s 679). Contravention of these prohibitions is a criminal offence (s 680). These rules are part of the controls on distributions to members. The rules prevent, for example, a sale of shares by a member of a company to another person, with the company paying the purchase price, which would be a return of capital to the vendor, with the shares still in issue even though they no longer represent any contributed capital. However, it has been very difficult to formulate the prohibition on financial assistance in a way which does not prevent entirely beneficial rearrangements of company finances. Before CA 2006 the prohibitions extended to financial assistance given by private companies as well, but were widely seen to be more trouble than they were worth. For criticism of the present law and proposals for reform, See S Mercouris, 'The prohibition on financial assistance: the case for a commercially pragmatic interpretation' (2014) 35 Co Law 321.

10.8.1.2 What constitutes financial assistance?

'Financial assistance' is defined in CA 2006, s 677, as meaning financial assistance given by way of gift, guarantee, security or loan and any other financial assistance which reduces, to a material extent, the net assets of the company giving the assistance, and any other financial assistance given by a company with no net assets.

Terms such as 'gift', 'guarantee', 'security' and 'indemnity' in s 677 must be restricted to their technical legal meaning (*British and Commonwealth Holdings plc v Barclays Bank plc* [1996] 1 WLR 1). In *British and Commonwealth Holdings plc v Barclays Bank plc* Aldous LJ said, at p 15:

> the section requires that there should be assistance or help for the purpose of acquiring shares and that that assistance should be financial.

In *Catley v Herbert* [1988] 1 NZLR 606 the New Zealand Court of Appeal held that 'financial assistance' has a wider meaning than 'monetary assistance' and can include a transfer of any of a company's assets. If financial assistance is given for the purpose of an acquisition of shares, it is prohibited by ss 678 to 680 regardless of whether it is given to the person acquiring the shares or to any other person (*Chaston v SWP Group Ltd* [2002] EWCA Civ 1999, [2003] 1 BCLC 675). In **Charterhouse Investment Trust Ltd v Tempest Diesels Ltd** [1986] BCLC 1, Hoffmann J said, at p 10, that when determining whether financial assistance has been given:

> One must examine the commercial realities of the transaction and decide whether it can properly be described as the giving of financial assistance by the company, bearing in mind that the section is a penal one and should not be strained to cover transactions which are not fairly within it.

In **Chaston v SWP Group Ltd** Arden LJ said, at [38]: 'It is clear . . . that the test is one of commercial substance and reality.'

Financial assistance is illegal if given either before or at the same time as an acquisition takes place (ss 678(1) and 679(1)). The prohibition of assistance before an acquisition includes assistance given in preparation for a proposed acquisition (*Chaston v SWP Group Ltd* at [42] to [44]). It is also illegal to give financial assistance after an acquisition has occurred (see **10.8.1.5**).

10.8.1.3 Exceptions

Various transactions are excepted from the prohibitions against financial assistance by CA 2006, ss 681 and 682.

A distribution of the company's assets by way of dividend lawfully made is excepted (s 681(2) (a)(i)). So it is legal to borrow money with which to acquire a controlling interest in a public company on the basis that the control will be used to declare a dividend from which the loan will be repaid. But the loan must not come from, or be secured by, the company itself or one of its subsidiaries.

Also excepted by s 681(2) are an allotment of bonus shares (see **10.4**), redemption (see **10.5**) and repurchase (see **10.6**) of shares, and reduction of capital by special resolution (see **10.7**).

Section 682 permits a company to lend money in the ordinary course of its money-lending business, provided the company is either a private company or, if it is a public company, the assistance does not reduce its net assets or is provided out of distributable profits. Section 682 also allows, with the same provisos, assistance for the purpose of employees' share schemes (see **10.9**).

10.8.1.4 Example

An example of illegal financial assistance is provided by *Belmont Finance Corporation v Williams Furniture Ltd (No 2)* [1980] 1 All ER 393. Belmont Finance Corporation bought all the issued shares of Maximum Finance Ltd from a Mr Grosscurth and his associates for £500,000. The shares were worth about £60,000. Grosscurth and associates used the money they got from Belmont to buy all the issued shares in Belmont from its parent company (so the directors of Belmont who caused it to give £500,000 to Grosscurth were also directors of the parent company which sold the shares in Belmont to Grosscurth). This was illegal financial assistance by Belmont for the purchase of its own shares. It made no difference that the Belmont directors genuinely believed that, under the direction of the persuasive Mr Grosscurth (who subsequently went bankrupt and left the country), Maximum Finance really was worth £500,000: the only purpose of buying Maximum

Finance was to provide Grosscurth with funds to buy the Belmont shares and this was well known to all concerned.

10.8.1.5 Discharging a liability of the purchaser

Where a person has acquired shares in a company (the target company) and incurred a liability for the purpose, it is illegal for the company or one of its subsidiaries to give financial assistance for the purpose of reducing or discharging that liability if, at the time of giving the assistance, the target company is a public company (CA 2006, s 678(3)). There is a similar prohibition in s 679(3) in relation to acquisition of the shares of a private company which is a public company's holding company.

In *Heald v O'Connor* [1971] 1 WLR 497, Douglas and Margaret Heald sold Mr O'Connor all the shares in D E Heald (Stoke-on-Trent) Ltd for £35,000 but also lent him £25,000. The company gave the Healds a floating charge on all its assets as security for repayment of this loan (floating charges are described in **11.6**), the effect being that if Mr O'Connor did not pay for the shares, the company would. This was illegal financial assistance. In *Re Hill and Tyler Ltd* [2004] EWHC 1261 (Ch), [2005] 1 BCLC 41, there was illegal financial assistance when a company charged its property as security for a loan to it of money which it then lent to a purchaser of its shares to finance payment for them.

If a debt owed by a company was not incurred for the purpose of giving illegal financial assistance for the acquisition of the company's shares, repayment of that debt cannot be illegal financial assistance, even if the shares could not be acquired without payment of the debt (*Anglo Petroleum Ltd v TFB (Mortgages) Ltd* [2007] EWCA Civ 456, [2008] 1 BCLC 185). If repaying a debt is not illegal financial assistance, neither is borrowing money to repay it or giving security for that borrowing (*Anglo Petroleum Ltd v TFB (Mortgages) Ltd*).

In *MT Realisations Ltd v Digital Equipment Ltd* [2003] EWCA Civ 494, [2003] 2 BCLC 117, MT Realisations Ltd (MTR) had been a loss-making company in the Digital group of companies. It owed £8 million to another company in the group, repayable on demand. MTI Holdings (UK) Ltd bought all shares in MTR for £1 and bought the £8 million debt for £6.5 million, payable in instalments. It was claimed that when money owed to MTR was used to pay those instalments, financial assistance was given for the purchase of MTR's shares. This was rejected at first instance and by the Court of Appeal. It was held that: (a) the liability to pay the instalments was not incurred for the purpose of acquiring the shares; (b) MTR was only paying a debt which it already owed, so it was not giving assistance to MTI; (c) as it was not claimed that the shares were worth more than £1 or that MTI could not afford to pay £1, MTI did not need to be assisted in paying for the shares. The Court of Appeal made clear that these conclusions could be reached only because the method chosen for arranging the share purchase reflected the commercial realities of the deal and was not chosen so as to disguise financial assistance. For criticism of this case see Virginia Rylatt, 'Fixed or floating?' (2004) 154 NLJ 1298.

10.8.1.6 Assistance from outside the United Kingdom

CA 2006, ss 678 to 680, do not have extraterritorial effect, so they do not, for example, prohibit a company incorporated in Gibraltar giving financial assistance for the acquisition of shares in its holding company incorporated in England (*Arab Bank plc v Merchantile Holdings Ltd* [1994] Ch 71). The fact that the financial assistance given by the foreign subsidiary reduces the value of the subsidiary's shares held by the UK holding company, and so reduces the holding company's net assets, does not turn it into financial assistance given by the holding company (*AMG Global Nominees (Private) Ltd v Africa Resources Ltd* [2008] EWCA Civ 1278, [2009] 1 BCLC 281). This does not mean that a holding company can transfer assets to a foreign subsidiary so that they can be used to buy the holding company's shares: that would be indirect financial assistance by the holding company, which is prohibited by s 678.

10.8.1.7 Benefit to company

The fact that financial assistance given by a company is not detrimental to the company does not in itself mean that it is legal (*Chaston v SWP Group Ltd* [2002] EWCA Civ 1999, [2003] 1 BCLC 675, at [41]). For example, a loan by a company to a person to enable the person to acquire shares in the company is illegal even if it is on terms that are very advantageous to the company. The fact that directors of a company cause it to give financial assistance bona fide in the company's interests does not in itself make the assistance legal (*Chaston v SWP Group Ltd* at [46]). But CA 2006, s 678(2), provides that s 678(1) does not apply to financial assistance given by a company for the purchase of its shares (or shares in its holding company) if the assistance is given in good faith in the interests of the company and:

(a) the company's principal purpose in giving that assistance is not to give it for the purpose of any such acquisition; or

(b) the giving of the assistance for that purpose is only an incidental part of some larger purpose of the company.

Similar exemptions are provided by s 679(2) from the prohibition in s 679(1), and in ss 678(4) and 679(4) from the prohibitions in ss 678(3) and 679(3) respectively.

In *Brady v Brady* [1989] AC 755, it was held that the fact that financial assistance given by a company will produce a benefit for the company does not mean that producing the benefit is a 'larger purpose' which will validate the assistance. *Brady v Brady* concerned the Brady family which owned various companies. The family had quarrelled and divided into two factions. They decided to divide the family businesses into two—one for each faction. To do this, all the existing operating companies were made wholly owned subsidiaries of a holding company called Ovalshield Ltd in which the two factions had equal shareholdings. Then two companies, Motoreal Ltd and Activista Ltd, were created, the plan being that the factions would take one of these companies each. Motoreal and Activista both issued all their shares to Ovalshield in return for shares in the operating companies so that each operating company became wholly owned by either Motoreal or Activista. Motoreal acquired the shares in the most valuable operating company, T Brady and Sons Ltd, and had to acknowledge that it still owed Ovalshield part of the purchase price of those shares. The right to receive this money was transferred by Ovalshield to Activista to make up the difference between the value of the operating companies being acquired by Activista and the value of Activista's shares. Ovalshield ended up owning shares in two companies, Motoreal and Activista, of equal value. Ovalshield was then liquidated and its shares in Motoreal went to one faction (Jack and Robert Brady) while its shares in Activista went to the other faction (Bob and John Brady). The final stage was to be the transfer to Activista of some assets of T Brady and Sons Ltd which Activista would accept as discharging the debt owed by Motoreal. In other words, T Brady and Sons Ltd would discharge a debt which had been incurred in order to buy its shares. This was illegal financial assistance.

10.8.2 PENALTIES

If a company gives financial assistance for the acquisition of its shares or those of a holding company, without proper authorisation, it commits an offence for which the penalty is a fine for which there is no limit; and every officer of the company in default is guilty of an offence triable either way (CA 2006, s 680).

In *Re Continental Assurance Co of London plc* [1997] 1 BCLC 48, causing a company to give about £2 million of illegal financial assistance for the purchase of its shares was in itself sufficient to justify disqualifying its chairman and managing director under CDDA 1986, s 6 (see **20.13**).

When other misconduct was taken into account the disqualification period was set at nine years. A non-executive director who failed to notice the illegal financial assistance was also disqualified for incompetence (see **16.8.5**).

As with an illegal excessive dividend (see **10.3.9**), money given by a company as illegal assistance for share acquisition and which is in the hands of any person who knew or ought to have known of the circumstances which made paying it improper will be subject to a constructive trust in favour of the company. For example, in *Belmont Finance Corporation v Williams Furniture Ltd (No 2)* [1980] 1 All ER 393 (the facts of which are set out in **10.8.1.4**), the money received by Belmont's parent company for selling the shares to Grosscurth was held by it on constructive trust for Belmont because its directors knew that the money was paid to Grosscurth by Belmont as illegal assistance for the acquisition of Belmont's shares. (The knowledge of the directors of the parent company was treated as the parent company's knowledge under the identification theory, see **19.8**.)

The courts always have great difficulty in deciding how far to allow illegal contracts to be enforced. In *Heald v O'Connor* [1971] 1 WLR 497 (the facts of which are set out in **10.8.1.5**) it was held that any contract for the giving of illegal financial assistance is void (so the contract made by the company in *Heald v O'Connor* giving a floating charge on its assets as security was void). This disagreed with the earlier case of *Victor Battery Co Ltd v Curry's Ltd* [1946] Ch 242. As both *Heald v O'Connor* and *Victor Battery Co Ltd v Curry's Ltd* were High Court decisions, the difference would seem to be unresolved, but in two subsequent cases in the House of Lords (*Brady v Brady* [1989] AC 755; *Neilson v Stewart* 1991 SC (HL) 22) it was assumed without argument that the rule stated in *Heald v O'Connor* is correct. The question was considered again at first instance in *Re Hill and Tyler Ltd* [2004] EWHC 1261 (Ch), [2005] 1 BCLC 41, and again it was held that a contract entered into for the purpose of providing illegal financial assistance is void.

If a contract for the acquisition of a company's shares includes a provision for illegal financial assistance, the illegal provision may be severed and the contract may be enforced without it, provided the illegal provision was made for the exclusive benefit of the party seeking to enforce the contract (*Carney v Herbert* [1985] AC 301; *Neilson v Stewart*). In *Carney v Herbert*, illegal financial assistance for the purchase of shares had been given by way of security for payment of the purchase price. The purchaser was a company called Ilerain Pty Ltd, which was controlled by the defendant, who guaranteed payment of the purchase price. The shares were resold at an enormous profit but the defendant refused to honour his guarantee on the ground that the contract of sale of the shares to Ilerain was illegal. It was held that the contract was valid despite the ancillary illegal security, so the defendant was liable on his guarantee. In *Neilson v Stewart*, illegal security was given for a loan to enable the defender to purchase shares: it was held that, despite the illegality of the security, the defender had to repay the loan.

In *Anglo Petroleum Ltd v TFB (Mortgages) Ltd* [2007] EWCA Civ 456, [2008] 1 BCLC 185, there is discussion of the circumstances in which use of money lent to a company to give illegal financial assistance for the acquisition of shares will lead the court to refuse to order repayment of the loan. It was held that a loan contract will not be invalidated if it does not require the money to be used for an unlawful purpose and if a reasonable person in the position of the lender would regard it as an ordinary commercial transaction.

10.8.3 RESTRICTIONS AND DISCLOSURE

A person who has been given financial assistance by a *public company* to acquire that company's shares, and holds those shares as trustee (for example, as nominee) for the company, must not exercise any voting rights attached to the shares (CA 2006, s 662(1)(e), (5) and (6)). If the company fails to dispose of its interests in such shares within one year of their acquisition by its trustee, it must cancel the shares and reduce its share capital accordingly (s 662(1)(e), (2)(a) and (3)(c)). If it shows its interest in such shares as an asset in a balance sheet, the value of that interest must be transferred from distributable profits to a reserve fund that will not be available for distribution (s 669). The fund is called a reserve for own shares.

In the accounts of a company the same information must be given about own shares acquired by trustees for the company (whether with or without the company's financial assistance) as for own shares forfeited or surrendered (see **6.5.2.6**).

10.9 EXEMPTIONS FOR EMPLOYEES' SHARE SCHEMES

Some companies take the view that their employees should also be shareholders and so be able to appreciate directly the financial circumstances of the enterprise for which they work. Accordingly, companies have set up schemes under which some of their profits each year are devoted to assisting employees to purchase shares, either on the London Stock Exchange or by subscription for new shares. Such schemes also provide an element of profit-sharing as part of employees' remuneration.

An employees' share scheme is defined in CA 2006, s 1166, as:

a scheme for encouraging or facilitating the holding of shares in or debentures of a company by or for the benefit of—

    (a)   the bona fide employees or former employees of—

        (i)   the company,

       (ii)   any subsidiary of the company, or

      (iii)   the company's holding company or any subsidiary of the company's holding company, or

    (b)   the spouses, civil partners, surviving spouses, surviving civil partners, or minor children or step-children of such employees or former employees.

An unresolved problem with this definition is the extent to which persons within para (a) or (b) can be excluded from the scheme, for example, by requiring a minimum period of service as an employee.

Employees' share schemes, as defined in s 1166, are facilitated by several exemptions from the controls in CA 2006. The directors of a company do not require authority from the articles or a resolution to allot shares in pursuance of an employees' share scheme (s 549(2); see **6.3.4**) and shares can be allotted to be held under a scheme without also being offered to other members (s 566; see **6.3.5**). Shares allotted in pursuance of a scheme by a public company are exempt from the rule that at least one quarter of the nominal value must be paid up before allotment (s 586(2)) (shares allotted under this exemption are ignored when determining whether a new public company has satisfied the minimum capital requirement: s 761(3)). Financial assistance may be provided by a company for the purposes of an employees' share scheme without committing an offence (see **10.8.1.3**), if the financial assistance is provided in good faith in the interests of the company (s 682(2)(b)).

The following relaxations of controls apply to repurchases by a company of its own shares for the purposes of or pursuant to an employees' share scheme. Payment does not have to be made on purchase (s 691(3)). Instead of needing approval of each contract for an off-market purchase, general authority can be given in the same way as for market purchases (s 693A). The requirements for approval of, and publicity for, a payment out of capital to repurchase shares are reduced to those in ss 720A and 720B, instead of the requirements in ss 714, 716, 719 and 720.

Employee share ownership is also encouraged by tax concessions, which are available when a company appropriates shares to its employees, or acquires shares on their behalf, or grants share options (rights to acquire shares) to them. Tax concessions are available only in respect of benefits received under schemes which satisfy conditions set out in the Income Tax (Earnings and Pensions) Act 2003. A scheme complying with the 2003 Act may or may not be an employees' share scheme as defined by CA 2006, s 1166. To deal with this problem, additional exemptions from the prohibition of financial assistance for acquisition of shares are made by s 682(2)(c) and (d). Paragraph (c) exempts financial assistance given by a company for the purposes of, or in connection with, 'anything done by' the company to enable or facilitate any of its bona fide employees, former employees and family, to become beneficial owners of its shares. Paragraph (c) also extends to financial assistance by, and schemes to benefit employees and former employees of, other companies in the same group. Paragraph (d) exempts loans by a company to its employees, but not directors, to enable them to acquire its shares or those of its holding company, provided the shares are fully paid (loans to directors are subject to strict controls which are discussed in **16.13**).

Tax concessions are available for four types of employee share scheme under the Income Tax (Earnings and Pensions) Act 2003:

(a)   A share incentive plan (SIP) under ss 488 to 515 and sch 2.

(b)   An SAYE option scheme (also known as ShareSave), under ss 516 to 520 and sch 3.

(c)   A company share option plan (CSOP) under ss 521 to 526 and sch 4.

(d)   An option conferring rights to acquire shares conforming with ss 527 to 541 and sch 5 (enterprise management incentives).

In order to qualify for tax exemption, schemes of types (a), (b) and (c) must be approved in advance by HM Revenue and Customs. Schemes of types (a) and (b) can be approved only if they cover all eligible directors and employees of the company. Schemes of types (c) and (d) allow the company to choose which directors or employees to reward. Enterprise management incentives are available only for companies with gross assets not exceeding £15 million.

The Employment Rights Act 1996, s 205A, introduced the status of 'employee shareholder'. An individual who is, or becomes, an employee of a company acquires this status by agreement with the company to be issued or allotted fully paid shares in the company worth at least £2,000 (at the time of issue or allotment) in return for the employee giving up various employment rights, including unfair dismissal and redundancy payments. The first £2,000 of employee shareholder shares are exempt from income tax (Income Tax (Earnings and Pensions) Act 2003, s 226B) and the first £50,000 are exempt from capital gains tax (Taxation of Capital Gains Act 1992, ss 236B and 236C). The tax exemptions are not available if the employee has a 'material interest' in the company, that is, if the employee and connected persons can exercise 25 per cent or more of the voting rights in the company (Taxation of Capital Gains Act 1992, s 236D; Income Tax (Earnings and Pensions) Act 2003, s 226D).

An employees' share scheme to be introduced for the employees of a premium listed company or any of its subsidiaries must be approved by ordinary resolution of the company's members if it involves, or may involve, issuing new shares or transferring treasury shares (LR 9.4.1R).

11

BORROWING AND SECURITY

SUMMARY OF POINTS COVERED

- What is in this chapter
- Security for financial obligations
- Registration of non-possessory security contracts

- Priorities
- Recourse
- Floating charges
- Registration of charges on company property

11.1 WHAT IS IN THIS CHAPTER

Borrowing is an important method of financing the activities of companies in the United Kingdom. Nowadays by far the most important form of borrowing is an overdraft at a bank, but this is quite a recent phenomenon and much of the law on borrowing by companies was developed to deal with loans from private individuals.

A lender of money to a company usually insists on being granted a right of recourse against property of the company if the loan is not repaid on time. The right of recourse is 'security' for the repayment of the loan (see **11.2** to **11.5**).

Companies, like individuals, give security in the form of fixed charges (mortgages) over land and also over other fixed assets. Unlike individuals, companies commonly give security in the form of a floating charge (see **11.6**). A floating charge covers all the changing current assets of a company (such as stocks of goods for sale).

It is very important to anyone considering extending credit to a company to be aware of the extent to which its assets are already charged as security. This is why recording charges in the publicly accessible register at Companies House is compulsory (see **11.7**).

If a company is registered as a public company on its initial incorporation, it is an offence for it to exercise any borrowing powers unless Companies House has issued it a trading certificate or it has re-registered as a private company (CA 2006, s 761(1); see **6.7.1**).

Key legislation which you should be able to consult when reading this chapter:

- Insolvency Act 1986, ss 238, 245, 249, 435;
- CA 2006, ss 859A–859Q.

All that legislation is in *Blackstone's Statutes on Company Law.*

The following cases, which are considered in this chapter, are particularly significant and are recommended further reading:

- *Evans v Rival Granite Quarries Ltd* [1910] 2 KB 979;
- *Re Spectrum Plus Ltd* [2005] UKHL 41, [2005] 2 AC 680; and
- *Re Yorkshire Woolcombers Association Ltd* [1903] 2 Ch 284.

Your particular course of study may require you to read other source materials.

11.2 SECURITY FOR FINANCIAL OBLIGATIONS

11.2.1 SECURITY CONTRACTS

If A owes B a financial obligation, A and B may also make an associated contract under which, if A personally fails to meet the obligation, then B can have recourse to property owned by A and can obtain what is due by selling the property, or by receiving income (such as rents or royalties) earned by the property. This kind of parallel contract is called a 'contract of direct security' for a financial obligation.

If A owes B a financial obligation, then B may make a contract with a third party C, under which C promises to meet A's obligation to B if A fails to do so. This is called a 'guarantee' and C is called a 'guarantor'. C's guarantee may be reinforced by a charge on C's property. Guarantees, and charges as security for guarantees, are called contracts of 'collateral security'. A guarantee cannot be enforced unless there is a written memorandum of the terms of the guarantee signed by the guarantor or by the guarantor's authorised agent (Statute of Frauds 1677, s 4), though the memorandum need not state what consideration was to be given to the guarantor (Mercantile Law Amendment Act 1856, s 3). It is also possible for C's property to be charged as security for an obligation owed by A to B without any personal promise by C to meet the obligation (*Re Bank of Credit and Commerce International SA (No 8)* [1998] AC 214).

A person whose property is charged as direct security or who acts as guarantor for another's financial obligation is called a 'surety'. One financial obligation may be covered by any number of direct and collateral security contracts.

Security contracts are most commonly made to cover repayment of loans but they also occur in connection with other kinds of financial obligation, such as payment of rent or payment for goods or services supplied. Any company with the power to borrow money has an implied power to give security for its repayment (*Re Patent File Co* (1870) LR 6 Ch App 83).

11.2.2 TYPES OF SECURITY CONTRACT

11.2.2.1 Pledge and lien

Probably the simplest way of making a person's goods security for a financial obligation is to give possession of the goods to the creditor on condition that possession will be returned when the obligation is met. This is called 'pledging' the goods. It is a characteristic of a pledge of goods that the creditor's rights against the goods cease when the creditor ceases to have possession of them.

The term 'pledge' is usually used where the primary reason for giving possession of the property to a creditor is to provide security. The term 'possessory lien' is used when possession of goods is given to a creditor otherwise than as security, for example so that the goods can be stored, transported or repaired and the creditor has a right to retain them as security, especially where the creditors' rights against the goods cease when the creditor ceases to have possession of them. Possessory liens may be created by contract. There are also possessory liens (called customary liens) which are recognised by common law as arising in certain trades and professions to secure payment of fees or charges owed by a client or customer and there are possessory liens which are created by statute.

11.2.2.2 Mortgages and charges, legal and equitable

The types of security contract which create most legal complications give a creditor a security interest in property without the creditor necessarily taking possession of the property. This is advantageous for a business enterprise, which can grant a security interest in its business assets while still having them in its possession for use in its business.

In this book the term 'charge' is used to describe all the forms of security contract which give a creditor a security interest in property without the transfer of possession of the property. In that sense, pledges and liens are not charges (see **11.2.2.1**). This is the way in which the term 'charge' is used in CA 2006, part 25 (ss 859A to 894) (see **11.2.2.4**).

The security interest created by a charge may, like any other property interest, be legal or equitable. If it is a legal interest, it must be recognised by any person who subsequently acquires title to the property or any interest in it. If it is an equitable interest, it may be ignored by any person who subsequently acquires, bona fide and for value, a legal interest in or legal title to the property without notice (actual or constructive), at the time of acquisition, of the existence of the equitable interest.

The essence of a contractual charge to secure a financial obligation is that a specific item of property or a class of property is appropriated to, or made answerable for, meeting the obligation, so that the creditor is entitled to look to the property to meet the obligation, regardless of whether the creditor has possession of the property (*Re Cosslett (Contractors) Ltd* [1998] Ch 495; *Flightline Ltd v Edwards* [2003] EWCA Civ 63, [2003] 1 WLR 1200; *Smith v Bridgend County Borough Council* [2001] UKHL 58, [2002] 1 AC 336, at [41]), if the obligation is not met in some other way (*Re Bond Worth Ltd* [1980] Ch 228 at p 248).

The most effective way of charging property is to transfer to the creditor legal title to the property on condition that it will be given back when the obligation is met otherwise than by recourse to the charged property. This form of charge creates a legal interest in the property and, in this book, is called a 'legal mortgage'. Where the property is a legal estate in land it is not now possible to transfer the legal title as security: instead a legal security interest may be created under the Law of Property Act 1925, s 85(1) (if the estate is freehold), or s 86(1) (if it is leasehold), by a deed which is expressed to create a charge by way of legal mortgage on the estate. It is also possible to create a legal security interest in a legal estate in land by granting a lease, but this method is hardly ever used in practice.

A person who has only an equitable interest in property cannot grant a legal security interest in it. But transferring the equitable interest to a creditor on condition that it will be returned if the obligation is met otherwise than by recourse to the property creates an equitable security interest and is known as an equitable mortgage.

The term 'equitable mortgage' is also used to describe a specifically enforceable contract to create a legal mortgage.

All other forms of charge which create only equitable security interests are, in this book, called 'equitable charges'.

11.2.2.3 Summary

The classification of security contracts was summarised by Millett LJ in **Re Cosslett (Contractors) Ltd** [1998] Ch 495 at p 508 as follows:

> There are only four kinds of consensual security known to English law: (i) pledge; (ii) contractual lien; (iii) equitable charge and (iv) mortgage. A pledge and a contractual lien both depend on the delivery of possession to the creditor. The difference between them is that in the case of a pledge the owner delivers

possession to the creditor as security, whereas in the case of a lien the creditor retains possession of goods previously delivered to him for some other purpose. Neither a mortgage nor [an equitable] charge depends on the delivery of possession. The difference between them is that a mortgage involves a transfer of legal or equitable ownership to the creditor, whereas an equitable charge does not.

11.2.2.4 Terminology

Creditors have developed many different forms of security arrangement and an unfortunate consequence of this is that there is little agreement on terminology. Words which some people use to describe particular forms of security arrangement are used by others as generic terms to refer to all kinds of security arrangement. For example, the term 'mortgage' is used by many people to refer to a particular kind of security, but the Law of Property Act 1925 uses 'mortgage' throughout and in the 'definitions' (s 205(1)(xvi)) says:

'Mortgage' includes any charge or lien on any property for securing money or money's worth.

CA 2006, part 25 (ss 859A to 894), though, is drafted using 'charge' as the generic term and s 859A(7) says:

'charge' includes mortgage.

In IA 1986, an interpretation section (s 248) provides:

'security' means . . . any mortgage, charge, lien or other security.

This book uses the CA 2006, part 25, terminology. In that terminology a security interest in property which subsists only while the creditor has possession of the property is not a charge (*R A Barrett and Co Ltd v Livesey* (1980) 131 NLJ 1213 (pledge); *Waitomo Wools (NZ) Ltd v Nelsons (NZ) Ltd* [1974] 1 NZLR 484 (contractual possessory lien); *Re Hamlet International plc* [1998] 2 BCLC 164 (contractual possessory lien)).

As is usual in legal terminology, the suffix 'or' is added to the name of a security contract to give the term for the person who creates the security interest, and the suffix 'ee' produces the term for the creditor for whom the interest is created. So a 'chargor' creates a charge in favour of a 'chargee', a 'mortgagor' creates a mortgage in favour of a 'mortgagee', and so on.

11.2.2.5 Debentures

Among business people the word 'debenture' usually denotes a document by which a company gives security for the repayment of a loan. However, the courts have always held that 'debenture' means any document issued by a company acknowledging indebtedness, whether secured or not (*Lemon v Austin Friars Investment Trust Ltd* [1926] Ch 1), and this is the sense in which the word is used in CA 2006 (see s 738).

In the second half of the nineteenth century small companies often took loans from private investors in units of, say, £100. For each £100 (say) lent an investor was given a certificate specifying entitlement to interest and repayment of principal, and the holders of these certificates would all be given an equal right of recourse against the company's property if there was default in paying interest or repaying principal. A set of identical certificates like this issued by a company is called a *series of debentures*. Debentures in series feature in many court cases but are now virtually extinct.

Very large loans can be raised in capital markets where investors can buy and sell their interests in the loans. These are known as marketable loans and are considered separately in **Chapter 12**.

11.2.3 REDEMPTION

If a secured obligation is met without recourse to the security then the security contract automatically terminates, and the security is said to be 'redeemed' or 'discharged' (*Walker v Jones* (1866) LR

1 PC 50; *Rourke v Robinson* [1911] 1 Ch 480). Chancery developed the important principle that a person whose property has been charged as security for meeting some obligation and who fails to meet the obligation on the contracted day may nevertheless redeem the security by meeting the obligation on some later day (*Brown v Cole* (1845) 14 Sim 427). Preservation of the right to redeem means that a person whose property has been charged always retains an interest in that property, and this interest (which is called the 'equity of redemption') comes to an end only if:

(a) there is redemption, that is if the charge itself is ended because the secured obligation is met; or

(b) the right to redeem is ended (or 'foreclosed') by court order; or

(c) the chargee exercises a power to sell the charged property, or it is sold by court order.

On foreclosure or sale the equity of redemption comes to an end but is replaced by a right to be paid the amount by which the proceeds of sale exceed the secured debt (*Ultraframe (UK) Ltd v Fielding* [2005] EWHC 1638 (Ch), [2007] WTLR 835, at [1403]).

The courts protect the equity of redemption by declaring void any provision in a charge contract that has the effect of excluding the right to redeem. (Such a provision is called a 'fetter' or 'clog' on the equity of redemption.) See *G and C Kreglinger v New Patagonia Meat and Cold Storage Co Ltd* [1914] AC 25. However, if a registered company gives a charge and excludes its right to redeem the charge, or makes it redeemable only on the happening of a contingency (such as the winding up of the company), the clog on the equity will not be void (CA 2006, s 739). This provision was enacted so that companies could borrow on what are called 'perpetual debentures', with no fixed date for the repayment of principal. An investor with a perpetual debenture has a right to a regular payment of interest for as long as the company exists. (Perpetual debentures of this kind are rare. The term is also sometimes used for unsecured marketable loans—see **Chapter 12**.) Section 739 also makes enforceable a contract giving security for a debt owed by a company, under which the contractual date for payment of the secured debt (and therefore the earliest date for redemption of the security) is far distant—for example, 40 years (*Knightsbridge Estates Trust Ltd v Byrne* [1940] AC 613).

11.2.4 REALISATION

No action can be taken by a creditor to realise any security until the secured obligation is actually due to be met and there has been failure to meet it. So if a secured loan is not due to be repaid until a certain date, the security cannot be realised until that date has passed without repayment of the loan. Banks are in an especially strong position because nearly all their lending to companies is on overdraft which is repayable on demand by the bank. In **Williams and Glyn's Bank Ltd v Barnes** [1981] Com LR 205, Mr Barnes contested the bank's claim against him in debt for some £2 million. The claim arose from the crash of his company, Northern Developments Holdings Ltd, which Mr Barnes alleged came about because the bank unreasonably refused to continue financing. In particular, he alleged that the bank should not have demanded repayment of its overdraft when it knew that this would destroy the company whose future profits were the only means of paying the debt. Ralph Gibson J said:

> Where money is lent on overdraft by a bank, and there is no agreed date for repayment, and no special terms which require implication of a further term as to the date of repayment, then it is clear to me that the overdraft is repayable on demand.
>
> When a bank lends money to a customer there is no reason to suppose that, in the absence of agreement to that effect, the bank must regard the fulfilment of the customer's known purpose as the agreed, or only, source of repayment. Borrowing from a bank may be replaced by borrowing from another bank or money-lender. If the borrowing cannot be replaced, because of the parlous state of the borrower's business, or of the

market generally, I know of nothing in the ordinary contract of lending which requires the lender to share the borrower's misfortune.

11.3 REGISTRATION OF NON-POSSESSORY SECURITY CONTRACTS

Charging property, otherwise than by pledge or lien, does not in practice involve giving possession of the charged property to the chargee. There is a danger that a person who charges property without giving up possession of it will pretend to future creditors that the property is unencumbered and will borrow money on the strength of the apparent wealth conferred by the property. To provide protection against this, statutes have set up government-administered registers for recording non-possessory charges on the following types of property:

(a) Registered land—that is, any estate in land that has been registered in one of the district land registries in England and Wales under the Land Registration Act 2002. If land has been registered at a district land registry, a charge on it should be registered at the same registry.

(b) Unregistered land in England and Wales. A charge on unregistered land should be registered at the Land Charges Department of the Land Registry under the Land Charges Act 1972 unless the chargee takes possession of the title deeds to the land.

(c) British ships. A charge on a British ship or a share in a ship should be registered under the Merchant Shipping Act 1995, sch 1, para 7, at the Registry of Shipping and Seamen.

(d) Registered trade marks (Trade Marks Act 1994, s 25).

(e) Registered designs (Registered Designs Act 1949, s 19).

(f) UK patents (Patents Act 1977, s 32).

(g) Aircraft and hovercraft registered in the United Kingdom (Mortgaging of Aircraft Order 1972 (SI 1972/ 1268)).

In addition, if an individual or a partnership executes a document giving a non-possessory charge on things in possession (personal tangible property) then the document is a bill of sale and must be registered at the Supreme Court under the Bills of Sale Acts 1878 and 1882 (unless the charged property is a ship), and the charge will be void unless the document is in the form prescribed by the schedule to the 1882 Act. However, the provisions of the Bills of Sale Acts do not apply to a charge given by a registered company on its things in possession (Bills of Sale Act (1878) Amendment Act 1882, s 17; *Re Standard Manufacturing Co* [1891] 1 Ch 627).

A charge on property of a registered company must be registered at Companies House under CA 2006, part 25, Chapter A1 (ss 859A to 859Q) (see **11.7**). This registration is required in addition to any registration that may be necessary because of the nature of the property charged. For example, a charge on a UK-registered aircraft belonging to a company must be registered in the register of aircraft mortgages kept by the Civil Aviation Authority and in the register of charges kept at Companies House.

All these registers are open to public inspection for a modest fee. If a charge is registered in one of these registers, a buyer of the charged property has to recognise the claim of the chargee to the property, and if the property is charged a second time, the second chargee has to recognise the prior claim of the chargee who is already registered. On the other hand, if a charge that could be registered in one of these registers is not then it can be ignored by a subsequent buyer of the property, or subsequent second chargee of the property whose charge is registered, even if notice of the existence of the prior charge is given by some other means.

The Law Commission has recommended replacing the Bills of Sale Acts 1878 and 1882 with a new 'Goods Mortgages Act' (*Bills of Sale* (Law Com No 369) (2016)).

11.4 PRIORITIES

The distinction between a legal and an equitable charge (see **11.2.2.2**) may be important if the person who granted the charge (the surety) deals with property after charging it. If a surety sells charged property (for value) then:

(a) if the chargee has a legal charge, the property remains charged in the hands of the new owner, so the chargee can still have recourse to it if the obligation secured by the charge is not met; and

(b) if the chargee has an equitable charge, the property remains charged in the hands of the new owner only if, at the time of buying the property, the new owner had notice of the chargee's interest.

If a surety has charged property and subsequently grants a legal charge over the property to a second chargee (for value) then:

(a) if the first charge is a legal charge, the first chargee is entitled to have recourse to the property in priority to the second chargee; and

(b) if the first charge is an equitable charge, the first chargee is entitled to priority only if, at the time the second charge was created, the second chargee had notice of the first chargee's interest.

If two equitable charges are created over the same property, they take priority in order of creation.

Chargees may agree among themselves to vary these rules and do not need the surety's consent to any variation (*Cheah Theam Swee v Equiticorp Finance Group Ltd* [1992] 1 AC 472).

The rules on priorities of legal and equitable charges are of very much less importance where there is a system for registering charges, because registration is equivalent to notice to any subsequent buyer or chargee of the existence of the registered charge (whether it is legal or equitable), and failure to register means that the charge (whether legal or equitable) may be ignored by any subsequent chargee who does register or any subsequent buyer. Thus registration rather than the form of the charge is the key to enforcing the charge against third parties.

11.5 RECOURSE

11.5.1 RIGHT TO SELL

A pledgee has a right to sell pledged property if the obligation secured by the pledge is not met (*Re Hardwick* (1886) 17 QBD 690, per Bowen LJ at p 698 and Fry LJ at p 701), though there are statutory restrictions on this right in some circumstances under the Consumer Credit Act 1974, ss 116 to 121.

A legal mortgagee of stocks and shares traded on the London Stock Exchange has a right to sell them when the obligation secured by the mortgage is not met (*Wilson v Tooker* (1714) 5 Bro Parl Cas 193; *Deverges v Sandeman Clark and Co* [1902] 1 Ch 579).

A chargee has no right to sell charged property under other types of security contract, unless that right has been granted by a provision in the contract. If the security contract is made by deed, a right of sale is deemed by the Law of Property Act 1925, s 101, to be given by the contract, unless the contract provides otherwise.

If no right of sale is granted by the charge contract, the chargee may apply to the High Court or County Court for an order to sell the charged property.

The right of sale given by the Law of Property Act 1925, s 101, has been held to be not available to the holders of debentures in series (*Blaker v Herts and Essex Waterworks Co* (1889) 41 ChD 399, decided under legislation that was replaced by the Law of Property Act 1925, s 101, in substantially the same terms).

Any profit made on selling charged property, after the secured obligation is met, is held on trust for the surety (Law of Property Act 1925, s 105).

Equity does not permit charged property to be sold under the chargee's power of sale to the chargee, either as a sole purchaser or jointly with others, or to a trustee for the chargee (*Downes v Grazebrook* (1817) 3 Mer 200), though there can be a sale to a company in which the chargee is interested (*Tse Kwong Lam v Wong Chit Sen* [1983] 1 WLR 1349).

When exercising a power of sale of charged property a chargee has a duty to take reasonable care to obtain the true market value of the property (*Cuckmere Brick Co Ltd v Mutual Finance Ltd* [1971] Ch 949). However, a chargee is entitled to sell when the power of sale becomes exercisable (that is, when the secured obligation is due and has not been paid). If the market happens to be depressed at that time, the chargee is under no obligation to wait until it improves (*Bank of Cyprus (London) Ltd v Gill* [1980] 2 Lloyd's Rep 51). Liability for breach of this duty may be excluded by an appropriately worded provision of the charge contract (*Bishop v Bonham* [1988] 1 WLR 742, in which the wording of the contract was not effective to exclude the liability).

11.5.2 EXERCISE OF THE SECTION 101 POWER OF SALE

The Law of Property Act 1925, s 103, provides that the power of sale given by s 101 of the Act may be exercised only if:

(a) the surety has failed to comply with three months' notice to repay the principal debt secured; or

(b) interest payable on the secured debt is unpaid two months after becoming due; or

(c) there has been a breach of a term of the charge contract other than terms relating to repayment of principal or payment of interest.

The Law of Property Act 1925, s 101(3), permits these time limits to be varied by a term in the charge contract. It is usual for a charge contract to state that the power of sale will be exercisable immediately there is default in paying interest or repaying principal.

11.5.3 RIGHT TO TAKE POSSESSION

A legal chargee is given the legal title to the charged property (or, in the case of land, a legal estate) and therefore has an immediate right to possession of the property. As Harman J said in *Four-Maids Ltd v Dudley Marshall (Properties) Ltd* [1957] Ch 317 at p 320:

> The mortgagee may go into possession before the ink is dry on the mortgage unless there is something in the contract, express or by implication, whereby he has contracted himself out of that right.

The right to possession is exercisable whether or not the surety has defaulted, unless there is a contrary agreement (*Western Bank Ltd v Schindler* [1977] Ch 1). However, a chargee who takes possession of the charged property comes under a strict and heavy liability because of the 'wilful default rule' under which a chargee in possession must account to the surety for rents and profits which, but for the chargee's default or neglect, the surety might have received. As Romilly MR said in *Chaplin v Young (No 1)* (1864) 33 Beav 330 at pp 337–8:

> if [a chargee of a business] enter into possession, he becomes the owner of the business, and he stands exactly, as regards his powers, in the place of the mortgagor, and, accordingly, he is accountable to the owner of the equity of redemption for everything which he either has received or might have received, while he continued in such possession.

Accordingly, creditors developed a procedure by which security interests were enforced by appointing a 'receiver' to take possession of the charged property and sell it, with a term in the charge contract deeming the receiver to be the agent of the surety—see per Rigby LJ in *Gaskell v Gosling* [1896] 1 QB 559 at pp 691–3.

An equitable chargee has no right to possession of the charged property unless granted the right by a provision of the charge contract (*Tennant v Trenchard* (1869) LR 4 Ch App 537; *Vacuum Oil Co v Ellis* [1914] 1 KB 693, per Buckley LJ at 703). (For a strongly expressed view to the contrary, see Wade (1955) 71 LQR 204.) However, on application by an equitable chargee, the court may appoint a receiver to take possession of the charged property, as an officer of the court, pending an order by the court to sell it to meet the obligation owed to the chargee.

The distinction between the rights of an equitable and a legal chargee was summarised by Buckley J in *Re London Pressed Hinge Co Ltd* [1905] 1 Ch 576 at p 583:

> A legal mortgagee may take possession simply because he chooses. In so doing he accepts the responsibility of a mortgagee in possession. An equitable mortgagee must show good reason why the court should at his instance take possession by its receiver.

From the chargee's point of view the problem with a court-appointed receiver is that such a receiver is a neutral officer of the court whose task is to administer property that is the subject of proceedings for the benefit of all parties to those proceedings. A chargee obviously wants the property administered solely for the chargee's benefit. One way of achieving this is to insert in a contract of equitable charge a provision that the chargee may appoint a receiver to take possession of the charged property and sell it for the chargee's benefit, but acting as agent of the surety. The device of appointing a receiver as agent of the surety was used in the most common form of equitable charge given by companies, the floating charge (see **11.6.3**).

11.5.4 RIGHT TO APPOINT A RECEIVER OF INCOME

Where charged property is land that has been leased the best way of satisfying the chargee's claims may be to ensure that the rent is paid to the chargee instead of to the surety. This may be achieved by appointing a receiver of income. A power to appoint a receiver of income is given by the Law of Property Act 1925, s 101, to any chargee whose charge has been given in a deed. A receiver of income appointed under this power is deemed to be the agent of the surety (Law of Property Act 1925, s 109(2)) and so probably does not 'take' possession of the charged property, and so may be appointed by an equitable or a legal chargee. The s 101 power to appoint a receiver of income may be exercised only if the chargee is entitled to exercise the s 101 power of sale (Law of Property Act 1925, s 109(1)).

11.5.5 RIGHT TO FORECLOSURE

A chargee may ask the court to foreclose (bring to an end) the surety's right of redemption. A chargee granted foreclosure would become absolute owner of the charged property. In any claim for foreclosure the court may instead direct a sale of the charged property (Law of Property Act 1925, s 91(2)) and in practice usually does.

11.5.6 RIGHT TO SUE FOR PERFORMANCE OF THE OBLIGATION

A creditor who has been given security cannot be forced to utilise that security, and is permitted to keep it in reserve and enforce the observance of the secured obligation by, for example, an ordinary claim for debt. However, a contract which creates a charge as security for an obligation does not in itself confer a right to sue the surety for performance of that obligation. This is significant where the charge is given as collateral security for another person's obligation: the chargee's right under such a contract is against the charged property not the chargor personally (unless the charge contract provides otherwise) (*Tam Wing Chuen v Bank of Credit and Commerce Hong Kong Ltd* [1996] 2 BCLC 69; *Re Bank of Credit and Commerce International SA (No 8)* [1998] AC 214).

Once a charge has been foreclosed, the chargee loses the right to sue on any express or implied covenant in the charge contract to repay the secured debt, unless prepared (and able) to return the charged property (*Kinnaird v Trollope* (1888) 39 ChD 636; *Lloyds and Scottish Trust Ltd v Britten* (1982) 44 P & CR 249). This is because the value of the property already received by the chargee is not known and cannot be deducted from the debt. If, instead of foreclosure, there has been a sale of the charged property, under the chargee's power of sale or a court order, its value will be known and the chargee can sue for the balance of the debt without returning the property (*Gordon Grant and Co Ltd v Boos* [1926] AC 781).

11.6 FLOATING CHARGES

11.6.1 DEFINITION OF FLOATING CHARGE

Much of the property of a trading company is in the form of a continually changing collection of current assets employed by the company in its business. The form of security arrangement known as a 'floating charge' was invented as a means of charging such property—current assets used to be known as 'floating assets'. In a floating charge given by a company, the subject matter of the charge is a class of the company's assets—such as plant, machinery and tools or stocks of goods for sale—and the charge confers on the chargee the right to take for payment of the secured debt all the assets of that type that the company owns at the time when the charge 'crystallises'. Normally a floating charge on a company's assets crystallises when, after the company has failed to pay the secured debt when it is due, the chargee appoints an administrator, administrative receiver or receiver (see **11.6.3**), or when the company ceases business. For more on crystallisation see **11.6.4**. It is an important characteristic of a floating charge that until it crystallises, the company may buy, sell, replace and otherwise deal with assets of the charged class in the normal course of its business without reference to the chargee.

A 'fixed charge' is a charge that is not a floating charge. The typical fixed charge granted by a company is a charge on a specific asset owned by the company (fixed charges are often called specific charges), which the company cannot deal with at all unless it has the permission of the chargee. The exact distinction between fixed and floating charges can be disputed and is discussed in **11.6.6**.

A powerful creditor such as a bank usually takes a charge on all, or substantially all, of a company's assets. This is usually a composite charge which is expressed to be a fixed charge on specified fixed assets and a floating charge on the company's whole undertaking and property other than the items covered by the fixed charge.

A company whose only asset is a major fixed asset such as a ship or a building may create a fixed charge on that asset which will effectively be a fixed charge on its entire property, but normally a charge on the 'undertaking' of a company must be a floating charge (*Re Panama, New Zealand and Australian Royal Mail Co* (1870) LR 5 Ch App 318).

In ***Governments Stock and Other Securities Investment Co Ltd v Manila Railway Co Ltd*** [1897] AC 81 Lord Macnaghten gave the following description of a floating charge, at p 86:

> A floating security is an equitable charge on the assets for the time being of a going concern. It attaches to the subject charged in the varying condition in which it happens to be from time to time. It is of the essence of such a charge that it remains dormant until the undertaking charged ceases to be a going concern, or until the person in whose favour the charge is created intervenes. His right to intervene may of course be suspended by agreement. But if there is no agreement for suspension, he may exercise his right whenever he pleases after default.

And in ***Illingworth v Houldsworth*** [1904] AC 355 his Lordship said, at p 358:

> what I said [in the passage from the *Manila Railway* case just quoted] was intended as a description, not as a definition, of a floating security. I should have thought there was not much difficulty in defining what a floating charge is in contrast to what is called a specific charge. A specific charge, I think, is one that without more fastens on ascertained and definite property or property capable of being ascertained and defined; a floating charge, on the other hand, is ambulatory and shifting in its nature, hovering over and so to speak floating with the property which it is intended to affect until some event occurs or some act is done which causes it to settle and fasten on the subject of the charge within its reach and grasp.

It is an important feature of English security law that only an incorporated business can create a floating charge over its changing current assets. A sole trader or unincorporated partnership cannot do so because of the requirements of the Bills of Sale Acts 1878 and 1882. Gaining the ability to borrow money on the security of a floating charge has always been an important reason for incorporating a business as a limited company. The Law Commission concluded that its project to reform the Bills of Sale Acts could not be extended to enabling unincorporated businesses to create floating charges (*Bills of Sale. A Consultation Paper* (Consultation Paper No 225) (2015), Chapter 6 and appendix D).

11.6.2 MORE THAN ONE CHARGE ON THE SAME PROPERTY

The essence of a floating charge on assets of a company is that the company is free to deal with those assets in the ordinary course of its business. In a series of cases it was held that this included being able to create fixed charges on assets within the class covered by the floating charge, having priority over the floating charge, in order to secure borrowing in the ordinary course of the company's business (see *Wheatley v Silkstone and Haigh Moor Coal Co* (1885) 29 ChD 715).

The courts have recognised that the nature of a floating charge precludes a company which has created one over its assets from creating another floating charge over *all of the same assets* ranking equally with, or in priority to, the first floating charge, except with the first chargee's permission (*Re Benjamin Cope and Sons Ltd* [1914] 1 Ch 800). However, it is possible to create a second floating charge over *a part of the assets* with priority over the first charge (*Re Automatic Bottle Makers Ltd* [1926] Ch 412).

In response to this it has become standard practice to include in a contract of floating charge a 'negative-pledge' clause, providing that the company will not create any charge over the assets covered by the floating charge with priority over the floating charge.

If a company grants two floating charges over its property and business then, as equitable charges, they take priority in order of creation (*Re Benjamin Cope and Sons Ltd*), though priority may be lost by failure to register under CA 2006, part 25, Chapter A1 (ss 859A to 859Q) (see **11.7**) and see also the discussion of *Griffiths v Yorkshire Bank plc* [1994] 1 WLR 1427 in **11.6.4.3**.

11.6.3 APPOINTMENT OF AN ADMINISTRATOR, ADMINISTRATIVE RECEIVER OR RECEIVER

Floating charges are equitable charges and, when they were first invented in the mid-nineteenth century, were enforced by asking the court to appoint a receiver, because the chargee had no right to take possession (see **11.5.3**). Victorian lawyers then began to insert into floating-charge contracts a provision giving the chargee the right to appoint a receiver of the charged property, who would realise it for the benefit of the chargee, but as the agent of the company. The use of this device has caused resentment because it seems that such a receiver sells the company's assets as quickly as possible so as to pay the preferential debts (see **20.2.3**) and some of the debt secured by the floating charge, leaving other creditors with nothing, without stopping to consider whether the company's business could be rescued.

The Insolvency Act 1985 introduced what has become known as a 'rescue culture'. It created a procedure for the appointment of an administrator of a company in financial difficulties (see **20.3**). An administrator does not act in the interests of a particular creditor and is required to consider first whether the company's business may be rescued. The 1985 Act also began to limit the activities of chargee-appointed receivers. It defined an 'administrative receiver' as a receiver who is appointed under a floating charge (or a composite fixed and floating charge) to take control of the whole (or substantially the whole) of a company's property (or who would have done so had it not been for the appointment of another receiver over part of the property) (now IA 1986, s 29(2)).

The Enterprise Act 2002 made amendments to IA 1986 which introduced substantial reforms. When the assets of a company subject to a floating charge are realised, a certain proportion must be set aside for the unsecured creditors (IA 1986, s 176A; see **20.2.4**). It is not possible to appoint an administrative receiver under a floating charge created on or after 15 September 2003 (IA 1986, s 72A; SI 2003/2095), except in the cases specified in IA 1986, ss 72B to 72H (which cover special cases summarised later). Instead, the chargee has the right to appoint an administrator (IA 1986, sch B1, para 14; see **20.3**). An administrator is an officer of the court (sch B1, para 5) who performs his or her functions in the interests of the company's creditors as a whole (sch B1, para 3(2)).

A chargee with a floating charge created before 15 September 2003 retains the right to appoint an administrative receiver, but also has the option of appointing an administrator.

A chargee whose floating charge (whether alone or in conjunction with other fixed or floating charges) does not cover the whole (or substantially the whole) of a company's property can still appoint a receiver, who will, by definition, not be an administrative receiver, and such a chargee does not have the option of appointing an administrator.

The cases in which an administrative receiver can be appointed to enforce a floating charge created on or after 15 September 2003 are:

(a) where a debt of £50 million or more is financed by a marketable loan (s 72B);

(b) where a person has step-in rights in relation to a project company (that is, rights to take over responsibility for carrying out the project or arranging for it to be carried out: sch 2A, para 6) and the project is a public–private partnership project (s 72C), a utility project (s 72D), an urban regeneration project (s 72DA), or will involve £50 million or more of financing (s 72E)—a right to appoint an administrative receiver does not amount to step-in rights (*Feetum v Levy* [2005] EWCA Civ 1601, [2006] 2 BCLC 102);

(c) to enforce charges which secure payment for purchases on recognised investment exchanges (s 72F);

(d) where the company is a social landlord (s 72G); and

(e) where the company is a railway, water or air traffic control company (s 72GA).

An administrator, administrative receiver or receiver cannot be appointed by the holder of a floating charge unless the charge is enforceable. The primary condition for enforcing a charge is that the debt secured by the charge is due and unpaid (see 11.2.4). It is also usual for a floating-charge contract to provide that the secured debt will become due for payment on the happening of various events including:

(a) the company going into liquidation;

(b) appointment of an administrator, administrative receiver or receiver by another chargee;

(c) levy of execution or distress on the assets of the company;

(d) the company becoming unable to pay its debts within the meaning of IA 1986, s 122(1) (see 20.6.4);

(e) cessation of business by the company;

(f) notice by the chargee converting the charge into a fixed charge, if provision is made in the contract for such notices to be given (see 11.6.4.2); and

(g) any 'automatic crystallisation' events (see 11.6.4.2), if the charge contract provides for them.

11.6.4 CRYSTALLISATION

11.6.4.1 What is crystallisation?

A floating charge is a charge on a class of assets (usually, all assets that are not covered by fixed charges) of a company. The actual assets in that class owned by the company change from time to time. The assets that the chargee is entitled to utilise for payment of the secured debt are the assets in the class that the company owns at the time when the charge 'crystallises'. Crystallisation has been described as operating as an equitable assignment (by way of charge), to the chargee, of the assets that were subject to the floating charge at the time of crystallisation (*George Barker (Transport) Ltd v Eynon* [1974] 1 WLR 462 per Edmund Davies LJ at p 467, Stamp LJ at p 471, and Sir Gordon Willmer at p 475). On crystallisation a floating charge becomes a fixed (or specific) equitable charge—that is, a charge on the specific assets of the charged class owned by the company at the time of crystallisation (*Re Griffin Hotel Co Ltd* [1941] Ch 129). The company has an equity of redemption (*Ultraframe (UK) Ltd v Fielding* [2005] EWHC 1638 (Ch), [2007] WTLR 835, at [1401]).

11.6.4.2 When does crystallisation occur?

The most important situation in which a floating charge crystallises is when the chargee enforces the charge by appointing an administrator, administrative receiver or receiver (see 11.6.3).

Also, as the basis of a floating charge is that the company needs to deal with the charged assets in the course of its business, it is an implied term of the charge contract that the charge will crystallise if the company's business ceases (*Re Woodroffes (Musical Instruments) Ltd* [1986] Ch 366; *William Gaskell Group Ltd v Highley* [1994] 1 BCLC 197) or the company goes into liquidation (*Wallace v Universal Automatic Machines Co* [1894] 2 Ch 547; *Re Panama, New Zealand and Australian Royal Mail co* (1870) LR 5 Ch App 318; *Re Crompton and Co Ltd* [1914] 1 Ch 954). This implied term could be excluded by an express provision to the contrary (*Re Real Meat Co Ltd* [1996] BCC 254 (cessation of business); *Re Brightlife Ltd* [1987] Ch 200 at p 212 (liquidation)).

A floating-charge contract may also specify other circumstances in which the charge crystallises (*Stein v Saywell* (1969) 121 CLR 529; *Re Permanent Houses (Holdings) Ltd* [1988] BCLC 563; *Covacich v Riordan* [1994] 2 NZLR 502). In particular, the chargee may have the right to give the company notice that the charge is converted into a fixed charge and that the charge becomes enforceable on giving such notice (see *Re Brightlife Ltd*). It is not possible for a floating-charge contract to specify that the charge will crystallise when the directors of the company obtain or prepare for a moratorium while they propose a voluntary arrangement (IA 1986, sch A1, para 43).

Sometimes charge contracts specify that the charge will crystallise in circumstances, such as failure to adhere to financial limits, which are not readily ascertainable by the chargee, who may not even want the charge to crystallise when such an event actually happens. A provision that a floating charge is to crystallise on the happening of a certain event without any action by the chargee is usually described as providing for 'automatic crystallisation'. Automatic crystallisation in circumstances that are not readily ascertainable is inconvenient (see the discussion in the Cork Committee report (Cmnd 8558, 1982), paras 1570–81). Nevertheless, courts have no grounds on which they can refuse to give effect to contractual provisions for automatic crystallisation—see the judgments in *Re Brightlife Ltd* and *Covacich v Riordan*.

11.6.4.3 Two or more floating charges

In *Griffiths v Yorkshire Bank plc* [1994] 1 WLR 1427, Morritt J held that if a company creates two floating charges at different times and the second crystallises before the first then the fixed charge created on crystallisation of the second takes priority over the first charge even after that has crystallised. The opposite conclusion was reached in the Ontario case of *Re Household Products Co Ltd and Federal Business Development Bank* (1981) 124 DLR (3d) 325 which was not cited to Morritt J, whose decision seems to ignore the rule that equitable interests take priority in order of creation. See further A Walters, 'Priority of the floating charge in corporate insolvency: *Griffiths v Yorkshire Bank plc*' (1995) 16 Co Law 291.

Where a company's property is subject to two or more floating charges, crystallisation of one of them may cause cessation of the company's business and so crystallise the others, but whether this happens is a question of fact in each case. In *Federal Business Development Bank v Prince Albert Fashion Bin Ltd* [1983] 3 WWR 464 the appointment of an administrative receiver by the holder of one floating charge did cause the cessation of the company's business so that another floating charge crystallised. But in *National Australia Bank Ltd v Composite Buyers Ltd* (1991) 6 ACSR 94 it did not. In *Re Woodroffes (Musical Instruments) Ltd* [1986] Ch 366 one floating charge provided for the charge to crystallise when the chargee gave notice converting it into a fixed charge, but when this was done there was no cessation of the company's business and so another floating charge did not crystallise.

The Cork Committee (Cmnd 8558, 1982) recommended (para 1580) that a floating charge should crystallise on the appointment of a receiver under any other floating charge on any assets or property of the company, and did not mention what should happen if crystallisation of another floating charge occurred in some other way. If the decision in *Griffiths v Yorkshire Bank plc* that crystallisation of a second floating charge gives it priority over the first is correct then it will become normal for a floating-charge contract to provide that it will crystallise if any other floating charge given by the company crystallises by any means, whether or not it causes cessation of the company's business.

11.6.5 RIGHTS CONFERRED BY A FLOATING CHARGE BEFORE CRYSTALLISATION

The floating charge was invented in order to provide a means of charging a company's current assets. The essential feature of a current asset of a company is that the company intends to bring its ownership of the asset to an end as quickly as possible and convert it into cash, or a claim to cash, which will be used to acquire a new current asset, and so on. The continual selling of current assets is the means by which the company will earn income from which it can meet the obligation secured by the floating charge. A company that has given a floating charge over its assets must nevertheless be able to sell them and, moreover, the assets must not remain subject to a charge after they have been sold, otherwise nobody would be able to buy from the company with certainty. However, the fact that an individual asset may be freely sold without consulting a chargee and is not subject to a charge in the hands of the buyer is inconsistent with the asset being charged at all.

Yet it is usual to say that, before a floating charge crystallises, it is an existing charge. In *Evans v Rival Granite Quarries Ltd* [1910] 2 KB 979 Fletcher Moulton LJ said, at p 994:

> [A floating charge] is an existing charge, and is rightly termed so, but care must be taken to remember that it has not settled down and fastened on the property which is the subject of the charge.

This raises the question whether, before a floating charge has crystallised, it gives the chargee any interest in, or rights over, the assets in the class charged. The courts have recognised that the holder of a floating charge has an interest in the charged property before crystallisation of the floating charge in the following cases:

(a) If the class of assets covered by a floating charge includes land, the courts have recognised that, before the charge has crystallised, the chargee has an interest in land (*Driver v Broad* [1893] 1 QB 744; *Wallace v Evershed* [1899] 1 Ch 891; *Re Dawson* [1915] 1 Ch 626). In the last of these cases the Court of Appeal did acknowledge that the interest could properly be described as a contingent or future interest which would arise only if and when the charge crystallised, while emphasising that whether it was a present or future interest made no difference to the point raised in the case.

(b) A person with a floating charge over a company's assets can, before the charge crystallises, obtain an injunction to prevent the company dealing with the assets otherwise than in the normal course of its business (*Re Woodroffes (Musical Instruments) Ltd* [1986] Ch 366 per Nourse J at p 378).

(c) A person with a floating charge over a company's assets may ask the court to appoint a receiver if something expected to be done to the assets threatens the security (*Re London Pressed Hinge Co Ltd* [1905] 1 Ch 576, in which one of the company's creditors had obtained judgment against it and was in a position to have the property subject to the floating charge seized in execution).

(d) When a floating charge crystallises it brings into effect an equitable interest which was created when the contract of floating charge was made and this takes precedence over any equitable interest created after the contract of floating charge was made. This is demonstrated by the cases of *Re Opera Ltd* [1891] 3 Ch 260 and *Taunton v Sheriff of Warwickshire* [1895] 2 Ch 319, in which the equitable interest created when a writ of *fieri facias* is delivered to an enforcement officer was held to be subordinate to the interest of the holder of a floating charge created before delivery of the writ and crystallising after delivery, but before the enforcement officer (in those days, a sheriff) had sold the goods. The decision of the Divisional Court in *Davey and Co v Williamson and Sons Ltd* [1898] 2 QB 194 that the same applied even if the floating charge has not crystallised was disapproved by the Court of Appeal in *Evans v Rival Granite Quarries Ltd*.

(e) If a person who has a floating charge over a company's property lawfully takes the property, or the proceeds of its realisation, and applies it to reduce the debt secured by the charge, there is no disposition of the company's property, even if the charge has not crystallised (*Re Margart Pty Ltd* [1985] BCLC 314, in which a bank retained money paid into a company customer's overdrawn account).

But the courts seem to be unwilling to give a floating chargee any further interest in, or rights over, assets in the class covered by the floating charge before it crystallises. In *Biggerstaff v Rowatt's Wharf Ltd* [1896] 2 Ch 93 a firm owed Rowatt's Wharf Ltd a debt which was, in common with the rest of the company's property, subject to a floating charge. Subsequently, Rowatt's Wharf Ltd became liable to the firm for a larger sum in liquidated damages. Then the chargees appointed a receiver, which crystallised the floating charge. The firm claimed it could set off the two debts and so did not have to pay anything to Rowatt's Wharf Ltd. Against this it was claimed that as soon as the firm became indebted to Rowatt's Wharf Ltd the debt was assigned to the chargees by virtue of the floating charge and this occurred before the liability to the firm arose so that set-off could not be allowed. The Court of Appeal held that there had been no assignment to the chargees before crystallisation of the floating charge and so the firm was entitled to set off the two debts.

In *Evans v Rival Granite Quarries Ltd*, judgment had been given against the quarry company for a debt. The company was owed money by its bank so the judgment creditor obtained a garnishee order nisi (now called an interim third party debt order) against the bank. Evans had a floating charge on the quarry company to secure a debt which was due and payable, but Evans had never taken action to crystallise his charge. When he heard of the garnishee order he told the bank that as chargee of the company's property he was entitled to the money and it could not be attached by garnishee proceedings. It was held that Evans was not entitled to the money as he had no specific charge on any asset of the company. If he had wanted the money, he should have appointed a receiver in order to crystallise his floating charge on the whole property of the company (including the money at the bank) but he could not claim one asset only.

Two alternative legal analyses of floating charges have been offered to explain how they affect assets before the charge has crystallised. The first is that a floating charge on a class of assets of a company is a charge on each and every asset in the class during the time that it is owned by the company, but that the charge is coupled with a licence to the company to deal with each asset without reference to the chargee, though only in the normal course of the company's business. The alternative analysis is that a floating charge is not a charge on any individual asset until the floating charge crystallises. In *Evans v Rival Granite Quarries Ltd* the Court of Appeal soundly rejected the first theory in favour of the second. Fletcher Moulton LJ said, at p 997:

> While it is a floating security the company has a right, not a mere licence, to carry on its business until the debenture-holder intervenes.

Buckley LJ said, at pp 999–1000:

> A floating security is not a future security; it is a present security, which presently affects all the assets of the company expressed to be included in it. On the other hand, it is not a specific security; the holder cannot affirm that the assets are specifically mortgaged to him. The assets are mortgaged in such a way that the mortgagor can deal with them without the concurrence of the mortgagee. A floating security is not a specific mortgage of the assets, plus a licence to the mortgagor to dispose of them in the course of his business, but is a floating mortgage applying to every item comprised in the security, but not specifically affecting any item until some event occurs or some act on the part of the mortgagee is done which causes it to crystallise . . . [Counsel for Mr Evans] argued that it was competent to the mortgagee to intervene at any moment and to say that he withdrew the licence as regards any particular item. That is not in my opinion the nature of the security; it is a mortgage presently affecting all the items expressed to be included in it, but not specifically affecting any item till the happening of the event which causes the security to crystallise as regards all the items.

The idea that a floating charge gave any charge on specific assets before crystallisation was also rejected in cases involving debentures given by railway companies which conferred 'a charge upon the undertaking of the company' (*Attree v Hawe* (1878) 9 ChD 337) but it seems that an important factor in these cases was that it had been decided that an administrative receiver could not be appointed, only a receiver of income (because of the public importance of keeping the railway running) so that the debenture holders could never obtain possession of the charged property (see C Stebbings, 'Statutory railway mortgage debentures and the courts in the 19th century' (1987) 8 J Legal Hist 36).

It is usually argued that the cases which have given floating chargees rights over the charged property before crystallisation have depended on the specific charge and licence theory, and that they could not be decided in the same way since the rejection of that theory by the Court of Appeal in *Evans v Rival Granite Quarries Ltd* (see D M Hare and D Milman, 'Debenture holders and judgment creditors—problems of priority' [1982] LMCLQ 57). However, those cases have never been expressly overruled and must be regarded as still representing the law. It is probably more accurate to say that the cases discussed here (other than *Biggerstaff v Rowatt's Wharf Ltd* and *Evans v Rival Granite Quarries Ltd*) show that a floating chargee does have some interest in the charged assets before the charge crystallises, but the *Evans* case established that this interest is not as great as a specific charge. If the specific charge and licence theory were correct, it would be possible to say exactly what the interest before crystallisation amounts to, but as the theory was rejected in the *Evans* case it can only be said that the interest is whatever has been established in cases so far and that future cases may extend the interest, but not as far as making it into a specific charge. In some recent cases Australian courts have interpreted the *Evans* case as meaning that, before crystallisation, a floating charge over property does not confer any equitable interest in the property (*Tricontinental Corporation Ltd v Federal Commissioner of Taxation* (1987) 73 ALR 433; *Lyford v Commonwealth Bank of Australia* (1995) 130 ALR 267). But this probably goes too far (see the obiter discussion in *Wily v St George Partnership Banking Ltd* (1999) 161 ALR 1).

For discussion of these issues, see *R in Right of British Columbia v Federal Business Development Bank* [1988] 1 WWR 1; E Ferran, 'Floating charges—the nature of the security' [1988] CLJ 213; K J Naser, 'The juridical basis of the floating charge' (1994) 15 Co Law 11; S Worthington, 'Floating charges—an alternative theory' [1994] CLJ 81.

11.6.6 DETERMINING WHETHER A CHARGE IS FIXED OR FLOATING

11.6.6.1 Approach taken by the court

From the chargee's point of view, a floating charge has the disadvantages that the chargee's debt may be subordinated to the company's preferential debts and liquidation expenses (see **20.2.3**) and a percentage of the floating charge assets must be devoted to paying unsecured creditors (see **20.2.4**). A chargee whose charge was created as a fixed charge may realise the security ignoring preferential and unsecured creditors. Under a composite floating and fixed charge it is legitimate for the chargee to take the property subject to fixed charges and treat only the remainder as subject to the floating charge and therefore available to pay the preferential and unsecured creditors (*Re Lewis Merthyr Consolidated Collieries Ltd* [1929] 1 Ch 498). Accordingly, secured creditors want as many as possible of their security interests to be fixed charges, and it is common for contracts of charge to declare that they are creating fixed charges whether they are or not. However, the courts will not accept that the label that parties to a contract attach to it is a conclusive statement of its legal nature (*Street v Mountford* [1985] AC 809 per Lord Templeman at p 819; *Re ASRS Establishment Ltd* [2000] 2 BCLC 631 at p 638) and have sometimes found that contracts declared to be creating fixed charges in fact created floating charges. Unusually, in *Russell Cooke Trust Co Ltd v Elliott* [2007] EWHC 1443 (Ch), [2007] 2 BCLC 637, it was found that a charge described as 'floating' was in law fixed.

In analysing a charge contract to see whether it creates a fixed or a floating charge, the court's task is not to discover whether the parties intended to create a fixed or floating charge and then give effect to their intention. The court's task is to discover what rights the parties intended to create and then to decide whether, as a matter of law, those rights constitute a fixed or a floating charge (*Agnew v Commissioner of Inland Revenue* [2001] UKPC 28, [2001] 2 AC 710, at [32]; *Smith v Bridgend County Borough Council* [2001] UKHL 58, [2002] 1 AC 336, at [42] per Lord Hoffmann and [53] per Lord Scott of Foscote).

The courts have usually taken as their starting point a passage in the judgment of Romer LJ in **Re Yorkshire Woolcombers Association Ltd** [1903] 2 Ch 284 at p 295:

['Floating charge'] is not a legal term. It has recently been used in more than one statute; but when the courts have to consider whether the charge is a floating one within the meaning of the term as used in the

Acts of Parliament, and in particular within the meaning of the Companies Act 1900 [which introduced the requirement to register charges at Companies House discussed in 11.7], one must, I think, deal with the question of substance to be answered according to the circumstance of each particular case. I certainly do not intend to attempt to give an exact definition of the term 'floating charge', nor am I prepared to say that there will not be a floating charge within the meaning of the Act, which does not contain all the three characteristics that I am about to mention, but I certainly think that if a charge has the three characteristics that I am about to mention it is a floating charge. (1.) If it is a charge on a class of assets of a company present and future; (2.) if that class is one which, in the ordinary course of the business of the company, would be changing from time to time; and (3.) if you find that by the charge it is contemplated that, until some future step is taken by or on behalf of those interested in the charge, the company may carry on its business in the ordinary way as far as concerns the particular class of assets I am dealing with.

It is the third of these which is the crucial distinguishing feature of a floating charge (*Agnew v Commissioner of Inland Revenue* at [13]; *Re Spectrum Plus Ltd* [2005] UKHL 41, [2005] 2 AC 680). As Lord Scott of Foscote said in **Re Spectrum Plus Ltd** at [111]:

> the essential feature of a floating charge, the characteristic that distinguishes it from a fixed charge, is that the asset subject to the charge is not finally appropriated as a security for the payment of the debt until the occurrence of some future event. In the meantime the chargor is left free to use the charged asset and to remove it from the security.

The future event mentioned by Lord Scott (Romer LJ's 'future step') is usually crystallisation of the charge. A provision of the charge contract which prevents the company from withdrawing assets from the security does not make it a fixed charge if, in practice, it is not enforced until crystallisation (*Re G E Tunbridge Ltd* [1995] 1 BCLC 34). So a provision in the charge contract that the charge is fixed, but that all charged assets are released from the charge and instead subject to a floating charge until the chargee declares otherwise means that the charge is a floating charge from the outset, otherwise any floating charge could be declared to be a fixed charge (*Agnew v Commissioner of Inland Revenue* at [34]).

11.6.6.2 Charges on book debts

Until *Re Spectrum Plus Ltd* [2005] UKHL 41, [2005] 2 AC 680, there was a long-running controversy over what was required to make a charge on book debts a fixed charge. A debt owed to a company was analysed into three phases: (a) when the debt was owed to the company and unpaid; (b) payment of the debt and crediting the money to the company's bank account; and (c) withdrawal from the bank account of a sum equivalent to the amount of the debt. It had been common to use a form of charge which prohibited a company from dealing with a debt in phase (a) (by assigning or factoring it), required it to pay the debt into a specified bank account in phase (b), but permitted it to use the money in phase (c). In *Siebe Gorman and Co Ltd v Barclays Bank Ltd* [1979] 2 Lloyd's Rep 142 this was held to be a fixed charge. In *Re New Bullas Trading Ltd* [1994] 1 BCLC 485 a charge added a control on phase (c) by requiring the money in the bank account to be applied as directed by the chargee, but declared that if no directions were given, the money was released from the fixed charge and subject instead to a floating charge. It was held by the Court of Appeal that this made uncollected debts subject to a fixed charge. In *Re Spectrum Plus Ltd* the House of Lords held that a charge which allowed the company to use the money in phase (c) without the chargee's permission could not be a fixed charge. This is because the only point of charging a debt is so that the money it generates can be appropriated to paying what is owed to the chargee (*Re Spectrum Plus Ltd* per Lord Scott of Foscote at [110] and [114]). Both *Siebe Gorman and Co Ltd v Barclays Bank Ltd* and *Re New Bullas Trading Ltd* were overruled. This followed the Privy Council's disapproval of *Re New Bullas Trading Ltd* in *Agnew v Commissioner of Inland Revenue* [2001] UKPC 28, [2001] 2 AC 710.

The House of Lords in *Re Spectrum Plus Ltd* rejected the argument that phase (c) is legally separate because money which is paid into a bank account becomes the bank's money, not the account holder's (*Foley v Hill* (1848) 2 HL Cas 28), and money is withdrawn from a bank account under the contract between bank and customer governing use of the account. Lord Scott in *Re Spectrum Plus Ltd* said, at [116], that whether a charge is floating or fixed depends on what, if any, restrictions there are on the use the chargor can make of the credit to the account that reflects each payment in. It is the commercial nature and substance of the charge which determine its categorisation, not a formalistic analysis of the bank clearing system.

It is possible to create a charge only on the proceeds of collection of debts without charging the debts at all (*Re SSSL Realisations (2002) Ltd* [2004] EWHC 1760 (Ch), [2005] 1 BCLC 1).

11.6.6.3 Exploitation of an asset

If a company leases an item of its property to another person and gives a charge on the lease then that charge is a fixed charge (*Re Atlantic Computer Systems plc* [1992] Ch 505) even if it is expressed to cover any future lease of the same item of property (*Re Atlantic Medical Ltd* [1993] BCLC 386). A charge on a lease charges the rental payments receivable by the lessor. The court will not analyse the charge into two separate charges: one on the lease and one on the payments due under the lease (*Re Atlantic Medical Ltd*). In both *Re Atlantic Computer Systems plc* and *Re Atlantic Medical Ltd* the company was free to use the rental payments in its business without reference to the chargee, but this was held not to affect the fixed nature of the charge. Similarly, in *Arthur D Little Ltd v Ableco Finance LLC* [2002] EWHC 701 (Ch), [2003] Ch 217, a charge on shares owned by a company which also charged the dividends payable in respect of the shares, but permitted the company to receive the dividends, was held to be a fixed charge. The point appears to be that a fixed charge on an asset may allow the chargor to enjoy the fruits of the property, or, as it was put in *Agnew v Commissioner of Inland Revenue* [2001] UKPC 28, [2001] 2 AC 710, at [37], exploit the characteristics inherent in the nature of the asset itself. For an argument that the charge considered in *Re Atlantic Computer Systems plc* should now be classified as a floating charge see C Addy, '*Re Spectrum Plus*, a year (and a bit) on—what conclusions can now be drawn?' (2007) 22 BJIBFL 67.

11.6.7 AVOIDANCE OF A FLOATING CHARGE SECURING A DEBT INCURRED BEFORE THE CHARGE WAS CREATED

11.6.7.1 By a liquidator

The Insolvency Act 1986, s 245, is intended to prevent an unsecured creditor of a company obtaining a floating charge to secure the existing debt and thus gain an advantage over other unsecured creditors. It enables a liquidator of a company to call in question floating charges created by the company in a certain period before the commencement of the winding up. The period is 12 months for charges granted to persons not connected with the company but two years for charges granted to persons who are connected.

The following are connected with a company (s 249):

(a) a director or shadow director of the company;

(b) an associate of a director or shadow director of the company; and

(c) an associate of the company.

Section 435 of IA 1986 defines who is an associate of a person. The section is long and detailed, and should be read in its entirety, but, in summary, the associates of a person include that person's spouse and relatives, business partners and their spouses and relatives, and companies of which the person and the person's associates have control. Two companies are associates of each other if they are under the control of one person or of a number of associated persons. Employer and employee are associated with each other (s 435(4)). A person who holds shares in a company as a bare trustee for another is not entitled to exercise 'voting power' and so cannot, under s 435(10), be associated with the company (*Re Kilnoore Ltd* [2005] EWHC 1410 (Ch), [2006] Ch 489).

A liquidator cannot avoid a floating charge given to a person *not connected with* the company unless the company was unable to pay its debts when it gave the charge or became unable to do so 'in consequence of the transaction under which the charge is created' (s 245(4)). Whether or not a company is unable to pay its debts is to be determined by the criteria set out in s 123 (see 20.6.4). If a floating charge was given to a person *connected with* the company within the two years preceding commencement of winding up then it can be avoided regardless of the company's financial position at the time. (If the company has been under administration then financial position is also irrelevant when considering a charge given within the 12 months preceding commencement of winding up to a person not connected with the company if it was given in the period while the petition on which the administration order was made was pending.)

The effect of s 245 is that, when a company is being wound up, the property charged by a floating charge that can be avoided under the section cannot be utilised by, or on behalf of, the chargee to pay anything other than:

(a) The value of so much of the consideration for the creation of the charge as consists of money paid, or goods or services supplied, to the company at the same time as, or after, the creation of the charge.

(b) The value of so much of that consideration as consists of the discharge or reduction, at the same time as, or after, the creation of the charge, of any debt of the company.

(c) The amount of such interest (if any) as is payable on amounts falling within (a) or (b) in pursuance of any agreement under which the money was so paid, the goods or services were so supplied or the debt was so discharged or reduced.

For the purposes of this provision, the value of goods or services supplied is the amount of money which, at the time they were supplied, could reasonably have been expected to be obtained for supplying them in the ordinary course of business on the same terms (apart from consideration) as those on which they were supplied to the company (s 245(6)). In the past it had been thought that money paid, or goods or services supplied, before the charge was created but in anticipation of and in reliance on it being created would be covered by the charge (*Re Fairway Magazines Ltd* [1993] BCLC 643) but the Court of Appeal in *Power v Sharp Investments Ltd* [1994] 1 BCLC 111 has held that this is not so.

If the floating charge crystallised before commencement of winding up and the property has already been utilised for paying amounts not permitted by s 245 then the liquidator cannot recover the money because s 245 comes into operation only in liquidation (ss 238(1)(b) and 245(1); *Mace Builders (Glasgow) Ltd v Lunn* [1987] Ch 191; *Power v Sharp Investments Ltd*).

The debts which s 245 does not permit to be paid using charged property are debts incurred before the floating charge was created. If the person who was granted a floating charge which is invalid under s 245 was previously an unsecured creditor of the company, then the charged property cannot be utilised to repay money advanced for the purpose of reducing the previously unsecured obligation. It is not permitted to substitute a secured loan for an unsecured one—see *Re G T Whyte and Co Ltd* [1983] BCLC 311, in which the new secured loan was made by a wholly owned subsidiary of the unsecured creditor but it was found that the floating charge was 'in substance' created to secure the past indebtedness to the unsecured creditor: it is submitted that the case would be decided in the same way under the new legislation. In *Re Fairway Magazines Ltd* the person who had been granted a floating charge which was invalid under s 245 advanced money for the specific purpose of reducing a debt of the company which he had guaranteed: it was held that this was a substitution of a secured debt for an unsecured obligation (the obligation to reimburse whatever was paid under the guarantee) and the charged property could not be used to repay the advance.

Although charged property cannot be used for paying certain debts if a charge is avoided under this provision, the debts themselves are still payable (*Re Parkes Garage (Swadlincote) Ltd* [1929] 1 Ch 139).

The intention of the chargee is irrelevant to the question of whether the charge is valid, and a charge may be declared invalid even though the chargee was not connected with the company and did not know it was insolvent; likewise it is unnecessary to show that the conduct of the chargee was underhand (*Re G T Whyte and Co Ltd*).

The legislation permits an unsecured creditor of an insolvent company to obtain a fixed charge but not a floating charge. The Cork Report (Cmnd 8558, 1982) suggested that it was acceptable to allow a creditor to take a fixed charge on property already owned by the company but not to take a floating charge which, on crystallisation, will attach property acquired by the company after giving the charge and probably acquired on credit. The Report pointed out that there may be advantages in permitting a creditor to take a charge and allow the company to continue in business rather than press immediately for payment: this is in line with its view that companies in difficulty should be given the opportunity of working their way out of the difficulty wherever possible.

If a bank obtains a floating charge over the property of an insolvent company as 'continuing security' for 'all present or future indebtedness to the bank on current account', then each payment out of the account after the charge is given is money paid to the company in consideration for the charge. If the account was overdrawn at the time the charge was given, payments into the account are presumed to pay off the existing overdraft on a first-in-first-out basis (*Devaynes v Noble, Clayton's Case* (1816) 1 Mer 572) and the bank will be left with debts incurred after the charge was created and for which the charge may be utilised (*Re Yeovil Glove Co Ltd* [1965] Ch 148).

11.6.7.2 By an administrator

The provisions of the Insolvency Act 1986, s 245, invalidating floating charges given to secure existing debts (see **11.6.7.1**) apply with the necessary changes to a company in administration (ss 238(1)(a) and 245(1)). A chargee whose floating charge could be avoided under this provision cannot veto the making of an administration order (sch B1, para 39; see **20.3.3.1**).

A floating charge on a company's property may be avoided by the company's administrator if it was created at any time within the period of 12 months before the date of presentation of the petition on which the administration order was made, or during the time that the petition was pending, and this period is extended to two years for charges given to persons connected with the company (see **11.6.7.1**).

11.7 REGISTRATION OF CHARGES ON COMPANY PROPERTY

11.7.1 INTRODUCTION

A person contemplating giving credit to a company may be encouraged to do so by the value of its assets, which could be seized in execution of any judgment obtained against the company. But the value of assets to one creditor is reduced or nullified if they have already been charged to another creditor. Accordingly, CA 2006 makes a charge on a company's property ineffective in administration or winding up unless it is registered for public inspection at Companies House. Copies of a company's charge contracts must be delivered to Companies House and the company must also keep copies available for inspection. The legislation on the subject is in CA 2006, part 25, Chapter A1 (ss 859A to 859Q).

Registration of charges with the registrar of companies began on 1 January 1901. CA 1862 had required each limited company to keep at its registered office a register of charges on its own property. However, only members of the company and existing creditors had a right to inspect this register, and if a charge was not entered in the register, it did not become ineffective in any way (*Wright v Horton* (1887) 12 App Cas 371) though fines could be imposed on company officers for failure to register.

The introduction in 1901 of registration of charges at Companies House, where the register may be inspected by anyone, and the sanction that an unregistered charge is ineffective, gave a great improvement in protection for creditors.

11.7.2 REGISTRATION AT COMPANIES HOUSE

When a company creates a charge, the company, or any person interested in the charge, may register it at Companies House within 'the period allowed for delivery' (CA 2006, s 859A(1) and (2)). That period is 21 days beginning with the day after the date of creation of the charge (s 859A(4)). For various kinds of security, the date of creation is defined in s 859E. For example, a charge that is created or evidenced by a deed, which has been executed and has immediate effect on execution and delivery, is created on the date of delivery. In practice, registration is effected by the chargee.

There are similar rules where a company creates a series of debentures containing a charge, or giving a charge by reference to another instrument (usually a trust deed) (s 859B).

Where a company acquires property or an undertaking which is already subject to a charge, that charge may be registered by the company or any person interested in it without time limit (s 859C).

11.7.3 EFFECT OF FAILURE TO REGISTER

If a charge, which a company has created over its own property, is unregistered at Companies House when the time limit has expired then the chargee's right of recourse against the charged property becomes 'void (so far as any security on the company's property or undertaking is conferred by it) against' a liquidator, administrator or creditor of the company (CA 2006, s 859H(1)–(3)). If the company commences winding up, the liquidator can take the property and sell it without regard to the unregistered charge: the proceeds of the sale will then be available for the benefit of the company's creditors generally, and the unregistered chargee loses the priority which would otherwise have been conferred by the charge. If the company goes into administration, the administrator can sell the property without regard to the unregistered charge. A liquidator or administrator deals with property as an agent of the company. The company owns the property and the charge contract is with the company. So 'void . . . against' a liquidator or administrator should be understood as 'void against the company acting by its liquidator or administrator' (*Smith v Bridgend County Borough Council* [2001] UKHL 58, [2002] 1 AC 336, at [21] to [23], [29] to [32] and [67]). Section 859H(3) (c) refers to an unregistered charge being void against 'a creditor of the company'. Creditors benefit from non-registration if the company goes into liquidation or administration, but otherwise registration or non-registration has no effect on a creditor, unless the creditor has a registered charge on the same property. A creditor with a registered charge on property, which is also subject to an unregistered charge, can ignore the unregistered charge completely, whether or not the company is in liquidation or administration, and even if the registered charge was registered in the knowledge that the unregistered charge existed (*Re Monolithic Building Co* [1915] 1 Ch 643).

An unregistered chargee may be able to retrieve the situation by obtaining a court order to extend the deadline for registration. But this will not affect rights acquired by other chargees and an order will not be made if the company is in administration or liquidation (see **11.7.9**). If there is no insolvency or subsequent charge, a missed deadline for registering a charge is usually dealt with by executing a new charge contract.

The Law Commission's view is that depriving a chargee of the benefit of the charge for non-registration is not incompatible with the European Convention on Human Rights, Protocol 1, art 1, in the Human Rights Act 1998, sch 1. This is because the sanction is imposed for the important purpose of securing publicity for charges which may have a serious effect on third parties and the sanction can be easily avoided by registering the charge. See Law Commission, *Registration of Security Interests* (Consultation Paper 164, 2002), para 3.43; *Company Security Interests* (Law Com No 296, Cm 6654, 2005), para 3.77.

An unregistered charge is void as against a liquidator, administrator or other creditor only: it is not, for example, void as against the company while it is not in administration or being wound up (*Re Monolithic Building Co* per Lord Cozens-Hardy MR at p 667 and Phillimore LJ at p 667; *Smith v Bridgend County Borough Council* at [21] and [65] to [66]). So CA 2006 provides that when a charge becomes void, the money secured by the charge becomes immediately payable (s 859H(4)).

The disabilities of non-registration cannot apply until the time limit for registration has expired. If a company creates a charge over its property and, before the time limit for its registration has expired, sells the property or creates another charge over it then priorities will be determined by the rules set out in **11.4** (*Re Ehrmann Brothers Ltd* [1906] 2 Ch 697; *Watson v Duff Morgan and Vermont (Holdings) Ltd* [1974] 1 WLR 450).

Until 6 April 2013, the legislation provided a criminal sanction against a company, and any officer of the company in default, if a charge on the company's property was not registered. The present legislation no longer makes this provision, assuming that making the charge ineffective is a sufficient incentive.

If a company acquires property subject to a charge created by a previous owner, and fails to register the charge, there are no sanctions and the charge remains effective as against all persons.

11.7.4 REGISTRATION PROCEDURE

In order to register a charge, it is necessary to deliver to Companies House the particulars specified in CA 2006, s 859D, and a certified copy of the instrument (if there is one) by which the charge is created or evidenced (s 859A(2) and (3)). If the instrument is not in English, it must be accompanied by a certified translation into English (s 1105). The copy of the instrument delivered for registration may be redacted to exclude (s 859G(1)):

(a) personal information relating to an individual (other than the individual's name);

(b) the number or other identifier of a bank or securities account of a company or individual; and

(c) a signature.

If an unredacted document is presented, Companies House is not required to check whether the failure to redact is intentional (s 859G(2)). The court has a power in s 859N to order Companies House to replace an unredacted copy with a redacted one.

11.7.5 REGISTRATION OF A CHARGE DOES NOT GIVE NOTICE OF THE TERMS OF THE CHARGE

Registration of a charge in the register of charges constitutes notice to the whole world that a charge of a particular type exists but does not constitute notice of the terms and conditions of the charge (*Wilson v Kelland* [1910] 2 Ch 306; *G and T Earle Ltd v Hemsworth Rural District Council* (1928) 44 TLR 605 at p 608). For charges created before 6 April 2013, this meant that there was no notice of a negative pledge in a contract giving a floating charge (see **11.6.2**). When a charge created on or after 6 April 2013 is registered, the statement of particulars required by CA 2006, s 859D, must state whether any of the terms of the charge prohibit or restrict the company from creating further security that will rank equally with or ahead of the charge (s 859D(2)(c)). This statement will give constructive notice of any negative pledge.

In *Ian Chisholm Textiles Ltd v Griffiths* [1994] 2 BCLC 291, the learned deputy judge expressed a 'tentative view' that a person who acquires an interest in property of a company while actually, rather than constructively, informed that the property had been charged would be deemed to be informed of all provisions of the charge contract (in particular, a negative pledge clause) because a reasonably prudent purchaser acting on skilled advice would have taken the trouble to read the contract.

11.7.6 CERTIFICATE OF REGISTRATION

After registering a charge at Companies House, the registrar is required to give a certificate which is 'conclusive evidence that the documents required by [s 859A or 859B] were delivered to the registrar before the end of the relevant period for delivery' (CA 2006, s 859I(6)). This wording is different from the provision before 6 April 2013 that the registrar's certificate was conclusive evidence that the requirements as to registration had been satisfied (s 869(6)). However, as the only 'requirements as to registration' are that the required documents are delivered in time, it is submitted that there has been no change in the effect of the provision. In cases decided before the wording was changed, the courts always held that, once a certificate had been issued, there could be no challenge to the registration of a charge, because the registrar's certificate was conclusive evidence that it was correctly registered. The courts took the view that everyone inspecting the register had to be confident that it was accurate and could not be altered to their detriment. It is submitted that this position has not changed. The following cases decided before 6 April 2013 illustrate this position.

The conclusiveness of the registrar's certificate of registration of a charge means that the charge must be treated as validly registered, even if it was not, and even if the registrar issued the certificate by mistake (*Ali v Top Marques Car Rental Ltd* [2006] EWHC 109 (Ch), *The Times*, 10 February 2006). For example, if the s 859D statement of particulars is inaccurate but the registrar nevertheless issues a certificate of registration, the certificate cannot be challenged. Any person inspecting the register will see inaccurate information and will be misled but the actual charge as created by the company is deemed to have been duly registered and so must be observed by the company's creditors and its liquidator or administrator (*National Provincial and Union Bank of England v Charnley* [1924] 1 KB 431; *Re Mechanisations (Eaglescliffe) Ltd* [1966] Ch 20). The registrar's certificate is conclusive evidence that the charge has been registered within 21 days of creation, even if the instrument creating the charge has been falsely postdated (*Re C L Nye Ltd* [1971] Ch 442).

It is impossible for there to be proceedings for judicial review of the registrar's decision to register a charge, because such proceedings would involve giving evidence that the requirements as to registration were not complied with (*R v Registrar of Companies, ex parte Central Bank of India* [1986] QB 1114). See G McCormack, 'Conclusiveness in the registration of company charge procedure' (1989) 10 Co Law 175.

11.7.7 REGISTRATION OF FURTHER INFORMATION

Once a charge has been registered at Companies House the following further information relating to the charge may be registered:

(a) A statement that the company is acting as trustee of the property or undertaking which is the subject of the charge (CA 2006, s 859J). This statement may be registered by the company or any person interested in the charge (s 859J(1)).

(b) Notification of an addition or amendment to the charge which adds a negative pledge (see **11.6.2**) or varies, or otherwise regulates the order of, the ranking of the charge in relation to any other charge (s 859O). This statement (which must be accompanied by a certified copy of the instrument effecting the amendment, variation or regulation) may be registered by the company that created the charge or the person taking the benefit of the charge (or any charge whose relative ranking has changed) (s 859O(2)).

(c) Notice of enforcement of the charge by the appointment of a receiver or manager (s 859K). This notice must be given, within seven days of the appointment, by the person who made the appointment or obtained a court order for it (s 859K(1) and (2)). There is a criminal sanction for failure to give this notice (s 859K(6) and (7)).

(d) Notice of ceasing to act as a receiver or manager (s 859K). This notice must be given by the person ceasing to act (s 859K(3)). There is a criminal sanction for failure to give this notice (s 859K(6) and (7)).

(e) A statement that the debt for which the charge was given has been paid or satisfied in whole or in part (s 859I). A person delivering this statement must indicate their interest in the charge (s 859I(4)(a)).

(f) A statement that all or part of the property or undertaking charged has been released from the charge or has ceased to form part of the company's property or undertaking (s 859I). A person delivering this statement must indicate their interest in the charge (s 859I(4)(a)).

11.7.8 INSPECTION OF THE REGISTER

Anyone may inspect the register at Companies House on payment of the appropriate fee (see **4.2.2**). Inspection of the register will not necessarily reveal all valid charges existing at the time of inspection, because of the 21 days allowed for registration. This is called the 21-day invisibility problem.

11.7.9 EXTENSION OF TIME LIMITS AND RECTIFICATION OF THE REGISTER

Under CA 2006, s 859F, the court has power to permit registration of a charge at Companies House outside the 21-day time limit. Under s 859M the court has a power to rectify an omission or misstatement in any statement or notice delivered to the registrar under Part 25, Chapter A1. The court may not act under these provisions unless it is satisfied (ss 859F(1)(b) and (2) and 859M(1)(b) and (2)):

(a) that the failure to deliver documents in time or the omission or misstatement in a statement or notice that was delivered

  (i) was accidental or due to inadvertence or to some other sufficient cause, or

  (ii) is not of a nature to prejudice the position of creditors or shareholders of the company; or

(b) that on other grounds it is just and equitable to grant relief.

These powers are discretionary and an application to the court to exercise either of them must be supported by full evidence of the reasons for non-registration or mistaken registration (*Re Kris Cruisers Ltd* [1949] Ch 138). The underlying guide to the exercise of the court's discretion is whether it would be just and equitable to grant relief (*Re Braemar Investments Ltd* [1989] Ch 54).

The court has a power under s 859N to order that a copy of an instrument or debenture which has been registered is to be removed and replaced if:

(a) the copy contains material which could have been redacted under s 859G (see **11.7.4**);

(b) the wrong instrument or debenture was registered; or

(c) the copy was defective.

The court's power under s 859M to order rectification of registration of a charge is limited to correcting omissions or misstatements within an entry. It cannot order removal of an entire entry (*Exeter Trust Ltd v Screenways Ltd* [1991] BCLC 888).

If the court makes an order extending the time for registration of a charge and the charge is registered accordingly and a certificate of registration is issued then the certificate is conclusive evidence that the charge has been duly registered, even if the court's order permitting registration is overruled (*Wilde v Australian Trade Equipment Pty Ltd* (1981) 145 CLR 590; *Exeter Trust Ltd v Screenways Ltd*).

When making an order under s 859F or 859M, the court may impose 'such terms and conditions as seem to the court just and expedient' (ss 859F(3) and 859M(3)). When a late registration is permitted the court usually makes a standard proviso that the registration is to be without prejudice to the rights of any parties acquired prior to the time when the charge is actually registered (*Re Joplin Brewery Co Ltd* [1902] 1 Ch 79; *Re I C Johnson and Co Ltd* [1902] 2 Ch 101). As a charge cannot become ineffective until after the time limit for registration has expired, the standard proviso applies only to rights acquired after the normal time limit expired (*Watson v Duff Morgan and Vermont (Holdings) Ltd* [1974] 1 WLR 450). This proviso will be modified to preserve any agreement about priorities which other creditors have already made with the creditor whose charge is to be registered out of time (*Re I C Johnson and Co Ltd* [1902] 2 Ch 101 (agreement to rank equally with unregistered charge); *Barclays Bank plc v Stuart Landon Ltd* [2001] 2 BCLC 316 (agreement to rank after unregistered charge)).

The standard proviso does not apply to a person who became an unsecured creditor while the charge was unregistered, because such a creditor has not acquired any rights in relation to the charged property (*Re Ehrmann Brothers Ltd* [1906] 2 Ch 697), unless the company has adopted a resolution for voluntary winding up or a winding-up order has been made (*Re Spiral Globe Ltd* [1902] 1 Ch 396; *Re Anglo-Oriental Carpet Manufacturing Co* [1903] 1 Ch 914). On the making of a winding-up resolution or order, the creditors acquire the right to have the company's assets realised and distributed among them in accordance with insolvency law. The courts have consistently held that nothing should be added to the proviso to protect unsecured creditors if there is no winding up, taking the view that any person who becomes an unsecured creditor of any debtor does so with the risk that the debtor's property will subsequently be validly charged, and that this outweighs the function which the registration regime has of providing information to creditors to enable them to decide the terms on which they will give credit (*Re Cardiff Workmen's Cottage Co Ltd* [1906] 2 Ch 627; *Re MIG Trust Ltd* [1933] Ch 542 per Romer LJ at pp 569–72; *Re Kris Cruisers Ltd*).

A person may benefit from the standard proviso, even if the interest which the person has was acquired knowing that the unregistered charge existed (*Re Monolithic Building Co* [1915] 1 Ch 643). However, in two reported cases the court has excluded from the protection of the standard proviso an interest acquired by a director of the company who knew that the unregistered charge existed (*Re Fablehill Ltd* [1991] BCLC 830; *Confiance Ltd v Timespan Images Ltd* [2005] EWHC 1557 (Ch), [2005] 2 BCLC 693). It seems that this is what should have been done in *Re Monolithic Building Co*.

The court will refuse an application to extend time to register a charge on a company's property if the application is heard after the company has adopted a resolution for voluntary winding up or an order has been made for the company to be wound up (*Re S Abrahams and Sons* [1902] 1 Ch 695; *Re Resinoid and Mica Products Ltd* [1983] Ch 132; *Re Ashpurton Estates Ltd* [1983] Ch 110), or the company is in administration and it is inevitable that it will proceed to insolvent liquidation (*Re Barrow Borough Transport Ltd* [1990] Ch 227). The fact that liquidation is imminent when the application is heard is a factor which the court will take into account when deciding whether to extend time for registration (*Re Resinoid and Mica Products Ltd*; *Re Ashpurton Estates Ltd*) and an order extending time when liquidation is imminent will usually include a term giving any subsequently appointed liquidator or administrator the right to challenge the order (known as a *Re Charles* term' as it was first used in *Re L H Charles and Co Ltd* [1935] WN 15). It is implicit in a *Re Charles* term that Companies House must not issue a certificate of registration until the court has ruled on any application for reconsideration of the order or no application has been made within the time limit set in the *Re Charles* term: when a certificate is issued the court is no longer able to reconsider the order (*Ali v Top Marques Car Rental Ltd* [2006] EWHC 109 (Ch), *The Times*, 10 February 2006). The factors to be considered by the court when dealing with an application for late registration of a charge created by a company which is now close to liquidation are discussed in *Barclays Bank plc v Stuart Landon Ltd* [2001] EWCA Civ 140, [2001] 2 BCLC 316.

For a detailed discussion see G McCormack, 'Extension of time for registration of company charges' [1986] JBL 282.

11.7.10 PROBLEMS IN DECIDING WHETHER AN INTEREST SHOULD BE REGISTERED

If a person acquires rights over a company's property that do not have to be registered at Companies House, the rights will not become void against subsequent chargees or an administrator or liquidator of the company. Arguments over whether or not an acquisition of rights should have been registered resolve into three questions:

(a) Were the rights created by the company (see **11.7.11**)?

(b) Do the rights constitute a charge (see **11.7.12**)?

(c) If the rights constitute a charge, is it exempt from registration (see **11.7.13**)?

11.7.11 RIGHTS NOT CREATED BY THE COMPANY

A right against the property of a company that arises by operation of law (such as a solicitor's lien or a vendor's lien) is not created by the company and so is not registrable (*London and Cheshire Insurance Co Ltd v Laplagrene Property Co Ltd* [1971] Ch 499).

In *Tatung (UK) Ltd v Galex Telesure Ltd* (1988) 5 BCC 325, Phillips J said that the fact that a retention of title agreement provided that the purchaser was to deal with the goods as agent of the supplier, as security for the payment of debts owed to the supplier, did not mean that the purchaser's obligation to account for the proceeds of reselling the goods arose only by operation of law (as one of the legal incidents of an agency relationship), and did not mean that it was not a right created by the purchaser. In his Lordship's view the supplier's rights against resale proceeds arose out of the security arrangement created by the purchaser and therefore constituted a registrable charge created by the purchaser on its book debts.

11.7.12 DO THE RIGHTS CONSTITUTE A CHARGE?

11.7.12.1 Agreement to create a charge

An agreement to give a charge is itself a charge (and so may be registrable) if it is immediately enforceable but not if it is contingent (*Re Jackson and Bassford Ltd* [1906] 2 Ch 467). For an example of an agreement to create a charge which was contingent and so not registrable, see *Williams v Burlington Investments Ltd* (1977) 121 SJ 424.

11.7.12.2 Contractual lien on goods

A contractual right to retain possession of a company's goods until payment has been received for transporting, storing or working on them (a contractual lien) is not a charge, even if the contract gives a right to sell the goods if the debt is not paid (*Re Hamlet International plc* [1998] 2 BCLC 164).

11.7.12.3 Charge or sale?

It is sometimes difficult to distinguish between a contract giving a mortgage or charge over property and a contract for the sale of property. In *Welsh Development Agency v Export Finance Co Ltd* [1992] BCLC 148, Dillon LJ said (at p 161) that 'there is no one clear touchstone' for making the distinction, though in the past it has been emphasised that a mortgage or charge is regarded by the parties as only one method of satisfying a financial obligation, and if the obligation is met in some other way then the mortgage or charge ceases to have any effect. As Slade J said in *Re Bond Worth Ltd* [1980] Ch 228 at p 248:

> In my judgment, any contract which, by way of security for the payment of a debt, confers an interest in property defeasible or destructible upon payment of such debt, or appropriates such property for the discharge of the debt, must necessarily be regarded as creating a mortgage or charge, as the case may be.

11.7.12.4 Charge or payment?

The cases which have caused the greatest difficulty have been where a company has assigned to one of its creditors its right to receive money from one of its debtors. If this is done simply to pay the creditor, the assignment is not a charge on the debt and need not be registered. If the assignment is made as security for payment of the creditor, contemplating that on payment of the creditor in some other way the assignment would be cancelled, the assignment is a charge and will be void against a liquidator, administrator or other creditor unless registered.

In *Re Kent and Sussex Sawmills Ltd* [1947] Ch 177, the company's bank allowed it an overdraft to finance work on a large contract for the Ministry of Fuel and Power. The bank required the company to write to the Ministry in the following terms:

> [W]e hereby authorise you to remit all moneys due [under the contract] direct to this company's account at Westminster Bank Ltd, Crowborough, whose receipt shall be your sufficient discharge. These instructions are to be regarded as irrevocable unless the said bank should consent to their cancellation in writing.

The bank contended that this was an outright assignment of the debts due under the contract and so the bank's failure to register the agreement as a charge did not render it ineffective. The court held that the transaction was a charge, for otherwise there would be no need to make any statement about revocation.

By contrast, in *Siebe Gorman and Co Ltd v Barclays Bank Ltd* [1979] 2 Lloyd's Rep 142, Siebe Gorman had supplied goods to a company called R H McDonald Ltd and was owed over £8,000 for them. But R H McDonald Ltd had bills of exchange, for just less than the amount of the debt, which were payable over a period of six months. These bills had been handed to the bank for collection. R H McDonald Ltd executed a deed assigning the bills to Siebe Gorman 'as security for' the debt owed to Siebe Gorman, and sent a letter to the bank instructing the bank to pay the proceeds of the bills direct to Siebe Gorman. The letter to the bank was expressed to be an irrevocable instruction. Slade J decided that the assignment was made in order to pay the debt and so held that the transaction was an absolute assignment and was not a contract of charge.

In *Orion Finance Ltd v Crown Financial Management Ltd* [1996] 2 BCLC 78, Atlantic Computer Systems Ltd had bought a computer on hire-purchase from Orion and leased it to Crown, assigning to Orion the rental payments due under the lease. The elaborate documents governing this deal (and numerous other similar transactions) repeatedly described the assignment as 'security' for the payment of the hire-purchase instalments, and stated that the rental payments were 'charged'. However, the contract had never been registered as a charge on Atlantic's book debts. The Court of Appeal held that there was no reason not to accept that the wording of the contract was the correct description of the transaction as intended by the parties, so the assignment was a charge on Atlantic's book debts and should have been registered as such (though this begs the question why, if it intended that the assignment should be by way of charge, Orion did not register it). The lease contract between Atlantic and Crown gave Crown an option to require Atlantic to make the lease payments for the last two years of the lease term. When Crown exercised this option, Atlantic was in insolvent liquidation. Orion's counsel put forward several extraordinarily ingenious arguments why Crown should be required to make the last two years' lease payments to Orion, but they were all rejected (*Orion Finance Ltd v Crown Financial Management Ltd (No 2)* [1996] 2 BCLC 382).

11.7.12.5 Charge-back

In banking it is common for a bank to obtain security for a loan by means of a 'charge-back', which works as follows. A customer of a bank, with an account in credit, agrees that if a specified obligation owed to the bank (either by the customer or another person) is not met, the bank can use the balance in the account to meet it and is relieved from its contractual obligation to repay the credit balance to the customer. The legal categorisation of this agreement is difficult and has been the subject of much argument. In *Re Bank of Credit and Commerce International SA (No 8)* [1996] Ch 245, CA, [1998] AC 214, HL, the question was argued by counsel and, though it was not necessary for the decision in the case, both the Court of Appeal and the House of Lords gave views on it. Unfortunately, their views were totally opposed. In the Court of Appeal Millett LJ repeated the view he had expressed, when a High Court judge, in *Re Charge Card Services Ltd* [1987] Ch 150, at p 175, that 'a charge in favour of a debtor of his own indebtedness to the chargor is conceptually impossible'. On this view a charge-back is merely a term of the banking contract between bank and customer and does not require registration as a charge. In the House of Lords, Lord Hoffmann forcefully rejected this view and said that a charge-back is a charge. Lord Hoffmann saw a bank with a charge-back on a deposit as having an obligation to repay the deposit when required to do so by the customer and, separately, a charge on the customer's right to demand that repayment. The fact that the charge would be enforced merely by making entries in accounts does not, in Lord Hoffmann's view, mean that the banking contract and the security contract are merged. The other Law Lords said that they had read Lord Hoffmann's speech and agreed with his disposal of the appeal, without expressing any dissent from his view that a charge-back is a registrable charge, so that view carries great authority, even though it is obiter. For opposing commentaries see the casenotes by R Calnan (1998) 114 LQR 174 (in favour of Lord Hoffmann) and R Goode (1998) 114 LQR 178 (against Lord Hoffmann). Lord Hoffmann's view was applied in *Fraser v Oystertec plc* [2004] EWHC 1582 (Ch), [2006] 1 BCLC 491 (which was not concerned with registration).

11.7.12.6 Lien on sub-freights

When a cargo-carrying ship is hired out (chartered) by its owner to another operator, who intends to use it to carry other persons' cargoes, it is usual to include in the contract of hire (which is called a charterparty) a provision that the owner has a right to intercept and collect the charges for the cargoes before they are paid to the charterer. This is called a lien on sub-freights and it secures payment for the hire of the ship. In *Re Welsh Irish Ferries Ltd* [1986] Ch 471, Nourse J heard that shipowners had been including provisions for liens on sub-freights throughout the world since 1913 and it had never been thought necessary to register them as charges on book debts in England or the many other jurisdictions with security registration requirements. Nevertheless, his Lordship held that the lien is a registrable charge on book debts. In *Agnew v Commissioner of Inland Revenue* [2001] UKPC 28, [2001] 2 AC 710, the Privy Council disapproved that decision, saying that a lien on sub-freights cannot be a charge, because it gives no proprietary rights in the sub-freights to the shipowner: any other person, including the charterer, can collect the sub-freights, even after being informed of the existence of the lien, without having to pay any attention to the shipowner's lien.

11.7.12.7 Retention of title by a seller

A contract of sale of goods may include a term stipulating that the property in the goods is not to pass until payment has been received by the seller (Sale of Goods Act 1979, s 19(1)). Here 'property' means the general property in the goods (Sale of Goods Act 1979, s 61), that is, the legal title to them. Terms of sale of this nature are called retention of title agreements.

There have been several cases in which retention of title agreements have been examined but care must be exercised in drawing general conclusions from them because each decision has been made in the light of the wording of the particular contract involved and the commercial situation in which the dispute arose (per Robert Goff LJ in *Clough Mill Ltd v Martin* [1985] 1 WLR 111).

If A sells goods to B for resale by B or for incorporation in B's products, a retention of title agreement must include a provision permitting B to use the goods in this way before title passes. Such a provision is not inconsistent with the legal title remaining with A (*Clough Mill Ltd v Martin*). Resale under such a provision is assumed to be for B's own account, not for the account of, or as agent for, A (*E Pfeiffer Weinkellerei-Weineinkauf GmbH & Co v Arbuthnot Factors Ltd* [1988] 1 WLR 150). Without such a provision a resale is without actual authority and is a conversion of A's goods: nevertheless, provided the subpurchaser is acting in good faith, the contract of resale is made valid by the Factors Act 1889, s 9, and the Sale of Goods Act 1979, s 25, so that when its conditions concerning transfer of title are satisfied the subpurchaser acquires title to the goods and A's retained title is extinguished.

This simple form of retention of title agreement does not constitute a charge on property of B because rights are not granted over B's own property: the goods are not B's property until paid for (*Aluminium Industrie Vaassen BV v Romalpa Aluminium Ltd* [1976] 1 WLR 676; *Armour v Thyssen Edelstahlwerke AG* [1991] 2 AC 339; see the definition in IA 1986, s 251). Similarly, a conditional sale agreement is not a charge (*Paintin and Nottingham Ltd v Miller Gale and Winter* [1971] NZLR 164).

In *Re Bond Worth Ltd* [1980] Ch 228, a supplier of goods to Bond Worth Ltd had tried a different type of condition of sale. The sale contract provided that 'equitable and beneficial ownership shall remain with us [the supplier] until full payment has been received'. It was held that the supplier could not claim to pass legal title in goods to Bond Worth Ltd while retaining 'equitable and beneficial ownership'. The 'equitable and beneficial ownership' must have been granted to the supplier by Bond Worth when Bond Worth became legal owner of the goods, and this was equivalent to creating a charge on the goods which should have been registered. As it had not been registered Bond Worth's liquidator could ignore it. It has been argued that the theoretical basis of this decision was removed by the House of Lords in *Abbey National Building Society v Cann* [1991] 1 AC 56—see, for example, D Turing, 'Retention of title: how to get value from a bad penny' (1995) 16 Co Law 119—but this argument was rejected in *Stroud Architectural Systems Ltd v John Laing Construction Ltd* [1994] 2 BCLC 276.

In *Re Curtain Dream plc* [1990] BCLC 925, Curtain Dream plc sold its entire stock of curtaining fabric to Churchill Merchanting Ltd for cash under an arrangement which entitled Curtain Dream plc to repurchase the stock immediately on 90 days' credit (which is what happened) subject to retention of title by Churchill Merchanting Ltd until it received payment. There was no physical movement of the stock corresponding to the separate components of this transaction. It was held that what happened should be analysed as one global transaction, in which in fact the retention of title constituted a charge on Curtain Dream plc's fabric as security for a loan made by Churchill Merchanting Ltd. It was not a retention by Churchill Merchanting Ltd of title to its own fabric. As this charge had not been registered it was void as against the administrative receivers of Curtain Dream plc.

If goods subject to a retention of title agreement are used by the buyer in such a way that they lose their separate identity, there will be nothing in which the seller can retain title. It may be difficult to decide whether goods subject to a retention of title agreement lose their separate identity while in the buyer's possession. In *Hendy Lennox (Industrial Engines) Ltd v Grahame Puttick Ltd* [1984] 1 WLR 485 it was held that an engine incorporated in a generator set could be so easily disconnected and removed that it remained separate and subject to a retention of title agreement.

In *Re CKE Engineering Ltd* [2007] BCC 975 ingots of zinc were supplied subject to a retention of title agreement, when buyer and seller knew that they would be immediately added to a tank of molten zinc, some of which had been supplied by another seller. The court held that it was intended that the seller should have title to a proportion of the contents of the tank. This would mean that the retention of title was not a registrable charge, but registration was not in issue in the case.

It is possible to include a provision in a contract of sale of goods that anything made by the buyer from the goods will belong to the seller, but this will normally be regarded as a charge on the buyer's goods (see the discussion of *Re Peachdart Ltd* [1984] Ch 131 and *Modelboard Ltd v Outer Box Ltd* [1993] BCLC 623 in the following paragraph). In *Ian Chisholm Textiles Ltd v Griffiths* [1994] 2 BCLC 291, an agreement that a seller of cloth should retain title to the cloth apparently contained no term specifying what was to happen when the cloth lost its separate identity by being made into garments. Curiously, the company conceded that the retention of title agreement still applied in some way to the garments, and it was held that it created a charge on the garments in favour of the seller (which charge was void for non-registration). It is submitted that the true position is that the seller could not have had any interest in the garments unless the contract of sale provided for an interest to be created.

A supplier of goods who has stipulated for retention of title to the goods usually wishes to obtain some control over the proceeds of resale of the goods. A simple provision that the purchaser's rights against customers arising from reselling the goods are to be assigned to the supplier as security for the payment of the purchase price is a registrable charge on the book debts of the purchaser (*E Pfeiffer Weinkellerei-Weineinkauf GmbH & Co v Arbuthnot Factors Ltd*; *Re Weldtech Equipment Ltd* [1991] BCLC 393). Some suppliers have tried a more sophisticated approach in which the purchaser, instead of being treated as trading on its own account, is turned into a mere agent for the supplier, or a mere bailee of the goods supplied, with a fiduciary obligation to account to the supplier for anything gained by dealing with the supplier's goods. There has to be an express provision to that effect: a retention of title agreement does not automatically make the buyer an agent or bailee of the seller (*Borden (UK) Ltd v Scottish Timber Products Ltd* [1981] Ch 25). However, the essence of such a contract is that the agency relationship is terminated when the debt to the supplier is paid and so it must be regarded as entered into as security for the payment of the debt. Accordingly, the supplier's rights under such an arrangement, to money owed to the purchaser by its customers on dealing with the goods, constitute a registrable charge on the purchaser's book debts (*Tatung (UK) Ltd v Galex Telesure Ltd* (1988) 5 BCC 325; *Compaq Computer Ltd v Abercorn Group Ltd* [1993] BCLC 602). For further discussion, see S Wheeler, '*Pfeiffer v Arbuthnot*; good news for financiers of receivables' (1989) 10 Co Law 151; and J de Lacy, 'Proceed with care' (1989) 10 Co Law 188. Similarly, a provision that any articles made by the buyer from the supplier's materials are to be the property of the supplier is really a charge because it is made on the basis that ownership of the articles will revert to the buyer as soon as the supplier has been paid (*Re Peachdart Ltd*; *Modelboard Ltd v Outer Box Ltd*). It seems that it is not possible for a retention of title agreement to give control over proceeds of resale without creating a charge that must be registered—see A Hicks, '*Romalpa* is dead' (1992) 13 Co Law 217. For criticism of this result, asserting that the courts have misinterpreted such agreements, see J de Lacy, 'When is a *Romalpa* clause not a *Romalpa* clause? When it is a charge on book debts' (1992) 13 Co Law 164.

11.7.13 CHARGES THAT ARE EXEMPT FROM REGISTRATION

Some types of charge are excluded from registration at Companies House under CA 2006, s 859A. They are:

(a) a charge in favour of a landlord on a cash deposit given as a security in connection with the lease of land (s 859A(6)(a));

(b) a charge created by a member of Lloyd's to secure its obligations in connection with its underwriting business at Lloyd's (s 859A(6)(b)); and

(c) financial collateral arrangements entered into on financial markets (SI 2003/3226, reg 4(4)).

11.7.14 REGISTRATION IN PROPERTY REGISTERS

If a company registered in England and Wales charges its land situated in England or Wales, its UK-registered aircraft, its British ships or its UK patents then, the chargee should ensure that the charge is registered in the appropriate register for the kind of property charged as well as at Companies House.

A floating charge is not a charge on any particular asset and so, even though a company that grants a floating charge may own registered land, ships, aircraft and patents, the charge cannot be registered in the registers for those kinds of property. (Articles 2(2) and 4(1) of SI 1972/1268 expressly provide that a floating charge cannot be registered in the Register of Aircraft Mortgages.) Conversely, if a charge is registered in a property register as a charge on specific items of property, it would imply that dealings in those items could not take place without reference to the chargee, which would imply that the charge was a fixed charge on those items of property. The exception is unregistered land. The Land Charges Act 1972 permits the registration of 'a general equitable charge' (s 2(4)(iii)) 'affecting land' (s 2(1)), and this is wide enough to include a floating charge. However, in this case double registration is unnecessary, because it is provided in the Land Charges Act 1972, s 3(7) and (8), that registration of a floating charge at Companies House is equivalent to registration in the Land Charges Register.

11.7.15 COMPANY MUST KEEP COPIES FOR INSPECTION

Every company must keep available for inspection a copy of every instrument creating a charge that is capable of being registered at Companies House and a copy of every instrument effecting any variation or amendment of such a charge (CA 2006, ss 859P and 859Q; see **4.4.2.8**).

11.7.16 REGISTRATION OF FLOATING CHARGES IN SCOTLAND

Scots law on floating charges is very different from English law and this has raised questions about, for example, whether a floating charge created under English law by a company registered in England can be effective against its property (other than land) in Scotland. The Scottish Law Commission recommended that there should be a separate Scottish register of floating charges kept, not at Companies House, but by the Keeper of the Registers of Scotland. It also recommended that English companies with property in Scotland must register floating charges there as well as in England. See *Report on Registration of Rights in Security by Companies* (Scot Law Com No 197) (Edinburgh: Stationery Office, 2004). These proposals have been enacted in the Bankruptcy and Diligence etc (Scotland) Act 2007 (asp 3), part 2. Arrangements can be made that registration in the Scottish floating charges register will also count as registration at Companies House for the purposes of Scots law (CA 2006, s 893; BIS, *Registration of Charges Created by Companies and Limited Liability Partnerships* (URN 10/697), paras 136–40). However, there has been considerable annoyance that lenders to companies registered in England will have to incur the extra expense of registering both an English floating charge at Companies House and a separate Scottish charge in the Scottish register. As a result, part 2 of the 2007 Act has never been brought into force. A technical working group reported to the Scottish Government in August 2011 on the options of implementing the Act unchanged, implementing it with various amendments (some of them quite drastic) or repealing it. That report is still under consideration. See **www.scotland.gov.uk/Topics/Justice/law/damages/company**.

12

MARKETABLE LOANS

SUMMARY OF POINTS COVERED

- What is in this chapter
- Stock
- Trustees
- Stock certificates
- Contracts for the allotment of debt securities

- Information for debenture holders
- Convertibles
- Meetings
- Prospectuses and listing particulars

12.1 WHAT IS IN THIS CHAPTER

This chapter deals with arrangements by which a company borrows a large sum of money long term. The money is put up by a number of investors who are entitled to receive interest payments (usually twice a year) and, at the end of the term of the loan, repayment of principal. Sale of all or part of an investor's entitlements is possible and arrangements are usually made for trading on a stock exchange. Marketable loans were once issued to the general public in the same way as shares, but nowadays they are usually held in large quantities by financial institutions and specialist investors. They are described as 'wholesale' rather than 'retail' investments. Interests in marketable loans are called 'debt securities', or 'bonds', or, in CA 2006, 'debentures'. Transfers of debt securities (unless they are convertibles—see **12.7**) are generally exempt from stamp duty (Finance Act 1986, s 79).

Key legislation which you should be able to consult when reading this chapter:

- FSMA 2000, ss 79–82, 86;
- CA 2006, ss 423, 431, 432, 580, 738, 740, 749, 859B, 859P, 859Q.

All that legislation is in *Blackstone's Statutes on Company Law*.

- The Listing Rules (LR) and the Prospectus Rules (PR) in the FCA Handbook, which is at **handbook.fca.org.uk**.

The following cases, which are considered in this chapter, are particularly significant and are recommended further reading:

- *Assénagon Asset Management SA v Irish Bank Resolution Corp Ltd* [2012] EWHC 2090 (Ch), [2013] Bus LR 266
- *Azevedo v Imcopa Importação, Exportação e Indústria de Óleos Ltda* [2013] EWCA Civ 364, [2015] QB 1

Your particular course of study may require you to read other source materials.

12.2 STOCK

For the purpose of measuring each investor's interest, when a company arranges a marketable loan it is nowadays usual to regard the whole amount borrowed as a 'stock' having a certain nominal value. This nominal value may be equal to, less than, or even greater than the amount actually loaned.

Each investor is regarded as being interested in a proportion of the stock, having a certain nominal value.

The nominal value of a particular investor's stockholding is normally the same as the amount of principal to be paid to that investor by the company at the end of the term of the loan. In some marketable loans, the company promises that when it repays principal it will additionally pay a certain percentage of the principal as a bonus, known as a redemption premium.

It is permissible to issue marketable loan securities at a discount, that is, for less than their nominal value (*Re Anglo-Danubian Steam Navigation and Colliery Co* (1875) LR 20 Eq 339). Usually, the amount of the discount is written off over the term of the loan.

12.3 TRUSTEES

If debt securities are to be listed, it is usual for a trust to be constituted for the duration of the loan, with a trustee, or trustees, whose duty is to look after the interests of the stockholders. A trust for stockholders is invariably constituted in a deed.

A major advantage of a trust for a marketable loan is that security can be given for the loan by means of a contract between the company and the trustees. (Not all marketable loans are secured: those that are not are usually described as 'unsecured loan stock'.) The contract of security is normally incorporated in the deed constituting the trust, and it normally gives a floating charge on the company's business and property, and a fixed charge on the company's land.

When a trust has been constituted, the contract to pay interest and repay principal must be between company and trustee, not company and stockholder (*Re Uruguay Central and Hygueritas Railway Co of Monte Video* (1879) 11 ChD 372; *Re Dunderland Iron Ore Co Ltd* [1909] 1 Ch 446). The practical result of this is that only the trustee may take proceedings against the company, and this preserves the equality of the stockholders. Where security has been given in a contract with a trustee, only the trustee may enforce that security, for example by appointing an administrator. If a trustee is dilatory, any stockholder (as beneficiary of the trust) may ask the court to order performance of the trustee's duties.

If the trust deed gives security, any stockholder must, on request, be sent a copy, for which the company may charge a fee, of the trust deed covering the stock (CA 2006, s 749).

If the trust deed creates a charge on the company's property or undertaking, it must be registered at Companies House and a certified copy of the deed must be delivered (s 859B; see 11.7.2) and the company must keep a copy of the deed available for inspection (ss 859P and 859Q).

12.4 STOCK CERTIFICATES

A stock certificate is a certificate given by a company that a person is the holder of stock to a specified nominal value.

A stock certificate issued in connection with a marketable loan is a written acknowledgement of a company's indebtedness and is therefore a 'debenture' for the purposes of CA 2006 (see 11.2.2.5). CA 2006, s 738, says that the meaning of 'debenture' is to include debenture stock.

A stock certificate for a marketable loan may be made out to bearer and be transferable by delivery alone. Such a document is judicially recognised as being a negotiable instrument (*Bechuanaland Exploration Co v London Trading Bank Ltd* [1898] 2 QB 658). Bearer debentures are exempt from stamp duty on issue and transfer (Finance Act 1986, s 79(2)). Normally, issue and transfer of debenture stock and unsecured loan stock are through a register operated in the same way as a company's register of members. Normally a trust deed covering a marketable loan requires the company to maintain a register of stockholders.

If a company maintains a register of debenture holders, it must observe the same rules on where it must be kept, on provision of copies, and on permitting inspection of the register as apply to the register of members (see **4.4.2.6**). A stockholder, whether or not also a member, may not be charged a fee for inspecting the register.

12.5 CONTRACTS FOR THE ALLOTMENT OF DEBT SECURITIES

Company marketable loans are company securities and the law stated in **Chapter 7** applies to them, except that:

(a) There is no limitation on the payment of underwriting commission on marketable loans—CA 2006, s 552 (see **7.8**), does not apply to debt securities.

(b) An allotment may be made however small a response there is to the offer—CA 2006, s 578 (see **7.9**), does not apply to issues of debt securities.

It was held in *South African Territories Ltd v Wallington* [1898] AC 309 that a contract for the allotment of debentures would not be enforced by an order for specific performance, and so CA 2006, s 740, gives a statutory power to the courts to order specific performance.

12.6 INFORMATION FOR DEBENTURE HOLDERS

The holder of any debenture of a company (that is, any document it has issued evidencing indebtedness) is entitled to ask for a copy of the company's most recent annual accounts as submitted to its members (CA 2006, ss 431(1) and 432(1)). Under s 423(1), a company must send a copy of its annual accounts and reports to every holder of its debentures (unless it is unaware of a holder's address: s 423(2)). See **9.6.1**. Holders of debt securities are rarely, if ever, entitled to attend members' meetings.

12.7 CONVERTIBLES

Unsecured loan stock, or occasionally secured debenture stock, may carry a right to exchange the stock at a future date for shares of the company that issued the stock.

The trust deed covering the loan would specify how the number of shares to be allotted is to be related to the nominal value of stock given in exchange. Often there are several different dates on which conversion may be made, with a different exchange rate for each conversion period.

The issue of convertible securities is subject to the rules on authority to allot, discussed in **6.3.4** (CA 2006, s 594(2)(b)). The issue of securities convertible into equity shares is subject to the rules on members' pre-emption rights, discussed in **6.3.5** (s 560(2)(a)).

The terms of issue of a convertible security must not result in the company receiving less than the nominal value of the shares issued (*Mosely v Koffyfontein Mines Ltd* [1904] 2 Ch 108; CA 2006, s 580).

12.8 MEETINGS

The terms of issue of debt securities often make provision for meetings of the holders of the securities which can, for example, agree to a change in the terms on which the securities were issued. As with meetings of shareholders, it is usually provided that a majority vote at such a meeting binds all holders of the securities, whether they attended the meeting or not. As with meetings of shareholders (see **14.10.5**), a majority decision which oppresses the minority is invalid. Two recent cases have tested what may be a quite widespread practice of a borrowing company offering an incentive to vote in the way favoured by the company.

In *Azevedo v Imcopa Importação, Exportação e Indústria de Óleos Ltda* [2013] EWCA Civ 364, [2015] QB 1, the Court of Appeal held that a company may make cash payments to holders of debt securities who vote in favour of a resolution restructuring the loan so that its terms are more favourable to the company. This is known as consent solicitation and the payments are called consent payments. Lloyd LJ, at [63], said that he could see:

> nothing wrong or unlawful, in general terms, in a process of putting to all members of a class a proposal which offers benefits open to all who vote in favour of the resolution, but not to the others. No member of the class is thereby excluded from participation in the offered benefits except by his own choice as to whether, and if so how, to vote.

The availability of the advantage to all voters was sufficient to distinguish the case from *Menier v Hooper's Telegraph Works* (1874) LR 9 Ch App 350 (discussed at **14.10.5**), where the dissenting minority could not have gained any benefit from voting for the resolution ([2013] EWCA Civ 364 at [66]).

This decision may be contrasted with *Assénagon Asset Management SA v Irish Bank Resolution Corp Ltd* [2012] EWHC 2090 (Ch), [2013] Bus LR 266. There it was held that what is known as 'exit consent' cannot be used. Exit consent is a technique for forcing bondholders to exchange their current securities for new ones with terms that are more favourable to the borrowing company. It is used when the existing securities have a poor market value, reflecting the issuer's inability to pay interest and repay the amount borrowed on the original securities. The technique works as follows. Bondholders are invited to exchange their bonds for the new ones before a deadline. They can only make the exchange if they commit, irrevocably, to voting in favour of a resolution at a meeting of bondholders to be held after the deadline. The resolution will change the terms of the existing bonds so that they are worthless. The resolution does not affect those who have exchanged their bonds for new ones, but will destroy any remaining value of bonds which have not been exchanged. Holders who consider that if they refuse to exchange, the issuer can and will offer a better deal, cannot do so unless they are certain that the resolution will not be passed. If the bonds are in bearer form, they will not even be able to contact other holders to find out how they are going to act. Declaring that this is an invalid oppression of the minority, Briggs J said, at [85]–[86]:

> 85. This form of coercion is in my judgment entirely at variance with the purposes for which majorities in a class are given power to bind minorities, and it is no answer for them to say that it is the issuer which has required or invited them to do so. True it is that, at the moment when any individual member of the class is required (by the imposition of the pre-meeting deadline) to make up his mind, there is at that point in time no defined minority against which the exit consent is aimed. But it is inevitable that there will be a defined (if any) minority by the time when the exit consent is implemented by being voted upon, and its only purpose is to prey upon the apprehension of each member of the class (aggravated by his relative inability to find out

the views of his fellow class members in advance) that he will, if he decides to vote against, be part of that expropriated minority if the scheme goes ahead.

86. Putting it as succinctly as I can, oppression of a minority is of the essence of exit consents of this kind, and it is precisely that at which the principles restraining the abusive exercise of powers to bind minorities are aimed.

In *Azevedo v Imcopa Importação, Exportação e Indústria de Óleos Ltda*, Lloyd LJ said, at [37], that its facts were too far away from *Assénagon Asset Management SA v Irish Bank Resolution Corp Ltd* for the decision in that case to be of assistance. Although the test of benefit being available to all voters applies to both consent payment and exit consent, it may be that the deprivation of the property of the dissenting voters is what distinguishes exit consent and makes it unlawful.

12.9 PROSPECTUSES AND LISTING PARTICULARS

12.9.1 PROSPECTUSES

The requirements for form and content of prospectuses for debt securities in Commission Regulation (EC) No 809/2004 make a distinction between the retail market (the general public) and the wholesale market (professional investors) which applies to debt securities (recital 14). The criterion used in the Regulation to distinguish between retail and wholesale debt securities is nominal value (or minimum investment if there is no nominal value). Securities with a nominal value or minimum investment of less than €100,000 (or equivalent in another currency) are regarded as intended for the retail market (art 7); securities with a nominal value or minimum investment greater than or equal to €100,000 (or equivalent) are regarded as intended for the wholesale market (art 12). On the London Stock Exchange, the wholesale market for debt securities and convertibles is the Professional Securities Market (PSM).

A prospectus is not required for a public offer of wholesale debt securities (Directive 2003/71/EC, art 3(2)(c) and (d); FSMA 2000, s 86(1)(c) and (d)). A prospectus is required for admission to trading on a regulated market, but the summary in non-technical language can be omitted (Directive 2003/71/EC, art 5(2); PR 2.1.3R) and the content requirements are simpler than for shares. The content requirements for wholesale debt securities are set out in Regulation (EC) No 809/2004, art 12 and annex IX (registration document) and art 16 and annex XIII (securities note). These requirements are reproduced in the FCA Handbook, PR 2.3.1EU and PR App 3EU.

A prospectus is not required for admission to trading on the Professional Securities Market of the London Stock Exchange, because the PSM is not a regulated market. Instead, the LSE requires securities traded on the PSM to be listed and the FCA classifies PSM securities as 'specialist securities' for which it requires listing particulars, which give the same information as a prospectus (see **12.9.2**).

12.9.2 LISTING PARTICULARS FOR THE PROFESSIONAL SECURITIES MARKET

'Specialist securities' are defined in the FCA Handbook Glossary as:

> securities which, because of their nature, are normally bought and traded by a limited number of investors who are particularly knowledgeable in investment matters.

LR 4 contains special rules for any application for listing of specialist securities for which a prospectus is not required. In practice it seems that the only securities issued by UK companies to which LR 4 will apply are wholesale debt securities to be admitted to the London Stock Exchange's Professional Securities Market. A prospectus is not required for a public offer of wholesale debt securities (Directive 2003/71/EC, art 3(2)(c) and (d); FSMA 2000, s 86(1)(c) and (d)) and is not required for admission to the PSM, because it is not a regulated market, but admission to trading on the PSM is restricted to listed securities.

A specialist security which is exempt from the prospectus requirement cannot be listed unless FCA-approved listing particulars have been published (FSMA 2000, s 79; LR 2.2.11R, 4.1.1R, 4.1.2G and 4.1.3R). Listing particulars fulfil the same function as a prospectus, but are regulated domestically rather than by EU legislation. However, LR 4.2 draws the requirements for the form and content of listing particulars from the requirements for prospectuses. Listing particulars, like a prospectus (see **7.4.3**), are subject to a general duty to disclose all information required by investors to make an informed assessment of the securities (FSMA 2000, s 80). Exemptions from disclosure, corresponding to those available under s 87B for a prospectus (see **7.4.3**), are available under s 82 for listing particulars. Supplementary listing particulars are required by s 81 in circumstances corresponding to those for which a supplementary prospectus is required (see **7.4.4**), but there is no provision for withdrawal of agreement to buy or subscribe for the securities on publication of supplementary listing particulars.

The option to publish listing particulars is not available for issues for less than €2.5 million (FSMA 2000, s 87(3); LR 4.1.1R), because there already is an option to publish a prospectus for such an issue (see **7.4.5.3**). However, it is unclear whether this option applies when the issue is for less than €100,000.

13

MARKET ABUSE

SUMMARY OF POINTS COVERED

- What is in this chapter
- Market abuse regulation
- Disclosure to the public
- Closed period for PDMRs

- Sanctions
- Offence of insider dealing
- Offence of creating a false market
- Fiduciary duty

13.1 WHAT IS IN THIS CHAPTER

Chapter 13 is concerned only with *public companies*. It is concerned with the buying and selling of company shares in regulated markets such as the London Stock Exchange Main Market (see **7.3.4.3**).

Chapter 7 examined how a company offers its shares to the public so that the shares can be traded on a regulated market. **Chapter 13** discusses how the law can encourage public confidence in regulated markets.

A stock exchange is a marketplace for buying and selling company shares and other securities. Like any marketplace, people will be more inclined to use it if they believe that prices in it correctly represent the value of what is bought and sold. A person who buys something which turns out to be worth less than the price paid for it will feel aggrieved. So will a person who sells something for less than its real value.

In principle, deals in a market are more likely to be at a price correctly reflecting value if all the information used in valuation is available to both buyers and sellers. Two main kinds of information are used in valuing company shares:

(a) Information about the economy of the nation, world trade and the particular market in which the company is trading.

(b) Information about how the company itself is handling its affairs.

Investors are expected to get information of type (a) from the financial press, reports of economists and government statistics, and it is assumed to be available to all. New information of type (b) is usually first known to people close to the company itself and is therefore known as 'inside information'. People with inside information are in a position to deal in the company's shares before the rest of the market has had an opportunity to revalue them in the light of the fresh information. Acting in this way is known as 'insider dealing'.

Disclosure of inside information to selected individuals, so that they can take advantage of knowing more about the value of the shares than the people they will buy from or sell to, is an extended form of insider dealing.

Taking advantage of inside information is a fraud on other investors, and is likely to lower public confidence in the market. It is also seen as a breach of trust, especially when directors use the information they gain from their position to swindle the shareholders who appointed them. The most effective ways of preventing insider dealing are to require companies to publish all information affecting the value of their publicly traded shares and to require insiders to declare their dealings (see **13.3**).

Another way in which public confidence in a market can be damaged is by spreading false information likely to affect the value of shares, creating a false market. This is known as 'market manipulation'.

Insider dealing, selective disclosure of insider information and market manipulation are collectively known as 'market abuse'. There are two regimes for controlling market abuse. The first regime imposes civil sanctions. It is set out in Regulation (EU) No 596/2014, which is directly effective EU legislation. It prohibits market abuse in various forms (see **13.2**), requires earliest possible disclosure of market-sensitive information (**13.3**), prohibits a company's senior managers from dealing in its shares during the 30 days before financial results are announced (**13.4**) and is enforced in the United Kingdom by the Financial Conduct Authority (FCA), which can impose administrative sanctions (**13.5**). The second regime imposes criminal sanctions and is contained in the Criminal Justice Act 1993, part V (see **13.6**) and the Financial Services Act 2012, s 90 (**13.7**).

If insider dealing is an abuse of a fiduciary position, equitable principles may be applied to recover profits or compensate for losses (see **13.8**).

For the history of controls on insider dealing in the United Kingdom see J Davies, 'From gentlemanly expectations to regulatory principles: a history of insider dealing in the UK' (2015) 36 Co Law 132 and 163.

Key legislation which you should be able to consult when reading this chapter:

- Criminal Justice Act 1993, ss 52–64, sch 1, sch 2;
- FSMA 2000, ss 123–131AE;
- Financial Services Act 2012, s 90.

Relevant provisions of the Criminal Justice Act 1993, FSMA 2000 and the Financial Services Act 2012 are in *Blackstone's Statutes on Company Law*.

- Regulation (EU) No 596/2014, which is at the EUR-Lex website, **www.eur-lex.europa.eu.**

- MAR 1, MAR 2, DTR 2, DTR 6 in the FCA Handbook, which is at **handbook.fca.org.uk.**

The following case, which is considered in this chapter, is particularly significant and is recommended further reading:

- *Percival v Wright* [1902] 2 Ch 421.

Your particular course of study may require you to read other source materials.

13.2 MARKET ABUSE REGULATION

13.2.1 GENERAL DESCRIPTION

Regulation (EU) No 596/2014 (the Market Abuse Regulation) is EU legislation which is directly effective in the United Kingdom and the rest of the EU (it has not yet been extended to the rest of the EEA). The regulation prohibits forms of market abuse (arts 14 and 15) and requires issuers of shares traded on regulated markets to disclose information (arts 17 to 19). It requires member States to empower competent authorities to take appropriate administrative sanctions and other administrative measures in relation to infringements (art 30). Guidance on the regulation is given in the FCA Handbook, MAR 1.

13.2.2 INVESTMENTS COVERED INCLUDE SHARES

Regulation (EU) No 596/2014 covers trading in 'financial instruments' as defined in Directive 2014/65/EU, art 4(1)(15) and annex I, s C (see Regulation 596/2014, art 3(1)(1)). That definition means that 'financial instruments' include 'transferable securities' (as defined in Directive 2014/65/EU, art 4(1)(44)), which in turn include company shares and debt securities. To simplify the discussion, **Chapter 13** only considers the application of Regulation 596/2014 to company shares.

13.2.3 MARKETS COVERED

In relation to company shares, Regulation (EU) No 596/2014 applies to trading on regulated markets such as the London Stock Exchange Main Market (see 7.3.4.3) and on multilateral trading facilities (MTFs) (art 2(1)).

13.2.4 INSIDER DEALING AS MARKET ABUSE

13.2.4.1 Insider dealing and improper disclosure defined to be market abuse

Regulation 596/2014/EU, art 14, provides that:

> A person shall not:
>
> (a) engage or attempt to engage in insider dealing;
>
> (b) recommend that another person engage in insider dealing or induce another person to engage in insider dealing; or
>
> (c) unlawfully disclose inside information.

Article 8 explains the first two of these prohibitions as follows:

1. . . . insider dealing arises where a person possesses inside information and uses that information by acquiring or disposing of, for its own account or for the account of a third party, directly or indirectly, financial instruments to which that information relates. The use of inside information by cancelling or amending an order concerning a financial instrument to which the information relates where the order was placed before the person concerned possessed the inside information, shall also be considered to be insider dealing.

2. . . . recommending that another person engage in insider dealing, or inducing another person to engage in insider dealing, arises where the person possesses inside information and:

    (a) recommends, on the basis of that information, that another person acquire or dispose of financial instruments to which that information relates, or induces that person to make such an acquisition or disposal, or

    (b) recommends, on the basis of that information, that another person cancel or amend an order concerning a financial instrument to which that information relates, or induces that person to make such a cancellation or amendment.

3. The use of the recommendations or inducements referred to in paragraph 2 amounts to insider dealing. . . where the person using the recommendation or inducement knows or ought to know that it is based upon inside information.

The 'persons' referred to in art 8(1) to (3) are the persons prohibited from insider dealing by art 14. They are limited to the persons (usually described as 'insiders', though the term is not used in the regulation) defined in art 8(4), as follows:

4.   This Article applies to any person who possesses inside information as a result of:

(a)   being a member of the administrative, management or supervisory bodies [ie, being a director] of the issuer . . . ;

(b)   having a holding in the capital of the issuer [ie, holding the issuer's shares] . . . ;

(c)   having access to the information through the exercise of an employment, profession or duties; or

(d)   being involved in criminal activities.

This Article also applies to any person who possesses inside information under circumstances other than those referred to in the first subparagraph where that person knows or ought to know that it is inside information.

Article 10 explains 'unlawful disclosure' as follows:

1.   For the purposes of this Regulation, unlawful disclosure of inside information arises where a person possesses inside information and discloses that information to any other person, except where the disclosure is made in the normal exercise of an employment, a profession or duties.

This paragraph applies to any natural or legal person in the situations or circumstances referred to in Article 8(4).

2.   For the purposes of this Regulation the onward disclosure of recommendations or inducements referred to in Article 8(2) amounts to unlawful disclosure of inside information under this Article where the person disclosing the recommendation or inducement knows or ought to know that it was based on inside information.

For an example of the form of market abuse defined by art 8(1) see *Massey v Financial Services Authority* [2011] UKUT 49 (TCC), [2011] Lloyd's Rep FC 459, in which a penalty of £150,000 was imposed (the amount of the profit made plus 50 per cent) (see Financial Services Authority (FSA) press release FSA/PN/021/2011).

13.2.4.2 Definition of inside information

In relation to company shares, Regulation (EU) No 596/2014, art 7(1), defines 'inside information' as follows:

1.   For the purposes of this Regulation, inside information shall comprise the following types of information:

(a)   information of a precise nature, which has not been made public, relating, directly or indirectly, to one or more issuers or to one or more financial instruments, and which, if it were made public, would be likely to have a significant effect on the prices of those financial instruments or on the price of related derivative financial instruments; . . .

(d)   for persons charged with the execution of orders concerning financial instruments, it also means information conveyed by a client and relating to the client's pending orders in financial instruments, which is of a precise nature, relating, directly or indirectly, to one or more issuers or to one or more financial instruments, and which, if it were made public, would be likely to have a significant effect on the prices of those financial instruments, the price of related spot commodity contracts, or on the price of related derivative financial instruments.

Article 7(4) adds that information which is likely to have a significant effect on prices means 'information a reasonable investor would be likely to use as part of the basis of his or her investment decisions'. Where it is intended that circumstances will come into existence or an event will occur as the result of a protracted process, the intermediate steps of that process may be deemed to be precise information (art 7(2) and (3)).

13.2.4.3 Market soundings

Inside information can be disclosed in the course of a 'market sounding' (Regulation (EU) No 596/2014, art 11). This where a person intending to make a transaction, such as a takeover bid, provides information about it to potential investors so as to gauge what interest there would be in participating. The recipients of the information must be informed that it is inside information which the recipient cannot make use of (art 11(5)). Full written records must be kept. Article 11 is supplemented by Commission Delegated Regulation (EU) 2016/959 and Commission Delegated Regulation (EU) 2016/960.

If all the conditions of art 11 and the delegated regulations are complied with, the disclosure will be deemed to be made in the normal exercise of a person's employment, profession or duties so that it is excepted by Regulation (EU) No 596/2014, art 10(1).

13.2.5 MARKET MANIPULATION AS MARKET ABUSE

13.2.5.1 Forms of market manipulation defined to be market abuse

Regulation (EU) No 596/2014, art 15, provides that 'A person shall not engage in or attempt to engage in market manipulation'. In relation to trading in shares, art 12(1) identifies the following forms of market manipulation:

(a) entering into a transaction, placing an order to trade or any other behaviour which:

  (i) gives, or is likely to give, false or misleading signals as to the supply of, demand for, or price of, a financial instrument . . .; or

  (ii) secures, or is likely to secure, the price of one or several financial instruments . . . at an abnormal or artificial level;

  unless the person entering into a transaction, placing an order to trade or engaging in any other behaviour establishes that such transaction, order or behaviour have been carried out for legitimate reasons, and conform with an accepted market practice as established in accordance with Article 13;

(b) entering into a transaction, placing an order to trade or any other activity or behaviour which affects or is likely to affect the price of one or several financial instruments . . . which employs a fictitious device or any other form of deception or contrivance;

(c) disseminating information through the media, including the internet, or by any other means, which gives, or is likely to give, false or misleading signals as to the supply of, demand for, or price of, a financial instrument . . . or secures, or is likely to secure, the price of one or several financial instruments . . . at an abnormal or artificial level, including the dissemination of rumours, where the person who made the dissemination knew, or ought to have known, that the information was false or misleading [see **13.2.5.2**].

No accepted market practices have been established to provide an exception to point (a) (FCA Handbook, MAR 1, annex 2).

Regulation (EU) No 596/2014, art 12(1), is supplemented by annex I, which lists factors that may indicate the employment of a fictitious device or any other form of deception or contrivance and indicators of false or misleading signals and price securing. There are further details in Commission Delegated Regulation (EU) 2016/522, art 4 and annex II. Regulation (EU) No 596/2014, art 12(1), is also supplemented by art 12(2), which lists specific behaviours which are to be considered as market manipulation. These include cornering, making an unrealistic purchase or sale at the beginning or end of the day so as to mislead other investors, using high-frequency or algorithmic trading so as to overload or destabilise a trading system and using traditional or electronic media to circulate an opinion about the value of securities in which one has already taken a position.

13.2.5.2 Journalists

For the purposes of Regulation (EU) No 596/2014, art 12(1)(c), it is provided in art 21 that disclosure or dissemination of information for the purpose of journalism or other form of expression in the media shall be assessed taking into account the rules governing the freedom of the press and freedom of expression in other media and the rules or codes governing the journalist profession, unless:

(a) the persons concerned, or persons closely associated with them, derive, directly or indirectly, an advantage or profits from the disclosure or the dissemination of the information in question; or

(b) the disclosure or the dissemination is made with the intention of misleading the market as to the supply of, demand for, or price of financial instruments.

The principal code covering the profession of journalism is the Editors' Code of Practice. In the version published by the Independent Press Standards Organisation which took effect from 1 January 2016, cl 13 (financial journalism) states:

(i) Even where the law does not prohibit it, journalists must not use for their own profit financial information they receive in advance of its general publication, nor should they pass such information to others.

(ii) They must not write about shares or securities in whose performance they know that they or their close families have a significant financial interest without disclosing the interest to the editor or financial editor.

(iii) They must not buy or sell, either directly or through nominees or agents, shares or securities about which they have written recently or about which they intend to write in the near future.

13.2.6 EXCEPTIONS

The Market Abuse Regulation prohibitions on insider dealing and market manipulation (Regulation (EU) No 596/2014, arts 14 and 15) do not apply to buy-back programmes (purchase of own shares, see **10.6**) and stabilisation (art 5) or to transactions, orders or behaviour in pursuit of monetary, exchange rate or public debt management policy by governments and EU institutions (art 6). Article 5(1) to (3) specify conditions which buy-back programmes must meet. Article 5 is supplemented by Commission Delegated Regulation (EU) 2016/1052 which sets out regulatory technical standards for buy-back programmes and market stabilisation. FCA Handbook, MAR 1.10, refers to Regulation 596/2014/EU, art 5, and says that acting in accordance with certain provisions of the Takeover Code is unlikely, of itself, to amount to market abuse.

13.2.7 REPORTING AND INVESTIGATION

13.2.7.1 Reporting suspicious transactions

Any person professionally arranging or executing transactions, who has a reasonable suspicion that an order or transaction in any financial instrument, whether placed or executed on or outside a trading venue, could constitute actual or attempted insider dealing or market manipulation must notify the FCA without delay (Regulation (EU) No 596/2014, art 16(2); FCA Handbook, SUP 15.10.4G and 15.10.7G). Such a report does not breach any restriction on the disclosure of information (FSMA 2000, s 131A).

13.2.7.2 Investigation

The FCA or the Secretary of State may, under FSMA 2000, s 168(3), appoint one or more investigators if it is apparent to them that there are circumstances suggesting that market abuse may have
taken place (s 168(2)(d)). See **18.8.3.3** and FCA Handbook, EG 3 and EG 4.

13.3 DISCLOSURE TO THE PUBLIC

13.3.1 DISCLOSURE OF INSIDE INFORMATION BY AN ISSUER

Regulation (EU) No 596/2014, art 17(1), requires an issuer of shares admitted to trading on a
regulated market (see **7.3.4.3**) to inform the public as soon as possible of inside information
(see **13.2.4.2**) which directly concerns that issuer. Disclosure of inside information must not be
combined with marketing the issuer's activities (art 17(1)).

The detailed requirements for effecting disclosure are set out in the FCA Handbook, DTR 6.3.

The issuer must post and maintain on its website for a period of at least five years, all inside
information it is required to disclose publicly (Regulation (EU) No 596/2014, art 17(1)).

An issuer may, under Regulation (EU) No 596/2014, art 17(4), delay disclosure of inside
information if:

(a) immediate disclosure is likely to prejudice the legitimate interests of the issuer;

(b) delay of disclosure is not likely to mislead the public;

(c) the issuer is able to ensure the confidentiality of that information.

Where disclosure of information has been delayed under art 17(4), disclosure must be made
immediately the confidentiality of the information is no longer ensured (art 17(7)). This includes a
situation where a rumour is circulating which is sufficiently accurate to indicate that confidentiality is no longer ensured (art 17(7)).

There is guidance on delaying disclosure in FCA Handbook, DTR 2.5.1AEU to 2.5.5G.

If any inside information is disclosed to any third party in the normal course of the exercise of an
employment, profession or duties, there must be simultaneous public disclosure unless the person
receiving the information owes a duty of confidentiality (Regulation 596/2014/EU, art 17(8); for
guidance see DTR 2.5.6AEU to 2.5.9G).

13.3.2 INSIDER LISTS

A company which has issued securities that are admitted to trading on a regulated market (or are
the subject of an application for admission) must draw up and maintain an insider list (Regulation (EU) No 596/2014, art 18(1)). An issuing company's insider list is a list of persons who have
access to inside information (see **13.2.4.2**) and who are working for the issuer under a contract
of employment, or otherwise performing tasks through which they have access to inside information, such as advisers, accountants or credit rating agencies (art 18(1)(a)). It must contain the
information specified in art 18(3). It must be updated promptly whenever there is a change in
the reason for including a person already on the list, whenever a new person has access to inside
information and whenever a person ceases to have access (art 18(4)). There must also be insider
lists for persons acting on behalf, or on account, of an issuer and the issuer is ultimately responsible for ensuring that they are maintained (art 18(1) and (2)). An insider list of a person acting
on behalf, or on account, of an issuer is a list of that person's workers who have access to inside
information relating, directly or indirectly, to the issuer. Workers must be included whether they

work under a contract of employment or otherwise, and whether their access to inside information is regular or occasional.

Insider lists must be provided to the FCA as soon as possible on request (art 18(1)(c)). The original and each update of an insider list must be kept for at least five years (art 18(5)).

An issuer must take all reasonable steps to ensure that every person on its insider list acknowledges in writing the legal and regulatory duties entailed and is aware of the sanctions applicable to insider dealing and unlawful disclosure of inside information (art 18(2)). The same must be done for workers on the insider lists of persons acting on the issuer's behalf or account (art 18(2)).

13.3.3 NOTIFICATION OF TRANSACTIONS BY PDMRS AND CONNECTED PERSONS

The directors and senior executives (PDMRs, see later) of a company which has issued securities that are admitted to trading on a regulated market (or which are the subject of an application for admission to trading) must notify all transactions conducted on their own account in the company's shares, and derivatives and other financial instruments relating to those shares (Regulation (EU) No 596/2014, art 19(1)). Transactions of €5,000 or less in a calendar year need not be notified (art 19(8)).

The notification must be made to the company and electronically to the FCA and must be made promptly and no later than three business days after the day on which the transaction occurred (art 19(1) and (2)). The company must ensure that information about a PDMR transaction notified to it is made public promptly and no later than three business days after the transaction (art 19(3)).

The persons within a company who are required to disclose transactions are known as 'persons discharging managerial responsibilities' (PDMRs). By art 3(1)(25), a PDMR is a person within a company who is:

(a) a member of the administrative, management or supervisory body of the company, which in the UK means any director; or

(b) any senior executive who is not a director but:

 (i) has regular access to inside information relating, directly or indirectly, to the company, and

 (ii) has power to make managerial decisions affecting the company's future development and business prospects.

The persons connected with a PDMR within a company are defined in art 3(1)(26) as applied to the United Kingdom by FSMA 2000, s 131AC, as:

(a) a spouse, or a partner considered to be equivalent to a spouse in accordance with national law;

(b) a dependent child, in accordance with national law;

(c) a relative who has shared the same household for at least one year on the date of the transaction concerned; or

(d) a legal person, trust or partnership, the managerial responsibilities of which are discharged by a person discharging managerial responsibilities or by a person referred to in point (a), (b) or (c), which is directly or indirectly controlled by such a person, which is set up for the benefit of such a person, or the economic interests of which are substantially equivalent to those of such a person.

13.3.4 OTHER MARKETS

Companies whose securities are admitted to trading only on markets which are not EU regulated markets are not subject to the extensive requirements of Directive 2003/6/EC. Other markets do, however, impose their own requirements for prompt disclosure of significant information.

A company with securities admitted to trading on AIM must notify an RIS of any developments which, if made public, would be likely to lead to a substantial movement in the price of those securities (AIM Rules, r 11). A company with securities admitted to trading on the ISDX Growth Market must notify an RIS of any changes which would be likely to have a significant effect on the price of its securities (ISDX Growth Market Rules for Issuers, r 32).

13.4 CLOSED PERIOD FOR PDMRS

A PDMR within a company (see **13.3.3**) must not conduct any transactions relating to the company's shares during a closed period of 30 calendar days before the announcement of an interim financial report or a year-end report (Regulation (EU) No 596/2014, art 19(11)). This covers transactions on the PDMR's own account and transactions for third parties. The announcement referred to in art 19(11) is the public statement whereby the company announces the information included in an interim or a year-end financial report. The announcement may be made before the report as a whole is published, but as soon as it is made, the closed period ends (European Securities and Markets Authority, *Questions and Answers on the Market Abuse Regulation*).

The company may allow a PDMR to conduct transactions in the closed period where there are exceptional circumstances, such as severe financial difficulty, which require the immediate sale of shares (art 19(12)(a)). There can also be transactions made under, or related to, an employee share scheme (art 19(12)(b)).

13.5 SANCTIONS

13.5.1 ADMINISTRATIVE SANCTIONS

FSMA 2000, ss 123, 123A and 123B, provide the FCA with a range of sanctions which can be imposed on a person for contravening Regulation (EU) No 596/2014. The FCA may:

(a) impose a financial penalty, of such amount as it considers appropriate (s 123(2);

(b) instead of imposing a financial penalty, publish a statement censuring the person (s 123(3));

(c) impose a temporary prohibition on an individual holding an office or position involving responsibility for taking decisions about the management of an investment firm (s 123A(2)(a))—the prohibition can refer to a particular firm, all firms of a particular type or all firms (s 123A(5)) and it may be permanent if the individual has contravened Regulation (EU) No 596/2014, art 14 (prohibition of insider dealing and of unlawful disclosure of inside information) or 15 (prohibition of market manipulation) (FSMA 2000, s 123A(3));

(d) impose a temporary prohibition on the individual acquiring or disposing of financial instruments, whether on his or her own account or the account of a third party and whether directly or indirectly (s 123A(2)(b));

(e) suspend and/or limit or otherwise restrict the person's permission to carry on a regulated activity, for up to 12 months (s 123B(2) and (4)).

The FCA may impose any one or more of these sanctions in relation to the same contravention (s 123C), except that it must choose between sanctions (a) and (b).

Sanctions under ss 123, 123A and 123B may be imposed if the FCA is satisfied that a person (s 123), an individual (s 123A) or an authorised person (s 123B):

(a) has contravened Regulation (EU) No 596/2014, art 14 or 15;

(b) has contravened, or been knowingly concerned in the contravention of a provision of Regulation (EU) No 596/2014 other than art 14 or 15 or a provision of a Commission Delegated Regulation providing regulatory technical standards to supplement Regulation (EU) No 596/2014.

The FCA does not have to be satisfied to the criminal standard of proof (beyond reasonable doubt), but must be satisfied to the civil standard (the balance of probabilities) (*Mohammed v Financial Services Authority* (FS & M Tribunal 29 March 2005)).

The imposition of a penalty does not make any transaction void or unenforceable (s 131). Details of the FCA's disciplinary and enforcement arrangements are in the Enforcement Guide (EG) in the FCA Handbook. See especially EG 7 (financial penalties and public censures).

13.5.2 INJUNCTION OR RESTITUTION ORDER

FSMA 2000, s 381, empowers the High Court (s 381(5)), on the application of the FCA, to issue an injunction restraining apprehended or continuing contravention of Regulation (EU) No 596/2014, art 14 (prohibition of insider dealing and of unlawful disclosure of inside information) or 15 (prohibition of market manipulation) (FSMA 2000, s 381(1)). The court may order a person to take steps to remedy or mitigate contravention in which the person has engaged (s 381(2) and (6)). If the court is satisfied that a person may be, or may have been, engaged in contravening art 14 or art 15, it has a power to issue a freezing injunction restraining the person from disposing of, or dealing with, assets (s 381(3) and (4)).

The FCA may make a restitution order against a person who has engaged in contravention of art 14 or 15, or who has required or encouraged another to do so (s 384) or may apply to the High Court (s 383(8)) for it to make an order (s 383). A restitution order may be made against a person only if either that person has profited as a result of the contravention or one or more other persons have suffered loss or been otherwise adversely affected as a result (ss 383(1) and (2) and 384(2) and (3)). The money which is paid under a restitution order goes to the person or persons to whom the profits are attributable or who have suffered the loss or adverse effect (ss 383(5) and (10) and 384(6)) and the amount is determined having regard to the size of the profit or loss (ss 383(4) and 384(5)).

On an application to the court under s 381 for an injunction, or under s 383 for a restitution order, the FCA may ask the court to consider imposing an administrative sanction on the person to whom the application relates (s 129).

In Scotland the Court of Session replaces the High Court (ss 381(5) and 383(8)).

13.5.3 REFERENCE TO THE UPPER TRIBUNAL

If the FCA decides to take action against a person under FSMA 2000, ss 123, 123A, 123B or 384 (see 13.5.1 and 13.5.2), that person may refer the matter to the Upper Tribunal (ss 127(4) and 386(3)).

13.6 OFFENCE OF INSIDER DEALING

13.6.1 INTRODUCTION

In addition to the legislation which enables the FCA and the High Court to impose civil penalties for insider dealing as market abuse (see **13.2**), there is older legislation, the Criminal Justice Act 1993, part V, which makes insider dealing a criminal offence. Unfortunately, the concepts of regulated market (see **13.6.3**), inside information (see **13.6.4** and **13.6.5**) and insider dealing (see **13.6.6** and **13.6.7**) used in the 1993 Act are slightly different from the ones used in the market abuse legislation.

Unlike market abuse, the offence of insider dealing can be committed only by an individual, not by a company.

13.6.2 SECURITIES

The Criminal Justice Act 1993, part V, protects from insider dealing the securities listed in sch 2 to the Act. These include company shares and stock (sch 2, para 1) and debt securities (sch 2, para 2), so both those categories of investment are protected both by the market abuse legislation in FSMA 2000, part VIII, and by the Criminal Justice Act 1993, part V.

13.6.3 REGULATED MARKETS

The protection from insider dealing given by the Criminal Justice Act 1993, part V, is given to what the Act calls 'regulated markets', but these are not defined in the same way as the regulated markets in EU legislation (see **7.3.4.3**). For the purposes of the Criminal Justice Act 1993, part V, a 'regulated market' is a market identified as such in an order made by the Treasury under s 60(1). The relevant order is SI 1994/187, which states that any market which is established under the rules of any of 45 investment exchanges in Europe listed in the schedule to the order is a regulated market for the purposes of the 1993 Act. The list of exchanges running regulated markets includes the London Stock Exchange and ISDX, which are RIEs and NASDAQ, which is an overseas RIE.

13.6.4 DEFINITION OF INSIDE INFORMATION

For the purposes of the statutory definition of the criminal offence of insider dealing, the term 'inside information' is defined in the Criminal Justice Act 1993, s 56(1), to mean information which:

(a) relates to particular securities or to a particular issuer of securities and not to securities generally or to issuers of securities generally;

(b) is specific or precise;

(c) has not been made public; and

(d) if it were made public would be likely to have a significant effect on the price of any securities.

Securities whose price would be likely to be significantly affected if an item of inside information were made public are known as 'price-affected securities' in relation to that information, and the information is called 'price-sensitive information' in relation to them (s 56(2)).

In s 56, 'price' includes value (s 56(3)).

Information must be treated as relating to a company not only where it is about the company but also where it may affect the company's business prospects (s 60(4)).

Section 58 gives some guidance on when information is to be regarded as made public, but s 58(1) states that the section's provisions are not exhaustive. By s 58(2), information is made public if:

(a) it is published in accordance with the rules of a regulated market for the purpose of informing investors and their professional advisers;

(b) it is contained in records which by virtue of any enactment are open to inspection by the public;

(c) it can be readily acquired by those likely to deal in any securities

   (i) to which the information relates, or

   (ii) of an issuer to which the information relates; or

(d) it is derived from information which has been made public.

By s 58(3), information may be treated as made public even though:

(a) it can be acquired only by persons exercising diligence or expertise;

(b) it is communicated to a section of the public and not to the public at large;

(c) it can be acquired only by observation;

(d) it is communicated only on payment of a fee; or

(e) it is published only outside the United Kingdom.

13.6.5 HAVING INFORMATION AS AN INSIDER

The basic idea of the definition of the offence of insider dealing in the Criminal Justice Act 1993, s 52, is to restrict what may be done by a person who is described in the section as 'an individual who has information as an insider'. According to s 57(1), an individual has information as an insider if and only if:

(a) the information is, and he or she knows that it is, inside information (which was defined in **13.6.4**); and

(b) he or she has the information, and knows that he or she has it, from an inside source.

Section 57(2) goes on to explain that a person has information from an inside source if and only if:

(a) he or she has it through

   (i) being a director, employee or shareholder of an issuer of securities, or

   (ii) having access to the information by virtue of his or her employment, office, or profession; or

(b) the direct or indirect source of his or her information is a person within para (a).

Paragraph (a)(i) covers persons who are directors, employees or shareholders of *an* issuer of securities, not necessarily the issuer of the securities whose price is affected by the inside information. Paragraph (a)(ii) is very wide-ranging: it would, for example, cover a financial journalist or an employee of a firm which prints offer documents for takeover bidders. Persons within para (b) are sometimes known as 'tippees' (people who have been 'tipped off' by persons within para (a)). An alternative terminology is to refer to people within para (a) as 'primary insiders' and people within para (b) as 'secondary insiders'. It is important to bear in mind that one essential element of the definition of inside information is that it is information which has not been made public. Once a primary insider makes his or her inside information public it ceases to be inside information and anyone who receives that information is not a secondary insider.

13.6.6 RESTRICTIONS ON INSIDERS

13.6.6.1 Restriction on dealing

The first restriction on an individual who has information as an insider is that he or she will commit an offence by *dealing* in 'securities that are price-affected securities in relation to the information' (Criminal Justice Act 1993, s 52(1)). This is explained in s 56(2):

> securities are 'price-affected securities' in relation to inside information . . . if and only if the information would, if made public, be likely to have a significant effect on the price of the securities.

By s 55(1), a person deals in securities if he or she:

(a) acquires or disposes of the securities (whether as principal or agent); or

(b) procures, directly or indirectly, an acquisition or disposal of the securities by any other person.

Other subsections of s 55 extend the definition of dealing further, for example prescribing that agreeing to acquire or dispose of securities counts as dealing.

Because it is marketplaces that are protected by the legislation, subsections (1) and (3) of s 52 provide that an offence under s 52(1) can be committed only if the acquisition or disposal in question occurs on a 'regulated market' (see **13.6.3**), or the person dealing relies on a 'professional intermediary' or is acting as a professional intermediary.

The term 'professional intermediary' is defined in s 59(1), (2) and (3) as follows:

(1) For the purposes of this part, a 'professional intermediary' is a person—

    (a) who carries on a business consisting of an activity mentioned in subsection (2) and who holds himself out to the public or any section of the public (including a section of the public constituted by persons such as himself) as willing to engage in any such business; or

    (b) who is employed by a person falling within paragraph (a) to carry out any such activity.

(2) The activities referred to in subsection (1) are—

    (a) acquiring or disposing of securities (whether as principal or agent); or

    (b) acting as an intermediary between persons taking part in any dealing in securities.

(3) A person is not to be treated as carrying on a business consisting of an activity mentioned in subsection (2)—

    (a) if the activity in question is merely incidental to some other activity not falling within subsection (2); or

    (b) merely because he occasionally conducts one of those activities.

Dealing in securities whose price would be affected by one's inside information if it were to be made public is what most people would consider to be the principal form of insider dealing. But dealing is punished only where necessary to protect a marketplace identified by the Treasury as a regulated market. People who do not use regulated markets are not protected from insider dealing: any primary or secondary insider who is not a professional intermediary is at liberty to exploit his or her inside information in sales or purchases made outside a regulated market.

The dealing prohibited by s 52(1) is an offence under the Act if the insider was within the United Kingdom at the time of doing any act constituting or forming part of the alleged dealing, no matter where in Europe the regulated market was on which the acquisition or disposal took place, or, if the dealing relied on a professional intermediary, no matter where the intermediary was (s 62(1)(a)). Dealing is also an offence under the Act, wherever the insider was located, if the dealing occurred on a regulated market identified by the Treasury as a market regulated in the United Kingdom (s 62(1)(b)). Those markets are identified in SI 1994/187, art 10, and include any market established under the rules of the London Stock Exchange or ISDX.

Dealing relying on a professional intermediary is an offence under the Act, wherever the insider was located, if the intermediary was within the United Kingdom at the time of doing anything by which the offence is alleged to have been committed (Criminal Justice Act 1993, s 62(1)(c)).

13.6.6.2 Restriction on encouraging others to deal

The second restriction on an individual who has information as an insider is that he or she will commit an offence by *encouraging another person to deal* in securities that are price-affected securities in relation to that information (Criminal Justice Act 1993, s 52(2)(a)). Gain to the insider is irrelevant to this offence which clearly exists only to protect marketplaces. Accordingly, it is provided by s 52(2)(a) and (3) that an offence under s 52(2)(a) can be committed only by an insider who knows or has reasonable cause to believe that the dealing being encouraged would occur on a regulated market, or the person dealing would rely on a professional intermediary or would be acting as a professional intermediary.

The encouragement to deal prohibited by s 52(2)(a) is an offence under the Act if the insider was within the United Kingdom at the time when he or she is alleged to have encouraged dealing, no matter where in Europe the regulated market was on which the dealing might occur or where the intermediary might be located (s 62(2)(a)). Encouragement is also an offence under the Act, wherever the insider was located, if the alleged recipient of the encouragement was within the United Kingdom at the time of receiving it, again wherever the market or intermediary might be (s 62(2)(b)).

13.6.6.3 Restriction on disclosing inside information

The third restriction on an individual who has information as an insider is that he or she will commit an offence by *disclosing the information*—otherwise than in the proper performance of the functions of his or her employment, office or profession—to another person (Criminal Justice Act 1993, s 52(2)(b)). This is the widest form of restriction. Again it is intended to protect marketplaces, and an individual has a defence to a charge under s 52(2)(b) by showing that he or she did not at the time expect any person, because of the disclosure, to deal in securities on a regulated market, or to deal in securities relying on a professional intermediary or to deal in them acting as a professional intermediary (s 53(3)(a)).

The disclosure prohibited by s 52(2)(a) is an offence under the Act if the insider was within the United Kingdom at the time when he or she is alleged to have disclosed the information, no matter where in Europe the regulated market was on which the dealing might occur or where the intermediary might be located (s 62(2)(a)). Disclosure is also an offence under the Act, wherever the insider was located, if the alleged recipient of the information was within the United Kingdom at the time of receiving it, again wherever the market or intermediary might be (s 62(2)(b)).

13.6.6.4 General defences

It is a defence to a charge of any form of insider dealing to show that one did not expect the dealing, which one had done, or encouraged others to do, or which might result from disclosing one's inside information, to result in a profit attributable to the fact that the information was 'price-sensitive information in relation to the securities' (Criminal Justice Act 1993, s 53(1)(a), (2)(a) and (3)(b)). 'Profit' here includes avoidance of a loss (s 53(6)). By s 56(2) and (3), inside information is price-sensitive information in relation to securities if and only if the information would, if made public, be likely to have a significant effect on the price or value of the securities.

Under s 53(1)(b) and (c) and (2)(b) and (c) it is a defence to a charge of dealing or encouraging others to deal while having information as an insider to show either:

(a) that one believed, on reasonable grounds, that the information had been disclosed widely enough to ensure that none of those taking part in the dealing would be prejudiced by not having the information; or

(b) that one would have done what one did even if one had not had the information.

13.6.6.5 Exemption for market makers

Market makers on regulated markets, and their employees, are exempt from the prohibitions on dealing or encouraging others to deal, provided they act in good faith in the course of the market-making business (Criminal Justice Act 1993, s 53(4) and sch 1, para 1). They are not exempt from the prohibition on disclosure. Thus a market maker can encourage others to act on the basis of inside information but must not say what that information is.

13.6.6.6 Acting within buy-back or price stabilisation rules

Under the Criminal Justice Act 1993, s 53(4) and sch 1, para 5, it is a defence to a charge of dealing or encouraging to deal that the defendant was acting in conformity with Regulation (EU) No 596/2014, art 5 (buy-back and price stabilisation, see **13.2.6**) or with the FCA's price stabilising rules (see FCA Handbook, MAR 2).

13.6.7 USE OF MARKET INFORMATION

The term 'market information' is defined in the Criminal Justice Act 1993, sch 1, para 4. Essentially it is information about dealings in securities that have occurred or are being considered or negotiated, limited to the identity of the securities, the number involved, the price (or range of prices) and the identity of the buyers and sellers. It also covers information that an acquisition or disposal of securities will not take place. Schedule 1, para 2(1), provides that an individual who has market information as an insider will have a defence to a charge of dealing or encouraging to deal if he or she can show that it was reasonable for an individual in his or her position to have acted as he or she did despite having that information as an insider at the time. Paragraph 2(2) says that, in determining the reasonableness of an individual dealing or encouraging to deal while having market information as an insider, account must be taken of:

(a) the content of the information;

(b) the circumstances and capacity in which the individual first had the information; and

(c) the capacity in which the individual now acts.

It remains to be seen whether the Crown Prosecution Service will ever want to argue before a jury about what constitutes reasonable behaviour by stock market investors.

Schedule 1, para 3, provides a defence to a charge of dealing or encouraging to deal for an individual whose inside information was only market information arising directly out of his or her involvement in the consideration or negotiation of an acquisition or disposal (or series of acquisitions and disposals) and that the dealing or encouragement to deal was in connection with, and was with a view to facilitating, that transaction or series of transactions.

13.6.8 PENALTIES

An offence under part V of the Criminal Justice Act 1993 is triable either way. On indictment the penalty can be imprisonment for up to seven years and/or a fine for which there is no limit (s 61(1)). There are restrictions on the commencement of prosecutions. In England and Wales the FCA may institute proceedings under FSMA 2000, s 402 (*R (Uberoi) v Westminster Magistrates' Court* [2008] EWHC 3191 (Admin), [2009] 1 WLR 1905), but otherwise a prosecution can be started only by, or with the consent of, the Secretary of State or the Director of Public Prosecutions (Criminal Justice Act 1993, s 61(2)). The role of the FCA in investigating and prosecuting insider dealing is examined by Michael Filby in 'The enforcement of insider dealing under the Financial Services and Markets Act 2000' (2003) 24 Co Law 334.

The longest prison sentence imposed so far is three years and four months (on a guilty plea) for eight offences committed over a period of eight years. See FSA press release FSA/PN/018/2011, which details other prosecutions by the FSA.

A contract that is entered into in contravention of s 52 is not void or unenforceable by virtue of that section (s 63(2)). Normally, however, the court will refuse to enforce such a contract because of the doctrine *ex turpi causa non oritur actio* (an action does not arise from a base cause) (*Chase Manhattan Equities Ltd v Goodman* [1991] BCLC 897). See **13.8** for a discussion of possible civil remedies.

13.6.9 INVESTIGATION

Either the FCA or the Secretary of State may appoint investigators under FSMA 2000, s 168(3), if a breach of the Criminal Justice Act 1993, part V, is suspected (see **18.8.3.3**).

13.7 OFFENCE OF CREATING A FALSE MARKET

13.7.1 INTRODUCTION

In addition to the legislation which enables the FCA and the High Court to impose civil penalties for market manipulation as market abuse (see **13.2**), the Financial Services Act 2012, s 90, makes creating a false market a criminal offence.

13.7.2 DEFINITION OF THE OFFENCE

The Financial Services Act 2012, s 90, makes it a criminal offence for any person to do any act, or engage in any course of conduct, which creates a false or misleading impression as to the market in, or the price or value of, any relevant investments. But doing such an act or engaging in such conduct is an offence only if:

(a) (the s 90(2) offence) the person intends to create the impression and does so with the intention of

    (i) inducing another person to acquire, dispose of, subscribe for or underwrite those investments, or to refrain from doing so, or

    (ii) inducing another person to exercise, or refrain from exercising, any rights conferred by those investments; or

(b) (the s 90(3) offence) the person knows that the impression is false or misleading or is reckless as to whether it is, and intends by creating the impression to produce one of the following results, or is aware that creating the impression is likely to produce one of them, namely

(i) to make a gain personally or for another, or

(ii) to cause a loss to another person or expose another person to the risk of loss.

Imprisonment for up to seven years may be imposed for an offence under s 90 (s 92).

Relevant investments are defined in s 93(5) and SI 2013/637, art 1(2) and 4, as the 'controlled investments' listed in SI 2005/1529, sch 1, paras 12 to 28. The list includes company shares and stock (para 14) and debt securities (para 15), subscription warrants (para 17) and options (para 21).

13.7.3 GEOGRAPHICAL JURISDICTION

The offence of creating a false market, defined in the Financial Services Act 2012, s 90, is, by s 90(10), committed if:

(a) the act is done, or the course of conduct is engaged in, in the United Kingdom; or

(b) the false or misleading impression is created there.

13.7.4 DEFENCES

The following defences to a charge of creating a false market, contrary to the Financial Services Act 2012, s 90, are provided by s 90(9):

(a) that the defendant reasonably believed that the conduct in question would not create a false or misleading impression as to the market in, or the price or value of, any relevant investments (this defence applies only to the s 90(2) offence);

(b) that the defendant acted or engaged in the conduct for the purpose of stabilising the price of investments and in conformity with the FCA's price stabilising rules in FCA Handbook, MAR 2;

(c) that the defendant acted or engaged in the conduct in conformity with the FCA's control of information rules in FCA Handbook, SYSC 10.2.2R (Chinese walls, also called ethical walls); or

(d) that the defendant acted or engaged in the conduct in conformity with the relevant provisions of Regulation (EU) No 596/2014, art 5 (see **13.2.6**).

13.8 FIDUCIARY DUTY

A director's duty to avoid conflicts of interest (CA 2006, s 175; see **16.9**) applies in particular to the exploitation of any information (s 175(2)). It would seem to follow that, if a director of a company buys and sells its shares as a result of information about the company obtained by virtue of the directorship, the profit made (perhaps, even, a loss avoided) belongs to the company unless the company agrees that the director should retain it. This has been held to be the law in the USA— see *Diamond v Oreamuno* (1969) 248 NE 2d 910—and the Privy Council has accepted that it is arguable that it is the law of England as well (*Walsh v Deloitte and Touche Inc* [2001] UKPC 58, 59 WIR 30).

In **Percival v Wright** [1902] 2 Ch 421, the joint holders of some shares in an unlisted colliery company offered them for sale to the company's chairman and two other directors. The price at which they were offered was determined by an independent valuer at £12 10s each. The sale of the shares was concluded but then it was discovered that while negotiating to purchase these shares the chairman had been discussing selling the whole colliery at a price that would have made each share in the company worth considerably more than £12 10s. In fact, the colliery never was sold and the court found from the evidence that the board of directors never intended to sell it. Percival and his co-shareholder asked for the sale of their shares to be set aside on the ground that the chairman had a duty to disclose that he was negotiating for the sale of the colliery at a price which implied that the valuation price of the shares was wrong. It was held that there was no such duty. In a remarkable passage, Swinfen Eady J said, at p 426:

> The contrary view would place directors in a most invidious position, as they could not buy or sell shares without disclosing negotiations, a premature disclosure of which might well be against the best interests of the company. I am of opinion that directors are not in that position.

In *Re Chez Nico (Restaurants) Ltd* [1992] BCLC 192, Browne-Wilkinson V-C said, at p 208, that he considered *Percival v Wright* to be 'very doubtful authority' for the proposition that directors of a company may purchase shares in the company without disclosing pending negotiations for the sale of the company's undertaking. His Lordship continued: 'I consider the law to be that . . . in certain special circumstances fiduciary duties, carrying with them a duty of disclosure, can arise which place directors in a fiduciary capacity vis-à-vis the shareholders'. His Lordship approved the decision of the New Zealand Court of Appeal in *Coleman v Myers* [1977] 2 NZLR 225. This concerned an old-established unlisted New Zealand company, Campbell and Ehrenfield Co Ltd. Shares in the company were held by various members of three generations of the Myers family but very few shares were held by young Mr Douglas Myers, the chairman's son, when he took over as managing director. He indicated to his father that he did not want the tough job of chief executive unless he had a sizeable equity stake in the company. So Douglas, with his father's assistance, contracted to purchase two large blocks of shares in the company on condition that he did not have to pay for them for six months. During those six months he intended to use the control given to him by holding those blocks of shares to force the company to sell valuable buildings and lend him the cash obtained thereby: he would then use the cash to pay for the shares. Other shareholders began to attack him so he launched a full-scale takeover bid in order that he could compulsorily purchase the shares of the dissentient minority (see 8.7.2). The price at which he offered to purchase shares was arrived at by an independent valuer who, however, was unaware that the company's buildings were dramatically undervalued in the company's books. All the deals actually went through and Douglas made a small fortune because the sale of the company's buildings yielded vastly more money than was necessary to buy the shares at the price that had been agreed. Minority shareholders who had been compulsorily purchased eventually brought an action alleging fraud, breach of fiduciary duty, negligence and breach of statutory duty (using the company's money to finance purchase of its shares). On the issue of fiduciary duty, it was held that Douglas and his father, as managing director and chairman, owed fiduciary duties to the shareholders which arose from the family character of the company, their high degree of inside knowledge and the way in which they conducted the takeover. Their duty was to disclose material facts. The court refused to follow *Percival v Wright*, on which Woodhouse J commented, at pp 324–5:

> the standard of conduct required from a director in relation to dealings with a shareholder will differ depending upon all the surrounding circumstances and the nature of the responsibility which in a real and practical sense the director has assumed towards the shareholder. In the one case there may be a need to provide an explicit warning and a great deal of information concerning the proposed transaction. In another there may be no need to speak at all . . . while it may not be possible to lay down any general test as to when the fiduciary duty will arise for a company director or to prescribe the exact conduct which will

always discharge it when it does, there are nevertheless some factors that will usually have an influence upon a decision one way or the other. They include . . . dependence upon information and advice, the existence of a relationship of confidence, the significance of some particular transaction for the parties and, of course, the extent of any positive action taken by or on behalf of the director or directors to promote it.

Special circumstances justifying the imposition on a director of a fiduciary duty to a shareholder were found in *Platt v Platt* [1999] 2 BCLC 745. The sole director of a company, and only owner of its ordinary shares, falsely represented to the owners of its preference shares that the company would have to be sold, because of its (truly) bad financial situation, that a sale would not be possible because of the continuing obligation to pay preference dividends, that the preference shares were worthless and that their holders (who were his brothers) should sell them to him for £1. In fact he had no intention of selling the company at that time and knew that its finances would improve quite soon. Four years later it was sold for about £2 million. At first instance, the court accepted counsel's submission that the director owed a fiduciary duty to the shareholders because he controlled the company's affairs and the other shareholders were dependent on him for information about the company, its business and the value of their shareholdings. The point was not considered on appeal [2001] 1 BCLC 698, but the members of the Court of Appeal went out of their way to state that this did not imply approval of the first-instance decision (at pp 704 and 719). So it seems that it may be too early to write off *Percival v Wright* in this jurisdiction, even though it has been abandoned in New South Wales (*Brunninghausen v Glavanics* [1999] NSWCA 199, 46 NSWLR 538). See R Goddard, 'Percival v Wright: the end of a "remarkable career"?' (2000) 116 LQR 197; 'The last rites for *Percival v Wright*?' (2000) 21 Co Law 261.

In *Allen v Hyatt* (1914) 30 TLR 444, directors of a company found a potential buyer of all its shares. They obtained from the company's other shareholders options to purchase their shares by representing that this would facilitate the sale to the potential buyer. In fact the price at which the directors exercised their options was lower than the price they had agreed with the purchaser, and the directors made a handsome profit. It was held that the directors were the agents of the shareholders for the purpose of selling their shares, and so owed the profit to their principals, the shareholders.

PART 4

GOVERNANCE

14

SHAREHOLDERS

SUMMARY OF POINTS COVERED

- What is in this chapter
- Definition
- Register of members
- Shareholder democracy
- Written resolutions of private companies
- Meetings
- Annual general meetings
- Notice of meetings
- Quorum and chair

- Voting
- Adjournment of meetings
- Records of resolutions, meetings and decisions
- Decision-making without meeting or written resolution
- Alteration of class rights
- Holding and subsidiary companies
- Authorisation of political donations

14.1 WHAT IS IN THIS CHAPTER

A company has a dual nature as an association of its members and as a person separate from its members. Membership of a commercial limited company is based on holding shares in the company which are issued in return for contributed capital. The member-shareholders benefit from the company, if it is successful, by taking annual profit dividends, or by sharing in a surplus of assets if the company is wound up while solvent. One of the principal reasons for the popularity of the company as a legal form for business enterprise is that it enables the member-shareholders to contribute capital and earn returns without taking part in the management of the company. It is assumed in company law that the constitution of a company will assign all management powers to the company's directors (see **Chapter 15**). The member-shareholders must be assured that handing over so much power to the directors will not deprive them altogether of their interest in the company. Mandatory rules of company law reserve for the members many important decisions on a company's affairs (see **14.4.4**). Company directors are constrained by their duty to act in the way they consider, in good faith, would be most likely to promote the success of the company for the benefit of its members as a whole (CA 2006, s 172; see **Chapter 16**).

This chapter starts with a discussion of the rules which determine who is a member of a company (**14.2**) and the information on its members which must be recorded by a company (**14.3**). Much of the rest of the chapter is concerned with the way in which members take decisions on their company's affairs. The members of a private company may take decisions by written resolution using a statutory procedure. Members of public companies will usually (and members of private companies may) take decisions at general meetings of members. Members of any kind of company may take decisions unanimously without meeting or going through the statutory procedure for written resolutions. The distinctive feature of the statutory procedure for written resolutions and the law of meetings is that they allow majority decisions. We have included a detailed discussion of the technical rules on meetings, because, in practice, many arguments about the validity of decisions depend on whether these rules have been complied with.

In some companies the membership is divided into two or more separate classes with differing membership rights and the alteration of class rights in such companies is considered in **14.14**.

A company may itself be a member of another company. If membership of another company gives control of that company, the relationship of holding company and subsidiary may be created. The definitions of holding company, subsidiary and wholly owned subsidiary are considered in **14.15**.

Key legislation which you should be able to consult when reading this chapter:

- CA 2006, ss 112, 113, 121–127, 153, 281–379, 527, 629–640, 1159, sch 6; and
- the model articles for private companies limited by shares and for public companies in SI 2008/3229.

All that legislation is in *Blackstone's Statutes on Company Law*.

- the Uncertificated Securities Regulations 2001 (SI 2001/3755), which are at the Online Resource Centre for *Blackstone's Statutes on Company Law*: **global.oup.com/uk/orc/law/company/company_statutes**.

The following cases, which are considered in this chapter, are particularly significant and are recommended further reading:

- *Allen v Gold Reefs of West Africa Ltd* [1900] 1 Ch 656 (also a key case for **Chapter 3**);
- *Re Duomatic Ltd* [1969] 2 Ch 365 (also a key case for **Chapter 16**);
- *Enviroco Ltd v Farstad Supply A/S* [2011] UKSC 16, [2011] 1 WLR 921;
- *Re Express Engineering Works Ltd* [1920] 1 Ch 466;
- *Menier v Hooper's Telegraph Works* (1874) LR 9 Ch App 350; and
- *North-West Transportation Co Ltd v Beatty* (1887) 12 App Cas 589.

Your particular course of study may require you to read other source materials.

14.2 DEFINITION

The definition of a member of a company is contained in CA 2006, s 112:

(1) The subscribers of a company's memorandum are deemed to have agreed to become members of the company, and on its registration become members and must be entered as such in its register of members.

(2) Every other person who agrees to become a member of a company, and whose name is entered in its register of members, is a member of the company.

The fact that a person's name has been entered in a company's register of members is not in itself sufficient to make that person a member of the company: the person must have *agreed* to become a member. This means that entry of the person's name in the register must have been assented to or authorised by the person but it does not mean that the register entry must have been made as a result of a *contract* between the person and the company (*Re Nuneaton Borough Association*

Football Club Ltd [1989] BCLC 454). Agreement is deemed in the case of a subscriber of the memorandum (s 112(1)). If the name of a person has been put on a company's register of members without that person's agreement, an application may be made to rectify the register (see **14.3.3**). Equally, if the name of a person who has agreed to be a member of a company has not been entered on the company's register of members, rectification may be sought either by the person who wishes to be a member (so as to participate in the company or sell shares) or by the company (if it wishes to claim payment for shares). See the summary of the law by Slade J in *Re Compañia de Electricidad de la Provincia de Buenos Aires Ltd* [1980] Ch 146 at p 182.

The fact that a person buys a share certificate as a scripophilist interested in the certificate as a collectable object does not in itself mean that the person has agreed to buy the shares and be a member of the company (*Re Baku Consolidated Oilfields Ltd* [1994] 1 BCLC 173).

Membership of a company limited by shares is normally based on shareholding but s 112 is drafted to apply to any sort of company. This may have the unexpected result that a person may be a member of a company limited by shares by virtue of s 112 without holding any shares. In *Re Nuneaton Borough Association Football Club Ltd*, Mr Shooter believed that he had been allotted 10,000 of the company's shares and that he had purchased a further 10,000 from a Mr Gallagher. His name was entered on the company's register of members accordingly. He believed that all 20,000 shares had been created by the company adopting a resolution to increase its authorised share capital. In fact, because of procedural irregularities, the authorised share capital had not been increased and Mr Shooter's shares did not exist. Nevertheless, the Court of Appeal held that he was a member of the company by virtue of being registered as such with his agreement.

A member who is registered in a false or fictitious name is nevertheless a member (*Re Hercules Insurance Co, Pugh and Sharman's Case* (1872) LR 13 Eq 566).

If a share in a company is held jointly by two or more persons, each of them is a member of the company (*Permanent Trustee Co of New South Wales Ltd v Palmer* (1929) 42 CLR 277).

If a company is an issuer of uncertificated shares, a person whose name is entered in the company's issuer register of members (see **14.3.2**) is not a member unless shown by the issuer register to be the holder of certificated shares in the company or by the Operator register to be the holder of uncertificated shares in the company (SI 2001/3755, reg 24(3)). A person whose shares are in the process of being converted from uncertificated to certificated form, or from certificated to uncertificated form, is deemed to be a member despite the shares being temporarily not entered in either register (regs 32(6)(b) and 33(8)(b)). This means that, in a company that has issued uncertificated shares, all members must be shareholders.

14.3 REGISTER OF MEMBERS

14.3.1 COMPANIES WITHOUT UNCERTIFICATED SHARES

CA 2006, s 113, requires every company which is not the issuer of uncertificated shares to keep a register of its members and to enter in it the particulars required by s 113. The register must be kept available for inspection for a proper purpose (ss 114 to 120; see **4.4**). Private companies will be able to keep this register at Companies House (see **4.4.2.9**).

The register of members of any company which is not the issuer of uncertificated shares must give the following basic information about its members:

(a) the names and addresses of the members (s 113(2)(a))—the names of all joint holders of a share must be given, but only one address (s 113(5));

(b) the date on which each person was registered as a member (s 113(2)(b)); and

(c) the date at which any person ceased to be a member (s 113(2)(c)) (an entry for a member must be kept for ten years after cessation of membership, but may be deleted then: s 121).

In addition, the register of members of a company with a share capital (such as a company limited by shares), which does not have any uncertificated shares, must contain:

(d) a statement of the shares held by each member, identifying, if relevant, the numbers of the shares held (numbering of shares is required by s 543 unless all the shares of a class are fully paid and rank equally for all purposes) and the class of shares held, if there is more than one class (s 113(3)(a)); and

(e) a statement of the amount paid or agreed to be considered as paid on the shares of each member (s 113(3)(b)).

A company which holds shares as treasury shares (see **10.6.6**) must enter itself in the register as the member holding those shares (s 724(4)). Provision for companies which have converted shares into stock is made in s 113(4). Section 113(3) does not apply to companies which do not have a share capital (which may be guarantee or unlimited companies), but if such a company has more than one class of members, its register must specify to which class each member belongs (s 113(6)). The entries to be made in the register of members on the issue of a share warrant to bearer are set out in s 122.

If a company is the issuer of uncertificated shares, s 113 does not apply to it (SI 2001/3755, sch 4, para 2(4)). Instead, there must be an issuer register of members and an Operator register of members, as required by SI 2001/3755, reg 20(4), and described in **14.3.2**.

The register of members of a limited company must state that it has only one member, if that is the case (Directive 2009/102/EC, art 3; CA 2006, s 123). The statement must give the date on which the company became a single-member company (unless it is the date of registration or of re-registration from unlimited to limited) and the date when it ceased to have only one member.

There is no requirement that the addresses recorded for individual members in the register must be their residential addresses: for any member an accommodation address is sufficient (*Hemmerling v IMTC Systems* (1993) 109 DLR (4th) 582). However, the recorded address must be the one supplied by the member: the company cannot itself substitute an accommodation address so as to limit publicly available information about its members (*POW Services Ltd v Clare* [1995] 2 BCLC 435 at p 451). The register may also record only the name and address of a nominee and not the beneficial owner of shares (see **8.6.1**). These factors may reduce the usefulness of the register as a means of identifying and communicating with shareholders. In public companies, the register of substantial interests (see **8.8**) may reveal more information about the beneficial ownership of shares, as may the new PSC register of people with significant control.

14.3.2 COMPANIES WITH UNCERTIFICATED SHARES

CA 2006, s 113 (see **14.3.1**), does not apply to a company if it is an issuer of uncertificated shares (SI 2001/3755, sch 4, para 2(4)). Instead, its register of members is in two parts (SI 2001/3755, reg 20(1)):

(a) The company's 'issuer register of members', which is maintained by the company itself or (usually) by an enterprise (called a 'registrar') which provides registration services for public companies (reg 20(1)(a)). The issuer register of members lists all the company's members but gives details of their holdings of certificated shares only.

(b) The company's 'Operator register of members', which is maintained by Euroclear (see **8.3.3.1**) in the CREST computer system (reg 20(1)(b)). The Operator register of members contains details of the holders of the company's uncertificated shares. The company, or its registrar, must keep a copy of its Operator register of members. This copy is called the company's 'record of uncertificated shares' (reg 20(6)).

If a company is an issuer of uncertificated shares, any reference in any enactment or instrument to its register of members is to be construed as a reference to its issuer register of members and its Operator register of members (reg 20(4)). The provisions discussed in **14.3.1** are adapted by SI 2001/3755 to apply to companies with uncertificated shares as described in the following paragraphs.

The issuer register of members of a company which issues uncertificated shares must, by SI 2001/3755, reg 20(2) and sch 4, para 2(1), record the same basic information about all its members (whether they have certificated or uncertificated shares) as is required in any other company's register of members, that is:

(a) the names and addresses of the members (sch 4, para 2(1)(a));

(b) the date on which each person was registered as a member (sch 4, para 2(1)(b)); and

(c) the date at which any person ceased to be a member (sch 4, para 2(1)(c)) (an entry for a member must be kept for 10 years after cessation of membership, but may be deleted then: sch 4, para 2(6)).

In relation to points (a), (b) and (c), if there is any inconsistency between the issuer register and the Operator register, the Operator register prevails (regs 20(5) and 24(2)).

With respect to the shareholdings of members, an issuer register of members is limited to describing their holdings of certificated shares, as follows:

(d) a statement of the certificated shares held by each member, identifying, if relevant, the numbers of the shares held and/or the class of shares held (sch 4, para 2(2)(a)); and

(e) a statement of the amount paid or agreed to be considered as paid on the certificated shares of each member (sch 4, para 2(2)(b)).

Provision for companies which have converted shares into stock is made in sch 4, para 2(3). Entries which have to be made in the register when the number of members of a private limited company falls to one and when the number increases to more than one (CA 2006, s 123) and when share warrants to bearer are issued (s 122) are to be made in the issuer register if the company has uncertificated shares (SI 2001/3755, sch 4, paras 3 and 8).

A company's Operator register of members must record (SI 2001/3755, reg 20(3) and sch 4, para 4):

(a) the names and addresses of the members who hold uncertificated shares in the company; and

(b) for each member, a statement of the uncertificated shares held by that member, if necessary, identifying which class of shares is held.

The registration of a member's shares is moved from the Operator register to the issuer register when the shares are converted from uncertificated into certificated form (or 'rematerialised') (see regs 28 and 32). Registration is moved in the other direction when shares are 'dematerialised' (see reg 33).

A company's record of uncertificated shares must contain the same particulars, so far as practicable, as are required to be in the Operator register of members, plus a statement of the amount paid or agreed to be considered as paid on the uncertificated shares of each member (sch 4, para 5(1)).

A company must ensure that its record of uncertificated shares is regularly reconciled with the Operator register of members, unless it is impracticable to do so by virtue of circumstances beyond the company's control (sch 4, para 5(2)).

It is an offence to fail to comply with the requirements for keeping a record of uncertificated shares (sch 4, para 5(4)).

A company's issuer register of members and its record of uncertificated shares must at all times be kept at the same place (sch 4, para 6(2)), which must be the company's registered office or the place where the register or record is made up (sch 4, para 6(1)). A company registered in England and Wales may not keep its register and record outside England and Wales (sch 4, para 6(1)). Unless the register and record are at all times kept at the company's registered office, the company must notify Companies House of the place where they are kept and of any change in that place (sch 4, paras 6(3) and (4)).

When a company has uncertificated shares the rules concerning inspection of the register of members apply to the issuer register of members and the record of uncertificated shares: the Operator register of members is not open to inspection (see 4.4).

14.3.3 EFFECT OF THE REGISTER OF MEMBERS AND RECTIFICATION

By CA 2006, s 127, or (where a company has uncertificated shares) SI 2001/3755, regs 24(1) and (4), a company's register of members (meaning, where the company has uncertificated shares, its issuer and Operator registers: SI 2001/3755, reg 3(1)) is prima facie evidence of any matters which are directed or authorised to be inserted in it by CA 2006 or SI 2001/3755, as the case may be. However, where a company has uncertificated shares, the Operator register of members prevails if there is any inconsistency between the issuer register and the Operator register in relation to the names and addresses of members, the date on which a person was registered as a member or the date on which a person ceased to be a member (SI 2001/3755, reg 24(2)). A central register (where the company has opted to keep its register of members at Companies House) is prima facie evidence of any matters about which a company is required to deliver information to Companies House under CA 2006, ss 128A to 128K (s 128H).

If there is an error in a company's register of members, the company may correct it if it is clear what must be done and the rights of other persons are not affected. In the case of a company with uncertificated shares, the company cannot correct the issuer register of members in a way that would involve altering the Operator register of members unless Euroclear consents to the correction (SI 2001/3755, regs 25(1) and (2)).

If there is any difficulty in correcting the register, it may be necessary to apply to the court claiming the equitable remedy of an order for the rectification of a document. An application for this purpose may be made under CA 2006, s 125, in two circumstances specified in s 125(1):

If—

(a)   the name of any person is, without sufficient cause, entered in or omitted from a company's register of members, or

(b)   default is made or unnecessary delay takes place in entering on the register the fact of any person having ceased to be a member.

An application under s 125 for rectification of a company's register of members may be made by any member of the company or by the company itself (s 125(1)). An application under s 125 is conducted under the Civil Procedure Rules 1998, Part 8, and is only suitable where there is no substantial dispute about facts. CA 2006, s 125, can only be used by an applicant who claims an immediate right to rectification. Where a right to rectification will only arise if another dispute is decided in the applicant's favour, s 125 cannot be used to try that other dispute (*Nilon Ltd v Royal Westminster Investments SA* [2015] UKPC 2, [2015] 3 All ER 372, where the real dispute was about whether the applicant was entitled to an order for specific performance of an alleged oral contract to procure the issuance of shares). The court's power to order rectification is discretionary. The court will not act on an application under s 125 if injustice would be caused to other members who have not been represented (*Re Sussex Brick Co* [1904] 1 Ch 598 per Vaughan Williams LJ at pp 606–7).

The court has jurisdiction under s 125 to rectify the register in respect of part only of a member's shareholding (*Re Transatlantic Life Assurance Co Ltd* [1980] 1 WLR 79). The order may be retrospective so that the court can declare that a person was or was not a member of a company as from a particular date (*Re Sussex Brick Co* [1904] 1 Ch 598; *Barbor v Middleton* 1988 SLT 288).

In *Re Data Express Ltd* (1987) *The Independent*, 13 April 1987, the company's register of members had been inadvertently deposited in a skip and irretrievably lost. The court treated the company as having a register which was erroneous because it was blank, and it rectified the register by inserting the names of the shareholders.

On an application under s 125, the court is empowered to decide any question relating to the title to shares of any person who is a party to the application, and generally may decide any question necessary or expedient to the question of rectification (s 125(3)). If the court orders rectification of the register, it will also order notice of the rectification to be given to Companies House (s 125(4)).

Information about the membership of a company is provided to Companies House in the annual confirmation statement (see **4.2.5**).

14.4 SHAREHOLDER DEMOCRACY

14.4.1 DECISION-MAKING BY MEMBERS

It is an important feature of company law that it allows for changes in companies—directors may be dismissed and replaced; capital structure may be altered; a company may change its name, its articles of association and so on. The legislation provides that decisions to make changes on many matters concerning a company may be taken only by the company's members (see **14.4.4** and **15.10.5**).

Decisions of members are embodied in statements known as 'resolutions'.

14.4.2 WRITTEN RESOLUTIONS, MEETINGS AND UNANIMOUS APPROVAL

Nineteenth-century company law, which was designed for public companies with a substantial number of members, all of them individuals, relied heavily on meetings as the mode of decision-making by members. In the twentieth century it became increasingly clear that written decisions are more convenient for small private companies. Brief provision for written resolutions was included in the model articles for private companies from 1948, and more extensive provision was introduced in CA 1989. CA 2006 has gone further and assumes that written resolutions will be the normal mode of decision-making by members of private companies, but that meetings are still the normal mode for public companies.

Both private and public companies must hold a meeting if a sufficient number of members request one (see **14.8.14**).

By s 281, a resolution of the members (or a class of members) of a private company may be passed either as a written resolution in accordance with ss 288 to 300 or at a meeting of members (s 281(1)). The only exceptions are that a meeting must be held to pass a resolution removing a director from office under s 168, or removing an auditor from office under s 510 (s 288(2)). The procedure in ss 288 to 300 for a written resolution is not available to public companies, which must, therefore, pass resolutions at meetings (s 281(2)). None of this affects the common law rule (see **14.13**) that the unanimous assent of members to a decision is effective, whether or not they meet or write it down (s 281(4)(a)). This common law rule applies to both private and public companies.

14.4.3 ORDINARY AND SPECIAL RESOLUTIONS

If it is necessary for the members of a company to decide on some matter and all the members entitled to vote on that matter in fact assent to the decision, then the decision is effective and it does not matter whether the members' assents were given separately or while they were gathered together (see **14.13.1**). However, in any company with more than a handful of members it will often be difficult to get every member to assent to a decision. Therefore, as a general rule, the assent of a majority of members is effective to make a decision that binds all members whether they took part in the decision-making or not.

The normal rule is that a resolution is passed if more votes are cast for it than against it (usually called a 'simple majority'). If the votes are equal, the resolution is not passed. Rules governing decision-making may require larger majorities (sometimes called 'super-majorities') for some types of resolution.

CA 2006 calls a resolution which may be passed by a simple majority an 'ordinary' resolution (s 282), but requires resolutions on many important topics to be 'special' resolutions, for which 75 per cent of the votes cast must be in favour (s 283).

Until 30 October 1929, a special resolution passed by a meeting had to be confirmed by a simple majority at a second, separately convened meeting. This inconvenient requirement was abolished by CA 1928, s 25. Before CA 2006, it was necessary to give 21 days' notice of intention to propose a special resolution, but there was also a separate category of 'extraordinary' resolutions for which a special period of notice was not required and which never required a confirmatory resolution.

When CA 2006 requires a decision to be taken by a resolution of the members without specifying whether it is to be ordinary or special, an ordinary resolution is sufficient, but the articles may specify a larger majority or unanimity (s 281(3)).

For written resolutions, majorities are majorities of the total voting rights of eligible members (ss 282(2) and 283(2); see **14.5.1**). At a meeting, majorities are majorities of votes cast by persons entitled to vote (ss 282(3) and 283(4)).

Anything that may be done by ordinary resolution may also be done by special resolution (s 282(5)). For the controversy over whether unanimous agreement without meeting and without following the statutory procedure for written resolutions is as effective as a special resolution, see **14.13.4**.

On some matters where there is a particular danger of a minority being treated unfairly, even though a special resolution is passed, a dissentient minority can apply to the court to have the resolution cancelled (s 98 (re-registration of public company as a private company), s 633 (alteration of class rights) and s 721 (private company making a payment out of capital for the redemption or purchase of its own shares)).

14.4.4 DECISIONS RESERVED FOR MEMBERS AND DECISIONS WHICH NEED SPECIAL RESOLUTIONS

CA 2006 and IA 1986 state that a large number of questions relating to a company's affairs can be decided only by the members. Many of these questions must be decided by special resolution (that is, by 75 per cent majority, see **14.4.3**). The decisions which are reserved for the members, and the decisions which require a special resolution, are decisions:

(a) to amend the company's articles of association (s 21(1)—special resolution required);

(b) to resolve to re-register (ss 88 (become or cease to be a Welsh company); 90(1)(a) (private to public); 97(1)(a) (public to private limited); 102(1)(a) (private limited to unlimited); 105(1)(a) (unlimited to private limited); 109(1)(a) (public limited to private unlimited)—all requiring a special resolution, except for a decision to re-register a limited company as an unlimited company, which requires the consent of all the members: ss 102(1)(a) and 109(1)(a));

(c) to approve a service contract of a director or shadow director of the company if it guarantees employment for more than two years with the company or within the group of which the company is the holding company (s 188(2))—a resolution is not required if the company is a wholly owned subsidiary (s 188(6));

(d) to approve a substantial property transaction with a director or shadow director of the company or of its holding company or a person connected with such a director (s 190(1))—a resolution is not required if the company is a wholly owned subsidiary (s 190(4));

(e) to approve loans to, quasi-loans to and credit transactions with a director or shadow director of the company or its holding company, or a person connected with such a director (ss 197(1) and (2), 198(2) and (3), 200(2), 201(2) and (3) and 203(1) and (2))—a resolution is not required if the company is a wholly owned subsidiary (ss 197(5), 198(6), 200(6), 201(6) and 203(5)) and the requirements for approval of transactions other than loans, giving security for loans and arrangements related to loans, do not apply to private companies;

(f) to approve compensation to a director or shadow director of the company, or of its holding company, for loss of office (ss 217(1) and (2), 218(1) and (2), and 219(1) and (2))—a resolution is not required if the company is a wholly owned subsidiary (ss 217(4), 218(4) and 219(6));

(g) to ratify conduct by a director amounting to negligence, default, breach of duty or breach of trust in relation to the company (s 239(2))—the directors may authorise something which would otherwise infringe the duty to avoid conflicts of interest (s 175(4)(b), (5) and (6));

(h) if the company is a traded company for the purposes of part 13 (see **7.3.4.6**), to authorise less than 21 days' notice of a general meeting (other than an AGM) (s 307A(4)—special resolution required);

(i) to authorise political donations in excess of £5,000 a year or political expenditure, by the company or its subsidiaries (s 366(1) and (2))—a resolution is not required if the company is a wholly owned subsidiary (s 366(3));

(j) if the company is a public company, to appoint an auditor (s 489(4)), though the directors may appoint the company's first auditor, or the first after a period of being exempt from audit, or fill a casual vacancy;

(k) unless the company is a private company with only one class of shares, to authorise the directors to allot shares (ss 549 to 551): such authority may alternatively be given in the company's articles of association, though if it is, the members can revoke it (s 551(8));

(l) to disapply members' pre-emption rights when shares are issued (ss 569 to 571—special resolution required): this may alternatively be done by the company's articles of association;

(m) if the company is public, to approve an agreement to acquire non-cash assets from founder members, in certain circumstances (s 601(1)(a)—see **17.7.3.3**);

(n) to subdivide or consolidate share capital (s 618(3));

(o) to reconvert stock into shares (s 620(2));

(p) to redenominate share capital (s 622(1))—if this involves reducing share capital, a special resolution is required (s 626(2));

(q) to reduce share capital (s 641(1)—special resolution required);

(r) to authorise the terms of a proposed contract for an off-market purchase by the company of
     its own shares; to vary, revoke or renew any such authority; and to vary an existing contract
     of purchase (s 694(2) and (4));

(s) to authorise the proposed release by the company of its rights under a contract for an off-
     market purchase; or to vary, revoke or renew any such authority (s 700(2) and (3));

(t) to approve a market purchase by the company of its own shares (s 701(1));

(u) to approve a payment out of the company's capital for the redemption or purchase of any of
     its own shares (s 716(1)—special resolution required)—such payments may not be made by
     public companies;

(v) to opt in to or opt out from automatic suspension of potential barriers to takeovers when
     there is a takeover bid (see **8.7.3**) (s 966(1) and (5)—special resolution required);

(w) to resolve that the company be wound up voluntarily (IA 1986, s 84(1)—special resolu-
     tion required unless the members are invoking a provision of the articles that the company
     should be wound up after a fixed time or on the happening of a specified event); and

(x) to approve the acceptance by a liquidator in a members' voluntary liquidation of shares of
     another company to which assets of the company in liquidation are to be transferred (IA
     1986, ss 110(2), (3) and (4) and 111(3)—special resolution required).

In addition, a special resolution is required to petition for the company to be wound up by the
court (IA 1986, s 122(1)(a)) but other persons, including the directors (s 124(1)), also have a power
to present a petition.

14.4.5 WHOSE DECISION IS IT?

A company has a dual aspect as an association of its members and a person separate from its
members. It is natural to think of the members of a company making decisions as representing the
company in its association aspect and, because the association and the separate corporate person
are but two aspects of the same thing, a decision of the members must also be a decision of the
company as a separate person. This would accord with the idea that a general meeting of members
of a company is an 'organ' of the company by which the company acts, as suggested by the realist
theory of corporate personality (see **5.5.2**). In CA 2006, for example, s 622(1) has the words 'A limited company . . . may by resolution redenominate its share capital', treating a resolution adopted
by the members as a resolution of the company. A requirement for 'the company' to take a decision
means that the members are to take the decision (*Re Duomatic Ltd* [1969] 2 Ch 365 at p 374). The
model articles for private companies, art 30(1), and the model articles for public companies, art
70(1), in SI 2008/3229, provide that 'The company may by ordinary resolution declare dividends'.
This provision enables a general meeting of the members to create a debt owed by the company,
as a separate person, to each of its members who is entitled under the articles to participate in the
dividend. In *Re Devala Provident Gold Mining Co* (1883) 22 ChD 593, legal proceedings were being
taken against a company, alleging that there had been a misrepresentation in its prospectus. It was
sought to give evidence that the company's chairman, as its agent, had admitted, at a general meeting of the company, that there was an error in the prospectus. A statement by an agent is regarded
as an admission by the principal if made to someone other than the principal, but it was held that in
this case the chairman was only reporting to his own principal because the meeting was identified
with the company as a separate person, and so his statement was not an admission by the company.

In *Northern Counties Securities Ltd v Jackson and Steeple Ltd* [1974] 1 WLR 1133, unusually, the
company as a legal person was separated from its members who made its decisions. The defendant company had failed to fulfil its obligations under a contract and had been ordered by the court
to perform those obligations. The company was required by the Stock Exchange to obtain its

members' approval before performing the contract (a point which apparently had been overlooked by the directors when they made the contract). The claimant argued that if the members failed to approve the contract, they would be in contempt of court, but this was rejected by Walton J, who pointed out that it was the company as a separate person which was subject to the court order, not the members. The members could take a decision that would effectively prevent the company complying with the order but it would then be the company that was in contempt not the members. The lack of liability of the members of a company for its contempt of court may be contrasted with the duty which its directors have to ensure that it complies with court orders (*Attorney-General for Tuvalu v Philatelic Distribution Corporation Ltd* [1990] 1 WLR 926) and a company's vicarious liability for contempt of court caused by its employees' actions (*Director General of Fair Trading v Pioneer Concrete (UK) Ltd* [1995] 1 AC 456). The *Northern Counties Securities* case may also be contrasted with *Re Arthur Rathbone Kitchens Ltd* [1997] 2 BCLC 280, in which it was held, at p 295, that the members of a company which makes a voluntary arrangement (see **20.4**) are bound by it, and referred to the members breaking the terms of the arrangement by adopting a resolution for voluntary winding up.

The circumstances in which a resolution of company members can create a contract binding the company are discussed at length in P Jaffey, 'Contractual obligations of the company in general meeting' (1996) 16 LS 27. See also **3.6.4** and **3.7** on the interaction between contracts made by a company and resolutions by the company's members to amend its articles.

14.5 WRITTEN RESOLUTIONS OF PRIVATE COMPANIES

14.5.1 PROCEDURE FOR PASSING A WRITTEN RESOLUTION

14.5.1.1 Principle

CA 2006, ss 288 to 300, provide a statutory procedure for passing written resolutions of private companies. This procedure is the normal mode of decision-making for members of private companies, because they are not required to hold meetings (s 281(1)), except to exercise the statutory power in s 291 to remove a director or the power in s 510 to remove an auditor (s 288(2)).

The required majority for an ordinary resolution is a simple majority of the total voting rights of eligible members (s 282(1) and (2)). For a special resolution, it is 75 per cent of the total voting rights of eligible members (s 283(1) and (2)). Thus a majority is a majority of the votes entitled to be cast, rather than, as at a meeting, a majority of votes actually cast.

The 'eligible members' are defined as the members entitled to vote on the resolution on the circulation date (see **14.5.1.2**), or at the time of first circulation, if there is a change of membership during the course of the circulation date (s 289).

14.5.1.2 Proposal and circulation

A written resolution may be proposed by the directors of a private company (CA 2006, ss 288(3)(a) and 291). A proposed resolution must be sent to every eligible member in hard copy form, in electronic form, or by means of a website (s 291(2) and (3)(a)). Alternatively, if it will not cause undue delay, a single document can be passed from one member to another (s 291(3)(b)). A combination of methods of circulation can be used (s 291(3)). The terms 'hard copy form' and 'electronic form' are defined in s 1168. Publication on a website must be in accordance with s 299. A document sent by a company must be sent in accordance with the provisions of sch 5 (ss 1143 and 1144(2)). Default deemed times of delivery for the various methods of sending documents are set out in s 1147 but they can be modified by a company's articles (s 1147(6)(a)).

A resolution sent to members must be accompanied by a statement informing the member how to signify agreement to the resolution (see s 296, see **14.5.1.3**) and the date by which the resolution must be passed (see s 297, see **14.5.1.3**). If a resolution is being proposed as a special resolution, that fact must be stated, and it may only be passed as a special resolution (s 283(3)).

The circulation date of a written resolution is the date on which copies are sent or submitted, as required by the legislation (or the first such date) (s 290).

The company's auditor is entitled to receive all communications relating to a written resolution which ss 288 to 300 require to be supplied to a member (s 502(1)).

14.5.1.3 Signifying agreement

A member's agreement to a written resolution is signified when the company receives an authenticated document (either hard copy or electronic) which identifies the resolution and indicates the member's agreement (CA 2006, s 296(1) and (2)). The means of authentication are specified in s 1146. Once signified, agreement cannot be revoked (s 296(3)). A written resolution is passed when the required majority of eligible members have signified their agreement to it (s 296(4)). This must occur within 28 days of the circulation date, or such other period (longer or shorter) as is specified in the company's articles (s 297). If a resolution is not passed before the deadline, it lapses (s 297(1)) and any member's agreement which is subsequently signified is ineffective (s 297(2)).

14.5.2 MEMBERS' RIGHT TO HAVE THEIR RESOLUTIONS PROPOSED

Members of a private company with the requisite percentage of voting rights may require the company to circulate a resolution which they propose and an accompanying statement (CA 2006, ss 288(3)(b) and 292 to 295). The requisite percentage is 5 per cent unless the articles specify a lower percentage (s 292(5)). A statement cannot be more than 1,000 words (s 292(3)). The members who request circulation of a resolution must pay the company's costs of doing so, unless the company resolves otherwise (s 294(1)), and the company is not required to circulate the resolution until it has received a sum reasonably sufficient to meet the expenses, unless it resolves otherwise (s 294(2)).

Members cannot (s 292(1) and (2)) require circulation of a resolution which:

(a) would, if passed, be ineffective (whether by reason of inconsistency with any enactment or the company's constitution or otherwise);

(b) is defamatory of any person; or

(c) is frivolous or vexatious.

A company, or any person who claims to be aggrieved, can obtain a court order to prevent circulation of a members' statement if the court is satisfied that the rights to require circulation of a resolution and statement are being abused (s 295).

14.6 MEETINGS

14.6.1 TECHNICAL RULES

If there is dissension over whether a particular decision should be taken, the technical rules governing meetings may be of crucial importance. When legislation requires a decision to be taken at a meeting of members of a company, the decision must be taken at a meeting held and conducted in accordance with CA 2006, ss 301 to 340, and with the company's articles (s 301).

If members who do not attend a meeting are to be bound by the meeting's decisions, all members must be given a reasonable opportunity of attending the meeting—that is, they must be given proper notice (s 301; see **14.8**)—and the meeting itself must be properly conducted: there must be a quorum, see **14.9**, and voting must be properly conducted, see **14.10**.

Members attending a meeting have only themselves to blame if they do not use the rules governing the meeting to their own advantage: no one at a meeting has a duty to explain the rules to the members—in particular, the auditor does not have such a duty (*Re Hockerill Athletic Club Ltd* [1990] BCLC 921). A resolution is not invalid merely because members who disagreed with it might have made more effective opposition had they known the rules better (*Re Hockerill Athletic Club*).

There is no requirement in CA 2006 that a company registered under the Act must hold its meetings in the jurisdiction in which it is incorporated (England and Wales, Northern Ireland or Scotland), but the constitution of a company may specify where its meetings are to be held.

14.6.2 GENERAL AND CLASS MEETINGS

A meeting that all members of a company are entitled to attend is called a 'general' meeting, whereas a meeting which only one class of members may attend is called a 'class' meeting. Class meetings are important for decision-making on class rights (see **14.14**). The law relating to meetings, and in particular the provisions of CA 2006, ss 301 to 333, applies to class meetings as it does to general meetings with exceptions which will be noted in the following discussion (s 334). The provisions of the model articles of association for public companies (SI 2008/3229) relating to general meetings apply to class meetings (art 42).

14.6.3 SPECIAL RULES FOR TRADED COMPANIES

CA 2006, part 13 (ss 281 to 361), includes special rules concerning the meetings of 'traded companies'. These rules implement Directive 2007/36/EC, the Shareholder Rights Directive. For the purposes of CA 2006, part 13, a traded company is defined in s 360C as a company any shares of which:

(a) carry rights to vote at general meetings; and

(b) are admitted to trading on a regulated market in an EEA State by or with the consent of the company.

14.6.4 NEED FOR PERSONAL ATTENDANCE

The underlying reason for requiring a company to hold meetings is that members shall be able to attend in person so as to debate and vote on matters affecting the company (*Byng v London Life Association Ltd* [1990] Ch 170 per Browne-Wilkinson V-C). It is not necessary for all the persons attending the meeting to be together in the same room provided there are adequate audio-visual links to enable everyone attending to see and hear what is going on in all the rooms being used (*Byng*). At first, the courts were unwilling to accept that a telephone conversation, lacking a visual link, could be a meeting (*Re Associated Color Laboratories Ltd* (1970) 12 DLR (3d) 338; *Higgins v Nicol* (1971) 18 FLR 343 at p 357; *Magnacrete Ltd v Douglas-Hill* (1988) 48 SASR 567). However, in *Re GIGA Investments Pty Ltd* (1995) 17 ACSR 472, it was held in the Federal Court of Australia that two people can hold a meeting by ordinary telephone connection, and more than two can meet using telephone conference facilities. Since 3 August 2009, CA 2006, s 360A(1), now provides that nothing in part 13 of the Act is to be taken to preclude persons attending, speaking and voting at a meeting by electronic means. If a traded company (see **14.6.3**) gives members a right to participate in a general meeting by electronic means, the only restrictions it can place on that right are necessary and proportionate restrictions to ensure identification of those taking part and security of the electronic communication (s 360A(2)). The model articles of association in SI 2008/3229 provide for meetings of members to be attended by individuals who are not all in the same place (model articles for private companies, art 37; model articles for public companies, art 29).

14.6.5 ATTENDANCE BY PROXY OR CORPORATE REPRESENTATIVE

14.6.5.1 Proxies

At common law a person who cannot attend a meeting does not have an absolute right to appoint a proxy to attend the meeting in his, her or its stead—a proxy may be appointed only if permitted by the rules governing the meeting (*Harben v Phillips* (1882) 23 ChD 14 per Cotton LJ at p 32 and Bowen LJ at pp 35–6). In CA 2006 there is a mandatory requirement that a member of a company is entitled to appoint a proxy to exercise all, or any, of the member's rights to attend, speak and vote at a meeting of the company (s 324(1)). Notices of meetings must state the right to appoint proxies (s 325). A member with more than one share is entitled to appoint more than one proxy to exercise the rights attached to different parts of the shareholding but there cannot be more than one proxy per share (s 324(2)).

A notice of appointment, or termination of appointment, of a proxy for a meeting of a traded company (see **14.6.3**) must be in writing (ss 327(A1) and 330(A1)). A traded company must provide for such notices to be given electronically (s 333A). This can be done through the CREST system. If notice of termination of a proxy's authority is not received before a meeting commences, or before an earlier time specified in a company's articles, it does not affect the validity of a vote given by the proxy (s 330(3)). In practice, processing proxy appointments and terminations before a meeting of a large public company is a very big task and articles usually require appointments and terminations to be delivered some time before a meeting. There is a mandatory rule in s 327 that a company's articles cannot require appointments of proxies to be delivered earlier than 48 hours before the meeting, counting only hours which are in working days. The same applies to the latest time for delivering notice of termination of a proxy's authority (s 330(6)).

Proxy voting is of great practical importance, in particular because very few members of public companies attend meetings. Usually the directors convening a meeting will want one of their number appointed proxy and able to vote as they want, so proxy forms sent out with notices will have the name of the directors' preferred proxy (usually the chairman) already printed on them. CA 2006, s 326, makes it an offence to send out such prepared proxy forms at the company's expense to just some of the members.

14.6.5.2 Corporate representatives

The right to appoint proxies is conferred on all company members whether natural or legal persons but CA 2006, s 323, also gives a corporate member of a company a right to appoint a human 'representative' who can act on behalf of the corporation at meetings of the company with the same powers as the corporation could exercise if it were an individual. The appointment must be made by resolution of the corporate member's directors or other governing body. A corporation may appoint more than one representative to exercise the rights attached to different parts of its shareholding.

14.7 ANNUAL GENERAL MEETINGS

14.7.1 REQUIREMENT TO HOLD ANNUAL GENERAL MEETINGS

From the earliest days of chartered and joint-stock companies, in which investors contributed capital to companies to be managed by directors, it has been considered important to hold regular meetings of members to which the directors are required to report. The constitutions of early companies usually required these meetings to be held once every three or six months, and they were known as 'ordinary general meetings', but in the mid-nineteenth century it became usual to require a general meeting to be held once a year with the title of 'annual general meeting' (AGM). A general meeting which is not an ordinary or annual general meeting is called an extraordinary general meeting (EGM), though that term is not used in CA 2006.

Under CA 2006, a *private company* is not required to hold AGMs at all, unless it is a traded company (see **14.6.3**). *Public companies*, and private companies that are traded companies, are required to hold AGMs linked to the reporting cycle, so as to ensure that members have a timely opportunity to hold the directors to account. A public company's AGM must be held in the period of six months beginning with the day following a company's accounting reference date (s 336(1)). Six months after the end of the accounting reference period is also the deadline for laying a public company's reports and accounts before a general meeting, which is called the 'accounts meeting' (s 437; see **9.6.3**) and for filing them at Companies House (s 442; see **9.6.4**). Normally, the AGM will be the accounts meeting. A private traded company's AGM must be held within nine months after its accounting reference date (s 336(1A)).

14.7.2 BUSINESS OF AN ANNUAL GENERAL MEETING

The AGM of a company provides an opportunity for members to discuss the company's affairs. The following matters would usually be considered at a public company's AGM:

(a) The directors lay before the company the annual accounts and reports for the most recent financial year of the company, thus making the AGM the accounts meeting (CA 2006, s 437(3)) (see **9.6.3**). The directors of a quoted company must ensure that a resolution approving the directors' remuneration report is put to the vote at the meeting (s 439). A premium listed company (see **7.6**) is required to propose a resolution relating to the annual accounts (UK Corporate Governance Code, para E.2.1) and this is usually done in other companies (see **9.6.3**).

(b) The auditor's term of office ends at the end of the meeting (assuming the annual accounts and reports have been laid), so the auditor must be reappointed or a new auditor appointed instead (see **17.4.1.3**).

(c) The accounts for the financial year must be accompanied by a directors' report, which must contain the directors' recommendation of the dividend to be paid to shareholders (see **9.9.4.4**), and a resolution will be proposed that the amount recommended be paid as dividend. (The model articles for public companies, art 70, in SI 2008/3229, requires dividends to be declared by ordinary resolution but without exceeding the amount recommended by the directors.)

(d) In companies whose articles require directors to retire by rotation (as the model articles for public companies, art 21, does, see **15.6.2**), some directors will retire at each AGM and will have to be re-elected or replaced (see **15.5.3.2**).

(e) Under the model articles for public companies, art 21(2), a person appointed to be a director by the other directors must retire at the AGM following appointment (see **15.5.3.3**) and so cannot continue in office unless reappointed by the members.

Members may be able to have their own resolutions placed on the agenda for an AGM under CA 2006, s 314—see **14.8.12**.

14.7.3 ANNUAL GENERAL MEETINGS AND SHAREHOLDER RELATIONS

Although AGMs are compulsory for public companies and traded companies, their meetings are in practice not very successful in terms of providing an opportunity for the membership to discuss company business. There are several reasons for this. First, the members of most traded companies are very widely dispersed throughout the world and most find it impractical to attend a meeting. Secondly, because of this, all questions to be voted on at meetings are decided beforehand by members who appoint company officials as proxies to vote for them. Thirdly, up to 80 per cent of the shares of a traded company will be held by financial institutions such as pension funds, insurance companies and investment companies, which rely on personal discussions with the company's directors to inform themselves of its progress and how to instruct proxies to vote and so think it unnecessary to attend the AGM. Fourthly, because of the current technical requirements of the CREST system, many small shareholdings in traded companies are held for the beneficial owner by a system-member as trustee. Because only the trustee can be recorded as a member of the company (see **8.6.1**), the beneficial owner cannot vote at meetings. Dealing with this problem is known as indirect investor enfranchisement and is being achieved partly by mandatory provisions and partly by encouraging voluntary enfranchisement.

It is hoped that traded companies will introduce into their articles provisions enabling a member (who will usually be a bare trustee) to nominate another person (the indirect investor) as entitled to exercise the registered member's membership rights. Often the trustee will be holding shares on behalf of more than one investor and will want to make several nominations in respect of different parts of the shareholding.

CA 2006, s 145(2), makes nomination provisions in a company's articles more effective by providing that:

> So far as is necessary to give effect to that provision, anything required or authorised by any provision of the Companies Acts to be done by or in relation to the member shall instead be done, or (as the case may be) may instead be done, by or in relation to the nominated person (or each of them) as if he were a member of the company.

Section 145(3) lists some provisions of the Act conferring rights on shareholders to which s 145(2) applies. It is clear that this list is not exhaustive.

In the absence of a provision in a company's articles, the court cannot extend shareholder rights to persons who are not registered holders of shares (*Re DNick Holding plc* [2013] EWHC 68 (Ch), [2014] Ch 196).

In one respect, recognition by companies of nominated persons is compulsory, when a company has shares admitted to trading on a regulated market (see **7.3.4.3**). By s 146, such a company must send to a nominated person all communications which it sends to its members generally, or to the class which the nominated person's shares are in. This includes the annual accounts and reports, and a nominated person is entitled to exercise the right under s 431 or 432, as appropriate, to demand an additional copy of the accounts and reports.

Section 151 gives the Secretary of State power to amend s 146 so as to extend compulsory rights for nominated persons. This power may be used if traded companies do not amend their articles to provide these rights.

Indirect investors also have the right, under s 153, to make requests under s 314 (circulation of members' statement), s 338 (notice of resolution for annual general meeting), s 342 (independent report on poll) and s 527 (website publication of audit concerns).

The DTI's notes on the draft Bill (para E4) said that there was careful consideration of whether anything in what is now CA 2006, s 126 (see **8.6.1**), would be an obstacle to indirect investor enfranchisement, but it has been concluded that no amendment of that section is required.

The UK Corporate Governance Code, main principle E.2, says that the board of a listed company 'should use the AGM to communicate with investors and to encourage their participation'. (See **15.2.7**.)

CA 2006, s 319A, may strengthen shareholders' involvement in company meetings. It provides that, at a general meeting of a traded company, the company must cause to be answered any question relating to the business of the meeting put by any member attending the meeting (s 319A(1)). There is no minimum shareholding qualification. An answer need not be given if (s 319A(2)):

(a) answering would interfere unduly with the preparation for the meeting;

(b) answering would involve disclosing confidential information;

(c) the answer has already been given on a website in the form of an answer to a question; and

(d) it is undesirable in the interests of the company or the good order of the meeting that the question be answered.

14.8 NOTICE OF MEETINGS

14.8.1 INTRODUCTION

The principle of the law of meetings is that a majority of members voting, in person or by proxy, at a meeting can take a decision which is binding on the members who did not attend, in person or by proxy. It follows that a decision of a meeting can be valid only if everyone with the right to attend the meeting was given notice of it and the notice was given in sufficient time, and gave sufficient details of the business to be transacted at the meeting, to enable each member to decide whether to attend.

For a resolution of the members of a company to be validly passed at a general meeting, notice of the meeting and of the resolution must be given in accordance with CA 2006, ss 301 to 335 (and, if it is a public company's annual general meeting, ss 336 to 340), and with the company's articles (s 301).

14.8.2 WHO MAY GIVE NOTICE?

The directors of a company may call a general meeting of the company (CA 2006, s 302). The directors' power to call general meetings is subject to the general duty to exercise powers only for the purposes for which they are conferred (s 171; see **16.5**) (*Pergamon Press Ltd v Maxwell* [1970] 1 WLR 1167). The members of a company may, under s 303, require its directors to call a general meeting (see **14.8.14**). The directors of a public company must convene a general meeting if half or more of the company's capital has been lost (s 656; see **10.7.7**). In the model articles for public companies (in SI 2008/3229), art 28 provides that, if the company has fewer than two directors and a remaining director (if there is one) is unable or unwilling to call a general meeting to appoint further directors, two or more members may call a general meeting. If it is impracticable to call a meeting (for example, because there are no directors of a private company), the court may order one to be called in accordance with its directions (s 306; see **14.8.15**).

A notice of a meeting issued by a person who does not have authority to issue such notices is void and even if the meeting takes place its decisions will be void (*Re Haycraft Gold Reduction and Mining Co* [1900] 2 Ch 230; *Re State of Wyoming Syndicate* [1901] 2 Ch 431). But the court will not intervene if it is clear the decisions would have been the same had the correct procedure been followed (*Browne v La Trinidad* (1887) 37 ChD 1; *Southern Counties Deposit Bank Ltd v Rider* (1895) 73 LT 374; *Boschoek Proprietary Co Ltd v Fuke* [1906] 1 Ch 148; *Bentley-Stevens v Jones* [1974] 1 WLR 638; see **18.5**).

14.8.3 WHO SHOULD BE GIVEN NOTICE AND HOW?

The default rule is that notice of a general meeting of a company must be sent to every member and every director of the company (CA 2006, s 310(1)), including every person to whom shares have been transmitted on death or bankruptcy of the holder (s 310(2) and (3)). A company's articles may make different provision (s 310(4)(b)). There is also a mandatory rule that the notice must be sent to the company's auditor (s 502(2)(a)). An auditor who has been removed from office by resolution under s 510 (see **17.4.3**) must be given notice of the general meeting at which his term of office would otherwise have expired, or the meeting at which it is proposed to fill the vacancy caused by removing him (s 513(1)).

It is submitted that s 310(1) must be treated literally, so that even members who are not entitled to vote at a meeting must be sent notice of it. It may be that, at common law, a restriction on the right to vote disentitles a member from receiving notice. This seems to have been the view of Astbury J in *Re Mackenzie and Co Ltd* [1916] 2 Ch 450 (though his Lordship thought the point immaterial to the case before him). In *John Shaw and Sons (Salford) Ltd v Shaw* [1935] 2 KB 113 (which concerned the equivalent point in relation to a directors' meeting) Greer LJ thought such a member was not entitled to notice but Slesser LJ thought he was: the third member of the court expressed no opinion on the point. However, an express requirement that all members are to receive notice of meetings may override any such common law rule. In *Royal Mutual Benefit Building Society v Sharman* [1963] 1 WLR 581 and in *Re Compaction Systems Pty Ltd* [1976] 2 NSWLR 477, such an express requirement was held to mean that members not entitled to vote at a meeting were nevertheless entitled to notice of it—however, there was no discussion of *Re Mackenzie and Co Ltd* or *John Shaw and Sons (Salford) Ltd v Shaw*.

14.8.4 LENGTH OF NOTICE

14.8.4.1 Minimum notice periods

For companies that are not traded companies (see **14.6.3**), the mandatory rule is that at least 14 clear days' notice must be given of a general meeting (CA 2006, s 307(A1) and (1)), except for an AGM of a public company, for which at least 21 clear days' notice is required (s 307(2)).

A traded company must give at least 21 clear days' notice of any general meeting (s 307A(1)(b)).

A company's articles may require a longer period of notice (ss 307(3) and 307A(6)). For the meaning of 'clear days' see **14.8.4.2**. A listed company should give at least 20 working days' notice of an AGM (UK Corporate Governance Code, para E.2.4).

14.8.4.2 Clear day rule

The minimum periods of notice required by CA 2006, ss 307 and 307A, are clear days, that is the day on which the notice is given and the day of the meeting are excluded (s 360). This clear day rule applies to other minimum periods listed in s 360(1).

14.8.4.3 Agreement to shorter notice

A general meeting of a company that is not a traded company may be called by shorter notice than is required by CA 2006, s 307, or the company's articles if the members agree by the required majority (s 307(4)). For a general meeting other than a public company's AGM, the majority in favour of shorter notice must be a majority in number of the members having the right to attend and vote at the meeting, who also hold the requisite percentage in nominal value of the shares which give that right (excluding treasury shares) (s 307(5)). The requisite percentage for a private company is 90 per cent, or a higher percentage (but not more than 95 per cent) specified in its articles (s 307(6)(a)). For a public company the requisite percentage is 95 per cent (s 307(6)(b)). For the AGM of a public company, all members entitled to attend and vote must agree to shorter notice (ss 307(7) and 337(2)). Those agreeing must appreciate that they are agreeing to short notice (*Re Pearce Duff and Co Ltd* [1960] 1 WLR 1014). *Re Pearce Duff and Co Ltd* was not cited in *Re a Company (No 004377 of 1986)* [1987] 1 WLR 102, in which it was held that voting at a meeting implies acceptance of short notice for it, which cannot, it is submitted, be correct.

The members of a traded company may, at one general meeting, adopt a special resolution reducing the minimum notice for a subsequent general meeting (provided it is before the next AGM) to a period not less than 14 clear days (s 307A(1)(a), (2), (4) and (5)). This cannot be done unless there is a facility for members to vote electronically (s 307A(3)). That facility may be a facility to appoint a proxy at a website (s 307A(3)).

14.8.5 HOW NOTICE IS TO BE GIVEN

Notice of a general meeting must be given in hard copy form, in electronic form, or by means of a website, or partly by one of these means and partly by another (CA 2006, s 308, which cannot be altered by articles). The terms 'hard copy form' and 'electronic form' are defined in s 1168. Notice given on a website must be in accordance with s 309. A notice given by a company must be sent in accordance with the provisions of sch 5 (ss 1143 and 1144(2)). Default deemed times of delivery for the various methods of giving notice are set out in s 1147 but they can be modified by a company's articles (s 1147(6)(a)).

14.8.6 EFFECT OF FAILURE TO GIVE NOTICE; WAIVER OF NOTICE

14.8.6.1 General principles

There is a long-established rule of the law of meetings that failure to give notice of a meeting to a member entitled to notice invalidates the proceedings of the meeting (the rule was applied to companies in *Musselwhite v C H Musselwhite and Son Ltd* [1962] Ch 964). At common law, a person who does not receive proper notice of a meeting, or of a particular item of business, but who attends the meeting may waive the entitlement to notice. But CA 2006, s 301, makes the validity of a resolution passed at a meeting depend on notice being given and does not allow for waiver of notice. Even so, it is likely that the court will not permit a member who has attended and voted at a meeting to object that it was invalid because he did not receive notice.

In *Re Pearce Duff and Co Ltd* [1960] 1 WLR 1014, a special resolution for reduction of capital was adopted at a meeting for which the notice was shorter than was required at that time by statute. The meeting was not attended by all members entitled to vote, and it was not realised at the time of the meeting that the notice was inadequate. After the meeting, all members entitled to vote on the matter agreed in writing (without meeting) that the special resolution should be treated as valid. It was held that the court could confirm the reduction of capital since no member was now entitled to object to it.

14.8.6.2 Accidental omission of notice

Accidental failure to give notice to one or more persons is to be disregarded for the purpose of determining whether notice is duly given (CA 2006, s 313(1)). This rule may be modified by a company's articles, except in relation to notice of a general meeting requested by members (whether called by the directors or by the requesting members) (see **14.8.14**) and notice of a resolution requested by members to be moved at a public company's AGM (see **14.8.12**) (s 313(2)).

Section 313(1) refers to accidental omission to give notice of meetings (as in *Re West Canadian Collieries Ltd* [1962] Ch 370 where a few members did not receive a notice because their address plates were inadvertently not put in an addressing machine). In *Musselwhite v C H Musselwhite and Son Ltd* [1962] Ch 964, the company deliberately failed to give notice of its annual general meeting to the claimants, in the mistaken belief that the claimants were not entitled to attend the meeting because they had sold their shares in the company even though the purchaser had not yet been entered in the register of members. It was held that the claimants, as registered holders of the shares, were entitled to attend the meeting and that, accordingly, the annual general meeting was invalid for want of notice to the claimants.

14.8.6.3 Member's request not to be given notice

A member's request not to be given notice of meetings must be ignored. This is because a meeting will be invalid if notice is deliberately not given to a member (unless that member attends anyway), even if the member has asked not to be given notice (*Re Portuguese Consolidated Copper Mines Ltd* (1889) 42 ChD 160; *Young v Ladies' Imperial Club Ltd* [1920] 2 KB 523).

14.8.7 CONTENTS OF NOTICE AND CIRCULARS

14.8.7.1 Fundamentals

Notice of a general meeting of a company must state the time and date of the meeting, and the place of the meeting (CA 2006, s 311(1)). For companies that are not traded companies (see **14.6.3**) the default provision, which may be modified by the articles, is that the notice must state the general nature of the business to be dealt with at the meeting (s 311(2)). For a traded company: (a) s 311(2) is mandatory, (b) a notice must also include the details required by s 311(3), and (c) the information listed in s 311A(1) must be freely accessible on a website. A notice given by any company must include 'with reasonable prominence' a statement of a member's right to appoint a proxy (s 325). If it is intended to propose a resolution as a special resolution, that intention must be stated in the notice together with the text of the resolution (s 283(6); see **14.8.9**).

It is not permissible to give conditional notice—that is, notice that a meeting will be held only if some condition is fulfilled (*Alexander v Simpson* (1889) 43 ChD 139, a case concerning the requirement, now abolished, for confirmation of a special resolution, see **14.4.3**). Once a meeting of a company has been summoned it cannot be postponed or cancelled unless the company's articles provide a power to do so, which the model articles in SI 2008/3229 do not (*Smith v Paringa Mines Ltd* [1906] 2 Ch 193; *Bell Resources Ltd v Turnbridge Pty Ltd* (1988) 13 ACLR 429).

14.8.7.2 Circulars

It is usual for the notice of a meeting to be a brief formal document but to send out with it a more discursive document, called a 'circular', setting out the background to items of business on the agenda. Holders of equity shares with a premium listing must be sent an explanatory circular with a notice of any meeting that includes business other than ordinary business at an AGM (FCA Handbook, LR 13.8.8R(1)). What constitutes ordinary business must be decided by each company in the light of its articles of association but is likely to include the items mentioned in **14.7.2**.

For statutory provisions requiring circulars in specific circumstances, see CA 2006, s 169(3) in **15.6.3** (representations of director sought to be dismissed), s 314(1) in **14.8.11** (members' statement concerning business of annual general meeting), ss 511(4) and 515(5) in **17.4.3** (representations of retiring auditor whom it is not proposed to reappoint or of auditor sought to be dismissed), s 571(7) in **6.3.5.3** (disapplication of pre-emption rights in relation to a particular allotment of equity shares) and s 897 (effect of compromise or arrangement).

If a notice is accompanied by a circular, the two documents can and should ordinarily be treated as one document (*Tiessen v Henderson* [1899] 1 Ch 861 at p 867; *Re Moorgate Mercantile Holdings Ltd* [1980] 1 WLR 227 at p 242).

14.8.7.3 Enabling members to decide whether to attend

The notice of a meeting and any accompanying circular must give sufficient information to allow shareholders to decide whether they will attend the meeting or not. As Kekewich J said in *Tiessen v Henderson* at pp 866–7:

> A shareholder may properly and prudently leave matters in which he takes no personal interest to the decision of the majority. But in that case he is content to be bound by the vote of the majority; because he knows

the matter about which the majority are to vote at the meeting. If he does not know that, he has not a fair chance of determining in his own interest whether he ought to attend the meeting, make further inquiries or leave others to determine the matter for him.

And see similar remarks by the same learned judge in *Young v South African and Australian Exploration and Development Syndicate* [1896] 2 Ch 268.

In *Re Teede and Bishop Ltd* (1901) 70 LJ Ch 409, notice of an extraordinary general meeting described its purpose as consideration of a resolution for voluntary winding up in order to carry out a reconstruction. In fact only a resolution for voluntary winding up was adopted and this was held to be ineffective because it was not covered by the description of the business given in the notice: a shareholder might not have troubled to go to a meeting to consider reconstruction but would have gone to one proposing a complete liquidation of the company.

It is particularly important for directors to disclose in a circular their own interests in matters being put before a meeting (*Kaye v Croydon Tramways Co* [1898] 1 Ch 358; *Tiessen v Henderson*; *Baillie v Oriental Telephone and Electric Co Ltd* [1915] 1 Ch 503; *Pacific Coast Coal Mines Ltd v Arbuthnot* [1917] AC 607). In **Baillie v Oriental Telephone and Electric Co Ltd**, Lord Cozens-Hardy MR said, at p 515, that in such circumstances a notice would not be effective unless it 'substantially put the shareholders in the position to know what they were voting about'.

In **Kaye v Croydon Tramways Co**, a notice convened a meeting of the company to approve the sale of its undertaking to another company without disclosing that the members would have to approve the receipt by their directors of a large payment from the purchasing company. The meeting was held and the resolution adopted but the Court of Appeal held that it was ineffective because of what Lindley MR, in a much quoted phrase, described (at pp 369–70) as a 'tricky notice'. See also *Baillie v Oriental Telephone and Electric Co Ltd* [1915] 1 Ch 503 per Lord Cozens-Hardy MR at p 515.

In *Pacific Coast Coal Mines Ltd v Arbuthnot*, Viscount Haldane noted that the uninformative notice in the case had been particularly inappropriate for the members who had appointed as their proxies at the meeting the directors who wanted the resolution adopted and who would benefit from it.

14.8.7.4 Explaining subject matter

Directors have a duty to give to members sufficient information for them to make informed decisions about proposals which the directors recommend they approve at meetings.

FCA Handbook, LR 13.3.1R, requires that any circular sent by a premium listed company to holders of its listed securities must, among other things:

(a) provide a clear and adequate explanation of its subject matter;

(b) if voting or other action is required, contain all information necessary to allow the holders of the securities to make a properly informed decision; and

(c) where voting is required, contain a recommendation from the directors as to the voting action security holders should take, indicating whether or not the proposal described in the circular is, in the opinion of the directors, in the best interests of the security holders as a whole.

In *Rackham v Peek Foods Ltd* [1990] BCLC 895, Templeman J said, at p 899, that directors owe 'a duty conscientiously to report to the shareholders and to furnish facts and information to enable the shareholders to decide whether to approve or disapprove' a resolution to be put to the meeting.

When directors of a premium listed company arrange for it to enter into a significant transaction with another person, the Listing Rules require that the transaction must be conditional on the approval of the company's shareholders (see **15.10.6**). It is usual for directors to promise to the other party that they will use all reasonable endeavours to obtain that approval. Such an undertaking is subject to the directors' duty to give their honest opinion of what is in the interests of the company to the company's members (*Rackham v Peek Foods Ltd*; *John Crowther Group plc v Carpets International plc* [1990] BCLC 460). In *Northern Counties Securities Ltd v Jackson and Steeple Ltd* [1974] 1 WLR 1133 the defendant company's directors had caused it to enter into a significant transaction unconditionally, apparently in ignorance of the need for shareholder approval. The court ordered the company to complete the contract and its directors were ordered to issue a circular to members recommending that they approve the transaction because if they did not the company would be liable to damages for breach of contract.

Directors have a right and a duty to advise members about resolutions proposed or supported by the directors (*Campbell v Australian Mutual Provident Society* (1908) 77 LJ PC 117) and accordingly the expenses of preparing and distributing information are payable from company funds (*Peel v London and North Western Railway Co* [1907] 1 Ch 5). However, the power to use company funds for this purpose is limited by directors' fiduciary duty to exercise a power only for the purposes for which it was conferred (CA 2006, s 171; see **16.5**).

In **Dawson International plc v Coats Patons plc** 1988 SLT 854, Lord Cullen said, at p 861:

> If . . . directors take it upon themselves to give advice to current shareholders . . . they have a duty to advise in good faith and not fraudulently, and not to mislead whether deliberately or carelessly. If they fail to do so the affected shareholders may have a remedy, including the recovery of what is truly the personal loss sustained by them as a result.

See also *Gething v Kilner* [1972] 1 WLR 337 per Brightman J at p 341 (duty to be honest and not to mislead) and *Goldex Mines Ltd v Revill* (1974) 54 DLR (3d) 672 at p 679 ('shareholders have a right to expect that the information sent to them is fairly presented, reasonably accurate, and not misleading').

14.8.8 MEMBERSHIP CHANGES AFTER NOTICE OF A MEETING IS GIVEN

A company with uncertificated shares is permitted to specify in a notice of a meeting a time by which a person must be entered on the register of members to be eligible to attend or vote at the meeting: the time must not be more than 48 hours before the time fixed for the meeting (SI 2001/3755, regs 41(1) and (2)). A company with uncertificated shares is also permitted to determine that only persons on the register at the close of business on a day determined by the company are entitled to notice of a meeting (reg 41(3)) though that day must not be more than 21 days before the day on which the notices of the meeting are sent (reg 41(4)).

14.8.9 NOTICE OF SPECIAL RESOLUTION

A resolution passed at a meeting is not a special resolution unless the notice of the meeting included the text of the resolution and specified the intention to propose it as a special resolution (CA 2006, s 283(6)(a)). Once that notice has been given, the resolution may only be passed as a special resolution (s 283(6)(b)).

In *Re Moorgate Mercantile Holdings Ltd* [1980] 1 WLR 227 it was held that the notice must set out the text or the entire substance of the resolution, and the resolution actually adopted by the meeting must be the same as that specified in the notice. Corrections of clerical or grammatical errors are allowed, or the resolution may be given a more formal wording, provided nothing of substance is altered. This means that no amendments of substance, however trivial, can be made by the meeting. It follows that a minor error of substance in the notice of a special resolution may mean that a new meeting has to be convened. However, the model articles for public companies, art 40(2) (SI 2008/3229), provides that a special resolution may be amended, by ordinary resolution, provided the chair of the meeting proposes the amendment and it does not go beyond what is necessary to correct an obvious error. C Baker, 'Amending special resolutions' (1991) 12 Co Law 64, discusses an unreported case (*Re Fenner plc* (1990)) in which the court did not follow *Re Moorgate Mercantile Holdings Ltd*.

14.8.10 SPECIAL NOTICE

Any person proposing to move any of four specific types of resolution at a general meeting of a company must give special notice of that intention to the company. Special notice is required of a resolution:

(a) to dismiss a director under CA 2006, s 168, by ordinary resolution of a general meeting (s 168(2));

(b) to appoint a person to fill the vacancy caused by the dismissal of a director under s 168 at the same meeting (s 168(2));

(c) to dismiss an auditor (s 511(1)); or

(d) to appoint as auditor a person other than a retiring auditor (s 515).

Special notice must be given to the company not less than 28 clear days before the meeting at which it is intended to move the resolution (s 312(1)). For the meaning of 'clear days' see **14.8.4.2**. The fact that special notice of intention to move a resolution has been given does not in itself require the conveners of the meeting to put it on the agenda: only members who request a meeting under s 303 (see **14.8.14**) or a resolution at an AGM under s 338 (see **14.8.12**) can force an item on to the agenda (*Pedley v Inland Waterways Association Ltd* [1977] 1 All ER 209). If, after special notice of the intention to move a resolution at a meeting has been given to the company, that meeting is then called for a date 28 days or less after the notice has been given, the special notice is deemed to have been properly given (s 312(4); *Fenning v Fenning Environmental Products Ltd* (1981) 79 LS Gaz 803). If a company has received special notice of intention to move a resolution at a meeting, and if that resolution is to be included in the business of the meeting, the company must give its members notice of that resolution at the same time and in the same manner as it gives notice of the meeting (s 312(2)) or, if that is not practicable, by advertisement or in any other mode allowed by the company's articles, at least 14 days before the meeting (s 312(3)).

14.8.11 MEMBERS' STATEMENT CONCERNING BUSINESS OF MEETING

Under CA 2006, s 314, a sufficiently large group of members of a company may require it to circulate a statement before a meeting with respect to:

(a) a matter referred to in a proposed resolution to be dealt with at the meeting; or

(b) other business to be dealt with at the meeting.

The statement must not be more than 1,000 words (s 314(1)).

A group is sufficiently large to have a statement circulated if it:

(a) represents at least 5 per cent of the total voting rights of all the members who have a relevant right to vote—excluding treasury shares, which cannot be voted anyway (s 314(2)); or

(b) includes 100 members who have a relevant right to vote and hold shares on which there has been paid up an average of £100 or more per member (s 314(2)(b)).

The relevant right to vote is the right to vote on the resolution to which the statement relates, or, if it relates to other business, to vote at the meeting (s 314(3)). Where shares which could be counted under s 314(2)(b) are held, in the course of a business, by a member on behalf of an indirect investor, who is entitled to instruct the registered member on how to vote them, the request may be made by the indirect investor under s 153, which prescribes a statement which the indirect investor must make.

A company, or any person who claims to be aggrieved, can obtain a court order to prevent circulation of a members' statement if the court is satisfied that the rights to require circulation are being abused (s 317).

Unless there is a court order under s 317, the company must circulate the statement in the same manner as the notice of the meeting and at the same time, or as soon as reasonably practicable after, giving notice of the meeting (s 315). A traded company must include it in the information made available on its website under s 311A (see **14.8.7.1**).

The members who request circulation of a statement must pay the company's costs of doing so, unless the company resolves otherwise (s 316(2)(a)), and the company is not required to circulate the statement until it has received a sum reasonably sufficient to meet the expenses, unless it resolves otherwise (s 316(2)(b)). This does not apply to circulating a statement about business at a public company's AGM, provided the statement is received before the end of the financial year preceding the meeting (s 316(1)).

14.8.12 MEMBERS' PROPOSALS AND AGENDA ITEMS FOR ANNUAL GENERAL MEETING

Under CA 2006, s 338, a sufficiently large group of members of a public company may require it to give notice of a resolution which they intend to move at the next AGM. A sufficiently large group of members of a traded company (see **14.6.3**) may require it to include in the agenda of an AGM any matter (other than a proposed resolution) (s 338A).

The same conditions (5 per cent of relevant voting rights or 100 members with £100 of shares each) must be satisfied as for a request to circulate a statement (ss 153, 338(3) and 338A(3); see **14.8.11**). For a request to put a resolution on the agenda, the relevant voting rights are rights to vote on that resolution. For a request to put other business on the agenda, the relevant voting rights are rights to vote at the meeting.

There is the same exception for ineffective, defamatory, frivolous or vexatious resolutions or other business as there is in the equivalent provision for private companies (ss 338(1) and (2) and 338A(1) and (2); see **14.5.2**).

Notice of a members' resolution or other business must be given in the same manner as the notice of the meeting and at the same time, or as soon as reasonably practicable after, giving notice of the meeting (ss 339 and 340A). A traded company must include it in the information made available on its website under s 311A (see **14.8.7.1**).

The rules on members paying the cost of giving notice of a resolution or other business are the same as for circulating a statement (ss 340 and 340B; see **14.8.11**).

14.8.13 WEBSITE PUBLICATION OF AUDIT CONCERNS IN RELATION TO QUOTED COMPANY

Under CA 2006, s 527, a sufficiently large group of members of a quoted company (see **9.5.2**) may require it to publish on a website a statement setting out any matter relating to:

(a) the audit of the company's accounts (including the auditor's report and the conduct of the audit) that are to be laid before the next accounts meeting; or

(b) any circumstances connected with an auditor of the company ceasing to hold office since the previous accounts meeting (see **17.4.3**), that the members propose to raise at the next accounts meeting of the company (which will usually be the next AGM). This provision applies where the company was a quoted company for the purpose of preparing the accounts to be presented at the next accounts meeting, even if it has subsequently ceased to be one (s 531).

The same conditions (5 per cent of relevant voting rights or 100 members with £100 of shares each) must be satisfied as for a request to circulate a statement (ss 153 and 527(2); see **14.8.11**), except that the relevant voting rights are rights to vote at the accounts meeting (s 527(3)).

The company, or any person who claims to be aggrieved, can obtain a court order to prevent publication of a members' statement if the court is satisfied that the rights to require publication are being abused (s 527(5)).

14.8.14 REQUEST BY MEMBERS FOR MEETING

Under CA 2006, s 303, a sufficiently large group of members of a company (private or public) may require the directors, within 21 days (s 304(1)), to call a general meeting. A group is sufficiently large to require a meeting if it represents at least 5 per cent of such of the paid-up capital of the company as carries the right of voting at general meetings—excluding treasury shares, which cannot be voted anyway (s 303(2)).

The request must state the general nature of the business to be dealt with at the meeting, and may include the text of a resolution intended to be moved at the meeting (s 303(4)). There is the same exception for ineffective, defamatory, frivolous or vexatious resolutions as there is in relation to a request by members of a private company to require circulation of a written resolution (s 303(4) and (5); see **14.5.2**).

On receipt of a valid request, notice must be given to the members of a general meeting to be held on a date not more than 28 days after the date of the notice (s 304(1)). The company must bear the cost.

If the directors do not proceed duly to convene a meeting, the members who requested it may convene one instead (s 305(1)) and must be repaid by the company the reasonable expenses of doing so (s 305(6)). The company can, in turn, deduct the expenses from any fees or other remuneration due to the defaulting directors (s 305(7)).

Sections 303 to 305 cannot be used to call a class meeting (s 334(2)).

In Canada, it has been held that, pending the holding of a requested meeting, there is no rule to preclude the directors from exercising their powers in such a way as to render nugatory the stated purpose of the members who requested it, provided the directors are not otherwise abusing their powers (see **16.5**) (*Shield Development Co Ltd v Snyder* [1976] 3 WWR 44). In Australia, though, it has been suggested that directors in this situation are 'caretaker directors', who must maintain the status quo pending the members' decision (*Woonda Nominees Pty Ltd v Chng* (2000) 34 ACSR 558). The court will not order members to reconsider their request in the light of changed circumstances (*Rose v McGivern* [1998] 2 BCLC 593).

Members other than those who requested the meeting have no right to have business put on the agenda for it, but the directors who convene the meeting may put their own business on the agenda (*Ball v Metal Industries Ltd* 1957 SC 315).

For the requisition of a meeting by the offeror in a 75 per cent successful takeover offer for an opted-in company, see **8.7.3.4**. For the requisition by a resigning auditor of a general meeting under s 518 to consider the circumstances of the resignation, see **17.4.3**.

14.8.15 COURT'S POWER TO ORDER MEETINGS

Under CA 2006, s 306, if, for any reason, it is 'impracticable' to call a meeting of a company in any manner in which meetings of that company may be called, or to conduct a meeting in any manner prescribed by the articles or by CA 2006, the court may order a meeting to be called, held and conducted in any manner the court thinks fit. In particular, the court may direct that one member of the company present in person or by proxy be deemed to constitute a meeting (s 306(4)). The court may make such an order of its own motion or on the application of any director of the company or of any member who would be entitled to vote at the meeting (s 306(2)). When making such an order, the court may give such ancillary or consequential directions as it thinks expedient (s 306(3)). Section 306 cannot be used to call a class meeting (s 334(2)).

This power only arises where it is 'impracticable' to call a meeting. In *Re El Sombrero Ltd* [1958] Ch 900, Wynn-Parry J said:

> It is conceded that the word 'impracticable' is not synonymous with the word 'impossible'; and it appears to me that the question necessarily raised by the introduction of that word 'impracticable' is merely this: examine the circumstances of the particular case and answer the question whether, as a practical matter, the desired meeting of the company can be conducted, there being no doubt, of course, that it can be convened and held.

The power has been used to remove practical obstacles. For example, in *Edinburgh Workmen's Houses Improvement Co Ltd* 1935 SC 56 the court reduced the quorum for general meetings from 13 to 5 of the company's 54 geographically widespread members. In *Re Beckers Pty Ltd* (1942) 59 WN (NSW) 206, one member and director of the company had died, leaving only two members to attend general meetings for which the quorum was three and only one director to attend board meetings for which the quorum was two. Furthermore, the company's articles did not provide for a surviving director to make appointments to the board to make up a quorum. The court ordered a general meeting to be convened (to consider filling the vacancy on the board of directors) at which two members present in person or by proxy would be sufficient to constitute a quorum.

Minority members of a company whose presence at general meetings is essential in order to form a quorum may deliberately stay away in order to prevent the adoption of an unwelcome resolution, for example a resolution dismissing them from directorships. The court may resolve this situation by an order under s 306 (typically reducing the number of members required to form a quorum) if the minority are in effect attempting to exercise a veto power which is not commensurate with their shareholding. See, for example, *Re El Sombrero Ltd*, in which two members holding 5 per cent of the votes each were refusing to attend meetings so as to prevent the only other member, with 90 per cent of the votes, dismissing them from their directorships. *Re H R Paul and Son Ltd* (1973) 118 SJ 166 and *Re Opera Photographic Ltd* [1989] 1 WLR 634 were similar cases in which a minority shareholder was not allowed to frustrate meetings. In *Ross v Telford* [1998] 1 BCLC 82, on the other hand, the member who was frustrating the holding of a meeting had 50 per cent of the voting rights and so was entitled to block any resolutions, and the court would not make an order taking away that entitlement.

The court will not enable the adoption of a resolution which is contrary to an agreement between the members (*Alvona Developments Ltd v Manhattan Loft Corporation (AC) Ltd* [2005] EWHC 1567 (Ch), [2006] BCC 119; *Monnington v Easier plc* [2005] EWHC 2578 (Ch), [2006] 2 BCLC 283).

When ordering a meeting under s 306, the court may vary the rules which would normally apply to meetings, so as to remove a practical obstacle, whether those rules are in the company's articles or in a unanimous shareholders' agreement (*Union Music Ltd v Watson* [2003] EWCA Civ 180, [2003] 1 BCLC 454). The court must not override a class right intended to protect the interests of members of that class (*Harman v BML Group Ltd* [1994] 1 WLR 893), but the mere fact that if any member does not attend there will not be a quorum at a meeting does not mean that any member has a class right—they all have the same rights (*Union Music Ltd v Watson*).

When a minority in a company are frustrating the holding of meetings they may also be taking proceedings under s 994 (relief of unfairly prejudicial conduct of a company's affairs, see **18.6**). The court will take into account the existence of such proceedings when deciding whether to make an order under s 306 on the application of the majority. In *Re Sticky Fingers Restaurant Ltd* [1992] BCLC 84 the majority made the s 306 application after the s 994 proceedings were commenced, and the object of the meeting was to appoint additional directors who could overrule the s 994 petitioner. A meeting was ordered, but on condition that the new board would not act to prejudice the position of the s 994 petitioner until the petition was disposed of. On the other hand, if s 994 proceedings are commenced by the minority after a s 306 application by the majority, they may be seen as merely a device to frustrate the s 306 application, in which case the court will ignore the s 994 proceedings (*Re Whitchurch Insurance Consultants Ltd* [1993] BCLC 1359). The possibility that s 994 proceedings might be taken in the future did not provide the court in *Re Woven Rugs Ltd* [2002] 1 BCLC 324 with sufficient evidence to show that it would be inequitable to order a meeting. The court would refuse to order a meeting of a company on the application of the majority if convinced that it would be used to conduct the company's affairs in a way which would be unfairly prejudicial to the interests of the minority, but usually an application under s 306 is not an appropriate forum for deciding questions which ought to be litigated in s 994 proceedings (*Vectone Entertainment Holding Ltd v South Entertainment Ltd* [2004] EWHC 744 (Ch), [2004] 2 BCLC 224).

14.9 QUORUM AND CHAIR

14.9.1 QUORUM

CA 2006, s 318, sets out rules on quorum for meetings of a company in terms of the presence of one or two 'qualifying persons'. A qualifying person is (s 318(3)):

(a) an individual who is a member of the company;

(b) a representative of a corporate member; and

(c) a proxy for a member.

The mandatory rule for a limited company with only one member is that one qualifying person present at a meeting is a quorum (s 318(1)). The default rule for any other company is that two qualifying persons present are a quorum, unless they are both representatives of the same corporate member or proxies of the same member (s 318(2)). The default rule can be modified by a company's articles.

A quorum can be formed only from persons entitled to vote (*Henderson v James Loutitt and Co Ltd* (1894) 21 R 674; Table A, art 40).

An inquorate meeting is incapable of transacting business, by definition (*Re Cambrian Peat, Fuel, and Charcoal Co Ltd, De La Mott's and Turner's Case* (1875) 31 LT 773). However, the model articles of association in SI 2008/3229 provide that no business other than the appointment of a chair can be transacted at an inquorate meeting (model articles for private companies, art 38; model articles for public companies, art 30). The chair must adjourn the meeting if a quorum is not present within half an hour of the time at which the meeting was due to start (model articles for private companies, art 41(1); model articles for public companies, art 33(1)).

14.9.2 SINGLE-MEMBER MEETINGS

A meeting is not properly constituted unless at least two individuals entitled to attend it are present. As Lord President Clyde said in *Neil M'Leod and Sons Ltd* 1967 SC 16 at p 21: 'a meeting is not properly constituted if only one individual is present, for there is no one for him to meet'. The leading case is *Sharp v Dawes* (1876) 2 QBD 26 in which Mellish LJ said:

> It is clear that, according to the ordinary use of the English language, a meeting could no more be constituted by one person than a meeting could have been constituted if no shareholder at all had attended. No business could be done at such a meeting.

One individual alone does not constitute a meeting, even if he or she represents two or more members, for example by being both a member and a proxy for another member (*Re Sanitary Carbon Co* [1877] WN 223; *Re M J Shanley Contracting Ltd* (1979) 124 SJ 239) or by being a member both in his or her own right and as trustee for another (*James Prain and Sons Ltd* 1947 SC 325).

The rule that a meeting is not properly constituted by only one individual entitled to attend is modified in the following circumstances:

(a) If the court exercises its power under CA 2006, s 306(4) (see **14.8.15**), to direct that one member present at a meeting which it has ordered is deemed to constitute a quorum. In **Re London Flats Ltd** [1969] 1 WLR 711, Plowman J described what is now s 306(4) as exceptional (at p 719) and held that it did not displace the general rule that 'a single shareholder cannot constitute a meeting' (at p 717).

(b) As s 318(1) provides for the quorum of a single-member limited company to be one member present in person by corporate representative or by proxy, a meeting of such a company attended by one individual is properly constituted and its proceedings are valid.

14.9.3 CHAIR

It is usual to appoint a chair to supervise the proceedings at a meeting. The identity of the chair may be crucial if the chair has a casting vote. The model articles of association in SI 2008/3229 give the directors first choice of chair, because they provide that the person the directors have appointed to chair their own meetings (the company's chairman) must chair any general meeting he or she attends (model articles for private companies, art 39; model articles for public companies, art 31). If there is no company chairman, or the company chairman is not present within ten minutes of the time at which the meeting was due to start, the directors present at the meeting must appoint someone to chair it. If no directors are present, the meeting must make the appointment. It may be necessary for someone to act as chair temporarily for the purpose of organising the election of a chair. There is a default rule that an individual who is present as a proxy for a member may be appointed chair (CA 2006, s 328(1)), but this may be modified by a company's articles (s 328(2)).

In **National Dwellings Society v Sykes** [1894] 3 Ch 159, Chitty J said, at p 162:

> Unquestionably it is the duty of the chairman, and his function, to preserve order, and to take care that the proceedings are conducted in a proper manner, and that the sense of the meeting is properly ascertained with regard to any question which is properly before the meeting.

The chair of a meeting has authority to decide all incidental questions arising at the meeting concerning its proceedings which require decision at the time: the onus is therefore on a person challenging such a decision to show that it was wrong (*Re Indian Zoedone Co* (1884) 26 ChD 70). Traditionally, companies manage their own affairs and do not call upon an independent outsider to chair meetings. The chair of a company general meeting is usually a member, or at least a director, of the company and will therefore be personally interested in all the procedural questions he or she has to decide. Accordingly, it is misleading to describe the chair of a company general meeting as occupying a quasi-judicial position. This is because a person in a judicial position would not be permitted to be judge in his or her own cause whereas it is an inevitable consequence of the tradition of self-government that a company chair is not disqualified by self-interest. When deciding questions, a chair must act honestly and fairly to all sectional interests, and in the interests of the company (*Blair v Consolidated Enfield Corp* (1995) 128 DLR (4th) 73 at p 87).

14.10 VOTING

14.10.1 RIGHT TO VOTE

14.10.1.1 General principle

Normally, each individual at a meeting has one vote which is exercised by a show of hands. However, companies normally allow members to have a number of votes proportional to the number of shares held, but such weighted voting rights can be exercised only when voting is by poll (*Re Horbury Bridge Coal, Iron and Waggon Co* (1879) 11 ChD 109; see **14.10.2**).

Under the model articles of association in SI 2008/3229 an objection to the qualification of any voter must be raised at the meeting or adjourned meeting at which the vote objected to is tendered (model articles for private companies, art 43; model articles for public companies, art 35). An objection must be referred to the chair, whose decision is final and conclusive. Every vote not disallowed at the meeting shall be valid.

14.10.1.2 Members

CA 2006, s 286 provides a default rule that, if a share is jointly held and votes are tendered by more than one of the joint holders, only the vote of the 'senior' will be accepted and seniority is determined by the order of the names in the register of members. Joint holders therefore have a right to instruct the company on the order in which their names are to appear in the register (*Re T H Saunders and Co Ltd* [1908] 1 Ch 415). The default rule may be modified by a company's articles (s 286(3)).

If a share has been sold but, at the date of a meeting, the transfer has not been completed because the share has not been paid for, the unpaid vendor retains the right to vote in respect of the share (*Musselwhite v C H Musselwhite and Son Ltd* [1962] Ch 964). If a vendor of a share has not been paid for it but the transfer has been registered, the buyer must vote in accordance with the unpaid vendor's instructions (*Musselwhite*).

If a share is held as a treasury share (see **10.6.6**), the rights to attend and vote at meetings in respect of the share are suspended and any purported exercise of those rights is void (s 726(1) and (2)).

14.10.1.3 Trustees in bankruptcy and personal representatives

Under the model articles of association in SI 2008/3229, a person who holds a share as a trustee in bankruptcy or a personal representative, though entitled under CA 2006, s 310(2), to notice of company meetings, is not, unless registered as a member in respect of a share, generally entitled to exercise any right conferred by membership in relation to company meetings (SI 2008/3229, model articles for private companies, art 27(3); model articles for public companies, art 66(2)). A bankrupt who is still registered as a member in respect of his or her shares remains entitled to attend and vote at company meetings though obliged to vote in accordance with the directions of his or her trustee in bankruptcy because the trustee has the beneficial interest in the shares (*Wise v Lansdell* [1921] 1 Ch 420; *Morgan v Gray* [1953] Ch 83).

14.10.1.4 Trustees

Under the model articles of association in SI 2008/3229, the only interest in one of its shares that a company will recognise is an absolute right of the registered shareholder to the whole share, except as otherwise provided by the articles or by law (model articles for private companies, art 23; model articles for public companies, art 45). By CA 2006, s 126, a company is not affected by notice that any of its shares are held on trust (see **8.6.1**). Therefore, if a share in a company is held on trust, a beneficiary of the trust cannot insist that the company accept their vote instead of the vote of the trustee who is the registered holder of the share. The court can, however, order a company not to act on a resolution adopted by means of votes cast in breach of trust (*McGrattan v McGrattan* [1985] NI 28).

14.10.1.5 Freezing orders

While investigations are in progress about the true ownership of shares in a company, those shares may be subjected to restrictions, imposed by the court or the Secretary of State, which, *inter alia*, prevent the votes attached to those shares being exercised. For details, see **8.8.5** and **18.8.3.2**.

14.10.1.6 Non-members

It has been held in Australia that a provision in a company's articles cannot give a non-member a right to vote at members' meetings (other than as a proxy or corporate representative) because such a provision would be inconsistent with the companies legislation (*Shears v Phosphate Co-operative Co of Australia Ltd* (1988) 14 ACLR 747). The provisions of CA 2006 concerned with company meetings are concerned only with resolutions of members (or of a class of members) (see, for example, ss 281 to 285), and s 324(1) confers the right to appoint a proxy only on members.

14.10.2 METHOD OF VOTING

14.10.2.1 Show of hands or poll

CA 2006, ss 282 to 284, provide for two methods of voting:

(a) *A show of hands.* Voters in favour of a resolution are asked to raise a hand each and are counted; the same is done for voters against the motion. Each voter can be counted only once, unless voting both in person and as a proxy or voting as a proxy for two or more absent members. The default rule in s 285(1) and (2) is that a proxy appointed by two or members can vote both for and against if so instructed by different members.

(b) *A poll.* A written record is made of each voter's vote and the numbers for and against the motion are counted. The default rule in s 284(3) is that, on a poll, every member has one vote for every share held, subject to any rights or restrictions attached to shares. On a poll, a member entitled to more than one vote need not use all of them, and may cast some for and some against the resolution (s 322)—this enables a member holding shares as nominee for two or more beneficial owners to cast votes as they wish.

The default rules apply to a company unless its articles provide otherwise.

By s 282(3), an ordinary resolution is passed at a meeting on a show of hands if it is passed by a simple majority of the votes cast by persons entitled to vote. By s 283(4) a special resolution is passed on a show of hands if it is passed by not less than 75 per cent of the votes cast by persons entitled to vote.

An ordinary resolution is passed on a poll if it is passed by members representing a simple majority of the total voting rights of members who (being entitled to do so) vote in person, by proxy or in advance on the resolution (s 282(4)). A special resolution is passed on a poll if it is passed by members representing not less than 75 per cent of the total voting rights of those persons (s 283(5)).

It is common for poll votes to be cast in advance of a meeting and a company's articles may make specific provision for this (s 322A(1)). A company cannot require advance votes to be received earlier than 48 hours before a meeting, counting only hours that are in working days (s 322A(3) and (4)).

14.10.2.2 Proxy voting

A member appointing a proxy may instruct the proxy on how to vote or may leave it to the proxy's discretion. A proxy must vote in accordance with any instructions given (CA 2006, s 324A).

14.10.2.3 Casting vote

A casting vote is a vote which the chair has, in addition to any other vote he or she can exercise, but which can be used only when there is otherwise an equality of votes for and against an ordinary resolution. There is no common law right to a casting vote: if the rules governing a meeting do not provide for a casting vote, an ordinary resolution on which there is an equality of votes is lost. The articles of some companies deliberately do not provide for a casting vote so as to preserve equality between joint venturers.

CA 2006, s 282, does not permit an ordinary resolution of the members of a company to be passed by means of a casting vote. The section defines an ordinary resolution as one that is passed by a simple majority (s 282(1)) and the definitions of 'simple majority' in s 282(2) to (4) do not mention the use of a casting vote. This seems to have been an unexpected consequence of the section. As late as July 2007, the draft model articles for companies to be registered under CA 2006 gave a casting vote to the chair of a meeting of members of a company. Eventually, the government decided to validate any provision for a casting vote that was in any company's articles of association before 1 October 2007 (SI 2007/3495, sch 5, para 2(1) and (5)). This validation took effect on 14 January 2008 (SI 2007/3495, art 2(6)). In addition any company that deleted a provision for a casting vote that was in its articles before 1 October 2007 (on learning that such a provision was ineffective) can put it back, on or after 14 January 2008. However, as from 3 August 2009, a provision for a casting vote at meetings of members of a traded company (see **14.6.3**) is ineffective (SI 2007/2194, sch 3, para 23A(4), inserted by SI 2009/1632, reg 22).

14.10.2.4 Need for a demand for a poll

Because there is only one vote each on a show of hands but one vote per share on a poll, the two methods of voting can, and often do, produce opposite results. It is therefore very important to know which method of voting is to be used on any particular question. The articles of a company may not exclude the right to demand a poll, except on the questions of who is to chair a meeting and whether a meeting is to be adjourned (CA 2006, s 321(1)). Under the model articles of association in SI 2008/3229, a decision is to be taken by show of hands unless there is a demand for a poll (model articles of association for private companies, art 42; model articles for public companies, art 34). A poll on a resolution may be demanded before there is a show of hands (and even before the meeting starts) or immediately after the result of a show of hands is declared (model articles of association for private companies, art 44(1); model articles for public companies, art 36(1)).

If there is no demand for a poll, the chair's declaration of the result of a show of hands and a statement of that declaration entered in the minutes are conclusive evidence of the fact stated (CA 2006, s 320).

In *Re Horbury Bridge Coal, Iron and Waggon Co* (1879) 11 ChD 109 a question had to be decided at a company general meeting and only an ordinary resolution (simple majority) was required. On a show of hands, three voters holding altogether 50 shares voted in favour and two voters holding altogether 65 shares voted against. No poll was demanded but the chairman declared that those voting against had won. It was held that this was wrong because if no poll was demanded, the question had to be determined by show of hands only, ignoring the weighted voting rights which were available only when voting was by poll. There was then no statutory provision equivalent to s 320 and the company's articles did not make such a provision, so the chairman's declaration of the result was not conclusive—see *Arnot v United African Lands Ltd* [1901] 1 Ch 518.

For meetings of premium listed companies, proxy appointment forms instruct the proxy how to vote, so the balance of those votes is usually known before the meeting starts. The UK Corporate Governance Code, para E.2.2, says that all proxy votes should be counted and the level of proxies for and against each resolution (and number of abstentions) should be indicated after the resolution has been dealt with by show of hands, unless a poll has already been demanded.

14.10.2.5 Who may demand a poll?

It is common for articles to provide that a demand for a poll is ineffective unless supported by a significant proportion of the membership. CA 2006, s 321, permits such conditions within limits: the articles must at least provide that the following persons may demand a poll (s 321(2)):

(a) not less than five members having the right to vote on the resolution; or

(b) a member or members representing not less than 10 per cent of the total voting rights of all the members having the right to vote on the resolution (excluding treasury shares, see **10.6.6**); or

(c) a member or members holding shares in the company conferring a right to vote on the resolution (excluding treasury shares), being shares on which an aggregate sum has been paid up equal to not less than 10 per cent of the total sum paid up on all the shares conferring that right.

A proxy for a member has the same right to demand a poll as that member has (s 329).

The model articles of association in SI 2008/3229, are more generous in that they allow a poll to be demanded by two members rather than five and also allow a poll to be demanded by the chair of the meeting (model articles of association for private companies, art 44(2); model articles for public companies, art 36(2)). The chair of a meeting is given a power to demand a poll in order that he or she can ascertain the sense of the meeting upon a matter before them (*Second Consolidated Trust Ltd v Ceylon Amalgamated Tea and Rubber Estates Ltd* [1943] 2 All ER 567). It would seem therefore that the chair must exercise the power whenever he or she is aware that a poll would reverse a decision obtained by show of hands.

In private companies it is usual to modify model articles to provide that any one member present in person or by proxy may demand a poll: this modification is necessary because private companies usually have a small membership. For an example of extraordinary results that can follow from not having an article on demands for a poll that is appropriate to the company's circumstances, see *Siemens Brothers and Co Ltd v Burns* [1918] 2 Ch 325, discussed in **18.5**.

In addition to the right to demand a poll conferred by CA 2006, s 321(2), if rights attached to a class of shares are to be varied pursuant to s 630 (see **14.14.2**), any holder of shares of the class in question who is present at a class meeting may demand a poll (s 334(6)). Notwithstanding anything in a company's articles, any member of the company may, in person or by proxy, demand a poll on a special resolution to confer, revoke or renew authority for an off-market purchase of its own shares (s 695(4)(b) and (c)) or on a special resolution approving a payment out of the company's capital for the redemption or purchase of any of its own shares (s 717(4)(b) and (c)).

14.10.2.6 Polls taken by quoted companies

Whenever a poll is taken at a meeting of a company that is a traded company (see **14.6.3**) or is quoted (see **7.3.4.6**) but not traded, the text of the resolution and the results of the voting must be published on a website (CA 2006, s 341). If there is a failure to comply with this requirement, every officer of the company in default will be liable to a fine.

Under s 342, a sufficiently large group of members of a quoted company may require the company to appoint an independent assessor to report on any poll taken, or to be taken, at a general meeting. The same conditions (5 per cent of relevant voting rights or 100 members with £100 of shares each) must be satisfied as for a request to circulate a statement (ss 153 and 338(3); see **14.8.11**), except that the relevant voting rights are rights to vote on the matter to which the poll relates. There are detailed provisions in ss 343 to 351.

14.10.3 CONFLICT OF INTEREST AND DUTY WHEN VOTING

As will be explained in **16.9**, a director of a company is under a duty to avoid conflicts of interest (CA 2006, s 175). However, it has often been stated that a member of a company is not, when voting as a member, subject to any no-conflict rule, because a member of a company is not a fiduciary for the company. In *Peters' American Delicacy Co Ltd v Heath* (1939) 61 CLR 457, Dixon J said, at p 504:

> The shareholders are not trustees for one another, and, unlike directors, they occupy no fiduciary position and are under no fiduciary duties. They vote in respect of their shares, which are property, and the right to vote is attached to the share itself as an incident of property to be enjoyed and exercised for the owner's personal advantage.

It follows that a member who is also a director is not subject to the no-conflict rule when voting as a member (*North-West Transportation Co Ltd v Beatty* (1887) 12 App Cas 589; *Re Express Engineering Works Ltd* [1920] 1 Ch 466; *Baird v J Baird and Co (Falkirk) Ltd* 1949 SLT 368). In **North-West Transportation Co Ltd v Beatty**, Sir Richard Baggallay said, at p 593:

> Unless some provision to the contrary is to be found in the charter or other instrument by which the company is incorporated, the resolution of a majority of the shareholders, duly convened, upon any question with which the company is legally competent to deal, is binding upon the minority, and consequently upon the company, and every shareholder has a perfect right to vote upon any such question, although he may have a personal interest in the subject-matter opposed to, or different from, the general or particular interests of the company.

In the same vein, Jessel MR in **Pender v Lushington** (1877) 6 ChD 70 observed, at p 75:

> a man may be actuated in giving his vote by interests entirely adverse to the interests of the company as a whole. He may think it more for his particular interest that a certain course may be taken which may be in the opinion of others very adverse to the interests of the company as a whole, but he cannot be restrained from giving his vote in what way he pleases because he is influenced by that motive.

Also widely quoted is Lord Maugham's remark in *Carruth v Imperial Chemical Industries Ltd* [1937] AC 707 at p 765:

> the shareholders' vote is a right of property, and prima facie may be exercised by a shareholder as he thinks fit in his own interest.

These remarks focus on the freedom of a member of a company to benefit from membership. Majority members are not so free to use their voting power to damage the interests of the minority, as will be seen in **14.10.4** and **14.10.5**. One area in which a decision by members may be declared to be invalid by the courts, alteration of the articles of association, has already been discussed in **3.6.5**.

There are the following statutory restrictions on self-interested voting on members' resolutions:

(a) When counting votes in favour of ratifying a director's negligence, default, breach of duty or breach of trust, unless the resolution is passed unanimously, votes by the directors and any member connected with the director must be ignored (CA 2006, s 239(3), (4) and (6)).

(b) When counting votes in favour of a special resolution to confer, vary, revoke or renew authority to make an off-market purchase of its own shares, to vary a contract for the purchase of its own shares or to release the company's rights under such a contract, votes attaching to the shares to be purchased must be ignored (ss 695, 698 and 700(5)).

(c) When counting votes in favour of a special resolution of a private company to make a payment out of capital to redeem or repurchase its shares, votes attaching to the shares to be redeemed or repurchased must be ignored (s 717(2) and (3)).

14.10.4 VOTING BONA FIDE FOR THE BENEFIT OF THE COMPANY AND FOR A PROPER PURPOSE

In some cases, the courts have sought to prevent misuse of the power of a majority to bind a minority by ruling that members of a company are required to vote bona fide in what they consider to be the interests of the company (for example, *Allen v Gold Reefs of West Africa Ltd* [1900] 1 Ch 656; see **3.6.5.1**) and not for an improper purpose (*Re Western Mines Ltd* (1975) 65 DLR (3d) 307 at p 313). These limitations are expressed in the same terms as the fiduciary duties of directors which, under CA 2006, have been reformulated as statutory duties to act within powers (s 171; see **16.5**) and to promote the success of the company (s 172; see **16.6**). In the case of directors, the fiduciary duties applied, and the statutory duties now apply, to every exercise of their powers. Members of a company do not have a fiduciary relationship with it, nor does a majority of members of a company have a fiduciary relationship with the minority (*Brant Investments Ltd v KeepRite Inc* (1991) 80 DLR (4th) 161). So, limitations on the exercise of members' power to vote at general and class meetings have been imposed only in certain circumstances.

The circumstances in which members are required to vote bona fide in what they consider are the interests of the company and not for an improper purpose are:

(a) When the members are exercising the company's statutory power to amend its articles of association: then an alteration must be bona fide for the benefit of the company as a whole (see **3.6.5.1**, where it is noted that this condition may be inappropriate where the alteration affects only the rights of members *inter se*).

(b) An appointment of a director must be made for the benefit of the company as a whole and not for any ulterior purpose (*Re H R Harmer Ltd* [1959] 1 WLR 62 per Jenkins LJ at p 82). See further **15.5.3.2**.

(c) At a class meeting the power of the majority to bind the minority must be exercised for the purpose of benefiting the class as a whole, not only particular members (*British America Nickel Corporation Ltd v M J O'Brien Ltd* [1927] AC 369 per Viscount Haldane at p 371). The importance of this rule is illustrated by *Re Holders Investment Trust Ltd* [1971] 1 WLR 583. The company sought to reduce its capital by cancelling all of its redeemable preference shares (which were due for redemption in ten months' time) and issuing unsecured loan stock (redeemable in 15 to 20 years' time) to the holders in exchange for their preference shares. The exchange had been approved at a class meeting of the preference shareholders but the majority voting in favour were also holders of ordinary shares in the company and it was proved that they voted in favour of the exchange only because it would improve the position of ordinary shareholders. Megarry J held that they had not given an effective approval of the reduction of capital. However, L S Sealy, 'Equitable and other fetters on the shareholder's freedom to vote', in N E Eastham and B Krivy (eds), *The Cambridge Lectures 1981* (Toronto: Butterworths, 1982), attacked the rule as wrong and based on a misinterpretation of previous authorities. The rule has been affirmed, at least in relation to class meetings ordered by the court under CA 2006, s 899, to consider a compromise or arrangement, in *Re Dee Valley Group plc* [2017] EWHC 184 (Ch), [2017] WLR (D) 85.

(d) When voting on whether the company should take legal proceedings to enforce its rights against persons in control of the company in respect of a matter that is illegal or *ultra vires* or is of a fraudulent character, members must vote bona fide in the interests of the company and not for an improper purpose, in particular, a member must not vote with a view to supporting the intended defendants to the claim rather than securing benefit to the company (*Taylor v National Union of Mineworkers (Derbyshire Area)* [1985] BCLC 237 at p 255; *Smith v Croft (No 2)* [1988] Ch 114 at p 186). See also **16.16.2** on disinterested voting when ratifying directors' breach of duty.

There have been two cases, *Phillips v Manufacturers' Securities Ltd* (1917) 86 LJ Ch 305 and *Harris v A Harris Ltd* 1936 SC 183, in which the judges seem to have disagreed over whether it was appropriate to ask whether the resolution in question had been adopted bona fide for the benefit of the company and for a proper purpose, or whether it was sufficient to ask whether the resolution was *ultra vires*, fraudulent or oppressive (see **14.10.5**). However, in both cases the resolutions in question were upheld by the courts so that the form of the test to be applied was not crucial to the outcome of the cases.

14.10.5 *ULTRA VIRES*, FRAUDULENT OR OPPRESSIVE RESOLUTIONS

Minority members of a company may bring a claim to question a decision of the majority that is *ultra vires*, fraudulent or oppressive (*MacDougall v Gardiner* (1875) 1 ChD 13 per James LJ at pp 21–2). Claims to question *ultra vires* decisions will be considered in **18.4.6**.

A decision that is fraudulent or oppressive towards shareholders who oppose it is often referred to as a 'fraud on the minority'. The general principle was stated in *Arrow Nominees Inc v Blackledge* [2000] 2 BCLC 167 by Chadwick LJ at p 197: equity imposes on majority shareholders an obligation not to use the powers attached to their shares to obtain a benefit at the expense of the company or the minority. A leading example is **Menier v Hooper's Telegraph Works** (1874) LR 9 Ch App 350, in which the major shareholder in a company had contracted to make and lay a submarine telegraph cable for the company but found that it was more advantageous to do the work for another person and so caused the company to abandon the contract. James LJ said, at p 353:

> The minority of the shareholders say in effect that the majority has divided the assets of the company, more or less, between themselves, to the exclusion of the minority. I think it would be a shocking thing if that could be done, because if so the majority might divide the whole assets of the company, and pass a resolution that everything must be given to them, and that the minority should have nothing to do with it. Assuming the case to be as alleged ... then the majority have put something into their pockets at the expense of the minority. If so, it appears to me that the minority have a right to have their share of the benefits ascertained for them in the best way in which the court can do it, and given to them.

In **Estmanco (Kilner House) Ltd v Greater London Council** [1982] 1 WLR 2 the company had been formed to carry into effect an agreement with the council. The directors instituted a claim in the company's name for specific performance of the agreement but a shareholders' meeting (at which the council was the only shareholder entitled to vote) instructed the directors to discontinue the claim. It was accepted that this instruction was effective (for the controversy on this issue, see **15.10.3**). But Megarry V-C said, at p 16:

> No right of a shareholder to vote in his own selfish interests or to ignore the interests of the company entitles him with impunity to injure his voteless fellow shareholders by depriving the company of a cause of action and stultifying the purpose for which the company was formed.

His Lordship therefore permitted a voteless shareholder to continue the claim in her own name as a derivative claim (see **18.4.2.4** for the effect of changes in the law on the procedure taken in this case).

In **Clemens v Clemens Bros Ltd** [1976] 2 All ER 268, the two shareholders in Clemens Bros Ltd were Miss Clemens (who had 55 per cent of the votes) and her niece, the claimant in the case (who had 45 per cent). They had inherited their shares. The claimant had resigned her directorship after disagreements with her aunt. Miss Clemens had remained a director and there were four other directors who the claimant thought aligned themselves with her aunt against her.

Miss Clemens exercised her voting rights so as to secure the passing of a resolution authorising the issue of new shares to directors other than herself and to an employee trust scheme. (The case occurred before the enactment of the provisions on members' pre-emption rights to subscribe for new shares discussed in **6.3.5**.) The effect of the issue was to reduce the claimant's holding in the company to under 25 per cent (thus preventing her from being able to stop the passing of extraordinary and special resolutions) and to reduce the value of her rights under the company's articles to purchase any shares which other members wanted to sell. She applied to the court to have the resolution set aside. Foster J found (at p 279) that the number of new shares to be issued had been deliberately chosen so as to reduce the claimant's holding to less than 25 per cent. His Lordship said, at p 282:

> in such a case as the present Miss Clemens is not entitled to exercise her majority vote in whatever way she pleases. The difficulty is in finding a principle, and obviously expressions such as 'bona fide for the benefit of the company as a whole', 'fraud on a minority' and 'oppressive' do not assist in formulating a principle.
>
> I have come to the conclusion that it would be unwise to try to produce a principle, since the circumstances of each case are infinitely varied. It would not, I think, assist to say more than that in my judgment Miss Clemens is not entitled as of right to exercise her votes as an ordinary shareholder in any way she pleases. To use the phrase of Lord Wilberforce [in *Ebrahimi v Westbourne Galleries Ltd* [1973] AC 360 at p 379], that right is 'subject . . . to equitable considerations . . . which may make it unjust . . . to exercise [it] in a particular way'. Are there then any such considerations in this case?
>
> I do not doubt that Miss Clemens is in favour of the resolutions and knows and understands their purport and effect; nor do I doubt that she genuinely would like to see the other directors have shares in the company and to see a trust set up for long service employees. But I cannot escape the conclusion that the resolutions have been framed so as to put into the hands of Miss Clemens and her fellow directors complete control of the company and to deprive the [claimant] of her existing rights as a shareholder with more than 25 per cent of the votes and greatly reduce her [rights to purchase other members' shares]. They are specifically and carefully designed to ensure not only that the [claimant] can never get control of the company but to deprive her of what has been called her negative control. Whether I say that these proposals are oppressive to the [claimant] or that no one could honestly believe they are for her benefit matters not. A court of equity will in my judgment regard these considerations as sufficient to prevent the consequences arising from Miss Clemens using her legal right to vote in the way that she has and it would be right for a court of equity to prevent such consequences taking effect.

Clemens v Clemens Bros Ltd may be contrasted with *Greenhalgh v Arderne Cinemas Ltd* [1946] 1 All ER 512. The shares of Arderne Cinemas Ltd were originally all 10s (50p) shares. Its articles provided that on a poll a member had one vote for each share held. Mr Greenhalgh had contributed capital to the company under an agreement which provided that the shares allotted to him would be subdivided into 2s (10p) shares so that he would have five times as many votes for his money as the other members. Two other members of the company made a contract with him that they would always vote their shares with him. Two years later, however, they transferred nearly all their shares to opponents of Mr Greenhalgh. In earlier proceedings, the Court of Appeal had held that this transfer was permitted by the articles and was not a breach of the voting contract (*Greenhalgh v Mallard* [1943] 2 All ER 234). Then a general meeting of the company resolved to subdivide all the remaining 10s shares into 2s shares so that in future Mr Greenhalgh would be outvoted. The Court of Appeal refused to declare the subdivision resolution invalid. It pointed out that when he invested in the company, Mr Greenhalgh could have protected himself from such a move by insisting on changes being made in the articles. The case was argued on the basis of implying a term into Mr Greenhalgh's agreement with the company that the company would not alter his voting control, but the court held that such a term was not implied. In *Clemens v Clemens Bros Ltd* it was thought appropriate to invoke equitable principles of conscionability and fairness but *Greenhalgh v Arderne Cinemas Ltd* was confined to legal questions concerning the interpretation of contracts.

The idea that equitable considerations may make it unjust for a company member to exercise a vote in a particular way also appears in cases in which the court has given relief for conduct of a company's affairs in a manner unfairly prejudicial to the interests of a member. The court can give relief in cases where the exercise of the vote is contrary to non-contractual agreements and understandings between members in quasi-partnership companies (see **18.6.5** and **18.6.9**). See also **12.8** concerning meetings of holders of debt securities.

14.10.6 FURTHER READING

For further discussion of *Clemens v Clemens Bros Ltd* [1976] 2 All ER 268, see the casenotes by D D Prentice, 'Restraints on the exercise of majority shareholder power' (1976) 92 LQR 502 and V Joffe, 'Majority rule undermined?' (1977) 40 MLR 71. The whole topic of restrictions on voting rights has been examined in three articles by P G Xuereb, 'The limitation on the exercise of majority power' (1985) 6 Co Law 199, 'Remedies for abuse of majority power' (1986) 7 Co Law 53, and 'Voting rights: a comparative review' (1987) 8 Co Law 16, and one by G R Douglas, 'What are the voting duties of company members?' (1987) 131 SJ 796. L S Sealy, 'Equitable and other fetters on the shareholder's freedom to vote', in N E Eastham and B Krivy (eds), *The Cambridge Lectures 1981* (Toronto: Butterworths, 1982), vigorously attacks such fetters.

S J Burridge, 'Wrongful rights issues' (1981) 44 MLR 40 describes and comments on an unreported case with many similarities to *Clemens v Clemens Bros Ltd.*

14.10.7 VOTING AGREEMENTS

Shareholders may enter into agreements restricting or determining the way in which they exercise their voting rights. Such agreements are valid and may be enforced by mandatory injunction (*Puddephatt v Leith* [1916] 1 Ch 200). Thus, in *Greenwell v Porter* [1902] 1 Ch 530, the defendants bound themselves by agreement to do all things within their power to secure the election of two named persons as directors of a company and thereafter to vote for their re-election. When the defendants subsequently tried to oppose the re-election of one of the two as a director, the court granted an injunction restraining them from voting in any way inconsistent with the agreement.

Shareholder agreements of this nature bind only the parties to the agreement. As Lord Greene MR said in **Greenhalgh v Mallard** [1943] 2 All ER 234 at p 239:

> If the contract is such that it only imposes an obligation to vote in respect of whatever shares the contracting parties happen to have available, it follows that directly they sell their shares the contract is at an end—until possibly they acquire more shares.
>
> If the contract on its true construction ceases to operate when the shares are sold, then in the hands of the purchaser there can be no question of a continuing obligation which runs with the shares.

Shareholder agreements may be the subject of a separate contract between the shareholders involved, but they may also arise out of the contract formed by the articles. Thus, a director may be given a right of veto in relation to certain transactions, as in *Salmon v Quin and Axtens Ltd* [1909] AC 442 (see **3.4.2.9**), or different voting rights may attach to certain shares on specified matters, as in *Bushell v Faith* [1970] AC 1099 (see **3.6.2.3**). Contracts in the articles are, however, subject to the difficulties of enforcement and to the problems of amendment discussed in **3.4** and **3.5**.

In *Halton International Inc (Holdings) Sàrl v Guernroy Ltd* [2005] EWHC 1968 (Ch), [2006] 1 BCLC 78, one member of a company was given a power of attorney authorising it to exercise the votes of all the other members for the purpose of raising fresh capital, in any manner which it, 'in its absolute discretion', considered fit. It used the votes to disapply the pre-emption rights in the company's articles and in CA 2006, s 561 (see **6.3.5**), and to authorise the directors to allot new shares to itself, to friends of its controller, and to the company's chairman. It was held that the voting agreement authorised this and excluded the imposition of any fiduciary duty not to profit from being an agent of the other shareholders.

Shareholder agreements restricting, enlarging or determining the exercise of voting rights are generally concerned with specified matters. It is not uncommon, however, for different rights to be attached by agreement, to certain classes of shares. The protection of these class rights is considered in **14.14**.

14.11 ADJOURNMENT OF MEETINGS

A meeting is said to be 'adjourned' if, at a time when its business has not been completed, the meeting is discontinued with the intention that there will be a continuation of the meeting at a subsequent time. When the meeting reassembles it is described as an 'adjourned meeting'. Rules on adjournment are provided in the model articles for private companies, art 41, and the model articles for public companies, art 33 (SI 2008/3229).

The persons who attend an adjourned meeting may not be the same as the persons who attended when the meeting first assembled. In particular, it is possible to appoint new proxies to attend an adjourned meeting. The rules in CA 2006, s 327 (see **14.6.5.1**), about when proxy appointments can be delivered, apply to adjourned meetings.

Section 332 prohibits a company from deeming that a resolution passed at an adjourned general or class meeting was adopted at an earlier date than the date on which it was in fact passed. If the question was decided by poll and the result of the poll was ascertained after the adjourned meeting, the date of the resolution is the date on which the result of the poll is ascertained (*Holmes v Keyes* [1959] Ch 199).

14.12 RECORDS OF RESOLUTIONS, MEETINGS AND DECISIONS

14.12.1 COMPANY'S RECORDS

By CA 2006, s 355, every company must keep records comprising:

(a) copies of all resolutions of members passed otherwise than at general meetings;

(b) minutes of all proceedings of general meetings; and

(c) details of decisions of a sole member (see **14.12.2**).

This is extended by s 359 to resolutions and meetings of holders of a class of shares. The records must be kept for at least ten years from the date of the resolution, meeting or decision (s 355(2)). There are criminal sanctions for failure to comply (s 355(3) and (4)). The records have some evidential value (s 356). They must be kept available for inspection (s 358; see **4.4**).

14.12.2 SOLE MEMBER'S DECISIONS

Where a limited company has only one member and that member takes any decision which may be taken by the company in general meeting and which has effect as if agreed by the company in general meeting (under the principle of *East v Bennett Brothers Ltd* [1911] 1 Ch 163, see **14.13.6**), the member must provide the company with details of the decision (CA 2006, s 357) for its records. There are criminal sanctions for failure to comply (s 357(3) and (4)), but the failure does not affect the validity of the decision (s 357(5)). Section 357 does not apply where a sole member's decision is made as a written resolution of a private company. Section 357 implements Directive 2009/102/EC, art 4.

14.12.3 REGISTRATION OF RESOLUTIONS

Some resolutions of a company are of such importance as to affect persons other than its members, for example, debtors, creditors and prospective shareholders. Accordingly, CA 2006, s 30, and some other sections require copies of certain resolutions or agreements to be forwarded to Companies House within 15 days of being passed or made (s 30(1)). These resolutions and agreements are part of the company's constitution (s 17), and a copy of every such resolution or agreement must accompany every copy of the articles issued after passing the resolution, or making the agreement, for as long as the resolution or agreement is in force, unless its effect has been incorporated in the articles by amendment (s 36).

The resolutions or agreements involved are:

(a) special resolutions (s 29(1)(a));

(b) resolutions and agreements agreed to by all the members of a company (see **14.13**) which, if there had not been unanimity, would have been ineffective unless they were special resolutions (s 29(1)(b));

(c) resolutions or agreements agreed to by all the members of a class of shareholders which, if there had not been unanimity, would have been ineffective unless they had been adopted by some particular majority or otherwise in some particular manner (s 29(1)(c));

(d) all resolutions or agreements which effectively bind all members of any class of shareholders though not agreed to by all of them (s 29(1)(d));

(e) a resolution giving, varying, renewing or revoking directors' powers to allot shares or issue convertible securities or grant share options (s 551(9); see **6.3.4.3**);

(f) a resolution redenominating share capital (s 622(8));

(g) a directors' resolution converting a public company into a private one because holdings of its own shares have reduced its allotted share capital below the authorised minimum (s 664(1); see **6.5.2.7**);

(h) a resolution conferring, varying, revoking or renewing authorisation for market purchases of a company's own shares (s 701(8); see **10.6.3**);

(i) a directors' resolution that a company's securities should be traded in uncertificated form through CREST and a members' resolution vetoing such a decision (s 790; see **8.2.1**);

(j) a resolution that the company may send or supply documents or information to members by making them available on a website (sch 5, para 10(5)); and

(k) a resolution requiring a company to be voluntarily wound up under IA 1986, s 84(1)(a) (because the duration of the company fixed by its articles has expired or an event has occurred on which the articles provide that the company is to be dissolved) (IA 1986, s 84(3)).

In addition, a copy of any resolution approving an acquisition by a public company of non-cash assets from certain founding members must be delivered to Companies House with the valuer's report (s 602; see **17.7.3.3**), but does not form part of the company's constitution.

Section 29(1)(b) shows that it is contemplated in CA 2006 that a decision which the Act requires to be taken by special resolution at a meeting may alternatively be taken by unanimous agreement without meeting (*Re M J Shanley Contracting Ltd* (1979) 124 SJ 239; but see **14.13.4**).

14.13 DECISION-MAKING WITHOUT MEETING OR WRITTEN RESOLUTION

14.13.1 UNANIMOUS ASSENT

If all members of a company actually agree to a particular decision, the decision is binding and effective without meeting. As Cotton LJ said in **Baroness Wenlock v River Dee Co** (1883) 36 ChD 675 n at pp 681–2 n:

> the court would never allow it to be said that there was an absence of resolution when all the shareholders, and not only a majority, have expressly assented to that which is being done.

In **Re Duomatic Ltd** [1969] 2 Ch 365, at p 373, Buckley J stated the principle as follows:

> where it can be shown that all shareholders who have a right to attend and vote at a general meeting of the company assent to some matter which a general meeting of the company could carry into effect, that assent is as binding as a resolution in general meeting would be.

And as Astbury J observed in **Parker and Cooper Ltd v Reading** [1926] Ch 975:

> I do not think it matters in the least whether that assent is given at different times or simultaneously.

Various statements of the principle have differed over whether every member must agree or just the members entitled to vote on the matter. In *Re Duomatic Ltd* Buckley J held that it is only necessary to have the agreement of those who can vote on the matter and in this form the principle has come to be known as the '*Duomatic* principle'.

The members of a company cannot, by unanimous agreement, overcome prohibitions imposed on the company by the general law or the Companies Acts. For example, they cannot give the company's property to themselves in a way not authorised by law (see **10.2**) (*Jalmoon Pty Ltd v Bow* [1996] QCA 516, [1997] 2 QdR 62). Members of a company cannot consent to theft of the company's property by themselves (see **19.8.5**). So in **Salomon v A Salomon and Co Ltd** [1897] AC 22, Lord Davey expressed the rule as: 'the company is bound in a matter *intra vires* by the unanimous agreement of its members' (at p 57). Many of the cases are concerned with agreement to release a director from liability for breach of duty. For restrictions on when this can be done see **16.16.4**.

The principle applies to class meetings as well as general meetings (*Re Torvale Group Ltd* [1999] 2 BCLC 605).

In *Re Duomatic Ltd*, two directors drew sums as salary according to their personal needs, and accounts showing these sums were signed and approved by them as directors at the time when they were also the only ordinary shareholders (though there were also non-voting preference shareholders). Subsequently the company went into liquidation and the liquidator sought repayment of the salaries on the ground that they had not been voted in general meeting as required by a provision of the company's articles. Buckley J held that the payments were valid since they had been approved by the unanimous assent of all shareholders entitled to vote on the matter.

Unanimous agreement without meeting is not effective if the persons who give the assent could not have made the decision at a meeting, for example, because there are not enough of them to form a quorum (*Re New Cedos Engineering Co Ltd* [1994] 1 BCLC 797). It would seem to follow that where a share is held on trust, only the registered owner of the share (the trustee) can validly assent to a decision without meeting. The assent of the beneficial owner should not be sufficient. This is the position taken in Australia (*Jalmoon Pty Ltd v Bow*). In England, however, the *Duomatic* principle has been extended so that agreement by the beneficial owner of a share is effective where it is found that the trustee could be compelled to vote in accordance with the beneficial owner's wishes (*Deakin v Faulding* (2001), *The Times*, 29 August 2001; *Shahar v Tsitsekkos* [2004] EWHC 2659 (Ch), *The Times*, 30 November 2004, at [67]). But if there are two or more beneficial owners, the assent of only some of them is not sufficient (*Re Tulsesense Ltd, Rolfe v Rolfe* [2010] EWHC 244 (Ch), [2010] 2 BCLC 525, at [43]).

In *Demite Ltd v Protec Health Ltd* [1998] BCC 638 Park J said that the agreement of the two individuals who controlled Demite Ltd was not a resolution of Demite in general meeting, because the persons registered as members of Demite were not those two individuals but two companies which they controlled. In this case no evidence was given of the precise relationship between the registered member companies and the individuals who controlled them. There is a hint in Park J's judgment that if it had been proved that the companies held their Demite shares as bare nominees of the individual controllers then the agreement of those individuals might have been effective.

For the *Duomatic* principle to apply it is necessary to show that everyone entitled to vote on the question applied his or her mind to it and decided in favour of the step taken. The agreement may be 'express or by implication, verbal or by conduct, given at the time or later, but nothing short of unqualified agreement, objectively established, will suffice' (**Schofield v Schofield** [2011] EWCA Civ 154, [2011] 2 BCLC 319, at [32]). A member's agreement cannot be established objectively if it is not expressed in any way by the member. A mere internal decision cannot count (*Re Tulsesense Ltd, Rolfe v Rolfe* at [41]). In *Re D'Jan of London Ltd* [1994] 1 BCLC 561 the court found that a director of the company, who held 99 per cent of its shares, had been negligent in the conduct of his directorial duties. He claimed that the court should regard this negligence as having been forgiven by the members, before the company went into liquidation, since he, as holder of 99 per cent of the shares, would have forgiven it. The other 1 per cent of the shares were held by his wife, who never disagreed with him on business matters. It was held that as the wife had never in fact considered whether to forgive her husband's negligence, before the company's liquidation, it could not be said that there had been an agreement without meeting sufficient to bind the company. Where an individual holds some shares personally and others as a trustee or executor, that individual's agreement is to be taken as applying only to the shares held personally, unless it is expressed to apply to the other shares as well (*Re Tulsesense Ltd, Rolfe v Rolfe* at [40]).

Joint holders of a share are only entitled to one vote for that share, so the assent of the 'senior' holder (see **14.10.1.2**) is sufficient for the application of the *Duomatic* principle (*Re Gee and Co (Woolwich) Ltd* [1975] Ch 52).

14.13.2 ASSENT GIVEN AS DIRECTORS

Where all members of a company are directors of it, a unanimous decision which they make as directors, in the erroneous belief that they are entitled to do so in that capacity, will be treated as a unanimous decision made in their capacity as members, if doing so would validate the decision (*Re Express Engineering Works Ltd* [1920] 1 Ch 466).

In *Re Express Engineering Works Ltd* a company was formed with five shareholders who were also directors. The company's articles prevented any director from voting on a contract in which he might be interested. At a meeting of the five, which was ostensibly a board meeting, they unanimously approved a contract by which the company purchased property from themselves and also approved the issue to themselves of debentures securing payment to them of the purchase money. The company went into liquidation and the liquidator argued that, as all the directors were disqualified from voting on the purchase and security contracts, no board meeting had ever bound the company to those contracts. It was too late to rescind the purchase contract because the company could not restore the property to the directors, but the liquidator sought a declaration that the debentures were invalid. The Court of Appeal held that the company was bound by the unanimous assent of the shareholders.

Counsel for the liquidator conceded that the members had power to issue the debentures, but R Grantham, 'The unanimous consent rule in company law' [1993] CLJ 245, points out that the juridical basis for this is unclear since members of a company are normally thought of as having no power to manage the company (see **15.10**) and no authority to make contracts for it (see **15.1**). It is submitted that there are two alternative ways of dealing with this problem. First, when there is no board capable of acting in a matter, the directors' powers of management revert to the members, and the members must be regarded as agents of the company for the purpose of exercising those powers (see **15.10.7**). Secondly, if directors of a company act outside their authority, the members may supply the missing authority by ratifying the act (see **19.5.7**) and it might be considered that the five shareholder directors of Express Engineering Works Ltd were acting as its directors when they issued the debentures and simultaneously acted as members ratifying the unauthorised act of themselves as directors: this was the view taken by the New Zealand Court of Appeal in *Wairau Energy Centre Ltd v First Fishing Co Ltd* (1991) 5 NZCLC 67,379.

The principle of *Re Express Engineering Works Ltd* has been extended to the situation in which all members of a company are either individuals who are directors or are corporations that have appointed directors: in such a situation a decision taken by all the directors is a decision of all the members (*Bobbie Pins Ltd v Robertson* [1950] NZLR 301; *Multinational Gas and Petrochemical Co v Multinational Gas and Petrochemical Services Ltd* [1983] Ch 258).

14.13.3 ACQUIESCENCE

Unanimous agreement by members of a company to a decision may be proved by their acquiescence to it, provided that sufficient information has been made available to all members (*Phosphate of Lime Co v Green* (1871) LR 7 CP 43; *Ho Tung v Man On Insurance Co Ltd* [1902] AC 232). In **Re Bailey Hay and Co Ltd** [1971] 1 WLR 1357, the company had five shareholders. A general meeting of the company was called by a notice which was one day short of the notice period required by the company's articles, though all five shareholders attended. At the meeting, a resolution for voluntary winding up of the company was adopted. Three of the shareholders abstained from voting on the resolution, but over five years later questioned its validity. Brightman J held that the acquiescence of these shareholders must be taken as an assent to the resolution so that it should be deemed to have been passed by the shareholders unanimously. His Lordship said at p 1367:

> The conclusion is that they outwardly accepted the resolution to wind up as decisively as if they had positively voted in favour of it. If corporators attend a meeting without protest, stand by without protest while their fellow-members purport to pass a resolution, permit all persons concerned to act for years on the basis that that resolution was duly passed and rule their own conduct on the basis that the resolution is an established fact, I think it is idle for them to contend that they did not assent to the purported resolution.

In *Schofield v Schofield* [2011] EWCA Civ 154, [2011] 2 BCLC 319, one member of a company stated his objection to a gathering being treated as a general meeting of the company because insufficient notice had been given. Other persons present insisted on going ahead with the purported meeting and the objector took part in the proceedings. However, as he had never unconditionally agreed to the short notice, those proceedings were of no effect.

In **EIC Services Ltd v Phipps** [2003] EWHC 1507 (Ch), [2003] 1 WLR 2360, the effects of *Re Duomatic Ltd* [1969] 2 Ch 365 and *Re Bailey Hay and Co Ltd* were combined in the following statement by Neuberger J at [122]:

> The essence of the *Duomatic* principle . . . is that, where the articles of a company require a course to be approved by a group of shareholders at a general meeting, that requirement can be avoided if all members of the group, being aware of the relevant facts, either give their approval to that course, or so conduct themselves as to make it inequitable for them to deny that they have given their approval. Whether the

approval is given in advance or after the event, whether it is characterised as agreement, ratification, waiver, or estoppel, and whether the members of the group give their consent in different ways at different times, does not matter.

In *EIC Services Ltd v Phipps* the shareholders were not aware of the crucial fact that their approval was required, so their acquiescence did not count as unanimous assent.

14.13.4 PROCEDURAL REQUIREMENTS

CA 2006, s 281, provides that a resolution of the members of a company must be passed at a meeting or (in the case of a private company) by the statutory written resolution procedure. However, s 281(4) states that this does not affect any 'rule of law as to things done otherwise than by passing a resolution'. This wording shows that a unanimous agreement without meeting, though it may be an effective agreement, is not a 'resolution' as defined in CA 2006. In *Re Barry Artist Ltd* [1985] 1 WLR 1305, Nourse J said that the court would not normally accept a unanimously adopted decision in place of the special resolution required by statute to reduce a company's capital (see **10.7.6**). Nevertheless, unanimous assent without meeting has been accepted as effective in other circumstances where the legislation says that there should be a special resolution (*Ho Tung v Man On Insurance Co Ltd* [1902] AC 232; *Cane v Jones* [1980] 1 WLR 1451; *Re Home Treat Ltd* [1991] BCLC 705) or an extraordinary resolution (*Re M J Shanley Contracting Ltd* (1979) 124 SJ 239). All these cases were decided before the statutory provisions on written resolutions of private companies, discussed in **14.5**, were enacted. A special resolution of a private company may now be adopted as a written resolution in accordance with those provisions. Use of unanimous agreement in place of a special resolution is contemplated in s 29(1)(b) (see **14.12.3**).

Several provisions of CA 2006 prescribe special procedures for provision of information to members when passing particular kinds of resolution, either at meetings or as written resolutions of private companies. Before CA 2006, it was held that a decision may be taken without meeting and without following the formal procedures if those procedures exist only to protect the interests of the members of the company who take the decision (*Wright v Atlas Wright (Europe) Ltd* [1999] 2 BCLC 301; *Re Torvale Group Ltd* [1999] 2 BCLC 605; *Euro Brokers Holdings Ltd v Monecor (London) Ltd* [2003] EWCA Civ 105, [2003] 1 BCLC 506). In relation to three kinds of resolution (to approve directors' long-term service contracts; to confer, vary, revoke or renew authority for off-market purchase of own shares; and to vary a contract for off-market purchase of own shares), CA 2006, ss 188(5), 696(5) and 699(6), now provide that they are not validly passed if the information procedures have not been followed. Section 188(5) overrules *Wright v Atlas Wright (Europe) Ltd*. Section 696(5) overrules *BDG Roof-Bond Ltd v Douglas* [2000] 1 BCLC 401.

The principle that members can waive procedures which exist only to protect their interests applies to special procedures prescribed otherwise than by CA 2006, for example in articles of association (*Re Torvale Group Ltd*) or in a shareholders' agreement (*Euro Brokers Holdings Ltd v Monecor (London) Ltd*). As Mummery LJ said in *Euro Brokers Holdings Ltd v Monecor (London) Ltd*, at [62], the *Duomatic* principle allows the members of a company:

> to reach an agreement without the need for strict compliance with formal procedures, where they exist only for the benefit of those who have agreed not [to] comply with them . . , It does not matter whether the formal procedures in question are stipulated for in the articles of association, in the Companies Acts or in a separate contract between the members of the company concerned. What matters is that all the members have reached an agreement. If they have, they cannot be heard to say that they are not bound by it because the formal procedure was not followed.

It is submitted that the special procedures in ss 169 and 511, which provide an opportunity for directors and auditors to protest against resolutions removing them from office (see **15.6.3** and **17.4.3**), cannot be waived by the members, because they exist for the protection of the person sought to be removed. Therefore, a resolution under s 168 removing a director or under s 510 removing an auditor cannot be adopted by unanimous agreement without meeting. Such resolutions cannot be adopted using the statutory procedure for written resolutions of private companies (s 288(2); see **14.5**).

14.13.5 JURIDICAL BASIS

The accepted explanation of the courts' refusal to declare members' decisions invalid just because they were not taken at a meeting is that given by Oliver J in **Re New Cedos Engineering Co Ltd** [1994] 1 BCLC 797. His Lordship's view was that it is inequitable to allow the company to rely on a mere irregularity of procedure when exactly the same decision would have been reached if the correct procedure had been followed. He said, at p 814:

> the *ratio* of Buckley J's decision [in *Re Duomatic Ltd* [1969] 2 Ch 365] is that where that which has been done informally could, but for an oversight, have been done formally and was assented to by 100 per cent of those who could have participated in the formal act, if one had been carried out, then it would be idle to insist upon formality as a precondition to the validity of the act which all those competent to effect it had agreed should be effected.

This was approved by Potter LJ (with whom the other members of the Court of Appeal agreed) in *Wright v Atlas Wright (Europe) Ltd* [1999] 2 BCLC 301 at pp 314–15. A similar view was taken by the New Zealand Court of Appeal in *Westpac Securities Ltd v Kensington* [1994] 2 NZLR 555 at p 563.

The earlier views of the Court of Appeal in **Re George Newman and Co** [1895] 1 Ch 674 seem to have been abandoned. In that case the Court of Appeal held that decisions taken by the members of George Newman and Co without meeting were ineffective. Mr George Newman had been a director and chairman of the company and had made a profit of £3,000 selling to it property which he knew it required. Newman had also used £3,500 of the company's money for improvements to his own house. Keeping these sums was contrary to the no-profit rule (see **16.9.2**) but Mr Newman claimed that all the shareholders (except those who were minors) approved of the payments so that they were ratified (see **16.16.2**), which, if true, would have meant that the company was no longer entitled to recover the money. The Court of Appeal held that there had been no effective ratification, saying, at p 686:

> Individual assents given separately may preclude those who give them from complaining of what they have sanctioned; but for the purpose of binding a company in its corporate capacity individual assents given separately are not equivalent to the assent of a meeting. The company is entitled to the protection afforded by a duly convened meeting, and by a resolution properly considered and carried and duly recorded. It may be true, and probably is true, that a meeting, if held, would have done anything which Mr George Newman desired; but this is pure speculation, and the liquidator, as representing the company in its corporate capacity, is entitled to insist upon and to have the benefit of the fact that even if a general meeting could have sanctioned what was done, such sanction was never obtained.

This reason for finding that the decisions were invalid was said to be only an alternative to the court's principal reason which was that the payments were illegal gifts out of capital and so could not have been validated by the members at all (see **10.1**). Subsequently, this principal reason has been taken to be the only *ratio* for the court's decision and it has been assumed that the court's remarks about decision-making without meeting were only saying that members could not make an *ultra vires* illegal decision without meeting. George Newman had been an associate of the large-scale swindler Jabez Balfour, who had escaped to South America, leaving Newman and others to suffer both this civil claim and a prison sentence. See David McKie, *Jabez: The Rise and Fall of a Victorian Rogue* (London: Atlantic Books, 2004).

14.13.6 ONLY ONE MEMBER

If there is only one member of a body of persons, a requirement that a decision of the body must be taken at a meeting will normally be interpreted as meaning that the decision can be taken by that one member without calling a meeting (*East v Bennett Brothers Ltd* [1911] 1 Ch 163, in which one person held all the preference shares of a company and a decision taken by him was as effective as a decision taken by a meeting of the preference shareholders; *Re Torvale Group Ltd* [1999] 2 BCLC 605). This is subject to the exception noted in **14.13.4** for procedural requirements which exist for the protection of persons other than the member concerned.

Directive 2009/102/EC, art 4(1), requires member States to provide that the sole member of a single-member private limited company shall exercise the powers of the general meeting of the company. Under CA 2006, s 281(1)(a), the sole member of such a company may take decisions by written resolution, provided a written record of the decision is given to the company (s 357, see **14.12.2**). But that procedure cannot be used to dismiss a director under s 168 or to dismiss an auditor under s 510. For any kind of decision, a meeting may be held at which the quorum will be one by virtue of s 318(1).

14.14 ALTERATION OF CLASS RIGHTS

14.14.1 CLASS RIGHTS

The capital structure of a company may involve the existence of different classes of shares, for example, ordinary shares and preference shares. Class rights may be defined as the rights which attach to a particular class of shares but not to another class or to shareholders generally. Such rights may be created by the articles of association of a company, by the terms of issue of shares or by a unanimous shareholders' agreement, and may relate to such matters as the right to a dividend, the right to share in surplus assets if the company is wound up and the right to attend and vote at company meetings.

The very nature of class rights requires that safeguards be provided to prevent one class being deprived of its rights by the votes of other classes, and the enactments which provide these safeguards will now be considered.

14.14.2 VARIATION OF CLASS RIGHTS

14.14.2.1 Introduction

Where a company's shares are of different classes, the variation of the class rights is governed by CA 2006, s 630, which 'is concerned with the variation of the rights attached to a class of shares in a company having a share capital' (s 630(1)). Section 630 also applies to the variation of rights of a class of members, where the rights do not depend on holding particular shares (*Cumbrian Newspapers Group Ltd v Cumberland and Westmorland Herald Newspaper and Printing Co Ltd* [1987] Ch 1). Section 631 makes provision for companies without a share capital.

The model articles of association in SI 2008/3229 are drafted for a company with only one class of shares and so make no provision for variation of class rights.

14.14.2.2 Method of variation

If a company's articles provide for the variation of class rights (whenever the provision was introduced into the articles), the rights may be varied only in accordance with those provisions of the articles (CA 2006, s 630(2)(a)).

If there is no provision in the articles for the variation of class rights, s 630(2)(b) and (4) provides that the rights may be varied if, but only if, the variation is approved by a three-quarters majority of that class. Class approval may be given either (a) at a class meeting by special resolution (75 per cent majority; see **14.4.3**) or (b) in writing by the holders of three-quarters in nominal value of the issued shares of the class excluding treasury shares (see **10.6.6**).

14.14.2.3 Conduct of meetings

Any meeting of shareholders of a company in connection with the variation of class rights must be conducted in accordance with CA 2006, ss 301 to 303 (s 334), with two special rules (s 334(3) to (6)):

(a) The quorum, other than at an adjourned meeting, is two persons holding or representing by proxy at least one third in nominal value of the issued shares of the class in question (excluding any shares of that class held as treasury shares; see **10.6.6**). At an adjourned meeting the quorum is one person holding shares of the class in question or his proxy.

(b) Any holder of shares of the class in question present in person or by proxy may demand a poll.

At a class meeting the power of the majority to bind the minority must be exercised for the purpose of benefiting the class as a whole, not only particular members (*Re Holders Investment Trust Ltd* [1971] 1 WLR 583, see **14.10.4**).

14.14.2.4 Application to cancel variation

Notwithstanding the safeguards provided by CA 2006, s 630, a further right is given by s 633. Where class rights have been varied, the holders of not less than 15 per cent of the issued shares of the class in question (not counting shares held by the company as treasury shares—see **10.6.6**), who did not consent to or vote in favour of the variation, may apply to the court to have the variation cancelled, and the variation does not then take effect until it is confirmed by the court (s 633(1) to (3)). The application must be made within 21 days after the variation was made, and may be made on behalf of the shareholders entitled to apply by one or more of their number appointed by them in writing (s 633(4)). The court must have regard to all the circumstances of the case and if it is satisfied that the variation would unfairly prejudice the holders of the class rights concerned it may disallow the variation, but must, if not so satisfied, confirm the variation, and in any event the court's decision is final (s 633(5)).

14.14.2.5 Meaning of variation

All statutory provisions in this area make it clear that 'variation' includes abrogation of rights (CA 2006, ss 334(7)(b), 630(6) and 633(6)). Further, by ss 334(7)(a) and 630(5):

> Any amendment of a provision contained in a company's articles for the variation of the rights attached to a class of shares, or the insertion of any such provision into the articles, is itself to be treated as a variation of those rights.

Apart from these express provisions, one must look to the judiciary for guidance on the meaning of 'variation', and it seems that the judges are reluctant to describe most changes of class rights as a variation. It may be thought that one of the most drastic 'variations' would be to issue more shares of the same class, thereby 'diluting' or 'watering down' the effective rights of the existing members of that class. In *White v Bristol Aeroplane Co Ltd* [1953] Ch 65, the company wanted to issue new preference shares and ordinary shares as bonus shares to the existing ordinary shareholders only and it was argued that this would vary the existing preference shareholders' voting rights since one vote would be a much smaller proportion of the total after the issue than before. The Court of Appeal held that there was no variation. Evershed MR explained, at p 74:

> It is no doubt true that the enjoyment of, and the capacity to make effective, those rights is in a measure affected; for as I have already indicated, the existing preference stockholders will be in a less advantageous

position on such occasions as entitle them to register their votes, whether at general meetings of the company or at separate meetings of their own class. But there is to my mind a distinction, and a sensible distinction, between an affecting of the rights and an affecting of the enjoyment of the rights, or of the stockholders' capacity to turn them to account.

Romer LJ said, at pp 81–2:

> The position then will be precisely the same as now—namely, that the holder of preference stock will have on a poll one vote for every £1 of preference stock held by him. It is quite true that ... the total voting power of the class, will, or may, have less force behind it, because it will *pro tanto* be watered down by reason of the increased total voting power of the members of the company; but no particular weight is attached to the vote, by the constitution of the company, as distinct from the right to exercise the vote, and certainly no right is conferred on the preference stockholders to preserve anything in the nature of an equilibrium between their class and the ordinary stockholders or any other class.

The same result will obtain if preference shares are issued to the detriment of ordinary shareholders (*Re John Smith's Tadcaster Brewery Co Ltd* [1953] Ch 305). Similarly, if shares of one class are subdivided, thereby increasing voting rights as against another class there will be no variation (*Greenhalgh v Arderne Cinemas Ltd* [1946] 1 All ER 512, where 50p shares of one class were subdivided into 10p shares).

A class right is not varied by making it worthless. For example, if preference shareholders have a right to participate in surplus assets on winding up, the company does not vary that right by ensuring that all surplus assets are distributed to the ordinary shareholders before winding up (*Dimbula Valley (Ceylon) Tea Co Ltd v Laurie* [1961] Ch 353). In *Adelaide Electric Supply Co Ltd v Prudential Assurance Co Ltd* [1934] AC 122 a preferential dividend payable in England became, as a result of an amendment, payable in Australia. The Australian pound was worth less than the pound sterling, so the preferential dividend diminished. The House of Lords held that this was not a variation of the preference shareholders' rights.

In *Re Mackenzie and Co Ltd* [1916] 2 Ch 450, preference shareholders were entitled to a dividend of 4 per cent on the amount paid up on their shares. The full nominal value of £20 had been paid on each share but a general meeting of the company (at which preference shareholders were not entitled to vote) approved a reduction of capital which would reduce the nominal value of each share to £12 so that the preference dividend would be reduced from £8 per share to £4.80 per share. This was held not to be a variation of the preference shareholders' rights.

In all these cases, the class rights involved remained the same—to have one vote per share, to participate in surplus assets, to be paid a dividend in pounds, to be paid a 4 per cent dividend—and they could not therefore be said to be varied, even though as a result of a change those rights became worthless. In *House of Fraser plc v ACGE Investments Ltd* [1987] AC 387, House of Fraser plc reduced its capital by returning all capital to a class of preference shareholders, thus expelling them from the company. It was held that this was not a variation of the preference shareholders' rights. Thus, for class rights to be protected in the event of a variation, the nature of those rights, rather than their enjoyment, must be affected, for example, by changing voting rights from one per share to one per member, or by removing completely the right to share in surplus assets on a winding up.

14.14.2.6 Transparency

A company must give notice to Companies House within one month of:

(a) assigning a name or other designation, or a new name or other designation, to any class or description of its shares (CA 2006, s 636); and

(b) varying the rights attached to any of its shares (s 637).

Where a notice under s 636 or 637 relates to a public company, Companies House must give public notice of receiving it (ss 1077 and 1078(3); see **4.3**).

Where an application is made under s 633 (see **14.14.2.4**), the company must deliver a copy of the court's order to Companies House within 15 days of the making of the order (s 635).

14.15 HOLDING AND SUBSIDIARY COMPANIES

For the purposes of CA 2006, the terms 'holding company', 'subsidiary' and 'wholly owned subsidiary' are defined in s 1159. There are similar provisions in s 1162 defining 'parent undertaking' and subsidiary undertaking' for the purposes of group accounts (see **9.8.2**).

By s 1159(2), a company is a wholly owned subsidiary of another company (which we will call the owning company) if all its members are in one or more of the following categories:

(a) the owning company;

(b) persons acting on behalf of the owning company;

(c) other wholly owned subsidiaries of the owning company; and

(d) persons acting on behalf of other wholly owned subsidiaries of the owning company.

In this definition, 'company' includes any body corporate (s 1159(4)). Thus a body corporate that is not a registered company (for example, a company incorporated outside the United Kingdom) can be counted as one of a registered company's wholly owned subsidiaries if the exclusive membership criterion of s 1159(2) is met. A wholly owned subsidiary is obviously very closely tied to its owning company. The owning company is the only effective member of a wholly owned subsidiary.

Sometimes it is necessary to know whether two companies are in the relationship of subsidiary and holding company. A subsidiary is closely tied to its holding company but there may be one or more effective members or directors apart from the holding company. Under s 1159(1), there are four ways in which the relationship of holding company and subsidiary may arise:

(a) under s 1159(1)(a), where the holding company holds a majority of the voting rights in the subsidiary;

(b) under s 1159(1)(b), where the holding company is a member of the subsidiary and has the right to appoint or remove a majority of its board of directors;

(c) under s 1159(1)(c), where the holding company is a member of the subsidiary and controls alone, pursuant to an agreement with other shareholders or members, a majority of the voting rights in the subsidiary; and

(d) under the final clause of s 1159(1), where the subsidiary is a subsidiary of a company which is itself a subsidiary of the holding company.

As with the definition of wholly owned subsidiary, 'company' includes any body corporate (s 1159(4)).

It is common to call a holding company and its subsidiaries a 'group' (for example, in s 188(1)(b) and in part 15—see s 474(1)).

The definition of the relationship of subsidiary and holding company in s 1159 is explained and supplemented by sch 6, in which, again, 'company' includes any body corporate (s 1159(4)).

By sch 6, para 4(1), rights which are exercisable only in certain circumstances shall be taken into account only:

(a) when the circumstances have arisen, and for so long as they continue to obtain; or

(b) when the circumstances are within the control of the person having the rights.

By para 4(2), rights which are normally exercisable but are temporarily incapable of exercise must continue to be taken into account.

Rights held by a person in a fiduciary capacity (see **16.3.2**) are to be treated as not held by that person (para 5). If shares in a company are sold but the transfer is not completed by registration in the company's register of members, the seller remains entitled to exercise any votes attached to the shares. The seller holds the shares on trust for the buyer, and holds the voting rights in a fiduciary capacity for the purposes of para 5 (*Michaels v Harley House (Marylebone) Ltd* [2000] Ch 104).

Paragraphs 6 to 8 of sch 6 attribute to a company rights held on its behalf by others or held by its subsidiaries.

Rights must be treated as held by a company if they are held by any of its subsidiaries (para 8(1)). Rights held by a person as nominee for another must be treated as held by the other (para 6(1)). Rights are to be regarded as held as nominee for another if they are exercisable only on the other's instructions or with that other's consent or concurrence (para 6(2)) (though this is not to be construed as requiring rights held by a company to be treated as held by any of its subsidiaries (para 8(2))). By para 8(3), rights must be treated as being exercisable in accordance with the instructions or in the interests of a company if they are exercisable in accordance with the instructions of or, as the case may be, in the interests of:

(a) any subsidiary or holding company of that company; or

(b) any subsidiary of a holding company of that company.

Paragraph 7 deals with rights attached to shares held by way of security (see **11.2**). If a holding company transfers its shares in a subsidiary to be held by a creditor as security, the holding company ceases to be a member of the subsidiary and so the relationship of holding company and subsidiary is ended, despite the provisions of para 7 (*Enviroco Ltd v Farstad Supply A/S* [2011] UKSC 16, [2011] 1 WLR 921). This is because, in the definition of holding company and subsidiary, there is no equivalent to the provision in s 1162(3)(b) (parent and subsidiary undertakings, see **9.8.2**) that company P is to be treated as a member of company S if shares in S are held by a person acting on behalf of P. Lord Collins said that the Supreme Court could not be 'abundantly sure' that this was an error which it could correct. The court could not be certain that the deeming provision was incorrectly omitted from what is now s 1159 or whether it was incorrectly inserted in what is now s 1162.

Voting rights in a company must be reduced by any rights held by the company itself (para 9).

References in any provision of paras 5 to 9 to rights held by a person include rights falling to be treated as held by that person by virtue of any other provision in those paragraphs (para 10). But references in any provision of paras 5 to 9 to rights held by a person do not include rights which, by virtue of any other provision in those subsections, are to be treated as not held by that person (para 10).

Another group of paragraphs define precisely what is meant by voting rights and rights to appoint directors.

'Voting rights' in a company are the rights conferred on shareholders in respect of their shares (or, in the case of a company not having a share capital, on members) to vote at general meetings of the company on all, or substantially all, matters (para 2).

A 'right to appoint or remove a majority of a company's board of directors' means the right to appoint or remove directors holding a majority of the voting rights at meetings of the board on all, or substantially all, matters (para 3(1)). A company must be treated as having the right to appoint to a directorship if (para 3(2)):

(a) a person's appointment to the directorship follows necessarily from his appointment as director of the company; or

(b) the directorship is held by the company itself.

By para 3(3), a right to appoint or remove which is exercisable only with the consent or concurrence of another person shall be left out of account unless no other person has a right to appoint or, as the case may be, remove in relation to that directorship. The appointment and dismissal of directors, and voting at board meetings, are dealt with in **Chapter 15**.

14.16 AUTHORISATION OF POLITICAL DONATIONS

14.16.1 INTRODUCTION

The Political Parties, Elections and Referendums Act 2000 introduced extensive provisions for UK political parties to reveal the sources of their funding and restricts the persons from whom they may accept donations. One aspect of this is the legislation which is now in CA 2006, part 14 (ss 362 to 379), headed 'Control of political donations and expenditure'.

The broad principle of part 14 is that a company must not make political contributions exceeding £5,000 a year unless authorised by a resolution of members, and it must not spend any money at all on its own political activities unless authorised by a members' resolution. If contributions or expenditures are made without authority, the directors at the time they were made are liable to reimburse the company, with interest. Contributions and expenditure by a company and its subsidiaries must be reported in the directors' report each year (see **9.9.4.10**).

14.16.2 DONATIONS AND EXPENDITURE FOR WHICH AN AUTHORISING RESOLUTION IS REQUIRED

By CA 2006, s 366(1), an authorising resolution (see **14.16.6**) is required for:

(a) any political donation (see **14.16.4**) to a political party or other political organisation (see **14.16.3**), or to an independent election candidate, except that, by s 378(1), a total of up to £5,000 may be donated by a group of companies over a period of 12 months without an authorising resolution; and

(b) any political expenditure (see **14.16.5**).

14.16.3 DONEES COVERED

Political donations (see **14.16.4**) are subject to CA 2006, part 14, only if they are made to a political party, a political organisation or an independent election candidate to which part 14 applies. Part 14 applies to a political party if (s 363(1)):

(a) the party is registered under the Political Parties, Elections and Referendums Act 2000, part 2, which requires registration with the Electoral Commission of all parties that intend to contest any national, regional, local and European elections held in the United Kingdom (apart from parish and community elections); or

(b) the party carries on, or proposes to carry on, activities for the purposes of, or in connection with, its participation in any election or elections to public office held in any EU State other than the United Kingdom.

Part 14 applies to a political organisation if (s 363(2)) the organisation carries on, or proposes to carry on, activities that are capable of being reasonably regarded as intended:

(a) to influence public support for a political party or an independent election candidate; or

(b) to influence voters in relation to any national or regional referendum held under the law of the United Kingdom or any other EU State.

Trade unions (s 374(2)) and all-party parliamentary groups (s 376) are not political organisations.

14.16.4 AUTHORISATION OF POLITICAL DONATIONS

By CA 2006, s 364, 'political donation' means anything that would constitute a donation for the purpose of the Political Parties, Elections and Referendums Act 2000, part 4, Chapter 1 (ss 50 to 53), or would do so if that chapter applied to all the donees to which CA 2006, part 14, applies rather than just to registered political parties. Sections 50 to 52 of the 2000 Act define 'donation' widely to include, among other things, gifts, sponsorship, subscriptions and provision of property, services, facilities or personnel at uncommercial rates. By CA 2006, s 363(4), the term also includes a loan at an uncommercial rate.

A donation to a trade union, other than a donation to its political fund, is not a political donation (s 374(1)).

A membership subscription to a trade association is not a political donation (s 375(1)). By s 375(2), 'trade association' means an organisation formed for the purpose of furthering the trade interests of (a) its members, or (b) of persons represented by its members. Category (b) covers international federations of national trade associations. But also, by s 375(2), a payment to a trade association for the purpose of financing any particular activity of the association is not a subscription. This means that, for example, special contributions to political fighting funds may count as political donations.

14.16.5 POLITICAL EXPENDITURE

By CA 2006, s 365(1), 'political expenditure' by a company means any expenditure incurred by the company:

(a) on preparing, publishing or disseminating any advertising or any other promotional or publicity material which is capable of being reasonably regarded as intended to affect public support for a political party, political organisation or independent election candidate (see **14.16.3**);

(b) any activities capable of being reasonably regarded as intended to affect public support for any political party, political organisation or independent election candidate; or

(c) any activities capable of being reasonably regarded as intended to influence voters in relation to any national or regional referendum in the EU.

Under s 377 the Secretary of State has made an order (SI 2007/2081) which provides that a company whose ordinary course of business includes publishing news material in any medium does not need authorisation for expenditure on preparing, publishing and disseminating its publications. So, for example, a newspaper publishing company does not need authorisation for the cost of publishing its newspaper just because the newspaper urges its readers to vote for a particular party. The government has been persuaded that it would be 'impractical' for such a company to comply with the requirements for authorisation (*Implementation of Companies Act 2006: A Consultative Document* (DTI, 2007), para 2.120). Given the great importance of newspapers in forming voting habits, this is a significant gap in the coverage of CA 2006, part 14.

14.16.6 AUTHORISING RESOLUTION

The authorising resolution which is required by CA 2006, s 366, before political donations (above £5,000 per 12 months) or political expenditure may be made by a company, must be expressed in general terms and must not purport to authorise particular donations or expenditure (s 367(5)). However, it must specify the maximum amount that may be donated or expended in the period for which it has effect (s 367(6)). That period is four years beginning when the resolution is passed, unless the directors determine, or the articles require, a shorter period (s 368(1)). The articles can restrict the directors' power to determine a shorter period (s 368(2)). Authorisation must, by s 367(3) and (4), be divided into authorisations for:

(a) donations to political parties or independent election candidates;

(b) donations to political organisations other than political parties; and

(c) political expenditure.

There must be separate financial limits for each category (s 367(6)).

An authorising resolution must be a resolution of the members of the company which will make donations or incur expenditure, unless it is a wholly owned subsidiary of a UK-registered company (s 366(2) and (3)). If the donating or expending company is a subsidiary of another UK-registered company, authorisation is also (or, in the case of a wholly owned subsidiary, solely) required from the members of its 'relevant holding company'. This means the company registered in the United Kingdom which is its holding company and is also not a subsidiary of another UK-registered company (s 366(2), (3) and (4)). (See **14.15** for definitions of the terms, 'subsidiary', 'holding company' and 'wholly owned subsidiary'.)

An authorising resolution passed by the members of a holding company can relate to the company itself and/or one or more of its subsidiaries (s 367(1)). It can also relate to the company and all its subsidiaries without naming them (s 367(2)).

An authorising resolution must be passed before any donation it authorises is made or expenditure incurred (s 366(5)(b)). Where a donation is made, or expenditure is incurred, in pursuance of a contract, the resolution must be passed before the company enters into the contract (s 379(2)).

14.16.7 LAWFULNESS OF DONATIONS

Nothing in CA 2006, s 366, enables a company to be authorised to do anything that it could not otherwise do lawfully (s 366(6)). Whether or not political donations are within the objects of a company is discussed in **3.8.5.3**. Whether or not a donation may be lawfully accepted by a registered party is determined by the Political Parties, Elections and Referendums Act 2000, ss 54 to 61. A registered party must not accept a donation made by a person who is not a permissible donor (s 54(1)) and, by s 54(2)(b), a company registered in the United Kingdom can be a permissible donor only if it carries on business in the United Kingdom. A company which does not carry on business in the United Kingdom may, however, reimburse the expenses of a member or officer of a registered party travelling abroad (s 55(3) and (4) of the 2000 Act).

14.16.8 REMEDIES FOR BREACH OF PROHIBITIONS

Sections 369 to 373 of CA 2006 contain detailed provisions on the remedies available when a company has made any donation or incurred any expenditure in contravention of any of the provisions of s 366 (which provides that donations and expenditure must not be made without advance approval by members).

Every person who was a director of the company at the relevant time is liable to reimburse the company the amount of the unauthorised donation or expenditure, with interest, and compensate the company for any loss or damage it sustained as a result of the contravening payment (s 369(2)). The interest rate is 8 per cent a year (SI 2007/2242). Directors of a relevant holding company (see **14.16.6**) are liable to the same extent for unauthorised donations or expenditures of its subsidiaries, if they failed to take all reasonable steps to prevent the donation being made or the expenditure incurred (s 369(4)).

Section 370 allows what it calls an 'authorised group' of members of a company to bring a claim against directors if the company refuses to do so. An authorised group may be formed by the holders of 5 per cent or more of the nominal value of the company's issued share capital, or 50 or more of its members, or, if there is no share capital, 5 per cent or more of its members (s 370(3)). A claim under these provisions is like a derivative claim, except that it is brought in the name of the company. The court may order the company to indemnify the authorised group in respect of their costs (s 372) and order the company to disclose information to them (s 373). The group must give the company 28 days' notice of the proceedings (s 371(1)). Under s 371(2) the company may get proposed proceedings under s 370 halted by the court on the ground that:

(a) the unauthorised amount has been made good to the company; or

(b) proceedings to enforce the liability have been brought and are being pursued with due diligence by the company; or

(c) the members proposing to bring the proceedings do not constitute an authorised group.

15

DIRECTORS

SUMMARY OF POINTS COVERED

- What is in this chapter
- Directors and corporate governance
- Definitions
- Minimum number of directors
- Appointment of directors
- Termination of office

- Transparency
- The board of directors
- Remuneration
- Powers of management
- Legal categorisation of directors
- Directors are not agents of members

15.1 WHAT IS IN THIS CHAPTER

A company as an artificial person cannot perform its own acts: it needs real people to represent it and act on its behalf. The registered company was invented to provide a legal form which would enable investors to put their money into a business without being responsible for managing it. Instead, management was to be conducted by directors, who would also represent the company in its dealings with others. Early companies legislation did not actually require companies to have directors, but it was generally assumed that they would have them and the courts quickly gave directors the right to represent their company to the exclusion of members. In *Ferguson v Wilson* (1866) LR 2 Ch App 77, Cairns LJ said, at pp 89–90: 'The company itself cannot act in its own person . . . it can only act through directors'. In **Ernest v Nicholls** (1857) 6 HL Cas 401, Lord Wensleydale said, at p 419: '[The shareholders] can only act through their directors, and the acts of the individual shareholders have no effect whatever on the company at large'. And, at p 423, his Lordship said:

> for the purposes of contract, the company exists only in the directors and officers acting by and according to the deed [ie, the deed of settlement, equivalent in those days to the articles of association]; and by the statute law the company is no more liable than a corporation by charter for the act of one or more of its members, who are distinct persons by law.

CA 2006, s 154, now requires every private company to have at least one director and every public company to have at least two directors (see **15.4**). This mandatory rule exists despite the fact that nowadays in very many private companies the only people who manage and represent the company are its shareholders. The rule ensures that every company has a designated representative to deal with other persons and CA 2006 requires information about directors to be sent to Companies House.

UK companies legislation does not require a company's directors to manage its business, leaving matters of management to be determined by the members in their articles of association. But the model articles of association in SI 2008/3229 do include this requirement (model articles for private companies, art 3; model articles for public companies, art 3) and so put directors at the centre of what is known as 'corporate governance', that is the system by which companies are directed and controlled (see **15.2**).

Rules on appointment and removal of directors are considered in **15.5** and **15.6**. There must be public disclosure of the names of a company's directors, but their residential addresses are disclosed only to public authorities and credit reference agencies (see **15.7**).

Directors work and take decisions together as a board (see **15.8**). They may be remunerated for their work (see **15.9**) and their powers of management are usually set out in the articles of association (see **15.10**). In **15.11** and **15.12** there is a discussion of the legal categorisation of directors, whether as fiduciaries, agents or trustees.

Key legislation which you should be able to consult when reading this chapter:

- CA 2006, ss 154–169, 215–230, 240–246, 248–251; and
- the model articles for private companies limited by shares and for public companies in SI 2008/3229;

All that legislation is in *Blackstone's Statutes on Company Law*.

- UK Corporate Governance Code, which is at **www.frc.org.uk/Our-Work/Corporate-Governance-Reporting/Corporate-governance.aspx**

The following cases, which are considered in this chapter, are particularly significant and are recommended further reading:

- *Bushell v Faith* [1969] 2 Ch 438 and [1970] AC 1099 (also a key case for **Chapter 3**);
- *Howard Smith Ltd v Ampol Petroleum Ltd* [1974] AC 821 (also a key case for **Chapter 16**);
- *Lee v Lee's Air Farming Ltd* [1961] AC 12 (also a key case for **Chapter 5**); and
- *Morris v Kanssen* [1946] AC 459.

Your particular course of study may require you to read other source materials.

15.2 DIRECTORS AND CORPORATE GOVERNANCE

15.2.1 INTRODUCTION

Everyone connected with a company, whether as member, employee, supplier, customer or director, wants it to be well managed, or at least managed for their own benefit. Of these, the only group actually in a position to ensure that the company is managed for their own benefit are the directors and the only group who have the opportunity to control the directors are the members. It follows that the relationship between directors and members is of great importance and this is reinforced by the prevalent shareholder-centred view of the company discussed in **1.6.4.2**. The UK Corporate Governance Code (**15.2.2**) attempts to set out principles of corporate governance in the interests of members. The shareholder-centred view of the company entails a belief that the members are entitled to the company's profits and leads to the directors being seen as stewards for the members (**15.2.5**). Economists suggest that market forces control directors' behaviour. In 1932, Berle and Means in the USA suggested that it is unrealistic to believe that shareholders of large public companies have any control over their directors (**15.2.6**) and they and others suggested that the profits of a business should reward those who undertake entrepreneurial functions, rather than shareholders who passively contribute capital. The rise of very large institutional shareholders may be returning power over public companies to their members (**15.2.7**).

15.2.2 THE UK CORPORATE GOVERNANCE CODE

The current edition of the UK Corporate Governance Code was issued by the Financial Reporting Council (FRC) in April 2016. It applies to premium listed companies (see **7.6**) in relation to financial years beginning on or after 17 June 2016. It is a guide to a number of key components of effective board practice. There are similar codes elsewhere in Europe. See the website of the European Corporate Governance Institute, **www.ecgi.org**.

Every company with premium listed shares is subject to listing rules which require an annual statement of how it has applied the main principles of the Code (FCA Handbook, LR 9.8.6R(5)). This must be followed by a statement of whether or not the company has complied with the principles throughout the accounting period being reported on (LR 9.8.6R(6)). The company must give reasons for any non-compliance. This is known as the 'comply or explain' philosophy.

The European Commission has established a European Corporate Governance Forum to encourage the coordination and convergence of national corporate governance codes. If a company has transferable securities admitted to trading on a regulated market (see **7.3.4.6**), Directive 2013/34/EU, art 20, requires its annual financial report to include a corporate governance statement (see **9.9.3**).

15.2.3 EXECUTIVE AND NON-EXECUTIVE DIRECTORS

In practice a distinction is often drawn between executive directors and non-executive directors. A non-executive director of a company typically does not devote his or her whole working time to the company and receives a relatively small director's fee. An executive director of a company typically devotes his or her whole working time to the company (or a number of companies in a group), often as an employee of the company, and has a significant personal interest in the company as a source of income. The distinction between executive and non-executive directors has no significance in company law though it may cause difficult problems in employment law.

Many people believe that non-executive directors (NEDs) can be effective in ensuring that the board of a company acts in the interests of the company rather than a member or members of the board. However, *Re Polly Peck International plc (No 2)* [1994] 1 BCLC 574, which is discussed in **20.13.6.9**, shows how unrealistic it is to expect non-executive directors to control a determined and powerful managing director. See also Elke Hellinx, 'Steeplechase in the boardroom: the obstacles for non-executive directors to fulfil their role in public companies' (2017) 38 Co Law 15. For premium listed companies, the UK Corporate Governance Code (see **15.2.2**) states (supporting principles B.1):

> The board should include an appropriate combination of executive and non-executive directors (and, in particular, independent non-executive directors) such that no individual or small group of individuals can dominate the board's decision taking.

Main principle A.4 states:

> As part of their role as members of a unitary board, non-executive directors should constructively challenge and help develop proposals on strategy.

The independent non-executive directors should be listed in the company's annual report and it is for the board to determine whether a director is 'independent in character and judgement' (UK Corporate Governance Code, para B.1.1). If any of seven factors listed in B.1.1, which could compromise independence of character and judgement, exists, the annual report should state why the board considers that the director is nevertheless independent. The seven factors are:

(a) being an employee of the company in the past five years;

(b) having a material business relationship with the company in the past three years, either directly or as a partner, shareholder, director or senior employee of a body that has such a relationship;

(c) receiving remuneration from the company other than a director's fee, including participating in a share-option scheme or being a member of the company's pension scheme;

(d) having close family ties with any of the company's advisers, directors or senior employees;

(e) holding cross-directorships or having other significant links with other directors through involvement in other companies (cross-directorships are where executive directors of two companies serve as non-executive directors on each other's boards);

(f) representing a significant shareholder (this reverses the effect of *Re Astec (BSR) plc* [1998] 2 BCLC 556); and

(g) serving on the board for more than nine years.

If a company is in the FTSE 350 (see **7.3.3.3**), at least half of its directors (excluding the chair) should be independent (B.1.2). Smaller companies should have at least two independent directors (B.1.2). One of the independent directors should be appointed senior independent director (A.4.1).

The UK Corporate Governance Code gives a special role to independent non-executive directors in controlling executive directors by recommending that independent non-executive directors form the majority on the nomination committee recommending appointments of directors (see **15.5.3.2**) and that the remuneration committee and audit committee should consist entirely of independent non-executive directors (see **15.8.7**).

15.2.4 TWO-TIER BOARDS

In the United Kingdom and USA, the non-executive directors of a company participate in regular board meetings equally with the executive directors, though they meet separately in the remuneration and audit committees from which executive directors are normally excluded. In Germany and the Netherlands, the general idea is that the non-executive directors form a separate board, known as the 'supervisory board' (the board of executive directors being known as the 'management board'). In those countries a two-tier structure of supervisory and management boards is mandatory for large public companies, and a supervisory board has statutory functions. Two of the functions of the supervisory board are appointing the members of the management board and determining their remuneration. In the United Kingdom the fact that these are appropriate functions for non-executive directors has been recognised in the UK Corporate Governance Code concerning the nomination and remuneration committees (see **15.8.7**).

In Germany, supervisory boards have an important role in the German system of worker participation in management, known as 'co-determination'. In most German public companies, one-third of the members of the supervisory board must be elected by the employees of the company while the other two-thirds are elected by the shareholders. In the Netherlands, appointments to a company's supervisory board are by co-optation but the company's works council may veto an appointment.

The constitution of a European public limited-liability company (SE) must adopt either the one-tier or the two-tier system (Council Regulation (EC) No 2157/2001, art 38). In the one-tier system for SEs the equivalent of the board of directors of a UK company is called the administrative organ. In the two-tier system there is a supervisory organ and a management organ. Articles 39 to 51 of Regulation 2157/2001 prescribe the structure and functions of these organs. An SE is formed by cooperation between at least two existing EU companies governed by the laws of different member States. The form of employee involvement in an SE is to be determined by negotiation between the management or administrative organs of the existing companies and representatives of their companies' employees (Directive 2001/86/EC; implemented by SI 2009/2401). The rules in Directive 2001/86/EC seek to ensure that if participation rights exist in one or more companies establishing an SE, they will be transferred to the SE, unless there is agreement to the contrary.

15.2.5 SHAREHOLDER PRIMACY

In the shareholder-centred view a company's directors are required to act in the interests of the shareholders exclusively. Shareholder primacy supports the idea that a company's shareholders are entitled to its profits, which continues the view of the capitalist held by the classical economists. For example, J S Mill, in a passage first published in 1848, talked of:

> the share of the capitalist; the profits of capital or stock; the gains of the person who advances the expenses of production—who, from funds in his possession, pays the wages of the labourers, or supports them during the work; who supplies the requisite buildings, materials, and tools or machinery; and to whom, by the usual terms of the contract, the produce belongs, to be disposed of at his pleasure. After indemnifying him for his outlay, there commonly remains a surplus, which is his profit; the net income from his capital. (*Principles of Political Economy* (London: John W Parker, 1848), vol 2, Ch 15, s 1)

Normally, the directors of a company are not required to own any of its shares (see **15.5.8**). Economists have analysed the problems which may arise when the people managing a business do not own all of it. Managers in this position are believed to manage the business less efficiently than if they did own it. Rather than treating this as a consequence of the fact that wealth owners are not necessarily good business managers and good business managers are not necessarily wealth owners, the analysis adopted in the shareholder-primacy view of the company is that the inefficiency of managers is a detriment for providers of capital, for whom the managers are treated as 'agents'. The role model for directors seems to be the eighteenth or nineteenth-century steward or land-agent managing an estate for a temporarily absent landlord who might be expected to return to retake control. This was how the leading classical economist Adam Smith put it in a passage first published in 1784:

> The directors of such companies, however, being the managers rather of other people's money than their own, it cannot well be expected, that they should watch over it with the same anxious vigilance with which the partners in a private copartnery frequently watch over their own. Like the stewards of a rich man, they are apt to consider attention to small matters as not for their master's honour, and very easily give themselves a dispensation from having it. Negligence and profusion, therefore, must always prevail, more or less, in the management of the affairs of such a company. (*An Inquiry into the Nature and Causes of the Wealth of Nations*, R H Campbell and A S Skinner (eds) (Oxford: Clarendon Press, 1976), p 741)

In this analysis, the efficiency losses, the costs incurred by investors in monitoring managers and the so-called 'bonding costs' incurred by managers to demonstrate that they really are working in the investors' interests are known collectively as 'agency costs'. Controlling agency costs is seen as central to the relationship between shareholders and directors of a company (see M C Jensen and W H Meckling, 'Theory of the firm: managerial behavior, agency costs and ownership structure' (1976) 3 J Fin Econ 305). In law, though, directors are not agents of members (see **15.12**).

Law and economics analysts who favour explanations in terms of markets suggest that economic forces are significant in controlling the behaviour of directors of companies whose shares are publicly traded: they think that when the stock market is informed that the directors of a company are not acting in the best interests of its shareholders, the price of the company's shares will fall and it will be taken over by new owners who will install new directors to run the business more efficiently (H G Manne, 'Mergers and the market for corporate control' (1965) 73 J Pol Econ 110). They believe that directors will be so frightened of this happening, because they will lose their jobs and will not be employed in such good jobs again, that they will realise that it is in their own interests to act in the interests of the shareholders. It is said that the market for corporate control and the market for directors' employment will align the interests of directors and shareholders. However, it is admitted that in some cases a director may be able to make more by diverting money from the company than he or she can hope to make legitimately and that such a director would not be deterred from taking the company's money merely by fear of losing legitimate earnings (H N Butler, 'The contractual theory of the corporation' (1989) 11 Geo Mason U L Rev 99).

15.2.6 SEPARATION OF OWNERSHIP AND CONTROL

It is often claimed that the concept of shareholders as owners and directors as stewards does not correctly describe the actual relationship between directors and shareholders of public companies. The whole idea of the public company has always been that it offers the opportunity to invest in a company without any involvement in management. Public company shareholders treat their *shares* as their property which they can do what they like with, but they see ownership of shares in a company as separate from ownership of the company. Usually a person buying company shares on a stock exchange does not obtain them from the company and does not give the company money for them—normally shares are bought from other shareholders. It is alleged that in many public companies, the widespread of ownership of shares means that no one shareholder or group of shareholders can exercise effective control over the directors and that if owners of the shares in a company do not like what its directors are doing then, rather than try to influence the directors, they sell the shares. This situation was described as a 'separation of ownership and control' in an influential book by **A A Berle Jr and G C Means, *The Modern Corporation and Private Property*** (New York: Commerce Clearing House, 1932). (The title of a more recent book by M J Roe, *Strong Managers, Weak Owners* (Princeton, NJ: Princeton University Press, 1994), has provided another apt catchphrase.) Berle and Means noted that venturing capital in business and controlling or managing the business are two different functions, both of which need to be encouraged if economic activity is to be promoted. They argued that the shareholder-centred model of the company and the traditional view that the profits of an enterprise should go to the providers of its capital arose at a time when individual business people both provided capital for and directed their enterprises, so that profits, though the reward and incentive for both investment and direction, went to a single owner who combined both functions. The separation of ownership and control separated the two functions, which meant that the shareholder providers of capital could no longer claim the exclusive need to be incentivised by profits. Berle and Means made the not altogether obvious leap from this argument to the proposal that large American corporations in which ownership and control had been separated should serve 'all society' (p 356) and that:

> the 'control' of the great corporations should develop into a purely neutral technocracy, balancing a variety of claims by various groups in the community and assigning to each a portion of the income stream on the basis of public policy rather than private cupidity.

Once again, the directors are given a self-effacing role working purely for others.

Even classical economists acknowledged that a business's profits reward the successful direction of the business, by what they called the 'entrepreneur', as well as the passive supply of funds. This became clearer when capital markets developed and appeared to establish a price (rate of return) for the supply of capital, dependent on the riskiness of the investment. Investors could be regarded as supplying capital for a fixed return (at least, fixed from time to time by the capital market) just as workers worked for a fixed wage, and, some would argue, the balance of profits should go to the entrepreneur, though there is much room for disagreement over exactly which entrepreneurial function deserves the reward.

A different approach sees a business organisation as a coalition of individuals, including managers, workers, shareholders, suppliers, customers, lawyers, tax collectors and industry regulators (R M Cyert and J G March, *A Behavioral Theory of the Firm*, 2nd edn (Cambridge, Mass: Blackwell, 1992), p 31). Sharing the profits may be a matter of bargaining between these groups. For an exploration of companies in terms of bargaining between managers and shareholders, analysed using game theory, see M A Utset, 'Towards a bargaining theory of the firm' (1995) 80 Cornell L Rev 540.

E F Fama, 'Agency problems and the theory of the firm' (1980) 88 J Polit Econ 288 suggested that 'ownership of capital should not be confused with ownership of the firm' (at p 290). Capital is just one input supplied to a company for the purpose of its operations and each input is owned by some person. Management is just another input. Using the nexus of contracts image discussed in **5.5.4**, Fama went on to say in that article:

> The firm is just the set of contracts covering the way inputs are joined to create outputs and the way receipts from outputs are shared among inputs. In this 'nexus of contracts' perspective, ownership of the firm is an irrelevant concept.

But in a later article, E F Fama and M C Jensen, 'Separation of ownership and control' (1983) 26 J Law and Econ 301, re-established shareholder primacy by describing the equity shareholders of a company as the 'residual claimants'—that is, they are entitled to whatever is left of the company's assets after its debts have been paid. They may receive any amount from zero upwards, but in a limited company, provided their shares are fully paid, they will not be required to pay anything more. Fama and Jensen offer the alternative description 'residual risk bearers' and this has become a popular description, but it may perhaps exaggerate the heroism of shareholders. Members of companies risk losing their investment, but this is no different from the risk that all creditors of limited companies bear of not being paid. The 'residual risk' that members bear is just the risk of not receiving the return that they expect on their investments. The idea of equity shareholders as residual claimants rather than owners allows for other claimants such as creditors in whose interests the company may be operated. But as residual claimants, equity shareholder members can argue that the company ought to be run in such a way as to maximise their residue and that may not be in the interests of other constituencies.

For a restatement of the view that the shareholders of a company should not be seen as its owners, either economically or legally, see R Sappideen, 'Ownership of the large corporation: Why clothe the emperor?' (1996–7) 7 King's College LJ 27. Professor Sappideen argues that the only owner of a company is the company itself so that it is meaningless to talk of a separation of ownership and control.

15.2.7 RISE OF THE LARGE INSTITUTIONAL SHAREHOLDER

Some commentators prefer to think of control of a company as a variety of political process (A A Berle Jr, '"Control" in corporate law' (1958) 58 Colum L Rev 1212 at p 1215; **A A Berle, 'Modern functions of the corporate system'** (1962) 62 Colum L Rev 433 at p 445: 'In fact, a large corporation is a variety of non-statist [meaning, apparently, non-State] institution'). J Pound, 'The rise of the political model of corporate governance and corporate control' (1993) 68 NYU L Rev 1003, observes that in democratic politics, influence may be exerted by discussion and lobbying as well as by intermittently changing the government by general election, and claims that in the USA in the early 1990s changes in board personnel and policies were more often brought about by the lobbying of large investors than by takeovers, which Pound claims are an inefficiently drastic method of correcting mismanagement.

The increase in shareholder activism in the USA, where large public employee pension funds are particularly significant shareholders, is discussed by B S Black, 'Shareholder passivity reexamined' (1990) 89 Mich L Rev 520. Black notes that shareholding is becoming more concentrated as institutions such as pension funds invest large amounts in the leading companies whose shares are publicly traded. It is possible for large institutional shareholders to control enough shares to overcome the separation of ownership and control in large public companies and have a direct influence on their management. For similar comments in the British context see J Farrar and M Russell, 'The impact of institutional investment on company law' (1984) 5 Co Law 107. However, several commentators have pointed out that active participation in the management of companies is an inappropriate activity for many institutional investors, such as pension funds and insurance companies, which have duties to their own members or customers requiring them to avoid risk (see R Sappideen, 'Ownership of the large corporation: Why clothe the emperor?' (1996–97) 7 King's College LJ 27; T A Smith, 'Institutions and entrepreneurs in American corporate finance' (1997) 85 Calif L Rev 1).

From a high point of about 60 per cent in 1993, domestic institutional investment in UK companies has declined somewhat, to around 45 per cent in 2008. This has been accompanied by an increase in overseas investment, including overseas pension funds and sovereign wealth funds.

For premium listed companies, the UK Corporate Governance Code (see 15.2.2), main principle E.1, states that the board and institutional shareholders should enter into a dialogue based on mutual understanding of objectives. The FRC has issued the UK Stewardship Code. The principles which are stated and explained in the Code are that institutional investors should:

(a) publicly disclose their policy on how they will discharge their stewardship responsibilities;

(b) have a robust policy on managing conflicts of interest in relation to stewardship and this policy should be publicly disclosed;

(c) monitor their investee companies;

(d) establish clear guidelines on when and how they will escalate their stewardship activities;

(e) be willing to act collectively with other investors where appropriate;

(f) have a clear policy on voting and disclosure of voting activity; and

(g) report periodically on their stewardship and voting activities.

A statement on an investing institution's website should:

(a) describe how each of the principles has been applied;

(b) disclose the specific information requested in the guidance to the principles; and

(c) provide an explanation of why any of these elements of the Code have not been complied with.

The board of a premium listed company should appoint one of the independent non-executive directors to be the senior independent director, who should be available to shareholders if they have concerns, which they cannot communicate to, or have failed to resolve with, the chairman, chief executive or another executive director (UK Corporate Governance Code, para A.4.1). The board should keep in touch with shareholder opinion in whatever ways are most practical and efficient (UK Corporate Governance Code, supporting principle E.1) and there should be a statement in the annual financial report of the steps taken to ensure that members of the board, particularly non-executive directors, develop an understanding of the views of major shareholders (UK Corporate Governance Code, para E.1.2).

The trustees of occupational pension schemes are required by the Pensions Act 1995, s 35, to produce a statement of their investment principles. As from 3 July 2000 this must state the trustees' policy in relation to the exercise of voting rights attaching to investments (SI 1996/3127, reg 11A(b)). The same requirement has been imposed on authorities administering pension funds for local government employees in England and Wales (SI 1998/1831, reg 9A(2)(g)) and Scotland (SI 1998/2888, reg 9A(2)(g)). There is also legislation in Northern Ireland to the same effect.

15.3 DEFINITIONS

15.3.1 INTERPRETATION OF 'DIRECTOR' IN LEGISLATION

By CA 2006, s 250, the expression 'director', when used in CA 2006, includes any person occupying the position of director, by whatever name called. The same provision is made in IA 1986, s 251; CDDA 1986, s 22(4); and FSMA 2000, s 417(1).

15.3.2 *DE JURE* AND *DE FACTO* DIRECTORS

A person is described as a *de jure* director of a company if:

(a) the person has been appointed to the office of director in accordance with the rules governing such appointment (see **15.5**);

(b) the person has agreed to hold office;

(c) the person is not disqualified from being a director of the company (see **20.13**); and

(d) the person has not vacated office (see **15.6**).

A person who acts as a director of a company but is not a *de jure* director of it is called a *de facto* director. Whether a *de facto* director is a director for the purposes of a legislative provision depends on context (*Re Lo-Line Electric Motors Ltd* [1988] Ch 477). Until the 1980s '*de facto* director' was used to refer to a director who had been appointed but whose appointment was in some way defective (see **15.5.5**) or a director who had been properly appointed but who carried on acting as a director after the appointment had terminated. More recently '*de facto* director' has also been used to describe people whom the courts have treated as directors despite never being appointed as such at all. This has happened most often in the context of disqualification proceedings (see **20.13.6.5**). The history of the term '*de facto* director' is examined in detail by Lord Collins in *Commissioners of HM Revenue and Customs v Holland* [2010] UKSC 51, [2010] 1 WLR 2793, at [58]–[93]. His Lordship said (at [93]) that the term could have different meanings in different contexts.

In fact, the only settled definition of the term '*de facto* director' is the one given by Lord Collins in *Commissioners of HM Revenue and Customs v Holland* at [93], which was for the purpose of deciding whether a person is subject to the fiduciary duties of a director (now codified as statutory duties, see **16.2**). For that purpose, it must be shown that the person was part of the corporate governing structure and assumed a role in the company sufficient to impose those duties. The question of how to determine whether a person is a *de facto* director for the purpose of imposing statutory duties is considered in **16.4**.

15.3.3 SHADOW DIRECTORS

In relation to a company, the term 'shadow director' means a person in accordance with whose directions or instructions the directors of the company are accustomed to act (CA 2006, s 251(1)). Advice given in a professional capacity does not make the adviser a shadow director (s 251(2)(a)). Also excluded are instructions, directions, guidance or advice given by a person exercising a function conferred by or under an enactment (s 251(2)(b)) and guidance or advice given by a person in his or her capacity as a Minister of the Crown (s 251(2)(c)). The same definition is given in IA 1986, s 251, and CDDA 1986, s 22(5). In FSMA 2000 the term 'director' is to be interpreted as including a shadow director (s 417(1)).

A person is a shadow director of a company only if 'the directors of the company' are 'accustomed' to act in accordance with that person's directions or instructions (s 741(2)). This means that at least a consistent governing majority of the directors must be accustomed to act in that way (*Ultraframe (UK) Ltd v Fielding* [2005] EWHC 1638 (Ch), [2007] WTLR 835, at [1272]). The fact that only a minority of the company's directors are accustomed so to act is not enough to make the person a shadow director (*Kuwait Asia Bank EC v National Mutual Life Nominees Ltd* [1991] 1 AC 187 at p 223; *Re Unisoft Group Ltd (No 3)* [1994] 1 BCLC 609 at p 620; *Lord v Sinai Securities Ltd* [2004] EWHC 1764 (Ch), [2005] 1 BCLC 295). A person will not be a shadow director of a company unless the directors of that company act on the person's directions or instructions as a matter of regular practice, over a period of time (*Re Unisoft Group Ltd (No 3)* at p 620).

A person does not become a shadow director of a company until its directors act in accordance with his or her directions or instructions: just giving the directions or instructions is not enough (*Ultraframe (UK) Ltd v Fielding* at [1278]). There may be a period before a person becomes a shadow director when directors act in accordance with the person's directions or instructions but are not yet 'accustomed' so to act (*Ultraframe (UK) Ltd v Fielding* at [1273]–[1277]).

The Court of Appeal considered the definition of shadow director in *Secretary of State for Trade and Industry v Deverell* [2001] Ch 340. It was held that, in order to establish that a person is a shadow director of a company:

(a) it is not necessary to show that the person gives directions or instructions on every matter on which the directors act, but it must be shown that the person has a real influence in the company's corporate affairs;

(b) whether any particular communication should be classed as a direction or instruction is for the court to determine objectively;

(c) advice (provided it is not professional advice) may be a direction or instruction;

(d) it is not necessary to show that the directors adopted a subservient role or surrendered their discretion; and

(e) despite the use of the term 'shadow director' it is not necessary to characterise the person as 'lurking in the shadows': it is possible for a person to be a shadow director quite openly.

A person may act partly as a shadow director and partly as a *de facto* director, for example by carrying out the functions of a director in relation to marketing or finance, and giving directions or instructions to the board on other matters (*Re Mea Corporation Ltd* [2006] EWHC 1846 (Ch), [2007] 1 BCLC 618, at [89]). The earlier view that a person cannot be both a shadow director and a *de facto* director (*Re Hydrodam (Corby) Ltd* [1994] 2 BCLC 180 at p 183) has been overtaken by the extension of the concept of *de facto* directorship (*Commissioners of HM Revenue and Customs v Holland* [2010] UKSC 51, [2010] 1 WLR 2793, at [91]).

The fact that the directors of a company are obliged to conduct it in accordance with requirements laid down by a major lender or customer for the protection of that person's interests does not necessarily make that person a shadow director (*Ultraframe (UK) Ltd v Fielding* at [1267]–[1269]).

For an extensive and detailed discussion, see C Noonan and S Watson, 'The nature of shadow directorship: ad hoc statutory intervention or core company law principle?' [2006] JBL 763.

15.3.4 CORPORATE DIRECTORS

It is currently possible for a company to have another company as a *de jure* director (*Re Bulawayo Market and Offices Co Ltd* [1907] 2 Ch 58). CA 2006, s 155, introduced a rule that every company had to have at least one director who is a natural person. When s 156A comes into force it will allow only natural persons to be appointed as company directors (s 156A(1)). An appointment in contravention of this requirement will be void (s 156A(3)) and an offence will have been committed by the company which made the appointment, the company appointed and officers of both companies who are in default (s 156A(6)). Companies will have 12 months to replace existing corporate directors, after which any corporate directors still in office will be deemed to have ceased to be directors (s 156C). These provisions will not prevent a person being a director as a corporation sole or otherwise by virtue of an office (s 156A(2)). The Secretary of State has the power to make regulations creating other exceptions (s 156B), but there has been difficulty in deciding what exceptions should be made. See J Ellis, 'The continued appointment of corporate directors' (2016) 37 Co Law 203.

A company which cannot be a *de jure* director can nevertheless be a *de facto* or shadow director (s 156A(4)). It is possible for a parent company to be a shadow director of a subsidiary company (but not necessarily, see *Gramophone and Typewriter Ltd v Stanley* [1908] 2 KB 89), and CA 2006, s 251(3), makes some special provisions for such cases, see **15.9.4**, **16.12.2** and **19.5.8**.

Any action taken in exercising the powers of a company, D, which is a *de facto* or shadow director of a company, C, must be taken by a human being acting on D's behalf. Whether such an individual thereby becomes a *de facto* or shadow director of C is a question of fact in each case. It does not automatically follow that a director of company D is a *de facto* or shadow director of C (*Re Hydrodam (Corby) Ltd* [1994] 2 BCLC 180; *Secretary of State for Trade and Industry v Hall* [2006] EWHC 1995 (Ch), [2009] BCC 190; *Commissioners of HM Revenue and Customs v Holland* [2010] UKSC 51, [2010] 1 WLR 2793; see **16.4**). A director of D who takes no part in the affairs of C cannot be a *de facto* or shadow director of C (*Secretary of State for Trade and Industry v Hall*).

15.4 MINIMUM NUMBER OF DIRECTORS

CA 2006, s 154(1), requires every private company to have at least one director. Section 154(2) requires every public company to have at least two directors.

If a public company which should, by statute, have at least two directors has only one, that one director cannot act (*Jalmoon Pty Ltd v Bow* [1996] QCA 516, [1997] 2 QdR 62), except to appoint another director, if the power to do so is available (*Channel Collieries Trust Ltd v Dover St Margaret's and Martin Mill Light Railway Co* [1914] 2 Ch 506; *Macson Development Co Ltd v Gordon* (1959) 19 DLR (2d) 465; *APT Group Services Pty Ltd v Ferguson* (1991) 6 ACSR 231). Power for a sole director to appoint another director is given in the model articles of association in SI 2008/3229 (model articles for private companies, arts 11(3)(a) and 17(1)(b); model articles for public companies, art 11, discussed in **15.5.3.3**).

CA 2006, s 156, gives the Secretary of State a power to require a company, which has fewer than the statutory minimum number of directors, or has no natural person as a director, to make the necessary appointments within a specified period of one to three months. Failure to comply is an offence.

If a company has fewer directors in office than the minimum number prescribed for the company by its articles, the directors in office cannot act (*Re Alma Spinning Co, Bottomley's Case* (1880) 16 ChD 681) unless there is a provision in the articles which permits them to act (*Re Scottish Petroleum Co* (1883) 23 ChD 413) or they are exercising a power to appoint directors to make up the minimum number (*Channel Collieries Trust Ltd v Dover St Margaret's and Martin Mill Light Railway Co*; *Macson Development Co Ltd v Gordon*; *Re Sly, Spink and Co* [1911] 2 Ch 430 at p 436). The articles of Scottish Petroleum Co, which required the company to have at least four directors, provided that 'The continuing directors or a sole continuing director may act notwithstanding any vacancies in their number'. Only two directors were left because of resignations. It was held that the acts of those two were valid. However, it seems that a provision in the articles of association worded in this way applies only when the number of directors has been reduced below the minimum and does not cover a situation in which the minimum number of directors never have taken office because of a failure to appoint the minimum number on registration of the company (*Re British Empire Match Co Ltd* (1889) 59 LT 291; *Re Sly, Spink and Co*).

For premium listed companies, the UK Corporate Governance Code says (supporting principles B.1):

> The board should be of sufficient size that the requirements of the business can be met and that changes to the board's composition and that of its committees can be managed without undue disruption, and should not be so large as to be unwieldy.

15.5 APPOINTMENT OF DIRECTORS

15.5.1 WHO APPOINTS?

The Companies Act 2006 does not prescribe who is to be responsible for appointing the directors of a company though it requires the first directors to be appointed by a statement signed by, or on behalf of, the subscribers of the memorandum (see **15.5.2**) and it gives the company's members a right to dismiss directors of the company (see **15.6.3**). Provision for appointment is normally made in a company's articles. In the absence of any provision, directors are to be appointed by the company's members (*Woolf v East Nigel Gold Mining Co Ltd* (1905) 21 TLR 660; *Harman v Energy Research Group Australia Ltd* [1986] WAR 123). The members have an inherent power to appoint directors (*Worcester Corsetry Ltd v Witting* [1936] Ch 640), which may be exercised by ordinary resolution (*Link Agricultural Pty Ltd v Shanahan* (1998) 28 ACSR 498). The articles may limit this power. For example, in *Blair Open Hearth Furnace Co Ltd v Reigart* (1913) 108 LT 665 it was held that the power to appoint additional directors had been given by the company's articles to the board of directors to the exclusion of members, though in *Worcester Corsetry Ltd v Witting*, with only a slight change in wording of the articles, this was held not to have happened. In a company which has two or more classes of members, each entitled to appoint its own directors, the power of the whole company in general meeting to appoint directors is probably excluded (*Berlei Hestia (NZ) Ltd v Fernyhough* [1980] 2 NZLR 150 at p 155).

An appointment of a person as a director of a company does not take effect unless the person agrees to the appointment (*Re British Empire Match Co Ltd* (1888) 59 LT 291). Consent given by a drug addict who did not appreciate what she was doing was held to be insufficient in *Re CEM Connections Ltd* [2000] BCC 917.

The model articles of association in SI 2008/3229 give the power to appoint directors both to the members and to the existing directors (model articles for private companies, art 17(1); model articles for public companies, art 20). Under the model articles for public companies, an appointment by the directors lasts only until the next annual general meeting, at which the co-opted director may offer him or herself for reappointment by the members (art 21(2)).

The model articles for a private company provide that if, as a result of death, the company has no shareholders and no directors, the personal representatives of the last shareholder to have died have the right to appoint a director (art 17(2) and (3)).

15.5.2 FIRST DIRECTORS

An application for registration of a company must include a statement of proposed officers (CA 2006, s 9(4)(c)), which must contain the required particulars of the person who is, or the persons who are, to be the first director or directors of the company (s 12(1)(a) and (2)(a)) and a statement that each has consented to act as a director (s 12(3); see **2.2.1.8**). The person or persons named in the statement are deemed to have been appointed director or directors as from the date of the company's incorporation (s 16(6)). These provisions were introduced by CA 1976. As the subscribers to a company's memorandum are, by definition, the company's first members (CA 2006, s 112(1)), these provisions accord with the common law rule that, in the absence of any provision in a company's constitution about the appointment of its first directors, an appointment made by its members is valid, and if they are unanimous then they can make appointments without meeting (*Perseus Mining NL v Landbrokers (Perth) Pty Ltd* [1972] WAR 12).

Under the model articles for a public company, art 21(1), in SI 2008/3229, at the first annual general meeting of the company all its directors must retire. So none of the first directors can continue in office beyond the first annual general meeting unless they are reappointed by the members.

15.5.3 SUBSEQUENT DIRECTORS

15.5.3.1 Circumstances in which appointments are made

After a company's first directors have been appointed, it may be necessary to make new appointments, either to fill a vacancy when a director vacates office (see **15.6**) or to increase the size of the board by appointing one or more additional directors.

15.5.3.2 Appointment by the members

The model articles of association in SI 2008/3229 empower the members to appoint a person by ordinary resolution to be a director, but say that only a person who is willing to act, and is permitted by law to do so, may be appointed (model articles for private companies, art 17(1); model articles for public companies, art 20).

The power of the majority to appoint directors must 'be exercised for the benefit of the company as a whole and not to secure some ulterior advantage' (*Re H R Harmer Ltd* [1959] 1 WLR 62 at p 82; *Re Broadcasting Station 2GB Pty Ltd* [1964–5] NSWR 1648 at p 1662). In *Theseus Exploration NL v Mining and Associated Industries Ltd* [1973] QdR 81, the court issued an interim injunction to prevent members of a company electing certain persons as directors because there was sufficient evidence that those persons intended to use the company's assets solely for the benefit of the majority shareholder.

The model articles for a public company, art 21(1), provides that all the first directors must retire at the first annual general meeting. Article 21(2) also provides a system of retirement by rotation for directors, under which each director must offer him or herself for re-election at every third annual general meeting (see **15.6.2**).

The term of office of a director whose appointment has been put to the vote will not commence until it has been ascertained that the vote is in favour of the appointment (*Holmes v Keyes* [1959] Ch 199).

At a general meeting of a public company, a motion for the appointment of two or more persons as directors by a single resolution must not be made, unless a resolution that it shall be so made has first been agreed to by the meeting without any vote being given against it (CA 2006, s 160(1)). A resolution in contravention of s 160(1) is void even if no one objected to it at the time (s 160(2)). However, the fact that appointments of directors of a company are deemed to be void by s 160(2) does not bring into operation a provision in the company's articles for the automatic reappointment of a retiring director in default of another appointment, and the acts of the directors are validated by s 161 (see **15.5.5**).

For premium listed companies, main principle B.2 of the UK Corporate Governance Code (see **15.2.2**) states that 'There should be a formal, rigorous and transparent procedure for the appointment of new directors to the board'. A premium listed company's board should establish a nomination committee (see **15.8.7**), to make recommendations to the board on all new board appointments (para B.2.1). A majority of the members of the nomination committee should be independent non-executive directors, and the chair should be either the chairman of the board or an independent non-executive director (para B.2.1). Code provision B.7.1 requires all directors of FTSE 350 companies (see **7.3.3.3**) to submit themselves for re-election annually. Directors of other premium listed companies should submit themselves for re-election at least every three years, and annually after serving for nine years (B.7.1). Sufficient biographical details should be supplied about persons submitted for election or re-election as directors to enable shareholders to take an informed decision on their election (B.7.1).

15.5.3.3 Appointment by the directors

The model articles of association in SI 2008/3229 empower the directors to appoint a person to be a director, but only a person who is willing to act, and is permitted by law to do so, may be appointed (model articles for private companies, art 17(1); model articles for public companies, art 20). This power may be exercised, even if there is only one director, to make the number of directors up to the minimum required by statute (*Channel Collieries Trust Ltd v Dover St Margaret's and Martin Mill Light Railway Co* [1914] 2 Ch 506; *Macson Development Co Ltd v Gordon* (1959) 19 DLR (2d) 465; *APT Group Services Pty Ltd v Ferguson* (1991) 6 ACSR 231), or by the articles (*Channel Collieries Trust Ltd v Dover St Margaret's and Martin Mill Light Railway Co*; *Macson Development Co Ltd v Gordon*; *Re Sly, Spink and Co* [1911] 2 Ch 430 at p 436), or needed to form a quorum (*Channel Collieries Trust Ltd v Dover St Margaret's and Martin Mill Light Railway Co*; *APT Group Services Pty Ltd v Ferguson*; model articles for public companies, art 11).

Under the model articles for public companies, art 21(2), a director appointed by the directors holds office only until the next annual general meeting.

15.5.4 DISQUALIFICATION

15.5.4.1 Introduction

A significant aspect of the control of companies for the public interest is the prohibition of certain persons from acting as company directors. In recent years Parliament has considerably extended the circumstances in which the courts can declare a person disqualified from directing or managing companies. This is done by making disqualification orders or accepting disqualification undertakings under the Company Directors Disqualification Act 1986 (CDDA 1986)—see **20.13**. Other circumstances in which a person must not be a company director are examined in the following paragraphs. It is notable that an individual who becomes personally insolvent and is declared bankrupt will automatically commit an offence if he or she acts as director of a company (see **15.5.4.2**). However, an individual who directs a company into insolvency is entitled to set up a new company immediately unless and until a court, in its discretion, makes a disqualification order. This is a striking example of the way in which incorporation of a company to carry on a business separates an individual's personal and business affairs.

15.5.4.2 By personal insolvency

From the time when an individual is adjudged bankrupt until the bankruptcy is discharged (which is usually one year) or annulled it is an offence triable either way for the undischarged bankrupt to act as director of, or directly or indirectly to take part in or be concerned in the management of, a company unless he or she has the leave of the court that made the bankruptcy order (CDDA 1986, ss 11 and 13; for discussion of sentencing see *R v Theivendran* (1992) 13 Cr App R (S) 601 and *R v Ashby* [1998] 2 Cr App R (S) 37). This applies wherever in the United Kingdom the bankruptcy order was made. The offence is one of strict liability, that is the prosecution only have to prove that the accused did the prohibited act and do not have to prove an intention to offend (*R v Brockley* [1994] 1 BCLC 606; *R v Doring* [2002] EWCA Crim 1695, [2003] 1 Cr App R 143). Annulment of an individual's bankruptcy order does not relieve the individual from liability for acting as a director before the order was annulled (*Commissioners of Inland Revenue v McEntaggart* [2004] EWHC 3431 (Ch), [2006] 1 BCLC 476). In four cases reported on applications by bankrupts for leave to take part in the management of companies, leave was refused (*Re Kingsgate Rare Metals Pty Ltd* [1940] QWN 42; *Re Altim Pty Ltd* [1968] 2 NSWR 762; *Re McQuillan* (1988) 5 BCC 137; *Re Ansett* (1990) 3 ACSR 357).

In addition, an individual who has been adjudicated bankrupt may be made subject to a bankruptcy restrictions order or undertaking for a period of two to 15 years (IA 1986, s 281A and sch 4A, and similar provisions in Scotland and Northern Ireland). This is similar to the system of director disqualification orders and undertakings (see **20.13**). It is an offence for a person, in respect of whom a bankruptcy restrictions order or undertaking is in force, to act as director of a company or directly or indirectly to take part in or be concerned in the promotion, formation or management of a company, without the leave of the court which adjudged him or her bankrupt (CDDA 1986, ss 11 and 13; IA 1986, sch 4A, para 8: it is submitted that 'in force' in CDDA 1986, s 11(2)(b), is synonymous with 'has effect' in IA 1986, sch 4A, para 8).

CDDA 1986, s 11, also applies to a person who is subject to a debt relief restrictions order or undertaking or a moratorium period under a debt relief order made in England and Wales or Northern Ireland (s 11(2)(c) and (d)).

If an administration order (under which an individual judgement debtor's estate is administered by the County Court under the County Courts Act 1984, part VI) is revoked because the individual has failed to make a payment required by the order, the court may order that CDDA 1986, s 12, is to apply to that individual (IA 1986, s 429(2)(b)). The individual is then prohibited from acting as director of, or directly or indirectly taking part or being concerned in the management of, a company without leave of the court which ordered CDDA 1986, s 12, to apply: contravention of the prohibition is an offence triable either way (s 13).

In CDDA 1986, 'director' includes any person occupying the position of director, by whatever name called (s 22(4); see **15.3.1**). What amounts to taking part in the management of a company is discussed in **20.13.1.3**.

15.5.4.3 By being auditor

An individual who is a director of a company is disqualified from acting as its auditor: in other words, the individual must choose to be either auditor or director (CA 2006, s 1214(1) and (2)).

15.5.4.4 By being too young

CA 2006, s 157, introduced a new rule from 1 October 2008 that an individual under the age of 16 cannot be appointed a director of a company (s 157(1)), except by an appointment which is not to take effect until his or her sixteenth birthday (s 157(2)). The Secretary of State has a power to make regulations specifying exceptions from this rule (s 158), but no regulations have been made. The rule does not affect the liability of any *de facto* or shadow director who is under 16 (s 157(5)).

15.5.4.5 By not being human

When CA 2006, s 156A, comes into force, directors must be natural persons. See **15.3.4**.

15.5.5 DEFECTIVE APPOINTMENTS

By CA 2006, s 161(1):

> The acts of a person acting as a director are valid notwithstanding that it is afterwards discovered—
>
> (a)   that there was a defect in his appointment;
>
> (b)   that he was disqualified from holding office;
>
> (c)   that he had ceased to hold office;
>
> (d)   that he was not entitled to vote on the matter in question.

In particular, the acts of directors of a public company whose appointment is deemed to be void by s 160(2) (prohibition of single motion for appointment of more than one director) are validated (s 161(2)).

Section 161(1) validates acts done by directors in relation to members (such as making calls and forfeiting shares) as well as transactions with outsiders (*Dawson v African Consolidated Land and Trading Co* [1898] 1 Ch 6).

An earlier version of s 161(1) was considered by the House of Lords in *Morris v Kanssen* [1946] AC 459, where Lord Simonds said, at pp 471–2:

> There is, as it appears to me, a vital distinction between (a) an appointment in which there is a defect or, in other words, a defective appointment, and (b) no appointment at all. In the first case it is implied that some act is done

which purports to be an appointment but is by reason of some defect inadequate for the purpose; in the second case there is not a defect, there is no act at all. The section does not say that the acts of a person acting as director shall be valid notwithstanding that it is afterwards discovered that he was not appointed a director . . . These observations apply equally where the term of office of a director has expired, but he nevertheless continues to act as a director. [This has now been dealt with by s 161(1), which does now validate the acts of directors afterwards found to have vacated office] . . . the section . . . being designed as machinery to avoid questions being raised as to the validity of transactions where there has been a slip in the appointment of a director, cannot be utilised for the purpose of ignoring or overriding the substantive provisions relating to such appointment.

In the case, Kanssen and Cromie were a company's only directors. Cromie claimed falsely that a third person, Strelitz, had been appointed a director and a minute of the appointment was falsely recorded. By the operation of the rule in *Re Consolidated Nickel Mines Ltd* [1914] 1 Ch 883 (see **15.6.2**), all the company's directors (real or false) automatically vacated office when the company failed to hold annual general meetings. (Unlike s 161(1), the legislation then in force did not validate the acts of directors afterwards found to have vacated office.) Subsequently, Cromie and Strelitz purported to hold a board meeting at which they appointed Mr Morris a 'director' of the company. Cromie, Strelitz and Morris then purported to hold a board meeting at which shares of the company were allotted which were acquired by Morris. Morris claimed that this allotment was validated by what is now s 161(1). The House of Lords held that the provision did not apply because the persons whose acts were sought to be validated had not been appointed directors at all. Morris could not rely on the indoor management rule (see **19.5.4.6**) to validate the allotment because he had himself acted as a director (that is, he was a *de facto* director) in making the allotment (see **19.5.4.10**).

A person seeking to rely on validation provisions must have acted in good faith (*Channel Collieries Trust Ltd v Dover, St Margaret's and Martin Mill Light Railway Co* [1914] 2 Ch 506, per Lord Cozens-Hardy MR at p 512). In particular, the defect must not have been known at the time of the appointment, though persons are not, in this context, presumed to know the law. This means that the validation provisions can apply where the facts which rendered the appointment invalid were known to the people involved at the time of the appointment but they honestly failed to appreciate that the legal effect was to render the appointment invalid (*British Asbestos Co Ltd v Boyd* [1903] 2 Ch 439; *Channel Collieries Trust Ltd v Dover, St Margaret's and Martin Mill Light Railway Co*). As Farwell J put it in **British Asbestos Co Ltd v Boyd**, at pp 444–5, the object of these provisions:

> is to make the honest acts of *de facto* directors as good as the honest acts of *de jure* directors . . . although there may be some slip which has been overlooked, if it has been bona fide overlooked, then the acts of the *de facto* directors are as good as the acts of the *de jure* directors.

A person cannot rely on the validation provisions to validate some acts of a *de facto* director and also seek to denounce other acts of that director on the ground that he was not a director *de jure* (*Levin v Clark* [1962] NSWR 686).

Where minutes have been made, in accordance with s 248 of a board meeting or s 355 of a general meeting, at which a director was appointed then, until the contrary is proved, the meeting is deemed duly held and convened, and the director's appointment is deemed to be valid (ss 249(2) and 356(5)).

15.5.6 ALTERNATE DIRECTORS

The model articles for a public company, art 25, in SI 2008/3229, permits a director to appoint an alternate—that is a person who can attend meetings that the appointing director is unable to attend, and can generally act in place of the appointing director. A director may appoint another present member of the board as alternate or may appoint another person, provided that other person is approved by resolution of the directors (art 25). By art 26, an alternate is not deemed to be the agent of the director by whom he or she was appointed but is responsible for his or her own acts and defaults. An alternate vacates office when the director who appointed him or her vacates office, except where the appointor retires by rotation and is immediately reappointed (art 27).

15.5.7 NOMINEE DIRECTORS

A shareholder with a significant investment in a private company who is not an executive director of the company usually ensures that he has the right to appoint one or more directors. This can best be done by dividing the company's shares into two classes: class A being those of the major investor and class B those of the other members. The articles are then amended to provide that a certain number of directors may be appointed and removed by notice given by holders of the majority of class A shares, and a certain number appointed similarly by the B shareholders. This creates class rights which can be varied only in accordance with CA 2006, s 630 (see **14.14.2**).

15.5.8 SHARE QUALIFICATION

It was common at one time for a company's articles of association to require its directors each to hold a certain number of shares in the company. Share qualifications are now much less common and the model articles of association in SI 2008/3229 do not mention them.

15.5.9 GENDER DIVERSITY

It is notorious that there have been few women directors of large companies in the United Kingdom. At the end of February 2012, 112 of the FTSE 250 companies had no women directors. However, this was the first time that companies with all-male boards were in the minority in the FTSE 250. The coalition government appointed Lord Davies of Abersoch (former Chairman of Standard Chartered plc and trade minister in the Labour government) to review the situation and make recommendations. Lord Davies recommended that all FTSE 350 companies should set targets for the percentage of women on their boards in 2013 and 2015. The target for FTSE 100 companies should be at least 25 per cent. That target was reached in October 2015 when 26.1 per cent of FTSE 100 directors were women. Lord Davies has recommended a new target of 33 per cent of women on FTSE 350 boards by 2020 (*Improving the Gender Balance on British Boards. Women on Boards Davies Review Five Year Summary October 2015*). For financial years ending on or after 30 September 2013, the strategic report of a quoted company must state the number of persons of each sex who were directors of the company and also give the gender balance of senior managers and all employees (CA 2006, s 414C(8)(c); see **9.9.2**). Following another of Lord Davies's recommendations the UK Corporate Governance Code, B.2.4, says that the section of the annual financial report dealing with the work of the nomination committee should include a description of the board's policy on diversity, including gender, any measurable objectives that it has set for implementing the policy and progress on achieving the objectives. The Code also says that consideration of diversity, including gender, should be part of a board's own annual review of its performance (B.6, supporting principles).

15.6 TERMINATION OF OFFICE

15.6.1 VACATION OF OFFICE DEEMED BY THE ARTICLES

The model articles for a private company, art 18, and the model articles for a public company, art 22, in SI 2008/3229, provide that a person ceases to be a director as soon as:

(a) that person ceases to be a director by virtue of any provision of CA 2006 or is prohibited from being a director by law;

(b) a bankruptcy order is made against that person;

(c) a composition is made with that person's creditors generally in satisfaction of that person's debts;

(d) a registered medical practitioner who is treating that person gives a written opinion to the company stating that that person has become physically or mentally incapable of acting as a director and may remain so for more than three months; and

(e) a notification to the company that that person is resigning or retiring from office as director is received by the company and has taken effect in accordance with its terms.

When one of these circumstances or events affects a director, the director's office is vacated automatically: there is no need for the other directors or the members to consider the matter or adopt a resolution. The other directors cannot waive the effect of such a provision (*Re Bodega Co Ltd* [1904] 1 Ch 276). A person who is removed from office by such a provision can be reappointed a director when no longer affected by the disqualifying circumstance (*Re Bodega Co Ltd*).

For the statutory prohibition on undischarged bankrupts acting as company directors, see **15.5.4.2**. For disqualification orders, see **20.13**.

15.6.2 RETIREMENT BY ROTATION

The model articles for public companies, art 21, in SI 2008/3229, provides for retirement of directors by rotation. It requires all the directors to retire at the first annual general meeting (art 21(1)). At subsequent annual general meetings, any directors appointed by the directors (see **15.5.3.3**) since the previous annual general meeting must retire (art 21(2)(a)). From the third annual general meeting on, every director who was not appointed at the two previous general meetings must retire (art 21(2)(b)).

In *Re Consolidated Nickel Mines Ltd* [1914] 1 Ch 883 it was held that, with articles like these, if an annual general meeting for a particular year is not held in that year, the directors due to retire at that meeting automatically vacate office at the end of the year. CA 2006, s 161(1) deals with this by providing that acts done by a person acting as a director shall be valid even if it is afterwards discovered that he or she had ceased to hold office. This provision validates only decisions taken before an irregularity is discovered. Once it is found that a director has vacated office, he or she cannot take part in decision-making until properly reappointed.

For the requirements of the UK Corporate Governance Code, B.7.1, see **15.5.3.2**.

15.6.3 DISMISSAL FROM OFFICE

Provision for the removal of directors is made by CA 2006, s 168. A company may, by ordinary resolution, remove a director before the expiration of the director's period of office, notwithstanding anything in any agreement between the company and the director (s 168(1)). Special notice (see **14.8.10**) is required of any resolution under s 168 to remove a director (s 168(2)) and a copy of the special notice must be sent by the company to the director concerned (s 169(1)). A resolution under s 168 may propose the dismissal of more than one director (*National Roads and Motorists' Association Ltd v Scandrett* [2002] NSWSC 1123, 43 ACSR 401).

A director sought to be dismissed by a resolution under s 168 is entitled under s 169 to communicate to the members. The director may make written representations, of a reasonable length, and, if received in time, the company must, when giving members notice of intention to propose the dismissal resolution, state that the representations have been received and send them to all members entitled to notice. If there is no time to do this (or the company defaults), the director is entitled to require the representations to be read out at the meeting. The director is entitled to speak on the resolution at the meeting, even if not a member of the company (s 169(2)). Because of the director's right to speak at the meeting it is doubtful whether a decision to dismiss a director arrived at by unanimous agreement without meeting could be effective under s 168 (see **14.13.4**). The procedure provided to private companies by s 288 for agreement to written resolutions cannot be used to dismiss a director under s 168 (s 288(2)(a)). Because of the rights to make representations, a resolution under s 168 to dismiss a director cannot be adopted in advance of the director's appointment (*National Roads and Motorists' Association Ltd v Scandrett*).

There seems to be no reason why the members for the time being of a company should not provide in a unanimous shareholders' agreement that they will not use s 168 to dismiss some or all of the company's directors. However, the articles of a company (which bind all members present and future) cannot exclude the members' statutory right to dismiss a director, because of the principle that any provision of a company's articles that is inconsistent with the law governing companies is void (see **3.3.3(b)**). Previous versions of s 168 stated expressly that the right to dismiss a director existed notwithstanding any provision in the company's articles (CA 1985, s 303(1)). The absence of this express statement in CA 2006, s 168, has led to speculation that articles may now take away the statutory right (A Cockerill and J Mendelsohn, 'Directors and the missing "articles"' (2008) 152(2) SJ 20). It is submitted that this would be inconsistent with the cases cited at **3.3.3(b)**.

In *Bushell v Faith* [1970] AC 1099, the company's 300 shares were held equally between the claimant, the defendant and their sister. The claimant and defendant were the company's only directors. The company's articles weighted the voting rights attached to the shares from one per share to three per share where the issue before a general meeting of the company was the removal of the director holding those shares. The claimant and her sister purported to remove the defendant from his office. The House of Lords upheld the validity of the voting rights by a 4–1 majority, and the resolution seeking the defendant's removal was therefore defeated by 300 votes (the defendant's weighted votes) to 200 (the claimant and her sister's combined unweighted votes). Lord Upjohn explained:

> Parliament has never sought to fetter the right of the company to issue a share with such rights or restrictions as it may think fit. There is no fetter which compels the company to make the voting rights or restrictions of general application and it seems to me clear that such rights or restrictions can be attached to special circumstances and to particular types of resolution. This makes no mockery of [s 168]; all that Parliament was seeking to do thereby was to make an ordinary resolution sufficient to remove a director. Had Parliament desired to go further and enact that every share entitled to vote should be deprived of its special rights under the articles it should have said so in plain terms by making the vote on a poll one vote one share.

This decision has been subjected to a good deal of criticism, but is clearly justified by the wording of s 168. P V Baker said in a casenote (1970) 86 LQR 155, at p 157: 'Either there are sound reasons of public policy why a bare majority of shareholders in general meeting should have ultimate control over the board of directors, or there are not. If there are, [*Bushell v Faith* shows] that [s 168] needs strengthening. If there are not, it should be repealed.' Professor Schmitthoff saw the decision in *Bushell v Faith* as justified by the fact that the company in question was a quasi-partnership company. See C M Schmitthoff, 'How the English discovered the private company', in *Quo vadis ius societatum*, P Zonderland (ed) (Deventer: Kluwer, 1972), pp 183–93.

A person cannot be appointed to fill the vacancy caused by the removal of a director under s 168 *at the same meeting* unless special notice of the appointment resolution has been given (s 168(2)). If, however, the vacancy is not filled at the same meeting then, under s 168(3), 'it may be filled as a casual vacancy'. The term 'casual vacancy' means a vacancy occurring otherwise than by retirement by rotation (*Munster v Cammell Co* (1882) 21 ChD 183 at p 187). The model articles of association in SI 2008/3229 do not make separate provision for filling casual vacancies so an appointment may be made by the members (see **15.5.3.2**) or by the directors (see **15.5.3.3**). Section 168(4) prescribes how provisions in articles for retirement of directors by rotation are to operate in relation to a person who replaces a director removed under s 168. The rotation provisions are to operate as if the replacement director had been appointed on the day on which the dismissed director was last appointed. It is submitted that this does not override the provision in the model articles for public companies, art 21(2)(a), that a replacement appointed by the directors under that article must be confirmed in office by the next annual general meeting.

Nothing in s 168 derogates from any other power to remove a director (s 168(5)(b)). Thus, articles could provide for dismissal of a director without special notice and without permitting the director to make representations (*Browne v Panga Pty Ltd* (1995) 120 FLR 34). If a company's articles provide for its directors to be dismissed by the members without formalities which can be carried out only at a meeting, the dismissal may be by unanimous agreement without meeting, and in a private company may be by written resolution under s 288. Some articles provide that a director's office is to be vacated if all the other members of the board make a written request for the director's resignation. Directors must act in the best interests of the company, and not for an ulterior motive, when making such a request but the fact that they are acting for an ulterior motive does not invalidate a request (*Lee v Chou Wen Hsien* [1984] 1 WLR 1202).

Removal of a person from the office of director of a company may be in breach of a contract between that person and the company. It may breach the contract under which the person acts as director if the contract is for a fixed period which has not expired or if the director is entitled to a period of notice. However, if the provision for a minimum period of service or notice is only in the articles of the company, rather than in a separate contract with the director concerned, it may be held to be subject to any power of removal also provided by the articles, so that using that power of removal does not breach the contract (as in *Shuttleworth v Cox Brothers and Co (Maidenhead) Ltd* [1927] 2 KB 9).

Removal of a person from the office of director of a company, whether or not breaching the contract under which the person serves as a director, may breach a second contract if the person can perform the second contract only by being a director. The leading cases have concerned removal from directorships of persons who served as managing director. It has been common for the articles of association of a company to provide that the appointment of a person as managing director of a company terminates if he or she ceases to be a director of the company. In *Southern Foundries (1926) Ltd v Shirlaw* [1940] AC 701 and in *Shindler v Northern Raincoat Co Ltd* [1960] 1 WLR 1038, removal of a director from office prevented him from continuing as managing director and caused a breach of the contract of appointment as managing director because, in both cases, the appointment as managing director was for a fixed term of ten years which had not expired. On the other hand, in *Read v Astoria Garage (Streatham) Ltd* [1952] Ch 637 there was nothing in the contract under which the plaintiff served as managing director to give him a fixed term of employment or even a period of notice so that summary removal from his directorship did not cause any breach of the contract of appointment as managing director. For the purposes of the Employment Rights Act 1996, s 98 (unfair dismissal), removal of a person from the board which causes loss of that person's job, which can only be held if the person is a director, is a dismissal for a substantial reason (*Cobley v Forward Technology Industries plc* [2003] EWCA Civ 646, [2003] ICR 1050). Whether or not it is an unfair dismissal depends on all the circumstances. Mr Cobley failed in his claim for unfair dismissal. He had been removed from the board, and so lost his job as chief executive, after a takeover battle for his employer in which he had been the unsuccessful bidder.

By CA 2006, s 168(5)(a), the fact that a company which dismisses a director under the s 168 procedure is using a power which is statutory and therefore overrides any contract with the director does not absolve the company from liability to pay the director compensation or damages for the dismissal.

If a director of a company is an employee of the company then removing the director from the directorship may mean terminating the contract of employment, which may involve a large compensation payment. Accordingly, provision has been made to ensure that members can discover the terms of their directors' contracts of service (s 228; see **4.4.4.1**). Compensation payments may be particularly heavy if a director has a fixed-term contract and so fixed-term contracts (whether contracts of service or contracts for services) for terms in excess of two years are subject to approval by the members (s 188; see **15.9.4**). A non-contractual termination payment must be approved by the members (ss 215 to 222; see **15.9.2**).

15.6.4 RESIGNATION

A director of a company is entitled to relinquish the office at any time by giving notice to the company. The director's resignation is effected by the notice and does not depend on acceptance of the resignation by the company, because the company cannot refuse acceptance. However, once notice has been given it cannot be withdrawn except by agreement with the company (*Glossop v Glossop* [1907] 2 Ch 370). It is not necessary to give the notice in advance of the day on which it is to take effect, that is, no period of notice is required (*O.B.C. Caspian Ltd v Thorp* 1998 SLT 653). All these rules may be altered by the terms of a director's contract of service. In particular, it is common to require an executive director to give a significant period of notice of resignation. In the absence of agreement, a reasonable term of notice is implied in a contract of employment. In *CMS Dolphin Ltd v Simonet* [2001] 2 BCLC 704, for example, it was held that three months was a reasonable period of notice for an executive director of an advertising agency.

The meaning of a resignation notice must be determined objectively by considering how a reasonable recipient would have understood it, taking into account the relevant objective contextual scene (*Quarter Master UK Ltd v Pyke* [2004] EWHC 1815 (Ch), [2005] 1 BCLC 245, applying *Mannai Investment Co Ltd v Eagle Star Life Assurance Co Ltd* [1997] AC 749).

Even though a person's resignation from his or her directorship of a company may seriously damage the company, it is not a breach of the director's fiduciary duty to the company (*CMS Dolphin Ltd v Simonet*). However, an executive director who breaches his or her contract of employment by leaving without giving the required period of notice may be liable to the company for loss it suffers as a result (see, for example, *CMS Dolphin Ltd v Simonet*).

15.6.5 DISPUTES ABOUT WHO HOLDS OFFICE AS A DIRECTOR

In a number of English cases a member of a company has successfully brought a claim to restrain a person who is acting as a director of the company, but has not been properly appointed, from continuing to act (*Catesby v Burnett* [1916] 2 Ch 325; *Spencer v Kennedy* [1926] 1 Ch 125; see also *Oliver v Dalgleish* [1963] 1 WLR 1274, in which a declaration that the defendants were not directors was given). The company also may bring such a claim (*Latchford Premier Cinema Ltd v Ennion* [1931] 2 Ch 409; *Worcester Corsetry Ltd v Witting* [1936] Ch 640). This raises the question whether the right of action in such a case belongs to the company or its members; see **18.4.5**.

A person who has been properly appointed director of a company may obtain an injunction to restrain the company or other directors from preventing him or her acting as such (*Pulbrook v Richmond Consolidated Mining Co* (1878) 9 ChD 610; *Munster v Cammell Co* (1882) 21 ChD 183; *Foster v Greenwich Ferry Co Ltd* (1888) 5 TLR 16). (In particular, an injunction may be issued to restrain directors from using their power to delegate to a committee as a device to exclude a particular director; *Kyshe v Alturas Gold Ltd* (1888) 4 TLR 331 and other cases cited in **15.8.7**.) In deciding whether to grant an interim injunction, the court will take into account the opinion of the members of the company, expressed in general meeting, on whether or not they wish the claimant to act as a director (*Harben v Phillips* (1883) 23 ChD 14; *Bainbridge v Smith* (1889) 41 ChD 462; *Clifton v Mount Morgan Ltd* (1940) 40 SR (NSW) 31). Such opinion would carry even more weight now that the members have a statutory right, under CA 2006, s 168, to dismiss a director by ordinary resolution—a right which was not available when any of the three last-mentioned cases was decided. In *Currie v Cowdenbeath Football Club Ltd* 1992 SLT 407, the club had commenced proceedings to prevent two men acting as its directors, claiming that they had resigned. The other directors decided to resolve the situation by convening an extraordinary general meeting to consider a resolution to dismiss each of the men under what is now s 168, 'if, as a matter of fact, [he] is presently a director'. Remarkably, Lord Penrose granted the men an interim interdict (the Scottish equivalent of an interim injunction) against the holding of the meeting, saying that it was an attempt to usurp the court's jurisdiction over the dispute and that it is not possible to pass a contingent resolution under what is now s 168. In a similar case in Western Australia, though, Ipp J took the opposite view and held that members do have a power to decide whether or not they want particular persons to be directors (*Browne v Panga Pty Ltd* (1995) 120 FLR 34). It is submitted that Ipp J's view is preferable.

In *Hayes v Bristol Plant Hire Ltd* [1957] 1 WLR 499, the extent of a claimant's proprietary interest in his or her office as a director required to justify the court granting an injunction was questioned. It was held that, in Mr Hayes's case, his shareholding and the possibility of being paid fees as a director were sufficient. It remains questionable whether a non-shareholding director could have a sufficient interest.

Exclusion of a director may also be conduct of the company's affairs in a manner unfairly prejudicial to the interests of members (see the discussion of *Re H R Harmer Ltd* [1959] 1 WLR 62 in **15.8.1.1**).

15.7 TRANSPARENCY

15.7.1 REGISTERS

Every company is required to keep a register of directors (CA 2006, s 162(1) and (3)). A company must also keep a register of its directors' residential addresses (s 165). The register of directors is open to public inspection (s 162(5); see **4.4.2.3**) but the register of directors' residential addresses is not. Private companies will be able to keep either or both of these registers at Companies House (see **4.4.2.9**). The register of directors must contain the required particulars of each person who is a director of the company (s 162(2)). The required particulars depend on whether the director is an individual (s 163), a company registered in an EEA State and of a type to which Directive 2009/101/EC applies (s 164, which refers to an earlier version of the Directive), any other company (s 164), or a firm that is a legal person under the law by which it is governed (s 164). Entries are required in the register of directors' residential addresses only for directors who are individuals (s 165(6)).

15.7.2 NOTIFICATION TO COMPANIES HOUSE AND IN THE *GAZETTE*

An application for registration of a company must include a statement of proposed officers (CA 2006, s 9(4)(c)), which must contain the required particulars of the person who is, or the persons who are, to be the first director or directors of the company (s 12(1)(a)). The required particulars are, by s 12(2)(a), the particulars that will have to be stated in the company's register of directors and register of directors' residential addresses (see **15.7.1**).

A company must notify Companies House within 14 days of any change in its directors or in the particulars contained in its register of directors or register of directors' residential addresses (s 167(1)). Any notice to Companies House of the appointment of a new director must be accompanied by a statement by the company that the person has consented to act in that capacity (s 167(2)). Companies House must give public notice (see **4.3**) of receipt of any notification of a change among the directors of a company (ss 1077 and 1078(2)). Section 1079 prevents a company from relying on a change in its directors until public notice has been given.

Companies House must notify everyone named as a director in a notice of appointment of a new director (CA 2006, s 1079B). Anyone so notified may advise Companies House that they did not consent to act as a director and ask for their name to be removed from the register (s 1095(4A) to (4D)).

The information about a company director that must be delivered to Companies House under CA 2006, s 12 (when a company is registered) or s 167 (when a new director is appointed), includes the director's date of birth. For information delivered on or after 10 October 2015, only the month and year of the date of birth will be available for public inspection at Companies House (ss 1087A and 1087B). The day of the date of birth must still be available for inspection on the company's own register (see 15.7.1) and that will apply whether the register is kept by the company or at Companies House. In addition, Companies House can reveal the day of the date of birth to a vast number of public officials and to credit reference agencies (see SI 2015/1694).

The fact that a person is (or is not) recorded at Companies House as being a director of a company does not determine whether the person actually is (or is not) a director of that company (*POW Services Ltd v Clare* [1995] 2 BCLC 435). However, the fact that a company has permitted a person to be registered as one of its directors is a representation to others that the person is a director which the company may not be allowed to deny.

15.7.3 RESIDENTIAL ADDRESSES

15.7.3.1 Introduction

It has always been considered very important that creditors, the police and regulatory authorities should be able to locate company directors and this is why every individual who is a director of a company must reveal his or her usual residential address in the company's register of directors and secretaries and in the company's records filed at Companies House. Directors have, however, been increasingly concerned that revealing their residential addresses endangers them and their families, in particular because of the tactics used by campaigners against various uses of animals in, for example, biomedical research. A limited system of confidentiality orders to protect directors who could demonstrate specific risk was introduced in 2002, but under CA 2006 there is a complete system of confidentiality for all directors' residential addresses (see 15.7.3.2).

15.7.3.2 Protection from disclosure of directors' residential addresses

A company's register of directors must state a service address for each of its directors who is an individual (CA 2006, s 163(1)(b)). The service address may be 'The company's registered office' (s 163(5)). The register of directors must also identify the country or State, or part of the United Kingdom, where the director is usually resident (s 163(1)(c)). The director's usual residential address must be stated in the company's register of directors' residential addresses (s 165(2)). An entry for a director in the register of directors' residential addresses can simply state that the address is the same as the service address, if that is the case, but this is not permitted if the service address is 'The company's registered office' (s 165(3)).

There is no requirement for a register of directors' residential addresses to be open to inspection. The information in the register of directors and the register of directors' residential addresses must be supplied to Companies House (see 15.7.2).

The usual residential address of a director, or the fact that a director's service address is his or her usual residential address, is 'protected information' (s 240). It remains protected information after the director ceases to hold office (s 240(3)). A company must not use or disclose protected information about any of its directors except (s 241):

(a) to communicate with the director;

(b) when reporting changes in the register to Companies House;

(c) to comply with a court order; and

(d) with the director's consent.

Companies House must withhold protected information from public inspection, provided it has been supplied as protected information, that is, on the form for reporting changes in directors' residential addresses (s 242). Companies House is under no obligation to identify protected information which happens to be on other documents (s 242(2)).

Under s 243, Companies House may disclose protected information if required to do so by a court order or:

(a) to a public authority specified in SI 2009/214, sch 1; or

(b) to a credit reference agency.

SI 2009/214, sch 2, specifies the conditions under which disclosure may be made to a public authority or credit reference agency. SI 2009/214 also provides a system under which an individual can obtain a decision from the registrar that his or her protected information is not to be disclosed to a credit reference agency (reg 4). The grounds for such a decision are either (a) there is a serious risk of the individual, or someone who lives with the individual, being subjected to violence or intimidation, or (b) the individual is or has been employed by a police force or the security services (reg 5(2)). The risk of violence or intimidation must result from the activities of a company of which the individual is, is going to be or has been a director.

If all individual directors of a company have the benefit of a decision that their protected information is not to be disclosed to a credit reference agency, the company is not required to display its name at any of its places of business other than its registered office and an inspection place (SI 2015/17, reg 22(5)).

A court order for disclosure of protected information by a company or by Companies House may be made if (s 244):

(a) there is evidence that service of documents at a service address is not effective to bring them to the director's notice; or

(b) the information is required for the enforcement of a court order.

Companies House can be ordered to disclose the usual residential address of a director of a company only if the company does not have it or the company has been dissolved (s 244(2)). A disclosure order must specify the persons to whom, and purposes for which, disclosure is authorised (s 244(4)).

Under ss 245 and 246, Companies House can change a director's service address to his or her usual residential address if:

(a) communications sent by Companies House to the director have remained unanswered; or

(b) there is evidence that service of documents at a service address is not effective to bring them to the director's notice.

Notice of intention to do this must be given to the director and to every company of which he or she is director, so far as is known to Companies House.

15.7.4 LISTED COMPANIES

A premium listed company must notify a regulatory information service (RIS) of any change in its board of directors, including any important change in the role, functions or responsibilities of a director (LR 9.6.11R). Whenever a new director is appointed, a premium listed company must notify an RIS of the director's name and whether the position is executive, non-executive or chair and the nature of any specific function or responsibility of the position (LR 9.6.11R(1)). Within five business days the following information about a new director must be notified (LR 9.6.13R):

(a) details of all directorships he or she has held in any other publicly quoted company in the previous five years, indicating whether the position is still held;

(b) any unspent convictions in relation to indictable offences;

(c) details of any insolvencies which have been suffered by any company of which he or she was an executive director, or of any partnership in which he or she was a partner; and

(d) details of any public criticism of the director by statutory or regulatory authorities and whether he or she has ever been disqualified from being a director.

Notification is required of any change in these details in relation to an existing director (LR 9.6.14R).

15.8 THE BOARD OF DIRECTORS

15.8.1 GENERAL LEGAL PRINCIPLES

15.8.1.1 Directors must act collectively but may be permitted to delegate

The directors of a company are appointed to act collectively and all may take part in decision-making. In *Re Marseilles Extension Railway Co, ex parte Crédit Foncier and Mobilier of England* (1871) LR 7 Ch App 161, Mellish LJ said, at p 168, 'a director is simply a person appointed to act as one of a board, with power to bind the company when acting as a board, but having otherwise no power to bind them'.

The model articles of association in SI 2008/3229 permit directors to delegate any of their powers to such persons as they think fit (model articles for private companies, art 5; model articles for public companies, art 5). For premium listed companies, the UK Corporate Governance Code (see **15.2.2**), para A.1.1, says that there should be a formal schedule of matters specifically reserved for the board's decision, and the annual financial report should summarise which types of decision are to be taken by the board and which are delegated to management.

In *Re H R Harmer Ltd* [1959] 1 WLR 62, Romer LJ said, at p 87:

> [M]embers are entitled to expect that their board shall perform its functions as a board, and that the proceedings of the directors shall be carried out in a normal and orthodox manner. They are entitled to the benefit of the collective experience of the directors and to expect that the directors and each of them can freely express their views at board meetings, and that regard shall be had to what they say and to resolutions duly passed.

Accordingly, exclusion of a director from participation in directors' meetings may be conduct unfairly prejudicial (see **18.6**) to the interests of that director as a member or of the members who appointed him under a right of appointment conferred by the articles (per Romer LJ, *Re H R Harmer Ltd*).

Conversely, a director 'has a right by the constitution of the company to take part in its management, to be present, and to vote at the meetings of the board of directors' (*Pulbrook v Richmond Consolidated Mining Co* (1878) 9 ChD 610 per Jessel MR at p 612—see further **15.6.5**).

15.8.1.2 Decisions must be taken at a meeting unless they are unanimous

It used to be thought that the decisions of the directors of a company with more than one director had to be taken at a meeting (*D'Arcy v Tamar, Kit Hill, and Callington Railway Co* (1867) LR 2 Ex 158; *Re Haycraft Gold Reduction and Mining Co* [1900] 2 Ch 230; *Re Associated Color*

Laboratories Ltd (1970) 12 DLR (3d) 338). However, it would often be the case that the indoor management rule would preclude a company from claiming that it was not bound by a decision because it was not taken at a meeting (*Re Bonelli's Telegraph Co, Collie's Claim* (1871) LR 12 Eq 246; see **19.5.4.6**).

Since at least the 1980s, decisions of directors of a company have been accepted as binding the company even though not taken at a meeting, provided all the directors agreed to or acquiesced in the decision (*Charterhouse Investment Trust Ltd v Tempest Diesels Ltd* [1986] BCLC 1 at p 9; *Runciman v Walter Runciman plc* [1992] BCLC 1084; *Hunter v Senate Support Services Ltd* [2004] EWHC 1085 (Ch), [2005] 1 BCLC 175, at [103]; *Base Metal Trading Ltd v Shamurin* [2004] EWCA Civ 1316, [2005] 1 WLR 1157, at [83]–[84]).

Procedural informality is acceptable when all the directors agree to a decision. For a decision of some only of a company's directors to be effective, it must be taken at a meeting convened and conducted in accordance with the company's constitution.

15.8.2 DECISION-MAKING IN PRIVATE COMPANIES UNDER THE MODEL ARTICLES

15.8.2.1 General rule

In the model articles for a private company in SI 2008/3229, art 7(1) says that the general rule is that any decision of the directors must be taken either unanimously under art 8 (see **15.8.2.2**) or by a majority at a directors' meeting (see **15.8.4**), though this obviously does not preclude a meeting passing a resolution unanimously.

The rules in the model articles relating to directors' decision-making do not apply if the company has only one director (provided its articles do not require the decision to be taken by more than one director) (art 7(2)).

15.8.2.2 Unanimous decisions

The model articles for a private company in SI 2008/3229 provide that a unanimous decision is taken when all eligible directors indicate to each other, by any means, that they share a common view on a matter (art 8(1)). A unanimous decision may be in the form of a resolution in writing, which each eligible director has signed or has otherwise indicated agreement to in writing (art 8(2)). In relation to any decision, a director is an eligible director if he or she would have been entitled to vote on the matter had it been proposed as a resolution at a directors' meeting (art 8(3)). A decision cannot be taken under art 8 if there are not enough eligible directors to form a quorum at a directors' meeting (art 8(4)).

15.8.3 DECISION-MAKING IN PUBLIC COMPANIES

15.8.3.1 General rule

The model articles for public companies in SI 2008/3229, art 7, provides that directors' decisions may be taken either at a directors' meeting (see **15.8.4**) or in the form of a directors' written resolution (see **15.8.3.2**). Article 19 provides that, subject to the articles, directors may make any rule which they think fit about how they take decisions.

For premium listed companies, the UK Corporate Governance Code (see **15.2.2**), para A.1.1, says, 'The board should meet sufficiently regularly to discharge its duties effectively'. The annual financial report of a premium listed company should record the number of board meetings and directors' attendance (para A.1.2).

15.8.3.2 Written resolutions

In the model articles for public companies in SI 2008/3229, arts 17 and 18 make detailed provisions for written resolutions of directors. Article 17 deals with giving notice of a proposed resolution. A resolution is adopted when all the directors who would have been entitled to vote on the resolution at a directors' meeting have signed one or more copies of it, provided they could form a quorum at a meeting (art 18(1)). Although notice of a proposed resolution must specify a time by which it is to be adopted (art 17(4)(b)), it is immaterial whether a resolution is signed before or after that time (art 18(2)).

An adopted written resolution must be treated as if it had been taken at a directors' meeting in accordance with the articles (art 18(3)).

15.8.4 DIRECTORS' MEETINGS

15.8.4.1 Technical rules

For a majority decision taken at a directors' meeting to be valid, the technical rules of the law of meetings must be complied with, just as with members' meetings (see **14.6.1**). Notice must be given; a quorum must be present; and voting must be properly conducted.

The model articles of association in SI 2008/3229 allow for a meeting of directors to be carried on without the directors all being in the same place. The model articles for private companies, art 10(1), and the model articles for public companies, art 9(1), refer to directors 'participating' in a meeting, which occurs when:

(a) the meeting has been called and takes place in accordance with the articles; and

(b) they can each communicate to the others any information or opinions they have on any particular item of the business of the meeting.

In determining whether directors are participating in a directors' meeting, it is irrelevant where any director is or how they communicate with each other (model articles for private companies, art 10(2); model articles for public companies, art 9(2)).

15.8.4.2 Notice

Under the model articles of association in SI 2008/3229, any director may call a directors' meeting by giving notice to the directors or by authorising the company secretary (if there is one) to do so (model articles for private companies, art 9(1); model articles for public companies, art 8(1) to (3)). Notice must be communicated to each director, but does not have to be in writing (private companies, art 9(3); public companies, art 8(5)). The fact that notice of a meeting has not been given to a director will not invalidate the proceedings of the meeting if the director waives entitlement to notice of it, not later than seven days after the meeting is held (private companies, art 9(4); public companies, art 8(6)). Notice of the waiver must be given to the company (private companies, art 9(4); public companies, art 8(6)).

It is unsettled whether a director who is not entitled to vote at a board meeting must nevertheless be given notice of it. In *John Shaw and Sons (Salford) Ltd v Shaw* [1935] 2 KB 113, Greer LJ thought such a director was not entitled to notice, but Slesser LJ thought he was: the third member of the court expressed no opinion on the point. See the discussion in **14.8.3**.

Notice of any directors' meeting must indicate (private companies, art 9(2); public companies, art 8(4)):

(a) its proposed date and time;

(b) where it is to take place; and

(c) if it is expected that directors will not be in the same place for the meeting, how it is proposed that they should communicate with each other.

If all the directors participating in a meeting are not in the same place, they may decide that the meeting is to be treated as taking place wherever any of them is (private companies, art 10(3); public companies, art 9(3)).

There is no requirement in CA 2006 that the directors of a company registered under the Act must hold board meetings in the jurisdiction in which the company is incorporated, but the constitution of a company may specify where directors' meetings are to be held.

15.8.4.3 Quorum

The model articles of association in SI 2008/3229 provide that the quorum for a directors' meeting is two unless the directors decide otherwise and that the directors cannot make the quorum less than two (model articles for private companies, art 11(2); model articles for public companies, art 10(2)). This provision does not apply when a private company has only one director (model articles for private companies, art 7(2)).

When there are not enough directors to form a quorum, the director or directors in office may appoint sufficient directors to make up a quorum or may call a general meeting to make the necessary appointments (private companies, art 11(3); public companies, art 11).

A decision taken at an inquorate board meeting is invalid and does not bind the company (*Re Greymouth Point Elizabeth Railway and Coal Co Ltd* [1904] 1 Ch 32; *Re North Eastern Insurance Co Ltd* [1919] 1 Ch 198). However, if the decision is to enter into a transaction with some person who is not a director, the company will usually be precluded by the indoor management rule from claiming that it is not bound by the transaction (*County of Gloucester Bank v Rudry Merthyr Steam and House Coal Colliery Co* [1895] 1 Ch 629; *Re Bank of Syria, Owen and Ashworth's Claim* [1901] 1 Ch 115; see **19.5.4.6**).

A quorum can be formed only by directors capable of voting on the business of the meeting (model articles for private companies, art 14(1); model articles for public companies, art 16(1); *Re Greymouth Point Elizabeth Railway and Coal Co Ltd* [1904] 1 Ch 32; see **16.11.3**).

15.8.4.4 Chair

Under the model articles of association in SI 2008/3229, the directors may appoint a director to chair their meetings (model articles for private companies, art 12(1); model articles for public companies, art 12(1)). The model articles insist that that person is to be known as the 'chairman' (private companies, art 12(2), public companies, art 12(2)). The directors may terminate the chairman's appointment at any time (private companies, art 12(3); public companies, art 12(4)). For public companies only, there is provision for the appointment of deputy or assistant chairmen to chair meetings in the chairman's absence (model articles for public companies, art 12(3)).

Where, as in the model articles, the power to appoint a chairman is vested in the directors, the members cannot make an appointment (*Clark v Workman* [1920] 1 IR 107).

If the appointed chairman, or a public company's deputy or assistant chairman, is not participating within ten minutes of the starting time for a meeting, the participating directors must appoint one of themselves to chair it (private companies, art 12(4); public companies, art 12(5)).

Under the model articles, the chair of a directors' meeting has a casting vote (private companies, art 13(1); public companies, art 14(1)). But this cannot be exercised if, under the articles, the chair is not to be counted as participating for quorum, voting or agreement purposes (private companies, art 13(2); public companies, art 14(2)).

The chairman of a public company must chair general meetings of members at which he or she is present, if willing to do so (model articles for public companies, art 31(1)).

The chairman of a premium listed company should be an independent non-executive director, at least at the time of appointment (UK Corporate Governance Code, para A.3.1).

15.8.4.5 Voting

The model articles of association for public companies in SI 2008/3229 state that a decision is taken at a directors' meeting by a majority of the votes of the participating directors (art 13(1)). Each participating director has one vote (art 13(2)). A director who is also an alternate for another director has an additional vote if the appointor is not present, provided the appointor would be entitled to vote on the matter (art 15). The chair of the meeting has a casting vote (art 14).

The model articles for private companies do not deal with these points and do not provide for the appointment of alternates.

Where there is no provision for a casting vote, the general rule is that, if there is an equality of votes for and against a board resolution, it is not adopted (*Moodie v W and J Shepherd (Bookbinders) Ltd* [1949] 2 All ER 1044).

15.8.4.6 Minutes

Every company must record minutes of all proceedings at directors' meetings (CA 2006, s 248(1)). Minutes of a meeting must be kept for at least ten years from the date of the meeting (s 248(2)). Minutes of a meeting which purport to be authenticated by the chair of the meeting, or of the next meeting, are evidence of the proceedings at the meeting (s 249(1)). Where minutes have been made of a directors' meeting, until the contrary is proved, the meeting is deemed duly held and convened, all proceedings at the meeting are deemed to have duly taken place, and all appointments at the meeting are deemed valid (s 249(2)).

The model articles of association in SI 2008/3229 also require resolutions adopted without meeting to be recorded and kept for ten years (model articles for private companies, art 15; model articles for public companies, art 18(4)).

A decision of directors is not invalidated by failure to minute it (*Re North Hallenbeagle Mining Co, Knight's Case* (1867) LR 2 Ch App 321).

15.8.5 EXECUTIVE DIRECTORS; MANAGING DIRECTOR

The model articles of association in SI 2008/3229 provide that a director 'may undertake any services for the company that the directors decide' (model articles for private companies, art 19(1); model articles for public companies, art 23(1)) and may be paid for such services (private companies, art 19(2)(b); public companies, art 23(2)(b)). These provisions permit the appointment of executive directors (see **15.2.3**) to whom the directors may delegate powers (private companies, art 5; public companies, art 5).

A chief executive officer, or managing director, may be appointed under the same provisions. In the absence of any express delegation of directors' powers, such an appointment impliedly delegates the powers that would ordinarily be exercisable by a CEO or MD. Where a CEO or MD carries out functions without needing to obtain specific directions from the board, the power to exercise those functions has been implicitly delegated (*Smith v Butler* [2012] EWCA Civ 314, [2012] Bus LR 1836, at [28]). In *Smith v Butler*, the MD of a company did not have an implied power to 'suspend' the chairman from his position, even where there was a suspicion that the chairman had defrauded the company.

In the twentieth century, courts took differing views on the role of a managing director. In *Re Newspaper Proprietary Syndicate Ltd* [1900] 2 Ch 349, Cozens-Hardy J said that 'A managing director is only an ordinary director entrusted with some special powers'. Other judges saw a managing director as a manager who happened also to be a director (Lord President Normand in *Anderson v James Sutherland (Peterhead) Ltd* 1941 SC 203 at p 217). In *Southern Foundries (1926) Ltd v Shirlaw* [1940] AC 701, Viscount Maugham said, at p 712, that 'the two positions, that of director and that of manager, involve different qualifications, duties and responsibilities'. These differing opinions reflect the fact that the position of managing director of a company is defined not so much by company law as by the company's articles, the managing director's service contract, and what the managing director makes of the position. A managing director's role can vary from autocrat to hired functionary. For example, in *Harold Holdsworth and Co (Wakefield) Ltd v Caddies* [1955] 1 WLR 352, Mr Caddies was appointed managing director of the appellant company under an agreement which required him to 'perform the duties and exercise the powers in relation to the business of the company and the businesses (howsoever carried on) of its existing subsidiary companies at the date hereof which may from time to time be assigned to or vested in him by the board of directors'. The board of the appellant company subsequently resolved that Mr Caddies should devote his attentions entirely to one of its subsidiaries. It was held that this was not a breach of the company's agreement with him.

15.8.6 MANAGING DIRECTOR AND CHAIRMAN

For premium listed companies, the UK Corporate Governance Code (see **15.2.2**), main principle A.2, states that 'There should be a clear division of responsibilities at the head of the company between the running of the board and the executive responsibility for the running of the company's business. No one individual should have unfettered powers of decision'. Code provision A.3.1 accordingly provides that the chairman should be an independent non-executive director when appointed: this seems to allow for the chairman to become more closely associated, especially financially, with management after appointment. Code provision A.2.1 states that one person should not be both chairman and chief executive and that the division of responsibilities should be agreed by the board and set out in writing. Supporting principle A.3 is:

> The chairman is responsible for setting the board's agenda and ensuring that adequate time is available for discussion of all agenda items, in particular strategic issues. The chairman should also promote a culture of openness and debate by facilitating the effective contribution of non-executive directors in particular and ensuring constructive relations between executive and non-executive directors.
>
> The chairman is responsible for ensuring that the directors receive accurate, timely and clear information. The chairman should ensure effective communication with shareholders.

15.8.7 COMMITTEES

It may not always be possible or convenient for the full board of directors to consider certain issues relating to the company's affairs, or it may happen that the expertise of some directors lends itself to a separate consideration by them of various problems and decisions. The model articles of association in SI 2008/3229 therefore envisage delegation of the directors' powers to committees (model articles for private companies, arts 5 and 6; model articles for public companies, arts 5 and 6).

The power to delegate to a committee must not be used as a device to exclude a particular director (*Great Western Railway Co v Rushout* (1852) 5 De G & Sm 290, which concerned a statutory company; *Kyshe v Alturas Gold Ltd* (1888) 4 TLR 331; *Bray v Smith* (1908) 124 LT Jo 293; *Trounce v NCF Kaiapoi Ltd* (1985) 2 NZCLC 99,422).

The UK Corporate Governance Code (see **15.2.2**) says that the board of a premium listed company should establish:

(a) a nomination committee, with a majority of independent non-executive directors, to make recommendations to the board on all new board appointments (para B.2.1; see **15.5.3.2**);

(b) a remuneration committee, composed exclusively of independent non-executive directors (para D.2.1), to set the remuneration of executive directors and the chairman and recommend and monitor the level and structure of remuneration for senior management (para D.2.2; see **15.9.1.4**); and

(c) an audit committee of independent non-executive directors, to review the scope and results of internal and external audits (paras C.3.1 and C.3.2; see **17.4.5.3**).

A meeting of one of these committees can be attended only by its members and chair and persons they invite (UK Corporate Governance Code, supporting principles B.1). The membership and chairmanship of these committees should be stated in the annual financial report, which should also record the numbers of meetings held and members' attendances (UK Corporate Governance Code, para A.1.2). The terms of reference of these committees should be made available, for example on the company's website (UK Corporate Governance Code, paras B.2.1, C.3.3 and D.2.1). The chairmen of these committees should be available to answer questions at the AGM (UK Corporate Governance Code, para E.2.3).

15.9 REMUNERATION

15.9.1 REMUNERATION

15.9.1.1 No prima facie entitlement to remuneration

A director of a company does not have a right to be remunerated for any services performed for the company except as provided by its constitution or approved by the company's members (*Dunston v Imperial Gas Light and Coke Co* (1832) 3 B & Ad 125; *Hutton v West Cork Railway Co* (1883) 23 ChD 654; *Guinness plc v Saunders* [1990] 2 AC 663). This is an aspect of the no-profit rule (see **16.9.2**).

In *Hutton v West Cork Railway Co* (1883) 23 ChD 654, Bowen LJ said, at p 672:

> A director is not a servant [ie, employee]. He is a person who is doing business for the company, but not upon ordinary terms. It is not implied from the mere fact that he is a director, that he is to have a right to be paid for it. In some companies . . . there is a special provision for the way in which the directors should be paid; in others there is not. If there is a special provision for the way in which they are to be paid, you must look to the special provision to see how to deal with it. But if there is no special provision their payment is in the nature of a gratuity.

The directors of a company have no authority to pay the company's money to themselves or any one of their number, unless they are given authority by the company's constitution or the payment is approved by the members (*Re George Newman and Co* [1895] 1 Ch 674). This rule was extended to cover a payment to the widow of a director in *Re Lee Behrens and Co Ltd* [1932] 2 Ch 46.

15.9.1.2 Provisions in articles for payment of directors' fees

In practice it is accepted that the directors of a company are to be paid fees for holding office, and provision for such fees is usually made in the articles of association. The model articles of association in SI 2008/3229 authorise the directors to determine their own remuneration for their services to the company as directors (model articles for private companies, art 19(2)(a); model articles for public companies, art 23(2)(a)).

If the articles of a company provide how the remuneration of its directors is to be determined then the court will not make its own determination of remuneration (*Re Richmond Gate Property Co Ltd* [1965] 1 WLR 335; *Guinness plc v Saunders* [1990] 2 AC 663). The court will not award a *quantum meruit* (see **3.4.2.7**) nor will it make an 'equitable allowance' by analogy with its power to authorise a trustee to charge for services rendered. In both *Re Richmond Gate Property Co Ltd* and *Guinness plc v Saunders* the remuneration of the director concerned was to be determined by the company's directors but no determination was made: in each case, therefore, the director concerned was not entitled to anything.

15.9.1.3 Expenses

Under the model articles of association in SI 2008/3229, a company may pay any reasonable expenses which directors properly incur in connection with the exercise of their powers and the discharge of their responsibilities in relation to the company (model articles for private companies, art 20; model articles for public companies, art 24).

15.9.1.4 Remuneration for other services

The model articles of association in SI 2008/3229 provide that a director 'may undertake any services for the company that the directors decide' (model articles for private companies, art 19(1); model articles for public companies, art 23(1)) and may be paid such remuneration as the directors determine for those services (private companies, art 19(2)(b); public companies, art 23(2)(b)).

The directors of a company should limit payments to executive directors to what the company can afford. Failure by a director to ensure that the board fixes affordable salaries may show the director's unfitness and be a ground for a disqualification order, as in *Secretary of State for Trade and Industry v Van Hengel* [1995] 1 BCLC 545. It is not correct that the company must pay the going rate for the job (*Van Hengel*).

For premium listed companies, the UK Corporate Governance Code (see **15.2.2**), main principle D.2, states:

> There should be a formal and transparent procedure for developing policy on executive remuneration and for fixing the remuneration packages of individual directors. No director should be involved in deciding his or her own remuneration.

A premium listed company's board of directors should establish a remuneration committee (see **15.8.7**), consisting only of independent non-executive directors (UK Corporate Governance Code, para D.2.1), to determine the remuneration of executive directors and the chairman and recommend and monitor the level and structure of remuneration for senior management (para D.2.2). The remuneration of the non-executive directors should be set by the board itself, or a committee of the board, unless the articles require their remuneration to be determined by the shareholders (para D.2.3).

In *Newcastle International Airport Ltd v Eversheds LLP* [2013] EWCA Civ 1514, [2014] PNLR 13, the Court of Appeal was told that in practice a company's solicitors are instructed to draft the contracts of executive directors by the directors themselves on the basis that the draft will be reviewed by the remuneration committee. Rimer LJ described this as 'less than ideal' (at [78]). It was held that, in this situation, the solicitors' duty to their client, the company, involves taking reasonable steps to ensure that the remuneration committee properly understand the effect of the draft contract (at [83]). In this case, communication of that information to the chair of the committee would have made no difference, because she had made it clear that she never read contracts or legal documents, so the company was awarded only nominal damages of £2.

All quoted companies must produce a directors' remuneration report, which must list the membership of the remuneration committee, if the company has one (see **15.9.3.4**).

15.9.1.5 Employment status of directors

The fact that a person is a director of a company does not in itself make that person an employee (what used to be called a 'servant') of the company (*Dunston v Imperial Gas Light and Coke Co* (1832) 3 B & Ad 125; *Hutton v West Cork Railway Co* (1883) 23 ChD 654). Being a director of a company is usually categorised as 'holding an office' rather than being an employee (*McMillan v Guest* [1942] AC 561). The same applies to being a managing director (*Goodwin v Brewster* (1951) 32 TC 80). (For an explanation of the term 'public company' as used in the income tax legislation discussed in *McMillan v Guest* and *Goodwin v Brewster*, see **4.2.5**. For a discussion of the distinction between office and employment, see J Ward, '"What can it matter? Why should it matter?": the taxation of offices and employments' [1989] BTR 281.) Whereas an employee serves under a contract of service, the appointment of a person as a director of a company does not in itself form any contract between the person and the company (*Newtherapeutics Ltd v Katz* [1991] Ch 226). Indeed the non-contractual nature of an appointment as a director is an indicator that it is an office rather than an employment. However, it is possible for the holder of an office to be considered to be also an employee. Whether a person who provides services is an employee depends on the conditions under which the services are provided, and is a notoriously difficult question of employment law and depends on the facts of each case (see *Montgomery v Johnson Underwood Ltd* [2001] EWCA Civ 318, [2001] ICR 819). Deciding whether a particular director is serving under a contract of service is especially difficult where the director also owns or controls the majority of the company's shares. The law has been reviewed most recently by the Court of Appeal in *Secretary of State for Business, Enterprise and Regulatory Reform v Neufeld* [2009] EWCA Civ 280, [2009] ICR 1183. It is an essential feature of a contract of employment that in performing services the employee is subject to the employer's control. In *Lee v Lee's Air Farming Ltd* [1961] AC 12 the Privy Council pointed out that it is possible for a company to control an employee, even if that control is exercised by the employee, acting as a director of the company. There is no reason why a director of a company who owns or controls the majority of shares in the company cannot be an employee of the company, even if he or she is the company's only director and owns or controls all of its shares (*Secretary of State for Business, Enterprise and Regulatory Reform v Neufeld* at [80]). Whether or not such a director is an employee is a question of fact, which may involve two issues:

(a) whether the alleged contract is a genuine contract or a sham (in the sense defined in *Snook v London and West Riding Investments Ltd* [1967] 2 QB 786 at p 802; see **5.3.6.4**); or

(b) if the contract is genuine, whether it amounts to a contract of employment rather than, for example, a contract for services (*Secretary of State for Business, Enterprise and Regulatory Reform v Neufeld* at [81]).

Guidance on dealing with these issues is given in *Secretary of State for Business, Enterprise and Regulatory Reform v Neufeld* at [82]–[90].

If a director of a company makes a contract with the company establishing the terms on which he or she will serve and the director is not serving under a contract of service, the contract is a contract for the supply of a service (also called a contract for services).

There is no implied term in a contract for the supply of services as a director in which remuneration is not settled that the company will pay a reasonable charge (Supply of Goods and Services Act 1982, ss 15 and 16(1)). If a person performs services as a director of a company without there being any agreement about remuneration, a *quantum meruit* (see **3.4.2.7**) will not be awarded (*Woolf v East Nigel Gold Mining Co Ltd* (1905) 21 TLR 660).

In *Craven-Ellis v Canons Ltd* [1936] 2 KB 403, Mr Craven-Ellis was one of the first directors of Canons Ltd. He and all the company's other directors automatically vacated office on failing to acquire qualification shares. Nevertheless, they continued to act as directors. Eighteen months after vacating office, the acting directors appointed Mr Craven-Ellis managing director and purported to make a contract with him agreeing his remuneration. The Court of Appeal held that there was no binding contract between the company and Mr Craven-Ellis, and awarded him a *quantum meruit*. There was no argument about whether the fact that he had acted as a director of the company made him subject to the fiduciary duties of a director so that he was not entitled to profit from his office. In *Guinness plc v Saunders* [1990] 2 AC 663, Lord Templeman said, at p 693, that because Mr Craven-Ellis was not a director, there was no conflict between his claim to remuneration and the no-profit rule (see **15.9.1.1**).

15.9.2 PAYMENTS FOR LOSS OF OFFICE

15.9.2.1 Payments requiring approval

A voluntary (see **15.9.2.2**) payment to a director of a company for loss of office must not, without approval by the members, be made:

(a) by the company itself (CA 2006, s 217(1)); or

(b) by anyone in connection with the transfer of the whole or any part of the undertaking or property of the company (s 218(1)) or of a subsidiary (s 218(2)); or

(c) by anyone in connection with a transfer of shares in the company, or in a subsidiary of the company, resulting from a takeover bid (s 219(1)).

A payment by a subsidiary company to a director of its holding company requires the approval of members of both companies (s 217(2)), unless the subsidiary is wholly owned (s 217(4)(b)). Approval of a payment in connection with share transfers resulting from a takeover bid must be given by a resolution of the 'relevant shareholders' (s 219(1)). This means the holders of the shares to which the bid relates and any holders of other shares of the same class (s 219(3)), but the person making the bid is not entitled to vote, nor is any associate of that person as defined in s 988 (see **8.7.2.10**) (s 219(4)).

The term 'payment for loss of office' is defined in detail in ss 215 and 216. A memorandum setting out particulars of the proposed payment must be made available to members (ss 217(3), 218(3) and 219(3)). In the case of a written resolution, the memorandum must be sent or submitted to every eligible member (see **14.5.1.1**) before or when sending or submitting the proposed resolution. In the case of a resolution at a meeting, the memorandum must be made available for inspection by members at the company's registered office for at least 15 days before the meeting and at the meeting itself.

A payment made without approval is, by s 222(1), (2) and (3), held on trust:

(a) in the case of a s 217 payment, for the paying company;

(b) in the case of a s 218 payment, for the company whose undertaking or property is, or is proposed to be, transferred; or

(c) in the case of a s 219 payment, for persons who have sold their shares as a result of the offer made.

If a payment contravenes more than one section, priorities are determined by s 222(4) and (5). Any director who authorised an unapproved s 217 payment is jointly and severally liable to indemnify the company that made the payment for any loss resulting from it (s 222(1)(b)).

For the purposes of these provisions, a shadow director is treated as a director (s 223(1)), but references to loss of office as a director do not apply in relation to loss of a person's status as a shadow director (s 223(2)).

15.9.2.2 Payments not requiring approval

Approval is not required under CA 2006, s 217, 218 or 219 (see **15.9.2.1**), for a payment made in good faith:

(a) in discharge of an existing legal obligation, unless it was entered into in connection with, or in consequence of, the event giving rise to a s 217 payment or the transfer to which a s 218 or s 219 payment is connected;

(b) by way of damages for breach of such an obligation;

(c) by way of settlement or compromise of any claim arising in connection with the termination of a person's office or employment; or

(d) by way of pension in respect of past services.

There is also an exemption in s 221 for a total payment of £200 in connection with any one event causing loss of office or any one transfer of undertaking, property or shares.

For control of contractual termination payments see **15.9.4**.

15.9.3 DISCLOSURE IN ACCOUNTS OF PAYMENTS TO DIRECTORS

15.9.3.1 Introduction

Regulations have been made under CA 2006, s 412, requiring large and medium-sized companies to give information about directors' remuneration and other benefits in notes to their annual accounts (see **15.9.3.2** and **15.9.3.3**). The requirements for the individual and group accounts of large and medium-sized companies are in SI 2008/410, reg 8 and sch 5. Quoted companies (defined at **9.5.2**) are subject to extra requirements. In particular, CA 2006, s 420, requires every quoted company to produce a directors' remuneration report for each financial year, and s 421 enables the Secretary of State to make regulations prescribing the information to be contained in the report. Those regulations are in SI 2008/410, reg 11 and sch 8.

An important feature of these provisions is that a quoted company's directors' remuneration report must identify payments to each director by name, whereas the information required by the regulations made under CA 2006, s 412, is only statistical information which is not specifically linked to named directors.

15.9.3.2 Disclosure of aggregate benefits

SI 2008/410, sch 5, para 1, requires every medium-sized and large company to give, in a note to its annual accounts:

(a) the total amount of directors' remuneration;

(b) if the company is quoted or has shares admitted to trading on AIM, the total gains made by directors on the exercise of share options;

(c) the total amount of money or assets received or receivable by directors under long-term incentive schemes; and

(d) the total value of company contributions to directors' pension schemes.

In addition, unquoted large and medium-sized companies are required by SI 2008/410, sch 5, paras 4 and 5, to state:

(a) aggregate payments made to directors or past directors for loss of office (see **15.9.2**); and

(b) aggregate sums paid to third parties in respect of directors' services (for an interpretation of what is 'in respect of' a director's services which is very generous to the director, see *Re Dominion International Group plc (No 2)* [1996] 1 BCLC 572).

An unquoted large or medium-sized company must disclose the aggregate amount of excess retirement benefits (meaning the amount by which directors' pensions exceed what they were entitled to on the later of 31 March 1997 or when the pensions first became payable) (SI 2008/410, sch 5, para 3).

15.9.3.3 Information about highest-paid director

An unquoted large or medium-sized company is required by SI 2008/410, sch 5, para 2, to give the following information about its highest-paid director, without identifying who that is:

(a) the overall total of remuneration, gains made in the exercise of share options and long-term incentives;

(b) pension scheme contributions by the company; and

(c) the amount at the end of the year of the director's accrued pension and accrued lump sum under a defined benefits pension scheme.

This information is not required if the total of item (a) for all directors is less than £200,000.

15.9.3.4 Quoted company's directors' remuneration report

A *quoted company* must give, in addition to the statement of aggregate directors' remuneration, etc in the notes to the accounts (see **15.9.3.2**), a separate directors' remuneration report giving information about the following matters, as specified in SI 2008/410, sch 8:

(a) the board's remuneration committee;

(b) the company's policy on directors' remuneration;

(c) a statement of how pay and employment conditions of employees of the company and other undertakings in the group were taken into account when determining directors' remuneration;

(d) a performance graph comparing, over the five years ending with the one reported on, total shareholder return on the company's equity shares and the return that would have been obtained on a hypothetical holding of shares from which a 'broad equity market index' (such as the FTSE 100) is calculated;

(e) directors' service contracts;

(f) emoluments and compensation for loss of office paid to each director;

(g) each director's share options;

(h) each director's interest in a long-term incentive scheme;

(i) each director's pension rights;

(j) excess retirement benefits;

(k) compensation to past directors for loss of office; and

(l) sums paid to third parties in respect of directors' services.

The company's auditor must report on items (f) to (l) (known as the 'auditable part' of the directors' remuneration report) and state whether, in the auditor's opinion, the auditable part has been properly prepared in accordance with the statutory requirements.

The directors' remuneration report of a company for a financial year must be approved by the board of directors and signed on behalf of the board by a director or the secretary of the company (s 422(1)). There is a criminal sanction for knowingly or recklessly approving a report that does not comply with the requirements of CA 2006 (s 422(2) and (3)).

The directors must ensure that a resolution approving the directors' remuneration report is put to the vote at the accounts meeting (CA 2006, s 439). The accounts meeting is normally the AGM (see **9.6.3** and **14.7.1**). This does not imply that any entitlement to remuneration depends on the resolution being passed (though director and company might agree that in a particular case) (s 439(5)). The resolution is therefore usually described as 'advisory'. This resolution does not apply to the part of the report containing the directors' remuneration policy, which is subject to a separate binding vote every three years (ss 439(1) and 439A; see **15.9.3.5**).

A premium listed company must give further information as required by the FCA Handbook, LR 9.8.6R(7) and 9.8.8R (see LR 9.8.9G), and that information must be reviewed by the auditor (LR 9.8.11R).

15.9.3.5 Quoted company's binding directors' remuneration policy

A quoted company's directors' remuneration policy, as stated in its directors' remuneration report, must be approved by ordinary resolution of its members every three years (CA 2006, s 439A). A directors' remuneration policy is the policy of a quoted company with respect to the making of remuneration payments and payments for loss of office (ss 226A(1) and 421(2A)). The term 'remuneration payment' is defined in s 226A(1) as:

any form of payment or other benefit made to or otherwise conferred on a person as consideration for the person—

(a) holding, agreeing to hold or having held office as director of a company, or

(b) holding, agreeing to hold or having held, during a period when the person is or was such a director—

  (i)   any other office or employment in connection with the management of the affairs of the company, or

  (ii) any office (as director or otherwise) or employment in connection with the management of the affairs of any subsidiary undertaking of the company,

other than a payment for loss of office;

'Payment for loss of office' has the same definition as for the provisions discussed at **15.9.2** (s 226A(1)) except that it also includes (s 226A(2) to (4)) the following payments to a director when made in connection with a takeover of the company or a sale of the whole or any part of its or its subsidiary's undertaking or property:

(a) the difference between the price paid for the director's shares and the price which could have been obtained by other shareholders; or

(b) any valuable consideration given to the director by a person other than the company.

A quoted company may not make a remuneration payment to a person who is, or is to be or has been, one of its directors, unless the payment is consistent with its approved directors' remuneration policy or is specifically approved by ordinary resolution of the members (s 226B). No payment for loss of office may be made by any person to a director, or former director, of a quoted company, unless the payment is consistent with its approved directors' remuneration policy or is specifically approved by ordinary resolution of the members (s 226C). Any obligation to make a payment in contravention of s 226B or 226C has no effect (s 226E(1)).

If a payment is made in contravention of s 226B or 226C, it is deemed to be held by the recipient on trust for, usually, the company or other person making the payment (s 226E(2)(a)). A payment in connection with the transfer of the company's, or its subsidiary's, property or undertaking, is held on trust for the company whose property is, or is proposed to be, transferred (s 226E(3)). An excess payment for the director's shares in a takeover bid is held on trust for the other shareholders who sold their shares as a result of the takeover, and the profiting director must bear the cost of distributing the money to those other shareholders (s 226E(4)).

Any director of a company who authorised a payment in contravention of s 226B or 226C is jointly and severally liable to indemnify the company for any resulting loss (s 226E(2)(b)).

The court can grant relief from these consequences to a director who acted honestly and reasonably (s 226E(5); see **16.16.6**).

When anyone ceases to be a director of a quoted company, all remuneration payments and payments for loss of office made, or to be made, to him or her must be disclosed on the company's website. The disclosure must state the amount paid and how it was calculated (s 430(2B)).

A quoted company's directors' remuneration policy can be revised after less than three years (s 422A(1)). The revision must be approved by the board of directors (s 422A(1)) and set out in a document signed on behalf of the board by a director or the company secretary (s 422A(3)). There is a criminal sanction for knowingly or recklessly approving such a document that does not comply with the requirements of CA 2006 (s 422(2) and (3) applied by s 422A(5)). Section 463 (director's liability for untrue or misleading statements or omissions; see **9.5.3**) applies to such a document (s 422A(5)). The document must be made available on the company's website (s 430(2A)). No payments can be made under the revised policy until it has been approved by the members by ordinary resolution at a general meeting as contemplated by s 439A(7)(b)(ii).

For a survey of how the requirements for disclosure and shareholder voting have been used see E Ndzi, 'UK shareholder voting on directors' remuneration: has binding vote made any difference?' (2017) 38 Co Law 139. The Department for Business, Energy and Industrial Strategy has put out for discussion a Green Paper, *Corporate Governance Reform* (November 2016) which is largely devoted to this topic.

15.9.4 INSPECTION AND APPROVAL OF DIRECTORS' SERVICE CONTRACTS

Every company must keep available for inspection (see **4.4.4.1**) a copy of every director's service contract with the company or any of its subsidiaries (CA 2006, s 228). If a service contract is not in writing, a written memorandum setting out its terms must be available for inspection (s 228(1)(b)). Availability for inspection must continue for at least one year from the date of termination or expiry of the contract (s 228(3)). This provision applies to shadow directors (s 230).

In relation to a company, the term 'service contract' is defined in s 227 to mean a contract under which:

(a) a director of the company undertakes personally to perform services (as director or otherwise) for the company, or for a subsidiary of the company; or

(b) services (as director or otherwise) that a director of the company undertakes personally to perform are made available by a third party to the company, or to a subsidiary of the company.

The term is not restricted to a contract relating to services as an executive director: it covers a contract relating only to the ordinary duties of a director (s 227(2)). A letter of appointment, setting out the terms of appointment of a person as a director, is a service contract (s 227(2)).

Qualifying indemnity provisions (see **16.16.5**) are also required to be available for inspection (s 237).

Under s 188, a director of a company cannot have a guaranteed term of employment with the company or any of its subsidiaries for more than two years unless it has been approved by resolution of the company's members.

A memorandum setting out the proposed contract incorporating the provision for a guaranteed term must be made available to members (s 188(5)). In the case of a written resolution, the memorandum must be sent or submitted to every eligible member (see **14.5.1.1**) before or when sending or submitting the proposed resolution. In the case of a resolution at a meeting, the memorandum must be made available for inspection by members at the company's registered office for at least 15 days before the meeting and at the meeting itself.

A provision for a guaranteed term of more than two years which is agreed to without members' approval is void, and the contract is deemed to contain a term entitling the company to terminate it at any time by giving reasonable notice (s 189).

A provision in a contract for a guaranteed term of more than two years must be approved before the contract is made (*Wright v Atlas Wright (Europe) Ltd* [1999] 2 BCLC 301 at p 314). In relation to employment within a group of companies of a director of the holding company, s 188 contemplates that the agreement may be made either by the holding company or a subsidiary: if it is made by a subsidiary that is not a wholly owned subsidiary, the provision must be approved by a general meeting of the subsidiary as well (s 188(2) and (6)).

A contract for services supplied by a parent company to its subsidiary does not have to be approved in accordance with s 188 if the only reason for treating the parent company as a shadow director of the subsidiary is that the subsidiary's directors are accustomed to act in accordance with the parent company's directions or instructions (s 251(3)).

For premium listed companies, the UK Corporate Governance Code (see **15.2.2**), para D.1.5, states:

> Notice or contract periods [for directors] should be set at one year or less. If it is necessary to offer longer notice or contract periods to new directors recruited from outside, such periods should reduce to one year or less after the initial period.

Very large payments in lieu of notice, given even when a director is dismissed for poor performance (reward for failure) have angered shareholders, employees and the general public. The UK Corporate Governance Code, para D.1.4, says:

> The remuneration committee should carefully consider what compensation commitments (including pension contributions and all other elements) their directors' terms of appointment would entail in the event of

early termination. The aim should be to avoid rewarding poor performance. They should take a robust line on reducing compensation to reflect departing directors' obligations to mitigate loss.

A company is, however, always bound by the contract which it entered into when trying to attract an executive it thought would be of great value. For example, in *Mallone v BPB Industries plc* [2002] EWCA Civ 126, [2002] ICR 1045, a company, which dismissed the managing director of its Italian subsidiary for poor performance, was unable to prevent him exercising share options which he had been granted three years previously when he was apparently doing very well.

15.10 POWERS OF MANAGEMENT

15.10.1 DIVISION OF POWER BETWEEN MEMBERS AND DIRECTORS

Directors' authority to manage their company has been reinforced by the principle, which the courts have adopted, that the articles divide the company's powers between the directors and the members, and the members cannot instruct the directors on how to exercise the powers assigned to them.

In *Howard Smith Ltd v Ampol Petroleum Ltd* [1974] AC 821, Lord Wilberforce, delivering the judgment of the Privy Council, said, at p 837:

> The constitution of a limited company normally provides for directors, with powers of management, and shareholders, with defined voting powers having power to appoint the directors, and to take, in general meeting, by majority vote, decisions on matters not reserved for management . . . it is established that directors, within their management powers, may take decisions against the wishes of the majority of shareholders, and indeed that the majority of shareholders cannot control them in the exercise of these powers while they remain in office.

In *Grundt v Great Boulder Proprietary Mines Ltd* [1948] Ch 145, Cohen LJ said, at p 157:

> there is nothing unusual in the shareholders not being allowed to interfere in matters which have been deliberately placed under the control of the directors.

In *Towcester Racecourse Co Ltd v Racecourse Association Ltd* [2002] EWHC 2141 (Ch), [2003] 1 BCLC 260, Patten J said, at [19]:

> in the absence of articles permitting the members to control the board, it is entitled to govern the company and exercise its powers without interference. If the directors act unlawfully, then they will be accountable for their actions and for any losses suffered by the company as a result . . . the proper claimant in such proceedings is the company and not the shareholders. [see **18.4**]

The principle of division of powers is often described as achieving a 'separation of ownership and control'. It is important to bear in mind that only some companies are affected by this: in the vast majority of private companies the directors and the members are the same persons.

The law gives directors freedom to exercise the powers assigned to them but this freedom is subject to their duty to exercise powers only for the purposes for which they are conferred (CA 2006, s 171) and their duty to act in the way they consider, in good faith, would be most likely to promote the success of the company for the benefit of its members as a whole (s 172) (see **Chapter 16**). Within these limits, directors' actions cannot be controlled by the members.

The members are not, however, entirely without influence: since 1948 the members of a company have had a statutory right to dismiss any of the company's directors, by ordinary resolution (s 168; see **15.6.3**). Cases decided before 1948 should always be considered in the light of the rule, in force at that time, that directors could not be removed unless there was a power in the articles to dismiss (*Imperial Hydropathic Hotel Co, Blackpool v Hampson* (1882) 23 ChD 1) and, where such a power was given by the articles, it was usual to require a special resolution.

No statutory power of dismissal was available to the members in *Teck Corporation Ltd v Millar* (1972) 33 DLR (3d) 288, in which the majority of members of a company authorised legal proceedings against its directors, seeking to halt an allotment of shares by the directors on the ground that it would be a misuse of their powers. Berger J, however, found that the allotment would not be an abuse of the directors' powers so that it could not be prevented. Berger J, at pp 307–8, adopted the following statement by Barwick CJ in *Ashburton Oil NL v Alpha Minerals NL* (1971) 123 CLR 614 at p 620:

> Directors who are minded to do something which in their honest view is for the benefit of the company are not to be restrained because a majority shareholder or shareholders holding a majority of shares in the company do not want the directors so to act.

15.10.2 DIRECTORS' GENERAL POWER OF MANAGEMENT

15.10.2.1 Model articles

In the model articles of association in SI 2008/3229, the directors' general power of management is conferred by art 3 of both the model articles for private companies and the model articles for public companies:

> Subject to the articles, the directors are responsible for the management of the company's business, for which purpose they may exercise all the powers of the company.

This general power of management applies only to managing the company as a going concern (see **15.10.2.2**) and is expressed to be subject to the provisions of the company's articles (see **15.10.2.3**). It does not imply a power to pay bribes to secure business for the company (*E Hannibal and Co Ltd v Frost* (1987) 4 BCC 3). What is controversial is whether the members have a general supervisory power: the courts have generally adopted the theory that they do not (see **15.10.2.5**).

15.10.2.2 Management as a going concern

It has been said that the general power of management conferred by art 3 of the model articles for private and for public companies and similar provisions is a power to carry on the company's business only as a going concern (*Re Standard Bank of Australia Ltd* (1898) 24 VLR 304; *Re Galway and Salthill Tramways Co* [1918] 1 IR 62—a case concerning a statutory company with power of management governed by the Companies Clauses Consolidation Act 1845, s 90, see **15.10.2.5**). Accordingly, it does not give the directors power to petition for the winding up of the company (*Re Galway and Salthill Tramways Co*; *Re Emmadart Ltd* [1979] Ch 540) or to oppose the restoration to the register of a company struck off by the registrar (*Re Regent Insulation Co Ltd* (1981), *The Times*, 5 November 1981). However, the directors of a company now have a statutory power to petition for its winding up (IA 1986, s 124(1)).

15.10.2.3 Subject to the articles

The general power of management conferred by art 3 of the model articles for private and for public companies is expressed to be subject to the articles. In *Salmon v Quin and Axtens Ltd* [1909] 1 Ch 311, the articles of Quin and Axtens Ltd conferred a general power of management on the directors (art 75) but art 80 made directors' decisions on certain matters subject to the veto of either of two named shareholders (who between them held the bulk of the company's shares). These two named shareholders were also appointed directors and managing directors of the company by the articles. The Court of Appeal upheld the validity of a veto issued by one of the named shareholders under art 80 and held that an ordinary resolution of the members was ineffective to override the veto because it was an attempt to amend art 80 by ordinary resolution instead of special resolution. The Court of Appeal's decision was affirmed by the House of Lords (sub nom *Quin and Axtens Ltd v Salmon* [1909] AC 442).

Matters which the articles expressly allot to the members are not within art 3 of the model articles (*Foster v Foster* [1916] 1 Ch 532).

15.10.2.4 Shareholders' reserve power

In the model articles both for private companies and for public companies, art 4 (which is titled 'shareholders' reserve power' in the model for private companies and 'members' reserve power' in the model for public companies) provides that:

(1) The shareholders [members in the model for public companies] may, by special resolution, direct the directors to take, or refrain from taking, specified action.

(2) No such special resolution invalidates anything which the directors have done before the passing of the resolution.

This article appears to confer a specific rather than a general supervisory power. Directors may wish to have a resolution passed under this article to make clear to persons they are dealing with that they have actual authority to enter into some unusual transaction. In practice, it is unlikely that this article would be used contrary to directors' wishes. Members who have disagreed so seriously with their directors that they have to adopt a special resolution under art 4, to tell them to do something they do not want to do, might just as well adopt an ordinary resolution under CA 2006, s 168, to dismiss the directors.

15.10.2.5 Members' general supervisory power

In versions of model articles prior to 1985, the general power of management (for example, in CA 1948, sch 1, Table A, art 80) was expressed to be subject 'to such regulations . . . as may be prescribed by the company in general meeting' (that is, by ordinary resolution). The articles of some companies provided that the general power of management was subject to regulations made by extraordinary resolution. Such provisions would appear to give members a general supervisory power over directors. However, judges have taken the view that these provisions are not enough to confer on members a general supervisory power: to do that it would be necessary to use the formula adopted for statutory companies in the Companies Clauses Consolidation Act 1845, s 90, which makes directors' exercise of their powers 'subject also to the control and regulation of any general meeting specially convened for the purpose' (for the operation of this provision, see *Exeter and Crediton Railway Co v Buller* (1847) 5 Ry & Can Cas 211; *Isle of Wight Railway Co v Tahourdin* (1883) 25 ChD 320). The absence of words as strong as this in the model articles for registered companies shows that directors of a registered company have a different status from those of statutory companies and that the members of registered companies do not have a general supervisory power (*Automatic Self-Cleansing Filter Syndicate Co Ltd v Cuninghame* [1906] 2 Ch 34 per Collins MR at p 43 and per Cozens-Hardy LJ at p 46; *Salmon v Quin and Axtens Ltd* [1909] 1 Ch 311 per Farwell LJ at p 320; *Breckland Group Holdings Ltd v London and Suffolk Properties Ltd* [1989] BCLC 100; *Rose v McGivern* [1998] 2 BCLC 593; see also *Charter Oil Co Ltd v Beaumont* (1967) 65 DLR (2d) 112 at pp 119–20 where it was said that a majority of members do not have a right to manage the company).

If a company's directors are of the opinion that a particular course of action is not in the company's best interests, they may refuse to pursue that course of action, even though the entire membership wants it to be pursued and even though the agreement of the entire membership would relieve the directors from liability for breach of duty (see **16.16.2**) if they did pursue it (*Lonrho Ltd v Shell Petroleum Co Ltd* [1980] 1 WLR 627 per Lord Diplock at p 634).

The court will not add implied terms to the articles of association of a company concerning the manner in which a general power of management is to be exercised by the directors (*Towcester Racecourse Co Ltd v Racecourse Association Ltd* [2002] EWHC 2141 (Ch), [2003] 1 BCLC 260).

Directors of a company are not regarded as delegates of its members; the members cannot hold meetings to tell the directors what to do. As Buckley LJ said in *Gramophone and Typewriter Ltd v Stanley* [1908] 2 KB 89, at pp 105–6:

> The directors are not servants to obey directions given by the shareholders as individuals; they are not agents appointed by and bound to serve the shareholders as their principals.

The courts have generally ruled provisions in articles making the general management power of directors subject to directions given by ordinary resolution ineffective because they are inconsistent with the principle of division of powers (*John Shaw and Sons (Salford) Ltd v Shaw* [1935] 2 KB 113; *Scott v Scott* [1943] 1 All ER 582; *Macson Development Co Ltd v Gordon* (1959) 19 DLR (2d) 465 at p 470; *Black White and Grey Cabs Ltd v Fox* [1969] NZLR 824; *Winthrop Investments Ltd v Winns Ltd* [1975] 2 NSWLR 666, per Samuels JA at p 683; *National Roads and Motorists' Association v Parker* (1986) 6 NSWLR 517). To the contrary are *Marshall's Valve Gear Co Ltd v Manning Wardle and Co Ltd* [1909] 1 Ch 267 and *Dowse v Marks* (1913) 13 SR (NSW) 332 following an obiter remark by Warrington J in *Thomas Logan Ltd v Davis* (1911) 104 LT 914—see later. Also to the contrary is *Credit Development Pte Ltd v IMO Pte Ltd* [1993] 2 SLR 370.

Similarly, a provision making the general power subject to extraordinary resolution is ineffective (*Queensland Press Ltd v Academy Instruments No 3 Pty Ltd* [1988] 2 QdR 575). And in *Re Coachman Tavern (1985) Ltd* [1988] 2 NZLR 635, Gallen J said, at p 639: 'In terms of the theories enunciated in the leading cases, it would be difficult to justify a contention that the company in general meeting could usurp powers reserved to the directors by using a special resolution.'

The principles of division of powers, and separation of ownership and control, are not universally popular. Many critics believe that directors should be subject to members' control and should be regarded more as members' delegates than as company officers. This is, in particular, crucial to proposals that in some companies, directors should be appointed to represent the interests of employees—see G R Sullivan, 'The relationship between the board of directors and the general meeting in limited companies' (1977) 93 LQR 569.

Critics of the division of powers principle have regarded statements of the principle by judges as obiter. This was the view taken by Neville J in *Marshall's Valve Gear Co Ltd v Manning Wardle and Co Ltd*, in which his Lordship held that members of a company have an inherent right to supervise directors by ordinary resolution unless the articles specify otherwise. According to this theory, a provision in articles that the power of management is subject to regulations prescribed by the company in general meeting merely restates the general law, and so does s 90 of the Companies Clauses Consolidation Act 1845. His Lordship distinguished *Automatic Self-Cleansing Filter Syndicate Co Ltd v Cuninghame* on the ground that the general management article in that case had subjected the power of management to regulations made by extraordinary resolution and thereby disentitled the members from interfering by ordinary resolution.

However, Neville J was answered within a month by Farwell LJ in the Court of Appeal in *Salmon v Quin and Axtens Ltd* [1909] 1 Ch 311, who argued that a minority who had become members of a company 'on the footing that the business should be managed by the board of directors' should not have to suffer that management being interfered with by 'a bare majority very inimical to [their] interests'. Farwell LJ was deploying an argument used by Neville J himself in *Horn v Henry Faulder and Co Ltd* (1908) 99 LT 524 to hold that directors could not agree to someone who was not a director having autonomous control over a division of the company's business.

Treating the principle of division of powers as a mere *obiter dictum*, critics assert that there is no basis for the decisions that provisions in articles subjecting directors' powers of management to regulations made by ordinary resolution are ineffective. Several commentators offer lengthy discussions of the true construction of such articles and conclude that they do give members the right to control directors. This was the view taken by the learned judicial commissioner in *Credit*

Development Pte Ltd v IMO Pte Ltd [1993] 2 SLR 370. In our view, however, the principle of division of powers is the reason for holding such provisions ineffective.

In *Salmon v Quin and Axtens Ltd* at first instance (1908) 25 TLR 64 and in *Thomas Logan Ltd v Davis* at first instance (1911) 104 LT 914, Warrington J, apparently differing from his view in *Cuninghame*'s case at first instance, said that an express provision that the members could give directions by ordinary resolution on matters of general management was effective. In *Salmon v Quin and Axtens Ltd* his Lordship was overruled on appeal. In *Thomas Logan Ltd v Davis*, he said that the directors had not acted under the general power of management but under a specific power granted by a different article which was not expressly subject to a power of the members to give directions: therefore, the directors' decision could not be altered by the members by ordinary resolution. This seems to contradict Neville J's theory that the members have an inherent right to control the directors by ordinary resolution. It is a pity that the Court of Appeal is not reported as saying anything about this when it affirmed ((1911) 105 LT 419) Warrington J's decision on the substantive point of the case.

The principle of separation of powers seems to have been generally adopted by the courts in recent years (see, for example, *Breckland Group Holdings Ltd v London and Suffolk Properties Ltd* and *Towcester Racecourse Co Ltd v Racecourse Association Ltd*) but criticism of it has continued in academic writings. In addition to the article by Sullivan mentioned earlier, discussion of the point will be found in the following articles: K A Aickin, 'Division of power between directors and general meeting as a matter of law, and as a matter of fact and policy' (1967) 5 MULR 448; B Slutsky, 'The relationship between the board of directors and the shareholders in general meeting' (1968) 3(3) Univ of Br Columbia Law Rev 81–95; G D Goldberg, 'Article 80 of Table A of the Companies Act 1948' (1970) 33 MLR 177; C J Cohen, 'The distribution of powers in a company as a matter of law' (1973) 90 SALJ 262; M S Blackman, 'Article 59 and the distribution of powers in a company' (1975) 92 SALJ 286; J-A MacKenzie, '"Who controls the company?"—the interpretation of Table A' (1983) 4 Co Law 99; M Stokes, 'Company law and legal theory', in W Twining (ed), *Legal Theory and Common Law* (Oxford: Blackwell, 1986), pp 155–83; L Flynn, 'The power to direct' (1991) 13 DULJ 101.

In debates about how companies should be governed by their members and directors, the company is often viewed, consciously or unconsciously, as a microcosm of the State, and writers on the topic often take over political theories. For a discussion of this, see R Romano, 'Metapolitics and corporate law reform' (1984) 36 Stan L Rev 923.

15.10.3 POWER TO LITIGATE

The power to litigate in the name of a registered company is one of the general powers of management assigned to the directors by art 3 of the model articles for private and for public companies in SI 2008/3229. So it cannot be exercised by the members (*John Shaw and Sons (Salford) Ltd v Shaw* [1935] 2 KB 113; *Alexander Ward and Co Ltd v Samyang Navigation Co Ltd* [1975] 1 WLR 673; *Breckland Group Holdings Ltd v London and Suffolk Properties Ltd* [1989] BCLC 100; *Mitchell and Hobbs (UK) Ltd v Mill* [1996] 2 BCLC 102). This statement is supported by the leading cases which are discussed in the following paragraphs. However, it has been subject to some controversy, which is a particular instance of the more general controversy over division of powers discussed in 15.10.2.5.

John Shaw and Sons (Salford) Ltd v Shaw concerned an established family company. Two members of the family, Peter and John Shaw, who were directors of the company, had admitted responsibility for 'deficiencies' of just over £25,000. Their brother, Percy, also a director, had previously admitted responsibility for a deficiency of £13,150. There were two other directors. (The brothers had presumably been putting the company's takings directly into their own pockets in order to evade tax.)

Part of a complicated arrangement for repaying these deficiencies to the company was that three additional directors were appointed and the articles of association were changed so that these three were named 'permanent directors'. The other five directors remained in office but as 'ordinary directors' and at board meetings they were to have 'such rights of voting . . . as may from time to time be conferred upon them by the permanent directors' (art 87). In addition, Peter, John and Percy Shaw had no control over, and no right to deal with, the debts due from them (art 86A). Article 95 was the article conferring general powers of management on the directors, in this company subject to 'regulations' adopted by ordinary resolution.

The three permanent directors held a board meeting and resolved to sue Peter and John Shaw for their debt to the company. They did not give notice of this meeting to the other directors on the ground that the other directors were not entitled to vote on the matter (see **14.8.3**). A shareholders' meeting resolved that the claim against Peter and John should be discontinued and the Court of Appeal had to consider Peter and John's application that the claim should be struck out on the grounds, *inter alia*, that:

(a) the directors' meeting was not properly convened; and

(b) the directors' decision had been overruled by the members.

Greer LJ (at p 133) held that the directors' meeting was properly convened but Slesser LJ (at pp 138–42) held that it was not. Roche LJ said that the defendants had failed to fulfil their burden of proof that the meeting was improperly convened.

On point (b), both Greer and Slesser LJJ held that the members had no power to overrule the directors (at pp 134 and 143). Roche LJ did not mention the point but his Lordship's agreement with Greer and Slesser LJJ is implicit in his conclusion that the claim should not be struck out.

In some earlier cases, the courts did permit members of a company to decide whether or not legal proceedings should be brought in the company's name.

In *Duckett v Gover* (1877) 6 ChD 82, a member of a company (who was also a director) commenced a derivative claim (see **18.4.2**) with the company as co-defendant but was allowed to amend the pleadings to make the company co-claimant. Later the directors resolved to sanction the proceedings (25 WR 554 at p 555). (See also the comments on the case by Jessel MR in *Mason v Harris* (1879) 11 ChD 97 at p 106.)

In *Harben v Phillips* (1883) 23 ChD 14, Mr Harben, who was a member of a company, claimed to have been elected a director and so joined the company as co-claimant in his claim to restrain the other directors from excluding him from board meetings. But the company's name was struck out after a shareholders' meeting disapproved of it being used (per Cotton LJ at p 38).

In *Marshall's Valve Gear Co Ltd v Manning Wardle and Co Ltd* [1909] 1 Ch 267 the majority of the directors of a company were not allowed to have struck out a claim made in the company's name by the majority of its members, Neville J taking the view that the members could instruct the directors to make the claim (cf *Pender v Lushington* (1877) 6 ChD 70 per Jessel MR at p 79). (In relation to statutory companies governed by the Companies Clauses Consolidation Act 1845, s 90—see **15.10.2.5**—it was established that the members could maintain a claim in the company's name to restrain directors from acting contrary to the members' ordinary resolutions: *Exeter and Crediton Railway Co v Buller* (1847) 5 Ry and Can Cas 211.)

However, these pre-1935 cases have not been followed since the Court of Appeal's decision in *John Shaw and Sons (Salford) Ltd v Shaw*, which was discussed earlier in this section.

In *Breckland Group Holdings Ltd v London and Suffolk Properties Ltd*, the facts were similar to those in *Marshall's Valve Gear Co Ltd v Manning Wardle and Co Ltd*. A claim had been made in the name of London and Suffolk Properties Ltd by solicitors acting on the instructions of a man who controlled a company which owned 51 per cent of the shares in London and Suffolk Properties Ltd. It was admitted that the claim was not properly authorised but contended that either a board meeting or a general meeting of members of London and Suffolk Properties Ltd could adopt it. Harman J held that the general meeting did not have power to adopt the claim, because only the board of directors had that power. His Lordship chose not to follow *Marshall's Valve Gear Co Ltd v Manning Wardle and Co Ltd* and the view taken in that case must now be regarded as abandoned.

15.10.4 POWERS CONFERRED ON DIRECTORS BY ARTICLES OTHER THAN AN ARTICLE CONFERRING A GENERAL POWER OF MANAGEMENT

In addition to an article conferring a general power of management on directors there may be other articles conferring specific powers. The wording of such an article may be construed as conferring the power on the directors to the exclusion of the members. See, for example, *Thomas Logan Ltd v Davis* (1911) 104 LT 914 (power to appoint a managing director) and *Blair Open Hearth Furnace Co Ltd v Reigart* (1913) 108 LT 665 (power to appoint additional directors).

G Hornsey, 'Some aspects of the law relating to company control' (1950) 13 MLR 470 at p 476, claimed that the decision in *Automatic Self-Cleansing Filter Syndicate Co Ltd v Cuninghame* [1906] 2 Ch 34, that the members of the company did not have power by ordinary resolution to instruct the directors to sell the company's property (see **15.10.2.5**), depended on the fact that the power to sell the company's property was a separate power given by an article (art 97) other than the article conferring the general power of management (art 96). This argument was not raised before the court and it is very doubtful that it is correct. Article 96 referred to 'the powers and authorities by these presents expressly conferred upon [the directors]' and stated that the directors 'may exercise all such powers', thus treating art 97 as merely an enumeration of some of the general powers of management. This is the way the matter was treated by Collins MR in *Cuninghame*'s case at p 42.

Hornsey's view is, however, shared by Goldberg (1970) 33 MLR 177 at p 179 and Sullivan (1977) 93 LQR 569 at p 574.

15.10.5 POWERS EXERCISABLE ONLY BY THE MEMBERS

The members of a company are given, by CA 2006 and by IA 1986, a large number of powers which only they can exercise. The powers are listed in **14.4.4**.

The members of a company also have statutory powers which, although not unique to them, cannot be taken away from them, and may be important in controlling their directors. These include the power to dismiss directors (CA 2006, s 168—see **15.6.3**) and the power to petition for a compulsory liquidation (IA 1986, s 122(1)(a)—special resolution required). In addition, any member may petition the court for relief of unfairly prejudicial conduct of the company's affairs under CA 2006, ss 994 to 999 (see **18.6**), or (provided the company is solvent) for compulsory liquidation on the ground that it is just and equitable (IA 1986, s 122(1)(g)—see **18.7**). Members holding 5 per cent of the total voting rights may insist on their resolution being put to other members, either as a written resolution if the company is private (CA 2006, s 292; see **14.5.2**) or at an annual general meeting if the company is public (s 338; see **14.8.12**), and members of a public company holding 10 per cent of votes may request a general meeting (s 303; see **14.8.14**) or ask the Secretary of State to appoint inspectors (CA 1985, s 431; see **18.8.3.1**).

15.10.6 APPROVAL BY MEMBERS OF A LISTED COMPANY'S LARGE-SCALE TRANSACTION

The listing rules require that a premium listed company must not undertake a large-scale transaction without the prior approval of its shareholders in general meeting (LR 10), and any agreement effecting the transaction must be conditional upon such approval being obtained (LR 10.5.1R). The transactions which require shareholder approval are known as 'class 1 transactions' and 'reverse takeovers'. A transaction is a class 1 transaction if any one of five financial ratios which compare the size of the transaction with the size of the company is 25 per cent or more (LR 10.2.2R). An acquisition is a reverse takeover if any of the ratios is 100 per cent or more or if the transaction would result in a fundamental change in the company's business or a fundamental change in board or voting control of the company (LR 5.6.4R). The most significant of the ratios used to classify a transaction is the ratio of the gross assets which are the subject of the transaction to the company's gross assets—the other ratios are listed in LR 10 Annex 1. In the typical reverse takeover of a company, the company acquires new assets (usually another company) by issuing so many of its own shares to the vendors that they end up with voting control of the company. A reverse takeover used to be a way for a financier to acquire a company with a stock exchange listing without having to disclose any information about himself. Now the FCA will generally cancel the listing of any company which completes a reverse takeover and will require it to apply again for listing (LR 5.2.3G).

15.10.7 REVERSION OF POWERS TO THE MEMBERS

If for some reason the directors are unable or unwilling to exercise their powers of management, those powers revert to and can be exercised by the members of the company. For instance, if no board of directors exists, the members may assume control of management (*Alexander Ward and Co Ltd v Samyang Navigation Co Ltd* [1975] 1 WLR 673). In this case, the respondent company had been registered in Hong Kong and its articles contained a provision that:

> The business of the company shall be managed by the directors, who . . . may exercise all such powers of the company as are not by the [Hong Kong] Ordinance or by these articles required to be exercised by the company in general meeting.

It was argued that this provision meant that, at a time when the company had no directors, it did not have capacity to take legal proceedings. This was rejected by the House of Lords. Lord Hailsham of St Marylebone said, at pp 678–9:

> In my opinion, at the relevant time the company was fully competent . . . to raise proceedings . . . The company could have done so either by appointing directors, or, as I think, by authorising proceedings in general meeting, which in the absence of an effective board, has a residual authority to use the company's powers.

Power similarly reverts to the general meeting where the board cannot act because its meetings are inquorate (*Foster v Foster* [1916] 1 Ch 532). It seems that the members must be regarded as agents of the company for the purpose of transacting any business when there are no directors.

In *Barron v Potter* [1914] 1 Ch 895, the company had two directors who were given power to appoint additional directors. The company's business came to a halt because one of the directors refused to attend any board meeting at which the other was present. Warrington J said, at p 903:

> If directors having certain powers are unable or unwilling to exercise them—are in fact a non-existent body for the purpose—there must be some power in the company to do itself that which under other circumstances would be otherwise done. The directors in the present case being unwilling to appoint additional directors under the power conferred on them by the articles, in my opinion, the company in general meeting has power to make the appointment.

It would therefore seem that power reverts to the general meeting where a deadlock exists between the directors which renders them incapable of exercising their powers of management. The situation in *Barron v Potter*, where the deadlock arose from an inability to act, must be distinguished from a situation like that in *Salmon v Quin and Axtens Ltd* [1909] AC 442.

The members of a company cannot exercise directors' powers if there is a potentially functioning board, even if the directors cannot be traced (*Re Frontsouth (Witham) Ltd* [2011] EWHC 1668

(Ch), [2011] BCC 635). It is difficult to reconcile this with the statement in *Barron v Potter* that if directors are 'unwilling' to exercise their powers, those powers revert to the members. Making oneself unavailable to act as a director must surely show an unwillingness to act.

R Grantham, 'The unanimous consent rule in company law' [1993] CLJ 245, argues that to allow the members of a company to exercise the directors' powers of management is a denial of the company's separate personality.

15.11 LEGAL CATEGORISATION OF DIRECTORS

In *Imperial Hydropathic Hotel Co, Blackpool v Hampson* (1882) 23 ChD 1, Bowen LJ said, at p 12:

> when persons who are directors of a company are from time to time spoken of by judges as agents, trustees, or managing partners of the company, it is essential to recollect that such expressions are used not as exhaustive of the powers or responsibilities of those persons, but only as indicating useful points of view from which they may for the moment and for the particular purpose be considered—points of view at which they seem for the moment to be either cutting the circle or falling within the category of the suggested kind. It is not meant that they belong to the category, but that it is useful for the purpose of the moment to observe that they fall *pro tanto* within the principles which govern that particular class.

In **Chapter 19** we will look at directors as agents of the company, a viewpoint that is useful when considering the company's liability for its directors' acts; in **Chapter 16** we will look at directors as fiduciaries for the company, a viewpoint that is useful when considering the duties of directors.

In the nineteenth century it used to be said that directors of a company were trustees of the company's property, especially in the context of what is now IA 1986, s 212, which provides for 'misfeasance proceedings' to be taken against any past or present officer of a company in liquidation. Before 1986, misfeasance proceedings could be taken for any 'breach of trust'. In *Re National Funds Assurance Co* (1878) 10 ChD 118, Jessel MR said (at p 128) that directors who had paid dividends out of capital had been guilty of a breach of trust for the purposes of misfeasance proceedings.

However, unlike true trustees, directors of a company do not hold the legal title to the company's property, and in *Re Exchange Banking Co, Flitcroft's Case* (1882) 21 ChD 519, another case of dividends being paid out of capital, Jessel MR preferred to call the directors 'quasi trustees' (at p 534). In *Regal (Hastings) Ltd v Gulliver* [1967] 2 AC 134, Lord Porter said, at p 159: 'Directors, no doubt, are not trustees, but they occupy a fiduciary position towards the company whose board they form'. The misfeasance provision has now been reworded, and instead of 'breach of trust' now refers to 'breach of fiduciary or other duty'. It would seem to be no longer necessary to refer to directors as trustees (but see **16.15.9**).

15.12 DIRECTORS ARE NOT AGENTS OF MEMBERS

As Buckley LJ pointed out in the passage from *Gramophone and Typewriter Ltd v Stanley* [1908] 2 KB 89 quoted in **15.10.2.5**, directors of a company do not, when acting as such, act as agents of the members of the company. Even a director who is an employee of a shareholder and was nominated to his directorship by that shareholder does not act as agent for that shareholder when acting as a director of the company (*Kuwait Asia Bank EC v National Mutual Life Nominees Ltd* [1991] 1 AC 187) and does not owe a duty to that shareholder under company law (*Hawkes v Cuddy* [2009] EWCA Civ 291, [2009] 2 BCLC 427, at [32]). It follows that a member of a company cannot be vicariously liable for wrongs committed by a director of the company on the basis of being a principal liable for the wrongs of his agent.

It is possible that particular circumstances may make a director of a company the agent of members of the company. This occurred, for example, in two cases where directors acted for members in selling their shares: *Allen v Hyatt* (1914) 30 TLR 444 and *Briess v Woolley* [1954] AC 333. In *Allen v Hyatt* the directors of a company made an undisclosed profit from selling the shares of the members of the company and were held liable to them (see **13.8**). In *Briess v Woolley*, the managing director of a company made a fraudulent misrepresentation when arranging the sale of the shares of members of the company and the members were held liable as principals to the purchasers for their agent's fraud.

16

DIRECTORS' DUTIES

SUMMARY OF POINTS COVERED

- What is in this chapter
- Codification of directors' general duties
- Fiduciary duty
- Shadow and *de facto* directors
- Duty to act within powers
- Duty to promote the success of the company
- Duty to exercise independent judgement
- Duty to exercise reasonable care, skill and diligence
- Duty to avoid conflicts of interest

- Duty not to accept benefits from third parties
- Duty to declare interest in proposed transaction or arrangement
- Substantial property transactions
- Loans, quasi-loans and credit transactions
- Connected persons and associated companies
- Remedies
- Relief from liability
- Secondary liability

16.1 WHAT IS IN THIS CHAPTER

The law on directors' duties has been transformed by CA 2006, which has put the whole subject on a statutory basis for the first time (see **16.2**). The new general duties stated in ss 171 to 177 are based on the equitable principles relating to fiduciary duties (see **16.3**) and the common law of negligence. The Secretary of State is to make regulations determining the extent to which the duties apply to shadow directors (see **16.4**). The seven general duties are:

- duty to act within powers (see **16.5**);
- duty to promote the success of the company (see **16.6**);
- duty to exercise independent judgement (see **16.7**);
- duty to exercise reasonable care, skill and diligence (see **16.8**);
- duty to avoid conflicts of interest (see **16.9**);
- duty not to accept benefits from third parties (see **16.10**); and
- duty to declare interest in proposed transaction or arrangement (see **16.11**).

There are also statutory requirements for shareholder approval of substantial property transactions between a company and its directors (see **16.12**) and loans and other credit facilities provided by a company to its directors (see **16.13**). Many of the statutory provisions apply not only to the company of which a person is a director but also to other companies in the same group, known as 'associated companies', and also to persons 'connected' with a director: these terms are defined in **16.14**. The equitable remedies for breach of duty are discussed in **16.15** and the ways in which directors can be relieved of liability in **16.16**. Secondary liability is the liability of other persons who have received property which was transferred in breach of duty or who have assisted in a breach (see **16.17**).

Key legislation which you should be able to consult when reading this chapter:

- CA 2006, ss 170–214, 232–239.

All this legislation is in *Blackstone's Statutes on Company Law*.

The following cases, which are considered in this chapter, are particularly significant and are recommended further reading:

- *Belmont Finance Corporation v Williams Furniture Ltd (No 2)* [1980] 1 All ER 393 (also a key case for **Chapter 10**);

- *Bhullar v Bhullar* [2003] EWCA Civ 424, [2003] 2 BCLC 241;

- *Bristol and West Building Society v Mothew* [1998] Ch 1;

- *Commissioners of HM Revenue and Customs v Holland* [2010] UKSC 51, [2010] 1 WLR 2793;

- *Cook v Deeks* [1916] 1 AC 554;

- *Re Duomatic Ltd* [1969] 2 Ch 365 (also a key case for **Chapter 14**);

- *Howard Smith Ltd v Ampol Petroleum Ltd* [1974] AC 821 (also a key case for **Chapter 15**);

- *Industrial Development Consultants Ltd v Cooley* [1972] 1 WLR 443;

- *Kuwait Asia Bank EC v National Mutual Life Nominees Ltd* [1991] 1 AC 187;

- *Regal (Hastings) Ltd v Gulliver* [1967] 2 AC 134; and

- *West Mercia Safetywear Ltd v Dodd* [1988] BCLC 250.

Your particular course of study may require you to read other source materials.

16.2 CODIFICATION OF DIRECTORS' GENERAL DUTIES

Before CA 2006 the duties of directors of a company to the company were mostly governed by the equitable principles of fiduciary duty and the common law of negligence. One of the most significant changes made by CA 2006 is to codify, in ss 170 to 181, the equitable principles of fiduciary duty and the common law of negligence as they apply to directors. Sections 171 to 177 state seven general duties, which will be considered separately in **16.5** to **16.11**. More than one of the general duties may apply in any case (s 179). Section 170(3) states that the general duties specified in ss 171 to 177:

> are based on certain common law rules and equitable principles as they apply in relation to directors and have effect in place of those rules and principles as regards the duties owed to a company by a director.

Within the limits allowed by the rules of precedent, courts can develop and adjust equitable principles and common law rules in a way which they are not normally allowed to do with the words of a statute. The courts will continue to develop the equitable principles of fiduciary duty and the common law of negligence as they apply other than to company directors. Codification risks losing this adaptability in exchange for the certainty and accessibility of fixed statutory wording. Section 170(4) attempts to have the best of both worlds by saying:

> (4) The general duties shall be interpreted and applied in the same way as common law rules or equitable principles, and regard shall be had to the corresponding common law rules and equitable principles in interpreting and applying the general duties.

This is a new way of interpreting a statute and it will be interesting to see how the courts take to it. It seems that they are required to regard ss 171 to 177 more as principles set out in a very authoritative judgment or textbook than as statutory rules.

Section 178 provides that the remedies for breaches of the principles in ss 171 to 177 are to be the same as if the corresponding common law rule or equitable principle were breached. Remedies for breaches of fiduciary duties are considered at **16.15**.

Codification was recommended by the Law Commission and the Scottish Law Commission in *Company Directors: Regulating Conflicts of Interests and Formulating a Statement of Duties* (Law Com No 261, Cm 4436) (London: Stationery Office, 1999), part 4. The Company Law Review Steering Group published a draft in *Modern Company Law for a Competitive Economy: Final Report*, vol 1 (URN 01/942) (London: DTI, 2001), annex C, with extensive commentary. For a critical assessment of the work of the Steering Group see S Worthington, 'Reforming directors' duties' (2001) 64 MLR 439. The primary reason for recommending codification was to make the rules accessible. The Law Commission and the Scottish Law Commission even recommended that every new director should be required to sign the code (Law Com No 261, paras 4.52 to 4.61), but the government decided against that (*Modernising Company Law* (Cm 5553–I, 2002), part II, paras 3.15 to 3.17). Signature would not make the duties any more binding than they are already and might mislead directors into believing that the code would be an exhaustive statement of their only legal responsibilities. The government also abandoned an intention to publish plain-language guidance explaining the statutory duties.

16.3 FIDUCIARY DUTY

16.3.1 EQUITABLE PRINCIPLES ON WHICH STATUTORY DUTIES ARE BASED

CA 2006, ss 171 to 173 and 175 to 177, are based on the equitable principles of fiduciary duty which applied to directors until those sections came into force and the sections must be interpreted and applied in the same way as those principles (s 174 codifies the common law of negligence).

16.3.2 DIRECTORS AS FIDUCIARIES

The word 'fiduciary' refers to trust and confidence. A fiduciary is someone who acts for, or on behalf of, another person, in a relationship of trust and confidence, which equity protects by imposing on the fiduciary a duty of loyalty (*Bristol and West Building Society v Mothew* [1998] Ch 1 per Millett LJ at p 18). The fiduciary duty of loyalty is a duty not to utilise the fiduciary position in a way which is adverse to the interests of the person for whom the fiduciary is acting (*Arklow Investments Ltd v Maclean* [2000] 1 WLR 594).

Some relationships are held to be always and inevitably fiduciary. These include the relationship of trustee to beneficiary (which is the archetypal fiduciary relationship), and the relationship of director to company (*Imperial Mercantile Credit Association v Coleman* (1873) LR 6 HL 189; *Regal (Hastings) Ltd v Gulliver* [1967] 2 AC 134, in which Lord Porter said, at p 159: 'Directors, no doubt, are not trustees, but they occupy a fiduciary position towards the company whose board they form').

There are some differences in the content of fiduciary duties for different fiduciary relationships (*Henderson v Merrett Syndicates Ltd* [1995] 2 AC 145 per Lord Browne-Wilkinson at p 206). Where there is both a contractual and a fiduciary relationship, the contract determines the extent and nature of the fiduciary duties owed (*Hospital Products Ltd v United States Surgical Corporation* (1984) 156 CLR 41 per Mason J at p 97; *Henderson v Merrett Syndicates Ltd* per Lord Browne-Wilkinson at p 206). The most onerous duties are imposed on trustees. A trustee has the legal title to property which must be dealt with for the benefit of the beneficiaries of the trust, not for the trustee's benefit. The directors of a company must deal with the company's property for the benefit of the company, not for their own benefit, but they do not have the legal title to the property, which belongs to the company as a separate person. So directors are not trustees, but they have trustee-like responsibilities, because they have the power and the duty to manage the company's business in the interests of the company (*Bairstow v Queens Moat Houses plc* [2001] 2 BCLC 531 per Robert Walker LJ at p 549).

A characteristic feature of a fiduciary duty is that the remedies provided by equity for breach of the duty are designed to deter breaches rather than compensate for loss (see **16.15.2**). The primary remedy for a breach of a director's fiduciary duty to the company is to confiscate any profit made by the director from the breach and hand it over to the company, regardless of whether the company has suffered any loss.

In equity, breach of fiduciary duty is described as 'fraud', even though no dishonesty or recklessness need be present (*Nocton v Lord Ashburton* [1914] AC 932 per Viscount Haldane LC at pp 945–58; *Armitage v Nurse* [1998] Ch 241). This sense of the term 'fraud' (sometimes described as 'equitable fraud') is much wider than fraud in common law (see the discussion of *Derry v Peek* (1889) 14 App Cas 337 in **6.8.6.2**).

Fiduciary duties are owed by persons who act as directors but have not been formally appointed as such (*Canadian Aero Service Ltd v O'Malley* (1973) 40 DLR (3d) 371; *DPC Estates Pty Ltd v Grey* [1974] 1 NSWLR 443). However, a person who has been elected a director of a company but has not yet taken up office does not owe fiduciary duties to the company, nor does a director of a holding company owe fiduciary duties to a subsidiary of the company if the subsidiary has an independent board (*Lindgren v L and P Estates Ltd* [1968] Ch 572).

A director of a company holds an office not an employment, and is on duty all the time while holding the office: there are no off-duty hours when the director is free from his or her fiduciary duties (*Gwembe Valley Development Co Ltd v Koshy* [1998] 2 BCLC 613 at p 621). In *In Plus Group Ltd v Pyke* [2002] EWCA Civ 370, [2002] 2 BCLC 201, it was held that a director of a company did not owe fiduciary duties to a company after he was excluded from any participation in its affairs.

16.3.3 DUTY OWED TO COMPANY ONLY

Fiduciary duties are owed by a director of a company to the company simply by virtue of being a director, but they are owed to (and can be enforced by) the company only. A director of a company does not, by virtue only of being a director, owe any fiduciary duties:

(a) to the members of the company (*Multinational Gas and Petrochemical Co v Multinational Gas and Petrochemical Services Ltd* [1983] Ch 258 per Dillon LJ at p 288; *Brant Investments Ltd v KeepRite Inc* (1991) 80 DLR (4th) 161); or

(b) to its creditors (*Re Wincham Shipbuilding, Boiler, and Salt Co, Poole, Jackson, and Whyte's case* (1878) 9 ChD 322; *Western Finance Co Ltd v Tasker Enterprises Ltd* (1979) 106 DLR (3d) 81; *Brant Investments Ltd v KeepRite Inc*), present or future (*Multinational Gas and Petrochemical Co v Multinational Gas and Petrochemical Services Ltd* at p 288) (see **16.6.9.2**); or

(c) to fellow directors (*Brant Investments Ltd v KeepRite Inc*; *Kohn v Meehan* (2003) LTL 4/6/2003).

It makes no difference that any of these roles are doubled up. For example, in *Western Finance Co Ltd v Tasker Enterprises Ltd* the fiduciary duties which a director of one company owed to that company were not also owed to a creditor of that company, which was itself a company of which he was a director. In *Kohn v Meehan* the fact that both claimant and defendant were directors and members of a company did not mean that the defendant owed fiduciary duties to the claimant.

The fact that a director of a company has been appointed by a particular member of that company does not, in itself, impose any duty on the director owed to the nominator (*Hawkes v Cuddy* [2009] EWCA Civ 291, [2009] 2 BCLC 427, at [32]). It is possible for the directors of a company to owe fiduciary duties to one or more members of the company by virtue of special transactions the directors enter into involving those members. Some examples are given in **13.8**. Another example is *Elliott v Wheeldon* [1993] BCLC 53, in which it was held to be arguable that where two persons pursue a joint venture as partners through the medium of a company of which they are directors, each person's actions as a director are subject to the fiduciary duties owed to the other as a partner. These are duties arising from special circumstances and are quite separate from the duties considered in this chapter which are duties owed by all directors to their companies by virtue of being a company director (*Peskin v Anderson* [2001] 1 BCLC 372).

A company does not owe fiduciary duties to its members (*Esplanade Developments Ltd v Dinive Holdings Pty Ltd* [1980] WAR 151).

16.3.4 SHOULD DIRECTORS BE SUBJECT TO FIDUCIARY DUTIES?

Some people argue that it is inappropriate to apply the concept of a fiduciary, which is derived from the concept of a trustee, to company directors. Trustees are supposed to be prudent, risk-averse people whose priority is to preserve the capital value of trust assets, whereas company directors are supposed to be risk-taking entrepreneurs. In response it may be argued that prohibition of risk-taking is not central to the law on fiduciary duties—it is a feature of the law on trustees, but in the law on company directors, courts have consistently stated that they will not judge the commercial sense of directors' decisions (see **16.6.3** and **18.3.3.1**). What is, and should be, central to the law on fiduciaries is that fiduciaries should be prevented from exercising their powers or discretions in a manner detrimental to those for whom they act and from abusing the trust and confidence reposed in them. It may also be said that economic theory suggests that executive directors of public companies should be more risk-averse than shareholders. An executive director has only one job which he or she will be careful to preserve whereas the typical shareholder has a diversified portfolio of investments so as to be more able to withstand losses on individual shares.

16.4 SHADOW AND *DE FACTO* DIRECTORS

CA 2006, s 170(5), provides:

> (5) The general duties [in ss 171 to 177] apply to a shadow director of a company where and to the extent that they are capable of so applying.

The Secretary of State has been empowered to make regulations providing for prescribed duties to apply to shadow directors with adaptations and for prescribed duties not to apply to them (Small Business, Enterprise and Employment Act 2015, s 89(2) to (5)). No steps have been taken to exercise this power.

In relation to *de facto* directors, there is no provision equivalent to s 170(5). So whether the general duties in ss 171 to 177 apply to *de facto* directors depends on whether the word 'director' used in those sections is construed as including *de facto* directors. Case law concerning events which occurred before ss 171 to 177 came into force has established a definition of who is to be treated as a *de facto* director for the purposes of imposing equitable fiduciary duties. It is submitted that the same definition should be used to determine who is a director for the purposes of the codified statutory duties. In *Commissioners of HM Revenue and Customs v Holland* [2010] UKSC 51, [2010] 1 WLR 2793, it was held that a person cannot be treated as a *de facto* director of a company, so as to be subject to equitable fiduciary duties to the company, unless it is shown that the person was part of the corporate governing structure and assumed a role in the company sufficient to impose fiduciary duties. This happened in *Primlake Ltd v Matthews Associates* [2006] EWHC 1227 (Ch), [2007] 1 BCLC 666. Mr Matthews controlled Primlake and ran the company's entire business. He was not named as a director for tax reasons. He was held to owe the company equitable fiduciary duties as a *de facto* director. In another case concerning events which occurred before ss 171 to 177 came into force, Arden LJ characterised a *de facto* director as a person who was 'one of the nerve centres from which the activities of the company radiated' (*Re Mumtaz Properties Ltd* [2011] EWCA Civ 610, [2012] 2 BCLC 109, at [47]).

In *Commissioners of HM Revenue and Customs v Holland* the Supreme Court had to decide whether a human director H of a company D, which was a corporate director of company C, owed equitable fiduciary duties as a *de facto* director of C. In this case, which concerned events occurring before 2006, D was the only director of C. (When CA 2006, s 156A, is brought into force, a company cannot be a *de jure* director of another company but can be a *de facto* or shadow director.) It was argued that when H, acting as a director of D, caused D to exercise its powers as a director of C, H acted as a *de facto* director of C. A majority in the Supreme Court rejected this argument. Lord Hope, at [42], and Lord Collins, at [96], said that if H does nothing other than discharge the duties of a director of D, then H is not a part of the corporate governance of C and has not assumed fiduciary duties to C. It is D that has exercised the powers of a director of C, not H. In that sense, it is D that is part of C's corporate governance, not H. For Lord Saville, at [97]–[99], treating H as acting as a director of D rather than C is an inevitable consequence of D's separate legal personality (see also Lord Hope at [25]). The approach of Lord Hope and Lord Collins is consistent with the approach to liability of a company director for a tort committed by the company, which is discussed at **19.7.1**.

In *Smithton Ltd v Naggar* [2014] EWCA Civ 939, [2015] 1 WLR 189, Mr Naggar was chairman of a company which owned 50.1 per cent of the claimant company's shares. He was also the claimant company's second largest client. He took a close interest in the claimant company's affairs. It was alleged that he acted as a *de facto* or shadow director of it. Mr Naggar did not deny that he performed directorial acts, but asserted that he always did so in his capacity as chairman of the holding company or as a client and never as a director of the claimant company. The trial judge and the Court of Appeal accepted this assertion and held that he was not a *de facto* or shadow director. Arden LJ, at [33]–[45], listed a number of points which are of general practical importance in determining who is a *de facto* director.

16.5 DUTY TO ACT WITHIN POWERS

16.5.1 STATUTORY DUTY

CA 2006, s 171, provides:

> A director of a company must—
> (a) act in accordance with the company's constitution, and
> (b) only exercise powers for the purposes for which they are conferred.

16.5.2 EQUITABLE PRINCIPLE ON WHICH STATUTORY DUTY IS BASED

CA 2006, s 171(b), is based on the equitable principle that a director of a company has a duty to exercise the company's powers for the purposes for which they were given. Under the model articles of association in SI 2008/3229, directors of a company have authority to exercise all its powers in the management of the company's business (model articles for private companies, art 3; model articles for public companies, art 3).

An exercise of a power for a purpose which is outside the purposes for which the power has been given (and which is variously described as an improper, extraneous or collateral purpose) is voidable. In older cases, such an exercise of a power was called a fraud on the power (*Spackman v Evans* (1868) LR 3 HL 171 at p 190).

In *Re Cameron's Coalbrook Steam Coal, and Swansea and Lougher Railway Co, Bennett's Case* (1854) 5 De G M & G 284, Turner LJ said, at p 298:

> in the exercise of the powers given to them ... [directors] must, as I conceive, keep within the proper limits. Powers given to them for one purpose cannot, in my opinion, be used by them for another and different purpose. To permit such proceedings on the part of directors of companies would be to sanction not the use but the abuse of their powers. It would be to give effect and validity to an illegal exercise of a legal power.

Where a company has restricted objects, use of a power for a purpose which is outside those objects is an example of using a power for an improper purpose.

Sometimes the limits on the exercise of a power may be found in the articles of association. In general, however, it is not possible to lay down in advance, as rules of law, the limits beyond which directors may never pass in exercising a particular power. Every case depends upon a scrutiny, in context, of its own relevant facts (*Advance Bank of Australia Ltd v FAI Insurances Australia Ltd* (1987) 9 NSWLR 464 per Kirby P at p 485).

In *Howard Smith Ltd v Ampol Petroleum Ltd* [1974] AC 821, Lord Wilberforce, giving the judgment of the Privy Council, said, at p 835:

> To define in advance exact limits beyond which directors must not pass is, in their lordships' view, impossible. This clearly cannot be done by enumeration, since the variety of situations facing directors of different types of company in different situations cannot be anticipated. No more, in their lordships' view, can this be done by the use of a phrase—such as 'bona fide in the interest of the company as a whole', or 'for some corporate purpose'. Such phrases, if they do anything more than restate the general principle applicable to fiduciary powers, at best serve, negatively, to exclude from the area of validity cases where the directors are acting sectionally, or partially: ie, improperly favouring one section of the shareholders against another.
>
> In their lordships' opinion it is necessary to start with a consideration of the power whose exercise is in question ... Having ascertained, on a fair view, the nature of this power, and having defined as can best be done in the light of modern conditions the, or some, limits within which it may be exercised, it is then necessary for the court, if a particular exercise of it is challenged, to examine the substantial purpose for which it was exercised, and to reach a conclusion whether that purpose was proper or not. In doing so it will necessarily give credit to the bona fide opinion of the directors, if such is found to exist, and will respect their judgment as to matters of management; having done this, the ultimate conclusion has to be as to the side of a fairly broad line on which the case falls.

In many cases, directors' exercise of a power leads to two or more effects, achieving one or more of the effects is a proper purpose and achieving the remainder is an improper purpose. The court is therefore required to find whether achieving the improper effects was the 'substantial' purpose, or the 'dominant' purpose (a phrase used in *Whitehouse v Carlton Hotel Pty Ltd* (1987) 162 CLR 285 at p 294) or 'the moving cause' (a phrase used by Lord Shaw in *Hindle v John Cotton Ltd* (1919) 56 SLR 625 at p 631). Thus the fact that a directors' exercise of power benefits themselves does not invalidate the exercise of the power if the self-benefit was not the dominant purpose (*Hirsche v Sims* [1894] AC 654; *Richard Brady Franks Ltd v Price* (1937) 58 CLR 112; *Mills v Mills* (1938) 60 CLR 150). In *Hindle v John Cotton Ltd*, Viscount Finlay said, at pp 630–1:

> Where the question is one of abuse of powers, the state of mind of those who acted, and the motive on which they acted, are all important, and you may go into the question of what their intention was, collecting from the surrounding circumstances all the materials which genuinely throw light upon that question of the state of mind of the directors so as to show whether they were honestly acting in discharge of their powers in the interests of the company or were acting from some by-motive, possibly of personal advantage, or for any other reason.

It has been said in the High Court of Australia that an improper purpose would invalidate the exercise of a power if the power would not have been exercised had that purpose not been present (*Mills v Mills*, per Dixon J at p 186; *Whitehouse v Carlton Hotel Pty Ltd*, per Mason, Dean and Dawson JJ at p 294). The concept of a dominant purpose is not easy to apply in practice. For a discussion see D M J Bennett, 'The ascertainment of purpose when bona fides are in issue—some logical problems' (1989) 12 Syd LR 5.

Acting bona fide in the interests of the company is not an excuse for acting for a dominant improper purpose, especially where the directors are acting in their own self-interest (*Ashburton Oil NL v Alpha Minerals NL* (1971) 123 CLR 614 per Menzies J at p 627; *Howard Smith Ltd v Ampol Petroleum Ltd* at p 834, though the contrary was held in *Olson v Phoenix Industrial Supply Ltd* (1984) 9 DLR (4th) 451). In *Advance Bank of Australia Ltd v FAI Insurances Australia Ltd*, Kirby P said, at p 485:

> statements by the directors about their subjective intention, whilst relevant, are not conclusive of the bona fides of the directors or of the purposes for which they acted as they did. In this sense, although the search is for the subjective intentions of the directors, it is a search which must be conducted objectively as the court decides whether to accept or discount the assertions which the directors make about their motives and purposes: cf Megarry V-C in *Cayne v Global Natural Resources plc* (12 August 1982 unreported).

In *Howard Smith Ltd v Ampol Petroleum Ltd*, Lord Wilberforce said, at p 832:

> when a dispute arises whether directors of a company made a particular decision for one purpose or for another, or whether, there being more than one purpose, one or another purpose was the substantial or primary purpose, the court, in their lordships' opinion, is entitled to look at the situation objectively in order to estimate how critical or pressing, or substantial or, *per contra*, insubstantial an alleged requirement may have been. If it finds that a particular requirement, though real, was not urgent, or critical, at the relevant time, it may have reason to doubt, or discount, the assertions of individuals that they acted solely in order to deal with it, particularly when the action they took was unusual or even extreme.

Changing a company's constitutional restrictions on the purposes for which directors may exercise their powers (for example, changing the company's objects) is not an improper purpose, and the directors may spend the company's money on investigating and planning for such a change (*Peskin v Anderson* [2001] 1 BCLC 372).

In *Eclairs Group Ltd v JKX Oil and Gas plc* [2015] UKSC 71, [2015] Bus LR 1395, Lord Sumption (with whom Lord Hodge agreed) discussed the problem of identifying a substantial or dominant purpose (at [14]–[24]). Lord Sumption expressed approval for the 'but for' test: that an improper purpose will invalidate the exercise of a power if, but for the existence of that purpose, the power would not have been exercised. This is the test stated by the High Court of Australia in *Mills v Mills* (1938) 60 CLR 150 at p 186 and in *Whitehouse v Carlton Hotel Pty Ltd* (1987) 162 CLR 285 at p 294. However, the other three Justices said that the point had not arisen in this case and they preferred not to express any opinion on it. One problem is that CA 2006, s 171(b), requires directors to exercise powers only for proper purposes. This would seem to forbid exercise for an improper purpose, even if it is only an incidental purpose. However, this would probably make the provision unworkable in practice, because business decisions inevitably have many foreseen and unforeseen effects. It seems that s 171(b) must be applied, as s 170(4) requires, in the same way as the equitable principle, ignoring incidental improper purposes.

It cannot be an answer to an abuse of directors' powers to say that the victims of the improper use of the power have only themselves to blame (*Eclairs Group Ltd v JKX Oil and Gas plc* at [39]).

16.5.3 POWER TO ALLOT SHARES

Many of the cases in which the question of an improper use of a power has arisen are concerned with directors using their power to allot shares in order to give votes to their friends and so prevent a change in the control of the company, and it is in these cases that the proper-purposes doctrine has been most fully explored in recent years.

In UK company law the directors' power to allot shares is now restricted by CA 2006 as described in **6.3.4** and **6.3.5**. Before these restrictions came into force it was established that:

(a) If directors allot shares for the dominant purpose of preserving their own control of the management of the company (by ensuring that there is a majority of votes in their favour) then the allotment is invalid (*Fraser v Whalley* (1864) 2 Hem & M 10; *Punt v Symons and Co Ltd* [1903] 2 Ch 506; *Piercy v S Mills and Co Ltd* [1920] 1 Ch 77; *Hogg v Cramphorn Ltd* [1967] Ch 254; *Ashburton Oil NL v Alpha Minerals NL* (1971) 123 CLR 614).

(b) If directors allot shares for the dominant purpose of manipulating voting power by favouring one shareholder or group of shareholders at the expense of another non-consenting shareholder or group, the allotment will be invalid (*Howard Smith Ltd v Ampol Petroleum Ltd* [1974] AC 821; *Whitehouse v Carlton Hotel Pty Ltd* (1987) 162 CLR 285).

(c) If directors allot shares for the dominant purpose of benefiting themselves financially, the allotment will be invalid (*Ngurli Ltd v McCann* (1953) 90 CLR 425).

See further, K E Lindgren, 'The fiduciary nature of a company board's power to issue shares' (1971–2) 10 West Aust L Rev 364.

In *Re Looe Fish Ltd* [1993] BCLC 1160, a director who allotted himself shares in order to provide himself with sufficient votes to defeat a motion to appoint further directors of whom he disapproved was disqualified from being a director for two and a half years.

In the *Howard Smith Ltd* case (an appeal from New South Wales), a company was being threatened with a takeover by two associates who between them held 55 per cent of the company's shares. The company needed more capital but proposed to obtain it by issuing 4.5 million shares to members other than the takeover bidders: this allotment would have reduced the takeover bidders to a minority in the company and was held to be a misuse of the directors' powers. (Pre-emption rights, see **6.3.5**, are important in preventing manoeuvres like this.)

16.5.4 RESPONSE TO TAKEOVER BIDS

A takeover bid is an offer to acquire the shares of a company's members and it is up to them to decide whether or not to accept. Directors who seek to prevent a bid succeeding will almost inevitably be thought to be acting primarily with a view to maintaining themselves in office. Many of the cases on directors' exercise of their power to allot shares have concerned allotments made to defeat unwelcome takeover bids. In the United Kingdom, the pre-emption rules which ensure that new shares are allotted to members in proportion to their existing shareholdings have reduced the incidence of such cases.

There is no legal principle that it is improper for directors to take action designed to defeat a takeover offer (per Clarke JA in *Darvall v North Sydney Brick and Tile Co Ltd* (1989) 16 NSWLR 260 at p 335; *347883 Alberta Ltd v Producers Pipelines Inc* (1991) 80 DLR (4th) 359). However, it may be difficult to make an arrangement which is proportionate to the actual threat of a particular takeover bidder without detrimental effects, such as entrenching the current directors in office. A disproportionate arrangement may be a misuse of directors' powers. In *Criterion Properties plc v Stratford UK Properties LLC* [2004] UKHL 28, [2004] 1 WLR 1846, the former managing director of the claimant plc had caused it to enter into a contract which left it with a 'poison pill' in the form of a right by an outsider to demand a potentially crippling payment if control of the company should change hands or if the managing director or chairman should leave office. Lord Scott of Foscote pointed out that this payment would have to be made even if the directors voluntarily resigned or there was a wholly beneficial takeover, and questioned whether the managing director had authority to make the contract.

Where there are rival takeover bids the directors must not exercise their powers in such a way as to prevent the members obtaining the best price for their shares (*Heron International Ltd v Lord Grade* [1983] BCLC 244 (use of power to refuse to register transfers); *Re a Company (No 008699 of 1985)* [1986] BCLC 382 (use of power to provide information)). In **Howard Smith Ltd v Ampol Petroleum Ltd** [1974] AC 821 Lord Wilberforce said, at pp 837–8:

> The right to dispose of shares at a given price is essentially an individual right to be exercised on individual decision... Directors are of course entitled to offer advice, and bound to supply information, relevant to the making of such a decision.

However, where there are competing offers, the directors are not under a positive duty to recommend and facilitate the implementation of the higher offer (*Re a Company (No 008699 of 1985)*; *Dawson International plc v Coats Patons plc* 1988 SLT 854).

The question has been posed whether directors can validly issue shares in order to defeat a takeover by an asset-stripper, a rival or an incompetent manager who would ruin the company. In **Cayne v Global Natural Resources plc** (12 August 1982 unreported) Megarry V-C said:

> I cannot see why that should not be a perfectly proper exercise of fiduciary powers by the directors of [the company]. The object is not to retain control as such, but to prevent [the company] from being reduced to impotence and beggary, and the only means available to the directors for achieving this purpose is to retain control. This is quite different from directors seeking to retain control because they think they are better directors than their rivals would be.

On the other hand, Hoffmann J, in **Re a Company (No 005136 of 1986)** [1987] BCLC 82, said that: 'The company is not particularly concerned with who its shareholders are' (at p 84). A sale of shares in a company by one of its members is not something that relates to the conduct of the company's affairs for the purposes of CA 2006, s 994 (*Re Leeds United Holdings plc* [1996] 2 BCLC 545). But in **Dawson International plc v Coats Patons plc** 1988 SLT 854, Lord Cullen said, at p 860:

> I do not accept as a general proposition that a company can have no interest in the change of identity of its shareholders upon a takeover. It appears to me that there will be cases in which its agents, the directors, will see the takeover of its shares by a particular bidder as beneficial to the company. For example, it may provide the opportunity for integrating operations or obtaining additional resources. In other cases the directors will see a particular bid as not in the best interests of the company.

See also per Mahoney JA in *Darvall v North Sydney Brick and Tile Co Ltd* (1989) 16 NSWLR 260 at pp 324–5. These conflicting opinions raise the crucial issue of how a company's interests are to be judged.

If directors of a company allow the company to be taken over by persons who ruin it, the company cannot, it seems, sue those directors, because members are free to pursue foolish or even negligent policies (*Multinational Gas and Petrochemical Co v Multinational Gas and Petrochemical Services Ltd* [1983] Ch 258). See further the discussion of *Heron International Ltd v Lord Grade* [1983] BCLC 244 in C Baxter, 'The true spirit of *Foss v Harbottle*' (1987) 38 NILQ 6 at p 29, n 96.

16.5.5 OTHER POWERS

Although the most extensive discussion recently of directors' duties when exercising powers has been in relation to the power to allot shares, the duties have been examined in other cases, notably in relation to:

(a) Power to refuse to register a transfer of shares (see **8.3.4.2**).

(b) Power to circulate information to shareholders (see **14.8.7.4**).

(c) Power to borrow and give security (see *Rolled Steel Products (Holdings) Ltd v British Steel Corporation* [1986] Ch 246).

(d) Power to forfeit shares (see **6.5.2.4**).

(e) Power to make calls on partly paid shares (*Anglo-Universal Bank v Baragnon* (1881) 45 LT 362; *Savoy Corporation Ltd v Development Underwriting Ltd* [1963] NSWR 138).

(f) Power to determine the terms and conditions on which shares are issued (*Alexander v Automatic Telephone Co* [1900] 2 Ch 56).

(g) Power to determine which competing bids from members for shares being offered by a member under pre-emption provisions of articles should succeed (*T C Newman (Qld) Pty Ltd v DHA Rural (Qld) Pty Ltd* [1988] 1 QdR 308).

(h) Power to call general meetings (*Pergamon Press Ltd v Maxwell* [1970] 1 WLR 1167).

(i) Power to cause the company to enter into contracts (*Lee Panavision Ltd v Lee Lighting Ltd* [1992] BCLC 22; *Neptune (Vehicle Washing Equipment) Ltd v Fitzgerald (No 2)* [1995] BCC 1000).

16.6 DUTY TO PROMOTE THE SUCCESS OF THE COMPANY

16.6.1 STATUTORY DUTY

CA 2006, s 172, expresses what is undoubtedly the central obligation of a director:

(1) A director of a company must act in the way he considers, in good faith, would be most likely to promote the success of the company for the benefit of its members as a whole, and in doing so have regard (amongst other matters) to—

  (a) the likely consequences of any decision in the long term,

  (b) the interests of the company's employees,

  (c) the need to foster the company's business relationships with suppliers, customers and others,

  (d) the impact of the company's operations on the community and the environment,

  (e) the desirability of the company maintaining a reputation for high standards of business conduct, and

  (f) the need to act fairly as between members of the company.

(2) Where or to the extent that the purposes of the company consist of or include purposes other than the benefit of its members, subsection (1) has effect as if the reference to promoting the success of the company for the benefit of its members were to achieving those purposes.

(3) The duty imposed by this section has effect subject to any enactment or rule of law requiring directors, in certain circumstances, to consider or act in the interests of creditors of the company.

It may be that, if a majority of directors of a company, in breach of their duty under s 172, refuse to agree to a course of action that would promote the company's success for the benefit of its members as a whole, the minority can make a valid decision to take that action. In *Fusion Interactive Communication Solutions Ltd v Venture Investment Placement Ltd (No 2)* [2005] EWHC 736 (Ch), [2005] 2 BCLC 571, directors of a company, in breach of their duty to the company, refused to agree to its taking legal proceedings that would have benefited it. The court treated as properly authorised, proceedings brought in the company's name by directors who did not have a majority of votes on the board.

16.6.2 EQUITABLE PRINCIPLE ON WHICH STATUTORY DUTY IS BASED

CA 2006, s 172, is based on the equitable fiduciary duty which was formulated, in combination with the duty to act within powers (see **16.5**), by Lord Greene MR in *Re Smith and Fawcett Ltd* [1942] Ch 304. The Master of the Rolls said, at p 306, that directors of a company must act:

> bona fide in what they consider—not what a court may consider—is in the interests of the company, and not for any collateral purpose.

In *J J Harrison (Properties) Ltd v Harrison* [2001] EWCA Civ 1467, [2002] 1 BCLC 162, Chadwick LJ, also combining the two duties, said, at [25]:

> the powers to dispose of the company's property, conferred upon the directors by the articles of association, must be exercised by the directors for the purposes, and in the interests, of the company.

In *Item Software (UK) Ltd v Fassihi* [2004] EWCA Civ 1244, [2005] ICR 450, at [41], Arden LJ spoke of:

> the fundamental duty to which a director is subject, that is the duty to act in what he in good faith considers to be the best interests of his company... The duty is expressed in these very general terms, but that is one of its strengths: it focuses on principle not on the particular words which judges or the legislature have used in any particular case or context. It is dynamic and capable of application in cases where it has not previously been applied but the principle or rationale of the rule applies. It reflects the flexible quality of the doctrines of equity.

Section 172(1) states that a duty of a director of a company to act in the way he or she considers, in good faith, would be most likely to promote the success of the company for the benefit of its members as a whole. It lists a number of matters to which, among other matters, the directors must have regard when considering which way of acting would be most likely to do this. Section 172(1) expresses the duty to act in the interests of the company as a duty to find what has the highest probability of promoting the company's success and provides a specification of what interests of a company are to be promoted.

16.6.3 WHAT IS THE TEST?

CA 2006, s 172(1), requires a director to act in the way that *the director considers*, in good faith, would be most likely to promote the company's success, not the way which *the court considers*, in the light of expert evidence, would be most successful. This reflects the way in which the equitable principle was applied, as stated in the dictum of Lord Greene MR quoted in **16.6.2**. As Lord Wilberforce said in *Howard Smith Ltd v Ampol Petroleum Ltd* [1974] AC 821, at p 832:

> There is no appeal on merits from management decisions to courts of law: nor will courts of law assume to act as a kind of supervisory board over decisions within the powers of management honestly arrived at.

In *Regentcrest plc v Cohen* [2001] 2 BCLC 80, Jonathan Parker J said, at p 105:

> The question is not whether, viewed objectively by the court, the particular act or omission which is challenged was in fact in the interests of the company; still less is the question whether the court, had it been in the position of the director at the relevant time, might have acted differently. Rather, the question is whether the director honestly believed that his act or omission was in the interests of the company. The issue is as to the director's state of mind. No doubt, where it is clear that the act or omission under challenge resulted in substantial detriment to the company, the director will have a harder task persuading the court that he honestly believed it to be in the company's interest; but that does not detract from the subjective nature of the test.

An act done in the unreasonable belief that it was in the interests of the company is not in breach of fiduciary duty, provided the belief was held honestly (*Extrasure Travel Insurance Ltd v Scattergood* [2003] 1 BCLC 598 at [90] and [97]). In determining whether an act by a director was bona fide in what the director considered to be in the interests of the company, the question whether the director would personally benefit from the act is irrelevant (*Australian Growth Resources Corporation Pty Ltd v Van Reesema* (1988) 13 ACLR 261).

If directors of a company have acted without separately considering the company's interests, their action may nevertheless be considered to have been bona fide in what they considered to be in the interests of the company if it satisfies the objective test formulated by Pennycuick J in **Charterbridge Corporation Ltd v Lloyds Bank Ltd** [1970] Ch 62, at p 74:

> The proper test, I think, in the absence of actual separate consideration, must be whether an intelligent and honest man in the position of a director of the company concerned, could, in the whole of the existing circumstances, have reasonably believed that the transactions were for the benefit of the company.

If, therefore, a director of a company has acted without separately considering the company's interests and there is no basis on which a director could reasonably have concluded that the action was in the company's interests, the court will find that the director was in breach of duty (*Item Software (UK) Ltd v Fassihi* [2004] EWCA Civ 1244, [2005] ICR 450, at [44]).

16.6.4 SUCCESS OF THE COMPANY

A company has a dual aspect as an association of its members and as a person separate from its members. CA 2006, s 172(1), neatly brings in the interests both of the company as a separate person and of its members by expressing a director's duty in terms of promoting 'the success of the company for the benefit of its members as a whole'. The Company Law Review Steering Group said (**Modern Company Law for a Competitive Economy: Developing the Framework** (URN 00/656) (London: DTI, 2000), para 3.51):

> We believe there is value in inserting a reference to the success of the company, since what is in view is not the individual interests of members, but their interests as members of an association with the purposes and the mutual arrangements embodied in the constitution; the objective is to be achieved by the directors successfully managing the complex of relationships and resources which comprise the company's undertaking.

The following cases suggest that, sometimes, the interests of the company as a separate person may be preferred to the interests of the members, or at least some of them.

In **Mutual Life Insurance Co of New York v Rank Organisation Ltd** [1985] BCLC 11, Goulding J said, at p 21, that provisions of a company's constitution conferring powers on its directors are subject to two implied terms:

> First, the time-honoured rule that the directors' powers are to be exercised in good faith in the interests of the company, and secondly, that they must be exercised fairly as between different shareholders.

The directors of the Rank Organisation had decided to issue new shares and part of the issue was made available to existing shareholders at a favourable price, but shareholders living in North America were excluded so as to save the company the high cost of complying with US and Canadian legislation concerning public offers of shares in those countries. It was held that the directors had not acted in breach of duty in preferring the interests of the company as a separate person to the interests of some of its members. This was followed by Arden J in *Re BSB Holdings Ltd (No 2)* [1996] 1 BCLC 155. Her Ladyship said, at p 251: 'The law does not require the interests of the company to be sacrificed in the particular interests of a group of shareholders.'

CA 2006, s 172(1)(f), says that, in fulfilling the general duty to promote the success of the company for the benefit of its members, a director must have regard to the need to act fairly as between members of the company who have different interests.

In *Gaiman v National Association for Mental Health* [1971] Ch 317, Megarry J observed, at p 330, that as a company is an artificial legal entity, it is not easy to determine what is in its best interests without paying due regard to its present and future members as a whole. Nevertheless, his Lordship went on to decide, at pp 335–6, that whereas persons exercising a power of expelling members from an unincorporated association may have a duty to the persons sought to be expelled to observe the rules of natural justice, what distinguished a registered company from an unincorporated association is precisely that:

> Where there is corporate personality, the directors or others exercising the powers in question [in this case, the board of directors was described as the 'council'] are bound not merely by their duties towards the other members, but also by their duties towards the corporation. These duties may be inconsistent with the observance of natural justice.
>
> Where, as in the present case, their duty [to the corporation] may impel the council to exercise the power with great speed, whereas natural justice would require delay, I think that that indicates that the council is intended to be able to exercise its powers unfettered by natural justice.

16.6.5 BENEFIT OF THE MEMBERS

It is usually assumed that the only benefit the members of a company derive from it is the return on their investments. However, this is not necessarily easy to define. Do the directors have to ensure the company pays the highest possible annual dividends, or that the market price for its shares is as high as possible, or should they ensure the long-term growth and stability of the company? How risky should the shareholders' investment be?

In Delaware, in *Paramount Communications Inc v Time Inc* (1990) 571 A 2d 1140, the court accepted that it was legitimate for the directors of Time Inc to decide that it was in the best interests of their company to go ahead with a merger with another company and not to allow shareholders the opportunity of selling their shares to an unwelcome takeover bidder, even though the bidder was offering considerably more than the current market price for the company's shares and many shareholders would have found the bid attractive. It is possible to interpret this case in terms of a preference for long-term increase in the company's value over short-term gain for the shareholders, but the court said, at p 1150:

> we think it unwise to place undue emphasis upon long-term versus short-term corporate strategy ... the question of 'long-term' versus 'short-term' values is largely irrelevant because directors, generally, are obliged to chart a course for a corporation which is in its best interests without regard to a fixed investment horizon.

It seems that the court was defining the directors' duties in terms of the interests of the company as a separate person ('*its* best interests'). The court expressly rejected the idea that the directors' duty was simply to maximise shareholder value in the short term.

A common criticism of British business people is that their approach is too short term, preferring immediate profits to long-term growth, and that this is bad for the British economy. See Commission on Public Policy and British Business, *Promoting Prosperity: a Business Agenda for Britain* (London: Vintage, 1997).

CA 2006, s 172(1)(a), states that, in fulfilling the statutory duty to promote the success of the company for the benefit of its members as a whole, a director must have regard to the likely consequences of any decision in the long term. This is a clear change from the draft cl B3(3) which the government published in its White Paper, *Company Law Reform* (Cm 6456, 2005), which required a director to take into account 'the likely consequences (short and long term) of the actions open to the director'. Of course, pointing out that both short and long-term consequences must be taken into account does not decide whether the short or the long term is more important. Parliament has clearly decided it is the long term that is more important.

The assumption that shares are acquired only for financial reward may not be correct. If a company's shareholders take account of other considerations when deciding whether to hold shares in the company, the company will serve their interests by advancing those other considerations. The presence of non-financial reasons for holding shares was recognised by the court in *CAS (Nominees) Ltd v Nottingham Forest FC plc* [2002] 1 BCLC 613, which concerned a public company, whose shares were traded on AIM, which owned all shares in a private company which ran the Nottingham Forest professional football club. The private company issued shares, in return for much-needed cash, which gave a new investor a majority holding. The owners of a large minority of shares in the plc claimed that this had unfairly prejudiced their interests (see **18.6**) by diminishing the value of their shares, but the court could find no rational basis for assessing what difference the action had made to that value. Hart J said, at p 641:

> The primary driver of value of a controlling interest in a football club is the desire of individuals (or a group of individuals) to control or have significant influence over the club. That desire would not arise from any expectation on the part of the investor that he would see a financial return. It was simply the desire to own or control a football club for its own sake. [An expert witness] described the valuation principle applicable to this as the valuation of a consumable, rather than an investment.

As there was no competition for control of the club, no price could be put on it.

In relation to the statutory duty to promote the success of the company, CA 2006, s 172(2), provides that, if a company is established for purposes other than the benefit of its members, the duty is to act in the way the director considers, in good faith, would be most likely to achieve those purposes.

16.6.6 OTHER CONSTITUENCIES

16.6.6.1 Interests to be considered by directors

For a long time, there has been discussion over whether the directors of a company should consider the interests of persons other than the company as a separate person and the members of the company. The introduction into British company law in the 1980s of duties to consider the interests of employees (see **16.6.7**) and creditors (see **16.6.9**) was a notable development but there have been many suggestions that directors should consider the interests of other groups (or 'constituencies' or 'stakeholders').

16.6.6.2 In the USA

In the USA many state legislatures, beginning with Pennsylvania in 1983, have enacted provisions allowing corporate directors to consider the interests of employees, customers, creditors, suppliers and communities in which the corporation has facilities, as well as national and state economies and other community and societal considerations. Provisions of this kind are usually known as 'other constituencies statutes'. They have usually been enacted to enable directors to take action in defence against hostile takeover bids where it is expected that the bidder, if successful, will change drastically the taken-over company's operations on which the other constituencies depend. However, the statutes are not expressed to be limited to that situation.

The other constituencies statutes enacted in the USA acknowledge the continuing importance that a company may have for many persons other than its members. It is argued that companies must acknowledge these responsibilities and act as good citizens in a socially responsible way (see E M Dodd, 'For whom are corporate managers trustees?' (1932) 45 Harv L Rev 1145; J B White, 'How should we talk about corporations? The languages of economics and of citizenship'

(1985) 94 Yale LJ 1416; C M Slaughter, 'Corporate social responsibility: a new perspective' (1997) 18 Co Law 313). If acting in a socially responsible way is a citizenship duty of a company as a separate person then directors who cause it to act in that way are acting in the interests of the company.

Dodd's article prompted a response by A A Berle, 'For whom corporate managers *are* trustees' (1932) 45 Harv L Rev 1365, who vigorously opposed the idea that corporate managers should have a free hand to use shareholders' money to promote the managers' own ideas of what was socially desirable (see also M Friedman, *Capitalism and Freedom* (Chicago: University of Chicago Press, 1962), pp 133–6). Berle's 1932 view was maintained by the courts in the USA but arguments for and against social responsibility continued: see, for example, Lord Wedderburn of Charlton, 'The social responsibility of companies' (1985) 15 MULR 4; Lord Wedderburn of Charlton, 'Trust, corporation and the worker' (1985) 23 Osgoode Hall LJ 203; C D Stone, 'Corporate social responsibility: what it might mean if it were really to matter' (1986) 71 Iowa L Rev 557; H J Glasbeek, 'The corporate social responsibility movement—the latest in Maginot Lines to save capitalism' (1988) 11 Dalhousie LJ 363. Berle eventually admitted that in practice when corporate managers in the USA had acted in the public interest they had acted wisely and had forestalled the need for government action ('Modern functions of the corporate system' (1962) 62 Colum L Rev 433 at pp 442–4). The Committee on Corporate Laws, 'Other constituencies statutes: potential for confusion' (1990) 45 Bus Law 2253 asserts that Berle's 1932 view should still prevail and points out that the other constituencies statutes which have been enacted may not have much practical significance because they do not provide any mechanism by which representatives of the other constituencies can require directors to take them into consideration. It seems that the stock market in the USA has not reduced share prices in response to the enactment of other constituencies statutes, possibly because of a general perception that they are practically ineffective (R Romano, 'Comment: what is the value of other constituency statutes to shareholders?' (1993) 43 UTLJ 533). For a full discussion see the special issue of the *University of Toronto Law Journal* entitled 'The corporate stakeholder debate: the classical theory and its critics', vol 43, No 3 (Summer 1993).

16.6.6.3 In the UK

The Commission on Public Policy and British Business, *Promoting Prosperity: a Business Agenda for Britain* (London: Vintage, 1997) recommended that British companies legislation should be amended along the lines of the Pennsylvania law, to enable directors to take a broader view of their responsibilities (p 107). The Company Law Review Steering Group rejected this option (which they called the pluralist approach). One important reason for rejecting it was expressed by the **Committee on Corporate Governance**, *Final Report* (London: Gee, 1997), para 1.17:

> From a practical point of view, to redefine the directors' responsibilities in terms of the stake-holders would mean identifying all the various stakeholder groups; and deciding the nature and extent of the directors' responsibility to each. The result would be that the directors were not effectively accountable to anyone since there would be no clear yardstick for judging their performance. This is a recipe neither for good governance nor for corporate success.

The route which has been taken in CA 2006, s 172(1), is to require directors to consider other constituencies in the context of promoting the benefit of the members. This is described as promoting enlightened shareholder value (see **1.6.4.3**). Section 172(1) provides that, when considering how to act in a way that would be most likely to promote the success of the company for the benefit of its members as a whole, a director must have regard (among other matters) to:

(a) the likely consequences of any decision in the long term;

(b) the interests of the company's employees;

(c) the need to foster the company's business relationships with suppliers, customers, and others;

(d) the impact of the company's operations on the community and the environment;

(e) the desirability of the company maintaining a reputation for high standards of business conduct; and

(f) the need to act fairly as between members of the company.

In the debate on report in the House of Lords, the Attorney-General, Lord Goldsmith, said that the government's intention is that the duty to have regard to these factors should be subordinate to the overriding duty to act in what the director considers, in good faith, would be most likely to promote the company's success (Hansard HL, 9 May 2006, col 845). The Attorney-General went on to say (col 846):

> We want the director to give such consideration to the factors identified as is necessary for the decision that he has to take, and no more than that. We do not intend a director to be required to do more than good faith and the duty of skill and care would require, nor do we want it to be possible for a director acting in good faith to be held liable for a process failure where it could not have affected the outcome.

16.6.7 INTERESTS OF EMPLOYEES

CA 2006, s 172(1)(b), provides that, when considering how to act in a way that would be most likely to promote the success of the company for the benefit of its members as a whole, a director must have regard to the interests of the company's employees. It is noticeable that the interests of employees are to be considered only in the context of benefit to members. This provision replaces an earlier independent requirement (CA 1985, s 309, first enacted in 1980) that directors were to have regard to the interests of the company's employees in general as well as the interests of its members.

The Company Law Review Steering Group believed that s 309 should be repealed because they saw a danger that it might be interpreted as enabling directors to prefer employees' interests to those of shareholders, which would threaten the principle of shareholder primacy. They believed that directors should consider employees' interests only in the process of promoting shareholders' interests (*Modern Company Law for a Competitive Economy: The Strategic Framework* (London: DTI, 1999), paras 5.1.20 to 5.1.23). Lord Wedderburn of Charlton, 'Employees, partnership and company law' (2002) 31 ILJ 99, sees this as a culmination of a long-term shift of power from labour to capital, resulting in labour being treated in company law as a commodity.

The interests of employees have traditionally been given scant attention in British company law: see B Bercusson, 'Workers, corporate enterprise and the law', in R Lewis (ed), *Labour Law in Britain* (Oxford: Basil Blackwell, 1986); Lord Wedderburn of Charlton, 'Companies and employees: common law or social dimension?' (1993) 109 LQR 220.

16.6.8 SOCIAL, ENVIRONMENTAL AND ETHICAL CONSIDERATIONS

CA 2006, s 172(1), provides that, when considering how to act in a way that would be most likely to promote the success of the company for the benefit of its members as a whole, a director must have regard to:

(d) the impact of the company's operations on the community and the environment,

(e) the desirability of the company maintaining a reputation for high standards of business conduct.

These are known as social, environmental and ethical (SEE) considerations and they are of interest to pension funds, which are very significant as shareholders of listed companies. The trustees of occupational pension schemes are required by the Pensions Act 1995, s 35, to produce a statement of their investment principles. As from 3 July 2000 this must state the extent to which (if at all) social, environmental or ethical considerations are taken into account in the selection, retention and realisation of investments (SI 1996/3127, reg 11A(a)). The same requirement has been imposed on authorities administering pension funds for local government employees in England and Wales (SI 1998/1831, reg 9A(2)(f)) and Scotland (SI 1998/2888, reg 9A(2)(f)). There is also legislation in Northern Ireland to the same effect. A company which itself takes into account SEE considerations will be serving the interests of pension fund shareholders which themselves take into account SEE considerations. The National Association of Pension Funds has commented:

> Over time, this requirement [that pension fund trustees must state what attention they pay to SEE considerations] is likely to have a significant impact on UK governance practices as institutional investors seek to establish the extent and nature of corporate activity in these areas in order that their impact on long-term shareholder value can be better assessed. At the same time, boards of directors will increasingly incorporate these concepts into corporate strategy and companies will strive to respond to investor concerns. Companies should now ensure that they report to shareholders on these developments. (*Towards Better Corporate Governance* (London: NAPF, 2000), p 10)

16.6.9 INTERESTS OF CREDITORS

16.6.9.1 Duty to consider the interests of creditors

The creditors of a company are not expressly listed in CA 2006, s 172(1), as a constituency to whose interests the directors must have regard, though some of the constituents who are listed (employees, suppliers and customers) will be creditors. Section 172(3) provides that the duty to promote the success of the company has effect, subject to any enactment or rule of law requiring directors, in certain circumstances, to consider or act in the interests of creditors of the company. This is a reference to the common law principle that directors of an insolvent company must have regard to the interests of its creditors (see **16.6.9.2**) and the provisions of IA 1986, ss 214 and 246ZB, concerning wrongful trading (see **16.6.9.3**).

16.6.9.2 Common law duty

In *West Mercia Safetywear Ltd v Dodd* [1988] BCLC 250, the Court of Appeal held that a director of an insolvent company must have regard to the interests of its creditors. The court adopted into English law a principle which had previously been enunciated in Australia and New Zealand in such cases as *Walker v Wimborne* (1976) 137 CLR 1; *Nicholson v Permakraft (NZ) Ltd* [1985] 1 NZLR 242; and *Kinsela v Russell Kinsela Pty Ltd* (1986) 4 NSWLR 722. Dillon LJ in *West Mercia Safetywear Ltd v Dodd* approved the following statement by Street CJ in **Kinsela v Russell Kinsela Pty Ltd** at p 730:

> In a solvent company the proprietary interests of the shareholders entitle them as a general body to be regarded as the company when questions of the duty of directors arise. If, as a general body, they authorise or ratify a particular action of the directors, there can be no challenge to the validity of what the directors have done. But where a company is insolvent the interests of the creditors intrude. They become prospectively entitled, through the mechanism of liquidation, to displace the power of the shareholders and directors to deal with the company's assets. It is in a practical sense their assets and not the shareholders' assets that, through the medium of the company, are under the management of the directors pending either liquidation, return to solvency, or the imposition of some alternative administration.

Earlier, in **Lonrho Ltd v Shell Petroleum Co Ltd** [1980] 1 WLR 627 Lord Diplock had explained, at p 634, that in relation to the principle that directors of a company must act in the best interests of the company, 'These are not exclusively those of its shareholders but may include those of its creditors.'

It has been held in Australia that a director of a company also has a duty to the company to consider the interests of the company's creditors when the company is not insolvent but where, to the knowledge of the director, there is a real risk of insolvency (*Grove v Flavel* (1986) 43 SASR 410).

In *Colin Gwyer and Associates Ltd v London Wharf (Limehouse) Ltd* [2002] EWHC 2748 (Ch), [2003] 2 BCLC 153, at [74], the deputy High Court judge expressed the principle as follows:

> Where a company is insolvent or of doubtful solvency or on the verge of insolvency and it is the creditors' money which is at risk the directors, when carrying out their duty to the company, must consider the interests of the creditors as paramount and take those into account when exercising their discretion.

Accordingly, if directors of a company, at a time when the company is insolvent, or of doubtful solvency or on the verge of insolvency, deal with its property in a way that is prejudicial to the interests of creditors then they are in breach of their fiduciary duty to the company. This is especially so if the purpose of the transaction is to place the company's assets beyond the reach of the creditors (*Kinsela v Russell Kinsela Pty Ltd*; *Australian Growth Resources Corporation Pty Ltd v Van Reesema* (1988) 13 ACLR 261).

In practice it may be very difficult for directors to decide what to do for the best, and easy to criticise them with hindsight (see **20.11.3**). As Scott V-C said in *Facia Footwear Ltd v Hinchliffe* [1998] 1 BCLC 218, at p 228:

> the boundary between an acceptable risk that an entrepreneur may properly take and an unacceptable risk the taking of which constitutes misfeasance is not always, perhaps not usually, clear-cut.

An insolvent company can sue its directors for breach of their duty to consider the interests of creditors, even if the breach consisted of using the company to defraud creditors (*Bilta (UK) Ltd v Nazir (No 2)* [2015] UKSC 23, [2016] 1 AC 1). The rule that the court will not hear a claim that is based on the claimant's wrongdoing (*ex turpi causa non oritur actio*) does not come into operation, because the directors' wrongdoing cannot be attributed to the company for the purpose of bringing the rule into action (*Bilta (UK) Ltd v Nazir (No 2)*). As the company is insolvent, any damages recovered will be used to pay the defrauded creditors. In *Stone and Rolls Ltd v Moore Stephens* [2009] UKHL 39, [2009] AC 1391, it was held that the *ex turpi causa* principle prevented an insolvent company from suing its auditor for negligently failing to advise the company that it was acting fraudulently, even though any damages recovered would have been used to pay the victim of the fraud as a creditor of the company (see **17.5.1**). In *Bilta (UK) Ltd v Nazir (No 2)* Lord Neuberger concluded (at [24]) that the decision in *Stone and Rolls Ltd v Moore Stephens* applies only to the particular facts of that case, in particular, that all members and directors of the company were parties to the fraud (at [26]).

The common law duty is owed to the company only, not to its creditors. As Lord Lowry said in *Kuwait Asia Bank EC v National Mutual Life Nominees Ltd* [1991] 1 AC 187 at p 217: 'A director does not by reason only of his position as director owe any duty to creditors or to trustees for creditors of the company.' See also *Yukong Line Ltd v Rendsburg Investments Corporation (No 2)* [1998] 1 WLR 294 and *Spies v R* [2000] HCA 43, 201 CLR 603.

See further, V Finch, 'Directors' duties towards creditors' (1989) 10 Co Law 23; C A Riley, 'Directors' duties and the interests of creditors' (1989) 10 Co Law 87; R Grantham, 'The judicial extension of directors' duties to creditors' [1991] JBL 1; J S Ziegel, 'Creditors as corporate stakeholders: the quiet revolution—an Anglo-Canadian perspective' (1993) 43 UTLJ 511. For criticism of the concept of a duty to consider the interests of creditors see an article and a casenote by L S Sealy, 'Directors' "wider" responsibilities—problems conceptual, practical and procedural' (1987) 13 Mon LR 164; 'Directors' duties—an unnecessary gloss' [1988] CLJ 175. **Andrew Keay, 'The duty of directors to take account of creditors' interests: has it any role to play?'** [2002] JBL 379, finds that a claim against directors for breach of the duty 'can play an important part in curbing the abuses of trust of directors and compensating creditors of insolvent companies' (at p 409).

16.6.9.3 Statutory duty

In Britain, the common law duty of directors of a company to consider the interests of the company's creditors has, since 28 April 1986, been put on a statutory basis by what is now IA 1986, s 214 (wrongful trading). Under this section, the court may declare a director or shadow director of a company in liquidation liable to contribute to the assets of the company if the director knew, or ought to have concluded, that the company had no reasonable prospect of not going into insolvent liquidation and did not take every step he or she ought to have taken to minimise the potential loss to the company's creditors.

This duty arises only where the company has no reasonable prospect of not going into insolvent liquidation, which is similar to the limitation on the circumstances in which the common law duty arises.

Since 1 October 2015, similar provision is made by s 246ZB for a company entering insolvent administration.

There is full consideration of ss 214 and 246ZB in **20.12**.

16.6.10 INTERESTS OF PERSONS FOR WHOM THE COMPANY IS A FIDUCIARY

Directors of a company are not directly in a fiduciary relationship with persons for whom the company is a fiduciary (*Bath v Standard Land Co Ltd* [1911] 1 Ch 618). However, this case has not been followed in New Zealand (*Lion Breweries Ltd v Scarrott* (1986) 3 NZCLC 100,042) and may be compared with *Re The French Protestant Hospital* [1951] Ch 567, in which it was held that directors of a chartered corporation which held property on charitable trusts should themselves be treated as trustees of the charity. See further A R Coleman, 'Duties of directors of corporate trustees to beneficiaries' (1984) 2 C & SLJ 147; R I Barrett, Companies—Directors' fiduciary duties' (1985) 59 ALJ 46.

The fiduciary duties of the directors of a company may be enforced by the beneficiaries of a trust of which the company is trustee (*Baden v Société Générale pour Favoriser le Développement du Commerce et de l'Industrie en France SA* [1993] 1 WLR 509, point not considered on appeal). But the directors' fiduciary duties do not include a duty to ensure that the company does not breach its fiduciary duties. So if a corporate trustee breaches its fiduciary duties, the beneficiaries cannot make a 'dog-leg' claim against the corporate trustee's directors (*Gregson v HAE Trustees Ltd* [2008] EWHC 1006 (Ch), [2008] 2 BCLC 542).

16.6.11 DUTY TO TAKE INTO ACCOUNT ALL MATERIAL CONSIDERATIONS

CA 2006, s 172(1), says that, in fulfilling the duty to promote the success of the company for the benefit of its members as a whole, a director must have regard to a number of matters listed in s 172(1), 'amongst other matters'. This may amount to a duty to take into account all material considerations, which has been recognised in one case at first instance (*Hunter v Senate Support Services Ltd* [2004] EWHC 1085 (Ch), [2005] 1 BCLC 175). This is an application of what the Court of Appeal referred to in **Edge v Pensions Ombudsman** [2000] Ch 602 at p 627 as:

> the ordinary duty which the law imposes on a person who is entrusted with the exercise of a discretionary power: that he exercises the power for the purpose for which it is given, giving proper consideration to the matters which are relevant and excluding from consideration matters which are irrelevant.

The Court of Appeal went on to note that this duty is part of what in public and administrative law is the duty to take decisions rationally, notably discussed by Lord Greene MR in *Associated*

Provincial Picture Houses Ltd v Wednesbury Corporation [1948] 1 KB 223, and said ([2000] Ch 602 at p 628):

> It seems to us no coincidence that courts, considering the exercise of discretionary powers by those to whom such powers have been entrusted (albeit in different contexts), should reach similar and consistent conclusions; and should express those conclusions in much the same language.

Hunter v Senate Support Services Ltd was concerned with a decision to forfeit a member's shares for non-payment of a call and it may well be that the courts will be cautious about what other kinds of decisions of directors will be subject to review for failure to consider all relevant matters. It seems highly unlikely that the courts will want to be involved in reviewing commercial decisions in this way (see **16.6.3**).

16.6.12 CONFLICT OF INTERESTS

A great problem for a director who is required to consider the interests of several different persons is what to do where those interests conflict, whether it is a conflict between groups, for example between members and creditors, or a conflict within a group, for example between different members.

As far as a conflict of interest between creditors and any other group is concerned, it seems that creditors' interests have to be given priority where there is no reasonable prospect of the company not going into insolvent liquidation and that this is the only situation in which there is a duty to consider creditors' interests. Also, if a company goes into insolvent liquidation, the creditors have the right to appoint the liquidator and thus take control of the company. Nevertheless, in **Re Welfab Engineers Ltd** [1990] BCLC 833, Hoffmann J held that it is not correct to say that the duty of directors is to act 'to the best advantage of creditors': their duty is not to act in a way that would leave creditors in a worse position than on liquidation. See further R Grantham, 'Directors' duties and insolvent companies' (1991) 54 MLR 576.

In both *Mutual Life Insurance Co of New York v Rank Organisation Ltd* [1985] BCLC 11 and *Re BSB Holdings Ltd (No 2)* [1996] 1 BCLC 155 the directors of a company were permitted to prefer the interests of the company as a separate person to the interests of a minority of its members (see **16.6.4**).

A director who has been appointed by a particular member is entitled to take into account that member's interests, but the duty to the company under CA 2006, s 172, is paramount (*Hawkes v Cuddy* [2009] EWCA Civ 291, [2009] 2 BCLC 427, at [33]). Where there is a conflict between members it seems that the favoured solution is to require one group to buy out the other on an application for relief of unfairly prejudicial conduct of the company's affairs (see **18.6**).

16.6.13 OBLIGATION TO DISCLOSE MISCONDUCT

It is an equitable principle that a director of a company who acts in breach of his or her fiduciary duty to the company is under an obligation to disclose the breach to the company, if disclosure is required by the equitable duty to act bona fide in what the director considers to be the interests of the company (*Item Software (UK) Ltd v Fassihi* [2004] EWCA Civ 1244, [2005] ICR 450). This means that the duty is to disclose what the director considers, not what a court may consider, is in the interest of the company to know (*Fulham Football Club (1987) Ltd v Tigana* [2004] EWHC 2585 (QB), LTL 17/11/2004, at [103], point not considered on appeal; J Armour and M Conaglen, 'Directorial disclosure' [2005] CLJ 48). If the director has not separately considered the company's interests and there is no basis on which a director could reasonably have concluded that disclosure was not in the company's interests, the court will find that the director was in breach of duty (*Item Software (UK) Ltd v Fassihi* at [44]; *GHLM Trading Ltd v Maroo* [2012] EWHC 61 (Ch), [2012] 2 BCLC 369, at [194]).

The statutory duty to promote the success of the company is based on the equitable duty to act in the company's interests, and regard must be had to the corresponding equitable principle in interpreting it. So, it would seem that a director who is in breach of his or her statutory general duties is under an obligation to disclose the breach to the company, if disclosure is required by the duty to promote the success of the company.

In *Item Software (UK) Ltd v Fassihi* the defendant, Mr Fassihi, was sales and marketing director of the claimant company ('Item'), which distributed the products of a software house ('Isograph'). While still a director of the claimant company, and without informing it, he set up his own company ('RAMS') to take over the distribution business, at the same time advising the claimant company to take a tough stance in its own negotiations for a new contract with Isograph. The defendant never considered whether it was in the interests of the company to disclose his breach of duty. So the test (see **16.6.3**) was whether an intelligent and honest person in Mr Fassihi's position could, in the whole of the existing circumstances, reasonably have believed that it was in the company's interest to know of his breach of duty. Arden LJ said, at [44]:

> there is no basis on which Mr Fassihi could reasonably have come to the conclusion that it was not in the interests of Item to know of his breach of duty... he could not fulfil his duty of loyalty in this case except by telling Item about his setting up of RAMS, and his plan to acquire the Isograph contract for himself.

Failure to comply with the obligation to disclose misconduct may mean loss of employment benefits, such as pension rights and share options, and may provide a justification for summary dismissal (*Tesco Stores Ltd v Pook* [2003] EWHC 823 (Ch), [2004] IRLR 618; *Fulham Football Club (1987) Ltd v Tigana*).

A director of a company who does not disclose to the company his or her own breaches of duty may be in further breach of duty if he or she fails to act as if the breach had been disclosed. In *Simply Loans Direct Ltd v Wood* (2006) LTL 4/7/2006 the sole director of a company had been stealing money from it by paying fictitious employees' salaries. He then awarded himself a salary increase. It was held that he could not have thought it to be in the company's interest to give a pay rise to an employee who was stealing from the company and he was therefore liable to return the extra pay to the company.

A director also has a duty to disclose breaches of duty by fellow directors, if to do so would be bona fide in what the director considers to be the interests of the company (*British Midland Tool Ltd v Midland International Tooling Ltd* [2003] EWHC 466 (Ch), [2003] 2 BCLC 523). In *British Midland Tool Ltd v Midland International Tooling Ltd*, four directors of a company planned to establish a rival company. One of them retired. He began to set up the new company and invited key employees of the old company to join it. The other three directors continued in their old employment without informing other directors of their plans. It was held that this was in breach of their fiduciary duty and amounted to a conspiracy to injure the company by unlawful means.

The decision in *Item Software (UK) Ltd v Fassihi* that a director has an equitable duty to disclose misconduct has been controversial because it is said to violate a supposed principle that equitable fiduciary duties should be proscriptive not prescriptive. This 'proscribe not prescribe' rule has been adopted in Australia (*Breen v Williams* (1996) 186 CLR 71), where *Item Software (UK) Ltd v Fassihi* has not been followed (*P & V Industries Pty Ltd v Porto* [2006] VSC 131, 14 VR 1). See L Ho and P-W Lee, 'A director's duty to confess: a matter of good faith?' [2007] CLJ 348.

16.7 DUTY TO EXERCISE INDEPENDENT JUDGEMENT

16.7.1 STATUTORY DUTY

CA 2006, s 173, provides:

(1) A director of a company must exercise independent judgment.

(2) This duty is not infringed by his acting—

(a) in accordance with an agreement duly entered into by the company that restricts the future exercise of discretion by its directors, or

(b) in a way authorised by the company's constitution.

16.7.2 EQUITABLE PRINCIPLE ON WHICH STATUTORY DUTY IS BASED

CA 2006, s 173, reflects the equitable principle that it is legitimate for the directors of a company to enter into a binding agreement that they will act as directors in a particular way if, at the time of making the agreement, they bona fide consider that it is in the interests of the company (*Thorby v Goldberg* (1964) 112 CLR 597; *Fulham Football Club Ltd v Cabra Estates plc* [1994] 1 BCLC 363). Having made such an agreement bona fide in the interests of the company, the directors will be held to it even if they consider that circumstances have changed and it would be in the interests of the company for them to act in a different way.

It is different if a company director makes a contract to carry out directorial duties in a certain way regardless of whether it is in the interests of the company to do so. That would be an agreement to act, if required by the contract, in a way that was not in the interests of the company. The courts would not enforce the contract by ordering the director to act contrary to the interests of the company (*Motherwell v Schoof* [1949] 4 DLR 812). It has sometimes been said that the whole of such a contract would be illegal and void and such contracts are described as 'fettering' a director's discretion. In **Boulting v Association of Cinematograph, Television and Allied Technicians** [1963] 2 QB 606, Lord Denning MR said, at p 626:

> It seems to me that no one, who has duties of a fiduciary nature to discharge, can be allowed to enter into an engagement by which he binds himself to disregard those duties or to act inconsistently with them. No stipulation is lawful by which he agrees to carry out his duties in accordance with the instructions of another rather than on his own conscientious judgment; or by which he agrees to subordinate the interests of those whom he must protect to the interests of someone else.

However, in Australia it has been said that if all the members of a company agree that its directors are to act in a certain way (as is common in unanimous shareholders' agreements), one member will not be able to prevent the agreement being implemented on the ground that it is illegal (*Thorby v Goldberg* (1964) 112 CLR 597). It may even be possible to obtain an order of specific performance of such an agreement (*Davidson v Smith* (1989) 15 ACLR 732 at p 736). For a detailed discussion see T B Courtney, 'Fettering directors' discretion' (1995) 16 Co Law 227.

16.8 DUTY TO EXERCISE REASONABLE CARE, SKILL AND DILIGENCE

16.8.1 STATUTORY DUTY

CA 2006, s 174, provides:

(1) A director of a company must exercise reasonable care, skill and diligence.

(2) This means the care, skill and diligence that would be exercised by a reasonably diligent person with—

(a) the general knowledge, skill and experience that may reasonably be expected of a person carrying out the functions carried out by the director in relation to the company, and

(b) the general knowledge, skill and experience that the director has.

Section 174(2) imposes what is known as a 'dual' or 'twofold', 'objective/subjective' standard for the statutory duty of care, skill and diligence. The objective standard is in s 174(2)(a) and the subjective in s 174(2)(b). In cases in the late nineteenth and early twentieth centuries, only a subjective standard was used. So, in *Re City Equitable Fire Insurance Co Ltd* [1925] Ch 407, Romer J said, at p 428:

> A director need not exhibit in the performance of his duties a greater degree of skill than may reasonably be expected from a person of his knowledge and experience.

At the end of the twentieth century, the courts realised that this was too low a standard and they adopted the dual objective/subjective standard from IA 1986, s 214(4) (wrongful trading; see **20.12**) (*Norman v Theodore Goddard* [1991] BCLC 1028; *Re D'Jan of London Ltd* [1994] 1 BCLC 561; *Base Metal Trading Ltd v Shamurin* [2004] EWCA Civ 1316, [2005] 1 WLR 1157, per Arden LJ at [86]). CA 2006, s 174(2), has now given it statutory force.

The courts also have to consider the standard of care and diligence required of directors in disqualification cases (see **20.13**) where the dual objective/subjective standard has also been adopted (*Re Landhurst Leasing plc* [1999] 1 BCLC 286 at p 344) and several such cases are cited in the following discussion to show the courts' current approach.

There is no statutorily implied term in a contract for the supply of services as a director that the director will carry out the services with reasonable care and skill, because directors have been exempted from the Supply of Goods and Services Act 1982, s 13, by SI 1982/1771. Members of a company have no right to expect a reasonable standard of general management from the company's managing director: it is one of the normal risks of investing in a company that its management may turn out not to be of the highest quality (*Re Elgindata Ltd* [1991] BCLC 959 at p 994).

16.8.2 COMMON LAW RULES AND EQUITABLE PRINCIPLES ON WHICH STATUTORY DUTY IS BASED

CA 2006, s 174, is based on both common law rules and equitable principles. According to the general analysis of liability for negligence made by the House of Lords in *Henderson v Merrett Syndicates Ltd* [1995] 2 AC 145, the duty of care owed by a director of a company to the company arises from the circumstance that the director assumes responsibility for the property or affairs of the company (per Lord Browne-Wilkinson at p 205). It is a duty both in equity and in the common law of tort (*Bristol and West Building Society v Mothew* [1998] Ch 1 at pp 16–17; *Base Metal Trading Ltd v Shamurin* [2004] EWCA Civ 1316, [2005] 1 WLR 1157, at [19]). The equitable duty of skill and care is not a fiduciary duty (*Henderson v Merrett Syndicates Ltd*; *Bristol and West Building Society v Mothew*). The common law duty does not depend on any contract, though an underlying contract may determine the extent and nature of the duty, and could exclude it (*Henderson v Merrett Syndicates Ltd*), except that CA 2006, s 232 (see **16.16.5**), limits contracting out by directors of a company from liability for breach of duty to the company.

16.8.3 KNOWLEDGE OF THE COMPANY'S BUSINESS

In *Re Brazilian Rubber Plantations and Estates Ltd* [1911] 1 Ch 425, Neville J said, at p 437:

> A director's duty has been laid down as requiring him to act with such care as is reasonably to be expected from him, having regard to his knowledge and experience. He is, I think, not bound to bring any special qualifications to his office. He may undertake the management of a rubber company in complete ignorance of everything connected with rubber, without incurring responsibility for the mistakes which may result from such ignorance.

Insofar as this is based on the subjective standard of care, this statement must be regarded as no longer correct, now that a dual objective/subjective standard is imposed by CA 2006, s 174. In the director disqualification case of **Re Barings plc (No 5)** [2000] 1 BCLC 523, at pp 535–6, the Court of Appeal agreed with the following statement by Jonathan Parker J at first instance:

> (i) Directors have, both collectively and individually, a continuing duty to acquire and maintain a sufficient knowledge and understanding of the company's business to enable them properly to discharge their duties as directors.

16.8.4 RELIANCE ON COMPANY OFFICIALS AND OTHERS

The courts have recognised that, except in the smallest of companies, directors must rely on employees to inform them accurately of what is going on in the company. In **Dovey v Cory** [1901] AC 477, the Earl of Halsbury LC said, at pp 485–6:

> The charge of neglect appears to rest on the assertion that Mr Cory, like the other directors, did not attend to any details of business not brought before them by the general manager or the chairman [who were both defrauding the company], and the argument raises a serious question as to the responsibility of all persons holding positions like that of directors, how far they are called upon to distrust and be on their guard against the possibility of fraud being committed by their subordinates of every degree. It is obvious if there is such a duty it must render anything like an intelligent devolution of labour impossible... I cannot think that it can be expected of a director that he should be watching either the inferior officers of the [company] or verifying the calculations of the auditors himself. The business of life could not go on if people could not trust those who are put into a position of trust for the express purpose of attending to details of management.

In **Re City Equitable Fire Insurance Co Ltd** [1925] Ch 407, Romer J said, at p 429:

> In respect of all duties that, having regard to the exigencies of business, and the articles of association, may properly be left to some other official, a director is, in the absence of grounds for suspicion, justified in trusting that official to perform such duties honestly.

However, directors must carry out their supervisory duties. The statement of Jonathan Parker J quoted in **16.8.3**, which the Court of Appeal agreed with in **Re Barings plc (No 5)** [2000] 1 BCLC 523, continues:

> (ii) Whilst directors are entitled (subject to the articles of association of the company) to delegate particular functions to those below them in the management chain, and to trust their competence and integrity to a reasonable extent, the exercise of the power of delegation does not absolve a director from the duty to supervise the discharge of the delegated functions.
>
> (iii) No rule of universal application can be formulated as to the duty referred to in (ii) above. The extent of the duty, and the question whether it has been discharged, must depend on the facts of each particular case, including the director's role in the management of the company.

See also per Scott V-C in *Re Barings plc* [1998] BCC 583 at p 586.

In **Equitable Life Assurance Society v Bowley** [2003] EWHC 2263 (Comm), [2004] 1 BCLC 180, Langley J agreed with the principles stated by Jonathan Parker J and said, at [41], that he did not think the aforementioned statement by Romer J, represented 'the modern law at least if... it means unquestioning reliance upon others to do their job'. Langley J agreed with Jonathan Parker J that the way in which the courts will define directors' duties in this area will be developed by examining the facts of particular cases.

In *Re Queens Moat House plc (No 2)* [2004] EWHC 1730 (Ch), [2005] 1 BCLC 136, Sir Donald Rattee applied the dual objective/subjective standard of care and said, at [35], that the duty of the defendant as chairman and joint managing director of a company to question accounts prepared by its finance director, who was a qualified accountant, was limited to matters which should have been apparent to a man of the chairman's business experience and knowledge of the company's affairs as being of at least doubtful accuracy or propriety. The defendant did not have a duty to check the performance of functions delegated to the finance director which were properly within the expertise of an accountant and which the defendant had no reason to doubt were being properly performed. It was held that the defendant had been grossly negligent in approving seriously misleading annual accounts and he was disqualified (see **20.13**) for six years.

In *Re Bradcrown Ltd* [2001] 1 BCLC 547 the finance director of a company, who was a chartered accountant, claimed that he had not considered the propriety of a transaction, by which nearly all the company's assets were transferred to other companies for no consideration, because he relied on the company's solicitors to advise the board of any problems. Disqualifying him for two years, Lawrence Collins J said, at p 561:

> He asked no questions and sought no advice. He simply did what he was told, and abdicated all responsibility. In these circumstances he cannot seek refuge in the fact that professional advisers were involved in the transactions.

In *Norman v Theodore Goddard* [1991] BCLC 1028, Mr Quirk, a chartered surveyor, was a director of a property company. The shares in the company were the principal assets of a trust administered by Theodore Goddard, a leading firm of solicitors. It was held that it was not negligent for Mr Quirk to rely on the advice of a partner in Theodore Goddard that tax would be saved if the company's surplus cash were lent on deposit to a company which the partner claimed was controlled by Theodore Goddard. In fact the company was controlled by that partner personally and was one of the devices he used to steal money from trust funds administered by his firm.

16.8.5 ATTENDANCE TO THE COMPANY'S AFFAIRS

In *Re Westmid Packing Services Ltd* [1998] 2 All ER 124 the Court of Appeal said:

> It is of the greatest importance that any individual who undertakes the statutory and fiduciary obligations of being a company director should realise that these are inescapable personal responsibilities.

If a director's duty to the company requires the performance of a particular action, the director is liable for the consequences of not doing it (*Lexi Holdings plc v Luqman* [2009] EWCA Civ 117, [2009] 2 BCLC 1).

In *Lexi Holdings plc v Luqman* the managing director of a company was found to have stolen £59.6 million which banks had lent the company for use in its business. His sisters were directors of the company and the elder sister was the registered holder of its shares. They knew that their brother had served two terms of imprisonment for deception. They should have known that statements in the company's accounts that their family had lent millions of pounds to the company were fictitious. They should have informed the auditor and other directors of these facts, which would have brought an end to their brother's dishonest dealings with the company's money. As they did not, they were liable (jointly with their brother) for the stolen money.

In *Brumder v Motornet Service and Repairs Ltd* [2013] EWCA Civ 195, [2013] ICR 1069, Mr Brumder was the sole director of the defendant company. He had paid no attention whatsoever to health and safety issues and this was a breach of his duty under CA 2006, s 174. It led to the company breaching its duty under health and safety regulations, which caused Mr Brumder himself to lose a finger. It was held that he could not sue the company for its breach of duty. He was the only person who could have prevented the company's breach of duty and he failed to do so. He could not make the company liable to him for his own wrongdoing. Even if he could sue the company for its breach of duty, the company would have an equal and opposite claim against him for his breach of duty.

In *Re Park House Properties Ltd* [1997] 2 BCLC 530 Mr Carter was a director of Park House Properties Ltd and so were his wife, son and daughter. Mr Carter's misconduct as a director justified disqualifying him for four years. His wife took no part at all in the conduct of the company. His children were employed by the company but took no part in running it as directors. Their 'complete inactivity in relation to, and complete uninvolvement with, the running of the company' justified disqualifying each of them for two years. Neuberger J said, at pp 556–7:

> A person who knowingly is a director of a company and takes no part whatever in the management of the company, no steps whatever to keep him or herself informed of the affairs of the company and leaves everything to another director who makes the sort of errors Mr Carter has made is, in my judgement, unfit in the absence of special circumstances.

16.9 DUTY TO AVOID CONFLICTS OF INTEREST

16.9.1 STATUTORY DUTY

CA 2006, s 175, provides:

(1) A director of a company must avoid a situation in which he has, or can have, a direct or indirect interest that conflicts, or possibly may conflict, with the interests of the company.

(2) This applies in particular to the exploitation of any property, information or opportunity (and it is immaterial whether the company could take advantage of the property, information or opportunity).

(3) This duty does not apply to a conflict of interest arising in relation to a transaction or arrangement with the company.

(4) This duty is not infringed—

    (a) if the situation cannot reasonably be regarded as likely to give rise to a conflict of interest; or

    (b) if the matter has been authorised by the directors.

(5) Authorisation may be given by the directors—

    (a) where the company is a private company and nothing in the company's constitution invalidates such authorisation, by the matter being proposed to and authorised by the directors; or

    (b) where the company is a public company and its constitution includes provision enabling the directors to authorise the matter, by the matter being proposed to and authorised by them in accordance with the constitution.

(6) The authorisation is effective only if—

    (a) any requirement as to the quorum at the meeting at which the matter is considered is met without counting the director in question or any other interested director, and

    (b) the matter was agreed to without their voting or would have been agreed to if their votes had not been counted.

(7) Any reference in this section to a conflict of interest includes a conflict of interest and duty and a conflict of duties.

Section 175(3) excludes transactions and arrangements with the company because they are dealt with by other statutory provisions which are considered in **16.12** and **16.13**.

Authorisation (s 175(4)(b), (5) and (6)) is considered in **16.16.2**.

16.9.2 EQUITABLE PRINCIPLE ON WHICH STATUTORY DUTY IS BASED

CA 2006, s 175, is based on two equitable principles, the no-conflict and no-profit rules, though it treats the no-profit rule as part of the no-conflict rule, as several of the cases do. The most significant circumstance in which the no-conflict and no-profit rules are applied in equity, to dealings between a fiduciary and the person to whom the fiduciary duties are owed, is also dealt with in separate statutory provisions (see **16.12** and **16.13**).

The fundamental principle was stated by Lord Herschell in *Bray v Ford* [1896] AC 44 at pp 51–2:

> It is an inflexible rule of a court of equity that a person in a fiduciary position ... is not, unless otherwise expressly provided, entitled to make a profit [the no-profit rule]; he is not allowed to put himself in a position where his interest and duty conflict [the no-conflict rule]. It does not appear to me that this rule is ... founded upon principles of morality. I regard it rather as based on the consideration that, human nature being what it is, there is danger, in such circumstances, of the person holding a fiduciary position being swayed by interest rather than by duty, and thus prejudicing those whom he was bound to protect. It has, therefore, been deemed expedient to lay down this positive rule.

Furthermore, a fiduciary for one person must not enter into a position which imposes conflicting fiduciary duties to another person, without the informed consent of both persons (*Clark Boyce v Mouat* [1994] 1 AC 428). This is known as the double employment rule (*Bristol and West Building Society v Mothew* [1998] Ch 1 at p 19) and it follows from the no-conflict rule. See the discussion of competing directorships in **16.9.5**.

The principle can be traced back to the case of ***Keech v Sandford*** (1726) Sel Cas t King 61, in which, under the will of a deceased lessee of some property, the leasehold interest had been given to a trustee to hold for the benefit of a child. When the lease came up for renewal the lessor refused to grant a new lease to the child because of the child's contractual incapacity, so the trustee obtained a renewal of the lease for himself. Lord King LC ordered the trustee to assign the new lease to the child. His Lordship said:

> I do not say there is a fraud in this case, yet he should rather have let it run out, than to have had the lease to himself. This may seem hard, that the trustee is the only person of all mankind who might not have the lease: but it is very proper that rule should be strictly pursued, and not in the least relaxed; for it is very obvious what would be the consequence of letting trustees have the lease, on refusal to renew to [the beneficiary of the trust].

For further discussion of the origins of the no-conflict and no-profit rules see G Jones, 'Unjust enrichment and the fiduciary's duty of loyalty' (1968) 84 LQR 472.

The strict enforcement of the equitable no-conflict rule is illustrated by *Towers v Premier Waste Management Ltd* [2011] EWCA Civ 923, [2012] 1 BCLC 67, which concerned events which occurred before CA 2006, ss 171 to 177, came into force. A director of a company had received a benefit from one of its customers, without disclosure to, or approval by, the other members of the board. Counsel for the director invited the Court of Appeal to find that there was no conflict of interest, because, among other things, there was no corrupt motive and the cash value of the benefit had been small (£5,200). The Court of Appeal held that these factors were irrelevant because the requirement of loyalty and the no-conflict rule are strict. A conflict of interest had arisen when the director took a benefit from a customer. The director had disloyally deprived the company of the ability to consider whether or not it objected.

16.9.3 NOMINEE DIRECTORS

A nominee director of a company may be put into an impossible position by a conflict of interests of the company and his nominator. In *Scottish Cooperative Wholesale Society Ltd v Meyer* [1959] AC

324 the Scottish CWS owned 4,000 of the 7,900 issued shares of Scottish Textile and Manufacturing Co Ltd. The society exercised its right under the company's articles of association to appoint three of its five directors. The other two directors were the minority shareholders in the company. The society decided to operate in the company's line of business in competition with the company, and deliberately set out to destroy the company. The society's nominee directors did nothing to protect the company's interests. Lord Denning said, at p 366, 'so soon as the interests of the two companies were in conflict, the nominee directors were placed in an impossible position'. At p 367, his Lordship said:

> They probably thought that 'as nominees' of the co-operative society their first duty was to the co-operative society. In this they were wrong.

There was no attempt in this case to make the nominee directors personally liable. The result of their wrongful preference of the interests of their nominator was that a petition by the minority shareholders for relief of prejudicial conduct of the company's affairs—see **18.6**—succeeded and the society was required to purchase the minority's shares.

In *Kuwait Asia Bank EC v National Mutual Life Nominees Ltd* [1991] 1 AC 187, Kuwait Asia Bank EC was beneficially interested in about 40 per cent of the shares of a New Zealand company called AIC Securities Ltd ('AICS') and appointed its employees House and August as two of the five directors of AICS. The Privy Council said, at p 222:

> In the performance of their duties as directors ... House and August were bound to ignore the interests and wishes of their employer, the bank. They could not plead any instruction from the bank as an excuse for breach of their duties to AICS.

However, in *Re Broadcasting Station 2GB Pty Ltd* [1964–5] NSWR 1648, Jacobs J expressed the view that a nominee director of a company is entitled to follow the wishes of his nominator, provided he bona fide believes that the interests of the nominator are identical with the interests of 'the company as a whole'. A nominee director would be wrong, however, to act in his nominator's interests either when they are contrary to the company's interests or without any regard to the interests of the company. His Honour said, at p 1663:

> I realise that, upon this approach, I deny any right in the company as a whole to have each director approach each company problem with a completely open mind, but I think that to require this of each director is to ignore the realities of company organisation. Also, such a requirement would, in effect, make the position of a nominee or representative director an impossibility.

See further P Redmond, 'Nominee directors' (1987) 10 UNSWLJ 194; E Boros, 'The duties of nominee and multiple directors' (1989) 10 Co Law 211, (1990) 11 Co Law 6; P Crutchfield, 'Nominee directors: the law and commercial reality' (1991) 12 Co Law 136.

16.9.4 CORPORATE OPPORTUNITY DOCTRINE

16.9.4.1 Introduction

CA 2006, s 175(2), provides that the duty to avoid conflicts of interest applies in particular to the exploitation of any property, information or opportunity. This is based on the equitable corporate opportunity doctrine, that there is a breach of fiduciary duty if a director of a company pursues for his or her own benefit a business opportunity which would be regarded in equity as belonging to the company (*Cook v Deeks* [1916] 1 AC 554; *Bhullar v Bhullar* [2003] EWCA Civ 424, [2003] 2 BCLC 241; *Ultraframe (UK) Ltd v Fielding* [2005] EWHC 1638 (Ch), [2007] WTLR 835, at [1332]–[1355]). The breach is not avoided by resigning the directorship (*Industrial Development Consultants Ltd v Cooley* [1972] 1 WLR 443; *Canadian Aero Service Ltd v O'Malley* (1973) 40 DLR (3d) 371; *CMS Dolphin Ltd v Simonet* [2001] 2 BCLC 704). The latter point has been codified in s 170(2)(a), which provides that a person who ceases to be a director continues to be subject to the duty to avoid conflicts of interest as regards the exploitation of any property, information or opportunity of which he became aware at a time when he was a director. In *Foster Bryant Surveying Ltd v Bryant* [2007] EWCA Civ 200, [2007] Bus LR 1565, at [69], Rix LJ said that, where a director's profit has been received after leaving office in order to pursue a business opportunity of which the director became aware while in office, the liability to account for the profits results from the breach of the no-conflict rule while in office, because the profits are causally connected with that breach.

16.9.4.2 Examples

In *Cook v Deeks* [1916] 1 AC 554 the holders of three-quarters of the shares in the Toronto Construction Co Ltd, who were three of the company's directors, fell out with the fourth director and shareholder, Cook. The company had completed several successful contracts for the Canadian Pacific Railway Co and the majority directors were only known to the railway company because of their association with Toronto Construction Co. Negotiations for a new contract with the railway company were conducted by the majority directors without informing Cook and when the contract was awarded the majority directors formed a new company to carry it out. The Privy Council ordered the majority directors and the new company to account to the Toronto Construction Co for the profits made out of the contract. Lord Buckmaster LC said, at p 563:

> the real question [is] whether [the transaction] was one into which, consistently with their duty, they were at liberty to enter.
>
> Men who assume the complete control of a company's business must remember that they are not at liberty to sacrifice the interests which they are bound to protect, and, while ostensibly acting for the company, divert in their own favour business which should properly belong to the company they represent.

In *Industrial Development Consultants Ltd v Cooley* [1972] 1 WLR 443, Mr Cooley was managing director of the plaintiff company, which acted as a project manager in the construction industry. During 1968 he had sought contracts for the company from the Eastern Gas Board. However, at that time the Gas Board decided not to go ahead with the work. In the next year the Gas Board reconsidered the position and this became known to Cooley personally through discussion with the Gas Board's deputy chairman. The Gas Board objected 'in principle to the set-up' of Industrial Development Consultants and other companies in the same group but were willing to employ Cooley himself. During the weekend of 14/15 June 1969, Cooley prepared a tender for the contracts. On 16 June he went to see the chairman of Industrial Development Consultants and pretended that he was on the verge of a breakdown and had to be released from his job—immediately—this was agreed to. On 17 June he submitted the tender. He was awarded the contract, which Roskill J found was substantially the same contract as Industrial Development Consultants had been trying to get the previous year. His Lordship said, at p 446:

> There can be no doubt that the defendant got this Eastern Gas Board contract for himself as a result of work which he did whilst still the plaintiffs' managing director.

And at p 451:

> From the time he embarked upon his course of dealing with the Eastern Gas Board ... he embarked upon a deliberate policy and course of conduct which put his personal interest as a potential contracting party with the Eastern Gas Board in direct conflict with his pre-existing and continuing duty as managing director of the plaintiffs.

It did not make any difference that when talking to the Gas Board in early June, Cooley said that he was acting for himself, not for Industrial Development Consultants. Roskill J said, at p 451:

> The defendant had one capacity and one capacity only in which he was carrying on business at that time. That capacity was as managing director of the plaintiffs.

Accordingly, Cooley was trustee for the plaintiffs of his profits on the Gas Board contract. Incidentally, it should be pointed out that Roskill J's extempore judgment is reported in some respects more fully at [1972] 2 All ER 162.

In *Canadian Aero Service Ltd v O'Malley* (1973) 40 DLR (3d) 371, the first two defendants, O'Malley and Zarzycki, had the job titles of 'president and chief executive officer' and 'executive vice-president and director' of Canadian Aero Service Ltd (usually referred to as 'Canaero'), which was a wholly owned subsidiary of an American company. Because of failure by the parent company to comply with formalities of Canadian company law, the defendants had not formally been appointed directors of Canaero. The Supreme Court of Canada, however, held this made no difference since they were clearly 'top management' of the company and so should be subject to the same fiduciary obligations as directors. (Liability was imposed in a similar situation in *DPC Estates Pty Ltd v Grey* [1974] 1 NSWLR 470.)

Canaero was engaged in aerial surveying and had been attempting to get a government contract for this work in Guyana from 1962 to 1966. Zarzycki, a widely respected expert on aerial survey techniques, visited Guyana on Canaero's behalf in 1962 and 1965 and prepared a proposal which was submitted to the relevant government agencies. On 9 July 1966, O'Malley and Zarzycki met the prime minister of Guyana and reported to Canaero that it was certain to get the contract. The next month the two men resigned from the company and set up a new company of their own, which tendered for the Guyana contract the following month and was awarded it in November 1966. The tender price was exactly that stated by Zarzycki in his 1965 proposal.

The Supreme Court of Canada held that O'Malley and Zarzycki were liable to Canaero for breach of fiduciary duty.

16.9.4.3 Company's alleged lack of interest irrelevant

The liability of a company director for personally pursuing one of the company's business opportunities is not diminished by the fact that the company itself would not have pursued the opportunity (CA 2006, s 175(2); *Industrial Development Consultants Ltd v Cooley* [1972] 1 WLR 443; *Consul Development Pty Ltd v DPC Estates Pty Ltd* (1975) 132 CLR 373 per Gibbs J at p 395; *Bhullar v Bhullar* [2003] EWCA Civ 424, [2003] 2 BCLC 241, at [41]).

16.9.4.4 Which opportunities?

It seems that the reason for holding a director of a company liable for diverting a business opportunity is that the opportunity should, in equity, be treated as belonging to the company (*CMS Dolphin Ltd v Simonet* [2001] 2 BCLC 704 at p 733; *Lindsley v Woodfull* [2004] EWCA Civ 165, [2004] 2 BCLC 131, per Arden LJ at [26] and [30]; *Ultraframe (UK) Ltd v Fielding* [2005] EWHC 1638 (Ch), [2007] WTLR 835, at [1355] and [1360]). The problem is to identify which opportunities should be treated in that way. In *Balston Ltd v Headline Filters Ltd* [1990] FSR 385, at p 412, Falconer J expressed the test as being whether the company had a 'specific interest' in the opportunity. But in ***Bhullar v Bhullar*** [2003] EWCA Civ 424, [2003] 2 BCLC 241, Jonathan Parker LJ said, at [28], it would be 'too formalistic and restrictive' to make the central question whether the company 'had some kind of beneficial interest in the opportunity'. In *Bhullar v Bhullar* the deciding factor was that 'it would have been "worthwhile" for the company to have acquired the property' which the directors acquired for themselves (at [41]). In ***Lindsley v Woodfull*** (which concerned the fiduciary relationship of a partner to his firm) a diverted opportunity was treated as an asset of the firm because it 'clearly fell within the partnership's area of business' (per Arden LJ at [26]).

In many cases the court has concentrated on the director's duty to inform the company of the opportunity. In ***DPC Estates Pty Ltd v Grey*** [1974] 1 NSWLR 443, Huntley JA said, at p 465:

> [Grey's] agreement required him to devote himself exclusively to the business of working manager of the associated companies, and one of his principal duties was to find avenues for real estate development. It is a notorious fact that such information comes from many sources, for example, from tips in clubs and on social

occasions. In my opinion, any information which he obtained in relation to real estate matters within the scope of the business of the associated companies could only be used by him for the benefit of those companies.

In *Industrial Development Consultants Ltd v Cooley* [1972] 1 WLR 443 Roskill J said, at p 451:

> Information which came to [Cooley] while he was managing director and which was of concern to [the company of which he was managing director] and was relevant for the [company] to know, was information which it was his duty to pass on to the [company] because between himself and the [company] a fiduciary relationship existed.

It is clear that a company director's duty to inform the company of a business opportunity arises when it is clearly within the company's normal line of business (as in *Industrial Development Consultants Ltd v Cooley*). In *Bhullar v Bhullar* the company, Bhullar Bros Ltd, primarily operated retail grocery stores, but it also owned a commercial property which was let to tenants, one of which used part of an adjacent property as a customer car park. When one of the directors of Bhullar Bros Ltd saw a 'for sale' sign on the adjacent property, he and a fellow director (his brother) caused another company which they controlled to buy it, for their self-administered pension scheme, without telling the other directors of Bhullar Bros Ltd. It was held (at [41]) that they were under a duty to communicate the opportunity to Bhullar Bros Ltd, because it would have been 'worthwhile' for that company to acquire the adjacent property. They were ordered to procure the transfer of the property from their own company to Bhullar Bros Ltd for the price which their company had paid for it and to account to Bhullar Bros Ltd for profits made from the property. For commentary on the significance of *Bhullar v Bhullar* in establishing a test for which business opportunities are subject to the duty to avoid conflicts of interest see D D Prentice and J Payne, 'The corporate opportunity doctrine' (2004) 120 LQR 198.

In *Canadian Aero Service Ltd v O'Malley* (1973) 40 DLR (3d) 371 the Supreme Court of Canada took, at p 391, a more general approach to the problem:

> The general standards of loyalty, good faith and avoidance of a conflict of duty and self-interest to which the conduct of a director or senior officer must conform, must be tested in each case by many factors which it would be reckless to attempt to enumerate exhaustively. Among them are the factor of position or office held, the nature of the corporate opportunity, its ripeness, its specificness and the director's or managerial officer's relation to it, the amount of knowledge possessed, the circumstances in which it was obtained and whether it was special or, indeed, even private, the factor of time in the continuation of fiduciary duty where the alleged breach occurs after termination of the relationship with the company, and the circumstances under which the relationship was terminated, that is whether by retirement or resignation or discharge.

It is certainly a breach of duty for a director of a company, while still a director, to invite its existing customers to cease dealing with the company and to deal instead with the director's own business (*Aubanel and Alabaster Ltd v Aubanel* (1949) 66 RPC 343; *Mordecai v Mordecai* (1988) 12 NSWLR 58).

16.9.4.5 When should a director leave?

In practice, the corporate opportunity doctrine puts directors in a very difficult position, and the courts have often found difficulty in balancing the freedom of an individual to exploit his or her own managerial and entrepreneurial abilities against the ethic of fiduciary loyalty which is intended to protect the company of which that individual is a director. In some cases, the law's policy against restraints on trade has been invoked to limit the liability of a director of a company for pursuing one of the company's corporate opportunities after leaving the company (see *Island Export Finance Ltd v Umunna* [1986] BCLC 460). A former director of a company must be allowed to compete with the company after leaving it, subject to any reasonable restraints in his or her contract of employment. What is objectionable is leaving the company in order to pursue an opportunity arising while with the company (*Industrial Development Consultants Ltd v Cooley* [1972] 1 WLR 443; *CMS Dolphin Ltd v Simonet* [2001] 2 BCLC 704).

A director's position with a company will naturally provide the director with information about the markets in which the company operates. However, such information becomes part of the director's general fund of knowledge and stock in trade, and, because of the policy of the law against restraints on trade, after leaving the company, the director cannot be held accountable for exploiting that information for his or her own or a new employer's benefit. In ***Balston Ltd v Headline Filters Ltd*** [1990] FSR 385 Falconer J said, at p 412:

> In my judgment an intention by a director of a company to set up business in competition with the company after his directorship has ceased is not to be regarded as a conflicting interest within the context of the [no-conflict rule], having regard to the rules of public policy as to restraint of trade, nor is the taking of any preliminary steps to investigate or forward that intention so long as there is no actual competitive activity, such as, for instance, competitive tendering or actual trading, while he remains a director.

In ***British Midland Tool Ltd v Midland International Tooling Ltd*** [2003] EWHC 466 (Ch), [2003] 2 BCLC 523, Hart J qualified this, saying, at [89]:

> A director who wishes to engage in a competing business and not to disclose his intentions to the company ought, in my judgment, to resign his office as soon as his intention has been irrevocably formed and he has launched himself on the taking of preparatory steps.

In *Shepherds Investments Ltd v Walters* [2006] EWHC 836 (Ch), [2007] IRLR 110, Etherton J said, at [108], that this statement may be too prescriptive, because the point at which a director should either resign or seek permission to pursue the business opportunity depends on the facts of each case. Nevertheless, Etherton J held, at [107], that Falconer J was wrong, in the passage from *Balston Ltd v Headline Filters Ltd* quoted earlier, to suggest that the policy against restraints on trade could override the equitable principles of fiduciary duty. Those principles require a director to act bona fide in what he or she considers to be in the interests of the company.

In ***Foster Bryant Surveying Ltd v Bryant*** [2007] EWCA Civ 200, [2007] Bus LR 1565, Rix LJ said, at [76]–[77], that it is difficult accurately to encapsulate the circumstances in which a director who is leaving office may or may not be found to have breached his or her fiduciary duty. The no-conflict rule must be applied to directors leaving office with care and with sensitivity to both the facts and to other principles, such as that of personal freedom to compete, on one hand, and misuse of the company's business opportunities or trade secrets, on the other hand. His Lordship concluded that courts have adopted pragmatic solutions based on common sense and the merits of the case. His Lordship summarised the cases as follows:

> At one extreme (*In Plus Group Ltd v Pyke* [2002] EWCA Civ 370, [2002] 2 BCLC 201) the defendant is director in name only. At the other extreme, the director has planned his resignation having in mind the destruction of his company or at least the exploitation of its property in the form of business opportunities in which he is currently involved (*Industrial Development Consultants Ltd v Cooley*; *Canadian Aero Service Ltd v O'Malley* (1973) 40 DLR (3d) 371; *CMS Dolphin Ltd v Simonet*; *British Midland Tool Ltd v Midland International Tooling Ltd*). In the middle are more nuanced cases which go both ways: in *Shepherds Investments Ltd v Walters* the combination of disloyalty, active promotion of the planned business and exploitation of a business opportunity, all while the directors remained in office, brought liability; in *Island Export Finance Ltd v Umunna*; *Balston Ltd v Headline Filters Ltd*, and *Framlington Group plc v Anderson* [1995] 1 BCLC 475, however, where the resignations were unaccompanied by disloyalty, there was no liability.

16.9.5 COMPETING DIRECTORSHIPS

The double employment rule, which follows from the no-conflict rule, is that someone owing fiduciary duties to one person cannot enter into a position which imposes conflicting fiduciary duties to another person, without the informed consent of both persons (*Clark Boyce v Mouat* [1994] 1 AC 428). Informed consent means consent given in the knowledge that there is a conflict and that fiduciary duty to one person may prevent the fiduciary passing on information, or giving advice, which might be useful to the other (*Clark Boyce v Mouat*).

In *London and Mashonaland Exploration Co Ltd v New Mashonaland Exploration Co Ltd* [1891] WN 165 the court refused to grant an injunction to prevent one of the claimant company's directors from acting as director of a rival company without the claimant company's consent. It is unfortunate that we have only an abbreviated report of this case, which does not mention fiduciary duties at all. Instead, Chitty J is reported as saying that there was nothing in the articles or any contract with the director prohibiting him from being a director of another company, and this absence of contractual prohibition was treated as the crucial point by the reporter. The case is usually cited as authority for the proposition that a director of a company may be a director of a competing company, unless prohibited by contract (per Lord Blanesburgh in *Bell v Lever Brothers Ltd* [1932] AC 161 at p 195). More recently, it has been said, obiter, that holding the contrary would be a substantive extension of directors' duties (*Item Software (UK) Ltd v Fassihi* [2004] EWCA Civ 1244, [2005] ICR 450, at [63] per Arden LJ). There is an obvious inconsistency between this and the double employment rule.

In the *Mashonaland* case it was found that there was no actual or threatened damage to the claimant company. The director concerned, the 7th Earl of Mayo, was (as was common in those days) an inactive figurehead, a 'Lord on the board', whose name was supposed to impress anyone thinking of subscribing for the company's shares. It may be that the authority of the case should be confined to such a situation, which would probably now be covered by CA 2006, s 175(4)(a), but where there is a real possibility of conflict, a competing directorship will be in breach of duty (see the judgment of Sedley LJ in *In Plus Group Ltd v Pyke* [2002] EWCA Civ 370, [2002] 2 BCLC 201).

See E Boros, 'The duties of nominee and multiple directors. Part II' (1990) 11 Co Law 6; M Christie, 'The director's fiduciary duty not to compete' (1992) 55 MLR 506 (which argues that the *Mashonaland* case was wrongly decided); R Grantham, 'Can directors compete with the company?' (2003) 66 MLR 109; R Goddard, 'Competing directorships' (2004) 25 Co Law 23; D D Prentice and J Payne, 'The corporate opportunity doctrine' (2004) 120 LQR 198.

16.10 DUTY NOT TO ACCEPT BENEFITS FROM THIRD PARTIES

CA 2006, s 176, provides:

(1) A director of a company must not accept a benefit from a third party conferred by reason of—

   (a) his being a director, or

   (b) his doing (or not doing) anything as director.

(2) A 'third party' means a person other than the company, an associated body corporate or a person acting on behalf of the company or an associated body corporate.

(3) Benefits received by a director from a person by whom his services (as a director or otherwise) are provided to the company are not regarded as conferred by a third party.

(4) This duty is not infringed if the acceptance of the benefit cannot reasonably be regarded as likely to give rise to a conflict of interest.

(5) Any reference in this section to a conflict of interest includes a conflict of interest and duty and a conflict of duties.

A person who ceases to be a director continues to be subject to the duty not to accept benefits from third parties as regards things done or omitted by him before ceasing to be a director (s 170(2)(b)).

16.11 DUTY TO DECLARE INTEREST IN PROPOSED TRANSACTION OR ARRANGEMENT

16.11.1 STATUTORY DUTY

16.11.1.1 Principle

CA 2006, s 177, provides:

(1) If a director of a company is in any way, directly or indirectly, interested in a proposed transaction or arrangement with the company, he must declare the nature and extent of that interest to the other directors.

(2) The declaration may (but need not) be made—

   (a) at a meeting of the directors, or

   (b) by notice to the directors in accordance with—

      (i) section 184 (notice in writing), or

      (ii) section 185 (general notice).

(3) If a declaration of interest under this section proves to be, or becomes, inaccurate or incomplete, a further declaration must be made.

(4) Any declaration required by this section must be made before the company enters into the transaction or arrangement.

(5) This section does not require a declaration of an interest of which the director is not aware or where the director is not aware of the transaction or arrangement in question.

For this purpose a director is treated as being aware of matters of which he ought reasonably to be aware.

(6) A director need not declare an interest—

   (a) if it cannot reasonably be regarded as likely to give rise to a conflict of interest;

   (b) if, or to the extent that, the other directors are already aware of it (and for this purpose the other directors are treated as aware of anything of which they ought reasonably to be aware); or

   (c) if, or to the extent that, it concerns terms of his service contract that have been or are to be considered—

      (i) by a meeting of the directors, or

      (ii) by a committee of the directors appointed for the purpose under the company's constitution.

This is backed up by s 182, which requires a declaration of interest in a transaction or arrangement which has been entered into by the company, to the extent that the interest has not already been declared under s 177. The s 182 obligation is subject to the same exceptions as in s 177 for interests of which the director is unaware (s 182(5)), or which are unlikely to give rise to a conflict of interest (s 182(6)(a)), or which are already known to the other directors (s 182(6)(b)) or are terms of a service contract (s 182(6)(c)). An interest as a bare trustee with no duties to perform is an interest which is unlikely to give rise to a conflict of interest and need not be declared (*Cowan de Groot Properties Ltd v Eagle Trust plc* [1991] BCLC 1045).

16.11.1.2 Sole directors

Sections 177(1) and 182(1) of CA 2006 require disclosure 'to the other directors' and so, according to the Explanatory Notes to the Act, para 352, no disclosure is required where the company has only one director. However, if the company should have more than one director, a declaration of an existing interest under s 182 must be recorded in writing (s 186).

16.11.1.3 Shadow directors

A shadow director is required to declare an existing interest by notice in writing (CA 2006, s 187).

16.11.1.4 Supplementary details

If company A proposes to contract with company B, and a director of company A is a member of company B, the membership is an interest which must be disclosed to the other directors (*Re British America Corporation Ltd* (1903) 19 TLR 662). Subject to the exceptions in CA 2006, ss 177(6) (c) and 182(6)(c)), a director's interest in his or her own service contract is an interest which has to be disclosed (*Toms v Cinema Trust Co Ltd* [1915] WN 29; *Runciman v Walter Runciman plc* [1992] BCLC 1084). Disclosure is not limited to contracts which are considered by the board (*Neptune (Vehicle Washing Equipment) Ltd v Fitzgerald* [1996] Ch 274).

A general notice under s 185 is a notice to the effect that a director has an interest in a specified body corporate or firm and is to be regarded as interested in any transaction or arrangement which may, after the date of the notice, be made with that body or firm, or that the director is to be regarded as interested in any contract which may after the date of the notice be made with a specified person with whom the director is connected (see **16.14**). Such a general notice is not effective unless it is given at a directors' meeting or the director concerned takes reasonable steps to secure that it is brought up and read at the next meeting of the directors after it is given (s 185(4)).

If a company has made a contract in which a director is interested, that interest must be declared when a variation of the contract is considered (*Runciman v Walter Runciman plc*).

16.11.1.5 Sanctions

There are criminal sanctions for failure to declare an existing interest (CA 2006, s 183), but there is probably no right to claim damages for breach of s 182 (*Coleman Taymar Ltd v Oakes* [2001] 2 BCLC 749).

16.11.2 EQUITABLE PRINCIPLE ON WHICH STATUTORY DUTY IS BASED

CA 2006, s 177, is based on an equitable principle that when a company is entering into a transaction, a director of the company must disclose to it any interest which that director has in the transaction (*Bentinck v Fenn* (1887) 12 App Cas 652 at pp 661, 667 and 671). In *Gwembe Valley Development Co Ltd v Koshy (No 3)* [2003] EWCA Civ 1478, [2004] 1 BCLC 131, the Court of Appeal said, at [145], that the duty to disclose arises from the no-profit rule, but in *Item Software (UK) Ltd v Fassihi* [2004] EWCA Civ 1244, [2005] ICR 450, Arden LJ said, at [41], that she preferred to base directors' fiduciary obligations of disclosure on what she called 'the fundamental duty' to act bona fide in what the director considers is in the interests of the company and not for a collateral purpose (see **16.6.2**). In other words, the obligation is to pass on to the company information which it is in the interests of the company to have, and not to withhold that information for the collateral purpose of furthering the director's interests. For another example of a fiduciary obligation to pass on valuable information see **16.9.4.4**.

16.11.3 PROHIBITION ON VOTING

If a director of a company is interested in an actual or proposed transaction or arrangement with the company, the model articles of association in SI 2008/3229 prohibit the director from participating in the decision-making process concerning it (model articles for private companies, art 14(1); model articles for public companies, arts 13(3) and 16(1)). This does not apply if the director's interest cannot reasonably be regarded as likely to give rise to a conflict of interest (model articles for private companies, art 14(2) and (3)(b); model articles for public companies, art 16(2) and (3)(b)), but then the director does not have to declare it (CA 2006, ss 177(6)(a) and 182(6)(a)).

This provision cannot be evaded by appointing an alternate director to vote instead, because alternates are subject to the same restrictions as their appointors (model articles for public companies, art 13(3) and 26(2)(c)).

A director who is disqualified by an interest from voting on a resolution cannot be counted towards the quorum for the resolution (model articles for private companies, art 14(1), model articles for public companies, art 16(1); *Re Greymouth Point Elizabeth Railway and Coal Co Ltd* [1904] 1 Ch 32; *Re North Eastern Insurance Co Ltd* [1919] 1 Ch 198). Where a transaction in which two directors, A and B, are interested is in reality a single transaction, it is not permissible for directors at a meeting to evade the disinterested quorum requirement by considering it first as a transaction relating to A, on which A does not vote but B does, and secondly as a transaction relating to B, on which B does not vote but A does (*Re North Eastern Insurance Co Ltd*; *Ireland Alloys Ltd v Dingwall* 1999 SLT 267). It is not permissible for the board to reduce its quorum temporarily to overcome this difficulty (*Re North Eastern Insurance Co Ltd*).

Under the model articles of association, the members may, by ordinary resolution, disapply the prohibition on voting (model articles for private companies, art 14(2) and (3)(a); model articles for public companies, art 16(2) and (3)(a)).

Under the model articles of association, there are three 'permitted causes' on which directors may vote despite an interest (model articles for private companies, art 14(2), (3)(c) and (4); for public companies, art 16(2), (3)(c) and (4)).

The prohibition is from voting at board meetings: it does not apply, where the director is a member of a company, to voting at members' meetings (*Re Express Engineering Works Ltd* [1920] 1 Ch 466 discussed in **14.13.2**; *Baird v J Baird and Co (Falkirk) Ltd* 1949 SLT 368), but a vote of an interested director at a members' meeting in favour of ratifying a breach of duty will be counted only if there is unanimous agreement (CA 2006, s 239).

16.12 SUBSTANTIAL PROPERTY TRANSACTIONS

16.12.1 STATUTORY REQUIREMENT FOR APPROVAL BY MEMBERS

Under CA 2006, ss 177 and 182, a company director's interests in a company transaction need be disclosed only to the other directors. Section 190 (first enacted in CA 1980, s 48) goes further and requires approval by a resolution of the members for certain transactions, which the title of the section calls 'substantial property transactions'.

The remedies in s 195 for failure to obtain approval are statutory versions of the equitable remedies of rescission and account of profits (see **16.15**).

16.12.2 WHICH TRANSACTIONS REQUIRE APPROVAL?

A transaction requires approval under CA 2006, s 190, if (s 190(1)) it is an 'arrangement' under which:

(a) a director of a company, or of its holding company, or a person connected with (see **16.14**) such a director, acquires, or is to acquire, from the company, a substantial non-cash asset; or

(b) the company acquires, or is to acquire, a substantial non-cash asset from such a person.

Indirect as well as direct acquisition is covered. The word 'arrangement' used in s 190(1) includes an agreement or understanding which does not have contractual effect (*Re Duckwari plc* [1999] Ch 253). The words 'is to acquire' do not mean 'may acquire' (*Smithton Ltd v Naggar* [2014] EWCA Civ 939, [2015] 1 WLR 189).

Shadow directors are treated as directors for the purposes of these provisions (s 223(1)), though a parent company is not to be treated as a shadow director of its subsidiary only because the subsidiary's directors are accustomed to act in accordance with its directions or instructions (s 251(3)).

Section 190 does not apply to an arrangement between a company and a member of the company qua member, or between a holding company and any of its wholly owned subsidiaries, or between wholly owned subsidiaries, of the same holding company (s 192), or if the value of the non-cash asset is less than £5,000 (s 191(2)(a)).

A non-cash asset is any property, or interest in property, other than cash (of any currency) (s 1163(1)). A non-cash asset is substantial if its value, at the time the arrangement is entered into, exceeds the lesser of £100,000 or 10 per cent of the amount of the company's net assets as shown in its most recent statutory accounts (or of its called-up share capital if it has not yet produced accounts) (s 191; *Joint receivers and managers of Niltan Carson Ltd v Hawthorne* [1988] BCLC 298). In Scotland it has been held that, if a non-cash asset is of special value to the person acquiring it (for example, because it enhances the value of property already owned by that person), that special value is the asset's value for the purposes of s 191 (*Micro Leisure Ltd v County Properties and Developments Ltd (No 2)* 1999 SLT 1428). For an interest in property to be a non-cash asset, it must be legally enforceable, but a right to compel someone else (for example, a trustee) to exercise a right over property is not an interest in that property (*Granada Group Ltd v Law Debenture Pension Trust Corp plc* [2016] EWCA Civ 1289, [2017] Pens LR 5). There is detailed discussion in *Ultraframe (UK) Ltd v Fielding* [2005] EWHC 1638 (Ch), [2007] WTLR 835, at [1362]–[1410] of whether various items are non-cash assets and how they should be valued, illustrating the complex issues of property law which may be involved in such questions.

A transaction effected by a director, or a person connected with a director, on a recognised investment exchange (see **7.3.4.2**) does not require approval if it is effected through the agency of an 'independent broker'—that is, a person who, independently of the director, or any person connected with the director, selects the person with whom the transaction is to be effected (s 194).

The provisions on substantial property transactions do not apply to entitlements under a director's service contract or to payments for loss of office which require approval under the provisions discussed in **15.9.2** (s 190(6)).

16.12.3 WHO MUST GIVE APPROVAL?

A substantial property transaction between a company and any of its directors, or any person connected with any of its directors (see **16.14**), must be approved by a resolution of the members of the company or made conditional on such approval being obtained (CA 2006, s 190(1)).

If a company is a subsidiary, a substantial property transaction between it and a director of its holding company, or a person connected with such a director, requires approval by resolution of the members of both the company (unless it is a wholly owned subsidiary) and the holding company (s 190(1), (2) and (4)(b)).

Approval by a company's members is not required if the company is in administration or being wound up, unless it is a members' voluntary winding up (s 193).

Approval is not effective unless the members approved all important terms of the transaction, especially the price (*Demite Ltd v Protec Health Ltd* [1998] BCC 638).

Where an arrangement is conditional on approval being given, the company must not be subject to any liability for failure to obtain the approval (s 190(3)).

16.12.4 EXAMPLE

In *British Racing Drivers' Club Ltd v Hextall Erskine and Co* [1996] 3 All ER 667, the company, which was a guarantee company whose members were present or former motor racing drivers, was persuaded by one of its directors, Mr Walkinshaw, to invest £5.3 million in his retail motor business. The business had been making losses for some years in a period of recession in the motor trade. The judge described the director as having a 'dominant position' on the board, whose members regarded him as having a 'Midas touch'. Mr Walkinshaw did not want the members of the company consulted about the investment in advance, because he said that some of them were his commercial rivals who would be prejudiced against him. The company's solicitors negligently advised that it was not necessary to obtain the members' approval for the transaction. After the investment was made and revealed to the members (without disclosing the price paid), dissenting members were advised by Mary Arden QC (now Arden LJ) that the approval of a general meeting should have been obtained under what is now CA 2006, s 190. At a subsequent general meeting, a motion to approve the transaction was defeated by 82 per cent of those voting. Eventually, litigation against Mr Walkinshaw was settled by his repurchasing the investment for £3.2 million, so the club lost £2.1 million. It was, however, able to recover this from its solicitors in a claim for damages for their negligence.

16.13 LOANS, QUASI-LOANS AND CREDIT TRANSACTIONS

16.13.1 LOANS AND COLLATERAL: STATUTORY REQUIREMENT FOR APPROVAL BY MEMBERS

CA 2006, s 197(1), requires approval by resolution of members of any company for a loan to a director of the company or of its holding company. A loan by a company to a director of its holding company requires the approval by resolution of the members of both the company (unless it is a wholly owned subsidiary) and the holding company (s 197(2) and (5)(b)). The same applies to guaranteeing or giving security in connection with a loan made by any other person (s 197(1)). Approval may be given within a reasonable period after a transaction or arrangement is entered into (s 214).

Before an approval resolution is adopted, a memorandum must be prepared setting out (s 197(4)):

(a) the nature of the transaction;

(b) the amount of the loan and the purpose for which it is required; and

(c) the extent of the company's liability under any transaction connected with the loan.

If an approval resolution is to be adopted as a written resolution, the memorandum must be sent or submitted to every eligible member before or with the resolution; if the resolution is to be adopted at a meeting, the memorandum must be available for inspection by members at the company's registered office for 15 days before the meeting and at the meeting (s 197(3)).

The remedies in s 213 for failure to obtain approval are statutory versions of the equitable remedies of rescission and account of profits (see **16.15**).

Before CA 2006, loans were prohibited and subject to criminal sanctions. The Law Commission and the Scottish Law Commission examined the prohibition on loans to directors and discussed it in *Company Directors: Regulating Conflicts of Interests and Formulating a Statement of Duties* (Law Commission Consultation Paper No 153) (London: Stationery Office, 1998), part 6. They said (para 6.1):

> As we see it the reason for the prohibition is to protect creditors and minority shareholders from the depletion in corporate assets through the making of loans, which if they were being made on arm's length terms, could usually be raised from third parties.

16.13.2 RELATED ARRANGEMENTS

A related arrangement is an arrangement under which another person makes a loan (or gives collateral) for a director of a company or its holding company in return for a benefit from the company or an associated (see **16.14**) body corporate. An arrangement under which a company will have assigned to it, or will assume, any rights, obligations or liabilities under a loan to, or collateral for, one of its or its holding company's directors is also a related arrangement. Any related arrangement requires approval under CA 2006, s 203, in the same away as a loan or collateral under s 197.

16.13.3 PUBLIC COMPANIES: APPROVAL OF OTHER KINDS OF TRANSACTIONS

In addition to approval of loans and collateral under CA 2006, s 197, a public company needs members' approval for four further types of financial arrangement for its and its holding company's directors:

(a) Quasi-loans to such a director (s 198). 'Quasi-loan' means an arrangement under which a company meets some financial obligations of a person on the understanding that it will be reimbursed later (s 199).

(b) Loans or quasi-loans to a person connected with such a director (s 200). See **16.14** for the meaning of 'connected'.

(c) Credit transactions under which land, goods or services are supplied on credit to such a director or a person connected with such a director (s 201).

(d) Related arrangements under which another person enters into a transaction of type (a), (b) or (c) which would otherwise require approval (s 203).

The requirements for approval of each of these types of transaction follow the same pattern as approval for loans under s 197, including a requirement for a memorandum of basic information about the transaction.

16.13.4 EXCEPTIONS

Sections 204 to 209 of CA 2006 make exceptions from the requirement for approval of loans, quasi-loans and (except in s 209) credit transactions. Where loans etc are exempt from the approval requirements, related arrangements are also exempt. The descriptions of loans, etc which are exempt are:

(a) Loans etc to meet a director's expenditure on company business, up to a limit of £50,000 (CA 2006, s 204).

(b) Loans etc to fund a director's defence of legal proceedings (civil or criminal) in connection with any alleged negligence, default, breach of duty or breach of trust in relation to the company or an associated company (see **16.14**), provided the money is to be repaid if the director loses the case (s 205).

(c) Loans etc to fund a director's defence of an investigation, or action proposed, by a regulatory authority, whether or not successful (s 206).

(d) Loans and quasi-loans up to a total of £10,000 (s 207(1)).

(e) Credit transactions up to a total of £15,000 (s 207(2)).

(f) Credit transactions made in the ordinary course of the company's business, provided the size of the transaction is not greater than, and the terms no more favourable than, the company would have offered to an unconnected person of the same financial standing (s 207(3)).

(g) Intra-group transactions (s 208).

(h) Loans and quasi-loans made by a moneylending company in the ordinary course of its business, provided the size of the transaction is not greater than, and the terms no more favourable than, the company would have offered to an unconnected person of the same financial standing (s 209(1) and (2)).

(i) Home loans made by a moneylending company in the ordinary course of its business for the borrower's principal private residence on the company's usual terms for lending to employees (s 209).

16.14 CONNECTED PERSONS AND ASSOCIATED COMPANIES

By CA 2006, s 252, the persons 'connected with' a director of a company (company A) are:

(a) members of the director's family (as defined in s 253);

(b) any body corporate with which the director is connected (as defined in s 254);

(c) a trustee of any trust under which the director or any person mentioned in (a) or (b) could benefit, apart from an employees' share scheme or a pension scheme;

(d) any partner (in a business or profession) of the director or of any person mentioned in (a), (b), (c) or (d), and the firm itself if it has separate legal personality.

However, any such person who is also a director of company A is not treated as being connected (otherwise one would go round in circles). This means that a director cannot be connected with him or herself acting in another capacity (for example, as a trustee) (*Clydebank Football Club Ltd v Steedman* 2002 SLT 109 at p 119).

Bodies corporate are 'associated' if one is a subsidiary of the other, or both are subsidiaries of the same body corporate (s 256(a)). Companies are associated if one is a subsidiary of the other, or both are subsidiaries of the same body corporate (s 256(b)).

16.15 REMEDIES

16.15.1 INTRODUCTION

The remedies for breach of one of the general duties of directors set out in CA 2006, ss 171 to 177, are the same as would apply if the corresponding equitable principle or common law rule applied.

The equitable remedies are described in **16.15.2** to **16.15.8**. They apply to fiduciaries generally, but are expressed here in terms of the general duties owed by a director of a company to the company. Statutory versions of these remedies are provided in CA 2006, s 195, for contravening the requirement for approval of substantial property transactions (see **16.12**), and in s 213 for contravening the requirement for approval of loans, quasi-loans and credit transactions (see **16.13**).

16.15.2 RETURN OF PROPERTY AND CONFISCATION OF PROFITS

A director of a company who has taken its property in breach of duty holds that property in trust for the company and may be ordered to restore it to the company (*J J Harrison (Properties) Ltd v Harrison* [2001] EWCA Civ 1467, [2002] 1 BCLC 162, at [27]–[30]).

When a director of a company has profited from a breach of duty to the company, the principal objective of the equitable remedies for the breach is to confiscate that profit and give it to the company (*Murad v Al-Saraj* [2005] EWCA Civ 959, [2005] WTLR 1573, per Arden LJ at [56] and Jonathan Parker LJ at [108]). The remedies are given to deter directors from breaching their duty (*Murad v Al-Saraj* per Arden LJ at [74] and Jonathan Parker LJ at [107]–[108]), not to compensate the company for loss (*United Pan-Europe Communications NV v Deutsche Bank AG* [2000] 2 BCLC 461 at p 484; see M Conaglen, 'Strict fiduciary loyalty and accounts of profits' [2006] CLJ 278). Compensation for loss is considered at **16.15.7**.

The principal remedy is a requirement to account for profits, known informally as 'disgorgement' of profits (per Arden LJ in **Charter plc v City Index Ltd** [2007] EWCA Civ 1382, [2008] Ch 313, at [74]). The profits that must be accounted for have been defined as profits made as a result of the breach of duty (*Gwembe Valley Development Co Ltd v Koshy (No 3)* [2003] EWCA Civ 1478, [2004] 1 BCLC 131, at [142]) or as profits from a transaction which has involved a breach of duty (*Murad v Al-Saraj* at [111]–[112]).

A director in breach of fiduciary duty is not liable to account for profits which are not attributable to the breach (*Murad v Al-Saraj* at [77]–[79] and [85]). There is a particular problem where a business opportunity has been diverted to a director's own business. Can the court assess what proportion of the profits of the director's business is attributable to the diverted opportunity? *Warman International Ltd v Dwyer* (1995) 182 CLR 544 concerned a breach of fiduciary duty by a senior executive of a company in diverting part of the company's business to companies of his own. The High Court of Australia decided that his account of profits should be limited to the first two years of operations, which would roughly ensure that he would not be accounting for profits which were the product of his own skill and effort rather than the claimant company's.

Only the profits made by the defendant are subject to confiscation: in general, a defendant is not jointly liable for profits made by another person (such as a company in which the director is interested) (*Regal (Hastings) Ltd v Gulliver* [1967] 2 AC 134; *Ultraframe (UK) Ltd v Fielding* [2005] EWHC 1638 (Ch), [2007] WTLR 835, at [1550]–[1576], disagreeing with *CMS Dolphin Ltd v Simonet* [2001] 2 BCLC 704). However, the other person may have secondary liability for knowing receipt or dealing or as an accessory (see **16.17**). A director is jointly liable for the whole of profits made, as a result of the director's breach of duty, by a partnership of which the director is a member (*Imperial Mercantile Credit Association v Coleman* (1873) LR 6 HL 189). In *Trustor AB v Smallbone (No 2)* [2001] 1 WLR 1177 the managing director of a company paid an enormous amount of its money to another company he controlled. The court decided that the recipient company was being used by the director as his agent or nominee (see **5.3.6.1**) and so he was made personally liable to restore the money to the defrauded company.

16.15.3 IRRELEVANT CONSIDERATIONS

As equitable remedies for breach of the general duties of directors are given to deter rather than to compensate, the principle that a claimant can claim only for a loss caused by the defendant's wrongdoing is irrelevant (*United Pan-Europe Communications NV v Deutsche Bank AG* [2000] 2 BCLC 461 at p 484; *Murad v Al-Saraj* [2005] EWCA Civ 959, [2005] WTLR 1573, per Arden LJ at [59], [72] and [73]). So a director of a company may have to account for a profit made in breach of fiduciary duty to the company even though the company has suffered no loss (*Parker v McKenna* (1874) LR 10 Ch App 96 per Lord Cairns LC at p 118; *Murad v Al-Saraj* per Arden LJ at [58]; *Foster Bryant Surveying Ltd v Bryant* [2007] EWCA Civ 200, [2007] Bus LR 1565, at [88] and [101]). Similarly, the fact that the director could have made the profit without breaching any duty is no defence (*Murad v Al-Saraj* per Arden LJ at [67]). It also follows that the director's profit will be confiscated and given to the company even if the company could not have made the profit itself (*Regal (Hastings) Ltd v Gulliver* [1967] 2 AC 134 per Lord Russell of Killowen at pp 149–50; *Murad v Al-Saraj* per Arden LJ at [59]–[66]; and cases cited in **16.9.4.3**). It is also no defence to prove that the company would have consented to the director keeping the profit if it had been asked: only actual consent counts (*Regal (Hastings) Ltd v Gulliver* per Lord Russell of Killowen at p 150; *Murad v Al-Saraj* per Arden LJ at [71]).

The position was summarised as follows by Lord Russell of Killowen in **Regal (Hastings) Ltd v Gulliver** at pp 144–5:

> The rule of equity which insists on those, who by use of a fiduciary position make a profit, being liable to account for that profit, in no way depends on fraud, or absence of bona fides; or upon such questions and considerations as whether the profit would or should otherwise have gone to the plaintiff, or whether the profiteer was under a duty to obtain the source of the profit for the plaintiff, or whether he took a risk or acted as he did for the benefit of the plaintiff, or whether the plaintiff has in fact been damaged or benefited by his action. The liability arises from the mere fact of a profit having, in the stated circumstances, been made. The profiteer, however honest and well-intentioned, cannot escape the risk of being called upon to account.

If a company has actually suffered a loss from a director's breach of duty, it may claim equitable compensation for that loss (see **16.15.7**) in addition to confiscation of the profits made by the director.

16.15.4 RELIEF FOR HONEST AND REASONABLE DIRECTOR

In order to obtain a remedy for breach of fiduciary duty, it is not necessary to show that the director acted dishonestly or in bad faith (see **16.15.3**), but the court may, under CA 2006, s 1157, relieve the director of liability if he or she acted honestly and reasonably (*Coleman Taymar Ltd v Oakes* [2001] 2 BCLC 749; see **16.16.6**).

16.15.5 EQUITABLE ALLOWANCE

The general rule applying to confiscation of profit made in breach of fiduciary duty by all kinds of fiduciaries is that the court may make allowance for the fiduciary's own expenditure in obtaining the profit, at least where there is no dishonesty (*Patel v Brent London Borough Council* [2003] EWHC 3081 (Ch), LTL 3/12/2003, at [29]). An allowance is unlikely where there has been dishonesty (*Crown Dilmun v Sutton* [2004] EWHC 52 (Ch), [2004] 1 BCLC 468, at [213]). However, in *Guinness plc v Saunders* [1990] 2 AC 663 the House of Lords was very much against making any allowance to a director. The House of Lords held that the more important principle is that a director is not entitled to remuneration except as allowed under the company's constitution (per Lord Templeman at pp 689–94 and Lord Goff of Chievely at p 701). Lord Goff acknowledged that in the case of a trustee an allowance might be made (as was done in *Boardman v Phipps* [1967] 2 AC 46), provided it would not have the effect of encouraging trustees in any way to put themselves in a position where their interests conflict with their duties. But his Lordship reserved the question whether this could ever be done in the case of a director. This hard line was followed in *Quarter Master UK Ltd v Pyke* [2004] EWHC 1815 (Ch), [2005] 1 BCLC 245, at [76]–[77].

16.15.6 RESCISSION

A transaction of a company which is in breach of a director's fiduciary duty is voidable at the company's option and may be rescinded. The transaction is not void (*Spackman v Evans* (1868) LR 3 HL 171; *Bamford v Bamford* [1970] Ch 212; *Hely-Hutchinson v Brayhead Ltd* [1968] 1 QB 549).

Rescission of a transaction involves each party returning to the other what was transferred in the transaction. A claimant cannot be awarded restitution from the defendant without being able to give counter-restitution (what used to be called *restitutio in integrum*) to the defendant (*Erlanger v New Sombrero Phosphate Co* (1878) 3 App Cas 1218 per Lord Blackburn at p 1278). For example, in *Bentinck v Fenn* (1887) 12 App Cas 652 it was not possible to rescind the purchase by a company of three mining properties in which one of its directors was interested, because the company had already resold them. Usually, when a contract of sale of property by a director of a company to the company is rescinded, what the director returns to the company includes whatever profit the director made from the transaction. The fact that property which is to be returned in rescission has declined in value is no bar to rescission (*Armstrong v Jackson* [1917] 2 KB 822).

If the transaction was with a person other than the defaulting director, rescission may be awarded if the company can show that the other party to the transaction was informed of, or wilfully refused to receive information about, the director's breach of duty (*Logicrose Ltd v Southend United Football Club Ltd* [1988] 1 WLR 1256).

The remedies of rescission and account of profits are independent (*Logicrose Ltd v Southend United Football Club Ltd*) and are suited to different circumstances.

16.15.7 EQUITABLE COMPENSATION

A court may award equitable compensation for any loss which is not compensated by the remedies of account, constructive trust or rescission for breach of fiduciary duty (*Extrasure Travel Insurance Ltd v Scattergood* [2003] 1 BCLC 598; *Gwembe Valley Development Co Ltd v Koshy (No 3)* [2003] EWCA Civ 1478, [2004] 1 BCLC 131, at [142]). Unlike the other remedies, equitable compensation is awarded to make good a loss which can be seen (using hindsight and common sense) to have been caused by the breach of duty, so it will not be awarded either if the company has not suffered a loss or if it is probable that the loss would have been suffered even if there had been no breach of duty (*Target Holdings Ltd v Redferns* [1996] 1 AC 421; *Gwembe Valley Development Co Ltd v Koshy (No 3)*). The loss must be measured as at the time of trial, not the time of the breach of duty (*Target Holdings Ltd v Redferns*). The test of whether a loss was caused by the breach of duty is the 'but for' test: compensation is awarded for a loss which would not have occurred but for the breach (*Target Holdings Ltd v Redferns*).

16.15.8 LIABILITY FOR KNOWINGLY ALLOWING BREACH

Where a director of a company repeatedly breaches his or her duty to the company, another director who knowingly permitted that practice will be jointly and severally liable, despite not having actual knowledge of every individual breach (*Neville v Krikorian* [2006] EWCA Civ 943, [2007] 1 BCLC 1; *Queensway Systems Ltd v Walker* [2006] EWHC 2496 (Ch), [2007] 2 BCLC 577).

16.15.9 LIMITATION

The normal limitation period for a claim in respect of breach of fiduciary duty by a director is six years, unless the provisions of the Limitation Act 1980, s 21(1), apply, in which case there is no limitation period (*Gwembe Valley Development Co Ltd v Koshy (No 3)* [2003] EWCA Civ 1478, [2004] 1 BCLC 131, at [111]). Section 21(1) applies in two situations in which a director is treated as a trustee:

(a) Under s 21(1)(a) there is no limitation period where the director was a party to any fraud or fraudulent breach of trust (as was the case in *Gwembe Valley Development Co Ltd v Koshy (No 3)*).

(c) Under s 21(1)(b) there is no limitation period for recovery of company property, or proceeds of company property, either (i) in a director's possession, or (ii) previously received by a director and converted to the director's use. A director of a company who obtains its property by misuse of directorial powers and sells it has converted the property and so a claim to recover the proceeds will not be subject to a limitation period (*J J Harrison (Properties) Ltd v Harrison* [2002] 1 BCLC 162).

Section 21(1) does not apply to a constructive trustee (*Williams v Central Bank of Nigeria* [2014] UKSC 10, [2014] AC 271). So it does not apply to secondary liability (see **16.17**), for example, for dishonest assistance (*Alpha Sim Communications Ltd v CAZ Distribution Services Ltd* [2014] EWHC 207 (Ch), [2014] STI 743).

16.15.10 CRIMINAL LIABILITY

The fact that equity would regard a director as constructive trustee of benefits or gains does not mean that the director's taking of those benefits or gains constitutes the offence of theft (*Attorney-General's Reference (No 1 of 1985)* [1986] QB 491). However, an agreement by a director with others dishonestly to conceal such benefits or gains so as to prevent the company recovering them does constitute the offence of conspiracy to defraud (*Adams v The Queen* [1995] 1 WLR 52).

16.16 RELIEF FROM LIABILITY

16.16.1 WAYS IN WHICH LIABILITY MAY BE RELIEVED

A company director may be relieved from liability for an act in breach of duty to the company in three ways:

(a) If the company gives permission for the director to act, either before or after the act, the company will not have a cause of action and will not be able to bring a claim against the director (see **16.16.2** to **16.16.4**). Permission to act in breach of duty is often called 'ratification' of the breach or, especially when given before the act, 'authorisation'.

(b) By a qualifying indemnity provision, which can only cover liability to third parties (see **16.16.5**).

(c) If the company does bring a claim, the court may, under CA 2006, s 1157, relieve the director from liability if it finds that the act was honest and reasonable (see **16.16.6**).

16.16.2 RATIFICATION

Ratification by a company of a breach of duty by one of its directors means that the company has no cause of action in respect of the breach and cannot bring a claim in respect of it. CA 2006, s 239, deals with ratification by a company of conduct by a director amounting to negligence, default, breach of duty or breach of trust in relation to the company (s 239(1)), and so covers breaches of the general duties in ss 171 to 177. Section 175(5) deals with prospective ratification of a breach of s 175 (duty to avoid conflicts of interest).

Unless s 175(5) applies (see later), ratification of a company director's act in breach of duty to the company must be by resolution of the company's members (s 239(2), (3) and (4)). The same applies to the ratification of acts of a former director or a shadow director (s 239(5)(b) and (c)). Unless the decision is unanimous (s 239(6)(a)), only disinterested members' votes can be counted (s 239(3) and (4)). Where the resolution is proposed as a written resolution, the requirement of a disinterested majority is achieved by s 293(3). This provides that neither the director whose conduct is to be ratified, nor any member connected with that director (see **16.14**), including a fellow director, is an eligible member. Where the resolution is proposed at a meeting, it is passed only if the necessary majority is obtained disregarding votes in favour by the director (if a member) and any member connected with him (s 239(4)). The director, and persons connected with the director, can attend the meeting, can be counted towards the quorum, and can take part in the proceedings (s 239(4)). As s 239(4) disallows votes cast by a director 'if a member' rather than 'as a member', it would seem that votes cast by the director as proxy must not be counted if the director is a member, but must be counted if the director is not a member. When s 239 came into force on 1 October 2007, it was new to company law. It does not affect any rule of law as to acts that are incapable of being ratified by the company (s 239(7); see **16.16.4**). It would seem that it also does not affect the rule that ratification must be fully informed (see **16.16.3**).

Section 175(5) permits disinterested directors of a *private company* to give a director prospective authorisation to act in breach of s 175 (duty to avoid conflicts of interest), unless the company's constitution forbids them from doing so (s 175(5)(a)). Section 175(5)(b) permits a *public company* to include in its constitution a provision enabling its directors to give prospective authorisation, but the model articles for public companies in SI 2008/3229 do not make such a provision. When directors (whether of private or public companies) decide to authorise a breach of CA 2006, s 175, the director who is being authorised and any other interested directors cannot be counted in the quorum for making the decision (s 175(6)(a)), nor can their votes be counted (s 175(6)(b)).

16.16.3 FULLY INFORMED CONSENT

In *Phosphate of Lime Co v Green* (1871) LR 7 CP 43 Willes J said, at pp 56–7:

> The principle by which a person on whose behalf an act is done without his authority may ratify and adopt it, is as old as any proposition known to the law. But it is subject to one condition: in order to make it binding, it must be either with full knowledge of the character of the act to be adopted, or with intention to adopt it at all events and under whatever circumstances.

Consent may be informal and failure to object may amount to consent (*Sharma v Sharma* [2013] EWCA Civ 1287, [2014] BCC 73).

Even though the members of a company have given their consent to transactions by the company's directors which would otherwise be a breach of duty, the court may permit the company to claim remedies for the breach from the directors if it considers that it is fair and equitable to do so because of the members' failure to understand fully what they were consenting to (*Knight v Frost* [1999] 1 BCLC 364). The court will consider all the circumstances in which consent was given (*Knight v Frost*). The directors will be safe if the members fully understood what they were consenting to, even if they did not know that it was a breach of a duty (*Knight v Frost*). A director of a company seeking permission to bid for its property at auction must specify the maximum price he or she would be willing to bid, and seek permission to buy the property for less than that price if other bidders do not reach it (*Newgate Stud Co v Penfold* [2004] EWHC 2993 (Ch), [2008] 1 BCLC 46, at [227]).

The most common circumstance in which consent is found not to be fully informed is where the directors obtained the consent without fully disclosing what they were to gain from the transaction. In *Kaye v Croydon Tramways Co* [1898] 1 Ch 358 a resolution approving a contract of sale of the company's undertaking was set aside because the notice convening the meeting and a circular sent by the directors to shareholders had failed to disclose that the purchaser would make a substantial payment to the selling company's directors. In *Baillie v Oriental Telephone and Electric Co Ltd* [1915] 1 Ch 503 a resolution authorising the company's directors to receive remuneration from one of the company's subsidiaries was set aside because the directors had failed to disclose that it would allow them to keep more than £40,000 that they had already received. See also *Tiessen v Henderson* [1899] 1 Ch 861.

16.16.4 ACTS WHICH CANNOT BE RATIFIED

CA 2006, s 239, does not affect any rule of law as to acts that are incapable of being ratified by the company (s 239(7)). In **North-West Transportation Co Ltd v Beatty** (1887) 12 App Cas 589 Sir Richard Baggallay said, at pp 593–4, that ratification may be made, provided it: 'is not brought about by unfair or improper means, and is not illegal or fraudulent or oppressive towards those shareholders who oppose it'. It was held in *Franbar Holdings Ltd v Patel* [2008] EWHC 1534 (Ch), [2009] 1 BCLC 1, that CA 2006, s 239(7), preserves this exception. In **Bowthorpe Holdings Ltd v Hills** [2002] EWHC 2331 (Ch), [2003] 1 BCLC 226, at [50], Morritt V-C said that the transaction to be ratified 'must be bona fide or honest'. In **Madoff Securities International Ltd v Raven** [2011] EWHC 3102 (Comm), [2012] 2 All ER (Comm) 634, it was held, at [123] (without reference to CA 2006), that a transaction cannot be ratified if it 'is not honest, bona fide and in the best interests of the company'.

The court should consider whether it should refuse to recognise ratification because of public policy considerations, for example where contravention of a statutory provision has been ratified (*Cox v Cox* [2006] EWHC 1077 (Ch), [2006] BCC 890).

A company's members cannot ratify a transaction which is likely to jeopardise the company's solvency or cause loss to its creditors (*Bowthorpe Holdings Ltd v Hills* at [51]). It may be that this is just an example of the rule that a ratified transaction must be bona fide or honest (*Bowthorpe Holdings*) and in some cases the phrase 'fraud on creditors' has been used (for example, **Rolled Steel Products (Holdings) Ltd v British Steel Corporation** [1986] Ch 246 at p 296). In *Kinsela v Russell Kinsela Pty Ltd* (1986) 4 NSWLR 722, the Court of Appeal of New South Wales emphasised that there is a difference between a solvent and an insolvent company. If the actions of directors damage a solvent company, then it is the interests of the members that are damaged and the members can decide whether or not to forgive the directors. In an insolvent company, however, actions of directors that damage the company damage the interests of the creditors, not the members, and therefore the members cannot be allowed to preclude action being taken against the directors to recover property for distribution among the creditors. This approach was approved by Dillon LJ in *West Mercia Safetywear Ltd v Dodd* [1988] BCLC 250.

See **18.4.2.7** for discussion of the theory that a breach of duty is incapable of being ratified if it could have been the subject of a derivative claim before ss 260 to 264 came into force.

16.16.5 INDEMNIFICATION AND EXCLUSION OF LIABILITY

In *Re Brazilian Rubber Plantations and Estates Ltd* [1911] 1 Ch 425, the terms of directors' appointments, contained in the company's articles of association, provided that the company could not sue a director for 'any … loss, damage, or misfortune whatever which shall happen in the execution of the duties of his office or in relation thereto, unless the same happen through his own dishonesty'. Neville J held that this was lawful and prevented the company's liquidator from taking proceedings against the directors for alleged negligence (though his Lordship also found that there was no negligence). *Re City Equitable Fire Insurance Co Ltd* [1925] Ch 407 concerned a company with a similar provision in its articles of association so that, although directors were found to have been negligent in some respects, they were not liable to the company.

Following these cases, CA 1928, s 78, was enacted to limit contracting out from directors' liability. The current legislation is in CA 2006, s 232. This declares void any provision which purports to exempt, to any extent, a director of a company from any liability in connection with any negligence, default, breach of duty or breach of trust by that director in relation to the company (s 232(1)). Any indemnity provided by a company for any of its own directors, or any director of an associated company (see **16.14**), against any such liability is also void, unless it is provided by means of a qualifying indemnity provision or by buying insurance (s 232(2)).

There are two kinds of qualifying indemnity provision: a qualifying third party indemnity provision (s 234), and a qualifying pension scheme indemnity provision (s 235).

A qualifying third party indemnity provision is defined in s 234 as a provision indemnifying a director against his or her liability which:

(a) does not cover liability to the company or any associated company, or the costs of unsuccessfully defending civil proceedings brought by the company or any associated company (that is, it only indemnifies against liabilities to third parties and the costs of successfully defending proceedings brought by the company);

(b) does not indemnify against a fine in criminal proceedings or a penalty payable to a regulatory authority for 'non-compliance with any requirement of a regulatory nature';

(c) does not apply to the costs of unsuccessfully defending criminal proceedings; and

(d) does not apply to the costs of an unsuccessful application for relief by the court under s 661(3) or (4) or s 1157 (see **16.16.6**).

A qualifying pension scheme indemnity provision (s 235) may be used where a company is a trustee of an occupational scheme. It indemnifies a director of the company against liability incurred in connection with the company's activities as trustee. To be a qualifying provision it must not provide any indemnity against a fine in criminal proceedings, or a penalty payable to a regulatory authority or the costs of unsuccessfully defending criminal proceedings.

Qualifying indemnity provisions must be available for inspection by members in the same way as directors' service contracts (ss 237 and 238; see **4.4.4.2**) and must be disclosed in the directors' report (s 236; see **9.9.4.1**). A company can fund a director's defence of civil, criminal or regulatory proceedings without approval by the members, provided the money has to be repaid if the defence is unsuccessful (ss 205 and 206; see **16.13.4**).

The UK Corporate Governance Code (see **15.2.2**) says that a premium listed company should arrange appropriate insurance cover in respect of legal action against its directors (para A.1.3). This kind of insurance is known as directors and officers (D and O) insurance. A guidance note from the Institute of Chartered Secretaries and Administrators, *Directors and Officers Insurance* (Reference No 030925) gives some idea of what is 'appropriate insurance cover'. It points out that the typical policy covers damages awarded for any error, misstatement, misleading statement, act, omission, neglect or breach of duty committed by a director, but not any fraudulent, dishonest or illegal act.

16.16.6 RELIEF BY THE COURT

16.16.6.1 Principle

CA 2006, s 1157, empowers a court which finds an officer of a company or a person employed by a company as auditor (whether or not an officer of the company) liable in respect of negligence, default, breach of duty or breach of trust to relieve the officer or auditor, either wholly or partly, from liability. Relief from liability may be given under s 1157 if the court finds that the officer or auditor has acted honestly and reasonably, having regard to the circumstances of the case, including those connected with his or her appointment.

There is a similar provision in s 226E(5) for relief from liability for remuneration and loss of office payments made without approval and in s 661(3) and (4) for relief from liability imposed under s 661(2) for calls made by a company on shares held for it by a nominee.

A company may fund or indemnify a successful application by a director under s 661(3) or (4) or s 1157 without breaching the prohibition against protection from liability (s 234) or the prohibition against providing loans and collateral to directors (s 205(1)(a)(ii) and (5)). A successful application under s 1157 by an auditor may be indemnified (s 533).

16.16.6.2 Scope

CA 1985, s 1157, applies to a liability to account for profits (see **16.15.2**) just as much as to a liability to pay damages (*Coleman Taymar Ltd v Oakes* [2001] 2 BCLC 749).

Section 1157 does not apply to a statutory liability of an officer or auditor of a company to answer for the company's default (*Commissioners of Customs and Excise v Hedon Alpha Ltd* [1981] QB 818), for example under CDDA 1986, s 15 (*Commissioners of Inland Revenue v McEntaggart* [2004] EWHC 3431 (Ch), [2006] 1 BCLC 476) or IA 1986, s 217 (*First Independent Factors and Finance Ltd v Mountford* [2008] EWHC 835 (Ch), [2008] 2 BCLC 297).

In *Re Produce Marketing Consortium Ltd* [1989] 1 WLR 745, Knox J held that s 1157 does not apply to liability under the Insolvency Act 1986, s 214 (wrongful trading, see **20.13**), because he thought that the two provisions adopt inconsistent approaches (which he described, at p 750, as 'objective' (s 214) and 'subjective' (CA 2006, s 1157)) to assessing liability, which he thought had to be applied 'at the same time' (at p 751). However, it is submitted that s 1157, is applied only after liability has been established, and that the process of deciding whether liability should be mitigated is entirely independent from the process of establishing liability. So it is difficult to follow why s 1157 cannot apply to liability for wrongful trading.

16.16.6.3 Court's approach

It would require an extremely powerful case to persuade a court to relieve from liability an officer or auditor who obtained a material personal benefit through the breach of duty (*Re In a Flap Envelope Co Ltd* [2003] EWHC 3047 (Ch), [2004] 1 BCLC 64, at [64]).

In *Re Duomatic Ltd* [1969] 2 Ch 365 the test of whether a director acted reasonably which was used (at p 377) was whether:

> he was acting in the way in which a man of affairs [that is, a right-hand man who can be trusted to carry out important transactions for someone] dealing with his own affairs with reasonable care and circumspection could reasonably be expected to act in such a case.

It is possible to find that a defendant acted reasonably even if it has been found that he or she acted negligently (*Re D'Jan of London Ltd* [1994] 1 BCLC 561). But a director of a company who has paid no attention at all to the company's affairs cannot claim to have acted reasonably (*Lexi Holdings plc v Luqman* [2007] EWHC 2652 (Ch), LTL 30/11/2007).

In determining whether a defendant has acted reasonably, it may be important to consider whether the company or the defendant should have obtained legal advice and, if legal advice was obtained, what that advice was (*Murray v Leisureplay plc* [2004] EWHC 1927 (QB), LTL 5/8/2004, at [121]). The court will regard not taking legal advice as acting reasonably unless the question for decision is sufficiently obviously one requiring expert legal consideration (*Re Brian D Pierson (Contractors) Ltd* [2001] 1 BCLC 275 at p 301).

In *Re Produce Marketing Consortium Ltd* [1989] 1 WLR 745 Knox J described the approach under CA 2006, s 1157 as 'subjective'. However, it is only the officer or auditor's honesty which should be assessed subjectively: reasonableness, by its very nature, must be assessed objectively (*Coleman Taymar Ltd v Oakes* [2001] 2 BCLC 749; *Re MDA Investment Management Ltd* [2004] EWHC 42 (Ch), [2005] BCC 783, at [14]–[17]).

Because the court must consider the circumstances before granting relief under s 1157, there must, other than in a quite exceptional case, be a full trial of the allegations: the court will not strike out a claim without a hearing on the basis that it would, under s 1157, relieve the defendant of liability entirely (*Equitable Life Assurance Society v Bowley* [2003] EWHC 2263 (Comm), [2004] 1 BCLC 180). Nevertheless, there is provision in s 1157(2) for an officer or auditor to apply to the court for relief in advance of proceedings even being brought.

16.16.6.4 Example

Re Duomatic Ltd [1969] 2 Ch 365 is an example of the operation of CA 2006, s 1157. The articles of Duomatic Ltd prescribed that directors' remuneration had to be approved by the members. Mr Elvins was a director of the company and, until part way through its last financial year, held the majority of the ordinary shares. Directors drew salaries from the company without prior authorisation by a general meeting, but in every year except the last all members entitled to attend and vote at general meetings in fact approved the directors' drawings and this was held to be equivalent to approval by a general meeting (see **14.13.1**). In the last year, Mr Elvins continued to draw a salary at a rate agreed with his fellow directors at the beginning of the year, but there was no approval by the members with or without meeting. It was not suggested that Mr Elvins had acted dishonestly. Buckley J held that he had acted reasonably and ought fairly to be relieved of liability to repay the agreed final year's salary. However, the judge refused to excuse Mr Elvins in respect of another breach of duty: Mr Elvins and a co-director wished to dismiss a third director, Mr Hanly, with whom they had quarrelled; Mr Hanly threatened to sue the company and so Mr Elvins agreed that the company should make Mr Hanly a severance payment of £4,000. This was illegal because it was not approved under s 217 (see **15.9.2.1**). Buckley J held that Mr Elvins should not have agreed to this payment without seeking legal advice to discover whether Mr Hanly actually had any claim against the company. Because he had not sought legal advice, Mr Hanly had not acted reasonably and ought not to be excused.

16.17 SECONDARY LIABILITY

16.17.1 CONSTRUCTIVE TRUST OF WRONGFULLY DISPOSED PROPERTY

If directors of a company act in breach of their fiduciary duties to the company then a person outside the company may be liable as a constructive trustee of property, which has been misappropriated by the directors, in two circumstances, namely where:

(a) in breach of the directors' fiduciary duties, company property is transferred to the outsider who knows that the transfer is a breach of duty or where the outsider receives company property, otherwise than as a bona fide purchaser for value, and deals with the property in a manner inconsistent with such fiduciary duties (usually called 'knowing receipt or dealing'); or

(b) the outsider dishonestly assists in or procures the directors' breach of fiduciary duty even though not personally receiving company property (liability as an accessory).

This is a general principle which applies wherever there is a breach of fiduciary duty. If misappropriated property has been converted into money, or money has been used to buy other assets, or the property has passed through several hands, it may be necessary to carry out the legal process of tracing. This is the process by which a person from whom property has been taken identifies the persons who have handled or received it, or converted it from non-monetary to monetary form, or vice versa, and justifies a claim to the return of the property or whatever it has been converted into (see per Millett LJ in *Boscawen v Bajwa* [1996] 1 WLR 328 at p 334).

The outsider is also liable to account for profits made personally from the breach of duty, but is not jointly liable for the profits that the delinquent director has made (*Ultraframe (UK) Ltd v Fielding* [2005] EWHC 1638 (Ch), [2007] WTLR 835, at [1595]–[1601]).

For general discussions see *Ultraframe (UK) Ltd v Fielding* at [1476]–[1510]; B Strong, 'Civil asset recovery procedures: how equity deters fraud' (1992) 13 Co Law 44.

16.17.2 KNOWING RECEIPT OR DEALING

The law on liability for knowing receipt or dealing was summarised in the following terms by Buckley LJ in *Belmont Finance Corporation Ltd v Williams Furniture Ltd (No 2)* [1980] 1 All ER 393 at p 405:

> in consequence of the fiduciary character of their duties the directors of a limited company are treated as if they were trustees of those funds of the company which are in their hands or under their control, and if they misapply them they commit a breach of trust (*Re Lands Allotment Co* [1894] 1 Ch 616 per Lindley LJ at p 631 and Kay LJ at p 638). So, if the directors of a company in breach of their fiduciary duties misapply the funds of their company so that they come into the hands of some stranger to the trust who receives them with knowledge (actual or constructive) of the breach, he cannot conscientiously retain those funds against the company unless he has some better equity. He becomes a constructive trustee for the company of the misapplied funds.

In *Rolled Steel Products (Holdings) Ltd v British Steel Corporation* [1986] Ch 246, Slade LJ said, at p 298:

> The *Belmont* principle thus provides a legal route by which a company may recover its assets in a case where its directors have abused their fiduciary duties and a person receiving assets as a result of such abuse is on notice that they have been misapplied.
>
> the *Belmont* principle must, in my opinion, be equally capable of applying in a case where the relevant misapplication of the company's assets by the directors has consisted either of an application for purposes not authorised by [a statement in the company's articles of its objects] or an application in breach of the company's articles of association, eg, pursuant to a board resolution passed at an inquorate meeting of the directors.

For cases in which persons have been held liable as constructive trustees of companies under the knowing receipt or dealing head see *Belmont Finance Corporation Ltd v Williams Furniture Ltd (No 2)*; *International Sales and Agencies Ltd v Marcus* [1982] 3 All ER 551; and *Rolled Steel Products (Holdings) Ltd v British Steel Corporation*.

Liability for knowing receipt or dealing can arise only in respect of a transfer that was itself in breach of duty, not for a transfer which was occasioned by a breach of duty (*Brown v Bennett* [1999] 1 BCLC 649).

In order to establish a person's liability for knowing receipt or dealing, it is not necessary to prove that the person acted dishonestly (*Bank of Credit and Commerce International (Overseas) Ltd v Akindele* [2001] Ch 437).

In order to be liable for knowing receipt of, or dealing, with, company property transferred in breach of directors' fiduciary duties, an outsider must know that the property is the subject matter of directors' fiduciary duties and that the transfer of the property is in breach of those duties. The most controversial area of the law on secondary liability is the definition of the circumstances in which an outsider who does not have actual knowledge of these matters is nevertheless to be held liable because of what is called constructive knowledge, that is because the court decides that a defendant should be treated as having knowledge which the defendant should have sought but did not. A defendant in this situation is usually described as having been 'put on inquiry'. In *Papadimitriou v Crédit Agricole Corporation and Investment Bank* [2015] UKPC 13, [2015] 1 WLR 4265, the Gibraltar branch of the defendant bank had accepted a deposit of money in a newly opened account of a Virgin Islands company controlled by Mr Robin Symes. The money had come from a Panamanian company via a Liechtenstein foundation. The only apparent purpose of the deposit was to provide a guarantee for a loan made by the bank's London branch to another of Mr Symes's companies. The money was in fact most of the proceeds of sale of stolen property. The question was whether, if the bank had given adequate consideration to the commercial purpose of the transaction, it would have concluded that it was improper and so had constructive notice of the right of the true owner of the stolen property to the money. The Privy Council held that it did have constructive notice. Lord Clark said, at [20]:

> on the one hand, the bank's knowledge of facts indicating the mere possibility of a third party having a proprietary right would not be enough to put the bank on inquiry but, on the other hand, it is not necessary for the bank to conclude that [the third party] probably had such a right. The test is somewhere in between. It may be formulated in this way. The bank must make inquiries if there is a serious possibility of a third party having such a right or, put in another way, if the facts known to the bank would give a reasonable banker in the position of the particular banker serious cause to question the propriety of the transaction.

Lord Sumption said, at [33], that the same test should be applied to accountability as a constructive trustee for knowing receipt.

16.17.3 DISHONEST ASSISTANCE

In order to establish a defendant's liability for dishonest assistance in a director's breach of fiduciary duty, it must be proved that the defendant was dishonest, but it is not necessary to show that the director was dishonest (*Royal Brunei Airlines Sdn Bhd v Tan* [1995] 2 AC 378; *Satnam Investments Ltd v Dunlop Heywood and Co Ltd* [1999] 3 All ER 652; *Twinsectra Ltd v Yardley* [2002] UKHL 12, [2002] 2 AC 164). Dishonesty is established by a combined objective and subjective test in which it must be proved that the defendant's conduct was dishonest by the ordinary standards of reasonable and honest people (objective element) and that the defendant had knowledge of those elements of the conduct which made it dishonest by ordinary standards (subjective element) (*Barlow Clowes International Ltd v Eurotrust International Ltd* [2005] UKPC 37, [2006] 1 WLR 1476). The type of knowledge required for liability as an accessory is either actual knowledge or blind eye knowledge (suspicion combined with a conscious decision not to make inquiries which might result in knowledge) (*Barlow Clowes International Ltd v Eurotrust International Ltd* at [10]).

In *Twinsectra Ltd v Yardley* Lord Hoffmann described what the defendant must be proved to have known in the following terms, at [24]:

> A person may dishonestly assist in the commission of a breach of trust without any idea of what a trust means. The necessary dishonest state of mind may be found to exist simply on the fact that he knew perfectly well that he was helping to pay away money to which the recipient was not entitled.

This was affirmed by the Privy Council in *Barlow Clowes International Ltd v Eurotrust International Ltd*. It has been suggested that, in order to find a defendant liable for dishonestly assisting a director's breach of fiduciary duty, it must be found that the defendant was aware that what he or she was doing was dishonest. In *Barlow Clowes International Ltd v Eurotrust International Ltd* the Privy Council, in an appeal from the Isle of Man, rejected this suggestion. In *Starglade Properties Ltd v Nash* [2010] EWCA Civ 1314, [2011] Lloyd's Rep FC 102, it was held that this is the law in England and Wales as well.

17

CORPORATE OFFICERS
AND PROMOTERS

SUMMARY OF POINTS COVERED

- What is in this chapter
- Liability of officers
- Company secretaries
- Auditors

- Auditors' liability
- Managers
- Promoters

17.1 WHAT IS IN THIS CHAPTER

The law relating to directors is considered in **Chapters 15** and **16**. **Chapter 20** will deal with insolvency office-holders. This chapter considers some other categories of person who have responsibilities and liabilities in relation to a company: the company secretary (**17.3**), auditors (**17.4** and **17.5**), managers (**17.6**) and promoters (**17.7**). The term 'officers' of a company is considered in **17.2** in the context of responsibility for criminal offences.

Key legislation which you should be able to consult when reading this chapter:

- CA 2006, ss 270–280, 485–539, 598–604, 1121, 1132, 1173. All this legislation is in *Blackstone's Statutes on Company Law*.
- UK Corporate Governance Code, which is at **www.frc.org.uk/Our-Work/Corporate-Governance-Reporting/Corporate-governance.aspx.**
- Regulation (EU) No 537/2014, which is at **eur-lex.europa.eu**.

The following cases, which are considered in this chapter, are particularly significant and are recommended further reading:

- *Caparo Industries plc v Dickman* [1990] 2 AC 605 (also a key case for **Chapter 9**).
- *Stone and Rolls Ltd v Moore Stephens* [2009] UKHL 39, [2009] AC 1391 (also a key case for **Chapter 19**).

Your particular course of study may require you to read other source materials.

17.2 LIABILITY OF OFFICERS

There are many provisions of CA 2006 which impose criminal sanctions for breach of its requirements. Where a company is required to do something, for example deliver a document to Companies House, it is usual to impose a criminal sanction, for failing to comply, on the company itself
and on 'every officer of the company who is in default'. See, for example, s 26(3) (failure to send
Companies House a copy of amended articles).

By s 1121(3), an officer is 'in default' if he or she authorises or permits, participates in,
or fails to take all reasonable steps to prevent, the contravention. By s 1121(2), 'officer' in this
context includes any director, manager or secretary. But CA 2006 also speaks of the auditor of
a company as a person who 'holds office' (see, for example, s 487(1)). The probable explanation
for not including auditors in the list in s 1121(2) is that, although an auditor appointed to report
on a company's annual accounts as required by s 495 is an officer (*R v Shacter* [1960] 2 QB 252;
Mutual Reinsurance Co Ltd v Peat Marwick Mitchell and Co [1997] 1 BCLC 1), it is possible for a
company to appoint other people called 'auditors' (for example, internal auditors or people who
conduct transfer audits in connection with registration of shareholdings) who are not officers of
the company.

On the other hand, managers are listed in s 1121(2), but this does not mean that everyone in a
company whose job title includes the word 'manager' is covered, because there is a general principle that a provision fixing a manager of a company with criminal responsibility should be interpreted narrowly to apply only to a person who has the management of the whole affairs of the
company, is in a position of real authority and has the power and responsibility to decide corporate
policy and strategy (*R v Boal* [1992] QB 591).

In other contexts, s 1173(1) says that, when the Act refers to the officers of a body corporate,
this includes a director, manager or secretary, and 'manager' here may have a wider meaning.
For example, s 1132 applies when there is shown to be reasonable cause to believe that a person
has, while an officer of a company, committed an offence in connection with the management
of the company's affairs. If that fact is shown, the court makes an order for the production and
inspection of documents for the purpose of investigating and obtaining evidence of the offence. In
Re a Company [1980] Ch 138 it was held that a departmental manager of a company was covered
by s 1132 as a manager who was an officer of the company. Shaw LJ said, at p 144, that for the
purposes of s 1132:

> The expression 'manager' should not be too narrowly construed. It is not to be equated with a managing
> or other director or a general manager. As I see it, any person who in the affairs of the company exercises a
> supervisory control which reflects the general policy of the company for the time being or which is related
> to the general administration of the company is in the sphere of management. He need not be a member of
> the board of directors. He need not be subject to specific instructions from the board.

17.3 COMPANY SECRETARIES

17.3.1 APPOINTMENT AND QUALIFICATIONS

Every *public company* must appoint a secretary (CA 2006, s 271). An application for registration of
a public company must give particulars of the person who is to be its first secretary (or the persons
who are to be its first joint secretaries) (s 12(1)(c)) and the person or persons so named take office
when the company is registered (s 16(1) and (6)). The Secretary of State may, under s 272, direct

a public company which appears not to have a secretary to appoint one within a specified period of one to three months, and there are criminal sanctions for failure to comply with a direction (s 272(6) and (7)).

Section 273 imposes a duty on the directors of a public company to ensure that the company's secretary is adequately qualified and experienced, and lists specific qualifications which a public company secretary should have.

For premium listed companies, the UK Corporate Governance Code (see **15.2.2**) states (supporting principles B.5):

> Under the direction of the chairman, the company secretary's responsibilities include ensuring good information flows within the board and its committees and between senior management and non-executive directors, as well as facilitating induction and assisting with professional development as required.
>
> The company secretary should be responsible for advising the board through the chairman on all governance matters.

And para B.5.1 says:

> All directors should have access to the advice and services of the company secretary, who is responsible to the board for ensuring that board procedures are complied with. Both the appointment and removal of the company secretary should be a matter for the board as a whole.

It is not mandatory for a private company to have a secretary, but a private company may appoint one (CA 2006, s 270). Accordingly, when applying to register a private company, it is only necessary to notify details of the first secretary if it is intended that there should be one (s 12(1)(b)). If a private company does not have a secretary, any requirement to give something to, send it to or serve it on the company by its secretary is satisfied by giving it to, sending it to or serving it on the company (s 270(3)(a)), and anything which must be done by or to the secretary may be done by or to a director or a person authorised for the purpose by the directors (s 270(3)(b)).

If the office of secretary is vacant, or for any reason the secretary is not capable of acting, then, under s 274, an assistant or deputy secretary may act or the directors can authorise any officer of the company to act in place of the secretary generally or specially.

Any provision requiring or authorising a thing to be done by or to a director and the secretary is not satisfied by being done by or to the same person acting both as director and as, or in place of, the secretary (s 280).

17.3.2 REGISTER AND NOTIFICATION TO COMPANIES HOUSE

Every private company which has a secretary and every public company must keep a register of its secretaries available for inspection (CA 2006, s 275; see **4.4**). Private companies will be able to keep this register at Companies House instead (see **4.4.2.9**). In respect of each individual who is a secretary or joint secretary of the company, the register must state the individual's Christian name or forename, and surname (and former names used for business purposes, excluding names changed or disused before the individual became 16 or more than 20 years previously) and his or her service address (s 277). For an individual who is a peer or is usually known by a title, the register may state the title instead of, or in addition to, his Christian name or forename and surname, or either of them, and it is not necessary to give the name by which he or she was known before the adoption of, or succession to, the title, unless it is not a British title (s 277(2) and (4)(a)).

An individual's service address may be stated to be 'The company's registered office'. Unlike the position with directors, there is no register at all of company secretaries' residential addresses.

If a corporation (or a partnership which has corporate personality) is a secretary or joint secretary, the register must state the corporate name and registered or principal office (s 278(1)(a) and (b)). Where all the partners in a firm are joint secretaries, the register may give the name and principal office of the firm instead of details of each individual partner (s 278(2)). For a corporate secretary registered in an EEA State, the registry in which it is registered and its registration number must be given.

An application to register a new company must give, for the person who is to be the company's first secretary (or the persons who are to be its first joint secretaries), the information about them which will be required to be entered in the company's register of secretaries (s 12(1) and (2)(b)). A company is required to notify Companies House of any change in its secretary or of any change in the particulars in the register of secretaries within 14 days of the change; and, if the change is the appointment of a new secretary or joint secretary, the notice must contain a statement by the company that the person has consented to act as secretary (s 276).

17.3.3 DUTIES

The company secretary performs many of the administrative duties imposed upon companies, for instance delivering documents to Companies House, but CA 2006 does not actually require any specific duties to be performed by the secretary. In *Re Maidstone Buildings Provisions Ltd* [1971] 1 WLR 1085, Pennycuick V-C said:

> So far as the position of a secretary as such is concerned, it is established beyond all question that a secretary, while merely performing the duties appropriate to the office of secretary, is not concerned in the management [of] the company. Equally I think he is not concerned in carrying on the business of the company. On the other hand, it is equally well established, indeed it is obvious, that a person who holds the office of secretary may in some other capacity be concerned in the management of the company's business.

The Cadbury Committee saw the company secretary as a kind of impartial civil servant offering advice to the board on procedures and responsibilities. It said (***Report of the Committee on the Financial Aspects of Corporate Governance*** (London: Gee, 1992), para 4.25):

> The company secretary has a key role to play in ensuring that board procedures are both followed and regularly reviewed. The chairman and the board will look to the company secretary for guidance on what their responsibilities are under the rules and regulations to which they are subject and on how those responsibilities should be discharged. All directors should have access to the advice and services of the company secretary.... It should be standard practice for the company secretary to administer, attend and prepare minutes of board meetings.

17.4 AUDITORS

17.4.1 APPOINTMENT AND REAPPOINTMENT

17.4.1.1 General requirement

Every company must appoint an auditor or auditors for each financial year, unless the directors reasonably resolve otherwise on the ground that audited accounts are unlikely to be required (CA 2006, ss 485(1) (private companies) and 489(1) (public companies)). By s 475, a company's annual accounts for a financial year must be audited unless, for that financial year, the company is a small company (see **9.4.6**; public companies cannot be small companies) or a dormant company (see **9.4.7**). There are also non-profit-making companies in the public sector which do not appoint auditors because they are audited by the Comptroller and Auditor General (or equivalent officers in Scotland and Northern Ireland) (ss 482 and 483).

A person appointed auditor as required by s 485(1) or s 489(1) is called a 'statutory auditor' (s 1210(1)). Where a partnership firm is appointed the appointment is of the firm and not of the partners even if the firm does not have legal personality (s 1216(2)).

17.4.1.2 Private companies

For a private company, CA 2006, s 485(2), defines the 'period for appointing auditors' as the period of 28 days beginning with either the end of the period for sending out copies of the company's annual accounts and reports (see **9.6.1.1**) or, if it is earlier, the day on which they are actually sent out.

During a period for appointing auditors, the members may, by ordinary resolution, appoint an auditor for the next financial year (s 485(4)(a)). An auditor for the first financial year can be appointed by the directors at any time before the company's first period for appointing auditors (s 485(3)(a)), though the members may make the appointment, by ordinary resolution, if the directors do not (s 485(4)(c)). An auditor ceases to hold office at the end of the next period for appointing auditors, unless reappointed (s 487(1)(b)). By s 487(2), an auditor is deemed to be reappointed, unless:

(a) a replacement is appointed; or

(b) the auditor was appointed by the directors; or

(c) the company's articles require actual reappointment; or

(d) notice is served by members under s 488.

The directors of a private company also have a power to appoint an auditor after a period during which the company was exempt from audit (s 485(3)(b)) or to fill a casual vacancy (s 485(3)(c)). The term 'casual vacancy' means a vacancy occurring otherwise than by expiration of the term of office (*Munster v Cammell Co* (1882) 21 ChD 183 at p 187).

Under s 488, members holding at least the requisite percentage of votes can serve notice that a private company's auditor is not to be deemed to be reappointed at the end of the next period for appointing auditors. The notice must be received before the end of the accounting reference period after which the reappointment would be deemed to take effect. The requisite percentage is 5 per cent or such lower percentage as is specified in the company's articles. It is a percentage of the total voting rights of all members who would be entitled to vote on a resolution that the auditor should not be reappointed.

17.4.1.3 Public companies

The auditor for a public company's first financial year may be appointed by the directors at any time before the first accounts meeting (see **9.6.3**) (CA 2006, s 489(3)(a)), though the members may make the appointment, by ordinary resolution, if the directors do not (s 489(4)(c)). Thereafter, the auditor for each financial year must be appointed by the members, by ordinary resolution, at the accounts meeting at which the company's annual accounts and reports for the previous financial year are laid. An auditor of a public company ceases to hold office at the end of the next accounts meeting following appointment, unless reappointed (s 491(1)(b)), but there is no provision for deemed reappointment as there is for private companies.

As with private companies (see **17.4.1.2**), the directors of a public company may appoint an auditor after a period during which the company was exempt from audit (s 489(3)(b)) or to fill a casual vacancy (s 489(3)(c)).

17.4.1.4 Public interest entities

The statutory audit of public interest entities is governed by Regulation (EU) No 537/2014 (the Audit Regulation). This is EU legislation with direct effect in the United Kingdom and the rest of the EU (it has not yet been extended to the rest of the EEA), but detailed implementation is made by provisions of CA 2006 and other UK legislation. Public interest entities (PIEs) are entities whose transferable securities are admitted to trading on a regulated market anywhere in the EU (see **7.3.4.3**) plus credit institutions and insurance undertakings (Directive 2006/43/EC, art 2(13), applied by Regulation (EU) No 537/2014, art 3).

In addition to the rules in **17.4.1.2** or **17.4.1.3** as the case may be, the following rules apply to the appointment of auditors of a PIE, unless it is a small or medium-sized enterprise (defined for this purpose by Directive 2003/71/EC, art 2(1)(f)). At least once every ten years, a PIE must carry out a selection procedure in accordance with Regulation 537/2014, art 16(3), to choose an auditor (or auditors) to propose for appointment by the members. The selection procedure is to be carried out by the audit committee if there is one, otherwise by the directors. In the other nine out of ten years, the audit committee or directors can propose the reappointment of the current auditor. An auditor of a PIE cannot serve for more than ten consecutive financial years (the 'maximum engagement period'), unless there is, within those ten years, a selection procedure which results in a reappointment, but even if this happens there is a maximum term of 20 years. An auditor who has served for the maximum engagement period cannot be reappointed until four years have elapsed. These rules are in Regulation 537/2014, arts 16 and 17, as implemented, in excruciating detail, by CA 2006, ss 485A, 485B and 485C (private companies), 489A, 489B and 489C (public companies) and 494ZA. The rules apply in relation to financial years beginning on or after 17 June 2016 and there are transitional provisions in s 494ZA which may apply up to 2023. The selection procedure is usually known as tendering. See Financial Reporting Council (FRC), *Audit Tenders. Notes on Best Practice* (February 2017).

17.4.1.5 Contractual restrictions on who may be appointed

A contractual term which restricts a company to choosing an auditor from a specified category or list is of no effect (Regulation (EU) No 537/2014, art 16(6) (PIEs); SI 2016/649, reg 12 (other companies)). Such terms used to be very common in loan and other financing agreements.

17.4.1.6 Failure to appoint

If a company fails to appoint an auditor for a financial year for which one should be appointed, it must give notice to the Secretary of State within one week of the end of the time during which an appointment must be made (CA 2006, ss 486(2) (private companies) and 490(2) (public companies)). There are criminal sanctions for failure to give notice (ss 486(3) and (4) and 490(3) and (4)). The Secretary of State has power (whether or not the notice is given) to appoint one or more persons to fill the vacancy (ss 486(1) and 490(1)).

17.4.2 ELIGIBILITY FOR APPOINTMENT AS A COMPANY AUDITOR

17.4.2.1 Approval and public oversight

Directive 2006/43/EC requires that a statutory audit can be carried out only by approved auditors (art 3(1)), who must be subject to public oversight (art 32(2)). Each member State must designate competent authorities responsible for approval (art 3(2)). In the United Kingdom, public oversight is provided by the Financial Reporting Council (FRC). In order to be eligible for appointment as a statutory auditor, an individual or firm must, by CA 2006, s 1212(1), be:

(a) a member of a recognised supervisory body (RSB); and

(b) eligible for appointment under the rules of that body.

'Firm' means any entity, whether or not a legal person, that is not an individual (s 1261(1)). An individual or firm is treated as a member of a supervisory body if subject to its rules in seeking appointment or acting as a company auditor, whether or not a member of the body (s 1217(2)).

A supervisory body is 'recognised' by means of a recognition order made under CA 2006, sch 10, by the FRC (to which the Secretary of State's functions have been delegated by SI 2012/1741, arts 2 and 7). The recognised supervisory bodies are the Institute of Chartered Accountants in England and Wales, the Institute of Chartered Accountants of Scotland, the Association of Chartered Certified Accountants, the Association of Authorised Public Accountants and Chartered Accountants Ireland.

17.4.2.2 Registration

Directive 2006/43/EC requires member States to create a public register of statutory auditors and audit firms (arts 15 to 20). The UK audit register is at **www.auditregister.org.uk**.

It is an offence for a person whose name does not appear on the register to describe himself as a registered auditor or so to hold himself out as to indicate, or be reasonably understood to indicate, that he is a registered auditor (CA 2006, s 1250(2); penalty in s 1250(6); diligence defence in s 1250(8)).

17.4.2.3 Ineligibility for lack of independence

A person is, by CA 2006, s 1214(1), (2) and (3), ineligible for appointment as auditor of a company if:

(a) an officer or employee of the company; or

(b) a partner or employee of such a person, or a partnership of which such a person is a partner; or

(c) ineligible by virtue of (a) or (b) for appointment as auditor of any associated undertaking of the company.

So that two partners can be appointed auditors of the same company, it is provided that, for the purposes of this provision, an auditor of a company is not to be regarded as an officer or employee of the company (s 1214(5)).

By s 1214(6), an 'associated undertaking' of a company is:

(a) a parent undertaking or subsidiary undertaking of the company; or

(b) a subsidiary undertaking of any parent undertaking of the company.

17.4.2.4 Effect of ineligibility

No person may act as a company auditor if ineligible for appointment to the office (CA 2006, s 1213(1)). A person who acts as company auditor though ineligible commits an offence triable either way (s 1213(3) and (4)), though it is a defence to show that one did not know and had no reason to believe that one was ineligible for appointment (s 1213(8)).

Sections 1248 and 1249 make provisions for requiring a company whose auditing has been conducted by a person who was ineligible for appointment to have the audit work reviewed or done again by an eligible person.

17.4.3 REMOVAL, RESIGNATION AND REPLACEMENT

A company may, by ordinary resolution, at any time, remove an auditor from office (CA 2006, s 510(1)). Special notice (see **14.8.10**) must be given of such a resolution (s 511(1)) and the company must send a copy of the notice to the auditor sought to be removed (s 511(2)). The auditor is entitled to make representations in writing (not exceeding a reasonable length), which the company must send to every member of the company to whom notice of the meeting is sent, though if the representations are received by the company too late for distribution to members, the auditor may (in addition to a right under s 502(2) to be heard at the meeting) require that the written representations be read out at the meeting (s 511(3), (4) and (5)). Because of the auditor's right under s 511 to make representations to members it is doubtful whether a decision to dismiss an auditor arrived at by unanimous agreement without meeting could be effective. The procedure provided to private companies by ss 288 to 300 for written resolutions cannot be used to dismiss an auditor under s 510 (s 288(2)(b)).

Notice of removal of an auditor at a general meeting must, subject to criminal sanctions, be given to Companies House within 14 days (s 512).

The policy of CA 2006 is that an auditor of a company who is critical of the company has a statutory right to bring that criticism to the attention of members. Dismissing an auditor cannot be used as a means of silencing such criticism. The provisions are elaborately detailed to deal with a variety of different circumstances in which an auditor may cease to hold office. They make a distinction between 'public interest' and 'non-public interest' companies. A company is a public interest company if it is a public interest entity (see **17.4.1.4**) (CA 2006, s 519A(1) and (2)).

An auditor of a company who is ceasing to hold office must send to the company a statement of reasons for leaving office (s 519(1)). If the company is a non-public interest company, this statement is not required if the auditor's term of office has simply expired at the end of a period for appointing auditors (private company, see **17.4.1.2**) or at the end of an accounts meeting (public company, see **17.4.1.3**) (s 519(2) and (2A)). The statement is also not required in the case of a non-public interest company if the reasons for ceasing office are all exempt reasons specified in s 519A(3) (these are all technical reasons such as the company becoming exempt from audit) and there are no matters that the auditor considers need to be brought to the attention of members or creditors of the company (s 519(2) and (2B)). Where there are matters connected with the auditor's ceasing to hold office that the auditor considers need to be brought to the attention of members or creditors of the company, the statement of reasons must include details of those matters (s 519(3A)). In the case of a non-public interest company, there must be a statement that there are no such matters, if that is the case (because that will excuse the company from circulating the statement) (s 519(3B)). There are criminal sanctions for failure to send a notice (s 519(5) and (7)), but there is a due diligence defence in s 519(6).

Unless, in the case of a non-public interest company, there is a s 519(3B) statement that there are no circumstances to be drawn to members' and creditors' attention, (a) the company must send a copy of the statement of reasons to every person who, under s 423, is entitled to be sent copies of the accounts, or apply to the court (s 520; there are criminal sanctions, subject to a due diligence defence), and (b) the auditor may requisition a general meeting to consider the circumstances (s 518) and, after waiting 21 days to allow for an application by the company to the court, must send a copy of the statement of reasons to Companies House (s 521). An application to the court may claim that the auditor is using the provisions of s 519 to secure needless publicity for defamatory matter. If the court agrees, it must direct that copies of the statement need not be sent out, and the company must instead send a statement setting out the effect of the court's order (s 520(4)).

In addition to sending a statement of reasons to the company in accordance with s 519, an auditor ceasing to hold office must send a copy of it to the FRC (ss 522 and 525; SI 2012/1741, arts 2 and 8).

If an auditor of a company ceases to hold office before the expiry of a term of office, and not for an exempt reason, the company too must inform the FRC and provide a copy of the auditor's statement of reasons, if there is one, or its own statement of the reasons for the auditor ceasing to hold office, where it does not agree with the auditor's statement (CA 2006, s 523). The FRC may in turn inform its Conduct Committee and the Secretary of State of the fact of an auditor ceasing to hold office, sending them, if it thinks fit, a copy of the auditor's and the company's statements of reasons (s 524).

When an auditor of a quoted company ceases to hold office, s 527 entitles members holding at least 5 per cent of the total voting rights to require the company to publish on a website their statement relating to circumstances connected with the auditor's departure which they propose to raise at the next accounts meeting.

See also **18.6.8.9**.

An auditor of a company may resign by sending a notice to that effect to the company (s 516(1)). However, where the company is a public interest company, the notice is not effective unless it is accompanied by the statement required by s 519 (s 516(2)).

A person who has been appointed auditor of a company but who becomes ineligible to hold that office must thereupon vacate the office, and must forthwith give written notice to the company of vacating the office because of ineligibility (s 1213(2)). Failure to do so is an offence triable either way (s 1213(3) and (4)) though it is a defence to show that one did not know and had no reason to believe that one had become ineligible for appointment (s 1213(8)).

If there is a casual vacancy in the office of auditor of a company, any surviving or continuing auditor may continue to act while the vacancy continues (s 526).

By s 515, special notice (see **14.8.10**) is required of a resolution at a general meeting of a company appointing a new auditor to replace an auditor whose term of office is expiring or who has left office before the term expired (the 'outgoing auditor'). A copy of the notice must be sent by the company forthwith to both the outgoing auditor and the person proposed to be appointed (s 515(3)). The outgoing auditor has a right to require representations to be circulated, subject to a court order if the representations are defamatory (s 515(4) to (7)). For a private company appointing a new auditor by written resolution, a copy of the resolution must be sent to the outgoing auditor (s 514). These provisions do not apply if the auditor resigned or has been removed from office by a resolution of the company.

The court may remove from office an auditor of a public interest company if satisfied that there are proper grounds for doing so (s 511A). Divergence of opinions on accounting treatments or audit procedures are not proper grounds for removal (s 511A(6)). An application to the court for removal under s 511A can be made only by the FRC (s 511A(2)) or by members of the company representing not less than 5 per cent of the voting rights at general meeting or 5 per cent of the nominal value of the company's share capital (s 511A(3) to (5)).

17.4.4 REMUNERATION

The remuneration of a company's auditor appointed by the members must be fixed by the members by ordinary resolution, or in such manner as the members may by ordinary resolution determine (CA 2006, s 492(1)). The remuneration of a company's auditor appointed by the directors must be fixed by the directors (s 492(2)). The Secretary of State fixes the remuneration of any auditor he or she appoints (s 492(3)).

Every large and medium-sized company must disclose, in a note to its annual accounts, the fee for auditing those accounts (s 494; SI 2008/489, regs 4(1)–(3) and 5(1)(a), (2) and (3)).

17.4.5 INTEGRITY AND INDEPENDENCE

17.4.5.1 General requirements

Directive 2006/46/EC requires member States to ensure the integrity and independence of statutory auditors in various respects (arts 21 to 25). CA 2006, sch 10, para 9, places these requirements on recognised supervisory bodies, mostly in wider terms than those used in the Directive.

The FRC has issued Ethical Standard 2016 Integrity, Objectivity and Independence.

17.4.5.2 Non-audit work

One point that has been of significant concern for some time is that the accountancy firms that act as company auditors also provide many other accountancy and financial and management consultancy services to the companies for which they are auditors. There can be suspicion that an auditor who is given a lot of remunerative non-audit work by a company's management will be reluctant to find fault with the management in the audit. Directive 2006/46/EC requires member States to ensure that adequate rules are in place which provide that fees for statutory audits are not influenced or determined by the provision of additional services to the audited entity and that they cannot be based on any form of contingency (art 25). Recognised supervisory bodies are required to have such rules by CA 2006, sch 10, para 9(1)(e). In addition, every large company (see **9.4.2**) must disclose, in a note to its annual accounts, all remuneration receivable by its auditor for the supply of services to the company, its subsidiaries and associated pension schemes, in respect of the period to which the accounts relate (SI 2008/489, reg 5). This includes remuneration receivable by associates of the auditor, as defined in SI 2008/489, sch 1. The payments must be analysed by type of service in accordance with SI 2008/489, sch 2A.

If a premium listed company's auditor provides non-audit services, the company's annual financial report should contain an explanation of how auditor objectivity and independence are safeguarded (UK Corporate Governance Code, para C.3.8).

For public interest entities (PIEs, see **17.4.1.4**), Regulation (EU) No 537/2014, art 5, prohibits the auditor of a company from supplying it (or its parent company or companies it controls) with any of a long list of specified non-audit services. Article 4 limits earnings from permitted non-audit services to 70 per cent of the audit fee (averaged over three years) and prohibits contingent fees. These rules are amplified in the FRC's Ethical Standard 2016 Integrity, Objectivity and Independence, s 5. The FRC can grant an exemption from the 70 per cent limit in exceptional circumstances (Regulation 537/2014, art 4(2); SI 2016/649, reg 13).

CA 2006, s 493, has given the Secretary of State a new power to make regulations requiring disclosure of auditors' terms of appointment and remuneration (engagement letters) (s 493). It is not intended to exercise this power yet.

17.4.5.3 Audit committees

Although a company's auditor is supposed to be appointed by, and is required to report to, the members of the company, in practice the auditor's only communication is with the directors. It is potentially easy for an auditor to adopt the board's attitudes to the company and to overlook negligence and fraud which the directors ignore or are party to. Directive 2006/43/EC requires every public interest entity (see **17.4.1.4**) to have an audit committee (art 39(1)), which must (art 39(6)):

(a) inform the board of directors of the outcome of the statutory audit and explain how the statutory audit contributed to the integrity of financial reporting and what the role of the audit committee was in that process;

(b) monitor the financial reporting process and submit recommendations or proposals to ensure its integrity;

(c) monitor the effectiveness of the company's internal control, internal audit and risk management systems;

(d) monitor the statutory audit;

(e) review and monitor the auditor's independence and the auditor's provision of non-audit services;

(f) be responsible for the procedure for the selection of the company's statutory auditor and recommend the statutory auditor to be appointed (see **17.4.1.4**).

Article 39 is transposed by rules in the FCA Handbook, DTR 7.1.1R to 7.1.5R.

Premium listed companies are subject to the UK Corporate Governance Code (see **15.2.2**). This requires the board of a listed company to establish an audit committee (see **15.8.7**) of independent non-executive directors, at least one of whom has recent and relevant financial experience (Code provision C.3.1). Code provision C.3.2 requires the audit committee, among other things, to monitor the integrity of the company's financial statements, review its internal financial controls and internal audit, make recommendations on the appointment of external auditors and review their independence, objectivity and effectiveness. These Code provisions are supported by the lengthy FRC Guidance on Audit Committees (revised April 2016).

17.4.6 CONTENTS OF AN AUDITOR'S REPORT

The principal function of a company's auditor is to report on the accounts for a financial year of the company, as described in **9.5.5** (CA 2006, s 495). It is sufficient if they deliver their report to the company secretary: they are not required personally to ensure it is supplied to the members (*Re Allen, Craig and Co (London) Ltd* [1934] Ch 483).

An auditor's report must include an introduction which identifies the annual accounts which have been audited and the financial reporting framework (Companies Act or IAS, see **9.5.7.4**) that has been applied in their preparation (s 495(2)(a) to (c)). The introduction must describe the scope of the audit and identify the auditing standards in accordance with which it was conducted (s 495(2)(d)). The report must state clearly whether, in the auditor's opinion, the annual accounts give a true and fair view (s 495(3)(a)) and have been properly prepared in accordance with CA 2006 and (if they are IAS accounts) Regulation (EC) No 1606/2002, art 4 (CA 2006, s 495(3)(b)). The report must be either unqualified or qualified (s 495(4)(a)). It must refer to any matters to which the auditor wishes to draw attention, by way of emphasis, without qualifying the report (s 495(4)(b)). Such a reference is called an emphasis of matter paragraph. The report 'must include a statement on any material uncertainty relating to events that may cast significant doubt about the company's ability to continue to adopt the going concern basis of accounting' (s 495(4)(c)). A company's accounts prepared on a going concern basis show the company's financial position on the assumption that it will continue in business for the foreseeable future, which is at least 12 months from the end of the financial year reported on (IAS 1 Presentation of Financial Statements, paras 25 and 26).

An auditor who expresses doubts about certain matters in the accounts must state whether there is doubt about the legality of the dividend proposed in the directors' report (see **10.3.8**). If the requirements of the regulations under s 412 concerning disclosure of payments to directors (see **15.9.3.1** to **15.9.3.3**) have not been complied with, the auditor must include in the report, so far as reasonably practicable, a statement giving the required particulars (s 498(4)).

An auditor must report on the strategic report (if any), the directors' report, and any separate corporate governance statement (ss 496 and 497A; see **9.9.1**).

An auditor's report must state, if it is so, that, in the auditor's opinion:

(a) adequate accounting records have not been kept (s 498(2)(a));

(b) returns adequate for the audit have not been received from branches not visited by the auditor (s 498(2)(a)); or

(c) the company's individual accounts are not in agreement with the accounting records and returns (s 498(2)(b)).

The report must also state, if it is so, that the auditor has failed to obtain all the information and explanations which, to the best of the auditor's knowledge and belief, are necessary for the purposes of the audit (s 498(3)).

An auditor must make a statement in the report if, in the auditor's opinion, the directors have wrongly taken advantage of the small companies regime or the small companies exemption in respect of the strategic report or directors' report (s 498(5)).

In a report on annual accounts of a quoted company, the auditor must:

(a) report on the auditable part of the directors' remuneration report (see **15.9.3.4**) (s 497); and

(b) state whether, in the auditor's opinion, the auditable part of the directors' remuneration report has been prepared in accordance with CA 2006 (s 497(1)(b)) and state if it is not in agreement with the accounting records and returns (s 498(2)(c)).

A qualified auditor's report and any qualified statement made under s 496 must be repeated in the supplementary material accompanying the strategic report when it is sent out instead of the full accounts and reports (s 426A(2)(c) and (d); see **9.6.1.3**). Non-statutory accounts must state whether the auditor's report on the statutory accounts was qualified or unqualified, or referred to any matters to which the auditor drew attention or contained a statement under s 498(2) or (3) (s 435(1)(c); see **9.6.7**).

An auditor's report must state the name of the auditor and be signed and dated (s 503(1)). Where the auditor is a partnership firm, the report must be signed by the senior statutory auditor, in his or her own name, for and on behalf of the auditor (s 503(3)). No additional civil liability will be incurred by the senior statutory auditor merely because of signing the report (s 504(3)). The senior statutory auditor must be identified in accordance with guidance issued by the Auditing Practices Board in its Bulletin 2008/6 (s 504(1); SI 2012/1741, arts 2, 15 and 16(2)). The name of a company's auditor or of its senior statutory auditor can be withheld if the company has adopted a resolution to that effect on the ground that disclosure would create, or be likely to create, a serious risk that the auditor, senior statutory auditor or any other person, would be subject to violence or intimidation (CA 2006, s 506). Notice of the resolution must be given to the Secretary of State (s 506(2)(b)).

17.4.7 INVESTIGATIVE POWERS

In order to prepare an auditor's report, investigations must be carried out which are sufficient to enable the auditor to form an opinion on whether adequate accounting records have been kept by the company and on whether the accounts for the financial year and the directors' remuneration report (if the company is a quoted company) agree with those accounting records (CA 2006, s 498(1)). The report must state any reservations the auditor has on these matters (s 498(2)).

An auditor of a company has a right of access, at all times, to the company's books, accounts and vouchers, in whatever form they are held (s 499(1)(a)).

An auditor of a company is entitled to require persons listed in s 499(2) to provide whatever information and explanations the auditor thinks necessary for the performance of his or her duties as an auditor (s 499(1)(b)). The persons listed in s 499(2) are:

(a) any officer or employee of the company;

(b) any person holding or accountable for any of the company's books, accounts or vouchers;

(c) any subsidiary undertaking of the company which is a body corporate incorporated in the United Kingdom;

(d) any officer, employee or auditor of any such subsidiary undertaking or any person holding or accountable for any books, accounts or vouchers of any such subsidiary undertaking;

(e) any person who fell within any of paragraphs (a) to (d) at a time to which the information or explanations required by the auditor relates or relate.

It is an offence to fail to comply with such a requirement without delay (s 501(3) and (5)), unless it can be shown that it was not reasonably practicable to comply (s 501(3)). It is an offence, for which a prison sentence of up to two years may be imposed, to provide, knowingly or recklessly, information or explanations which are misleading, false or deceptive in a material particular (s 501(1) and (2)).

An auditor of a parent company, which has a subsidiary undertaking which is not a body corporate incorporated in the United Kingdom, may require the parent company to obtain information or explanations from the undertaking and its officers, employees, auditors, etc (s 500(1) and (2)) and the parent company must take all such steps as are reasonably open to it to obtain the required information or explanations (s 500(3)). It is an offence under s 501(4) to fail to comply with s 500.

If an auditor has failed to obtain all the information and explanations which, to the best of the auditor's knowledge and belief, are necessary for the purposes of the audit, that fact must be stated in the auditor's report (s 498(3)). Every director of a company must make a statement in the directors' report concerning provision of information to the company's auditor (s 418; see **9.9.4.2**).

17.5 AUDITORS' LIABILITY

17.5.1 AUDITOR'S LIABILITY TO THE COMPANY FOR NEGLIGENCE

The contract under which the work of a company's auditor is performed is with the company as a separate person. Like anyone who renders professional services for reward, a company's auditor owes the company an implied contractual duty of care in and about the manner in which the audit is performed (*Equitable Life Assurance Society v Ernst and Young* [2003] EWCA Civ 1114, [2003] 2 BCLC 603, at [108]). Auditors also have a liability in tort for negligent misstatement (see **17.5.2** to **17.5.4**).

The nature of an auditor's duty of care in the performance of an audit was considered by Lopes LJ in *Re Kingston Cotton Mill Co (No 2)* [1896] 2 Ch 279 at pp 288–9:

> It is the duty of an auditor to bring to bear on the work he has to perform that skill, care, and caution which a reasonably competent, careful, and cautious auditor would use. What is reasonable skill, care, and caution must depend on the particular circumstances of each case. An auditor is not bound to be a detective, or, as was said, to approach his work with suspicion or with a foregone conclusion that there is something wrong. He is a watchdog, but not a bloodhound. He is justified in believing tried servants of the company in whom confidence is placed by the company. He is entitled to assume that they are honest, and to rely upon their representations, provided he takes reasonable care. If there is anything calculated to excite suspicion he should probe it to the bottom; but in the absence of anything of that kind he is only bound to be reasonably cautious and careful.
>
> [An auditor] does not guarantee the discovery of all fraud.

As Lord Denning put it in *Fomento (Sterling Area) Ltd v Selsdon Fountain Pen Co Ltd* [1958] 1 WLR 45, at p 61:

> An auditor is not to be confined to the mechanics of checking vouchers and making arithmetical computations. He is not to be written off as a professional 'adder-upper and subtractor'. His vital task is to take care to see that errors are not made, be they errors of computation, or errors of omission or commission, or downright untruths. To perform this task properly he must come to it with an inquiring mind—not suspicious of dishonesty, I agree—but suspecting that someone may have made a mistake somewhere and that a check must be made to ensure that there has been none.

In *Barings plc v Coopers and Lybrand* [1997] 1 BCLC 427 Leggatt LJ said, at p 435:

> The primary responsibility for safeguarding a company's assets and preventing errors and defalcations rests with the directors. But material irregularities, and a fortiori fraud, will normally be brought to light by sound audit procedures, one of which is the practice of pointing out weaknesses in internal controls. An auditor's task is so to conduct the audit as to make it probable that material misstatements in financial documents will be detected.

Auditors can refute a charge of negligence by showing that they have acted in accordance with a practice accepted as proper by a body of responsible and skilled professional opinion (*Lloyd Cheyham and Co Ltd v Littlejohn and Co* [1987] BCLC 303).

A company auditor's duty of care is owed to the company in the interests of its shareholders (*Stone and Rolls Ltd v Moore Stephens* [2009] UKHL 39, [2009] AC 1391, per Lord Philips of Worth Matravers at [19]). The scope of an auditor's duty of care in tort encompasses anything which the company in general meeting could, having regard to the statutory scheme for annual accounts and audit, be expected to do on the strength of the auditor's report (*Johnson v Gore Wood and Co* [2003] EWCA Civ 1728, [2003] NPC 147, per Arden LJ at [98]).

If a company's auditor performs an audit negligently, it is the company that is the proper claimant to sue for loss: members of the company are not proper claimants. In **Caparo Industries plc v Dickman** [1990] 2 AC 605, Lord Bridge of Harwich said, at p 626:

> The shareholders of a company have a collective interest in the company's proper management and in so far as a negligent failure of the auditor to report accurately on the state of the company's finances deprives the shareholders of the opportunity to exercise their powers in general meeting to call the directors to book and to ensure that errors in management are corrected, the shareholders ought to be entitled to a remedy. But in practice no problem arises in this regard since the interest of the shareholders in the proper management of the company's affairs is indistinguishable from the interest of the company itself and any loss suffered by the shareholders, eg, by the negligent failure of the auditor to discover and expose a misappropriation of funds by a director of the company, will be recouped by a claim against the auditors in the name of the company, not by individual shareholders.

In a number of reported cases the problem has been to establish what harm was actually caused by auditors' negligence, and this calls into question what is meant by causation in the law of negligence. In *Berg Sons and Co Ltd v Adams* [1993] BCLC 1045, the auditors of a company were found to have carried out their audit negligently in that they failed to state in their report that an important part of the company's assets consisted of bills payable by a person whose creditworthiness could not be evaluated by the auditors. However, this fact was well known to Mr Golechha, who was the only person beneficially interested in the company's shares and who was its only active director. Accordingly, the company had not suffered from the auditors' negligence (because Mr Golechha was identified with the company—see **19.8**) and so was entitled only to nominal damages. In *Galoo Ltd v Bright Grahame Murray* [1994] 1 WLR 1360 it was alleged that a company's auditors had negligently failed to recognise that its accounts were erroneous in showing that it was solvent when in fact it was insolvent and that the company would have ceased trading had it been known that it was insolvent. The company tried to sue the auditors for the losses incurred in continuing to trade when insolvent. It was held that the auditors had not caused these losses: failure to report that the company was insolvent merely gave the company an opportunity to continue trading and incur losses. The Court of Appeal said that its decision was based on common sense, but, speaking extra-curially, Lord Hoffmann said that the real question in the case was whether the scope of the auditors' duty under the law of negligence extended to protecting persons from unwittingly extending credit to the company when it was insolvent (*Common Sense and Causing Loss: Lecture to the Chancery Bar Association* (15 June 1999), **www.chba.org.uk**). A similar claim was struck out in **Bank of Credit and Commerce International (Overseas) Ltd v Price Waterhouse** [1999] BCC 351, in which Laddie J pointed out, at p 371, that an auditor of a company could not be regarded as insuring it against all possible future trading losses. His Lordship said, at p 369:

> The skill [an auditor] offers and for which he is paid is the skill in looking at the company's accounts and the underlying information on which they are or should be based and telling the shareholders whether the accounts give a true and fair view of the company's financial position. He is not in possession of facts nor qualified to express a view as to how the business should be run, in the sense of what business to undertake,

what prices to charge, what lines of credit to extend and so on. Not only does he not normally have the necessary expertise but those are areas in respect of which his advice is not sought. When the company engages an auditor, it is not seeking his help in steering the management into making better management decisions.

However, in *Equitable Life Assurance Society v Ernst and Young* the Court of Appeal said, at [129]:

> When auditors undertake for reward to perform services . . . and are found to be negligent in the way they perform those services we do not understand the law to require the client to ask for specific advice before it can recover damages for the foreseeable losses it later suffers.

It was held that a client could argue that if it had had the correct information from the auditors about its financial position, it would have asked them for advice which would have prevented it from acting in a way that incurred loss, and so that loss would be recoverable.

A company may not sue its auditor for negligently failing to detect that the company itself has committed a fraud, if all persons beneficially interested in the company's shares were complicit in the fraud. Such a claim is barred by the rule, *ex turpi causa non oritur actio* (an action does not arise from a base cause) (*Stone and Rolls Ltd v Moore Stephens* [2009] UKHL 39, [2009] AC 1391; see **19.8.3**). In *Stone and Rolls Ltd v Moore Stephens* Lord Phillips of Worth Matravers said that the fact that the company had gone into liquidation (so that any damages recovered would have to be paid to the company's defrauded creditors) made no difference, because the duty of a company's statutory auditor is owed only to the company in the interests of its members, not to the company's creditors (*Al Saudi Banque v Clark Pixley* [1990] Ch 313) or to persons that the company might defraud. There is extensive discussion of this case in *Bilta (UK) Ltd v Nazir (No 2)* [2015] UKSC 23, [2016] 1 AC 1 (see **16.6.9.2**).

For auditors' liabilities to other persons, see **17.5.2** to **17.5.4**.

17.5.2 AUDITOR'S LIABILITY FOR NEGLIGENT MISSTATEMENT

A person who buys shares in a company on the basis of accounts which erroneously suggest the shares are worth more than they are may try to seek compensation for the error. The usual target has been the company's auditor for issuing a report on the accounts which negligently failed to state that those accounts were erroneous. The general principle of the law of negligence is that liability to compensate a person for damage caused by negligence depends on there being a duty not to cause that type of damage to that person. That duty is called a 'duty of care'. Negligence may have unending consequences. But the law should not impose on a person 'liability in an indeterminate amount for an indeterminate time to an indeterminate class' (per Cardozo CJ in *Ultramares Corporation v Touche* (1931) 174 NE 441 at p 444). The common law has always sought to limit the scope of the tort of negligence so as to make the system workable. As Lord Bridge of Harwich said in *Caparo Industries plc v Dickman* [1990] 2 AC 605 at pp 617–18, a necessary ingredient in any situation giving rise to a duty of care is that: 'the situation should be one in which the court considers it fair, just and reasonable that the law should impose a duty of a given scope upon the one party for the benefit of the other'.

The 'scope' of a duty of care owed by D to C is the extent of the damage which D must save C from, and which D must compensate C for if it occurs as a result of D breaching the duty of care. The courts have always said, for example, that liability will not be imposed for losses which are characterised as being too 'remote' from the breach of duty or which are 'unforeseeable'. The common law has been especially reluctant to hold that it is within the scope of a duty of care to save a person from what are called 'economic losses', that is damage other than injury to individuals' health or injury to tangible property (see *Murphy v Brentwood District Council* [1991] 1 AC 398). Since the landmark case of *Hedley Byrne and Co Ltd v Heller and Partners Ltd* [1964] AC 465, it has been possible to sue for purely economic losses caused by a person's negligent misstatements if the person who made the misstatement owed a duty of care to the person who suffered loss.

An auditor of a company is employed by the company as a separate person and the primary liability of the auditor for negligence is to the company as a separate person (see **17.5.1**). Cases in which damages have been claimed for paying too much for shares in reliance on audited accounts have depended on establishing that a company's auditor owes a duty of care to persons contemplating buying the company's shares.

In *Caparo Industries plc v Dickman*, Lord Bridge said, at p 621, that in order to establish a duty of care in a claim for negligent misstatement, the claimant must prove:

> that the defendant knew that his statement would be communicated to the [claimant], either as an individual or as a member of an identifiable class, specifically in connection with a particular transaction or transactions of a particular kind (eg in a prospectus inviting investment) and that the [claimant] would be very likely to rely on it for the purpose of deciding whether or not to enter upon that transaction or upon a transaction of that kind.

This formulation gives the impression that the test is subjective, but, as Lord Oliver of Aylmerton pointed out at p 638, what the defendant knew includes not only actual knowledge but such knowledge as would be attributed to a reasonable person placed as the defendant was placed. So it is not necessary to prove that the defendant intended that the claimant should rely on the statement, or that the defendant's purpose in supplying the statement was that the claimant should rely on it (*Royal Bank of Scotland plc v Bannerman Johnstone Maclay* 2005 SLT 579).

Similarly, the formulation of the test, which is commonly used, that the defendant assumed responsibility to the claimant is, as Lord Slynn of Hadley pointed out in *Phelps v Hillingdon London Borough Council* [2001] 2 AC 619, at p 654, misleading if it suggests that liability depends on the defendant having knowingly and deliberately accepted responsibility. In fact, the test of liability is objective. Lord Slynn preferred to discuss the test of whether a duty of care was owed in terms of whether there was a sufficient nexus between claimant and defendant. On the other hand, Lord Steyn, in *Williams v Natural Life Health Foods Ltd* [1998] 1 WLR 830 at p 837, said that there is no better rationalisation of this species of tort liability than assumption of responsibility. Assumption of responsibility is not the unique criterion for liability for pure economic loss, though it is a sufficient reason for concluding that it is fair, just and reasonable to impose liability (*Commissioners of Customs and Excise v Barclays Bank plc* [2006] UKHL 28, [2007] 1 AC 181, per Lord Bingham of Cornhill at [4]–[8], Lord Hoffmann at [35]–[38]). In some cases it is not an appropriate criterion (Lord Rodger of Earlsferry at [49]–[52], Lord Mance at [85]–[93]). Where it is not appropriate, the court may apply the 'threefold' test, which Lord Bingham stated, at [4]:

> whether loss to the claimant was a reasonably foreseeable consequence of what the defendant did or failed to do; whether the relationship between the parties was one of sufficient proximity; and whether in all the circumstances it is fair, just and reasonable to impose a duty of care on the defendant towards the claimant.

17.5.3 LIABILITY OF A COMPANY'S AUDITOR TO PERSONS CONTEMPLATING BUYING ITS SHARES

To establish that a company's auditor is liable to persons contemplating buying the company's shares, it must be proved that the auditor knew, or ought to have known, that its opinion on the company's accounts was being communicated to those persons for the purpose of deciding whether to buy the shares and how much to pay for them (see **17.5.2**). Normally, the only purpose for which an auditor's report on a company's annual accounts is given is the purpose for which that report is required by statute. In *Caparo Industries plc v Dickman* [1990] 2 AC 605 Lord Jauncey of Tullichettle, at pp 661–2, identified this purpose as enabling shareholders, collectively, to question the past management of the company, vote for or against appointment of directors and take other decisions affecting the company, and to influence future policy and management. See also per Lord

Bridge of Harwich at p 626 and Lord Oliver of Aylmerton at p 654. An auditor's report is not normally given for the purpose of advising people how much they should pay for the company's shares, or how much existing members should sell them for. So, unless it can be shown that the auditor knew, or ought to have known, of some special purpose for which the opinion was required, the auditor owes no duty of care, not to make negligent misstatements, to members of the public at large who rely upon the accounts in deciding to buy shares in the company. Nor does the auditor owe a duty to save existing members from losses caused by buying further shares at an overvalue.

The fact that a company is vulnerable to a takeover bid does not mean that the auditor owes a duty of care to potential takeover bidders who would very probably rely on the audited accounts (*Caparo Industries plc v Dickman*). Similarly, the fact that it is highly probable that the company will need to borrow money does not make the auditor liable to potential lenders (*Al Saudi Banque v Clark Pixley* [1990] Ch 313, approved by Lord Bridge in *Caparo Industries plc v Dickman* at p 623 and by Lord Jauncey at p 662; *R Lowe Lippmann Figdor and Franck v AGC (Advances) Ltd* [1992] 2 VR 671; *Berg Sons and Co Ltd v Adams* [1993] BCLC 1045). A company's auditor does not owe a duty of care to the beneficiaries of a trust of which the company is trustee (*Anthony v Wright* [1995] 1 BCLC 236).

17.5.4 LIABILITY FOR SPECIALLY COMMISSIONED REPORT

If a company's auditor is asked to prepare a special report on its accounts specifically for a person to whom the company's controllers wish to sell their shares, the auditor will be liable to that investor for negligent misstatements in that report, even if it was commissioned by the company rather than the investor. In *Caparo Industries plc v Dickman* [1990] 2 AC 605 Lord Bridge of Harwich, at p 625, and Lord Oliver of Aylmerton, at p 648, thought that this might have been the situation in *JEB Fasteners Ltd v Marks, Bloom and Co* [1983] 1 All ER 583. In that case, JEB Fasteners Ltd had taken over a company whose accounts were erroneous: the error had not been detected by the company's auditor. However, it was found that the real reason JEB Fasteners took over the company was to acquire the services of its directors, and the amount paid was not determined by the company's financial position, which was well known to be poor, so the claimant company's loss was not *caused* by the auditor's negligence, and the auditor was not liable for it.

In *James McNaughton Paper Group Ltd v Hicks Anderson and Co* [1991] 2 QB 113, the claimant company failed to convince the court that accounts which it had relied on were prepared specifically for it. There had been a takeover by the claimant company of a group of companies known as the MK Paper group. This takeover had been negotiated by the claimant company's chairman and the chairman of MK. In deciding on the takeover the claimant company's chairman had relied on draft annual accounts prepared by Hicks Anderson and Co. These accounts were erroneous and the claimant company claimed £75,000 damages for the accountants' negligence. Although the chairman of the MK group had asked for the draft accounts to be prepared quickly when the negotiations were under way, they were prepared for him, not for any potential buyer of the group, according to Neill LJ. They were clearly labelled 'draft' accounts and, again according to Neill LJ, the claimant's chairman was not entitled to treat them as final accounts, and the accountants could not be expected to foresee that they would be so treated.

The concept of assumption of responsibility was expressly relied on in **Abbott v Strong** [1998] 2 BCLC 420, which concerned a company called Resort Hotels plc. Mr Strong was chairman of the company and his co-defendant, Mr Feld, was its managing director. Among other co-defendants were the accountants Coopers and Lybrand Deloitte ('Coopers'). The company had invited its shareholders to subscribe for a rights issue and had issued a circular, dated 30 April 1992, which included a forecast of the company's profits for the year ended 30 April 1992. Coopers had assisted in the preparation of this forecast, but had relied on forged and fraudulent documents prepared by Mr Feld (who was subsequently sent to prison) and substantially overstated the company's profits. The fact that Coopers had assisted in the preparation of the circular was not disclosed in it. More than 200 shareholders who had subscribed for shares on the basis of the erroneous circular sued Coopers for negligence in preparing it, but the claim was struck out, because it was held that Coopers had not assumed responsibility to them. Ferris J said, at p 428:

> I do not find it comprehensible that a person (X) who makes a statement or gives advice to another (Y) for the purpose of assisting Y to make representations to a third party (Z), is to be regarded as owing a duty of care to Z when the participation of X in the preparation of Y's statement is unknown to Z. It does not seem to me that, in these circumstances, X is assuming any degree of responsibility for Z.

In two reported cases at first instance, purchasers of shares in a company who relied on erroneous accounts have been able to make the company's accountants liable: in both cases the accountants attended meetings between the vendors of the shares and the purchasers and were persuaded to give verbal assurances to the purchasers that the accounts were accurate. In *Peach Publishing Ltd v Slater and Co* [1996] BCC 751 the accounts relied on were unaudited but in *ADT Ltd v BDO Binder Hamlyn* [1996] BCC 808 they were audited annual accounts. In *ADT Ltd v BDO Binder Hamlyn* the accountants were held liable to pay £65 million in damages. However, on appeal in *Peach Publishing Ltd v Slater and Co* [1998] BCC 139 it was held that the accountants were not liable for the representation made at the meeting: it was found that the partner who attended the meeting did so as an adviser to the vendor of the shares, not as an independent expert, and it was held that he did not assume responsibility to the purchaser. The partner's statement verifying the accuracy of the accounts was elicited by the purchaser only for the purpose of persuading the vendor to warrant that the accounts were accurate and did not directly persuade the purchaser to buy the shares. This seems to be a very fine distinction. These cases should make accountants very wary about commenting on the work they have done for a company or its controlling shareholders when attending meetings with potential purchasers of shares.

17.5.5 RELIEF FROM LIABILITY

CA 2006, s 532, declares void any exemption of an auditor of a company from any liability which the auditor would otherwise have for negligence, default, breach of duty or breach of trust in relation to the company, occurring in the course of auditing accounts, unless it is given by an authorised liability limitation agreement. It also declares void any indemnity against any such liability, which is given by the company, unless it is given in the terms of s 533. Section 533 permits an indemnity against an auditor's liability incurred in successfully defending civil or criminal proceedings or successfully applying for relief under s 1157. These provisions are similar to those made in ss 232 and 234 relating to directors, which are discussed in **16.16.5**.

A liability limitation agreement is defined in ss 534(1) and 535(1)(b) as an agreement that purports to limit the liability of a company's auditor to the company in respect of negligence, default, breach of duty or breach of trust occurring in the course of auditing the accounts for a specified financial year. A liability limitation agreement can only be for one financial year (s 535(1)(a)). A liability limitation agreement must, by s 534(2)(b), be authorised by the company in accordance with s 536. By s 536(2) and (3), a company may adopt a resolution, before it enters into the agreement, approving the agreement's principal terms (as defined in s 536(4)) or it may adopt a resolution, after it enters into the agreement, approving the agreement. A *private company* may, by s 536(2)(a), adopt a resolution, before it enters into a liability limitation agreement, waiving the need to approve the agreement.

Section 537 provides that a liability limitation agreement can only effectively limit the auditor's liability to such an amount as is fair and reasonable in all the circumstances of the case, having regard to:

(a) the auditor's responsibilities under the legislation;

(b) the nature and purpose of the auditor's contractual obligations to the company; and

(c) the professional standards expected of the auditor.

Despite this rule, a liability limitation agreement is not required to express the limit on liability as a fixed amount or an amount to be determined by a formula (s 535(4)). This permits the use of so-called proportional liability agreements. These overcome the usual principle of English law that, if two or more persons are liable to the same claimant for the same damage, each of them is liable for the whole amount of compensation awarded for that damage. The claimant need only sue one of the persons responsible (naturally choosing the wealthiest), leaving that person to seek contribution from the others by joining them as co-defendants. A defendant who is ordered to pay compensation for damage for which other persons are also liable may seek a contribution from any other liable person of an amount found by the court to be just and equitable, having regard to the extent of that person's responsibility for the damage in question (Civil Liability (Contribution) Act 1978, s 2(1)). The idea is that the person who should bear the risk of not being able to recover a contribution should be a person who wronged the claimant rather than the claimant. Under a proportional liability agreement between a company and its auditor, the company will take on this risk, by agreeing that the auditor will only be liable for its own proportion of any compensation awarded.

A company which has entered into a liability limitation agreement must disclose, in a note to its annual accounts, the principal terms of the agreement and the date of the resolution approving it (or, in the case of a private company, waiving the need for approval) (SI 2008/489, reg 8).

The FRC intends to publish guidance on the use of liability limitation agreements.

The provisions of CA 2006, s 1157, which empowers the court to relieve persons of liability for negligence, default, breach of trust, etc, if they have acted honestly and reasonably (see **16.16.6**), apply to 'an officer of a company or a person employed by a company as auditor (whether he is or is not an officer of the company)'. Whether an auditor is an officer is considered in **17.2**.

17.5.6 CRIMINAL LIABILITY FOR INACCURATE AUDITORS' REPORTS

CA 2006, s 507(1), creates a criminal offence of knowingly or recklessly causing an auditor's report to include any matter that is misleading, false or deceptive in a material particular. Section 507(2) creates an offence of knowingly or recklessly causing an auditor's report to omit a statement of directors' failings required by s 498(2)(b), (3) or (5) (see **17.4.6**).

Only the persons specified in s 507(3) can be guilty of these offences. Where the auditor is an individual, s 507(3)(a) specifies that individual and any employee or agent of that individual who is eligible for appointment as auditor of the company. Where the auditor is a partnership firm, s 507(3)(b) specifies any director, member, employee or agent of the firm who is eligible for appointment.

When used in statutory provisions defining crimes, the term 'recklessly' does not have any special legal meaning but is used in its ordinary everyday sense (*Commissioner of Police of the Metropolis v Caldwell* [1982] AC 341) though this may be modified by the context (*R v Reid* [1992] 1 WLR 793 per Lord Ackner at p 805). If the definition of 'reckless' given by Lord Diplock in *Caldwell* at p 354 (and affirmed by the House of Lords in *R v Reid*) is applied to s 507, it means that a person who has caused an auditor's report to be inaccurate in any of the ways specified in s 507(1) or (2) will have done so recklessly if there was an obvious risk that the report would include the misleading, false or deceptive matter, or omit a required statement, but the person either failed to give any thought to that risk or caused the report to be issued despite having recognised the risk.

Only a fine, and not a custodial sentence, may be imposed as a penalty for the offences (s 507(4)).

17.6 MANAGERS

A manager of a company may be sufficiently senior to be in a fiduciary relationship with the company. In *Agip (Africa) Ltd v Jackson* [1991] Ch 547, the chief accountant of a company was held to be in a fiduciary relationship with it. In *Canadian Aero Service Ltd v O'Malley* (1973) 40 DLR (3d) 371, two employees of the company (which was a wholly owned subsidiary) who had the jobs of 'president and chief executive officer' and 'executive vice-president and director', but whose appointments as directors were formally defective, were held to owe the same fiduciary duties as directors. In *DPC Estates Pty Ltd v Grey* [1974] 1 NSWLR 470 the defendant was employed as 'manager' of a group of companies and acted as director of one of them though his appointment as director was formally defective. He was held to owe the same fiduciary duties as a director. In *Green v Bestobell Industries Pty Ltd* [1982] WAR 1, the company was organised in four divisions and each division had a branch in each State of Australia. The branches were operated separately and to some extent autonomously. Mr Green was the manager of the Victoria branch of one of the divisions with 'the complete control of all human, financial and contractual resources within the branch' according to his letter of appointment. He was held to owe the same fiduciary duties as a director.

Senior managers are therefore subject to the fiduciary duties on which the statutory general duties of directors are based (see **16.3**). There is a difference, however, in that the rule that a director of a company is not entitled to remuneration except as provided by its constitution or approved by the company's members does not apply to senior managers or even to persons who act as directors without being properly appointed—see the discussion of *Craven-Ellis v Canons Ltd* [1936] 2 KB 403 in **15.9.1.5**.

17.7 PROMOTERS

17.7.1 INTRODUCTION

When an individual has an idea for a new business venture, he or she may set about interesting others in the venture and persuade them to contribute capital to a company to be incorporated for the purpose of carrying on the venture. The individual will then be described as a 'promoter' of the company. In the nineteenth century there were no restrictions on advertising immediately to the public inviting them to take shares in new companies, and some promoters took advantage of their position and the gullibility of the public. The most common forms of misbehaviour were:

(a) A promoter of a company would transfer his own property to the company for a consideration—either in cash (ie, the capital contributed by others) or in fully paid shares— that greatly overvalued the property. By taking shares with a nominal value greater than the value of the property sold, the promoter could obtain for himself a large cash profit by reselling the shares if a sufficient public demand for them could be stimulated or, if he kept the shares, a disproportionate share of dividends if the company was successful; deeming the shares to be fully paid meant he had no liability for the company's debts if it was unsuccessful. Most promoters took a combination of cash and shares. (It is now an offence for a plc to allot shares for a non-cash consideration unless an independent valuation report has certified that there is no overvaluation—see **6.6.4.2**.)

(b) A promoter of a company would undertake to acquire for the new company an essential asset, such as land for development, mining rights or a patent, without disclosing that he personally would profit from the deal, either by buying the asset first on his own account and then reselling at a profit to the company or by taking a commission from the vendor.

Often an individual promoter did not have sufficient resources to purchase a property and resell it to the promoted company, so he would form a 'syndicate' of investors to finance that stage of the promotion. Sometimes the syndicate would itself be incorporated as a company.

During most of the twentieth century, people refused to buy shares in newly incorporated companies with no trading history and so disreputable company promoters have disappeared. An important factor in eliminating them has been the authorities' refusal (other than in exceptional cases) to list the shares of a company until it can show the results of a substantial period of trading (currently three years: see **7.6.2.1**). However, this has meant that genuine new businesses have been unable to use contributed capital, beyond the usually small resources of their founders, and have had to rely instead on bank overdrafts as finance in their early years. There has been an increase in public offers of unlisted shares including shares in companies with new businesses and it may be that the law relating to company promoters is due for a revival.

17.7.2 DEFINITION

The activities of a promoter are so varied that no comprehensive definition of the term has ever been formulated, though judges have from time to time offered broad guidelines. For example, in *Whaley Bridge Calico Printing Co v Green* (1880) 5 QBD 109, Bowen J said:

> The term promoter is a term not of law, but of business, usefully summing up in a single word a number of business operations familiar to the commercial world by which a company is generally brought into existence.

In later cases the Court of Appeal expressed a dislike of the term 'promoter', preferring to concentrate on what was done by a person to put him in a fiduciary relationship with a company being formed. In *Lydney and Wigpool Iron Ore Co v Bird* (1886) 33 ChD 85 the court said, at p 93:

> it is necessary to ascertain in each case what the so-called promoter really did before his legal liabilities can be accurately ascertained. In every case it is better to look at the facts and ascertain and describe them as they are.

See also per Cotton LJ in *Ladywell Mining Co v Brookes* (1887) 35 ChD 400 at pp 407 and 411. For a detailed discussion, see J H Gross, 'Who is a company promoter?' (1970) 86 LQR 493.

17.7.3 DUTIES OF PROMOTERS

17.7.3.1 Fiduciary duty

The relationship between a promoter of a company and the company is fiduciary (*Erlanger v New Sombrero Phosphate Co* (1878) 3 App Cas 1218 per Lord Cairns at p 1236). The meaning of this equitable concept is examined in more detail in **16.3**, because nowadays its most important application in company law is to the relationship between a director of a company and the company. The principal fiduciary duty affecting promoters is the no-profit rule (see **16.9.2**), which typically arises in relation to a transaction into which the promoted company enters and from which the promoter will profit, either as a vendor or by being paid a commission. A big problem in many of the cases is determining whether the promoter's interest was acquired in a fiduciary capacity (see **17.7.4**).

As with directors (see **16.11.2**), a promoter of a company selling property to the company has a duty to disclose any interest in it (see **17.7.3.2**), and a promoter's undisclosed profit is usually called a 'secret profit'. Where there is a failure to disclose the interest of a company's promoter in a transaction with the company, it is voidable at the company's option (*Erlanger v New Sombrero Phosphate Co*). The company may rescind the transaction (see **16.15.6**).

If a secret profit cannot be recovered by rescission (for example, where it is a commission on a transaction with some other person), the promoter may be ordered to account for it (see **16.15.2**) to the company (*Emma Silver Mining Co v Grant* (1879) 11 ChD 918; *Lydney and Wigpool Iron Ore Co v Bird* (1886) 33 ChD 85; *Gluckstein v Barnes* [1900] AC 240). Equitable compensation may be awarded for the difference between the price paid by the company for assets, acquired in a transaction in which a promoter had an undisclosed interest, and the market value of those assets (*Re Leeds and Hanley Theatres of Varieties Ltd* [1902] 2 Ch 809). There is a dispute among commentators over whether equitable compensation is available where the only breach of fiduciary duty is a non-fraudulent failure to disclose an interest which was not acquired in a fiduciary capacity (see **17.7.4**).

The characterisation of promoters as fiduciaries seems to have been first made by Wigram V-C in *Foss v Harbottle* (1843) 2 Hare 461 at p 489. *Foss v Harbottle* established the important rule that any wrong done by a promoter of an incorporated company is done to the company as a separate person so that action against the promoter must be taken by the company not by its members.

17.7.3.2 Disclosure and approval

The rules on disclosure and approval of a promoter's interest and profit are based on the idea that everyone who is intended by the promoter to become a member of the promoted company must be involved in the disclosure and approval process. If the promoter's scheme is that the company is to be a private company with only certain persons as members then disclosure to and approval by all those persons is sufficient, even if subsequently other persons become members (*Re Ambrose Lake Tin and Copper Mining Co* (1880) 14 ChD 390; *Re British Seamless Paper Box Co* (1881) 17 ChD 467; *Salomon v A Salomon and Co Ltd* [1897] AC 22).

Where the promoter's scheme is to invite the general public to become members of the company, the promoter may either disclose to and obtain approval from a board of directors whose members are independent of the promoter or make the disclosure to the subscribers of the memorandum and in the material published to prospective shareholders inviting them to take shares, so that persons only become members of the company in full knowledge of the promoter's interest (*Erlanger v New Sombrero Phosphate Co* (1878) 3 App Cas 1218; *Lagunas Nitrate Co v Lagunas Syndicate* [1899] 2 Ch 392; *Gluckstein v Barnes* [1900] AC 240).

17.7.3.3 Statutory duty

CA 2006, ss 598 to 604, require independent valuation (s 599) of non-cash assets sold to a public company by persons who were its first members either because they were the subscribers of its memorandum (if it was registered as a public company) (s 598) or because they were members at the time it re-registered as a public company (s 603). The valuer's report must state that it is worth at least as much as the consideration being given for it by the company (s 600(3)(d)). In addition, the agreement for sale must be approved by ordinary resolution of the members (s 601) and a copy of this resolution and the valuation report must be sent to Companies House within 15 days of adoption (s 602). Companies House gives public notice of receipt of the report (ss 1077 and 1078(3); see **4.3**).

These requirements apply for the period of two years after the date of a public company's trading certificate or its re-registration (ss 598(1) and (2) and 603). They do not apply to a sale in the normal course of the company's business (s 598(4)) or to a sale for a consideration that is less than 10 per cent of the nominal value of the company's allotted share capital at the time of the agreement for transfer of the assets (s 598(1)(c)).

If an agreement with a member for the transfer of non-cash assets is made without following this procedure and the member knew, or ought to have known, of the contravention, the company is entitled to recover any consideration it has given, and the agreement, so far as unperformed, is void (s 604).

17.7.4 LEGITIMATE AND WRONGFUL PROFITS OF PROMOTERS

There is an important distinction between a promoter who enters into a transaction in his or her capacity as a promoter and profits from it, and one who acquired an interest in property before promoting and makes a profit when the property is sold to the promoted company. In the former circumstance the profit is made in breach of fiduciary duty whereas in the second circumstance the profit is legitimate (*Erlanger v New Sombrero Phosphate Co* (1878) 3 App Cas 1218 per Lord Cairns LC at pp 1234–5). As James LJ said in **Re Coal Economising Gas Co, Gover's Case** (1875) 1 ChD 182, at p 187:

> It is surely open to any man, in point of law, to sell his property to a joint stock company, and to invite persons to form themselves into a joint stock company to purchase from him, just as it is open to any man to sell to any persons in the world the right to become his partners in any property or undertaking. Until the formation of the partnership he is simply a vendor of the wares; he may ask what price he likes, and obtain what price he can.

(His Lordship went on to say that such a vendor need not disclose the price paid for the property, but it is clear that the full and frank disclosure required of a fiduciary's interest includes quantification of the value of the interest: see *Re Lady Forrest (Murchison) Gold Mine Ltd* [1901] 1 Ch 582.)

The distinction between the two types of profit is set out clearly by Lord Parker in *Jacobus Marler Estates Ltd v Marler* (1913) 85 LJ PC 167.

The difficulty of deciding whether or not a promoter acquired an interest in a fiduciary capacity will be apparent from nearly all the cases on promoters' liabilities, but see especially *Re Coal Economising Gas Co, Gover's Case*; *Ladywell Mining Co v Brookes* (1887) 35 ChD 400; *Omnium Electric Palaces Ltd v Baines* [1914] 1 Ch 332.

The distinction between legitimate and wrongful profits is not relevant if the profit was not disclosed and the contract can be rescinded. In those circumstances the non-disclosure of the promoter's interest renders the contract voidable, whether or not the interest was acquired in a fiduciary capacity. Rescission means returning the property to the promoter, who must return what the company paid for it, including the promoter's profit, whether legitimate or wrongful. If, however, the contract can no longer be rescinded, a promoter is not liable to account for a legitimate profit (*Re Cape Breton Co* (1885) 29 ChD 795, CA, affirmed by HL sub nom *Bentinck v Fenn* (1887) 12 App Cas 652; *Ladywell Mining Co v Brookes*; *Re Lady Forrest (Murchison) Gold Mine Ltd*), but can be ordered to account for a wrongful profit. In all the cases cited in this paragraph the person sought to be made liable as a promoter of a company had been one of the company's first directors.

It has been argued (for example, in *Bentinck v Fenn* (1887) 12 App Cas 652) that, even though a promoter did not acquire an interest in a fiduciary capacity, and so is entitled in equity to profit from the interest, failure to disclose the interest to the company before it entered into the transaction may have deprived it of the opportunity to make a better bargain, because, for example, it might have realised that the property it was buying was not worth what was being paid for it. The argument continues that equitable compensation could be claimed from the promoter for a loss of this kind.

There is no reported case in which equitable compensation has been awarded when there was a non-fraudulent failure to disclose an interest not acquired in a fiduciary capacity. In *Bentinck v Fenn* this was partly because it was not proved that there had been non-disclosure (per Lord Herschell at p 661, Lord FitzGerald at p 667, Lord Macnaghten at p 671), but mainly because there was no evidence that the properties were worth less than the company paid for them (per Lord Herschell at pp 659–61, Lord Watson at p 666, Lord FitzGerald at pp 667–8, Lord Macnaghten at p 671), so no loss was proved for which compensation could be claimed. This was also the principal basis of the decision when the case was before the Court of Appeal (sub nom *Re Cape Breton Co* (1885)

29 ChD 795), and the Court of Appeal followed that decision in *Ladywell Mining Co v Brookes* (1887) 35 ChD 400 (see especially per Cotton LJ at p 408). In *Re Lady Forrest (Murchison) Gold Mine Ltd* [1901] 1 Ch 582 Wright J concluded from these cases that there is no liability to account for profits, but did not mention the possibility of equitable compensation for the company's losses.

Some commentators have suggested that the absence of awards of equitable compensation for non-disclosure of an interest not acquired in a fiduciary capacity is because of a rule against awarding compensation in such circumstances. This controversy is reviewed by M D J Conaglen in 'Equitable compensation for breach of fiduciary dealing rules' (2003) 119 LQR 246. Mr Conaglen concludes that there is no such limitation and the Court of Appeal has noted his view without dissenting from it (*Gwembe Valley Development Co Ltd v Koshy (No 3)* [2003] EWCA Civ 1478, [2004] 1 BCLC 131, at [143]).

For further discussion of the liabilities of promoters, see J Gold, 'The liability of promoters for secret profits in English Law' (1943) 5 UTLJ 21 and B E McCrea, 'Disclosure of promoters' secret profits' (1968) 3(3) Univ of Br Columbia Law Rev 183–216.

18

REMEDIES FOR MALADMINISTRATION

SUMMARY OF POINTS COVERED

- What is in this chapter
- Action against company officers
- The rule in *Foss v Harbottle*
- Proper claimant principle

- Irregularity principle
- Unfairly prejudicial conduct of the company's affairs
- Winding up
- Company investigations

18.1 WHAT IS IN THIS CHAPTER

Chapters 14 to **16** examined the roles of members and directors in the governance of a company. **Chapter 18** examines what can be done, and by whom, when something has gone wrong.

The existence of the company as a separate person is very important in this. It is necessary to analyse whether a wrong has been done to that separate person or to individual members.

If the wrong is to the company as a separate person, only the company can claim a remedy for it: this is the proper claimant principle established in *Foss v Harbottle* (1843) 2 Hare 461 (see **18.2** to **18.4**). The practical problem is that usually the people who are causing harm to the company also control it and so can prevent it taking action to remedy the harm. In this situation, it may be possible for a member to make a derivative claim on behalf of the company (see **18.4.2**).

If a member of a company is wronged, that member can make a claim to vindicate a personal right (see **18.4.5** to **18.4.8**). But a wrong to a member that merely reflects a wrong done to the company (for example, loss in share value caused by damage to the company) does not give the member a claim (see **18.4.3**). The courts also wish to leave questions of internal management to the members themselves to sort out in general meeting (see **18.4.4**). In particular, the courts will not hear claims about mere informality or irregularity in decision-making which could be dealt with by taking the decision again with the correct procedure (see **18.5**).

Rather than making a traditional legal claim as described in **18.2** to **18.4**, it may be better for a member to petition the court for relief under CA 2006, part 30 (ss 994 to 999) (see **18.6**). Part 30 provides the court with a very wide-ranging jurisdiction to remedy conduct of a company's affairs 'that is unfairly prejudicial to the interests of its members generally or of some part of its members'. Part 30 is primarily concerned with finding remedies that enable the company to continue, and the most common remedy sought is an order that the petitioning member is to be bought out at a fair price. Winding up a company (see **18.7**) ends a company's existence, but may be the only way of dealing with deadlock and other serious problems.

The public interest in the consequences of maladministration may justify the intervention of the Secretary of State (**18.8**), especially where companies are being used for fraudulent or illegal purposes. The Secretary of State has extensive investigatory powers, and investigations can lead to criminal proceedings, a petition for winding up or an application for director disqualification.

Key legislation which you should be able to consult when reading this chapter:

- CA 1985, ss 431–457;

- Insolvency Act 1986, ss 112, 122, 124, 124A, 125, 165, 167, sch 1, sch 4; and

- CA 2006, ss 260–264, 994–999.

All the legislation listed here is in *Blackstone's Statutes on Company Law*.

The following cases, which are considered in this chapter, are particularly significant and are recommended further reading:

- *Browne v La Trinidad* (1887) 37 ChD 1;

- *Burland v Earle* [1902] AC 83;

- *Foss v Harbottle* (1843) 2 Hare 461, 67 ER 189;

- *Johnson v Gore Wood and Co* [2002] 2 AC 1;

- *MacDougall v Gardiner* (1875) 1 ChD 13;

- *O'Neill v Phillips* [1999] 1 WLR 1092;

- *Prudential Assurance Co Ltd v Newman Industries Ltd (No 2)* [1982] Ch 204.

Your particular course of study may require you to read other source materials.

18.2 ACTION AGAINST COMPANY OFFICERS

If an actionable wrong has been done to a company by its officers, the company has a cause of action which it can pursue like any other person in legal proceedings. In practice the major difficulty is that the offending officers may themselves be able to block action through being in control of board meetings and/or holding sufficient shares to control members' meetings. Often, action is taken only when a company goes into liquidation and comes under the control of an independent liquidator.

As with any other person who has suffered an actionable wrong, there is no legal requirement that a company must pursue the wrongdoer through the courts to the bitter end. It may decide that no purpose would be served by pursuing a claim, and even if it does bring a claim it may compromise it or even abandon it. As Vinelott J said in *Taylor v National Union of Mineworkers (Derbyshire Area)* [1985] BCLC 237 at pp 254–5:

> it is open to a majority of the members, if they think it is right in the interests of the corporate body to do so, to resolve that no action should be taken to remedy the wrong done to the corporate body and such a resolution, if made in good faith and in what they considered to be for the benefit of the corporate body, will bind the minority. The majority of the members of a trading company, for instance, might properly take the view that the publicity, costs and the inevitable loss, let us say, of the services of a managing director, who would be the defendant, would outweigh the benefit to the company of successfully prosecuting an action and might properly decide not to pursue it; although, of course, a contractual release of the right of action, as compared with a decision simply not to institute proceedings, would require to be supported by some consideration.

As explained in **16.16.2**, a company may preclude a cause of action arising by authorising or ratifying a director's actions.

In most companies the directors have control of the company's litigation (see **15.10.3**). The considerations outlined by Vinelott J apply to decisions by directors as well as to decisions by members.

Of course, some members may disapprove of the company not bringing a claim against a delinquent officer. The possibility of action being taken at the instance of a dissentient member is discussed in **18.4**.

18.3　THE RULE IN *FOSS V HARBOTTLE*

18.3.1　STATEMENT OF THE RULE

The big problem for a member of a company seeking to cure maladministration of the company by legal action is that the courts have usually tried to avoid hearing such claims. The term 'the rule in *Foss v Harbottle*' is used to describe the policy of the courts of not hearing a claim concerning the affairs of a company brought by a member or members of the company. The title of the rule is taken from the case of *Foss v Harbottle* (1843) 2 Hare 461 (see **18.4.1.2**).

In *Burland v Earle* [1902] AC 83, Lord Davey said, at pp 93–4:

> It is an elementary principle of the law relating to joint stock companies that the court will not interfere with the internal management of companies acting within their powers, and in fact has no jurisdiction to do so. Again, it is clear law that in order to redress a wrong done to the company or to recover moneys or damages alleged to be due to the company, the action should prima facie be brought by the company itself . . . It should be added that no mere informality or irregularity which can be remedied by the majority will entitle the minority to sue, if the act when done regularly would be within the powers of the company and the intention of the majority of shareholders is clear.

Three principles can be taken from this statement:

(a) If a wrong is done to a company (as a person separate from its members), only the company may sue for redress. This is the significant principle stated by Wigram V-C in *Foss v Harbottle* itself and is known as the 'proper claimant' principle (see **18.4**). CA 2006, s 260, permits derivative claims (see **18.4.2**) as an exception to this principle.

(b) The court will not interfere with the internal management of companies acting within their powers. This is called the 'internal management' principle. The internal management principle has a 'proper claimant aspect', which is that the court will not determine a question concerning what it regards as the internal management of a company except in proceedings brought by the company itself. This is considered in **18.4.4**.

(c) A member cannot sue to rectify a mere informality or irregularity if the act when done regularly would be within the powers of the company and if the intention of the majority of members is clear. This is called the 'irregularity' principle. It is considered in **18.5**.

The proper claimant principle and the proper claimant aspect of the internal management principle apply to any association that can sue in its own name, for example a trade union (*Cotter v National Union of Seamen* [1929] 2 Ch 58), a building society (*Farrow v Registrar of Building Societies* [1991] 2 VR 589), or a partnership (*Watson v Imperial Financial Services Ltd* (1994) 111 DLR (4th) 643).

In *Edwards v Halliwell* [1950] 2 All ER 1064 Jenkins LJ referred to the rule in *Foss v Harbottle* as applying only where a wrong had been done to the company as a separate person and said that it had two elements: (a) the proper claimant principle and the proper claimant aspect of the internal management principle, as mentioned earlier, and (b) a principle that if a wrong done to a company is ratifiable by a simple majority of members (see **16.16.2**) then a member cannot sue in respect of it because when it has been ratified it is no longer a wrong and if the members decide against ratification there is no valid reason why the company itself should not sue (the 'ratifiability principle').

In *Prudential Assurance Co Ltd v Newman Industries Ltd (No 2)* [1982] Ch 204, the Court of Appeal said, at pp 210–11, that Jenkins LJ's judgment in **Edwards v Halliwell** stated the 'classic definition of the rule in *Foss v Harbottle*' but pointed out that the rule 'also embraces' the irregularity principle as a 'related principle'. Australian courts, on the other hand, still regard the judgment of the Privy Council in *Burland v Earle* as containing the 'classic statement' of the rule (per Street J in *Hawkesbury Development Co Ltd v Landmark Finance Pty Ltd* (1969) 92 WN (NSW) 199 at p 206; King CJ in *Hurley v BGH Nominees Pty Ltd* (1982) 31 SASR 250 at p 252).

18.3.2 ACADEMIC AND JUDICIAL COMMENT

The rule in *Foss v Harbottle* is the deepest mystery of company law but is of great practical importance. A lawyer must be able to determine whether his or her client's claim will or will not be heard by the court. So if the client's claim concerns the affairs of a company of which the client is a member, the lawyer must determine whether the claim is an exception to the rule. Unfortunately there is disagreement over defining the rule itself, let alone its exceptions, and the topic has been, and will continue to be, the subject of a vast amount of academic and judicial comment.

The best discussion is the lucid and comprehensive account in Law Commission, *Shareholder Remedies* (Consultation Paper No 142) (London: Stationery Office, 1996).

Some cases and articles are particularly important. K W Wedderburn, 'Shareholders' rights and the rule in *Foss v Harbottle*' [1957] CLJ 194, [1958] CLJ 93 is a very important article as are two by S M Beck, 'An analysis of *Foss v Harbottle*', in J S Ziegel (ed), *Studies in Canadian Company Law* (Toronto: Butterworths, 1967) and 'The shareholders' derivative action' (1974) 52 Can Bar Rev 159. Leading cases include *Foss v Harbottle* (1843) 2 Hare 461; *Burland v Earle* [1902] AC 83; *Edwards v Halliwell* [1950] 2 All ER 1064; and the lengthy and expensive suit of *Prudential Assurance Co Ltd v Newman Industries Ltd (No 2)*, in which, at first instance ([1981] Ch 257), Vinelott J examined previous case law in great detail. However, his Lordship's analysis and judgment were attacked by Professor Lord Wedderburn of Charlton, 'Derivative actions and *Foss v Harbottle*' (1981) 44 MLR 202, and by the Court of Appeal ([1982] Ch 204). (See also the casenotes by L S Sealy [1981] CLJ 29, [1982] CLJ 247.) Subsequently, Vinelott J was defended by G R Sullivan, 'Restating the scope of the derivative action' [1985] CLJ 236, and Colin Baxter carried out a very interesting review of the whole area in 'The true spirit of *Foss v Harbottle*' (1987) 38 NILQ 6.

For the history of the rule, see B S Prunty Jr, 'The shareholders' derivative suit: notes on its derivation' (1957) 32 NYU L Rev 980; A J Boyle, 'The minority shareholder in the 19th century: a study in Anglo-American legal history' (1965) 28 MLR 317 and D Linehan, 'Derivative suits in American, English and Irish law' (1974) 9 Irish Jurist 265. Linehan makes the point that derivative claims are much more important in the USA than in England or Ireland because English jurisprudence has placed greater emphasis on the so-called 'personal rights' of members—see **18.4.5**. Accordingly, the US experience is not always relevant to the law on this side of the Atlantic.

18.3.3 REASONS FOR THE RULE

There appear to be three reasons for the court's policy of not hearing a claim by a member of a company concerning the affairs of the company:

(a) refusal to be involved in disputes over business policy;

(b) disputes among members should be settled by the members themselves in general meeting where the majority should prevail; and

(c) a fear of multiplicity of claims.

18.3.3.1 Refusal to decide business policy

Judges have repeatedly said that a court determines questions of law not questions of business judgement. A court will not review the merits of a lawful decision of the members or directors of a company. See, in particular, the remarks of Scrutton LJ in *Shuttleworth v Cox Brothers and Co (Maidenhead) Ltd* [1927] 2 KB 9 at pp 22–4, and those of Lord Wilberforce in *Howard Smith Ltd v Ampol Petroleum Ltd* [1974] AC 821 quoted in **16.6.3**. The view is an old one. Lord Eldon LC was clearly horrified when, in **Waters v Taylor** (1808) 15 Ves Jr 10, the endlessly disputing partners of the Italian Opera asked him to appoint a manager to carry on the opera house and decide their disputes. Making such an appointment, said his Lordship (at p 25), would 'justify an expectation, that this court is to carry on every brewery, and every speculation in the kingdom'. Four years later, in **Carlen v Drury** (1812) 1 Ves & B 154, his Lordship *was* asked to appoint a manager of a brewery and made his much-quoted remark (at p 158): 'This court is not to be required on every occasion to take the management of every playhouse and brewhouse in the kingdom.'

Thus, in *Lord v Governor and Co of Copper Miners* (1848) 2 Ph 740 the court would not review a decision by the members to make an assignment for the benefit of creditors generally. In *Inderwick v Snell* (1850) 2 Mac & G 216, the members had dismissed directors under a provision in the company's articles that directors could be removed for 'reasonable cause': the court held that this meant what the members considered a reasonable cause not what the court thought was reasonable. In both cases the plaintiffs attempted to characterise the members' decisions as fraudulent but failed to convince the courts that any fraud was involved. See also *Odessa Tramways Co v Mendel* (1878) 8 ChD 235 and *Anglo-Universal Bank v Baragnon* (1881) 45 LT 362, which concerned directors' decisions and are discussed in **6.5.2.2**.

A more recent example is *Sandys v House of Fraser plc* 1985 SLT 200, in which a director of House of Fraser plc, who represented Lonrho plc's interest in the company, failed to obtain an interim interdict requiring an extraordinarily detailed analysis of the company's activities to be put before its board of directors as part of Lonrho's attempts to buy from House of Fraser the London department store Harrods.

18.3.3.2 Majority rule

There is a long-standing opinion that membership of any kind of association involves an obligation to settle disputes within the association and to abide by majority decisions. In **Cooper v Gordon** (1869) LR 8 Eq 249 (a case concerning a dissenting congregation), Stuart V-C said:

> The submission of the minority is the principle on which civil society is founded. It is a principle essential for that reasonable harmony which is necessary for the coherence of all societies, great or small, civil or religious.

As Lord Wilberforce said in **Re Kong Thai Sawmill (Miri) Sdn Bhd** [1978] 2 MLJ 227, at p 229: 'Those who take interests in companies limited by shares have to accept majority rule.'

The principle of majority rule is thought by commentators to be the basis of the rule in *Foss v Harbottle*.

Wedderburn's theory is that the ratifiability principle applies both where the company could be claimant and where it could be defendant: a member cannot complain to a court about an act that is ratifiable by a simple majority of members, but there is a class of acts which cannot be ratified by a simple majority, and a member can complain to a court about any act of that class. So he says ([1957] CLJ 194 at p 198): 'there is, after all, one "rule in *Foss v Harbottle*"; and the limits of that rule lie along the boundaries of majority rule'. The two problems with this approach are, first, that one is left to find out what is and is not 'ratifiable', of which Wedderburn said: 'We know that a shareholder can sue to challenge [directors' breaches of duty] and that they can be ratified, but not why' ('Unreformed company law' (1969) 32 MLR 563 at p 564). The second problem is that there is doubt about the existence of a category of acts which cannot be ratified at all (see **18.4.2.7**).

Beck's theory is that majority rule is the foundation of the rule in *Foss v Harbottle* because the internal management principle is based on the idea that matters of internal management are conclusively settled by majority decision and so not reviewable by the courts and the proper plaintiff principle is based on a supposed common law rule that the majority in general meeting have the right to decide on whether or not to litigate in the company's name (see **15.10.3**).

18.3.3.3 Multiplicity of claims

Of the many judicial comments on this, perhaps the most frequently quoted is that of Mellish LJ in *MacDougall v Gardiner* (1875) 1 ChD 13 at p 25:

> Looking to the nature of these companies, looking at the way in which their articles are formed, and that they are not all lawyers who attend these meetings, nothing can be more likely than that there should be something more or less irregular done at them—some directors may have been irregularly appointed, some directors as irregularly turned out, or something or other may have been done which ought not to have been done according to the proper construction of the articles. Now, if that gives a right to every member of the company to file a bill to have the question decided, then if there happens to be one cantankerous member, or one member who loves litigation, everything of this kind will be litigated; whereas, if the bill must be filed in the name of the company, then, unless there is a majority who really wish for litigation, the litigation will not go on. Therefore, holding that such suits must be brought in the name of the company does certainly greatly tend to stop litigation. [In the Chancery procedure of the time, a bill was the equivalent of a claim form and particulars of claim.]

And see per Lord Campbell LC in *Orr v Glasgow, Airdrie and Monklands Junction Railway Co* (1860) 3 Macq 799 at pp 802–3, and per James LJ in *Gray v Lewis* (1873) LR 8 Ch App 1035 at pp 1050–1.

18.3.3.4 Floodgates

The reasons for the rule in *Foss v Harbottle* are typical 'floodgates' arguments which the courts use to refuse jurisdiction—that courts should not deal with matters with which they are not familiar, and for which a domestic settlement procedure exists, and that allowing one claim would lead to an overwhelming number of similar claims (see F K H Maher and R C Evans, '"Hard" cases, floodgates and the new rhetoric' (1985) 8 U Tas LR 96). As in other circumstances in which floodgates arguments are used to justify not hearing a class of cases: (a) the courts make exceptions, and (b) the legislature has intervened to require the courts to deal with cases. The exception which the courts made to allow a member of a company to pursue a derivative claim on the company's behalf has now been put on a statutory basis (see **18.4.2**). Another major legislative intervention is now in CA 2006, part 30 (protection of company's members against unfair prejudice) see **18.6**. There are also provisions for a dissentient minority to apply to the court in respect of decisions on certain matters—see the final paragraph of **14.4.3**.

Despite the function of the rule in *Foss v Harbottle* of holding back a flood of litigation, it may be that sometimes a case which could have been barred by the rule has been heard simply because no defendant sought to invoke the rule to have the case stopped. In *Advance Bank of Australia Ltd v FAI Insurances Australia Ltd* (1987) 9 NSWLR 464, counsel for Advance Bank of Australia Ltd conceded that, on appeal, it was too late to challenge the standing of a member of the company to make a claim in respect of the company's affairs when standing had not been questioned at first instance (see per Kirby P at pp 470–1 and Mahoney JA at p 492). See also per Mahoney JA in *Darvall v North Sydney Brick and Tile Co Ltd* (1989) 16 NSWLR 260 at p 332. So not every case in which a company's affairs were considered by a court at the instance of a member can be regarded as a precedent on the applicability of the rule in *Foss v Harbottle*.

18.3.4 THE RATIFIABILITY PRINCIPLE

The ratifiability principle was stated by Wigram V-C in *Bagshaw v Eastern Union Railway Co* (1849) 7 Hare 114 at p 130 in the following form:

> if the act, though it be the act of the directors only, be one which a general meeting of the company could sanction, a bill by some of the shareholders, on behalf of themselves and others, to impeach that act cannot be sustained, because a general meeting of the company might immediately confirm and give validity to the act of which the bill complains. [In the Chancery procedure of the time, a bill was the equivalent of a claim form and particulars of claim.]

See also *Davidson v Tulloch* (1860) 3 Macq 783 per Lord Campbell LC at p 792 and Lord Cranworth at p 796.

In *Edwards v Halliwell* [1950] 2 All ER 1064, Jenkins LJ took the view that the ratifiability principle is a vital component of the rule in *Foss v Harbottle* (see **18.3.1**). Academic discussions of the rule often accord the ratifiability principle the central position which Jenkins LJ thought it had. See, for example, R Gregory, 'What *is* the rule in *Foss v Harbottle*?' (1982) 45 MLR 584.

18.4 PROPER CLAIMANT PRINCIPLE

18.4.1 THE COMPANY IS THE PROPER CLAIMANT TO ENFORCE ITS RIGHTS

18.4.1.1 Statement of principle

The legal rights of a company belong to the company as a separate person and not to its members. The members of a company do not have standing to enforce its rights by legal action. As the Court of Appeal explained in *Prudential Assurance Co Ltd v Newman Industries Ltd (No 2)* [1982] Ch 204, at p 210, it is an:

> elementary principle that A cannot, as a general rule, bring an action against B to recover damages or secure other relief on behalf of C for an injury done by B to C. C is the proper plaintiff because C is the party injured, and, therefore, the person in whom the cause of action is vested. This is sometimes referred to as the rule in *Foss v Harbottle* (1843) 2 Hare 461 when applied to corporations, but it has a wider scope and is fundamental to any rational system of jurisprudence.

Whether or not a company sues to enforce its legal rights must be decided by the persons who, under the company's constitution, have authority to institute legal proceedings in the company's name. This will normally be the directors (*Breckland Group Holdings Ltd v London and Suffolk Properties Ltd* [1989] BCLC 100; see **15.10.3**).

The principle that a company is the only person able to claim redress for injury to itself is known as the proper claimant principle. It prevents a member of a company claiming redress on behalf of the company. The principle cannot be avoided by claiming redress for a loss (for example, in the value of shares) suffered by the member as a result of the company's loss (see **18.4.3**). There are exceptions where the company is prevented by the wrongdoer from taking action itself (see **18.4.2** and **18.4.3.2**).

The proper claimant principle does not infringe art 6 (right to a fair trial) of the European Convention on Human Rights in the Human Rights Act 1998, sch 1 (*Agrotexim v Greece* (application 14807/89) (1995) 21 EHRR 250 at para 73).

The proper claimant principle applies even if a majority of members support a claim by a member to enforce a right of the company (*Mozley v Alston* (1847) 1 Ph 790) and even if all the members are claiming (*Hawkesbury Development Co Ltd v Landmark Finance Pty Ltd* (1969) 92 WN (NSW) 199).

18.4.1.2 *Foss v Harbottle*

In *Foss v Harbottle* (1843) 2 Hare 461, Mr Foss and Mr Turton, who were members of a statutory company called the Victoria Park Co, alleged that various people, including five directors of the company (one of whom was Mr Harbottle), had made secret profits as promoters of the company (see **17.7.3**) and that the directors had breached their fiduciary duties to the company by causing it to enter into improper and fraudulent transactions. Foss and Turton commenced an action against the alleged wrongdoers, 'on behalf of themselves and all other the proprietors of shares except the defendants'. Wigram V-C said, at p 490:

> The Victoria Park Co is an incorporated body, and the conduct with which the defendants are charged in this suit is an injury not to the plaintiffs exclusively; it is an injury to the whole corporation.

His Honour observed that there was no doubt that proceedings to remedy this wrong could have been brought in the name of the company but these proceedings had been:

> brought by two individual corporators, professedly on behalf of themselves and all other members of the corporation, except those who committed the injuries complained of—the plaintiffs assuming to themselves the right and power in that manner to sue on behalf of and represent the corporation itself.

The plaintiffs were treating the company just as an association of its members, so that they could represent the company if they represented the members, but this ignored the fact that the company was also a separate person:

> It was not, nor could it successfully be, argued that it was a matter of course for any individual members of a corporation thus to assume to themselves the right of suing in the name of the corporation. In law the corporation and the aggregate members of the corporation are not the same thing for purposes like this.

18.4.2 DERIVATIVE CLAIMS

18.4.2.1 Definition

Sometimes the court permits a right of action of a company to be pursued in proceedings brought in the name of a member of the company, as an exception to the proper claimant principle. At first such proceedings were treated, like the unsuccessful proceedings in *Foss v Harbottle* (1843) 2 Hare 461 (see **18.4.1.2**), as being brought by the company as an association of its members, and were expressed to be brought on behalf of the claimant and all other members of the company except (if they were also members) the defendants. More recently, following US jurisprudence, a member of a company bringing proceedings to enforce a right of the company is said to be deriving a right of action from the company. Accordingly, such proceedings are called 'derivative claims' (*Schiowitz v IOS Ltd* (1971) 23 DLR (3d) 102 at p 121; *Estmanco (Kilner House) Ltd v Greater London Council* [1982] 1 WLR 2 at p 10).

A derivative claim is defined in CA 2006, s 260(1), as a proceeding by a member of a company:

(a) in respect of a cause of action vested in the company; and

(b) seeking relief on behalf of the company.

In this provision, 'member' includes a person to whom shares in the company have been transferred, or have been transmitted by operation of law (see **8.5**), but who is not a member of the company (because of not being registered as the holder of the shares) (s 260(5)(c)).

The company must be joined as a co-defendant so that if its rights are vindicated it will be able to enforce the judgment (Civil Procedure Rules 1998, r 19.9(3)). Before the changes of terminology made by the Civil Procedure Rules 1998, derivative claims were known as derivative actions.

18.4.2.2 When is a derivative claim required?

The need for a derivative claim arises only where the claim cannot be brought in the company's name. Unless a company is subject to an insolvency or liquidation procedure (see **18.4.2.10**), authority to institute litigation in a company's name normally lies with its directors (see **15.10.3**). So, outside of liquidation and insolvency, a derivative claim is necessary only where there is a dispute between a member of a company and its directors over the merits of bringing a claim. A dissentient member must normally accept the decision of those who under the company's constitution have the authority to decide on litigation. So a derivative claim is allowed only if the court is willing to ignore the company's decision not to sue. The usual reason for asking a court to ignore a company's decision not to sue is that it was taken by the very persons who should be sued. Under the law before CA 2006, a decision not to sue in respect of a wrong done to a company (or, equivalently, to ratify the wrong) was described as a fraud on the minority (that is, the member or members who wished to bring a claim) if the wrong was of a fraudulent character or beyond the powers of the company and the persons sought to be sued used their own influence over the company (for example, as directors or major shareholders) to prevent the company suing them. In *Burland v Earle* [1902] AC 83, Lord Davey said, at p 93:

> But an exception is made to the [proper claimant principle], where the persons against whom the relief is sought themselves hold and control the majority of the shares in the company, and will not permit an action to be brought in the name of the company. In that case the courts allow the shareholders complaining to bring an action in their own names. This, however, is mere matter of procedure in order to give a remedy for a wrong which would otherwise escape redress.

Where a wrong has been done to a subsidiary of a company, the parent company is the person who should bring a derivative claim when the subsidiary's directors refuse to do so. Normally, however, the same directors control both parent and subsidiary and the person who wishes to bring a claim to vindicate the subsidiary's rights is a member of the parent company. In this situation, a multiple derivative claim is required in which the member of the parent company sues on behalf of the subsidiary (see *Universal Project Management Services Ltd v Fort Gilkicker Ltd* [2013] EWHC 348 (Ch), [2013] Ch 551).

18.4.2.3 Statutory derivative claims

A derivative claim by a member of a company may now be brought only under CA 2006, part 11, Chapter 1 (ss 260 to 264), or in pursuance of a court order under s 996(2)(c) (see **18.6.11.1**) (s 260(2)). This restriction is new to CA 2006. Previously, the court decided whether it would permit a derivative claim, which generated a large quantity of case law. A derivative claim brought under ss 260 to 264 is usually described as a statutory derivative claim.

A claim can be brought under ss 260 to 264 only in respect of the causes of action specified in s 260 (see **18.4.2.4**) and the claimant must obtain the court's permission to continue the claim (s 261(1); see **18.4.2.5**).

A multiple derivative claim (see **18.4.2.2**) may be brought at common law and has not been abolished by CA 2006 (*Universal Project Management Services Ltd v Fort Gilkicker Ltd* [2013] EWHC 348 (Ch), [2013] Ch 551).

18.4.2.4 Causes for which derivative claims are allowed

A member of a company may bring a statutory derivative claim under CA 2006, part 11, Chapter 1 (ss 260 to 264), only in respect of a cause of action specified in s 260. The cause of action must be vested in the company (s 260(1)). It must arise from an actual or proposed act or omission which involves negligence, default, breach of duty or breach of trust by a director, former director or shadow director of the company (s 260(3), (5)(a) and (b)). The cause of action may be against the director, or another person or both (s 260(3)). It may have arisen before the claimant became a member of the company (s 260(4)): this rule arises from the principle that it is the company's claim which is being pursued, not the member's (*Seaton v Grant* (1867) LR 2 Ch App 459).

Before CA 2006, derivative claims were allowed in respect of acts which were of a fraudulent character or *ultra vires*. Under the old law a derivative claim could be brought in respect of an act by a member (*Estmanco (Kilner House) Ltd v Greater London Council* [1982] 1 WLR 2; see **14.10.5**). A derivative claim could not now be brought under ss 260 to 264 in respect of an act by a member, but the act might be the subject of a petition for relief of unfairly prejudicial conduct of the company's affairs (see **18.4.2.11**). Under the old law a derivative claim could not be brought in respect of a director's negligence if it did not benefit the director personally (*Pavlides v Jensen* [1956] Ch 565). The fact that this restriction is not stated in s 260 has caused fears of a flood of litigation in respect of directors' negligence.

18.4.2.5 Permission to continue a statutory derivative claim

A member of a company who brings a statutory derivative claim under CA 2006, part 11, Chapter 1 (ss 260 to 264), must apply to the court for permission to continue it (s 261(1)). For the first time, s 263 gives guidance on how the court should approach deciding whether to give permission. The principal matters to be taken into account are:

(a) whether the company has decided not to pursue the claim (s 263(3)(e); see **18.4.2.6**);

(b) the views of disinterested members (s 263(4); see **18.4.2.6**);

(c) whether the claim would promote the company's success (s 263(2)(a) and (3)(b); see **18.4.2.6**);

(d) whether there has been, or could be, authorisation or ratification of the act or omission giving rise to the claim (s 263(2)(b) and (c) and (3)(c) and (d); see **18.4.2.7**); and

(e) the good faith of the derivative claimant (s 263(3)(a); see **18.4.2.8**).

In response to fears that putting derivative claims on a statutory basis would open the floodgates of litigation (see **18.3.3.4** and **18.4.2.4**), s 261 requires the court to consider an application for permission to continue a derivative claim in two stages. At the first stage it considers only the evidence presented by the claimant and must dismiss the application if this evidence does not disclose a prima facie case for giving permission. If the court decides that there is a prima facie case, it will give directions for the company to file evidence for a contested hearing of the application.

18.4.2.6 Decision by the company not to sue

If those with authority to conduct a company's litigation (usually the directors) have decided not to pursue a claim which a member is seeking to bring on the company's behalf, the underlying question for the court is whether it should override that decision (see **18.4.2.2**). Usually, the obvious reason for overriding a decision not to sue is that it was taken by those liable to be sued. So CA 2006, s 263(4), requires the court to have 'particular regard' for the views of members of the company who have no personal interest, direct or indirect, in the matter. There is always a possibility that it is not in the interests of the company to waste time and money on litigation or that the matter can be settled satisfactorily out of court (see **18.2**). So s 263(3)(b) asks the court to take into account, in particular, the importance that a person acting in accordance with s 172 (duty to promote the success of the company) would attach to continuing the claim. Section 263(2)(a) goes further and requires the court to refuse permission if satisfied that such a person would not seek to continue the claim.

A derivative claim may be available to a member of a company without showing that those in control of the company's litigation have made a positive decision not to sue. This may occur if it is not possible to reach a decision on the question because the parties sought to be sued can block decision-making, for example, because they have exactly the same number of votes as the parties seeking to sue or they can prevent meetings being quorate by refusing to attend (*Ingre v Maxwell* (1964) 44 DLR (2d) 764; *Glass v Atkin* (1967) 65 DLR (2d) 501; *Fargro Ltd v Godfrey* [1986] 1 WLR 1134; *Anglo-Eastern* (1985) *Ltd v Knutz* [1988] 1 HKLR 322). In such a case, the member bringing the derivative claim may not have a minority of votes but will be in the same position as a minority (*Glass v Atkin* at p 504).

18.4.2.7 Authorisation or ratification

A decision by those who have authority to conduct a company's litigation not to pursue a cause of action arising from an act or omission may be based on a belief that the act or omission has been, or will be, authorised or ratified by the company. If a decision to ratify an act is effective, a derivative claim is not possible, because the act will be deemed by the ratification not to be a wrong to the company and so there will be no right of action which a member can enforce on the company's behalf (*Kent v Jackson* (1851) 14 Beav 367; affirmed (1852) 2 De G M & G 49).

If a derivative claim arises from an act or omission that is yet to occur, the court deciding whether to permit the claim to continue must take into account whether the act or omission could be authorised by the company before it does occur, or could be ratified afterwards, and whether, in the circumstances, one of these things is likely to happen (CA 2006, s 263(3)(c)). If it is satisfied that the act or omission has been authorised, it must refuse permission to continue (s 263(2)(b)).

If a derivative claim arises from an act or omission that has already occurred, the court deciding whether to permit the claim to continue must take into account whether the act or omission could be ratified by the company, and whether, in the circumstances, it would be likely to be ratified (s 263(3)(d)). If it is satisfied that the act or omission has been authorised or ratified, it must refuse permission to continue (s 263(2)(c)).

Before ss 260 to 264 came into force, the courts sometimes allowed a derivative claim in respect of an act even though the act had been ratified. These were cases in which the court held that the ratification was invalid (see **16.16.2** to **16.16.4**). In other cases the courts refused to allow a derivative claim on behalf of a company in respect of an act which had been ratified by the members of the company, even where the ratification depended on the votes of interested members. These were cases in which the court held that ratification was valid despite being made by interested persons. The unresolved question is whether the validity of ratification depended on the character of the act (the first theory) or on whether ratification was by disinterested persons (the second theory). The first theory is particularly associated with Lord Wedderburn of Charlton. See K W Wedderburn, 'Shareholders' rights and the rule in *Foss v Harbottle*' [1957] CLJ 194, [1958] CLJ 93. The first theory predicts that the causes of action in respect of which derivative claims will be allowed are those arising from acts which cannot be ratified. However, the only way of discovering which acts cannot be ratified is by observing which causes of action are allowed to be the subject of derivative claims. The courts seemed to move towards adopting a second theory, that any act could be ratified, provided the ratification was effected by the votes of disinterested members (*Smith v Croft (No 2)* [1988] Ch 114; *Taylor v National Union of Mineworkers (Derbyshire Area)* [1985] BCLC 237). As Vinelott J said in not the nature of the act. (No 2) [1981] Ch 257 at p 307:

> there is no obvious limit to the power of the majority to authorise or ratify an act or transaction whatever its character provided that the majority does not have an interest which conflicts with the company.

For Lord Wedderburn's criticism of this statement, see 'Derivative actions and *Foss v Harbottle*' (1981) 44 MLR 202 at pp 207–8. The courts never took the second theory to its logical conclusion by overruling earlier decisions that some acts could be ratified by interested votes. However, this has now been done by CA 2006, s 239 (see later).

If the second theory is correct, the fact that an act could be ratified would not in itself have prevented a derivative claim being allowed before CA 2006, ss 260 to 264, came into force. This is because, under the second theory, it was the nature of the ratification (disinterested or not) which was crucial, not the nature of the act. In *Regal (Hastings) Ltd v Gulliver* [1967] 2 AC 134 the company was, properly, the claimant in proceedings concerning a wrong done to it. Lord Russell of Killowen, at p 143, said that the defendants' liability was considered on the footing that they acted with bona fides, intending to act in the interest of the company, and that an attempt at first instance to make out a case of wilful misconduct or fraud on their part had failed. At p 150 his Lordship said that the five directors against whom the case had been brought 'could, had they wished, have protected themselves by a resolution (either antecedent or subsequent) of the Regal shareholders in general meeting'. There were (according to his Lordship, at p 140) 20 shareholders in all, and they never considered whether to resolve to allow the directors to keep their profit from the transaction in question: accordingly, whether there had been authorisation or ratification by the votes of disinterested members was never an issue in the case. The first theory would deduce that a director's profit from a transaction to which the company is not a party could not have been the subject of a derivative claim before ss 260 to 264 came into force, because it could have been ratified (Lord Wedderburn of Charlton, 'Derivative actions and *Foss v Harbottle*' (1981) 44 MLR 202 at pp 206 and 210–11). Under the second theory, whether or not it could have been the subject of a derivative claim would have depended on whether it was ratified by the votes of disinterested members.

For critical discussion see F H Buckley, 'Ratification and the derivative action under the Ontario Business Corporations Act' (1976) 22 McGill LJ 167; G R Sullivan, 'Restating the scope of the derivative action' [1985] CLJ 236 at pp 239–44; and P StJ Smart, 'Misuse of confidential information: the company's and minority shareholder's remedies' [1987] JBL 464. At p 248 of his article, Sullivan attempts to unravel the mystery surrounding Lord Russell's remark in *Regal (Hastings) Ltd v Gulliver*. The rest of his article defends Vinelott J's analysis, which Smart (at n 42) dismisses as wrong.

Now CA 2006, s 260(3), defines the acts or omissions on which statutory derivative claims may be based as those involving negligence, default, breach of duty or breach of trust. However, ratification is still relevant because, by s 263(2)(b) and (c), ratification or authorisation prevents a derivative claim proceeding (see **18.4.2.6**). Section 239 requires ratification of any conduct by a director of a company which amounts to negligence, default, breach of duty or breach of trust in relation to the company to be by the votes of disinterested members (the second theory), unless it is unanimous. But s 239(7) provides that s 239 does not affect any rule of law as to acts that are incapable of being ratified by a company. It was held in *Franbar Holdings Ltd v Patel* [2008] EWHC 1534 (Ch), [2009] 1 BCLC 1, that this means the court must ask whether the ratification has the effect that the claimant is being improperly prevented from bringing the claim on behalf of the company (citing *Smith v Croft (No 2)* [1988] Ch 144 at p 185). This could happen where the ratification has been obtained by the votes of a member who is associated with the director sought to be sued but is not connected with that director for the purposes of s 239(4). This seems to concentrate on the nature of the ratification (second theory) rather than the character of the act being ratified (first theory).

The cases in which ratification by a majority which included interested members was permitted before s 239 came into force were:

(a) negligence by a director which did not benefit the director personally (*Pavlides v Jensen* [1956] Ch 565);

(b) sale by a director to the company of an asset which was not acquired by the director in a fiduciary capacity (*North-West Transportation Co Ltd v Beatty* (1887) 12 App Cas 589; *Burland v Earle* [1902] AC 83; as explained in *Cook v Deeks* [1916] 1 AC 554; see **17.7.4**); and

(c) a director's profit from a transaction to which the company was not a party (see the earlier discussion of *Regal (Hastings) Ltd v Gulliver*).

In all these cases, ratification, by a majority including an interested member, of a director's negligence or breach of duty (in (b) the duty to declare an interest in a transaction with the company) is now not permitted by s 239.

18.4.2.8 Good faith

The court will usually not allow a derivative claim to proceed if, rather than being pursued bona fide for the benefit of the company, the claim has been brought for an ulterior purpose (*Barrett v Duckett* [1995] 1 BCLC 243; *Portfolios of Distinction Ltd v Laird* [2004] EWHC 2071 (Ch), [2004] 2 BCLC 741), or if there is another adequate remedy (*Barrett v Duckett*; *Cooke v Cooke* [1997] 2 BCLC 28; *Portfolios of Distinction Ltd v Laird*; *Mumbray v Lapper* [2005] EWHC 1152 (Ch), [2005] BCC 990). In *Barrett v Duckett* the plaintiff was pursuing a derivative claim against her former son-in-law primarily in retribution for his treatment of her daughter, but she apparently could not afford to continue with the claim and it was found that putting the company into liquidation, so that an independent liquidator could take over the litigation, would be better than continuing with the derivative claim.

In *Cooke v Cooke* the court stayed all proceedings in a derivative claim because the claimant had also petitioned for relief of unfairly prejudicial conduct of the company's affairs (see **18.6**), making substantially the same factual allegations, and it was assumed that the unfair prejudice petition was the better means of dealing with the issues.

The court will not allow a derivative claim to be brought by a person who participated in the wrongful act complained of (*Whitwam v Watkin* (1898) 78 LT 188). In *Towers v African Tug Co* [1904] 1 Ch 558, the company had paid an illegal dividend because of an honest mistake by its directors. Two shareholders, who had received the illegal dividend in respect of their shares, sought to bring a derivative claim against the directors to compel them to pay the amount of the illegal dividend to the company. It was held that they were not entitled to bring the claim. Another example is *Nurcombe v Nurcombe* [1985] 1 WLR 370.

18.4.2.9 Blocking proceedings by company

If those with authority to conduct a company's litigation fear a derivative claim, they may try to block it by causing the company to bring a claim but with no intention of genuinely pursuing it. CA 2006, s 262, therefore permits a member of a company to apply to the court for permission to take over a claim brought by the company and continue it as a derivative claim on the ground that:

(a) the manner in which the company commenced or continued the claim amounts to an abuse of the process of the court;

(b) the company has failed to prosecute the claim diligently; and

(c) it is appropriate for the member to continue the claim as a derivative claim.

18.4.2.10 Insolvency and liquidation

If a company is subject to an insolvency or liquidation procedure (other than voluntary arrangement), the insolvency office-holder can bring proceedings in its name (Insolvency Act 1986, s 165(2) and sch 4, para 4 (liquidator in voluntary winding up); s 167(1) and sch 4, para 4 (liquidator in a compulsory winding up); sch 1, para 5 (administrator, administrative receiver)). In relation to a company being wound up, it has been held that a member who disagrees with the liquidator's decision not to pursue one of its causes of action cannot bring a derivative claim: the dispute must be dealt with in an application to the court to review the liquidator's decision (*Ferguson v Wallbridge* [1935] 3 DLR 66; *Fargro Ltd v Godfroy* [1986] 1 WLR 1134). Such an application is made under s 167(3) in a winding up by the court or s 112 (asking the court to exercise its powers under s 167(3)) in a voluntary winding up.

18.4.2.11 Unfair prejudice claim

If a company's claim against a person, which the company will not pursue, arises from unfairly prejudicial conduct of the company's affairs, a member may petition under CA 2006, s 994 (see **18.6**), asking the court to give the company a remedy against that person, as an alternative to bringing a derivative claim (*Re a Company (No 005287 of 1985)* [1986] 1 WLR 281; *Lowe v Fahey* [1996] 1 BCLC 262; *Clark v Cutland* [2003] EWCA Civ 810, [2004] 1 WLR 783; *Anderson v Hogg* 2002 SC 190). Section 996(2)(c) also empowers the court, on hearing a petition under s 994, to authorise the bringing of a derivative claim: this power may be useful where it is not possible to determine the merits of the claim in the s 994 proceedings.

In *Whyte* 1984 SLT 330 a company called Liquid Gas Equipment Ltd ('LGE') had instituted proceedings against another company, which was controlled by LGE's majority shareholder. That shareholder threatened to use its majority vote to discontinue the proceedings, but a minority shareholder in LGE petitioned under s 994 and obtained an interim order preventing the majority carrying out that threat.

18.4.2.12 Costs

Before a derivative claim is heard, the court may order the company to indemnify the claimant for liability in respect of costs, whether the claim is successful or not (Civil Procedure Rules 1998, r 19.9E). This is sometimes called a pre-emptive costs order. It is also called a *Wallersteiner* order, because it was first suggested in *Wallersteiner v Moir (No 2)* [1975] QB 373. When deciding whether to make a pre-emptive costs order in favour of a claimant making a derivative claim on behalf of a company, the court will take into consideration the effect on the defendant's interest in the company: it may be unfair that a successful defendant who is not required to pay the unsuccessful claimant's costs should nevertheless have to bear a substantial loss in the value of shares when the company pays the costs (*Halle v Trax BW Ltd* [2000] BCC 1020; *Mumbray v Lapper* [2005] EWHC 1152 (Ch), [2005] BCC 990). Despite obiter indications to the contrary in *Halle v Trax BW Ltd*, there is no rule that a successful derivative claimant has a lien, for costs, on assets recovered in the claim (*Qayoumi v Oakhouse Property Holdings plc* [2002] EWHC 2547 (Ch), [2003] 1 BCLC 352).

18.4.3 NO REFLECTIVE LOSS PRINCIPLE

18.4.3.1 Statement of principle

The proper claimant principle discussed in **18.4.1** is that if a company has a right of action against a person, D, to claim compensation for loss which D has caused the company, then legal proceedings making that claim must be in the name of the company, and neither a member of the company, nor anyone else, can claim that compensation from D. (Though, in limited circumstances a member may be permitted to bring a derivative claim—see **18.4.2** to **18.4.4**—to claim compensation for the company.) The damage which D has inflicted on the company may affect, for example, its ability to pay dividends to its members, or return their capital in winding up, or its ability to pay its employees and other creditors, and the price at which members can sell their shares may be diminished. But these ill effects should be put right when the company recovers what is due to it from D. The no reflective loss principle is that members and others cannot themselves sue D to recover losses which merely reflect the losses D has caused to the company which the company could recover from D (*Prudential Assurance Co Ltd v Newman Industries Ltd (No 2)* [1982] Ch 204 at pp 222–3; *Johnson v Gore Wood and Co* [2002] 2 AC 1; *Gardner v Parker* [2004] EWCA Civ 781, [2004] 2 BCLC 554).

The no reflective loss principle ensures that D can only be sued once for the same loss. It prevents a person other than the company suing even if that person has a cause of action against D and even if that cause of action differs from the company's (*Day v Cook* [2001] EWCA Civ 592, [2002] 1

BCLC 1, at [79]). It applies whether the cause of action lies in common law or equity, and whether the remedy is damages or restitution (*Gardner v Parker*). It applies to prevent a member suing whether the member has a controlling or a minority interest (*Gardner v Parker*, rejecting doubts expressed in *Humberclyde Finance Group Ltd v Hicks* (2001) LTL 19/11/2001 and *Floyd v John Fairhurst and Co* [2004] EWCA Civ 604, [2004] PNLR 41, at [77]). The no reflective loss principle is not an infringement of the European Convention on Human Rights, protocol 1, art 1 (protection of property), in the Human Rights Act 1998, sch 1 (*Humberclyde Finance Group Ltd v Hicks*).

The principle has been held to apply to payments which might have been made in the shareholder's capacity as an officer or employee. In *Johnson v Gore Wood and Co* a member of a company, who controlled it, claimed, among other things, for contributions which the company failed to make to his pension fund when it did not have enough money because of losses allegedly caused by the defendants' negligence. Lord Bingham of Cornhill thought it 'plain that this claim is merely a reflection of the company's loss' (at p 36) and it was struck out.

In *Stein v Blake* [1998] 1 All ER 724, Mr Stein owned half the shares in a number of companies. The first defendant owned the other half and was sole director of the companies. It was alleged that the first defendant misappropriated assets from the companies and he was sued for the loss in value of Mr Stein's shares resulting from that misappropriation. The companies could have sued the first defendant for the value of the misappropriated assets. It seems that Mr Stein brought his personal claim because all the companies had gone into liquidation and the liquidators were not taking action. Mr Stein's claim was struck out because the companies were the proper claimants in respect of the wrong allegedly done to them. As all the companies were insolvent it was their creditors who were primarily interested in recovery of their assets, not Mr Stein. It made no difference that Mr Stein alleged that the other director owed him a duty personally: the damage allegedly caused by breach of that duty was to the companies and was caused in breach of the defendant's duty to the companies. The loss caused to Mr Stein was only a reflection of the companies' loss, which the companies were the proper claimants to recover for the benefit of their creditors.

By analogy with the no reflective loss principle, if a defendant's wrongful act is found to have caused both a loss to a claimant and a gain to a company in which the claimant is a shareholder, the claimant's loss and the company's gain must be set off (*Floyd v John Fairhurst and Co*).

If a company whose shares are publicly traded claims damages for an injury done to it, a fall in the market price of its shares is not acceptable to the court as a measure of the damages: if the market really has accurately valued the company's shares, it should have taken into account the award of damages (*Collins Stewart Ltd v Financial Times Ltd* [2004] EWHC 2337 (QB), [2005] EMLR 5).

See C Mitchell, 'Shareholders' claims for reflective loss' (2004) 120 LQR 457.

18.4.3.2 Company's failure to recover its loss

If a company with a right to sue a person, D, to recover a loss fails to recover all or part of that loss, for example because it settles the claim before trial, or refuses to take any action at all, it will not be possible for the company to pay members all or part of their reflective losses. This does not give the members a right to sue D for the unrecovered amount of the reflective losses, because the shortfall in recovery is caused by the company, not D (*Johnson v Gore Wood and Co* [2002] 2 AC 1). There is an exception if it is D's wrongdoing which has caused the company to be unable to sue, for example, because that wrongdoing has left it without enough money to fund litigation (*Giles v Rhind* [2002] EWCA Civ 1428, [2003] Ch 618). In *Giles v Rhind*, Mr Giles was a member of a company which, as a result of Mr Rhind's wrongdoing, had become insolvent, gone into administration and then into liquidation. Just before going into administration the company had commenced a claim against Mr Rhind, but its administrator had been forced to discontinue the claim for lack of funds and had undertaken that the company would not recommence the claim. The Court of Appeal held that, as the company's inability to sue had been caused by the same wrongdoing for which compensation was sought, Mr Giles should be allowed to claim instead.

It has been suggested that a defendant applying to strike out a claim, on the ground that it reflects a loss which a company could have sued for, but did not, must show that the supposed claim by the company would have been likely to succeed (*Perry v Day* [2004] EWHC 1398 (Ch), [2005] BCC 375, at [65]).

18.4.3.3 Company without a cause of action

The mere fact that D has caused a company to suffer loss does not give a holder of shares in that company a right of action to sue for the diminution in share value resulting from that loss. However, it is possible for a company to suffer loss because of something done by D but have no right of action against D while a shareholder does have a right of action against D. In such a case, the shareholder is permitted to claim for loss in value of the shareholding due to a loss which the company has no cause of action to recover (*George Fischer (Great Britain) Ltd v Multi Construction Ltd* [1995] 1 BCLC 260; *Gerber Garment Technology Inc v Lectra Systems Ltd* [1997] RPC 443).

In *George Fischer (Great Britain) Ltd v Multi Construction Ltd* a company sued for breach of a contract to supply equipment for its warehouse. The breach of contract had disrupted the activities of its wholly owned subsidiaries which used the warehouse, and the company sued for the resulting loss in value of its shares in those subsidiaries. It was held that damages for breach of contract could be recovered for this loss. As the subsidiaries were not parties to the contract, they had no right of action in respect of any breach of it.

In *Bank Mellat v HM Treasury (No 2)* [2013] UKSC 39, [2014] AC 700, it was held that the Treasury had unlawfully deprived Bank Mellat of its property, contrary to the European Convention on Human Rights, protocol 1, art 1, and the Human Rights Act 1998, s 6(1). Bank Mellat is claiming damages for that loss of property under s 8 of the Human Rights Act. When determining damages a UK court must take into account the principles applied by the European Court of Human Rights in relation to the award of compensation under art 41 of the Convention (Human Rights Act 1998, s 8(4)). Deciding preliminary issues, in *Bank Mellat v HM Treasury* [2015] EWHC 1258 (Comm), [2016] 1 All ER (Comm) 766, Flaux J held that the rule against claiming reflective loss is part of the ECHR's jurisprudence. That would prevent Bank Mellat from suing for the loss of value of shares in a subsidiary, which resulted indirectly from the defendant's wrongdoing. However, as only a 'victim' who is directly affected by a breach of convention rights has standing to sue for compensation, the subsidiary has no cause of action for its losses. Flaux J held that in those circumstances, Bank Mellat can sue for the loss of value of the shares in the subsidiary.

18.4.3.4 Losses which are not reflective

It is possible, when both company and shareholder have causes of action against the same defendant, that some of the shareholder's claims are not for reflective losses and can be pursued by the shareholder personally. For example, in *R P Howard Ltd v Woodman Matthews and Co* [1983] BCLC 117 a solicitor acted for both a company and its controlling shareholder. The solicitor negligently failed to ensure that the company applied in time to enforce its statutory right to renew its tenancy of business premises. As a result the company had to accept a new tenancy on significantly worse terms and the shareholder had to agree not to sell his controlling interest without the landlord's permission. It was held that the company could recover from the solicitor the increased rent it had to pay, and the shareholder could recover the loss in value of his shares caused by the restriction on selling them. The shareholder's loss was not a reflection of any loss by the company and so could be recovered by the shareholder personally.

In *Pearce v European Reinsurance Consultants and Run-off Ltd* [2005] EWHC 1493 (Ch), [2005] 2 BCLC 366, the claimant's shares in a company had been compulsorily purchased under provisions of the company's articles which required the purchase price to be determined by the company's auditor, acting on the company's instructions. The claimant alleged breach of duty to himself by the auditor in carrying out this valuation and claimed the difference between what he alleged was the correct valuation and the amount he was actually paid for the shares. It was held that this was not a claim for a reflective loss. The claimant had also alleged that the shares had declined in value since the valuation, but this allegation was made so as to justify not claiming rescission of the sale and did not affect the nature of the claim in respect of the incorrect valuation.

Determining whether a claim by a shareholder is unsustainable because it is only for a loss which could have been made good in a claim made by the company requires close scrutiny of the facts (per Lord Bingham in *Johnson v Gore Wood and Co* [2002] 2 AC 1 at p 36). For an illustration of how difficult this may be see *Day v Cook* [2001] EWCA Civ 592, [2002] 1 BCLC 1. For a more straightforward case see *Ellis v Property Leeds (UK) Ltd* [2002] EWCA Civ 32, [2002] 2 BCLC 175.

18.4.3.5 Judicial review

The no reflective loss principle has not been acknowledged in judicial review proceedings. The Administrative Court is willing to recognise that a member or officer of a company has a sufficient interest in a decision affecting the company to claim judicial review of that decision, even if the company declines to make such a claim (*R (Wildman) v Office of Communications* [2005] EWHC 1573 (Admin), *The Times*, 28 September 2005 (claim by company secretary); *R (Grierson) v Office of Communications* [2005] EWHC 1899 (Admin), [2005] EMLR 37 (claim by member and managing director)). The more important an arguable issue, the stronger its apparent merits, the more ready should the court be to grant standing (*Grierson* at [23]), but it is highly relevant that relief is sought in favour of a company which does not want it (*Grierson* at [22]). Neither Mr Wildman nor Mr Grierson succeeded in their claims to overturn decisions not to award their companies commercial radio licences.

18.4.3.6 Non-shareholder claimants

The no reflective loss principle applies to prevent a non-shareholder from claiming redress for a loss which reflects a loss by a company for which the company has a right of action, even if it is a different right of action and even if the company has not pursued it (*Shaker v Al-Bedrawi* [2002] EWCA Civ 1452, [2003] Ch 350). In *Shaker v Al-Bedrawi* all shares in a company incorporated in Pennsylvania, USA, were held by Mr Al-Bedrawi and by his wife as his nominee. It was alleged that 70 per cent of the shares were held on trust for the claimant and a fellow investor. It was held that the claimant could not sue for an account of profits made by Mr Al-Bedrawi in breach of that trust, to the extent that the company could have sued for the same money as an illegal dividend.

18.4.4 THE COMPANY IS THE PROPER CLAIMANT IN A MATTER CONCERNING ITS INTERNAL MANAGEMENT

The internal management principle is that the court will not interfere with the internal management of companies acting within their powers. The proper claimant aspect of this principle is that the court will not determine a question concerning what it regards as the internal management of a company except in proceedings brought by the company itself.

The proper claimant aspect of the internal management principle is derived from the Court of Appeal's decision in **MacDougall v Gardiner** (1875) 1 ChD 13, in which James LJ said, at pp 21–2:

> I think it is of the utmost importance in all these companies that the rule which is well known in this court as the rule in . . . *Foss v Harbottle* should be always adhered to; that is to say, that nothing connected with internal disputes between the shareholders is to be made the subject of a bill by some one shareholder on behalf of himself and others, unless there be something illegal, oppressive, or fraudulent—unless there is something *ultra vires* on the part of the company qua company, or on the part of the majority of the company, so that they are not fit persons to determine it; but that every litigation must be in the name of the company, if the company really desire it. [In the Chancery procedure of the time, a bill was the equivalent of a claim form and particulars of claim.]

Claims to challenge majority decisions that are fraudulent or oppressive are considered in **14.10.5**; see also **18.4.2** on decisions not to sue company controllers. Claims in respect of a company's *ultra vires* acts are considered in **18.4.6**.

In *MacDougall v Gardiner*, Colonel Gardiner had chaired a meeting of members of a company. He knew that he and his colleagues would win votes taken by show of hands but lose votes taken by poll. So, before any resolutions that he did not like could be put to the meeting, Colonel Gardiner accepted a resolution to adjourn the meeting which had been adopted by show of hands, and refused a demand for a poll on the resolution. (As was usual at that time, the articles of the company did not contain a provision like art 37(4) of the model articles for public companies in SI 2008/3229 that a poll on a question of adjournment must be taken forthwith. Some lawyers thought that it was unnecessary to make this provision explicitly because in their view it merely stated a common law rule. Other lawyers—including those advising Colonel Gardiner—said that there was no such common law rule, and argued that as, without such a provision, any demand for a poll on a question of adjournment could be rendered ineffective by directing that the poll be held after the meeting, it followed that not making such a provision implied that a poll could not be demanded on a question of adjournment. The disagreement has never been settled. See *R v Vestry of St Pancras* (1839) 11 Ad & El 15; *R v D'Oyly* (1840) 12 Ad & El 139.) The Court of Appeal in *Mac-Dougall v Gardiner* dismissed a member's action seeking to question Colonel Gardiner's refusal of the demand for a poll. The court had two reasons for dismissing the action. First, it observed that the member did not seek any substantive relief. At that time, the court had no power to make a declaration on a question of law where the plaintiff was not seeking any other relief. Accordingly the court did not have jurisdiction. Secondly, and more controversially, the court said that the company was the only proper plaintiff because, as James LJ put it at p 23:

> The whole question comes back to a question of internal management; that is to say, whether the meeting ought or ought not to be held in a particular way . . . if [the affairs of the company] are being managed in a way in which they ought not to be managed, the company are the proper persons to complain of that . . . this was a bill which, if it was to be sustained at all, could only be sustained by the company.

In *Cotter v National Union of Seamen* [1929] 2 Ch 58 it was said that the internal management principle applied to everything '*intra vires* the corporation' (per Laurence LJ at pp 107–8 and Russell LJ at p 111). (Incidentally the claim in *Cotter v National Union of Seamen* could have been dismissed by invoking the irregularity principle without reference to the internal management principle. Lord Hanworth MR, at p 100, described the claimants' complaints as 'matters really of irregularity, and no more'.)

The importance of the internal management principle in relation to a claim by a member of a company against the company has been considerably diminished by the courts recognising 'personal rights' exceptions (see **18.4.5**).

18.4.5 CLAIM BY A MEMBER TO VINDICATE A PERSONAL RIGHT

Despite the internal management principle, the courts do sometimes allow a member of a company to take legal proceedings in respect of matters internal to the company and which are not regarded as vindicating the company's rights.

A person is not debarred from obtaining damages or other compensation from a company by reason only of holding or having held shares in the company (CA 2006, s 655). In *Prudential Assurance Co Ltd v Newman Industries Ltd (No 2)* [1982] Ch 204, the Court of Appeal, at p 222, gave the following example:

> if directors convene a meeting on the basis of a fraudulent circular, a shareholder will have a right of action to recover any loss which he has been personally caused in consequence of the fraudulent circular; this might include the expense of attending the meeting.

If a claim brought by a member of a company is not in respect of the company's rights (so the member is not pursuing a derivative claim), it must be enforcing the legal rights of the member. Accordingly the cases in which members of companies are allowed to bring proceedings in respect of their companies' internal affairs are often regarded as being concerned with the 'personal rights' of the members. For example, a member of a company may bring a claim in respect of:

(a) A decision to enter into a transaction beyond the company's objects (*Simpson v Westminster Palace Hotel Co* (1860) 8 HL Cas 712).

(b) A decision to enter into a transaction contrary to the general law or the Companies Acts (*Hope v International Financial Society* (1876) 4 ChD 327; *Bisgood v Henderson's Transvaal Estates Ltd* [1908] 1 Ch 743).

(c) A members' resolution which was required to be adopted as a special resolution but had not received the requisite majority (*Young v South African and Australian Exploration and Development Syndicate* [1896] 2 Ch 268; cf *Edwards v Halliwell* [1950] 2 All ER 1064).

(d) A members' decision to pay dividends in the form of bonds though the articles required dividends to be paid in cash (*Wood v Odessa Waterworks Co* (1889) 42 ChD 636).

(e) A directors' decision which, under a provision in the articles, had been effectively vetoed (*Quin and Axtens Ltd v Salmon* [1909] AC 442).

(f) A special resolution to amend the company's articles (*Allen v Gold Reefs of West Africa Ltd* [1900] 1 Ch 656 and other cases discussed in **3.6.5**).

(g) A resolution that was not properly adopted because votes against it were improperly rejected (*Pender v Lushington* (1877) 6 ChD 70 and other cases discussed in **18.5**).

(h) A decision by directors to allot shares for an improper purpose (*Fraser v Whalley* (1864) 2 Hem & M 10; *Punt v Symons and Co Ltd* [1903] 2 Ch 506; *Residues Treatment and Trading Co Ltd v Southern Resources Ltd* (1988) 51 SASR 177).

(i) Failure of directors to provide adequate notice of meetings (*Baillie v Oriental Telephone and Electric Co Ltd* [1915] 1 Ch 503 and other cases discussed in **14.8.7.3** and **14.8.7.4**).

(j) Whether or not a preference dividend was cumulative under the articles and terms of issue (*Webb v Earle* (1875) LR 20 Eq 556) or by the company's old-style memorandum (*Staples v Eastman Photographic Materials Co* [1896] 2 Ch 303). (In neither of these cases was the rule in *Foss v Harbottle* pleaded as a defence.)

(k) A decision of the members to pay a dividend that was less than was required to be paid by the old-style memorandum (*Evling v Israel and Oppenheimer Ltd* [1918] 1 Ch 101) or by the articles (per Wynn-Parry J in *Godfrey Phillips Ltd v Investment Trust Corporation Ltd* [1953] Ch 449 at p 457).

(l) An irregular forfeiture of shares by directors (*Sweny v Smith* (1869) LR 7 Eq 324 and other cases discussed in **6.5.2.4**).

(m) The proper conduct of elections of directors or other officers (*Ryan v South Sydney Junior Rugby League Club Ltd* (1974) 3 ACLR 486; *Pappaioannoy v Greek Orthodox Community of Melbourne* (1978) 3 ACLR 801; *Link Agricultural Pty Ltd v Shanahan* (1998) 28 ACSR 498; but *Watt v Commonwealth Petroleum Ltd* [1938] 4 DLR 701 shows that a contrary view is taken in Canada).

(n) Decision-making by the board of directors contrary to natural justice (*St Johnstone Football Club Ltd v Scottish Football Association Ltd* 1965 SLT 171).

Although cases in which members challenge a decision to act *ultra vires* or a decision not taken by special majority which should have been ((a), (b) and (c) in this list) are traditionally discussed separately, it would seem that they are examples of the personal rights exception.

In *Fulloon v Radley* [1992] 2 QdR 290, it was held that a person with only an equitable interest in shares of a company could not bring a derivative claim in respect of a wrong alleged to have been done to the company. It was argued that, in nineteenth-century cases such as *Bagshaw v Eastern Union Railway Co* (1850) 2 Mac & G 389, equitable owners had been permitted to bring derivative claims but the court observed that they were all cases to prevent companies acting *ultra vires* and therefore were not derivative claims but were claims to protect the personal rights of shareholders.

There does not seem to be any generally accepted test of what is and what is not a personal right in respect of which an exception will be made to the internal management principle (see **18.4.8**).

In some situations it is disputed whether wrongful conduct of a company's affairs is a wrong to the company or to its members or both. For example, if a person acts as a director of a company without being properly appointed then in Canada it has been held that the wrong is to the company only (*Watt v Commonwealth Petroleum Ltd* [1938] 4 DLR 701; *Schiowitz v IOS Ltd* (1971) 23 DLR (3d) 102). But in Australia it has been held that such a situation affects the personal rights of the company's members for which they may take action personally (*Australian Coal and Shale Employees' Federation v Smith* (1937) 38 SR (NSW) 48; *Kraus v J G Lloyd Pty Ltd* [1965] VR 232). In the English cases on a person wrongfully acting as a director of a company, both the company (*Latchford Premier Cinema Ltd v Ennion* [1931] 2 Ch 409; *Worcester Corsetry Ltd v Witting* [1936] Ch 640) and members (*Catesby v Burnett* [1916] 2 Ch 325; *Spencer v Kennedy* [1926] 1 Ch 125; *Oliver v Dalgleish* [1963] 1 WLR 1274) have been claimants but the standing of the members who brought proceedings was never questioned (see **15.6.5**).

18.4.6 *ULTRA VIRES* TRANSACTIONS

Any one member of a company may ask a court to restrain it from doing something that is *ultra vires*, in the sense of being (a) beyond the company's restricted objects (*Simpson v Westminster Palace Hotel Co* (1860) 8 HL Cas 712; see **3.8.2.2**) or (b) contrary to the general law or the Companies Acts (*Hope v International Financial Society* (1876) 4 ChD 327). Such a claim is permitted as an exception to the proper claimant aspect of the internal management principle. This is an example of the court permitting a claim in respect of a member's interest in having the affairs of the company conducted constitutionally—see **18.4.8**—and it seems that such a claim should not be classified as a derivative claim (see *Fulloon v Radley* [1992] 2 QdR 290 discussed in **18.4.5**).

In *Powell v Kempton Park Racecourse Co Ltd* [1899] AC 143, in order to determine whether the company was breaking the law by allowing bookmakers to operate at its racecourse, a member of the company brought a claim to restrain the company, its agents and employees from permitting bookmakers to use the course. The House of Lords decided by a majority that the company was not breaking the law and so refused to grant the injunction.

There are, it seems, limits on the standing of a member of a company to prevent the company acting illegally. In **Anderson v Midland Railway Co** [1902] 1 Ch 369, a member of the company alleged that the company was charging one of its regular customers less than the company's standard rate for carrying freight and that this was forbidden by a statutory provision which required all customers to be treated alike. Under the relevant statutory provision, a customer who suffered from undue preference to another customer was entitled to bring the matter before the Railway and Canal Commissioners. Buckley J held that the member did not have standing to complain because (at p 377):

> The breach, if there be a breach, of the Act of Parliament is not one which gives rise to any rights as between the corporator and the corporation, but one which gives rise to rights as between the corporation and other customers of the corporation. There is nothing *ultra vires* in the act which is done by the corporation towards the particular customer of which the corporator can complain; it is an act of which other customers of the corporation may complain.

It follows that it may be doubted, for example, whether a member of a company could restrain the company from trading contrary to consumer protection or environmental protection legislation.

If an *ultra vires* transaction has been completed, the proper claimant to recover property transferred under the transaction is the company itself (*Russell v Wakefield Waterworks Co* (1875) LR 20 Eq 474 at p 479; *Nankivell v Benjamin* (1892) 18 VLR 543; *Hawkesbury Development Co Ltd v Landmark Finance Pty Ltd* (1969) 92 WN (NSW) 199). It is competent for the company to decide not to recover property which has been transferred *ultra vires*, provided the decision is taken in good faith in the company's interests (*Taylor v National Union of Mineworkers (Derbyshire Area)* [1985] BCLC 237; *Smith v Croft (No 2)* [1988] Ch 114 at 139; cf *Gray v Lewis* (1873) LR 8 Ch App 1035; but *Cockburn v Newbridge Sanitary Steam Laundry Co Ltd* [1915] 1 IR 237 seems to be to the contrary). A derivative claim may be allowed to recover such property (for example, *Salomons v Laing* (1850) 12 Beav 377; *Simmonds v Heffer* [1983] BCLC 298; see the discussion in *Russell v Wakefield Waterworks Co* and in *Smith v Croft (No 2)* [1988] Ch 114 at pp 168–77).

18.4.7 RATIFIABILITY AS THE BASIS OF THE PERSONAL RIGHTS EXCEPTIONS

The ratifiability principle asserts that any matter which can be ratified by the members must be one which the court will consider only in proceedings brought by the company, either because it is a question of internal management or because a derivative claim is not allowed. Our view is that the question whether a matter can be ratified by the members of a company and the question whether members of a company have standing to sue in respect of the matter are separate issues which are not logically connected, and that the ratifiability principle does not accurately summarise the law on standing to sue.

It has now been held in South Australia that the fact that a decision, though unlawful, is capable of being ratified is not a bar to a claim until the infringement has been expunged by ratification (*Residues Treatment and Trading Co Ltd v Southern Resources Ltd* (1988) 51 SASR 177 at p 205). Even where ratification has occurred it is still open to challenge as a fraud on the minority.

In *Hogg v Cramphorn Ltd* [1967] Ch 254, a member of a company challenged the lawfulness of an allotment of shares by the directors of the company. Having found that the allotment was unlawful, Buckley J stood over the action so that a meeting of the members could be held to ratify the allotment, the allottees having undertaken not to vote their shares at that meeting. In *Southern Resources Ltd v Residues Treatment and Trading Co Ltd* (1990) 56 SASR 455, a member of Southern Resources Ltd challenged a decision of its directors to take over a company in which the chairman of Southern Resources had a substantial interest. The takeover was to be by share exchange which would give the chairman a controlling interest in Southern Resources Ltd. A general meeting of Southern Resources Ltd ratified the directors' decision but it was held that the decision was unlawful because it was made for the improper purpose of increasing the directors' control over the company, and the ratification by the members was held to be an oppressive fraud on the minority. Accordingly Southern Resources Ltd was ordered not to go ahead with the takeover. These two cases show that it is not the ratifiability of a decision which determines whether the court will hear a member's claim to question the decision. However, in the past, commentators have usually proposed that ratifiability should be the criterion: see K W Wedderburn, 'Shareholders' control of directors' powers: a judicial innovation?' (1967) 30 MLR 77 and 'Unreformed company law' (1969) 32 MLR 563; C J H Thomson, 'Share issues and the rule in *Foss v Harbottle*' (1975) 49 ALJ 134; H Mason, 'Ratification of directors' acts: an Anglo-Australian comparison' (1978) 41 MLR 161; R Baxt, 'Judges in their own cause: the ratification of directors' breaches of duty' (1978) 5 Mon LR 16.

For other discussions of the personal rights exceptions to the rule in *Foss v Harbottle* see N A Bastin, 'The enforcement of a member's rights' [1977] JBL 17; R J Smith, 'Minority shareholders and corporate irregularities' (1978) 41 MLR 147; C Baxter, 'The role of the judge in enforcing shareholder rights' [1983] CLJ 96.

18.4.8 LAWFULNESS OF DECISION-MAKING AS THE BASIS OF THE PERSONAL RIGHTS EXCEPTIONS

A decision of a company (either of the members or of the directors) may be unlawful in the sense that it fails to comply with the general law or with the constitution of the company or with the Companies Acts. If the lawfulness of a decision of a company is in question, two separate interests are usually involved:

(a) The interests of the company as a separate person. If the decision has already been implemented, the company has an interest in any property lost as a result of the decision, which it may be able to recover by having the decision rescinded. If the decision has not been implemented, the company has an interest in not having to enter into transactions that are voidable.

(b) The interests of the members who disagree with the decision. As Romer LJ said in *Re H R Harmer Ltd* [1959] 1 WLR 62 at p 87:

shareholders are entitled to have the affairs of a company conducted in the way laid down by the company's constitution.

So both the company and a member may be claimants in respect of their separate interests (as in *Pender v Lushington* (1877) 6 ChD 70). The company is the proper claimant in respect of its interests. A claim to enforce the interests of the members is a claim against the company, which one would expect to be barred by the proper claimant aspect of the internal management principle, but in fact it rarely is—see **18.4.5**.

For example, if directors propose to allot shares for an improper purpose (that is, in breach of their duty to the company under CA 2006, s 171), a member has standing to bring a claim to prevent the proposed allotment (*Fraser v Whalley* (1864) 2 Hem & M 10; *Punt v Symons and Co Ltd* [1903] 2 Ch 506; *Residues Treatment and Trading Co Ltd v Southern Resources Ltd* (1988) 51 SASR 177). If an allotment has been made in breach of fiduciary duty, the company is the proper claimant to sue for rescission of it (*Bamford v Bamford* [1970] Ch 212 per Harman LJ at p 238, Russell LJ at p 242). If an allotment made in breach of fiduciary duty has been ratified by the members, a member is not permitted to bring a derivative claim for rescission unless there has been a fraud on the minority (see **18.4.2**) as there was in *Ngurli Ltd v McCann* (1953) 90 CLR 425 (see further *Residues Treatment and Trading Co Ltd v Southern Resources Ltd*; *Re a Company (No 005136 of 1986)* [1987] BCLC 82; J Birds, 'No costs for minority shareholder' (1987) 8 Co Law 131).

It is especially difficult to analyse cases where the chairman of a meeting of members has made a wrong decision. In *MacDougall v Gardiner* (1875) 1 ChD 13, James LJ (at p 22) thought that the wrong in such a case was only to the company as a separate person, but in *Pender v Lushington*, Jessel MR said that a wrongful refusal to count a member's votes was a wrong to the member personally. In *Breay v Browne* (1897) 41 SJ 159, Wright J said that the wrongful refusal of the chairman of a members' meeting to put to the meeting a motion proposed by a member did not damage the member personally: her right was not a personal one but belonged to her as a member of the company. The appropriate remedy was an order compelling the company to convene a fresh meeting and forbidding the chairman of the fresh meeting repeating the mistake. The chairman of a meeting is not personally liable to pay damages for his or her mistaken decisions (*Breay v Browne*; *Bluechel v Prefabricated Buildings Ltd* [1945] 2 DLR 725). Thus, the claim is properly against the company to prevent it acting on the wrong decision: there is no order for the court to make against the chairman who made the wrong decision (*Turner v Canadian Pacific Ltd* (1979) 107 DLR (3d) 142).

We suggest that the common factor in the personal rights cases is that a member is alleging that a decision is unlawful in the sense that it fails to comply with the general law or with the constitution of the company or with the Companies Acts. We suggest that a member of a company has standing to challenge the lawfulness of any decision of the members or the directors or the chairman of a meeting of members, subject only to the irregularity principle (see **18.5**). The recognition of a member's standing to challenge the lawfulness of company decisions would, we suggest, provide a means of enforcing the entitlement of shareholders 'to have the affairs of a company conducted in the way laid down by the company's constitution' which Romer LJ recognised in **Re H R Harmer Ltd** [1959] 1 WLR 62 at p 87.

In **Dunn v Banknock Coal Co Ltd** (1901) 9 SLT 51, Lord Stormonth Darling said, at p 52, 'any shareholder is entitled to object to a material deviation from what is the law of the company, without the necessity of showing that the thing done is hurtful to the interests of the company'. His Lordship identified 'the law of the company' as its old-style memorandum and articles and the Companies Acts. We would add that deviation from the general law, such as breaches of the rule that a decision must be taken in the interests of the company, can also be grounds for a member's claim. We would also explain the term 'material deviation' as meaning a breach to which the irregularity principle does not apply.

The Company Law Review Steering Group proposed that the approach which we have suggested here (it was first stated in the sixth edition of this work in 1989) should be the basis for a statutory definition of personal rights (*Modern Company Law for a Competitive Economy: Completing the Structure* (URN 00/1335) (London: DTI, 2000), paras 5.70 to 5.74; *Modern Company Law for a Competitive Economy: Final Report*, vol 1 (URN 01/942) (London: DTI, 2001), paras 7.34 to 7.40). However, the government decided against including such a list in CA 2006.

18.5 IRREGULARITY PRINCIPLE

The court will reject a claim that a decision taken by the members (or directors) of a company is invalid if the only factor alleged to invalidate it is a mere informality or irregularity and the intention of the members (or directors) is clear (*Burland v Earle* [1902] AC 83 per Lord Davey at pp 93–4). This principle is often expressed in terms of ratification: where only a mere informality or irregularity is alleged to invalidate a decision, a claim may not be brought questioning its validity if it is clear that, on going through the correct procedure, the decision would be ratified. In *MacDougall v Gardiner* (1875) 1 ChD 13 Mellish LJ said, at p 25:

> In my opinion, if the thing complained of is a thing which in substance the majority of the company are entitled to do, or if something has been done irregularly which the majority of the company are entitled to do regularly, or if something has been done illegally which the majority of the company are entitled to do legally, there can be no use in having a litigation about it, the ultimate end of which is only that a meeting has to be called, and then ultimately the majority gets its wishes.

A commonly occurring application of the irregularity principle is that a court will not consider claims that attempt to invalidate the proceedings of meetings on the ground of mere mistakes in procedure if there is no evidence that the decision would have been different had the correct procedure been observed. As Cotton LJ said in *Browne v La Trinidad* (1887) 37 ChD 1 at p 10:

> a court of equity refuses to interfere where an irregularity has been committed, if it is within the power of the persons who have committed it at once to correct it by calling a fresh meeting and dealing with the matter with all due formalities.

In *Browne v La Trinidad*, there was a purported meeting of directors of La Trinidad Ltd at which it was resolved to summon an extraordinary general meeting of the members. At first instance it was found that the directors' meeting itself had been improperly convened because inadequate notice was given to one of the directors, Mr Browne, who was ultimately removed from office by the extraordinary general meeting of the members. The Court of Appeal judges doubted that the notice to Mr Browne was inadequate but were unwilling to overturn the finding of the judge below on this ground. The Court of Appeal refused to rule that the proceedings of the members' meeting had been invalidated by the irregularity. They observed that Mr Browne had had plenty of time to call another directors' meeting and argue his point of view but had not done so and that the decision of the members had been unanimous. Clearly, there was no point in going through the procedure again. For other examples see *Southern Counties Deposit Bank Ltd v Rider* (1895) 73 LT 374; *Boschoek Proprietary Co Ltd v Fuke* [1906] 1 Ch 148; *Bentley-Stevens v Jones* [1974] 1 WLR 638.

In both *Re Haycraft Gold Reduction and Mining Co* [1900] 2 Ch 230 and *Re State of Wyoming Syndicate* [1901] 2 Ch 431 a meeting of members had been summoned and had adopted a resolution for voluntary winding up. However, in both cases the notice convening the meeting had been issued by the secretary of the company without the authority of the directors, which was not permitted by the articles of association. In both cases the court held it would be going too far to hold that this was a mere irregularity and so the resolutions for voluntary winding up were declared to be invalid.

An error in the proceedings of a meeting which has affected whether a resolution was adopted or not is more than a mere irregularity and the court will declare that the erroneously taken decision is invalid. An example is *Siemens Brothers and Co Ltd v Burns* [1918] 2 Ch 324, which concerned a company called Siemens Brothers Dynamo Works Ltd, which had been registered at a time when every company had to have at least seven members. Of its 20,000 shares, seven were held by seven individuals who held one share each. The remaining 19,993 were in the joint names of Burns (whose name was first on the register) and another person. By the company's articles if shares were in joint names then only the person named first in the register could vote in respect of the shares. A meeting was held at which it was proposed to pass a special resolution to amend the company's articles. The matter was voted on by a show of hands on which the amendment was adopted by seven votes (those of the members with one share each) to one (that of Burns with 19,993 shares). Burns demanded a poll but the chairman ruled that he lacked entitlement under the articles to demand a poll. The Court of Appeal held that for the purposes of the article relating to a demand for a poll, Burns and his co-holder were 'members holding . . . together at least 300 shares' and so could demand a poll. Clearly this case involved a procedural error that affected the outcome of a very important decision of the meeting.

For other examples see *Pender v Lushington* (1877) 6 ChD 70; *Shaw v Tati Concessions Ltd* [1913] 1 Ch 292; *Marks v Financial News Ltd* (1919) 35 TLR 681.

18.6 UNFAIRLY PREJUDICIAL CONDUCT OF THE COMPANY'S AFFAIRS

18.6.1 COURT'S POWER TO GIVE RELIEF FOR UNFAIRLY PREJUDICIAL CONDUCT

Part 30 (ss 994 to 999) of CA 2006 gives the court a wide-ranging power to remedy conduct of a company's affairs 'that is unfairly prejudicial to the interests of its members generally or of some part of its members'. The most common complaint is that a controlling majority of members have unfairly prejudiced the minority, and the most common remedy sought is an order that the majority must purchase the minority's shares at a price which reflects their proportion of the company's value. Section 994(1) sets out the court's jurisdiction:

A member of a company may apply to the court by petition for an order under this Part on the ground—

(a) that the company's affairs are being or have been conducted in a manner that is unfairly prejudicial to the interests of members generally or of some part of its members (including at least himself), or

(b) that an actual or proposed act or omission of the company (including an act or omission on its behalf) is or would be so prejudicial.

The courts have had to examine carefully the meaning of the terms 'interests of members' (see **18.6.5**) and 'unfairly prejudicial' (see **18.6.6**).

Most of the cases on unfair prejudice have concerned quasi-partnership companies (see **2.7**), but the provisions apply to all types of company (*Re a Company (No 00314 of 1989)* [1991] BCLC 154).

18.6.2 WHO MAY PETITION?

18.6.2.1 Main principle

Under CA 2006, s 994(1), a petition for relief of unfairly prejudicial conduct of a company's affairs may be presented by a member of the company in respect of conduct which unfairly prejudices the interests of: (a) the members generally, or (b) a section of the membership which includes at least the petitioner (in many petitions the petitioner is the only member claiming to have been prejudiced).

18.6.2.2 Supplementary details

A person to whom shares in a company have been transferred, or have been transmitted by operation of law (see **8.5**), but who is not a member of the company (because of not being on the register of members) is treated as a member for the purposes of CA 2006, s 994(1), and references to a member or members must be construed accordingly (s 994(2)).

The word 'transferred' in s 994(2) requires at least that a proper instrument of transfer should have been executed and delivered to the transferee or the company in respect of the shares in question. It is not sufficient that there is an agreement for transfer (*Re a Company (No 003160 of 1986)* [1986] BCLC 391; *Re Quickdome Ltd* [1988] BCLC 370).

The phrase 'transmitted by operation of law' in s 994(2) refers to a legal process by which the legal title passes and does not cover the creation of an equitable interest, for example under a trust (*Re a Company (No 007828 of 1985)* (1985) 2 BCC 98,951).

Under s 995 the Secretary of State has standing to present a petition for the relief of what appears to him, from an inspectors' report or from a confidential investigation, to be unfairly prejudicial conduct of a company's affairs (see **18.8.5.4**).

A petition for relief of unfairly prejudicial conduct of a company's affairs may be presented by a person who joined the company in the knowledge that its affairs were being conducted in the manner complained of (*Bermuda Cablevision Ltd v Colica Trust Co Ltd* [1998] AC 198).

A nominee shareholder, holding shares as a bare trustee, may petition under s 994, because the interests of such a shareholder include the economic and contractual interests of the beneficial owners of the shares (*Atlasview Ltd v Brightview Ltd* [2004] EWHC 1056 (Ch), [2004] 2 BCLC 191).

The rule that he who comes to equity must come with clean hands does not apply to s 994. In other words, a petitioner's own misconduct is not in itself a reason for rejecting the petition, though it may show that the petitioner was not unfairly prejudiced or may affect the remedy given by the court (*Re London School of Electronics Ltd* [1986] Ch 211).

The legislation does not give a former member standing to petition (*Re a Company (No 00330 of 1991)* [1991] BCLC 597). D D Prentice has argued that it should ('The theory of the firm: minority shareholder oppression: sections 459–461 of the Companies Act 1985' (1988) 8 Oxford J Legal Stud

55 at p 64). In *Re a Company (No 00330 of 1991)*, an injunction was granted to prevent the other members of the company operating a provision in the company's articles entitling them to compulsorily purchase the petitioner's shares and thus deprive him of his standing before the petition was heard.

A person who cannot show prima facie evidence of standing will not be allowed to petition: the question of standing must be settled first. In *Re Quickdome Ltd*, a company had been bought off the shelf and the original members (the company registration firm which had sold it) had executed transfers of their shares without naming the transferees. Unfortunately, the purchasers never registered any share transfers and when one of them petitioned under s 994 she could not prove any agreement that she should be a shareholder. It was held that the dispute over who should be the company's shareholders would have to be settled before a petition under s 994 could be presented. (This does not mean that disputes over the ownership of shares cannot be the subject of s 994 proceedings. In *Re Garage Door Associates Ltd* [1984] 1 WLR 35, a person who was the registered holder of one share in the company was permitted to bring s 994 proceedings to challenge the allotment of 799 of the company's other 800 shares: the one share registered in his name gave him standing.)

18.6.2.3 Time limits

No limitation period applies to a petition for the relief of unfairly prejudicial conduct of a company's affairs. However, the court has a discretion whether to grant relief and it was held in *Re Grandactual Ltd* [2005] EWHC 1415 (Ch), [2006] BCC 73, that no court would grant relief for events which happened nine years ago and which the petitioner had cooperated in.

18.6.3 HISTORY

Sections 994 to 999 of CA 2006 were originally enacted as CA 1980, s 75, to replace a provision in CA 1948, s 210, which provided a remedy only if the affairs of a company were being conducted in a manner oppressive to some part of the members. The term 'oppressive' was given a restricted interpretation by the courts which also insisted that relief could be given only in respect of continuing conduct. Furthermore, it was necessary under s 210 to show that the circumstances of the company were such that it was just and equitable that the company should be wound up (see **18.7**). These restrictions meant that only a handful of petitions under s 210 succeeded. The new provisions have given the courts power to intervene in relation to a much wider range of conduct and similar provisions have been enacted in many Commonwealth jurisdictions. In order to succeed with a petition for the relief of unfairly prejudicial conduct of a company's affairs it is not necessary to show that the circumstances justify winding up the company (*O'Neill v Phillips* [1999] 1 WLR 1092 per Lord Hoffmann at pp 1099–100).

18.6.4 PROBLEMS AND PROPOSALS FOR REFORM

There has been some disquiet about the way the unfair prejudice provisions have operated in practice, especially about the cost of proceedings.

In *Re Unisoft Group Ltd (No 3)* [1994] 1 BCLC 609, Harman J said, at p 611:

> Petitions under [CA 2006, s 994], have become notorious to the judges of this court—and I think also to the Bar—for their length, their unpredictability of management, and the enormous and appalling costs which are incurred upon them particularly by reason of the volume of documents liable to be produced.

The unreported case of *Re Freudiana Music Co Ltd* (1993) occupied 165 days of court time. The court heard petitions from both of the principal shareholders (a musician and a theatrical producer) in a group of companies which produced a musical on the life of Sigmund Freud. The length of the hearing was not helped when, on day 85, the musician (who eventually lost the case) dispensed with his professional advisers and conducted the rest of his case in person. After the case was decided there was a lengthy battle over who should pay costs (*Re Freudiana Holdings Ltd* (1995), *The Times*, 4 December 1995).

Unfortunately, lawyers presenting a case on unfair prejudice in a company often deal with the whole history of the company in detail, so as to build up an overall picture of prejudice, and this is countered by equally extensive evidence and cross-examination from the other side. The result can easily be that costs exceed the value of the assets being fought over, as in *Re Elgindata Ltd* [1991] BCLC 959, discussed in **18.6.8.2**, where costs of £320,000 were incurred arguing over shares worth a mere £24,600. The fact that litigants continue with these cases may reflect more on the depth of personal animosity involved than a desire for compensation for financial loss, but it is an important criticism of the legal system that it cannot provide a simpler method of dealing with such disputes and requires so much publicly funded court resources to be devoted to them (see L Sealy, 'No relief for the minority shareholder' (1995) 16 Co Law 178). In *Re a Company (No 00836 of 1995)* [1996] 2 BCLC 192, the petition was struck out because a reasonable offer to buy the petitioner's shares had been made, but the judge commented (at p 205) that striking out might also be justified if it appeared that the proceedings were being conducted in pursuit of a family feud rather than for commercial reasons. The two sides in the case had already incurred costs of between £1 million and £2 million in another case, *Re Macro (Ipswich) Ltd* [1994] 2 BCLC 354, which is discussed in **18.6.8.2**.

The threat of long, expensive and uncertain legal proceedings of any kind can be used to extract a payment to settle a claim which, if it went to a hearing, might not succeed. The notorious expense of unfair prejudice petitions makes them particularly likely to be used as a means of oppression (per Hoffmann J in *Re a Company (No 007623 of 1984)* [1986] BCLC 362 and in *Re a Company (No 004377 of 1986)* [1987] 1 WLR 102 at p 111).

Where a petition for the relief of unfairly prejudicial conduct of a company's affairs arises from a personal dispute between members of the company, it is a misapplication of the company's money to pay any costs of the proceedings except for those necessarily incurred in representing the company as a separate person (*Re Kenyon Swansea Ltd* [1987] BCLC 514; *Re Elgindata Ltd*). An injunction will be granted to prevent the company paying such costs (*Re Milgate Developments Ltd* [1993] BCLC 291; *Re a Company (No 004502 of 1988)* [1992] BCLC 701). The court may order the company to indemnify the petitioner for the costs of obtaining an order (see **18.6.11.1**) in favour of the company as a separate person (*Clark v Cutland* [2003] EWCA Civ 810, [2004] 1 WLR 783; A Reisberg, 'Indemnity costs orders under s 459 petition?' (2004) 25 Co Law 116). The company may, as permitted by CA 2006, s 234 (see **16.16.5**), voluntarily indemnify a director who successfully defends an allegation of negligence, default, breach of duty or breach of trust contained in an unfair prejudice petition (*Branch v Bagley* [2004] EWHC 426 (Ch), LTL 15/3/2004).

In its report, *Shareholder Remedies* (Law Com No 246, Cm 3769) (London: Stationery Office, 1997), the Law Commission considered ways of reforming unfair prejudice proceedings. Its principal recommendation is that the problems of excessive length and cost should be dealt with primarily by active case management by the courts. The courts have indicated that the new powers of case management which they have under the Civil Procedure Rules 1998 will be used to control proceedings on unfair prejudice petitions (*North Holdings Ltd v Southern Tropics Ltd* [1999] 2 BCLC 625; *Re Rotadata Ltd* [2000] 1 BCLC 122). One aspect of the overriding objective of the Civil Procedure Rules which is relevant to cases like *Re Elgindata Ltd* is that the court should deal with a case in a way which is proportionate to the amount of money involved (r 1.1(2)(c) (i)). In ***Allmark v Burnham*** [2005] EWHC 2717 (Ch), [2006] 2 BCLC 437, after court-directed mediation had failed, the court directed instruction of single joint experts on accountancy and land valuation and adopted 'a fairly robust or even rough and ready approach', which nevertheless produced a judgment of 145 paragraphs to value the petitioner's shares at £30,500 and establish liability for repayment to him of a debt of £65,000. The Law Commission also recommended that there should be a time limit within which proceedings for unfair prejudice may be brought, time starting to run from the date when the petitioner ought reasonably to have known the relevant facts (see **18.6.2.3**). It also recommended that, in the most common type of case, exclusion from the management of a quasi-partnership, statutory presumptions should apply, which it hoped would simplify proceedings (see **18.6.9**).

The Company Law Review Steering Group made quite elaborate suggestions for an arbitration scheme to deal with disputes which might otherwise be taken to court under s 994 (*Modern Company Law for a Competitive Economy: Developing the Framework* (URN 00/656) (London: DTI, 2000), paras 7.44 to 7.69; *Modern Company Law for a Competitive Economy: Final Report*, vol 1 (URN 01/942) (London: DTI, 2001), paras 4.10 to 4.12). For discussion of how ADR could be used, see J Corbett and R Nicholson, 'Mediation and section 459 petitions' (2002) 23 Co Law 274.

The Company Law Review Steering Group and some judges have taken the view that Lord Hoffmann's judgment in *O'Neill v Phillips* [1999] 1 WLR 1092 has restricted the circumstances in which a finding of unfair prejudice can be made, and that this will help to restrict litigation under s 994, but it will be argued in **18.6.10** that Lord Hoffmann's judgment does not have the claimed effect.

18.6.5 MEANING OF 'INTERESTS OF MEMBERS'

The interests of members which are claimed to be unfairly prejudiced in a petition under CA 2006, s 994, need not necessarily be interests in their capacity as members, though they must be sufficiently connected with membership (*Gamlestaden Fastigheter AB v Baltic Partners Ltd* [2007] UKPC 26, [2007] Bus LR 1521). It has been held, for example, that a loan by a member of a company to the company, to provide it with working capital, is an interest of the member which may be the subject of an unfair prejudice petition (*Gamlestaden Fastigheter AB v Baltic Partners Ltd*), but a lease of land is not (*Re J E Cade and Son Ltd* [1992] BCLC 213; *Brown v Scottish Border Springs Ltd* 2002 SLT 1213). In *Gamlestaden Fastigheter AB v Baltic Partners Ltd* the company was a joint venture and the Privy Council said (at [34]) that what distinguished the case from *Re J E Cade and Son Ltd* was that the loans were made pursuant to and for the purposes of the joint venture. For criticism of *Re J E Cade and Son Ltd* see S Griffin, 'Defining the scope of a membership interest' (1993) 14 Co Law 64.

Disputes among members of a company about dealings in their shares cannot normally involve unfairly prejudicial conduct of the company's affairs (*Re Unisoft Group Ltd (No 3)* [1994] 1 BCLC 609).

The rights of a member of a company are defined by the company's constitution and the Companies Acts but the word 'interests' is wider than the term 'rights' (*Re a Company (No 00477 of 1986)* [1986] BCLC 376) and members may have different interests even if their rights as members are the same (*Re Sam Weller and Sons Ltd* [1990] Ch 682).

Conduct that affects all members may be prejudicial to the interests of some of them only (as in *Re Cumana Ltd* [1986] BCLC 430, in which it was known that a rights issue on apparently favourable terms could not be taken up by a minority shareholder because of his financial position and would have had the desired effect of squeezing him out of the company—see also the earlier proceedings in the same case [1985] BCLC 80). However, until an amendment was made by CA 1989, sch 19, para 11, the court did not have jurisdiction to deal with conduct that was indiscriminately prejudicial to the interests of all the members of a company (*Re a Company (No 00370 of 1987)* [1988] 1 WLR 1068; cf *Re Carrington Viyella plc* (1983) 1 BCC 98,951 at p 98,959). It may be that the court in *Re a Company (No 00370 of 1987)* was mistaken in not recognising that the conduct complained of affected different members in different ways and could have been found to have been unfairly prejudicial to some of them—see *Re Sam Weller and Sons Ltd*; *McGuiness v Black* 1990 SC 21 at p 24.

In *Jaber v Science and Information Technology Ltd* [1992] BCLC 864, a number of persons claimed that they had been wrongfully excluded from membership of a company. They could not petition under s 994 in respect of that wrong because they were not members. An individual who supported them and was actually a member could not petition in respect of that wrong because it was held that a member of a company does not have an interest in the recognition of voting rights of other persons claiming to be members. Disputes about membership have to be resolved by a claim for rectification of the register of members (see **14.3.3**).

18.6.6 MEANING OF 'UNFAIRLY PREJUDICIAL'

In *Re Saul D Harrison and Sons plc* [1995] 1 BCLC 14, Neill LJ said, at pp 30–1:

> The words 'unfairly prejudicial' are general words and they should be applied flexibly to meet the circumstances of the particular case.
>
> The conduct [being complained of] must be both prejudicial (in the sense of causing prejudice or harm to the relevant interest) and also unfairly so: conduct may be unfair without being prejudicial or prejudicial without being unfair, and it is not sufficient if the conduct satisfies only one of these tests.

The prejudice must be 'harm in a commercial sense, not in a merely emotional sense' (per Harman J in *Re Unisoft Group Ltd (No 3)* [1994] 1 BCLC 609 at p 611). However, CA 2006, s 994, cannot be limited to cases in which the value of members' shareholdings has been seriously diminished or jeopardised (per Nourse J in *Re R A Noble and Sons (Clothing) Ltd* [1983] BCLC 273 at p 291; *Re Elgindata Ltd* [1991] BCLC 959).

In *O'Neill v Phillips* [1999] 1 WLR 1092, Lord Hoffmann emphasised that equitable jurisdiction must be exercised in a principled way, saying, at p 1098:

> In [s 994] Parliament has chosen fairness as the criterion by which the court must decide whether it has jurisdiction to grant relief. It is clear . . . that it chose this concept to free the court from technical considerations of legal right and to confer a wide power to do what appeared just and equitable. But this does not mean that the court can do whatever the individual judge happens to think fair. The concept of fairness must be applied judicially and the content which it is given by the courts must be based upon rational principles.
>
> Although fairness is a notion which can be applied to all kinds of activities, its content will depend upon the context in which it is being used.

It is not easy to agree with Lord Hoffmann that a court's concept of fairness should vary from context to context, and the examples which his Lordship gave of contexts in which he asserted that concepts of fairness differ (business, family, cricket, love and war) do not seem to be relevant to the content of judicial fairness. Lord Hoffmann went on to say that the context in which an evaluation of the fairness of prejudicial conduct of a company's affairs must be made is that:

> a company is an association of persons for an economic purpose, usually entered into with legal advice and some degree of formality.

This:

> leads to the conclusion that a member of a company will not ordinarily be entitled to complain of unfairness unless there has been some breach of the terms on which he agreed that the affairs of the company should be conducted.

However:

> there will be cases in which equitable considerations make it unfair for those conducting the affairs of the company to rely upon their strict legal powers. Thus unfairness may consist in a breach of the rules or in using the rules in a manner which equity would regard as contrary to good faith.

In *Re Guidezone Ltd* [2000] 2 BCLC 321, Jonathan Parker J said, at p 355, that it has been established by *O'Neill v Phillips* that:

'unfairness' for the purposes of [s 994] is not to be judged by reference to subjective notions of fairness, but rather by testing whether, applying established equitable principles, the majority has acted, or is proposing to act, in a manner which equity would regard as contrary to good faith.

In the Court of Session in Scotland, Lord Coulsfield has expressed agreement with Jonathan Parker J's summary (*Anderson v Hogg* 2002 SC 190 at p 198).

A situation which a member can get rid of immediately by exercising voting control (for example, by dismissing a director) cannot be unfairly prejudicial to that member's interests (*Re Baltic Real Estate Ltd (No 2)* [1993] BCLC 503). See also *Re Legal Costs Negotiators Ltd* [1999] 2 BCLC 171.

An infringement of a member's rights under the articles may not in itself be unfairly prejudicial (*Re Carrington Viyella plc* (1983) 1 BCC 98,951). Section 994 was not intended to cover trivial or technical infringements of the articles (per Hoffmann LJ in *Re Saul D Harrison and Sons plc* at p 19).

18.6.7 UNWRITTEN AGREEMENTS

In some cases the court recognises that a member of a company has a legitimate expectation that the company's affairs will be conducted in a particular way, even though there is nothing to that effect in the company's constitution or in CA 2006, and that failure to run the company in the expected way is unfairly prejudicial to that member's interests. The type of company in which such expectations will be taken into account is known as the 'quasi-partnership company' (see **2.7**).

In the case of a public company, the court is highly unlikely to pay attention to understandings and agreements that are not recorded in the documents available to outside investors (*Re Blue Arrow plc* [1987] BCLC 585; *Re Tottenham Hotspur plc* [1994] 1 BCLC 655). In *Re Astec (BSR) plc*, Jonathan Parker J said, at p 589:

If the market in a company's shares is to have any credibility members of the public dealing in that market must it seems to me be entitled to proceed on the footing that the constitution of the company is as it appears in the company's public documents, unaffected by any extraneous equitable considerations and constraints.

Even in a private company, if the petitioner became a member of the company by virtue of a complex set of formal written agreements, it will be assumed that the petitioner's rights and expectations are defined exhaustively in those agreements (*Re Elgindata Ltd* [1991] BCLC 959 at p 985).

The type of unwritten agreement which the court will recognise when considering whether there has been unfairly prejudicial conduct of a company's affairs typically limits the rights of members and/or directors under the company's articles. The most common example is an understanding that the petitioner will not be removed from his or her directorship despite the provisions of CA 2006, s 168 (see **15.6.3**).

In *O'Neill v Phillips* [1999] 1 WLR 1092, Lord Hoffmann emphasised that the term 'legitimate expectation' refers to an expectation that the company's affairs will be conducted in the manner agreed by all the members, not a personal hope of the petitioner that other members will do something which they have not in fact agreed to do. His Lordship approved the following statement by Jonathan Parker J in *Re Astec (BSR) plc* [1998] 2 BCLC 556 at p 588:

in order to give rise to an equitable constraint based on 'legitimate expectation' what is required is a personal relationship or personal dealings of some kind between the party seeking to exercise the legal right and the party seeking to restrain such exercise, such as will affect the conscience of the former.

Lord Hoffmann in *O'Neill v Phillips* went on to say ([1999] 1 WLR at p 1101):

This is putting the matter in very traditional language, reflecting in the word 'conscience' the ecclesiastical origins of the long-departed Court of Chancery . . . I think that one useful cross-check in a case like this is to ask whether the exercise of the power in question would be contrary to what the parties, by word or conduct, have actually agreed. Would it conflict with the promises which they appear to have exchanged? . . . In a quasi-partnership company, [these promises] will usually be found in the understandings between the members at the time they entered into association. But there may be later promises, by words or conduct, which it would be unfair to allow a member to ignore. Nor is it necessary that such promises should be independently enforceable as a matter of contract. A promise may be binding as a matter of justice and equity although for one reason or another (for example, because in favour of a third party) it would not be enforceable in law.

The court will only take into account understandings between the members, not a belief by some members that others will be externally constrained to act in a particular way. Thus, in *Re Carrington Viyella plc* (1983) 1 BCC 98,951, the holder of 49.36 per cent of the issued ordinary shares of the company had given undertakings to the government to reduce its holding to not more than 35 per cent, and not to exercise votes in excess of 35 per cent meanwhile, in return for the government not making a reference to the Monopolies and Mergers Commission. Vinelott J held that a petition could not be presented for relief of unfairly prejudicial conduct based on allegations of past and proposed breaches of these undertakings because the undertakings should not be treated as part of the constitution of the company or as in any way affecting the rights of shareholders *inter se*. In any case, other shareholders must have known that the undertakings 'were never intended to be immutable' and were always 'subject to change in the light of changed circumstances'.

The court will take account of an understanding between all the members, but not an understanding between some members and the directors, where there are other members who are not directors: the directors cannot be regarded as entering into an understanding on behalf of the non-director members (*Re Benfield Greig Group plc* [2001] BCC 92, point not considered on appeal).

Members of a quasi-partnership company may agree, or acquiesce in, operation of the company in a way that does not comply with the requirements of its articles of association, and operation of the company in that way will then not be unfairly prejudicial (*Fisher v Cadman* [2005] EWHC 377 (Ch), [2006] 1 BCLC 499). Members who have acquiesced in non-compliance with provisions of the articles which protect their interests may at any time insist on enforcing those requirements, and from then on failure to comply will be unfairly prejudicial (*Fisher v Cadman*).

When dealing with claims that agreements have been breached the courts have emphasised that they will only enforce what was actually agreed: they will not try to create a better agreement. In ***Re Posgate and Denby (Agencies) Ltd*** [1987] BCLC 8, Hoffmann J said, at p 14:

Section [994] enables the court to give full effect to the terms and understandings on which the members of the company become associated but not to rewrite them.

This was followed by Warner J in *Re J E Cade and Son Ltd* [1992] BCLC 213, who held that where there are agreements and understandings between a company's members which are not expressed in its constitution, the court will not supplement them with further rights and obligations to accord with its own concept of fairness. If the provisions of the constitution do not conflict with other rights, expectations and understandings, a member cannot complain about conduct in accordance with the constitution, unless it can be shown that there is bad faith or impropriety or, possibly, that the constitution is itself unfair (per Hoffmann J in *Re a Company (No 004377 of 1986)* [1987] 1 WLR 102 at p 110).

18.6.8 EXAMPLES OF CONDUCT ON WHICH A PETITION MAY BE GROUNDED

18.6.8.1 Majority taking financial benefits from minority

In *Re London School of Electronics Ltd* [1986] Ch 211, a petition was presented under what is now CA 2006, s 994, by the holder of 25 per cent of the shares in the company, whose business was providing further education courses. The other 75 per cent of the shares were held by a company called

City Tutorial College Ltd. Two directors of London School of Electronics Ltd, who were also directors and principal shareholders in City Tutorial College Ltd, caused London School of Electronics to transfer many of its students to City Tutorial College thus depriving the petitioner of his 25 per cent share in the profits to be made from those students. This was held to be prejudicial conduct and the court ordered City Tutorial College to buy the petitioner's shares, which should be valued as if the students had not been transferred.

In *Re Cumana Ltd* [1986] BCLC 430 the court gave effect to an oral agreement between the two owners of the company that they should share the profits of their business ventures in the ratio two-thirds to one-third. The man who was to get two-thirds devised various schemes to cut the other out of his share. One (as in *Re London School of Electronics Ltd*) was to divert some of the company's business to another company controlled by himself. Another scheme was to make a large rights issue of shares, which, although priced favourably, he knew the minority member could not afford to take up. Thirdly, he got the company to pay him an excessive bonus and to pay an excessive contribution to his pension fund. All three matters were held to be unfairly prejudicial conduct. The rights issue was restrained in interim proceedings ([1985] BCLC 80).

In *Re Little Olympian Each-Ways Ltd (No 3)* [1995] 1 BCLC 636, the petitioner was Supreme Travel Ltd, which was a substantial but minority holder of preference shares in the company which was the subject of the petition. The controller of Supreme had lost interest in the investment, because of its poor performance, and then died, after which the company was unable to contact Supreme. The majority of the shares in the company came under the control of three new directors who improved its business greatly though it suffered from heavy debts. In a restructuring they transferred their shares to a new company (referred to in the judgment as 'Newco') which they controlled and then caused the company to sell all its assets to Newco for £1. Subsequently they sold their shares in Newco for £10 million. It was found that this was conduct prejudicial to the interests of Supreme, and Newco was ordered to buy Supreme's shares and to pay for them what Supreme would have got if the company had itself received the £10 million and then been wound up. The directors acted negligently and in breach of trust when they sold the assets for only £1 and their knowledge of this breach of trust would be attributed to Newco because they were directors of Newco and under a duty to inform it that the transaction was tainted by breach of trust (see *Belmont Finance Corporation v Williams Furniture Ltd (No 2)* [1980] 1 All ER 393 discussed in **19.8.3**). That made Newco responsible.

A policy of paying excessive remuneration to director shareholders and not distributing profits as dividends despite the company not having any use for retained profits in its business (apart from paying the directors) is unfairly prejudicial to shareholders who are not directors (*Re a Company (No 004415 of 1996)* [1997] 1 BCLC 479). Failure of directors, who are well remunerated in other ways, even to consider whether dividends should be paid is unfairly prejudicial to the interests of shareholders who are not directors (*Re McCarthy Surfacing Ltd* [2008] EWHC 2279 (Ch), [2009] 1 BCLC 622). A member of a company does not lose the right to complain about excessive remuneration by failing to examine annual accounts which disclosed the amounts paid (*Maidment v Attwood* [2012] EWCA Civ 998, [2013] Bus LR 753).

18.6.8.2 Mismanagement

The hearing in *Re Elgindata Ltd* [1991] BCLC 959 lasted 43 days during which almost every aspect of the company's affairs was minutely examined. The petitioners made numerous allegations of bad management by the company's managing director and principal shareholder. Warner J said (at p 993) that although, in an appropriate case, serious mismanagement of a company's affairs would constitute unfairly prejudicial conduct, the court would normally be very reluctant to accept that managerial decisions can amount to unfairly prejudicial conduct. It is not for the court to resolve differences of commercial judgement (see **18.3.3.1**). It is not unfair for a member of a company to suffer the consequences of poor management of the company: it is one of the normal risks of investing in a company that its management may turn out not to be of the highest quality. The petitioners had no right to expect a reasonable standard of general management from the managing director. However, the evidence showed that the managing director used assets of the company for his personal benefit and for the benefit of his family and friends. This was unfairly prejudicial conduct by its very nature rather than because it reduced the value of the petitioners' shares, and the managing director was ordered to buy the petitioners' shares. In *Re Macro (Ipswich) Ltd* [1994] 2 BCLC 354, though, it was found that mismanagement of the two companies involved had been so serious that the court should order the majority shareholder and sole director of the two companies to buy out the minority and that the value of the shares should be increased to take account of what the companies had lost through the mismanagement. The hearings in *Re Macro (Ipswich) Ltd* occupied 25 days and ranged over 40 years of the companies' history. The difference between the mismanagement in *Re Macro (Ipswich) Ltd* (where the companies had shown a consistent growth in profits) and that in *Re Elgindata Ltd* (which had declined into loss-making) is difficult to characterise and shows how difficult it is for legal advisers to predict the outcome of these lengthy and expensive proceedings.

18.6.8.3 Share value

It is prejudicial to the interests of a holder of shares in a company to be prevented from selling those shares at the best price. Thus, a misleading letter from the chairman of a company asserting that the lower of two rival takeover bids for the company should be accepted because the other 'cannot succeed' (when this was not in fact the case) is capable of being unfairly prejudicial conduct (*Re a Company (No 008699 of 1985)* [1986] BCLC 382).

18.6.8.4 Criminality

It is permissible for a petition to complain that a company's affairs are being conducted in contravention of criminal law: such a petition does not infringe the principle that the criminal law should not be enforced by civil proceedings (*Bermuda Cablevision Ltd v Colica Trust Co Ltd* [1998] AC 198).

18.6.8.5 Oppressive conduct under former law

Under CA 1948, s 210, it was necessary to show that the affairs of a company were being conducted in a manner oppressive to some part of the members. It would seem that conduct which is oppressive must be unfairly prejudicial so that conduct which was held to be oppressive under CA 1948, s 210, would certainly be unfairly prejudicial under CA 2006, s 994 (per Slade J in *Re Bovey Hotel Ventures Ltd* (ChD 31 July 1981 unreported); adopted by Nourse J in *Re R A Noble and Sons (Clothing) Ltd* [1983] BCLC 273).

In *Scottish Cooperative Wholesale Society Ltd v Meyer* [1959] AC 234, the Scottish CWS appealed to the House of Lords against the Scottish court's decision that it should purchase from Dr Meyer and Mr Lucas their minority interest in its subsidiary, Scottish Textiles and Manufacturing Co Ltd, on the ground that its affairs had been conducted in a manner oppressive to Dr Meyer and Mr Lucas. The subsidiary had been formed in 1946 to exploit Dr Meyer's ability to obtain a government licence to produce rayon, production of which was strictly controlled at the time. The CWS controlled the company by holding a majority of shares and appointing a majority of directors. The arrangement was that a factory owned by CWS would weave cloth which the subsidiary would dye and finish. The subsidiary made considerable profits for five years but when production controls were lifted the CWS decided that it had served its purpose and should be liquidated. Accordingly, it diverted its supplies of woven cloth to its own dyeing and finishing department, to which it sold cloth at low prices, leaving the subsidiary to buy cloth (which was then in short supply) at uneconomically high prices. The House of Lords dismissed the appeal, finding that the CWS's policy of destroying the company was, in effect, carried out by its nominee directors who failed to do anything to defend the company and failed to use their own position in the CWS to persuade the CWS to change its policy: the conduct of the subsidiary's affairs was in the hands of these nominee directors because they were in a majority on the board.

In *Re H R Harmer Ltd* [1959] 1 WLR 62 the company had been formed in 1947 to conduct the long-established philatelic business of Mr Harmer, then aged 77. The shares were owned by Mr Harmer, his two sons (who had spent their working lives in the business) and their wives. Mr Harmer senior and his wife held 78.6 per cent of the voting shares but only about 10 per cent of the total share capital (most of the shares were non-voting). By the time the petition was heard, Mr Harmer senior was 88, very deaf, and had difficulty comprehending questions put to him at the hearing. He took the view that he was entitled to disregard board decisions because he controlled so many voting shares. He often acted against the board's wishes in important matters which were detrimental to the interests of the company and acted foolishly, doubtless because of his advancing age. The Court of Appeal upheld Roxburgh J's order that the company should appoint Mr Harmer senior its salaried philatelic consultant and give him the title of president for life (an office carrying no rights or duties) in return for his not interfering with the business of the company except in accordance with board decisions.

For another example of a finding of oppressive conduct, see *Caratti Holding Co Pty Ltd v Zampatti* (1978) 52 ALJR 732, discussed in **3.4.3**.

18.6.8.6 Other companies in group

In *Nicholas v Soundcraft Electronics Ltd* [1993] BCLC 360, the petitioner was a minority shareholder in a subsidiary company. The parent company acted as overseas agent for the subsidiary and also effectively controlled its finances—for example, all cheques drawn on the subsidiary's bank account had to be signed by a director of the parent company. The parent company got into grave financial difficulties and refused to pass on to the subsidiary money earned from overseas sales of the subsidiary's products. The Court of Appeal held that this amounted to conduct of the subsidiary's affairs but that it was not unfairly prejudicial to the petitioner because the subsidiary depended on the parent company, and the parent company was entitled to use the resources of the group to keep both companies going.

The way in which the affairs of a wholly owned subsidiary of a company, with common directors, are conducted is capable of being unfairly prejudicial conduct of the parent company's affairs, as it will affect the value of the parent company's investment in the subsidiary (*Rackind v Gross* [2004] EWCA Civ 815, [2005] 1 WLR 3505).

In *Re Grandactual Ltd* [2005] EWHC 1415 (Ch), [2006] BCC 73, Sir Donald Rattee said, at [29], that the essence of these two decisions is that:

> it may in certain cases be possible to say that conduct of the affairs of one company also constitutes conduct of the affairs of another when the first company either is controlled by or has control of the other.

If one of two companies does not control the other, the fact that they are both controlled by the same persons does not mean that conduct of the affairs of one company is conduct of the affairs of the other (*Re Grandactual Ltd*).

18.6.8.7 Affairs of company and affairs of members

A petition under CA 2006, s 994, will complain of conduct by persons in *de facto* control of the company but it can only complain of their conduct of the company's affairs, not of their own affairs which happen to affect the company (*Re a Company (No 001761 of 1986)* [1987] BCLC 141, in which it was held that the fact that a director had purchased a debt owed by the company without informing the company and the fact that she had asked other members of the company to transfer their shares to her and resign as directors could not support a petition under s 994; *Re Leeds United Holdings plc* [1996] 2 BCLC 545, in which it was held that an alleged understanding that major shareholders would not sell their shares without consulting each other could not relate to conduct of the company's affairs).

In *Re Legal Costs Negotiators Ltd* [1999] 2 BCLC 171, three of the four directors of a quasi-partnership company had dismissed the fourth from his employment and he had resigned as a director but continued to hold one-quarter of the shares. The remaining three director-members petitioned under s 994 for an order that the former director sell his shares to them, claiming that his continued membership of the company was unfairly prejudicial to them. It was held that the retention of his shares was not conduct of the company's affairs or an act or omission of the company, so that s 994 did not apply.

18.6.8.8　Conduct past, future, continuing and isolated

A petition for relief of prejudicial conduct of a company's affairs may be grounded on conduct that has occurred in the past (*Re a Company (No 005287 of 1985)* [1986] 1 WLR 281) including conduct which occurred before the petitioner was a member of the company (*Lloyd v Casey* [2002] 1 BCLC 454).

A petition may be grounded on proposed prejudicial conduct (*Whyte* 1984 SLT 330), and it is no answer to such a petition to say that the immediate threat of the proposal was withdrawn before the petition was heard: the proposal might be made again and it is for the court to decide, on hearing the petition, whether an order is necessary to protect the petitioner's interests (*Re Kenyon Swansea Ltd* [1987] BCLC 514; D Milman, 'Anticipated unfair prejudice' (1987) 8 Co Law 272). But the court will not act on a mere fear that something prejudicial might be done by people whom the petitioner does not trust: the petitioner must identify a specific threatened prejudicial act (*Re Astec (BSR) plc* [1998] 2 BCLC 556).

It is not essential to allege a course of action—a single act or omission may be sufficient (*Re Marchday Group plc* [1998] BCC 800 at p 816). But it is necessary for a petitioner to allege a prejudicial act. For example, the mere fact that a listed company is not complying with the UK Corporate Governance Code by not having enough independent directors (see **15.2.3**) is not prejudicial conduct of the company's affairs, though a decision by the board, which was unconstrained by the lack of independent directors, could be (*Re Astec (BSR) plc*).

18.6.8.9　Improper removal of auditor

Removing a company's auditor from office, on grounds of divergence of opinions on accounting treatments or audit procedures, or on any other improper grounds, must be treated as being unfairly prejudicial to the interests of some part of the company's members (CA 2006, s 994(1A)).

18.6.9　EXCLUSION FROM A QUASI-PARTNERSHIP COMPANY

Many petitions under CA 2006, s 994, arise because of a disagreement among members of quasi-partnership companies (see **2.7**). As will be seen in **18.7**, one method of dealing with a dispute in a quasi-partnership company is to wind up the company, but in many cases this is an undesirably drastic remedy. What is usually required is for one of the disputing factions to leave the company, but this involves fixing an acceptable price at which the departing interest is to be bought out. What a departing member really wants is the proportion of the total value of the company represented by the shareholding being given up, but this is usually far greater than the market price of the shares, because, usually, they will not give an outside buyer any opportunity to influence the company's affairs.

Dismissal of a member of a quasi-partnership company from a directorship is capable of being unfairly prejudicial conduct (*Re a Company (No 00477 of 1986)* [1986] BCLC 376; *Re Ghyll Beck Driving Range Ltd* [1993] BCLC 1126; *Brownlow v G H Marshall Ltd* [2000] 2 BCLC 655), if it breaches a mutual understanding that a particular member is to be a director. However, dismissal will not be unfair if it was caused by the director's own misconduct which threatened the company's viability (*Woolwich v Milne* [2003] EWHC 414 (Ch), LTL 14/2/2003). A breach of an otherwise enforceable mutual understanding is not unfair if it is to protect the company from conduct which is detrimental to the company or its assets (*Grace v Biagioli* [2005] EWCA Civ 1222, [2006] 2 BCLC 70, at [64]). It cannot be unfairly prejudicial to exclude a person from management of a company if taking part in management would be unlawful, for example because it would contravene IA 1986, s 216 (see **20.14**) (*Hawkes v Cuddy* [2007] EWCA Civ 1072, [2008] BCC 125). A director who is justifiably dismissed is not unfairly prejudiced by more lenient treatment of a fellow director who is equally culpable (*Mears v R Mears and Co (Holdings) Ltd* [2002] 2 BCLC 1).

However, a breakdown in relations between members of a quasi-partnership company, making it impossible for them to work together, is not in itself unfairly prejudicial conduct of the company's affairs, if it is a normal hazard of business relationships between people with conflicting personalities (*Re a Company (No 007623 of 1984)* [1986] BCLC 362; *O'Neill v Phillips* [1999] 1 WLR 1092), though it may justify winding up the company (see **18.7.5.2**). In *O'Neill v Phillips* the petitioner, who was a minority shareholder and director, had lost confidence in, and could no longer work with, the only other shareholder and director. But this was because of actions by the other director which the court found were not unfair, so there was no ground for relief of unfairly prejudicial conduct. In contrast, in *Re Baumler (UK) Ltd* [2004] EWHC 1763 (Ch), [2005] 1 BCLC 92, the petitioner's loss of confidence in his fellow director was caused by that director's breach of fiduciary duty and underhand behaviour, which was unfairly prejudicial, so that relief could be ordered.

A member cannot force other members to buy him out simply because he wants to realise his interest in the company (*Re a Company (No 004475 of 1982)* [1983] Ch 178) or realise it for its proportionate share of the company's value (*Re Phoenix Office Supplies Ltd* [2002] EWCA Civ 1740, [2003] 1 BCLC 76).

If one member of a quasi-partnership company is asked to leave, because of a failure of the business relationship which has not been caused by unfairly prejudicial conduct of the company's affairs, the question is whether it is reasonable for that member to be the one who is to go and whether the terms on which that member is to be bought out are unfairly prejudicial (*Re a Company (No 007623 of 1984)*; *Re a Company (No 004377 of 1986)* [1987] 1 WLR 102). It is nearly always clear from the outset which party should leave the company (*Re a Company (No 004377 of 1986)* at p 110) and *Re a Company (No 003096 of 1987)* (1987) 4 BCC 80 shows that even where there was originally equality between the factions the one that has lost practical control to such an extent as to think it necessary to petition the court for relief is likely to be the one that will have to go. It would be very unusual for the court to order someone who is actively concerned in the management of a company and owns the majority of its shares to sell those shares to a minority shareholder when the majority shareholder is willing and able to buy out the minority shareholder at a fair price (*Re a Company (No 006834 of 1988)* [1989] BCLC 365).

In *Re Ghyll Beck Driving Range Ltd* the petitioner had joined three other men who were all to be equal partners in a joint venture in which they would each invest £25,000. All were to take part in management but the petitioner thought the others were not pulling their weight financially or managerially and quarrelled with them after which he was excluded from management. It was held that the petitioner was unjustifiably excluded, and the other three were ordered to buy his shares for a quarter of the going-concern value of the company. This may be contrasted with *Re Phoenix Office Supplies Ltd*, in which one of three men in a quasi-partnership company announced that he was leaving the company to start a new life, which he did within a few weeks. The fact that the other directors then treated him as having resigned his directorship and refused him access to management of the business was not unfairly prejudicial to him, and the other two could not be ordered to buy his shares at their full proportionate value.

In its report, *Shareholder Remedies* (Law Com No 246, Cm 3769) (London: Stationery Office, 1997), the Law Commission recommended that, if a member of a private company who is petitioning under s 994 shows that he or she has been removed as a director, or has been prevented from carrying out substantially all functions as a director, the court must presume there has been unfairly prejudicial conduct of the company's affairs unless the contrary is shown. This presumption would apply only if the petitioner held at least 10 per cent of the voting rights in the company and substantially all other members of the company were directors. The Law Commission further recommended that if, in such a case, the court decides to make an order for the purchase of the petitioner's shares, a statutory formula for fixing the price will be used unless the court orders otherwise. The Commission hoped that these presumptions would focus the parties' attention on the real dispute between them and reduce the cost of solving that dispute. This recommendation has not been acted on.

18.6.10 IS CONDUCT UNFAIRLY PREJUDICIAL ONLY IF IT BREACHES AN AGREEMENT?

In the passage from Lord Hoffmann's judgment in *O'Neill v Phillips* [1999] 1 WLR 1092 at p 1101, quoted in **18.6.7**, his Lordship said:

> I think that one useful cross-check in a case like this is to ask whether the exercise of the power in question would be contrary to what the parties, by word or conduct, have actually agreed.

Some people have taken this to mean that conduct cannot be unfairly prejudicial unless it is contrary to an existing agreement. This is despite the fact that Lord Hoffmann said that the cross-check was useful only in a case like the one before him, and despite the fact that he went on to say:

> I do not suggest that exercising rights in breach of some promise or undertaking is the only form of conduct which will be regarded as unfair for the purposes of [CA 2006, s 994].

Nevertheless, the Company Law Review Steering Group took the view that the result of *O'Neill v Phillips* is that:

> the basis for a claim [that conduct of a company's affairs is unfairly prejudicial] should be a departure from an agreement, broadly defined, between those concerned, to be identified by their words or conduct. This is necessary in the interests of certainty and the containment of the scope of [s 994] actions. (*Modern Company Law for a Competitive Economy: Final Report*, vol 1 (URN 01/942) (London: DTI, 2001), para 7.41.)

It is difficult to believe that Parliament intended s 994 to be restricted in this way, and it is submitted that this is not the effect of Lord Hoffmann's judgment (see also A J Boyle, '"Unfair prejudice" in the House of Lords' (2000) 21 Co Law 253). It is submitted that the preferable view is that of Arden J in *Re BSB Holdings Ltd (No 2)* [1996] 1 BCLC 155 at p 243:

> But the words of [s 994] are wide and general and . . . the categories of unfair prejudice are not closed. The standards of corporate behaviour recognised through [s 994] may in an appropriate case thus not be limited to those imposed by enactment or existing case law.

In *Arrow Nominees Inc v Blackledge* [2000] 2 BCLC 167, which was heard after *O'Neill v Phillips*, the Court of Appeal did not disagree with the following statement by the judge at first instance ([2001] BCC 591 at p 618):

> it is plain that Lord Hoffmann was not restricting the right to relief under ss [994 and 996] to circumstances where it could be shown that the respondent was exercising his control of the company to the disadvantage of the petitioner in breach of some contract or understanding between them which the court would regard as either contractually binding or sufficiently binding in conscience so that the court could treat its breach as being unfair. Lord Hoffmann plainly acknowledges the right, long established by authority under CA 1948,

s 210, and [CA 2006, s 994], for a minority shareholder to petition where a majority exercised its power to the disadvantage of the minority in their capacity as shareholders. Such conduct can be rationalised as a breach of the express or implied terms of the articles of association binding on the shareholders.

However, the Court of Appeal held that, in this case, the powers attached to the majority shareholder's shares had not been exercised, or threatened to be exercised, to the disadvantage of the minority.

In *O'Neill v Phillips*, Lord Hoffmann, at pp 1101–2, gave the following example of unfairly prejudicial conduct which does not involve a breach of some promise or undertaking:

> there may be some event which puts an end to the basis upon which the parties entered into association with each other, making it unfair that one shareholder should insist upon the continuance of the association. The analogy of contractual frustration suggests itself. The unfairness may arise not from what the parties have positively agreed but from a majority using its legal powers to maintain the association in circumstances to which the minority can reasonably say it did not agree: *non haec in foedera veni* [it was not this that I promised to do].

In *Hale v Waldock* [2006] EWHC 364 (Ch), [2007] 1 BCLC 520, Mann J said, at [90]:

> Lord Hoffmann was demonstrating that unfairness does not arise only out of a failure to comply with prior agreements or to fulfil prior expectations. The relationships between shareholders are more subtle than that, and Lord Hoffmann was recognising that unfairness can come out of a situation where the game has moved on so as to involve a situation not covered by the previous arrangements and understanding. In those circumstances the conduct of the affairs of the company can be unfairly prejudicial within [s 994] notwithstanding the absence of the prior arrangements, and the court can thus intervene.

18.6.11 ORDERS THE COURT MAY MAKE

18.6.11.1 Statutory powers

If the court is satisfied that a petition under CA 2006, s 994, is well founded, it is empowered by s 996(1) to 'make such order as it thinks fit for giving relief in respect of the matters complained of'. More particularly, under s 996(2), the court may:

(a) regulate the conduct of the company's affairs in the future; this could include altering the company's constitution or preventing the company from making any, or any specified, alteration to the constitution without the court's leave;

(b) require the company to refrain from doing or continuing an act complained of by the petitioner or to do an act which the petitioner has complained it has omitted to do;

(c) authorise civil proceedings to be brought in the name and on behalf of the company by such person or persons and on such terms as the court may direct (see **18.4.2**);

(d) require the company not to make any, or any specified, alterations in its articles without the leave of the court; and

(e) provide for the purchase of the shares of any members of the company by other members or by the company itself and, in the case of a purchase by the company itself, the reduction of the company's capital accordingly.

The petitioner must specify the relief sought, and it must be appropriate to the conduct of which the petition complains (*Re J E Cade and Son Ltd* [1992] BCLC 213 at p 223) though it need not be directed solely towards remedying the particular things that have happened (*Re Hailey Group Ltd* [1993] BCLC 459 at p 472). The court is required to make the order that is appropriate at the time of the hearing (*Re Hailey Group Ltd*, p 472). The court is not limited to reversing or putting right the conduct found to be unfairly prejudicial: it should consider the overall situation, past, present and future (*Grace v Biagioli* [2005] EWCA Civ 1222, [2006] 2 BCLC 70, at [73]). The court is not limited to giving the relief asked for by the petitioner (*Hawkes v Cuddy* [2009] EWCA Civ 291, [2009] 2 BCLC 427). The court can only enforce the actual agreement between the members, taking into account, if appropriate, legitimate understandings of how that agreement would be implemented: it cannot substitute a different agreement which is thought to be fairer (*Re J E Cade and Son Ltd*). The court has jurisdiction to make orders against persons who are not members of the company or who are not involved in the conduct complained of (provided they have been made parties to the proceedings) (*Re Little Olympian Each-ways Ltd* [1994] 2 BCLC 420).

The court has a power under s 996(1) to make such orders as it considers will enable the company, for the future, to be properly run, and for its affairs to be under the conduct of somebody who shareholders generally can be confident will conduct the affairs of the company properly (*Re a Company (No 00789 of 1987)* [1990] BCLC 384 per Harman J at p 395, followed in *Re Hailey Group Ltd*).

The appropriate remedy to deal with a dispute between the members of a small private company is normally to order the other members to purchase the petitioner's shares at a price to be fixed by the court. Such an order will free the petitioner from the company. The petitioner will take out a fair share of the value of the company's business and assets in return for giving up a share in its future. The company will be preserved for the other members free from the petitioner's claims and free from future conflict with the petitioner. The alternative of requiring the petitioner to stay, making orders to regulate the future conduct of the company is unlikely to be effective to preserve the peace and protect the petitioner's interests (*Grace v Biagioli* at [75]).

If unfairly prejudicial conduct of a company's affairs has resulted in the company having a right of action against a person, a petition by a member under s 994 may join that person as a respondent and ask the court to give the company remedies for its cause of action (*Re a Company (No 005287 of 1985)* [1986] 1 WLR 281; *Lowe v Fahey* [1996] 1 BCLC 262; *Anderson v Hogg* 2002 SC 190; *Clark v Cutland* [2003] EWCA Civ 810, [2004] 1 WLR 783). A petition asking for a remedy against a third party in favour of the company serves the same function as a derivative claim (see **18.4.2** to **18.4.4**).

18.6.11.2 Share purchase orders

The most common order made on petitions under CA 2006, s 994, is an order that the majority shareholders must buy the petitioner's shares (s 996(2)(e)). Exceptionally, in *Re Brenfield Squash Racquets Club Ltd* [1996] 2 BCLC 184, the majority shareholder was ordered to sell its shares to the petitioner. It is inconceivable that the court would order any person other than the company or its members to buy shares (*Re Little Olympian Each-ways Ltd* [1994] 2 BCLC 420).

For discussion of the way in which shares are priced when purchase is ordered under s 996(2)(e) see *Profinance Trust SA v Gladstone* [2002] 1 WLR 1024; G Shapira, 'Valuation of shares in buyout orders' (1995) 16 Co Law 11; D D Prentice, 'Minority shareholder oppression: valuation of shares' (1986) 102 LQR 179; G Sim, 'Shareholders in dispute' (2003) 153 NLJ 876.

A petitioner who wishes to ask for a share purchase order must not do so without first attempting to exercise any rights given by the company's articles to offer the shares to the other members at a fair price (*Re a Company (No 007623 of 1984)* [1986] BCLC 362; *Re a Company (No 004377 of 1986)* [1987] 1 WLR 102). The Law Commission has recommended strengthening such 'exit rights' (see **18.6.13**). If a reasonable offer to purchase the petitioner's shares has already been made, the petition will be struck out as an abuse of process: a petitioner is not entitled to insist on the court carrying out a valuation which can be performed more cheaply by an accountant (*Re a Company (No 00836 of 1995)* [1996] 2 BCLC 192). There is a helpful discussion of what counts as a reasonable offer to purchase a petitioner's shares in *O'Neill v Phillips* [1999] 1 WLR 1092 at pp 1107–8. An offer is not reasonable if the offeror cannot finance it (*West v Blanchet* [2000] 1 BCLC 795). In many cases the petitioner contends that the value of the shares has been diminished by the conduct complained of in the petition and some way has to be found for a valuer to take this into account. Valuing the petitioner's shares as if the company had been compensated for wrongs done to it is a legitimate way of compensating the petitioner for a reflective loss (see **18.4.3**) (*Atlasview Ltd v Brightview Ltd* [2004] EWHC 1056 (Ch), [2004] 2 BCLC 191; G Sim, 'Shareholders in dispute' (2003) 153 NLJ 876). If the value of the shares depends on the answer to a question of law, the question should be left for the court to decide (*North Holdings Ltd v Southern Tropics Ltd* [1999] 2 BCLC 625).

18.6.12 INTERIM ORDERS

It is desirable that the status quo should be preserved in the time between presentation and hearing of a petition under CA 2006, s 994, and the court will grant injunctions to achieve this (*Re a Company (No 002612 of 1984)* [1985] BCLC 80; *Re a Company (No 00330 of 1991)* [1991] BCLC 597; *Re a Company (No 003061 of 1993)* [1994] BCC 883). See also the discussion in **14.8.15** of the interaction between a petition by a minority under s 994 and an application by the majority under s 306 to overcome the minority's frustration of meetings. As usual when considering whether to grant an interim injunction, the court will not do so if the balance of convenience is against it (*Rutherford* [1994] BCC 876).

18.6.13 EXIT RIGHTS IN ARTICLES

In its report, *Shareholder Remedies* (Law Com No 246, Cm 3769) (London: Stationery Office, 1997), the Law Commission recommended that model articles should include a provision providing a minority shareholder with 'exit rights' to demand to be bought out by the other members at a fair valuation in certain circumstances, such as on being dismissed from a directorship. A draft article is set out in Appendix C to the report. The Commission believed that many unfair-prejudice petitions litigated before their report would have been unnecessary if such exit rights had been available. Exit rights are not included in the model articles of association in SI 2008/3229.

18.7 WINDING UP

18.7.1 AVAILABILITY OF WINDING UP AS A REMEDY

If members of a company are dissatisfied with the way in which it is being run, one, rather drastic, way of dealing with the situation is to end the company's existence by having it wound up. There is a statutory provision in the Insolvency Act 1986, s 84(1)(b), permitting members of a company to adopt a resolution for voluntary winding up, but this has to be a special resolution, which requires a three-quarters majority of those voting. (It is only an accident of the legislative process that this provision is in an Act concerned with insolvency. A solvent company may be wound up under s 84(1)(b).)

The usual practical difficulty for a dissatisfied member is the inability to get the majority needed for a special resolution for a voluntary winding up. The alternative provided by the legislation is for such a member to ask the court to order that the company be wound up. A present member of a company has standing to make such an application under the Insolvency Act 1986, s 124, by virtue of being a 'contributory' of the company, as will be explained in **20.1.6**.

The court cannot make a winding-up order unless it is shown that one of the circumstances listed in the Insolvency Act 1986, s 122(1), exists. The circumstance that dissatisfied members invariably rely on is s 122(1)(g): 'the court is of the opinion that it is just and equitable that the company should be wound up'. In *Re Blériot Manufacturing Aircraft Co Ltd* (1916) 32 TLR 253, Neville J said, at p 255:

> The words 'just and equitable' are words of the widest significance, and do not limit the jurisdiction of the court to any case. It is a question of fact, and each case must depend on its own circumstances.

A contributory petitioning under s 122(1)(g) may rely 'upon any circumstances of justice or equity which affect him in his relations with the company, or . . . with the other shareholders' (per Lord Wilberforce in *Ebrahimi v Westbourne Galleries Ltd* [1973] AC 360 at p 375).

Unless the articles of association of a company provide otherwise, a member cannot make it wind up voluntarily other than by obtaining a three-quarters majority at a general meeting. A person must accept, on joining a company, that leaving the company is subject to this fundamental restriction. A contributory presenting a just and equitable petition is claiming that it is just and equitable to waive this restriction. The essential question on a contributory's petition is whether members who do not desire to stay in a company should be entitled to be released (per Harman J in *Re a Company (No 00370 of 1987)* [1988] 1 WLR 1068 at p 1075).

Some problems have appeared repeatedly in reported cases over the years and illustrate the sorts of situations in which the court will regard it as just and equitable to order a company to be wound up. These include:

(a) Cases in which the company was promoted fraudulently (see **18.7.2**).

(b) Cases in which there is a 'deadlock' (see **18.7.3**).

(c) Cases in which the management and conduct of the company are such that it is unjust and inequitable to require the petitioner to continue as a member (see **18.7.4**).

(d) Cases in which the company is a quasi-partnership company and there has been a sufficiently serious breach of mutual understandings not expressed in the company's constitution (see **18.7.5**).

(e) Cases in which the company's substratum has gone (see **3.8.3** and **3.8.6**).

A winding-up order will not be made on a member's petition unless the petitioner has a sufficient interest in having the company wound up (*Re Rica Gold Washing Co* (1879) 11 ChD 36). The interest that a member must have is known as a 'tangible interest', a phrase used by Jessel MR in *Re Rica Gold Washing Co* at p 43. Thus a member whose shares are all fully paid up cannot petition unless it appears there will be a dividend for members in the winding up (*Re Rica Gold Washing Co*; *Re Bellador Silk Ltd* [1965] 1 All ER 667; *Re Othery Construction Ltd* [1966] 1 WLR 69; *Re Expanded Plugs Ltd* [1966] 1 WLR 514; *Re Chesterfield Catering Co Ltd* [1977] Ch 373).

Those opposing a member's petition may point out to the court that even if the court takes the view that the petitioner is entitled to relief from a situation that is unjust and inequitable, there is a remedy available, other than winding up the company. However, IA 1986, s 125(2), requires the court, if it is of opinion that the petitioner is entitled to relief, to decide whether it is just and equitable that the company should be wound up, *ignoring* the possibility of other forms of relief. If it comes to the conclusion that in the absence of any other remedy it would be just and equitable that the company should be wound up then it *must* make a winding-up order unless it is of opinion that the petitioner is acting unreasonably in seeking a winding-up order rather than pursuing some alternative remedy (see *Re a Company (No 002567 of 1982)* [1983] 1 WLR 927 per Vinelott J at p 932; *Vujnovich v Vujnovich* [1990] BCLC 227 at p 232). It cannot be unreasonable of the petitioner not to pursue an alternative remedy that has already been refused (*Vujnovich v Vujnovich*). The alternative remedy that is usually appropriate is an application under CA 2006, s 994 (see **18.6**). A reasonable offer by other members of the company to buy out the petitioner's interest is also an alternative remedy (*Re a Company (No 002567 of 1982)* [1983] 1 WLR 927; *Re a Company (No 003843 of 1986)* [1987] BCLC 562; *Re a Company (No 003096 of 1987)* (1987) 4 BCC 80).

It is not unreasonable to refuse an offer to buy the petitioner's shares if the person who will value them is not, or cannot be seen to be, wholly independent (*Re Boswell and Co (Steels) Ltd* (1988) 5 BCC 145). In *Re a Company (No 001363 of 1988)* [1989] BCLC 579, it was not unreasonable of the petitioner to refuse an offer to buy the one share registered in his name because one of the claims of his petition was that he was entitled to 3,250 shares. It is not unreasonable of a petitioner to refuse an offer to buy his shares if he fears that the valuation will be wrong, because, for example, the valuer will apply a discount to reflect the fact that the shareholding is not large enough to give control of the company or will be unable to deal properly with disputed claims against the company (*Virdi v Abbey Leisure Ltd* [1990] BCLC 342).

Even so, as Lord Wilberforce said in *Cumberland Holdings Ltd v Washington H. Soul Pattinson and Co Ltd* (1977) 13 ALR 561, at pp 566–7: 'to wind up a successful and prosperous company and one which is properly managed must clearly be an extreme step and must require a strong case to be made'.

In *Ebrahimi v Westbourne Galleries Ltd* [1973] AC 360, Lord Cross of Chelsea said at p 387:

> A petitioner who relies on the 'just and equitable' clause must come to court with clean hands, and if the breakdown in confidence between him and the other parties to the dispute appears to have been due to his misconduct he cannot insist on the company being wound up if they wish it to continue.

18.7.2 FRAUDULENT PROMOTION

It is just and equitable to wind up a company on a contributory's petition if the company was promoted fraudulently, for example for the purpose of taking money from subscribers for shares without any intention of carrying on any substantial business (*Re London and County Coal Co* (1866) LR 3 Eq 355; *Re Neath Harbour Smelting and Rolling Works Ltd* (1886) 2 TLR 336; *Re Thomas Edward Brinsmead and Sons* [1897] 1 Ch 406). Such companies are usually described as 'bubbles' (see also *Mahony v East Holyford Mining Co Ltd* (1875) LR 7 HL 869 per Lord Cairns LC at p 886 and Lord Chelmsford at p 889) or 'shams'. The entire scheme of the company must be fraudulent in order to justify compulsory liquidation: the fact that the company has been defrauded is not sufficient because normally action should be taken in the name of the company against persons, such as promoters, who have defrauded it (*Foss v Harbottle* (1843) 2 Hare 461; *Re Anglo-Greek Steam Co* (1866) LR 2 Eq 1; *Re Haven Gold Mining Co* (1882) 20 ChD 151; *Re Nylstroom Co Ltd* (1889) 60 LT 477; *Re Othery Construction Ltd* [1966] 1 WLR 69). The appropriate remedy for a person who has been misled into subscribing for shares is not winding up but rescission of the allotment of the shares (*Re Bwlch y Plym Co Ltd* (1867) 17 LT 235).

18.7.3 DEADLOCK

In *Ng Eng Hiam v Ng Kee Wei* (1964) 31 MLJ 238, Lord Donovan said, at p 240:

> The principle is clear that if the court is satisfied that complete deadlock exists in the management of a company the jurisdiction [to wind up a company if the court thinks it just and equitable to do so] will be exercised . . . It may be that the jurisdiction will be more readily exercised where . . . although the business is carried on by means of a private limited company, the case is not unlike one of a partnership.

Exactly what is meant by 'deadlock' in this context is unclear. Lord Donovan in *Ng Eng Hiam v Ng Kee Wei* said, at p 240: 'The question whether such a deadlock exists as makes it just and equitable to wind the company up is a question predominantly of fact in each case.' It seems that deadlock involves a division of the membership and directors into two opposed and uncooperative factions which inhibits decisions on matters crucial to the company's prosperity. Deadlock has been described as 'an impasse in the corporate decision-making process'

(J O'Donovan and G W O'Grady, 'Company deadlocks: prevention and cure' (1982) 1 C & SLJ 67 at p 67).

In *Ng Eng Hiam v Ng Kee Wei*, deadlock was alleged but the Privy Council refused to disturb the decision of the courts below not to wind up the company because 'there seems to be reasonable hope of reconciliation and cooperation if ordinary good sense is employed' (at p 240, quoting the words of Hill JA in the Malaya Court of Appeal (1962) 29 MLJ 73 at p 77). In *Re Goodwealth Trading Pte Ltd* [1991] 2 MLJ 314, Yong Pung How CJ said, at pp 318–19, that this was an 'extraordinary opinion . . . which was against the evidence'. The Chief Justice thought that the evidence showed there was 'what can only be described as a Chinese family feud of considerable intensity'.

It has been said that there is no deadlock if there is any procedure under the company's constitution or the general law by which one faction could get decisions made (for example, by appointing additional directors, using casting votes, going to arbitration, dismissing directors or asking the court to summon a general meeting and directing that one member may be a quorum) (*Re Furriers' Alliance Ltd* (1906) 51 SJ 172; *Re Expanded Plugs Ltd* [1966] 1 WLR 514 at p 519; *Ebrahimi v Westbourne Galleries Ltd* [1973] AC 360 per Lord Cross of Chelsea at p 383). If a company is a quasi-partnership company, the court will recognise that it may be unjust and inequitable for one faction to exercise its legal rights to overrule the petitioner (*Ebrahimi v Westbourne Galleries Ltd*). The factor determining whether it is just and equitable to wind up a company may be whether it is just and equitable to leave the petitioner to submit to the exercise by an opposing faction in the company of their legal rights rather than invoke equitable considerations to release the petitioner (*Ebrahimi v Westbourne Galleries Ltd*). This accounts for the fact that, as Lord Donovan pointed out in the passage from *Ng Eng Hiam v Ng Kee Wei* quoted earlier, a company is more likely to be wound up for deadlock if it is a quasi-partnership company than if it is not.

Deadlock in a quasi-partnership company inevitably involves cessation of trust and confidence among the quasi-partners, which is in itself a recognised ground for winding up a quasi-partnership company (see **18.7.5.2**).

18.7.4 MANAGEMENT AND CONDUCT OF THE COMPANY: OPPRESSION

18.7.4.1 Principle

It may be just and equitable to order the compulsory winding up of the company if the management and conduct of the company are such that it is unjust and inequitable to require the petitioner either to continue as a member or to leave on unjust terms.

18.7.4.2 Directors' lack of probity

In many reported cases the significant factor making it just and equitable to order the winding up of a company on a contributory's petition was that directors whom the petitioner could not remove appeared to have shown a lack of probity in the conduct of the company's affairs. See, for example, *Loch v John Blackwood Ltd* [1924] AC 783; *Re Straw Products Pty Ltd* [1942] VLR 272; *Re Concrete Column Clamps Ltd* [1953] 4 DLR 60 (in which the controlling director had systematically stolen a vast sum of money from the company over many years and had sold its principal revenue-earning assets to a new company owned by himself and his son); *Re Maritime Asphalt Products Ltd* (1965) 52 DLR (2d) 8 (in which the company and its controlling directors had been fined for numerous tax offences); *Re Worldhams Park Golf Course Ltd* [1998] 1 BCLC 554 (in which one director had got his position by lying about his qualifications and had stolen the company's retail takings: this was characterised, at p 556, as 'gross misconduct').

Lack of probity may be shown by a persistent disregard of an obligation to act in the interests of the company (*Thomson v Drysdale* 1925 SC 311; *Re Wondoflex Textiles Pty Ltd* [1951] VLR 458).

In *Loch v John Blackwood Ltd* [1924] AC 783, Lord Shaw of Dunfermline said, at p 788:

> It is undoubtedly true that at the foundation of applications for winding up, on the 'just and equitable' rule, there must lie a justifiable lack of confidence in the conduct and management of the company's affairs. But this lack of confidence must be grounded on conduct of the directors, not in regard to their private life or affairs, but in regard to the company's business. Furthermore the lack of confidence must spring not from dissatisfaction at being outvoted on the business affairs or on what is called the domestic policy of the company. On the other hand, wherever the lack of confidence is rested on a lack of probity in the conduct of the company's affairs, then the former is justified by the latter, and it is under the statute just and equitable that the company be wound up.

The fact that directors are unwise, inefficient and careless in the performance of their duties does not show lack of probity and does not justify winding up (*Re Five Minute Car Wash Service Ltd* [1966] 1 WLR 745, especially at p 752; see also per Plowman J in *Re Surrey Garden Village Trust Ltd* [1965] 1 WLR 974 at p 981).

Misconduct by directors is not enough to justify winding up if it could be remedied by a claim brought by the company against the directors, or a derivative claim brought by a member (*Re Anglo-Greek Steam Co* (1866) LR 2 Eq 1 per Lord Romilly MR at p 5; *Re Diamond Fuel Co* (1879) 13 ChD 400 per Baggallay LJ at p 408; *Re Kitson and Co Ltd* [1946] 1 All ER 435 per Lord Greene MR at p 441; *Re Surrey Garden Village Trust Ltd* [1965] 1 WLR 974 per Plowman J at p 981).

18.7.4.3 Oppression

In many cases in which a member of a company petitions for it to be wound up, it is alleged that the affairs of the company are being conducted in a manner oppressive to the petitioner. This terminology was used in CA 1948, s 210 (repealed), which provided that if a member could prove this state of affairs and the court found that the oppression justified the making of a winding-up order, the court could instead make other orders (the most useful of which was an order that the other shareholders buy out the petitioner). Similar provisions were enacted in other Commonwealth jurisdictions. Oppressive conduct justifying winding up was found in *Scottish Co-operative Wholesale Society Ltd v Meyer* [1959] AC 324; *Re H R Harmer Ltd* [1959] 1 WLR 62; and a number of Commonwealth cases. Experience of the operation of CA 1948, s 210, and the similar Commonwealth provisions revealed many companies in which there were dissatisfied members who wished to leave but where the situation was not bad enough to be called oppressive and to justify winding up the company. Eventually, the provisions which are now CA 2006, ss 994 to 999, were enacted, providing relief short of winding up for conduct which is unfairly prejudicial, rather than oppressive (see **18.6**).

18.7.4.4 Controller treating the company as his or her own

In several cases in which winding up has been ordered on the just and equitable ground, the courts have commented that one individual in *de facto* control of the company has treated it as his or her own, typically failing to give proper information to other members and withdrawing excessive remuneration or other benefits (*Baird v Lees* 1924 SC 83; *Thomson v Drysdale* 1925 SC 311; *Loch v John Blackwood Ltd* [1924] AC 783 at p 794). In *Thomson v Drysdale*, Lord President Clyde said, at p 315:

> in any case in which the shareholders who hold a preponderating interest in a company make it manifest that they intend to set at naught the security provided by company procedure, and to treat the company and its affairs as if they were their own property, it is impossible that the minority should retain any confidence in the impartiality or probity of the company's administration, and—according to the circumstances of each particular case—it becomes a question whether the minority are not entitled, as a matter of 'justice and equity' within the meaning of [the Insolvency Act 1986, s 122(1)(g)], to have the company wound up.

18.7.5 QUASI-PARTNERSHIP COMPANIES

18.7.5.1 Recognition of legitimate expectations outside the company's constitution

If a company is a quasi-partnership company (see **2.7**), it may be just and equitable to order its compulsory liquidation on a contributory's petition if there has been a breach of mutual understandings by the members not expressed in the company's constitution. The breach must be sufficiently serious to justify winding up and most of the cases so far fall into three categories:

(a) Cases in which there was a mutual understanding that the company would be conducted on the basis of a personal business relationship between members involving mutual confidence and that relationship has irretrievably broken down (see **18.7.5.2**).

(b) Cases in which the petitioner has been unjustifiably excluded from management in breach of a mutual understanding that he or she would participate in managing the company while a member of it (see **18.7.5.3**).

(c) Cases in which there was a mutual understanding that the company would engage in one venture only, which venture has now been completed or abandoned (*Virdi v Abbey Leisure Ltd* [1990] BCLC 342; *Bernhardt v Beau Rivage Pty Ltd* (1989) 15 ACLR 160) (see **3.8.6**).

If the articles specifically provide a procedure to deal with a breakdown of the business relationship in the company or the removal of the petitioner from management (typically by providing for the petitioner to be bought out at a fair price), it is not just and equitable to wind up the company if the petitioner unjustifiably refuses to follow that procedure (see *Re a Company (No 004377 of 1986)* [1987] 1 WLR 102). But it may be unjust and inequitable to insist that the petitioner must be confined to following that procedure (*Virdi v Abbey Leisure Ltd* [1990] BCLC 342).

It is the members' mutual understandings which the court takes into account, not its own view of what would be fair (*Re J E Cade and Son Ltd* [1992] BCLC 213 at p 227).

18.7.5.2 Cessation of trust and confidence

In *Symington v Symingtons' Quarries Ltd* (1905) 8 F 121, Lord M'Laren, at p 129, referred to the principle of partnership law that 'incompatibility between the views or methods of the partners' justifies a decree of dissolution and said that this was applicable by analogy to divisions among shareholders of a quasi-partnership company. In that case there was continual quarrelling 'directed . . . to points not only of substance, but to points of an absolutely trivial description' (per Lord President Dunedin at p 128).

In *Re Yenidje Tobacco Co Ltd* [1916] 2 Ch 426, the company had two shareholders, Weinberg and Rothman, who had equal votes as members and who were both directors for life. At board meetings, by the articles of the company, no casting vote could be exercised. The two were not on speaking terms. Rothman had sued Weinberg alleging fraudulent misrepresentation. Disagreement between the two over the dismissal of a factory manager had been referred to a lengthy and expensive arbitration, but Rothman had refused to accept the result. Despite this the company was increasingly successful and made considerable profits. The Court of Appeal affirmed a winding-up order made on Weinberg's petition. Lord Cozens-Hardy MR said, at p 432:

> I think the circumstances are such that we ought to apply, if necessary, the analogy of the partnership law and to say that this company is now in a state which could not have been contemplated by the parties when the company was formed and which ought to be terminated as soon as possible.

18.7.5.3 Exclusion from management

It is just and equitable to order the compulsory liquidation of a quasi-partnership company on a contributory's petition if the petitioner has been unjustifiably excluded from management of the company contrary to a legitimate expectation of participating in that management (*Re Davis and Collett Ltd* [1935] Ch 693; *Re Wondoflex Textiles Pty Ltd* [1951] VLR 458; *Re Lundie Brothers Ltd* [1965] 1 WLR 1051; *Ebrahimi v Westbourne Galleries Ltd* [1973] AC 360; *Tay Bok Choon v Tahansan Sdn Bhd* [1987] 1 WLR 413). These cases are sometimes called 'expulsion' cases.

In *Ebrahimi v Westbourne Galleries Ltd* [1973] AC 360, Mr Ebrahimi and Mr Nazar had carried on business in partnership dealing in Persian and other carpets. They shared equally in management and profits. In 1958 they formed a private company carrying on the same business and were appointed its first directors. Shortly after the company's incorporation, Mr Nazar's son, George, became a director. Mr Nazar and his son between them held the majority of votes exercisable at general meetings. The company made good profits which were all distributed as directors' remuneration: no dividends were ever paid. In 1969 Mr Ebrahimi was removed from his directorship by a resolution of a general meeting under what is now CA 2006, s 168 (see **15.6.3**), and a provision of the company's articles. The House of Lords upheld Plowman J's decision to order the company to be wound up on Mr Ebrahimi's petition, because of his inability after his dismissal to participate in the company's management and profits.

18.7.6 FURTHER DISCUSSION

Ebrahimi v Westbourne Galleries Ltd [1973] AC 360 provoked a considerable amount of academic comment. See M R Chesterman, 'The "just and equitable" winding up of small private companies' (1973) 36 MLR 129; D D Prentice, 'Winding up on the just and equitable ground: the partnership analogy' (1973) 89 LQR 107; B A K Rider, 'Partnership law and its impact on "domestic companies"' [1979] CLJ 148. Since then, the provisions that are now CA 2006, ss 994 to 999, have been enacted (see **18.6**) and it may be that the court can provide better remedies for disputes in quasi-partnership companies under those provisions than by the drastic method of winding up.

The winding-up and unfair prejudice jurisdictions overlap, but are not identical (*Hawkes v Cuddy* [2009] EWCA Civ 291, [2009] 2 BCLC 427, at [107], overruling *Re Guidezone Ltd* [2000] 2 BCLC 321). The statutory provisions are differently worded and they ask the court to consider different questions: on a winding-up petition, the question is whether the company's existence should be ended; on an unfair prejudice petition, the question is how the company's existence should be continued. In many, if not most, cases conduct of a company's affairs may justify relief under both jurisdictions. It is not necessary to show that the circumstances justify winding up a company in order to succeed with a petition for the relief of unfairly prejudicial conduct of its affairs (*Re a Company (No 00314 of 1989)* [1991] BCLC 154; *O'Neill v Phillips* [1999] 1 WLR 1092 per Lord Hoffmann at pp 1099–100). In some quasi-partnership cases, prejudicial conduct cannot be found but a just and equitable winding up can be ordered as in *Re R A Noble (Clothing) Ltd* [1983] BCLC 273 and *Re a Company (No 00370 of 1987)* [1988] 1 WLR 1068. In *Re Phoneer Ltd* [2002] 2 BCLC 241 one of two members of a company petitioned for it to be wound up, the other petitioned for relief of unfairly prejudicial conduct of the company's affairs: although unfairly prejudicial conduct was found, it was held that winding up was the only appropriate remedy. On the other hand, a petitioner seeking a just and equitable winding up may be defeated by the clean hands rule or the tangible interest rule, neither of which applies to a petition for relief of unfairly prejudicial conduct (see **18.6.2.2**).

18.8 COMPANY INVESTIGATIONS

18.8.1 INTRODUCTION

Registered companies, unlike individuals and partnerships, are subject to having their affairs investigated by civil servants or specially appointed inspectors, who may use extensive powers to collect evidence and pass it on to regulatory or prosecuting authorities. There are two different forms of investigation: (a) a confidential investigation (**18.8.2**), and (b) an investigation by inspectors (**18.8.3** and **18.8.4**).

A confidential investigation is an informal, unpublicised enquiry, usually conducted by officials of the Insolvency Service, which is an executive agency of the Department for Business, Energy and Industrial Strategy. A confidential investigation is similar to a police enquiry, but backed by powers, usually not available to the police, to require people to provide information on pain of prosecution. The Service aims to complete an inspection within six months. For contact details see **www.gov.uk/complain-about-a-limited-company.**

An investigation by inspectors is a much more serious affair, often lasting several years. It is usual to appoint two inspectors, one a QC, the other an accountant. The appointments are publicly announced and the result of the investigation is usually a published report.

Investigations are still governed by provisions of CA 1985.

18.8.2 CONFIDENTIAL INVESTIGATION

The Insolvency Service conducts confidential investigations under CA 1985, s 447. Action is usually taken under s 447(3), which empowers the Secretary of State, in relation to a company, to authorise an investigator to require the company, or any other person, to produce documents or provide information specified by the investigator. Alternatively, under s 447(2), the Secretary of State may direct the company to produce specified documents or provide specified information. Failure to comply with a requirement under s 447 may be punished as a contempt of court (s 453C). Knowingly or recklessly providing information which is false in a material particular is an offence under s 451.

The term 'documents' includes information recorded in any form (s 447(8)). Information not in hard copy form must, if required, be produced in hard copy form, or in a form from which a hard copy can be readily obtained (s 447(9)). The investigator or the Secretary of State may take copies of or extracts from documents produced in response to a s 447 requirement (s 447(7)).

Section 447A prevents a statement made by a person in response to a s 447 requirement being referred to at a criminal trial of that person and is in similar terms to s 434(5), (5A) and (5B), which are discussed in **18.8.4.2.**

Documents for which legal professional privilege could be claimed are exempt from disclosure and cannot be seized (s 452(2)), but a lawyer may be required to disclose the name and address of his or her client (s 452(5)). By s 452(3) and (4), a person carrying on the business of banking cannot be required to produce a document relating to a customer's affairs, or provide information about those affairs, except as necessary for investigating the bank's own affairs, or where the customer is the subject of a requirement either under s 447 or under FSMA 2000, s 171 or 173.

If there are reasonable grounds for believing that there are, on any premises, documents required under s 447 to be produced, but which have not been produced, a search warrant, which will be executed by the police, may be obtained from a justice of the peace under s 448.

An investigator who is authorised by the Secretary of State may require entry to premises which the investigator believes are used, wholly or partly, for the purposes of a company's business, and remain on those premises, if the investigator thinks that to do so will materially assist the exercise of his or her functions in relation to the company (s 453A). The investigator may be accompanied by such other persons as he or she thinks appropriate (s 453A(4)). It is an offence to obstruct, intentionally, a person lawfully exercising the power to enter and remain on premises (s 453A(5)). No magistrates' warrant is necessary. For strong criticism of the lack of judicial control see M Griffiths, 'DTI: power to enter and remain' (2005) 155 NLJ 738.

Section 448A gives immunity from a claim for breach of confidence to a whistle-blower who gives information to the Secretary of State to show that an investigation is required.

18.8.3 INVESTIGATION BY INSPECTORS

18.8.3.1 Investigation into a company's affairs

The Secretary of State may appoint one or more inspectors to investigate a company's affairs and to report thereon under either s 431 or 432 of CA 1985.

Under s 431, inspectors may be appointed to investigate and report on a company's affairs on an application by the company itself or a sufficient number of its shareholders (s 431(1) and (2)). The sufficient number is either 200 or more shareholders or shareholders holding at least 10 per cent of the company's issued share capital (other than treasury shares; see **10.6.6**) (s 431(2)). The application must be supported by such evidence as the Secretary of State may require for the purposes of showing that the applicants have good reason for requiring the investigation (s 431(3)). If an investigation is undertaken, the applicants may be liable to pay for it (s 439(5)) and so the Secretary of State may require applicants to give security for up to £5,000 (s 431(4)).

Under s 432(2), inspectors may be appointed to investigate and report on a company's affairs if it appears to the Secretary of State that:

(a) the company's affairs are being or have been conducted with intent to defraud its creditors or the creditors of any other person or otherwise for a fraudulent or unlawful purpose or in a manner which is unfairly prejudicial to some part of its members (including a person who is not a member but to whom shares have been transferred or transmitted by operation of law, such as a personal representative or trustee in bankruptcy: s 432(4)), or any actual or proposed act or omission of the company or on its behalf is or would be so prejudicial, or it was formed for any fraudulent or unlawful purpose; or

(b) persons concerned with the company's formation or management of its affairs have been guilty of fraud, misfeasance, or other misconduct towards the company or its members; or

(c) the company's shareholders have not been given all the information with respect to its affairs which they might reasonably expect.

The Secretary of State may exercise this power even if the company is in the course of being voluntarily wound up (s 432(3)). There is no requirement that the Secretary of State must provide to the company, or the persons thought to have misconducted its affairs, the material which appears to show the grounds specified in s 432(2) or must provide an opportunity for representations to be made before deciding whether to appoint inspectors (*Norwest Holst Ltd v Secretary of State for Trade* [1978] Ch 201).

The Secretary of State must appoint one or more inspectors to investigate and report on a company's affairs if the court by order declares that its affairs ought to be investigated by an inspector (s 432(1)).

These provisions are only used in the most serious cases and when they are used, the investigations are lengthy and expensive. The investigation into Barlow Clowes Gilt Managers Ltd, for example, cost £6.25 million and the investigation into Atlantic Computers plc cost £6.5 million. The Barlow Clowes report was published in July 1995. Since then only six investigations have been completed and published: Guinness plc in 1997, Chancery plc in 1998, Mirror Group Newspapers plc in 2001, TransTec plc in 2003, Queens Moat Houses plc in 2004, and Phoenix Venture Holdings Ltd, MG Rover Group Ltd and 33 other companies in 2009.

18.8.3.2 Investigation of ownership or control

The Secretary of State, if satisfied that there is good reason to do so, may appoint one or more inspectors to investigate and report on the 'membership of any company, and otherwise with respect to the company, for the purpose of determining the true persons who are or have been financially interested in the success or failure (real or apparent) of the company or able to control or materially to influence its policy' (CA 1985, s 442(1)).

An application may be made to the Secretary of State by members of the company for such an investigation to be undertaken with respect to particular shares or debentures of the company (s 442(3)). If the application is by 200 or more members of the company, or by members holding 10 per cent or more of the company's issued shares, the Secretary of State must appoint inspectors unless satisfied that the application is vexatious or that it would be sufficient to carry out an investigation under s 444 (see the following paragraph) (s 442(3), (3A) and (3C)). The Secretary of State is entitled to exclude from the inspectors' terms of reference any matter which the members want included if satisfied that it is unreasonable for the matter to be investigated (s 442(3A)). If an investigation is undertaken, either by inspectors or under s 444, the applicants may be liable to pay for it (s 439(5)) and so the Secretary of State may require applicants to give security for up to £5,000 (s 442(3B)).

Where the Secretary of State is satisfied that there is good reason to investigate the ownership of any shares in or debentures of a company but that it is unnecessary to appoint an inspector for the purpose, a requirement may be imposed under s 444 on persons to give information which they have, or are able to obtain, about the present and past interests in those shares or debentures, and the names and addresses of the persons interested and of any persons who act or have acted on their behalf in relation to those shares or debentures. Such a requirement may be imposed on any person whom the Secretary of State has reasonable cause to believe has or is able to obtain the information. Under s 444(2), the persons who are deemed to be interested in shares and debentures include persons who have any right to acquire or dispose of them, or of any interest in them, or to vote in respect of them, and any person whose consent is necessary for the exercise of any of the rights of other persons interested in them. If persons interested in shares or debentures can be required, or are accustomed, to exercise their rights in accordance with another person's instructions then that other person is deemed to be interested in those shares or debentures. It is an offence not to give information required by s 444 or, in giving it, knowingly or recklessly to make a statement which is false in a material particular (s 444(3)).

Where an investigation is proceeding under s 442 or 444 and it appears to the Secretary of State that there is some difficulty in finding out the relevant facts about any shares, the Secretary of State may order that the shares be subject to restrictions (s 445). Provisions about restrictions orders (usually known as freezing orders) are in ss 454 to 457. A share subject to a freezing order may not be transferred, the votes attached to it may not be exercised, no dividend may be paid on it, there can be no return of capital unless the company is wound up and no pre-emptive subscription rights may be exercised (s 454). There is a right to appeal to the court against a refusal to lift a freezing order (s 456).

The investigation of Mirror Group Newspapers plc, published in 2001, was under both s 432(2) and s 442. Only one other investigation under s 442 (into Wace UK Holdings Ltd and two other companies) has been started since 1990.

18.8.3.3 Investigations under the Financial Services and Markets Act 2000

Sections 97 and 167 to 169 of FSMA 2000 confer on the FCA, the PRA and the Secretary of State various powers to appoint one or more competent persons to conduct an investigation. Persons so appointed are referred to in the Act as 'investigators', but their role and powers are very similar to inspectors under CA 1985, part XIV. Most of these powers are concerned with investigating breaches of provisions of FSMA 2000 which are not covered in this book, but the following powers are relevant to company law.

Under s 97, the FCA may appoint one or more investigators if it is apparent to it that there are circumstances suggesting that:

(a) there may have been a contravention of a provision of part VI or of Part 6 rules or a provision otherwise made in accordance with Directive 2003/71/EC (see **7.4**, **7.6**);

(b) a person who was at the material time a director of a person mentioned in s 91(1) (see **7.6.4.2**) or s 91(1A) (see **7.4.6.2**) has been knowingly concerned in a contravention by that person of one of the provisions listed in (a); and

(c) there may have been a contravention of s 85 (requirement for a prospectus; see **7.4.2.1**) or s 87G (requirement for a supplementary prospectus; see **7.4.4**).

Under s 168(3), the FCA, the PRA or the Secretary of State (the investigating authority: s 168(6)) may appoint one or more investigators if it appears to the investigating authority that there are circumstances suggesting that:

(a) an offence may have been committed under the Criminal Justice Act 1993, part V (insider dealing) (FSMA 2000, s 168(2)(a)); or

(b) market abuse may have taken place (s 168(2)(d)).

The investigating authority may appoint one of their own employees to be an investigator (s 170(5)). See FCA Handbook, EG, Chapters 3 and 4.

18.8.4 CONDUCT OF AN INVESTIGATION

18.8.4.1 Form of investigation

Investigating inspectors have wide powers to require persons to give them oral evidence on oath (see **18.8.4.2**). They are not, however, limited to considering sworn oral evidence. They themselves decide on the course of their investigation and what questions to ask witnesses, and they draw their own conclusions from the evidence they collect. Their function is purely investigative and is in no way judicial: they do not decide any person's legal rights or obligations (*Re Pergamon Press Ltd* [1971] Ch 388; *Fayed v United Kingdom* (1994) 18 EHRR 393). The investigation must be conducted in private (*Re an Inquiry into Mirror Group Newspapers Ltd* [2000] Ch 194), but investigations, other than insider dealing investigations, usually result in a published report (see **18.8.5.1**).

The Secretary of State may, under CA 1985, s 446A, give directions to inspectors appointed under CA 1985 as to the subject matter of the investigation or may require them to take, or not take, specified steps in their investigation.

18.8.4.2 Collection of evidence

An investigating inspector has a right to call on persons:

(a) To produce all documents of, or relating to, a company under investigation (or relating to the company in whose securities insider dealing is suspected, or the securities of that company).

(b) To attend before the inspector.

(c) Otherwise to give the inspector all assistance with the investigation which they are reasonably able to give.

In any investigation an inspector has a right to call on any person if the inspector considers that person may be able to provide relevant information (CA 1985, s 434(2) (investigation under s 431, 432 or 433(1)) and s 443(1) (investigation under s 442); FSMA 2000, s 173 (insider dealing investigation under FSMA 2000, s 168(3)).

In some investigations an inspector has an absolute right to call on certain persons. In an investigation under CA 1985, s 431, 432, 433(1) or 442, an inspector may call on all past and present officers and agents (including auditors, solicitors and bankers) of the company under investigation (s 434(1)). In an investigation under s 442, an inspector may call on all persons who are or have been: (a) financially interested in the success or failure (or apparent success or failure) of the company under investigation, or (b) able to control or materially influence its policy (s 443(2)).

An inspector (other than an investigator appointed under FSMA 2000, s 168(3)) may examine on oath any person, and may personally administer oaths (CA 1985, s 434(3)).

A person is not required to disclose any information that is subject to legal professional privilege except a client's name and address (CA 1985, s 452(1) and (5); FSMA 2000, s 175(4)).

Inspectors may not require a bank to disclose information about the affairs of any customer other than the company under investigation unless the Secretary of State authorises the requirement (CA 1985, s 452(1A); FSMA 2000, s 175(5), under which authority may also be given by the FCA or the PRA). This does not apply if the bank is the subject of the investigation, provided the investigation is under CA 1985, s 431, 432 or 433 (s 452(1B)) or FSMA 2000 (s 175(5)).

Any person who fails to cooperate with an inspector when properly required to do so may be reported to the court by the inspector and the court may punish the person as if he or she were in contempt of court (CA 1985, s 436; FSMA 2000, s 177(1) and (2)). Before punishing for contempt, the court must first inquire into the case and hear witnesses and a statement in defence (CA 1985, s 436(2)). This gives an opportunity to question whether the inspectors were right to ask for the information which has been refused by the alleged contemnor. See, for example, *Re an Inquiry into Mirror Group Newspapers plc* [2000] Ch 194, in which the court did not punish for contempt, but laid down guidelines for the future conduct of the examination. In **Re an Inquiry into Mirror Group Newspapers plc**, Scott V-C emphasised that s 434(1) requires a person to give the inspectors the assistance which he or she 'is reasonably able to give'. The individual whom the inspectors wished to interview in their investigation of the flotation of Mirror Group Newspapers was Kevin Maxwell, son of the late Robert Maxwell. He had already been interviewed by the administrators and liquidators of various insolvent companies which his father controlled, by the Serious Fraud Office, and by his own trustee in bankruptcy, and had given evidence at his own trial, which lasted for 131 days and which resulted in his acquittal. In these exceptional circumstances the court indicated that the inspectors should keep their questioning of Kevin Maxwell to a minimum and should assist him by identifying relevant answers he had given in previous interviews.

In an insider dealing investigation it is an offence triable either way for a person, in purported compliance with a requirement to give information to an inspector or investigator, to provide information knowing it to be false or misleading in a material particular or recklessly to provide information which is false or misleading (FSMA 2000, s 177(4) and (5)).

If there are reasonable grounds for believing that there are, on any premises, documents required by an inspector to be produced, but which have not been produced, a search warrant, which will be executed by the police, may be obtained from a justice of the peace under CA 1985, s 448 or (in an insider dealing investigation) FSMA 2000, s 176.

An inspector acting under CA 1985, who is authorised by the Secretary of State, may require entry to premises which the inspector believes are used, wholly or partly, for the purposes of a company's business, and remain on those premises, if the inspector thinks that to do so will materially assist the exercise of his or her functions in relation to the company (s 453A). The inspector may be accompanied by such other persons as he or she thinks appropriate (s 453A(4)). It is an offence to obstruct, intentionally, a person lawfully exercising the power to enter and remain on premises (s 453A(5)).

18.8.4.3 Opportunity to correct

The usual practice in relation to interviews by inspectors is that a transcript of the interview is sent to the interviewee, who may then correct any mistake in the answers given, provide additional explanation to avoid a misleading impression and add new information to the answers. When inspectors are drafting their report and intend to criticise an interviewee they usually send a draft to the interviewee so that he or she can make further submissions. This process is called 'Maxwellisation' as it was examined by the Court of Appeal in two cases brought by the late Robert Maxwell, *Re Pergamon Press Ltd* [1971] Ch 388 and *Maxwell v Department of Trade and Industry* [1974] QB 523. The Court of Appeal was anxious to ensure that a criticised person should not be able to turn the process into a full-scale trial of each criticism. It rejected a claim that the inspectors should supply the evidence on which their criticisms were based, including documents and transcripts of other interviews. As Lord Denning MR put it in **Re Pergamon Press Ltd** at pp 399–400:

> The inspectors can obtain information in any way they think best, but before they condemn or criticise a man, they must give him a fair opportunity for correcting or contradicting what is said against him. They need not quote chapter and verse. An outline of the charge will usually suffice.

See also *R (Clegg) v Secretary of State for Trade and Industry* [2002] EWCA Civ 519, [2003] BCC 128.

18.8.4.4 Other uses of answers given in interviews

CA 1985, s 434(5), provides that an answer which a person gives to an inspector may be used in evidence against that person. It was held in *R v Seelig* [1992] 1 WLR 148 and *R v Saunders* [1996] 1 Cr App R 463 that s 434(5) meant that, if a person admitted commission of a criminal offence to inspectors, that admission could be used in evidence on the person's trial for that offence, despite the fact that the admission was made under threat of punishment for contempt of court for not making it. The European Court of Human Rights held that a trial of a person for a criminal offence which heard evidence of that person's confession to the offence extracted under threat of punishment for not confessing is not a fair trial as required by art 6 of the European Convention for the Protection of Human Rights (*Saunders v United Kingdom* (1996) 23 EHRR 313). As from 14 April 2000 subsections (5A) and (5B) of s 434 provide that, on a person's trial for a criminal offence, the prosecution cannot adduce evidence, or ask a question relating to, that person's answer given to inspectors, unless the answer is first referred to by or on behalf of the accused. This does not apply to a trial for perjuriously giving a false answer under oath to the inspectors. Similar provisions are made in FSMA 2000, s 174, in relation to insider dealing investigations. However, documents or other evidence whose existence is revealed by an individual's compelled answers may be given in evidence by the prosecution at a criminal trial of that individual (*Attorney-General's Reference (No 7 of 2000)* [2001] 1 WLR 1879).

The DTI decided that, despite *Saunders v United Kingdom*, transcripts of compelled evidence will be used in director disqualification proceedings in the civil courts under ss 6 to 10 of the Company Directors Disqualification Act 1986. In *R v Secretary of State for Trade and Industry, ex parte McCormick* [1998] BCC 379 the Court of Appeal refused to declare that this decision is unlawful. The court found that it was not irrational, unreasonable or inconsistent for the Secretary of State to take the view that director disqualification proceedings are not criminal proceedings and that what is required by art 6 of the Human Rights Convention to achieve a fair trial in civil proceedings is not the same as in criminal proceedings. Although the European Court of Human Rights has agreed that proceedings under CDDA 1986, s 6, are civil, not criminal proceedings, it has so far accepted that it is fair to use compulsorily obtained evidence in such proceedings only where the evidence is not contested and is not a significant part of the applicant's case (*DC v United Kingdom* (application 39031/97) [2000] BCC 710).

The court may order disclosure and inspection of transcripts of interviews for use in civil proceedings (*British and Commonwealth Holdings plc v Barclays de Zoete Wedd Ltd* [1999] 1 BCLC 86).

Questioning by inspectors must not be conducted in public, but an interviewee is entitled to make public what he or she has told inspectors (*Re an Inquiry into Mirror Group Newspapers plc* [2000] Ch 194, in which the former practice of requiring interviewees to sign comprehensive confidentiality undertakings was held to be unreasonable).

18.8.4.5 Investigation of related companies

An inspector appointed to investigate a company under CA 1985, s 431, 432 or 442, may, if he or she thinks it necessary, extend the investigation to the company's holding company or any subsidiary of the company or of its holding company. The inspector may also investigate any corporation which, at any relevant time, has been a subsidiary or holding company of the company under investigation, or a subsidiary of its holding company or a holding company of its subsidiary (ss 433(1) and 443(1)).

18.8.4.6 Termination of investigations

The Secretary of State may direct inspectors to take no further steps in their investigation (CA 1985, s 446B(1); FSMA 2000, s 170(7) and (8)). The Secretary of State may not terminate a CA 1985, s 432 or 442, investigation unless it appears that matters have come to light in the investigation suggesting the commission of criminal offences and those matters have been referred to the appropriate prosecuting authority (s 446B(2)).

18.8.5 CONSEQUENCES OF INSPECTION OR INVESTIGATION

18.8.5.1 Inspectors' reports

At the end of an investigation, inspectors (or investigators appointed under FSMA 2000, s 97 or s 168) must make a final report to whoever appointed them (the Secretary of State, the FCA or the PRA); they may also make interim reports and must do so if their appointer directs them to (CA 1985, ss 437(1) and 443(1); FSMA 2000, s 170(6), (7) and (8)). The Secretary of State must send a copy of any report prepared by an inspector appointed by order of the court under CA 1985, s 432(1), to the court (s 437(2)).

When inspectors are appointed under s 432(2) their terms of appointment may specify that their report is not for publication (s 432(2A)). If their appointment was not on those terms, or if they were appointed under any other provision of CA 1985, the Secretary of State may have their report printed and published, send a copy of the report to the company's registered office, and send a copy, on request and payment of a fee, to any member of the company which was the subject of the report, the applicants for the investigation, the company's auditor, any person whose conduct is referred to in the report, and any person whose financial interests appear to be affected by matters dealt with in the report (ss 437(3) and 443(1)).

Under s 446A(3), the Secretary of State may give directions in relation to CA 1985 investigations to secure that a report:

(a) includes the inspector's views on a specified matter;

(b) does not include any reference to a specified matter;

(c) is made in a specified form or manner; or

(d) is made by a specified date.

Such a direction may be given at the inspector's request (s 446A(4)).

It has long been the practice to publish reports submitted by inspectors under s 437 as being matters of public interest. However, what is now the Department for Business, Energy and Industrial Strategy has always been cautious to delay publication until any legal proceedings arising from the issues dealt with in the report are complete. In practice, this may mean many years' delay in the publication of inspectors' reports, by which time the affair which caused the inspection has been largely forgotten. In *R v Secretary of State for Trade and Industry, ex parte Lonrho plc* [1989] 1 WLR 525, Lonrho plc attempted to challenge this cautious practice by means of judicial review of the Secretary of State's decision that publication of a report into House of Fraser Holdings plc should be delayed until after the report had been considered by the Serious Fraud Office and the completion of any prosecutions. Lonrho plc had lost to the brothers Mohamed, Ali and Salah Fayed in their rival attempts to take over House of Fraser plc (which owned the famous London department store, Harrods). Lonrho plc considered that it had been defeated by unfair means and mistaken government decisions concerning references to the Monopolies and Mergers Commission: it wished to maintain public awareness of its grievances. The House of Lords, however, found no fault in the way in which the Secretary of State exercised his discretion. He was entitled and obliged to decide for himself whether or not to publicise or postpone publication of the report in the public interest. The report was eventually published in March 1990 after the Serious Fraud Office decided not to prosecute anyone and the Secretary of State decided not to apply for disqualification orders against the Fayed brothers. The Fayed brothers objected to the criticisms made of them in the report but were unable to sue the inspectors for libel because publication of the report was privileged. The European Court of Human Rights ruled in *Fayed v United Kingdom* (1994) 18 EHRR 393 that it is in the public interest that inspectors should be able to report freely. The inspectors' procedure was fair and the Fayeds had been given adequate opportunities to respond to the allegations made against them. The investigation did not involve a denial of the Fayeds' right of access to a court because judicial review was available to control any unfairness in the inspectors' procedure. As the inspectors' findings were not a judicial determination, they were not subject to art 6(1) of the European Convention on Human Rights requiring a fair and public hearing for the determination of civil rights and obligations. The report is discussed by G McCormack, 'The House of Fraser inspectors' report' (1994) 15 Co Law 40.

There is no provision for publication of FSMA 2000 investigations. The results of an inspection of documents under CA 1985, s 447, are never collected in a formal report and are never published, but may be used as a basis for further action.

18.8.5.2 Cooperation with other regulatory authorities

Any information obtained under CA 1985, s 447, 448A or 453A, can be disclosed to a person specified in sch 15C, or any officer or employee of such a person (s 449(1), (2)(a) and (8)). The persons specified in sch 15C include the Secretary of State, the Treasury, the DPP, the FCA, the PRA and any constable. Information can also be disclosed for any of the purposes listed in sch 15D, which has 52 paragraphs listing a wide variety of regulatory functions (s 449(2)(b)). Any other disclosure is a criminal offence (s 449(6)).

Investigations under FSMA 2000 are subject to similar rules in FSMA 2000, ss 348 to 353.

Inspectors appointed under CA 1985 may inform the Secretary of State, at any time, of any matters coming to their knowledge as a result of their investigations (and can be directed by the Secretary of State to do so) (CA 1985, ss 437(1A) and 443(1)). By s 451A the Secretary of State may disclose any information obtained from inspectors to any person to whom, or for any purpose for which, disclosure is permitted under s 449. The Secretary of State can also authorise such disclosure directly by the inspectors. An inspector is authorised by s 451A(3) to disclose information to any other inspector or to any investigator authorised under s 447.

18.8.5.3 Petition for winding up

The Secretary of State may petition for a company to be wound up by the court under the Insolvency Act 1986 (IA 1986), s 124(4)(b), if the case falls within IA 1986, s 124A. A case falls within s 124A if the company is not already in compulsory liquidation (s 124A(2)) and it appears to the Secretary of State that it is expedient in the public interest that the company should be wound up, this being apparent from, among other matters (s 124A(1)):

(a) any report made or information obtained under CA 1985, part XIV (ss 431 to 453C) (company investigations etc), apart from information obtained from a whistle-blower under s 448A,

(b) any report made under FSMA 2000, s 168 (investigation into insider dealing), or

(c) any information obtained under CA 1989, s 83 (powers exercisable for purpose of assisting overseas regulatory authorities).

Petitions in cases falling within s 124A are called 'public-interest petitions', because the Secretary of State necessarily acts not in his or her own interest but in the interests of the public at large (per Megarry J in *Re Lubin, Rosen and Associates Ltd* [1975] 1 WLR 122 at pp 128–9). Only the Secretary of State may petition on the ground that it is in the public interest that a company should be wound up (*Re Millennium Advanced Technology Ltd* [2004] EWHC 711 (Ch), [2004] 1 WLR 2177). Section 124A defines cases in which the Secretary of State has standing to present a public-interest petition. However, the court has jurisdiction to make a winding-up order only if one of the circumstances listed in s 122(1) is proved to exist, and s 124A(1) confines the court, when considering a public-interest petition, to considering whether it is just and equitable that the company should be wound up (s 122(1)(g)).

The Secretary of State has standing to present a petition for the compulsory liquidation of a company only after forming the opinion that it is expedient in the public interest that the company be wound up. In accordance with general principles of constitutional law, it is competent for an official of the Department for Business, Energy and Industrial Strategy to form that opinion and decide to present a petition: the matter does not have to be considered by the Secretary of State personally (*Re Golden Chemical Products Ltd* [1976] Ch 300).

The court must be careful not to be influenced too much by the very fact that a public-interest petition is presented by a person of such significance as the Secretary of State. This fact means that it is highly unlikely that the petition has been presented frivolously or vexatiously, but it does not mean that the court is relieved of its function of determining judicially whether or not a winding-up order should be made. Nicholls LJ in ***Re Walter L Jacob and Co Ltd*** said, at p 353:

> the court will take note that the source of the submissions that the company should be wound up is a government department charged by Parliament with wide-ranging responsibilities in relation to the affairs of companies. The department has considerable expertise in these matters and can be expected to act with a proper sense of responsibility when seeking a winding-up order. But the cogency of the submissions made on behalf of the Secretary of State will fall to be considered and tested in the same way as any other submissions. His submissions are not *ipso facto* endowed with such weight that those resisting a winding-up petition presented by him will find the scales loaded against them.

Equally the court should not indulge a prejudice against civil servants as being incapable of understanding the realities of business life, though, regrettably, such a lack of understanding seems to have occurred in *Re a Company (No 5669 of 1998)* [2000] 1 BCLC 427 with disastrous consequences.

It may be in the public interest to wind up a company as a matter of punishment for past misbehaviour and to set an example to others (*Re Walter L Jacob and Co Ltd* [1989] BCLC 345). Even the fact that a company is no longer able to continue its former business because, for example, of the withdrawal of a licence should not persuade the court that a winding-up order is not required in order to express disapproval and serve as an example. The wishes of the company's controllers, that the company should remain extant for other purposes, should normally carry little weight (*Re Walter L Jacob and Co Ltd* per Nicholls LJ at p 360).

Many public-interest petitions are concerned with stopping companies which trade in a way that is seriously detrimental to people who do business with them. Several recent public-interest petitions have concerned companies running so-called pyramid or snowball schemes, in which people are persuaded to pay to join a scheme on the basis that they can take a proportion of the joining fees of people whom they persuade to join after them. Such schemes are illegal under part XI of the Fair Trading Act 1973 and are also usually found to be illegal lotteries, and a company running one will be wound up because its business is illegal. There are full examinations of these schemes in *Secretary of State for Trade and Industry v Hasta International Ltd* 1998 SLT 73 (which was heard before part XI of the Fair Trading Act 1973 came into force) and *Re Delfin International (SA) Ltd* [2000] 1 BCLC 71, which were hearings of winding-up petitions, and *Re Senator Hanseatische Verwaltungsgesellschaft mbH* [1996] 2 BCLC 562, which was concerned with steps to protect the public pending the hearing of a petition.

There have been several reported cases of petitions against companies conducting insurance business illegally. In *Re Secure and Provide plc* [1992] BCC 405, *Re a Company (No 007923 of 1994) (No 2)* [1995] 1 BCLC 594, and *Re a Company (No 007816 of 1994)* [1995] 2 BCLC 539 the petitions failed because the court refused to accept that the breaches were serious enough to justify winding up. In *Re Sentinel Securities plc* [1996] 1 WLR 316, on the other hand, a company was wound up for carrying on insurance business without being authorised to do so.

In *Re Market Wizard Systems (UK) Ltd* [1998] 2 BCLC 282 a company was wound up for giving investment advice without being authorised under the Financial Services Act 1986.

18.8.5.4 Unfair prejudice petition

The Secretary of State has power under CA 2006, s 995, to petition under s 994 (see **18.6**) for the relief of any prejudicial conduct of a company's affairs which is revealed by a report under CA 1985, s 437 (see **18.8.5.1**), or documents produced under s 447 or s 448 (see **18.8.2**), or from an investigation under FSMA 2000 (see **18.8.3.3**). Until 1996, this power (which was first enacted in CA 1980, s 75(2)) had never been exercised (Law Commission, *Shareholder Remedies* (Consultation Paper No 142) (London: Stationery Office, 1996), p 118, n 20) and there have been no reported cases since 1996.

18.8.5.5 Recovery of expenses

The expenses of, and incidental to, a CA 1985 investigation are in the first instance borne by the Secretary of State. However, the Secretary of State is entitled to demand reimbursement from any person who is convicted of an offence as a result of the investigation (to such extent as the convicting court may order), by any company dealt with by an inspectors' report (unless the company itself applied for the investigation or the inspectors were appointed on the Secretary of State's own motion), or by the applicants under s 431 or s 442(3) (to such extent as the Secretary of State may direct) (s 439(1) to (5)).

19

ACTING FOR A COMPANY: AGENCY AND ATTRIBUTION

SUMMARY OF POINTS COVERED

- What is in this chapter
- Authentication and execution of documents
- Company contracts
- Contractual capacity
- Authority of a company's agents
- Pre-incorporation and post-dissolution contracts
- Liabilities of principal and agent
- Attribution by a court so as to impose liability on a company
- Companies in court

19.1 WHAT IS IN THIS CHAPTER

A company's property is owned by the company as a separate person, not by the members; the company's business is conducted by the company as a separate person, not by the members. Therefore it is the company as a separate person that enters into contracts in relation to the company's business and property.

Any physical act that has to be done in order to make a company a party to a voluntary transaction has to be done by a human being acting on the company's behalf. It is necessary to establish rules which determine the circumstances in which the acts of one or more individuals are to be regarded as the acts of a company. In *Meridian Global Funds Management Asia Ltd v Securities Commission* [1995] 2 AC 500, Lord Hoffmann described these rules as 'rules of attribution' (at p 506). For each company, what Lord Hoffmann called 'primary rules of attribution' are established by its constitution, which will state, for example, the rules governing general meetings, at which the members may take decisions which are the decisions of the company as a separate person (see **14.4.5**), and the rules on appointment of directors, who are given authority by a provision in the articles to exercise all the powers of the company in the management of its business (see **15.10.2**). Lord Hoffmann also included in the category of primary rules, general rules of company law such as those on decision-making without meeting (see **14.13**), or the execution of documents (see **19.2.4**).

For the purposes of making a company a party to legal relationships such as contracts, the legal concept of agency is used to establish whose acts are to be attributed to the company. The legal relationship of agency exists between two persons, called the principal and the agent, if the agent has authority or capacity to create legal relationships between the principal and third parties. Whether one person is an agent of another is a question of fact, and agency can be inferred from surrounding circumstances, though it can only be established by the consent of the principal and the agent (*Garnac Grain Co Inc v H M F Faure and Fairclough Ltd* [1968] AC 1130). An agent can execute a document for a company (see **19.2**) or otherwise cause it to enter into contracts (see **19.3**). The acts of an agent of a company are attributed to the company only if the agent was acting within his or her authority (see **19.5**), which used to be limited by the company's capacity (see **19.4**). There can be no agency if the company does not in fact exist, either because it has not yet been registered or because it has been dissolved (see **19.6**). In civil law, an agent is not necessarily liable for what his or her principal does (see **19.7.1**), but a principal is usually vicariously liable for anything its agent does (see **19.7.2**).

There are many situations in which it is necessary to apply to a company legal concepts that are formulated in human terms, involving, for example, knowledge, intention, criminality, residence or opinion. The courts have done this by attributing to a company the knowledge etc of one or more humans they identify with the company (see **19.8**). This is particularly important for the purpose of imposing criminal liability on a company (see **19.8.4** to **19.8.6**).

The ways in which companies can be represented and give evidence in court proceedings, and who must pay costs if a company is unsuccessful are discussed in **19.9**.

In relation to company contracts, there has always been great difficulty in reconciling two opposing principles: the first is that the members of a company should be protected from misapplication of the money they have invested in it; the second is that dealings with a company should not be hindered or discouraged. Companies would be less useful as means of carrying on business if people would not deal with them because of uncertainty about the security of their transactions, or if security of transaction could be ensured only by making extensive inquiries.

The early attitude of the courts was that members' investments in a company should be protected by insisting that every person was deemed to be informed of the contents of the old-style memorandum and articles of the company (or, under the Joint Stock Companies Act 1844, its deed of settlement) (per Lord Wensleydale in *Ernest v Nicholls* (1857) 6 HL Cas 401 at p 419; per Lord Hatherley in *Mahony v Easy Holyford Mining Co Ltd* (1875) LR 7 HL 869 at p 893). Having made every person who dealt with a company cognisant of the restrictions which its constitution placed on the use of its funds, the courts could then make such persons responsible for seeing that the restrictions were observed by insisting that they bear the loss when those restrictions were not observed. One important consequence of this philosophy was the '*ultra vires* rule' which is discussed in **19.4.1**.

People who dealt with companies naturally thought it unfair that they should have the burden of making inquiries to ensure that companies' funds were not misapplied. The courts responded initially with the 'rule in *Turquand*'s case', subsequently developed as the 'indoor management rule', which limited the inquiries that had to be made (see **19.5**). The indoor management rule was largely replaced by the concept of the ostensible authority of a person acting for a company, but complete reform had to wait until Parliament enacted CA 1989, which nullified the *ultra vires* rule (s 108(1)) (see **19.4**). In addition, s 142 would have abolished the doctrine of deemed notice, but this reform was never brought into force and was repealed by CA 2006, sch 16. It seems that, without the *ultra vires* rule, the doctrine of deemed notice has become ineffective anyway.

Key legislation which you should be able to consult when reading this chapter:

- CA 2006, ss 39 to 52; and
- the model articles for private companies limited by shares and for public companies in SI 2008/3229.

All that legislation is in *Blackstone's Statutes on Company Law*.

The following cases, which are considered in this chapter, are particularly significant and are recommended further reading:

- *Lennard's Carrying Co Ltd v Asiatic Petroleum Co Ltd* [1915] AC 705;
- *Meridian Global Funds Management Asia Ltd v Securities Commission* [1995] 2 AC 500;

- *Stone and Rolls Ltd v Moore Stephens* [2009] UKHL 39, [2009] AC 1391 (also a key case for **Chapter 17**);
- *Tesco Supermarkets Ltd v Nattrass* [1972] AC 153;
- *Williams v Natural Life Health Foods Ltd* [1998] 1 WLR 830; and
- *Bilta (UK) Ltd v Nazir (No 2)* [2015] UKSC 23, [2016] 1 AC 1.

Your particular course of study may require you to read other source materials.

19.2 AUTHENTICATION AND EXECUTION OF DOCUMENTS

19.2.1 INTRODUCTION

An individual shows that a document expresses his or her intention by signing it and thereby authenticating it. Where the document is intended to have some legal effect, this is an expression of an intention to accept that legal effect. Acceptance of the legal effect of a document may be expressed more solemnly by executing it as a deed. If a company as a separate person is to accept the legal effect of documents, ways have to be found of showing that acceptance which are equivalent to those used by individuals. How this may be done will be considered in **19.2**.

19.2.2 A COMPANY'S COMMON SEAL

As a body corporate a company is entitled to a 'common seal' for authenticating documents (CA 2006, s 45(1)). However, a company may do without a common seal (s 45(1)), because signature of a document can be equivalent to sealing it (s 44(4); see **19.2.4**).

A company seal is usually a die which is used to emboss an engraved design on to paper. A company which has a common seal must, under penalty, have its name engraved in legible characters on the seal (s 45(2)). Affixing a company's common seal to a document is sufficient to execute it as a document of the company (s 44(1)), and a company may be made a party to a written contract by affixing its common seal to the contract (s 43(1)). See *OTV Birwelco Ltd v Technical and General Guarantee Co Ltd* [2002] EWHC 2240 (TCC), [2002] 4 All ER 668, discussed in **4.5.2**. Executing a document under seal is not in itself sufficient to make the document a deed (see **19.2.5**).

Under the model articles of association in SI 2008/3229, the directors may decide how the seal is to be used, but the model articles provide a default rule which applies unless the directors decide otherwise (model articles for private companies, art 49; model articles for public companies, art 81). The default rule in the model articles is that when a company's common seal is affixed to a document, the document must also be signed by an authorised person in the presence of a witness who attests the signature. An 'authorised person' is:

(a) any director of the company;

(b) the company secretary (a private company need not have a secretary); or

(c) any other person authorised by the directors for the purpose of signing documents to which the company's seal is applied (this is not the same as being authorised, for the purposes of CA 2006, s 44, to sign documents that are not sealed).

Section 44(1) refers only to affixing a company's seal without mentioning that use of a company's seal may be governed by the company's own rules, such as those in the model articles, which require officers' signatures. It is clear that s 44(1) does not override a company's articles. In other words, if the articles require signatures, s 44(1) does not provide authority for a document to be executed by sealing without signature (Law Commission, *The Execution of Deeds and Documents by or on behalf of Bodies Corporate* (Law Com No 253, 1998), paras 3.34 to 3.39).

A company that has a common seal may also have an official seal for use abroad (s 49) and/or a securities seal (s 50; see **8.2.1**).

19.2.3 CONTRACTUAL FORMALITIES

Any formalities required by law in the case of a contract made by an individual also apply, unless a contrary intention appears, to a contract made by or on behalf of a company (CA 2006, s 43(2)). Few formal requirements are nowadays imposed in relation to contracts, but, for instance, a contract for the sale, or other disposition, of an interest in land can only be made in writing (Law of Property (Miscellaneous Provisions) Act 1989, s 2(1)), and a disposition of an equitable interest in any property must be in writing (Law of Property Act 1925, s 53(1)(c)). Bills of exchange, cheques and promissory notes are by definition written (Bills of Exchange Act 1882, ss 3(1), 73 and 83(1)). An instrument creating a power of attorney must be executed as a deed (Powers of Attorney Act 1971, s 1(1)).

19.2.4 EXECUTION OF DOCUMENTS

One way in which a document may be executed by a company is by affixing its common seal (CA 2006, s 44(1); see **19.2.2**). Another way is by signing the document in accordance with s 44(2), which applies whether or not a company has a common seal. Section 44(2) provides that a document is validly executed by a company if it is signed on behalf of the company by:

(a) two authorised signatories; or

(b) a director of the company in the presence of a witness who attests the signature.

If the document is also expressed, in whatever words, to be executed by the company, it will have the same effect as if executed under the company's common seal (s 44(4)). Every director of the company is an authorised signatory and so is the company secretary (or any joint secretary) (s 44(3)). A *private company* is not required by statute to have a secretary (though its articles may require it to have one). A director or secretary which is a firm signs a document when it is signed by an individual who is authorised to sign on the firm's behalf (s 44(7)).

A signature is effective for the purposes of s 44(2) even if it is not expressed to be for and on behalf of the company (*Williams v Redcard Ltd* [2011] EWCA Civ 466, [2011] Bus LR 1479). However, it is always sensible to use words to that effect so as to make the effect of the signature clear, in particular, to exclude personal liability of the signatory (see **19.2.6**).

A document is expressed to be executed by a company, for the purposes of s 44(4), if the company's name appears next to the signatures of authorised persons or the attested signature of a director. It has also been held to be sufficient if some term which is used in the contract to describe the company appears next to such a signature (*Williams v Redcard Ltd*, in which the company was defined to be one of the 'sellers' who were parties to the contract and the word 'seller' was next to the authorised persons' signatures).

Where a document is to be executed by two or more companies by being signed by one individual who is a director or secretary of them all, that individual must sign separately on behalf of each company (s 44(6)). There is no equivalent rule when an individual signs on his or her own behalf and on behalf of a company, and in that case one signature is sufficient (*Williams v Redcard Ltd*). However, this does not apply if the signature is expressed to be for and on behalf of the company. If words to that effect are used, the signature will not bind the signer in his or her personal capacity, and a second signature will be required for that purpose.

In favour of a 'purchaser', a document is deemed to have been duly executed by a company if it purports to be signed by a director and the secretary of the company, or by two directors of the company (s 44(5)). A 'purchaser' for this purpose means a purchaser in good faith for valuable consideration and includes a lessee, mortgagee or other person who for valuable consideration acquires an interest in property (s 44(5)).

Under the Law of Property Act 1925, s 74(2), the board of directors of a company may, by resolution or otherwise, appoint an agent, either generally or in any particular case, to execute on behalf of the company any agreement or other instrument which is not a deed in relation to any matter within the company's powers.

19.2.5 EXECUTION OF DEEDS

A document is not a deed unless it has been validly executed as a deed by the person making it, or by one or more of the parties to it, or by a person authorised to execute it in the name or on behalf of the maker or one or more parties (Law of Property (Miscellaneous Provisions) Act 1989, s 1(2)). In order to validly execute a document as a deed, a company must execute it, as described in **19.2.4**, and deliver it as a deed (CA 2006, s 46(1)). Lord Denning MR explained in *Vincent v Premo Enterprises (Voucher Sales) Ltd* [1969] 2 QB 609 at p 619:

> 'Delivery' in this connection does not mean 'handed over' to the other side. It means delivered in the old legal sense, namely, an act done so as to evince an intention to be bound.

By s 46(2), a document is presumed to be delivered on being executed, unless a contrary intention is proved. This gives the option of stating, on executing a deed, that it will not be delivered (and so executed as a deed) until some condition is fulfilled. In effect, s 46(2) means that, unless a company wants execution of a deed to be conditional, there is no difference between executing a document and executing a document as a deed. The old rule that a seal was essential for the valid execution of a deed was abolished by the Law of Property (Miscellaneous Provisions) Act 1989, s 1(1)(b): a seal is now optional. The one defining characteristic of a deed now is that it must make clear on its face that it is intended to be a deed by the person making it or, as the case may be, by the parties to it (whether by describing itself as a deed or expressing itself to be executed or signed as a deed or otherwise) (Law of Property (Miscellaneous Provisions) Act 1989, s 1(2)). The fact that it is executed under seal does not in itself satisfy this requirement (s 1(2A)).

19.2.6 SIGNATURE

A requirement that a document is to be 'signed by' a company means that it is to be executed as described in **19.2.4** (*Hilmi and Associates Ltd v 20 Pembridge Villas Freehold Ltd* [2010] EWCA Civ 314, [2010] 1 WLR 2750).

An individual who signs a company document with his or her own name for the purpose of authenticating it as an act of the company or in order to make it signed by the company does not incur any personal liability. However, it must be clear that it is a company document that is being signed, otherwise there is a danger that the individual's signature on the document will be taken as establishing personal liability.

If there is no other evidence that a document signed by an individual is a company document then words added to the signature which merely describe the signer ('AB, director of CD Ltd') may be insufficient to exclude personal liability. It is necessary to add words which establish that the signer has signed only as an agent or in a representative capacity, and is not personally liable ('AB, director of CD Ltd, for and on behalf of CD Ltd').

In *Badgerhill Properties Ltd v Cottrell* [1991] BCLC 805, Badgerhill Properties Ltd used the trading name 'The Plumbing Centre'. Mrs Cottrell entered into a contract on the basis of an estimate written on notepaper headed 'The Plumbing Centre' with the company's name (misspelled) at the bottom. The estimate ended 'Yours faithfully, The Plumbing Centre, B Twigg, Director'. All Mrs Cottrell's dealings had been with Mr Twigg, and she argued that she had contracted with him personally (it seemed likely that the company would be unable to pay the damages she claimed). The Court of Appeal rejected this argument. Woolf LJ said, at p 809:

> So far as those documents are concerned, their contents establish that Mrs Cottrell was accepting the estimates of the Plumbing Centre and that she was contracting with whoever was trading as the Plumbing Centre.

Once it was established that the documents were the documents of the company which was trading as the Plumbing Centre, Mr Twigg's signature could be on them only for the purpose of authenticating them as company documents.

19.3 COMPANY CONTRACTS

CA 2006, s 43(1), sets out two ways in which a company may become contractually bound to another person (a 'contractor'). The first is by a written contract to which the company's common seal is affixed (s 43(1)(a)). Whether or not a company has a common seal, if a written contract is signed by two authorised signatories, or by a director in the presence of an attesting witness, and is expressed (in whatever form of words) to be executed by the company, it has the same effect as if executed under the company's common seal (s 44(2) and (4)). Any director, secretary or joint secretary of the company is an authorised signatory (s 44(3)).

The second means by which a company may become contractually bound to a contractor is where a person who was acting under the express or implied authority of the company has made a contract on behalf of the company (s 43(1)(b)). The main problem for the contractor is to know whether the person who has acted for the company did so with the company's authority (see **19.5**). There used to be another danger for a contractor in that a contract might be beyond the company's contractual capacity because it was not capable of being within the company's objects. This difficulty was removed by CA 1989 but, because of its historical importance, will be discussed briefly in **19.4**.

19.4 CONTRACTUAL CAPACITY

19.4.1 THE *ULTRA VIRES* RULE

In *Ashbury Railway Carriage and Iron Co Ltd v Riche* (1875) LR 7 HL 653 the House of Lords decided that a registered company did not have the contractual capacity to enter into contracts outside its objects, which, at that time, had to be stated in the company's old-style memorandum. This came to be known as the '*ultra vires* rule'. A similar rule had been established in relation to statutory companies (see, for example, *East Anglian Railways Co v Eastern Counties Railway Co* (1851) 11 CB 775 and the general discussion by Lord Cranworth LC in *Shrewsbury and Birmingham Railway Co v North-Western Railway Co* (1857) 6 HL Cas 113 at pp 135–8).

A transaction entered into by a company outside of its legal capacity is not enforceable in law. The company does not have to carry out its side of the bargain even if the other party's obligations have been completely performed. The fact that the members of the company approve the transaction cannot cure the company's lack of capacity, even if they approve it unanimously (*Ashbury Railway Carriage and Iron Co Ltd v Riche*). However, since the Companies (Memorandum of Association) Act 1890, the members of a company have been able to alter any restriction on its objects.

The objects of the Ashbury Railway Carriage and Iron Co Ltd were to make and sell, or lend on hire, railway carriages and wagons, and all kinds of railway plant, fittings, machinery and rolling stock; to carry on the business of mechanical engineers etc. The directors entered into a contract to buy a concession for the construction of a railway in Belgium, subcontracting the construction work to Mr Riche's firm. The company's shareholders disapproved of the deal and the company repudiated Mr Riche's contract. The House of Lords held that constructing a railway, as opposed to railway carriages and rolling stock, was not within the objects of the company and that the company did not have capacity to enter into a contract to build a railway. As the contract was void, Mr Riche was not entitled to damages for breach of it.

In *Rolled Steel Products (Holdings) Ltd v British Steel Corporation* [1986] Ch 246, the Court of Appeal held that if an act was capable of being within the objects of a company then it would be within the company's contractual capacity. This covers acts, such as borrowing money, which do not have an implicit purpose so that the contractor does not know whether the act is for the purpose of pursuing the company's objects or not (see **19.5.4.4**).

Although the Law Lords in *Ashbury Railway Carriage and Iron Co Ltd v Riche* were convinced that they were protecting creditors by insisting on certainty about the extent of a company's capacity, in practice the *ultra vires* rule was very unfair to persons contracting with companies. It assumed that a person contracted with a company only after reading its old-style memorandum to ascertain whether the contract was for a purpose within its objects. In practice, however, few persons have ever bothered to read the memorandum of a company they were contracting with, and drafters tried to counter the *ultra vires* rule by producing lengthy and wide-ranging objects clauses.

CA 1989, s 108(1), nullified the *ultra vires* rule (except for charitable companies; see **19.4.2**) by introducing, from 4 February 1991, what is now CA 2006, s 39(1):

> The validity of an act done by a company shall not be called into question on the ground of lack of capacity by reason of anything in the company's constitution.

The effect of this provision is that a company, other than a charitable company, cannot refuse to honour a contract simply because it is incapable of being within the company's objects, as it could have done under the old *ultra vires* rule. However, any limit in a company's articles on its objects does limit the authority of the company's directors, which may cause a contract to be not binding if the other party was not dealing with the company in good faith (s 40; see **19.5.5**). Any director of a company who is responsible for it entering into a transaction outside its restricted objects has breached the duty to act within powers (s 171) and is liable to replace the money the company expended on the transaction (*Re Lands Allotment Co* [1894] 1 Ch 616), unless the members of the company ratify the transaction (see **16.16.2** to **16.16.4** and **19.5.7**). See also **3.8**.

In addition, s 40(2)(b)(i) provides that a party to a transaction with a company is not bound to inquire whether there is any limitation on the power of the board of directors to bind the company, or authorise others to do so.

19.4.2 CHARITABLE COMPANIES

CA 2006, s 39 (which generally nullifies the *ultra vires* rule, see **19.4.1**), does not, by s 42, apply to the acts of a company which is a charity, except in favour of a person who:

(a) does not know at the time the act is done that the company is a charity; or

(b) gives full consideration in money or money's worth in relation to the act in question and does not know (as the case may be)

    (i) that the act is not permitted by the company's constitution, or

    (ii) that the act is beyond the powers of the directors.

Accordingly, charitable companies are required to make it clear to persons who deal with them that they are charities (see **4.5.5**).

In *Rosemary Simmons Memorial Housing Association Ltd v United Dominions Trust Ltd* [1986] 1 WLR 1440 it was held that it is beyond the capacity of an incorporated charity to give away its assets to a non-charitable body (presumably this does not refer to gifts to the objects of the charity). See J Warburton, 'Charitable companies and the *ultra vires* rule' [1988] Conv 275.

See also **19.5.10**.

19.5 AUTHORITY OF A COMPANY'S AGENTS

19.5.1 ACTING UNDER A COMPANY'S AUTHORITY

As an artificial person, a company cannot make contracts or enter into transactions by itself: it has to act through agents.

The rule of agency law is that an agent can act only within what is known as the agent's 'authority': the principal of an agent is not bound by any legal relationship which the agent purports to put the principal into if it was outside the agent's authority (though the principal may choose to 'ratify'—that is adopt the contract and retrospectively supply the missing authority). The authority under which a contract made by an agent on behalf of a company will become binding on the company may be actual (see **19.5.2**) or ostensible (see **19.5.3** and **19.5.4**). Any legal relationship which a company is put into by an agent within the actual or (with exceptions) ostensible authority of the agent is binding on the company. But an agent of a company who purports to make a contract on behalf of the company which is outside the scope of the agent's actual or ostensible authority has not made a contract by which the company is bound: a contractor who suffers loss as a result may sue the agent for breach of warranty of authority.

19.5.2 ACTUAL AUTHORITY

19.5.2.1 Definition

The actual authority of an agent of a company is the authority conferred on the agent by the contract governing the agency which has been agreed between the agent and the company. As Diplock LJ said in ***Freeman and Lockyer v Buckhurst Park Properties (Mangal) Ltd*** [1964] 2 QB 480, at pp 502–3:

> An 'actual' authority is a legal relationship between principal and agent created by a consensual agreement to which they alone are parties. Its scope is to be ascertained by applying ordinary principles of construction of contracts, including any proper implications from the express words used, the usages of the trade, or the course of business between the parties. To this agreement the contractor is a stranger; he may be totally ignorant of the existence of any authority on the part of the agent. Nevertheless, if the agent does enter into a contract pursuant to the 'actual' authority, it does create contractual rights and liabilities between the principal and the contractor.

Thus, if any person acting within the scope of his or her actual authority makes a contract on behalf of a company then the company will be bound by it.

19.5.2.2 Company's constitution

The most notable limitation which a company's constitution may place on the actual authority of its directors (and so, on any agent to whom the directors may delegate authority) is where the articles limit the company's objects. If that is done, the directors are limited to acting for the purpose of, or reasonably incidental to, attaining or pursuing the company's objects as set out in its articles (*Rolled Steel Products (Holdings) Ltd v British Steel Corporation* [1986] Ch 246 per Slade LJ at p 295). There may be other constitutional limitations on what directors may do. For example, it used to be common for the articles of a company to limit the amount that its directors could commit it to borrowing.

A company's constitution will also usually impose procedural requirements which must be met before directors are authorised to act, for example setting a quorum for board meetings.

CA 2006, s 40 (see **19.5.5**), has severely curtailed the effect on the enforceability of a company's contracts of limitations made by a company's constitution on the actual authority of its agents.

19.5.2.3 Directors' duty

The actual authority of the directors of a company is limited to acting in accordance with their statutory duty to promote the success of the company (CA 2006, s 172), which is based on the former fiduciary duty to act in the company's interests (*Hopkins v T L Dallas Group Ltd* [2004] EWHC 1379 (Ch), [2005] 1 BCLC 543, at [88]).

19.5.3 OSTENSIBLE AUTHORITY

Ostensible, or apparent, authority is the authority of an agent as it appears to others. As Byles J said in *Totterdell v Fareham Blue Brick and Tile Co Ltd* (1866) LR 1 CP 674, at pp 677–8:

> a principal is bound, not only by such acts of the agent as are within the scope of the agent's *actual* authority, but by such acts as are within the larger margin of an apparent or *ostensible* authority derived from the representations, acts, or default of the principal.

In *Armagas Ltd v Mundogas SA* [1986] AC 717, Lord Keith of Kinkel said, at p 777:

> Ostensible authority comes about where the principal, by words or conduct, has represented that the agent has the requisite actual authority, and the party dealing with the agent has entered into a contract with him in reliance on that representation.

Having represented that the agent has the requisite authority, the principal is precluded (or 'estopped') from claiming that the agent actually did not have authority. The principal may withdraw a representation of an agent's ostensible authority, but third parties may continue to rely on the agent's ostensible authority until the withdrawal is communicated to them (*AMB Generali Holding AG v Manches* [2005] EWCA Civ 1237, [2006] 1 All ER 437).

Ostensible authority can only be relied on by someone who does not know that the agent has no actual authority (*Criterion Properties plc v Stratford UK Properties LLC* [2004] UKHL 28, [2004] 1 WLR 1846, at [31]). The doctrine of ostensible authority means that a contractor who does not know that the contract is outside the agent's actual authority is under no obligation to inquire whether it might be, unless the transaction is abnormal or there are other circumstances giving rise to suspicion (*Hopkins v T L Dallas Group Ltd* [2004] EWHC 1379 (Ch), [2005] 1 BCLC 543, at [94]). The detailed conditions under which a company is bound by ostensible authority are discussed in **19.5.4**.

19.5.4 PROTECTION OF THE CONTRACTOR WHEN ACTUAL AUTHORITY IS EXCEEDED: COMMON LAW

19.5.4.1 Doctrine of ostensible authority

The general rule (see **19.5.3**) is that a principal is bound by an agent's exercise of ostensible authority even if that exceeds the agent's actual authority. The details of how the doctrine of ostensible authority works when the principal is a company were set out by Diplock LJ in *Freeman and Lockyer v Buckhurst Park Properties (Mangal) Ltd* [1964] 2 QB 480 at p 506. His Lordship said that a contract made by an agent (or a person represented to be an agent) of a company outside the agent's actual authority would be binding on the company if:

(a) The ostensible authority of the person acting as agent to make such a contract was represented to the contractor (see **19.5.4.2**).

(b) The representation was made by a person or persons who had actual authority to manage the business of the company, either generally or in respect of the matters to which the contract relates (see **19.5.4.2**).

(c) The contractor actually relied on the representation as a reason for entering into the contract (see **19.5.4.3**).

(d) Under its constitution:

  (i) the company had capacity to enter into the contract; and

  (ii) the company was not precluded from authorising the person acting as agent to make the contract in question on its behalf.

Because of CA 2006, s 40 (which was first enacted in 1972; see **19.5.5**), point (d) is no longer relevant to a contractor who deals with a company in good faith, unless the company is charitable (see **19.5.10**).

Whether it is unconscionable for a contractor to rely on ostensible authority is irrelevant (*Criterion Properties plc v Stratford UK Properties LLC* [2004] UKHL 28, [2004] 1 WLR 1846).

19.5.4.2 Representation

Points (a) and (b) in the list in **19.5.4.1** were elaborated upon by Diplock LJ in *Freeman and Lockyer v Buckhurst Park Properties (Mangal) Ltd* [1964] 2 QB 480 at p 505:

> The commonest form of representation by a principal creating an 'apparent' authority [Diplock LJ used the term 'apparent authority' as an alternative to 'ostensible authority'] of an agent is by conduct, namely, by permitting the agent to act in the management or conduct of the principal's business. Thus, if in the case of a company the board of directors who have 'actual' authority under the memorandum and articles of association to manage the company's business permit the agent to act in the management or conduct of the company's business, they thereby represent to all persons dealing with such agent that he has authority to enter on behalf of the corporation into contracts of a kind which an agent authorised to do acts of the kind which he is in fact permitted to do usually enters into in the ordinary course of such business. The making of such a representation is itself an act of management of the company's business. Prima facie it falls within the 'actual' authority of the board of directors.

In this case, Kapoor and Hoon formed a company to buy and resell the Buckhurst Park estate. The two of them, and a nominee of each, were appointed directors. The company's articles conferred full powers of management on the directors, and also gave power to appoint a managing director, though none was ever appointed. Kapoor instructed architects to carry out certain work in connection with the development of the estate, and the architects subsequently sued the company for the payment of their fees. In holding the company liable, the Court of Appeal explained that the directors knew that Kapoor had in fact been acting as managing director and had permitted him to do so, and by that conduct had represented that he had authority to enter into contracts of a kind which a managing director or an executive director would in the normal course be authorised to enter into on the company's behalf. The board had actual authority to manage the business under the terms of the articles. The two conditions were thus satisfied.

There is a problem, however, identified by Lord Pearson in *Hely-Hutchinson v Brayhead Ltd* [1968] 1 QB 549, at p 593, in showing how a representation by conduct is made by the directors to the contractor:

> Now there is not usually any direct communication in such cases between the board of directors and the outside contractor. The actual communication is made immediately and directly, whether it be express or

implied, by the agent to the outside contractor. It is, therefore, necessary in order to make a case of ostensible authority to show in some way that such communication which is made directly by the agent is made ultimately by the responsible parties, the board of directors. That may be shown by inference from the conduct of the board of directors in the particular case by, for instance, placing the agent in a position where he can hold himself out as their agent and acquiescing in his activities, so that it can be said they have in effect caused the representation to be made. They are responsible for it and, in the contemplation of law, they are to be taken to have made the representation to the outside contractor.

In determining what representations have been made of the ostensible authority of a company's agent it is necessary to look at the entire conduct of those making the representations (*Ebeed v Soplex Wholesale Supplies Ltd* [1985] BCLC 404). For more on representations of ostensible authority see **19.5.4.7** and **19.5.4.11**.

In *First Energy (UK) Ltd v Hungarian International Bank Ltd* [1993] BCLC 1409, the manager of the bank's Manchester branch had made an offer of financing facilities to First Energy (UK) Ltd. He did not have either actual or ostensible authority to decide to make such an offer himself but it was found that he had ostensible authority to communicate such offers. Accordingly the bank was bound when the offer was accepted.

19.5.4.3 Reliance

It may be inferred that a contractor did not rely on the ostensible authority of a company's agent if the contractor knew, or had reason to believe, that the contract was contrary to the commercial interests of the company (*Criterion Properties plc v Stratford UK Properties LLC* [2004] UKHL 28, [2004] 1 WLR 1846, at [31]).

19.5.4.4 Non-obvious misuse of powers

If a company's articles limit its objects, persons acting for the company cannot have actual authority to cause it to enter into any transaction which is not for the purpose of, or reasonably incidental to, attaining or pursuing objects within those limits (*Rolled Steel Products (Holdings) Ltd v British Steel Corporation* [1986] Ch 246 per Slade LJ at p 295). A person contracting with a company cannot always tell whether or not the contract is for an *intra vires* purpose. For example, when a company borrows money, there may be no implication that the money will be used for any particular purpose. The courts have recognised that a contractor should not be required to inquire whether an apparently authorised transaction is in fact for an *intra vires* purpose. The purpose for which an agent of a company causes it to enter into a transaction, if unknown to the contractor, cannot put the transaction outside the agent's ostensible authority, provided the transaction is of a category which is *capable* of being reasonably incidental to the attainment or pursuit of the company's objects (*Rolled Steel Products (Holdings) Ltd v British Steel Corporation* per Slade LJ at p 295, Browne-Wilkinson LJ at p 306). In *Rolled Steel Products (Holdings) Ltd v British Steel Corporation*, Slade LJ summarised the law as follows, at pp 295–6:

> A company holds out its directors as having *ostensible* authority to bind the company to any transaction which falls within the powers expressly or impliedly conferred on it by its [constitution]. Unless he is put on notice to the contrary, a person dealing in good faith with a company which is carrying on an *intra vires* business is entitled to assume that its directors are properly exercising such powers for the purposes of the company as set out in its [constitution]. Correspondingly such a person in such circumstances can hold the company to any transaction of this nature.
>
> If, however, a person dealing with a company is on notice that the directors are exercising the relevant power for purposes other than the purposes of the company, he cannot rely on the ostensible authority of the directors and, on ordinary principles of agency, cannot hold the company to the transaction.

So that a contractor could enforce a transaction entered into for an *ultra vires* purpose, but within ostensible authority, it was necessary to relax the old *ultra vires* rule (see **19.4.1**) and treat the transaction as within the company's contractual capacity (*Rolled Steel Products (Holdings) Ltd v British Steel Corporation* per Slade LJ at p 295).

For an example of enforcement of a contract entered into for an *ultra vires* purpose see *Re David Payne and Co Ltd* [1904] 2 Ch 608. Money was borrowed by a company, not for its own purposes, but to pay the personal debts of its controller. It was held that the lender was not bound to inquire how the borrowing company would use the money and that the loan was enforceable.

Now, under CA 2006, s 40 (see **19.5.5**), a contract between a company and a contractor made through the agency of the company's board of directors, or any person authorised by the board, is enforceable by the contractor despite not being for the purpose of, or reasonably incidental to attaining or pursuing the company's objects, provided the contractor dealt with the company in good faith. Section 40 does not apply:

(a) if the contractor does not deal with the company in good faith; or

(b) in some circumstances, if the company is a charity (see **19.5.10**).

If s 40 does not apply and the contractor knew that the contract was outside the company's objects, and therefore outside the actual authority of the agent of the company who made the contract on its behalf, the contractor cannot rely on the agent's ostensible authority and the contract is unenforceable (*Re Introductions Ltd* [1970] Ch 199; *Rolled Steel Products (Holdings) Ltd v British Steel Corporation*).

19.5.4.5 Rule in *Turquand*'s case

The doctrine of ostensible authority had been developing for a century before *Freeman and Lockyer v Buckhurst Park Properties (Mangal) Ltd* [1964] 2 QB 480. Early cases were not expressed in terms of ostensible authority, and it is sometimes difficult to fit them in to the modern rules based on that concept. The first case to deal with the protection of a person contracting with agents of a company who were exceeding their actual authority was *Royal British Bank v Turquand* (1856) 6 El & Bl 327. The 'rule in *Turquand*'s case' was expressed by Wood V-C in **Fountaine v Carmarthen Railway Co** (1868) LR 5 Eq 316 at p 322 as follows:

> If . . . as in the case of *Royal British Bank v Turquand*, the directors have power and authority to bind the company, but certain preliminaries are required to be gone through on the part of the company before that power can be duly exercised, then the person contracting with the directors is not bound to see that all these preliminaries have been observed. He is entitled to presume that the directors are acting lawfully in what they do.

The rule in *Turquand*'s case was originally intended to limit the inquiries that persons dealing with companies had to make. In *Royal British Bank v Turquand*, the directors of a company had, on its behalf, borrowed money from the Royal British Bank and had affixed the company's seal to a bond for £2,000 to secure repayment of the borrowing. Under the company's deed of settlement, borrowings had to be approved by resolution of the members, and the company (through its liquidator, Mr Turquand) claimed that no resolution had been adopted to cover this borrowing. When the bank sued on the bond, it was argued that the company should not be liable because the bank was deemed to be informed of the contents of the company's deed of settlement and should have inquired whether the appropriate resolution had been adopted. The argument was that as the bank had not inquired, it should bear the loss. The court thought this was requiring too many inquiries from persons dealing with companies: they were at that time, as Jervis CJ said, at p 332, 'bound to read the statute and the deed of settlement. But they are not bound to do more.' The Chief Justice explained that:

> the party here, on reading the deed of settlement, would find not a prohibition from borrowing, but a permission to do so on certain conditions. Finding that the authority might be made complete by a resolution, he would have a right to infer the fact of a resolution authorising that which on the face of the document appeared to be legitimately done.

Nowadays, *Royal British Bank v Turquand* would be covered by CA 2006, s 40, which renders ineffective any limitation in a company's constitution on the power of its directors to bind the company (see **19.5.5**). It would seem that the rule in *Turquand*'s case has been completely replaced by s 40. However, s 40 does not apply to charitable companies (see **19.5.10**), and the rule in *Turquand*'s case is still relevant to them. Also s 40 does not operate in favour of a person who is not acting in good faith, but it seems unlikely that the courts would give such a person the benefit of the rule in *Turquand*'s case either.

19.5.4.6 Indoor management rule

The rule in *Turquand*'s case (see **19.5.4.5**) was subsequently developed by the courts as the indoor management rule, which was described in the following terms by Lord Hatherley in **Mahony v East Holyford Mining Co Ltd** (1875) LR 7 HL 869 at p 894:

> all that the directors do with reference to what I may call the indoor management of their own concern, is a thing known to them and known to them only.
>
> . . . when there are persons conducting the affairs of the company in a manner which appears to be perfectly consonant with the articles of association, then those so dealing with them, externally, are not to be affected by any irregularities which may take place in the internal management of the company. They are entitled to presume that that of which only they can have knowledge, namely, the external acts, are rightly done, when those acts purport to be performed in the mode in which they ought to be performed.

Under the indoor management rule, if a decision that a company should enter into an obligation has purportedly been made by the company's board of directors, the company cannot escape from the obligation by claiming that the board meeting was inquorate (*County of Gloucester Bank v Rudry Merthyr Steam and House Coal Colliery Co* [1895] 1 Ch 629; *Re Bank of Syria, Owen and Ashworth's Claim* [1901] 1 Ch 115) or that there was no board meeting (*Re Bonelli's Telegraph Co, Collie's Claim* (1871) LR 12 Eq 246). As Atkin LJ said in **Kreditbank Cassel GmbH v Schenkers Ltd** [1927] 1 KB 826 at p 844:

> When . . . a certain thing . . . can be done by the company in board meeting, and there purports to be a resolution authorising it, you are not obliged to inquire whether or not the forms of the company required by the articles as to the constitution of the board, the quorum and so forth, have been actually complied with.

19.5.4.7 Ostensible authority conferred by position or job title

A person's job title or official position is nowadays the most important factor determining the content of his or her ostensible authority. Business people generally expect that a managing director of a company, for example, has a certain range of authority to make contracts on the company's behalf by virtue of being its managing director. As Lord Keith of Kinkel said in **Armagas Ltd v Mundogas SA** [1986] AC 717, at p 777:

> In the commonly encountered case, the ostensible authority is general in character, arising when the principal has placed the agent in a position which in the outside world is generally regarded as carrying authority to enter into transactions of the kind in question. Ostensible general authority may also arise where the agent has had a course of dealing with a particular contractor and the principal has acquiesced in this course of dealing and honoured transactions arising out of it.

A person appointed to an office in a company has ostensible authority to make contracts on behalf of the company that are usually made by persons in that office. This ostensible authority exists whether or not an express delegation of authority has been made by the board of directors under a provision of the articles like the model articles for private companies, art 5, and the model articles for public companies, art 5, in SI 2008/3229. A person who is permitted by a company to act as though holding a particular office in the company also has the ostensible authority of that office

(*Freeman and Lockyer v Buckhurst Park Properties (Mangal) Ltd* [1964] 2 QB 480). If, for example, it is not intended that a particular individual associated with a company should have the authority associated with the title 'managing director' then the individual must not be given that title, or allowed to act as a managing director: if the company gives the individual the title of 'managing director' or allows him or her to act as such then it will be bound by all contracts that the individual enters into on its behalf within the usual authority that managing directors have.

Normally, the actual authority of a person in a particular position is the same as the ostensible authority which people in such a position usually have. There are two possible reasons for the actual authority of a person in a particular position being less than the person's ostensible authority:

(a) the person was never in fact appointed to the position which the principal represents that the person holds; and

(b) the person's authority has actually been limited by the principal so that it is less than the person's ostensible authority.

In **Re County Life Assurance Co** (1870) LR 5 Ch App 288, the company was held to be bound to pay the sum assured by a life assurance policy which was signed by three men who acted as directors of the company but had never been appointed as such, and countersigned by a man who acted as secretary but had never been appointed: the court heard that about 350 other policies had been issued in the same way. Giffard LJ said, at p 293:

> The company is bound by what takes place in the usual course of business with a third party where that third party deals bona fide with persons who may be termed *de facto* directors, and who might, so far as he could tell, have been directors *de jure*.

In *Mahony v East Holyford Mining Co Ltd* (1875) LR 7 HL 869 it was held that the bank at which the East Holyford Mining Co Ltd had its account was justified in honouring cheques drawn by persons who had been represented as being the directors and secretary of the company even though they had never been appointed as such. See also *Totterdell v Fareham Blue Brick and Tile Co Ltd* (1866) LR 1 CP 674 and *Duck v Tower Galvanizing Co Ltd* [1901] 2 KB 314.

For an example of a case in which the ostensible authority conferred by a job title was found not to cover the transaction which the contractor wanted the company to be bound by, see *British Bank of the Middle East v Sun Life Assurance of Canada (UK) Ltd* [1982] BCLC 78, which concerned the ostensible authority of a branch manager of an insurance company. See also *Kreditbank Cassel GmbH v Schenkers Ltd* [1927] 1 KB 826 discussed in **19.5.4.11**.

Sometimes a company may represent that a person's authority to act for the company is greater than that normally conferred by the person's job title or position in the company. For example, *Ebeed v Soplex Wholesale Supplies Ltd* [1985] BCLC 404 concerned a transaction entered into by the documentary credit manager of a bank. There was conflicting evidence over whether the transaction in question would be within the ostensible authority of a documentary credit manager of a merchant bank or trading bank, but it was also found that in this instance the directors had regularly allowed their documentary credit manager to act for the company over a wide field of business beyond that normally associated with the work of an official with that job title, and so he did have ostensible authority in relation to the transaction in question. In *Commissioners of Inland Revenue v Ufitec Group Ltd* [1977] 3 All ER 924, Mr Zhilka was a director of Ufitec Group Ltd and chairman of the board. On 10 March 1971, Mr Zhilka signed a contract, in which he was described as 'the duly authorised representative' of Ufitec Group Ltd, to sell one of its major assets. The contract had been drawn up by the company's solicitors, a well-known London firm, and the sale had been negotiated by Mr Zhilka and by a partner in that firm of solicitors over a period of months. The negotiations were known to the other directors of the company. Unfortunately it had been forgotten that the company was supposed to retain beneficial ownership of the asset until

18 April 1971 in order to qualify for an important tax relief. When the Revenue denied the company the tax relief, the company pointed out that making a contract to sell a company's major asset is outside the ostensible authority of one member of the company's board of directors and that the Revenue could not prove that Mr Zhilka had ever been given actual authority to make the contract by Ufitec's board, and so could not prove that the contract was effective. However, it was held that by allowing Mr Zhilka and the solicitor to conduct the negotiations the company had represented that Mr Zhilka had authority to make the contract and he therefore had ostensible authority to make it so that the contract was effective.

A company which has represented that a person has ostensible authority to act for it (for example, by representing that the person holds a particular position) may withdraw the representation, but third parties may continue to rely on the person's ostensible authority until the withdrawal is communicated to them (*AMB Generali Holding AG v Manches* [2005] EWCA Civ 1237, [2006] 1 All ER 437).

19.5.4.8 Ostensible authority or implied actual authority

An alternative way of looking at the authority of a person in a particular office or job in a company is to say that in making the appointment the company impliedly authorised the person to do everything within the usual scope of the office or job. Such implied authority would be *actual* authority. This was the line taken by the Court of Appeal in *Hely-Hutchinson v Brayhead Ltd* [1968] 1 QB 549 and *SMC Electronics Ltd v Akhter Computers Ltd* [2001] 1 BCLC 433. The difference between these two ways of looking at the authority attached to an office is crucial if the company itself wishes to show that it is bound by the act of a particular officer. For example, in *Re Qintex Ltd (No 2)* (1990) 2 ACSR 479, the managing director of Qintex Ltd instructed solicitors to oppose a petition for the compulsory winding up of his company which had been presented to the Tasmania Supreme Court by a company claiming to be a creditor of Qintex Ltd. On the application of another creditor supporting the petition, it was held that the managing director of a company does not have implied actual authority to make crucial decisions following the presentation of a petition to wind up the company, and, in particular, does not have implied actual authority to instruct solicitors to oppose the petition. As there was no decision of the board of directors to give the instructions, it was held that the court could not recognise the solicitors as acting for the company and could not hear the counsel they had instructed. (The board was unable to ratify the managing director's acts because there were no longer enough directors to form a quorum.) The company could not rely on the doctrine of ostensible authority because that doctrine can only be invoked to bind the company to a contract by the other party to that contract. It cannot be invoked by the company itself to make itself bound by a contract purportedly made by an agent of the company outside his actual authority.

19.5.4.9 No representation by the company

If a person purporting to act as agent of a company acts outside any actual or ostensible authority then the company is not bound. If such a person acts by way of making and issuing a document purporting to be a document of the company when it is not (because of the person's lack of actual authority to make the document) then the document is a forgery and, provided the company has never represented that the person has ostensible authority to make the document, the company is not bound by it. This is what happened in *Ruben v Great Fingall Consolidated* [1906] AC 439 and *South London Greyhound Racecourses Ltd v Wake* [1931] 1 Ch 496, which are discussed in **8.2.2**. In ***Ruben v Great Fingall Consolidated***, the stockbrokers who had been issued the forged share certificate argued that the company was bound by it because of the indoor management rule. Lord Loreburn LC said, at p 443:

I cannot see upon what principle your Lordships can hold that the defendants are liable in this action. The forged certificate is a pure nullity. It is quite true that persons dealing with limited liability companies are not bound to inquire into their indoor management, and will not be affected by irregularities of which they had no notice. But this doctrine, which is well established, applies only to irregularities that otherwise might affect a genuine transaction. It cannot apply to a forgery.

In *Northside Developments Pty Ltd v Registrar-General* (1990) 170 CLR 146, a mortgage of the company's land was purportedly executed by Robert Sturgess, who was one of the company's three directors, and by a person acting as the company secretary who had never been appointed as such. They attached the company's seal to the mortgage deed and countersigned it though they did not have the requisite authority of a board resolution to do so. The mortgage was given not to secure any indebtedness of the company but to secure debts of other companies controlled by Sturgess. A majority of the High Court of Australia held that the mortgage was a forgery which did not bind the company. The minority preferred to say that the indoor management rule did not apply to bind the company to observe the mortgage because a person taking a mortgage of a company's property that was not for the benefit of the company should make inquiries to satisfy itself that the persons who executed the mortgage were authorised to do so, and the bank had not made such inquiries. This division of opinion reflects a long-running debate about the nature of the 'forgery exception' to the indoor management rule—the debate is fully explored in the judgments delivered by the High Court in the case.

If the representation that a person holds a particular office in a company is made falsely by that person, and there is no representation to that effect by the company, then the person does not have the ostensible authority of that office. In *First City Capital Ltd v 105383 BC Ltd* (1985) 28 BLR 274, a man who was secretary and general manager of a company pretended to be its president for the purpose of leasing a car. The British Columbia Court of Appeal held that the company was not bound by the lease. Curiously, according to *Panorama Developments (Guildford) Ltd v Fidelis Furnishing Fabrics Ltd* [1971] 2 QB 711 (see **19.5.9**), the man would have had ostensible authority as company secretary to bind the company to a contract for the hire of a car.

19.5.4.10 Knowledge of the lack of actual authority

The doctrine of ostensible authority only protects a contractor who was unaware of the agent's lack of actual authority (*Criterion Properties plc v Stratford UK Properties LLC* [2004] UKHL 28, [2004] 1 WLR 1846, at [31]). On this point a contractor is protected by CA 2006, s 40(2)(b)(i), which provides that a contractor is not bound to inquire whether there is any limitation on the powers of the board of directors to bind the company or authorise others to do so.

The fact that the questions specified in s 40(2)(b)(i) have not been asked cannot be a reason for refusing to allow reliance on ostensible authority, whatever the circumstances of the case. However, the court can deny reliance on ostensible authority if other questions have not been asked and the court finds that, in the circumstances of the case, they should have been asked. Section 40 does not, for example, protect a contractor who did not deal with the whole board of directors and did not inquire whether the person who purported to act for the company had been authorised by the board where the circumstances suggested such an inquiry should be made (*Wrexham Association Football Club Ltd v Crucialmove Ltd* [2006] EWCA Civ 237, [2008] 1 BCLC 508, at [47]). In *Hopkins v T L Dallas Group Ltd* [2004] EWHC 1379 (Ch), [2005] 1 BCLC 543, Lightman J said, at [94], that if a transaction, which an agent of a company proposes to cause it to enter into, is 'abnormal or there are other circumstances giving rise to suspicion', the contractor should make such inquiries as ought reasonably to be made to ensure that the agent's authority is sufficient to bind the company. The transactions in question in *Hopkins v T L Dallas Group Ltd* were found to be abnormal, because they gave rise to unusual and onerous obligations which did not form part of the company's business (at [95]). Lightman J also found that 'the circumstances gave rise to suspicion as to the propriety of the conduct and the existence of the necessary authority to enter into them' (at [95]). The contractor, who dealt with the company's deputy managing director, should have required confirmation from the managing director of the 'propriety and regularity' of the transactions (at [96]). As this was not done, the ostensible authority of the deputy managing director could not be relied on. A contractor's lack of belief that an agent had actual authority to make a contract may be inferred from the contractor's knowledge, or reason to believe, that the contract was contrary to the commercial interests of the agent's principal (*Criterion Properties plc v Stratford UK Properties LLC* at [31]).

In *Mahony v East Holyford Mining Co Ltd* (1875) LR 7 HL 869, Lord Hatherley said, at p 895, that the indoor management rule is subject to the assumption that 'All those ordinary inquiries which mercantile men would, in the course of their business make . . . would have to be made on the part of the persons dealing with the company'. For cases in which it was held that the rule could not be relied on because of failure to ask questions that the court decided should have been asked, see *A L Underwood Ltd v Bank of Liverpool and Martins* [1924] 1 KB 775 and *B Liggett (Liverpool) Ltd v Barclays Bank Ltd* [1928] 1 KB 48, all of which were decided before the provisions now in s 40 were first enacted.

If a company did not give actual authority for the making of a contract, a person who, as a director of the company, or acting as such, took part in attempting to act for the company in making the contract, cannot rely on the indoor management rule (*Re Patent Ivory Manufacturing Co* (1888) 38 ChD 156; *Morris v Kanssen* [1946] AC 459) or on s 40 (*Smith v Henniker-Major and Co* [2002] EWCA Civ 762, [2003] Ch 182). As Lord Simonds said in *Morris v Kanssen* at p 476:

> His duty as a director is to know; his interest, when he invokes the rule, is to disclaim knowledge. Such a conflict can be resolved in only one way.

Transactions to which directors are party are now subject to statutory rules discussed in **19.5.8**.

19.5.4.11 Powers of delegation do not confer ostensible authority

At first, cases on ostensible authority were argued in the context of provisions in companies' articles for delegation of authority. The indoor management rule was interpreted as meaning that any contractor with whom a contract was made on behalf of the company by a person to whom authority *could have been delegated* under a provision in the articles was entitled to assume that there had been delegation, and this meant that the person had ostensible authority to make the contract on behalf of the company. For example, in *Biggerstaff v Rowatt's Wharf Ltd* [1896] 2 Ch 93, which concerned the ostensible authority of Mr Davy, the managing director of the defendant company, to assign to other persons debts owed to the company, Lopes LJ said, at pp 103–4:

> There is no doubt that Mr Davy was the managing director and acted as such, and according to the articles the directors could have given him the power which he purported to exercise.
>
> It cannot be said but that Mr Davy was acting within the limits of his apparent authority.

In *Dey v Pullinger Engineering Co* [1921] 1 KB 77 this argument was adopted to hold that the managing director of a company had what was called 'implied authority' to draw and endorse a bill of exchange on behalf of the company.

However, in *J C Houghton and Co v Nothard, Lowe and Wills Ltd* [1927] 1 KB 246 and *Kreditbank Cassel GmbH v Schenkers Ltd* [1927] 1 KB 826, the Court of Appeal switched to the view that it is the general understanding of the authority usually held by a person in a particular position which determines the ostensible authority of a person in that position. If a person in a particular position acts outside the usual authority of a person in such a position then the act is outside the person's ostensible authority and it makes no difference that under the articles of that particular company there was a theoretical possibility that actual authority for the act could have been conferred. In *J C Houghton and Co v Nothard, Lowe and Wills Ltd*, Sargant LJ said, at p 267, that in *Biggerstaff v Rowatt's Wharf Ltd*:

> the act done was one within the ordinary ambit of the powers of a managing director in the transaction of the company's affairs. It is I think clear that the transaction there would not have been supported had it not

been in this ordinary course, or had the agent been acting merely as one of the ordinary directors of the company.

Similarly, in *Freeman and Lockyer v Buckhurst Park Properties (Mangal) Ltd* [1964] 2 QB 480, Diplock LJ said, at p 509, that the contract in *Biggerstaff v Rowatt's Wharf Ltd* 'was a normal contract, that is of a kind which a director managing the affairs of the company . . . would be authorised to enter into'. Accordingly, the only relevance of the articles of association was that there was nothing in them to *prevent* delegation of authority to enter into such a contract on behalf of the company.

It seems that the argument based on the internal management rule was dropped because, as articles usually permit delegation to any agent, the argument would lead to the result that any agent could make any contract on the company's behalf and this was contrary to the principle that the members of a company should be protected from misapplication of the money they have invested in it. As Sargant LJ said in *J C Houghton and Co v Nothard, Lowe and Wills Ltd* at p 266:

> in my opinion this is to carry the doctrine of presumed power far beyond anything that has hitherto been decided, and to place limited companies, without sufficient reason for so doing, at the mercy of any servant or agent who should purport to contract on their behalf. On this view, not only a director of a limited company with articles founded on Table A, but a secretary or any subordinate officer might be treated by a third party acting in good faith as capable of binding the company by any sort of contract, however exceptional, on the ground that a power of making such a contract might conceivably have been entrusted to him.

See also per Atkin LJ in *Kreditbank Cassel GmbH v Schenkers Ltd* at pp 842–3.

In *J C Houghton and Co v Nothard, Lowe and Wills Ltd*, the claimants were a firm of fruit brokers. They had wanted to gain the right to sell all fruit imported by the defendant company and retain 70 per cent of the net proceeds of sale of that fruit as repayment of a loan they had made to a company associated with the defendant company. They had an oral agreement with the chairman of the board of the defendant company to that effect but wanted written confirmation from the company. The only document they ever received, though, was a letter from the company's secretary purporting to confirm the arrangement. The secretary had no actual authority to make such a contract on behalf of the company and the Court of Appeal rejected the argument that as there was a power in the articles to delegate such an authority the claimants were entitled to assume under the indoor management rule that it had been delegated.

In *Kreditbank Cassel GmbH v Schenkers Ltd*, the manager of the defendant company's branch office in Manchester had purported to draw and endorse bills of exchange on behalf of the company but did not have actual authority to do so. The defendant company's articles empowered its directors to determine who should be entitled to draw and endorse bills on its behalf. The Court of Appeal held that the claimant bank could not argue that because of the indoor management rule it could assume that authority to draw and endorse bills had been delegated to the Manchester branch manager. The manager of a branch of a business does not have ostensible authority to draw and endorse bills of exchange on behalf of the owner of the business.

These two cases show that it is the nature of the office which determines the ostensible authority of an officer of a company not the existence in the company's articles of a provision for the delegation of authority.

It follows that a contractor may be able to rely on the ostensible authority attaching to a particular company office whether or not the contractor was aware that the authority could have been expressly delegated. For example, in *British Thomson-Houston Co Ltd v Federated European Bank Ltd* [1932] 2 KB 176 the chairman of the board of directors of the bank made a contract on behalf of the bank to guarantee some debts owed to the claimant company. It was held that the claimant company dealt with the chairman in a matter in which normally a director would have power to act and therefore the bank was bound by the guarantee. Under the bank's articles, the board could have expressly delegated authority to the chairman to enter into guarantees on the bank's behalf but had never done so. The claimant company had not actually been informed of the contents of the bank's articles and so did not rely on the possibility of delegation. *Freeman and Lockyer v Buckhurst Park Properties (Mangal) Ltd* is a similar case.

In both *J C Houghton and Co v Nothard, Lowe and Wills Ltd* and *Kreditbank Cassel GmbH v Schenkers Ltd*, the claimants were not informed of the contents of the companies' articles when dealing with them and so could not even claim that there was a representation on which they had relied that the officers with whom they dealt had, under the articles, been delegated the authority on which they relied.

19.5.4.12 A company cannot rely on its agent's ostensible authority

A person dealing with a company can use the ostensible authority doctrine to prevent the company denying the contract, but a company cannot use the doctrine to ratify a contract made without its authority. It might try to do this where ratification by resolution of the directors or members is no longer possible because, for example, a quorum cannot be assembled (*Re Qintex Ltd (No 2)* (1990) 2 ACSR 479, which is discussed in **19.5.4.8**) or ratification will not be allowed because it would prejudice another person (*NM Superannuation Pty Ltd v Baker* (1992) 7 ACSR 105).

19.5.5 PROTECTION OF THE CONTRACTOR WHEN ACTUAL AUTHORITY IS EXCEEDED: STATUTE

19.5.5.1 Section 40 and the First Directive

The old attitude of English law was that the investments of the members of a company should be protected by making everyone who dealt with a company responsible for seeing that restrictions imposed by its constitution on the use of its assets were observed. The present-day attitude is that a person dealing in good faith with a company should not have to be concerned at all with its constitution. The common law had moved some way in this direction by developing the rule in *Turquand's* case, the indoor management rule and the doctrine of ostensible authority (see **19.5.4**). A substantial change had to be made when the United Kingdom joined what was then the EEC, where the First Company Law Directive (68/151/EEC, now codified as Directive 2009/101/EC) was already in force. In CA 1989, Parliament made a further important move towards security of transaction for persons dealing with companies by nullifying the *ultra vires* rule (s 108(1); see **19.4.1**). The preamble to Directive 2009/101/EC states that:

> The protection of third parties must be ensured by provisions which restrict to the greatest possible extent the grounds on which obligations entered into in the name of the company are not valid.

Article 10(2) of the Directive provides:

> The limits on the powers of the organs of the company, arising under the statutes or from a decision of the competent organs, may never be relied on as against third parties, even if they have been disclosed.

It seems that the articles of association of a UK company are its 'statutes', the memorandum of such a company being its 'instrument of constitution'. Article 10(2) of the Directive is implemented by CA 2006, s 40. The Directive was drafted before the United Kingdom joined what was then the EEC, and uses the unfamiliar concept of an 'organ' of a company, in the sense of an instrumentality by which acts of the company are performed. In the UK implementing legislation the board of directors of a company is given the role of the 'competent organ'. See further **19.5.6** and V Edwards, '*Ultra vires* and directors' authority—an EC perspective' (1995) 16 Co Law 202. Section 40 provides:

> (1) In favour of a person dealing with a company in good faith, the power of the board of directors to bind the company, or authorise others to do so, is deemed to be free of any limitation under the company's constitution.

(2) For this purpose—
 (a) a person 'deals with' a company if he is a party to any transaction or other act to which the company is a party,
 (b) a person dealing with a company—
  (i) is not bound to enquire as to any limitation on the powers of the directors to bind the company or authorise others to do so,
  (ii) is presumed to have acted in good faith unless the contrary is proved, and
  (iii) is not to be regarded as acting in bad faith by reason only of his knowing that an act is beyond the powers of the directors under the company's constitution.
(3) The references above to limitations on the directors' powers under the company's constitution include limitations deriving—
 (a) from a resolution of the company in general meeting or a meeting of any class of shareholders, or
 (b) from any agreement between the members of the company or of any class of shareholders.

Section 40 operates only in favour of a person dealing with a company. The company itself cannot enforce a transaction which has been entered into without its actual authority unless it ratifies the transaction (see **19.5.7**).

The provisions of s 40 were first enacted in the European Communities Act 1972, s 9(1), in different words. The original version caused some problems of interpretation which the present version is intended to solve (see **19.5.5.3** and **19.5.5.4**).

19.5.5.2 Limits on the scope of s 40

A person cannot invoke CA 2006, s 40, to make a transaction or other act binding on a company:

 (a) if the person did not become a party to the transaction etc in good faith (s 40(1); see **19.5.5.4**); or

 (b) if the person is not one of the third parties whom Directive 2009/101/EC, art 10(2), is intended to protect.

In *Smith v Henniker-Major and Co* [2002] EWCA Civ 762, [2003] Ch 182, a majority (Carnwath and Schiemann LJJ) of the Court of Appeal held that a director of a company who caused it to enter into the transaction or act which the director is seeking to enforce is not a person protected by art 10. Schiemann LJ also rejected the argument that CA 2006, s 40, protects such a director even though the Directive does not. There are special provisions in s 41 concerning transactions involving directors (see **19.5.8**). In *EIC Services Ltd v Phipps* [2004] EWCA Civ 1069, [2005] 1 WLR 1377, it was said, at [37], that neither the company itself nor any of its members is a person whom Directive 2009/101/EC, art 10(2), is intended to protect, but, strictly, this statement is obiter, and *EIC Services Ltd v Phipps* is authority only for the statement that a member of a company is not protected by CA 2006, s 40, in relation to an issue of bonus shares.

If a company is a charity, special conditions must be satisfied before the benefit of s 40 can be claimed (s 42; see **19.5.10**).

Directive 2009/101/EC, art 10(2), is concerned to prevent the validity of a transaction with a company from depending on the company's own constitution: it does not affect laws which make company contracts invalid for other reasons, such as conflict of interest on the part of the directors who made the contract (see **16.9**; *Coöperatieve Rabobank 'Vecht en Plassengebied' BA v Minderhoud* (case C-104/96) [1998] ECR I-7211) or, it is submitted, breach of duty by the directors (see **19.5.2.3**).

A person who cannot rely on CA 2006, s 40, to enforce a transaction or other act, to which a company was made a party by individuals acting outside the board's actual authority, may still be able to rely on those individuals' ostensible authority, though this will not be possible if the person knew that the act was beyond actual authority (*Criterion Properties plc v Stratford UK Properties LLC* [2004] UKHL 28, [2004] 1 WLR 1846, at [31]). Knowledge of lack of actual authority will often be present in a case of bad faith, even though such knowledge cannot by itself demonstrate bad faith (s 40(2)(b)(iii)).

19.5.5.3 Dealing with a company

If someone claiming to act on behalf of a company acts without its authority to make it a party to a transaction with another person, it is sometimes argued that the company is not a party to the transaction, so that the other person has not, by CA 2006, s 40(2)(a), dealt with the company, and so cannot claim the protection of s 40. But if that were true, s 40 would have no application at all. So it is clear that 'party' and 'transaction or other act' in s 40(2)(a) must be interpreted more widely to include the purported transactions or acts which the section was enacted to validate (*TCB Ltd v Gray* [1986] Ch 621, point not considered on appeal). A more restricted form of this argument is that where the persons who exercised a power of a company's board of directors were not entitled to do so, for example because the power was exercised at an inquorate board meeting, that power has not been exercised, so s 40 does not apply to it. This argument (which attempts to distinguish between 'substantive' and 'procedural' limitations on a board's powers) was rejected in *Smith v Henniker-Major and Co* [2002] EWCA Civ 762, [2003] Ch 182.

These arguments raise the question whether a transaction or other act could be so defective (for example, where an impostor had pretended to act for the company) that s 40 would not apply—whether there is an 'irreducible minimum that must be established in order to obtain protection under [s 40]' (*Smith v Henniker-Major and Co* at [28]). Unfortunately, the two members of the Court of Appeal (Robert Walker and Carnwath LJJ) who dealt with that question in **Smith v Henniker-Major and Co** disagreed on the answer, and the third member of the court did not discuss it at all. Robert Walker LJ, at [41], looking at the question from the company's point of view, sought to distinguish between a procedural irregularity, which would not take the transaction or act outside the protection of s 40, and a nullity or non-event, which would. He said that the irreducible minimum is:

> a genuine decision taken by a person or persons who can on substantial grounds claim to be the board of directors acting as such, even if the proceedings of the board are marred by procedural irregularities of a more or less serious character.

Carnwath LJ, at [103] to [108], disagreed. Looking at the question from the point of view of the person dealing with the company, he said, at [108]:

> A purposive approach to the section suggests a low threshold. The general policy seems to be that, if a document is put forward as a decision of the board by someone appearing to act on behalf of the company, in circumstances where there is no reason to doubt its authenticity, a person dealing with the company in good faith should be able to take it at face value.

It is submitted that Carnwath LJ's opinion better reflects the policy of Directive 2009/101/EC, art 10(2).

For discussion of these questions see P Heatherington and J Knapp, 'How much of a "person" is a director?' (2003) 153 NLJ 640; C Howell, 'Companies Act 1985, s 35A and 322A: *Smith v Henniker-Major* and the proposed reforms' (2003) 24 Co Law 264; and C Twigg-Flesner, 'Sections 35A and 322A revisited: who is a "person dealing with a company"?' (2005) 26 Co Law 195.

The definition of 'deals with' a company in CA 2006, s 40(2)(a), overrules the decision in *International Sales and Agencies Ltd v Marcus* [1982] 3 All ER 551. In that case, cheques were drawn on the company's bank account by a director in order to pay a debt incurred by a deceased fellow director for which the director who drew the cheques felt responsible but for which the company was not responsible. It was held that the recipient of the cheques was not a person dealing with the company under the differently worded European Communities Act 1972, s 9(1), which was a precursor of CA 2006, s 40.

19.5.5.4 Good faith

The provision of CA 2006, s 40(2)(b)(iii), that a person is not to be regarded as acting in bad faith by reason only of his knowing that an act is beyond the directors' powers under the company's constitution overrules the opinion of Lawson J in *International Sales and Agencies Ltd v Marcus* [1982] 3 All ER 551 at p 559. It is reinforced by the provision in s 40(2)(b)(i) that a party to a transaction with a company has no duty to inquire whether there is any limitation on the powers of the board of directors to bind the company or authorise others to do so. Section 40(2)(b)(i) means that, when a person invokes s 40 to validate an irregular transaction of a company, it cannot be said that s 40 does not apply because the circumstances were such that the person ought to have inquired about the matters specified in s 40(2)(b)(i). It does not protect against a failure to inquire about other matters which circumstances suggest should be asked about, for example, where the dealing has not been with the whole board of directors, whether the person who purported to act for the company had been authorised by the board (*Wrexham Association Football Club Ltd v Crucialmove Ltd* [2006] EWCA Civ 237, [2008] 1 BCLC 508, at [47]).

For a person who deals with a company when actually knowing the contents of its constitution, s 40(2)(b)(i) is irrelevant. By s 40(2)(b)(iii), such a person cannot be regarded as acting in bad faith simply because of knowing the contents of the constitution, but what else would show bad faith? The only relevant judicial comment is an obiter statement by Nourse J which was on the European Communities Act 1972, s 9(1), which was a precursor of CA 2006, s 40, and still seems to be relevant to s 40. His Lordship said, in ***Barclays Bank Ltd v TOSG Trust Fund Ltd*** [1984] BCLC 1, at p 18, that 'a person acts in good faith if he acts genuinely and honestly in the circumstances of the case', but in order to show that he acted in good faith it is not necessary to show that he acted reasonably. (The remark was obiter because his Lordship found that it was unnecessary to rely on the European Communities Act 1972, s 9(1), to validate the transactions in question in the case and this was not pursued on appeal.)

In *Harrison v Teton Valley Trading Co Ltd* [2004] EWCA Civ 1028, [2004] 1 WLR 2577, the Court of Appeal considered the meaning of 'bad faith' in another Directive, concerned with trade mark law. Sir William Aldous said, at [20], that bad faith includes dishonesty but is a wider concept. Bad faith is a mental state and must be judged by a combined subjective/objective test: there is bad faith when there is a realisation (subjective element) that reasonable persons applying the correct standard (objective element) would regard behaviour as in bad faith. The correct standard is that of acceptable commercial behaviour observed by reasonable and experienced persons in the particular commercial area being examined (at [33]).

19.5.6 AUTHORITY OF A BOARD OF DIRECTORS

In *Heiton v Waverley Hydropathic Co Ltd* (1877) 4 R 830, Lord President Inglis said, at p 843:

> The fundamental doctrine of the law of partnership in the case of ordinary mercantile companies is, that every individual partner of the company may bind the company in all ordinary transactions, and that each partner has an implied mandate to that effect. But in the case of a joint-stock company . . . there is no room for such a presumption as that, because the very nature of the association renders it indispensable that there should be a directorial body to carry on the business of the company, and the constitution of the body of directors of course takes away at once the power of any individual member of the company to bind the company. But it does more than that, for it creates a presumption of a different kind—a presumption that the whole business of the company is to be done by the directors and by nobody else, and in no other way; and the public are entitled to expect that everything that the directors do shall be valid and binding upon the company.

In *Ferguson v Wilson* (1866) LR 2 Ch App 77, Cairns LJ said at pp 89–90:

> The company itself cannot act in its own person . . . it can only act through directors, and the case is, as regards those directors, merely the ordinary case of principal and agent.

This statement is not consistent with the idea that the board of directors of a company is an organ of the company which acts as the company rather than as agent for it, as suggested by the realist theory of corporate personality (see **5.5.2**). A director acting for a company, in making a contract, for example, is acting in right and on behalf of the company. The director is the means whereby the company, as an artificial creation, acts. It cannot be said that the director is instructing the company to act (*Group Seven Ltd v Allied Investment Corporation Ltd* [2013] EWHC 1509 (Ch), [2014] 1 WLR 735, at [67]).

The directors must act as a board, unless they delegate their powers. In **Re Marseilles Extension Railway Co, ex parte Crédit Foncier and Mobilier of England** (1871) LR 7 Ch App 161, Mellish LJ said, at p 168, 'a director is simply a person appointed to act as one of a board, with power to bind the company when acting as a board, but having otherwise no power to bind them'. Articles of association may permit the directors to delegate their powers (see model articles for private companies, art 5, and model articles for public companies, art 5, in SI 2008/3229). In *Mitchell and Hobbs (UK) Ltd v Mill* [1996] 2 BCLC 102, one of two directors of a company instructed solicitors to bring legal proceedings in the name of the company. There was no evidence that he had been delegated authority to do this by the board and there had been no board meeting to ratify his action, which was in fact opposed by the other director. Accordingly, the proceedings were struck out as unauthorised.

CA 2006 treats the board of directors of a company as primarily authorised to make contracts on behalf of the company. By virtue of s 40(1), in favour of a person dealing with a company in good faith, the company cannot claim that the actual authority of its board to make contracts on its behalf is limited in any way by the company's constitution or (s 40(3)) by a resolution of or agreement between the members.

19.5.7 RATIFICATION OF ACTS OUTSIDE ACTUAL AUTHORITY

If an act of a company's agent is outside the agent's actual authority, it is possible for the act to be ratified by the company: ratification supplies the lacking authority and adopts the act as an act of the company.

The general rule is that if the board of directors of a company have acted on behalf of the company outside their actual authority, the act may be ratified by the members in general meeting by ordinary resolution (*Grant v United Kingdom Switchback Railways Co* (1888) 40 ChD 135). Ratification must be by the members at the time of ratifying, not those at the time of the act which is to be ratified (*EIC Services Ltd v Phipps* [2003] EWHC 1507 (Ch), [2003] 1 WLR 2360, at [144]).

To the extent that ratification is of conduct amounting to breach of duty (for example, the duty to act within powers), or negligence, default or breach of trust, it must be in accordance with CA 2006, s 239 (see **16.16.2**). Under that section, unless the decision is unanimous (s 239(6)(a)), only disinterested members' votes can be counted (s 239(3) and (4)).

If some person other than the board of directors has acted outside actual authority, the board of directors may ratify the act if it is within the board's actual authority (*Macari v Celtic Football and Athletic Co Ltd* 1999 SLT 138). Similarly, the acts of an agent appointed, under delegated authority, by any person other than the board of directors may be ratified by that person if within that person's actual authority.

For example, in *Irvine v Union Bank of Australia* (1877) 2 App Cas 366 there was no limitation on the company's borrowing powers but the directors were limited to borrowing a sum equal to half the company's paid-up capital. The Privy Council held that the company in general meeting could ratify borrowing by the directors in excess of their borrowing powers. Ratification by the members of a contract in respect of which the directors were disqualified from voting was allowed by the

Court of Appeal in *Grant v United Kingdom Switchback Railways Co.* Corporate litigation which is instituted without authority may be ratified by the company in general meeting (*Danish Mercantile Co Ltd v Beaumont* [1951] Ch 680).

It is necessary in this connection to distinguish the ratification of past acts which were not authorised by the articles, and which is effected by ordinary resolution, and the authorisation of future acts which are not permitted by the articles, which is not ratification but an amendment of the articles and must be effected by special resolution (see **3.5.1**) (*Irvine v Union Bank of Australia* at pp 375–6). As Cotton LJ said in *Grant v United Kingdom Switchback Railways Co* at p 138:

> The ratifying a particular contract which had been entered into by the directors without authority, and so making it an act of the company, is quite a different thing from altering the articles. To give the directors power to do things in future which the articles did not authorise them to do, would be an alteration of the articles, but it is no alteration of the articles to ratify a contract which has been made without authority.

The members may ratify a contract which an individual director has entered into when it should have been decided on by the entire board (*Re Horsley and Weight Ltd* [1982] Ch 442).

19.5.8 TRANSACTIONS INVOLVING DIRECTORS

In general, if the board of directors of a company enter into a transaction, on the company's behalf, with a person who is dealing with the company in good faith then the fact that the board have exceeded any limitation on their powers under the company's constitution does not entitle the company to repudiate the transaction. This is because, by virtue of CA 2006, s 40(1), the power of the board of directors to bind the company is, in such circumstances, deemed to be free of any limitation under the company's constitution (see **19.5.5**). However, by s 41, a transaction is voidable, at the option of the company, on the ground that the directors have exceeded a limitation on their powers under the company's constitution (such as the limitation to act only within the company's objects) if the parties to the transaction include:

(a) a director of the company or of its holding company; or

(b) a person connected with such a director or a company with whom such a director is associated (for the meaning of 'connection' and 'association' in this context see **16.14**).

The persons listed in paragraphs (a) and (b) will be referred to in this discussion as 'insiders'. 'Transaction' includes any act (s 41(7)(a)).

Section 41 makes a transaction to which an insider is a party voidable if, or to the extent that, its validity depends on s 40 (see **19.5.5**) (s 41(1)). In other words, s 41 prevents an insider from relying on s 40.

So what the company can avoid under s 41 is its own obligations under the transaction. In a wide-ranging discussion of the relationship between what are now ss 40 and 41, Christian Twigg-Flesner argues that this is a misuse of the concepts of transaction and avoidance ('Sections 35A and 322A revisited: who is a "person dealing with a company"?' (2005) 26 Co Law 195).

If an insider is party to a transaction in connection with which the board exceeded their powers under the company's constitution, the transaction ceases to be voidable if (s 41(4)):

(a) restitution of any money or other asset which was the subject matter of the transaction is no longer possible; or

(b) the company is indemnified for any loss or damage resulting from the transaction; or

(c) rights acquired bona fide for value and without actual notice of the directors' exceeding their powers by a person who is not party to the transaction would be affected by the avoidance; or

(d) the transaction is affirmed by the company.

Whether or not a transaction of a company to which an insider is a party is avoided, any insider who is party to the transaction, and any director of the company who authorised the transaction is liable, by s 41(3):

(a) to account to the company for any gain which he has made directly or indirectly by the transaction; and

(b) to indemnify the company for any loss or damage resulting from the transaction.

A person other than a director of the company is not liable under s 41(3) if he shows that at the time the transaction was entered into he did not know that the directors were exceeding their powers (s 41(5)).

Section 41 does not affect the protection given by s 40 to any party who is not an insider (s 41(6)). If a transaction is voidable under s 41 but valid under s 40, an application may be made to the court, which may affirm, sever or set aside the transaction on such terms as appear to it to be just (s 41(6)). In *Re Torvale Group Ltd* [1999] 2 BCLC 605 the court, under s 41(6), affirmed a transaction between a company and the five trustees of its pension fund, who included a director of the company who did not personally benefit from the transaction.

If a limited company has only one member who is also a director or shadow director of the company, s 231 requires that any contract between the company and the director/member otherwise than in the ordinary course of the company's business must be recorded in writing. If the contract itself is not in writing, its terms must be set out in a written memorandum or recorded in the minutes of the first board meeting after the contract is made. Failure to comply does not affect the validity of the contract (s 231(6)) but the company and every officer who is in default will have committed an offence (s 231(3); penalty in s 231(4)). A contract between a subsidiary company and its holding company is not subject to s 231 if the only reason for treating the holding company as a shadow director of the subsidiary is that the subsidiary's directors are accustomed to act in accordance with the holding company's directions or instructions (s 251(3)). The source of s 231 is Directive 2009/102/EC, art 5).

19.5.9 AUTHORITY OF A COMPANY SECRETARY

In *Panorama Developments (Guildford) Ltd v Fidelis Furnishing Fabrics Ltd* [1971] 2 QB 711, the claimant company carried on a car hire business. The defendant company's secretary hired cars from the claimant company apparently for use in the course of the defendant company's business. The hire agreements were in the secretary's name and signed by him as 'Company Secretary'. The cars were used for the secretary's own purposes and not by the defendant company. The claimant company sued the defendant company for non-payment of the hire charges. The Court of Appeal held that the company secretary had apparent or ostensible authority to enter into contracts connected with the administrative side of the defendant company's affairs, including the hiring of cars. The defendant company was accordingly liable to pay the hire charges. Lord Denning MR said of a company secretary:

> He is an officer of the company with extensive duties and responsibilities. This appears not only in the modern Companies Acts, but also by the role which he plays in the day-to-day business of companies. He is no longer a mere clerk. He regularly makes representations on behalf of the company and enters into contracts on its behalf which come within the day-to-day running of the company's business. So much so that he may be regarded as held out as having authority to do such things on behalf of the company. He is certainly entitled to sign contracts connected with the administrative side of a company's affairs, such as employing staff, and ordering cars, and so forth. All such matters now come within the ostensible authority of a company's secretary.

Panorama Developments (Guildford) Ltd v Fidelis Furnishing Fabrics Ltd has not altered the rule that the secretary of a company does not have authority, other than by specific delegation, to institute legal proceedings in the company's name (*Daimler Co Ltd v Continental Tyre and Rubber Co (Great Britain) Ltd* [1916] 2 AC 307; *Club Flotilla (Pacific Palms) Ltd v Isherwood* (1987) 12 ACLR 387) nor the rule that the secretary does not have authority to decide what entries to make in the company's register of members (*Re Zinotty Properties Ltd* [1984] 1 WLR 1249, see **8.3.4**).

19.5.10 CHARITABLE COMPANIES

CA 2006, s 40 (see **19.5.5.1**) does not, by s 42, apply to the acts of a company which is a charity, except in favour of a person who:

    (a) does not know at the time the act is done that the company is a charity (see **4.5.5**); or

    (b) gives full consideration in money or money's worth in relation to the act in question and does not know (as the case may be)

       (i) that the act is not permitted by the company's constitution, or

     (ii) that the act is beyond the powers of the directors.

By s 42(4), a ratification of a charitable company's transaction to which s 41 applies (see **19.5.8**) is ineffective without the prior written consent of the Charity Commission.

19.6 PRE-INCORPORATION AND POST-DISSOLUTION CONTRACTS

19.6.1 PERSONAL LIABILITY

When people wish to pursue a business opportunity and incorporate a company for the purpose, they may make contracts relating to the intended company's affairs before the company is incorporated. Sometimes a 'pre-incorporation contract', agreed between a person acting in anticipation of incorporating a company and another contractor, may apparently name the intended company as a party to the contract, even though it is not possible for a non-existent person to be a party to a contract. English common law attempted to distinguish two possibilities:

    (a) that it was intended that the contract should be between the contractor and the person who was acting in anticipation of incorporating the company, in which case the contract would exist and the person who apparently acted as an agent for a non-existent principal would be liable on the contract; and

    (b) that it was intended that the contract should be between the contractor and the company, in which case, the company being non-existent, there was no contract at all and no one was liable on it.

In *Kelner v Baxter* (1866) LR 2 CP 174, the person acting in relation to the non-existent company was held liable on the contract, and it used to be thought that this imposed an absolute rule that a person purporting to make a contract for a non-existent company would always be personally liable. However, in *Newborne v Sensolid (Great Britain) Ltd* [1954] 1 QB 45, the supposed contract was held to have been with the non-existent company and therefore not a contract at all. That the position depends on the intention of the parties when the contract was formed was suggested by Oliver LJ in *Phonogram Ltd v Lane* [1982] QB 938 and has been applied by the Court of Appeal in *Cotronic (UK) Ltd v Dezonie* [1991] BCLC 721.

    One of the objectives of the First Company Law Directive (68/151/EEC, which was adopted before the United Kingdom joined what was then the EEC and has now been codified as Directive

2009/101/EC) is to protect third parties by restricting 'to the greatest possible extent the grounds on which obligations entered into in the name of the company are not valid'. Directive 2009/101/EC, art 8, provides:

> If, before a company being formed has acquired legal personality, action has been carried out in its name and the company does not assume the obligations arising from such action, the persons who acted shall, without limit, be jointly and severally liable therefor, unless otherwise agreed.

This was implemented in the law of England and Wales by the European Communities Act 1972, s 9(2), which has been re-enacted, with slight changes, as CA 2006, s 51(1):

> A contract that purports to be made by or on behalf of a company at a time when the company has not been formed has effect, subject to any agreement to the contrary, as one made with the person purporting to act for the company or as agent for it, and he is personally liable on the contract accordingly.

Section 51(1) applies to both of the situations distinguished by the common law (*Phonogram Ltd v Lane*). It applies even if the company is never in fact registered (*Phonogram Ltd v Lane*). It applies to a contract purportedly made by or on behalf of a company to be incorporated outside Great Britain, provided the contract is governed by the law of England and Wales or Scotland (SI 1994/950), even if the company is never in fact incorporated (*Hellmuth, Obata and Kassbaum Inc v King* (2000) LTL 25/10/2000). It applies to the making of a deed under the law of England and Wales or Northern Ireland as it applies to the making of a contract (CA 2006, s 51(2)). It applies to an inferred agreement to pay a reasonable sum for work or services performed, for example in preparation for a contract (*Hellmuth, Obata and Kassbaum Inc v King*).

In **Phonogram Ltd v Lane**, it was suggested that, for the purpose of s 51(1), a contract is 'purported' to be made by a company only when there has been a representation that the company is already in existence. Lord Denning MR (with whom Shaw and Oliver LJJ agreed) said, at p 943:

> I do not agree. A contract can purport to be made on behalf of a company, or by a company, even though that company is known by both parties not to be formed and that it is only about to be formed.

It may be concluded, therefore, that, subject to any agreement to the contrary, promoters are now personally liable in respect of pre-incorporation contracts made for the benefit of their unformed company, irrespective of the capacity in which they purport to contract and irrespective of their subjective beliefs.

It would seem that, like s 40 (see **19.5.5**), s 51 cannot be relied on by a contractor who is not one of the third parties whom Directive 2009/101/EC is intended to protect.

When a person acts in anticipation of the incorporation of a company to make a contract naming the company as party, s 51(1) provides that the contract 'has effect' as a contract made with that person. This makes that person liable on the contract (as the section points out) but also entitles that person to enforce the contract as against the other party (*Braymist Ltd v Wise Finance Co Ltd* [2002] Ch 273). However, this is subject to the normal rule of contract law that if a misrepresentation about who is to be one party to a contract induced the other party to enter into the contract, to that other party's detriment, then the other party is entitled to rescind it. In *Braymist Ltd v Wise Finance Co Ltd* a firm of solicitors made a contract, as agents of and solicitors for Braymist Ltd, for the sale of land. In fact Braymist Ltd had not been incorporated when the contract was made. It was found that the identity of the vendor was of no significance at all to the purchaser and so the solicitors could enforce the contract of sale.

If promoters make contracts before buying a company off the shelf then, provided the company they buy was in existence at the time the contracts were made, s 51 does not apply and the company can ratify the contracts, though the promoters must have made it clear that they were acting as agents for the company when they made the contracts. It makes no difference that the shelf company did not have the right name at the time the contracts were made (*Oshkosh B'Gosh Inc v Dan*

Marbel Inc Ltd [1989] BCLC 507). It is, however, easy to make mistakes in this situation. In *Cross v Aurora Group Ltd* (1988) 4 NZCLC 64,909, Mr Cross made a contract on behalf of 'Cross Property Management Ltd a company currently being formed'. He then bought a shelf company, which was in existence at the time the contract was made, and changed its name to Cross Properties Management Ltd. It was held that this company could not adopt the contract. It was not the company Mr Cross was purporting to act for because it had already been formed when the contract was made.

Persons who work together to form a registered company and order goods for the company and open a bank account, are not carrying on a business so as to be in partnership (*Keith Spicer Ltd v Mansell* [1970] 1 WLR 333).

Section 51 does not apply when a person purports to make a contract for a company which once existed but has been dissolved (*Cotronic (UK) Ltd v Dezonie*). However, the person purporting to represent the non-existent company can sue for a *quantum meruit* for any work he or she does under the supposed contract (*Cotronic (UK) Ltd v Dezonie*) or, if the obligations apparently undertaken by the non-existent company under the supposed contract are not performed, the person who purported to represent it can be sued for damages for breach of warranty of authority (*Royal Bank of Canada v Starr* (1985) 31 BLR 124).

19.6.2 AGREEMENT TO THE CONTRARY AND NOVATION

A person who makes a pre-incorporation contract, purporting to act for, or as agent for, a company which has not yet been registered, may avoid personal liability for the contract by entering into an 'agreement to the contrary' (CA 2006, s 51(1)). In *Phonogram Ltd v Lane* [1982] QB 938, it was suggested that if it was stated that a person making a pre-incorporation contract was acting as agent for the future company, it could be inferred that an agreement had been made excluding what is now s 51. The Court of Appeal firmly rejected this idea. Oliver LJ pointed out, at p 946, that the provision was specifically expressed to apply to a contract which purported to be made by a person as agent so that, rather than excluding the provision, stating that one is acting as agent in fact brings it into operation.

An express agreement simply to exclude s 51 from operating on a contract seems unlikely because it would mean that there would be no enforceable contract at all. What may be provided in a pre-incorporation contract is that the person making it will be released from liability on it if the company, after incorporation, enters into a second contract with the contractor in the same terms as the pre-incorporation contract. This is known as a 'novation'. The problem for the contractor is to prove that the company did make a new contract after incorporation—the general attitude of the courts seems to be to require very clear evidence (*Bagot Pneumatic Tyre Co v Clipper Pneumatic Tyre Co* [1902] 1 Ch 146). Simply acting in the mistaken belief that a pre-incorporation contract is binding is not enough (*Re Northumberland Avenue Hotel Co* (1886) 33 ChD 16). However, if a company, after incorporation, takes possession of property transferred to it in a pre-incorporation contract, the court may be able to infer that the only possible explanation is that a new contract was made after incorporation (*Re Patent Ivory Manufacturing Co* (1888) 38 ChD 156; *Heinhuis v Blacksheep Charters Ltd* (1987) 46 DLR (4th) 67).

The fact that the terms of a pre-incorporation contract are stated in the company's articles, giving authority to adopt the contract, is not in itself evidence that there actually was a novation (*Melhado v Pôrto Alegre, New Hamburgh, and Brazilian Railway Co* (1874) LR 9 CP 503; *Eley v Positive Government Security Life Assurance Co Ltd* (1876) 1 ExD 88; *Re Hereford and South Wales Waggon and Engineering Co* (1876) 2 ChD 621; *Browne v La Trinidad* (1887) 37 ChD 1; *Re Dale and Plant Ltd* (1889) 61 LT 206).

A company cannot simply ratify a contract purportedly made on its behalf before it was incorporated so as to make the contract in its original form valid: the contract could not have been a valid contract with the company when it was made because the company did not exist then, and the company cannot retrospectively supply the person who made the contract with authority to act as its agent because the company could not have had any agents when it did not exist (*Kelner v Baxter* (1866) LR 2 CP 174; *Re Empress Engineering Co* (1880) 16 ChD 125; *Natal Land and Colonization Co Ltd v Pauline Colliery and Development Syndicate Ltd* [1904] AC 120).

19.6.3 FURTHER READING

J H Gross, 'Pre-incorporation contracts' (1971) 87 LQR 367 gives an extensive survey of the law as it was before 1973, with references to the situation in the USA and Canada. When the new law was first enacted it was commented on in D D Prentice, 'Section 9 of the European Communities Act' (1973) 89 LQR 518 at pp 530–3. For an extended discussion of the new law, see N N Green, 'Security of transaction after *Phonogram*' (1984) 47 MLR 671 and A Griffiths, 'Agents without principals: pre-incorporation contracts and section 36C of the Companies Act 1985' (1993) 13 LS 241.

19.7 LIABILITIES OF PRINCIPAL AND AGENT

19.7.1 IMMUNITY WHEN ACTING FOR A COMPANY

It is a basic principle of agency law that when an agent acts to make his or her principal a party to a contract, the agent does not become a party to that contract, unless there is an express provision to that effect. It follows that the agent is not liable for any breach of the contract by the principal. So if a director of a company causes it to enter into a contract and subsequently causes it to breach the contract, it is the company, not the director, that is liable for the breach. It has also been held that a director of a company who causes a breach of a contract between the company and a third party is not liable for the tort of intentionally inducing the company to breach the contract. As an agent of the company, the director was acting for the company, not inducing the company to act (*Said v Butt* [1920] 3 KB 497; *Welsh Development Agency v Export Finance Co Ltd* [1992] BCLC 148; *Crystalens Ltd v White* (2006) LTL 15/9/2006). In *Said v Butt*, Mr Said had an acrimonious disagreement with a company that managed a theatre. He tried to obtain a ticket for the first night of a new production at the theatre, but the company refused to supply him with one. So he got someone else to obtain a ticket without revealing that it was to be used by him. When he arrived for the performance, the managing director of the company refused him entrance. Mr Said sued the managing director for inducing the company to break the contract to admit him to the performance. It was held that no contract had been made, because the company was mistaken about whom it was dealing with. Alternatively, it was held that the managing director was not personally liable, because he was acting within his authority as a director in the company's interest. The principle established in *Said v Butt* will not apply if the director is acting outside his or her authority (*Crystalens Ltd v White*).

The principle established in *Said v Butt* has been extended to torts and infringements of intellectual property rights committed by companies. A director of a company who acts for the company in causing it to commit a tort is not liable for the tort. However, in any particular case it may be very difficult to establish whether the director was acting only for the company and not for himself. As Slade LJ, giving the judgment of the Court of Appeal in **C Evans and Sons Ltd v Spritebrand Ltd** [1985] 1 WLR 317, said, at p 329:

> In every case where it is sought to make [a director] liable for his company's torts, it is necessary to examine with care what part he played personally in regard to the act or acts complained of.

In *Mancetter Developments Ltd v Garmanson Ltd* [1986] QB 1212, a director of Garmanson Ltd was held liable for an act of waste (ie, damage to property leased to the company) which was an act of the company but which was procured and directed by him. In *A P Besson Ltd v Fulleon Ltd* [1986] FSR 319, a director of a company was held liable, as a joint tortfeasor, for damages for an infringement of copyright committed by his company because of his personal involvement in the actual ordering or physical commission of the tort. In *Fairline Shipping Corporation v Adamson* [1975] QB 180, Mr Adamson owned a refrigerated store, which was used by a company of which he was managing director. That company contracted with Fairline Shipping Corporation to store perishable goods in Mr Adamson's store but the goods were ruined because of Mr Adamson's negligence. He was held to be personally liable to Fairline for his negligence. (The company which actually made the contract with Fairline had gone into liquidation and could not have paid any damages.)

The law was reviewed by Chadwick LJ in **MCA Records Inc v Charly Records Ltd** [2001] EWCA Civ 1441, [2003] 1 BCLC 93, at [29] to [53]. His Lordship drew four principles from the jurisprudence:

> [49] First, a director will not be treated as liable with the company as a joint tortfeasor if he does no more than carry out his constitutional role in the governance of the company—that is to say, by voting at board meetings . . . if all that a director is doing is carrying out the duties entrusted to him as such by the company under its constitution, the circumstances in which it would be right to hold him liable as a joint tortfeasor with the company would be rare indeed.
>
> [50] Second . . . if, in relation to the wrongful acts which are the subject of complaint, the liability of the individual as a joint tortfeasor with the company arises from his participation or involvement in ways which go beyond the exercise of constitutional control, then there is no reason why the individual should escape liability because he could have procured those same acts through the exercise of constitutional control.
>
> [51] Third . . . at least in the field of intellectual property . . . liability as a joint tortfeasor may arise where in the words of Lord Templeman in *CBS Songs Ltd v Amstrad Consumer Electronics plc* [1988] AC 1013 at p 1058 . . . the individual 'intends and procures and shares a common design that the infringement takes place'.
>
> [52] Fourth . . . an individual who does 'intend, procure and share a common design' that the infringement should take place may be liable as a joint tortfeasor.

Commenting on this in **Koninklijke Philips Electronics NV v Princo Digital Disc GmbH** [2003] EWHC 2588 (Ch), [2004] 2 BCLC 50, Pumfrey J said, at [7]:

> The essential part of this analysis is the emphasis on the need . . . to show on normal principles that [the director] was a joint tortfeasor with the company . . . the fact that he was an officer of the company is not a factor in his liability save to the extent to which it afforded him the opportunity to participate in the acts of the company to the extent necessary to fix him with liability as a joint tortfeasor.

In *Società Esplosivi Industriali SpA v Ordnance Technologies (UK) Ltd (No 2)* [2007] EWHC 2875 (Ch), [2008] 2 All ER 622, Lindsay J said, at [87], that it may be too much to expect that a practical test can be formulated for a director's or shareholder's liability in all cases. It is better to examine the facts of each case.

Where, in the course of a company's business, a tort such as negligent misstatement (see **17.5.2** to **17.5.4**) is committed, for which liability is only imposed where there is a duty (an assumption of responsibility) to the claimant, it is possible for a director, on whom the duty is not imposed, to be not liable while the company is liable. In *Williams v Natural Life Health Foods Ltd* [1998] 1 WLR 830 the claimants claimed damages for negligent advice given to them under a franchise agreement they had made with Natural Life Health Foods Ltd. They contended that the company's managing director was personally liable for this negligent advice, because the company's own advertising made clear that it relied on his expertise. The plaintiffs had not dealt with the managing director personally, though he had helped to prepare the negligent advice. The House of Lords held that the managing director did not owe a duty (had not assumed responsibility) to the claimants in respect of the advice and so was not liable. For wide-ranging commentary on this case see R Grantham and C Rickett, 'Directors' "tortious" liability: contract, tort or company law?' (1999) 62 MLR 133; J H Armour, 'Corporate personality and assumption of responsibility' [1999] LMCLQ 246.

For a species of tort, such as deceit, for which liability does not depend on the existence of a duty of care, a director who commits the wrong will be personally liable (*Standard Chartered Bank v Pakistan National Shipping Corporation (Nos 2 and 4)* [2002] UKHL 43, [2003] 1 AC 959). A director of a company who has made a deceitful representation that the company is creditworthy is liable for it, provided the representation is in writing and signed by the director as required by the Statute of Frauds (Amendment) Act 1828, s 6 (*Contex Drouzhba Ltd v Wiseman* [2007] EWCA Civ 1201, [2008] 1 BCLC 631). This is so even if the statement is signed by the director while he is acting as a director of the company. Such a representation may be implied by the director signing an agreement between the company and a supplier concerning the terms on which the company will pay for goods to be supplied. If, when signing the agreement, the director knows that the company will not be able to pay for the goods, the director will be personally liable for the loss the supplier suffers as a result.

19.7.2 VICARIOUS LIABILITY FOR TORTS OF EMPLOYEES AND AGENTS

When an employee commits a tort, the employer, whether an individual or a company, may be held vicariously liable for the tort committed by the employee, if there is a close connection between the tort and the employment making it just to hold the employer liable (*Mohamud v Wm Morrison Supermarkets plc* [2016] UKSC 11, [2016] AC 677, at [39] and [46]). The three principal reasons for imposing vicarious liability in this situation, identified by Lord Reed in *Cox v Ministry of Justice* [2016] UKSC 10, [2016] AC 660, at [22], are:

(a) the tort will have been committed as a result of activity being taken by the employee on behalf of the employer;

(b) the employee's activity is likely to be part of the business activity of the employer; and

(c) the employer, by employing the employee to carry on the activity, will have created the risk of the tort committed by the employee.

Similarly, a principal may be vicariously liable for a tort committed by an agent (*Credit Lyonnais Bank Nederland NV v Export Credits Guarantee Department* [2000] 1 AC 486 per Lord Woolf MR at p 494). A relationship other than one of employment or agency is in principle capable of giving rise to vicarious liability where harm is wrongfully done by an individual who carries on activities as an integral part of the business activities carried on by a defendant and for its benefit (rather than the activities being entirely attributable to the conduct of a recognisably independent business of the individual's own or of a third party) and where the commission of the wrongful act is a risk created by the defendant by assigning those activities to the individual in question (*Cox v Ministry of Justice* at [24]). 'Business' does not have to be a commercial activity for profit. It is sufficient that the defendant is carrying on activities in the furtherance of its own interests (*Cox v Ministry of Justice* at [30]).

A company's vicarious liability for someone else's tort does not mean that the company is regarded as having committed the tort: the company is liable for someone else's commission of the tort because of being that someone's employer or principal. The company's capacity to commit the tort is therefore irrelevant. For example, in *Citizens' Life Assurance Co Ltd v Brown* [1904] AC 423, the insurance company was held to be vicariously liable for a defamatory libel which one of its employees published in the course of his employment. The jury found that the employee had acted with what is known in libel law as 'express malice' so that he would not have been able to claim the defence of qualified privilege had he been sued personally. It was argued for the company that 'malice' had no meaning in relation to a company so it could claim qualified privilege as a defence, but this missed the point that the company was being made liable for its employee's actions and motives, not its own. Lord Lindley, giving the judgment of the Privy Council, said, at p 426:

> To talk about imputing malice to corporations appears to their Lordships to introduce metaphysical subtleties which are needless and fallacious. Their Lordships concur with the view of the Acting Chief Justice [of New South Wales] in this case that, if [the employee] published the libel complained of in the course of his employment, the company are liable for it on the ordinary principles of agency.

In *W B Anderson and Sons Ltd v Rhodes (Liverpool) Ltd* [1967] 2 All ER 850, Rhodes (Liverpool) Ltd acted as agent for a company called Taylors (Corn and Produce) Ltd making contracts by which Taylors bought potatoes. The employee of Rhodes who made the contracts told the sellers that Taylors was creditworthy but in fact it was not. That employee would only have known that Taylors was a bad payer if either Rhodes's manager or its bookkeeper had told him but they negligently did not. The manager and bookkeeper were not liable for negligent misrepresentation because they made no representations. The employee who did make the representations was not negligent. Even so, Rhodes was held vicariously liable for negligent misrepresentation. The court aggregated the negligence of two employees with the representation made by the third to create the employer's liability.

The fact that a company is made vicariously liable for the tort of an employee or agent does not make the employee or agent immune from being sued for what he or she did (*Standard Chartered Bank v Pakistan National Shipping Corporation (Nos 2 and 4)* [2002] UKHL 43, [2003] 1 AC 959).

Vicarious liability for crimes is considered in **19.8.4.7**.

For an argument that holding companies could be made vicariously liable for the torts of their subsidiaries, see P Morgan, 'Vicarious liability for group companies: the final frontier of vicarious liability?' (2015) 31 PN 276.

19.8 ATTRIBUTION BY A COURT SO AS TO IMPOSE LIABILITY ON A COMPANY

19.8.1 IDENTIFICATION THEORY

A legal penalty or detriment for an act—particularly a criminal liability—is usually considered to be deserved only by a person who consciously chose to act in the way that attracts the penalty. This is at the heart of the concept of *mens rea* in criminal law and is often reflected in the wording of legislation imposing penalties. A company, as an artificial legal person, does not have consciousness. So it has been found to be expedient to make a company liable to a penalty for a wrongful act by attributing to it the wrongful acts and thoughts of humans identified with the company.

Many civil law rights and liabilities attach only to persons who have requisite knowledge. To make these concepts applicable to companies as separate persons it is necessary to attribute to companies the knowledge of humans identified with them.

The rules of attribution by agency discussed so far in this chapter are not intended to cover these situations and so it is necessary for the courts to devise other appropriate rules.

For example, in ***Lennard's Carrying Co Ltd v Asiatic Petroleum Co Ltd*** [1915] AC 705, a shipowning company, Lennard's Carrying Co Ltd, attempted to claim the protection of the Merchant Shipping Act 1894, s 502. This provided that a shipowner was not liable for fire damage to goods on board the ship which happened 'without his actual fault or privity'. The company owned a ship which had carried a cargo of benzine consigned to the Asiatic Petroleum Co Ltd. The ship ran aground because its boilers were in such a poor state that there was not enough power to navigate the vessel. Grounding the ship damaged the cargo holds. The benzine escaped and exploded when it came into contact with the boiler fires. The evidence showed that Mr J M Lennard, a director of the shipowning company, knew, or ought to have known, that the ship was unseaworthy. Viscount Haldane LC said, at pp 713–14:

> did what happened take place without the actual fault or privity of the owners of the ship who were the appellants? . . . a corporation is an abstraction. It has no mind of its own any more than it has a body of its own; its active and directing will must consequently be sought in the person of somebody who for some purposes may be called an agent, but who is really the directing mind and will of the corporation, the very ego and centre of the personality of the corporation . . . If Mr Lennard was the directing mind of the company, then his action must, unless a corporation is not to be liable at all, have been an action which was the action of the company itself within the meaning of s 502 . . . It must be upon the true construction of that section in such a case as the present one that the fault or privity is the fault or privity of . . . somebody for whom the company is liable because his action is the very action of the company itself.

The company could have had the benefit of s 502 if it had shown that Mr Lennard's position was such that his fault was not the company's fault or a fault to which the company was privy. However, the burden of proving this was on the company and as it had not discharged that burden it was liable. The 'directing mind and will' has become the most important criterion for identifying humans with companies: see **19.8.2**.

The Admiralty Court developed an extensive case law on the liability of companies under s 502 of the Merchant Shipping Act 1894 and the similar s 503 (which limited liability for various matters including damage caused by improper navigation of the ship). See, for example, *The Lady Gwendolen* [1965] P 294 and *The Ert Stefanie* [1987] 2 Lloyd's Rep 371. There was a move away from the 'directing mind and will' criterion. In *The Lady Gwendolen*, Sellers LJ said, at p 333, that in order to show that something had been done without the actual fault or privity of a shipowning company it is necessary to show that it was done without the actual fault or privity of the person or persons in the company who were 'in charge of and responsible, in the capacity of the owners, for the running of the ships'. Willmer LJ, at p 343, said that this did not have to be a director, though in this case the court approved the finding of the judge at first instance that it was one of the company's assistant managing directors.

Sections 502 and 503 have since been repealed and shipowners' liability is now governed by an international convention. See the Merchant Shipping Act 1995, s 185 and sch 7.

19.8.2 WHOSE ACTS OR THOUGHTS WILL BE ATTRIBUTED TO A COMPANY?

19.8.2.1 Purpose of the attribution

In *Meridian Global Funds Management Asia Ltd v Securities Commission* [1995] 2 AC 500 at p 507, Lord Hoffmann emphasised that choosing whose human thoughts and/or actions will be attributed to a company for the purpose of applying a rule of law to it depends on interpreting that rule:

> Whose act (or knowledge, or state of mind) was *for this purpose* intended to count as the act etc of the company? One finds the answer to this question by applying the usual canons of interpretation, taking into account the language of the rule (if it is a statute) and its content and policy.

Meridian Global Funds Management Asia Ltd v Securities Commission concerned a New Zealand statute, which required a company to give notice of being a substantial holder of securities in a public company as soon as it knew or ought to have known that it had become one. The Privy Council held that the knowledge that had to be attributed to the company was the knowledge of the individual who had authority to acquire the securities for the company, regardless of whether that individual was the company's directing mind and will. However, Lord Hoffmann said, at p 511:

> But their Lordships would wish to guard themselves against being understood to mean that whenever a servant of a company has authority to do an act on its behalf, knowledge of that act will for all purposes

be attributed to the company. It is a question of construction in each case as to whether the particular rule requires that the knowledge that an act has been done, or the state of mind with which it was done, should be attributed to the company.

A case which is similar to *Meridian Global Funds Asia Ltd v Securities Commission* is *Moore v I Bresler Ltd* [1944] 2 All ER 515, in which it was held that a company had been rightly convicted of publishing false documents (which were statements, required by statute, of taxable transactions) with intent to deceive, because the company's secretary and a branch sales manager who had prepared the documents did so as 'the proper officers' of the company to make the statements.

Meridian Global Funds Asia Ltd v Securities Commission and *Moore v I Bresler Ltd* are examples of cases in which the acts or thoughts of an individual who is not part of a company's directing mind and will have been attributed to a company in order to make it criminally liable. By contrast, in *R v Rozeik* [1996] 1 WLR 159, it was held not to be appropriate to attribute to a company the state of mind of a person who was not part of its directing mind and will.

Mr Rozeik had received cheques from two companies and was convicted of obtaining them dishonestly, by deceiving the companies. On appeal the issue was whether the prosecution had proved that the companies had been deceived. To do this the prosecution had to prove that an individual whose state of mind could be attributed to the company was deceived. Which individuals might count for this purpose? The court said, at p 165 per Leggatt LJ:

> In cases in which the company is the victim the person or persons who stand for its state of mind may differ from those who do so in cases in which a company is charged with the commission of a criminal offence. The latter are [more] likely to represent what Viscount Haldane LC in *Lennard's Carrying Co Ltd v Asiatic Petroleum Co Ltd* called 'the directing mind and will' of the company. [Leggatt LJ has kindly confirmed to us that he meant 'more' rather than 'less' as printed in the report quoted.]

For the purposes of this particular crime, many junior employees who had been deceived did not count because it could not be said that the cheques had been 'obtained' from them. As the court said, at p 165:

> a cheque could only be obtained from the company from an employee who had authority to provide it. The deception had to operate on the mind of the employee from whom the cheque was obtained.

Employees who checked and typed a cheque were not persons from whom the cheque was obtained, but employees who signed it were. If an employee who signed a cheque knew that it was being issued fraudulently, that knowledge would be attributed to the company so that the company was not deceived, and it did not matter that the employee was not part of the directing mind and will of the company. It was part of the prosecution's case that a branch manager who had signed a cheque knew of the fraud. As this would have meant that the company was not deceived, the jury should not have convicted.

19.8.2.2 Directing mind and will

Although, as indicated in **19.8.2.1**, there have been cases in which a person who was not part of the directing mind and will of a company was identified with it, being part of the directing mind and will has always been the most common criterion for attribution, especially, as Leggatt LJ indicated in the passage from *R v Rozeik* [1996] 1 WLR 159 quoted in **19.8.2.1**, when what is being considered is the attribution of a state of mind to a company so as to make it liable for a criminal offence.

A famous description of the nature of a company's directing mind and will comes from a civil case. In *H L Bolton (Engineering) Co Ltd v T J Graham and Sons Ltd* [1957] 1 QB 159, a company applied for renewal of its lease of business premises under the provisions of the Landlord and Tenant Act 1954, part II. The landlord, T J Graham and Sons Ltd, sought to rely on s 30(1)(g) of the Act under which a landlord can oppose renewal of a lease on the ground that 'the landlord intends to occupy the holding for the purposes, or partly for the purposes, of a business to be carried on by him therein'. The tenant objected that the landlord did not in fact have that intention. There were three directors of the land-lord company, which was a wholly owned subsidiary of another company. The three directors only held board meetings once a year but they had all on many occasions discussed and approved an extensive redevelopment of the site in question. The judge at first instance found that the landlord company had evinced the necessary intention, and this finding was affirmed by the Court of Appeal, where Denning LJ, in a much quoted passage at p 172, indulged in some medieval anthropomorphism:

> A company may in many ways be likened to a human body. It has a brain and nerve centre which controls what it does. It also has hands which hold the tools and act in accordance with directions from the centre. Some of the people in the company are mere servants and agents who are nothing more than hands to do the work and cannot be said to represent the mind or will. Others are directors and managers who represent the directing mind and will of the company, and control what it does. The state of mind of these managers is the state of mind of the company and is treated by the law as such.

(For medieval anthropomorphic (or 'organological') conceptions of Church and State, see M Wolff, 'On the nature of legal persons' (1938) 54 LQR 494 at pp 498–9; E H Kantorowicz, *The King's Two Bodies* (Princeton NJ: Princeton University Press, 1957), Chapter 5.)

19.8.2.3 Delegation by the directing mind and will

In *Tesco Supermarkets Ltd v Nattrass* [1972] AC 153, Lord Reid said, at p 171:

> There have been attempts to apply Lord Denning's words to all servants of a company whose work is brain work, or who exercise some managerial discretion under the direction of superior officers of the company. I do not think that Lord Denning intended to refer to them. He only referred to those who 'represent the directing mind and will of the company, and control what it does'.
>
> I think that is right for this reason. Normally the board of directors, the managing director and perhaps other superior officers of a company carry out the functions of management and speak and act as the company. Their subordinates do not. They carry out orders from above and it can make no difference that they are given some measure of discretion. But the board of directors may delegate some part of their functions of management giving to their delegate full discretion to act independently of instructions from them. I see no difficulty in holding that they have thereby put such a delegate in their place so that within the scope of the delegation he can act as the company. It may not always be easy to draw the line but there are cases in which the line must be drawn.

In some cases it has been necessary to attribute to a company the acts or thoughts of individuals who were not part of its directing mind and will, because otherwise the persons who formed its directing mind and will could insulate the company from liability by delegating their functions. Two examples are *Director General of Fair Trading v Pioneer Concrete (UK) Ltd* [1995] 1 AC 456 and *Bank of India v Morris* [2005] EWCA Civ 693, [2005] 2 BCLC 328.

In *Director General of Fair Trading v Pioneer Concrete (UK) Ltd* the Director General had obtained a court order under the Restrictive Trade Practices Act 1976, s 35(3), against Pioneer Concrete and other companies restraining them from giving effect to agreements which restricted competition among them in the supply of ready-mixed concrete. The companies had been fined for being in contempt of court by disobeying these orders. By s 35(4) an order could only have been made against any of the companies if it was a 'person party to the agreement'. Pioneer claimed that the agreements in question had been entered into by its employees (an area manager and plant manager) with employees of the other companies, against the express prohibition of their employers. So it was claimed that Pioneer was not a party to the agreement and no order could have been made against it. The House of Lords rejected this argument. Lord Nolan said, at p 475:

> The Act is not concerned with what the employer says but with what the employee does in entering into business transactions in the course of his employment. The plain purpose of s 35(3) is to deter the

implementation of agreements or arrangements by which the public interest is harmed, and the subsection can only achieve that purpose if it is applied to the actions of the individuals within the business organisation who make and give effect to the relevant agreement or arrangement on its behalf.

(The Restrictive Trade Practices Act 1976 was repealed by the Competition Act 1998, which made new provision for controlling anti-competitive practices.)

In **Bank of India v Morris** the Court of Appeal considered whether the knowledge of someone who was not a director of a company should be attributed to it so as to make it liable under the Insolvency Act 1986, s 213, for knowingly being a party to another company's fraudulent trading. The court said:

[129] . . . the wording of, and policy behind, s 213 indicate that it would be inappropriate, in the case of a company, to limit attribution for its purposes to the board, or those specifically authorised by a resolution of the board. To limit it in such a way would be to ignore reality, and risk emasculating the effect of the provision.

[130] . . . it therefore must to some extent depend on the facts of each particular case whether an agent's knowledge should be attributed to the company for the purposes of s 213 . . . it must typically depend on factors such as these. The agent's importance or seniority in the hierarchy of the company: the more senior he is, the easier it is to attribute. His significance and freedom to act in the context of the particular transaction: the more it is 'his' transaction, and the more he is effectively left to get on with it by the board, the easier it is to attribute. The degree to which the board is informed, and the extent to which it can be said that it was, in the broadest sense, put on inquiry: the greater the grounds for suspicion or even concern or questioning, the easier it is to attribute, if questions were not raised or answers were too easily accepted by the board.

19.8.2.4 Terminology

Some commentators refer to the principle that one or more humans associated with a company form the directing mind and will of a company so that their actions, thoughts etc may be attributed to the company as the 'organic theory'. This was the terminology used in *Gower's Principles of Modern Company Law* (see fifth edn, pp 193–8, where it is explained that individuals identified with a company are treated as organic parts of the company), though it was dropped in the sixth edition. Other commentators refer to it as the 'alter ego theory', saying either that the person identified with the company is its alter ego (second self) or that the company is the alter ego of the person identified with it. In *UBAF Ltd v European American Banking Corporation* [1984] QB 713, the Court of Appeal said, at pp 719–20, that it found the description of a person as a company's 'alter ego', 'largely meaningless, save as an indication of some very wide but undefined authority'. In *Cristina v Seear* [1985] 2 EGLR 128, Purchas LJ was equally dubious about describing a company as an alter ego of its members.

19.8.3 WHEN ATTRIBUTION WILL NOT BE MADE

If a company has been the victim of wrongdoing by an individual who could otherwise be identified with the company, that wrongdoing will not be attributed to the company so as to prevent it claiming for the loss suffered as a result of the wrongdoing, at least where the company has gone into insolvent liquidation and the claim is made by the liquidator for the benefit of the creditors (*Bilta (UK) Ltd v Nazir (No 2)* [2015] UKSC 23, [2016] 1 AC 1). A solvent company may be able to ratify or consent to directors' breach of duty (see **16.16.2** to **16.16.4**).

In *Bilta (UK) Ltd v Nazir (No 2)* the liquidator of Bilta (UK) Ltd (which was insolvent) alleged that Bilta's directors had illegally conspired with a Swiss company and its chief executive to divert VAT, which Bilta collected from customers, to offshore bank accounts so that Bilta was unable to meet its obligation to remit the VAT to HMRC (a missing trader fraud). The Swiss company and its chief executive argued that the directors' dishonesty and knowledge of the fraud should be attributed to Bilta so that it could not recover compensation for what would be deemed to be its own dishonesty and illegal behaviour, (an illegality defence based on the rule, *ex turpi causa non oritur actio*, a legal claim does not arise from a base cause). The Supreme Court (agreeing with the courts below) held that attribution could not be made for that purpose. Similarly, in *Belmont Finance Corporation Ltd v Williams Furniture Ltd* [1979] Ch 250 it was held that knowledge by the claimant company's directors that they were part of a conspiracy to harm the company could not be attributed to the claimant company so as to make it one of the conspirators and therefore debar it from suing the others.

In *Re Hampshire Land Co* [1896] 2 Ch 743 the directors of Hampshire Land Co caused it to borrow money from the Portsea Island Building Society. Mr Wills was secretary of both the company and the building society, which, by the time this case was heard, were both being wound up. Under the company's constitution, its directors did not have actual authority to borrow as much as they did unless they were authorised by a general meeting. The appropriate resolution had been passed at a meeting, but the notice convening that meeting had not mentioned the resolution, as was required by the company's constitution. So the resolution was invalid and the borrowing was unauthorised. It seems that the error in the notice was Mr Wills's fault. As the law stood at that time, the building society could not recover an unauthorised loan unless it could rely on the indoor management rule (see **19.5.4.6**) to validate the loan. However, it could not rely on the indoor management rule if it knew that the directors lacked actual authority. The company claimed that Mr Wills's knowledge of the erroneous notice should be attributed to the building society of which he was secretary, so as to make the loan unenforceable. The court refused to do this. See also the similar case of *Re David Payne and Co Ltd* [1904] 2 Ch 608 (the facts of which are given in **19.5.4.4**). In those cases, and in *J C Houghton and Co v Nothard Lowe and Wills Ltd* [1928] AC 1, the reason given for not making the attribution was that the wrongdoer could not be expected to disclose the information to the company (through its directors) voluntarily and so should not be regarded as having a duty to disclose the information. This is inconsistent with the rule that breach of duty to a company by one of its directors must be disclosed to the company even though it would not be disclosed voluntarily (*Item Software (UK) Ltd v Fassihi* [2004] EWCA Civ 1244, [2005] ICR 450; see **16.6.13**). Also, in *Belmont Finance Corporation v Williams Furniture Ltd (No 2)* [1980] 1 All ER 393 (the facts of which are given in **10.8.1.4**), it was held that two directors and the secretary of City Industrial Finance Ltd were under a duty to disclose to it that they had arranged for it to sell its shares in a subsidiary for money provided by that subsidiary as illegal financial assistance for share purchase. Their knowledge was attributed to City Industrial Finance Ltd so that it could be declared to be a constructive trustee of the money it received for selling the shares. See also *Re Little Olympian Each-Ways Ltd (No 3)* [1995] 1 BCLC 636 discussed in **18.6.8.1**. Because of these inconsistencies it seems better to base the decision, whether or not to make an attribution, on the effect of the wrongdoing on the company rather than on absence of duty to the company.

It may be necessary to attribute an individual's knowledge of his or her own wrongdoing to a company in order to give effect to regulatory laws. See *Meridian Global Funds Management Asia Ltd v Securities Commission* [1995] 2 AC 500, discussed in **19.8.2.1** and *Moore v I Bresler Ltd* [1944] 2 All ER 515, discussed in **19.8.4.3**. This demonstrates that whether or not an individual's knowledge is attributed to a company depends on the purpose for which the attribution is to be made (per Lord Hoffmann in *Meridian Global Funds Management Asia Ltd v Securities Commission* at p 507).

An individual's knowledge of his or her own wrongdoing will be attributed to a company so that it can claim an illegality defence (*ex turpi causa non oritur actio*) if the individual is the only person beneficially interested in the company's shares (or if any other persons so interested are complicit in the wrongdoing) (*Stone and Rolls Ltd v Moore Stephens* [2009] UKHL 39, [2009] AC 1391). Stone and Rolls Ltd had been used by a Mr Stojevic, who was the only individual interested in its shares, to defraud a bank of over £90 million. It was held that a court could not hear a claim by the company suing its auditor for negligence in not discovering the fraud, because to do so would be assisting the company to benefit from its own illegal conduct. The company had argued that it should not be regarded as being at fault for this purpose, because Mr Stojevic's knowledge and criminal intent should not be attributed to it, but the majority of the Law Lords rejected this argument. If Mr Stojevic had carried out his fraud in his own name, instead of using a company, it would have been obvious that he could not have sued his own accountant for damages for not spotting the fraud. In the opinion of the majority, the same principle meant that a claim could not be made by a company which Mr Stojevic completely controlled. In *Bilta (UK) Ltd v Nazir (No 2)* the Supreme Court Justices discussed at length, and with considerable disagreement, the contrast between the case before them and *Stone and Rolls Ltd v Moore Stephens*. See also *Berg Sons and Co Ltd v Adams* [1993] BCLC 1045 discussed in **17.5.1**.

In Australia it has been held that it is not possible to aggregate the knowledge of various individuals identified with a company and infer from the aggregate knowledge that the company was dishonest (*Macquarie Bank Ltd v Sixty-fourth Throne Pty Ltd* [1998] 3 VR 133). This may be contrasted with aggregation in order to create vicarious liability for tort (see **19.7.2**).

19.8.4 CORPORATE CRIMINAL LIABILITY

19.8.4.1 Can a company be prosecuted for a criminal offence?

Two early cases involving statutory companies established that it is possible to bring criminal proceedings against a body corporate (*R v Birmingham and Gloucester Railway Co* (1842) 3 QB 223; *R v Great North of England Railway Co* (1846) 9 QB 315).

It may be argued that there is something about a particular offence which prevents a company being charged with it. For example, it may be said that the offence can be committed only by someone performing some physical action, which a company is incapable of—for example, a company cannot be convicted of an offence which can be committed only by driving a lorry (*Richmond London Borough Council v Pinn and Wheeler Ltd* [1989] RTR 354). It has been said that where the only punishment that can be ordered for an offence is corporal (such as the mandatory sentence of life imprisonment, custody for life or detention during Her Majesty's pleasure which must be ordered for murder), a court would not 'stultify itself by embarking on a trial [of a company for the offence] in which, if a verdict of guilty is returned, no effective order by way of sentence can be made' (*R v ICR Haulage Ltd* [1944] KB 551 at p 554). Whether or not a company may be guilty of a crime must be decided for each crime separately (*R v P and O European Ferries (Dover) Ltd* (1990) 93 Cr App R 72 per Turner J at p 84). Many would say that Parliament is the proper forum for deciding such fundamental questions of criminal liability but Parliament has given no general guidance on the question, and the courts have proceeded cautiously.

In New Zealand, homicide is defined by statute as the killing of a human being by another human being, and it was held in *R v Murray Wright Ltd* [1970] NZLR 476 that this statutory wording precluded the indictment of a non-human entity for manslaughter.

In Canada it has been held that a company on trial for a criminal offence cannot call evidence that it is of good character: it is in the nature of a corporation that it does not have a character and the character of humans associated with the corporation cannot be attributed to it (*R v Deslauriers* [1993] 2 WWR 401).

It used to be thought that a company could not be charged with an offence which had a mental element requiring proof of a criminal state of mind (*mens rea*) (see per Channell J in *Pearks, Gunston and Tee Ltd v Ward* [1902] 2 KB 1 at p 11). However, in *Director of Public Prosecutions v Kent and Sussex Contractors Ltd* [1944] KB 146, it was held that the identification theory (see **19.8.1**) could be used to make a company liable for such an offence. In ***Director of Public Prosecutions v Kent and Sussex Contractors Ltd***, the company's transport manager had signed a false statement of the distance that had been travelled by one of the company's vehicles, presumably in order to obtain an increased allocation of petrol under the rationing scheme then in force. The company was charged with two offences under the Defence (General) Regulations 1939: that, for the purposes of the petrol-rationing scheme, it had made use of a document which was false in a material particular, with intent to deceive; and that, in furnishing information for the purposes of the scheme, it made a statement which it knew to be false in a material particular. The magistrates' court refused to convict, saying that a limited company could not have an 'intent to deceive' and could not 'know' that a statement was false. The divisional court allowed the prosecutor's appeal. Macnaghten J at p 156, said:

> It is true that a corporation can only have knowledge and form an intention through its human agents, but circumstances may be such that the knowledge and intention of the agent must be imputed to the body corporate.

Viscount Caldecote CJ said, at p 155: 'The officers are the company for this purpose'. See further *R v ICR Haulage Ltd* [1944] KB 551, in which the Court of Criminal Appeal held that the company had been rightly convicted of a common-law conspiracy to defraud. Use of the identification theory to make a company criminally liable had been approved in the Canadian courts before it was adopted in England: see *R v Fane Robinson Ltd* [1941] 3 DLR 409, which was also a case of conspiracy to defraud. The possibility of using the identification theory to make a company criminally liable had been put forward in an article by C R N Winn, 'The criminal responsibility of corporations' (1929) 3 CLJ 398.

In *Tesco Supermarkets Ltd v Nattrass* [1972] AC 153, Lord Reid said, at p 170:

> A living person has a mind which can have knowledge or intention or be negligent and he has hands to carry out his intentions. A corporation has none of these: it must act through living persons, though not always one or the same person. Then the person who acts is not speaking or acting for the company. He is acting as the company and his mind which directs his acts is the mind of the company ... He is an embodiment of the company or, one could say, he hears and speaks through the persona of the company, within his appropriate sphere, and his mind is the mind of the company. If it is a guilty mind then that guilt is the guilt of the company.

At p 173, Lord Reid criticised a statement in *R v ICR Haulage Ltd* at p 559 that the liability of a company for a criminal act of an individual identified with the company depends on the nature of the charge. In Lord Reid's view:

> If the guilty man was in law identifiable with the company then whether his offence was serious or venial his act was the act of the company but if he was not so identifiable then no act of his, serious or otherwise, was the act of the company itself.

19.8.4.2 Whose acts or thoughts will be attributed to a company to make it criminally liable?

As is clear from what Lord Reid said in *Tesco Supermarkets Ltd v Nattrass* [1972] AC 153 at p 170, quoted in **19.8.4.1**, being part of, or constituting, the directing mind and will of the company is the usual criterion for identifying an individual with a company for the purpose of making it criminally liable (see **19.8.2.2**).

In *Tesco Supermarkets Ltd v Nattrass*, the company was charged under the Trade Descriptions Act 1968, s 11, with the offence of advertising goods for sale at a price less than that at which they were in fact offered for sale. The offence was committed at the company's store at Northwich near Manchester. The company would have had a defence to the charge if it could prove that the commission of the offence was due to the act or default of 'another person' and that it took all reasonable precautions and exercised all due diligence to avoid the commission of such an offence by itself or any person under its control (Trade Descriptions Act 1968, s 24(1)). The prosecutor said that the company could not claim this defence because the manager of its Northwich store, who the prosecutor claimed should be identified with the company, had clearly not avoided committing the offence. The House of Lords allowed Tesco's appeal against conviction, saying that the store manager was not identified with the company but was 'another person', and the people who were identified with the company had taken all reasonable precautions and exercised all due diligence. The crucial factor in these findings seems to have been that the company had more than 800 store managers. The bigger the company the easier it is to escape liability. The Trade Descriptions Act 1968, s 11, has since been repealed. Provisions concerning misleading pricing are now made by the Consumer Protection Act 1987, part III (ss 20 to 26). The 1987 Act provides a due diligence defence in s 39. An offence under the new provisions can be committed by a person only 'in the course of any business of his'. Where a business owner has employees, anything they do which results in misleading pricing of the business's goods will be done in the course of the owner's business not the employees' business and so the employees cannot be guilty of offences under the new provisions (*R v Warwickshire County Council, ex parte Johnson* [1993] AC 583). As a large corporate employer (in *Ex parte Johnson* it was Dixons) will usually be able to escape liability under the principles laid down in *Tesco Supermarkets Ltd v Nattrass*, many instances of misleading pricing cannot now be prosecuted (see I Brown, 'Corporate criminal liability and consumer protection' [1993] LMCLQ 158).

It has been said that prosecutors are dealing with the problem of making large companies criminally liable by seeking to persuade the courts to identify more junior employees with their companies (G Forlin, 'Directing minds: caught in a trap' (2004) 154 NLJ 326).

When determining whether a company has criminal liability the courts have been unwilling to make the knowledge of an employee about some subject the knowledge of the company merely because it was the employee's job to deal with that subject. *Moore v I Bresler Ltd* [1944] 2 All ER 515 and *Meridian Global Funds Management Asia Ltd v Securities Commission* [1995] 2 AC 500 (see **19.8.2.1**) are rare exceptions. In *John Henshall (Quarries) Ltd v Harvey* [1965] 2 QB 233, a weighbridge operator employed by John Henshall (Quarries) Ltd at one of its quarries permitted a lorry to leave the quarry even though it exceeded the maximum permitted weight. One of his duties was to see that lorries were not overweight, and the quarry manager periodically checked that this rule was being observed. The haulage contractor was convicted of the offence of using an overweight lorry and the quarry company was charged with aiding, abetting, counselling and procuring the contractor's offence. It was accepted that the weighbridge operator took no part in the general management of the company. The Divisional Court held that therefore he could not be identified with the company so that his knowledge that an offence had been committed by the contractor could not be attributed to the company. Accordingly the company could not be guilty of aiding, abetting, counselling and procuring the contractor's offence. In *Airtours plc v Shipley* (1994) 158 JP 835, the directors of a company had established what was admitted to be a good system for ensuring that no errors appeared in the company's holiday brochures but they never checked any brochures themselves, leaving that to persons employed to perform that task. When a mistake did appear in a brochure, contravening the Trade Descriptions Act 1968, s 14, it was held that the directors had not delegated to the responsible employee their management functions as envisaged in the statement by Lord Reid in *Tesco Supermarkets Ltd v Nattrass* quoted earlier. Accordingly no one who could be identified with the company had committed the offence and the company was not guilty of it.

It is often suggested that crimes are committed in the course of business conducted by companies because of organisational failures. The Corporate Manslaughter and Corporate Homicide Act 2007 seeks to deal with this by concentrating on the way in which a company's activities are managed or organised by its senior management (see **19.8.4.8**). But the organisation which is seen to fail is the organisation of the company's business, not the association of members which forms the company in law. The traditional approach of the courts has been to find a company liable for the criminal failings of its business organisation if either the crime was one for which the company could be held vicariously liable or the crime was intended by the directors who are at the interface of the company as it is conceived in law and the organisation which conducts the company's business.

19.8.4.3 Acting against the company

In *Moore v I Bresler Ltd* [1944] 2 All ER 515, it was held that a company had been rightly convicted of making false tax returns with intent to deceive when the company officials who had prepared the returns had falsified them in order to disguise their own fraud against the company. The Law Commission has proposed in its draft Criminal Code Bill (Law Com No 177) that a company should not be guilty of an offence by virtue of one of its officers acting with the intention of doing harm, or of concealing harm done by that officer, or another person, to the corporation (see cl 30(6) of the draft Bill). See also **19.8.3**.

19.8.4.4 Crime committed by an agent of a company

Just as an individual can be guilty of a crime if he or she instructs another to commit it, so a company which obtains the commission of a crime by an agent can be guilty of the crime. The agent who commits the criminal act may have no criminal intent and so be innocent but the company will be guilty if an individual identified with the company has the necessary criminal intent. In *Deutsche Genossenschaftsbank v Burnhope* [1995] 1 WLR 1580 it was accepted (though ultimately the point was not necessary for the decision in the case) that a company had been guilty of theft of property from a bank because the chairman of the company (who was identified with it) had the dishonest intention of permanently depriving the bank of the property, though the actual appropriation of the property was carried out by an innocent employee who was unaware of the chairman's plan. However, this point was obiter because the case was concerned with an insurer's liability for the bank's loss and it was held that the insurance policy did not cover thefts by companies. The policy referred to thefts by persons present on the bank's premises. The innocent employee had performed the appropriation on the bank's premises but the chairman was not with him. The bank argued that in the policy, the word 'person' included a company because of the Law of Property Act 1925, s 61, which provides that in contracts 'person' includes a corporation unless the context otherwise requires. But a majority of the House of Lords held that the context of this insurance policy did otherwise require: the policy was concerned only with physically present thieves not a thief deemed in law to be present by an application of the identification theory, and in any case Lords Keith of Kinkel, Lloyd of Berwick and Nicholls of Birkenhead thought that the innocent employee was not identified with the company so that it was not present on the bank's premises.

19.8.4.5 Other ways of imposing criminal liability on a company

It is often difficult to prosecute a company for a criminal offence using the identification theory, especially if the company is large (see **19.8.4.2**). Some criminal offences are defined in ways that avoid the need to use the identification theory. There are two general principles of criminal law which can be used for this purpose. They are strict liability (see **19.8.4.6**) and vicarious liability (see **19.8.4.7**). Recently two offences have been specially defined to impose criminal liability for organisational failure. They are corporate manslaughter (see **19.8.4.8**) and failure to prevent bribery (see **19.8.4.9**).

19.8.4.6 Strict liability

The usual principle of English criminal law is that there cannot be a conviction of a person accused of a crime without proving that the person had a criminal state of mind (*mens rea*) when performing the prohibited act. The identification theory is needed to attribute to a company the criminal state of mind of individuals. But there are many offences which do not have any mental element. They are often called offences of strict liability. For example, in *Alphacell Ltd v Woodward* [1972] AC 824, the company operated a factory in which paper was made. The layout of the plant was such that if two pumps failed, waste material from the paper-making process would be discharged into a river. The pumps failed and the river was polluted by the waste material. The House of Lords dismissed the company's appeal against conviction for causing polluting matter to enter a stream contrary to the Rivers (Prevention of Pollution) Act 1951, s 2 (since repealed and replaced by the Water Resources Act 1991, s 85). The company had caused the pollutant to enter the river and this was sufficient to make it guilty of the offence: it was not necessary to ask whether the company 'knew' that it was polluting the river.

If a company is accused of an offence of strict liability, it is unnecessary to prove that individuals who can be identified with the company were responsible for committing the offence. In *R v Gateway Foodmarkets Ltd* [1997] 3 All ER 78 the Court of Appeal dismissed Gateway's appeal against conviction of the offence of failing to ensure, so far as is reasonably practicable, the health, safety and welfare at work of all its employees, contrary to the Health and Safety at Work etc Act 1974, ss 2(1) and 33(1). The court held that this is an offence of strict liability. So it was irrelevant that the failure that had caused the commission of the offence was of a shop manager who, Gateway claimed, was not part of its directing mind and will. See also *R v British Steel plc* [1995] 1 WLR 1356 and *R v Nelson Group Services (Maintenance) Ltd* [1999] 1 WLR 1526 on s 3(1) of the 1974 Act. In order for a defendant company to show that it has done everything reasonably practicable to ensure compliance with s 2 or 3, it must do more than show just that people who form its directing mind and will have done everything reasonably practicable: it must show that all reasonable precautions were taken both by it and by its employees and agents on its behalf (*R v Gateway Foodmarkets Ltd*). However, the court is not permitted to conclude, from the mere fact that someone in the company's organisation has failed to do everything reasonably practicable, that the company has failed (*R v Nelson Group Services (Maintenance) Ltd*).

Unless the question is settled by statute, it is for the courts to decide whether an offence is one of strict liability. The courts have found strict liability particularly appropriate where criminal penalties are invoked to enforce regulation of economic activity of general public importance. This is the type of offence with which companies are most often charged and so strict liability is particularly important to companies. Nevertheless, strict liability is a characteristic of an offence and is a general concept of criminal law not company law. If an offence is one of strict liability, it is unnecessary to examine the mental state of any person on trial for the offence, whether the accused is a natural person or a company. Deciding to make an offence one of strict liability will facilitate the conviction of companies but will also affect the trials of natural persons.

19.8.4.7 Vicarious liability

Another concept of criminal law that is of great significance for companies is vicarious liability, which imposes criminal liability on the employer of an individual who commits an offence while acting within the course and scope of his or her employment. A company employer may be convicted of a vicarious-liability offence committed by its employee (see, for example, *Pearks, Gunston and Tee Ltd v Ward* [1902] 2 KB 1). As with strict liability (see **19.8.4.6**), whether an offence is one of vicarious liability must be decided by the courts unless the question is settled by statute. The courts tend to impose vicarious liability for the same sort of regulatory offences for which strict liability is imposed. For example, in *National Rivers Authority v Alfred McAlpine Homes East Ltd* [1994] 4 All ER 286 it was held that if a company's employees, acting within the course and scope of their employment, had caused polluting matter to enter controlled waters contrary to the Water Resources Act 1991, s 85, the company would be guilty of an offence under that section regardless of whether the employees were sufficiently senior to be part of its directing mind and will. The company would be vicariously liable for its employees' breach of the law, whatever their position in the company, not directly liable because of being identified with those employees. Nevertheless, in *Seaboard Offshore Ltd v Secretary of State for Transport* [1994] 1 WLR 541, in which the offence of failure by a shipowner to secure that a ship is operated in a safe manner (Merchant Shipping Act 1995, s 100) was held not to be a vicarious-liability offence, Lord Keith of Kinkel (at p 546) emphasised that vicarious and strict liability are separate concepts.

In relation to many vicarious-liability offences, Parliament has provided employers with a 'due diligence' defence—that is, the employer is relieved of liability if it is shown that the employer had exercised all due diligence to avoid commission of the offence; see *Tesco Supermarkets Ltd v Nattrass* [1972] AC 153 discussed in **19.8.4.2**.

In *Mousell Bros v London and North-Western Railway Co* [1917] 2 KB 836 a company was made vicariously liable for an offence committed by its employee even though the definition of the offence required it to be committed 'with intent'. According to Atkin J, at p 846, it was sufficient that the employee had the intent so that the offence was committed: the employer was then vicariously liable for the offence that had been committed. However, in *Vane v Yiannopoullos* [1965] AC 486 the House of Lords held that, unless otherwise specified by statute, there could be no vicarious liability for an offence with a mental element unless the employer's proprietary or managerial functions had been delegated to the employee who committed the offence. In **Vane v Yiannopoullos** Lord Evershed glossed over *Mousell Bros v London and North-Western Railway Co*, saying that intent, unlike knowledge, was not '*mens rea* in a real sense'.

Sometimes a statute creating an offence with strict and vicarious liability creates a defence for an employer which depends on the state of mind of the employee who carried out the prohibited act. For example, in *Tesco Stores Ltd v Brent London Borough Council* [1993] 1 WLR 1037, Tesco was convicted of supplying an 18 certificate video to a person under 18 contrary to the Video Recordings Act 1984, s 11. This is a strict-liability offence but s 11(2)(b) provides a defence if 'the accused' neither knew nor had reasonable grounds to believe that the person supplied was under 18. Tesco was vicariously liable for a supply made by a check-out operator but claimed that it was entitled to the s 11(2)(b) defence because none of the individuals who could be identified with it knew anything at all about the person supplied. It was held that 'the accused' in s 11(2)(b) had to be construed as meaning the employee who did the prohibited act, because otherwise a large company like Tesco could never be convicted. Indeed any owner of a business, whether a natural or a legal person, who did not serve customers personally could escape prosecution. The same view was taken in Australia in *Woolworths Ltd v Luff* (1988) 77 ACTR 1 (in relation to an offence of selling alcohol to a person under 18) and in England in *Chuter v Freeth and Pocock Ltd* [1911] 2 KB 832, which was not cited in either the *Tesco* or the *Woolworths* case. For further discussion see C Wells, 'Corporate liability and consumer protection: *Tesco v Nattrass* revisited' (1994) 57 MLR 817.

As with strict liability, vicarious liability is a concept of criminal law not company law. Whether an offence should be one of vicarious liability depends on whether employers generally should be required to control and take responsibility for the actions of their employees.

19.8.4.8 Corporate killing

Until 2008, a company could be guilty of manslaughter, that is, unintentionally killing an individual by an unlawful act or by gross negligence (*R v P and O European Ferries (Dover) Ltd* (1990) 93 Cr App R 72). However, a company could be found guilty of manslaughter only by being identified with an individual who was guilty of the crime (*Attorney-General's Reference (No 2 of 1999)* [2000] QB 796). In practice this will only happen where a company is controlled and operated entirely by one individual. In a larger company, a death may occur because unsafe practices are accepted generally in the company, but without any one individual being so directly involved in the death as to be guilty of manslaughter. After much public dissatisfaction with this situation, Parliament eventually passed the Corporate Manslaughter and Corporate Homicide Act 2007.

By s 1 of the 2007 Act, the offence of corporate manslaughter (corporate homicide in Scotland) is committed by a company if the way in which its activities are managed or organised:

(a) causes a person's death; and

(b) amounts to a gross breach of a relevant duty of care owed by the company to that person.

A 'gross breach' of a duty is defined as conduct falling 'far below' what can reasonably be expected of the company in the circumstances (s 1(4)(b)). A company is guilty of the offence only if the way in which its activities are managed or organised by its senior management is a substantial element in the breach of the duty of care (s 1(3)). 'Senior management' is defined in s 1(4)(c) as persons who play significant roles in:

(a) making decisions about how the whole or a substantial part of the company's activities are to be managed or organised; or

(b) the actual managing or organising of the whole or a substantial part of those activities.

The punishment for the offence is a fine (s 1(6)) and the court may order the company to take specified steps, within a specified time, to remedy the breach of duty and any other resultant cause of the victim's death (s 9). The court may also make a publicity order requiring the company to publicise the conviction, particulars of the offence, the amount of the fine and the terms of any remedial order (s 10). The Sentencing Council has published a definitive guideline on corporate manslaughter sentences (along with health and safety and food safety and hygiene offences) which has been effective since 1 February 2016. It seems that, in practice, fines have been lower than suggested by previous guidelines. See S Field and L Jones, 'The Corporate Manslaughter and Corporate Homicide Act 2007 and the sentencing guidelines for corporate manslaughter: more bark than bite?' (2015) 36 Co Law 327. The article also points out that the Act has so far only been used against small companies rather than the large companies for which it was designed.

19.8.4.9 Failure to prevent bribery

The Bribery Act 2010, s 7, creates a new offence of failure of a commercial organisation to prevent bribery. Only a 'relevant commercial organisation' can be prosecuted for this offence (s 7(1)). For this purpose relevant commercial organisations include a company or other body which is incorporated under the law of any part of the United Kingdom and which carries on a business (whether in the United Kingdom or elsewhere) (s 7(5)). Relevant commercial organisations also include a UK partnership which carries on a business anywhere in the world, and any foreign corporation or partnership which carries on a business in the United Kingdom (s 7(5)). A trade or profession is a business (s 7(5)).

The s 7 offence is committed by a relevant commercial organisation if a person 'associated' with the organisation bribes another person intending:

(a) to obtain or retain business for the organisation; or

(b) to obtain or retain an advantage in the conduct of business for the organisation (s 7(1)).

It is a defence for the organisation to prove that it had in place adequate procedures designed to prevent persons associated with it from undertaking such conduct (s 7(2)). It is because of this crucial defence that the offence is described as failure to prevent bribery.

For the s 7 offence to be committed, the bribe in question must itself be an offence under ss 1 to 6 of the Act, whether or not there is a prosecution for it (s 7(3)).

Any person who performs services for or on behalf of a relevant commercial organisation (apart from the bribe in question) is 'associated' with that organisation (s 8(1)). This can include employees (who are presumed to be associated, unless the contrary is shown), agents, and subsidiaries (s 8(3) and (5)).

The Secretary of State must publish guidance about procedures that relevant commercial organisations can put in place to prevent persons associated with them from bribing (s 9). This guidance was published by the Ministry of Justice (MoJ) in March 2011 and is available at the MoJ's website, **www.justice.gov.uk/downloads/legislation/bribery-act-2010-guidance.pdf**.

The Criminal Finances Act 2017, ss 45 and 46, create new 'failure to prevent' offences of failure to prevent facilitation of UK tax evasion and failure to prevent facilitation of foreign tax evasion. Again, government guidance must be published, this time by the Chancellor of the Exchequer (s 47).

19.8.4.10 Sentencing

The problems of finding an appropriate way of punishing a company are discussed in G Slapper, 'Corporate punishment' (1994) 144 NLJ 29. The Court of Appeal gave guidance on sentencing for offences under the Health and Safety at Work etc Act 1974 in *R v F Howe and Son (Engineers) Ltd* [1999] IRLR 434 and revisited the question in *R v Balfour Beatty Rail Infrastructure Services Ltd* [2006] EWCA Crim 1586, [2007] Bus LR 77. In between those cases, the Criminal Justice Act 2003, s 142, created a statutory statement of the purposes of sentencing as:

(a) the punishment of offenders;

(b) the reduction of crime (including its reduction by deterrence);

(c) the reform and rehabilitation of offenders;

(d) the protection of the public; and

(e) the making of reparation by offenders to persons affected by their offences.

In the ***Balfour Beatty*** case the Court of Appeal observed, at [41], that most of these can be applied to a company offender, but said that 'there are obvious difficulties' in looking for reform and rehabilitation. This is somewhat dispiriting, as companies convicted of offences typically continue to carry on their businesses after conviction.

In *R v Rollco Screw and Rivet Co Ltd* [1999] IRLR 439 the court observed that imposing a fine on a company necessarily punishes its shareholders. It is common for the shareholders and directors of a small company to be the same individuals. If both company and directors have been convicted of an offence and the directors are fined, the fine imposed on the company should not in effect be a double punishment of the shareholder-directors (*R v Rollco Screw and Rivet Co Ltd*). A large company should be required to pay a fine immediately (*R v B & Q plc* [2005] EWCA Crim 2297, *The Times*, 3 November 2005).

In *R v Thames Water Utilities Ltd* [2015] EWCA Crim 960, [2015] 1 WLR 4411, the Court of Appeal observed that a fine for environmental damage caused by a very large company could be as great as 100 per cent of the company's pre-tax net profit for the year in question, even if this would result in a fine of £100 million or more. The court described a £250,000 fine for the company's 163rd environmental offence (since 1991) as 'lenient' and said they 'would have had no hesitation in upholding a very substantially higher fine'. On 22 March 2017 at Aylesbury Crown Court the company was fined £9 million for one similar offence and £8 million for another. Further lesser offences brought the total penalty to £19.75 million plus costs (Environment Agency Press Release, 22 March 2017, 'Thames Water ordered to pay record £20 million for river pollution').

19.8.4.11 Responsibility of officers for a company's crime

The discussion so far in **19.8.4** has been concerned with the ways in which the criminal law makes a company liable for criminal acts committed in the course of its activities. Another problem for the criminal law is to ensure that when a criminal offence is committed in the course of a company's business, liability can be imposed on the human beings who caused it to commit the offence. Under the common law, it is an offence to aid, abet, counsel or procure the commission of any offence. Nevertheless, it is nowadays standard practice in statutes creating offences to make a provision like IA 1986, s 432(2), that the fact that a company is guilty of the offence does not preclude prosecution of 'any director, manager, secretary or other similar officer . . . or any person who was purporting to act in any such capacity' if the offence 'is proved to have been committed with the consent or connivance of, or to be attributable to any neglect' on his or her part. Such officer is deemed to be liable as a principal. Under such a provision, it would seem that if an individual who is identified with a company commits an offence then that individual and the company can both be convicted as principals in respect of the same act. This has been accepted under somewhat different provisions of Australian law (*Hamilton v Whitehead* (1988) 166 CLR 121). 'Manager' in such a provision means a person who has the management of the whole affairs of the company, is in a position of real authority and has the power and responsibility to decide corporate policy and strategy (*R v Boal* [1992] QB 591).

The court is sometimes willing to stretch legal concepts to impose criminal liability on company directors. *Brown v Director of Public Prosecutions* (1998) 162 JP 333 concerned the Sexual Offences (Amendment) Act 1976, s 4, which provided that if the name or address of the victim of a rape offence was published in England and Wales in a written publication available to the public, any proprietor, any editor and any publisher of the newspaper or periodical was guilty of an offence. A newspaper owned by a company published information in contravention of the provision and it was held that the company's managing director, who did not take part in the editing of the newspaper, had been rightly convicted as the 'publisher' of the newspaper. (As from 7 October 2004, s 4 of the 1976 Act has been repealed and replaced by more comprehensive provisions in amended sections of the Sexual Offences (Amendment) Act 1992. Like the 1976 Act, s 5(1)(a) of the 1992 Act also imposes liability on any proprietor, any editor and any publisher of a newspaper or periodical.) In *Jones v Hellard* [1998] PNLR 484 the chief executive of a company which provided adjudication and arbitration services wrote a letter on its notepaper setting out the terms on which he would act as arbitrator in a building dispute. He added to his signature the letters FRIBA, meaning fellow of the Royal Institute of British Architects. In fact his membership of the Institute and registration as an architect had lapsed. He was charged with practising or carrying on business under a name, style or title containing the word 'architect' while not registered with the Architects Registration Board, contrary to what is now the Architects Act 1997, s 20. The Divisional Court held that he was offering his own services, not his company's, so that he had used the false description while carrying on business.

Unusually, a penalty imposed on a company by the Competition and Markets Authority (CMA) for infringement of the Competition Act 1998, part 1, chapter 1 (prohibition of agreements preventing, restricting or distorting competition) is imposed on the company alone and not on the directors who may have caused the infringement. The company cannot sue its directors to recover the penalty from them, because such a claim is forbidden by the *ex turpi causa* principle (see **19.8.3**). The liability is imposed on the company directly by statute and not by attribution or vicarious liability (*Safeway Stores Ltd v Twigger* [2010] EWCA Civ 1472, [2011] Bus LR 1629). In *Bilta (UK) Ltd v Nazir (No 2)* [2015] UKSC 23, [2016] 1 AC 1, Lord Sumption (at [83]) thought that the only justification for the decision in *Safeway Stores Ltd v Twigger* is that the CMA could not have imposed a penalty on the directors (but it can bring director disqualification proceedings, see **20.13.2.10**). Lord Mance (at [52]) and Lords Toulson and Hodge (at [156] to [162]) expressed greater disquiet with the decision.

19.8.5 DOUBLE-COUNTING; THEFT FROM A COMPANY

The act of an individual who is identified with a company, because of being the directing mind and will of the company, the very ego and centre of the personality of the company, may be attributed to the company to create its liability for the act. The individual in question cannot then be guilty of conspiring with the company to commit the act: conspiracy requires two or more guilty minds but under the identification theory there is only one guilty mind, the mind of the human whose guilty thoughts are attributed to the company (*R v McDonnell* [1966] 1 QB 233). For a detailed exploration of this topic, including the difficult question of whether a company can conspire with two or more of its directors, see M R Goode, 'Corporate conspiracy: problems of *mens rea* and the parties to the agreement' (1975) 2 Dalhousie LJ 121.

There has been much debate about whether it is correct to convict, for theft, a person who owns all the shares in a company and has taken its property, otherwise than in a way permitted by company law. In England and Wales, the Court of Appeal decided in *Attorney-General's Reference (No 2 of 1982)* [1984] QB 624 and *R v Philippou* (1989) 89 Cr App R 290 that conviction for theft is possible if the accused acted dishonestly, which is a question for the jury. The Theft Act 1968, s 1(1), provides that a person is guilty of theft 'if he dishonestly appropriates property belonging to another with the intention of permanently depriving the other of it'.

If persons, who between them represent the directing mind and will of a company, dishonestly appropriate the company's property, they cannot rely on the doctrine that their minds are the minds of the company to deem that the company has consented to what they have done (*Attorney-General's Reference (No 2 of 1982)*) or authorised it (*R v Philippou*). As the Court of Appeal made clear in *Attorney-General's Reference (No 2 of 1982)* at p 640, the identification theory does not apply to offences committed against the company itself or to illegal or dishonest actions in relation to the company. In particular, they cannot rely on the Theft Act 1968, s 2(1)(b), which provides that 'A person's appropriation of property belonging to another is not to be regarded as dishonest . . . if he appropriates the property in the belief that he would have the other's consent if the other knew of the appropriation and the circumstances of it'. Persons who between them represent the directing mind and will of a company cannot rely on s 2(1)(b) to negate the dishonesty of their appropriation of the company's property if the only consent they can allege is the consent of themselves which they say should be deemed to be the company's consent by virtue of the identification theory, for in those circumstances there is no consent by an 'other', only their own consent (*Attorney-General's Reference (No 2 of 1982)*).

The Court of Criminal Appeal of Victoria took the opposite view in *R v Roffel* [1985] VR 511, saying that the accused can not only say that the company 'consented' to what they did because their consent can be attributed to the company, but also that the consent means that there has been no 'appropriation' as that term is used in the statutory definition of theft. The House of Lords has since made it clear in *Director of Public Prosecutions v Gomez* [1993] AC 442 that an action can be an appropriation of an owner's property for the purposes of the Theft Act 1968 despite the owner's consent to the action. Lord Browne-Wilkinson said, at pp 496–7, that in his judgment *R v Roffel* was wrongly decided and the law was correctly stated in *Attorney-General's Reference (No 2 of 1982)* and *R v Philippou*.

In *R (A) v Snaresbrook Crown Court* (2001) *The Times*, 12 July 2001, the Administrative Court held that a director of a company can be guilty of stealing property from the company, despite the taking of the property being authorised by all the company's directors, if the taking was dishonest, which is a question for the jury to decide.

Two articles discuss the question further. D W Elliott, 'Directors' thefts and dishonesty' [1991] Crim LR 732 suggests that where people who own all the shares in a company have taken its money, otherwise than in a way permitted by company law, they have not been dishonest so that there can be no conviction of theft. G Virgo, 'Stealing from the small family business' [1991] CLJ 464, on the other hand, believes that conviction for theft is possible and is a proper deterrent to abuse of the corporate form, especially where creditors are prejudiced.

19.8.6 FURTHER DISCUSSION OF CORPORATE CRIMINAL LIABILITY

The Law Commission's consultation paper, *Criminal Liability in Regulatory Contexts* (Consultation Paper No 195, 2010) is a wide-ranging discussion of many issues concerning corporate criminal responsibility. See especially Chapter 5 and appendices A, B and C by Professors Julia Black, Peter Cartwright and Celia Wells. There is another very good discussion of the principles of corporate criminal liability in the Law Commission's earlier paper, *Legislating the Criminal Code: Involuntary Manslaughter* (Law Com No 237, House of Commons Papers, Session 1995–6, 171) (London: HMSO, 1996).

The identification theory of corporate criminal liability sometimes seems too fragile to survive. Some commentators argue that it is merely a restricted version of the theory of vicarious liability (G R Sullivan, 'The attribution of culpability to limited companies' [1996] CLJ 515; R J Wickins and C A Ong, 'Confusion worse confounded: the end of the directing mind theory?' [1997] JBL 524). Some argue that a company is a person capable of moral responsibility and accountability, which can therefore be criminally liable (P A French, *Collective and Corporate Responsibility* (New York: Columbia University Press, 1984); M B Metzger and D R Dalton, 'Seeing the elephant: an organisational perspective on corporate moral agency' (1996) 33 Am Bus LJ 489; P A French, 'Integrity, intentions, and corporations' (1996) 34 Am Bus LJ 141), but this is rejected by Sullivan, 'The attribution of culpability to limited companies'. For some, companies should never be subject to criminal proceedings (D R Fischel and A O Sykes, 'Corporate crime' (1996) 25 J Legal Stud 319).

For other extensive discussions see L H Leigh, *The Criminal Liability of Corporations in English Law* (LSE Research Monographs 2) (London: London School of Economics and Political Science; Weidenfeld and Nicolson, 1969); *Tesco Supermarkets Ltd v Nattrass* [1972] AC 153; L H Leigh, 'The criminal liability of corporations and other groups' (1977) 9 Ottawa L Rev 247; *Canadian Dredge and Dock Co Ltd v R* (1985) 19 DLR (4th) 314; B Fisse and J Braithwaite, 'The allocation of responsibility for corporate crime: individualism, collectivism and accountability' (1988) 11 Syd LR 468; C Wells, *Corporations and Criminal Responsibility* (Oxford: Clarendon Press, 1993); C M V Clarkson, 'Kicking corporate bodies and damning their souls' (1996) 59 MLR 557.

19.8.7 RESIDENCE

19.8.7.1 Two tests

In order to apply the concept of residence to a company, the courts have formulated two tests:

(a) a company is resident where its central management and control is (it has become a tradition among lawyers that the apparently compound term 'central management and control' is treated as grammatically singular); and

(b) a company is resident (or present) in a particular location if its business, or other corporate activity, is carried on, either by itself or by an agent, at or from a fixed place of business in that location, for more than a minimal period of time.

The two tests focus on opposite ends of a company's operational structure. The central management and control test looks at the top of the company to find where its controllers are. It is used as a test of liability to tax (see **19.8.7.2**) and liability to give security for costs when bringing a legal claim (see **19.8.7.4**). The carrying on business test looks at the location of places where the company's everyday business is carried on. It is used to determine the jurisdiction of courts in civil matters (see **19.8.7.3**).

19.8.7.2 Taxation

In the United Kingdom, income tax was invented before registered companies, and the income tax legislation made liability to the tax depend on residence in the United Kingdom without saying how the residence of a company, as opposed to an individual, was to be determined. The courts filled the gap by adopting the test that a company is resident where its central management and control is, because that is where its real business is carried on (*De Beers Consolidated Mines Ltd v Howe* [1906] AC 455 (company registered in South Africa resident in the United Kingdom); *Unit Construction Co Ltd v Bullock* [1960] AC 351 (company registered in Kenya resident in the United Kingdom)). Applying this test it is possible to find that a company incorporated in the

United Kingdom is not resident here (*Egyptian Delta Land and Investment Co v Todd* [1929] AC 1). However, for taxation purposes that possibility was ended by the Finance Act 1988, s 66, which deems any company registered in the United Kingdom to be resident here (there are transitional provisions in sch 7 to deal with companies which had previously been regarded as resident outside the United Kingdom). The only exception is that a UK-registered company can rely on any provision of a double taxation agreement under which its residence is outside the United Kingdom, for the purpose of claiming relief from UK tax under that agreement (Finance Act 1994, s 249). Apart from the provisions of double taxation agreements, the test of whether a company incorporated outside the United Kingdom is resident in the United Kingdom for taxation purposes is still the central management and control test (see *Wood v Holden* [2006] EWCA Civ 26, [2006] 1 WLR 1393; Inland Revenue Statement of Practice SP 1/90).

The term 'place of effective management' is used in some double taxation agreements. It seems that this is the same as the place where a company's central management and control is (*Wood v Holden* at [6]).

If the central management and control of a company is divided, the company may be found to have two or more places of residence (*Swedish Central Railway Co Ltd v Thompson* [1925] AC 495).

It is possible to find that central management and control is exercised by people other than those who are supposed to exercise it under the company's constitution. In *Unit Construction Co Ltd v Bullock* a company registered in Kenya was managed by the board of its parent company in England, whereas its articles required it to be managed by its own directors in Kenya. When the tax disadvantage of this was noticed, it was claimed that the actions of the English board should be ignored because they were unconstitutional, but this argument was rejected by the House of Lords.

It is common in tax planning schemes for valuable assets to be held by a company which is incorporated in a lower-tax jurisdiction. The directors of that company, who act in that jurisdiction, are expected to follow instructions given by tax planners in the United Kingdom. Provided these instructions are expressed as professional advice, and it appears that the directors consider whether it would be in the interest of the company to follow the advice, the directors, not the tax planners, will be found to be the central management and control (*Wood v Holden*).

19.8.7.3 Jurisdiction

Apart from powers given by statute, a court in England and Wales has no power to exercise jurisdiction over anyone outside England and Wales (*Re Busfield* (1886) 32 ChD 123 per Cotton LJ at p 131). The test of whether a corporation formed elsewhere is here so as to be subject to the jurisdiction of the courts of England and Wales is whether its business, or other corporate activity, has been carried on, either by itself or by an agent, at or from a fixed place of business in England or Wales, for more than a minimal period of time (*Okura and Co Ltd v Forsbacka Jernverks AB* [1914] 1 KB 715; *Adams v Cape Industries plc* [1990] Ch 433). In the cases the terms 'residence' and 'presence' are used interchangeably to refer to this connection with the jurisdiction.

This common law rule is modified by Regulation (EU) No 1215/2012. The general rule under art 4 of the Regulation is that, if a company is domiciled in an EU State, it must be sued in the courts of that State, and not in the courts of any other EU State, whatever its connection with that other State. The same general rule applies to natural persons. In English common law, a company is domiciled where its registered office is (see **2.5.3**). The Regulation provides that, alternatively, a company is domiciled where it has its central administration or its principal place of business (art 63). The identification of a company's principal place of business is discussed in *The Rewia* [1991] 2 Lloyd's Rep 325 and *Ministry of Defence and Support of the Armed Forces for Iran v FAZ Aviation Ltd* [2007] EWHC 1042 (Comm), [2008] 1 All ER (Comm) 372. According to these authorities, a company's principal place of business must be its chief or most important place of business and is not necessarily where it carries out most of its business. It will usually be the place where its central management and control is located.

19.8.7.4 Security for costs

By commencing a claim in a court in England and Wales a company submits to the jurisdiction, but, if it is not resident in the EU, Iceland, Norway or Switzerland, it may be required to give security for a defendant's costs (Civil Procedure Rules 1998, rr 25.13(1) and (2)(a)). An earlier version of this rule, which was expressed in terms of ordinary residence rather than residence, was considered in *Re Little Olympian Each-Ways Ltd* [1995] 1 WLR 560 and it was held that the central management and control test was the appropriate test of ordinary residence for the purpose of deciding whether security should be required.

19.8.8 ENEMY CHARACTER

In time of war it is illegal for any person bound in loyalty to the Crown to trade with the enemy power or its subjects. A State is an enemy for the purposes of the law on trading with the enemy only if there has been a formal declaration of war against it by Her Majesty's government (HMG) (*Amin v Brown* [2005] EWHC 1670 (Ch), [2005] NPC 104). As there has been no declaration of war by HMG since the Second World War, the law on trading with the enemy has become obsolescent. However, cases decided before 1939 in which the court considered whether to attribute the enemy character of a company's shareholders to the company itself, so as to make it illegal to trade with the company, have been important in the historical development of the law on attribution of human characteristics to companies. The cases themselves have been superseded by statutory provisions in the Trading with the Enemy Act 1939. Under s 2(1) of that Act, any corporation controlled by an enemy is deemed to be an enemy itself.

In the First World War (1914–18), there was no legislative provision for determining whether a body corporate was an enemy and there were no common law rules because the use of registered companies for trading had developed since the United Kingdom was last engaged in a large-scale European war. The question came before the courts in the controversial case of *Daimler Co Ltd v Continental Tyre and Rubber Co (Great Britain) Ltd* [1916] 2 AC 307. Daimler Co Ltd claimed that it did not have to pay money it owed to the respondent company because to do so would be trading with the enemy (namely Germany). The respondent company was incorporated in England to sell tyres made by a German company. Of its 25,000 shares, only one was held by a person who was not German. All the directors were German and none of them had been in England since the outbreak of war. The company secretary had issued a writ in the company's name against Daimler Co Ltd but the House of Lords held he had no authority to control the company's litigation so that the writ was of no effect. The Law Lords also dealt with the question whether the respondent company was an enemy.

A majority (6–2) of the Law Lords thought that a company which was not incorporated in an enemy country could nevertheless have an enemy character. One of those in the majority, the Earl of Halsbury, thought that this enemy character could be determined simply by ignoring the company's separate personality and looking at the nationality of its shareholders, because it was they who had formed the company for the purpose of benefiting from its trading. The other five, however, thought that enemy character depended on the residence of the company as determined by the central management and control test (see **19.8.7**) (Lord Atkinson at pp 318–20; Lord Parker of Waddington at pp 339–40; Lord Sumner, Viscount Mersey and Lord Kinnear agreed with all of Lord Parker's judgment; see also *Re Hilckes* [1917] 1 KB 48). In *Daimler Co Ltd v Continental Tyre and Rubber Co (Great Britain) Ltd* there was no evidence that anyone other than the company secretary was managing, and acting for, the respondent company. For Lord Atkinson that was the end of the matter. But Lord Parker said, at pp 345–6, that in those circumstances the court would be entitled to consider whether the company secretary was in fact adhering to, taking instructions from or acting under the control of the shareholders who were enemies.

In two cases which followed Lord Parker's judgment in *Daimler Co Ltd v Continental Tyre and Rubber Co (Great Britain) Ltd*, ships owned by English companies whose shareholders were enemy aliens were held to be enemy ships (*The Polzeath* [1916] P 241 and *The St Tudno* [1916] P 291; see also *The Hamborn* [1919] AC 993, in which the shareholding was indirect).

The idea that the enemy status of a company's members may be attributed to the company may be compared with the general refusal to attribute to a company its members' religious or ethnic characteristics (see **19.8.9** and **19.8.10**). It may well be that *Daimler Co Ltd v Continental Tyre and Rubber Co (Great Britain) Ltd* is a product more of the extreme circumstances of the First World War than of any underlying principle of company law. For a detailed discussion of the background to the case see D Foxton, 'Corporate personality in the Great War' (2002) 118 LQR 428.

Even though a company registered in England and Wales has enemy character it is still an English company subject to English law: in particular it is not free to trade with the enemy (*Kuenigl v Donnersmarck* [1955] 1 QB 515).

19.8.9 IDENTIFICATION OF RELIGIOUS BELIEF

In *Adelaide Company of Jehovah's Witnesses Inc v Commonwealth* (1943) 67 CLR 116, Latham CJ said, at p 147, 'It is obvious that a company cannot exercise a religion.' A body corporate is incapable of public worship and cannot exercise itself in 'the duties of piety and true religion' as required by the Sunday Observance Act 1677 before it was repealed (*Rolloswin Investments Ltd v Chromolit Portugal Cutelarias e Produtos Metálicos SARL* [1970] 1 WLR 912). A statement that a company does or does not have a particular opinion is really only a statement that an individual who can be identified with the company has or does not have that opinion (*Lloyd v David Syme and Co Ltd* [1986] AC 350). In *Edwards Books and Art Ltd v R* (1986) 35 DLR (4th) 1, Dickson CJC said, at p 53:

> I have no hesitation in remarking that a business corporation cannot possess religious beliefs ... A more difficult question is whether a corporate entity ought to be deemed in certain circumstances to possess the religious values of specified natural persons. If so, should the religion of the directors or shareholders or even employees be adopted as the appropriate test? What if there is a divergence of religious beliefs within the corporation?

The Chief Justice did not find it necessary to rule on this question in the case before the court.

In *Re Northern Ireland Electricity Service's Application* [1987] NI 271, the High Court of Northern Ireland was concerned with Northern Ireland legislation which renders unlawful certain kinds of discrimination on the grounds of religious belief or political opinion. The Fair Employment Agency for Northern Ireland wished to investigate an allegation that, in making contracts with companies, the Northern Ireland Electricity Service (NIES) had unlawfully discriminated on the ground of religious belief or perceived political opinion. NIES sought to stop the investigation saying that there could be no discrimination to investigate because the dealings were with companies and companies could not have religious beliefs or political opinions. Nicholson J held that discrimination under the legislation was not restricted to discrimination against a person for that person's own beliefs. A person who is adversely affected by discrimination against others can complain about that discrimination. Accordingly a company could complain about being affected by discrimination against people connected with it. As this disposed of the case it was unnecessary for his Lordship to go on to deal with the question of whether a company could hold a religious belief or political opinion. However, he did so, at pp 288–9, saying that in his view the identification theory could be used to attribute to a company 'the religious belief (or supposed religious belief) of its governing body or chief officer or other superior officers who speak and act as' the company, and similarly a company can have a political opinion.

19.8.10 ETHNICITY

The US Supreme Court has declared that a corporation has no racial identity (*Village of Arlington Heights v Metropolitan Housing Development Corporation* (1977) 429 US 252 at p 263). It may be that this statement is obiter and the point could be fully argued in the Supreme Court in the future (*Oti Kaga Inc v South Dakota Housing Development Authority* (2002) 188 F Supp 2d 1148, (2003) 342 F 3d 871), but common law courts all over the world have taken the same view and have always refused to attribute the ethnicity of a company's members to the company itself. Thus a company whose members are all Indians is itself neither an Indian nor a band of Indians (*Reference re Stony Plain Indian Reserve No 135* (1981) 130 DLR (3d) 636 at p 657). A company whose members are all Indians entitled to exemption from taxation on their property is not itself a tax-exempt Indian (*Re Kinookimaw Beach Association* (1979) 102 DLR (3d) 333; *Northwest/Prince Rupert Assessor, Area No 25 v N and V Johnson Services Ltd* [1991] 1 WWR 527). A company whose members are all Africans is not an African entitled to sue in a court whose jurisdiction is limited to disputes between Africans (*Kajubi v Kayanja* [1967] EA 301). A company whose members are all Afro-Americans is not a 'person of African descent' or a 'coloured person' (*People's Pleasure Park Co Inc v Rohleder* (1908) 61 SE 794, in which owners of land had covenanted not to sell it to such persons). The State of California is not a white person, and so a Chinese individual could give evidence for another Chinese defending a criminal prosecution by the State despite a California statute (presumably now repealed) prohibiting members of various races from giving evidence against a white person (*People v Awa* (1865) 27 Cal 638).

19.9 COMPANIES IN COURT

19.9.1 REPRESENTATION

An individual engaged in civil litigation may personally appear in court to conduct the case. As an artificial person, appearance in court is not possible for a company, but the court may permit a company to be represented at trial by an employee whom it has authorised (Civil Procedure Rules 1998, r 39.6). Paragraph 5 of Practice Direction 39A supplementing the Civil Procedure Rules (PD 39A) states how r 39.6 is to operate in practice. PD 39A, para 5.3, says that permission for a company to be represented by an employee should be given by the court, 'unless there is some particular and sufficient reason why it should be withheld'. Permission should be obtained in advance of the hearing, preferably from the judge who is to hear the case (para 5.4). Permission may be obtained informally and without notice to other parties, but the judge should record the grant of permission in writing and supply a copy to the company and to any other party who asks for one (para 5.5). The company must provide a written statement of its representative's authority and other details set out in para 5.2. In considering whether to grant permission the court will take into account the complexity of the issues and the experience and position in the company of the proposed representative (para 5.3). In *Tracto Teknik GmbH v LKL International Pty Ltd* [2003] EWHC 1563 (Ch), [2003] 2 BCLC 519, a man was permitted to represent a company of which he was a full-time employee, but was not permitted to represent a co-defendant which had hired him for £1 a year as a legal adviser and which was obviously able to afford professional representation. The Admiralty and Commercial Courts Guide, para M3.1, warns that, because of the complexity of most cases in the Commercial Court, permission for employee representation will not usually be given. Permission should not normally be granted in jury trials or contempt proceedings (PD 39A, para 5.6). On the small claims track, a company has an unfettered right to be represented by an officer or employee (PD 27, para 3.2(4)) or a lay representative (para 3.2(1); *Avinue Ltd v Sunrule Ltd* [2003] EWCA Civ 1942, [2004] 1 WLR 634).

A company being represented by its officer is a litigant in person able to claim the officer's remuneration as costs under the Litigants in Person (Costs and Expenses) Act 1975 (Civil Procedure Rules 1998, r 46.5(6)(a)).

19.9.2 COSTS

A party to legal proceedings who is unsuccessful will usually be ordered to pay the successful party's costs (Civil Procedure Rules 1998, r 44.2(2)). If the party ordered to pay costs is unable to do so, the party awarded costs may ask for a third party costs order to be made against a person who caused the unsuccessful party to pursue the litigation. In particular, a third party costs order may be made where a company, which has been unsuccessful in litigation, is unable to meet other parties' costs that it has been ordered to pay.

A third party costs order will be made only if, in all the circumstances, it is just to do so (*Dymocks Franchise Systems (NSW) Pty Ltd v Todd* [2004] UKPC 39, [2004] 1 WLR 2807, at [25]). A third party costs order will not be made in an ordinary case in which a company has litigated in order to protect its own interests, even if it loses. There must be some exceptional factor which makes it just to order a third party to pay costs (*Mills v Birchall* [2008] EWCA Civ 385, [2008] 1 WLR 1829). If it is just to make a third party costs order, it may be made against a person who can be described as the real party who would have benefited if the litigation had been successful and who controlled and/or funded the litigation (*Goodwood Recoveries Ltd v Breen* [2005] EWCA Civ 414, [2006] 1 WLR 2723, per Rix LJ at [59]; *Petromec Inc v Petróleo Brasileiro SA* [2006] EWCA Civ 1038, [2007] 2 Costs LR 212, per Longmore LJ at [10]–[11]).

Legal aid is for individuals only (Legal Aid, Sentencing and Punishment of Offenders Act 2012, s 9(1)) and so litigation by companies cannot be publicly funded. It would seem that an individual suing on behalf of a company in a derivative claim is also not entitled to public funding (*Wallersteiner v Moir (No 2)* [1975] QB 373).

19.9.3 EVIDENCE

A company may be required to provide evidence concerning its affairs for the purposes of legal proceedings to which it is a party. Before trial it may be ordered to disclose and allow inspection of relevant documents and may be ordered to clarify or give additional information about any matter in dispute. A company cannot be ordered to attend, by an officer, for oral examination (*Penn-Texas Corporation v Murat Anstalt* [1964] 1 QB 40). Documents or further information must be transmitted by an officer or other agent of the company but will bind the company (*Welsbach Incandescent Gas Lighting Co v New Sunlight Incandescent Co* [1900] 2 Ch 1). Accordingly, privilege against incriminating the company can be claimed (*Triplex Safety Glass Co Ltd v Lancegaye Safety Glass (1934) Ltd* [1939] 2 KB 395). If the evidence would incriminate the particular officer or agent nominated to transmit it then that individual can refuse to provide it but the court can nominate another person to provide it (*Sociedade Nacional de Combustiveis de Angola UEE v Lundqvist* [1991] 2 QB 310).

Evidence about a company's affairs can also be given by an individual with knowledge of those affairs as the evidence of that individual and not as the evidence of the company (*Macmillan Inc v Bishopsgate Investment Trust plc (No 2)* [1993] ICR 385). The fact that the individual could be identified with the company does not in itself mean that he or she is giving evidence as or for the company (*R v N M Paterson and Sons Ltd* (1980) 117 DLR (3d) 517). So such an individual is not entitled to claim any privilege to which the company is entitled, such as the privilege against self-incrimination. For example, in *R v N M Paterson and Sons Ltd*, the company was charged with an offence. The prosecution wished to call as a witness a manager who could be regarded as the directing mind and will of the company under the identification theory. It was contended for the manager that his evidence would be the company's evidence and so he could refuse to testify because of the rule that a person charged with an offence cannot be compelled to give evidence at his own trial for that offence. However, the Supreme Court of Canada rejected this contention and held that the manager would be giving his own evidence not the company's evidence and so could be compelled to testify. These cases were not cited in *Kensington International Ltd v Republic of Congo* [2007] EWHC 1632 (Comm), [2007] 2 Lloyd's Rep 382, in which the question was left open.

In *Environment Protection Authority v Caltex Refining Co Pty Ltd* (1993) 178 CLR 477 the High Court of Australia refused to follow the English rule that companies can claim privilege against self-incrimination. The division of opinion on this issue reflects different views of the nature of corporate personality which are explored at length in the judgments in the case.

PART 5

INSOLVENCY AND LIQUIDATION

20
COMPANY INSOLVENCY AND LIQUIDATION

SUMMARY OF POINTS COVERED

- Introduction
- Administrative receivership and floating charges
- Administration
- Voluntary arrangements
- Voluntary winding up
- Winding up by the court
- Appointment of a provisional liquidator
- Commencement of winding up: going into liquidation

- Investigation of a company's affairs
- Control of insolvency and liquidation procedures by the court
- Liability for fraudulent trading
- Wrongful trading
- Directors' disqualification
- Use of insolvent company's name
- Order of application of assets in liquidation
- Dissolution

20.1 INTRODUCTION

20.1.1 NATURE OF COMPANY INSOLVENCY AND LIQUIDATION PROCEDURES

The governance of a company is normally entrusted to its directors. In certain circumstances, notably when a company is insolvent, the directors may be displaced by a qualified insolvency practitioner or (in a more restricted range of circumstances) an official receiver.

Several different procedures are available for putting a qualified insolvency practitioner or an official receiver in charge of a company. The different procedures are suitable for different circumstances. All but one of them are used to deal with insolvent companies and may conveniently be referred to as 'insolvency procedures'.

The insolvency procedures are administrative receivership, administration, voluntary arrangement, creditors' voluntary winding up, winding up by the court and the appointment of a provisional liquidator. Of these, only creditors' voluntary winding up and winding up by the court involve the liquidation of the company (see **20.1.2**) and may be called 'liquidation procedures'. Winding up by the court and appointment of a provisional liquidator can also be applied to a solvent company. The one other procedure available for putting a qualified insolvency practitioner in charge of a company, namely, members' voluntary winding up, is a procedure for the liquidation of a solvent company.

All the company insolvency and liquidation procedures involve the appointment of a qualified insolvency practitioner (or in some circumstances an official receiver) to a named office in relation to a company—the offices being those of administrative receiver, administrator, supervisor of a voluntary arrangement, liquidator and provisional liquidator. Persons holding any of these offices are known as 'office-holders' or 'insolvency office-holders'.

20.1.2 LIQUIDATION

The end result of the liquidation (or winding up, the terms are used interchangeably) of a company is that the company ceases to exist. The purpose of a liquidation procedure is to ensure that, before the company's existence ceases, all its affairs are dealt with (or 'wound up'), which means removing the company from all its legal relationships. Its contracts must be completed, transferred or otherwise brought to an end; it must cease carrying on business; its liabilities must be met, as far as possible; legal proceedings to which it is a party must be determined.

The members are entitled to benefit from any property remaining unless the articles provide otherwise. Surplus non-cash assets may be sold and the proceeds distributed to the members.

Finally the company must be removed from the register and dissolved.

20.1.3 LEGISLATION ON COMPANY INSOLVENCY AND LIQUIDATION

The statute law on company insolvency and liquidation is contained principally in the Insolvency Act 1986 (IA 1986). (Sections 252 to 385 of IA 1986 are concerned with the insolvency of natural persons (bankruptcy) and are not relevant to this work.)

The primary legislation is supplemented by secondary legislation made by the Lord Chancellor and the Secretary of State under IA 1986, s 411. The principal item of secondary legislation is the Insolvency (England and Wales) Rules 2016 (SI 2016/1024) (I(EW)R 2016). Company insolvency rules are made after consultation with the Insolvency Rules Committee (IA 1986, s 413). Its members are judges particularly concerned with insolvency matters, and an accountant, a barrister and a solicitor specialising in insolvency work.

20.1.4 QUALIFIED INSOLVENCY PRACTITIONERS

Any person who acts as an administrative receiver, nominee in relation to or supervisor of, a voluntary arrangement, liquidator or provisional liquidator of a company (known as 'acting as an insolvency practitioner in relation to the company') without being qualified to do so commits an offence punishable by imprisonment for up to two years and/or a fine (IA 1986, ss 388(1) and (4) and 389(1) and sch 10). This does not apply to official receivers (see 20.1.5) (s 389(2)). A person can be appointed administrator of a company only if qualified to act as an insolvency practitioner in relation to the company (sch B1, para 6).

There are two aspects to being qualified to act as an insolvency practitioner in relation to a company:

(a) qualification to act as an insolvency practitioner generally; and

(b) qualification to act in relation to the particular company concerned.

Qualification to act as an insolvency practitioner generally is obtained by being authorised to do so (s 390(2)). Authorisation is by recognised professional bodies. It may be authorisation to act in individual insolvencies (bankruptcy or individual voluntary arrangement) as well as company insolvencies or partial authorisation in relation to companies only or in relation to individuals only.

Qualification to act in relation to a specific company is by posting a bond under which a surety accepts liability for the proper performance of the practitioner's duties in relation to that company (IA 1986, s 390(3)).

Only an individual can act as an insolvency practitioner (s 390(1)): companies and partnerships are not eligible. An individual cannot act as an insolvency practitioner while an undischarged bankrupt, while subject to a director disqualification order or while lacking capacity under the mental health legislation (s 390(4)).

20.1.5 OFFICIAL RECEIVERS

Official receivers attached to the High Court and/or the County Court are appointed by, and act under the general authority and directions of, the Secretary of State (IA 1986, ss 399(2), (3), (5) and (6) and 400(2)). The same official receiver may be attached to both courts (s 399(5)).

The main tasks of an official receiver are to investigate the causes of insolvencies and to act as trustee in bankruptcy and as liquidator or provisional liquidator in compulsory liquidations of companies. Although the creditors of an insolvent person can put their own appointee (who must be a qualified insolvency practitioner) in place of the official receiver as trustee or liquidator, most insolvent estates are not sufficiently valuable to remunerate an insolvency practitioner.

An official receiver attached to a particular court is the person authorised to act as the official receiver in relation to every winding up falling within the jurisdiction of that court (s 399(4)). If there are two or more official receivers attached to a particular court, the Secretary of State may provide for the distribution of their business between or among them (s 399(6)) and may also authorise an official receiver attached to one court to act as the official receiver in relation to any case or description of cases falling within the jurisdiction of the other court (s 399(6)).

An official receiver exercises the functions of his or her office as an officer of the court in relation to which those functions are exercised (s 400(2)).

For the purposes of the IA 1986, 'the official receiver', in relation to any winding up, is the person who is authorised under s 399(4) or (6) to act as the official receiver in relation to that winding up (s 399(1)).

20.1.6 CONTRIBUTORIES

The principal tasks in the winding up of a company are to collect its assets and use them to settle its liabilities, and to distribute any surplus to the persons entitled to it. The assets consist of property owned by the company, including debts owed to it, and the money which the members of the company and other persons are liable to contribute in the event of winding up.

The persons who are liable to contribute to the assets of a company in the event of its being wound up are called the 'contributories' of the company (IA 1986, s 79(1)). The IA 1986, s 74(1), announces that 'every present and past member' of a company is liable to contribute to its assets when it is wound up, so every past and present member is a contributory of the company. But this is subject to the extensive limitations set out in the rest of s 74, the most significant of which is s 74(2)(d):

> in the case of a company limited by shares, no contribution is required from any member exceeding the amount (if any) unpaid on the shares in respect of which he is liable as a present or past member.

The legislation on the compulsory liquidation of companies, some of which dates back to the Joint Stock Companies Act 1856, gives the contributories, rather than the members, of a company a significant role. For example, the contributories of a company are entitled to petition for its compulsory liquidation (IA 1986, s 124(1)), contributories are entitled to nominate a person to be liquidator (s 139), and contributories may elect members of a liquidation committee (s 141). The emphasis on members as persons contributing to the assets of a company being wound up was very important in the early days of registered companies when shares were usually partly paid. When companies moved to having only fully paid up shares, whose holders, by IA 1986, s 74(2)(d), are not required to contribute anything to the assets in winding up, the courts took the pragmatic step of deciding that members with fully paid shares are nevertheless contributories for the purposes of the legislation, and have the same rights and duties as other contributories, except that they do not have to contribute anything (*Re National Savings Bank Association* (1866) LR 1 Ch App 547; *Re Anglesea Colliery Co* (1866) LR 1 Ch App 555; *Re Phoenix Oil and Transport Co Ltd* [1958] Ch 560).

As the status of contributory confers various rights to control the progress of a compulsory winding up, it is denied to persons who are ordered by the court to contribute to the assets of a company because of their past misdeeds. For example, IA 1986, s 79(2), denies the status of contributory to persons ordered to contribute to the assets under s 213 (liability for fraudulent trading) or s 214 (liability for wrongful trading), and the courts have held that persons ordered to contribute in misfeasance proceedings under s 212 are also not contributories (*Re AMF International Ltd* [1996] 1 WLR 77).

20.1.7 DECISION-MAKING BY CREDITORS

Where legislation requires a decision to be made by creditors, it can usually be made by the 'deemed consent procedure' (IA 1986, s 246ZF). Under this procedure creditors are deemed to have consented to any proposed decision put to them (usually by an office-holder) in a notice unless 10 per cent (in value) object to it (IA 1986, s 246ZF(1), (3) and (6)). If 10 per cent or more object, the decision is not made and it can only be asked for again by using a 'qualifying decision procedure' (s 246ZF(5)). Qualifying decision procedures are prescribed by I(EW)R 2016, r 15.3, as (a) correspondence; (b) electronic voting; (c) virtual meeting; (d) physical meeting; or (e) any other decision making procedure which enables all creditors who are entitled to participate in the making of the decision to participate equally. Legislation, or a court order, may require a qualifying decision procedure to be used instead of the deemed consent procedure (IA 1986, s 246ZF(1)). The qualifying decision procedure to be used to make any particular decision is to be chosen by the office-holder seeking the decision (s 246ZE(1) and (2)) but a meeting cannot be used unless expressly required or permitted for the decision by legislation or court order (s 246ZE(2) and (5)) or if 10 per cent of the voters (or ten of them) require the decision to be taken at a meeting (s 246ZE(2) to (4) and (7)). A creditor of a company can opt out of receiving notices from the company's office-holder (ss 246C and 248A).

In qualifying decision procedures, creditors' decisions are usually taken by a simple majority, *in value*, of the unsecured creditors who vote (I(EW)R 2016, r 15.34(1)). Values of votes are calculated according to the amount of each creditor's claim, as detailed in r 15.31, but the value of a wholly secured claim is nil (r 15.31(4)).

20.2 ADMINISTRATIVE RECEIVERSHIP AND FLOATING CHARGES

20.2.1 SUMMARY DESCRIPTION

As explained in **11.6.3**, an administrative receiver takes control of the whole (or substantially the whole) of a company's property so as to realise it for the purpose of paying one creditor who is secured by a floating charge (or sometimes a group of creditors who have common security in the form of a floating charge). No other interest groups are involved. Administrative receivership arises because of the security contract made between a company and one or more of its creditors (or a trustee for a group of creditors): by agreeing to a contract of that type with a creditor, the company confers on that creditor a special advantage over other creditors.

Administrative receivership is an insolvency procedure: it is usually invoked in relation to insolvent companies and not solvent companies.

Administrative receivership is not a liquidation procedure.

Except in rare cases, the involvement of the court is not required for initiating or confirming the use of this procedure.

As explained in **11.6.3**, appointments of administrative receivers are being replaced by appointments of administrators (see **20.3**) except for large-scale marketable loans, projects with step-in rights, financial market charges, social landlords and some utility companies. As administrative receivership has substantially declined in importance the rest of **20.2** will concentrate on the effect of insolvency and liquidation procedures generally on floating charges.

20.2.2 PROPERTY ACQUIRED AFTER CRYSTALLISATION

If a floating charge on a company's assets of a particular class is expressed to charge all present and future assets of that class then, after the floating charge has crystallised, any asset of that class subsequently acquired by the company will be subject to a fixed equitable charge as from the time of acquisition (*N W Robbie and Co Ltd v Witney Warehouse Co Ltd* [1963] 1 WLR 1324). Property acquired for the company's estate by the exercise of a statutory power given to a liquidator or administrator by IA 1986, s 213 (see **20.11**), 214 (see **20.12**), 238, 239, 244, 246ZA or 246ZB, is not the company's property and so cannot be subject to a floating charge (s 176ZB, which codifies case law such as *Re Oasis Merchandising Services Ltd* [1998] Ch 170). A liquidator or administrator may assign rights of action arising under these provisions, including the proceeds of a claim (s 246ZD).

20.2.3 PREFERENTIAL CREDITORS AND LIQUIDATION EXPENSES

A disadvantage of a floating charge, as far as the chargee is concerned, is that if an administrative receiver is appointed, or if the company is wound up before an administrative receiver is appointed, certain of the company's debts, called its 'preferential debts', must be paid out of the assets subject to the floating charge in priority to the chargee's debt (IA 1986, ss 40 and 175(2)(b)). The preferential debts are defined in s 386 and sch 6 (see **20.15.1**).

Furthermore, if a company goes into liquidation, the expenses of winding up have priority over any claims to property comprised in or subject to a floating charge, insofar as the expenses cannot be paid out of assets available for payment of general creditors (s 176ZA, which came into force on 6 April 2008 and overrules *Buchler v Talbot* [2004] UKHL 9, [2004] 2 AC 298). Litigation expenses exceeding £5,000 are not payable out of floating charge assets unless they have been approved by the charge holder or by the court (s 176ZA(3); I(EW)R 2016, rr 6.44 to 6.48).

If, in addition to the floating charge under which a receiver is appointed, property of the company is charged under a fixed charge that ranks in priority to, or equally with, the receiver's floating charge then that property cannot be utilised to pay the preferential debts or liquidation expenses, even if it is charged to secure the same debt as is secured by the receiver's charge (*Re Lewis Merthyr Consolidated Collieries Ltd* [1929] 1 Ch 498; *Re G L Saunders Ltd* [1986] 1 WLR 215). Creditors exploit this rule by obtaining a charge that combines a fixed charge over as many assets as possible and an equally ranking floating charge on the remainder. A receiver can be appointed under both fixed and floating elements of the charge but preferential debts are paid only out of the property charged by the floating charge. However, property subject to a floating charge and also a fixed charge which ranks *after* the floating charge must be utilised to pay preferential debts (*Re Portbase Clothing Ltd*). These rules apply where the other charge was created as a fixed charge, but there is disagreement over what happens if a prior charge was created as a floating charge. In *Griffiths v Yorkshire Bank plc* [1994] 1 WLR 1427 it was held that a floating charge created after the one under which the receiver was appointed acquired priority over it by crystallising first (the opposite conclusion was reached in *Re Household Products Co Ltd and Federal Business Development Bank* (1981) 124 DLR (3d) 325; see **11.6.4.3**), and, because no receiver was appointed under it, what is now IA 1986, s 40, did not apply to it and the preferential debts did not have priority over the debt it secured. This would seem to open the way for any floating chargee to collaborate with another creditor to avoid the operation of s 40. In *Re H and K (Medway) Ltd* [1997] 2 All ER 321 the chargee who had appointed the receiver had agreed (for legitimate business reasons) that another floating charge was to have priority and it was held that s 40 gave the preferential debts priority over both floating charges. The interpretation of s 40 adopted in *Re H and K (Medway) Ltd*, though very strained, would prevent avoidance of the section.

The expenses of an administrative receivership are payable in priority to the preferential debts (*Woods v Winskill* [1913] 2 Ch 303; *Re Glyncorrwg Colliery Co Ltd* [1926] Ch 951). The principle, as explained in **Batten v Wedgwood Coal and Iron Co** (1884) 28 ChD 317, is that: 'The man who has actually produced the fund for distribution is to have his costs of producing it paid in priority.'

However, a receiver has a duty not to incur expenses if to do so would lessen the amount available to pay preferential creditors (*Woods v Winskill*; *Westminster Corporation v Haste* [1950] Ch 442—both of which were concerned with liabilities incurred in carrying on the company's business).

A receiver who pays preferential debts is entitled to recoup the payment out of any assets of the company available for payment of general creditors (s 40(3)).

For a detailed study see H Anderson, 'Receivership preferential creditors' (1994) 15 Co Law 195.

20.2.4 STATUTORY SHARE OF ASSETS FOR UNSECURED CREDITORS

When a company whose assets are subject to a floating charge goes into administrative receivership, or any other insolvency or liquidation procedure (other than voluntary arrangement), the prescribed percentage of floating charge assets must be set aside to pay the company's unsecured creditors (IA 1986, s 176A). The prescribed percentage is (SI 2003/2097, art 3):

(a) 50 per cent of the first £10,000; and

(b) 20 per cent of the remainder,

up to a maximum of £600,000. It is possible to vary this rule by means of a voluntary arrangement (IA 1986, s 176A(4)). The rule does not apply:

(a) where the company's net property is less than £10,000 (s 176A(3)(a); SI 2003/2097, art 2); or

(b) where the costs of distribution to unsecured creditors would be disproportionate to the benefits (IA 1986, s 176A(3)(b)): the office-holder may apply to the court for an order stating that this is so (s 176A(5)).

If the office-holder has led unsecured creditors to believe that they will receive a distribution, but then obtains a court order under s 176A(5), the court will give the creditors an opportunity to apply to have the order set aside (*Re Hydroserve Ltd* [2007] EWHC 3026 (Ch), [2008] BCC 175). Exception (b) is available only where distribution costs are disproportionate for all unsecured creditors. Section 176A(3)(b) and (5) does not permit exclusion of only particular creditors whose share would be less than the cost of distributing to them (*Re Courts plc* [2008] EWHC 2339 (Ch), [2009] 1 WLR 1499).

If the debt secured by the floating charge is only partly paid, the unpaid part does not count as an unsecured debt that is to be paid from the statutory share of assets for unsecured creditors (*Re Permacell Finesse Ltd* [2007] EWHC 3233 (Ch), [2008] BCC 208; *Re Airbase (UK) Ltd* [2008] EWHC 124 (Ch), [2008] 1 WLR 1516).

20.3 ADMINISTRATION

20.3.1 SUMMARY DESCRIPTION

Administration is a statutory insolvency procedure, which was introduced by the Insolvency Act 1985. After 15 or so years' experience of the procedure, improvements were made by the Enterprise Act 2002, s 248. The statutory provisions on administration are now in IA 1986, s 8 and sch B1.

An administrator of a company is appointed by the court, by the holder of a floating charge relating to the whole or substantially the whole of the company's property, by the company itself or by the company's directors. An appointment by the court is made in response to an application made by the company itself or its directors or a creditor. A company's administrator is asked to formulate, if possible, a plan for dealing with the company otherwise than by putting it into liquidation. The administrator's proposals must, within eight weeks of his or her appointment, be submitted for the approval of the company's unsecured creditors.

Administration is an insolvency procedure: it can be invoked only in relation to a company that is, or is likely to become, insolvent.

Administration can be a liquidation procedure.

Proceedings in court are an optional method of appointing an administrator, but an out-of-court appointment must be reported to the court.

20.3.2 PURPOSE OF ADMINISTRATION

An administrator of a company is a person appointed under IA 1986, sch B1, to manage the company's affairs, business and property (sch B1, para 1(1)). An administrator must perform his or her functions with the objective of (para 3(1)):

(a) rescuing the company as a going concern; or

(b) achieving a better result for the company's creditors as a whole than would be likely if the company were wound up (without first being in administration); or

(c) realising property in order to make a distribution to one or more secured or preferential creditors.

This is the purpose of administration. Objective (a) must be given priority unless the administrator believes it is not reasonably practicable or that objective (b) would achieve a better result for the company's creditors as a whole (para 3(3)). Objective (c) may be pursued only if the administrator believes it is not reasonably practicable to achieve either objective (a) or objective (b) and the interests of the creditors of the company as a whole will not be harmed unnecessarily (para 3(4)). In practice, objective (a) is hardly ever pursued, because the usual solution to an insolvent company's problems is to sell its business to another person, leaving the company to be wound up.

An administrator is an officer of the court (para 5) who must perform his or her functions as quickly and efficiently as is reasonably practicable (para 4) and, unless pursuing objective (c), in the interests of the company's creditors as a whole (para 3(2)).

For a wide-ranging discussion see J M Wood, 'The objectives of administration' (2015) 36 Co Law 1.

20.3.3 APPOINTMENT OF AN ADMINISTRATOR

20.3.3.1 Methods of appointment

An administrator may be appointed:

(a) by the court making an administration order, on the application of the company itself, its directors, one or more creditors, the supervisor of a voluntary arrangement, or the designated officer for a magistrates' court following non-payment of a fine imposed on the company (IA 1986, s 7(4)(b) and sch B1, paras 10 and 12);

(b) by the holder of a floating charge over the whole or substantially the whole of the company's property (para 14); or

(c) by the company itself or its directors (para 22).

An appointment by the court or by the company or its directors cannot be made unless the company is, or is likely to become, unable to pay its debts (paras 11(b) and 27(2)(a)), and an appointment by the holder of a floating charge cannot be made unless the floating charge is enforceable, that is unless the company is unable to pay the debt secured by the charge (para 16).

An application to the court is required:

(a) if the company is being wound up voluntarily or by the court, in which case an administration application may be made only by the liquidator (IA 1986, sch B1, paras 8 and 38) or (if it is a winding up by the court) by the holder of a floating charge (paras 8 and 37); or

(b) if an administrative receiver of the company has been appointed, in which case the court will make an appointment only if the chargee who appointed the receiver consents or the court is satisfied that if an order were made the floating charge under which the receiver was appointed would be discharged or avoided or declared invalid by the court under ss 238 to 240 or 245 (see **11.6.7**) (sch B1, paras 17(b), 25(c) and 39). The administrative receiver must vacate office if an administrator is appointed (para 41(1)).

When the appointment of an administrator takes effect, the company is said to 'enter administration', and it will then be 'in administration' until the appointment of the administrator ceases to have effect (sch B1, para 1(2)).

20.3.3.2 Appointment by the company or its directors

An appointment of an administrator of a company may be made by the company itself or by its directors under IA 1986, sch B1, para 22. In practice, an appointment under para 22 is usually made by directors. No appointment may be made under para 22 if any insolvency or liquidation procedure (apart from a voluntary arrangement) is already in progress or there is a pending application for an administration or winding-up order (paras 7, 8 and 25).

An appointment may not be made under para 22 within 12 months of the ending of a previous administration initiated by the company or its directors (para 23) or within 12 months of a moratorium under sch A1 (see **20.4.4**) which failed to produce a workable voluntary arrangement (sch B1, para 24).

A qualified insolvency practitioner willing to act as administrator must be found. The directors must give at least five business days' written notice, naming the proposed administrator, to holders of floating charges who are entitled to appoint an administrative receiver or administrator (para 26). A copy of this notice must be filed with the court, accompanied by a statutory declaration stating, among other things, that the company is, or is likely to become, unable to pay its debts and that the conditions under which an appointment may be made are satisfied (para 27). Copies must also be given to the persons listed in I(EW)R 2016, r 3.23(4) (IA 1986, sch B1, para 26(2)), but directors do not have to give a copy to the company itself (*Re Virtualpurple Professional Services Ltd* [2011] EWHC 3487 (Ch), [2012] 2 BCLC 330). When the notice period has expired, if no floating charge-holder has appointed an administrator or administrative receiver or applied to the court for an administration or winding-up order, the administrator named in the notice may be appointed (para 28(1)). The appointment must be made within ten business days of filing the notice of intention with the court (para 28(2)). It is not necessary to wait until the end of the notice period if all floating charge-holders give their consent in writing (para 28(1)).

A notice of appointment must be filed in court with another statutory declaration in prescribed form stating, among other things, that the appointment is in accordance with sch B1 and with a statement from the administrator that he or she consents to the appointment and believes that the purpose of administration is reasonably likely to be achieved (para 29). The appointment takes effect when the notice of appointment is filed (para 31). After the notice of appointment has been filed the company or the directors who made the appointment must notify the administrator (para 32). Up until the filing of the notice of appointment, it is still possible for an administrator to be appointed by the court or by the holder of a floating charge, and, if this is done, the appointment by the company or its directors will not take effect (para 33).

20.3.3.3 Appointment by holder of floating charge

The holder of what the legislation calls a 'qualifying floating charge' over a company's property may appoint an administrator of the company under IA 1986, sch B1, para 14, when the floating charge is enforceable (para 16). This means that the charge must be enforceable when the notice of appointment is filed under para 18 (see later), for that is when the appointment is made (*Fliptex Ltd v Hogg* [2004] EWHC 1280 (Ch), [2004] BCC 870). The fact that there is a dispute about whether the charge is enforceable does not prevent an appointment being made (*BCPMS (Europe) Ltd v GMAC Commercial Financial plc* [2006] EWHC 3744 (Ch), LTL 21/2/2006).

No appointment may be made under para 14 if any insolvency or liquidation procedure (apart from a voluntary arrangement) is already in progress (paras 7, 8 and 17(b)). It is, though, possible to appoint under para 14 if an application is pending for a court appointment of an administrator or if an application for winding up is pending, unless a provisional liquidator has been appointed (para 17(a)). If no provisional liquidator has been appointed, a petition for a company to be wound up by the court will be suspended while the company is in administration under para 14 (para 40(1)(b)). The petition can be reactivated if creditors fail to approve any proposals made by the administrator (para 55). Alternatively a floating charge-holder can apply to the court in which the winding-up petition is pending for an administration order, as the court has power to dismiss the petition on making an administration order (para 40(1)(a)). Suspension does not occur if the petition was presented in the public interest by the Secretary of State, the FCA, or the PRA (para 40(2)), though it is usual on such a petition to appoint a provisional liquidator, so para 40 is unlikely to come into effect anyway.

A floating charge over a company's property is a qualifying floating charge if it alone, or in conjunction with other floating or fixed charges, covers the whole or substantially the whole of the company's property and the contract creating the floating charge states (para 14(2)):

(a) that para 14 applies to the charge; or

(b) that the holder has power to appoint an administrator; or

(c) that the holder has power to appoint an administrative receiver (whether using that term or not).

So the holder of an existing floating charge, which confers a power to appoint an administrative receiver may, instead, appoint an administrator under para 14. As from 15 September 2003, a power in any new qualifying floating charge contract to appoint an administrative receiver cannot be exercised (s 72A; SI 2003/2095) and the only option for the holder of the charge is to appoint an administrator (or ask the court to appoint one).

The holder of a floating charge cannot appoint an administrator unless the holders of qualifying floating charges which have priority are given two business days' written notice or have themselves given written consent to the appointment (sch B1, para 15).

Provided prior charge-holders have been dealt with, an appointment of an administrator under sch B1, para 14, is made by filing with the court a notice of appointment with a statutory declaration stating, among other things, that the appointment is in accordance with sch B1 and with a statement from the administrator that he or she consents to the appointment and believes that the purpose of administration is reasonably likely to be achieved (para 18). All these documents must be in prescribed form (para 18(5)). The appointment takes effect when the notice of appointment is filed (para 19). After the notice of appointment has been filed the person who made the appointment must notify the administrator (para 20).

There is an option to file a notice of intention to appoint, in prescribed form, up to five business days before making the appointment: if such a notice is filed, the company will benefit from a moratorium on creditors' actions and legal proceedings (para 44(2) and (3); see **20.3.8**).

20.3.3.4 Announcement of appointment

As soon as is reasonably practicable a newly appointed administrator of a company must send a notice of his or her appointment to the company, publish it in accordance with I(EW)R 2016, r 3.27, and notify Companies House (IA 1986, sch B1, para 46). The administrator must obtain a list of the company's creditors and send a notice to each creditor of whose claim and address the administrator is aware (para 46(3)). While a company is in administration, every business document issued by or on behalf of the company or the administrator must, under penalty, state the name of the administrator and that the affairs, business and property of the company are being managed by the administrator (para 45).

20.3.4 ADMINISTRATOR'S PROPOSALS

An administrator's first main job is to prepare proposals for achieving the purpose of administration (IA 1986, sch B1, para 49(1)). A statement of proposals must be sent to the registrar and to creditors and members of the company, insofar as the administrator is aware of their addresses (para 49(4)). This must be done within eight weeks of the company entering administration (para 49(5)), though the time limit may be extended by the court on application by the administrator (paras 49(8) and 107).

Creditors must be asked to approve the proposals within ten weeks of the company entering administration, subject to extension by the court on application by the administrator (para 51). This is not required if the administrator advises that the company can pay all creditors in full, or that it cannot pay unsecured creditors anything other than their statutory share of assets covered by a floating charge (see **20.2.4**), or that objectives (a) and (b) (see **20.3.2**) cannot be achieved (para 52(1)). Even then, 10 per cent (in value) of the creditors can require the administrator to ask the creditors whether they approve the proposals (para 52(2) to (4)).

The creditors may approve the administrator's proposals, approve the proposals with modifications (provided the administrator accepts the modifications) (para 53(1)) or fail to give any approval (para 55(1)(a)). The administrator must report the creditors' decision to the court and Companies House (para 53(2)). There is a criminal sanction for failing to do this (para 53(3)).

An administrator may propose a composition or arrangement (para 49(3)), but the creditors in administration cannot impose a composition or arrangement. They can only approve the administrator's proposals. Further steps must be taken under IA 1986, ss 1 to 7, or CA 2006, ss 895 to 901, as appropriate (*Re St Ives Windings Ltd* (1987) 3 BCC 634).

An administrator may not propose (except as part of a proposed compromise or arrangement) any action which affects the right of a secured creditor to enforce the security, or would affect the priority of any preferential creditors, unless the affected creditor consents (IA 1986, sch B1, para 73).

If creditors approve proposals, the administrator must manage the company's affairs, business and property in accordance with the proposals (sch B1, para 68). The creditors can establish a creditors' committee, which may ask the administrator to provide it with information about the exercise of his or her functions and require the administrator to attend its meetings at any reasonable time on seven days' notice (para 57). If the administrator thinks that a substantial revision to the proposals is necessary, the administrator can seek the creditors' approval of the proposed revision (para 54). If there is an urgent need to implement a substantial amendment before the creditors can be consulted, the court may give directions under para 63 to implement the amendment (*Re Smallman Construction Ltd* (1988) 4 BCC 784, in which the amendment had been unanimously approved by the creditors' committee).

If the creditors fail to approve any proposals, the court may end the administrator's appointment, adjourn proceedings, make an interim order, make a winding-up order if there is a suspended winding-up petition or make any other order it thinks appropriate (para 55).

20.3.5 POWERS OF AN ADMINISTRATOR

The very wide powers of an administrator are stated in IA 1986, sch B1, para 59(1):

> The administrator of a company may do anything necessary or expedient for the management of the affairs, business and property of the company.

An administrator has, by sch B1, para 60, the specific powers listed in sch 1.

In exercising his or her powers an administrator of a company is deemed to be acting as agent of the company (sch B1, para 69). A person dealing with an administrator of a company in good faith and for value is entitled to assume that the administrator is acting within his or her powers (para 59(3)).

The administrator of a company has power to call meetings of its members and seek a decision on any matter from its creditors (para 62).

On appointment, the administrator of a company shall take custody or control of all the property to which he or she thinks the company is entitled (para 67). Custody (of tangible property) or control (of intangible property) pass to the administrator by virtue of para 67 without any need for action on the administrator's part (*Katz v Bradney* [2012] EWHC 1018 (Ch), [2013] Bus LR 169).

The administrator of a company may dispose of any of its property that is subject to a charge which as originally created was a floating charge as if the property were not subject to the charge (para 70(1)) but then the chargee shall have the same priority in respect of any property of the company directly or indirectly representing the property disposed of as he would have had in respect of the property disposed of (para 70(2) and (3)).

The administrator of a company may apply to the court for authority to dispose of property subject to any charge other than a floating charge as if it were free from the charge, provided the proceeds of disposal go first to paying the obligation owed to the chargee (para 71). If the proceeds of disposal are less than the market value of the property, the court may order that the deficiency be paid to the chargee and the court must in any case be satisfied that making an order under para 71 would be likely to promote the purpose of the company's administration (para 71(2)(b)). For a detailed discussion, see *Re ARV Aviation Ltd* [1989] BCLC 664. An administrator may apply for a similar order in respect of property in the possession of the company under hire-purchase, conditional sale, chattel leasing or retention of title agreements (paras 72 and 111(1)). For such property the court's order will enable it to be sold as if the company owned it provided the true owner is paid what is owed to him out of the proceeds of sale (para 72(3)). An administrator may ignore a charge that should have been registered at Companies House but was not (see **11.7**).

20.3.6 PRE-PACKS

In the period between appointment and submission of proposals for approval by creditors, an administrator may exercise all the powers conferred by IA 1986, sch B1, para 59, and sch 1 (see **20.3.5**), including the power to sell the company's property. So if a company's administrator receives an offer for the company's assets before submitting proposals to creditors, and the offer must be accepted quickly, it may be accepted without the approval of the creditors or the court if the administrator considers this is in the best interests of the creditors (*Re Transbus International Ltd* [2004] EWHC 932 (Ch), [2004] 2 All ER 911, applying *Re T and D Industries plc* [2000] 1 WLR 646).

In practice a sale is usually negotiated before an administrator takes office and under the advice of the insolvency practitioner who is appointed administrator. This is known as a pre-packaged sale or 'pre-pack'. The fact that this is all done without consulting creditors gives rise to considerable suspicion, especially as it is usually the owners/directors of the distressed company who buy its business in a pre-pack sale, so that it is phoenixed: see **20.14**. The great advantage of a pre-pack is that it minimises the impact which going into administration has on financing arrangements, customer service and goodwill.

In response to disquiet, the regulatory authorities for insolvency practitioners issued Statement of Insolvency Practice 16 (E & W), which took effect from 1 January 2009. This emphasises that an administrator's functions must be performed in the interests of the company's creditors as a whole (para 7) and points out that the administrator must be able to explain and justify why this particular pre-pack sale was in their interests (para 2). It specifies a long list of matters which must be disclosed to creditors (para 9). Disquiet has, however, continued and, as a result, Parliament has given the Secretary of State power to make regulations controlling pre-packs (IA 1986, sch B1, para 60A), though no regulations have yet been made. See T Astle, 'Pack up your troubles: addressing the negative image of pre-packs' (2015) 28 Insolv Int 72. In addition, the Pre Pack Pool has been established. It is an independent body of experienced business people who will offer an opinion on the purchase of a business and/or its assets by connected parties to a company where a pre-packaged sale is proposed. Any proposed pre-pack that is submitted will be assessed by a member of the Pool. The most positive opinion that can be given is that it is not unreasonable to proceed with the sale.

20.3.7 EFFECT ON DIRECTORS

As with an administrative receiver, the appointment of an administrator of a company leaves its directors with very little to do. IA 1986, sch B1, para 64, provides that any power of the company or its officers that could be exercised in such a way as to interfere with the administrator's exercise of his or her powers is not exercisable except with the consent of the administrator. (This offers the curious possibility of an administrator consenting to the company interfering with his or her powers.) Furthermore, the administrator of a company is given a power to remove any of its directors from office and a power to appoint directors either to fill vacancies on the board or as additional directors (para 61).

20.3.8 MORATORIUM

While a company is in administration, IA 1986, sch B1, para 43, prevents creditors, unless they have the consent of the administrator or the permission of the court, from enforcing security, putting in execution or taking control of the company's goods. Also, no steps may be taken to repossess goods in the company's possession under any hire-purchase agreement, conditional sale agreement, chattel leasing agreement or retention of title agreement except with consent or permission. A landlord cannot exercise a right of forfeiture by peaceable re-entry in relation to premises let to the company, except with consent or permission (para 43(4)) and no one may take legal proceedings against the company, except with consent or permission (para 43(6)). The company cannot adopt a resolution to wind up and the court cannot make a winding-up order, except on a public-interest petition by the Secretary of State, the FCA or the PRA (para 42). This protection is known as a moratorium. The same protection applies (except that only the court can give permission) during the following periods of preparation for administration (para 44):

(a) from when an application is made to the court for an administration order until the court's administration order take effect or the application is dismissed;

(b) from when the holder of a floating charge files with the court a notice of intention to appoint an administrator until the appointment takes effect, provided this is within five business days; and

(c) from when a notice of intention to appoint an administrator is filed with the court by the company or its directors until the appointment takes effect, provided this is within ten business days.

Protection under para 44 is known as an interim moratorium. It does not prevent or require the court's permission for (para 44(7)):

(a) the presentation of a public-interest winding-up petition by the Secretary of State, the FCA or the PRA;

(b) the appointment of an administrator by the holder of a floating charge;

(c) the appointment of an administrative receiver; and

(d) the carrying out by an administrative receiver of his or her functions.

Guidance on dealing with applications for permission in administration was given by the Court of Appeal [1992] Ch 505 at pp 541-4.

20.3.9 END OF ADMINISTRATION

Administration automatically ends after one year, extended by consent of the creditors or order of the co

There can only be one extension by consent, w (paras 76(2)(b) and 78(4)(a)). Consent must be given (para 78(4)(b) and (c)). Consent must be given by e creditors (para 78(1)). If the administration has pr available for unsecured creditors is their statutory sh (see **20.2.4**), the consent required is of preferential cr creditors (para 78(2)).

[handwritten note: Interim Moratorium — Effect of freezing the rights of creditors to bring insolvency proceedings and other legal processes against the company.]

The court may make any number of extensions for any periods it thinks fit, but it can never revive a term of office that has already expired (paras 76(2)(a) and 77(1)).

An administrator whose term of office is extended must, under penalty, notify Companies House and, if the extension is by consent, the court (paras 77(2) and (3) and 78(5) and (6)).

An administrator may terminate the administration if he or she thinks that its purpose has been sufficiently achieved: this is done by application to the court if the administrator was appointed by court order (para 79(3)), or otherwise by notice to the court and to Companies House (para 80).

A court-appointed administrator must apply to the court for an order ending the appointment if he or she thinks that the purpose of the administration cannot be achieved or that the company should not have entered administration, or if the creditors decide that such an application must be made (para 79(2)).

A creditor can apply to the court to end an administration on the ground that the person who appointed the administrator or applied for a court appointment did so for an improper motive (para 81).

An administrator of a company who thinks that its secured creditors have been paid or provided for and that there is money to distribute to unsecured creditors may put the company into creditors' voluntary winding up by sending a notice to Companies House, filing a copy of it with the court and sending a copy to creditors (para 83). On registration of the notice at Companies House, the appointment of the administrator ceases to have effect (para 83(6)(a)) and the administrator becomes the liquidator, unless the creditors nominate someone else (para 83(7)). Provided the administrator was in office when the notice was sent, the fact that his or her term of office expires before the notice is registered does not affect the operation of para 83 (*Re E Squared Ltd* [2006] EWHC 532 (Ch), [2006] 1 WLR 3414).

An administrator of a company who thinks that it has nothing to distribute to its creditors must have it dissolved by sending a notice to Companies House, unless this obligation is disapplied by the court (see **20.16.2.8**) (para 84). The use of this procedure is not restricted to a company which never in the period of administration had any property to distribute (*Re Preston and Duckworth Ltd* (2005) LTL 11/11/2005; *Re GHE Realisations Ltd* [2005] EWHC 2400 (Ch), [2006] 1 WLR 287). So when the purpose of an administration has been achieved, the administrator can avoid the expense of putting the company into liquidation by making a distribution of all remaining assets and then proceeding to dissolution under para 84. To the extent that a distribution is to persons other than secured and preferential creditors it requires the permission of the court (para 65). This permission will be given if a distribution by the administrator rather than by a liquidator is in the interests of the company's creditors as whole (*Re GHE Realisations Ltd*).

A court-appointed administrator is not required to apply under para 79(3) for his or her appointment to cease to have effect in order to give notice under para 83 or para 84 (*Re Ballast plc* [2004] EWHC 2356 (Ch), [2005] 1 WLR 1928).

20.3.10 PRIORITY FOR ADMINISTRATION EXPENSES

The expenses of an administration have priority over a debt secured by a floating charge (IA 1986, sch B1, para 99). ('Floating charge' means a charge which was a floating charge on its creation: para 111(1).) But debts or liabilities arising out of a contract entered into by the administrator have priority (sometimes called 'super-priority') over the administrator's own remuneration and expenses (para 99(3) and (4)). If a company in administration is in rateable occupation of property, the non-domestic rates payable during the administration are 'necessary disbursements by the administrator in the course of the administration' and, under I(EW)R 2016, r 3.51, rank for payment before the administrator's remuneration (*Exeter City Council v Bairstow* [2007] EWHC 400 (Ch), [2007] Bus LR 813).

A sum payable under a contract of employment adopted by the administrator has super-priority, except to the extent to which it refers to anything done or occurring before the contract was adopted (IA 1986, sch B1, para 99(5)). Only payments of wages or salary have super-priority under this provision. This includes deductions for income tax and national insurance (*Re FJL Realisations Ltd* [2001] ICR 424). But compensation for wrongful dismissal does not have super-priority (*Re Leeds United Association Football Club Ltd* [2007] EWHC 1761 (Ch), [2007] ICR 1688). Wages to be paid in lieu of notice have super-priority, but only when the employee has been asked not to work during a period of notice, not when summary dismissal is permitted by the contract of employment on condition that a sum described as wages in lieu of notice is paid (*Re Huddersfield Fine Worsteds Ltd* [2005] EWCA Civ 1072, [2006] ICR 205). A protective award under the Trade Union and Labour Relations (Consolidation) Act 1992, s 189, for failure to consult before dismissing employees for redundancy, does not have super-priority (*Re Huddersfield Fine Worsteds Ltd*), nor does a statutory redundancy payment (*Re Allders Department Stores Ltd* [2005] EWHC 172 (Ch), [2005] ICR 867). Paragraph 99(6) of IA 1986, sch B1, explains how liability for holiday and sick pay is to be allocated.

Nothing done or omitted to be done during the first 14 days after an administrator's appointment is to be taken as showing that the administrator has adopted any contract of employment (para 99(5)(a)). After the first 14 days, there must be some conduct by the administrator which amounts to an election to treat a continued contract of employment as giving rise to a separate liability in the administration (*Powdrill v Watson* [1995] 2 AC 394 at p 449; *Re Antal International Ltd* [2003] EWHC 1339 (Ch), [2003] 2 BCLC 406). The fact that a contract of employment is not terminated during the 14-day period may lead inevitably to the conclusion that it has been adopted (*Powdrill v Watson*), but not where the administrator was unaware that it existed (*Re Antal International Ltd*).

20.4 VOLUNTARY ARRANGEMENTS

20.4.1 SUMMARY DESCRIPTION

In a voluntary arrangement a decision by those of a company's unsecured creditors who participate in a decision-making process imposes on all unsecured creditors a composition or scheme of arrangement that has been proposed by the company's directors (or its liquidator or administrator) and approved by its members.

Voluntary arrangement is an insolvency procedure: it is usually invoked in relation to insolvent companies and not solvent companies. Most of the law on voluntary arrangements is contained in IA 1986, part I (ss 1 to 7).

Voluntary arrangement is not a liquidation procedure.

A proposal for a voluntary arrangement must be reported to the court but does not require the court's approval.

There is a similar procedure for insolvent individuals. A voluntary arrangement entered into by a company is usually known as company voluntary arrangement or CVA, and an individual voluntary arrangement is known as an IVA.

20.4.2 PROPOSAL FOR A VOLUNTARY ARRANGEMENT

If a company is not in liquidation or administration, its directors may propose a composition or scheme (IA 1986, s 1(1)). The directors must nominate a qualified insolvency practitioner (see **20.1.4**) to be supervisor. That person is referred to as the 'nominee' in the legislation. The nominee must, within 28 days after being given notice of the proposal, submit a report to the court stating whether, in his or her opinion, the proposal should be considered by a meeting of the company's members and by the company's creditors, and whether it has a reasonable prospect of being approved and implemented (s 2(1) and (2)). The directors must provide the nominee with a statement of the company's affairs (s 2(3)) and any further information the nominee requires (I(EW)R 2016, r 2.6). If the nominee's opinion is that the scheme is worth submitting to members and creditors, the nominee must summon a meeting of the company's members and seek a decision from its creditors (IA 1986, s 3(1) and (3)).

If a company is in liquidation or administration, its liquidator or administrator (who must be a qualified insolvency practitioner) may propose a composition or scheme to be supervised by him or herself (s 1(3)). The administrator or liquidator may then put the proposal to members and creditors (s 3(2)) without reference to the court. Alternatively, a liquidator or administrator may nominate another insolvency practitioner to be supervisor and then a report is made to the court as if the proposal had been made by the directors using the procedure described in the preceding paragraph.

20.4.3 APPROVAL OF A PROPOSAL

When a proposal for a voluntary arrangement is put to members and creditors of a company (see 20.4.2), they must decide whether to approve the proposal, with or without modifications (IA 1986, s 4(1) and (1A)). The creditors' decision must be taken by a qualifying decision procedure (s 3(3)). A proposal is not approved by creditors unless three-quarters or more (in value) of those responding vote in favour of it (I(EW)R 2016, r 15.34(3)) and is not made if more than half of the total value of the unconnected creditors vote against it (r 15.34(4) and (5)). The persons who are connected with a company are defined in IA 1986, s 249 (see 11.6.7.1).

A proposal or a modification that deprives a secured creditor of the right to enforce the security cannot be approved unless that creditor agrees (s 4(3)). This means that, as with administration, no proposal can go forward without the consent of the holders of floating charges over the company's property. It is possible to approve a scheme of arrangement which will benefit secured creditors but has no realistic prospect of resulting in any payment to preferential or unsecured creditors (*Commissioners of Inland Revenue v Adam and Partners Ltd* [2001] 1 BCLC 222).

A proposal that affects the priority of any preferential debt cannot be approved unless the creditor concerned concurs (ss 4(4) and 387(2)). This also applies to any debt that would be preferential if the company had gone into liquidation when it entered administration (if it is in administration) or (if it is not in administration or liquidation) when the voluntary arrangement takes effect. Preferential debts are discussed in 20.15.1.

The decisions of the members and creditors must be reported to the court (IA 1986, s 4(6) and (6A)). If both members and creditors approve the proposal (either with the same modifications or without modification), the composition or scheme takes effect as if made by the company at the time the creditors decided to approve it and it binds every person who had notice of, and was entitled to vote in the qualifying decision procedure by which the creditors approved it (IA 1986, s 5(1) and (2)). The nominee becomes the supervisor of the voluntary arrangement (s 7(1) and (2)). However, during the period of 28 days beginning with the day on which the first of the reports required by s 4(6) is made to the court, any person entitled to vote as a member or creditor, the nominee or the company's liquidator or administrator (if there is one) may apply to the court, under s 6, on the ground:

(a) that the approved composition or scheme unfairly prejudices the interests of a creditor, member or contributory of the company; and/or

(b) that there has been some material irregularity at the company meeting or in relation to the relevant qualifying decision procedure.

The court may then revoke or suspend the approvals and make directions for revised proposals to be put to the members and creditors (s 6(4)). An approval is not invalidated by any irregularity in decision-making unless the approval is successfully challenged by proceedings under s 6 (s 6(7)). An irregularity is 'material' if there is a substantial chance that the arrangement would not have been approved in that form if the irregularity had not occurred (*Re Trident Fashions plc* [2004] EWHC 293 (Ch), [2004] 2 BCLC 35).

If members and creditors reach opposite conclusions, the view of the creditors will prevail, but, within 28 days, a member may apply to the court, which may overrule the creditors' decision or make such other order as it thinks fit (s 4A).

If a proposal is approved for a company that is in liquidation or administration then, when the 28-day period for lodging an objection has expired, and after the court has disposed of any objections that are made, the court may order that the proceedings in the winding up be stayed (that is, the winding up shall proceed no further) or provide for the appointment of the administrator to cease to have effect (s 5(3) and (4)).

20.4.4 ALTERNATIVE PROCEDURE FOR SMALL COMPANIES

One of the difficulties for a company in preparing a proposal for a voluntary arrangement is that when the proposal is circulated to creditors for their approval, any one creditor may wreck the proposal by taking individual action, for example appointing a receiver, repossessing hire-purchase goods or even presenting a winding-up petition. This can be prevented by going into administration, but the administration procedure is itself expensive. To deal with this problem, IA 1986, s 1A and sch A1, enable an 'eligible company' (which primarily means a small company) to obtain a moratorium on creditor action while a proposal for a voluntary arrangement is considered, without having to go into administration. A moratorium cannot be obtained until there is a viable proposal for an arrangement and a nominee has agreed to act.

A moratorium begins (sch A1, para 8(1)) when an eligible company files with the court the following documents (sch A1, para 7(1)):

(a) a document setting out the terms of the proposed voluntary arrangement;

(b) a statement of affairs;

(c) a statement that the company is eligible for a moratorium;

(d) a statement that the nominee (see **20.4.2**) has consented to act;

(e) a statement from the nominee that, in his or her opinion

    (i) the proposed voluntary arrangement has a reasonable prospect of being approved and implemented,

    (ii) the company is likely to have sufficient funds available during the moratorium to enable it to carry on its business, or

    (iii) the proposed voluntary arrangement should be considered by a meeting of the company and by the company's creditors.

The principal condition for eligibility for a moratorium is in sch A1, para 3, and is that in the year ending with the date of filing, or in the company's financial year (see **9.5.2**) which ended last before that date, the company satisfied two or more of the requirements for being a small company specified in CA 2006, s 382(3) (see **9.4.2**). A company is not eligible for a moratorium if it is the holding company of a group which did not qualify as a small or medium-sized group (see **9.4.5**) in the company's last financial year (IA 1986, sch A1, para 3(4)). A company is not eligible for a moratorium if it has a liability, under any agreement, of £10 million or more (sch A1, para 4C). By sch A1, para 4, a moratorium is not available to a company which is already subject to a liquidation or insolvency procedure (though the fact that a winding-up petition has been presented is not a bar to a moratorium, unless a provisional liquidator has been appointed). Also by sch A1, para 4, if a company's moratorium fails to produce a workable voluntary arrangement, the company cannot file for another moratorium for 12 months, and a company cannot file for a moratorium within 12 months of being in administration. The moratorium procedure is not available to insurance, banking and various financial services companies (sch A1, para 2), or to companies with liabilities under certain kinds of marketable loans valued at £10 million or more (sch A1, paras 4A, 4D, 4E, 4F, 4G and 4K) or to certain companies involved in public–private partnership projects (sch A1, paras 4B, 4H, 4I, 4J and 4K).

The directors must notify the nominee that the moratorium has begun (sch A1, para 9), and the nominee must advertise the fact and notify the registrar (sch A1, para 10).

The effects on creditors of a moratorium are specified in sch A1, para 12, and are substantially the same as the effects of an administration moratorium (see 20.3.8). The company must state that a moratorium is in force, and identify the nominee, in every invoice, order for goods or business letter, issued by or on its behalf, in or on which its name appears (sch A1, para 16). It must not obtain credit (which includes taking advance payments from customers) for more than £250 from a person who has not been informed that a moratorium is in force (sch A1, para 17).

It is not possible for a floating-charge contract to specify that obtaining or preparing for a moratorium crystallises the floating charge (sch A1, para 43).

The nominee must seek the approval of the proposal by the company's members and creditors in the same way as is described in 20.4.3 (sch A1, paras 31, 37, 38 and 39) within a period of 28 days beginning with the day on which the moratorium comes into force (sch A1, paras 8(3) and 29(1)). If not, the moratorium ends on the last day of that period (sch A1, para 8(4)). If the members' meeting is first held within the 28 days, the moratorium ends on the day of that meeting or on the day when the creditors decide whether to approve the proposal, whichever is later (sch A1, para 8(2)), unless the creditors decide to extend the moratorium (sch A1, paras 8(2), 32 and 36). An extension may not be for longer than two months (sch A1, para 32(2)). Members and creditors may decide to end an extended moratorium (sch A1, para 32(6)). If the members' meeting disagrees with a decision to extend the moratorium or to end an extended moratorium, a member may apply to the court, under sch A1, para 36, for an order substituting the members' decision.

When a moratorium ends the nominee must advertise the fact and notify the court, Companies House, and all of the company's creditors of whose claims he or she is aware (sch A1, para 11).

If a company's moratorium has ended without an effective voluntary arrangement, one or more creditors may petition for the company to be wound up by the court (ss 122(1)(fa) and 124(3A)).

20.4.5 FALSE REPRESENTATION OR FRAUD

It is an offence, punishable by up to seven years' imprisonment, for an officer of a company to make a false representation, or fraudulently to do or omit to do, anything, for the purpose of obtaining approval of a proposal for a voluntary arrangement (IA 1986, s 6A and sch 10).

20.5 VOLUNTARY WINDING UP

20.5.1 SUMMARY DESCRIPTION

20.5.1.1 Members' voluntary winding up

Members' voluntary winding up is a liquidation procedure (see 20.1.2). It is initiated when the members of a company adopt a resolution for voluntary winding up following a statutory declaration of solvency by the company's directors. The members appoint a qualified insolvency practitioner as liquidator of the company.

Members' voluntary winding up is not an insolvency procedure: it can be invoked only in relation to solvent companies. It is sometimes called solvent liquidation.

The involvement of the court is never required for initiating or confirming the use of this procedure.

20.5.1.2 Creditors' voluntary winding up

Creditors' voluntary winding up is a liquidation procedure (see **20.1.2**). It is initiated when the members of a company adopt a resolution for voluntary winding up without a statutory declaration of solvency by the company's directors. The company's unsecured creditors have the right to appoint a qualified insolvency practitioner as liquidator of the company and a liquidation committee may be appointed, with up to five representatives of creditors, to assist and supervise the liquidator.

Creditors' voluntary winding up is an insolvency procedure: it is usually invoked in relation to insolvent companies and not solvent companies.

The involvement of the court is never required for initiating the use of this procedure. Confirmation by the court is an optional procedure under I(EW)R 2016, rr 21.4 and 21.5, which will give the winding up recognition throughout the EU (apart from Denmark) under Regulation (EU) 2015/848: this will be appropriate where the company has assets located in another EU State (apart from Denmark).

20.5.2 RESOLUTION FOR VOLUNTARY WINDING UP

Voluntary winding up of a company is commenced by the members passing a resolution for voluntary winding up (IA 1986, s 84(1) and (2)). The resolution must normally be a special resolution (75 per cent majority). Only an ordinary resolution is necessary if the members are invoking a provision in the company's articles that it should cease operations on the expiry of a certain time, which has now expired, or on the happening of a particular event, which has now happened (s 84(1)(a)).

20.5.3 DECLARATION OF SOLVENCY

After the adoption of a resolution to wind up, the liquidation may proceed as a members' voluntary winding up only if, within the five weeks *preceding* the adoption of the resolution, a majority of the directors of the company made, at a board meeting, a statutory declaration of the company's solvency (IA 1986, s 89). The declaration may be made on the same day as the members' meeting provided it is made before the meeting (s 89(2)(a)).

If a directors' declaration of solvency is not made then the liquidation is a creditors' voluntary winding up (s 90).

The directors must, under penalty, file their declaration with the registrar before the expiry of the period of 15 days immediately following the date on which the winding-up resolution is adopted (s 89(3) and (6) and sch 10).

The requirement that the declaration must be made by a majority of directors means that there must be more directors making the declaration than not making it. So if the company has only two directors then both must make the declaration; and if it has only one director then that director must make the declaration (s 89(1)).

The declaration must state that the declaring directors have made a full inquiry into the affairs of the company, and have formed the opinion that the company will be able to pay its debts (including post-liquidation interest) in full within a specified period after the commencement of winding up. The specified period must not exceed 12 months (s 89(1)).

A declaration is of no effect unless it embodies a statement of the company's assets and liabilities as at the latest practicable date before the making of the declaration (s 89(2)(b)). It is not required that the statement be correct in every detail provided it can be fairly described as being a statement of assets and liabilities (*De Courcy v Clement* [1971] Ch 693).

A director making a declaration of solvency without reasonable grounds for the opinion expressed in it commits an offence triable either way (s 89(4) and sch 10). If the company's debts are not paid or provided for within the period stated in the declaration then the makers of the declaration are presumed not to have had reasonable grounds for making it (s 89(5)).

20.5.4 APPOINTMENT OF A MEMBERS' LIQUIDATOR

In a members' voluntary winding up the members in general meeting must appoint one or more liquidators (IA 1986, s 91(1)). The appointment would normally be made at the meeting at which the resolution to wind up is adopted and no notice is required of intention to propose a resolution to appoint a liquidator at that meeting (*Re Trench Tubeless Tyre Co* [1900] 1 Ch 408).

On the appointment of a liquidator of a company all the powers of its directors cease, though either the company in general meeting or the liquidator may allow some or all of the directors to continue to exercise some or all of their powers (s 90(2)). However, after the resolution to wind up is adopted, if the members fail to appoint a liquidator then the directors commit a summary offence if they exercise any of their powers without the sanction of the court (s 114) except for the purpose of disposing of goods that are perishable or likely to diminish in value if not immediately disposed of and for the purpose of protecting the company's assets (s 114(3)).

20.5.5 APPOINTMENT OF A CREDITORS' LIQUIDATOR

If no declaration of solvency is made by the directors of a company in the five weeks preceding the meeting at which it is proposed to adopt a resolution for voluntary winding up then the liquidation will be a creditors' voluntary winding up (IA 1986, s 90). If the creditors do not approve of the members' choice of liquidator, they may nominate a liquidator themselves, and their nominee becomes liquidator, unless the court orders otherwise (s 100). To prevent frustration of the creditors' right to choose a liquidator, s 166 makes it an offence for a liquidator nominated by the members in a creditors' voluntary liquidation to exercise any powers (except for the purpose of taking control of the company's property, disposing of perishable goods and goods likely to diminish in value unless immediately disposed of and protecting the company's assets) until the creditors have had an opportunity to make an appointment.

20.5.6 LIQUIDATION COMMITTEE

In a creditors' voluntary liquidation, the creditors may appoint a committee (known as a 'liquidation committee') of not more than five persons to act with the liquidator. If they do so, the members of the company may appoint up to five persons to the committee to represent shareholders' interests. However, the creditors may veto any or all of the persons appointed by the shareholders and this veto is effective unless the court orders otherwise, though the court may appoint some other person in place of a vetoed appointee (IA 1986, s 101).

The function of the liquidation committee is to assist and supervise the work of the liquidator and in particular it may:

(a) sanction the sale of the company's business to another company in exchange for shares of the purchasing company (s 110);

(b) sanction the continuance of the powers of the directors of the company (s 103);

(c) approve payment of the expenses of the statement of affairs to the liquidator or an associate of the liquidator (I(EW)R 2016, r 6.7(5));

(d) fix the liquidator's remuneration (r 18.20);

(e) receive reports and information from the liquidator (r 17.23) and inspect the liquidator's financial records (Insolvency Regulations 1986 (SI 1986/1994), reg 27(2));

(f) sanction committee members' dealings with the company (I(EW)R 2016, r 17.25);

(g) permit the liquidator to distribute the company's assets in kind to creditors (r 14.13); and

(h) resolve that the liquidator is to require costs, charges or expenses payable by the company to be assessed by the court (r 12.42(2)).

If a creditors' liquidator disposes of any property of the company to a person who is connected with the company (for the meaning of 'connected with' a company, see **11.6.7.1**), the liquidator must notify the liquidation committee (IA 1986, s 165(6)).

20.6 WINDING UP BY THE COURT

20.6.1 SUMMARY DESCRIPTION

Winding up by the court is a liquidation procedure (see **20.1.2**). It is a liquidation of a company by virtue of an order of a court (with appropriate jurisdiction: see **1.5.2.2**) that the company be wound up by that court. Winding up by the court is also called compulsory liquidation.

Compulsory liquidation may be applied to a solvent or an insolvent company, but, in practice, is most often invoked in relation to insolvent companies.

The involvement of the court is required for initiating this procedure.

20.6.2 CIRCUMSTANCES IN WHICH A WINDING-UP ORDER MAY BE MADE

A registered company may be wound up by the court only if it is shown that one of the circumstances listed in IA 1986, s 122(1), exists. In practice, nowadays, only circumstances (f) and (g) are relied on. They are:

(f) the company is unable to pay its debts; and

(g) the court is of the opinion that it is just and equitable that the company should be wound up.

20.6.3 PETITION

An application to the court for a winding-up order must be made by petition under IA 1986, s 124. The persons who may petition for the compulsory liquidation of any company are:

(a) any creditor or creditors of the company (including any contingent or prospective creditor or creditors) (s 124(1));

(b) any contributory or contributories of the company (s 124(1));

(c) the company itself (s 124(1));

(d) the directors of the company (s 124(1));

(e) a supervisor of a voluntary arrangement of the company (s 7(4)(b));

(f) the designated officer for a magistrates' court (if the company has failed to pay a fine) (s 124(1));

(g) a liquidator (within the meaning of Council Regulation (EC) No 1346/2000, art 29(b)) appointed in proceedings by virtue of art 3(1) of the Regulation, or a temporary administrator (within the meaning of art 38 of the Regulation) (IA 1986, s 124(1));

(h) all or any of the parties listed in (a) to (g) together or separately (s 124(1));

(i) the Secretary of State (s 124(4));

(j) an official receiver (though only if the company is already in voluntary liquidation) (s 124(5));

(k) an administrator of the company (sch B1, para 60 and sch 1, para 21)—an administrator of a company is deemed to act as the company's agent (sch B1, para 69); and

(l) an administrative receiver of the company (s 42(1) and (2); sch 1, para 21)—an administrative receiver of a company is deemed to act as the company's agent (s 44(1)).

In practice, about 95 per cent of petitions are by creditors (see **20.6.4**). Contributories' petitions are considered in **18.7**, and petitions by the Secretary of State in **18.8.5.3**.

Other statutes confer standing on other persons to petition in relation to special classes of companies, such as charitable companies and financial services companies, but this chapter will concentrate on the provisions of IA 1986.

20.6.4 CREDITORS' PETITIONS

Usually a creditor petitions for the winding up of a company by the court on the ground that the company is unable to pay its debts (IA 1986, s 122(1)(f)). Although s 122(1)(f) is expressed in terms of the company's inability to pay its debts generally, this may be proved by showing that the company has failed to pay one debt (usually the petitioner's). Section 123 assists a petitioner by defining a number of circumstances which the court will take as sufficient evidence of a company's inability to pay its debts:

(a) if the company fails to comply with a written demand in prescribed form (known as a statutory demand) for payment of a debt exceeding £750 (s 123(1)(a));

(b) if execution of a judgment against the company anywhere in the United Kingdom fails wholly or partly (s 123(1)(b), (c) and (d));

(c) if it is proved to the satisfaction of the court that the company is unable to pay its debts as they fall due (s 123(1)(e)); or

(d) if it is proved that the company's assets are less than its liabilities, taking into account prospective and contingent liabilities (s 123(2)).

Under s 123(1)(e) the court will accept evidence that the company has failed to pay the petitioner's debt as proof that it is unable to pay its debts as they fall due (*Taylors Industrial Flooring Ltd v M and H Plant Hire (Manchester) Ltd* [1990] BCLC 216).

A person claiming to be a creditor of a company cannot petition for it to be wound up by the court if there is a bona fide dispute on substantial grounds over whether the debt actually exists (*Mann v Goldstein* [1968] 1 WLR 1091; *Stonegate Securities Ltd v Gregory* [1980] Ch 576; *Re Selectmove Ltd* [1995] 1 WLR 474). This is because a dispute about the existence of the petitioner's debt is generally thought to be a dispute about the petitioner's standing to petition and must normally be resolved before the petition can be heard. However, proceedings on a winding-up petition are not appropriate for determining a dispute about the existence of a debt, and so the practice is to refuse to allow such a petition to proceed, leaving the petitioner to establish the debt, and thus standing to petition, in a more appropriate forum.

If the fact that a company is indebted to a person who is petitioning as a creditor for the company to be wound up is not disputed, but the amount to be paid, and/or the time at which it is to be paid, is disputed (in particular, if only part of the petitioner's debt is disputed) then the petitioner's standing is not in question (*Re Tweeds Garages Ltd* [1962] Ch 406). However, if the size of the creditor's debt is not known with certainty, a statutory demand for it cannot be served (*Re a Company (No 003729 of 1982)* [1984] 1 WLR 1090) and the petitioner must be able to prove the company's inability to pay its debts otherwise than by neglect to comply with a statutory demand for the petitioner's debt.

IA 1986, s 123(1)(a), comes into operation only when a creditor of a company has served a statutory demand on the company 'by leaving it at the company's registered office' (IA 1986, s 123(1)(a)). This contrasts with the provision of CA 2006, s 1139(1), that: 'A document may be served on a company registered under this Act by leaving it at, or sending it by post to, the company's registered office'. Accordingly, Nourse J, in *Re a Company* [1985] BCLC 37, took the view that IA 1986, s 123(1)(a), does not operate if a statutory demand has been sent by post. The same view was taken (without reference to *Re a Company* [1985] BCLC 37) by Sheriff Principal N D MacLeod QC in *Craig v Iona Hotels Ltd* 1988 SCLR 130, ruling that a statutory demand sent by recorded delivery was not effective. However, in *Re a Company (No 008790 of 1990)* [1991] BCLC 561, Morritt J observed that s 123(1)(a) does not specify who is to leave the demand at the registered office, and held that it can be left there by any agent of the person making the demand, including the Post Office: the important point is that it must be proved that the demand was left; there is no presumption that a posted demand has been delivered; however, a demand sent by registered post which the company admitted had been delivered was effective. It is submitted that Morritt J's decision is correct. It accords with the view of Wynn-Parry J in *Stylo Shoes Ltd v Prices Tailors Ltd* [1960] Ch 396 that the act of sending a letter by ordinary post is equivalent to leaving it for the proposed recipient at the place to which the letter is delivered. In *Re a Company* [1985] BCLC 37, Nourse J held that a demand transmitted by telex was not properly served.

20.6.5 APPOINTMENT OF A LIQUIDATOR

If the court orders a company to be wound up, the official receiver attached to the court automatically becomes the company's liquidator (IA 1986, s 136(1) and (2)).

In many cases the official receiver will find that the company's realisable assets will not cover the expenses of liquidation. If that is the case and the company's affairs do not require further investigation, the official receiver will notify Companies House for the company to be dissolved under s 202 (see **20.16.2.6**).

If there are substantial assets to be administered, an insolvency practitioner may be appointed liquidator in place of the official receiver. This may be achieved in three ways under ss 136 and 137:

(a) One-quarter, in value, of the company's creditors may request the official receiver to seek nominations from the company's creditors and contributories for the purpose of choosing a liquidator.

(b) The official receiver may seek nominations on his or her own initiative.

(c) The official receiver may apply to the Secretary of State to make an appointment.

Creditors and contributories may each nominate a person to be liquidator in place of the official receiver (s 139(2)). The person nominated by the creditors becomes the liquidator but if they do not nominate anyone, the person nominated by the members becomes liquidator (s 139(3)). However, if creditors and contributories nominate different persons, any contributory or even creditor may, within seven days after the date on which the nomination was made by the creditors, apply to the court to have the contributories' nominee appointed instead of or jointly with the creditors' nominee or to have someone else appointed instead of the creditors' nominee (s 139(4)). It is important to remember that only unsecured creditors vote.

There are special provisions in s 140 for an administrator of a company to continue as its liquidator if compulsory liquidation follows administration, and similar provisions for a supervisor of a voluntary arrangement.

20.6.6 LIQUIDATION COMMITTEE

Where the liquidator in a compulsory winding up is not the official receiver, the creditors and contributories may, under IA 1986, s 141, appoint a liquidation committee to assist and supervise the work of the liquidator. In particular, it may:

(a) sanction the making of a call by the liquidator (s 160(2));

(b) fix the liquidator's remuneration (I(EW)R 2016, r 18.20);

(c) receive reports and information from the liquidator (r 17.23) and inspect the liquidator's financial records (Insolvency Regulations 1986 (SI 1986/1994), reg 9(2));

(d) sanction committee members' dealings with the company (I(EW)R 2016, r 17.25);

(e) permit the liquidator to distribute the company's assets in kind to creditors (r 14.13); and

(f) resolve that the liquidator is to require costs, charges or expenses payable by the company to be assessed by the court (r 12.42(2)).

Where there is a liquidation committee in a winding up by the court, the liquidator must notify it of any disposition of the company's property to a person who is connected with the company (for the meaning of 'connected with' a company, see **11.6.7.1**), or any employment by the liquidator of a solicitor (IA 1986, s 167(2)).

20.6.7 EFFECT ON DIRECTORS

The functions of a compulsory liquidator of a company are to secure that the assets of the company are got in, realised and distributed to the company's creditors and, if there is a surplus, to the persons entitled to it (IA 1986, s 143(1)). The compulsory liquidator of a company 'shall take into his custody or under his control all the property and things in action to which the company is or appears to be entitled' (s 144(1)). Custody (of tangible property) or control (of intangible property) pass to the liquidator by virtue of s 144(1) without any need for action on the liquidator's part (*Katz v Bradney* [2012] EWHC 1018 (Ch), [2013] Bus LR 169). In a winding up by the court, the liquidator has the power to sell the company's property, use the company's seal, draw cheques on its bank account and carry on the business of the company so far as may be necessary for its beneficial winding up (s 167(1)). Clearly there is little left for the company's directors to do in these circumstances, but the Act never explicitly makes the important point that the powers of the directors cease on a compulsory winding up as it does in relation to a voluntary winding up. In *Re Farrow's Bank Ltd* [1921] 2 Ch 164, Lord Sterndale MR said:

> There is no express provision in the Act in the case of a compulsory liquidation as there is in the case of a voluntary liquidation, that the powers of the directors shall cease on the appointment of a liquidator, but they do in fact cease on the appointment of a liquidator in a compulsory liquidation. In that case the liquidator is imposed upon the company compulsorily by the court to do acts on behalf of the company and to carry on the business of the company so far as it shall be necessary for the purposes of the winding up. It is quite true that the company does not choose him; he is put there by the court; but he is put there to do the acts which the directors of the company did before their powers ceased: with this restriction, of course, that in all that he does he must have regard to the interests of the creditors of the company.

However, the directors may appeal against the winding-up order, because the suspension of their powers derives from the very order they dispute (*Re Diamond Fuel Co* (1879) 13 ChD 400).

In *Madrid Bank Ltd v Bayley* (1866) LR 2 QB 37, the bank was in compulsory liquidation and there was a dispute between its liquidator and a contributory over liability to calls. In legal proceedings concerning this dispute the contributory made a pre-trial request for further information. Since the other party to the dispute was a company, its 'officers' could be required to provide this information. Blackburn J held that individuals who were directors of the company when it went into liquidation 15 months previously still held office and so were required to provide the information. However, in *Re Ebsworth and Tidy's Contract* (1889) 42 ChD 23, Lord Esher MR said, at p 43, that he thought that on the appointment of a liquidator in the compulsory winding up of a company, the directors of the company 'have ceased to exist', and the decision in *Madrid Bank Ltd v Bayley* is inconsistent with the views of the Court of Appeal in **Measures Brothers Ltd v Measures** [1910] 2 Ch 248. Mr Measures had a fixed-term contract to be a director of the company until 26 June 1910, which he could then renew at his option for a further seven years. A winding-up order was made on 13 October 1909. Buckley LJ said (at p 256):

> by the operation of a winding-up order...the office itself came to an end...after that order was made the company could not employ him in the office...He has ceased to hold his office.

Kennedy LJ said, at p 257:

> The effect of the events of 1909...was unquestionably...to render the company admittedly and finally unable to fulfil its agreement for the continuance of the defendant as a director.

One problem with the theory that an order for the compulsory liquidation of a company abolishes the offices of the directors of the company is to determine what happens if the liquidation is stayed. Australian judges have taken the view that when a winding-up order is made, the directors remain in office but their powers are removed, and therefore if proceedings in the winding up are stayed, the directors continue in office and their powers are returned to them (*Re Country Traders Distributors Ltd* [1974] 2 NSWLR 135; *Austral Brick Co Pty Ltd v Falgat Constructions Pty Ltd* (1990) 21 NSWLR 389; *McAusland v Deputy Commissioner of Taxation* (1993) 118 ALR 577). In *Re Country Traders Distributors Ltd*, however, it was held that the directors of a company in liquidation could not be required to sign a document which the company was required by statute to prepare and which the statute directed should be signed by the company's directors: they could not be responsible for the preparation of the document and so should not be forced to authenticate it. And in *Lord Corporation Pty Ltd v Green* (1991) 22 NSWLR 532 it was held that a director of a company no longer holds a fiduciary position with respect to the company after it has gone into compulsory liquidation. It is submitted that these decisions show that it is artificial to regard directors of a company as still holding office after it has gone into compulsory liquidation and that the better view is that the winding-up order has the effect of removing them from office.

20.7 APPOINTMENT OF A PROVISIONAL LIQUIDATOR

At any time after a petition for the compulsory liquidation of a company has been presented to the court, and before the court disposes of the petition, any person with standing to petition for the company's compulsory liquidation may apply for the appointment by the court of a provisional liquidator (IA 1986, s 135; I(EW)R 2016, r 7.33). A provisional liquidator is appointed to take charge of the company's affairs, maintain the status quo and prevent prejudice either to those supporting the winding-up petition or to those against it, pending the court's decision on the petition. Like compulsory liquidation, to which it is closely linked, the procedure for appointing a provisional liquidator is mostly invoked in relation to insolvent companies and so may be considered an insolvency procedure, but there are also significant circumstances in which it may be applied to solvent companies.

Appointment of a provisional liquidator is not a liquidation procedure.

A provisional liquidator can be appointed only by the court.

20.8 COMMENCEMENT OF WINDING UP: GOING INTO LIQUIDATION

As winding up is a distinct and special period in the history of a company it is important to know when it commences. This is determined by two sections of IA 1986. By s 86, a voluntary winding up is deemed to commence at the time of the passing of the resolution for voluntary winding up. By s 129(1), if a winding-up order is made in respect of a company on a petition presented when the company was already in voluntary liquidation then the winding up is still deemed to have commenced at the time the resolution for voluntary winding up was passed. By s 129(2), in any other compulsory winding up, the date of commencement is the day on which the petition for winding up was presented.

The provision in CA 2006, s 332, that a resolution passed at an adjourned meeting of a company is to be treated as having been passed on the date on which it was in fact passed, was enacted in CA 1928 to stop companies backdating the commencement of winding up (see Report of the Company Law Amendment Committee 1925–26 (Cmd 2657, 1926), paras 36–7).

IA 1986 also uses the phrase 'to go into liquidation'. By s 247(2), a company goes into liquidation when it adopts a resolution for voluntary winding up or when a winding-up order is made against it (unless it had already passed a resolution for voluntary winding up, in which case the date of that resolution is the date of going into liquidation).

A company subject to compulsory winding up (not preceded by voluntary winding up) 'goes into liquidation' when the winding-up order is made but the winding up 'commenced' when the petition for the order was presented (*Re Walter L Jacob and Co Ltd* [1993] BCC 512).

20.9 INVESTIGATION OF A COMPANY'S AFFAIRS

20.9.1 INTRODUCTION

A person who is appointed as an office-holder in one of the company insolvency or liquidation procedures is usually unfamiliar with the company but must take charge of it very quickly. The legislation therefore makes several provisions for information about the company to be provided to the office-holder. A summary statement of the company's financial position, called a statement of affairs, must be prepared (**20.9.2**) and certain persons are required to provide information reasonably required by the office-holder (**20.9.3**). The customary liens which accountants and solicitors have on books and papers in their possession cannot deny the office-holder access to them (**20.9.4**). An insolvency office-holder is also required to investigate wrongdoing in relation to the company's affairs, in particular, for the purpose of instituting director disqualification proceedings (**20.9.6** to **20.9.8**). This may require formally recorded questioning of company officers (**20.9.5**).

20.9.2 STATEMENT OF AFFAIRS

In all the company insolvency procedures, the insolvency office-holder is entitled to require a person associated with the company to prepare a statement of affairs. This is a simple statement of the company's assets, debts and liabilities with a list of its creditors and details of the securities they hold. Except in the voluntary arrangement procedure, a statement of affairs must be verified by affidavit or, in administration, by a statement of truth.

An administrative receiver of a company may, under IA 1986, s 47, require a statement of its affairs from one or more persons connected with the company. The persons who may be required to submit the statement are listed in s 47(3), and s 47(6) makes it an offence to fail to comply without reasonable excuse. Similar provision is made in relation to an administrator by sch B1, para 47. On the making of a winding-up order against a company or the appointment of a provisional liquidator, the official receiver may require a statement of affairs (s 131). In a creditors' voluntary winding up, within seven days of passing the resolution for voluntary winding up, the directors must send a statement of the company's affairs to its creditors (s 99(1)) and must deliver it to the liquidator, when appointed (I(EW)R 2016, r 6.3(4)). If the directors of a company propose a voluntary arrangement, without asking for a moratorium, they must deliver a statement of affairs to the nominee (IA 986, s 2(3)(b); I(EW)R 2016, r 2.6). To obtain a moratorium while a proposal for a voluntary arrangement is under consideration, a statement of affairs must be filed with the court (IA 1986, sch A1, para 7).

In a members' voluntary winding up the directors' statutory declaration of solvency must include a statement of the company's assets and liabilities (IA 1986, s 89(2)(b)).

A person who is required by an administrative receiver to prepare a statement of affairs may claim a declaration that the receiver's appointment is invalid, even though this requires interpretation of the charge contract under which the receiver was appointed and to which the claimant is not a party (*Feetum v Levy* [2005] EWCA Civ 1601, [2006] 2 BCLC 102). Such a person is not only directly interested in the question of whether the receiver's appointment is valid, but is also directly affected by it, because refusal to comply with the requirement would be a criminal offence if the receiver were validly appointed.

In administration (I(EW)R 2016, r 3.32), administrative receivership (r 4.13(1) to (4)), members' voluntary winding up (IA 1986, s 89(3)) and creditors' voluntary winding up (I(EW)R 2016, r 6.2(3) and (4)), a copy of a statement of affairs must be filed at Companies House.

An office-holder or official receiver who thinks that allowing public inspection of the statement of affairs would prejudice the conduct of the procedure may apply to the court for an order of limited disclosure, under which the statement cannot be inspected without the court's permission (r 2.7 (CVA without moratorium), r 2.12 (CVA with moratorium), r 3.45 (administration); r 4.12 (administrative receivership); r 6.6 (creditors' voluntary winding up), r 7.43 (compulsory liquidation or appointment of provisional liquidator)). An order of limited disclosure is not available in voluntary winding up or during a moratorium while a proposal for a voluntary arrangement is considered. The nominee's report to the court on a proposal for a voluntary arrangement must include the directors' statement of affairs or a summary of it (r 2.9(1)).

20.9.3 DUTY TO COOPERATE WITH THE OFFICE-HOLDER

While a company is subject to any of the insolvency or liquidation procedures other than voluntary arrangement, certain persons connected with the company are, by IA 1986, ss 234(1) and 235, under an obligation:

(a) To give to the company's office-holder such information concerning the company and its promotion, formation, business dealings, affairs or property as the office-holder may, at any time after his or her appointment, reasonably require.

(b) To attend on the office-holder at such times as the office-holder may reasonably require.

'Reasonably' in this context means that the office-holder's request must be proportionate and relevant to the achievement of his or her objective (*Bishopsgate Investment Management Ltd v Maxwell* [1993] Ch 1 at p 57).

Failure, without reasonable excuse, to comply with an obligation imposed by s 235 is an offence triable either way (s 235(5) and sch 10).

The persons who have a duty under s 235 to cooperate with the office-holder are (s 235(3) and (4)):

(a) Persons who are or have at any time been officers of the company.

(b) Persons who have taken part in the formation of the company at any time within one year before a date defined in s 235(4), which is generally the date when the insolvency or liquidation procedure came into effect.

(c) Persons who are in the employment of the company, or have been in its employment within that year, and are, in the office-holder's opinion, capable of giving information which the office-holder requires.

(d) Persons who are, or have within that year been, officers of, or in the employment of, another company which is, or within that year was, an officer of the company in liquidation.

For these purposes, 'employment' includes employment under a contract for services.

By s 208(1)(a) to (c) it is an offence, triable either way, for a past or present officer or shadow director (s 208(3)) of a company in liquidation to keep from its liquidator any property, books or papers of the company. A sentence of up to seven years' imprisonment may be imposed (sch 10). It is a defence to prove that there was no intent to defraud (s 208(4)(a)).

20.9.4 BOOKS, PAPERS AND RECORDS

Under IA 1986, s 234(1) and (2), while a company is subject to any of the insolvency or liquidation procedures other than voluntary arrangement, the court may order any person who has what appears to be the company's books, papers or records to deliver them to the office-holder.

This power will be exercised only for the purpose of assisting the office-holder's work. So it could not be invoked by administrative receivers in order to obtain documents so as to assist in litigation being conducted by the chargee who appointed them (*GE Capital Commercial Finance Ltd v Sutton* [2004] EWCA Civ 315, [2004] 2 BCLC 662).

While a company is subject to any of the insolvency or liquidation procedures other than administrative receivership and voluntary arrangement, a lien on or other right to possession of, any of the books, papers or other records of the company is unenforceable to the extent that it would deny possession of them to the office-holder (s 246). This affects, for example, the right of an accountant in public practice or a solicitor to retain the books and papers of a client until paid for work done for the client. There is an exception for 'a lien on documents which give a title to property and are held as such' (s 246(3)). In this exception 'held as such' means 'held for the purpose of giving rise to a lien' rather than 'held for the purpose of giving title to property' (**Brereton v Nicholls** [1993] BCLC 593).

20.9.5 PRIVATE EXAMINATION

20.9.5.1 Nature of private examination

Under IA 1986, ss 234(1) and 236, while a company is subject to any of the insolvency or liquidation procedures other than voluntary arrangement, the office-holder may apply to the court for an order requiring a person:

(a) to appear before the court for oral examination on oath or by interrogatories (ss 236(2) and 237(4));

(b) to submit an affidavit to the court containing an account of his or her dealings with the company (s 236(3)); or

(c) to produce any books, papers or other records in his or her possession or under his or her control relating to the company or the promotion, formation, business, dealings, affairs or property of the company (s 236(3)).

The court's order may be backed by a warrant for arrest and seizure of books, papers, records, money and goods (s 236(5)).

In a winding up by the court the official receiver may make an application under s 236 whether or not he or she is the liquidator (s 236(1)).

The persons who may be required to provide information under s 236 are:

(a) any officer of the company;

(b) any person known or suspected to have in his or her possession any property of the company or supposed to be indebted to the company; or

(c) any person whom the court thinks capable of giving information concerning the promotion, formation, business, dealings, affairs or property of the company.

The court has power to order the production of books, papers or records which relate to the company even if they are not the company's property and the company itself could not have obtained them (*Re Trading Partners Ltd* [2002] 1 BCLC 655).

An inquiry under s 236 is intended primarily to obtain information and is not a stage in civil or criminal proceedings against the person summoned. Accordingly attendance at an oral examination is limited by the court and such an examination is known as a 'private examination' (*Re Greys Brewery Co* (1883) 25 ChD 400; *Re Norwich Equitable Fire Insurance Co* (1884) 27 ChD 515). An examinee is entitled to be attended and advised by solicitor and counsel who may re-examine the examinee and make representations on his or her behalf (I(EW)R 2016, r 12.20(4)). A written record must be made of the examination in such form as the court thinks proper (r 12.20(5)). It must be read over, either to or by the examinee, and signed by the examinee (r 12.20(5)). An examinee is not entitled to privilege against self-incrimination (*Bishopsgate Investment Management Ltd v Maxwell* [1993] Ch 1). There is a detailed discussion of the kinds of questions which may be put in examinations (either private or public) in *Re Richbell Strategic Holdings Ltd (No 2)* [2000] 2 BCLC 794.

The written record of an examination under IA 1986, s 236, is a private document for the use of the insolvency office-holder. Unless the court otherwise directs, the record is not filed in court and is not made available for public inspection (I(EW)R 2016, r 12.21). The court may give directions concerning the custody of the record (r 12.21(4)).

The court will order disclosure of the record of a private examination if it is required by the Secretary of State under the Company Directors Disqualification Act 1986, s 7(4), so that the Secretary of State may consider whether to institute disqualification proceedings against a present or past director of the company (*Re Polly Peck International plc* [1994] BCC 15). In *R v Clowes* [1992] 3 All ER 440, persons on trial on serious fraud charges in relation to the affairs of two companies were granted witness summonses ordering production of the record of private examinations conducted by the liquidators of the companies: the public interest in affording the accused every opportunity to defend themselves on serious charges outweighed the advantages of privacy of the examinations. A liquidator of a company may disclose information obtained under IA 1986, s 236, to the company's subsidiaries to enable them to recover or defend their assets for the benefit of themselves and the parent company (*Re Esal (Commodities) Ltd* [1989] BCLC 59).

Because answers to questions put to a person under s 236 are given under compulsion, they cannot be used in evidence against that person at a criminal trial, other than for offences relating to the giving of the answers, such as perjury (s 433). This protection was introduced as a result of the ruling of the European Court of Human Rights in *Saunders v United Kingdom* (1996) 23 EHRR 313 (see **18.8.4.4**). It applies to a person who answers questions after being told that if answers are not given an application will be made for an order under s 236 (*R v Sawtell* (2000) LTL 23/1/2001). However, documents or other evidence whose existence is revealed by an individual's compelled answers may be given in evidence by the prosecution at a criminal trial of that individual (*Attorney-General's Reference (No 7 of 2000)* [2001] 1 WLR 1879).

20.9.5.2 Geographical jurisdiction

The court can order a person within the jurisdiction to produce books, papers or records held outside the jurisdiction (*Re Mid East Trading Ltd* [1998] 1 All ER 577). In *McIsaac* [1994] BCC 410 it was held in Scotland that an order under IA 1986, s 236, may be made against an individual outside the jurisdiction, whereas in England, in *Re Tucker, ex parte Tucker* [1990] Ch 148, it was held that such an order could not be made under the corresponding provision in bankruptcy. *McIsaac* is criticised in P StJ Smart, 'Cross-border liquidations' (1996) 41 JLSS 141. The question was re-examined in detail by David Richards J (as he then was) in *Re MF Global UK Ltd (No 7)* [2015] EWHC 2319 (Ch), [2016] Ch 325. It was accepted (at [31]) that *McIsaac* was decided on an erroneous basis and could not be relied on. David Richards J held that the question has been decided authoritatively by the Court of Appeal in *Re Tucker, ex parte Tucker* and s 236 does not have extraterritorial effect. In *Re Omni Trustees Ltd* [2015] EWHC 2697 (Ch), [2015] BCC 906, HHJ Hodge QC, sitting as a High Court judge, refused to follow *Re MF Global UK Ltd (No 7)*, holding that there are material differences between the provisions in bankruptcy and in winding up. See Adrian Walters, 'Office-holder investigations in cross-border insolvencies: how far does s 236 of the Insolvency Act 1986 reach?' (2016) 37 Co Law 101; Ian Fletcher, 'Extra-territorial application of section 236 of the Insolvency Act 1986 — unfinished business for the English courts' (2016) 29 Insolv Int 113.

If the court has ordered that a person attend for oral examination, it may order the person not to leave the jurisdiction until the examination is completed (*Re Oriental Credit Ltd* [1988] Ch 204, in which the man sought to be examined was offered the alternative of posting a bond for £250,000; in *Re Bank of Credit and Commerce International SA (No 7)* [1994] 1 BCLC 455 security of £500,000 was required).

20.9.5.3 Purposes for which private examination may be ordered

The court has a discretion whether to make an order for a private examination on an application by an office-holder or official receiver under IA 1986, s 236. The powers conferred by s 236 are there to enable the court to help the applicant to discover the truth of the circumstances connected with the affairs of the company so that the applicant can complete his or her statutory functions as effectively as possible and with as little expense as possible (*British and Commonwealth Holdings plc v Spicer and Oppenheim* [1993] AC 426 per Lord Slynn of Hadley at p 438, approving a statement by Buckley J in *Re Rolls Razor Ltd* [1968] 3 All ER 698 at p 700). The statutory functions which may be assisted include providing information for the purpose of director disqualification proceedings (*Re Pantmaenog Timber Co Ltd* [2003] UKHL 49, [2004] 1 AC 158). The discretion to make an order must be exercised only after a careful balancing of the reasonable requirements of the insolvency office-holder against the oppressive effect that an order may have on the person sought to be examined (*British and Commonwealth Holdings plc v Spicer and Oppenheim* at p 439). The fact that the proposed examinee is under a duty to cooperate with the office-holder (see **20.9.3**) does not in itself mean that an order for examination must be made (*Shierson v Rastogi* [2002] EWCA Civ 1624, [2003] 1 WLR 586). It is prima facie oppressive to order examination of someone who is not under a duty to cooperate (*Re Westmead Consultants Ltd* [2002] 1 BCLC 384).

In *British and Commonwealth Holdings plc v Spicer and Oppenheim*, British and Commonwealth was in administration and its administrators were investigating the company's recent acquisition of Atlantic Computers plc. Atlantic had been bought for £420 million on the basis of accounts which had been audited by Spicer and Oppenheim. About 18 months after the acquisition, Atlantic had to be put into administration and it was revealed to have a deficiency in assets of about £279 million. The administrators of British and Commonwealth sought an order that Spicer and Oppenheim produce all books, papers and other records relating to their last two audits of Atlantic and to advice given to Atlantic in relation to the takeover. The House of Lords granted the order, saying that the administrators' need to find out how such a massive sum of money had been lost outweighed the interest of Spicer and Oppenheim in not providing the administrators with information which might reveal that their audits had been negligent and the disruption that would be caused by providing the documents sought. In *Re Arrows Ltd (No 2)* [1994] 1 BCLC 355, examination was ordered of a man who had been the chairman, managing director and sole beneficial shareholder of a company which had collapsed owing approximately £103 million and who had been arrested and charged with serious offences in relation to the company. The public interest in discovering what had happened to many millions of pounds outweighed the fact that the examinee might have to give incriminating answers to questions relating to the offences with which he had been charged.

In *Cloverbay Ltd v Bank of Credit and Commerce International SA* [1991] Ch 90 the balance was the other way. The administrators of Cloverbay Ltd suspected that BCCI had knowingly assisted Cloverbay's former managing director to defraud Cloverbay. Oral examination of officers of BCCI was refused since its apparent purpose was to force them to admit the fraud, whereas in a claim against BCCI the burden would be on the company to prove the fraud. (The case was heard before the widespread malpractices in BCCI were revealed to the public.)

Deciding whether examination is primarily required to assist the office-holder's work, and so allowable, or is primarily intended to give the office-holder an unfair advantage in litigation against the examinee, and so not allowable, seems to be a virtually impossible task, especially as it is legitimate for an office-holder to seek information in order to determine whether or not there is a case worth pursuing against the examinee (because finding that there is no such case will avoid wasting money on commencing proceedings) (see *Re Bishopsgate Investment Management Ltd (No 2)* [1994] BCC 732). The fact that litigation is already in progress against the person sought to be examined does not mean that an examination cannot be ordered: the court must control carefully the questions that are asked so as to ensure that the examination is not conducted in a way designed to give the office-holder an unfair advantage in litigation against the examinee (*Daltel Europe Ltd v Makki* [2004] EWHC 726 (Ch), [2005] 1 BCLC 594).

A company's liquidator should not ask for a private examination of a person claiming to be a creditor purely for the purpose of investigating the claim: the claimant has the onus of establishing the claim and a liquidator who doubts a claim should reject it and leave it to the claimant to establish it on appeal against the rejection (*Bellmex International Ltd v British American Tobacco Ltd* [2001] 1 BCLC 91).

20.9.6 PUBLIC EXAMINATION OF OFFICERS

In a compulsory liquidation of a company, an officer or promoter of the company may be ordered to attend the court for a public examination on the promotion, formation or management of the company, or the conduct of its business and affairs or his or her conduct and dealings in relation to the company (IA 1986, s 133). The Cork Committee believed that public examinations (which had not taken place in company liquidations since 1935) were very valuable and should be revived. The Committee took the view that a public examination should serve three purposes (Cmnd 8558, 1982, para 655):

(a) To form the basis of reports by the official receiver, for example on disqualification of directors (see **20.9.7**) or possible offences (see **20.9.9**).

(b) To obtain material information for the administration of the liquidation.

(c) To give publicity, for the information of creditors and the community at large, to the salient facts and unusual features connected with the company's failure.

A public examination is applied for by the official receiver (IA 1986, s 133(1)). An application must be made if requested by one-half, in value, of the company's creditors or three-quarters, in value, of the company's contributories (s 133(2)). The following persons may be summoned for public examination (s 133(1)):

(a) Any person who is or has been an officer of the company.

(b) Any person who has acted as liquidator or administrator of the company, or as receiver or manager of its property.

(c) Any other person who is or has been concerned, or has taken part, in the promotion, formation or management of the company.

An individual who is among those specified in s 133(1) may be summoned for a public examination in England and Wales whether or not he or she is within the jurisdiction at the time, and whether or not he or she is a British subject (*Re Seagull Manufacturing Co Ltd* [1993] Ch 345).

If satisfied that the proposed examinee is one of the persons liable under s 133(1) to be examined, the court must make an order for public examination, unless it is clear that the order would serve no purpose, for example because no questions could properly be put (*Re Casterbridge Properties Ltd* [2003] EWCA Civ 1246, [2004] 1 WLR 602).

The following may put questions during a public examination (IA 1986, s 133(4)):

(a) The official receiver.

(b) The liquidator of the company.

(c) Any person who has been appointed special manager of the company's property or business.

(d) Any creditor of the company who has tendered a proof.

(e) Any contributory of the company.

The person being examined may not claim privilege against self-incrimination (*Bishopsgate Investment Management Ltd v Maxwell* [1993] Ch 1 per Dillon LJ at pp 24–5, Stuart-Smith LJ at p 46, Mann LJ at p 62).

It seems that where a company is in voluntary liquidation, its liquidator or any creditor or contributory may apply under IA 1986, s 112(1), for the court to exercise its power under s 133 to order a public examination as if the company were in compulsory liquidation (*Re Campbell Coverings Ltd (No 2)* [1954] Ch 225; *Bishopsgate Investment Management Ltd v Maxwell* [1993] Ch 1 per Dillon LJ at p 24, Stuart-Smith LJ at p 46).

20.9.7 REPORT TO THE SECRETARY OF STATE ON CONDUCT OF DIRECTORS

When a company is subject to any of the insolvency or liquidation procedures other than voluntary arrangement or the appointment of a provisional liquidator, the office-holder (or, in a winding up by the court, the official receiver) must, under the Company Directors Disqualification Act 1986 (CDDA 1986), s 7A, submit a report to the Secretary of State on the conduct of everyone who was a director of the company in the three years preceding the insolvency date. This report must, in relation to each person, describe any conduct which may assist the Secretary of State in deciding whether to apply for a disqualification order under s 6 or accept a disqualification undertaking. It must be sent to the Secretary of State within three months of the insolvency date, unless the Secretary of State considers that a longer period is appropriate (s 7A(4)). The 'insolvency date' is defined in s 7A(10). The criteria for disqualification under s 6 are that the company has become insolvent and that the person's conduct as a director of the company, either in relation to that company alone or taken together with conduct as a director of another company, makes the person unfit to be concerned in the management of a company. 'Director' in these provisions includes a shadow director (CDDA 1986, ss 6(3C) and 7A(12)).

20.9.8 OFFICIAL RECEIVER'S INVESTIGATION AND REPORT

In a compulsory liquidation of a company, the official receiver attached to the court that made the winding-up order has a duty to investigate the promotion, formation, business, dealings and affairs of the company, and, if the company has failed, the causes of the failure (IA 1986, s 132(1)). The official receiver may, if he or she thinks fit, make a report to the court on these matters (s 132(1)). Such a report is prima facie evidence of facts stated in it (s 132(2)) and is absolutely privileged so that an official receiver always has a complete defence to an action for defamation based on statements made in a report (*Bottomley v Brougham* [1908] 1 KB 584).

20.9.9 SUSPECTED CRIMINAL OFFENCES

In a compulsory or voluntary liquidation of a company, IA 1986, s 218, imposes a duty on the liquidator to report any criminal offences apparently committed in relation to the company by any of its past or present officers or members. A compulsory liquidator, if not the official receiver, must make such a report to the official receiver (s 218(3)). A voluntary liquidator must report to the Secretary of State (s 218(4)), who is then entitled to exercise any of the extensive powers available to investigating inspectors (see **18.8.4**), for the purpose of investigating the matter reported and any other matters relating to the company's affairs which appear to require investigation (s 218(5)). The court, of its own motion, or on the application of any person interested in the winding up, may direct a liquidator to make a report under this section (s 218(1) and (6)).

There are similar provisions in s 7A where a moratorium has been obtained for a company or a voluntary arrangement has taken effect.

20.10 CONTROL OF INSOLVENCY AND LIQUIDATION PROCEDURES BY THE COURT

20.10.1 APPLICATION BY AN OFFICE-HOLDER FOR DIRECTIONS

An office-holder who is uncertain how to deal with any aspect of the insolvency or liquidation is entitled to apply to the court for directions (IA 1986, s 35 (administrative receiver); sch B1, para 63 (administrator); s 7(4)(a) (supervisor of a voluntary arrangement); sch A1, para 39(5)(a) (supervisor of a voluntary arrangement following a moratorium); s 112 (voluntary liquidator); s 168(3) (compulsory liquidator)).

20.10.2 APPLICATION TO THE COURT BY MEMBERS OR CREDITORS

When a company is the subject of any insolvency or liquidation procedure, apart from administrative receivership, the members or creditors of the company are entitled to apply to the court for relief from an action or decision of the office-holder which they consider to be wrong.

In administration, IA 1986, sch B1, para 74, gives members the right to apply to the court for relief of unfairly harmful acts by the company's administrator, and gives creditors the right to apply if the administrator is not performing his or her functions as quickly or as efficiently as is reasonably practicable.

Any creditor, or any other person, who is dissatisfied by any act, omission or decision of the supervisor of a voluntary arrangement may apply to the court under s 7(3) (or sch A1, para 39(3), if the arrangement followed a moratorium). The court may confirm, reverse or modify any act or decision of the supervisor; give the supervisor directions; or make such other order as it thinks fit. The same provision is made by sch A1, para 26, in relation to acts, omissions or decisions of a nominee during a moratorium.

Any person who is aggrieved by an act or decision of a liquidator in a winding up by the court may apply to the court under s 168(5). The court may confirm, reverse or modify the act or decision complained of, and make such order in the case as it thinks just.

In a voluntary winding up, any contributory or creditor may, like the liquidator, apply for directions under s 112, and may apply under that section for the court to exercise its power under s 168(5) to confirm, reverse or modify an act or decision of the liquidator.

20.11 LIABILITY FOR FRAUDULENT TRADING

20.11.1 PRINCIPLE

If a company is being wound up or is in administration, a person who is found to have been knowingly party to the carrying on of any business of the company with intent to defraud its creditors, or creditors of any other person, or for any fraudulent purpose, may be declared by the court to be liable to make such contributions (if any) to the company's assets as the court thinks proper (IA 1986, ss 213 and 246ZA). Furthermore, if the declaration is made under s 213 (in winding up), a disqualification order may be made under CDDA 1986, s 10 (see **20.13.2.9**). A person domiciled outside Great Britain may be made liable under s 213 (*Bilta (UK) Ltd v Nazir (No 2)* [2015] UKSC 23, [2016] 1 AC 1).

Only the company's liquidator or administrator can apply for a declaration.

A person who was knowingly party to a company's fraudulent trading may be made liable to contribute to its assets only when it is wound up or put into administration, but such a person may at any time be prosecuted for the criminal offence of knowingly being a party to fraudulent trading (CA 2006, s 993). The offence may be tried either way and, on indictment, a prison sentence of up to ten years may be imposed (s 993(3)(a)) and a disqualification order may be made under CDDA 1986, s 2 (see **20.13.2.1**). There is another power to disqualify a person where 'in the course of the winding up of a company, it appears that' the person has committed an offence under what is now CA 2006, s 993, even if not convicted (CDDA 1986, s 4(1)(a); see **20.13.2.3**). The variety and extent of these provisions show how seriously the use of companies for fraudulent purposes is regarded. The Company Law Review Steering Group said that what is now CA 2006, s 993, is:

> a valuable weapon in countering corporate crime. It enables the whole course of the defendant's conduct to be examined and thus a proper picture of the defendant's criminality to be given. (*Modern Company Law for a Competitive Economy: Completing the Structure* (URN 00/1335) (London: DTI, 2000), para 13.31)

20.11.2 ANALYSIS

It was held in *R v Kemp* [1988] QB 645 that the provisions of what are now CA 2006, s 993, and IA 1986, ss 213 and 246ZA, are concerned with three different practices (and so CA 2006, s 993, creates three separate offences), namely, carrying on the business of a company:

(a) with intent to defraud the creditors of the company;

(b) with intent to defraud the creditors of any person; or

(c) for any fraudulent purpose (which is not limited to fraudulence against creditors but may be, for example, against customers of the company as in *Kemp*'s case).

Under (a) or (b) the provisions may be invoked even if the fraudulence was against only one creditor or was in relation to only one transaction. As Templeman J said in **Re Gerald Cooper Chemicals Ltd** [1978] Ch 262 at p 268:

> It does not matter for the purposes of [CA 2006, s 993, and IA 1986, ss 213 and 246ZA] that only one creditor was defrauded, and by one transaction, provided that the transaction can properly be described as a fraud on a creditor perpetrated in the course of carrying on business.

This does not mean that the fact that one person is defrauded in the course of a company's business always means that the business was carried on with intent to defraud (*Morphitis v Bernasconi* [2003] EWCA Civ 289, [2003] Ch 552).

Under (a), 'creditors' includes persons whose debts are payable in the future as well as those presently payable (*R v Smith* [1996] 2 Cr App R 1).

Under (c), the fraudulent purpose does not have to be the sole or even the dominant purpose for which the company carries on business. The crucial question is whether what is done for a fraudulent purpose is carried out in the course of business. In *R v Philippou* (1989) 89 Cr App R 290, the two accused were the sole shareholders and directors of a company in the travel trade which could not carry on its business without an Air Travel Organiser's Licence issued by the Civil Aviation Authority. The Authority has to be satisfied that the persons to whom it issues licences have adequate financial resources. The accused concealed from the Authority the true financial position of their companies to avoid having the licence cancelled. Dismissing the accused's appeals against conviction for offences under what is now CA 2006, s 993, the Court of Appeal held that applying for, maintaining and renewing the licence were integral parts of the company's business, and doing those things fraudulently could amount to carrying on the company's business for a fraudulent purpose.

In order to make a person liable under CA 2006, s 993, or IA 1986, s 213 or 246ZA, it is necessary to prove three elements (*Re Bank of Credit and Commerce International SA (No 14)* [2003] EWHC 1868 (Ch), [2004] 2 BCLC 236, at [11]):

(a) that the business of the company has been carried on

    (i) with intent to defraud the creditors of the company, or

    (ii) with intent to defraud the creditors of any person, or

    (iii) for any fraudulent purpose (see **20.11.3**);

(b) that the defendant participated in the carrying on of the business in that manner (see **20.11.4**); and

(c) that the defendant participated knowingly, that is with knowledge that the business was being carried on with the intent or purpose specified in (a) (see **20.11.5**).

20.11.3 WHAT AMOUNTS TO FRAUD?

The phrases 'intent to defraud' and 'fraudulent purpose' used in IA 1986, ss 213 and 246ZA, imply that a person should be made responsible only for 'actual dishonesty involving, according to current notions of fair trading among commercial men, real moral blame' in the carrying on of a business (**Re Patrick and Lyon Ltd** [1933] Ch 786 per Maugham J; *Bernasconi v Nicholas Bennett and Co* [2000] BCC 921), that is only if there was conduct which was deliberately and actually dishonest according to the notions of ordinary decent business people (*Re EB Tractors Ltd* [1986] NI 165). It is also essential to prove dishonesty in order to secure a conviction under CA 2006, s 993 (*R v Cox* (1982) 75 Cr App R 291), though more recently it has been held that in a criminal case the jury should be directed to consider the standards of ordinary and honest people rather than 'commercial men' (*R v Lockwood* (1985) 2 BCC 99,333). In *A/S Dansk Skibsfinansiering v Brothers* [2001] 2 BCLC 324, though, Lord Hoffmann NPJ in the Hong Kong Court of Final Appeal said, at p 334:

> While I quite accept that a defendant cannot be allowed to shelter behind some private standard of honesty not shared by the community, I think there is a danger in expressing that proposition by invoking the concept of the hypothetical decent honest man. The danger is that because decent honest people also tend to behave responsibly, considerately and so forth, there may be a temptation to treat shortcomings in these respects as a failure to comply with the necessary objective standard. It seems to me much safer, at least in the context of an allegation of fraud, to concentrate upon the actual defendants and simply ask whether they have been dishonest. Judges and juries seldom have any conceptual difficulty in knowing what is meant by dishonesty.

Despite Lord Hoffmann's confidence that judges and juries can recognise dishonesty when they see it, the concept has been subject to further analysis in the context of secondary liability for breach of fiduciary duty, where a combined objective and subjective test has been adopted (see **16.17.3**). It would seem that this is an appropriate test to apply to fraudulent trading. See Andrew Keay, 'Fraudulent trading: the intent to defraud element' (2006) 35 Common Law World Review 121.

The Court of Appeal, in *R v Grantham* [1984] QB 675, considered the meaning of the phrase 'intent to defraud' in what is now CA 2006, s 993, and IA 1986, ss 213 and 246ZA, and noted a relevant dictum of Lord Radcliffe in **Welham v Director of Public Prosecutions** [1961] AC 103:

> Now, I think that there are one or two things that can be said with confidence about the meaning of this word 'defraud'. It requires a person as its object: that is, defrauding involves doing something to someone. Although in the nature of things it is almost invariably associated with the obtaining of an advantage for the person who commits the fraud, it is the effect upon the person who is the object of the fraud that ultimately determines its meaning.

In *R v Grantham* the Court of Appeal also noted that it had said in *R v Allsop* (1977) 64 Cr App R 29 that there is fraud if there is an intention to use deceit to induce a course of conduct in another which puts that other's economic interests in jeopardy, even if there is no intention that actual loss should ultimately be suffered by that other.

Whether there has been intent to defraud is a question of fact to be determined in every case and a person's intent usually has to be inferred from what the person did. The courts have said that some behaviour will usually give rise to an inference that there has been an intent to defraud. An example is inducing people to give credit to a company knowing that they will not be paid when they expect to be paid (*R v Grantham*). Similarly it can usually be inferred that there is intent to defraud if liability to 'involuntary creditors' such as HM Revenue and Customs is incurred when there is no honest belief that the liability will be discharged when due, or shortly thereafter (*Re a Company (No 001418 of 1988)* [1991] BCLC 197).

However, there is no rule that behaviour of a particular kind inevitably leads to a finding of intent of defraud. For example, there is no rule that continuing to trade while insolvent is fraudulent. In **Re White and Osmond (Parkstone) Ltd** (ChD 30 June 1960), Buckley J formulated what has become known as the 'sunshine' test:

> there is nothing to say that directors who genuinely believe that the clouds will roll away and the sunshine of prosperity will shine upon them again and disperse the fog of their depression are not entitled to incur credit to help them get over the bad time.

In *Re Continental Assurance Co of London plc* [2001] BPIR 733 Park J pointed out, at para 281, that:

> whenever a company is in financial trouble and the directors have a difficult decision to make whether to close down and go into liquidation, or whether instead to trade on and hope to turn the corner, they can be in a real and unenviable dilemma.

If they continue trading and there is no recovery, they are at risk of a claim for wrongful trading or, as in *Secretary of State for Trade and Industry v Gill* [2004] EWHC 933 (Ch), [2006] BCC 725, disqualification. If they close down immediately, there will inevitably be an insolvent liquidation and they will be criticised for not having had the courage to carry on, with the probability of trading out of difficulty. In *Re Continental Assurance Co of London plc* it was found that the decision of the directors to continue trading after large and unforeseen losses had caused a financial crisis which they were advised had not caused the company to be insolvent, was 'entirely appropriate' (at para 292). In *Secretary of State for Trade and Industry v Gill*, directors were not disqualified for making a commercial judgement to continue trading when 'they reasonably believed that there was a reasonable prospect of finding a corporate solution, thereby achieving a satisfactory outcome for all of the group's creditors' (at [157]).

Similarly, incurring a contingent liability, such as a warranty, knowing that it might not be possible to meet that liability, is not necessarily fraudulent (*Norcross Ltd v Amos* (1980) 131 NLJ 1213). It is not necessarily fraudulent for a company to pay some of its creditors ahead of others, even if it is clear that this will mean that some creditors will not be paid in full (*Re Sarflax Ltd* [1979] Ch 592). But it is dishonest to do this deliberately so that a particular creditor or creditors will not be paid (*Starglade Properties Ltd v Nash* [2010] EWCA Civ 1314, [2011] Lloyd's Rep FC 102).

In *Re Augustus Barnett and Son Ltd* [1986] BCLC 170, the company was a wholly owned subsidiary of a Spanish company, Rumasa SA. The subsidiary traded at a loss for some time but the parent company repeatedly issued statements that it would continue to support the subsidiary. Some of these statements were made in letters (known as 'comfort letters') written to the subsidiary's auditors and published in the subsidiary's annual accounts for three successive years. Eventually the parent company allowed the subsidiary to go into liquidation. Hoffmann J held that these facts did not show that the parent company intended to defraud the subsidiary's creditors; they were consistent with the parent company having an honest intention, at the time of making the statements, to support the subsidiary— the fact that it later altered this intention did not prove that its original statements were fraudulent.

The meaning of 'intent to defraud' is considered at length in M Beckman and S Ross, 'Fraudulent or wrongful trading' (1991) 141 NLJ 1744, (1992) 142 NLJ 62, 100.

20.11.4 WHO ARE PARTIES TO THE CARRYING ON OF THE BUSINESS?

In *Re Maidstone Buildings Provisions Ltd* [1971] 1 WLR 1085 it was held that a company secretary, who knew that the company was insolvent but failed to advise the company's directors that the company should cease trading, was not included among 'parties to the carrying on of the business' with intent to defraud creditors. Pennycuick V-C said:

> The expression 'parties to the carrying on of the business' is not, I think, a very familiar one but, so far as I can see, the expression 'party to' must on its natural meaning indicate no more than 'participates in', 'takes part in' or 'concurs in'. And that, it seems to me, involves some positive steps of some nature. I do not think it can be said that someone is party to carrying on a business if he takes no positive steps at all. So in order to bring a person within the section you must show that he is taking some positive steps in the carrying on of the company's business in a fraudulent manner.

The term 'parties to the carrying on of the business' includes both the directors and so on who actively carried on the company's business for a fraudulent purpose and persons such as financiers who encouraged the carrying on of the business for the fraudulent purpose without carrying on the business themselves (*Re Bank of Credit and Commerce International SA, Banque Arabe Internationale d'Investissement SA v Morris* [2001] 1 BCLC 263). It is essential to show that a person who actively carried on the business did so with fraudulent intent before any other party can be made liable (*Re Augustus Barnett and Son Ltd* [1986] BCLC 170). An employee of a company who did not exercise a controlling or managerial function and did not run the business cannot be liable for fraudulent trading (*R v Miles* [1992] Crim LR 657).

20.11.5 KNOWLEDGE

Where it has been proved that a company carried on a business with the intent to defraud or fraudulent purpose required to attract liability under CA 2006, s 993, and IA 1986, ss 213 and 246ZA, what is required to prove that a defendant was a knowing party was examined by Patten J in *Re Bank of Credit and Commerce International SA (No 14)* [2003] EWHC 1868 (Ch), [2004] 2 BCLC 236, at [11] and in *Re Bank of Credit and Commerce International SA (No 15)* [2004] EWHC 528 (Ch), [2004] 2 BCLC 279, at [13]. His Lordship concluded that:

(a) There must have been knowledge that the business to which the defendant was a party was carried on in the fraudulent manner which has been proved.

(b) This must have been realised at the time the defendant was a party; hindsight is not enough.

(c) A distinction must be drawn between a conscious appreciation of the true nature of the business being carried on and a failure, however negligent, to appreciate that fraud was being perpetrated: the liability is for participating in fraud, not for negligently failing to recognise fraud.

(d) Knowledge includes so-called blind-eye knowledge, which exists when there is a deliberate decision to avoid obtaining confirmation of well-founded suspicions.

20.11.6 NATURE OF LIABILITY

On finding a person liable under IA 1986, s 213 or 246ZA, the court may order that person to make contributions to the company's assets. Those contributions will be shared among the company's creditors, and so they should reflect, and compensate for, the loss caused to those creditors by carrying on the business in the manner which the court found was fraudulent (*Morphitis v Bernasconi* [2003] EWCA Civ 289, [2003] Ch 552, at [55]). It is not appropriate to add some amount as a penalty for the fraudulent conduct: penalties should be sought in criminal proceedings, for example under CA 2006, s 993 (*Morphitis*).

The court is allowed to give such further directions as it thinks proper for the purpose of giving effect to a declaration of liability to contribute, and may in particular make the liability under its declaration a charge on any debt or obligation due from the company to the person liable or on any mortgage or charge on any of the company's assets held by that person (s 215(2)). Furthermore, it can order that any debt owed by the company to the person declared liable shall rank in priority after all its other debts and the interest owed on all other debts (s 215(4)).

A person who is made liable under s 213(2) to contribute to the assets of a company is not one of the 'contributories' of the company (s 79(2)) and so does not acquire any right to influence the winding up.

If a company's liquidator or administrator does not take proceedings under s 213 or s 246ZA, against a person who has been a party to the company's fraudulent trading, it may be possible for a victim of the fraud to sue the person in tort. See, for example, *Contex Drouzhba Ltd v Wiseman* [2007] EWCA Civ 1201, [2008] 1 BCLC 631, discussed at **19.7.1**.

20.12 WRONGFUL TRADING

20.12.1 PRINCIPLE

According to its title, s 214 of IA 1986 is concerned with 'wrongful trading', though the phrase 'wrongful trading' is not used in the section. Briefly, the section empowers the court to declare a director of a company liable to contribute to the assets of the company if the director knew, or ought to have concluded, that the company had no reasonable prospect of not going into insolvent liquidation and did not take every step that ought to have been taken by that director to minimise the potential loss to the company's creditors. The section applies to shadow directors (s 214(7)) and to *de facto* directors as well as *de jure* directors (*Re Hydrodam (Corby) Ltd* [1994] 2 BCLC 180).

Section 214 comes into operation only if a company goes into liquidation (see **20.8**) at a time when its assets are insufficient for the payment of its debts and other liabilities and the expenses of winding up (s 214(1), (2)(a) and (6)) and it is for the company's liquidator to apply to the court for a declaration (s 214(1)). Similar provision is made in s 246ZB for a company entering insolvent administration.

Establishing liability under s 214 or 246ZB involves two elements (apart from the fact of insolvent liquidation or administration):

(a) knowledge, actual or constructive, that insolvent liquidation or administration was unavoidable (see **20.12.2** and **20.12.3**); and

(b) failure to take every step to minimise potential loss to creditors (see **20.12.4**).

20.12.2 DUAL OBJECTIVE/SUBJECTIVE STANDARD

In order to make a person liable under IA 1986, s 214, it must be proved that the person 'knew or ought to have concluded that' insolvent liquidation was unavoidable (s 214(2)(b)). But it is a defence to prove that the director 'took every step...he ought to have taken' to minimise creditors' losses (s 214(3)). Similar provision is made in relation to insolvent administration by s 246ZB(2) (b) and (3).

The phrases 'ought to have concluded that' and 'ought to have taken' imply that the legislation is referring to a standard of thinking and behaviour, and a director is to be penalised for not meeting that standard. Subsections (4) and (5) of ss 214 and 246ZB attempt to specify what that standard is. The court is asked to consider the facts which would be known or ascertained, the conclusions which would be reached and the steps which would be taken by a reasonably diligent person having both:

(a) the general knowledge, skill and experience that may reasonably be expected of a person carrying out the same functions as are carried out by the person against whom a declaration is sought in relation to the company that is in liquidation; and

(b) the general knowledge, skill and experience that that person has.

In other words, a person who is not sufficiently qualified for his or her job is to be tested by the standards of someone who is ideally qualified while someone who is overqualified is to be tested by the higher standards he or she happens to possess. Subsection (5) emphasises this by requiring the court to look at the ideal qualifications of a person doing the job with which the person against whom the declaration is sought was entrusted, even if he or she did not in fact carry out some or all of its functions.

This is the dual objective/subjective standard, which has since been extended to become a general standard of directors' duties of care, skill and diligence (see **16.8.1**).

20.12.3 WHEN IS IT WRONG TO TRADE WHILE INSOLVENT?

The fact that a company is trading while insolvent does not in itself mean that the trading is wrongful so as to create liability under IA 1986, s 214 or 246ZB. There is wrongful trading only if there is no reasonable prospect of not going into insolvent liquidation or administration. If there is a reasonable prospect of not going into insolvent liquidation or administration, liability for wrongful trading does not arise.

In *Secretary of State for Trade and Industry v Taylor* [1997] 1 WLR 407, Chadwick J said, at p 414, in relation to an application to disqualify a director:

> The companies legislation does not impose on directors a statutory duty to ensure that their company does not trade while insolvent; nor does that legislation impose an obligation to ensure that the company does not trade at a loss… Directors may properly take the view that it is in the interests of the company and of its creditors that, although insolvent, the company should continue to trade out of its difficulties. They may properly take the view that it is in the interests of the company and its creditors that some loss-making trade should be accepted in anticipation of future profitability. They are not to be criticised if they give effect to such views, properly held. But the legislation imposes on directors the risk that trading while insolvent may lead to personal liability. Section 214 imposes that liability where the director knew, or ought to have concluded, that there was no reasonable prospect that the company would avoid going into insolvent liquidation.

The difficulty of deciding, with hindsight, whether it was wrongful to continue trading, knowing of insolvency, is discussed in relation to fraudulent trading in **20.11.3**.

20.12.4 TAKING STEPS TO MINIMISE POTENTIAL LOSS

Once it has been established that a director of a company knew or ought to have concluded that there was no reasonable prospect that the company would avoid going into insolvent liquidation, the director will not be liable for wrongful trading if it is proved that the director took 'every step with a view to minimising the potential loss to the company's creditors as… he ought to have taken' (IA 1986, ss 214(3) and 246ZB(3)). The steps which ought to have been taken are (ss 214(4) and 246ZB(4)) those which would be taken by a reasonably diligent person having both:

(a) the general knowledge, skill and experience that may reasonably be expected of a person carrying out the same functions as are carried out by that director in relation to the company, and

(b) the general knowledge, skill and experience that that director has.

The defence is examined in detail in *Brooks v Armstrong* [2015] EWHC 2289 (Ch), [2015] BCC 661; see C Jenner, 'Wrongful trading: the elements of a successful claim' (2015) 28 Insolv Int 124. See also *Grant v Ralls* [2016] EWHC 243 (Ch), [2016] 1 Costs LR 185.

20.12.5 EXAMPLES

The first wrongful trading case to be reported was *Re Produce Marketing Consortium Ltd (No 2)* [1989] 2 BCLC 520. The company had acted as agent in relation to the import of fruit and, although it traded successfully for some time, gradually the number of directors, the turnover and the profitability shrank until it went into creditors' voluntary liquidation with an estimated deficit of £317,694 after approximately 16 years' trading. The general drift towards insolvency was evident from the audited accounts. They showed a decline from no overdraft, excess assets over liabilities, and no trading loss in 1980 to a large overdraft, excess of liabilities over assets, and a trading loss by 1984. These all continued to deteriorate until the liquidation in 1987. The gradual decrease in the company's overdraft in the later years was financed by increased indebtedness to the company's most important shipper who was owed £175,062 in the liquidation.

One of the directors admitted knowing in February 1987 that the liquidation of the company was inevitable but put forward, as justification for its continuing to trade until October of that year, that it enabled an advantageous realisation of the company's stock of perishable fruit in cold store. This was said to be an attempt within IA 1986, s 214(3), to minimise the potential loss to creditors.

Knox J held that the two directors were liable to contribute £75,000 to the company's assets. They ought to have concluded back in July 1986 that there was no reasonable prospect of avoiding insolvent liquidation because, although they did not have the accounts until January 1987, they had an intimate knowledge of the business and must have known that turnover was well down on the previous year, which would inevitably lead to an increase in the deficit of assets over liabilities. Furthermore, s 214 refers not only to facts which directors ought to know but also to facts which they ought to ascertain. Therefore the court assumed that the financial results for the year ending September 1985 were known at the end of July 1986. His Lordship said, at p 551:

> [Counsel for one of the directors] was not able to advance any particular calculation as constituting a basis for concluding that there was a prospect of insolvent liquidation being avoided. He is not to be criticised for that for in my judgment there was none available. Once the loss in the year ending 30 September 1985 was incurred PMC was in irreversible decline, assuming (as I must) that the [directors] had no plans for altering the company's business and proposed to go on drawing the level of reasonable remuneration that they were currently receiving.

In short, they should not have continued trading after July 1986. Also the directors had not taken the steps they ought to have taken under s 214(3) because they continued trading after July 1986, and even after February 1987, and that conduct was compounded by the fact that trading from February 1987 was not limited to realising the fruit in cold store as claimed.

Re Rod Gunner Organisation Ltd [2004] EWHC 316 (Ch), [2004] 2 BCLC 110, concerned a company whose main business was film production. It never traded profitably in its 30 months of existence. Its directors were taken in by 'a charming and thoroughly convincing man', who was represented by reputable London solicitors. He was appointed chief executive officer of the company in response to his repeated promises to refinance the company using enormous funds he claimed to control but which were pure fantasy. All the promises of finance were unfulfilled and he was subsequently made bankrupt. The judge found that for a while it was not unreasonable of the directors to believe that refinancing would take place and so it was not wrongful to continue trading despite insolvency. However, it was possible to identify a time when management accounts showed such a dramatic fall in turnover, and the promises of refinance became so unrealistic, that the directors should have realised that insolvent liquidation was unavoidable, and they were liable for wrongful trading beyond that point.

Re Sherborne Associates Ltd [1995] BCC 40 concerned three men who had set up a company to run an advertising agency. None of them had worked in an advertising agency but one of them was an accountant who had considerable business experience at a high level and had identified advertising as a profitable area to invest in. They relied on hiring employees with the necessary skills and client contacts but in fact none of the people they hired was able to contribute enough to make the business profitable and it was put into liquidation two years after it commenced trading. The liquidator alleged that, at a date one year before the liquidation, the directors ought to have concluded that there was no reasonable prospect that the company would avoid going into insolvent liquidation but the court decided that the liquidator had not shown that the directors were not entitled at that time to believe that the company could become profitable. This seems to have been a generous application of the sunshine test (see **20.11.3** and **20.12.3**).

20.12.6 NATURE OF LIABILITY

In *Re Produce Marketing Consortium Ltd (No 2)* [1989] BCLC 520, Knox J decided that the appropriate amount which the directors were to be ordered to contribute to the company's assets under IA 1986, s 214, was the amount by which its assets could be seen to have been depleted by the director's conduct which gave rise to the liability. In effect, the jurisdiction under s 214 is primarily compensatory rather than penal.

In *Re Purpoint Ltd* [1991] BCLC 491, Vinelott J rejected a submission that a director held liable for wrongful trading should pay all the company's creditors whose debts were incurred after he should have known that the company would go into insolvent liquidation. Money ordered to be paid under s 214 goes into the general assets of the company for distribution among all creditors: the court has no power to direct payment of the money to particular creditors. The right measure of the director's liability for wrongful trading in this case was the increase in the net liabilities of the company caused by the company continuing to trade after the director should have known that it would go into liquidation.

In *Re DKG Contractors Ltd* [1990] BCC 903 the amount which the directors were declared liable to pay for wrongful trading was the amount of trade debts incurred since they should have known that the company would go into insolvent liquidation, but this seems to be the wrong measure according to the decisions in *Re Produce Marketing Consortium Ltd (No 2)* and *Re Purpoint Ltd*.

There is further discussion of the measure of liability in *Grant v Ralls* [2016] EWHC 243 (Ch), [2016] 1 Costs LR 185.

In *Re Produce Marketing Consortium Ltd* [1989] 1 WLR 745 it was held that CA 2006, s 1157 (see **16.16.6**), does not apply to liability for wrongful trading, but it may be doubted whether this is correct (see **16.16.6.2**).

If the court makes a declaration of liability for wrongful trading against a person, it may give such further directions as it thinks proper for the purpose of giving effect to the declaration. In particular, it may make the liability under its declaration a charge on any debt or obligation due from the company to the person liable or on any mortgage or charge on any of the company's assets held by him (IA 1986, s 215(2)). Furthermore it can order that any debt owed by the company to the person declared liable shall rank in priority after all its other debts and the interest owed on all other debts (s 215(4)).

The court may make a disqualification order (see **20.13**) against a person when making a declaration under s 214(1) (CDDA 1986, s 10).

A person who is made liable, by a declaration under IA 1986, s 214(1), to contribute to the assets of a company is not one of the 'contributories' of the company (s 79(2)) and so does not acquire any right to influence the winding up.

20.12.7 GENERAL DISCUSSION

It seems that liquidators have been encouraged by the introduction of the wrongful trading provision to make much more detailed investigations into the past activities of directors—the judge in *Re Purpoint Ltd* [1991] BCLC 491 was concerned with what kind of car it was appropriate for the company to buy its director—and to make composite misfeasance and wrongful trading claims. It may be that misfeasance and wrongful trading claims carry rather less stigma than fraudulent trading claims or disqualification orders, and are therefore easier to sustain (see 'Company directors and insolvent companies: a new reality?' (1991) 12 Co Law 82). On the other hand, it must be recognised that most individuals against whom misfeasance and wrongful trading claims are upheld will be bankrupted by them.

For detailed discussions of IA 1986, s 214, see F Oditah, 'Wrongful trading' [1990] LMCLQ 205; D Milman, 'Personal liability and disqualification of company directors: something old, something new' (1992) 43 NILQ 1; A Hicks, 'Advising on wrongful trading' (1993) 14 Co Law 16, 55; A Keay, 'The duty of directors to take account of creditors' interests: has it any role to play?' [2002] JBL 379.

20.13 DIRECTORS' DISQUALIFICATION

20.13.1 DISQUALIFICATION ORDER

20.13.1.1 Definition

A disqualification order against a person is an order that the person shall not, without leave of a court (see **20.13.9**), be a director of a company or in any way, whether directly or indirectly, be concerned or take part in the management of a company (CDDA 1986, s 1(1)). The person is also banned from promoting or forming companies and from acting as an insolvency practitioner or a receiver of a company's property. In effect a disqualification order prevents a person from trading with limited liability, though a disqualified person may engage in business as a sole trader or in partnership. A disqualification undertaking (see **20.13.3**) has the same effect as a disqualification order but is made without court proceedings.

20.13.1.2 Details of disqualification orders

The acts which a disqualified person is prohibited from doing are listed in two paragraphs in CDDA 1986, s 1(1), but the only form of disqualification order which may be made is one disqualifying a person from doing all the things listed: it is not possible to disqualify from only a selection of them (*Official Receiver v Hannan* [1997] 2 BCLC 473; *R v Cole* [1998] 1 BCLC 234; *Re Adbury Park Estates Ltd* [2003] BCC 696). It is not possible to make a disqualification order limited to a particular class of companies, such as public companies (*R v Ward* (2001) *The Times*, 10 August 2001). Disqualification orders are not confined to individuals: companies may also be disqualified from being directors (*Official Receiver v Brady* [1999] BCC 258).

20.13.1.3 Penalties for contravention

Acting in contravention of a disqualification order is an offence triable either way (CDDA 1986, s 13). In addition a person who contravenes a disqualification order by being a director of a company, or being concerned, whether directly or indirectly, or taking part, in the management of a company, may be made personally liable for all debts and liabilities of the company incurred while so acting (s 15(1)(a), (3)(a) and (4)). A person liable under s 15 is jointly and severally liable with the company itself and with any other person who is also jointly and severally liable for the debts (whether under s 15 or some other provision) (CDDA 1986, s 15(2)).

Acting as a management consultant advising on financial management and restructuring of a company may constitute being directly or indirectly concerned in the management of the company for these purposes (*R v Campbell* (1983) 78 Cr App R 95). The concept of 'management' in this context includes activities which involve policy-making or decision-making affecting the company as a whole or a substantial part of it and which may have a significant effect on its financial standing (*Commissioner for Corporate Affairs v Bracht* [1989] VR 821). 'Taking part in' and 'being concerned in' are to be interpreted widely and include activities involving some responsibility and participation in the decision-making processes of the company as opposed to routine clerical or administrative duties which may be associated with management: to prove that a person contravened a disqualification order, it is not necessary to show that the person had ultimate control or responsibility (*Commissioner for Corporate Affairs v Bracht*; *Re Market Wizard Systems (UK) Ltd* [1998] 2 BCLC 282).

There is obviously great difficulty in catching people who act as shadow directors, managing companies through people who do what they are told. CDDA 1986, s 15, therefore also imposes personal liability for the debts of a company on any person involved in its management who is willing to act on instructions given by a person whom the person knows to be the subject of a disqualification order (s 15(1)(b), (3)(b) and (4)).

20.13.1.4 Other disabilities of disqualified persons

Other legislation imposes further restrictions on disqualified persons. For example, a disqualified person is also disqualified from being a charity trustee or trustee for a charity (Charities Act 2011, ss 178 to 184) and cannot be a trustee of an occupational pension scheme without the permission of the Occupational Pensions Regulatory Authority (Pensions Act 1995, s 29).

20.13.2 GROUNDS FOR DISQUALIFICATION

20.13.2.1 Conviction of indictable offence

Under CDDA 1986, s 2, a disqualification order may be made against a person who has been convicted of an indictable offence which was in connection with the promotion, formation, management, liquidation or striking off of a company, with the receivership of a company's property or with being an administrative receiver of a company. An order on these grounds may be made by the court which convicted the person (s 2(2)). A magistrates' court may disqualify for up to five years, the Crown Court for up to 15 years (s 2(3)). In addition, a disqualification order may be made by any court with jurisdiction to wind up the company in relation to which the offence was committed (s 2(2)) and that court may disqualify for up to 15 years (s 2(3)).

20.13.2.2 Persistent breaches of companies legislation

Under CDDA 1986, s 3, a disqualification order may be made against a person who has been persistently in default in providing returns, accounts or other documents required to be filed with the registrar of companies. A person is conclusively proved to be a persistent defaulter if it is shown that within five years there have been three instances of conviction for failing to provide information or of orders made requiring delivery of information (s 3(2) and (3)).

A disqualification order under s 3 may be made by any court with jurisdiction to wind up any company in relation to which the defendant has been in default (s 3(4)) and the disqualification period may be up to five years (s 3(5)).

20.13.2.3 Fraud

Under CDDA 1986, s 4, a disqualification order may be made against a person if it appears that, while that person was an officer or liquidator or administrative receiver of a company now in liquidation, or receiver of the company's property, he or she was guilty of:

(a) any fraud in relation to the company; or

(b) any breach of duty as such officer, liquidator, receiver or manager; or

(c) an offence (whether convicted of it or not) of knowingly being a party to fraudulent trading in contravention of CA 2006, s 993 (see **20.11**).

A disqualification order under s 4 may be made by any court with jurisdiction to wind up any company in relation to which fraud was committed (s 4(2)) and the disqualification period may be up to 15 years (s 4(3)).

20.13.2.4 Three convictions for failure to supply information to registrar

Under CDDA 1986, s 5, a disqualification order may be made against a person who has been found guilty in a magistrates' court of an offence triable only summarily that consists of failing to provide information to the registrar, and that, including the present offence, there have been three instances within the past five years of conviction for failing to provide information or of orders made requiring delivery of information.

A disqualification order under s 5 may be made by the magistrates' court when it makes the finding of guilt (s 5(2)) and the disqualification period may be up to five years (s 4(3)).

20.13.2.5 Disqualification for convictions abroad

Under CDDA 1986, s 5A, a disqualification order may be made against a person who has been convicted of a relevant foreign offence as defined in s 5A(3). These are serious offences committed outside Great Britain in connection with the promotion, formation or management of a company. The conviction must have occurred on or after 1 October 2015, but it does not matter when the act or omission which constituted the offence took place (Small Business, Enterprise and Employment Act 2015, s 104(2)).

20.13.2.6 Unfitness shown by conduct while director of a company which has become insolvent

Under CDDA 1986, s 6, a disqualification order may be made against a person who:

- (a) is, or has been, a director or shadow director (s 6(3C)) of a company (known as the 'lead company') which has 'become insolvent' (see later); and
- (b) is made unfit to be concerned in the management of a company by conduct as a director or shadow director of the lead company, either taken alone or taken together with conduct as a director or shadow director of any other company—known as a 'collateral company'.

For these purposes a company 'becomes insolvent' if (s 6(2)):

- (a) the company goes into liquidation (see **20.8**) at a time when its assets are insufficient for the payment of its debts and other liabilities and the expenses of the winding up; or
- (b) an administration order is made in relation to the company; or
- (c) an administrative receiver of the company is appointed.

The insolvency of the lead company may have occurred during or after the time when the person sought to be disqualified was its director or shadow director.

Collateral companies may be companies incorporated or formed outside Great Britain ('overseas companies': s 22(2A)).

A person cannot be disqualified under s 6 for less than two years; the maximum disqualification period is 15 years (s 6(4)).

Section 6 is the most important provision under which disqualification orders are made and is considered in detail in **20.13.3** to **20.13.7**.

20.13.2.7 Expedient in the public interest

The Secretary of State may, under CDDA 1986, s 8, apply for a disqualification order to be made against a person who is, or has been, a director, or shadow director, of a company, if it appears to the Secretary of State that it is expedient in the public interest for a disqualification order to be made.

A disqualification order under s 8 may be for up to 15 years (s 8(4)). Disqualification under s 8 is considered further in **20.13.3** to **20.13.7**.

20.13.2.8 Instructing unfit director

Where a disqualification order has been made against a person ('the main transgressor') under CDDA 1986, s 6 or 8, and any of the conduct for which the order was made against the main transgressor was the result of the main transgressor acting in accordance with another person's directions or instructions, that other person may be disqualified under s 8ZA (where the main transgressor's disqualification was under s 6) or s 8ZD (main transgressor's disqualification under s 8).

The maximum period of disqualification under s 8ZA or 8ZD is 15 years (ss 8ZA(4) and 8ZD(5)). Disqualification under s 8ZA must be for a minimum of two years (s 8ZA(4)).

20.13.2.9 Participation in wrongful trading

Under CDDA 1986, s 10, a disqualification order may be made against a person who has been found liable by the court to contribute to the assets of a company being wound up, either under IA 1986, s 213 (liability for fraudulent trading, see **20.11**) or IA 1986, s 214 (director's responsibility for company's wrongful trading, see **20.12**).

A disqualification order under CDDA 1986, s 10, may be made by the court which made the finding of liability (s 10(1)) and may be for a period of up to 15 years (s 10(2)).

20.13.2.10 Competition disqualification order

A competition disqualification order must be made by the court against a person who has been a director of a company which has breached competition law if the director's conduct makes him or her unfit to be concerned in the management of a company (CDDA 1986, s 9A). A competition disqualification order may be applied for by the Competition and Markets Authority or by any of the regulators listed in s 9E(2) and the application must be made to the High Court (s 9E(3)). A competition disqualification order may be for a period of up to 15 years (s 9A(9)).

20.13.3 DISQUALIFICATION UNDERTAKINGS

Instead of applying to the court for an order under CDDA 1986, s 5A, 6, 8, 8ZA or 8ZD, disqualifying a person from being a director, the Secretary of State may accept from the person a disqualification undertaking, if expedient in the public interest (ss 5A(4), 7(2A), 8(2A), 8ZC and 8ZE). A disqualification undertaking is an undertaking by a person not to do any of the things which are prohibited by a disqualification order, for a specified period of time (s 1A). The Secretary of State refuses to accept a disqualification undertaking unless it is accompanied by an agreed statement of the facts which showed the person's unfitness to be a director, and the Secretary of State is entitled to insist on such a statement (*Re Blackspur Group plc (No 3)* [2001] EWCA Civ 1595, [2002] 2 BCLC 263). Sections 13 and 15 apply to disqualification undertakings as well as disqualification orders, so that the penalties for breaching an undertaking are the same as for acting contrary to a disqualification order.

Instead of applying to the court for a competition disqualification order under s 9A, the Competition and Markets Authority, or one of the regulators listed in s 9E(2), may accept a disqualification undertaking (s 9B).

20.13.4 APPLICATION FOR DISQUALIFICATION UNDER SECTION 6 OR 8

20.13.4.1 Who may apply?

In order to obtain a disqualification order against a person under CDDA 1986, s 6 or 8, an application must be made to the appropriate court by the Secretary of State, though if the application is for an order under s 6 and the lead company is or has been in compulsory liquidation, the Secretary of State may direct the official receiver to make the application (s 7(1)). An application for a disqualification order can be made only if it appears to the Secretary of State that it is expedient in the public interest that an order should be made (ss 7(1) and 8(1)). Decisions on when to apply for disqualification orders are taken in the Disqualification Unit of the Insolvency Service, which is an executive agency of the Department for Business, Energy and Industrial Strategy (**www.gov.uk/government/ organisations/insolvency-service**).

An application for an order under s 6 may be made without the court's permission within three years of the lead company becoming insolvent, but the court's permission is required for an application after three years (s 7(2)). For companies which became insolvent before 1 October 2015, the period is two years.

20.13.4.2 Warning notice

By CDDA 1986, s 16(1), any person intending to apply to the County Court or the High Court for the making of a disqualification order must give not less than ten days' notice of that intention to the person against whom the order is sought. An application made without giving the correct period of notice is not a nullity (*Secretary of State for Trade and Industry v Langridge* [1991] Ch 402; followed in Scotland in *Secretary of State for Trade and Industry v Lovat* 1996 SC 32), but may be an abuse of process, for which one possible sanction would be to strike out the claim (*Re Finelist Ltd* [2003] EWHC 1780 (Ch), [2004] BCC 877, at [93]).

20.13.5 PURPOSE OF DISQUALIFICATION UNDER SECTIONS 6 AND 8

In *Re Sevenoaks Stationers (Retail) Ltd* [1991] Ch 164, Dillon LJ said, at p 176:

> It is beyond dispute that the purpose of CDDA 1986, s 6, is to protect the public, and in particular potential creditors of companies, from losing money through companies becoming insolvent when the directors of those companies are people unfit to be concerned in the management of a company.

See also *Re Lo-Line Electric Motors Ltd* [1988] Ch 477; *Re Westmid Packing Services Ltd* [1998] 2 All ER 124 at p 131. Protection is not necessarily limited to the British public (*Re Westminster Property Management Ltd (No 2)* [2001] BCC 305 at p 358).

A further, related purpose is to raise standards of responsibility among those who make use of limited liability (per Nicholls V-C in *Secretary of State for Trade and Industry v Ettinger* [1993] BCLC 896 at p 899). This was described by Scott V-C in *Re Barings plc* [1998] BCC 583 at p 590 as subsidiary to the main purpose of protection of the public.

In *Re Blackspur Group plc* [1998] 1 WLR 422 the Court of Appeal said, at p 426:

> The purpose of [CDDA 1986] is the protection of the public, by means of prohibitory remedial action, by anticipated deterrent effect on further misconduct and by encouragement of higher standards of honesty and diligence in corporate management, from those who are unfit to be concerned in the management of a company.

Other judges at first instance have taken raising standards to be the primary purpose of disqualification: see Lawrence Collins J in *Re Bradcrown Ltd* [2001] 1 BCLC 547 at p 550 (apparently misreading the mention of it in *Re Westmid Packing Services Ltd* at p 129 as a statement by the court of the law whereas in fact it was only a summary of counsel's argument) and Peter Smith J in *Re J A Chapman and Co Ltd* [2003] EWHC 532 (Ch), [2003] 2 BCLC 206, at [9]. That this is the primary purpose may be indicated by the rule that, if unfitness is proved, a disqualification order must be made under s 6 (which requires a disqualification period of at least two years), whether or not the court thinks that the defendant is a danger to the public (*Re Grayan Building Services Ltd* [1995] Ch 241).

Meting out retribution for aggrieved creditors is not the purpose of a disqualification order (*Re Cubelock Ltd* [2001] BCC 523 at p 536).

20.13.6 FACTORS THE COURT CONSIDERS IN AN APPLICATION UNDER SECTIONS 6 AND 8

20.13.6.1 Unfitness must be proved

The court cannot disqualify a person under CDDA 1986, s 6, unless it is satisfied that the person's conduct as a director or shadow director of a particular company—either taken alone or taken in conjunction with conduct as director or shadow director of any other company—makes that person unfit to be concerned in the management of a company. This means unfit to be concerned in the management of companies generally, though not necessarily every company in the country (*Re Polly Peck International plc (No 2)* [1994] 1 BCLC 574; *Re Barings plc (No 5)* [2000] 1 BCLC 523 at p 535): it is possible to give permission for a disqualified person to manage a particular company (see **20.13.9**). If the court does find that the defendant's past conduct renders the defendant unfit, it must make a disqualification order for at least two years, regardless of subsequent reform of character (*Re Grayan Building Services Ltd* [1995] Ch 241; *Re Migration Services International Ltd* [2000] 1 BCLC 666 at p 673). Subsequent reform of character may be taken into account when fixing the length of the disqualification period (see **20.13.7**).

On an application under s 8, the court may, at its discretion, disqualify a defendant whose conduct in relation to a particular company demonstrates unfitness to be concerned in the management of a company.

The following discussion concentrates on disqualification under s 6. Sections 6 and 8 are compared and contrasted in *Re J A Chapman and Co Ltd* [2003] EWHC 532 (Ch), [2003] 2 BCLC 206, at [2] to [9].

In *Re Sevenoaks Stationers (Retail) Ltd* [1991] Ch 164, Dillon LJ said, at p 176:

> The test laid down in s 6—apart from the requirement that the person concerned is or has been a director of a company which has become insolvent—is whether the person's conduct as a director of the company or companies in question 'makes him unfit to be concerned in the management of a company'. These are ordinary words of the English language and they should be simple to apply in most cases. It is important to hold to those words in each case.

20.13.6.2 Evidence

The matters by reference to which the defendant is alleged to be unfit (commonly known as the 'charges') must be specified by the claimant in a statement filed with the claim form (SI 1987/2023, r 3(3)). Whatever other evidence is before the court, its reasons for making a disqualification order must be limited to proved charges: this ensures the defendant knows what case has to be answered (*Re Deaduck Ltd* [2000] 1 BCLC 148 at pp 159 and 164–5; *Re Cubelock Ltd* [2001] BCC 523). Only proved charges may be taken into account when setting the period of disqualification (*Re Sevenoaks Stationers (Retail) Ltd* [1991] Ch 164 at p 177). But other evidence may show the context in which the proved misconduct occurred and influence the court's assessment of its gravity, either when deciding whether the proved charges demonstrate unfitness (*Re Deaduck Ltd* at pp 159 and 164–5) or (at least insofar as it provides mitigation) when determining the period of disqualification (*Re Sevenoaks Stationers (Retail) Ltd* at p 177).

Whether a defendant is unfit is a question of fact (*Re Sevenoaks Stationers (Retail) Ltd* at p 176). Determining that question:

> involves the evaluation of the seriousness of the charges which have been proved and a judgment of the trial judge as to whether, taking all the circumstances into account, including all matters of mitigation and extenuation, the director is or is not unfit. (*Re Hitco 2000 Ltd* [1995] 2 BCLC 63 at p 65)

Charges must be viewed cumulatively, so that it is no defence to say that no individual instance of misconduct merits disqualification (*Re Barings plc (No 5)* [2000] 1 BCLC 523 at p 535). Circumstances which may be taken into account include the defendant's health at the time of the alleged misconduct (*Re CEM Connections Ltd* [2000] BCC 917; *Secretary of State for Trade and Industry v Mitchell* 2002 SLT 658). It is irrelevant that some other remedy has been or might be obtained for the misconduct (*Re Grayan Building Services Ltd* [1995] Ch 241). General evidence of character is irrelevant (*Re Dawes and Henderson (Agencies) Ltd* [1997] 1 BCLC 329) though it may be relevant in determining the period of disqualification (*Re Barings plc* [1998] BCC 583 at p 590; *Re Westmid Packing Services Ltd* [1998] 2 All ER 124 at p 133). The standard of proof is the civil standard of balance of probabilities, but the more serious the charges, especially if they allege serious moral turpitude, the more the court will need the assistance of cogent evidence (*Re Living Images Ltd* [1996] 1 BCLC 348 at pp 355–6; *Re Dominion International Group plc (No 2)* [1996] 1 BCLC 572 at p 576; *Re Verby Print for Advertising Ltd* [1998] 2 BCLC 23).

A court hearing a director disqualification claim must consider:

(a) what the defendant did (see **20.13.6.3**);

(b) whether the defendant's actions were due to the defendant's lack of probity or incompetence or both (see **20.13.6.4**);

(c) whether the case against the defendant is serious enough to warrant disqualification (see **20.13.6.4**).

20.13.6.3 What the defendant did

The limitations on the conduct from which charges may be formulated are considered in **20.13.6.5** and **20.13.6.6**. The court must have regard to matters specified in CDDA 1986, sch 1 (see **20.13.6.7**). It may take into account matters not listed in sch 1 (*Re Bath Glass Ltd* [1988] BCLC 329 at p 332; *Re Sykes (Butchers) Ltd* [1998] 1 BCLC 110 at p 125) and the fact that they are not in the schedule does not mean that they are less significant than the matters that are in the schedule. Any allegation of unfitness must be considered on its merits irrespective of whether it is in the schedule (*Re Amaron Ltd* [2001] 1 BCLC 562 at p 568). In practice there are recurring themes in cases, notably the way in which defendants have financed trading while insolvent by using money owed to unsecured trade creditors and involuntary creditors such as HM Revenue and Customs (see **20.13.6.8**). In *Re Firedart Ltd* [1994] 2 BCLC 340, Arden J said, at p 351:

> there are a number of matters which if proved would generally lead me to the conclusion that a director was unfit to be concerned in the management of a company. They include: trading while insolvent; taking personal benefits over and above any proper remuneration; failing to keep proper accounting records.

For trading while insolvent see **20.13.6.8**. Arden J's reference to taking personal benefits is echoed by Lindsay J in *Re Polly Peck International plc (No 2)* [1994] 1 BCLC 574, who said that any breach of duty designed to benefit the defendant who owed the duty is likely to be regarded as serious enough to warrant disqualification, but a breach of duty which was not intended to benefit the defendant might not warrant disqualification (see also *Re Deaduck Ltd* [2000] 1 BCLC 148 at p 160). On failure to keep proper accounting records see per Nicholls V-C in *Secretary of State for Trade and Industry v Ettinger* [1993] BCLC 896 at p 900 cited in **9.1**.

In *Secretary of State for Trade and Industry v McTighe (No 2)* [1996] 2 BCLC 477, Morritt LJ said that persistent failure to cooperate with the liquidator and the official receiver would demonstrate unfitness.

20.13.6.4 Seriousness of case

In **Re Grayan Building Services Ltd** [1995] Ch 241, Hoffmann LJ said, at p 253, that the court must decide whether the defendant's conduct, 'viewed cumulatively and taking into account any extenuating circumstances, has fallen below the standards of probity and competence appropriate for persons fit to be directors of companies'. In *Re Landhurst Leasing plc* [1999] 1 BCLC 286, Hart J, at p 344, identified Hoffmann LJ's standard of probity and competence with the dual objective/subjective standard of care which Hoffmann LJ, in *Re D'Jan of London Ltd* [1994] 1 BCLC 561, had taken from the Insolvency Act 1986, s 214(4) (see **16.8.1**).

As the minimum period of disqualification under CDDA 1986, s 6, is two years, a disqualification order should not be made at all if the defendant's misconduct is not serious enough to merit two years' disqualification (*Re Polly Peck International plc (No 2)* [1994] 1 BCLC 574).

Although the mere fact that a defendant's misconduct is neither dishonest nor contrary to the law does not mean that it cannot render the director unfit (*Re Deaduck Ltd* [2000] 1 BCLC 148 at p 167), the courts have generally been more ready to disqualify for lack of probity than for incompetence. In *Re Lo-Line Electric Motors Ltd* [1988] Ch 477, Browne-Wilkinson V-C said, at p 486:

> Ordinary commercial misjudgment is in itself not sufficient to justify disqualification. In the normal case, the conduct complained of must display a lack of commercial probity, although I have no doubt that in an extreme case of gross negligence or total incompetence disqualification could be appropriate.

In *Re McNulty's Interchange Ltd* (1988) 4 BCC 533, Browne-Wilkinson V-C repeated that commercial misjudgement does not demonstrate unfitness and went on to say that an application for a disqualification order should not be made where all that was alleged was mere mismanagement. In *Re Sevenoaks Stationers (Retail) Ltd* [1991] Ch 164, Dillon LJ said, at p 184, that he did not think it was necessary for incompetence to be 'total', as suggested by Browne-Wilkinson V-C in *Re Lo-Line Electric Motors Ltd*, to render a director unfit: incompetence or negligence 'in a very marked degree' was sufficient in the case before him. In *Re Barings plc (No 5)* [1999] 1 BCLC 433, Jonathan Parker J, at pp 483–4, reconciled the two approaches by saying:

> Where … [the claimant's] case is based solely on allegations of incompetence … the burden is on [the claimant] to satisfy the court that the conduct complained of demonstrates incompetence of a high degree.

On appeal in *Re Barings plc (No 5)* [2000] 1 BCLC 523 the Court of Appeal, at p 535, said that it wished to emphasise what Jonathan Parker J had said. The Court of Appeal went on to suggest that it is unnecessary to require an exaggerated degree of incompetence to justify the penalty of disqualification, given that the court can give leave to act during a period of disqualification (see **20.13.9**). But it is surely better to adopt the view of Lindsay J in *Re Polly Peck International plc (No 2)* that the court's power to give leave is not something to be taken into account when deciding whether to disqualify. It is not right to deal with misconduct that is not serious enough to warrant the minimum period of two years' disqualification by disqualifying and then giving leave to act despite being disqualified: the right course is not to disqualify at all. In *Re Cubelock Ltd* [2001] BCC 523, Park J said, at p 536, that 'the Court of Appeal [in *Re Barings plc (No 5)*] did not to any appreciable extent diminish the level of incompetence which would be required to justify a disqualification'. Jonathan Parker J's formulation has been followed in *Re Bradcrown Ltd* [2001] 1 BCLC 547 and *Secretary of State for Trade and Industry v Walker* [2003] EWHC 175 (Ch), [2003] 1 BCLC 363.

For examples of incompetence of such seriousness as to amount to unfitness see *Re Barings plc* [1998] BCC 583 and *Re Barings plc (No 5)*.

20.13.6.5 *De facto* directorships included

To decide whether a defendant's conduct shows that a disqualification order should be made, the court considers conduct as a director whether properly appointed as such or not (*Re Eurostem Maritime Ltd* 1987 PCC 190; *Re Lo-Line Electric Motors Ltd* [1988] Ch 477; *Re Moorgate Metals Ltd* [1995] 1 BCLC 503). In *Re Lo-Line Electric Motors Ltd*, Browne-Wilkinson V-C said that Parliament's plain intention was to have regard to the conduct of a person acting as a director, whether validly appointed, invalidly appointed or just assuming to act as a director without any appointment at all. (A person who acts as a director without being properly appointed is known as a *de facto* director.) It may be very difficult to decide whether what a person has done, when he or she was not legally holding office as a director, amounts to acting as a director so as to make the individual liable to disqualification. In practice the question may be inextricably linked with whether what he or she has done in itself merits disqualification—see *Secretary of State for Trade and Industry v Tjolle* [1998] 1 BCLC 333. In *Re Kaytech International plc* [1999] 2 BCLC 351 the Court of Appeal refused to lay down a definition of *de facto* director, but found that in the case before it an individual had acted as a director. *Re Sykes (Butchers) Ltd* [1998] 1 BCLC 110 is another case in which a defendant was found to have been a *de facto* director. There is a full review of the authorities in *Secretary of State for Trade and Industry v Becker* [2002] EWHC 2200 (Ch), [2003] 1 BCLC 555.

20.13.6.6 Geographical coverage

The court may consider conduct that occurred outside England and Wales, and persons who are not British subjects or are not domiciled in England and Wales may be disqualified under CDDA 1986, s 6 (*Re Seagull Manufacturing Co Ltd (No 2)* [1994] Ch 91). This has been particularly important in cases involving people who earn a living by being nominee directors of companies to shield those who really run them (see *Re Kaytech International plc* [1999] 2 BCLC 351, concerning a resident of the Isle of Man, and *Official Receiver v Vass* [1999] BCC 516, concerning a resident of Sark who was a director of 1,313 UK companies and secretary of 513).

20.13.6.7 Statutory list of matters to be considered

When considering whether a person's conduct in relation to a company makes the person unfit to be a director, the court is required by CDDA 1986, s 12C, to have regard in particular to the matters mentioned in sch 1 to the Act. Where the person is or has been a director, these matters include:

(a) Any misfeasance or breach of any fiduciary duty by the director in relation to a company or overseas company (sch 1, para 5). A finding of breach of duty is neither necessary nor sufficient for a finding of unfitness: a defendant may be found to be unfit though no breach of duty has been proved, a defendant may be found not to be unfit even though a breach of duty is proved (*Re Barings plc (No 5)* [2000] 1 BCLC 523 at p 535).

(b) Any material breach of any legislative or other obligation of the director which applies as a result of being a director of a company or overseas company (sch 1, para 6).

Whether or not the person is or has been a director, the court must take into account:

(a) The extent to which the person was responsible for the causes of any material contravention by a company or overseas company of any applicable legislative or other requirement (sch 1, para 1).

(b) Where applicable, the extent to which the person was responsible for the causes of a company or overseas company becoming insolvent (sch 1, para 2). Responsibility is to be assessed broadly and not by reference to legal concepts of causation (*Re Barings plc (No 5)* at p 535).

(c) The nature and extent of any loss or harm caused, or any potential loss or harm which could have been caused, by the person's conduct in relation to a company or overseas company (sch 1, para 4).

The court must also take into account the frequency of conduct of the director which falls within sch 1, paras 1, 2, 5 or 6 (sch 1, paras 3 and 7).

The fact that particular matters are listed in sch 1 does not mean that the court may not have regard to other matters (see **20.13.6.3**).

20.13.6.8 Taking unwarranted risks with creditors' money

In *Secretary of State for Trade and Industry v Creegan* [2002] 1 BCLC 99 it was held that unfitness is not demonstrated merely by allowing a company to trade while knowing it to be insolvent: it must also be shown that the defendant knew or ought to have known that there was no reasonable prospect of meeting creditors' claims. The phrase 'taking unwarranted risks with creditors' money' is used in some of the cases to describe this kind of misconduct (see *Re Living Images Ltd* [1996] 1 BCLC 348; *Re City Pram and Toy Co Ltd* [1998] BCC 537).

A policy of not paying on time creditors who do not press for payment may demonstrate unfitness, especially where the money is used to finance trading while insolvent (*Re Sevenoaks (Stationers) Retail* [1991] Ch 164). A non-payment policy may demonstrate unfitness even if it is not shown that the defendant intended that the creditors would never be paid (*Secretary of State for Trade and Industry v McTighe (No 2)* [1996] 2 BCLC 477; *Re Structural Concrete Ltd* [2001] BCC 578), but the mere fact that debts are routinely paid late may not show unfitness (*Re Funtime Ltd* [2000] 1 BCLC 247). A non-payment policy may demonstrate unfitness if adopted while the company is solvent (*Re Hopes (Heathrow) Ltd* [2001] 1 BCLC 575). Although it is often so-called Crown debts (especially value added tax and employees' national insurance and tax contributions) that are the subject of a non-payment policy, the identity of the creditor is not the crucial factor demonstrating unfitness, and the court must consider the significance of the non-payment policy and whether the defendant was taking unfair advantage of the creditor's forbearance (*Re Sevenoaks (Stationers) Retail Ltd* at p 183; *Re Amaron Ltd* [2001] 1 BCLC 562 at pp 571–3).

20.13.6.9 Directors who do not stand up to a dominant board member

In *Re Polly Peck International plc (No 2)* [1994] 1 BCLC 574, the company had been dominated by Mr Asil Nadir, who owned 25 per cent of the shares and was widely regarded as one of the most successful entrepreneurs of his time. It was alleged that Mr Nadir had used the company, which was listed on the Stock Exchange, to raise enormous sums of money from shareholders and banks, which money was lent to subsidiary companies which did not in fact need much of the money but deposited it in banks in the Turkish Republic of Northern Cyprus (which is not recognised by the British government) from which the money could not be recovered. Mr Nadir had failed to appear for trial on criminal charges concerning his handling of the company's finances. The Secretary of State sought leave to commence proceedings out of time to seek the disqualification of the company's finance director, its former joint managing director and two non-executive directors. It was said that they should have made the company institute better financial controls to prevent Mr Nadir mishandling its funds and that they should have threatened to resign. Lindsay J pointed out that the four were a minority of the company's board of directors and could not have forced any decision. There was no evidence that a threat to resign would have had any effect on Mr Nadir, who was obviously planning to get rid of one of the four anyway. The finance director had in fact done a great deal to improve controls and was constantly pushing for better financial management. His Lordship described the Secretary of State's case as 'at best speculative and very weak' (at p 604) and refused leave to bring the proceedings out of time. Similarly, in *Secretary of State for Trade and Industry v Taylor* [1997] 1 WLR 407, unfitness was not demonstrated by the fact that a director did not resign when his advice that the company could not avoid insolvent liquidation and should cease trading was ignored by the majority of the board. But in *Re Westmid Packing Services Ltd* [1998] 2 All ER 124 the Court of Appeal emphasised that former directors of a company could not claim to be excused from failure to keep themselves properly informed of the company's position just because the board was dominated by another person:

> It is of the greatest importance that any individual who undertakes the statutory and fiduciary obligations of being a company director should realise that these are inescapable personal responsibilities. The appellants may have been dazzled, manipulated and deceived by Mr Griffiths [who controlled the company and was disqualified for nine years] but they were in breach of their own duties in allowing this to happen.

See also *Re Park House Properties Ltd* [1997] 2 BCLC 530 discussed in **16.8.5**.

20.13.7 PERIOD OF DISQUALIFICATION

In *Re Sevenoaks Stationers (Retail) Ltd* [1991] Ch 164, Dillon LJ accepted (at p 179) the following guidelines for disqualification under CDDA 1986, s 6:

(i) [T]he top bracket of disqualification for periods over ten years should be reserved for particularly serious cases. These may include cases where a director who has already had one period of disqualification imposed on him falls to be disqualified yet again. (ii) The minimum bracket of two to five years' disqualification should be applied where, though disqualification is mandatory, the case is, relatively, not very serious. (iii) The middle bracket of disqualification for from six to ten years should apply for serious cases which do not merit the top bracket.

The same principles apply to disqualification under s 8 (*Re Samuel Sherman plc* [1991] 1 WLR 1070).

When determining what the period of disqualification under s 6 should be, the court must take into account the matters set out in sch 1 (s 12C).

In a case under s 2, the Court of Appeal decided that fraudulent trading for four years result-ing in losses of about £0.75 million was a middle-bracket offence meriting eight years' disquali-fication (*R v Millard* (1993) 15 Cr App R (S) 445). In *Secretary of State for Trade and Industry v McTighe (No 2)* [1996] 2 BCLC 477, a case under s 6, the Court of Appeal imposed disqualification for 12 years on a 'particularly serious case' in which a man had caused three companies successively to trade at the risk of their creditors, ultimately leaving unpaid debts of well over £1 million. £1 to 2 million or more had been misappropriated in a way that was 'tantamount to theft' and the director had failed to cooperate with the liquidator or official receiver.

In **Re Westmid Packing Services Ltd** [1998] 2 All ER 124 there is an extensive review by the Court of Appeal of the approach to be taken when determining the period of disqualification. The Court of Appeal wants the process to be kept simple and disapproves of extensive citation from previous cases. The court should exercise its jurisdiction 'in a summary manner' (p 135). The Court of Appeal emphasised (at p. 132) that determining the length of a period of disqualification is little different from determining the sentence in a criminal case:

> The period of disqualification must reflect the gravity of the offence. It must contain deterrent elements. That is what sentencing is all about, and that is what fixing the appropriate period of the disqualification is all about.

The fact that the court has already decided to grant leave to act as a director during the period of disqualification (see **20.13.9**) should not affect the length of the period. The period of disqualifica-tion is a matter for the judge's discretion, which, like any exercise of judicial discretion, must be decided in the light of all relevant circumstances, which can include mitigating factors such as: 'the former director's age and state of health, the length of time he has been in jeopardy, whether he has admitted the offence, his general conduct before and after the offence, and the periods of disquali-fication of his co-directors that may have been ordered by other courts' (at p 134).

20.13.8 COMPENSATION ORDERS

For conduct occurring on or after 1 October 2015, new ss 15A, 15B and 15C of CDDA 1986 may have a considerable impact on director disqualification proceedings. Section 15A provides that if a person is subject to a disqualification order or undertaking, for conduct which has caused loss to one or more creditors of an insolvent company of which the person has, at any time, been a director, the Secretary of State can apply to the court for a compensation order against the disqualified person (s 15A). A compensation order (s 15B(1)) is an order requiring a person to pay a specified amount either:

(a) to the Secretary of State for the benefit of individual creditor(s) or class(es) of creditor; or

(b) as a contribution to the assets of a company.

The amount specified in the order must reflect the amount of the loss, the nature of the conduct which caused it, and whether the person has made any other financial contribution in recompense for the conduct (s 15B(3)).

An application for a compensation order has to be made within two years of the disqualification order being made or undertaking accepted (s 15A(5)).

Where a person is disqualified for instructing an unfit director, a compensation order may be based on losses caused by the main transgressor (s 15A(6)).

The Secretary of State may accept a compensation undertaking instead of applying for a court order (ss 15A(2) and 15B(2)).

A person subject to a compensation order or undertaking may ask the court to reduce the amount payable or revoke the order (s 15C(1)) The court must hear the Secretary of State on such an application (s 15C(2)).

20.13.9 LEAVE TO ACT DURING A PERIOD OF DISQUALIFICATION

A person subject to a disqualification order or undertaking may apply for permission to do any of the things which it prohibits, apart from acting as an insolvency practitioner (CDDA 1986, ss 1(1) and 1A(1)).

The Secretary of State must appear on a hearing of an application for leave, in order to call the court's attention to any relevant matters, and may give evidence or call witnesses (s 17(5)).

Leave will be given only where there is a need for it (*Re Cargo Agency Ltd* [1992] BCLC 686) and that must be the need of the company for the director's services not the director's need to work (*Re Gibson Davies Ltd* [1995] BCC 11). When the person who is applying for leave to manage a company is substantially the only person interested in the company's equity capital, it is difficult to find any company need that is separate from the applicant's. In those circumstances the question is, according to Rattee J in *Secretary of State for Trade and Industry v Barnett* [1998] 2 BCLC 64 at p 72:

> whether it is necessary for [the applicant] to be a director of a company in order to protect some legitimate interest of [the applicant] himself, or of any third party, which it is in all the circumstances of the case reasonable that the court should seek to protect. If it is so necessary, then the next question is whether that need can be met without infringing the protection of the public secured by the disqualification order.

Saving tax may be a legitimate interest for this purpose (*Re Dawes and Henderson (Agencies) Ltd (No 2)* [1999] 2 BCLC 317).

The principles to be applied when deciding whether to grant leave were reviewed by Scott V-C in *Re Barings plc (No 3)* [2000] 1 WLR 634. His Lordship said that leave should never be granted without serious consideration (at p 641). If leave is granted, the reasons for doing so must be consistent with the reasons for making the disqualification order (at p 640). In particular the court should ask whether the situation in which the disqualified person would be given leave to act would risk recurrence of the particular faults for which he or she had been disqualified (at p 641).

Adequate protection of the public must be provided. For example, an independent chartered accountant or solicitor must act as co-director (*Re Majestic Recording Studios Ltd* [1989] BCLC 1; *Secretary of State for Trade and Industry v Palfreman* [1995] 2 BCLC 301). In *Re Gibson Davies Ltd* ten protective undertakings were given. The court does not tolerate imperfect compliance with such undertakings (*Re Brian Sheridan Cars Ltd* [1996] 1 BCLC 327), but this raises the question of who is to check that the undertakings are being observed. In *Re Hennelly's Utilities Ltd* [2004] EWHC 34 (Ch), [2005] BCC 542, the court required the finance director, of the company which the disqualified person was applying to manage, to provide quarterly reports to the Department of Trade and Industry on the disqualified person's compliance with undertakings he had given. The learned deputy judge said, at [63]:

> the court has to balance any need for the director to act against the protection of the public from the conduct that led to the disqualification order. But the protection of the public (ie, creditors, employees, lenders, investors and all those with whom the company will do business) is ... paramount.

See further, D Milman, 'Partial disqualification orders' (1991) 12 Co Law 224; R Goddard, 'Leave to act and the disqualified director: *Re Hennelly's Utilities Ltd*' (2004) 25 Co Law 222.

It is not the policy of the Act to prevent a disqualified director from earning his or her living, only from doing so with the insulation from liability available to company directors. Being a member of an unlimited company imposes unlimited liability when the company is wound up and an application to be a director of an unlimited company of which the applicant will be substantially the only interested member may be looked on favourably by the court, provided there are undertakings to maintain the company's unlimited status (*Re Dawes and Henderson (Agencies) Ltd (No 2)*).

20.13.10 VARIATION OF DISQUALIFICATION UNDERTAKING

A person who has given a disqualification undertaking may apply under CDDA 1986, s 8A, for an order reducing or ending the period for which the undertaking is to be in force. On the hearing of the application, the Secretary of State must appear, in order to call the court's attention to any relevant matters, and may give evidence or call witnesses (CDDA 1986, s 8A(2)).

Disqualification undertakings were created in order to avoid court proceedings, so variation of an undertaking should be ordered only where circumstances have arisen since the undertaking was given which could not have been foreseen or which were not intended to be covered by the undertaking (*Re INS Realisations Ltd* [2006] EWHC 135 (Ch), [2006] 1 WLR 3433, at [39]–[40]). An application for variation should not normally be made just because the undertaking was given without legal advice or because other directors of the company were given shorter disqualification periods by the court (*Re INS Realisations Ltd* at [43]).

20.13.11 REGISTER OF DISQUALIFICATION ORDERS AND UNDERTAKINGS

The Secretary of State maintains a register of disqualification orders and undertakings, which is open to inspection free of charge (CDDA 1986, s 18). The register may be inspected at the Companies Houses in London, Cardiff and Edinburgh, and at the Royal Courts of Justice in London. The register may also be searched online at the Companies House website: **www.companieshouse.gov. uk**. Within 14 days of a disqualification order being made by a court a prescribed officer of the court must send prescribed particulars of the order to the Secretary of State for entry in the register (SI 2009/2471). Variations of orders or undertakings and grants of leave to act despite an order or undertaking must also be reported.

20.14 USE OF INSOLVENT COMPANY'S NAME

20.14.1 PRINCIPLE

A person who was a director or shadow director of a company that went into insolvent liquidation (defined in **20.14.2**) must not be a director of, or take part in the management of, a company with a similar name during the next five years (IA 1986, s 216). This applies regardless of whether a director disqualification order has been made. There is both a criminal penalty (**20.14.3**) and, under s 217, a civil liability for all debts and other liabilities of a company managed in contravention of s 216 (**20.14.4**). Contravention of s 216 can be avoided either by obtaining the leave of a court to act as director despite s 216 (**20.14.6**) or, in certain circumstances, if notice is given to the insolvent company's creditors (**20.14.7**). The primary purpose of the provision is to deal with what has become known as the 'phoenix syndrome', in which the directors of a company which has been wound up set up the same business, often on the same premises, with a similar name, often repeating the process several times. However, the application of s 216 is not restricted to those circumstances (*Ad Valorem Factors Ltd v Ricketts* [2003] EWCA Civ 1706, [2004] 1 All ER 894).

It applies, for example, where a man is director of two companies in the same group which have similar names, one of them goes into insolvent liquidation and he continues as director of the other (unless the exception described in **20.14.8** applies).

20.14.2 DETAILS

IA 1986, s 216, applies to any person who has been a director or shadow director of a company that has gone into insolvent liquidation and who occupied that position at any time within the period of 12 months ending with the day before it went into liquidation (s 216(1). The company that went into liquidation is referred to in the legislation as 'the liquidating company'. Any name by which the liquidating company 'was known' during those 12 months is a 'prohibited name'. So is any name which is so similar to a name by which it was known as to suggest an association with the liquidating company (s 216(2); see **20.14.5**). A company is known by the name under which it is registered and any name under which the company carries on business (s 216(6)). This includes a name under which part of the business is carried on and a name which is used as well as another name or names (*ESS Production Ltd v Sully* [2005] EWCA Civ 554, [2005] 2 BCLC 547).

A company goes into insolvent liquidation if it goes into liquidation (see **20.8**) at a time when its assets are insufficient for the payment of its debts and other liabilities and the expenses of the winding up (s 216(7)).

During the period of five years beginning with the day on which the company went into insolvent liquidation, the ex director or shadow director must not (s 216(3)):

(a) be a director of any other company that is known by a prohibited name; or

(b) in any way, whether directly or indirectly, be concerned or take part in the promotion, formation or management of any such company; or

(c) in any way, whether directly or indirectly, be concerned, or take part, in the carrying on of a business carried on (otherwise than by a company) under a prohibited name.

20.14.3 CRIMINAL PENALTY

Acting in contravention of IA 1986, s 216, is an offence triable either way (s 216(4) and sch 10). The offence is one of strict liability, that is the prosecution only have to prove that the accused did the prohibited act and do not have to prove an intention to offend (*R v Cole* [1998] 1 BCLC 234; *R v Doring* [2002] EWCA Crim 1695, [2003] 1 Cr App R 143).

20.14.4 CIVIL PENALTY

In addition to the possibility of a criminal penalty, a potentially severe civil penalty for contravention of IA 1986, s 216, is imposed by s 217. A person who acts as director etc of a company in contravention of s 216 is personally responsible for all debts and other liabilities of the company incurred while involved in its management (s 217(1)(a) and (3)(a)). Furthermore, any person who is 'involved in the management of' a company and acts, or is willing to act, on instructions given by a person whom he or she knows to be contravening s 216 is also personally responsible for debts and other liabilities of the company incurred while he or she was so acting or willing to act (s 217(1)(b) and (3)(b)). For the purposes of s 217, a person who is a director of a company, or is concerned, whether directly or indirectly, or takes part, in the management of the company is 'involved in the management of' the company (s 217(5)). A person liable under s 217 is jointly and severally liable with the company and with anyone else liable under the section (s 217(2)). For examples of the operation of s 217 see *Thorne v Silverleaf* [1994] 1 BCLC 637 and *Commissioners of Inland Revenue v Nash* [2003] EWHC 686 (Ch), [2004] BCC 150. It is not an abuse of process to buy outstanding debts with a view to enforcing them under s 217 (*First Independent Factors and Finance Ltd v Mountford* [2008] EWHC 835 (Ch), [2008] 2 BCLC 297). CA 2006, s 1157 (power of court to relieve director from liability; see **16.16.6**) does not apply to a claim under IA 1986, s 217 (*First Independent Factors and Finance Ltd v Mountford*).

20.14.5 SIMILAR NAMES SUGGESTING ASSOCIATION

In determining whether a company's name is so similar to a liquidating company's name as to suggest an association, the court must compare the two names:

> in the context of all the circumstances in which they were actually used or likely to be used: the types of products dealt in, the locations of the business, the types of customers dealing with the companies and those involved in the operation of the two companies (*Ad Valorem Factors Ltd v Ricketts* [2003] EWCA Civ 1706, [2004] 1 All ER 894, at [22]).
>
> … the similarity of the two names must be such as to give rise to a probability that members of the public, comparing the names in the relevant context, will associate the two companies with each other (*Ad Valorem Factors Ltd v Ricketts* at [30]).

Probability of association is sufficient: it is not necessary to show that anyone has actually been led to believe that the two companies are associated (*Commissioners of HM Revenue and Customs v Walsh* [2005] EWHC 1304 (Ch), [2005] 2 BCLC 455, at [16]). Because companies' names are looked at in the context of their operations, a court may find that an association is suggested by ordinary words of the English language, or common forenames or surnames. So, in the context in which they operated, the following pairs of companies were found to have names so similar as to suggest an association:

(a) two companies selling air compressors called Air Equipment Co Ltd and Air Component Co Ltd (*Ad Valorem Factors Ltd v Ricketts*);

(b) two companies, trading as building and civil engineering companies from the same address, called S G and T Walsh and Co Ltd and Walsh Construction Ltd (*Commissioners of HM Revenue and Customs v Walsh*);

(c) two companies called Williams Hair Studio Ltd and Williams and Xpress Ltd, which operated the same hairdressing salon (which was called Williams) (*Commissioners of HM Revenue and Customs v Benton-Diggins* [2006] EWHC 793 (Ch), [2006] 2 BCLC 255); and

(d) two companies called Classic Conservatories and Windows Ltd and Classic Roofs Ltd, the second describing itself as 'conservatory roof fabricators' (*First Independent Factors and Finance Ltd v Mountford* [2008] EWHC 835 (Ch), LTL 23/4/2008).

In *Commissioners of HM Revenue and Customs v Walsh* the court thought that association was not suggested by the companies having the same address for their registered offices or even by having an employee (the defendant's wife) in common, but the fact that the defendant was 'the face' of both companies was held to be significant. On the other hand, trading from premises in close proximity was held to suggest an association in *First Independent Factors and Finance Ltd v Mountford*, where it was also important that the same man's name appeared on letterheads and invoices of the two companies. In *Commissioners of HM Revenue and Customs v Walsh* similarity in the way in which the companies' names were presented on their letterheads was not thought to suggest association, where it was just an unimaginative use of stock typefaces. But presenting companies' names in different ways will not be seen as reducing the probability of suggesting an association (*Archer Structures Ltd v Griffiths* [2003] EWHC 957 (Ch), [2004] 1 BCLC 201).

It seems that people who are made liable by IA 1986, s 217, are caught more by their lack of imagination in devising names for their companies than by any specially bad treatment of creditors.

20.14.6 LEAVE OF COURT

The prohibition in IA 1986, s 216(3), against acting as a director etc of a company with a prohibited name is subject to leave being given by the High Court or County Court (s 216(5)).

For examples of applications for leave (which was granted), see *Re Bonus Breaks Ltd* [1991] BCC 546 and *Re Lightning Electrical Contractors Ltd* [1996] 2 BCLC 302. It is not right to refuse leave as a substitute for making a disqualification order where the facts of the case would not justify disqualification (*Penrose v Secretary of State for Trade and Industry* [1996] 1 WLR 482). The fact that the amount paid by the new company for the old company's business was determined by independent valuation will favour granting leave but the court should not require undertakings concerning adequate capitalisation of the new company or the appointment of independent directors as a condition for granting leave (*Penrose*). The most important consideration is whether there is any risk to creditors beyond that which is inherent in dealing with limited companies (*Penrose*). For detailed discussion see G Wilson, 'Delinquent directors and company names: the role of judicial policy-making in the business environment' (1996) 47 NILQ 345.

Provided application for leave is made not later than seven business days after the date of going into liquidation, the person applying for leave can act without that leave until six weeks after the date of going into liquidation, or until the application for leave is determined if earlier (I(EW)R 2016, r 22.6).

20.14.7 NOTICE BY SUCCESSOR COMPANY

If a company acquires the whole, or substantially the whole, of an insolvent company's business, under arrangements made by its insolvency office-holder, a director of the insolvent company can act as director etc of the acquiring company, despite IA 1986, s 216, if notice is given in accordance with I(EW)R 2016, r 4.228.

The notice must be given, by the director, within 28 days of the completion of the arrangements for acquiring the business (r 22.4(3)(a)). The notice must be given to all creditors of the insolvent company whose names and addresses are known to the director, and must be published in the *London Gazette* (r 22.4(2)). The notice must contain the details required by r 22.4(3)(b). The notice procedure can be used by someone who is already a director of the acquiring company at the time of giving notice (r 22.4(4)). For full discussion see A Deacock, 'Section 216 and phoenixism—let's hope no one notices' (2007) 23 Insolv L & P 134.

20.14.8 ESTABLISHED USE OF NAME

The prohibition in IA 1986, s 216(3), against acting as a director etc of a company with a prohibited name does not apply if the company has been known by that name throughout the 12 months preceding the day the liquidating company went into liquidation, provided it was not a dormant company (defined in CA 2006, s 1169) during that time (I(EW)R 2016, r 22.7). If the company uses more than one prohibited name, it is sufficient if one of them was used throughout the qualifying 12 months (*ESS Production Ltd v Sully* [2005] EWCA Civ 554, [2005] 2 BCLC 547). If the company was dormant in the relevant 12 months, this exception does not apply even if its name (without the word 'Ltd') was used for a business that did operate throughout that period (*First Independent Factors and Finance Ltd v Mountford* [2008] EWHC 835 (Ch), LTL 23/4/2008).

20.15 ORDER OF APPLICATION OF ASSETS IN LIQUIDATION

The matters considered in **20.15** apply in both voluntary and compulsory liquidations.

20.15.1 PRINCIPLES

The general rule is that if a company is insolvent so that creditors cannot be paid in full then all creditors must be paid equal percentages of their debts (IA 1986, s 107 (voluntary liquidation); I(EW)R 2016, r 14.12 (compulsory liquidation)). However, three further principles have to be taken into account. The first is the principle of salvage, that the expenses of collecting and realising the assets and distributing the proceeds must be paid out of those proceeds (*Batten v Wedgwood Coal and Iron Co* (1884) 28 ChD 317). The second principle is that certain debts are, by statute, made preferential and payable before other debts (though not before expenses). The provisions on preferential debts are contained in IA 1986, ss 175, 386 and 387 and sch 6. In s 175(2)(a), though, it is provided that the expenses of the winding up must be paid before the preferential payments. By s 115, all expenses properly incurred in a voluntary winding up, including the remuneration of the liquidator, are payable out of the assets of the company in priority to all other claims. The third principle is set-off of mutual debts. A creditor of an insolvent person who is also owed money by that person is likely to be very aggrieved if forced to pay the whole of the debt owed to the insolvent person in return for only a percentage of what the creditor is owed. Accordingly, insolvency law has long allowed for mutual debts to be set off. In the winding up of companies the provision currently permitting set-off of mutual debts is I(EW)R 2016, r 14.25. This rule normally benefits a creditor of a company being wound up who is also a debtor to the company but it also aids the administration of the winding up and it cannot be excluded by any agreement between a creditor and a company (*National Westminster Bank Ltd v Halesowen Presswork and Assemblies Ltd* [1972] AC 785).

From what has been said so far it emerges that, rather than all a company's liabilities being treated *pari passu*, there are at least three groups—expenses of the liquidation, preferential payments, other liabilities—each subject to its own rules. And it must not be forgotten that secured creditors with charges may take whatever property has been charged with payment of their debts and pay themselves out of the proceeds of sale of that property.

The result is that, ignoring secured creditors who look after themselves, a liquidator of a company is required to classify the claims against the company into groups. The groups are paid off one by one in an order prescribed by law. When the liquidator comes to a group that cannot be paid in full, all claimants in the group receive the same proportion (called a 'dividend') of their claims—that is, claimants in that group are treated *pari passu*—and subsequent groups receive nothing.

20.15.2 CONTRACTING OUT

It is possible for a creditor of a company to agree that if the company should go into liquidation, payment of the creditor's debt will be postponed until other specified debts, which would normally have equal or lower priority, are paid. This is known as 'subordination' of the debt. The creditors who are to be paid before the subordinated creditor are known as 'senior' creditors. A subordination agreement will be enforced by the courts (*Re Maxwell Communications Corporation plc* [1993] 1 WLR 1402; *United States Trust Co of New York v Australia and New Zealand Banking Group Ltd* (1995) 37 NSWLR 131). A subordination agreement is effective, whether it was entered into at the time the debt to be subordinated was created or subsequently when the debt to be given priority was created (*Re SSSL Realisations (2002) Ltd* [2004] EWHC 1760 (Ch), [2005] 1 BCLC 1). The effect of a subordination agreement is that any dividend due to the subordinated creditor is paid instead to the senior creditors. However, this does not mean that the subordination agreement is a charge on the subordinated debt (*United States Trust Co of New York v Australia and New Zealand Banking Group Ltd*; *Re SSSL Realisations (2002) Ltd*).

Agreeing that one's debt is to have a lower-than-normal priority is permitted because it does no harm to other creditors. Agreements which do affect what will be distributed to other creditors are limited to some extent by the anti-deprivation principle. This principle is that a company cannot agree that, if it goes into liquidation, its property is to go to another person and not be available for distribution to its creditors. The same principle applies in the bankruptcy of individuals. The way in which this principle should be applied has become controversial because there are many exceptions to it. For example:

(a) A company can charge its property to secure payment to a creditor. Provided the charge is properly registered, winding up does not affect the right of the creditor to seize the charged property and realise it to pay the secured debt (see **Chapter 11**).

(b) It is usual for a lease of land to provide that the lease will terminate if the lessee goes into liquidation or is adjudicated bankrupt. This has never been seen as contrary to the anti-deprivation principle.

The anti-deprivation principle was considered by the Supreme Court in *Perpetual Trustee Co Ltd v BNY Corporate Trustee Services Ltd* [2011] UKSC 38, [2012] 1 AC 383. The lead judgment given by Lord Collins reviewed the cases and concluded (at [78]) that the principle is applied only where there is a deliberate intention to evade the insolvency laws, and (at [104]) that it should not be applied 'to bona fide commercial transactions which do not have as their predominant purpose, or one of their main purposes, the deprivation of the property of one of the parties on [insolvency]'. The Supreme Court held that the case before it was in the second category so that the impugned provision should not be invalidated.

In *Folgate London Market Ltd v Chaucer Insurance plc* [2011] EWCA Civ 328, [2011] Bus LR 1327, a clause in an agreement was held to infringe the anti-deprivation principle. The agreement gave a company an indemnity for damages it had to pay in a particular case. The offending clause provided that the indemnity would cease if the company entered into any insolvency procedure. Approving this decision in *Perpetual Trustee Co Ltd v BNY Corporate Trustee Services Ltd*, Lord Collins (at [104]) described this agreement as 'a blatant attempt to deprive a party of property in the event of liquidation'.

20.15.3 ADJUSTING THE RIGHTS OF CONTRIBUTORIES

Where shares are partly paid and different amounts have been paid up, a call may have to be made on some shareholders (*Re Anglo-Continental Corporation of Western Australia* [1898] 1 Ch 327) and at this stage any amount owed by the company to a shareholder may be set off against a call made on that shareholder (IA 1986, s 149(3)). The process of equalising amounts paid up on shares and setting off against amounts owing to shareholders is referred to in the legislation as adjusting the rights of the contributories among themselves.

20.15.4 POST-LIQUIDATION INTEREST

By IA 1986, s 189, interest is payable on all debts proved in a liquidation once the proved debts have been paid. The rate payable is either the contractually agreed rate, if there is one, or the rate specified in the Judgments Act 1838, s 17, on the day the company went into liquidation, whichever is greater. The rate in the 1838 Act is altered from time to time by order of the Lord Chancellor under the Administration of Justice Act 1970, s 44. It is currently 8 per cent a year (SI 1993/564). The interest is paid on the amount of debt proved (which may include pre-liquidation interest) and the interest is payable for the period during which the debts have been outstanding since the company went into liquidation (IA 1986, s 189(2)).

20.15.5 PROVISION FOR EMPLOYEES

The liquidator of a company is empowered by IA 1986, s 187, to make provision for the benefit of persons employed or formerly employed by the company or any of its subsidiaries on the cessation or transfer of its business, though only after the company's liabilities have been fully satisfied and provision has been made for the costs of the winding up. Whether the winding up is compulsory or voluntary the liquidator must have the sanction of an ordinary resolution of the company, unless the company's articles impose more restrictive conditions on the exercise of the power in which case those restrictions must be complied with. In a compulsory liquidation the liquidator's exercise of this power is subject to the court's control and any creditor or contributory may apply to the court in respect of it (s 187(4)) and this provision applies also to a voluntary liquidation by virtue of s 112. If the company resolved to make provision for employees under what is now CA 2006, s 247, before the commencement of liquidation then the liquidator is empowered to put the resolution into effect (IA 1986, s 187(1)).

20.16 DISSOLUTION

20.16.1 INTRODUCTION

In the sense in which the term is used in the United Kingdom, the dissolution of a company is effected by Companies House removing the name of the company from the register. Dissolution of a company ends its legal personality and dissolves the relationship between company and members. The company ceases to be party to any legal relationship: if it has property at the time of dissolution, that property passes to the Crown or a royal duchy in the same way as the property of an intestate deceased individual who has no heirs (CA 2006, s 1012). If a company was holding property on trust for another at the time of its dissolution, a new trustee must be appointed to replace the company. If an individual has given a company property in his or her will but the company is dissolved before he or she dies, the gift lapses (*Re Servers of the Blind League* [1960] 1 WLR 564), unless the court can infer a general charitable intention so that it can make a scheme for applying the gift cy-pres (*Re Finger's Will Trusts* [1972] Ch 286). If an insurer compensated a company for a loss it suffered then, after dissolution of the company, the insurer loses the right of subrogation to sue in the company's name for recovery of the loss from the person who caused it (*M H Smith (Plant Hire) Ltd v Mainwaring* [1986] BCLC 342).

In European Union documents the term 'dissolution' is used in the sense in which that term is understood in Continental legal systems—that is, for what in the United Kingdom is called the commencement of winding up. On the Continent the transition from going concern to company in winding up is thought of as the point at which the company is 'dissolved'. In the United Kingdom the final end of a company's legal personality on completion of winding up is regarded as the point of dissolution but on the Continent this is regarded simply as the end of winding up.

20.16.2 METHODS OF DISSOLUTION

20.16.2.1 By Act of Parliament

Occasionally, a statute is necessary to end the legal relationships or duties of a company. A statute is usually necessary, for example, to transfer the business of one bank to another, so as to transfer to the acquiring bank the obligations owed to customers by the taken-over bank. Usually a bank merger Act provides that the registrar will strike a transferor company off the register at the request of the transferee company and that, by virtue of being struck off, the transferor company will be dissolved. For recent examples, see the HSBC Investment Banking Act 2002 and the Barclays Group Reorganisation Act 2002. A statute that moves a company from one domicile to another (see 2.5.3) will provide for the company to be struck off the register but this will not dissolve the company which continues in its new domicile.

20.16.2.2 By cancellation of registration

On an application by the Attorney-General for judicial review of the registrar's decision to register a company, the court may order the registrar to cancel the company's registration (see **2.2.3**).

Directive 2009/101/EC, art 12(b) (originally enacted in Directive 68/151/EEC), requires the laws of member States to provide that what the Directive calls 'nullity' of limited companies may be ordered by a court only on six grounds, namely:

(a) that no instrument of constitution (memorandum of association) was executed or that the rules of preventive control (such as the rules for vetting of sensitive names) or the requisite legal formalities were not complied with;

(b) that the objects of the company are unlawful or contrary to public policy (this was the ground relied on in *R v Registrar of Companies, ex parte Attorney-General* [1991] BCLC 476 discussed in **2.2.3**);

(c) that the instrument of constitution (the memorandum of association) or the statutes (the articles of association) do not state the name of the company, the amount of the individual subscriptions of capital, the total amount of the capital subscribed, or the objects of the company;

(d) failure to comply with the provisions of the national law concerning the minimum amount of capital to be paid up;

(e) the incapacity of all the founder members; and

(f) that, contrary to the national law governing the company, the number of founder members is less than two.

No UK legislation has been passed to implement this requirement. However, a UK court, as an authority of the State which was required to implement the Directive, must interpret its national law in the light of the wording and purpose of the Directive, and so must not declare the registration of a company to have been void on any ground other than those listed in art 12 (*Marleasing SA v La Comercial Internacional de Alimentación SA* (case C-106/89) [1990] ECR I-4135). The 'objects of the company' referred to in art 12(b)(ii) are the objects (if any) stated in its articles of association, not (if they are different) the objects actually pursued by the company (*Marleasing SA*).

The registration of a trade union as a company is void (Trade Union and Labour Relations (Consolidation) Act 1992, s 10(3)) and the annual reports of the Department of Trade and Industry on companies since 1974 show that three companies have been removed from the register because they were trade unions. It would seem that this was contrary to Directive 2009/101/EC, art 12(a), which requires that nullity must be ordered by a court of law: the registrar, as an authority of the State which was required to implement the Directive, should have complied with this provision.

Directive 2009/101/EC, art 13(3), requires that nullification of the incorporation of a company shall not of itself affect the validity of any commitments entered into by or with the company and art 13(2) requires that nullification shall entail the winding up of the company. No UK legislation has been enacted to implement the requirements of these paragraphs. It is submitted that the reversal by legal process of a decision on the ground that it was wrong operates to substitute a new decision as from the date of reversal but that acts done before that date which depend on the original decision remain valid. This point was made, in the context of an appeal reversing a judicial decision, by Megarry V-C in *Re D (J)* [1982] Ch 237 and it is submitted that it applies equally to judicial review reversing an administrative decision (see per Donaldson MR in *R v Panel on Takeovers and Mergers, ex parte Datafin plc* [1987] QB 815).

The problems of void registration are considered in more detail in R R Drury, 'Nullity of companies in English law' (1985) 48 MLR 644.

20.16.2.3 By order of the court

Under CA 2006, s 900(2)(d), the court may make an order dissolving without winding up any company which, under a compromise or arrangement sanctioned by the court under s 899, is transferring its business and property to another registered company. A company in relation to which such an order is made must, under penalty, deliver a copy of it to Companies House within seven days (s 900(6) to (8)).

20.16.2.4 By the registrar

The registrar may strike a defunct company off the register under CA 2006, s 1000.

Action may be taken under s 1000 if the company has not gone into liquidation but the registrar has reasonable cause to believe it is not carrying on business or is not in operation (s 1000(1)). The usual reasons for this belief are:

(a) Documents which the company should have sent to Companies House have not been received.

(b) Mail sent by Companies House to the company's registered office is returned undelivered.

Companies House sends a communication under s 1000(1) to the company inquiring whether it is carrying on business or in operation. If no reply is received to this communication within 14 days then, within a further 14 days, Companies House sends a second communication, under s 1000(2), warning that if no reply is received within 14 days, the next step in the process of dissolution will be taken. The next step is the publication of a notice in the *Gazette* that, two months after the date of the notice, the final step will be taken to dissolve the company unless cause is shown to the contrary. The final step is to strike the name of the company off the register (s 1000(4)) and to publish a notice in the *Gazette* that it has been struck off (s 1000(5)). The company is dissolved when this final notice is published (s 1000(6)).

If a company has commenced winding up but the registrar has reasonable cause to believe either that no liquidator is acting or that the affairs of the company are fully wound up, and six months have passed without the liquidator making any returns, the registrar can go straight to the publication of the two-month warning notice in the *Gazette* (s 1001). A copy of the notice must be sent to the company or, if there is one, to its liquidator at his or her last known place of business (ss 1001(1) and 1002(3)).

Under s 1003, the directors of a company, or a majority of them, may apply to the registrar to have the company struck off the register provided it has been inactive for three months. An application cannot be made unless a long list of activities specified in ss 1004 and 1005 have not occurred in the previous three months. These include trading or otherwise carrying on business or being the subject of any other insolvency or liquidation procedure. So, for example, a company cannot escape from a winding-up petition by applying to be dissolved. The registrar must give two months' notice in the *Gazette* of intention to act on an application to have a company struck off (s 1003(3)). The company is dissolved when the registrar publishes a notice in the *Gazette* that it has been struck off (s 1003(4) and (5)).

It is expressly provided that if a company is struck off by the registrar under s 1000, 1001 or 1003, the liability, if any, of every director, managing officer and member of the company shall continue and may be enforced as if the company had not been dissolved (ss 1000(7), 1001(5) and 1003(6)).

20.16.2.5 On completion of voluntary liquidation

The final stage of a voluntary winding up is the filing at Companies House of the liquidator's account of the winding up plus a statement of whether any of the company's creditors objected to the liquidator's release (IA 1986, s 106).

On receiving the account and statement Companies House must register them, and three months from the date of registration the company is dissolved unless the court orders deferment of dissolution (s 201(2) and (3)). Companies House must give public notice (see **4.3**) of receiving a liquidator's account and statement (CA 2006, ss 1077 and 1078(2), where the document is still described as a return of final meeting).

An application to the court to defer dissolution may be made by the liquidator or by any other person who appears to the court to be interested (IA 1986, s 201(3)). If the application is granted, the applicant must, under penalty, within seven days, file a copy of the court's order at Companies House (s 201(4) and sch 10), but Companies House is not required to give public notice of receiving it.

The process of dissolution under s 201 is effective even if the liquidator was mistaken in filing final accounts because the company actually had property that was not dealt with in the liquidation (*Re Cornish Manures Ltd* [1967] 1 WLR 807).

20.16.2.6 On application by the official receiver for early dissolution

An official receiver who is liquidator in the compulsory winding up of a company may notify Companies House for 'early dissolution' of the company under IA 1986, s 202. This may be done only if it appears to the official receiver that the realisable assets of the company are insufficient to cover the expenses of liquidation and that the affairs of the company do not require further investigation (s 202(2)). The official receiver must give 28 days' notice of intention to apply for early dissolution to the company's creditors and contributories and, if there is one, its administrative receiver (s 202(3)). Once that notice has been given the official receiver has no obligation to do anything else in relation to the company except put in an application for dissolution to Companies House (s 202(4)).

During the 28-day notice period fresh information may become apparent. The official receiver, any creditor, any contributory or an administrative receiver of the company may apply to the Secretary of State for directions to enable the liquidation to proceed as if no notice had been given (s 203).

If the official receiver applies for early dissolution, Companies House must register the application and, at the end of three months beginning with the day of registration, the company will be dissolved (s 202(5)). Again, however, if new information becomes apparent, the official receiver or any person who appears to the Secretary of State to be interested, may apply to the Secretary of State for directions to enable the winding up to continue and for the date of dissolution to be deferred (ss 202(5) and 203).

20.16.2.7 On completion of compulsory liquidation

If a liquidator in a compulsory liquidation who is not the official receiver forms the opinion that the winding up is for practical purposes complete, he or she must send to the court and to Companies House an account of the winding up plus a statement of whether any of the company's creditors objected to the liquidator's release (IA 1986, s 146). The liquidator vacates office when this has been done (s 172(8)). On receipt of that notice and statement Companies House must register them, and at the end of the period of three months beginning with the day of registration the company is dissolved unless the Secretary of State or, on appeal, the court, directs deferment of dissolution (IA 1986, s 205(1) to (4)).

Application for deferment of dissolution may be made by the official receiver or any other person who appears to the Secretary of State to be interested. A person for whom deferment of dissolution is directed must, under penalty, send Companies House a copy of the direction within seven days of it being given (s 205(6) and (7) and sch 10).

20.16.2.8 On completion of administration

An administrator of a company who thinks that it has nothing to distribute to its creditors must notify that fact to Companies House (IA 1986, sch B1, para 84(1)), unless the obligation to do so has been disapplied by the court (para 84(2)). The administrator must, under penalty, supply copies of a notice under para 84(1) to the court and to each creditor of whose claim and address he or she is aware (paras 84(5) and (9)). Companies House must register the notice (para 84(3)). On registration of the notice the administrator's appointment ceases (para 84(4)) and three months after registration the company is deemed to be dissolved (para 84(6)). The court may make an order delaying, suspending or disapplying the automatic dissolution (para 84(7)) and the administrator must notify any such order to Companies House (reg 84(8)).

INDEX